THE HISTORY OF PARLIAMENT

THE HOUSE OF COMMONS 1715-1754

Robert Walpole, 1st Earl of Orford
by J. M. Rysbrack, in the National Portrait Gallery

THE HISTORY OF PARLIAMENT

THE
HOUSE OF COMMONS
1715-1754

Romney Sedgwick

II
MEMBERS
E–Y

PUBLISHED FOR THE HISTORY OF PARLIAMENT TRUST
BY HER MAJESTY'S STATIONERY OFFICE, LONDON
1970

Printed in England for Her Majesty's Stationery Office by Unwin Brothers Limited, Woking and London

Contributors

E.C.	Eveline Cruickshanks (Mrs. D. Wyeth)
E.H.-G.	Edith, Lady Haden-Guest
J.B.L.	J. B. Lawson
R.S.L.	R. S. Lea
S.R.M.	Shirley Matthews
L.B.N.	Sir Lewis Namier
A.N.N.	A. N. Newman
J.B.O.	J. B. Owen
R.R.S.	Romney Sedgwick
J.M.S.	J. M. Simpson
P.D.G.T.	Peter D. G. Thomas
P.W.	Paula Watson

Abbreviations

In addition to standard and self-explanatory abbreviations, the following occur.

In the preliminary paragraphs:

abp.	archbishop
adv.	advocate
bp.	bishop
called	called to the bar
ch.	children
c.j.	chief justice
commr.	commissioner
c.p.	common pleas
contr.	contract
da.	daughter, daughters
dep.	deputy
e.	elder, eldest
E.I.	East Indies, East India
Ft.	regiment of Foot
[GB]	Great Britain, British
g.s.	grammar school
gd.-s., etc.	grandson, etc.
h.s.	high school
[I]	Ireland, Irish
jt.	joint
l.c.j.	lord chief justice
m.	married
M.P.	a Member of the House of Commons whose entire term of membership lies outside the period 1715–54
Mq.	Marquess
ret.	retired
s.	son, sons
[S]	Scotland, Scottish
S.C.J.	Senator of the College of Justice
suc.	succeeded
w.	wife
wid.	widow

In the footnotes:

Add.	Additional MSS, British Museum
AECP Angl.	Archives étrangères, correspondance politique, Angleterre, Ministry of Foreign Affairs, Paris
AEM & D Angl.	Archives étrangères, mémoires et documents, Angleterre, Ministry of Foreign Affairs, Paris
APC Col.	*Acts of the Privy Council, Colonial series*
Bodl.	Bodleian Library, Oxford
Burke LG	Burke's *Landed Gentry*
Burke PB	Burke's *Peerage and Baronetage*
Burnet	Gilbert Burnet, *History of his own Time* (1823)
Cal. Treas. Bks.	*Calendar of Treasury Books*
Cal. Treas. Pprs.	*Calendar of Treasury Papers*
CB	*Complete Baronetage*
Chandler	Richard Chandler, *The History and Proceedings of the House of Commons* (1742–4)
Chesterfield, *Letters*	*The Letters of Philip Dormer Stanhope, 4th Earl of Chesterfield* (1932)
CJ	*Journals of the House of Commons*
Coxe, *Walpole*	William Coxe, *Memoirs of the Life and Administration of Sir Robert Walpole* (1798)
Coxe, *Pelham*	William Coxe, *Memoirs of the Administration of the Rt. Hon. Henry Pelham* (1829)
CP	*Complete Peerage*
CSP Dom.	*Calendar of State Papers, Domestic series*
DNB	*Dictionary of National Biography*
Dodington Diary	*The Diary of the late George Bubb Dodington* (1784)
DWB	*Dictionary of Welsh Biography*
EHR	*English Historical Review*
Gent. Mag.	*The Gentleman's Magazine*
Harley Diary	Edward Harley's diary, 1734–41, Cambridge University Library
Hatsell	J. Hatsell, *Precedents of Proceedings in the House of Commons* (1818, unless an earlier ed. is indicated)
Hervey, *Mems.*	*Memoirs of the Reign of King George II* (1931)
Hist. Reg.	*The Historical Register*
HMC	used to introduce the short title of a publication of the Historical Manuscripts Commission
IHR Bull.	*Bulletin of the Institute of Historical Research*
Jnl.	*Journal*
Knatchbull Diary	*The Parliamentary Diary of Sir Edward Knatchbull* (Royal Historical Society, Camden 3rd series, vol. xciv)
Lib.	Library
LJ	*Journals of the House of Lords*
Luttrell	Narcissus Luttrell, *A Brief Historical Relation of State Affairs*
Mahon	Lord Mahon, *History of England from the Peace of Utrecht to the Peace of Versailles* (1858)

N. & Q.	*Notes and Queries*
New Hist. Northumb.	Northumberland County History Committee, *History of Northumberland* (1893–1940)
NLS	National Library of Scotland
NLW	National Library of Wales
n.s.	new series
N.S.	new style
Parl. Hist.	W. Cobbett, *The Parliamentary History of England from the earliest time to the year 1803*
PCC	Prerogative Court of Canterbury
Pol. State	A. Boyer, *The Political State of Great Britain*
PRO	Public Record Office
Ramsay of Ochtertyre	*Scotland and Scotsmen in the Eighteenth Century, from the mss of John Ramsay of Ochtertyre*
RO	Record Office
SHR	*Scottish Historical Review*
SRO	Public Record Office of Scotland
UCNW	University College of North Wales
VCH	*Victoria County History*
Vis.	*Visitation*
Walpole, *Mems. Geo. II*	Horace Walpole, *Memoirs of the Reign of King George II* (1847)
Walpole, *Mems. Geo. III*	Horace Walpole, *Memoirs of the Reign of King George III* (1894)
WO	War Office
Yorke, *Hardwicke*	Philip C. Yorke, *The Life and Correspondence of Philip Yorke, Earl of Hardwicke* (1913)
Yorke's parl. jnl.	Philip Yorke's parliamentary journal (Add. 35337), printed in *Parl. Hist.* xii. 102–1272

MEMBERS
E–Y

EARLE, Giles (c.1678–1758), of Eastcourt House, Crudwell, nr. Malmesbury, Wilts.

| CHIPPENHAM | 1715–1722 |
| MALMESBURY | 13 Dec. 1722–1747 |

b. c.1678, 6th s. of Sir Thomas Earle, M.P., mayor of Bristol, by Elizabeth Ellinor, da. of Joseph Jackson; bro. of Joseph Earle (q.v.). *educ.* M. Temple 1692. *m.* (1) lic. 20 May 1702, Elizabeth, da. and coh. of Sir William Rawlinson of Hendon House, Mdx., commr. of the great seal, wid. of William Lowther, 2nd s. of Sir John Lowther, 2nd Bt., M.P., 1s. 1da.; (2) Margaret, 1s. *d.v.p.*
Capt. 33 Ft. 1702; capt. R. Horse Gds. 1711–17; commissary of musters in Spain 1711; commissary-gen. of provisions in Spain 1711 and Minorca 1712–17; groom of the bedchamber to Prince of Wales 1718–20; clerk of Board of Green Cloth 1720–27; chairman of committee of privileges and elections 1727–41; commr. of Irish revenue 1728–37; ld. of Treasury 1737–42; high steward, Malmesbury 1741–2.

In 1677 Sir Thomas Earle, an eminent merchant of Bristol, inherited from his uncle, Giles Earle, lands in Crudwell, Wilts. On his death in 1696 he bequeathed these lands to his younger son, Giles,[1] who entered the army, serving in the Duke of Argyll's regiment and under him as commissary in Minorca. Returned as a Whig in 1715, he spoke in favour of the septennial bill in 1716, saying:

> I observe that certain people, who have consistently opposed the King and the good of their country, are against the bill; therefore without any other reason, I am heartily for it.[2]

Later in the year when, during the King's absence in Hanover, the Opposition were promoting addresses to the Prince of Wales as Regent, Walpole reported to Hanover that 'the Duke of Argyll's Earle' had personally presented an address from Gloucestershire to the Prince.[3] Next year he voted against the Government on the case of Argyll's rival, Lord Cadogan (q.v.), at the cost of losing both his place and his commission. Paying his court to the Prince's reputed mistress, Mrs. Howard,[4] he was compensated in 1718 with a place in the Prince's household, which he exchanged in 1720 for one under Argyll, who had returned to office as lord steward.

In 1722 Earle gained control of Malmesbury, near his estate, returning himself and another Member for the borough for a quarter of a century. A frequent speaker, with 'an odd violent way of expressing himself', he became chairman of the elections committee in 1727. Appointed a commissioner of Irish revenue in 1728, he supported proposals for the removal of the duty on Irish yarn, which he described on 12 Feb. 1734 as

> an affair of the greatest consequence to the trade and well being of England; the laws are already as severe as can be, and make what other you will, the people of Ireland will not execute them, the penalties are so severe, no jury in Ireland will find a person guilty, as was the case in England when it was made death to run. The only method to prevent it is to let Ireland into some small share of the trade, for their poor must be subsisted, and he knew nothing so capable to prevent their running as to take off the duty on their yarn.[5]

Next day, on an opposition motion to prevent the dismissal of army officers on political grounds, he said

> he himself had once been removed, and he was very sorry for it; but he was not for turning everything topsy turvy out of resentment.[6]

When in 1737 Earle was made a lord of the Treasury, Hervey wrote of him:

> This Earle was originally a dependent on the Duke of Argyll, a man of no great abilities, of a sordid avaricious temper, a very bad character, and as profligate in his discourse as his conduct, professing himself always ready, without examining what it was, to do anything a minister bid him; by which means he had worked himself so well into Sir Robert's good graces, that, merely by his own personal interest there (which even his attachment at the same time to the Duke of Argyll could not outweigh), he got himself preferred to this high post, the whole world exclaiming against such a prostitution of the office.[7]

Horace Walpole describes him as

> very covetous, and affected to be so more than he was; and his humour was set off by a whining tone, crabbed face, and very laughing eyes. One day as he was eating oysters, he said 'Lord God! what fine

things oysters would be if one could make one's servants live on the shells'.[8]

His unpopularity, aggravated by mordant witticisms 'dealt out largely against the Scotch and the Patriots',[9] contributed to his failure to secure re-election as chairman of the elections committee by four votes on 16 Dec. 1741, a blow from which Walpole never fully recovered. He lost his post on Walpole's fall but continued to support the Administration. Defeated at Malmesbury in 1747, he never stood again. He died 20 Aug. 1758.

[1] PCC 16 Hale; 241 Bond. [2] A. Corbière to Horace Walpole, 27 Apr. 1716, Cholmondeley (Houghton) mss. [3] Coxe, *Walpole*, ii. 77–78. [4] *Letters of Lady Suffolk*, i. 11–12, 15. [5] *HMC Egmont Diary*, i. 108; ii. 27. [6] Stuart mss 169/90. [7] Hervey, *Mems.* 740. [8] Note in Hanbury Williams, *Works*, i. 32. [9] Walpole to Mann, 16 Dec. 1741.

E.C.

EARLE, Joseph (c.1658–1730), of Bristol, Glos.

BRISTOL   1710–1727

b. c.1658, 1st s. of Sir Thomas Earle, M.P., mayor of Bristol, and bro. of Giles Earle (q.v.). *m.* (lic. 18 Nov. 1689) Elizabeth, da. of Sir Thomas Cann, merchant of Bristol, 1da. *d.v.p. suc.* fa. 1696.

Master of the Merchant Venturers of Bristol 1721–2.

Joseph Earle was a merchant of Bristol, which he represented in four Parliaments. Classed in 1715 as a Whig, he opposed the septennial bill, supported the repeal of the Occasional Conformity and Schism Acts, and was absent on the peerage bill. In 1719 he was one of the ministerial 'underlings' who opposed a Tory election petition till two in the morning.[1] Re-elected at the head of the poll in 1722, he lost his seat at the next general election, during which

old Earle came into the Hall the first day and demanded a poll which, being granted, he was asked who he chose to manage his election. He answered 'The Devil, by G-d'; so polled two men and went off![2]

He died 10 or 13 Mar. 1730 aged 72, leaving his property to his brothers, with remainder to the son of his daughter Eleanor by William Benson (q.v.).

[1] *HMC Portland*, v. 577. [2] Jas. Pearce to Humphry Morice, 9 Sept. 1727, Morice mss at Bank of England.

S.R.M.

EARLE, William Rawlinson (c.1703–74), of Eastcourt House, Crudwell, nr. Malmesbury, Wilts.

MALMESBURY   1727–1747
CRICKLADE   1747–1761
NEWPORT I.o.W.   7 Aug. 1762–1768

b. c.1703, 1st s. of Giles Earle (q.v.). *m.* 4 Jan. 1731 (with £20,000), Susannah, da. and h. of William White of Somerford, Wilts., 1s. 3da. *suc.* fa. 1758.

Clerk of deliveries in the Ordnance 1733–40; clerk of the Ordnance 1740–72.

For twenty years Earle represented Malmesbury jointly with his father. A staunch government supporter, he was given a post in the Ordnance, which he retained after Walpole's fall. Defeated at Malmesbury in 1747, he was successful at Cricklade, continuing to support the Administration. Resigning from the Ordnance in 1772, he died 10 Aug. 1774.

E.C.

EAST, William (c.1695–1737), of the Manor House, Kennington, Surr. and Hall Place, Hurley, Berks.

ST. MAWES   2 Mar. 1728–1734

b. c.1695, 1st s. of William East of the Manor House, Kennington, and the M. Temple by Elizabeth, da. of Jeremy Gough of London. *educ.* King's, Camb. 1714; M. Temple 1714. *m.* 30 Apr. 1724, Anne, da. of Sir George Cooke of Harefield, Mdx., chief prothonotary of court of common pleas, sis. of George Cooke (q.v.), 1s. 2da. *suc.* fa. 1726.

Commr. for wine licences 1719–27.

The son of a wealthy barrister, belonging to a prominent city of London family connected with the wine trade, East was appointed commissioner for wine licences under George I. Sir Philip Parker (q.v.), wrote to Walpole, 7 Aug. 1727:

My brother [-in-law] East, whom I took the liberty to recommend to your interest for to be in Parliament, informs me that Mr. Gibson [Thomas, q.v.] assures him of a certainty of his being elected at Marlborough in case he will comply with the demands of the electors, which he has agreed to in case you will please to permit him to resign his commissioner's place in the wine licence office to his brother, Mr. Gilbert East, who is a gentleman zealous for your Administration and every way qualified for the place.[1]

Permission was granted but the Marlborough deal fell through. Brought in instead for St. Mawes at a by-election by John Knight (q.v.), he voted with the Administration on the army in 1732 and on the repeal of the Septennial Act in 1734, when he did not stand. He died 7 Nov. 1737.

[1] Cholmondeley (Houghton) mss.

E.C.

EDEN, John (c.1678–1728), of West Auckland, co. Dur.

DURHAM CO.   1713–1727

b. c.1678, 1st s. of Sir Robert Eden, 1st Bt., M.P., of West Auckland by Margaret, da. and h. of John Lambton of Durham. *educ.* Queen's, Oxf. 1695. *m.* 31 Jan. 1715, Catherine, da. of Mark Shafto of

Whitworth, co. Dur., sis. of Robert and John Shafto (qq.v.), 1s. *suc.* fa. as 2nd Bt. May 1720.

Eden and his father represented Durham county from 1702 to 1727. Succeeding his father as a Tory in 1713, he voted against the Government in every recorded division of the 1715 Parliament. His name was sent to the Pretender in 1721 as a probable supporter in the event of a rising.[1] He owed his re-election in 1722 to a split among the Whigs,[2] who sank their differences in 1727, when he either withdrew or did not stand. He died 2 May 1728.

[1] Stuart mss 65/16. [2] E. Hughes, *N. Country Life in 18th Cent.* 280 n. 1.

R.R.S.

EDGCUMBE, Hon. George (1720–95), of Mount Edgcumbe, nr. Plymouth, Devon.

FOWEY   30 July 1746–10 May 1761

b. 3 Mar. 1720, 2nd s. of Richard Edgcumbe, 1st Baron Edgcumbe, and bro. of Hon. Richard Edgcumbe (qq.v.). *educ.* ?Eton 1732. *m.* 6 Aug. 1761, Emma, da. of Rt. Rev. John Gilbert, abp. of York, 1s. *suc.* bro. as 3rd Baron 10 May 1761; *cr.* Visct. Mount Edgcumbe 5 Mar. 1781; Earl of Mount Edgcumbe 31 Aug. 1789.
  Lt. R.N. 1739, capt. 1744, r.-adm. 1762; c.-in-c. Plymouth 1765–71; v.-adm. 1770, adm. 1778; v.-adm. Cornw. 1782.
  Clerk of duchy of Lancaster 1747–62; ld. lt. Cornw. 1761–*d.*; PC 26 July 1765; treasurer of the Household 1765–66; jt. vice-treasurer [I] 1770–72, 1784–93; capt. of gent. pensioners 1772–82.

George Edgcumbe was returned for Fowey by his father at a by-election in 1746. Re-elected in 1747, he was classed as a government supporter, but seems rarely to have attended owing to his absence at sea. He died 4 Feb. 1795.

E.C.

EDGCUMBE, Richard (1680–1758), of Mount Edgcumbe, nr. Plymouth, Devon.

CORNWALL	25 June–11 Nov. 1701
ST. GERMANS	1701–1702
PLYMPTON ERLE	1702–1734
LOSTWITHIEL	1734–1741
PLYMPTON ERLE	1741–20 Apr. 1742

bap. 23 Apr. 1680, 3rd s. of Sir Richard Edgcumbe, K.B., M.P., of Mount Edgcumbe, and Cotehele, Cornw. by Lady Anne Montagu, da. of Edward Montagu, M.P., 1st Earl of Sandwich. *educ.* Trinity, Camb. 1697. *m.* 12 Mar. 1715, Matilda, da. of Sir Henry Furnese, 1st Bt., M.P., of Waldershare, Kent. *suc.* e. bro. Piers to family estates 1694; *cr.* Baron Edgcumbe 20 Apr. 1742.
  Ld. of Treasury 1716–17 and 1720–4; jt. vice-treasurer [I] 1724–42; P.C. [I] 28 Nov. 1727;

ld. warden of the stannaries 1734–7; ld. lt. Cornw. 1742–*d.*; chancellor of duchy of Lancaster 1743–58; P.C. 25 Jan. 1744; col. of a regt. of Ft. 1745; maj-gen. 1755; c.j. in eyre north of Trent Jan. 1758–*d.*
  Recorder, Lostwithiel 1733–*d.*, capital burgess 1736, mayor 1738 and 1742.

Returned on the family interest at Plympton, Edgcumbe in 1717 went into opposition with Walpole, 'a most intimate friend'. When the opposition charges of corruption against Lord Cadogan (q.v.) were considered by a committee of the whole House on 4 June 1717, Walpole was successful in getting Edgcumbe chosen as chairman, instead of a government supporter. In 1720 he was entrusted by Walpole with the details of his secret negotiations with Sunderland and the Prince of Wales, indiscreetly supplying daily accounts of them to Pulteney, whose exclusion from them was the beginning of his estrangement from Walpole. On Walpole's return to office, Edgcumbe secured a seat at the Treasury board, from which he was promoted in 1724 to be joint vice-treasurer of Ireland, worth £3,000 a year. In 1725 Carteret, seeking to make his peace with Walpole, asked Edgcumbe to act as his intercessor, knowing, he wrote, 'your just and tender attachment to the person concerned' and trusting 'that you would be glad to facilitate my coming into that friendship, which you yourself are so happily engaged in'.[1]

During the 1727 election campaign Edgcumbe made a 'grand tour' of Cornwall, reporting 'success in every place where I have been'. Shortly before the next general election, Walpole chose him to succeed the 1st Lord Falmouth (q.v. under Boscawen, Hugh) as chief government manager in Cornwall, making him the 'disposer of the government's money for buying the Cornish elections for Members in Parliament.' Though he was successful in 1734, in 1741 the combined interests of the Prince of Wales and Lord Falmouth, together, it was alleged, with his own 'indolence and unskillfulness', led to unprecedented losses in the Cornish boroughs, which were one of the main causes of Walpole's fall. According to Falmouth, (to Frederick, Prince of Wales, 12 May 1741) 'there will now be but three Members returned to the ensuing Parliament from this county by his agency'.[2] Turned out of his office by Pulteney, who 'particularly hated' him as 'a particular friend' of Walpole's, Edgcumbe was made a peer to prevent his being examined by the secret committee of the House about the management of the Cornish elections. He was also appointed lord lieutenant of Cornwall by the King without consulting Pulteney, who did not conceal his annoyance. Regaining office in 1743, he managed the Cornish elections in 1747 and 1754, in association with the 2nd Lord Falmouth (Hugh Boscawen, b. 1707, q.v.). He had a natural interest in one seat only at Plympton, near Mount Edgcumbe. But in his capacity as manager of the government interest in Cornwall he was able to return two Members for Lostwithiel, for a time two for Grampound, and usually one each for Fowey, Penryn, and Bossiney, besides having a part-interest in Mitchell. His electoral influence in Cornwall, unlike that of the Boscawens, was the consequence rather than the cause of his being put in charge of the government interest there. He died 22 Nov. 1758, commemorated by Horace Walpole as 'one of the honestest and steady men in the world'.[3]

[1] Walpole to Mann, 9 Aug. 1784; Chandler, vi. 137; Coxe, *Walpole*, i. 356–7; ii. 488; *HMC Egmont Diary* ii. 33. [2] SP Dom. 36/2, ff. 147–8; *HMC Egmont Diary*, ii. 132; Stuart mss 219/91; Owen, *Pelhams*, 8–9; Royal archives. [3] Horace Walpole's ms poems, ex. inf. W. S. Lewis; Walpole to Mann, 15 Apr., 29 July 1742, 27 Nov. 1758.

E.C.

EDGCUMBE, Hon. Richard (1716–61), of Mount Edgcumbe, nr. Plymouth, Devon.

PLYMPTON ERLE 4 Dec. 1742–1747
LOSTWITHIEL 1747–1754
PENRYN 1754–22 Nov. 1758

b. 2 Aug. 1716, 1st s. of Richard Edgcumbe, 1st Baron Edgcumbe, and bro. of Hon. George Edgcumbe (qq.v.). *educ.* Eton 1725–32. *unm. suc.* fa. as 2nd Baron 22 Nov. 1758.

Ld. of Trade Apr. 1754–5; ld. of Admiralty 1755–6; P.C. 19 Nov. 1756; comptroller of the Household 1756–d.; ld. lt. Cornw. 1759–d.

Capital burgess, Lostwithiel 1743, mayor 1744, and 1756, recorder 1759–d.; recorder, Plympton Erle 1759–d.

'A martyr to gaming: with every quality to make himself agreeable', Edgcumbe 'did nothing but make himself miserable'. As a young man his practice of losing 'his daily twenty guineas'[1] at White's reduced him to such straits that Henry Pelham, a fellow-member, charitably procured him a secret service pension of £500 a year.[2] After some time on the dole he appealed to Pelham for a more satisfactory provision.[3] When he had last been named by the Duke of Newcastle to the King for a place, George II's answer was

'that he gave me something already:' which, I suppose, he intended should be a satisfactory one why he should give me nothing else. But I look upon that as extremely different from an employment; it was given me as an alms, for which I was, and ever shall be, very thankful. But though beggars (and I can't call myself much better) must not be choosers, yet a mere object of charity is what one would not wish to be for ever, and the question is,

whether my standing in life as well as in Parliament, joined to my future prospect, is not a pretension equal to those of my competitors—not that I claim anything as due to my own particular merit; but whatever was to be conferred on me, I should esteem, and would have the world do so too, as a grace bestowed upon our family, which may be allowed to be as well entitled the bounty of the Crown as another.

Then the secrecy which he was required to observe with regard to his pension exposed him to embarrassing enquiries as to why he was not provided for. His usual answer was 'that sons seldom are in their father's lifetime', but

when the same question is put to me by my father, accompanied with complaints, (as sometimes it is) then, Sir, I do assure you I suffer greatly to find myself obliged to leave him in his error.

Further, was it not possible that Lord Edgcumbe, who 'as chancellor of the duchy goes into the King sometimes . . . should apply to his Majesty?' Were the King to give him the same answer as he did the Duke of Newcastle, this

would be of infinite more prejudice to me than the bare refusal of a place; for I am sure my father would never forgive me if he knew I had done that, which I think I was in the right to do, though he would be so too to blame me for it.

Finally,

I find I am growing a middle-aged man, for I begin to feel symptoms of the passion of that state of life. But I hope you will not look upon it as a degree of ambition more than is laudable, to be desirous to keep pace with my equals, who if I don't start soon, will all distance me . . . Indeed, Sir, I am tired of absolute idleness and want some better food for my brain than what it now feeds upon. I shall be extremely happy to get into a better road, and to owe my happiness to you with double the joys.

In the event he did not obtain a place till shortly after Pelham's death, when he exchanged his pension for a seat on the board of Trade.[4]

He died 10 May 1761, appointing in his will his old friend, Horace Walpole, to be trustee for his mistress.[5]

[1] Horace Walpole to Mann, 14 May 1761; to Hanbury Williams, 7 July 1744. [2] Add. 33038, f. 415. [3] Rich. Edgcumbe to Pelham, 16 Nov. 1752, Newcastle (Clumber) mss. [4] Add. 33038, f. 352. [5] Horace Walpole's *Short Notes* of his life, Mar. 1761.

E.C.

EDWARDES, Francis (d.1725), of Johnston, nr. Haverfordwest, Pemb.

HAVERFORDWEST 1722–Dec. 1725

2nd s. of Owen Edwardes of Treffgarne, Pemb. by Damaris, da. of James Perrott. *m.* (1) *s.p.*; (2) Lady Elizabeth Rich, o. da. of Robert, 5th Earl of Warwick, 2s. 1da.

According to the 2nd Earl of Oxford,

Lady Elizabeth Rich had run out her fortune and retired to Wales, and there married Francis Edwardes, who was a younger son of a gentleman; he was a purser of a ship; got £60 per ann.[1]

On the death intestate in 1721 of her nephew, the 7th Earl of Warwick, she became heir-at-law to his estates, including considerable property in Kensington. A year later Edwardes was returned as a Tory for Haverfordwest.

He died 15 Dec. 1725.

[1] *N. & Q.* (ser. 8), i. 326.

R.R.S.

EDWARDES, William (c.1712–1801), of Johnston, nr. Haverfordwest, Pemb.

HAVERFORDWEST 1747–1784, 6 Feb. 1786–13 Dec. 1801

b. c.1712, 2nd s. of Francis Edwardes (q.v.). *m.* (1) his cos. Rachel (*d.* 14 Aug. 1760), da. of Owen Edwardes of Treffgarne Pemb., *s.p.*; (2) 10 June 1762, Elizabeth, da. and coh. of William Warren of Longridge, Pemb., 1s. *suc.* fa. to Haverfordwest estates 15 Dec. 1725; his e. bro. Edward Henry to Warwick estates, 18 Mar. 1738, including considerable property, in Kensington; *cr.* Baron Kensington [I] 28 July 1776. Sheriff, Pemb. 1745.

Soon after Edwardes's return the 2nd Lord Egmont wrote of Haverfordwest in his electoral survey: 'The best interest is in Edwardes, but his behaviour and life will probably beat him'—a notably incorrect forecast, possibly based on his first cousin, the 7th Earl of Warwick, who was said to have 'killed himself by his debauchery', and his elder brother, who 'drank himself to death'.[1]

In the 1747 Parliament Edwardes was classed by the ministry 'against', apparently as a Tory. But on 12 June 1753 Henry Fox, who had leased Holland House from him, wrote to Henry Pelham about a recommendation made relating to the filling of a government post in Pembrokeshire:

I understand Mr. Edwardes is opposed by Sir John Philipps (q.v.) at Haverfordwest, and I make no doubt may be brought to oppose Sir John Philipps's principles everywhere. But my application is not political. Wells, Windsor, Malmesbury all together cannot make me so desirous of procuring a favour, as does the regard I have for my landlord, of whom I want a bit of a waste, a lease, and 2 or 3 other small favours. If you can oblige me in this therefore I hope you will.[2]

Nevertheless in the next Parliament he continued to be classed as a Tory.

Though Edwardes represented Haverfordwest for over fifty years, never, so far as is known, voting against any Government, he died 13 Dec. 1801, without having attained his object, an English peerage.

[1] *N. & Q.* (ser. 8), i. 326. [2] Newcastle (Clumber) mss.

R.R.S.

EDWARDS, Samuel (c.1668–1738), of Frodesley, Salop.

WENLOCK 1722–12 June 1738

b. c.1668, s. of John Edwards of Pentre, Mont. *m.* (1) 24 Nov. 1699, Rebecca, da. of John Godolphin of Doctors' Commons, London, step-sis. of Col. Sidney Godolphin (q.v.) of Abertanat, Salop, 2s.; (2) Sept. 1723, Elizabeth Jones, da. of a Shropshire clergyman.[1]

Deputy teller of the Exchequer 1700–*d.*; trustee for keeper of Windsor Great Park 1709–*d.*

Edwards, a minor Exchequer official in 1697, married into the Godolphin family, with whom he thereafter maintained a close connexion, becoming a trustee for Charles Godolphin, M.P., looking after the affairs of Godolphin's widow, and acting as an executor of Col. Sidney Godolphin.[2] Early in 1700 he received promotion in the office of Francis Godolphin, later the 2nd Earl, then a teller of the receipt, retaining his place under subsequent holders of the office, and also holding other offices such as cashier and later paymaster of Exchequer bills, and director in several lotteries.[3] About this time he acquired land in Shropshire at Frodesley and on Wenlock Edge, near Wenlock,[4] for which he was returned after a contest as a Whig, probably on the joint interests of William Forester (q.v.) and Lord Bradford, whose brother had been made a teller in 1718. Re-elected in 1727 and 1734, he voted with the Government. His son Godolphin was mayor of Shrewsbury in 1730, in which year the town's South Sea stock was transferred to Edwards to hold in trust.[5] He died 12 June 1738, aged 70.

[1] *Hist Reg.* 1723, chron. p. 41. [2] *Cal. Treas. Bks.* xii. 270; F. G. Marsh, *The Godolphins*, 13, 22, 23. [3] *Cal. Treas. Bks.* xv. 56; xvii. 430; xxiv. 129, 201; xxvii. 400, 485. [4] PCC 304 Brodrepp. [5] *Salop Arch. Soc. Trans.* (ser. 8), xi. 208.

J.B.L.

EDWARDS, Thomas (?1673–1743), of the Middle Temple, London, and Filkins Hall, Oxon.

BRISTOL 1713–1715
WELLS 14 Dec. 1719–25 Mar. 1735

b. ?1673, 1st s. of Thomas Edwards of Broad St., Bristol, attorney-at-law, by his 1st w. *educ.* Balliol, Oxf. 29 Oct. 1691, aged 18; M. Temple 1693, called 1698, bencher 1724. *m.* bef. 1701, Mary, o. surv. da. and h. of Sir William Hayman, merchant and mayor of Bristol, by Mary, sis. of Edward Colston, M.P., the wealthy Bristol philanthropist (*d.* 1721), 3da. *suc.* fa. 1727.

Thomas Edwards, whose wife inherited a considerable fortune from her uncle, Edward Colston,[1] succeeded to Colston's Bristol seat in 1713. Described as a Tory who might often vote Whig, he was defeated in 1715, his petition, though read three times, making no progress. In 1719 he successfully contested a by-election at Wells, which had been represented under Queen Anne by his wife's cousin Edward Colston junior. Returned there at the next three general elections, he was unseated in 1735, never standing again. His only recorded vote was against the Government on the repeal of the Septennial Act in 1734. He died intestate about June 1743, when administration was granted to his daughter Sophia Ready, afterwards Colston.

[1] PCC 111 Degg, 236 Buckingham, 163 Farrant.

R.S.L.

EDWIN, Charles (c.1699–1756), of Llanmihangel Plas, Glam.

WESTMINSTER   31 Dec. 1741–1747
GLAMORGAN   1747–29 June 1756

b. c.1699, o.s. of Samuel Edwin (q.v.). *m.* 1 May 1736, Lady Charlotte Hamilton, da. of James, 4th Duke of Hamilton [S], *s.p. suc.* fa. 1722; and uncle Thomas Edwin to estate of Headley, Surr. and to lands in Northants. and Suss. 1735.
Sheriff, Northants. 1739–40.

Two days before the Westminster election of 1741 it was decided to put up Admiral Vernon (q.v.) for the city against the government candidates. 'Mr. Edwin, a gentleman of Wales, of good fortune, appearing accidentally at the meeting held for the purpose of the Admiral's nomination, was joined with him'.[1] The impression created by Edwin's candidature is shown by a letter written after the return of his opponents.

Poor Mr. Edwin's name at first turned the thing to a farce, but the poll has been carried on with great vigour and expense on both sides . . . Mr. Edwin having neither chance nor pretence his part is ridiculous enough, and those who really wish the Prince well are vexed there should be an opposition made with so little prospect of success, and by a man of so little eminence.[2]

On the annulment of the election by the Commons the Prince and the opposition leaders could not prevent Edwin, 'who accidentally was the person pitched upon by the mob for the first contest', from being re-nominated since 'it was impossible to suppose the people would depart from him in gratitude for the money he had spent'.[3] This time he was joined with Lord Perceval—'Lord Perceive-all and Mr. Perceive-nothing', as Horace Walpole called them[4]—with whom he was returned unopposed.

A Tory, Edwin, known to his friends as 'Numps',[5] voted with the Opposition. In 1743 he tried to steal a march on his fellow-Member by presenting, without Perceval's knowledge, an address from the

city of Westminster to the King, who refused to receive it, ordering Edwin to be told that 'he did not care to receive addresses presented by only one Member, when both were in town'.[6]

In 1747 Edwin was returned on the Tory interest for Glamorgan. He died 29 June 1756.

[1] *Hist. House of Yvery*, ii. 460. [2] *HMC Carlisle*, 197. [3] Egmont mss, Add. 47091. [4] To Mann, 7 Jan. 1742. [5] Walpole to Mann, 22 Jan. 1742; *HMC Denbigh*, v. 178. [6] *HMC Egmont Diary*, iii. 292.

E.C.

EDWIN, Samuel (1671–1722), of Llanmihangel Plas, Glam.

MINEHEAD   11 Apr.–23 May 1717

bap. 12 Mar. 1671, 1st s. of Sir Humphrey Edwin, ld. mayor of London 1697–8, by Elizabeth, da. of Samuel Sambrooke of London, merchant, sis. of Sir Jeremy Sambrooke, merchant, of St. Michael Bassishaw, London. *educ.* Pembroke, Oxf. 1687; L. Inn 1689. *m.* (lic. 20 Sept. 1697) Lady Catherine Montagu, da. of Robert Montagu, M.P., 3rd Earl of Manchester, 1s. 1da. *suc.* fa. 1707.
Usher of the receipt of the Exchequer and keeper of council chamber of Star Chamber 1698–*d.*

Edwin inherited a great fortune from his father, an eminent London merchant, who had acquired extensive properties in Westminster and Glamorgan. He stood for Minehead unsuccessfully, apparently as a Tory, in 1715. Returned for it in 1717, but unseated on petition, he was defeated on a third attempt in 1722. He died 27 Sept. 1722.

S.R.M.

EGERTON, Hon. Charles (?1694–1725).

CHIPPING WYCOMBE   1722–7 Nov. 1725

b. ?1694, yst. s. of John Egerton, M.P., 3rd Earl of Bridgwater, by Jane, da. of Charles Powlett, M.P., 1st Duke of Bolton; bro. of Hon. William Egerton (q.v.). *educ.* New Coll., Oxf. 9 Feb. 1712, aged 17. *m.* Catherine, da. of Hon. Francis Brooke and sis. of 6th and 7th Lords Brooke, 2s.

Egerton was returned as a Whig on his family's interest, with the support of the followers of the late Marquess of Wharton. He died soon afterwards, 7 Nov. 1725.

R.R.S.

EGERTON, Sir Thomas, 6th Bt. (?1721–56), of Heaton, Lancs.

NEWTON   1747–1754

b. ?1721, 2nd surv. s. of Sir Holland Egerton, 4th Bt., of Heaton by Eleanor, da. of Sir Roger Cave, 2nd Bt., M.P., of Stanford, Leics. by Mary. sis. of William Bromley (q.v.), Speaker of the House of Commons.

educ. B.N.C. Oxf. 28 Nov. 1740, aged 19. *m.* 14 June 1748, Catherine, da. of Rev. John Copley of Batley, Yorks., fellow of the collegiate church at Manchester and rector of Thornhill and Wakefield, Yorks., 2s. 1da. *suc.* bro. Sir Edward Egerton, 5th Bt., 16 Feb. 1744.

Egerton, a Tory country gentleman, was returned by Peter Legh of Lyme (q.v.). In November 1748 he and other members of the Newton Hunt were reported in the London press to have gone 'in a body, to the Market Cross at Newton, and proclaimed the Pretender, by the style and title of James the Third', wearing 'white cockades' and 'plaid waistcoats', and 'riding about to drink, and to force others to drink treasonable healths'. In January he arranged for a letter to be published in the *London Evening Post* denying these allegations and claiming that, when he had gone to complain to a neighbouring justice of repeated attacks by a Whig mob from Wigan on the Newton gentlemen's houses, he was merely told to 'repel force by force'. In February a friend reported,

> Sir Thomas goes down in a week's time, there being no great business for minoritarians to transact in Parliament, where they don't let them into any great secrets, being able to manage matters and moneys without their assistance.[1]

He declined to stand in 1754, 'preferring . . . the satisfaction of a private station', dying 7 Aug. 1756, aged 35.[2]

[1] *London Evening Post*, no. 3315, 28–31 Jan. 1749; *Remains of John Byrom* (Chetham Soc. xliv), ii (2), pp. 474–81, 486. [2] His M.I. quoted in J. Croston, *County Fams. of Lancs. and Cheshire*, 153.

E.C.

EGERTON, Hon. William (1684–1732).

BUCKINGHAMSHIRE 27 Feb. 1706–1708
BRACKLEY 1708–20 Apr. 1714
 1715–15 July 1732

b. 5 Nov. 1684, 4th s. of John Egerton, M.P., 3rd Earl of Bridgwater, and bro. of Hon. Charles Egerton (q.v.). *m.* Anna Maria, da. of Adm. Sir George Saunders (q.v.). commr. of the navy, 3da.
 Capt. 6 Ft. 1704; capt. and lt.-col. 1 Ft. Gds. 1705–Mar. 1714, Dec. 1714–June 1715; brevet col. 1711; col. 36 Ft. 1715–19, 20 Ft. 1719–*d.*

William Egerton, who had been forced to sell his company in the Guards in March 1714,[1] was reinstated after the Hanoverian succession and given a regiment in 1715. Returned for Brackley by his brother, the 1st Duke of Bridgwater, he voted with the Government in all recorded divisions till his death, 15 July 1732.

[1] *HMC Portland*, v. 408, 417.

R.R.S.

EGMONT, Earl of, *see* **PERCEVAL, John,** Visct. Perceval (*d.*1748); **PERCEVAL, John,** Visct. Perceval (*d.*1770)

ELDE, Francis (?1692–1760), of Seighford, nr. Stafford.

STAFFORD 19 Nov. 1724–4 Feb. 1725

b. ?1692, 1st s. of Francis Elde of Seighford by his 1st w. née Hunt of Worcs. *educ.* Trinity, Oxf. 18 July 1710, aged 18; M. Temple 1711, called 1718, bencher 1728. *unm.*
 Master in Chancery Feb. 1724–*d.*

Elde was appointed a master in Chancery by Lord Chancellor Macclesfield, giving him '5,000 guineas in gold and bank notes', shortly before Macclesfield's impeachment for selling such appointments.[1] He then stood for Stafford successfully against the 1st Viscount Chetwynd (q.v.), who petitioned. When the petition came before the House

> Thomas Foley [the other Member] said he was ordered by the borough to acquaint the House, that they could prove a bargain made for money, for Elde to resign his place [his seat] to Lord Chetwynd and that there were persons at the door to prove it and more at the town; so the report was put off for 10 days and those persons ordered to come up to prove their complaint at the Bar, and Mr. Elde not being in his place it was understood he must attend, though no order was made because it was only a complaint and not a charge.[2]

Expelled the House for having corruptly attempted to compromise the petition before it was heard by the elections committee, he was soon afterwards made a bencher of his Inn, but did not stand again. He died 5 Mar. 1760.

[1] Howell, *State Trials*, xvi. 871–2. [2] *Knatchbull Diary*, 23 Jan. 1725.

E.C.

ELFORD, Jonathan (1684–1755), of Bickham, Devon.

SALTASH 19 Dec. 1710–1715
FOWEY 1715–1722

bap. 11 Nov. 1684, 1st s. of of Jonathan Elford of Bickham by Amy, da. of Matthew Halse of Keynedon and Efford, Devon. *educ.* Ch. Ch. Oxf. 1702; M. Temple 1702. *m.* Anne, da. and h. of Sir Thomas Neville, 1st Bt., of Neville Holt, Leics., *s.p. suc.* fa. 1690.
 Commr. of public accounts June–Oct. 1714.

Returned as a Tory in 1715, Elford voted against the Administration in every recorded division. His name was sent to the Pretender as a Jacobite supporter in 1721.[1] He did not stand again. He died 10 Dec. 1755.

[1] Stuart mss 65/16.

E.C.

ELIOT, Edward (?1684–1722), of Port Eliot, nr. St. Germans, Cornw.

ST. GERMANS	4 Dec.	1705–1715
LOSTWITHIEL	26 Nov.	1718–11 June 1720
LISKEARD		12 Apr.–18 Sept. 1722

b. ?1684, 1st s. of William Eliot, R.N., of Cuddenbeak, Cornw. by Anne, da. of Lawrence Williams of Ireland; bro. of Richard Eliot (q.v.). *educ.* Exeter, Oxf. 9 Mar. 1703, aged 18. *m.* (1) Susan (bur. 4 Jan. 1714), da. of Sir William Coryton, 3rd Bt., M.P., of Newton Ferrers, Cornw., sis. of Sir John Coryton, 4th Bt. (q.v.), 1s. 1da.; (2) Apr. 1718, Elizabeth, da. and coh. of James Craggs, postmaster-gen., sis. and coh. of James Craggs (q.v.). *suc.* cos. Daniel Eliot, M.P., at Port Eliot 1702.

Receiver gen. of duchy of Cornwall Mar. 1715–20; commr. of victualling 1718–20, of excise June 1720–Apr. 1722.

Descended from the great Sir John Eliot, Eliot succeeded a cousin to an estate carrying control of two seats at St. Germans, which he represented as a Tory under Queen Anne. In 1715 he did not stand but brought in government supporters for St. Germans, in return for which he was appointed receiver-general of the duchy of Cornwall.[1] Marrying the sister of James Craggs (q.v.), he was returned in 1718 for Lostwithiel by the Government, with whom he voted on the repeal of the Occasional Conformity and Schism Acts and the peerage bill in 1719. He vacated his seat a year later on being appointed to a place, which he resigned in 1722 in favour of his brother Richard (q.v.) in order to be chosen for Liskeard, where he had established a controlling interest. He died five months later, 18 Sept. 1722.

[1] W. Moyle to Humphry Morice, 26 Mar. 1715, Morice mss at Bank of England.

E.C.

ELIOT, Edward (1727–1804), of Port Eliot, nr. St. Germans, Cornw.

ST. GERMANS	12 Dec.	1748–1768
LISKEARD		1768–1774
ST. GERMANS		1774–Nov. 1775
CORNWALL	15 Nov.	1775–13 Jan. 1784

b. 8 July 1727, 1st s. of Richard Eliot (q.v.). *educ.* Liskeard sch.; St. Mary Hall, Oxf. 1742; Grand Tour 1746–8. *m.* 25 Sept. 1756, Catherine, da. and h. of Edward Elliston of Gestingthorpe, Essex, capt. E.I. Co., 4s. *suc.* fa. 1748; *cr.* Baron Eliot 13 Jan. 1784.

Receiver gen. of duchy of Cornwall 1749–*d.*; ld. of Trade 1759–76.

On Richard Eliot's death his seat at St. Germans was filled by his son Edward, aged 21, who was also appointed to his father's place in the duchy of Cornwall by Frederick, Prince of Wales. After the Prince's death, Edward Eliot joined the Pelhams, under the aegis of his uncle by marriage, Robert Nugent (q.v.), with whom he voted against the clandestine marriages bill in June 1753.[1]

He died 17 Feb. 1804.

[1] C. Amyand to Newcastle, 4 June 1753, Add. 32732, f. 22.

E.C.

ELIOT, Richard (1694–1748), of St. Giles-in-the-Fields, Mdx.[1]

ST. GERMANS	29 Jan.	1733–1734
LISKEARD		1734–1747
ST. GERMANS		1747–19 Nov. 1748

bap. 28 Oct. 1694, 2nd s. of William Eliot, R.N., and bro. of Edward Eliot (q.v.). *educ.* Balliol, Oxf. 1712. *m.* 10 Mar. 1726, Harriot, illegit. da. of James Craggs (q.v.), 3s. 6da. *suc.* nephew James Eliot at Port Eliot 1742.

Sec. to Lord Carteret in Sweden Mar. 1719–20; commr. of excise 1722–May 1729; surveyor gen. of duchy of Cornwall Jan. 1730–8; receiver gen. of duchy Mar. 1738–*d.*; mayor, Liskeard 1741–2, 1746–7.

Eliot was appointed secretary of embassy to Carteret in Sweden in 1719, receiving £200 p.a. with no extraordinaries as he was to live with the ambassador.[2] After his brother's death in 1722 he managed the estates and parliamentary interest of his young nephew, whom he eventually succeeded. From 1733 he represented his family's boroughs, voting with the Administration on the excise bill in 1733 and the repeal of the Septennial Act in 1734. In 1738 he went into opposition with the Prince of Wales, under whom he held a duchy of Cornwall office, voting against the Spanish convention in 1739, for the place bill in 1740, but withdrawing on the motion to dismiss Walpole in February 1741. At the general election of 1741, he returned for St. Germans the son of Sir John Hynde Cotton (q.v.), the Tory leader, who wrote on 19 May thanking him 'for the great pains you and some others of your countrymen have taken to save a sinking constitution'. In the new Parliament he continued to act with the Prince of Wales's party, voting against the Administration on the chairman of the elections committee in December 1741, but going over to them after Walpole's fall till 1747, when he reverted to opposition with the Prince. He died 19 Nov. 1748 in financial difficulties caused, as his wife wrote on 29 Nov., by his duchy office, which had cost him '£7,000 since he has lived in the family [i.e. the Prince of Wales's household], the source of all our present woes, yea even of his death I do believe.'[3]

[1] PCC 261 Price. [2] SP Dom. 36/5, ff. 214–15. [3] Eliot mss at Port Eliot.

E.C.

ELIOTT, Sir Gilbert, 3rd Bt. (c.1680–1764), of Stobs, Roxburgh.

ROXBURGHSHIRE 1708–1715, 6 July 1726–1727

b. c.1680, 1st s. of Sir William Eliott, 2nd Bt., M.P. [S], of Stobs by his 2nd w. Margaret, da. of Charles Murray of Hadden, Roxburgh. *m.* 23 Apr. 1702, Eleanora, da. of William Elliot of Wells, Roxburgh, lace-maker of London, 10s. (inc. George, Lord Heathfield) 1da. *suc.* fa. 19 Feb. 1699.

Eliott, whose father, grandfather and great-grandfather had all represented Roxburghshire before the Union, sat for the county as a Whig in the British Parliament under Queen Anne. He did not stand in 1715 or 1722 but was again returned in July 1726 at a contested by-election caused by the elevation of his kinsman, Sir Gilbert Elliot (q.v.) of Minto, to the bench. A month later he quarrelled with Colonel Stewart of Stewartfield after dinner at an inn in Jedburgh, ran him through the stomach with fatal results, made his escape to Holland, and was outlawed at a meeting of local magistrates. His relations did all they could for him, obtaining the active help of Lord Ilay, who on 27 Aug. 1727 reported to Minto, 'I have very good hopes the King will pardon him'.[1] When this came about, Eliott returned to his estates, where he died, 27 May 1764.

[1] G. Tancred, *Rulewater and its People*, 26–27; *Annals of a Border Club*, 4–5; G. F. S. Elliot, *Border Elliots*, 310.

R.S.L.

ELLIOT, Sir Gilbert, 2nd Bt. (c.1693–1766), of Minto, Roxburgh.

ROXBURGHSHIRE 1722–June 1726

b. c.1693, 1st s. of Sir Gilbert Elliot, 1st Bt., M.P. [S], of Minto and Headshaw, Roxburgh, Lord Minto, S.C.J., by his 2nd w. Jean, da. of Sir Andrew Carre of Cavers, Roxburgh. *educ.* Utrecht 1712; adv. 1715. *m.* (contract 4 Aug. 1718) Helen, da. of Sir Robert Stewart, 1st Bt., M.P. [S], of Allanbank, Berwick, 5s. 8da. *suc.* fa. 1 May 1718. Ld. of session (Lord Minto) 1726–*d.*, ld. of justiciary 1733–*d.*, ld. justice clerk 1763–*d.*

Elliot's family was a junior branch to that of Stobs. Like his father, who owed his professional success to his ties with the house of Argyll,[1] he was closely associated with the Duke of Argyll and his brother, Lord Ilay, whose assistance he invoked in the case of his unfortunate namesake of Stobs (q.v.). Returned for his shire in 1722, he vacated the seat on elevation to the bench in 1726 but continued to take an active part on the Argyll side in local politics. Soon after the general election of 1747, Ilay, now Duke of Argyll, wrote to Newcastle about the bestowal of a government post 'at the desire of Lord Minto [Sir Gilbert Elliot] who

supported the court interest against Mr. [Lawrence] Dundas, the commissary, and Mr. [John] Murray of Philiphaugh [qq.v.]'.[2] Elliot's promotion to lord justice clerk in 1763 was owing to the good offices of his more famous son Gilbert (q.v.). 'Better acquainted with the belles lettres than with the quiddities of the feudal or municipal law',[3] he died 16 Apr. 1766.

[1] G. F. S. Elliot, *Border Elliots*, 314. [2] Add. 32712, f. 45. [3] Ramsay of Ochtertyre, *Scotland and Scotsmen in 18th Cent.* i. 81–82.

J.M.S.

ELLIOT, Gilbert (1722–77), of Minto, Roxburgh.

SELKIRKSHIRE 13 Dec. 1753–May 1765
ROXBURGHSHIRE 20 June 1765–11 Jan. 1777

b. Sept. 1722, 1st s. of Sir Gilbert Elliot (q.v.), 2nd Bt., of Minto, Lord Minto, S.C.J.; bro. of Adm. John Elliot, M.P. *educ.* Dalkeith 1732; Edin. Univ. 1735; Leyden; adv. 1743; Grand Tour (Holland, Germany) 1744–5. *m.* 15 Dec. 1746, Agnes, da. and h. of Hugh Dalrymple Murray Kynynmound of Melgund, Forfar, and Lochgelly and Kynynmound, Fife, 5s. 2da. *suc.* fa. as 3rd Bt. 16 Apr. 1766. Sheriff-depute, Roxburghshire 1748–53; ld. of Admiralty 1756–Apr. 1757, June 1757–1761; ld. of Treasury 1761–2; treasurer of the chamber 1762–70; P.C. 14 July 1762; keeper of the signet [S] 1766–*d.*; treasurer of the navy 1770–*d.*

Gilbert Elliot, a lawyer like his father and grandfather, came to the fore as one of the procurators for his uncle Archibald Stewart (q.v.), who was tried and acquitted in 1747 for neglect of duty, when lord provost of Edinburgh, during the Forty-five. His father's patron, the Duke of Argyll, found him a seat in Selkirkshire at a by-election in December 1753. He died 11 Jan. 1777.

E.H.-G.

ELLIOT, William (c.1704–1764), of Wells, Roxburgh.

CALNE 1741–1754

b. c.1704, 1st s. of William Elliot of Wells, Roxburgh, lace merchant of London, by his w. Eleanor. *m.* 4 June 1737, Lady Frances d'Auverquerque, 1st da. and coh. of Henry, Earl of Grantham, 1s. *d.v.p. suc.* fa. 1728. Cornet R. Horse Gds. 1722; capt. 10 Drags. 1723; maj. 2nd tp. Horse Gren. Gds. 1737, lt.-col. 1741; equerry to George II 1743–60.

William Elliot's father came from Scotland to London as a young man, made a fortune there in trade, and bought an estate in Scotland.[1] The son, mentioned by the 1st Lord Egmont as 'by family a gentleman, though son to a laceman',[2] became a professional soldier in one of the best regiments and married rank. In 1741 he succeeded his commanding officer William Duckett (q.v.) both in the regiment and as Member for Calne, soon afterwards obtaining a place at court and retiring from the army. Supporting the Administration in all recorded divisions, he described himself to Newcastle in 1751, in connexion with an application for the place of surveyor, as 'a hearty and steadfast well wisher to [your] Grace and family',[3] but he did not stand again. He died 7 June 1764.

[1] W. Elliot, *Elliots of Brugh and Wells*, 62, 64–66; G. Tancred, *Rulewater and its People*, 202–4. [2] *HMC Egmont Diary*, ii. 414. [3] 29 Apr. 1751, Add. 32724, f. 268.

R.S.L.

ELLIS, Welbore (1713–1802), of Tylney Hall, Hants.

CRICKLADE	24 Dec. 1741–1747
WEYMOUTH AND MELCOMBE REGIS	1747–1761
AYLESBURY	1761–1768
PETERSFIELD	1768–1774
WEYMOUTH AND MELCOMBE REGIS	1774–1790
PETERSFIELD	29 Apr. 1791–13 Aug. 1794

b. 15 Dec. 1713, o. surv. s. of Rt. Rev. Welbore Ellis, bp. of Kildare and (1731) Meath, by Diana, da. of Sir John Briscoe of Boughton, Northants. and Amberley, Suss. *educ.* Westminster 1727–32; Ch. Ch. Oxf. 1732. *m.* (1) 18 Nov. 1747, Elizabeth (*d.* 1 Aug. 1761), da. and h. of Sir William Stanhope (q.v.), *s.p.*; (2) 20 July 1765, Anne, da. of George Stanley of Paultons, Hants, sis. and coh. of Hans Stanley (q.v.), *s.p. suc.* fa. 1734; *cr.* Baron Mendip 13 Aug. 1794.
Ld. of Admiralty 1747–55; jt. vice-treasurer [I] 1755–62; P.C. 20 Mar. 1760; sec. at war 1762–5; jt. vice-treasurer [I] 1770–7; treasurer of the navy 1777–82; sec. of state for America Feb.-Mar. 1782.

In 1738 Welbore Ellis, aged 24, inherited a great fortune from his uncle, John Ellis, M.P., under-secretary of state to William III and Anne, who had acquired by Act of Parliament the forfeited Irish estates of his own brother, Sir William Ellis, secretary of state to James II in exile.[1] Entering Parliament for the venal borough of Cricklade after a double return in 1741, he was included, May 1742, in Pelham's list for a proposed public accounts commission, to which he was not elected.[2] In the Cockpit list of ministerial supporters, October 1742, he is put down as receiving the whip through his friend Henry Fox. Voting regularly with the Government, he spoke against an opposition motion for discontinuing the Hanoverian troops in British pay, 6 Dec. 1743, seconded the Address at the opening of the sessions of 1744 and 1745, supported the Hanoverians, 11 Apr. 1746, and spoke second for the Administration on the heritable jurisdictions bill, 14 Apr. 1747.[3] He was returned for

Weymouth and Melcombe Regis on Pelham's recommendation in 1747, when the Duke of Bedford, then first lord of the Admiralty, agreed to his succeeding George Grenville at that board.[4] He held office for over 30 years, a record rivalling that of his colleague, the 2nd Lord Barrington (q.v.), to whom Horace Walpole compares him:

> They were shades of the same character; the former [Barrington] a little brighter by better parts, the other a little more amiable by less interestedness.[5]

He died 2 Feb. 1802.

[1] PCC 173 Brodrepp; *HMC Egmont Diary*, iii. 350. [2] Horace Walpole to Mann, 26 May 1742. [3] Add. 35876, f. 250. [4] Hartington to Devonshire, 16 June 1747, Devonshire mss. [5] *Mems. Geo. II*, ii. 141–2.

R.R.S.

ELLISON, Cuthbert (1698–1785), of Hebburn, co. Dur.

SHAFTESBURY 1747–1754

b. 10 May 1698, 1st s. of Robert Ellison of Hebburn by Elizabeth, o. da. of Sir Henry Liddell, 3rd Bt., M.P., of Ravensworth Castle, co. Dur. *unm. suc.* fa. 1726.
Capt. 8 Drags. 1723, maj. 1731; lt.-col. 23 Ft. 1739–43; lt.-col. Drags. 1743–5; adjutant-gen. to Earl of Stair in England 1744; col. 1745; maj.-gen. 1755; lt.-gen. 1759; gen. 1772.

Ellison came from an old family of Newcastle-upon-Tyne merchants who acquired Hebburn, across the river, about 1650.[1] His great-grandfather Robert Ellison represented Newcastle in the Long Parliament and in 1660. A professional soldier, he saw service abroad from 1741 to 1744 and was present at Dettingen in 1743. He was also on the Duke of Cumberland's staff during the advance against Prince Charles Edward at Derby. After selling his regimental commission for £3,500 in 1745, he was nominated by Pelham and returned for Shaftesbury in 1747 on Lord Ilchester's interest. Shortly before the election he wrote:

> As I am supported by Lord Ilchester's interest and have the returning officer, most of the magistrates and better sort of the people by that means in my favour, I may hope for success, but my election will be dubious, troublesome and very expensive.

These expenses amounted to £2,700, of which Ellison spent £1,500 or £2,000 of his own and Pelham provided the rest.[2] He did not stand again. When he died, 11 Oct. 1785, he was the second senior general in the army.

[1] Surtees, *Durham*, ii. 76, 78–79. [2] E. Hughes, *N. Country Life in 18th Cent.*, 85–88, 282–3, citing Ellison mss in the Pub. Lib., Shipcote, Gateshead; Ilchester to Henry Fox, 7 Oct. 1747, Fox mss; Matthew Merefield to Pelham, 5 Apr. 1753, Newcastle (Clumber) mss.

R.S.L.

ELLYS, Richard (c.1674–1742), of Nocton, Lincs.

GRANTHAM   1701–1705
BOSTON   7 Dec. 1719–1734

> *b.* c.1674, 1st surv. s. of Sir William Ellys, 2nd Bt., M.P., of Wyham and Nocton, Lincs. by Isabella, da. of Richard Hampden, M.P., of Great Hampden, Bucks. *m.* (1) lic. 21 May 1714, Elizabeth (*d.*11 Aug. 1724), da. and coh. of Sir Thomas Hussey, 2nd Bt., M.P., of Honington and Doddington, Lincs., *s.p.*; (2) Sarah, da. and coh. of Thomas Gould of Iver, Bucks., *s.p. suc.* fa. as 3rd Bt. 6 Oct. 1727.

Ellys was descended on his mother's side from John Hampden, whose great-grandson, Richard (q.v.), married his sister. After sitting with his father for Grantham, he was returned as a Whig for Boston in 1719, defeating a Tory candidate. In 1727 he succeeded to the manors of Wyham, which had been in the family since the early 17th century, and Nocton, left to his father by Sir William Ellys, a judge of the common pleas under Charles II. Thereafter he voted against the Government till he retired in 1734. He had some pretensions to learning as the owner of a very expensive library, and as the author of *Fortuita Sacra*, published in 1727.[1] He died 14 Feb. 1742, leaving his estates worth £4,000 p.a. to his wife for life and thereafter to a son of John, Lord Hobart (q.v.), his cousin.[2]

[1] Hanbury Williams, *Works*, i. 47; Nichols, *Lit. Anecs.* vi. 83.
[2] PCC 50 Trenley.

P.W.

ELTON, Sir Abraham, 1st Bt. (1654–1728), of Clevedon Court and Whitestaunton, Som.

BRISTOL   1722–1727

> *bap.* 3 July 1654, 1st s. of Isaac Elton of St. Philip's and St. Jacob's, Barton Regis, Bristol by his w. Elizabeth. *m.* 11 Sept. 1676, Mary, da. of Robert Jefferies of Pile Green, Glos., 3s. 1da. *suc.* fa. 1695; *cr.* Bt. 31 Oct. 1717.
> Alderman, Bristol 1699, sheriff 1702–3, mayor 1710–11; treasurer, Merchant Venturers 1705–8, master 1708–9.

A Dissenter of humble origin, the son of a market-gardener,[1] Elton became one of the greatest commercial magnates of Bristol, 'a pioneer of its brass foundries and iron foundries, and . . . owner of its principal weaving industry, as well as of its glass and pottery works, besides largely contributing to the shipping of the port.'[2] Buying Clevedon Court in 1709 and Whitestaunton in 1714, he was created a baronet in 1717 in reward for his services in the rebellion of 1715. He sat as a Whig for his native city from 1722 to 1727, when he stood down

in favour of his son. He died 9 Feb. 1728, leaving a fortune estimated at £100,000.[3]

[1] J. Latimer, *Annals of Bristol in 18th cent.*, 162. [2] *GEC Baronetage*, v. 41. [3] Latimer, loc. cit.

S.R.M.

ELTON, Abraham (1679–1742), of Bristol and Clevedon Court, Som.

TAUNTON   18 Jan. 1724–1727
BRISTOL   1727–20 Oct. 1742

> *bap.* 30 June 1679, 1st s. of Sir Abraham Elton, 1st Bt. (q.v.). *m.* 14 May 702, Abigail, da. of Zachary Bayly of Charlcot House, nr. Westbury, Wilts. and Northwood Park, nr. Glastonbury, Som., 3s. 3da. *suc.* fa. as 2nd Bt. 9 Feb. 1728.
> Sheriff, Bristol 1710–11, mayor 1719–20, alderman 1723; master, Merchant Adventurers 1719–20.

A merchant and industrialist, Elton is said to have withdrawn to France in 1720 owing to his South Sea losses.[1] Four years later he was returned for Taunton on the Whig interest, standing unexpectedly two days before the poll.[2] At the next general election he succeeded his father at Bristol, paying the Tory candidate £1,000 to give up.[3] In the new Parliament he became a member of the gaols committee, and spoke in February 1730 against the African Company's petition to be relieved of the cost of maintaining their forts. He presented a petition from the city of Bristol, 27 Feb. 1730, to take off the duty on soap and candles which was rejected; and another from the Bristol merchants in February 1731, complaining of Spanish depredations, which led to an address for papers. During that year he spoke three times against the removal of the duties on the importation of Irish yarn, repeating his objections in 1734 and again in 1739. On the first reading of the excise bill in 1733 he

> made a bantering speech against the bill, proving out of the profits and revelations that merchants were the best and most honourable subjects, and the excise a wicked thing.

When constables were sent for by the magistrates to control the anti-excise mob outside the House, he and Sir John Hynde Cotton (q.v.)

> went out, and seeing that number of constables, asked, 'what is the meaning of all these constables? Did Sir Robert Walpole send you?' Which [it was observed] could not fail to spirit up this mob.[4]

Both in this and the next Parliament he voted with the Opposition in all recorded divisions; but in his last Parliament, after abstaining from the division on the chairman of the elections committee in December 1741, he was reported to be voting with the Government.[5] He died during the recess,

20 Oct. 1742, leaving the pottery, copper and glass works within the family.[6]

[1] J. Latimer, *Annals of Bristol in 18th cent.* 127. [2] Thos. Brodrick to Ld. Midleton, 25 Jan. 1724, Midleton mss. [3] Jas. Pearce to Humphry Morice, 9 Sept. 1727, Morice mss. [4] *HMC Egmont Diary*, i. 51, 55, 131, 150, 183, 186, 349-50, 361; ii. 27; iii. 36; *Knatchbull Diary*. [5] Hartington to Devonshire, 22 Dec. 1741, Devonshire mss. [6] PCC 195 Boycott.

S.R.M.

ELWES, Sir Hervey, 2nd Bt. (c.1683–1763), of Stoke, Suff.

SUDBURY   16 Dec. 1706–1710, 1713–1722

b. c.1683, s. of Gervase Elwes, M.P. Sudbury 1679–81, by Isabella, da. of Sir Thomas Hervey, M.P., of Ickworth, Suff. and sis. of John Hervey, M.P., 1st Earl of Bristol. *educ.* Queens', Camb. 1702. *unm. suc.* gd.-fa. as 2nd Bt. May 1706.

Elwes inherited estates so heavily encumbered that his uncle, Lord Bristol, advised him either to sell them or marry a rich wife. In 1715 Lord Bristol opened negotiations on his nephew's behalf for a lady with a portion of £10,000, which, he explained, was 'absolutely necessary to discharge the encumbrances left upon his estate by his grandfather',[1] but the scheme fell through. In the meantime Elwes had succeeded to the family seat at the neighbouring borough of Sudbury, which his father and grandfather had represented in most Parliaments for nearly thirty years. Though classed as a government supporter, all his recorded votes after George I's accession were against the Administration, except on the repeal of the Occasional Conformity and Schism Acts, on which he did not vote. He withdrew from politics in 1722, devoting the rest of his long life to restoring his fortune by practising an economy so drastic that his life has been described as 'perhaps the most perfect picture of human penury that ever existed'. He died 18 Sept. 1763, aged about 80, leaving at least a quarter of a million[2] to his nephew, John Elwes, M.P., who modelled his way of life on his uncle's.

[1] *Letter Bks. of John Hervey, 1st Earl of Bristol*, i. 304; ii. 10. [2] E. Topham, *Life of the late John Elwes* (1790), 6, 28.

R.R.S.

ELWILL, Sir John, 4th Bt. (*d*.1778), of Englefield Green, Surr.

GUILDFORD   1747–1768

o.s. of Sir Edmund Elwill, 3rd Bt., of Exeter, comptroller of the excise, by Anne, da. of William Speke of Beauchamp, Som. *educ.* Eton. *m.* 30 Nov. 1755, Selina, da. of Peter Bathurst (q.v.) of Clarendon Park, Wilts., wid. of Arthur Cole, 1st Baron Ranelagh [I], 1da. *suc.* fa. 2 Feb. 1740. His sis. Mary m. 16 May 1741, Richard Onslow (q.v.), 3rd Baron Onslow.

Elwill was returned by his brother-in-law, Lord Onslow, classed as a government supporter. In the 2nd Lord Egmont's electoral survey, c.1749–50, he is described as a possible supporter of Frederick's future government.

He died 1 Mar. 1778.

R.R.S.

ENGLAND, George (1679–1725), of Stokesby and Yarmouth, Norf.

GREAT YARMOUTH   1710–1722

b. Dec. 1679, s. of Thomas England of Yarmouth, merchant, by Ann, da. of Thomas Bulwer of Buxton, Norf. *educ.* Yarmouth; Caius, Camb. 1694; G. Inn 1696. *m.* bef. 1707, Alice, da. of John Jermy of Bayfield, Norf., 4s. 1da. *suc.* fa. 1693.
Mayor, Great Yarmouth 1715–16.

George England was the grandson of a leading citizen of Yarmouth, Sir George England, who was knighted by Charles II in 1671. One of his uncles, George, was M.P. Yarmouth, 1679–81 and 1689–1701; another, Benjamin, 1702–5. In 1710 he was returned unopposed as a Tory for the borough, succeeding in 1711 to the fortune of his uncle Benjamin, who had inherited that of his uncle George. Re-elected without a contest at both the next two general elections, after 1715 he voted consistently against the Government. In 1722 he was overwhelmed by the combined Townshend-Walpole influence, coming out bottom of the poll. By that time he was so hopelessly in debt that after his death, 12 June 1725, his estates were sold by an order of the court of Chancery, and his descendants sank into obscurity.

R.R.S.

ERLE, Thomas (?1650–1720), of Charborough, nr. Wareham, Dorset.

WAREHAM   1679–1681, 1685–1687, 1689–1698
PORTSMOUTH   1698–1701
WAREHAM   1701–Mar. 1718

b. ?1650, 2nd s. of Thomas Erle, M.P. (*d.v.p.* 1650), of Charborough by Susanna, da. of William Fiennes, 1st Visct. Saye and Sele. *educ.* Trinity, Oxf. 12 July 1667, aged 17; M. Temple 1669. *m.* 1675, Elizabeth, da. of Sir William Wyndham, 1st Bt., M.P., of Orchard Wyndham, Som., 1da. *suc.* e.bro. Walter bef. 1665 and gd.-fa. Sir Walter Erle, M.P., at Charborough 1665.
M.P. [I] 1703–13.
Sheriff, Wilts. 1679–80; capt. Dorset militia by 1679, maj. by 1688; col. new regt. of Ft. 1689–98, 19 Ft. 1691–1709; brig.-gen. 1693; gov. Portsmouth 1694–1712, 1714–18; maj.-gen. 1696; P.C. [I] 1701; c.-in-c. [I] 1701–5; one of the lds. justices [I] 1702–3, Mar.-Nov. 1704; lt.-gen. 1703; col. of Drags. [I] 1704–5; lt.-gen. of the Ordnance 1705–12, 1714–18; P.C. 3 May 1705; gen. of Ft. 1711.

Thomas Erle came from a Devonshire family, who acquired Charborough by marriage in the 16th century. His grandfather, Sir Walter Erle, was M.P. for Poole, Dorset, Lyme Regis, and, in the Long Parliament, Weymouth and Melcombe Regis; his father also sat in the Long Parliament for Wareham. Succeeding to his estates as a boy, Erle consolidated his interest at Wareham by buying the manor in 1697.[1] Though he did not become a professional soldier until the Revolution, when he was nearly 40, he played a distinguished part in all King William's campaigns both in Ireland and the Low Countries. After further service in Ireland as commander-in-chief there, he fought under the Earl of Galway at the battle of Almanza, in Spain, in 1707; and was in command of the projected descent on the French coast which was diverted to Ostend in 1708. Between 1679 and 1718 he sat in sixteen successive Parliaments, fourteen times for Wareham on his own interest and twice for Portsmouth, where he held an office, on the government interest. He was also returned for both boroughs in February and November 1701, 1702 and 1708. After the Hanoverian succession he regained his two military posts, of which the Tories had deprived him in 1712. He voted for the septennial bill in 1716 but next year took part in the attack on Lord Cadogan (q.v.), moving for papers relating to the Dutch troops and voting against the Government in the ensuing division, 4 June 1717. In December he supported Walpole in urging a reduction of the army from 16,000 to 12,000 men. Superseded by Cadogan as general of foot, he was forced to resign all his posts in March 1718 in return for a pension of £1,200 a year,[2] thereby vacating his seat. He died 23 July 1720.

[1] Hutchins, *Dorset*, i. 82; iii. 502. [2] Draft letter from Erle to the King, undated [1718], Erle-Drax mss at Churchill Coll., Cambridge; *Cal. Treas. Bks.* xxxii. 246.

R.S.L.

ERNLE, Sir Edward, 3rd Bt. (c.1673–1729), of Brimslade Park, nr. Marlborough; Etchilhampton, nr. Devizes, Wilts., and Charborough, nr. Wareham, Dorset.

DEVIZES		1695–1698
WILTSHIRE		1698–1700
WAREHAM		5 Mar.–11 Nov. 1701
HEYTESBURY		1701–1702
WAREHAM	22 Feb.	1704–1705
MARLBOROUGH	10 Dec.	1708–1710
WAREHAM	13 Dec.	1710–1713
PORTSMOUTH		1715–1722
WAREHAM		1722–31 Jan. 1729

b. c.1673, 2nd s. of Edward Ernle of Etchilhampton (who *d.v.p.*, s. and h. ap. of Sir Walter Ernle, 1st Bt., M.P.), by Anne, da. of Edward Ashe, M.P., of Heytesbury, Wilts. *m.* Frances, da. and h. of Gen. Thomas Erle (q.v.) of Charborough, 2da. *suc.* bro. as 3rd Bt. 1690.

Sir Edward Ernle came of a Wiltshire family seated near Devizes since the early part of the sixteenth century.[1] His grandfather was M.P. for that borough in 1679 and 1681. After sitting as a Whig in seven Parliaments under William III and Anne, he again offered opposition to the Tories in Wiltshire before the 1715 Parliament,[2] but did not go to a poll. Instead he was returned for the government borough of Portsmouth through the influence of the governor, his father-in-law, General Erle. In that Parliament he voted for the septennial bill in 1716, but went into opposition with Walpole the following year, voting against the repeal of the Occasional Conformity and Schism Acts and the peerage bill in 1719. On General Erle's death in 1720, he succeeded to his electoral interest at Wareham and was himself returned there for the fourth time in 1722 and again in 1727. He died 31 Jan. 1729.

[1] *Wilts. Arch. Mag.* xi. 192. [2] *HMC 15th Rep. VII*, 219.

R.S.L.

ERSKINE, Charles (1716–49).

AYR BURGHS 1747–25 June 1749

b. 21 Oct. 1716, 1st s. of Charles Areskine (q.v.). *educ.* Corpus Christi, Camb. 1733; M. Temple 1733, called 1739; L. Inn 1743. *unm.*

Returned by the Duke of Argyll for Ayr Burghs in 1747, Erskine, 'a most rising youth',[1] died 25 June 1749.

[1] *HMC Laing*, ii. 305.

R.R.S.

ERSKINE, Sir Henry, 5th Bt. (1710–65), of Alva, Clackmannan.

| AYR BURGHS | 29 Dec. 1749–1754 |
| ANSTRUTHER BURGHS | 1754–9 Aug. 1765 |

bap. 23 Dec. 1710, 2nd s. of Sir John Erskine, 3rd Bt., M.P., by Catherine, da. of Henry St. Clair, 10th Lord Sinclair [S]. *educ.* ?Eton 1725; L. Inn 1728. *m.* 16 May 1761, Janet, da. of Peter Wedderburn, Lord Chesterhall, S.C.J., sis. of Alexander Wedderburn, M.P., afterwards Lord Loughborough and Earl of Rosslyn, 2s. 1da. *suc.* bro. Charles 2 July 1747.

Ensign 22 Ft. 1735, lt. 1736; capt. 1 Ft. 1743; lt.-col. army 1746; dismissed Jan. 1756; re-instated and promoted maj.-gen. Nov. 1760, with effect from June 1759; col. 67 Ft. 1760–1, 25 Ft. 1761–2, 1 Ft. 1762–*d.*; lt.-gen. 1765.

Surveyor of the King's private roads 1757–60; sec. of the Order of the Thistle Apr. 1765–*d.*

Erskine's father, related to the Earl of Mar, was a Jacobite leader in the Fifteen, but received a full pardon in return for surrendering to the Treasury his silver mine near Alva.[1] Having subsequently dissipated his fortune in extravagant mining projects, he was employed as manager of the Scottish Mining Company, selling his estate to his brother, Charles Areskine (q.v.).

Erskine was intended for the English bar, but in 1735 joined the 22nd Foot commanded by his uncle James St. Clair (q.v.). In 1742, while stationed in Minorca, he fell foul of the lieutenant governor, General Philip Anstruther (q.v.), who, having been attacked by the Opposition for neglect of duty, arrested Erskine on suspicion of conspiring against him. Acquitted by court martial, Erskine transferred to the 1st Foot, now commanded by St. Clair, serving at L'Orient and Lauffeld, where his brother was killed.

In 1747 Erskine was supported by James Oswald (q.v.) and St. Clair as candidate for Dysart Burghs, but St. Clair, having lost Sutherland, required the seat for himself.[2] After accompanying St. Clair as aide-de-camp on his mission to Vienna and Turin in 1748, Erskine was returned for Ayr Burghs on the Argyll-Bute interest, in succession to his first cousin, Charles Erskine, in December 1749. Attaching himself to Leicester House, he soon acquired considerable reputation as an opposition speaker.

> This man [writes Horace Walpole], with a face as sanguine as the disposition of the commander in chief, had a gentle plausibility in his manner, that was not entirely surprising in a Scotchman, and an inclination to poetry, which he had cultivated with little success either in his odes, or from the patrons to whom they were dedicated; one had been addressed to the Duke, and another to an old gentlewoman at Hanover, mother of my Lady Yarmouth. Of late he had turned his talent to rhetoric and studied public speaking . . . at the Oratorical club in Essex street, from whence he brought so fluent, so theatrical, so specious, so declamatory a style and manner as might have transported an age and audience not accustomed to the real eloquence and graces of Mr. Pitt.

He joined on 20 Feb. 1751 in Egmont's attack on the mutiny bill, 'complaining of the exorbitant power of general officers on courts martial, instanced in his own case' by Anstruther's treatment of him in 1742. This led to a protracted dispute which further envenomed his relations with Anstruther.

After the death of the Prince of Wales, 20 Mar. 1751, Erskine supported the Administration, voted in December for the mutiny bill, spoke on 22 Jan. 1752 in favour of the Saxon treaty, and on 29 Jan. against the motion condemning subsidy treaties

in time of peace. When Egmont, in the debate on the mutiny bill, 9 Feb. 1753, again raised the question of courts martial, 'Sir Henry Erskine, the old companion of his chivalry, was now the first to oppose him'.[3] In 1754 he ousted his enemy, Anstruther, from Anstruther Burghs, which he represented till his death, 9 Aug. 1765.

[1] *Sc. Hist. Soc. Misc.* ii. 414–17; HMC Stuart, ii. 496–500 et passim; iii. 135, 369; v. 350; HMC 8th Rep. pt. 1, pp. 84–85. [2] Argyll to Pelham, 30 July 1747, Newcastle (Clumber) mss; Lady Morton to Ld. Morton, 13 Aug. 1747, Morton mss; *Letters of David Hume*, ed. Greig, i. 102. [3] Walpole, *Mems. Geo. II*, i. 41, 220, 243, 254, 295.

E.H.-G.

ERSKINE, James (1671–aft. 1745).

ABERDEEN BURGHS 21 Feb.–22 July 1715

b. 1671, 2nd but 1st surv. s. of David Erskine, M.P. [S], of Dun, Forfar by Margaret, da. of Sir James Lumsden of Innergellie, Fife, wid. of Thomas Ramsay of Bamff, Perth. *unm.*
Ensign 1 Ft. 1694, lt. 1701, capt. 1707-aft. 1715.

Erskine, whose father represented Forfarshire before the Union, was disinherited in favour of his younger brother, the judge, Lord Dun. After serving under Marlborough in the war of the Spanish succession, he was returned, after a contest, for Aberdeen Burghs in 1715, described as a Tory who might often vote Whig. When his defeated opponent, John Middleton (q.v.), petitioned, Erskine wrote to Lord Dun, 27 Mar. 1715:

> I hope, brother, that you'll make such answer to his (Middleton's) objections that he'll be ashamed of them. The Duke of Argyll stands his great friend. I'll endeavour all I can to counter-balance his interest, for which reason I've drawn upon you for thirty pound, yet I assure you much contrary to my inclination, for upon my word I have it not of my own. You know those things cannot be done without money. I hope to manage so that you shall have no reason to think me extravagant . . . I think to get some interest made with the Duke of Montrose and Lord Rothes. It is thought the petition will be brought before the bar of the House of Commons where little justice is to be expected but only interest determines, for though you're not named in the petition you will be brought in for bribery.

He was unseated, after which nothing more is known of him except that he took an active part at the age of 74 in the Forty-five.[1]

[1] V. Jacob, *Lairds of Dun*, 235–6, 249–55.

J.M.S.

ERSKINE, Hon. James (c.1678–1754), of Prestongrange, nr. Prestonpans, East Lothian.

CLACKMANNANSHIRE   1734–1741
STIRLING BURGHS   1741–1747

b. c.1678, 2nd s. of Charles Erskine, 5th Earl of Mar [S], by Lady Mary Maule, da. of George, 2nd Earl of Panmure [S]. *educ.* Utrecht c.1700; adv. 1705. *m.* Rachel, da. of John Chiesly of Dalry (executed 1689 for murdering President George Lockhart), 4s.

Principal keeper of the signet [S] 1705–7; ld. of session (Lord Grange) 1707–34; lord justice clerk 1710–14; sec. for Scotland to Prince of Wales Apr. 1738–45.

Provost of Stirling 1737–*d.*

'A good lawyer, a ready and forcible speaker',[1] Erskine was a strict Presbyterian and a prominent member of the General Assembly, with an interest in demonology and the reputation of being a secret libertine.[2] Dismissed as a Tory from the post of lord justice clerk at George I's accession, he took no part in the Fifteen rebellion headed by his brother, Lord Mar, after whose attainder he devoted himself to recovering his family's forfeited estates and honours. With this object he allied himself with Lord Ilay, Walpole's electoral manager for Scotland, placing at his disposal the Erskine interest in Stirlingshire, Aberdeenshire, and Clackmannan. In return, Ilay secured permission for him to purchase Lord Mar's forfeited estates for the benefit of his nephew, Thomas, Lord Erskine (q.v.), holding out further hopes of a pardon for Mar and the restoration of the family honours.

In 1728 Erskine was asked by his nephew to take steps to prevent Lady Mary Wortley Montagu from acquiring the legal custody of her lunatic sister, Lady Mar, thus depriving the impoverished Lord Mar of the use of her jointure of £1,000 p.a. Erskine responded by kidnapping Lady Mar, with a view to taking her to Scotland, but was intercepted on the way by Lady Mary, with a warrant from the lord chief justice ordering her return. He was more successful with his termagant wife, whom he kidnapped in 1732, keeping her prisoner in the Outer Hebrides till her death in 1745.[3]

By this time Erskine had become dissatisfied with Ilay for failing to fulfil his promises to obtain a pardon for Mar, who died in 1732, and the restoration of the family honours to Lord Erskine. He had also asked Lord Ilay for a pension for himself. Ilay offered to quarter him on his son-in-law's office of knight marshal [S], but he refused to be 'a louse feeding upon my friend'. In 1733 he decided to join forces with Ilay's opponents, the Squadrone, at the forthcoming general election, writing:

As we can make their elections go clear in several places, so can they ours, in spite of all that Ilay and his Jack Middletons [John, q.v.] and Milton [Andrew Fletcher, Lord] can do. And we have engaged to mutual assistance, in every place, and they to me in a particular manner, not only as to elections but other things, if Sir Robert tumbles.

Intending to stand himself as an opposition candidate, he arranged to correspond with Pulteney by messenger as his letters were being opened in the post office. On 10 Dec. 1733 he wrote to Lord Marchmont, the father of Alexander and Hugh Hume Campbell (qq.v.):

I meet with some odd unexpected things in my burghs and I see I must have much greater troubles and difficulties of different kinds than I expected . . . And I daily discover more of the acts and tricks and lies that were used against me in my absence. I know not any other private commoner that has more reason to wish he may be in Parliament against those people than I have, and I see it plainly that I must get in or be exposed many ways to their wrath.

And two days later:

I have begged lord president of the session, Mr. Robert Dundas [q.v.] and other lawyers to consider all the acts, Scots and British, since the Act 1681, concerning elections for shires or towns that a new act may be proposed in order to make the procedure at elections more certain and to prevent tricks of the sheriffs and clerks. Such an act may cut off one of the unjust ways which the courtiers plainly and barefacedly tell they are to use (as it has been expressly told to myself that they would do with Lord Erskine and me in particular) . . . Now that people are setting about the publishing things by the press the terror of prosecutions seizes them since they will be summarily whipt up by magistrates and tried without a jury and condemned and hurried to prison till payment of a fine. I spoke to your Lordship of getting a law made this winter enacting that all crimes, deliquencies and misdemeanours whatsoever should be tried before every competent court in Scotland by a jury as well as they are in England.

He immediately began to prepare materials for such a bill, which was brought in by Dundas in February 1734, when Pulteney wrote to him:

I doubt not but you are apprised of the clause intended to be added to the bill for regulating the elections in North Britain, to render the lords of session incapable of being elected members of Parliament . . . whether it will pass or not is very uncertain, though this favourite clause be added to it by Lord Ilay in honour of you . . . I take it for granted that you despise the maliciousness of this intention, and will render it of no effect by quitting the employment if it shall be necessary.

Resigning his judgeship, he stood unsuccessfully for Stirling Burghs, but was returned for Clackmannanshire. In his first session he was associated with Dundas in preparing a petition to the House of Lords against the methods used by Ilay to secure the election of the government list of representative peers, and in collecting evidence to support an impeachment of Ilay in the Commons, in each case without success. In the Commons he spoke against the army, 14 Feb. 1735, and supported a bill to reduce the number of playhouses, 5 Mar.

In the next session he covered himself with ridicule by 'a long canting speech' attacking a bill for repealing a statute of James I against witchcraft. On 16 May 1737 he spoke in a debate on the Porteous riots, opposing the bill of pains and penalties against Edinburgh, also publishing a pamphlet in defence of the Lord provost. But

> being so much absent from the courts here and at the time of best business breaks my employment . . . I once thought it would have been pretty good as others also thought, but I neither have youth nor ability enough to bear up at the bar under the continued oppression of the grand oppressors and their tools.

He appealed to Pulteney to procure some employment for him either in the city of London or about the Prince of Wales, who made him his secretary for Scotland in 1738. In October 1739 Pulteney asked him to see that all opposition Members from Scotland should be in London for the opening of the session, 'that joint and right measures may be taken'.[4] He supported the motion for the dismissal of Walpole in February 1741.

Meanwhile Erskine had become involved in the negotiations with the Pretender and the French government for a restoration of the Stuarts initiated in 1739 by Lord Lovat. The negotiations were conducted by his intimate friend Macgregor of Balhaldy, who consulted and kept him informed throughout. On 13 Mar. 1740 the Pretender wrote to him, thanking him for his 'zealous and loyal disposition', and on 27 Mar. 1741 Erskine sent a letter by messenger to Cardinal Fleury, asking for French help in restoring the Stuarts. Shortly before Walpole's fall the Pretender suggested that Erskine should assure his friends among the opposition Whigs that if they

> enter seriously and heartily into measures for bringing about my restoration . . . there is no reasonable demand they can make, either on behalf of themselves in particular, or of the country in general, that I shall not readily and cheerfully comply with.

Erskine decided to approach Pulteney, as 'there was none [he] had greater intimacy or freedom with', handing him a written pledge from the Pretender to safeguard English liberties and the Protestant religion, which Pulteney gave him back at their next meeting, saying 'take your papers, I do not love to have such papers'. Erskine then mentioned the dissatisfaction of the Tories, who formed the bulk of the Opposition, and how difficult it had been to hold it together.

> Mr. Pulteney answered that he had done exceeding well, but now he thanked God that they were out of the power of the Tories, for Sir Robert Walpole . . . had sent to them and agreed to resign his offices

and leave them to form a ministry such as they found proper.[5]

Erskine continued in the service of the Prince of Wales after Walpole's fall, though participating in the talks held in London in 1743 with an agent sent over by the French Government to concert arrangements for a rising.[6] He also absented himself from the divisions on the Hanoverians in 1742 and 1744, in which most of the Prince's followers supported the Government. In Apr. 1743 he informed the Pretender's representative in Paris that Pulteney, now Lord Bath, and Carteret had managed

> to draw the general hatred and execration on themselves more in the space of one year than Lord Orford [Walpole] purchased to himself in twenty;

adding that the Prince had

> given himself wholly to them and his countenance is changed towards those to whom once he showed great favour, but who continued true to their old principles, [and that] many think that all such will be quickly dismissed from his family and service, . . . though they should be allowed to hang about him some time longer.

He himself hung on to his post till May 1745, when he was replaced by Sir John Gordon (q.v.).

In June 1745 Erskine informed the Pretender that, with the Administration deeply divided and most of the troops out of the kingdom,

> there never was and never can be such a favourable opportunity to attempt your Majesty's restoration . . . If the Prince landed in the present circumstances with ten battalions, or even a smaller body of troops, there will be no opposition, but, on the contrary, that his Royal Highness will be received with blessings and acclamations.

But when he heard that the Young Pretender, tired of the delays in the French preparations, might come to Scotland without troops or arms, he condemned the project as 'very weak and very rash', predicting that 'some great misfortune will ensue'. He was in London during the whole of the rebellion, joining the English Jacobites in September in appealing for a body of French troops to be landed near London without delay.[7]

After the collapse of the rebellion, Erskine went over to the Government, voting for the Hanoverians in April 1746 when he was classed as a 'new ally' of the Pelhams. In March 1747, at the request of Ilay, now 3rd Duke of Argyll, he sent Hardwicke suggestions for the bill abolishing hereditary jurisdictions, so as to avoid debate on amendments which might prove embarrassing to the ministry,[8] speaking for the bill in April.[9] He did not stand in 1747. He may have been the 'Mr. Erskine' drawing a secret service pension of £400 p.a.

shown in a list of such pensions saved since April 1754,[10] when he died, 24 Jan., aged 75.

[1]Ramsay of Ochtertyre, *Scotland and Scotsmen in 18th Cent.* i. 83. [2] *Autobiog. of Dr. Alexander Carlyle* (1910 ed.), 18. [3] *Spalding Club Misc.* iii. 27–45; R. Halsband, *Life of Lady Mary Wortley Montagu*, 133–5; *Soc. of Antiq. of Scotland Proc.* xi. 593–608. [4] *HMC Mar and Kellie*, 529–31; *HMC Polwarth*, v. 73–75, 95–107, 144–5, 173; Carlyle, 10; *More Culloden Pprs.* iii. 133. [5] Stuart mss 221/52, 233/202, 232/160–2, 240/140; Browne, *Hist. of the Highlands*, ii. 443. [6] Murray of Broughton, *Memorials* (Sc. Hist. Soc. xxvii), 48, 61, 62–63. [7] Stuart mss 249/83, 268/5; Browne, ii. 464–5. [8] Add. 35446, ff. 151–5. [9] *HMC Polwarth*, v. 235. [10] Add. 33038, f. 352.

E.C.

ERSKINE, Thomas (?1706–66), of Alloa, Clackmannan.

STIRLING BURGHS 16 Mar. 1728–1734
STIRLINGSHIRE 6 Feb.–18 June 1747
CLACKMANNANSHIRE 1747–1754

b. ?1706, 1st s. of John Erskine, 6th Earl of Mar [S], by his 1st w. Lady Margaret Hay, da. of Thomas, 7th Earl of Kinnoull [S]. *educ.* Westminster May 1715, aged 8. *m.* 1 Oct. 1741, Lady Charlotte Hope, da. of Charles, 1st Earl of Hopetoun [S], *s.p.*
Capt. of Ft. 1729–34.

Erskine, commonly known as Lord Erskine, was at Westminster school during the rebellion which his father, Lord Mar, headed in 1715. Later, he joined his attainted father abroad, obtaining a company in one of the Irish regiments in the French service in 1724. In 1728 his uncle, the Hon. James Erskine (q.v.), who had purchased his father's forfeited estates on his behalf, took him home, introduced him to Walpole and Ilay, and brought him into Parliament. Given a commission in the army, he voted with the Administration on the Hessians in 1730 and on the army in 1732. According to his uncle, he was promised by Ilay that if he voted for the excise he 'would be restored to the honours of his family next session, but though he did so, going along with them as fully as their other slaves',[1] he was disappointed. With his uncle, he went into opposition, voting against the Administration on the repeal of the Septennial Act in 1734. He was defeated for Stirlingshire at the next general election. In 1747, after his uncle had returned to supporting the Administration, he was elected for Stirlingshire at a by-election and for Clackmannanshire at the general election as a government supporter. He did not stand in 1754. He died 16 Mar. 1766.

[1] *Spalding Club Misc.* iii. 28–31, 39.

E.C.

ERSKINE, William (1691–1754), of Torry, Fife.

PERTH BURGHS 27 Oct. 1722–1727

b. 19 Mar. 1691, 1st s. of Hon. William Erskine of Torry, M.P. [S], dep. gov. of Blackness castle, by Magdalen, da. of Sir James Lumsden of Innergellie, Fife. *m.* 10 Dec. 1725, Henrietta, 2nd da. of Sir William Baillie of Lamington, Lanark, wid. of Robert Watson of Muirhouse, Edinburgh, 1s. 2da. *suc.* fa. Apr. 1697.
Capt. 2 Drags. 1717, maj. 1723; lt.-col. 7 Drags. 1741, ret. 1751.

Erskine, a professional soldier, of a Fifeshire family, was awarded the Perth Burghs seat by the Commons after a double return against a Squadrone candidate, Charles Leslie, whose petition was referred to the elections committee, a motion for fixing a date for the hearing of the petition by the committee being rejected.[1] As one of the tellers against the motion was Lord Ilay's friend, Henry Cunningham (q.v.), it appears that Erskine belonged to the Argyll faction, but there is no record of his voting. He did not stand again. He served in the army for some thirty-four years, commanding his regiment at Fontenoy, where he is said to have strapped the regimental standard to his son's leg, telling him not to return without it.[2]

He died 2 May 1754.

[1] *CJ*, xx. 49, 51. [2] Dalton, *George I's Army*, ii. p. xiv.

J.M.S.

ERSKINE, *see also* **ARESKINE**

ESSINGTON, John (1689–1729), of Wandsworth, Surr.

NEW ROMNEY 1727–29 Apr. 1728

bap. 8 Dec. 1689, 4th s. of Peter Essington of Wandsworth, goldsmith of London, by his 1st w. Elizabeth. *educ.* I. Temple 1706. *m.* 10 Jan. 1713, Elizabeth Claphamson of Wandsworth, 3s. 8da.
Sheriff, Surr. 1724.

John Essington[1] (not to be confused with the Member for Aylesbury 1710–15) was returned as a Whig at New Romney in 1727 with the Duke of Dorset's 'privity'.[2] Unseated on petition, he died on 8 Apr. 1729, 'in Newgate where he was imprisoned for debt'.[3]

[1] *Misc. Gen. et Her.* (ser. 5), v. 326–9. [2] D. Papillon to Sir Philip Yorke, 1 Aug. 1727, Add. 35585, f. 71. [3] *Hist. Reg.* 1729, p. 24.

A.N.N.

ETTRICK, William (1651–1716), of Middle Temple, London.

POOLE 1685–1687
CHRISTCHURCH 1689–5 Dec. 1716

b. 15 Nov. 1651, 1st s. of Anthony Ettrick, M.P., of Holt Lodge, Dorset by Anne, da. of Edward Davenant of Gillingham, Dorset. *educ.* Trinity, Oxf. 8 Mar. 1667, aged 16; M. Temple 1669, called 1675, bencher 1699. *m.* (1) Elizabeth, da. of Sir Edmund Bacon,

4th Bt., M.P., of Redgrave, Suff., 1da.; (2) Frances, da. of Col. Thomas Wyndham, M.P., of Witham, Som., 1da. *suc.* fa. 1703.

Attorney to Prince George by 1692–1708; counsel to Admiralty 1711.

Ettrick, a practising lawyer, sat as a Tory for Christchurch from the Revolution to the Hanoverian accession. Re-elected unopposed in 1715, he voted against the septennial bill. He died 5 Dec. 1716.

P.W.

EUSTON, Lord, *see* FITZROY, George

EVANS, George, 1st Baron Carbery [I] (c.1680–1749), of Caharas, co. Limerick, and Laxton, Northants.

WESTBURY   1 June 1715–1722, 16 Mar. 1724–1727

b. c.1680, 1st s. of George Evans, P.C. [I], M.P. [I], of Bulgaden Hall, co. Limerick by Mary, da. of John Eyre of Eyre Court, co. Galway. *m.* 4 May 1703, Anne, da. of William Stafford of Blatherwycke, Northants., yr. sis. and coh. of William Stafford of Blatherwycke. *cr.* Baron Carbery [I] 9 May 1715; *suc.* fa. 1720.

M.P. [I] 1713–14.

Gov. Limerick castle, 1714–27, 1740–*d.*; P.C. [I] 1715.

According to the 1st Lord Egmont, Carbery's grandfather was a sergeant in Cromwell's army, who set up as a cobbler in co. Cork:

> but being a cunning, industrious and saving man, by buying army debentures and other opportunities that offered, laid the foundation of a large estate, which his son and grandson, the present lord, by parsimony have improved to near £6,000 a year.[1]

Carbery himself acquired the Laxton estate in England by marriage and had connexions with Wiltshire through his mother's family. In 1715 he and Charles Allanson (q.v.) were sent down to Westbury by Lord Cowper and other leading Whigs to challenge Lord Abingdon's Tory interest there. Though unsuccessful at the election, on petition he and Allanson were declared elected by the Whig House of Commons. In Parliament he voted for the septennial bill in 1716 and the peerage bill in December 1719, but was absent on the repeal of the Occasional Conformity and Schism Acts, January 1719. In 1722 he was again defeated but this time, though 'the merits of that election [were] undoubtedly against' his opponent, his petition failed on a technical point.[2] However, one of the sitting Members having elected to sit for Middlesex, Carbery came in at the ensuing by-election, despite a further petition. He did not stand again, dying 28 Aug. 1749.

[1] *HMC Egmont Diary*, ii. 388. [2] Cholmondeley (Houghton) mss 68, n.d.

R.S.L.

EVANS, Hon. George (*d.*1759), of Caharas, co. Limerick, and Laxton, Northants.

WESTBURY   1734–1747

2nd but 1st surv. s. of George Evans (q.v.), 1st Baron Carbery [I]. *m.* 23 May 1732, Frances, da. of Richard Fitzwilliam (q.v.), 5th Visct. Fitzwilliam of Merrion [I], 3s. 1da. *suc.* fa. as 2nd Baron Carbery [I] 28 Aug. 1749.

George Evans was narrowly returned for his father's former seat at Westbury in 1734 and by a big majority in 1741, in both cases defeating members of the Bertie family standing on Lord Abingdon's interest. He voted against the Spanish convention in 1739 but subsequently figures in a ministerial list of government supporters absent on 21 Nov. 1739. In the next Parliament he voted consistently with the Administration, and was classed as an Old Whig in 1746. Although on his marriage he had received his father's Laxton estate, worth £1,100 p.a., and an annuity of over £1,400 from the family estates in Ireland, he was in financial difficulties by September 1743, when among other debts he was £900 in arrears on an annuity of £200 payable to the 1st Earl of Egmont from March 1734.[1] He did not stand again but, after his father's death, took his seat in the Irish House of Lords, 22 Nov. 1749. He died 2 Feb. 1759.

[1] Cholmondeley (Houghton) mss 66; *HMC Egmont Diary*, ii. 59; iii. 273–4.

R.S.L.

EVANS, Richard (*d.*1762), of Queenborough, Kent.

QUEENBOROUGH   27 Jan. 1729—1754

m., 1s. 2da.

Capt. in Col. Richard Sutton's Ft. 1709; half-pay 1713; capt. of Invalids for Portsmouth 1715; lt.-gov. Sheerness 1725–*d.*

Evans, whose parentage has not been ascertained, was several times mayor of Queenborough, his father acting as his deputy in 1725.[1] Returned for the borough on his own interest with government support at a by-election in 1729, he was able to secure the return of himself with government nominees over the next 25 years. In Pelham's words he became 'the means of settling the interest in Whig hands', 'votes well, and has his reward'.[2] However, in 1750 he fell foul of some of the townsmen on the question of non-resident freemen.[3] Pelham wrote to Newcastle on 26 Oct. 1753: 'I hear Queenborough is in great danger of being lost both by jealousies and ill-management together with a strange fellow at the head of the corporation —I mean Captain Evans'.[4] After Pelham's death

Evans was induced by Newcastle to withdraw,[5] although he still on occasion advised Newcastle on local patronage.[6] He died 22 Nov. 1762,

> greatly despised by all his friends for giving all his personal estate to a Scotch girl, his tucker-in, and making her his executrix. He did not give his son a penny what he could hinder him of, and he never named his eldest daughter . . . (his younger daughter died a little time before . . .). The girl has pulled the house to pieces, sold all the family pictures and plate, goods, wine, etc. and gone off we don't know whither, without paying her testator's debts.[7]

[1] *Cal. Treas. Pprs.* 1720–28, p. 360. [2] Pelham to Bedford, 11 June 1747, Bedford mss; Evans to Walpole, 17 Dec. 1734, Cholmondeley (Houghton) mss. [3] See QUEENBOROUGH. [4] Add. 32733, f. 138. [5] Memo. 21 Mar. 1754, Add. 32995, f. 114. [6] See Evans to Newcastle, 13 Feb. 1755, Add. 32852, f. 446. [7] Unsigned letter to Geo. Wellard, town clerk of Queenborough, Wellard mss, Kent AO.

A.N.N.

EVELYN, George (1678–1724), of Rooksnest, nr. Bletchingley, Surr.

BLETCHINGLEY 1705–18 Oct. 1724

b. 26 Oct. 1678, 2nd s. of George Evelyn, M.P., of Nutfield, nr. Bletchingley by his 2nd w. Margaret, da. and h. of William Webb of Throgmorton St., London; bro. of William Glanville (q.v.), formerly Evelyn. *m.* (1) lic. 14 Aug. 1701, Rebecca Rollinson (*d.*1703), *s.p.*; (2) Anne (*d.* Oct. 1716), da. of Hon. Robert Paston, *s.p.*; (3) settlement 22 Aug. 1720, Mary, da. of Thomas Garth of Harrold, Beds., 3da.; she later m. Charles Boone, whose son Daniel (qq.v.) m. her da. Ann. *suc.* bro. 1702.
    Clerk of the household to Prince of Wales 1716–*d.*

In 1591 the Evelyns bought the manor of Godstone, near Bletchingley, which they thereafter frequently represented. Returned as a Whig on the family interest for the borough, George Evelyn obtained a post in the Prince of Wales's household after George I's accession, following the Prince into opposition in 1717, when he voted against the Government in the division of 4 June on the case of Lord Cadogan (q.v.), and was classed as 'Prince of Wales'. He remained in opposition till the reconciliation between the King and the Prince in 1720, voting against the Government on the Occasional Conformity and Schism Acts and on the peerage bill in 1719. After his death, intestate, 18 Oct. 1724, Godstone was sold for £24,000 in 1733 to his mother's second husband, Charles Boone, whose son Daniel sold it in 1751 to Sir Kenrick Clayton (q.v.).[1]

[1] U. Lambert, *Godstone*, 292–3.

R.R.S.

EVELYN, John (1706–67), of Wotton, Surr.

HELSTON	1727–1741
PENRYN	1741–1747
HELSTON	1747–1767

b. 24 Aug. 1706, 1st s. of Sir John Evelyn, 1st Bt., M.P., commr. of the customs, by Anne, da. of Edward Boscawen, M.P., sis. of Hugh Boscawen (q.v.), 1st Visct. Falmouth, and gd.-da. of Sir Francis Godolphin. *educ.* Eton 1718; Queen's, Oxf. 1725. *m.* 17 Aug. 1732, his cos. Mary, da. of Hugh Boscawen, 1st Visct. Falmouth. *suc. fa.* as 2nd Bt. 15 July 1763.
    Equerry 1731–3 and groom of the bedchamber 1733–51 to Frederick, Prince of Wales; clerk of the household to George, Prince of Wales, 1756–60; clerk of the Green Cloth, 1760–*d.*

Returned by Lord Godolphin at Helston, Evelyn entered the service of Frederick, Prince of Wales, voting with the Administration till 1738, when he followed Frederick into opposition. He was one of the opposition Whigs who withdrew on the motion for the removal of Walpole in February 1741. Returned by Lord Falmouth for Penryn in 1741, he continued to conform with the Prince's politics, supporting the Administration after Walpole's fall till 1747, when Frederick reverted to opposition. At the general election of that year, he was returned for Helston as a member of the Prince's party, Frederick contributing £300 towards his election expenses.[1] After Frederick's death, he went over to the Government, securing a place in the new heir apparent's household on its formation in 1756.
    He died 11 June 1767.

[1] *HMC Fortescue*, 120, 128.

E.C.

EVELYN, *see also* **GLANVILLE**

EVERSFIELD, Charles (c.1682–1749), of Denne Place, nr. Horsham, Suss.

HORSHAM	1705–1710
SUSSEX	1710–1713
HORSHAM	1713–16 June 1715, 12 June 1721–1741
STEYNING	1741–1747

b. c.1682, o.s. of Nicholas Eversfield of Charlton Court, nr. Steyning, Suss., M.P. Bramber 1679, by Elizabeth, da. and h. of Nicholas Gildridge of Eastbourne, Suss. *m.* (1) 21 July 1702, Mary, da. and h. of Henry Duncombe of Weston, Surr., 1s. 4da.; (2) 9 Aug. 1731, Henrietta Maria, da. and coh. of Charles Scarborough of Windsor, Berks., wid. of Sir Robert Jenkinson, 3rd Bt. (q.v.), of Walcot, Oxon., sis.-in-law of Henry Ingram (q.v.), 7th Visct. Irvine [S], *s.p. suc. fa.* 1684; uncle Anthony Eversfield (M.P. Horsham 1679–81, 1685–7, 1689) at Denne 1695.
    Paymaster and treasurer of the Ordnance 1712–14.
    Charles Eversfield inherited from his uncle an

interest at Horsham, for which he was returned to eight successive Parliaments, though in 1710 he chose to sit for the county. Originally a Tory, he obtained a place under Anne, which he lost on George I's accession. Having been defeated for the county and unseated on petition for Horsham in 1715, he came to an agreement with his opponents at Horsham, the Ingrams (qq.v.), to share the representation of that borough,[1] for which he was returned unopposed at a by-election in 1721. About the same time he went over to the Government, speaking for them in an army debate, 26 Oct. 1722, voting regularly with them, and co-operating with the Duke of Newcastle in county elections.[2] On the hearing of a Southwark election petition in February 1736 it was noted that the unsuccessful petitioner against George Heathcote (q.v.) 'had most wretched friends, Charles Eversfield being the chief manager, and his case most simply managed'.[3] In 1737 Eversfield sold his burgages at Horsham to the Ingrams,[4] after which he was returned for the neighbouring borough of Steyning, continuing to vote with the Government. Classed in 1746 as an Old Whig, he did not stand in 1747, dying 17 June 1749.

[1] W. Albery, *Parl. Hist. Horsham*, 71. [2] Add. 32689, f. 407; 32690, f. 66. [3] Harley Diary, 17 Feb. 1736. [4] Albery, 74–76.

J.B.L.

EWER, Charles (d.1742), of Lime St., London.

SHAFTESBURY 1741–20 June 1742

yr. s. of Thomas Ewer of Bushey Hall and the Lea, in Watford, Herts. by Mary, da. of Hon. James Montagu of Lackham, Wilts; bro. of Jane, Countess of Shaftesbury.[1] m. Catherine, s.p.
Alderman, London 1741–2.

Charles Ewer, a London grocer, came of a Hertfordshire family settled at the Lea since the time of Henry VIII.[2] In March 1741 he was chosen alderman for Broad St. ward, standing as a city radical[3] and anti-Walpole candidate, but his election was challenged and not confirmed till November following. Meanwhile he was returned to Parliament for Shaftesbury on the interest of his nephew, the 4th Earl of Shaftesbury. He died suddenly 20 June 1742.

[1] PCC 182 Trenley. [2] *VCH Herts.* ii. 183, 462. [3] Owen, *Pelhams*, 67, 69.

R.S.L.

EYLES, Francis (c.1679–1735), of Essex St., London, and Earnshill, nr. Taunton, Som.

DEVIZES 1715–28 Jan. 1721

b. c.1679, 2nd s. of Sir John Eyles of Southbroom, Wilts., M.P. Devizes 1679–81, by his w. Elizabeth

Cowper; 1st cos. of Sir John and Sir Joseph Eyles (qq.v.). m. s.p.s.[1]
Director, South Sea Co. 1715–21.

Eyles was the son of a lord mayor of London, who owned estates near Devizes, which the family represented in every Parliament from 1715 to 1741. Returned for Devizes as a Whig, he voted with the Government except on the peerage bill, on which he abstained. As a director of the South Sea Company he was expelled from the House after the collapse of the scheme and was included in the bill confiscating the estates of the chief culprits for the relief of their victims. He petitioned the Commons for lenient treatment on the ground that

> he was no ways concerned in promoting the scheme upon which the Act passed . . . nor was ever at any meeting of the directors . . . to consult or contrive the carrying on the scheme . . . nor privy to the giving or taking in any stock for any minister of state, or Member of either House of Parliament; . . . he never made any advantage of being a director . . . was absent in the country whilst many of the said matters were transacted, etc.[2]

The House took a comparatively favourable view of his case, allowing him to keep £20,000 out of estates valued at about £35,000. Like the other directors, he was also incapacitated from sitting again or holding public office. He died 19 Dec. 1735, leaving everything to his nephew, Francis Eyles (q.v.).

[1] The inventory of his estate in 1721 mentions his wife and children; his will dated 1731 does not mention them. [2] *CJ*, xix. 516.

R.R.S.

EYLES, Francis (c.1704–50) of Soho Sq., London, and Earnshill, nr. Taunton, Som.

DEVIZES 1727–July 1742

b. c.1704, 1st s. of John Eyles of Southbroom, Wilts. (e. bro. of Francis Eyles, q.v.) by Mary, da. of John Eyles of Chalford, Glos. suc. uncle Francis Eyles 1735.
Cornet 4 Drags. 1723, lt. 1726, capt. bef. 1731; commr. for victualling the navy 1734–42; superintendent of the King's foundries 1742–d.

Returned for Devizes on the Eyles interest Eyles became a member of the gaols committee of the House of Commons and a trustee for Georgia, voting with the Government. Described by the 1st Lord Egmont as one of Walpole's 'creatures',[1] he obtained a place worth £500 a year.[2] In 1734 he appears to have also stood unsuccessfully for Calne. After Walpole's fall he gave up his seat to George Lee (q.v.), exchanging his place for a sinecure appointment. He died 21 Sept. 1750.

[1] *HMC Egmont Diary*, iii. 168. [2] *Gent. Mag.* 1739, p. 305.

R.R.S.

EYLES, John (1683–1745), of Gidea Hall, Essex.

CHIPPENHAM   1713–1727
LONDON   1727–1734

b. 1683, 1st surv. s. of Sir Francis Eyles, 1st Bt., of London by Elizabeth, da. of Richard Ayley, London merchant; bro. of Joseph Eyles (q.v.). m. his cos. Mary, da. of Joseph Haskins Stiles by Sarah, sis. of Francis Eyles (q.v.), 1s. 1da. suc. fa. as 2nd Bt. 24 May 1716.

    Director, E. I. Co. 1710–14, 1717–21; director, Bank of England 1715–17; alderman, London 1716–d., lord mayor 1726–7; commr. for forfeited estates 1716–25; master, Haberdashers' Co. 1716–17; sub-gov. South Sea Co. Feb. 1721–33; pres. St. Thomas's Hospital 1737–d; jt. postmaster gen. 1739–d.

John Eyles, a Wiltshire mercer and wool stapler, had two sons, John and Francis, who made their fortunes as London merchants; became aldermen and, in John's case, lord mayor of London and M.P. Devizes 1679–81; and ended with a knighthood and a baronetcy respectively. Francis's eldest son, John, was a leading figure in the city of London when he was returned as a Whig in 1713 for Chippenham, not far from the Eyles estates in Wiltshire. Voting regularly with the Government after George I's accession, he was elected by the Commons to be a commissioner for the sale of the estates forfeited by English Jacobites in the 1715 rebellion. In 1721 he was called in to salvage the South Sea Company, over whose affairs he presided as sub-governor for the next 12 years, speaking frequently on the Company's behalf in Parliament.

On the third reading of the bill to regulate elections for London, 19 Mar. 1725, Eyles successfully proposed an amendment to alter the qualification for householders from 20s. to 30s., although the House had already debated and agreed to 20s. in committee. A year later, on a petition from Richard Hampden (q.v.) to compound for his debts as treasurer of the navy, Eyles asserted that Hampden so far from being a great loser in the South Sea bubble had actually gained £9,000, as appeared from the Company's books.[1]

At the general election of 1727 Eyles was returned at the head of the poll for the city of London, where he was 'the great support of the ministry interest'.[2] In 1732 he incurred a reprimand from the House of Commons for having authorized the secretary to the forfeited estates commission to sign for him in his absence, thus making possible the fraudulent sale of the Derwentwater estates (see Bond, Denis). In a public apology he wrote:

If the great weight of business which the disordered affairs of the South Sea Company laid upon him within that remarkable period of time be not forgot, he can not but hope to find a generous apology from

the breast of everyone before whom he is now in judgment.[3]

In the same session he was attacked by Edward Vernon (q.v.), who insinuated

that the directors of the Company had carried on a private trade, contrary to their oaths and hurtful to the company . . . having his eye all the time on Sir John Eyles (who by the universal vogue has been greatly guilty in this respect). Sir John, in his reply, took this as a charge levelled at himself, and said that gentleman had accused him in the House of what he dared not say to him out of it. Upon this several gentlemen interposed, and required the Speaker to enjoin both of them to give their words that nothing should ensue; accordingly they both declared they would not prosecute their resentment.[4]

Next January, presiding as sub-governor over a general meeting of the South Sea Company, he announced 'in a pathetic speech' that he

thanked the Company for the honours they had done him in choosing him four times successively into that post; that his close application to the Company's affairs had impaired his health to that degree as to determine him not to stand candidate at the next election for the station he was in; and therefore desired them to think of another.[5]

Voting against the excise bill in 1733, he did not stand for London in 1734 and was defeated at Chippenham. He became father of the city in 1737, but 'seldom or never' attended a corporation meeting.[6] Made joint postmaster general in 1739, he died 11 Mar. 1745.

[1] Knatchbull Diary, 19 Mar. 1725, 11 Mar. 1726. [2] HMC Egmont Diary, i. 247. [3] Case of Sir John Eyles. [4] HMC Egmont Diary, i. 263. [5] Gent. Mag. 1733, p. 44. [6] Stuart mss 254/134.

                                              R.R.S.

EYLES, Joseph (c.1690–1740), of Bishopsgate, London.

DEVIZES   1722–1727
SOUTHWARK 1727–1734
DEVIZES   1734–8 Feb. 1740

b. c.1690, 4th s. of Sir Francis Eyles, 1st Bt., and bro. of John Eyles (q.v.). m. Sarah, da. of Alderman Sir Jeffrey Jefferies, 1s. 2da. Kntd. 9 Dec. 1724.

    Director, E.I. Co. 1714–17, 1721–2; director, Bank of England 1717–21, 1730–3; sub gov. London Assurance Co.; sheriff, London 1724–5; master, Haberdashers' Co. 1724–5; alderman, London 1739–40.

A Turkey merchant, with extensive commercial interests in the Mediterranean, Joseph Eyles became one of the financial agents of the Government. On 15 July 1730 the Treasury board directed that 'Mr. Pelham, paymaster of the forces, is for the future to receive proposals from Sir Joseph Eyles for the remittances required for the forces in Minorca and Gibraltar, or any other foreign service'.[1] In 1739 his profits from this source were said to amount to £2,500 a year.[2]

Except in 1727, when he sat for Southwark, Eyles was returned on his family's interest for Devizes. He voted with the Government in all recorded divisions other than that on the excise bill in 1733, which both he and his brother, Sir John Eyles, opposed. His only known speech was made on 30 Mar. 1739, when he seconded a motion for the repeal of the Test Act.[3] He died 8 Feb. 1740.

[1] *Cal. Treas. Bks. and Pprs.* 1729-30, p. 409. [2] *Gent. Mag.* 1739, p.305. [3] *HMC Egmont Diary,* iii. 47.

R.R.S.

EYRE, Giles (1692–1750), of Brickworth, Wilts.

DOWNTON   2 Dec. 1715–1734

> *bap.* 27 May 1692, 1st s. of Giles Eyre of Brickworth by Mabel, da. of Alexander Thayne of Cowsfield, in Whiteparish, Wilts. *educ.* L. Inn 1715. *unm. suc.* fa. 1734.

Giles Eyre succeeded his uncle, John Eyre, at Downton, which he represented for over eighteen years, during which his only recorded votes were for the septennial bill in 1716 and the peerage bill in 1719. Retiring in 1734, he retained a diminishing number of burgages at Downton till his death, 7 June 1750.

R.S.L.

EYRE, John (1665–1715), of Lincoln's Inn and Brickworth, Wilts.

DOWNTON   23 May 1698–1701, 1705–2 Nov. 1715

> *bap.* 12 Apr. 1665, 2nd s. of Sir Giles Eyre, M.P., justice of the King's bench, by his 1st w. Dorothy, da. of Sir John Ryves of Ranston, Dorset. *educ.* Merton, Oxf. 1682; L. Inn 1682, called 1688, bencher 1715. *unm.*

In 1605 Giles Eyre, of an ancient Wiltshire family, bought the estate of Brickworth, near the borough of Downton, in which he and his descendants developed a strong interest. His great-grandson John Eyre, a Whig lawyer, sat for Downton in eight Parliaments till his death, 2 Nov. 1715, commemorated as 'a lover of liberty and independence, [who] served his country at his own expense and not . . . himself at the expense of his country'.[1]

[1] *Wilts. N. & Q.* v. 97–101.

R.S.L.

EYRE, Robert (c.1693–1752), of Newhouse, Wilts.

SOUTHAMPTON   1727–May 1729

> *b.* c.1693, 1st s. of Sir Robert Eyre, M.P., of Newhouse, c.j. of the common pleas, by Elizabeth, da. of Edward Rudge of Warley, Essex. *educ.* L.

Inn 1710, called 1723. *m.* Mary, da. of William Fellowes of Eggesford, Devon, 1s. *suc.* fa. 1735.

> Recorder, Southampton 1723–42; commr. of excise 1729–*d.*

Eyre was the son of an eminent lawyer, whom he succeeded as recorder of Southampton. Returned for Southampton in 1727, he voted with the Administration on the civil list arrears in 1729. In the following May he vacated his seat on being appointed a commissioner of excise. He was elected one of the trustees of the Georgia Society on 21 Mar. 1734 and a common councillor of it on 17 Mar. 1737.[1] He died 14 Dec. 1752.

[1] *HMC Egmont Diary,* ii. 66, 372.

P.W.

EYRE, *see also* **ARCHER, William**

EYTON, Thomas (?1682–1757), of Lower Leeswood, Flints.

FLINT BOROUGHS   10 June 1721–1727

> *b.* ?1682, s. of Thomas Eyton of Trimley, Flints. by Elizabeth, da. of Sir Thomas Powell, 2nd Bt., of Horsley, Denb. and Birkenhead, Cheshire. *educ.* Jesus, Oxf. 29 Oct. 1700, aged 18. *m.* 1707, Elizabeth, da. of Robert Davies of Gwyrsaney and Llanerch, Denb., 2s. 1da. *suc.* fa. to Trimley and uncle John Eyton to Lower Leeswood.

> Sheriff, Flints. 1711–12.

Eyton, the head of a prominent Flintshire family, was a fellow member with Sir Watkin Williams Wynn (q.v.) of the Jacobite Cycle of the White Rose. His name was sent to the Pretender in 1721 as a probable supporter in the event of a rising.[1] Returned for Flint without opposition at a by-election on the death of Sir John Conway (q.v.) in 1721, he was re-elected after a contest in 1722. He did not stand again, but continued to support Wynn's political activities in North Wales. He died in 1757.

[1] NLW, 14941 C; *Flints. Hist. Soc. Publ.* ix. 15; Stuart mss 65/16.

P.D.G.T.

FAGG, Robert (1704–40), of Wiston, nr. Steyning, Suss.

STEYNING   1734–14 Sept. 1740

> *bap.* 20 Sept. 1704, 3rd but o. surv. s. of Sir Robert Fagg, 3rd Bt., of Wiston by Christian, da. of Sir Cecil Bishopp, 4th Bt., M.P., of Parham, Suss. *m.* 1729, Sarah, da. of William Ward, M.D., of York, *s.p. suc.* fa. as 4th Bt. 22 June 1736.

Under William III Fagg's grandfather sat for Steyning, which his father, a leading Sussex Tory, contested unsuccessfully in 1722 and 1727. When Fagg stood for it in 1734, the 1st Duke of Chandos wrote:

I am for Lord Carnarvon (q.v.) joining openly with Mr. Fagg, who by the character I had of him, is really a very deserving gentleman and whose behaviour . . . has been such as will engage me on all occasions to be his humble servant.[1]

Returned with Carnarvon, standing jointly, Fagg voted with the Opposition against the Spanish convention in 1739, and for the place bill in 1740. He died 14 Sept. 1740, leaving the family estates to his sister Elizabeth, who afterwards married Sir Charles Goring, 5th Bt., son of Sir Henry Goring (q.v.).

[1] 7 Feb. 1734, Chandos letter bks.

J.B.L.

FAIRFAX, Hon. Robert (1707–93), of Leeds Castle, nr. Maidstone, Kent.

MAIDSTONE 15 Jan. 1740–1741, 1747–1754
KENT 1754–1768

b. 1707, 3rd s. of Thomas Fairfax, M.P., 5th Lord Fairfax [S], by Catherine, da. and h. of Thomas Colepeper, 2nd Baron Colepeper. *m.* (1) 25 Apr. 1741, Martha (bur. 17 Sept. 1743), da. and coh. of Anthony Collins of Baddow, Essex, 1s. *d.v.p.*; (2) 15 July 1749, Dorothy, da. of Maudistly Best of Boxley and Chatham, Kent, brewer, sis. of Thomas Best (q.v.), *s.p. suc.* cos. Bryan Fairfax 1749, and bro. as 7th Lord Fairfax [S] 12 Mar. 1782.
Cornet, R. Horse Gds. 1726, lt. 1737; capt. 1 Life Gds. 1739, maj. 1742, res. 1745.

Fairfax's father was cousin once removed to the 3rd Lord Fairfax, commander-in-chief of the parliamentary army. Through his mother the family acquired Leeds Castle, which was made over to him by his brother, the 6th Lord Fairfax. Returned at a by-election for the neighbouring borough of Maidstone in time to vote with the Government against the place bill in 1740, he did not stand again till 1747, when he was re-elected as a government supporter after a contest. Though in 1749 he inherited 'a very considerable fortune', he was in constant financial difficulties, which he attributed to his election expenditure, till his death, 15 Aug. 1793.[1]

[1] Namier, *Structure*, 409–14.

A.N.N.

FALCONER, John (1674–1764), of Phesdo, Kincardine.

KINCARDINESHIRE 1734–1741

b. 21 Oct. 1674, 1st s. of Sir James Falconer, M.P. [S], of Phesdo, Lord Phesdo, S.C.J., by his w. Elizabeth Trent. *educ.* adv. 1700. *unm. suc.* fa. 1705.
Commr. of justiciary for the Highlands 1701, 1702.

As a young man, Falconer lived many years in France, developing a great admiration and affection for it. Returned at the age of 60 for his county, he attracted Walpole's interest by voting 'steadily with us without asking anything or coming near me'. Duncan Forbes (q.v.) thereupon arranged for Falconer to dine with Walpole, later asking him why he had been so shy in paying his respects to the prime minister when he was so strenuous a supporter of his measures. Falconer is said to have replied:

I think the French the happiest people under the sun; nay, I like their government, which is a good one for one that minds his own business. In my opinion Sir Robert's measures bid fair to make Britain one day a province of France, which, I think, would be a blessing to us.

He did not stand again, dying 21 Nov. 1764, aged 90, 'bent like the segment of a circle, . . . a very keen golfer and a very facetious, pleasing companion'.[1]

[1] Ramsay of Ochtertyre, *Scotland and Scotsmen in the 18th Cent.* i. 56–57.

R.S.L.

FALL, James (*d.*1743), of Dunbar.

HADDINGTON BURGHS 1734–1741

3rd s. of Robert Fall, merchant, burgess and bencher of Dunbar, M.P. [S] Dunbar 1693–1702. *m.* c.1723, Jean, da. of Patrick Murray of Pennyland, Caithness, 1s. 2da.

Fall was one of four brothers, described as the most considerable merchants of their time in Scotland.[1] Reputedly of gypsy origin, the family were the chief magistrates of Dunbar, one of the Haddington district of burghs, for which Fall was returned after a contest as a government supporter in 1734. He is shown in a list of the division on the Spanish convention, for which he voted, as holding a lease in Holy Island.[2] Next year he voted with the Government on the place bill. During the ensuing election campaign Lord Ilay, the government manager in Scotland, sent a letter to Walpole 'by a servant 20 miles out of town to Mr. Fall's town, where the Duke of Argyll's attorney cannot get it'.[3] Fall himself stood again for Haddington Burghs, where there was a double return, on which he withdrew, leaving the seat to be awarded to his opponent. Appointed collector of the bishops' rents in Scotland on the day of Walpole's resignation,[4] he died 25 Dec. 1743.

[1] *Sc. Antiq.* xvi. 127–32. [2] *Gent. Mag.* 1739, p. 305. [3] 14 Sept. 1740, Cholmondeley (Houghton) mss. [4] *Cal. Treas. Bks. and Pprs.* 1742–5, p. 211.

R.R.S.

FANE, Hon. Charles (aft. 1708–66), of Basildon, nr. Reading, Berks.

TAVISTOCK   1734–1747
READING   1754–1761

b. aft. 1708, 1st s. of Charles Fane, M.P. [I], 1st Visct. Fane [I], by Mary, da. of Alexander Stanhope, sis. of James Stanhope (q.v.), 1st Earl Stanhope. *m.* 7 June 1749, Susanna, da. of John Marriott of Sturton Hall, Suff., wid. of Sir William Juxon, 2nd Bt., of Little Compton, Glos., *s.p. suc.* fa. as 2nd Visct. 7 July 1744.

Minister plenipotentiary, Florence, Feb. 1734–40.

Soon after being appointed to Florence, Fane was brought into Parliament by the 4th Duke of Bedford, whose follower he remained for the rest of his political life. In 1737 Walpole sent out Horace Mann as assistant to Fane, who had proved extremely unsatisfactory, once staying

> in bed six weeks because the Duke of Newcastle, in one of his letters, forgot to sign himself 'your very humble servant' as usual, and only put 'your humble servant'.[1]

Superseded by Mann, he returned to England in 1740, voting against the Government on the place bill. He strengthened his connexions with Bedford by the marriage of his sister in 1741 to the 4th Earl of Sandwich, Bedford's boon companion and political ally. During the last days of Walpole's Administration Horace Walpole wrote to Mann, 17 Dec. 1741:

> Your friend Mr. Fane would not come for us last night, nor will vote till after the Westminster election; he is brought into Parliament by the Duke of Bedford, and is unwilling to disoblige him in this.

After Walpole's fall Fane continued with Bedford in opposition, voting against the Hanoverian troops in 1742 and 1744, till Bedford joined the Government at the end of 1744, after which he voted for the Hanoverians in 1746 and was classed by the ministry as New Ally. Shortly before the general election of 1747, at which he did not stand, he told Bedford that 'my mind is now turned towards retreat',[2] but soon after it he applied unsuccessfully to Newcastle for the Lisbon embassy, having previously declined an offer of the Constantinople embassy because the terms were unsatisfactory.[3] A proposal that he should accompany Sandwich as minister plenipotentiary to Aix-la-Chapelle in 1748 also fell through.[4] On 19 Nov. 1750 Horace Walpole told Mann:

> Your friend Lord Fane some time ago had a mind to go to Spain: the Duke of Bedford, who I really believe is an honest man, said very bluntly, 'Oh! my Lord, nobody can do there but Keene [Benjamin, q.v.]'.

When Bedford and Sandwich broke with the Pelhams in 1751, Fane followed them into opposition,

comforting Sandwich. according to Horace Walpole, 'with an annuity of a thousand a year—scarcely for his handsome behaviour to his sister', Sandwich's wife.[5] In the meantime he cultivated his interest at Reading for which he was returned after a contest in 1754. He died 24 Jan. 1766.

[1] Walpole to Mann, 2 Feb. 1774. [2] *Bedford Corresp.* i. 210–11. [3] Add. 32707, f. 324. [4] Coxe, *Pelham,* i. 392. [5] To Mann, 19 Nov. 1750, 18 June 1751.

A.N.N.

FANE, Francis (c.1698–1757), of Brympton, nr. Yeovil, Som.

TAUNTON   1727–1741
PETERSFIELD 1741–1747
ILCHESTER   1747–1754
LYME REGIS 1754–27 May 1757

b. c.1698, 1st s. of Henry Fane of Bristol by Anne, da. of Thomas Scrope, a Bristol merchant, sis. and coh. (in her issue) of John Scrope (q.v.); bro. of Thomas Fane (q.v.), 8th Earl of Westmorland. *educ.* King's, Camb. 1715; M. Temple 1714, called 1721. *unm. suc.* fa. 1726.

Counsel to the board of Trade 1725–46; K.C. 1727; solicitor-gen. to the Queen 1730–7; chairman of committees of supply and ways and means 1739–51; ld. of Trade 1746–55.

In 1727 Fane was returned for Taunton, where he had inherited leasehold property,[1] making his first recorded speech on 24 Feb. 1730 in support of a bill to prevent loans to foreign powers without licence. Throughout his parliamentary career he voted with the Administration, except on the motion for the repeal of the Test Act in 1736, which he supported, as did his uncle, John Scrope, secretary of the Treasury, both of them having been elected on condition that they would do so. It was no doubt owing to his connection with Scrope that he was appointed in 1739 to the money chair, a post which he held till Scrope's death in 1752. In 1739 he seconded the Address.[2]

In 1741 Fane was defeated at Taunton but was returned on the Joliffe interest for Petersfield. On 11 Jan. 1744 he spoke for keeping the British troops in Flanders.[3] He did not resign with the Pelhams in February 1746, offering his services to Lord Bath (William Pulteney, q.v.), like his uncle, John Scrope.[4] Later in the year he was transferred, it was said against his wishes, to a seat on the board of Trade, his place of counsel to the board being given to Matthew Lamb (q.v.).[5]

On 20 Apr. 1752 Henry Pelham wrote to Newcastle that Scrope had died

> leaving a vast fortune to Frank Fane; he will have in all, at least £2,000 a year on land and above £100,000 in money, all in his own disposal, without any entail on his brothers, or even a recommendation; he is the

honestest man amongst 'em all and will continue to employ his whole credit for the service of the King.[6]

His inheritance included both seats at Lyme Regis. He died 27 May 1757, aged 59.

[1] *Cal. Treas. Bks. and Pprs.*, 1731–4, pp. 439, 452, 454. [2] *HMC Egmont Diary*, ii. 243; iii. 16; Coxe, *Walpole*, iii. 515. [3] Yorke's parl. jnl. *Parl. Hist.* xiii. 390. [4] Ilchester, *Lord Holland*, i. 125. [5] *HMC Polwarth*, v. 184. [6] Add. 32726, f. 393.

S.R.M.

FANE, Hon. John (1686–1762), of Mereworth, Kent.

HYTHE	1708–27 Jan. 1711
KENT	28 Sept. 1715–1722
BUCKINGHAM	1 Mar. 1727–1734

bap. 24 Mar. 1686, 4th son of Vere Fane, M.P., 4th Earl of Westmorland, by Rachel, da. and h. of John Bence, alderman of London; bro. of Hon. Mildmay Fane (q.v.). *educ.* Eton 1698, L. Inn 1703; Emmanuel, Camb. 1704. *m.* 5 Aug. 1716, Mary, da. and h. of Lord Henry Cavendish, M.P., 2nd s. of William, 1st Duke of Devonshire, *s.p. suc.* bro. Mildmay Fane (q.v.) at Burston 1715; *cr.* Baron Catherlough [I] 4 Oct. 1733; *suc.* bro. Thomas as 7th Earl of Westmorland 4 July 1736.

Capt. 5 Drag. Gds. 1709–14; lt.-col. 37 Ft. ?1714, col. 1715–17; col. 1 tp. Horse Gren. Gds. 1717–33; col. 1 tp. Life Gds. 1733–7; brig.-gen. 1735; maj.-gen. and lt.-gen. 1742, with effect from 1735 and 1739 respectively; gen. 1761.

High steward, Oxford Univ. 1754, chancellor 1759–*d.*

Fane, an army officer, served at Malplaquet, ending the war as lieutenant-colonel of the 37th Foot. On the outbreak of the Fifteen he bought the colonelcy of his regiment from its holder, who had been dismissed on security grounds. He is said in Horace Walpole's *Memoirs of George II* (iii. 167) to have commanded the troops sent to hold down Oxford during the rebellion, but in fact he was stationed at Chester, where he created an uproar by arresting the local officer of the Ordnance 'for refusing to provide coal and candles for the guards' of the castle and by placing the recorder under military confinement for protesting against this action. He was severely reprimanded, suspended from his command, and ordered to repair to London and remain under house arrest till further notice.[1] Two years later he bought the colonelcy of the 1st troop of Horse Grenadier Guards, vacant by the dismissal of Lord Lumley for adhering to the Prince of Wales in the quarrel in the royal family.[2]

Fane was returned as a Whig for Hythe by the Earl of Dorset as lord warden in 1708 and 1710, but lost his seat on petition in 1711. Succeeding his brother, Mildmay Fane, as knight of the shire for Kent at a by-election in 1715, he was one of the Whigs who voted against the septennial bill in 1716, subsequently voting with the Government on the repeal of the Occasional Conformity and Schism Acts but against them on the peerage bill in 1719. He put up again for Kent in 1722 but withdrew before the poll, remaining out of the House of Commons till 1727, when his friend, Lord Cobham, brought him in at a by-election for Buckingham.

On Cobham's dismissal from the army for opposing the excise bill Fane, who himself had voted for it, was informed by Newcastle that the King proposed to give him the colonelcy of the 1st troop of Life Guards, vacated by Lord Pembroke's appointment to Cobham's regiment, together with an Irish peerage. He replied:

> It would have been the last thing in my thoughts to have desired a succession arising from the removal of my Lord Cobham, with whom I have lived in the most perfect friendship, and from whom I have received several obligations . . . nevertheless . . . I understand it in such a manner, as that my duty calls upon me to bury all my scruples in a perfect obedience to his Majesty's gracious disposition.[3]

During the next session Fane, now Lord Catherlough, displeased the King and Walpole by supporting, 13 Feb. 1734, an opposition motion to prevent army officers from being dismissed on political grounds. No immediate action was taken against him, but at the general election that year, when he stood down for Kent in favour of the Duke of Dorset's son, Lord Middlesex (q.v.), on a promise by Dorset to bring him in for one of the Cinque Ports, Walpole, 'not apt to forgive any who oppose his measures . . . obliged the Duke to go off from his promise'.[4] In a letter to Henry Fox (q.v.), Hervey describes the results on the Kent county election:

> Lord Catherlough, who has acted very oddly in several things this year, is playing the devil there, roars out against the Duke of Dorset, and does all he can against Lord Middlesex (q.v.).[5]

He remained out of Parliament till 1737 when, having succeeded his elder brother as Earl of Westmorland, he spoke and voted in the Lords for an increase in the Prince of Wales's allowance. He was forthwith dismissed from the army, not being allowed to sell out, thus losing the £6,500 which he had paid for his regiment in 1717. Thenceforth he became one of Walpole's most vehement enemies, going so far as to subsidize mobs to burn him in effigy in 1742.[6] Though reinstated in the army after Walpole's fall, with retrospective promotion, he was not given another regiment, nor would the King agree to reimburse his £6,500, despite repeated applications based on the treatment of the officers from whom he had bought his regiments.[7] 'His resentment', Horace Walpole writes, 'led him to imbibe all the nonsensical tenets of the Jacobites'.[8] From 1743 onwards he was privy to the Jacobite negotiations with France, which led to the Forty-five. He was mentioned by the Pretender in December 1743 as one of his 'principal friends' in England; was included in the prospective council of the Young Pretender on becoming Regent of England;[9] was one of the prominent Tories who agreed to support the Prince of Wales's programme in 1747; and with the Duke of Beaufort (Lord Noel Somerset, q.v.) presided at a meeting of English Jacobites held during the Young Pretender's secret visit to London in September 1750.[10] He was also one of the few trusted with the secret of the Prussian plot of 1752–3.[11] In 1759 he was elected chancellor of Oxford University, where he was installed 'all be-James'd with true-blue ribbands'.[12] He died 26 Aug. 1762.

[1] Secretary at war to Fane, 29 Dec. 1715, Chester RO mss. [2] Westmorland to Pelham, 6 Feb. 1746, Newcastle (Clumber) mss. [3] Fane to Newcastle, 25 June 1733, Add. 32688, f. 15. [4] HMC Egmont Diary, ii. 101, 109, 415–16. [5] Ilchester, Lord Hervey and his Friends, 198. [6] Horace Walpole to Mann, 8 Apr. 1742. [7] Pelham to Westmorland and Westmorland to Pelham, 13 and 19 Feb. 1753, Newcastle (Clumber) mss. [8] Mems. Geo. II, iii. 167. [9] Stuart mss 254/104, 152. [10] Add. 35870, ff. 129–30; The Times, 2 Dec. 1864. [11] Politische Corresp. Friedrich's des Grossen, ix. 436–8. [12] Walpole to Montagu, 19 July 1759.

E.C.

FANE, Hon. Mildmay (1689–1715), of Burston, Kent.

KENT 8 Feb.–11 Sept. 1715

bap. 31 Oct. 1689, 5th s. of Vere Fane, M.P., 4th Earl of Westmorland, and bro. of Hon. John Fane (q.v.). *unm.* *suc.* cos. Thomas Fane, M.P., at Burston 1692.

After contesting Kent unsuccessfully in 1713, Fane was elected as a Whig in 1715. He died the same year, 11 Sept.

A.N.N.

FANE, Thomas (1700–71), of Bristol.

LYME REGIS 19 Jan. 1753–26 Aug. 1762

bap. 8 Mar. 1701, 2nd s. of Henry Fane and yr. bro. of Francis Fane (q.v.). *educ.* M. Temple 1729, called 1759. *m.* 8 Aug. 1727, Elizabeth, da. of William Swymmer, Bristol merchant, wid. of Samuel Kentish, clerk in Chancery, 2s. 2da. *suc.* bro. Francis (q.v.) 1757; his distant cos. John Fane (q.v.) as 8th Earl of Westmorland 26 Aug. 1762.

Originally an attorney and clerk of the Society of Merchant Venturers at Bristol (1726–57), Thomas Fane was returned for Lyme Regis by his brother Francis Fane (q.v.). He supported the Administration until his death, 25 Nov. 1771.

S.R.M.

FANSHAWE, Simon (1716–77), of Fanshawe Gate, Derbys. and Dengie Hall, Essex.

OLD SARUM 22 Nov. 1751–1754
GRAMPOUND 1754–1768

b. 4 Mar. 1716, 1st s. of Thomas Edward Fanshawe of Great Singleton, Lancs. by Elizabeth, da. of William Snelling of Bromley St. Leonards, by Bow, Mdx. *m.* 10 Oct. 1753, cos. Althea, da. of his mat. uncle William Snelling of Holborn, Mdx., 1s. 3da. *suc.* fa. 1726.

Comptroller of the household to George, Prince of Wales 1756–60; comptroller of the Green Cloth 1761–7.

Simon Fanshawe's father, of an old Derbyshire family, inherited Fanshawe Gate and Dengie in 1716 from the 5th Viscount Fanshawe.[1] As the friend of Lord Lincoln, the nephew of the Pelhams, he was brought in at Old Sarum in 1751 by Pelham, who had 'a thorough good opinion of him'.[2] He died 1 Jan. 1777.

[1] H. C. Fanshawe, Hist. Fanshawe Fam. 264 et seq. [2] Ld. Waldegrave to Newcastle, 27 Feb. 1756, Add. 32863, ff. 85–86.

R.S.L.

FARINGTON, Sir Richard, 1st Bt. (c.1644–1719), of Farington House, Chichester.

CHICHESTER 4 Jan.–28 Mar. 1681, 1698–1700, 1708–1713, 1715–7 Aug. 1719

b. c.1644, 2nd s. of John Farington, M.P. Chichester 1679, of Chichester by Anne, da. of John May of Rawmere, Suss. *m.* (1) lic. 28 Feb. 1671, aged 27, Elizabeth Merlott,[1] 1s. *d.v.p.*; (2) 24 May 1687, Elizabeth, da. and h. of John Peachey of Eartham, nr. Chichester,[2] *s.p.* *cr.* Bt. 17 Dec. 1697. Sheriff, Suss. 1696–7.

Farington, whose grandfather had been three times mayor of Chichester, succeeded his father in representing the borough in 1681. His son became its recorder at George I's accession.[3] Returned as a Whig in 1715, Farington voted with the Administration in every recorded division till his death at Bath, 7 Aug. 1719.

[1] Foster, London Marriage Licences. [2] PCC 44 Cann, 7 and 183 Browning. [3] Dallaway, Suss. City of Chichester, 140, 154.

E.C.

FARRER, William (?1656–1737), of Biddenham, Beds.

BEDFORD 1695–1698, 1701–1702, 1705–1713, 1715–1727

b. ?1656, s. of Thomas Farrer of Harrold, Beds. and Aylesbury, Bucks. by Helen, 1st da. of Sir

William Boteler of Biddenham and Harrold, Beds. *educ.* I. Temple 1667, called 1677; Trinity, Oxf. 16 Feb. 1672, aged 15. *m.* (1) 2 Mar. 1680, Mary da. and coh. of William Boteler of Biddenham 1s. 3da.; (2) Elizabeth, *s.p. suc.* fa. 1703.

Dep. recorder, Bedford; K.C. 1699; commr. for army debts 1700–5; chairman of committees of supply and ways and means 1708–10, 1715–27; clerk of the pipe 1710–11; master of St. Katherine's Hospital by the Tower 1715–27.

The Farrers, a legal family of the Inner Temple, acquired Harrold in 1556, intermarrying with the Botelers of Biddenham, an ancient Bedfordshire family.[1] William Farrer, after representing Bedford as a Whig on the Russell interest under William III and Anne, was again returned at contested elections in 1715 and 1722, voting with the Administration in all recorded divisions. Throughout this period he acted as chairman of supply and ways and means, except for a short time when, having been taken very ill in the chair of the supply committee, he was replaced temporarily by Sir Charles Turner (q.v.),[2] who succeeded him when he retired from Parliament in 1727. He died 12 Apr. 1737.

[1] *VCH Beds.* iii. 37, 66; *VCH Bucks.* iv. 325. [2] *Knatchbull Diary,* 2 Dec. 1724.

R.S.L.

FARRINGTON, Thomas (aft. 1687–1758), of Chislehurst, Kent.

WHITCHURCH	2 Feb.–5 Aug. 1727
MITCHELL	1727–1734
LUDGERSHALL	1747–1754

b. aft. 1687,[1] o.s. of Lt.-Gen. Thomas Farrington, M.P., of Chislehurst by Theodosia, da. of Richard Betenson, sis. and coh. of Sir Edward Betenson, 2nd Bt., of Scadbury, Chislehurst. *unm. suc.* fa. 1712.

Auditor of the land revenues for Wales 1733–56.

Thomas Farrington was connected with the Selwyns. His mother's sister was wife of Major-General William Selwyn, M.P., whose eldest son, John Selwyn (q.v.), married Farrington's sister Mary.[2] Returned at a by-election for Whitchurch in 1727, he succeeded his cousin Charles Selwyn (q.v.) at Mitchell in the general election of that year; but though he was re-elected in 1733 after obtaining a place, he was beaten there in 1734. He did not stand again till 1747, when he was brought in for Ludgershall by his brother-in-law John Selwyn. In Parliament he voted for the Administration in all recorded divisions and was classed by the ministry as 'for' in 1747. He died 29 Jan. 1758.

[1] His parents were married 18 Aug. 1687 at Chislehurst. [2] Webb, Miller & Beckwith, *Chislehurst,* 156.

R.S.L.

FAZAKERLEY, Nicholas (?1685–1767), of Prescot, Lancs.

PRESTON 24 Jan. 1732–Feb. 1767

b. ?1685, 1st s. of Henry Fazakerley of Fazakerley, Lancs. *educ.* perhaps Eton 1698; B.N.C. Oxf. 12 Mar. 1702, aged 17; M. Temple 1700, called 1707. *m.* 10 Oct. 1732, Anne, da. of Sir Thomas Lutwyche, M.P., 1s *d.v.p.* 1da. (who m. 1744, Lord Trentham q.v.).

Bencher, L. Inn 1736; counsel to Camb. Univ. 1738–57; recorder, Preston 1742–*d.*

Fazakerley first came before the public eye as counsel for the defence in the trial of the printer and publisher of *The Craftsman* in 1731. In 1732 he was returned unopposed as a Tory for Preston, which he continued to represent for the rest of his life. 'A long-winded lawyer',[1] he became one of the most frequent Tory speakers, voting against the Administration in every recorded division of the reign. On 30 Mar. he spoke in favour of a bill to declare void the sale of the Derwentwater estates[2] (see Bond, Denis), and on 5 Apr. 1736 he supported the mortmain bill,[3] which most of the Tories opposed. In spite of an exchange of personal compliments with Walpole in the debate on the Spanish convention in 1739, he spoke and voted for the motion for his removal in 1741. After Walpole's fall he was employed by the opposition leaders to draw up an impeachment against him, and elected to the secret committee of inquiry into his Administration.[4] He was one of the leading opponents of the new Government, signing the circular letter of 20 Dec. 1743 appealing to opposition Members to be present to vote against the Hanoverians when Parliament reassembled after Christmas.[5]

Though described by Horace Walpole as a Jacobite,[6] Fazakerley was not a party to the negotiations between the Jacobite leaders and the French Government from 1740 to 1745. On 11 Jan. 1744 he spoke against continuing British troops in Flanders. After the failure of the attempted French invasion at the beginning of 1744 he introduced a bill making it treasonable to correspond with the Pretender's sons, but strenuously opposed a government amendment instituting forfeiture of estates for such correspondence, describing it as 'one of the most pernicious and unconstitutional provisions ever devised'. In March 1745 he 'had the chief hand in the management' of a bill for the stricter enforcement of the Act regulating the qualification of the justices of the peace[7] (see Bramston, Thomas). During the Forty-five he subscribed £200 towards raising the Lancashire militia.[8] On 21 Dec. 1745 he followed Lord Gower, his daughter's father-in-law, by speaking 'most heartily' for the Hessians.[9] He was one of the prominent Tories who agreed to support the Prince of Wales's programme in 1747.[10] About 1750 the 2nd Lord Egmont wrote in his electoral survey:

> Fazakerley is very cordial with us at this time, and will so continue if upon the change he is not disappointed of the Duchy of Lancaster which is his great view—and which I apprehend he cannot have [it was reserved for Thomas Bootle, q.v.]—yet he is in great credit with the Tories, and if possible must be obliged in some way or other.

Egmont put him down as a commissioner of the great seal in the future reign but thought he would probably refuse that office.

Fazakerley took a leading part in the debates on the regency bill in 1751. On the clause for continuing the sitting Parliament to the end of the minority he 'made a tedious calculation, which he seemed to intend for humour, of how long the Parliament might possibly continue if every one of the late Prince of Wales's children should happen to die just at a given time'. He was alone in opposing a clause to prevent the young King from marrying as a minor without the consent of the Regent and the Council, showing 'the dangers that may arise from pronouncing the King's wife guilty of high treason, and her children illegitimate, and the mischiefs it may occasion, as he may marry her again after his majority'.[11] In 1753 he attacked Lord Hardwicke's marriage bill and the bill for the naturalization of the Jews.

He died in Feb. 1767.

[1] *Corresp. H. Walpole* (Yale ed.), xvii. 336 n. 9. [2] *HMC Egmont Diary*, i. 248. [3] *Harley Diary*. [4] Walpole to Mann, 18 Feb. and 1 Apr. 1742. [5] Add. 29597, f. 29. [6] *Mems. Geo. II*, i. 111. [7] Yorke's parl. jnl. *Parl. Hist.* xiii. 393, 1245; Coxe, *Pelham*, i. 147–8. [8] Thos. Starkie to Ld. Derby, 21 Oct. 1745, mss DDK/1741, Lancs. RO. [9] Ilchester, *Lord Holland*, i. 121–2. [10] Add. 35870, ff. 129–30. [11] *Mems. Geo. II*, i. 126–8, 144, 146.

E.C.

FEILDING, Hon. William (?1669–1723), of Ashtead, Surr.

CASTLE RISING   29 Nov. 1705–21 Sept. 1723

> b. ?1669, 2nd s. of William Feilding, 3rd Earl of Denbigh, by Mary, da. of Sir Robert King of Boyle Abbey, co. Roscommon, wid. of Sir William Meredith, 1st Bt., of Creenehill, co. Kildare. *educ.* Queen's, Oxf. 4 May 1686, aged 16. *m.* Lady Diana Newport, da. of Francis Newport, M.P., 1st Earl of Bradford, wid. of Thomas Howard, M.P., of Ashtead, Surr., *s.p.*[1]
> Lt. of yeomen of the guard 1704–8; clerk comptroller of the Green Cloth Feb. 1716–*d.*

Feilding, who was returned on his wife's interest, voted from 1715 with the Government in all recorded divisions till his death, 21 Sept. 1723.

[1] Manning & Bray, *Surr.* ii. 629–32.

R.R.S.

FELLOWES, Coulson (1696–1769), of Ramsey Abbey, Hunts. and Eggesford, Devon.

HUNTINGDONSHIRE   1741–1761

> b. 12 Oct. 1696, 1st s. of William Fellowes of Eggesford, master in Chancery, by Mary, da. and h. of Joseph Martin of St. Mary at Hill, London. *educ.* L. Inn 1714, called 1723; Ch. Ch. Oxf. 1716; Grand Tour (France, Italy) 1723–5. *m.* 20 Apr. 1725, Urania, da. of Francis Herbert of Oakley Park, Salop, sis. of Henry Arthur Herbert (qq.v.), 1st Earl of Powis, 2s. 3da. *suc.* fa. 1724.
> Sheriff, Devon 1727–8.

Coulson Fellowes's grandfather, a London merchant, married the sister and heir of Thomas Coulson, M.P. for Totnes, a director of the East India Company; his uncle, Sir John Fellowes, 1st Bt., was deputy governor of the South Sea Company; his father, a lawyer, acquired an estate in Devonshire.[1] Buying Ramsey Abbey in 1737,[2] he was returned for Huntingdonshire in 1741 as an opposition Whig, with the support of Lord Sandwich. He voted consistently against the Administration, even after Sandwich accepted office in 1744. None the less in 1747 Sandwich made his own candidate join with Fellowes,

> as I knew it would be a more certain method of securing great part of Mr. Fellowes's interest upon any other occasion by joining him, than by suffering him to connect and unite his personal friends with the Tory interest.[3]

In the new Parliament Fellowes was classed by the ministry as Opposition. Soon after the election, in recommending a place for a constituent, Sandwich wrote to the Duke of Bedford:

> If hereafter I should have any occasion (as may very likely be the case) to oppose Mr. Fellowes or his son, I shall by obliging this man be able to carry more than half his own town of Ramsey against him.

When at the end of 1751 John Proby (q.v.) became a candidate, Sandwich claimed to have prevailed upon Fellowes to decline in Proby's favour, provided that the latter joined Sandwich's brother, Captain William Montagu (q.v.). But on 18 Apr. 1753 Fellowes sent out a circular letter stating that Montagu, having declined standing at the next general election, 'recommended me to his friends for their votes and interests.'[4] Re-elected unopposed, he died 23 Feb. 1769.

[1] Polwhele, *Devon*, iii. 388. [2] *VCH Hunts.* ii. 194. [3] Sandwich to Devonshire, 10 Oct. 1746, Devonshire mss; *Bedford Corresp.* i. 281–2. [4] Sandwich to Bedford, 2 Feb. 1748 and 15 Dec. 1751, to Ld. Trentham, 15 Dec. 1751, Bedford mss.

R.S.L.

FENWICK, John (1698–1747), of Stanton, Brinkburn and Bywell, Northumb.

NORTHUMBERLAND   1741–19 Dec. 1747

b. 24 Feb. 1698, 1st s. of Roger Fenwick, M.P., of Stanton by Elizabeth, da. and h. of George Fenwick of Brinkburn. *educ.* at home and St. John's, Camb. 1716. *m.* 28 Jan. 1719, Margaret (bur. 10 June 1727), da. and coh. of William Fenwick of Bywell and sister of Isabella, w. of William Wrightson (q.v.), 2s. 1da.; (2) 5 Feb. 1730, Alice, da. of Thomas Errington of Beaufront, Northumb., 1da. *suc.* fa. 1701.

Sheriff, Northumb. 1727–8.

Fenwick, whose family had often represented Northumberland, was described by Lord Tankerville, its lord lieutenant, as a Jacobite, who 'ought not to represent the county'.[1] He certainly had Jacobite connexions: William Fenwick of Bywell, father of his first wife, sheltered Thomas Forster (q.v.); Thomas Errington, father of his second wife, was one of the rebel leaders and prisoners of the Fifteen.[2]

After standing unsuccessfully for Northumberland in 1734, he was returned unopposed in 1741 and 1747. He voted against the Government on the chairman of the elections committee in 1741 and the Hanoverians in 1744, but was absent from the divisions on them in 1742 and 1746. At the general election of 1747 he was 'in such a bad state of health' that he was not expected to 'last 12 months'.[3] He died 19 Dec. 1747.

[1] To Newcastle, 27 May 1747, Add. 32711, f. 124. [2] R. Patten, *Hist. Rebellion in 1715* (1745 ed.); *Pol. State*, x. 343, 543. [3] Ld. Tankerville to Newcastle, 14 June 1747, Add. 32711, f. 345.

E.C.

FENWICK, Nicholas (c.1693–1752), of Pilgrim St., Newcastle-on-Tyne, and Lemington, Northumb.

NEWCASTLE-UPON-TYNE 1727–1747

b. c.1693, 1st s. of Robert Fenwick, merchant, mayor of Newcastle 1708, by Isabella, da. of Cuthbert Ellison of Hebburn, co. Dur. *m.* (1) 21 Oct. 1713, Elizabeth (*d.* Mar. 1715), da. of George Baker of Crook, co. Dur., *s.p.*; (2) 9 May 1716, Elizabeth, da. and coh. of Sir James Clavering, 4th Bt., of Axwell, co. Dur., 6s. 7da.

Mayor, Newcastle 1726, 1736, 1746, 1747.

The grandson of Nicholas Fenwick, governor of the Merchant Adventurers 1697–1704, Fenwick was admitted to that Company in 1712. Representing Newcastle as a Tory for twenty years, he voted against the Administration in every recorded division. In 1733 he was given a vote of thanks by the Merchant Adventurers for his zeal in opposing the excise bill.[1] Through his second wife he had acquired Lemington, in Alnwick, where he practised forestry, for which he received a gold medal from the Society of Arts.[2] Retiring in 1747, he died in 1752 (buried 27 Feb.).

[1] J. Richmond to Walter Blackett (q.v.), 2 June 1733, Add. 27420, f. 62. [2] *Arch. Aeliana* (ser. 4), xxiii. 150.

E.C.

FENWICK, Robert (1688–1750), of Burrow Hall, Lancs.

LANCASTER 1734–1747

b. 5 Nov. 1688, o.s. of John Fenwick of Nunriding, nr. Morpeth, Northumb. by Jane, da. and h. of Nicholas Tatham of Burrow Hall, Lancs. *educ.* Burrow sch.; St. John's, Camb. 19 June 1706, aged 17; G. Inn 1705, called 1715, transferred to L. Inn 1725, bencher 1740. *suc.* fa. 1732.

Attorney-gen. of court of Chancery and King's serjeant for duchy of Lancaster Aug. 1727–Dec. 1749; v.-chancellor of the duchy July 1742–Jan. 1743.

In 1727 Fenwick stood for Morpeth, near his father's estate, with the support of the corporation, offering £25 a vote. Defeated by Lord Carlisle's candidate, Thomas Robinson (q.v.), he petitioned, but eventually withdrew his petition at the instance of the corporation and to oblige Lord Carlisle.[1] Returned for Lancaster as an independent Whig after a contest in 1734 and unopposed in 1741, he voted against the Administration in all recorded divisions except that for the dismissal of Walpole in 1741, when he withdrew. Retiring in 1747, he died 13 Feb. 1750.

[1] J. M. Fewster, 'Politics and Admin. of Morpeth in 18th Cent.' (Durham Univ. Ph.D. thesis), 56–59.

E.C.

FERGUSSON, Alexander (1685–1749), of Craigdarroch, Dumfries.

DUMFRIES BURGHS 1715–1722

b. 3 Nov. 1685, 1st surv. s. of John Fergusson of Craigdarroch by Elizabeth, da. of Alexander McGhie of Balmaghie, Kirkcudbright. *m.* 29 Aug. 1709, Anna ('Annie Laurie'), da. of Sir Robert Laurie, 1st Bt., of Maxwelton, Kirkcudbright, 2s. 2da. at least. *suc.* fa. 1689.

Fergusson, whose father was killed serving as a lieutenant-colonel of foot in King William's army at Killiecrankie, received the Duke of Argyll's letter of mobilization on the outbreak of the Fifteen rebellion,[1] during which he was engaged in the defence of Dumfries. Returned unopposed as a Whig in 1715 in succession to his uncle by marriage, Sir William Johnstone (q.v.), who had moved to the county seat, he voted with the Government on the septennial bill in 1716. His name does not appear in the list of Whigs voting against Lord Cadogan (q.v.) in June 1717, but three days later he was present at a dinner given by Cadogan's rival, the Duke of Argyll, one of whose followers describes him as having 'acted a prodigious honest part' in the affair.[2] He was absent from the division on the repeal of the Occasional Conformity and Schism Acts but voted for the peerage bill in 1719. Defeated in 1722, he was also unsuccessful for the county in 1734, petitioning without success on each occasion. He died 8 Mar. 1749.

[1] J. Fergusson & R. M. Ferguson, *Recs. of Clan and Name of Fergusson*, 387–8, 398–9. [2] *More Culloden Pprs.* ii. 175.

J.M.S.

FERGUSSON, Sir James, 2nd Bt. (c.1687–1759), of Kilkerran, Ayr.

SUTHERLAND   15 Feb. 1734–Nov. 1735

b. c.1687, 1st s. of Sir John Fergusson, 1st Bt., of Kilkerran by Jean, da. of James Whitefoord of Dunduff, Ayr, sis. of Sir Adam Whitefoord, 1st Bt. *educ.* ?Edinburgh; ?Leyden 1709; adv. 1711. *m.* (contr. 3 and 8 Sept. 1726) Jean, da. and h. of James, Visct. Maitland, gd.-da. of the 16th Earl of Sutherland [S], 9s. 5da. *suc.* fa. 14 Feb. 1729.
Ld. of session, Lord Kilkerran, 1735–*d.*; ld. of justiciary 1749–*d.*

Fergusson was brought in for Sutherland by the 17th Earl of Sutherland, his wife's first cousin, at a by-election in February 1734, voting with the Administration on the bill to repeal the Septennial Act a month later. At the ensuing general election that year he defeated Sir William Gordon (q.v.), whose petition alleged that Fergusson had not been enfeoffed in his qualifying estate within the shire until 27 Nov. 1733, less than the required year before the teste of the writ.[1] His appointment to be a lord of session in November 1735 vacated his seat before a hearing of the petition, which was later withdrawn. He died 20 Jan. 1759.

[1] *CJ*, xxii. 339.

R.S.L.

FERMANAGH, Visct., *see* VERNEY, John, VERNEY, Ralph (*b.* 1683), *and* VERNEY, Ralph (*b.* 1714)

FERMOR, John (1674–1722), of Sevenoaks, Kent.

MALMESBURY   13–29 Dec. 1722

b. 10 Oct. 1674,[1] 6th s. of William Fermor of Walshes, Suss. by his 3rd w. Martha, da. of Tristram Thomas of Kent; bro. of Sir Henry Fermor, 1st Bt. *unm.*
Ensign, Brudenell's Ft. 1694; capt. Orrery's Ft. 1706, maj. 1707; maj. 3 Ft. 1709; adjutant-gen. in Spain 1711; brevet-col. 1711; lt.-gov. Port Mahon. Minorca 1711; half pay 1713; lt.-col. Rich's Drags, 1715–18.

John Fermor, a professional soldier of an old Sussex family, was invalided home from Portugal in 1705, served in the Duke of Argyll's regiment (the Buffs) at Malplaquet 1709 and was appointed by the Duke to his staff in Spain 1711.[2] At the election of 1722 he was brought in at Malmesbury by Giles Earle (q.v.), who had also served in

Spain on Argyll's staff. Though defeated at the poll, he was seated by the House of Commons 16 days before his death from smallpox, 29 Dec. 1722.

[1] Add. 5697, f. 571. [2] Dalton, *Eng. Army Lists*, vi. 325–6.

R.S.L.

FERRERS, Thomas (c.1665–1722), of Bangeston, Pemb.

PEMBROKE BOROUGHS   1715–22 Oct. 1722

b. c.1665, 4th s. of John Ferrers of Cookham, Berks. by Anne, da. of John Kinsman of Isleworth, Mdx. *m.* c.1707, Elizabeth, da. and h. of Henry White of Bangeston, wid. of (i) Thomas Lort (s. of Sampson Lort, M.P. Pembroke 1659), and (ii) Richard Bulkeley, M.P., 3rd Visct. Bulkeley of Cashel [I], *s.p.*
Ensign 1 Ft. 1692, lt. 1695, capt. 1705; brevet-col. 1705; brig.-gen. 1710; col. 23 Drags. 1715; half-pay 1718; col. 39 Ft. 1719, transferred to 17 Ft. 1722.

Ferrers, whose family had settled at Cookham in the reign of Elizabeth, served under Marlborough at Ramillies and Malplaquet. By marriage he acquired property in Pembrokeshire, standing for Pembroke in 1710, but desisting.[1] Returned for it as a Whig in 1715, he voted with the Government on the septennial bill in 1716, but against them on the repeal of the Occasional Conformity and Schism Acts in 1719. He was to be spoken to by Craggs and George Treby (qq.v.) on the peerage bill, on which he did not vote. Again returned in 1722, he died that year, 22 Oct.

[1] *HMC Portland*, iv. 569.

E.C.

FINCH, Daniel, Lord Finch (1689–1769).

RUTLAND   1710–1 Jan. 1730

b. 24 May 1689, 1st surv. s. of Daniel Finch, M.P., 2nd Earl of Nottingham and 7th Earl of Winchilsea, by his 3rd w. Anne, da. of Christopher, 1st Visct. Hatton; bro. of Hon. Edward, Henry, John and William Finch (qq.v.). *educ.* Westminster; Ch. Ch. Oxf. 1704. Grand Tour 1706. *m.* (1) 28 Dec. 1729, Lady Frances Feilding (*d.* 24 Sept. 1734), da. of Basil, 4th Earl of Denbigh, 1da.; (2) 18 Jan. 1738, Mary, da. and coh. of Sir Thomas Palmer, 4th Bt. (q.v.), 4da. *suc.* fa. as 8th Earl of Winchilsea and 3rd Earl of Nottingham 1 Jan. 1730; K.G. 13 Mar. 1752.
Gent. of the bedchamber to Prince of Wales 1714–16: ld. of Treasury 1715–16; comptroller of the King's Household 1725–30; P.C. 1 June 1725; first ld. of Admiralty Mar. 1742–Dec. 1744 and Apr.–July 1757; ld. pres. of the Council 1765–6.

Daniel Finch, 2nd Earl of Nottingham and 7th Earl of Winchilsea (1647–1730), commonly called 'Dismal', had five surviving sons and seven surviving daughters, known from their swarthiness as 'the black funereal Finches'. All five sons were returned to Parliament, three of them by their sisters' husbands, the 'proud' Duke of Somerset and Sir Thomas Watson Wentworth (q.v.), successively created Earl of Malton and Marquess of Rockingham. Other sisters married Sir Roger Mostyn and William Murray, afterwards Lord Mansfield (qq.v.). As one of them, Isabella, said to her brother Edward (q.v.), 'the women of the family had been the credit and indeed the support of it'. When he asked her how, 'I told him', she wrote to her brother-in-law, Lord Malton,

> by the figure they had made in the world and the service they had done the brothers by having married people of fortune and interest, who had brought them into Parliament . . . He only replied that he had not his seat from any brother-in-law. I at him again and told him that had not you chose Henry [Henry Finch, q.v.], Cambridge would and then he would have been to seek for a place.[1]

On coming of age Lord Nottingham's eldest son, Lord Finch, was returned for his county, shortly before his father went over to the Whigs. Classed as a Whig at George I's accession, when he was appointed to the Prince's bedchamber, he seconded the motion for choosing Spencer Compton as Speaker and was a member of the secret committee of inquiry into the conduct of the late Queen's ministers, subsequently speaking in support of the Duke of Ormonde's impeachment (15 Aug. 1715). Promoted to the Treasury board in October 1715, he was one of the managers of the impeachment of the rebel lords (9 Jan. 1716); but when Lord Nottingham was turned out in March 1716 for sponsoring a parliamentary agitation for their reprieve, Finch resigned, 'only because', as he afterwards told his father, 'you was ill used, not for the things done'.[2] Going into opposition, he spoke against the septennial bill, declaring it to have been 'calculated to serve the avarice of a few persons' and calling the House a 'lick spittle Parliament for giving into it'.[3] In April 1717 he attacked the vote of supply for warlike preparations against Sweden, ascribing it to the fact that Bernstorff, the King's chief Hanoverian adviser, had lands in Mecklenburg, and suggesting that it would have been cheaper to have made him a present of £50,000.[4]

During the split in the Whig party (1717–20), Finch voted against the Government but dissociated himself from the discontented Whig leaders, in deference to Lord Nottingham, who considered that they had treated him as badly as the ministers had done. At or about the time of the re-union of the Whig party he appears to have reluctantly refused an attractive offer because, as he wrote to his father (5 Apr. 1720), 'your Lordship would not come into it and it was my duty to sacrifice my avarice to your commands . . . For myself I look upon the game to be up and ambition is as dead in me as if I were six foot under ground'. Ceasing to attend Parliament, he devoted himself to 'the only passion I have left . . . the advancement of my brothers in the world.' Having made some money in the South Sea bubble, he advanced his brother William (q.v.) £1,000 for his initial expenses in Sweden, paid his brother John's (q.v.) expenses on contesting Maidstone, and subsequently bought him a fine set of chambers in the Temple.[5] He was continually pressing on Lord Nottingham schemes for their advancement.

> For myself [he wrote, 8 Nov. 1722] I have no desire, I have no ambition, and if ever I was to stir in life it shall only be for them. There was a time, I own, I did imagine to have had a share in the government of this country before this time or to have fallen in the attempt. To serve them now, to raise their fortune, is my view, and if I do succeed in that I don't care what turn my own affairs take.

And again 31 Jan. 1723:

> The love I have had for my brothers and family is seriously the most real solid pleasure that I ever met with in this world. I have always founded and built my happiness, present and future, as to this world, upon theirs.

But a fortnight later he was writing to his father about the possibility of his being offered an important post abroad, presumably an embassy: ''tis recovering a rank which is lost by being out of it so long. Besides, there is no way so likely of coming into business at home as by such a foreign step.' He continued:

> I would either give up quite and not let any one action of my life look as if I was at all concerned in this ridiculous world or be something in it. But to be in a middle way is tedious and unpleasant. Besides all the younger sons would rise faster and better in proportion to the figure one makes than they could do any other way and really I can't help thinking, since this country must be governed, why one had not better govern than be governed.[6]

Though this particular post did not materialize, Finch made a return to politics by moving the Address at the opening of the next session and speaking in support of the army estimates a fortnight later. In April 1725 he presented to the House Bolingbroke's petition for the restitution of his estates, following it up with an implementing bill, which was supported by Walpole and passed into law. Appointed comptroller of the Household at the end of the session, he spoke in the next in defence of the treaty of Hanover, making his last recorded speech in the Commons in support of a vote of credit on 25 Mar. 1726. Soon after succeeding his father in 1730 he resigned with his friend Carteret, by whom, according to Hervey, he was usually governed, but who on this occasion was governed by him.[7] He spent most of the rest of his long political career in opposition in the Lords.

He died 2 Aug. 1769.

[1] 7 July 1744, Rockingham mss. [2] 4 Feb. 1724, Finch mss at HMC. [3] Coxe, *Walpole*, ii. 63. [4] W. Michael, *England under Geo. I*, ii. 273. [5] Ld. Finch to Ld. Nottingham, 12 Jan. 1718, 5 Apr. and 10 May 1720, 14 May 1723, 4 Feb. 1724; Ld. Nottingham to Ld. Finch, 3 Nov. 1724, Finch mss. [6] Finch mss. [7] Hervey, *Mems.* 120.

R.R.S.

FINCH, Hon. Edward (?1697–1771), of Kirby Hall, nr. Rockingham, Northants.

CAMBRIDGE UNIVERSITY 1727–1768

b. ?1697, 5th s. of Daniel Finch, 2nd Earl of Nottingham and 7th Earl of Winchilsea, and bro. of Daniel, Lord Finch, and Hon. Henry, John and William Finch (qq.v.). *educ.* Trinity, Camb. 10 Oct. 1713, aged 16; Grand Tour. *m.* 6 Sept. 1746, Elizabeth, da. and coh. of Sir Thomas Palmer, 4th Bt. (q.v.), 2s. 3da. *suc.* to estates of his gt.-aunt Hon. Anne Hatton 1764, and took add. name of Hatton.

Minister to imperial diet 1724–5, to Poland 1725–7; envoy to Sweden 1728–39; minister to Poland, Apr.–May 1740; envoy to Russia 1740–2; groom of the bedchamber 1742–56; master of the robes 1757–60; surveyor of the King's private roads 1760–d.

Edward Finch returned from his grand tour via Hanover, whence he reported to his father that Townshend and Carteret, who were there in attendance on the King, had 'assured me that rather than send me into Rutlandshire as your Lordship's bailiff . . . they will cook me up some secretary place in Italy. Of Lord Carteret's friendship for me your Lordship will not doubt and of Lord Townshend's good disposition of doing something for me I have all the reasons in the world to assure you. All depends on a vacancy'. 'I shall always call Ned the Protestant Envoy', Lord Finch (q.v.) observed, on learning that his brother had been assigned to the German diet at Ratisbon. 'My Lord Townshend once speaking to me of him did not give him in discussion the title of envoy but called him only the Protestant Thing'.[1] He spent most of his diplomatic career in Sweden, where in 1736 he pleased George II as elector but embarrassed Walpole by putting up a plan for an alliance between the northern and the maritime powers against Prussia.[2] In 1742 he retired on grounds of ill health, immediately after concluding an abortive treaty with Russia. Horace Walpole described him as combining the 'unpolished

sycophancy' of the Russian court with the 'formality of a Spaniard'.[3]

In an interval between two posts Finch was returned in 1727 for Cambridge University, for which his brother Henry (q.v.) had stood unsuccessfully at the previous general election. He continued to represent the university for over 40 years, founding jointly with his fellow Member, Thomas Townshend, the Members' prizes. While on foreign service he is recorded as having voted only once, against the place bill of 1740. On his return to England in 1742 he attached himself to Carteret, was appointed to the King's bedchamber, and spoke on the Address, 16 Nov. 1742, giving 'an account of all his negotiations, and the interest as well as the views of every court in Europe.'[4] He spoke warmly against the opposition motion of 6 Dec. 1743 for discontinuing the Hanoverian troops on British pay 'as reflecting on the King', for which he was called to order and told by the Speaker that he must 'not mention that great person in the debate'.[5] Next year he was recommended by Carteret for the surveyorship of works but was passed over in favour of his brother Henry, Pelham's candidate. After Carteret's dismissal he was allowed to retain his post at the personal request of the King (see Finch, William). He subsequently transferred his allegiance to the Pelhams, remaining faithful to Newcastle in the next reign.

He died 16 May 1771.

[1] 27 Aug. 1723 and 4 Feb. 1724, Finch mss at HMC. [2] Coxe, *Walpole*, i. 483. [3] Walpole, *Mems. Geo. II*, ii. 120. [4] Hen. Finch to Ld. Malton, 18 Nov. 1746, Fitzwilliam mss. [5] Yorke's parl. jnl. *Parl. Hist.* xiii. 191–2.

R.R.S.

FINCH, Heneage, Lord Guernsey (?1683–1757).

MAIDSTONE 3 Nov. 1704–1705
SURREY 1710–22 July 1719

b. ?1683, 1st s. of Heneage Finch, M.P., 1st Earl of Aylesford, by Elizabeth, da. and coh. of Sir John Banks, 1st Bt., M.P., of Aylesford, Kent; bro. of Hon. John Finch (*b.* ?1689, q.v.). *educ.* Westminster; Ch. Ch. Oxf. 27 June 1700, aged 17. *m.* 9 Dec. 1712, Mary, da. and h. of Sir Clement Fisher, 3rd Bt., of Packington, Warws., 1s. 3da. *suc.* fa. as 2nd Earl 22 July 1719.

Master of jewel office 1711–16.

Guernsey's father, a Hanoverian Tory, who had acquired by marriage the manor of Aylesford, carrying an interest at Maidstone where his family usually returned one Member, went over to the Whigs with his brother, the 2nd Earl of Nottingham, at the end of Anne's reign. Classed as a Tory who might often vote Whig, Guernsey was allowed to retain his place after George I's accession. At the outbreak of the rebellion of 1715 he declared to the Commons:

> It was well known that he had, on many occasions, differed from some Members in that House; but being now convinced that our liberty, religion and all that is dear to Englishmen were aimed at, he would, *laying his hand on his sword*, rather die with his sword in his hand, than survive the Pretender's coming in, though he were to enjoy the greatest honours and preferments.[1]

He subsequently told the 1st Lord Egmont that

> The Earl of Nottingham was as violent as any to turn out the Tories, and in a great wrath with him (who was then in the House of Commons) for voting with the Tories. My Lord told him he was sorry it displeased him, but that his violence [would] soon turn him out himself, which soon came to pass.[2]

Turned out of office with Lord Nottingham and the rest of the Finches at the beginning of 1716 for opposing the execution of the rebel lords, Guernsey spoke against the septennial bill, observing that 'if a man did not fall into all the measures of the ministry, and lap with them like the men of Gideon, he was immediately brow-beaten', which exposed him to the retort that 'he was of another opinion not many weeks before; so that what he now said must proceed either from resentment or disappointment'.[3] He also spoke against the vote of supply for measures against Sweden (8 Apr. 1717); suggested (12 May 1717) that on being ordered by the King to disband part of the army, the ministry had by mistake disbanded convocation; and moved for the insertion of a clause against Socinianism in the bill for the repeal of the Occasional Conformity and Schism Acts in 1719. Succeeding to his father's earldom in 1719 he became one of the Tory stalwarts in the Lords.[4]

He died 29 June 1757.

[1] Chandler, vi. 36. [2] *HMC Egmont Diary*, ii. 67. [3] Chandler, vi. 105. [4] Hervey, *Mems.* 120.

R.R.S.

FINCH, Heneage, Lord Guernsey (1715–77).

LEICESTERSHIRE   20 Dec. 1739–1741
MAIDSTONE   1741–1747
                                            1754–29 June 1757

b. 6 Nov. 1715, 1st s. of Heneage Finch (q.v.), 2nd Earl of Aylesford. *educ.* Westminister 1728–32; Univ. Coll. Oxf. 1732. *m.* 6 Oct. 1750, Lady Charlotte Seymour, da. of Charles, 6th Duke of Somerset, by his 2nd w. Lady Charlotte Finch, da. of Daniel, 2nd Earl of Nottingham and 7th Earl of Winchilsea, 8s. 4da. *suc.* fa. as 3rd Earl 29 June 1757.

Returned unopposed as a Tory at a by-election at the end of 1739, Guernsey voted against the Government on the place bill of 1740, and withdrew on the motion for the dismissal of Walpole in February 1741. After the death of his uncle, John Finch (q.v.), he transferred to Maidstone, voting against the Hanoverian troops in all three recorded divisions and speaking against them on 11 Apr. 1746. He lost his seat in 1747, by which time he had become associated with the Prince of Wales, appearing in Thomas Pitt's election papers,[1] and subsequently being put down for a seat at the Treasury in the 2nd Lord Egmont's lists of a future Government.

He died 9 May 1777.

[1] *HMC Fortescue*, i. 118.

A.N.N.

FINCH, Hon. Henry (?1694–1761).

MALTON 27 Nov. 1724–26 Apr. 1761

b. ?1694, 4th surv. s. of Daniel Finch, 2nd Earl of Nottingham and 7th Earl of Winchilsea, and bro. of Daniel, Lord Finch, and Hon. Edward, John and William Finch (qq.v.). *educ.* Eton 1707; Christ's, Camb. 19 Aug. 1712, aged 17. *unm.*

Receiver gen. of revenues of Minorca 1729–43; surveyor gen. of works 1743–60.

Henry Finch was nominated by his father a fellow of Christ's on the Finch and Baines foundation before taking his degree. In 1720 he stood unsuccessfully for the University on the Whig interest. After he had been over ten years at Cambridge his brother Lord Finch (q.v.) wrote to Lord Nottingham on 4 Feb. 1724:

> As for Harry I can only tell your Lordship this, that I think him capable of anything but the seat of the muses or retirement at Burley, which can lead to nothing nor contribute to no good. It is more than sufficient hardship that he has remained so long in the bosom of his Alma Mater after she proved so unnatural to him in disappointing him of his just pretensions to her favour . . . I have now in terms a direct offer from my brother W. [Thomas Watson Wentworth, q.v.] of a seat at Malton . . . But though upon discourse with your Lordship you seemed . . . to think a provision out of Parliament most agreeable to his circumstances, upon discoursing with my Lady upon what I wished for him, which is to send him abroad, she did not approve of it. I must beg leave to lay down my scheme for him before your Lordship, and [know] whether he shall be chose at Malton or shall now immediately go abroad. His going abroad to learn languages is not all, but to rub off the academical improvements and habits which in the course of ten years he must have made and contracted and to see a little of the world is the end I propose he should attain, and thereby qualify himself to make these future advantages of being in Parliament more than barely securing an employment . . . Otherwise Harry has not had fair play in the world.

And on 11 Feb.:

I don't pretend to fix any particular way for Harry, but I do desire he may be in the way of fortune in some manner or other, for I cannot agree that because he has no profession he therefore will never be able to live. Let him be tried as others have been before him, and if he fails he cannot be worse than in the way he is.[1]

Returned for Malton on the interest of his brother-in-law, Thomas Watson Wentworth (q.v.), he secured a 'provision out of Parliament' as receiver-general of the revenues of Minorca, where he for some time resided. In 1726 he was deprived of his college fellowship on the grounds of non-residence, and that as an M.P. he possessed more property than was permissible for a fellow; but soon afterwards he was reinstated. Unlike his brothers, he voted with the Government in every recorded division. In 1743 he was appointed surveyor of works on Pelham's recommendation, in preference to his brother Edward (q.v.), Carteret's candidate.[2] He was classed in 1747 as Old Whig and by the 2nd Lord Egmont about 1750 among 'the most obnoxious men of an inferior degree' in the House. He died 26 Apr. 1761.

[1] Finch mss at HMC. [2] Owen, *Pelhams*, 203.

R.R.S.

FINCH, Hon. John (?1689–1740), of the Inner Temple.

Maidstone 1722–1 Jan. 1740

b. ?1689, 2nd s. of Heneage Finch, M.P., 1st Earl of Aylesford, and bro. of Heneage, Lord Guernsey (b. ?1683, q.v.). *educ.* ?Westminster; Ch. Ch. Oxf. 1 Apr. 1709, aged 19; I. Temple 1710, called 1719. *m.* 30 Apr. 1726, Elizabeth, da. and h. of John Savile of Methley, Yorks., 1s. 1da.

Returned as à Tory on the family interest at Maidstone, John Finch, a lawyer, voted consistently with the Opposition. In February and March 1732 he twice paired with his cousin, Lord Perceval (q.v.), on Walpole's proposed salt duty, which he opposed.[1] He died 1 Jan. 1740.

[1] *HMC Egmont Diary*, i. 220, 234.

A.N.N.

FINCH, Hon. John (?1692–1763), of Bushey, Herts.

Higham Ferrers   20 Jan. 1724–1741
Rutland   1741–1747

b. ?1692, 3rd s. of Daniel Finch, 2nd Earl of Nottingham and 7th Earl of Winchilsea, and bro. of Daniel, Lord Finch, and Hon. Edward, Henry and William Finch (qq.v.). *educ.* Eton 1706–7; Ch. Ch. Oxf. 26 Jan. 1708, aged 15; I. Temple 1711, called 1719. *m.* Elizabeth Younger, actress, 1da. (born before marriage).

Solicitor gen. to Prince of Wales 1726–7; K.C. 1727.

On the night of 18 Dec. 1722 John Finch, a practising barrister, was stabbed by Sally Salisbury, a well known courtesan, at the Three Tuns tavern in Chandos Street, where she had been drinking with Lord Scarsdale. An attempt by his eldest brother, Lord Finch (q.v.), to keep the news from their father was foiled by an anonymous letter informing Lord Nottingham that

> the expectations of the town at this time are great what will be done with that creature in Newgate that stab[bed] your son, Mr. Finch. It is thought by all people your Lordship may punish her as you please and if you dont make an example of her you are highly to blame. Should she ever have her liberty again your son had better have died, for she will certainly ruin him, which may be prevented by your Lordship's known wise conduct, and will not only be a good to your own family but of infinite service to the public, for there is hardly a person but has suffered by her in son or husband. No one ever went there more than Mr. Finch and 'scaped death narrower than he, and from the hands of the highest monster in nature; one only permitted here to seduce and ruin mankind and to do the work of the devil.

Lord Finch reassured his father as to the steps which were being taken to deal with Sally:

> She is destroyed beyond the power of her friends ever to support her and the next sessions I conceive we shall have a sentence of imprisonment for a time certain, with a fine which being large amounts to perpetual imprisonment, since scarce anyone will be ready to pay the fine for her.

John Finch also wrote to his father:

> My intentions . . . were more than once determined to acquaint you with the whole truth. But my resolutions were vain for the nearer I approached you the consciousness of my guilt and your virtue always turned me back silent . . . Your tenderness to me in not confounding me face to face is so amiable that (were there no other inducements) it would always serve to animate me in the ways of virtue.
> On Thursday next the wretch will be upon her trial (I should tell your Lordship I am subpoenaed which I am not sorry for) and will I dare say meet with her just reward.

The defence was that the blow had been the result of 'a sudden heat of passion' occasioned by an opera ticket given by Finch to her blind sister, which she resented as an attempt to seduce her sister. Found guilty of assaulting and wounding, without intent to kill, she was sentenced to a year's imprisonment, to pay a fine of £100, and thereafter to give surety for two years good behaviour.[1] She died in Newgate 11 Feb. 1724, before her sentence had been completed.[2] For the rest of John Finch's life he was known as 'him who was stabbed by Sally Salisbury'.[3]

A month after the trial John Finch stood unsuccessfully for Maidstone on the interest of his cousin, the 2nd Lord Aylesford (Heneage Finch, q.v.). Next year he was returned for Higham Ferrers by his brother-in-law, Thomas Watson Wentworth (q.v.). Shortly after his return his elder brother, Lord Finch, wrote to Lord Nottingham:

> My fears for him arise from . . . his inadvisable modesty and bashfulness, which prevent his putting himself forward in the world and perhaps will continue to do it, and is the natural result of his education and his retired studious life, and it was for that very reason I spent my money at Maidstone and am glad he is chose at Higham that by bringing him into a higher form of acquaintance he by seeing more of the world, may know how to live in it before it is too late. For at present his happiness consists in the acquaintance of only two or three that have been bred up with him, nor can I get him even in the idle hours (if I may be allowed without an offence to say that the hardest student of law may have some) to see even those friends that might be of use to him.[4]

In Parliament he followed Lord Finch, seconding the Address in 1729 and accompanying him into opposition in 1730. After Walpole's fall, with the rest of his brothers, he supported the Government and was classed in 1746 as one of Granville's followers. In 1747 his elder brother, now Lord Winchilsea, intended to put him up again for Rutland, for which he had been returned in 1741, but desisted on finding that there was no prospect of success.[5] He never stood again. He died 12 Feb. 1763, leaving a natural daughter, whose presentation at court in 1747 led to lively dissensions in the family.[6]

[1] Her real name was Pridden but on being told that she looked like Lady Salisbury, she took that name. Ld. Finch to Ld. Nottingham, 22 Mar., 25 and 30 Apr. 1723, John Finch to Ld. Nottingham, 9 and 22 Mar., 21 Apr. 1723, Finch mss at HMC. [2] J. Caulfield, *Portraits of Remarkable Persons*, ii. 151–4. [3] Walpole to Mann, 10 Apr. 1747. [4] 4 Feb. 1724, Finch mss. [5] *HMC Rutland*, ii. 200. [6] Walpole to Mann, 10 Apr. 1747.

R.R.S.

FINCH, Hon. William (1691–1766), of Charlewood, Herts.

COCKERMOUTH 31 Jan. 1727–1747, 11 Dec. 1747–1754

BEWDLEY 5 Feb. 1755–1761

b. 18 Jan. 1691, 2nd surv. s. of Daniel Finch, 2nd Earl of Nottingham and 7th Earl of Winchilsea, and bro. of Daniel, Lord Finch, and Hon. Edward, Henry and John Finch (qq.v.). educ. Ch. Ch. Oxf. 1707. m. (1) 25 Jan. 1733, Lady Anne Douglas (d. 26 Oct. 1741), da. of James, 2nd Duke of Queensberry [S] and 1st Duke of Dover, s.p.; (2) 9 Aug. 1746, Lady Charlotte Fermor, da. of Thomas, 1st Earl of Pomfret, 1s. 4da.

Envoy to Sweden 1720–4; envoy to United Provinces 1724–8 and minister 1733–4; P.C. 13 July 1742; vice-chamberlain of the Household 1742–65.

William Finch owed his start in life to Lord Carteret, who when ambassador to Sweden 1719–20

took him with him as secretary, securing his appointment as envoy there after his own departure. In 1721 Carteret, now secretary of state, sent a friendly admonition to his protégé at Stockholm:

> I beg of you not to write such short letters, the King does really take notice of it, and when you have a whole week to prepare a despatch in you may certainly send all the occurrences . . . If you give occasion to reflect upon your want of diligence you will disconcert all my schemes for your service. I have often given you hints of this nature, which proceeded always from my affection to you and from observing that other people took notice of it. I know you think me pedantic but nothing is done in this world without pains and application, nothing but labour can set a man on his own feet.[1]

After Sweden Finch served for two spells at The Hague, where his 'indolent ministry' threw the Dutch 'entirely into the hands and under the direction of France'.[2] When in 1734 Walpole's brother, Horace (q.v.), was sent there with the rank of ambassador on a special mission, Finch

> desired to be recalled, and quitted the King's service; thinking his capacity (which was a very mean one) equal to the most delicate transactions of state, and not comprehending, though it had been as good as he thought it, that yet Sir Robert Walpole . . . might choose rather to confide in his own brother in an affair where the utmost secrecy was required than in a brother to my Lord Winchilsea, and one who was brought into the world by Lord Carteret, owed everything to his favour, and still lived with him in the strictest friendship.[3]

Finch, who had been brought into Parliament by his brother-in-law the Duke of Somerset, had previously voted with the Government, but now went over to the Opposition till Walpole's fall, when he and his brother Edward (q.v.) obtained posts in the royal Household as Carteret's adherents. On the dismissal of their patron in 1744 they were not molested, on the ground that it would be 'very indecent to ask the King to remove the people that are immediately about his person'. But after the abortive attempt by Carteret (now Granville) and Bath to form an Administration in 1746 the King was invited to agree that the Government should 'be purged of all their friends and dependents'. He agreed to everything, Newcastle told Chesterfield, 'except the Bedchamber', i.e. Edward Finch's dismissal, and to that of William Finch, which he

> begged us not to insist upon in such a manner, and said he should not take it so kindly if we did not do it, that in the opinion of everybody it would have been indecent to have pressed it. As to Ned Finch, we all thought the Bedchamber could not be attacked.

They therefore escaped, though Chesterfield considered it

a ridiculous and an indecent thing that Will Finch should every day by virtue of his office hear and see everything that is done in that backstairs room . . . As for Ned, I would rather he had a thousand pounds a year at the board of Trade than his present five hundred in the Bedchamber.[4]

A few years later they were both included by the 2nd Lord Egmont in a list of 'the most obnoxious men of an inferior degree' in the Commons.

William Finch retained his place till 1765, when he was pensioned off. In December of that year Mrs. Montagu

saw a very odd scene at the Prince of Wales drawing room, Mr. Finch, partly mad, had beat his wife, Lady Charlotte [governess to the royal children], and thrown her down stairs, upon which they were separated by articles, notwithstanding this he was talking to her as she sat in the drawing room with the youngest prince in her lap . . . he is certainly the first man who ever talked in public to a wife from whom he was separated.[5]

He died 25 Dec. 1766.

[1] 10 Nov. 1721, Finch mss at HMC. [2] Horace Walpole to Sir Robt. Walpole, 28 Oct. 1736, Coxe, *Walpole*, iii. 427. [3] Hervey, *Mems.* 367. [4] Lodge, *Private Corresp. Chesterfield and Newcastle* (R. Hist. Soc. Cam. 3rd. ser. xliv), 110-11, 115. [5] R. Blunt, *Mrs. Montagu*, 92.

R.R.S.

FINCH HATTON, *see* FINCH, Hon. Edward

FIREBRACE, Sir Cordell, 3rd Bt. (1712–59), of Long Melford, Suff.

SUFFOLK   5 Mar. 1735–28 Mar. 1759

b. 20 Feb. 1712, o.s. of Sir Charles Firebrace, 2nd Bt., of Stoke Golding, Leics. by Margaret, da. of Sir John Cordell, 2nd Bt., M.P., of Long Melford, sis. and h. of Sir John Cordell, 3rd Bt., M.P. *educ.* St. John's, Oxf. 1729. *m.* 26 Oct. 1737, Bridget, da. of Philip Bacon of Ipswich, wid. of Edward Evers of Ipswich, and Washingley, Lincs., *s.p. suc.* fa. 1727.

Sir Cordell Firebrace was the grandson of a London vintner. His father acquired by marriage the Cordell estates, including Long Melford. Returned unopposed for the county as a Tory, he was absent, probably owing to illness, from the divisions on the Spanish convention in 1739 and the place bill in 1740. Re-elected unopposed in 1741, he voted against the Government in all recorded divisions except on the Hanoverians in 1746, from which he was absent. On 14 Apr. 1747 he spoke against the bill to abolish hereditary jurisdictions in Scotland.[1]

During the contested county election of 1747 it was claimed on behalf of Firebrace that he had discharged his trust 'with great honour in the House of Commons'; that he 'did associate and subscribe to support his Majesty' with his 'life

and fortune' during the late rebellion; and that insinuations to the contrary were unjustified.[2] The 2nd Lord Egmont, who regarded him as one of 'the heads of the Tories',[3] wrote of him in his electoral survey of c.1749–50:

Is sincerely with us; as he is the greatest instrument to bring about what has hitherto happened with the Tories, so he is the man that will be most instrumental to keep them in a proper disposition. He has solemnly protested to me that he never was in the least disposed to the Pretender's interest. Yet he has a great deal of weight, as much as any body, with the Duke of Beaufort [Lord Noel Somerset, q.v.]. He has a good estate, £3,500 per annum and £30,000 in money.

Egmont adds that Firebrace had a very considerable interest at Ipswich, 'which he will give to the Prince, as in all other boroughs in this county'. In Egmont's lists of persons to receive office on Frederick's accession, Firebrace figures as a lord of the Admiralty. His only recorded speech in this Parliament was made in the debate of 19 Feb. 1753 on Nova Scotia.[4] He died 28 Mar. 1759.

[1] Add. 24120, f. 123; 35876, f. 250. [2] Robt. le Grys to Miles Barne, 8 July 1747, Barne mss. [3] Occasional memo., Add. 47073. [4] Walpole, *Mems. Geo. II*, i. 307.

R.R.S.

FISHER, Francis (1688–1763), of the Grange, Grantham, Lincs.

GRANTHAM   1722–1727

bap. 20 Dec. 1688, 4th but 1st surv. s. of Robert Fisher of the Grange by his w. Elizabeth. *educ.* Ch. Ch. Oxf. 1706. *m.* Jane, da. and coh. of John Digby of Mansfield Woodhouse, Notts., 3s. 4da. *suc.* fa. 1712.

Fisher was put up for Grantham in 1722 by Lord Cardigan, the head of the local Tories. He is described as

a gentleman of a small estate and encumbered, hardly qualified in case his debts [were] paid, but [Lord Cardigan] is to bear the expense.

Returned head of the poll, he did not stand in 1727, when he gave his interest to Sir Michael Newton (q.v.).[1] He died 21 Feb. 1763.

[1] J. Garner to Heathcote, 18 Mar. 1722, I. Ancaster mss 13/B/2; Newton to W. Archer, 2 July 1727, Monson mss 28B/10/82, Lincs. Archives Office.

P.W.

FITZPATRICK, John, 1st Earl of Upper Ossory [I] (?1719–58), of Ampthill, Beds.

BEDFORDSHIRE   5 Dec. 1753–23 Sept. 1758

b. ?1719, 1st s. of Richard Fitzpatrick, 1st Baron Gowran [I], by Anne, da. and coh. of Sir John Robinson, 2nd Bt., of Farmingwoods, Northants. *educ.* Queen's, Oxf. 16 June 1735, aged 15. *m.* 30 June 1744, Lady Evelyn Leveson Gower, da. of John, 1st Earl Gower, sis. of Gertrude (w. of John, 4th Duke of Bedford) and of Lord Trentham and Hon.

Richard Leveson Gower (qq.v.), 2s. 2da. *suc.* fa. as 2nd Baron 9 June 1727; and mother in the estates of Farmingwoods and Ampthill 1744; *cr.* Earl of Upper Ossory [I] 5 Oct. 1751.

Fitzpatrick inherited extensive Irish estates from his father, and from his mother Ampthill, which she had purchased in 1736. He bought the manor of Houghton Conquest, Bedfordshire, in 1741. At a by-election in 1753 he was put up by his brother-in-law, the Duke of Bedford, for the county, which he represented till his death, 23 Sept. 1758.

R.S.L.

FITZROY, Lord Augustus (1716–41).

THETFORD 10 Feb. 1739–28 May 1741

b. 16 Oct. 1716, 3rd s. of Charles Fitzroy, 2nd Duke of Grafton, and yr. bro. of George Fitzroy, Lord Euston (q.v.). *educ.* Eton 1728. *m.* March 1734, Elizabeth, da. of Col. William Cosby, gov. of New York, 3s.

Lt. R.N. by 1734, capt. 1736.

'This brave and gallant young man', writes Charnock, 'was of a very amorous disposition.'[1] As a naval lieutenant, aged 17, he contracted a marriage which his father refused to recognize. Three years later, now a captain, he told his wife 'the night before he left her to go to sea that he had received with much transport a letter' from the wife of Sir William Morice (q.v.) 'that she would lie with him the following night and go to sea with him'. The couple were caught *flagrante delicto* at an inn on the road to the harbour where his ship lay; Lady Morice was seized but made her escape to France; her husband secured a divorce and damages of £5,000 against Fitzroy; while the Duke of Grafton

> was so touched with the barbarity of his son that he went to see his daughter-in-law, which he had never done before, and assured her that he would be kind to her and never let her want while he lived.[2]

Returned for Thetford by the Duke of Grafton in 1739, Fitzroy was absent on active service from the division on the Spanish convention in March but voted with the Government against the place bill in January 1740. In April he took part in an engagement resulting in the capture of a Spanish man-of-war.[3] Sailing in October under Sir Chaloner Ogle (q.v.) to reinforce Admiral Vernon (q.v.) in the West Indies, he died in Jamaica of a disease contracted at Cartagena, 28 May 1741. He was the father of the 3rd Duke of Grafton, who became prime minister under George III.

[1] *Biog. Navalis*, iv. 308. [2] *HMC Egmont Diary* ii. 421; *Gent. Mag.* 1737, p. 762; *LJ*, 13 Mar. 1738. [3] H. W. Richmond, *Navy and the War of 1739–48*, i. 78.

R.R.S.

FITZROY (afterwards FITZROY SCUDAMORE), Charles (?1713–82), of Holme Lacy, Herefs.

THETFORD	1 Feb. 1733–1754
HEREFORD	1754–1768
HEYTESBURY	1768–1774
THETFORD	1774–Mar. 1782

b. ?1713, illegit. s. of Charles Fitzroy, 2nd Duke of Grafton. *educ.* Westminster, Nov. 1721, aged 8, left 1730. *m.* 1749, Frances, da. and h. of James Scudamore, 3rd and last Visct. Scudamore [I], div. w. of Henry Somerset, 3rd Duke of Beaufort, 1da. Assumed add. name of Scudamore by Act of Parliament 22 Mar. 1749.

Capt. 5 Ft. 1735; capt. and lt.-col. 1 Ft. Gds. 1740, second maj. 1747; ret. 1748.

Master of the King's tennis courts 1733–62; groom porter 1743–62; deputy cofferer of the Household 1765–70.

Charles Fitzroy was returned by his father, the Duke of Grafton, for Thetford, voting with the Government in all recorded divisions.

He died 22 Aug. 1782.

R.R.S.

FITZROY, George, Lord Euston (1715–47).

COVENTRY 12 Apr. 1737–1747

b. 24 Aug. 1715, 1st surv. s. of Charles Fitzroy, 2nd Duke of Grafton, ld. chamberlain of the Household to George I and George II, by Henrietta, da. of Charles Somerset, Mq. of Worcester, sis. of Henry, 2nd Duke of Beaufort; bro. of Lord Augustus Fitzroy (q.v.). *educ.* Eton 1728. *m.* 10 Oct. 1741, Lady Dorothy Boyle, da. and coh. of Richard, 4th Earl of Cork [I] and 3rd Earl of Burlington, *s.p.*

Lord Euston, whose father was recorder of Coventry, stood unsuccessfully for the town at a by-election in February 1737. Returned for it two months later, he was absent from the division on the Spanish convention in 1739 but voted with the Administration on the place bill in 1740. No further votes of his are recorded. In October 1741 he married Lady Dorothy Boyle, 'a girl of the softest temper, vast beauty, birth and fortune', whom he treated with the utmost brutality, till her death on 2 May 1742, in the words of her mother, delivered her 'from extremest misery'.[1] He was on the worst terms with the Duke of Grafton who, Horace Walpole wrote to Mann (29 June 1743),

> is so unhappy in his heir apparent, that he checks his hand in almost everything he undertakes. Last week he heard a new exploit of his barbarity. A tenant of Lord Euston in Northamptonshire brought him his rent, and the Lord said it wanted three and sixpence: the tenant begged he would examine the account, that it would prove exact—however, to content him, he would willingly pay him the three and sixpence. Lord E. flew into a rage and vowed

he would write to the Duke to have him turned out of a little place he has in the post office of thirty pounds a year. The poor man, who has six children, and knew nothing of my Lord's being on no terms of power with his father, went home and shot himself.

In August of that year he

> forced himself to the Duke of Grafton's house . . . threw himself at his feet, professed great remorse for his past conduct, and promised an entire reformation for the time to come. But the Duke told him he had tried him too often to be deceived any more and that God was his witness that no man ever loved his son more tenderly, and seen him lost with greater pain, but that was over now; that he attempted in vain to move the bowels of a father who had long since looked upon himself to have no son.[2]

In the autumn of 1744 he eloped to Italy with a Miss Nevill 'of a very ancient family in Lincolnshire, with eleven thousand pounds for her fortune, and a celebrated beauty',[3] giving her a promise of marriage,[4] which he never fulfilled. He was put up for Coventry in 1747, but before the election he died, 7 July, aged 31, to the relief of his father.[5]

[1] Walpole to Mann, 22 Oct. 1741 and 22 July 1744. [2] Lady Hertford to Ld. Beauchamp, 4 Dec. 1743, Northumberland mss. [3] HMC Denbigh, v. 257. [4] Add. 29601, f. 206. [5] Pelham to Hartington, n.d., Devonshire ms.

E.C.

FITZWILLIAM, John, Visct. Milton (c.1685–1728), of Milton, nr. Peterborough.

PETERBOROUGH 1710–28 Aug. 1728

> b. c.1685, o. surv. s. of William, 1st Earl Fitzwilliam [I], M.P., by Anne, da. and h. of Edmund Cremer of West Winch, Norf. m. 17 Sept. 1718, Anne, da. and h. of John Stringer of Sutton-upon-Lound, Notts., 1s. 3da. suc. fa. as 2nd Earl 28 Dec. 1719.
> Custos rot. Peterborough 1720–8.

The Fitzwilliams were the heads of the Whig interest at Peterborough, holding the politically important office of custos rotulorum, or lord lieutenant, of the city, which they represented in most Parliaments from the mid-17th century till they became English peers in 1742. Returned for Peterborough in 1710, Fitzwilliam after 1715 voted consistently with the Government, speaking for them in a debate on foreign affairs, 8 Mar. 1727. His sudden death of a malignant fever, 28 Aug. 1728, was described as 'a terrible blow' to the government interest at Peterborough.[1]

[1] Thos. Gibson to Jos. Banks, 30 Aug. 1728, Letters and Pprs. Banks Fam. ed. Hill (Lincoln Rec. Soc. xlv), 88–89.

R.R.S.

FITZWILLIAM, Richard, 5th Visct. Fitzwilliam [I] (c.1677–1743).

FOWEY 27 Jan. 1727–1734

> b. c.1677, o. s. of Thomas, 4th Visct. Fitzwilliam [I],

of Merrion, co. Dublin by Mary, da. of Sir Philip Stapleton, M.P., of Wighill, Yorks. m. (settlement 26 Feb. 1704) Frances, da. of Sir John Shelley, 3rd Bt., of Mitchelgrove, sis. of Sir John Shelley, 4th Bt. (q.v.), 3s. 2da. suc. fa. 20 Feb. 1705.
> P.C. [I] 15 Sept. 1715.

Fitzwilliam, a Roman Catholic, conformed to the established church, taking his seat in the Irish House of Lords on 25 May 1710. In 1715 he was a member of a committee of Irish Lords to congratulate George I on his accession.[1] Returned for Fowey as a Whig in 1727, he moved the Address on 13 Jan. 1730 in a studied but laboured speech,[2] on which Lord Hervey (q.v.) commented:

> Lord Fitzwilliam's performance was darker, thicker and heavier than the fog of this day . . . I am sorry when God thought fit to send such a piece of original obscurity and chaos into the world as that head, that he did not think fit to dispel the mists of it by the same methods which Moses tells us he made use of to enlighten the rest of the universe. Human aids, I am sure, can never bring it about.[3]

Never standing again, he died 6 June 1743.

[1] Lodge, Irish Peerage, iv. 319–20. [2] HMC Egmont Diary, i. 3. [3] Ilchester, Lord Hervey and his Friends, 44.

E.C.

FITZWILLIAM, William, 3rd Earl Fitzwilliam [I] (1720–56).

PETERBOROUGH 1741–19 Apr. 1742

> b. 15 Jan. 1720, o. s. of John, 2nd Earl Fitzwilliam [I] (q.v.). educ. Eton 1732, Grand Tour (Italy, Germany) 1740. m. 22 June 1744, Lady Anne Wentworth, da. of Thomas Watson Wentworth (q.v.), 1st Marquess of Rockingham, 2s. 6da. suc. fa. 28 Aug. 1728. cr. Lord Fitzwilliam, Baron Milton [GB] 19 Apr. 1742, Viscount Milton and Earl Fitzwilliam [GB] 6 Sept. 1746.
> Custos rot. Peterborough 1741–56; ld. of the bedchamber to George II 1751–6.

Returned for Peterborough on the Fitzwilliam interest after coming of age, Fitzwilliam was warm in support of Sir Robert Walpole during the last days of his Administration, weeping on his resignation. He was on the court list for the secret committee set up by the Commons to inquire into Walpole's Administration,[1] soon after which he was raised to the English peerage.

On his marriage he distinguished himself not only by the magnificence of his apparel and the 'new equipage . . . made in the chinese fashion being all over japanned' in which he took his bride to be presented at court, but also by making himself very ill by a surfeit of small beer and ices.[2]

On 2 July 1746 he successfully applied through Newcastle for an English earldom, with the support of Lord Rockingham.[3] Nevertheless the 2nd

Lord Egmont in his electoral survey, c.1749–50, noted under Peterborough:

> Lord Fitzwilliam has grumbled more than once to me being slighted notwithstanding what has been done for him when so young, and without any parliamentary merit, and not a very sure interest in this borough.

He died 10 Aug. 1756.

[1] Walpole to Mann, 17 Dec. 1741, 4 Feb. and 1 Apr. 1742. [2] HMC Denbigh, v. 180, 249. [3] Add. 32707, ff. 388, 395.

E.C.

FLEETWOOD, Henry (?1667–1746), of Penwortham, nr. Preston, Lancs.

PRESTON   1708–1722

b. ?1667, o. s. of Arthur Fleetwood of Lichfield, Staffs. and St. Margaret's, Westminster, sec. to the Earl of Danby, by Mary, da. and coh. of Sir Henry Archbold of Abbots Bromley and Lichfield, Staffs.[1]; cos. of Sir Christopher Musgrave (q.v.). educ. B.N.C. Oxf. 25 Oct. 1683, aged 16. m. (settlement 12 Feb. 1714) Sarah, da. of Roger Sudell of Preston, Lancs., s.p. suc. fa. 1677; his distant cos. Edward Fleetwood, M.P. for Preston 1660 and 1685, in Penwortham estates 1704.
Ensign 7 Ft. 1685, 2nd lt. 1687, lt. 1688.

Fleetwood served in the regiment of his maternal uncle, Lord Dartmouth, till the Revolution, when Dartmouth was deprived of all his offices. In 1704 he succeeded to an estate near Preston, which he represented as a Tory from 1708. A member of the Preston Jacobite club,[2] he was attached to the Duke of Hamilton, the head of the Lancashire Jacobites under Anne.[3] After George I's accession his only recorded vote was against the repeal of the Occasional Conformity and Schism Acts in 1719. Retiring in 1722 he gave up his interest at Preston to Thomas Hesketh (q.v.).[4] He died 22 May 1746. In 1747 a private Act of Parliament was passed, providing for the sale of his estates to discharge debts totalling £16,000.[5]

[1] N. & Q. (ser. 10), vii. 303. [2] H. W. Clemesha, Hist. Preston, 199. [3] Sir R. Bradshaigh to Geo. Kenyon, 18 Nov. 1712, HMC 14th Rep. IV, 449. [4] E. Hamilton to Sunderland, undated, Sunderland (Blenheim) mss. [5] VCH Lancs. vi. 59.

E.C.

FLEETWOOD, John (?1685–1745), of Missenden, Bucks.

BUCKINGHAMSHIRE   1713–1722

b. ?1685, 1st surv. s. of William Fleetwood of Missenden by his 2nd w. Sarah, da. of Thomas Bridgwood, citizen and embroiderer of London, wid. of William Whorwood of St. James's, Clerkenwell, Mdx. educ. Oriel, Oxf. 23 Mar. 1702, aged 16. m. 19 Jan. 1724, Elizabeth Seare, s.p. suc. fa. 1691.
Sheriff, Bucks, 1709–10.

John Fleetwood was descended from William

II—D

Fleetwood, M.P., Queen's serjeant and recorder of London, who acquired the reversion of the site of Missenden abbey in 1574.[1] Succeeding as a child to an estate of £1,000 p.a.,[2] he sat for the county as a Tory in the 1713 Parliament. Re-elected in 1715 unopposed on a compromise arranged by his cousin Lord Cheyne,[3] the late Tory lord lieutenant, he voted against the Administration in all recorded divisions. His name was sent to the Pretender in 1721 as a probable supporter in the event of a rising.[4] Never standing again, he died 17 Aug. 1745.

[1] Lipscomb, Bucks. ii. 377; VCH Bucks. ii. 351. [2] HMC Portland, iv. 459. [3] Verney Letters of 18th Cent. i. 315–20. [4] Stuart mss 65/16.

R.S.L.

FLEMING, Richard (c.1682–1740), of North Stoneham, nr. Southampton, Hants.

SOUTHAMPTON   1710–1722

b. c.1682, 2nd s. of Edward Fleming of North Stoneham by Margaret, da. of Thomas Bland. educ. L. Inn 1701. m. Anne, da. of Sir Ambrose Crowley of Greenwich, sis. of John Crowley (q.v.), s.p. suc. e. bro. Thomas Fleming 1708.

Richard Fleming inherited the manor of North Stoneham, which had been in his family since the sixteenth century.[1] A Tory and a member of the October Club, he was re-elected after a contest for Southampton in 1715, voting against the Administration in all recorded divisions. His name was sent to the Pretender in 1721 as a probable supporter in the event of a rising. He did not stand again, dying 4 Aug. 1740.

[1] VCH Hants, iii. 479. [2] Stuart mss 65/16.

P.W.

FLETCHER, Andrew (1722–79), of Saltoun, Haddington.

HADDINGTON BURGHS   1747–1761
HADDINGTONSHIRE   1761–1768

b. 1722, 1st s. of Andrew Fletcher of Saltoun, Lord Milton, S.C.J., lord justice clerk 1735–48, keeper of the signet 1746–66, by Elizabeth, da. of Sir Francis Kinloch, 2nd Bt., of Gilmerton. educ. Glasgow Univ. 1735; Ch. Ch. Oxf. 1739. m. 1764, Jeanie, da. of Sir Robert Myreton, 2nd Bt., of Gogar, Edinburgh, s.p. suc. fa. 1766.
Clerk of the pipe in the Exchequer [S] 1746–51; sec. to Duke of Argyll as keeper of the great seal [S], 1748–61; auditor gen. of the Exchequer [S] 1751–79 (£1,200 p.a.).

Fletcher was the son of 'the confidential friend and deputy' of Lord Ilay, afterwards Duke of Argyll,[1] who managed Scotland under Walpole and the Pelhams. In 1747, when the restored Argyll régime routed their opponents (see Craigie,

Robert), Fletcher, by an agreement between his father, Argyll, and Sir Hew Dalrymple (q.v.), was returned for Haddington Burghs.[2] In 1748 he secured the reversion of Dalrymple's office of auditor general of Scotland under a bargain by which his father gave up the office of lord justice clerk to Charles Areskine (q.v.), but 'retained the charge of superintending elections'.[3] At the same time he succeeded John Maule (q.v.) as Argyll's secretary and constant companion. He died 24 May 1779.

[1] Ramsay of Ochtertyre, *Scotland and Scotsmen in the 18th Cent.*, i. 87. [2] See HADDINGTON and HADDINGTON BURGHS. [3] Ramsay, 89.

R.R.S.

FLOYER, John (c.1681–1762), of Hints Hall, nr. Tamworth, Staffs.

TAMWORTH   1741–21 Mar. 1742

> b. c.1681, 1st s. of Sir John Floyer of Hints Hall by Mary, da. and coh. of Sir Henry Archbold of Abbots Bromley, Staffs., chancellor of the diocese of Lichfield, wid. of Arthur Fleetwood of Lichfield and mother of Henry Fleetwood (q.v.). m. Catherine, da. of Edward Littleton, M.P., of Pillaton Hall, Staffs., 1da. suc. fa. 1734.

Floyer, son of Sir John Floyer the physician, was descended from Ralph Floyer of the Middle Temple, who acquired Hints Hall in 1601. Returned as a Tory for Tamworth in 1741, he voted against the Government on the chairman of the elections committee, but was soon afterwards unseated on petition, never standing again. He appears in a list of leading Jacobite sympathizers prepared for the French foreign office in 1743.[1] He died 4 June 1762.[2]

[1] Stuart mss 248/151. [2] Shaw, *Staffs.* ii. 21.

R.R.S.

FOLEY, Edward (1676–1747).

DROITWICH   1701–June 1711, 15 Apr. 1732–1741

> bap. 23 Sept. 1676, 2nd s. of Thomas Foley, M.P., of Witley Court, Worcs. by Elizabeth, da. of Edward Ashe, M.P.; bro. of Thomas Foley, M.P., 1st Baron Foley, and Richard Foley (q.v.). educ. L. Inn 1717. unm. suc. bro. Richard 1732.
> Commr. for leather duties and land taxes, 1711–14.

The Foleys were descended from a Worcestershire ironmaster, who founded an immense fortune by introducing a Swedish method of splitting iron to make nails.[1] One of his grandsons, Thomas, of Witley Court, was M.P. for Worcestershire in six Parliaments and then for Droitwich, where the family controlled one seat, from 1698 to his death in 1701; another, Paul, of Stoke Edith Court, Herefordshire, was M.P. for Hereford in seven

Parliaments and Speaker of the House of Commons 1695–8; and a third, Philip, of Prestwood, Staffordshire, was M.P. for Bewdley in three Parliaments and then for Stafford 1689–90 and for Droitwich 1701. In conjunction with their connexions, the Harleys, they exercised considerable electoral influence in Herefordshire, as well as being the heads of the Worcestershire Tories. Thomas Foley's eldest son sat for Stafford from 1694 to 1712, when he was raised to the peerage by his brother-in-law Robert Harley, Earl of Oxford, as one of the 12 peers created to secure a Tory majority in the House of Lords. His second son, Edward, sat as a Tory for Droitwich from 1701 to 1711, when he surrendered his seat to his younger brother Richard. On Richard's death in 1732 he resumed the seat, voting with the Opposition until 1741, when he stood down in favour of his cousin, Thomas Foley (b.1716, q.v.), who in the meantime had come of age. He died 4 Apr. 1747.

[1] B. L. C. Johnson, 'The Foley Partnerships', *Econ. Hist. Review* (ser. 2), iv. 322–40.

A.N.N.

FOLEY, Paul (d.1739), of Newport, Herefs.

ALDBOROUGH   1713–1715
WEOBLEY   1 Feb.–18 June 1715

> b. aft. 1671, 2nd s. of Paul Foley, M.P., Speaker of House of Commons 1695–8, of Stoke Edith Court, Herefs., uncle of Edward Foley (q.v.), by Mary, da. of John Lane, alderman of London; yr. bro. of Thomas Foley I (q.v.). educ. I. Temple 1693; L. Inn 1706, called 1708; re-admitted I. Temple 1734, bencher 1738. m. (1) Susannah, da. of Sir William Massingberd, 2nd Bt., of Gunby, Lincs., sis. of Sir William Massingberd, 3rd Bt. (q.v.), s.p.; (2) lic. 13 Dec. 1722, Susannah, da. of Henry Hoare of Stourton Castle, Wilts., s.p.

In 1713 Paul Foley, a Tory, was returned for Aldborough by the dowager Duchess of Newcastle. Returned for Weobley in 1715, he was unseated on petition. In 1727 he canvassed Weobley but, though 'worth above £60,000',[1] declined before the poll. Again unsuccessful at Weobley in 1732, he died 28 Nov. 1739.

[1] Chandos to Walpole, 9 Aug. 1727, Chandos letter bks.

A.N.N.

FOLEY, Richard (1681–1732), of Lincoln's Inn, London.

DROITWICH   18 July 1711–27 Mar. 1732

> b. 19 Feb. 1681, 3rd s. of Thomas Foley, M.P., of Witley Court, Worcs., and bro. of Edward Foley (q.v.). educ. L. Inn 1695, called 1702, bencher 1726. unm.
> 2nd prothonotary court of common pleas 1703–d.

Returned as a Tory on the family interest at Droitwich, Richard Foley voted consistently with the Opposition. He died 27 Mar. 1732, bequeathing £100 to William Shippen (q.v.) 'for his services done his country'.[1]

[1] *Gent. Mag.* 1732, p. 679.

A.N.N.

FOLEY, Thomas (?1670–1737), of Stoke Edith Court, Herefs.

WEOBLEY 12 Nov. 1691–1698, 12 Dec. 1698–1700
HEREFORD 1701–1722
STAFFORD 1722–1727, 1734–10 Dec. 1737

b. ?1670, 1st s. of Paul Foley, M.P., and bro. of Paul Foley (q.v.). *educ.* Pemb. Oxf. 16 Oct. 1685, aged 15; I. Temple 1688. *m.* 12 July 1688, his 1st cos. Anne, da. and h. of Essex Knightley of Fawsley, Northants., 1s. 2da. *suc.* fa. 1699.
Ld. of Trade 1712–13; jt. auditor of the imprest 1713–*d.*

Returned as a Tory for Hereford, Foley was made joint auditor of the imprest for life by his cousin by marriage, Robert Harley, Earl of Oxford, the other auditor being Edward Harley (q.v.). After the Hanoverian accession he voted consistently with the Opposition, speaking against the impeachment of Lord Oxford in June 1715. In February 1718, Lord Mar, the Pretender's secretary of state, suggested that he should be asked for money for a project to restore the Stuarts with the help of Swedish troops (see Caesar, Charles).[1] Transferring to Stafford in 1722 to maintain his family's interest there, he 'spoke to nothing else but' praise of Lord Oxford's ministry,[2] in a debate on the treaty of Hanover in February 1726. He did not stand again till 1734, when he was returned once more for Stafford. He died 10 Dec. 1737, aged 67.

[1] *HMC Stuart*, v. 456. [2] *HMC Portland*, vii. 424.

A.N.N.

FOLEY, Thomas (?1695–1749), of Stoke Edith Court, Herefs.

HEREFORD 1734–1741
HEREFORDSHIRE 6 Jan. 1742–1747

b. ?1695, 1st s. of Thomas Foley (q.v. above). *educ.* Hereford; Trinity, Camb. 18 Sept. 1711, aged 16. *m.* (1) Hester (*d.* 1717), da. and h. of Thomas Andrews of St. Mary-at-Hill, London, 2s.; (2) Mary (*d.*Jan. 1721), da. of John Warters of Barbados, 1s. 1da.; (3) Elizabeth (*d.*1725), da. of Henry Wolstenholme, 1s.; (4) 1731, Elizabeth, da. of Robert Unitt of Birchwood, Herefs., *s.p.*; (5) 24 May 1744 (with £10,000), Catherine, da. of Francis Gwyn (q.v.), *s.p. suc.* fa. 1737.

After contesting Weobley unsuccessfully in 1718, Foley in 1722 stood for Hereford in succession to his father, but withdrew before the poll. Returned as a Tory for Hereford at the head of the poll in 1734, he voted with the Opposition. He did not stand at the general election of 1741 but shortly afterwards was returned for Herefordshire in place of his cousin, Edward Harley jun., who had succeeded to the earldom of Oxford. In this Parliament also he voted consistently with the Opposition, signing the opposition 'whip' of November 1743.[1] In 1747 he stood down in favour of Lord Oxford's son and heir. He died 3 Apr. 1749.

[1] Owen, *Pelhams*, 198.

A.N.N.

FOLEY, Thomas (1716–77), of Stoke Edith Court, Herefs.

DROITWICH 1741–1747, 9–16 Dec. 1747, 1754–1768
HEREFORDSHIRE 1768–20 May 1776

b. 8 Aug. 1716, 1st s. of Thomas Foley (q.v. above) by his 1st w. *educ.* Westminster 1724–32; Trinity, Camb. 1732. *m.* 29 Mar. 1740, Grace, da. and coh. of George Granville, M.P., 1st Baron Lansdowne, 3s. 4da. *suc.* fa. 1749, and to estates of cos. Thomas, 2nd Baron Foley, 1766. *cr.* Baron Foley 20 May 1776.

Thomas Foley was returned as a Tory by his cousin, the 2nd Lord Foley, in succession to Edward Foley (q.v.), voting consistently against the Administration. At the 1747 election he was again returned but was unseated on petition. In the 2nd Lord Egmont's electoral survey, c.1749–50, he is described as a likely candidate at either Leominster or Weobley, 'having a fair character in the county'. He died 18 Nov. 1777.

A.N.N.

FONNEREAU, Thomas (1699–1779), of Christ Church, Ipswich, Suff.

SUDBURY 1741–1768
ALDEBURGH 13 May 1773–20 Mar. 1779

b. 27 Oct. 1699, 1st s. of Claude Fonnereau, Hamburg merchant, by his 1st w. Elizabeth, da. of Philip Bureau of La Rochelle; bro. of Zachary Philip Fonnereau (q.v.). *unm. suc.* fa. 1740.

Thomas Fonnereau's father, a Huguenot naturalized in 1693, was a Hamburg merchant, who is said to have made his fortune in the linen trade. He left the estate of Christ Church, Ipswich, to Thomas, as well as large money legacies to him and the other children.[1] After standing unsuccessfully for Stamford in 1734, Fonnereau was returned unopposed for Sudbury, where he built up a strong interest. In Parliament he voted with the Government in all recorded divisions. On 15 Apr. 1745 he spoke in favour of regulating the choice of churchwardens and overseers of the poor, saying that under the present system a large part of the money raised was being misappropriated. He was given leave to bring in a bill, which reached the report stage and was then thrown out.[2] During the rebellion of 1745 he made a speech to the grand jury of Suffolk, which was distributed at their request.[3] In 1747 he extended his electoral influence to Aldeburgh, where he secured the return of his brother, Zachary Philip, against Pelham's candidate. He and his brother had a share in the contract for victualling the Gibraltar garrison.[4] He died 20 Mar. 1779.

[1] Agnew, *Protestant Exiles from France*, ii. 399–400, 485; *Gent. Mag.* 1740, p. 203. [2] *Parl. Hist.* xiii. 300–3. [3] Walpole, *Mems. Geo. III*, iii. 112 n. 2. [4] Add. 32866, ff. 393–4; 32868, ff. 170–1.

R.R.S.

FONNEREAU, Zachary Philip (1706–78), of Sise Lane, Bucklersbury, London.

ALDEBURGH 1747–1774

b. 31 Jan. 1706, 4th s. of Claude Fonnereau, and bro. of Thomas Fonnereau (q.v.). *m.* 13 Apr. 1738, Margaret, da. and coh. of George Martyn of Paternoster Row, London, and Odington, Glos., 10s. 3da.
Director, E. I. Co. 1753, 1754.

Fonnereau was returned on his brother's interest for Aldeburgh in 1747, contrary to Pelham's original arrangements. Nevertheless he was classed as a supporter in 1747, and acted with the Government. He died 15 Aug. 1778.

R.R.S.

FORBES, Sir Arthur, 4th Bt. (1709–73), of Craigievar, Aberdeen.

ABERDEENSHIRE 13 July 1732–1747

b. 1709, 6th but 1st surv. s. of Sir William Forbes, 3rd Bt., of Craigievar by Margaret, da. of Hugh Rose of Kilravock, Nairn, sis.-in-law of Duncan Forbes (q.v.). *educ.* Marischal Coll. Aberdeen c.1723–7. *m.* (1) 1729, Christian (*d.* 6 Oct. 1733), 1st da. of John Ross of Arnage, Aberdeen, provost of Aberdeen, 2da.; (2) Oct. 1749, Margaret, *née* Strachan, of Balgall, wid. of John Burnett of Elrick, Aberdeen, 5s. 4da. *suc.* fa. May 1722.
Rector of Marischal Coll. Aberdeen 1761–4.

Forbes, whose grandfather and great-grandfather had represented Aberdeenshire in the pre-Union Parliament of Scotland, succeeded at the age of 12 to an estate worth £728 a year, burdened with debts of £6,184 and annuities of £195.[1] Returned unopposed for his county in 1732 at a by-election caused by the expulsion from the House of Sir Archibald Grant (q.v.), he became a government supporter, though he was absent on the excise bill of 1733. Lord Ilay described him in August 1733 to James Erskine (q.v.), as 'a damned forward prattling boy [for repeating Ilay's private offer of support at the next election]; but really ... Sir Arthur behaved very firmly to us in Parliament, and is not a bad man'. Erskine, who was then supporting the candidature of his nephew Thomas Erskine, Lord Erskine (q.v.), wrote to a kinsman about the county election in 1734:

As to Sir Arthur ... consider: 1. That he promised at his last election to join for Lord Erskine if he should stand at the next, and yet sets up now against him. 2. That he has gone along in all the pernicious measures of last session, and, by these bad means, has recommended himself. 3. That, therefore, he must henceforth be the tool of a wicked party, that have oppressed ... us and the nation. 4. That he has insidiously joined Earl Ilay and become his slave. 5. That to continue him is to introduce Ilay's power into the shire ... The breach with him is not on our part but his own.[2]

Re-elected after a contest, he was still 'a friend' of the Administration in January 1738, when he obtained a commission for his brother through Sir William Yonge (q.v.), secretary at war;[3] but, following the Duke of Argyll, he changed sides soon afterwards, voting against the Government on the Spanish convention in 1739 and the place bill of 1740. The Jacobite Lord Lovat wrote to a kinsman in September 1740 that the Duke of Argyll

has a vast friendship for Sir Arthur Forbes, and he desired me to write to any friends that I had in [Aberdeenshire] to do what service they could to Sir Arthur ... I earnestly entreat that you will not only give your vote for Sir Arthur, but that you will go about and solicit for him ... among your friends; I promised to the Duke of Argyll that you would do this upon my account.[4]

Returned unopposed in 1741, Forbes voted against Walpole's candidate for the chairman of the elections committee in December. One of the group of opposition Members known as the Duke of Argyll's gang,[5] he voted against the Hanoverians in 1742 and 1744. In 1747 he retired in favour of his kinsman, Andrew Mitchell (q.v.). He died 1 Jan. 1773.

[1] *Cal. Treas. Pprs.* 1720–8, p. 278. [2] *Spalding Club Misc.* iii. 42–43, 48. [3] *More Culloden Pprs.* iii. 129. [4] *Spalding Club Misc.* ii. 8. [5] John Drummond to Ld. Morton, 2 and 4 Dec. 1742, Morton mss, SRO.

R.S.L.

FORBES, Duncan (1685–1747), of Edinburgh.

AYR BURGHS	2 Sept. 1721–1722
INVERNESS BURGHS	23 Oct. 1722–21 June 1737

b. 10 Nov. 1685, 2nd s. of Duncan Forbes of Culloden, M.P. [S], by Mary, da. of Sir Robert Innes of Innes, Elgin; yr. bro. of John Forbes (q.v.). *educ.* Inverness Royal Academy; Marischal Coll. Aberdeen 1699; Edinburgh 1702; Leyden 1705; adv. 1709. *m.* 21 Oct. 1708, Mary, da. of Hugh Rose of Kilravock, Nairn, 1s. *suc.* bro. at Culloden 1735.

Sheriff depute Edinburghshire 1714–16; dep. lt. Inverness-shire 1715–16; sheriff, Edinburghshire 1716–25; ld. advocate depute 1716–25; ld. advocate 1725–37; ld. pres. of court of session 1737-*d.*

Soon after the Fifteen, Duncan Forbes, not yet in Parliament but a rising lawyer, closely connected with the Duke of Argyll, whose estates in Scotland he managed during the Duke's absence, sent an anonymous letter to Walpole, remonstrating against the harsh treatment of the rebels as likely to defeat its object by increasing rather than diminishing disaffection in Scotland. Another 'false step' by the ministry in Scotland had been to give 'the management of it to a set of men hated and despised by almost all the King's friends . . . known here by the name of Squadrone'—a reference to the recent appointment of the Duke of Roxburghe to be secretary of state for Scotland. Finally, it was 'no small cause of discontent . . . to find that a ministry can be so designing, or so far imposed on, as to quit with the Duke of Argyll',[1] who had just been dismissed from his offices.

In 1721 Forbes was brought into Parliament by Argyll for Ayr Burghs, transferring next year to Inverness Burghs, where he was returned on petition, continuing to represent them for the rest of his parliamentary career on his family's interest. Two days after taking his seat, described as 'a very ingenious Scotch lawyer', he had the first of a series of encounters with Robert Dundas (q.v.), in a 'battle' between the friends of the Duke of Roxburghe, and those of the Duke of Argyll, over an Aberdeen Burghs election petition.[2] When in 1725 the Squadrone were dismissed for opposing the enforcement of the malt tax in Scotland, Forbes succeeded Dundas as lord advocate. His first assignment was to deal with the aftermath of the malt tax riots in conjunction with Argyll's brother, Lord Ilay, who described Forbes as 'very violent', while Forbes was 'uneasy' at Ilay's more diplomatic methods.[3] Commenting on the decision to abolish Roxburghe's office, Forbes wrote:

We shall not be troubled with that nuisance, which we so long have complained of, a Scots secretary, either at full length or in miniature; if any one Scotsman has absolute power, we are in the same slavery as ever, whether that person be a fair man or a black man, a peer or commoner, 6 foot or 5 foot high, and the dependence of the country will be on that man, and not on those that made him.[4]

When Ilay began to act as minister for Scotland, Forbes did his best to 'check' him and 'put spokes in his wheel'.[5]

In 1726 Forbes answered Dundas's speech on Daniel Campbell's (q.v.) petition for compensation for the destruction of his house in the malt tax riots: 'He laid all the blame on the lords of session and the magistrates of Glasgow, and set forth the affair in quite a different light'. A fortnight later he moved successfully that anything over £20,000 raised by the malt tax in Scotland should go to the improvement of manufactures in that country, which Dundas described as a job.[6] His only recorded speech in the next Parliament was against an opposition motion to make army officers not above the rank of colonel irremovable except by court martial or on an address from either House, 13 Feb. 1734. He claimed in 1735 that

since I first had the honour to serve the Crown, I never was one day absent from Parliament. I attended the first and last and every intermediate day of every session, whatever calls I had from my private affairs.[7]

In this Parliament he denied Dundas's charge that troops had been used to overawe the election of the representative peers of Scotland, 14 Feb. 1735; seconded a petition for a grant in aid of Georgia, 7 Mar. 1737;[8] and with most of his compatriots opposed the bill of pains and penalties against Edinburgh for the Porteous riots, 16 May and 9 June 1737. In the last speech he mentioned that he would probably never address the House again, referring to his impending appointment to the lord presidency of the court of session, the highest judicial position in Scotland.

Forbes's elevation to the bench took him out of politics, though he continued to look after his interest in Inverness Burghs. After Walpole's fall he declined an invitation to him and to Dundas, now himself a judge, to act as advisers to Ilay's successor, Lord Tweeddale, in matters relating to Scotland.[9] During the Forty-five he rendered great service to the Government by raising independent companies and using his personal influence with the chiefs to keep a considerable part of the Highlands loyal (see Macleod, Norman). After the rebellion he again came out strongly for clemency, at the cost of incurring the displeasure of the Duke of Cumberland, who said that 'the

President was no Jacobite but was a Highlander and carried that to very dangerous lengths'.[10]

He died 10 Dec. 1747.

[1] *Culloden Pprs.* 61–65. For other unsigned letters of this kind see WEST, James, and BUBB (Dodington), George. [2] Ld. Finch to Ld. Nottingham, 29 Oct. 1722, Finch mss at HMC. [3] Coxe, *Walpole,* ii. 454, 456. [4] *More Culloden Pprs.* ii. 322. [5] *Culloden Pprs.* 469–70. [6] *Knatchbull Diary,* 4, 18 Mar. 1726. [7] *More Culloden Pprs.* iii. 104–5. [8] *HMC Egmont Diary,* ii. 363–4. [9] *Culloden Pprs.* iii. 150–1, 175–85. [10] *HMC Polwarth,* v. 257.

R.R.S.

FORBES, George, Visct. Forbes (1685–1765), of Castle Forbes, co. Longford.

QUEENBOROUGH   19 Mar. 1723–1727
AYR BURGHS   1741–1747

b. 21 Oct. 1685, 3rd but 1st surv. s. of Arthur Forbes, 2nd Earl of Granard [I], by Mary, da. of Sir George Rawdon, 1st Bt., M.P. [I], of Moira, co. Down. *educ.* Drogheda g.s. *m.* 1709, Mary, da. of William Stewart, 1st Visct. Mountjoy [I], wid. of Phineas Preston of Ardsallagh, co. Meath, 2s. 1da. *suc.* to family estates on resignation of fa. 1717; *summ. v.p.* to Irish House of Lords as Lord Forbes 27 Feb. 1724; *suc.* fa. as 3rd Earl of Granard [I] 24 Aug. 1734.

Entered navy 1702; midshipman 1704; 2nd lt. Brig. Holt's regt. of marines 1704–11; lt. R.N. 1705; capt. R.N. 1706; brig. 4 tp. Horse Gds. Mar. 1708, exempt and capt. Nov. 1708, cornet and maj. 1712–17; cdr. of Drags. and Ft. in Constantine 1711; lt.-gov. Fort St. Philip, Minorca 1716–18; v.-adm. in Austrian navy 1719–21; P.C. [I] 6 May 1721; gov. Leeward Is. 1729–31; minister plenip. to St. Petersburg 1733–4; r.-adm. 1734; v.-adm. 1736; res. 1742; gov. co. Longford and co. Westmeath 1740–56.

Lord Forbes was closely connected with the 2nd Duke of Argyll, to whom he owed his military career and whom he followed politically. Holding commissions both in the army and the navy, he served with distinction in the war of the Spanish succession, taking part in several land actions. Meanwhile, in 1717, after Argyll had dissuaded him from buying the 4th troop of Horse Guards from Lord Dundonald for 10,000 guineas, he retired from the army in order to concentrate on his naval career. In the same year his father made over to him all the family estates in return for a pension of £700 and the payment of certain annuities. In 1719 the Emperor, whom he had known as the Archduke Charles during the Spanish succession war, summoned him to Vienna to build a navy based on Trieste. Forbes, however, ran into opposition from the imperial ministers and resigned this appointment after two years. Brought in by the Government for Queenborough at a by-election in 1723, he served afloat in the Mediterranean, 1726–7, and again for the last time in 1731. From 1729 to 1731 he was nominally

governor of the Leeward Islands, but never went there, on the ground that the refusal of the local assemblies to vote him a fixed salary would leave him 'at the mercy of those whom he was to govern by instructions from the King'. In 1733 he went to St. Petersburg to conclude a trade treaty, making such a good impression on the Empress Anna that she later offered him the command of the Russian navy, which he rejected. In 1738, now Lord Granard, he refused the governorship of New York, apparently because his friends were unable to obtain for him the order of the Thistle. According to his son, Walpole disliked him, 'giving for reason that he was a man too curious and busy'.[1] On the outbreak of war in 1739 he was asked to take a squadron to the West Indies but once more declined. When Edward Vernon (q.v.) was sent in his place, he considered himself to be superseded and refused to serve again. Up to this time no vote by him is recorded. Brought in by Argyll for Ayr Burghs in 1741, he voted against Walpole's candidate for the chairman of the elections committee in December. After Walpole's resignation, his name was included in a list of new lords of the Admiralty, which was rejected by the King.[2] Returning with Argyll into opposition, he was appointed to the secret committee of inquiry into Walpole's Administration,[3] voted against the Hanoverians in 1742 and 1744, and was a signatory of opposition whips in November and December 1743.[4] Soon after Argyll's death in 1743 Granard is said to have broken off 'all commerce with public men, and confined himself to the society of a very few friends'.[5] However, he attended the House during the parliamentary inquiry March–April 1745 into the indecisive action off Toulon the previous year, presumably because his son John was one of the few captains to give Admiral Thomas Matthews (q.v.) full support in the battle. On 14 Mar. he criticized Vice-Admiral Lestock's evidence and, on his recall before the committee, cross-questioned him closely, though, Philip Yorke (q.v.) commented, 'what passed between him and Lord Granard was but indifferently understood by those unversed in naval language and criticism'. When, on 10 Apr., an address was moved to court martial both admirals, Granard spoke in favour of omitting Matthews' name.[6]

He died 19 June 1765.

[1] *Mems. Earls of Granard,* 83–190, 266–92. [2] *HMC Egmont Diary,* iii. 260. [3] *Walpole to Mann,* 1 Apr. 1742. [4] Newdegate mss 2550, Warws. RO; Add. 29597, f. 29. [5] *Earls of Granard,* 261. [6] *Parl. Hist.* xiii. 1254, 1269.

R.S.L.

FORBES, John (c.1673–1734), of Culloden, Inverness.

NAIRNSHIRE 1713–1715
INVERNESS-SHIRE 1715–1722
NAIRNSHIRE 1722–1727

b. c.1673, 1st s. of Duncan Forbes of Culloden, M.P. [S], and bro. of Duncan Forbes (q.v.). *educ.* Inverness R. Acad.; Netherlands 1692. *m.* 1699, Jean, da. of Sir Robert Gordon of Gordonstoun, Elgin, M.P. [S], *s.p. suc.* fa. 1704.

 M.P. [S] Nairnshire 1704–7; dep. lt. Inverness-shire 1715–16; commr. of the equivalent 1716–17;[1] provost, Inverness 1716, 1721.

John Forbes was descended from an Inverness burgess Presbyterian family who, though they had represented Inverness, Inverness-shire, and Nairnshire since 1625, were regarded as parvenus by the local aristocracy. Lord Lovat called them 'the upstart offspring of a servant of Strehines and a burgher of Inverness, that no man in his senses can call a family, no more than a mushroom of one night's growth can be called an old oak tree of five hundred years' standing'.[2] Returned in 1713 as a Whig for Nairnshire, which he had represented in the pre-Union Parliament of Scotland, he transferred to Inverness-shire in 1715, when he obtained a place of £500 a year. With his brother, Duncan (q.v.), he took an active part on the government side in the Fifteen rebellion, deprecating the harsh treatment of the rebels, especially in the matter of forfeitures.[3] Attached like his brother to the Duke of Argyll, he voted against the Government on the motion of 4 June 1717 against Argyll's military rival, Lord Cadogan (q.v.), attending the dinner given by Argyll to his followers four days later.[4] Though turned out of his place, he voted with the Government in 1719, when Argyll returned to office. Defeated for the county in 1722, he was once more returned for Nairnshire, but never again secured a seat, though he stood for Inverness-shire in 1734, when he was a dying man. He died December 1734.

[1] See BOTELER, John. [2] Sir W. Fraser, *Chiefs of Grant*, ii. 327–8. [3] *Culloden Pprs.* 33. [4] *More Culloden Pprs.* ii. 175.

 J.M.S.

FORESTER, Brooke (1717–71), of Willey Park, Salop.

WENLOCK 14 Feb. 1739–1768

b. 7 Feb. 1717, 1st s. of William Forester (q.v.). *m.* (1) 4 May 1734, Elizabeth (*d.*Mar. 1753), da. and h. of George Weld of Willey Park, Wenlock, 4s.; (2) 1760, Elizabeth, da. of Robert Barnstone of Chester, 1da. *suc.* fa. 1758.

Brooke Forester, who resided at Willey Park 1734–59 and at Dothill thereafter, strengthened his family's interest at Wenlock by his marriage to the heiress of the Welds of Willey, whose estate was in the borough. Returned for Wenlock in 1739, he abstained with his father from voting on the Spanish convention, but subsequently regularly supported the Administration, and was classed in 1746 as an Old Whig. Like his father, he followed H. A. Herbert, Lord Powis (q.v.). He died 8 July 1771.

 J.B.L.

FORESTER, William (1690–1758), of Dothill Park, Salop.

WENLOCK 1715–1722, 1734–1741, 1754–12 Nov. 1758

b. 1690, 1st s. of Sir William Forester, M.P., of Dothill, clerk of the Green Cloth, by Lady Margaret Cecil, da. of James, 3rd Earl of Salisbury. *m.* 1714, Catherine, da. and h. of William Brooke of Clerkenwell, 3s. 3da. *suc.* fa. 1718.

William Forester, whose grandmother was sister of the 1st Earl of Bradford, inherited a predominant interest at Wenlock, for which his family were returned in almost every Parliament for three centuries. Succeeding his father at Wenlock, he voted with the Government in all recorded divisions. Whilst the South Sea bill was before Parliament he had dealings in South Sea stock and was credited by the Company with £1,000 stock at 272 on 25 Mar. 1720, but was able to show that he had subsequently paid for it.[1] Though he did not stand at the next two general elections, he returned his brother-in-law, John Sambrooke, in 1727, his son, Brooke, from 1739, and his son-in-law, Sir Bryan Delves, in 1741. Re-elected unopposed in 1734, he abstained from voting on the Spanish convention in 1739 but thereafter constantly voted with the Administration as one of the group of Shropshire Whigs associated with H. A. Herbert, Lord Powis (q.v.). He died 12 Nov. 1758.

[1] *CJ*, xix. 569.

 J.B.L.

FORSTER, Thomas (1683–1738), of Adderstone, Northumb.

NORTHUMBERLAND 1708–2 Feb. 1716

bap. 29 Mar. 1683, 1st s. of Thomas Forster of Adderstone, M.P., by Frances, da. of Sir William Forster of Bamburgh Castle. *educ.* Newcastle sch.; St. John's, Camb. 1700. *unm.*

Of an ancient Northumbrian family, Forster was the co-heir of his maternal uncle, Ferdinand Forster, M.P., of Bamburgh Castle, whose branch of the family represented Northumberland from

1689 till his murder in 1701. Returned for the county as a high church Tory in succession to his father in 1708, he continued to represent it till his expulsion from the House of Commons for participating in the rebellion of 1715.

On 21 Sept. 1715 Forster, then in London, was one of six Members whose arrest was ordered on a charge of being 'engaged in a design to support the intended invasion of the kingdom'.[1] Evading arrest, he made his way to Northumberland, where he joined Lord Derwentwater and at the head of 300 horse proclaimed the Pretender at Warkworth. After an unsuccessful attempt on Newcastle he joined another body of rebels north of the border and a detachment from Mar's army. Despite a complete lack of military experience he was chosen to command the combined force as a popular Protestant M.P., receiving a commission as general of all the Pretender's forces in England.[2] With a force of 1,500 men he marched into Lancashire, where he expected to find substantial support, but was surrounded at Preston by the government forces, and capitulated after a brief resistance. His chaplain, who accompanied him, describes him as 'better at his beads and prayers than at his business as a soldier', adding 'we all thought him fitter for a priest than a field officer'. Interrogated by Craggs, he refused to turn King's evidence, merely saying that 'he looked on the whole body of the Tories to be in it'.[3]

Taken to London with the other chief rebels, Forster was imprisoned in Newgate, from which he escaped a few days before the day fixed for his trial. The Government issued a description of him as 'one of middle-stature, inclined to be fat, well-shaped, except that he stoops in the shoulders, fair complexioned, his mouth wide, his nose pretty large, his eyes grey, speaks the northern dialect', and placed a reward of £1,000 upon his head.[4] He succeeded in making his way to Paris, where he was sent money by William Dicconson, the Pretender's treasurer. Next year he joined the English Jacobites at the Stuart court, where he was made steward of the Household.[5] Five years later (10 Jan. 1722) the Pretender wrote to the Duke of Ormonde,

> I have convinced Mr. Forster that it is reasonable for him not to think of leaving this place at least for some time. He is a mighty honest good man, and I am very glad to have him here and shall endeavour to make him as easy as I can as to money matters.

When the Pretender moved to Avignon from Rome he summoned Forster (16 Oct. 1727) to join him:

> You see honest Tom I am as good as my word, I have no sooner fixed my habitation here, but I send for you.

As Forster had been excepted from the Act of Indemnity, his brother John succeeded to Adderstone in 1725. Thereafter, he corresponded with the next heir, his nephew Thomas, who held out 'little hopes' of his 'getting anything from the succession'. In October 1738 he died at Boulogne, in France, awaiting news from his nephew.[6] His body was brought home and buried at Bamburgh Castle 7 Dec. 1738.

[1] *Pol. State*, x. 416. [2] *HMC Stuart*, i. 448. [3] *HMC Townshend*, 171. [4] R. Patten, *Hist. Rebellion in 1715* (1745 ed.), 96–97, 108. [5] *HMC Stuart*, ii. 148, 241; v. 429, 603; vii. 335. [6] Stuart mss 57/26, 111/68, 210/73, 134.

E.C.

FORTESCUE, Theophilus (c.1707–1746), of Castle Hill, Filleigh, nr. Barnstaple, Devon.

BARNSTAPLE 1727–1741
DEVON 1741–13 Mar. 1746

b. 1707, 3rd s. of Hugh Fortescue, M.P., of Filleigh by his 1st w. Bridget, da. of Hugh Boscawen of Tregothnan, Cornw. and coh. to barony of Clinton. *unm.*

Of an old Devonshire family, Fortescue was returned for Barnstaple on his family's interest in 1727 as an opposition Whig, transferring to the county in 1741. He voted against the Administration in every recorded division, except on the civil list arrears in 1729, when he was absent. In 1733 his elder brother, Hugh, 1st Earl Clinton, was dismissed as lord of the bedchamber and lord lieutenant of Devon for voting against the excise bill.[1] He died 13 Mar. 1746.

[1] *HMC Egmont Diary*, i. 363.

S.R.M.

FORTESCUE, William (1687–1749), of Buckland Filleigh, Devon.

NEWPORT I.o.W. 1727–17 Feb. 1736.

bap. 26 June 1687, o.s. of Henry Fortescue of Buckland Filleigh by Agnes, da. of Edward Dennis of Barnstaple. *educ.* Barnstaple g.s.; Trinity, Oxf. 1705; M. Temple 1710; I. Temple 1714, called 1715. *m.* 7 July 1709, Mary, da. and coh. of Edmund Fortescue of Fallapit, Devon, 1da. *suc.* fa. 1691.

Private sec. to Sir Robert Walpole as chancellor of the Exchequer c.1727–36; K.C. 1730; attorney-gen. to Prince of Wales 1730–36; baron of the Exchequer 1736–8; justice of the common pleas 1738–41; master of the rolls 1741–d.; P.C. 19 Nov. 1741.

Fortescue, a practising barrister, was distantly related to Margaret Rolle, the daughter-in-law of Sir Robert Walpole,[1] whose private secretary he became. Returned on the government interest at Newport, he voted with the Administration till he vacated his seat on being made a baron of the Exchequer in 1736. He spoke for the Government in February 1730 on the bill to prevent loans to foreign powers except with the King's permission, and next year on the Hessians.[2] The friend to whom Pope addressed his imitation of the first satire of the second book of Horace, he died 15 Dec. 1749.

[1] *Corresp. H. Walpole* (Yale ed.), xviii. 236 n. 1. [2] *HMC Egmont Diary*, i. 60, 126.

P.W.

FORTESCUE ALAND, John (1670-1746), of Stapleford Abbots, Essex.

MIDHURST   1715-24 Jan. 1717

b. 7 Mar. 1670, 2nd s. of Edmund Fortescue of Bierton, Bucks. by Sarah, da. of Henry Aland, sis. and coh. of Henry Aland of Waterford. *educ.* M. Temple 1688, called 1695; called I. Temple 1712, bencher 1714. *m* (1) lic. 19 Dec. 1707, Grace, da. of Sir John Pratt, l.c.j. of King's bench, sis. of Charles Pratt, M.P., 1st Earl Camden, 2s.; (2) 29 Dec. 1721, Elizabeth, da. and coh. of Sir Robert Dormer, M.P., justice of common pleas, 1s. *suc.* e. bro. 1704, taking add. name of Aland. Kntd. 24 Jan. 1717. *cr.* Baron Fortescue of Credan [I] 15 Aug. 1746.

K.C. 1714; solicitor-gen. to Prince of Wales 1714-15; solicitor-gen. 1715-17; baron of the Exchequer 1717-18; justice of King's bench 1718-27; justice of common pleas 1729-46.

Fortescue Aland was descended from Henry VI's chief justice, Sir John Fortescue, whose treatise on the difference between an absolute and a limited monarchy he prepared for publication. Appointed solicitor-general to the Prince of Wales at George I's accession, he was brought into Parliament by the Duke of Somerset in 1715, succeeding Nicholas Lechmere (q.v.) as solicitor-general, a post which he held till he was appointed a baron of the Exchequer, thereby vacating his seat, in 1717. In this capacity he was one of the judges who, during the quarrel between the King and the Prince of Wales, were asked whether the care and education of the Prince's children belonged to the King, expressing the opinion that it did. On George II's accession he wrote to Walpole, begging his protection 'if there should be any difficulty in renewing my patent', as a result of the new King's resentment of the opinion which Fortescue Aland had given 'upon an unhappy occasion'. He continued:

His Majesty has all along approved of my services, when I was his solicitor-general, whilst Prince of Wales; and when I was solicitor-general to his father; and himself made me a baron of the Exchequer by your recommendation; for he was regent and present in council when that was done.[1]

His patent was not renewed but after a few months he was restored to the bench of judges. He retired

with an Irish peerage in 1746, dying 19 Dec. that year.

[1] 1 Aug. 1727, Cholmondeley (Houghton) mss.

J.B.L.

FORTROSE, Lord, *see* MACKENZIE, Kenneth

FOSTER, Thomas (c.1720-65), of Elim, Jamaica, and Egham House, Surr.

BOSSINEY   12 May-11 Dec. 1741
            18 Mar. 1742-1747
DORCHESTER 1761-20 Oct. 1765

b. c.1720, 1st s. of Col. John Foster of Elim, Jamaica by his w. Elizabeth Smith of Barbados. *m.* 2 June 1741, Mary, da. and h. of John Helden of St. Kitts and Egham House, Surr., *s.p.. suc.* fa. 1731.

The grandson of Col. Thomas Foster of Northumberland who took part in the capture of Jamaica under Cromwell and was granted large tracts of land in the island,[1] Foster was a wealthy West Indian planter. Returned for Bossiney as an opposition Whig in 1741, he was unseated on petition by the Administration, but succeeded on a further petition after the fall of Walpole. He was absent from the division on the Hanoverians on 10 Dec. 1742, supported a motion to discharge them on 6 Dec. 1743,[2] voted for them on 18 Jan. 1744, and was absent from the division on them on 11 Apr. 1746, when he was classed by the ministry as 'doubtful'. In 1747 he was put up for Bossiney by Thomas Pitt (q.v.) but was unsuccessful.[3]

He died 20 Oct. 1765.

[1] *Gent. Mag.* 1741, p. 331; *Caribbeana*, iii. 230, 375. [2] Yorke's parl. jnl. *Parl. Hist.* xiii. 144. [3] *HMC Fortescue*, i. 108, 114, 120.

E.C.

FOWLER, Richard (1681-1731), of Harnage Grange, Salop.

RADNORSHIRE   1715-1722

b. 1681, 1st s. of Sir William Fowler, 1st Bt., by Mary, da. of Sir Robert Cotton, 1st Bt., of Combermere, Cheshire. *m.* 19 Sept. 1706, Sarah, da. of William Sloane of Portsmouth, niece of Sir Hans Sloane, 1st Bt., 3s. 1da. *suc.* fa. as 2nd Bt. Aug. 1717.

Commr. for stating army debts 1720-2.

Fowler, whose family had been seated at Harnage since the 16th century, was returned as a Whig for Radnorshire, wresting the seat from the Harleys. In Parliament he voted regularly with the Government and was put down in 1719 as 'Coningsby' (q.v.). Defeated in 1722 by another Whig, Sir Humphrey Howorth, he did not stand again. He died in 1731.

R.R.S.

FOWNES, John, jun. (?1687–1733), of Nethway and Kittery Court, nr. Dartmouth, Devon.

DARTMOUTH 1715–1722

b. ?1687, 1st s. of John Fownes, M.P. Dartmouth 1714–15, of Nethway by Anne, da. of Edward Yarde, M.P. Dartmouth 1681, of Churston Ferrers, Devon. *educ.* Hart Hall, Oxf. 10 Oct. 1702, aged 15. *m.* (1) 24 Jan. 1709, Elizabeth (*d.*23 Jan. 1719), da. and h. of Robert Berry of Plymouth, 1s. 4da.; (2) 9 May 1720, Anne, da. of Samuel Maddock of Tamerton Folliot, nr. Plymouth, Devon, 3s. *suc.* fa. 1731.

Fownes belonged to an old Plymouth family, who began to acquire landed property towards the end of the seventeenth century, purchasing Nethway in 1696, and Kingswear, near Dartmouth, in 1717.[1] Returned for Dartmouth as a Tory in 1715, he is only recorded as voting once, against the septennial bill. In 1721 his name was sent to the Pretender as a probable supporter in the event of a rising.[2] He did not stand again, dying 1 Oct. 1733. His elder son, Henry Fownes, married the daughter and heir of Alexander Luttrell (q.v.).

[1] *Trans. Dev. Assoc.* lxxxv. 78–79. [2] Stuart mss 65/16.

S.R.M.

FOX (afterwards FOX LANE), George (c.1696–1773), of Bramham Park, Yorks.

HINDON 1734–1741
YORK 21 July 1742–1761

b. c.1696, 1st surv. s. of Henry Fox by his 2nd w. Frances, da. of George Lane, 1st Visct. Lanesborough [I]. *m.* 12 July 1731, Harriet, da. and h. of Robert Benson, M.P., of Bramham Park, 1st Baron Bingley, 1s. *d.v.p.* 1da. *suc.* fa. 1719, and to estates of his uncle, James, 2nd Visct. Lanesborough [I], taking add. name of Lane 1751; *cr.* Baron Bingley, 13 May 1762.

Ld. mayor, York 1757.

George Fox is said to have obtained £100,000 by his marriage to the heiress of a former M.P. for York, together with estates, mostly in Yorkshire, worth £7,000 a year. Returned as a Tory for Hindon in 1734, after contesting it unsuccessfully in 1727, he voted against the Government. He did not stand in 1741 and was defeated at a by-election for Yorkshire in 1742, but later in the same year he was returned unopposed for York, continuing to vote with the Opposition. He died 27 Feb. 1773, aged 76.

R.R.S.

FOX, Henry (1705–74), of Holland House, Kensington.

HINDON 28 Feb. 1735–1741
WINDSOR 1741–1761
DUNWICH 1761–17 Apr. 1763

b. 28 Sept. 1705, 2nd surv. s. of Rt. Hon. Sir Stephen Fox, M.P., of Farley, Wilts. by his 2nd w. Christian, da. of Rev. Francis Hopes, rector of Haceby and subsequently Aswaby, Lincs.; bro. of Stephen Fox (q.v.). *educ.* Eton 1715; Ch. Ch. Oxf. 1720; L. Inn 1723. *m.* 2 May 1744, Lady Georgiana Caroline Lennox (*cr.* Baroness Holland of Holland 3 May 1762), da. of Charles, 2nd Duke of Richmond, 4s. (1 *d.v.p.*). *cr.* Baron Holland of Foxley 17 Apr. 1763.

Surveyor gen. of works 1737–43; ld. of Treasury 1743–6; P.C. 23 July 1746; sec. at war 1746–Oct. 1755; Cabinet councillor Dec. 1754; sec. of state for southern dept. Oct. 1755–Oct. 1756; granted Apr. 1757 reversion to sinecure post of clerk of the pells [I] for his life and those of his two elder sons (suc. to it July 1762); paymaster gen. June 1757–May 1765; 'Cabinet councillor and H.M.'s minister in the House of Commons', Oct. 1762–Apr. 1763.

Henry Fox stood unsuccessfully as a Tory for Hindon in 1727, soon after coming of age. On petition 'the whole power of the ministry was exerted' in favour of his opponent (George Heathcote, q.v.), who was confirmed in his seat, though Fox 'was generally supposed to have the fairer right'.[1] Next year he tried again at Thomas Pitt's borough of Old Sarum, 'losing the election', as his friend, Thomas Winnington (q.v.), wrote to him, 'by one vote only, for Pitt not suspecting any opposition, had but two voters there except the person who voted for you'.[2] In 1731, having dissipated his fortune 'in the common vices of youth, gaming included', he was obliged by his debts to go abroad, where he met 'a very salacious Englishwoman', Mrs. Strangways Horner, 'whose liberality restored his fortune, with several circumstances more to the honour of his vigour than his morals'. Succeeding his brother at Hindon in 1735, he returned to England with Mrs. Horner, who next year clandestinely married her 13 year old daughter to Stephen Fox. Eight years later he himself, the son of a footman, was to scandalize society by clandestinely marrying a King's great-grand-daughter.

In Parliament, Fox, now a Whig, supported the Government, developing into a useful though

> a most disagreeable speaker . . . inelegant in his language, hesitating and ungraceful in his elocution, but skilful in discerning the temper of the House, and in knowing when and how to press, or to yield.[3]

His claims to promotion were vigorously pressed by his friend, Lord Hervey (q.v.), who, by persistently importuning Walpole, succeeded in obtaining a minor place for him.[4] But about 1741, according to Horace Walpole,

> Lord Hervey persuaded Fox to make love to the Duchess of Manchester, in order to betray this amour to rich Mrs. Horner, who kept Mr. Fox; she quarrelled with Mr. Fox, and flung herself and her

presents into Lord Hervey's power, and the Duchess refused Mr. Fox, who broke with Lord Hervey.[5]

At the opening of the next Parliament, Fox took part in Walpole's defence, speaking against the appointment of a secret committee of inquiry into the Administration on 21 Jan. and again on 9 and 23 Mar. 1742. Consulted by Pelham on the compilation of the Cockpit list in October 1742, he spoke against the revival of the secret committee, 1 Dec. 1742.[6] 'Fox you cannot do without', Walpole now Orford, wrote, 25 Aug. 1743, to Pelham,[7] who brought him into the Treasury when the board was reconstituted in December 1743. Though occasionally differing from Pelham on matters cutting across normal parliamentary lines, he atoned by resigning with him in February 1746. On Winnington's death in April 1746, Fox would have liked to succeed him at the pay office, but had to give way there to Pitt, taking instead the war office, much against his own wishes. 'I fear I must take it', he wrote, 'to quarrel with the army and, hated, as I already am, by the Duke [of Cumberland], to do business from morning to night.'[8] In the event, however, he soon became so attached to his chief, the captain-general, that when Cumberland was passed over for the regency in 1751, Fox, though obliged as a member of the Government to declare himself for the regency bill, 'spoke against almost every part of it'.

Though since Winnington's death Fox had been Pelham's 'ostensible second' in the Commons, with 'the seeming right of succession', his relations with the chief ministers, already affected by his allegiance to Cumberland, were strained by his behaviour in the debates on the clandestine marriages bill in 1753. Resenting the bill as a slur on his own and his brother's marriages, he made a violent personal attack in the Commons on its author, Lord Chancellor Hardwicke; then, finding that he had gone too far, denied that he had intended his remarks to apply to Hardwicke, with great professions of regard for him; thus exposing himself to Hardwicke's rejoinder in the Lords: 'I despise the invective and I despise the recantation; I despise the scurrility . . . and I reject the adulation.' In this affair, writes Horace Walpole, Fox

> first discovered some symptoms of irresolution; and the time advanced but too fast when the provocation offered to Yorke [Hardwicke], and the suspicion of his want of a determined spirit, were of essential detriment to him.[9]

So it proved, for, when Pelham's death a few months later opened the way to the succession to the position of first minister, Hardwicke threw all his weight into the scale against Fox, whose

yellow streak, ever more apparent, became the determining factor in his future career.

He died 1 July 1774.

[1] *HMC Egmont Diary*, i. 27. [2] Ilchester, *Lord Holland*, i. 30. [3] Ld. Chesterfield, *Characters* (1777), 38–40; *HMC Egmont Diary*, ii. 150; see HORNER, Thomas. [4] Hervey, *Mems.* 453, 667–8, 740–1. [5] *Corresp. H. Walpole* (Yale ed.), xxx. 313. [6] Ilchester, i. 89–90, 92. [7] Coxe, *Pelham*, i. 91–93. [8] Ilchester, i. 113–14, 117–19, 129, 132. [9] Walpole, *Mems. Geo. II*, i. 132, 349–53, 379.

R.R.S.

FOX, Stephen (1704–76), of Redlynch, Som.

SHAFTESBURY   3 May 1726–1734
HINDON   1734–20 Feb. 1735
SHAFTESBURY   20 Feb. 1735–1741

b. 12 Sept. 1704, 1st surv. s. of Rt. Hon. Sir Stephen Fox, M.P., and e. bro. of Henry Fox (q.v.). *educ.* Eton 1715; Ch. Ch. Oxf. 1721; Grand Tour (Low Countries, France, Italy) 1723–5. *m.* 15 Mar. 1736, Elizabeth, da. of Thomas Strangways Horner (q.v.) of Mells, Som. by Susannah, da. and coh. of Thomas Strangways of Melbury, sis. and h. of Thomas Strangways, formerly Horner, of Melbury, Dorset, 3s. 4da. *suc.* fa. 1716; assumed add. name of Strangways Feb. 1758 on d. of his w.'s mother. *cr.* Lord Ilchester, Baron of Woodford Strangways, 11 May 1741; Lord Ilchester and Stavordale, Baron of Redlynch 12 Jan. 1747; Earl of Ilchester 17 June 1756.
Jt. sec. to Treasury June 1739–Apr. 1741; jt. comptroller of army accounts 1747–*d.*; P.C. 22 Apr. 1763.

Beginning life as a footman,[1] Sir Stephen Fox, the founder of the Fox family, made a great fortune under Charles II as paymaster of the forces, investing most of it in land in Wiltshire and Somerset. By his first wife he had one son, who succeeded him as paymaster but predeceased him; by his second, whom he married in his 77th year, he left two sons, Stephen and Henry (q.v.). The elder, Stephen, entered Parliament as a Tory for Shaftesbury in 1726, soon after he had come of age. Re-elected in 1727, he went to Italy in 1728 with Lord Hervey (q.v.), who confessed to feeling towards him more like 'a mistress than a friend'.[2] Returning with Hervey to England in 1729, he voted with the Opposition on the Hessians in 1730, but soon afterwards went over to the Government, seconding an address to the King on the Princess Royal's marriage in a speech 'got by heart', 8 Apr. 1733, and the Address at the opening of the session in 1734. He moved the Address in 1736, in which year he married clandestinely a 13 year old heiress, whose mother was keeping his brother, Henry. He spoke for the Government on the army estimates in 1737,[3] moving the Address again in 1738 in a speech described as 'masterly'.[4] His claims to recognition were strongly pressed by Hervey on

Walpole, who tried to stave him off with a promise of a peerage as soon as any peers were created, but was eventually forced, against his own inclination, to make him joint secretary to the Treasury,[5] dealing with the preparations for the general election.[6] In February 1741 he spoke against the motion for Walpole's removal, soon afterwards resigning his Treasury post on obtaining a peerage, in return for a payment to Lady Yarmouth, the King's mistress.[7] He took little further part in national politics, but kept up his interest at Shaftesbury, for which he received £400 a year from the secret service money under Pelham and Walpole.[8] In 1756 he secured an earldom through the influence of his brother, Henry.[9] He died 26 Sept. 1776.

[1] *HMC Egmont Diary*, iii. 260; Walpole to Mann, 29 May 1744. [2] Hervey, *Mems.* p. xxiii. [3] *HMC Egmont Diary*, i. 371; ii. 350; see HORNER, Thomas, and FOX, Henry. [4] *HMC 14th Rep. IX*, 10. [5] Hervey, *Mems.* 453, 667, 740-1; Walpole, *Mems. Geo. II*, i. 205. [6] Ilchester, *Lord Holland*, i. 78. [7] *HMC Egmont Diary*, iii. 260. [8] Namier, *Structure*, 228, 429 n. 7 et seq. [9] Ilchester, i. 344.

R.R.S.

FRANK, Robert (1660–1738), of Pontefract.

PONTEFRACT   1710–22 Mar. 1716

bap. 2 Feb. 1660. s. of John Frank of Pontefract by Mary, da. and coh. of William Harbred of Wistow, Yorks. *educ.* G. Inn 1678. *m.* 21 Feb. 1698, Elizabeth, da. of Ralph Lowther of Ackworth, Yorks., sis. of John Lowther (q.v.), 1s. *d.v.p.* 3da.
    Recorder, Pontefract.

Frank belonged to one of the leading families of Pontefract, where he owned 20 burgages[1] and was the recorder of the borough. Returned for Pontefract as a Tory in Anne's last two Parliaments, he was re-elected in 1715, when the mayor was his uncle, and the town clerk was his agent. On petition he was unseated on the ground that the mayor as returning officer, under the influence of Frank and his agent, had wrongfully rejected a number of his opponent's votes.[2]

He did not stand again, dying in 1738 (buried 6 Sept.).

[1] C. Bradley, 'Parl. Rep. of Pontefract, Newark and East Retford 1754-68' (Manchester Univ. M.A. thesis). [2] *CJ*, xviii. 409-10.

R.R.S.

FRANKLAND, Frederick Meinhardt (c.1694–1768), of Whitehall, Westminster.

THIRSK   1734–25 Mar. 1749

b. c.1694, 5th s. of Sir Thomas Frankland, 2nd Bt., M.P. Thirsk 1685-95 and 1698-1711, by Elizabeth, da. of Sir John Russell, 3rd Bt., of Chippenham, Wilts. by Frances, da. of Oliver Cromwell, wid. of Hon. Robert Rich; bro. of Sir Thomas Frankland,

3rd Bt. (q.v.). *educ.* Jesus, Camb. 1711; M. Temple 1711, called 1718. *m.* (1) his sis-in-law Elizabeth (*d.* 27 Jan. 1737), da. of René Baudouin, London merchant, wid. of William Frankland (*d.* 1714) and of Adam Cardonnel, Marlborough's secretary (*d.* 1719), 3s. *d.v.p.* 3da. one of whom *m.* Thomas Pelham of Stanmer (q.v.), later 1st Earl of Chichester; (2) Feb. 1739, Lady Anne Lumley, da. of Richard, 1st Earl of Scarbrough, *s.p.*
    Director, Bank of England 1736-8; commr. of revenue [I] Mar. 1749-53, of excise 1753-63.

A younger son, who went into business as a merchant, Frankland was returned for his family's borough, voting steadily with the Government. In 1739 he surprised his friends by separating from his recently married second wife, the sister of the Earl of Scarbrough, to whom 'he would give no reason but that she was his utter aversion'. According to the 1st Lord Egmont:

Mr. Frankland declared the same to his lady, who on her knees begged she might still have an apartment in his house though he should never speak to her; otherwise, that such an open separation would give occasion to the world to suspect her virtue or make what ill stories it pleased of her. But he would not consent. He has since settled £600 per annum upon her, which was the jointure agreed upon when he married her, has returned her fortune, which was £10,000, has given her £1,000 to furnish a house, and all her jewels, together with his plate.

This procedure is the more wondered at because they were playfellows and acquaintances from their youth, and it was a match of his own seeking, though she was then between forty and fifty years old, ugly, and as fat as most women. He . . . made a remarkable good husband to his first wife.[1]

He vacated his seat in 1749 by accepting an office incompatible with a seat in the House of Commons. About this time the 2nd Lord Egmont in his electoral survey observed that the Frankland family 'had some thoughts of selling' Thirsk, 'but extravagantly dear', on which the Prince of Wales commented 'The best way is to continue Fred Frankland in his place, and then we have the borough'.

Frankland died 8 Mar. 1768. It is not known how he came to acquire the name of Meinhardt, sometimes spelt 'Mynhard'.[2] He was returned and signed his letters as 'Frederick Frankland'.

[1] *HMC Egmont Diary*, iii. 72. [2] E.g. in Add. 33190.

R.R.S.

FRANKLAND, Thomas (c.1683–1747), of Thirkleby Park, nr. Thirsk, Yorks.

HARWICH   1708–1713
THIRSK   1713–17 Apr. 1747

b. c.1683, 1st s. of Sir Thomas Frankland, 2nd Bt., M.P., and bro. of Frederick Meinhardt Frankland (q.v.). *educ.* Jesus, Camb. 1700. *m.* (1) 5 June 1715,

Diana (*d.* 2 Feb. 1741), da. and h. of Francis Topham of Agglethorpe, Yorks., 2da.; (2) 9 July 1741, Sarah Moseley of Worcs., *s.p.s. suc.* fa. as 3rd Bt. 30 Oct. 1726.

Clerk of deliveries in the Tower 1714-15; sec. to master general of, and clerk of deliveries in, the Ordnance 1715-22; commr. of revenue [I] 1724-8; ld. of Trade 1728-30; ld. of Admiralty 1730-42.

Returned from 1713 for the family borough of Thirsk, Frankland from 1715 voted with the Government in all recorded divisions, except those on Lord Cadogan (q.v.) and the peerage bill, on which he voted with the Opposition. He lost his place on Walpole's fall, after which his only recorded vote was with the Opposition on the Hanoverians in 1744. Classed in 1746 by the ministry as 'doubtful', he died 17 Apr. 1747, leaving all his property absolutely to his second wife, 'a very pretty woman', 40 years younger than himself, who was said to have 'bedevilled' the 'superannuated old fool'.[1] The will was upset by the courts as made under undue influence and while of unsound mind; but under an earlier will, which was upheld, she inherited the Frankland property for her life. She held Thirkleby for 36 years, amassing a fortune of £35,000, which she left away from her husband's family.[2]

[1] *GEC Baronetage*, iii. 143. [2] Sir R. F. Payne-Gallwey, *Ped. Frankland of Thirkleby*.

R.R.S.

FRANKLAND, Thomas (1718-84), of Kirby Hall, Inkpen, Berks.

THIRSK 12 May 1747-1780, 3 Apr.-21 Nov. 1784

b. 26 June 1718, 2nd s. of Henry Frankland, gov. of Fort William, Bengal (bro. of Frederick Meinhardt and Sir Thomas Frankland, qq.v.), by Mary, da. of Alexander Cross, merchant. *m.* 27 May 1743, Sarah, da. of Judge William Rhett, c.j. and gov. of South Carolina, 5s. 8da. *suc.* bro. as 5th Bt. 11 Jan. 1768, and his uncle's wid. to Thirkleby estates 1783.

Entered navy 1731, capt. 1740, r.-adm. 1755, v.-adm. 1759, adm. 1770.

While serving in the West Indies in 1744 Frankland captured several ships, including one said to have been worth 'half a million of treasure'. As an agent for the sale of other captured ships, he dealt in very large sums of money.[1]

In 1747 he was brought in for the family borough, classed as a government supporter, sitting until 1780, and again in 1784, dying on 21 Nov.

[1] Sir R. F. Payne-Gallwey, *Ped. Frankland of Thirkleby*.

R.R.S.

FRASER, Hon. William (1691-1727), of Fraserfield, Aberdeen.

ELGIN BURGHS 1722-23 Jan. 1725

b. 19 Nov. 1691, 2nd s. of William, 12th Lord Saltoun [S] of Abernethy, by Margaret, da. of James Sharp, abp. of St. Andrews. *educ.* adv. 1713. *m.* 25 Oct. 1724, Lady Katherine Anne Erskine, da. of David, 9th Earl of Buchan [S], 1s. Bought estate of Balgownie from Lord Gray and called it Fraserfield 1721.

On 20 Oct. 1722 Lord Finch (q.v.) wrote to his father, Lord Nottingham:

I have this day heard and seen what I never expected to have met with i.e. that I should sit in a House of Commons that could be convinced by the debate and turned by the eloquence of any one man who was not in authority. But there is a Scotch gentleman, one Mr. Fraser, a friend of my Lord Aberdeen's, who is returned for the burghs of Elgin, Banff, Cullen, and Inverurie, against whom Col. John Campbell [of Mamore, q.v.], Mrs. Campbell's husband, petitions. This Mr. Fraser was in the rebellion, not long since pardoned that he might plead at the bar in Scotland. The House was as much set upon bringing in Jack Campbell as we were in the last Parliament, when I moved to have the return tried before the merits of the election against James Murray [q.v.], now secretary to the Pretender at Rome, and had Mr. Fraser been silent he had met the same fate, and left to petition, as Mr. Murray was. When he began to speak, the usual compliment of silence was paid to him as a new speaker but if the question had been put when he began, he would not have had 50 votes, for I don't believe he had ever seen five gentlemen of England that were of the House till the first meeting of the Parliament nor did he know the half of his own countrymen. But when he had done, Mr. Campbell's friends did not think fit to divide, for if they had I don't believe there would have been 50 for John Campbell with all the advantage of his acquaintance and friendship with the greatest part of the House. In short Mr. Fraser said everything that was necessary to enforce his cause, to convince his judges, and to persuade their favour, and not one word more than was necessary.[1]

The same day Knatchbull noted in his parliamentary diary:

Mr. Fraser, the sitting member, made a most handsome speech in his own defence and turned the whole House that seemed prepossessed against him.

Pending the decision of the elections committee, to whom the petition was referred, Fraser was active in the House on matters relating to Scotland, such as the malt tax and the alleged frauds on the customs by the Glasgow tobacco merchants, observing that 'it was necessary to keep the thing as much as possible off from a national footing, for then we were sure to lose it'.[2] However, on 10 Dec. 1724, when the committee of ways and means were debating the malt tax, he

insisted it was a breach of the Union in this point, and said he was one that protested against it as such. This being an unusual expression in the House of Commons, the attorney general first took notice of it and after Mr. Walpole saying it was such an expression he had never heard there, and if the person that used it had considered the consequence or knew it, he thought he would not have done it, but as he was a young member he would not insist on the consequence, only he could not let it go unobserved, and advised those gentlemen to acquiesce for though they were a minority to the English yet they would not put them in the case they had put themselves in in this debate, and that this way of raising money due from them was an indulgence to them since we took now not above £20,000 for £60,000 and they had behaved themselves as if they were a separate nation when now we are all one, so the question put and no division.[3]

Next month the elections committee decided against Fraser, who was unseated. Unsuccessful for Linlithgow Burghs at a by-election in April 1725, he died 23 March 1727.

[1] Finch mss at HMC. [2] SRO, Dalhousie mss 14/397. [3] *Knatchbull Diary*, 10 Dec. 1724.

J.M.S.

FREDERICK, Charles (1709–85), of Hammersmith, Mdx.

NEW SHOREHAM 1741–1754
QUEENBOROUGH 1754–1784

b. 21 Dec. 1709, 3rd s. of Sir Thomas Frederick, gov. of Fort St. David, Madras and director of South Sea Co., by Mary, da. of William Moncrieff; bro. of John and Thomas Frederick (qq.v.). *educ.* Westminster 1719–20; New Coll. Oxf. 1725; M. Temple 1728; Grand Tour with his bro. John (Italy, Constantinople, Near East, France) 1737–9. *m.* 18 Aug. 1746, Lucy, da. of Hugh Boscawen (q.v.), 1st Visct. Falmouth, 4s. 2da. K.B. 23 Mar. 1761.
    Clerk of deliveries in the Ordnance 1746–50; surveyor gen. of the Ordnance 1750–82.

Charles Frederick, an eminent antiquary, director of the Society of Antiquaries in 1736 and 1740, succeeded his brother John (q.v.) as Member for Shoreham in 1741, voting consistently with the Administration. In 1746 he was appointed to a place in the Ordnance, starting a 36 years' connexion with that office. Frances Boscawen, writing to her husband the Admiral (q.v.), describes Frederick and his wife, the Admiral's sister, in 1748:

Mr. and Mrs. Frederick are in Berkeley Square—he the busiest, she the idlest, mortal living. He is in the Green Park from 8 in the morning till 4 in the afternoon, has an office built there for him. The rest of the day he gives audiences and worries his spirits and his person till 'tis reduced to a shadow.[1]

Horace Walpole wrote to Henry Seymour Conway, 6 Oct. 1748:

Charles Frederick has turned all his *virtu* into fireworks, and, by his influence at the Ordnance, has prepared such a spectacle for the proclamation of the peace as to surpass all its predecessors of bounc-

ing memory. It is to open with a concert of fifteen hundred hands, and conclude with so many hundred thousand crackers all set to music . . . I wish you could see him making squibs of his *papillotes*, bronzed over with a patina of gunpowder, and talking to himself still hoarser on the superiority that his fireworks will have over the Roman *naumachia*.

He died 18 Dec. 1785.

[1] C. Aspinall-Oglander, *Admiral's Wife*, 123.

A.N.N.

FREDERICK, John (1708–83) of Burwood Park, Walton-on-Thames, Surr.

NEW SHOREHAM 24 Nov. 1740–1741
WEST LOOE 10 Dec. 1743–1761

b. 28 Nov. 1708, at Fort St. George, India, 2nd s. of Sir Thomas Frederick and bro. of Charles and Thomas Frederick (qq.v.). *educ.* Westminster 1719–20; New Coll. Oxf. 1725; M. Temple 1729; Grand Tour with his bro. Charles (Italy, Constantinople, Near East, France) 1737–9. *m.* 22 Oct. 1741, Susanna, da. of Sir Roger Hudson of Sunbury, Mdx., sis. and h. of Vansittart Hudson, 2s. 3da. *suc.* bro. Thomas 1740; his cos. as 4th Bt. 16 Dec. 1770.
    Commr. of customs 13 Mar. 1761–19 Mar. 1782.

John Frederick succeeded his brother Thomas at Shoreham but in 1741 gave up the seat to his younger brother, Charles, unsuccessfully contesting Chippenham jointly with his brother-in-law Alexander Hume (q.v.). With the support of the Government he and Hume presented an election petition, the defeat of which in the House of Commons finally decided Walpole to resign.[1]

In 1743 Frederick was brought in for West Looe by the Administration, with whom he consistently voted. For many years he was a constant but unsuccessful applicant for places and favours, on the ground that

our family have for many years served his Majesty with the most inviolable attachment, and at as great an expense as any commoners whatever.[2]

He died 9 Apr. 1783.

[1] Walpole to Mann, 4 Feb. 1742. [2] 5 Mar. 1750, Add. 32720, f.127.

A.N.N.

FREDERICK, Thomas (1707–40), of Burwood Park, Walton-on-Thames, Surr.

NEW SHOREHAM 1734–21 Aug. 1740

b. 26 Oct. 1707, at Fort St. George, India, 1st s. of Sir Thomas Frederick; bro. of Charles and John Frederick (qq.v.). *educ.* Westminster 1719–20; New Coll. Oxf. 1725. *unm. suc.* fa. 1731.

Thomas Frederick, whose great-grandfather, Sir Thomas Frederick, M.P., had been lord mayor of London in 1662, came of a family of wealthy merchants.[1] He was returned for Shoreham '(as his friends gave out) with the assistance of the Government',[2] with whom he consistently voted. He was on the council of the Georgia Society but ceased to attend meetings after the society incurred Walpole's displeasure, 'he being very great with my Lady Walpole, who is a great enemy to our colony'. On 22 Feb. 1737 he spoke in favour of the motion to settle £100,000 upon the Prince of Wales, and on 8 Mar. 1738 he seconded the motion for a grant for the further settlement of Georgia.[3] He died 21 Aug. 1740, leaving most of his property to his brother John (q.v.).

[1] E. H. Fellowes, *Hist. Frederick Fam.*, 28. [2] Undated mem. by the Duke of Richmond, Richmond mss. [3] *HMC Egmont Diary*, ii. 286, 469.

A.N.N.

FREIND, John (?1677–1728), of Hitcham, Bucks.

LAUNCESTON   1722–17 Mar. 1724
            29 Mar. 1725–1727

b. ?1677, 3rd s. of Rev. William Freind, rector of Croughton, Northants., by his w. Anne. *educ.* Westminster under Dr. Busby; Ch. Ch. Oxf. 7 July 1694, aged 17; M.B. 1703, M.D. 1707. *m.* 3 Dec. 1709, Anne, da. of Thomas Morice, paymaster of the British forces in Portugal, and cos. of Sir Nicholas Morice (q.v.), 1s.[1] Freind was bro.-in-law of Rev. William Morice, Atterbury's son-in-law.
    Fellow, R. Coll. of Physicians 1716; gov. Bridewell and Bethlehem Hospitals 1728.

Freind distinguished himself as a scholar at Christ Church, where he became the intimate friend of Francis Atterbury. Adopting the profession of medicine, in 1705 he accompanied the Earl of Peterborough as physician during the Spanish campaign; in 1712 he went to Flanders with the Duke of Ormonde in the same capacity. On his return, he became one of London's chief physicians, drawing his patients principally from among the Tories. He moved in high Tory political circles, dining with Harley and St. John, and contributing articles to *The Examiner*.[2]

After George I's accession Freind corresponded with the Stuart court at Rome, engaging an English nurse for the newly-born Young Pretender in 1720. Brought into Parliament in 1722 by Lord Lansdowne, one of the Pretender's representatives in France, he became deeply involved in the scheme for a Jacobite rising known as the Atterbury plot. On 30 Mar. of that year the Pretender wrote to Lord Strafford, who was to command the rising in the north:

I think you have done very well to let Dr. Freind into the secret of our present affair. He is a most worthy man and out of good will to me would have quitted both his practice and his country to have

attended me if I would have allowed him, which is a sufficient proof of his sincere attachment to me and the cause.

In April he seems to have been in charge of the 'military chest' formed to finance the rising, sending bills of exchange to the Pretender's banker in Paris by a London alderman and by another emissary to Ormonde to enable him to make the necessary preparations in Spain and Italy. Walpole later told Sir Dudley Ryder (q.v.) that had the scheme succeeded, Freind was to have been secretary of state. About this time he began to suspect Lord Mar, Lansdowne's colleague in France, of treachery, imparting his suspicions in a letter to Lansdowne, who gave it to Mar to decipher. Mar wrote at once to the Pretender:

God have mercy on an undertaking of this kind with Dr. Jo. Freind at the head of it . . . Earl Strafford has bred in and is imposed upon by Dr. Jo. Freind . . . Sir Henry Goring [q.v.] is entirely led by Dr. Jo. Freind.

When the Government got wind of the conspiracy Freind told Lansdowne that it was being 'asserted with great positiveness' that Mar had given 'an account of the design all along, and keeps a constant correspondence in cypher with Sir Robert Sutton [q.v.] and Lord Stair', the British ambassadors at Cambrai and Paris, adding: 'I hope he is injured in it, and am sure no one wishes him every way more clear than myself'.[3] Freind was not arrested with his fellow conspirators in August and September because, though frequently mentioned in intercepted correspondence under the name of Clinton, the government decipherers were unable to identify him.[4] But unfortunately for him the English nurse whom he had engaged for the Young Pretender 'became so uneasy' in Rome that she was sent back to England, where on 11 Mar. 1723 she admitted, on being questioned, that the expenses of her journey had been paid by Freind and that she had taken letters from him to persons in the Pretender's service.[5] Arrested the following day, but discharged without trial three months later, he received a letter from the Pretender assuring him that 'the many proofs you have already given me of your friendship will ever engage me to profess an eternal gratitude to you'.[6]

In Parliament, Freind spoke, 27 Nov. 1722, against a proposal to raise £100,000 from Roman Catholics. He was unseated on petition after a heated debate in March 1724, but recovered his seat at a by-election in 1725. On 20 Apr. 1725 he spoke in support of the bill for restoring Bolingbroke's estates 'in hopes it was an earnest for more and better'.[7] In a debate on foreign affairs in February 1726 he lashed the ministry and their whole conduct and said that no Englishman could give his approbation to the treaty of Hanover, if he had not renounced the interest of his native country, and sold himself a bond slave to foreigners. He exposed the treaty of Hanover and showed that the whole design of it was to guarantee the Hanover dominions which is directly against the Act of Settlement.

On the accession of George II Freind was appointed physician to Queen Caroline, whose children he had been summoned to attend in 1724, when she had treated him with high favour. He did not stand at the general election and forbad the Pretender's agent in London from ever speaking to him on his master's affairs.[8] An Oxford Tory wrote of his defection:

Had he excused himself from being physician in waiting, on account of its being inconsistent with his other business, as Radcliffe did to King William, but offered readily to attend when called upon any occasion, he might have had as much power and not much less money, and no one could have taken the least exception to it.[9]

On his death of a violent fever,[10] 26 July 1728, Atterbury observed:

I dare say, notwithstanding his station at court, he died of the same political opinions in which I left him. He is lamented by men of all parties at home, and of all countries abroad.[11]

[1] J. H. Glover, *Stuart Pprs.* pp. 1–li. [2] Swift, *Works.* v. 384: ix. 69; *Jnl. to Stella*, passim. [3] Stuart mss 46/149, 58/91, 58/116, 59/72, 60/26, 60/160; Harrowby mss 21 (L. Inn), 13 Feb. 1742; Stowe 250, f. 77; Howell, *State Trials*, xvi. 336–7, 395. [4] Stowe 250, ff. 5, 9, 13–14. [5] SP Dom. 35/42, ff. 34, 45; *State Trials*, 395. [6] Stuart mss 76/94. [7] *Knatchbull Diary.* [8] Stuart mss 90/128, 122/3. [9] *HMC Portland*, vii. 467. [10] Hearne, *Colls.* (Oxf. Hist. Soc.), x. 38. [11] Nichols, *Lit. Anecs.* v. 101.

E.C.

FREMAN, Ralph (c.1665–1742), of Aspenden Hall, Herts.

HERTFORDSHIRE 30 Dec. 1697–1727

b. c.1665, 1st s. of Ralph Freman, M.P., by Elizabeth, da. of Sir John Aubrey, 1st Bt., of Llantrithyd, Glam. *m.* Elizabeth, da. and coh. of Thomas Catesby of Ecton, Northants., 3s. *suc.* fa. 1714.

Chairman of committee of privileges and elections 1710–13.

Freman was the great-grandson of a London merchant, who bought the manor of Aspenden in Hertfordshire at the beginning of the 17th century. A Hanoverian Tory, he is said to have refused an offer of a seat on the Admiralty board by George I on his accession.[1] When it was moved that a loyal address should be presented on the outbreak of the rebellion in 1715, he proposed and the House agreed that at so important a juncture they should lose no time in drawing up an address but should forthwith lay the resolution before the King. Otherwise he spoke and voted consistently

with the Opposition, securing the withdrawal of the peerage bill in April 1719 by a call of the House, which led a large number of Members to return to town to oppose it.[2] After representing the county for 30 years, he was defeated by his brother-in-law, Charles Caesar, in 1727. According to his own account, when George II

came to the crown, his Majesty sent to him and told him he hoped that as he had always shown himself a friend to his family, he would be in the House in this first Parliament of his reign. Mr. Freman replied he did not think of standing, but if his Majesty thought it for his service, he would, but then he hoped his Majesty's servants would not oppose him. The King replied they should on the contrary assist him. So down he went, but when the election came on he found the Government's officers oppose him to a man in favour of Mr. Caesar, a much higher Tory than himself, who had gone all my Lord Bolingbroke's length in Queen Anne's reign, and whom the Jacobites now supported. Surprised at this, he caused those officers to be spoke to, who replied they dare not do otherwise, for it might cost them their employments. In a word, Mr. Freman lost the election, and being returned to London acquainted the King how he had been served. The King was very angry with Sir Robert. As he came out of his Majesty's closet he met Sir Robert going in, who, stopping him, expressed his surprise that he had not carried his election, asked him how it was possible, and declared nothing had surprised and vexed him more. Mr. Freman replied, 'Don't ask me how I lost it, you know that better than I', at which Sir Robert blushed up to his eyes, which, said Mr. Freman, is the only time I ever saw him blush.[3]

At the next general election Freman turned the tables on Caesar by joining with the Whigs to secure his defeat. He died 8 June 1742, aged 76.

[1] Worsley list. [2] *Pol. State*, xvii. 427–8. [3] *HMC Egmont Diary*, ii. 164–5.

A.N.N.

FRENCH, Jeffrey (c.1701–54), of Argyle Bldgs., London.

MILBORNE PORT 1741–1747
TAVISTOCK 24 Apr.–14 May 1754

b. c.1701, 6th s. of Arthur French of Cloonyquin, co. Roscommon, mayor of Galway, by his 2nd w. Sarah, da. and h. of Ulick Burke of Clare, co. Galway, wid. of Iriel Farrel of Cloonyquin. *educ.* M. Temple 1719, called 1724. *m.* Catherine, da. of Richard Lloyd of Croghan, co. Roscommon, Speaker of Upper House of Assembly and c.j. Jamaica.

French's family had extensive estates in western Ireland, but after his father's death in 1712 he went to London where he entered the inns of court. In February 1734 Egmont noted in connexion with an Irish popish solicitors' bill:

Two petitions have been presented . . . against it, one . . . by a lawyer here, named French, who petitioned on behalf of the Protestants of Ireland, as falling hard on the new converts who practice as solicitors.[1]

His wife, a vivacious woman, well known in London 'for her elegant assemblies, and bringing eminent characters together',[2] appears to have been unfaithful. On 6 Jan. 1743 Horace Walpole wrote to Mann:

> There is nothing new but the separation of . . . Mr. and Mrs. French . . . She has been fashionable these two winters; her husband has commenced a suit in Doctors' Commons against her boar-cat, and will, they say, recover considerable damages: but the lawyers are of the opinion that the kittens must inherit Mr. French's estate, as they were born in lawful wedlock.

The couple were reconciled, but in 1751 separated again.[3]

An account of French has been left by his nephew, Arthur Murphy, the author, who was educated at St. Omer in France at his expense. On his return, he had a meeting with his uncle:

> He talked with me for some time about indifferent things; and then, repeating a line from Virgil, asked me if I could construe it? I told him I had the whole of the *Aeneid* by heart. He made me repeat ten or a dozen lines, and then said, 'If I have fifty acres of land to plough, and can only get two labouring men to work at two acres per day, how many days will it take to do the whole?' 'Sir!' said I, staring at him; 'Can't you answer that question?' said he; 'Then I would not give a farthing for all you know. Get Crocker's Arithmetic; you may buy it for a shilling at any stall; and mind me, young man, did you ever hear *Mass* while you was abroad?' 'Sir, I did, like the rest of the boys.' 'Then, mark my words; let me never hear that you go to *Mass* again; it is a mean, beggarly, blackguard religion.' He then rose, stepped into his chariot, and drove away.[4]

French wanted Murphy to work on his plantation in Jamaica, but Murphy refused, whereupon French disowned him and eventually left him out of his will. Murphy revenged himself by satirising his uncle's character in the person of Wingate, a self-made, passionate old man, very fond of money and mathematics, in the comedy *The Apprentice*, which was acted at Drury Lane in 1756. The likeness was recognised by the public. Murphy remarked afterwards: 'So I made old Jeffrey at last extricate me from my difficulties'.[5]

French was returned in 1741 for Milborne Port, where he had bought an estate,[6] voting with the Administration until April 1746, when he voted against them on the Hanoverian troops, being classed as 'doubtful'. Losing his seat in 1747, he is described in the 2nd Lord Egmont's electoral survey, c.1749–50, as 'having been slighted utterly by this Administration'. He died 14 May 1754.

[1] *HMC Egmont Diary*, ii. 19. [2] Boswell's *Johnson*, iv. 48. [3] Walpole to Montagu, 30 May 1751. [4] Jesse Foot, *Life of Arthur Murphy* (1811), p. 9. [5] H. H. Dunbar, *Dramatic Career of Arthur Murphy* (New York 1946), pp. 20–22. [6] PCC 131 Pinfold. [7] Rigby to Bedford, 25 Apr. 1754, Bedford mss. [8] PCC 131 Pinfold.

E.C.

FULLER, John (?1679–1744), of Great Yarmouth, Norf.

PLYMPTON ERLE 29 Feb. 1728–1734

b. ?1679, 2nd but 1st surv. s. of Samuel Fuller, M.P., merchant and mayor of Yarmouth, by Rose, da. of Richard Huntington, M.P.[1] *educ.* Colchester and Yarmouth; Caius, Camb. 14 May 1695, aged 15. prob. *unm. suc.* fa. 1721.
    Consul at Leghorn c. 1718–22.

John Fuller, of a Yarmouth family, whose father had represented the borough in four Parliaments under William III, resigned his post at Leghorn in 1722[2] and returned to England after his father's death. Having unsuccessfully challenged the Townshend-Walpole interest at Yarmouth in the general election of 1727, he was apparently bought off with a government seat at Plympton six months later, but voted against the Administration in all recorded divisions. He did not stand again, dying 22 Mar. 1744. His nephew, Richard Fuller, contested Yarmouth without success in 1741, 1754, and 1756.

[1] Swinden, *Great Yarmouth*, 866. [2] *Pol. State*, xxiv. 499.

R.S.L.

FULLER, see also PARGITER FULLER

FURNESE, Henry (aft. 1688–1756), of Gunnersbury House, Mdx.

DOVER 20 Dec. 1720–1734
MORPETH 18 May 1738–1741
NEW ROMNEY 1741–30 Aug. 1756

b. aft. 1688,[1] 1st s. of George Furnese, an E. I. Co. factor, and 1st cos. of Sir Robert Furnese (q.v.). *unm.,* 1da. *suc.* fa. aft. Sept. 1709, and to personal estate of cos. Sir Henry Furnese, 3rd Bt. 1735.
    Sec. to Treasury, July–Nov. 1742; ld. of Treasury 1755–*d.*

Furnese, whose father died insane,[2] was apprenticed to a well-known London merchant, Moses Berenger, and became a member of the Lisbon factory.[3] Returned for Dover with government support in 1720, he bought Lathom Hall, near Wigan, in 1722. At the general election that year he declared himself a candidate for Wigan, but gave up before the poll.[4] Re-elected for Dover, he joined Lord Morpeth (q.v.) in attacking the directors of the South Sea Company at a meeting of the shareholders in 1723.[5] In 1723 and 1729 he obtained contracts for remitting money to the garrisons in Gibraltar and Minorca.[6] In the next Parliament, like his cousin, Sir Robert Furnese (q.v.), he went into opposition, losing his seat in 1734. He re-entered Parliament in 1738 for the seat vacated by his friend, Lord Morpeth, on succeeding to the peerage. In 1739 he bought Gunnersbury Park from Lord Hobart (q.v.).[7] Attaching himself to Pulteney, he voted with the Opposition against the Spanish convention in 1739 and for the place bill in 1740. In 1741 he was returned on the Furnese interest for New Romney, which he represented for the rest of his life.

On Walpole's fall Furnese was included in Pulteney's list of nominees to the secret committee, to which he was elected. He was one of the ten personal followers who went over with Pulteney to the Administration, all of them receiving places, in his case the joint secretaryship of the Treasury vice Henry Legge (q.v.), who complained that his livelihood was being taken away and an important office of business converted into a sinecure merely to add 'to the superfluities of one who is already possessed of a large estate'.[8] The appointment figures prominently in the contemporary libels and satires on Pulteney, now Earl of Bath, and his associates. One lampoon by Hanbury Williams (q.v.) suggests that Furnese was required to pay half his fees as secretary 'to Bath's ennobled doxy', i.e. Lady Bath; another taunts him with his low extraction:

> And see with that important face
> Berenger's clerk to take his place
> Into the Treasury come;
> With pride and meanness act thy part,
> Thou look'st at the very thing thou art,
> Thou Bourgeois Gentilhomme.[9]

When in the next session Bath declared himself opposed to a revival of the secret committee, Furnese took the opportunity to resign, inspiring a press statement to the effect that, his eyes having been opened to the true character of his colleagues and to the terms on which his 'lucrative post' had been given him, 'with a noble abhorrence of both he . . . made haste to quit a fellowship he thought injurious to his virtue'.[10] Though twice recommended to Newcastle by Chesterfield as a man who would be 'of infinite use to you, not only in . . . office, but in many other ways',[11] he remained in opposition, voting against the Government in all recorded divisions. In the next Parliament he attached himself to Dodington, through whom he secured from the Prince of Wales a promise of a seat at the Treasury board in the next reign. After Frederick's death he acted as intermediary in Dodington's abortive attempts to conclude a

political deal with Pelham.[12] In 1753 he wrote to his friend, Sir Francis Dashwood (q.v.), that he was 'obliged to live in a constant painful regularity, not sick enough to draw pity or compassion . . . nor well enough to do any one thing I have a mind to'.[13] After a brief term of office under Newcastle, he died 30 Aug. 1756.

[1] PCC 234 Barnes. [2] Wm. Boys, *Colls. Hist. Sandwich*, i. 486. [3] SP For. Portugal, 89, f. 86. [4] *Bull. Rylands Lib.* xxxvii. 150; *VCH Lancs.* iii. 252. [5] *Evening Post*, 23 Nov. 1723. [6] *Cal. Treas. Pprs*, 1720–8, p. 238; 1729–30, pp. 54, 90, 152. [7] *HMC Lothian*, 147. [8] *Bedford Corresp.* i. 2. [9] Walpole to Mann, 29 July, 11 Sept. 1742. [10] *Gent. Mag.* 1742, pp. 642, 659. [11] *Private Corresp. Chesterfield and Newcastle* (R. Hist. Soc. Cam. 3rd ser. xliv), 36, 101. [12] *Dodington Diary*, 6, 132, 225. [13] 13 Aug. 1753, Bodl. Dashwood mss.

A.N.N.

FURNESE, Sir Robert, 2nd Bt. (1687–1733), of Waldershare, Kent.

TRURO	1708–1710
NEW ROMNEY	1710–1727
KENT	1727–7 Mar. 1733

b. 1 Aug. 1687, o.s. of Sir Henry Furnese, 1st Bt., M.P., by his 1st w. Anne, da. of Robert Brough of St. Lawrence Jewry, London, linen draper. *educ.* Eton c.1697. *m.* (1) c.1708, Anne (*d.* 29 May 1713), da. of Anthony Balam by his stepmother Matilda, da. of Sir Thomas Vernon of London, merchant, 1da.; (2) 8 July 1714, Lady Arabella Watson (*d.* 5 Sept. 1727), da. of Lewis Watson, M.P., 1st Earl of Rockingham, sis. of Edward, Visct. Sondes (q.v.), 1s. 1da.; (3) 15 May 1729, Lady Anne Shirley, da. of Robert, 1st Earl Ferrers, 2da. *suc.* fa. 30 Nov. 1712.

The Furneses were descended from a Cromwellian sergeant of dragoons who settled at Sandwich as a tallow-chandler.[1] One son, Henry, moved to London; became prominent as a Flanders and East India merchant; remitted money to William III and Marlborough's forces in Flanders; and retired with a baronetcy to Waldershare, near Sandwich, for which he sat. His son, Robert, thought it 'right to get a little quality to so much riches',[2] two of his three wives being the daughters of earls, while his daughters found noble husbands. Re-elected as a Whig on his own interest at New Romney in 1715, he voted for the septennial bill, but followed Walpole into opposition in 1717, voting against the Government on Lord Cadogan (q.v.) in June 1717 and on the peerage bill in 1719.

In 1727 Furnese stood with government support for the county,[3] as well as for New Romney,

> as active as a fat man can be. He sits at home most part of the day surveying the field of battle, and reviewing his forces as they are drawn out on paper and gives his directions to his agents and attendants who are writing for his success and assure his Honour of success.[4]

Returned for the county, and, on petition, for New Romney, he chose to sit for Kent. From 1729 he voted against the Government. He 'went off delirious, roaring against the excise',[5] on 7 Mar. 1733, not having been 'sober for ten days before he was taken ill.'[6]

[1] Wm. Boys, *Colls. Hist. Sandwich*, i. 484. [2] *Arch. Cant.* v. 91. [3] Cal. SP Dom. Geo. II, iii. 41, 46. [4] Sir Geo. Oxenden to David Polhill, 12 July 1727, Polhill mss, Sevenoaks Pub. Lib. [5] Sir Adolphus Oughton to Edw. Hopkins, 17 Mar. 1733, Hopkins mss. [6] *HMC Hastings*, iii. 15.

A.N.N.

FYDELL, Richard (?1709–80), of Boston, Lincs.

BOSTON 1734–1741

b. ?1709, *s.* of Robert Fydell of London, brewer. *educ.* Charterhouse; Trinity, Camb. 9 July 1726, aged 16; M. Temple 1727. *m.* Jan. 1739, Elizabeth Hall, 3s. 3da.

Mayor, Boston 1739, 1753, 1776; judge of Admiralty, Boston 1745.

Fydell, a wine merchant of Boston, in partnership with his brother-in-law John Michell (q.v.), possessed considerable influence with the Boston corporation.[1] Returned for Boston in 1734 as a Tory, he voted against the Administration. He did not stand again, dying 11 Apr. 1780.

[1] P. Thompson, *Hist. Boston*, 456.

P.W.

GAGE, Thomas (c.1695–1754), of High Meadow, Glos.

MINEHEAD 11 Apr.–23 May 1717
TEWKESBURY 25 Oct. 1721–1754

b. c.1695, 1st *s.* of Joseph Gage of Sherborne Castle, Oxon. by Elizabeth, da. and eventually h. of Sir George Penruddock of Hale, Hants. *m.* (1) settlement 3 Oct. 1713, Benedicta Maria Teresa (*d.* 25 July 1749), da. and h. of Henry Benedict Hall of High Meadow, Glos., 2s. 1da.; (2) 26 Dec. 1750, Jane, da. of one Godfrey, wid. of Henry Jermyn Bond of Bury St. Edmunds, Suff., *s.p. cr.* Baron Gage of Castlebar and Visct. Gage of Castle Island [I] 14 Sept. 1720. *suc.* fa.-in-law to High Meadow, Dec. 1714; Sir Francis Fortescue, 4th Bt., to 'near £20,000', 9 Nov. 1729;[1] his cos. Sir William Gage, 7th Bt. (q.v.), to baronetcy and Firle, Suss. 23 Apr. 1744.

Verderer, Forest of Dean till May 1752; master of the household to Prince of Wales 1743–51.

Gage, like his first cousin, Sir William Gage (q.v.), a converted Roman Catholic, was returned for Minehead in 1717. Unseated on petition but returned for Tewkesbury in 1721, he made his first recorded speeches 23, 26 Nov. 1722, 6, 14 May 1723, against the special tax on Papists. In April 1727 he spoke for the motion for a vote of credit.

In the next Parliament Gage voted with the Government except on the excise bill, which he opposed. He was responsible for exposing the fraudulent sale of the Derwentwater estates, for which he was thanked by the House of Commons on 31 Mar. 1732, and awarded £2,000 under Act of Parliament 8 Geo. II, c.29, in 1735.[2] Horace Walpole states that he was 'constantly paid by the foreign ministers for intelligence' and 'did all kinds of jobs for Sir Robert Walpole in the same way'.[3] Described by Hervey as a 'petulant, silly, busy, meddling, profligate fellow',[4] he was prominent in the Irish peers' agitation for their right of precedence at the Princess Royal's wedding in 1734, on which he moved for 'a bill to relieve prisoners for debt' so 'that every part of his Majesty's subjects might rejoice on this occasion'. In 1736 he introduced a bill to prevent clandestine marriages, which was rejected. He was reported in 1738 to have been appointed governor of Barbados, in succession to Sir Orlando Bridgeman (q.v.), but the appointment did not materialize.[5] Going into opposition, he spoke against the Spanish convention of 1739 both in Parliament and at Tewkesbury, where his 'rhetoric and eloquence made them damn the convention and all who espoused it'.[6] In December 1739 he supported Pulteney's motion for a call of the House; but he was one of the opposition Whigs who withdrew on the motion for Walpole's removal in February 1741. In the last days of Walpole's Administration he is described as acting as 'a postilion' for the Prince of Wales, carrying 'messages and errands for him in order to concert measures for the . . . Opposition'.[7] According to Horace Walpole, who states that Gage depended on his privilege as a Member of Parliament for keeping out of gaol for debt, the Opposition also employed him

in getting together the party to the House and keeping watch at the door to prevent their going away. On the change, he was paid for staying away a whole sessions. At his house in the country, he would frequently leave his company to go and read letters from, or write them to the King and royal family. Soon after he was made master of the household to the Prince.[8]

With the rest of the Prince's party he voted with the Government till 1747 when he followed his master back into opposition, putting up his son, W. H. Gage (q.v.), against Newcastle's candidate at Seaford, so 'that he might have something to talk about at Leicester House'.[9] In the 2nd Lord Egmont's lists of future office-holders on Frederick's accession he is put down as comptroller of the Mint.

After the death of the Prince Gage made his peace with the Pelhams.[10] In 1753 he wrote to a local newspaper complaining that many of his friends at Tewkesbury were

> engaged in a scheme, which, if persisted in, must deprive me of the honour of representing them; although I flatter myself their resolution to choose no members but such as will give £1,500 each towards mending their roads, does not proceed from any personal dislike to me, but from the benefit they conceive the trade of Tewkesbury will receive by it.[11]

Refusing to accede to these terms, he and his son, Thomas, were defeated in 1754 at Tewkesbury, which he had represented for 33 years. He died shortly afterwards, 21 Dec. 1754.

[1] *Glos. N. & Q.* ii. 651. [2] *HMC Egmont Diary*, i. 244, 247, 250; Harley Diary, 6 May 1735. [3] *Corresp. H. Walpole* (Yale ed.), xvii. 252-3 n. 22. [4] Hervey, *Mems.* 265. [5] *HMC Egmont Diary*, i. 405, 409; ii. 63, 257; *Gent. Mag.* 1738, p. 325. [6] Robt. Tracy to Sir Robt. Walpole, 21 Sept. 1739, Cholmondeley (Houghton) mss. [7] T. Carte to O'Bryan, 6 Apr. 1742, Stuart mss 241/3. [8] *Corresp. H. Walpole*, loc. cit. [9] *HMC 10th Rep. I*, 296-7. [10] AECP Angl. 435, ff. 210-12. [11] Namier, *Structure*, 131.

R.R.S.

GAGE, Sir William, 7th Bt. (1695–1744), of Firle, Suss.

SEAFORD 1722–23 Apr. 1744

b. 1695, 3rd s. of Sir John Gage, 4th Bt., by his 2nd w. Mary, da. of Sir William Stanley, 1st Bt., of Hooton, Cheshire. *unm. suc.* bro. as 7th Bt. Oct. 1713. K.B. 27 May 1725.

Gage, a converted Roman Catholic, came of an old Sussex family, seated at Firle, half way between Lewes and Seaford. Returned for Seaford on Newcastle's recommendation, he voted regularly with the Government, looking after Newcastle's interests in both boroughs and reporting any local incidents of interest. For example:

> Yesterday the commonalty of Seaford dined with us and they are all extremely easy and satisfied. But there was a melancholy scene in the evening. A journeyman shoemaker that had been in Seaford about a month dropped off the form and died in less than a quarter of an hour's time, without making the least struggle for life. The poor man had eaten and drunk very hard.

When both the Members for Lewes died in 1743, it was Gage who advised Newcastle as to the probable local reactions to the various persons considered for the vacant seats and to whom Newcastle announced his final choice, for communication to the whole town, or only to the heads of it, as Gage should think proper.[1] On his death, 23 Apr. 1744, Firle passed to his first cousin, Thomas, 1st Viscount Gage [I] (q.v.).

[1] Add. 35584, f. 249; 32699, f. 606; 32701, ff. 271-3.

R.R.S.

GAGE, Hon. William Hall (1718–91), of Firle, Suss. and High Meadow, Glos.

SEAFORD 9 May 1744–1747, 1754–1780

b. 1 Jan. 1718, 1st s. of Thomas, 1st Visct. Gage [I] (q.v.). *educ.* Westminster 1728-35. *m.* 3 Feb. 1757, Elizabeth, da. of Sampson Gideon, sis of Sir Sampson Gideon, 1st Bt., M.P., *s.p. suc.* fa. as 2nd Visct. 21 Dec. 1754. *cr.* Baron Gage of Firle [GB] 17 Oct. 1780; Baron Gage of High Meadow [GB] 1 Nov. 1790, with sp. rem. to his nephew.

Equerry to Prince of Wales 1742–51; paymaster of pensions 1755–63, July 1765-Mar. 1782.

In 1744 William Gage was returned with the support of the Duke of Newcastle for Seaford, in succession to Sir William Gage (q.v.), whose estates had passed to his first cousin, Thomas, 1st Viscount Gage [I] (q.v.), William Gage's father. Like Lord Gage, a member of the Prince of Wales's party, William Gage voted with the Government till 1747, when they both followed the Prince into opposition. At the general election that year Newcastle informed Lord Gage that he could not recommend William Gage for re-election at Seaford.[1] On this, Lord Gage, with the Prince's support, put up William, standing jointly with Lord Middlesex (q.v.), for Seaford, where they were defeated by Newcastle's candidates, one of whom was William Pitt. The defeated candidates petitioned against the return, on the ground that Newcastle had infringed the privileges of the House of Commons by personally canvassing on behalf of the candidates and by sitting next to the returning officer at the poll to intimidate the voters, in contravention of a standing resolution of the House forbidding peers to intervene in elections. Treated with derision by Pitt, the petition was rejected by an overwhelming majority.

In the 2nd Lord Egmont's lists of persons to be brought into Parliament on Frederick's accession, William Gage is put down for Seaford, Monmouth, or Sussex. Going over to the Government after Frederick's death, he was returned by Newcastle for Seaford in 1754. He died 11 Oct. 1791.

[1] A. Stone to Hurdis, 10 June 1747, Add. 32711, f. 287.

R.R.S.

GALWAY, Visct., see MONCKTON, John, and Monckton, Hon. William

GAPE, Thomas (1685–1732), of Harpsfield Hall, nr. St. Albans, Herts.

ST. ALBANS 23 Mar. 1730–11 Dec. 1732

b. 17 Aug. 1685, 1st surv. s. of John Gape, M.P., by Susan, da. of Thomas Cowley of London. *educ.* Canterbury; Trinity, Camb. 1703; L. Inn 1703. *m.* 21 Feb. 1710, Elizabeth Baxter, 2s. *d.v.p.*

The Gapes were an old St. Albans family, figuring frequently as mayors from 1554. Gape's grandfather, who in 1676 bought the neighbouring estate of Harpsfield Hall, was returned for St. Albans in 1679 and his father sat for it as a Tory, 1701–5 and 1708–15. He himself played a prominent part on behalf of the opposition candidates in the St. Albans election of 1722 when, according to a petition lodged by the defeated candidates, 'the mob was encouraged by Mr. Gape, junior, who, with his drawn sword, began the riot on the election day, and caused the music to play "The King shall enjoy his own again" '. He also appears to have been responsible for the arrangements for bribing voters.

On a vacancy at St. Albans in 1730 Gape was asked by Sarah, Duchess of Marlborough, to support the candidature of her grandson John Spencer (q.v.). Instead he used her invitation as a bargaining factor with Lord Grimston (q.v.), on whose recommendation the St. Albans corporation unanimously adopted Gape himself as their representative.[1] According to an account of the election, he was escorted to the poll by Lord Grimston and the principal gentlemen of the county, attended by about 300 voters, all on horseback,

and the town was illuminated, bonfires made, and such great rejoicings made there as has not been seen for many years: which shews what regard is paid to those gentlemen who are elected with no other view than to serve their country.

In Parliament Gape voted against the Government on the army in 1732. On his death on 11 Dec. 1732 his estate of about £900 p.a. passed to his brother William, 'late a dry-salter'.[2]

[1] *HMC Verulam*, 119, 121–2; see also ST. ALBANS. [2] *St. Albans and Herts. Arch. Soc. Trans.* n.s. v(3), pp. 301–2.

R.R.S.

GARTH, John (1701–64), of Brownston (or Garth) House, Devizes.

DEVIZES 26 Feb. 1740–24 Dec. 1764

b. 1701, 2nd but 1st surv. s. of Lt.-Col. Thomas Garth of Harrold, Beds. by Elizabeth, da. of Thomas Colleton of Barbados (yr. s. of Sir John Colleton, 1st Bt., one of the original proprietors of S. Carolina). *educ.* Clare, Camb. 1719; L. Inn 1718; I. Temple 1727, called 1728. *m.* c.1730, Rebecca, da. and coh. of John Brompton of Whitton, Mdx., 3s. 3da. *suc.* fa. 1731.
Recorder, Devizes 1732-*d.*

John Garth came of a family settled in the 17th century at Bolam, co. Durham. His uncle, Sir Samuel Garth, was physician-general to the army and physician-in-ordinary to George I, author of

The Dispensary and a prominent member of the Kit-Cat Club. He may have owed his appointment as recorder of Devizes to his cousin, John Colleton, who married an Ernle, of the prominent Wiltshire family with estates in the neighbourhood of Devizes, and had business dealings with Sir Joseph Eyles, M.P. for the borough.[1] On Eyles's death in 1740 Garth was returned on his own interest for Devizes, which he represented unopposed till his death. In 1756 he could speak of 'constant attendance and steady concurrence in the support of the measures of Government in Parliament without any assistance or return.'[2] When he died, 24 Dec. 1764, he was succeeded by his son, Charles Garth, both as recorder and as M.P. for the borough.

[1] Namier, 'Charles Garth and his connexions', *EHR*, liv. 444–6. [2] Garth to Newcastle, 14 Apr. 1756, Add 32864, f. 263.

R.S.L.

GASCOIGNE, Joseph (d. 1728), of Chiswick, Mdx. and Weybridge, Surr.

WAREHAM 1722–1 Sept. 1728

m., 2da.
Agent victualler for Port Mahon 1709;[1] receiver gen. in Minorca 1712-*d.*[2]

Joseph Gascoigne was probably related to Joseph Gascoigne (*d.* 1685), chandler, of Chiswick, and Benjamin Gasoigne (*d.* 1731), also of Chiswick, father of Joseph and Sir Crisp Gascoigne, lord mayor of London in 1752. Holding a lucrative post in Minorca, he defeated the sitting Tory at Wareham, where he was a stranger, in 1722, standing as a government supporter. He was again successful in 1727 but no vote or speech of his has been recorded. In an undated letter to Sir Robert Walpole he thanked him for 'the liberty you have been pleased to give me to write to you in favour of some of my Wareham people for to make them tidesmen or some other small places in the customs'.[3] He was of Weybridge, Surrey, in June 1725, when he received a grant of arms. He died 1 Sept. 1728, administration being granted to his two daughters, Aline and Theodosia.

[1] *Queen Anne's Navy* (Navy Recs. Soc. ciii), 296. [2] *Cal. Treas. Bks.* xxxi. 151. [3] Cholmondeley (Houghton) mss 1200.

R.S.L.

GASCOIGNE NIGHTINGALE, Joseph (1695–1752), of Enfield, Mdx.

STAFFORD 1727–1734

bap. 19 Dec. 1695,[1] 1st s. of Rev. Joseph Gascoigne, vicar of Enfield, by Anne, da. and h. of Francis Theobald of Barking, Suff. by Anne, sis. of Sir Thomas Nightingale, 2nd Bt., of Newport Pond,

Essex. *educ.* Enfield; Trinity, Camb. 1712. *m.* 24 June 1725, Lady Elizabeth Shirley, da. and coh. of Washington, 2nd Earl Ferrers, 3s. 1da. *suc.* fa. 1721; yr. bro. Robert to estates of Sir Robert Nightingale, 4th Bt., 1722 and assumed add. name of Nightingale.

Nightingale succeeded to estates worth nearly £300,000 left by his first cousin, Sir Robert Nightingale. Shortly afterwards he married one of the daughters of the 2nd Earl Ferrers of Chartley, near Stafford, for which he was returned in 1727. He voted with the Opposition in every recorded division, did not stand again, and died 16 July 1752.

[1] *Westminster Abbey Reg.* 384.

A.N.N.

GASHRY, Francis (1702–1762), of Hollybush House, Parson's Green, London.[1]

ALDEBURGH 30 Mar.–27 Apr. 1741
EAST LOOE 1741–19 May 1762

b. 14 Nov. 1702, s. of Francis Gascherie, perfumer, of Lamb's St., Stepney by his w. Susanna, both natives of La Rochelle.[2] *m.* bef. 1747, Martha, sis. of Burrinton Goldsworthy (consul at Leghorn, and subsequently at Cadiz), aunt of Philip Goldsworthy, M.P., wid. of Charles Bolton, nephew of Adm. Charles Wager (q.v.)[3], *s.p. suc.* through his w. to manor of Rotherhithe, and to Kilmenath, nr. Looe, on death of Wager's wid. 1748.

Inspector of the captains' journals, sec. to Sir Charles Wager (first ld. of Admiralty 1732–42) and commr. for sick and hurt seamen 1737; asst. sec. to Admiralty 1738; commr. of the navy 1741–7; comptroller of victualling accounts 1744–7; director, South Sea Co. 1749–*d.*; treasurer and paymaster of the Ordnance 1751–*d.*

Gashry's father was naturalized in 1709 as 'Gascherie';[4] in the books of the Sun Fire Office in 1710 the name is anglicized into 'Gashery'.

Admiral Wager (q.v.) in his will refers to Gashry as 'my very good friend', and Gashry describes Wager as his 'Great Patron' on the monument which he raised to Wager in Westminster Abbey: it was under Wager's wing that he started his official and parliamentary career. Wager made him successor to George Purvis (q.v.), both as Member for Aldeburgh and as a commissioner of the navy; and from Wager's letter to the mayor of East Looe[5] it appears that there too, Gashry was Wager's candidate, on the interest of Edward Trelawny (q.v.). In 1742 he appeared before the secret committee appointed to inquire into Walpole's Administration to give evidence regarding the payment of secret service money during Wager's election for Westminster in 1741.[6] In 1747 he resigned his office which, under the Place Act of 1742, was about to become incompatible with a seat in the Commons. On Trelawny's departure for Jamaica as governor, Gashry became the

intermediary between the Government and the Trelawny family, and also personal agent for the governor.[7] Egmont wrote about the Looes in his electoral survey c.1749–50: 'Gashry has the management of these boroughs in Trelawny's absence'. The connexion, at first a business one, turned in time into a personal one, as Trelawny wrote to Gashry, 19 July 1753:

I look upon it as a thing fixed your being for one of the Looes. I must be so frank as to say that at first, when you were chosen, I was not for your being so but as one recommended by the ministry, so as they should be obliged to us for your being chosen, not reckon you as coming in by your own interest or at the desire of our family; but since I have entered into friendship with you, and you have given yourself a great deal of trouble in my affairs, and, as I apprehend, been of great service in them, the case is altered. As the matter now stands, I think neither Mr. Pelham nor myself can be against you, so that we may take you between us, both joining to recommend you, he to me, I to him, and both to the corporation.[8]

He continued to represent East Looe until his death, 19 May 1762.

[1] Ex inf. F. E. Hansford, chairman, executive committee, Fulham Hist. Soc. [2] *Reg. of La Patente, Spitalfields,* 1689–1785 (Huguenot Soc. London, xi), 35. [3] *VCH Surr.* iv. 88–89. [6] *Denizations and Naturalizations,* 1701–1800 (Huguenot Soc. London, xxvii), 84. [5] 25 Mar. 1741, East Looe Town Trust. [6] *CJ,* xxiv. 331. [7] Gashry to Trelawny, 25 July 1749 and 19 Mar. 1753, Add.19038, ff. 44–45 and 48–49; also Gashry to Trelawny's successor, Governor Knowles, 26 July 1753, ibid. ff. 50–51. [8] Vernon-Wager mss in Library of Congress.

E.C.

GAY, Robert (*d.*1738), of Hatton Gardens, Mdx. and Walcot, Bath.

BATH 22 Feb. 1720–1722, 1727–1734

b. c.1676. *educ.* Jesus, Camb. 1693. *m.* by 1708,[1] Margaret, da. of Sir Edward Farmer of Canons, in Great Parndon, Essex, 1s. 2da.

Treasurer, Christ's and St. Bartholomew's Hospitals, 1731.

Robert Gay, an eminent doctor and F.R.S., who acquired the manor of Walcot, on the northwest side of Bath, before 1707,[2] was returned as a Tory for Bath at a by-election in 1720, but was defeated in 1722. In 1725 John Wood, the architect, submitted to him plans for developing his property. He authorized Wood to go ahead, but in 1727, when he was standing again, he began to 'discountenance' the scheme, 'to preserve his interest' with the corporation, who regarded it as 'chimerical'. After his election, however, he leased to Wood sufficient land for the building of Queen Square and Gay Street, which was named in honour of him and in which he had a house. He also gave land for a new general hospital in Bath and for a chapel in Queen Square.[3] In his second

Parliament he voted consistently against the Government. He did not stand again, dying 31 Oct. 1738.

¹ PCC 11 Lane; Lysons, *Environs of London*, iv. 238. ² R. Warner, *Hist. Bath*, 274. ³ J. Wood, *Bath* (1749), i. 232; ii. 240-3, 284-5, 313.

S.R.M.

GAYER, Robert (1672–aft. 1737), of Stoke Park, Bucks.

NEW WINDSOR   26 Jan.–14 Apr. 1715

bap. 21 Jan. 1672,¹ 1st s. of Sir Robert Gayer, K.B., by his 1st w. Mary, da. of Sir Thomas Rich, 1st Bt., M.P., of Sonning, Berks. *m.* (1) lic. 8 Nov. 1694, Elizabeth (*d.* c.Dec. 1725),² da. of James Annesley, M.P., 2nd Earl of Anglesey, 1s. 3da.; (2) Elizabeth, *s.p. suc.* fa. 1702.
   Sheriff, Berks, 1735-7.

Robert Gayer was grandson of Sir John Gayer, lord mayor of London in 1647, who came of a Cornish family.³ His father's second wife was sister of the Jacobite exile, Thomas Bruce, M.P., 2nd Earl of Ailesbury. In September 1714, before the King's arrival,⁴ Gayer offered himself as a Tory candidate with Christopher Wren (q.v.), for the nearby borough of Windsor. He was returned by a majority of one vote, but was unseated on petition; and when he stood again in 1722, he received only three votes. To enable him to pay his father's legacies, he sold Stoke Park in 1723, going to live at Hurley, Berks.⁵ The date of his death has not been found.

¹ Stoke Poges par. reg. ² PCC 6 Plymouth. ³ Gayer, *Mems. of Fam. of Gayer*. ⁴ Memo. by Chas. Aldworth, 10-14 Sept. 1714, Berks. RO. ⁵ *VCH Bucks*. iii. 307; *Berks*. iii. 155.

R.S.L.

GEERS, Thomas (c.1697–1753), of Bridge Sollers, nr. Hereford, and Glasshampton, Worcs.

HEREFORD   1727–1734, 1741–1747
WORCESTER   1747–11 Feb. 1748

b. c.1697, 1st s. of Timothy Geers of Bridge Sollers by Mercy, da. of Henry Winford of Glasshampton, Worcs. *educ.* L. Inn 1719, called 1722. *m.* Apr. 1731, Sarah, 3rd da. and coh. of Thomas Lutwyche (q.v.) of Lutwyche Hall, Salop, 2da. *suc.* 1731 on his marriage to estates of his uncle, Sir Thomas Cookes Winford, 2nd Bt., M.P., taking the name of Winford. *suc.* fa. 1750.
   Town clerk, Worcester c.1745-d.

Geers's grandfather was a successful lawyer who sat for Hereford 1685-7. His father was one of the local gentry who successfully resisted the attempt of the Duke of Chandos and the Foleys to gain control of the borough in 1722. Returned as a Tory for Hereford on a compromise in 1727, he did not stand again till 1741, when he was returned

jointly with his cousin, Edward Hopton. In 1747 he was successful for Worcester but unseated on petition. He spoke occasionally¹ and voted consistently with the Opposition. On 4 Feb. 1730 he moved unsuccessfully that Dr. Samuel Croxall be thanked for his sermon preached on 30 Jan., the anniversary of Charles I's execution, on the text 'take the wicked [i.e. Walpole] from before the King and His throne shall be established as righteousness'.² He died 23 May 1753.

¹ *HMC Egmont Diary*, i. 126; iii. 330. ² *Knatchbull Diary*.

A.N.N.

GERMAIN, Lord George, *see* SACKVILLE (afterwards GERMAIN)

GERMAIN, Sir John, 1st Bt. (1650–1718), of Westminster, and Drayton, Northants.

MORPETH   1713–1715
TOTNES   22 Apr. 1717–11 Dec. 1718

b. 1650. *m.* (1) lic. 15 Sept. 1701, Mary (*d.* 17 Nov. 1705), *suo jure* Baroness Mordaunt, div. w. of Thomas Howard, 7th Duke of Norfolk, *s.p.*; (2) Oct. 1706, Lady Elizabeth Berkeley, da. of Charles Berkeley, M.P., 2nd Earl of Berkeley, 2s. 1da. all *d.v.p.* Kntd. 26 Feb. 1698; *cr.* Bt. 25 Mar. 1698.

'A Dutch gamester of mean extraction, who had gotten much by gaming',¹ Germain came to England with the Prince of Orange, subsequently serving under him in Holland and Flanders. In 1692 he was sued by the Duke of Norfolk 'for £100,000 for enticing away his duchess; the verdict was for the Duke but the jury gave but 100 marks [£66] damages to the wonder of all the court'. He later married the Duchess, who died in 1705 leaving him Drayton and other estates in Northamptonshire, worth £70,000.² He then married a daughter of the Earl of Berkeley, thirty years younger then himself. Returned as a Whig in Anne's last Parliament, Germain did not stand in 1715, but was later returned for Totnes, probably on the Duke of Bolton's interest. He died 11 Dec. 1718, leaving his property to his wife, subject to bequests *inter alia* of £20,000 to his brother, Philip Germain, £15,000 each to a second brother, Daniel, and to his sister, Judith Persode, and £50 to the poor of the congregation of the Dutch church in London.³ His widow, Lady Betty Germain, spent most of the rest of her life at Knole with the Duke and Duchess of Dorset, leaving her property to Lord George Sackville (q.v.).

¹ *Evelyn Diary*, ed. E. S. de Beer, v. 393-4. ² Luttrell, ii. 624-5; v. 613. ³ PCC 238 Tenison.

S.R.M.

GIBBON, Edward (1707–1770), of Putney, Surr.

PETERSFIELD   1734–1741
SOUTHAMPTON   1741–1747

b. Oct. 1707, o.s. of Edward Gibbon of Putney, linen draper, clothing contractor and bill broker, by Catherine, da. of Richard Acton of Leadenhall St., London, goldsmith. *educ.* Westminster 1716–20; Emmanuel, Camb. 1723; Grand Tour (France, Italy). *m.* (1) 3 June 1736, Judith (*d.* Dec. 1747), da. of James Porten of Putney, 6s. 1da.; (2) 8 Apr. 1755, Dorothea Patten. *suc.* fa. 1736.
    Alderman, London 1743.

Gibbon, the father of the historian, was the son of a South Sea Company director, who had theoretically been deprived of most of his money by the South Sea Sufferers Act of 1721, but in practice had managed to preserve most of his real property by settling it on his wife shortly before the passing of the Act. Returned as a Tory for Petersfield in 1734 on the interest of his father, who owned the manor, he voted against the Administration in all recorded divisions. In his son's words:

> without acquiring the fame of an orator or statesman, he eagerly joined in the great Opposition which, after a seven years chase hunted down Sir Robert Walpole, and in the pursuit of an unpopular minister he gratified a private revenge against the oppressor of his family in the South Sea persecution.

After his father's death he sold the manor of Petersfield, with his electoral influence there, to John Jolliffe (q.v.), in 1739. In 1741 he stood 'an expensive and successful' contest for Southampton,[1] continuing to act with the Tories against the Administration. On 4 May 1743 Thomas Carte, the Jacobite historian, wrote to the Pretender:

> In the Whiggish wards in the city [of London] that party does scarce pretend to make any opposition; for so the other day in Vintry ward, Mr. Gibbon, Member of Parliament for Southampton, was chosen alderman without opposition, though he had not been made a freeman above two months, and was not known to any man in the ward; but Alderman Benn's [an active Jacobite and future lord mayor] recommendation of him and his being son to Ned Gibbon (who when living was the most zealous man for your Majesty and the most capable of serving you of any in the city) were enough to carry the point without any difficulty.[2]

Gibbon was elected in 1744 to three of the key committees of the court of common council administering city affairs, but resigned in 1745, according to his son because the duties were 'repugnant to his inclination and habits'.[3] He did not stand in 1747, after which increasing financial difficulties, caused by extravagance and lack of business ability, forced him to retire to his estate

at Buriton, near Petersfield, where he died, 10 Nov. 1770.

[1] D. M. Law, *Edward Gibbon*; J. Murray, *Autobiog. of Edw. Gibbon*, 18, 30. [2] Stuart mss 249/113. [3] J. Murray, 31.

P.W.

GIBSON, Thomas (1667–1744), of Lothbury, London.

MARLBOROUGH   26 Oct. 1722–1734
YARMOUTH I.o.W.   23 Jan. 1736–21 Sept. 1744

b. 16 Mar. 1667,[1] 5th s. of John Gibson of Welburn, Yorks. by Joan, da. of James Pennyman of Ormesby, Yorks. *m.* Martha, 2da.
    Jt. surveyor of petty customs in London 1708–?22; cashier to the pay office 1714–July 1744.[2]

Descended from Sir John Gibson, who bought the manor of Welburn in 1597, Gibson was a partner in the firm of Gibson, Jacob, and Jacomb, of Lothbury, scriveners and bankers, Walpole's bankers and men of business (see Jacomb, Robert). In Walpole's early days Gibson is said to have saved him from the Fleet by a timely loan of £1,500.[3] When Walpole became paymaster he appointed Gibson his cashier. Heavily engaged in financing colliery undertakings in the north of England, Gibson was active in the coal trade lobby before he entered Parliament. Returned for Marlborough in 1722, he voted with the Government in all recorded divisions. He did not stand in 1734, when he appears to have been consulted by Walpole on north country elections,[4] but he was brought in by Walpole for Yarmouth in 1736, again voting steadily with the Administration. On 12 Feb. 1741 Sir George Wynne (q.v.) wrote to Walpole about the elections in Flintshire and Denbighshire, saying that the bishop of Salisbury and Gibson held mortgages on an estate of his and that the bishop was about to assign his mortgage to Sir Watkin Williams Wynn (q.v.), which would put it in his power to ruin him, 'yet Mr. Gibson seemed to pay no regard to my representation, though I pressingly importuned him to pay the bishop off that I might not fall into the enemy's hands'. After Walpole's fall Gibson applied to him, 16 July and 13 Aug. 1743, to secure his retention as cashier to the army under the new paymaster if Pelham became first lord of the Treasury, suggesting that if he were dismissed he might have to press for the amount that Walpole owed him, namely £7,741 0s. 7½d.[5] On 25 Aug. Walpole asked Pelham to 'insist upon continuing Mr. Gibson deputy. He has been there from the beginning of my time and is as solicitous about it as in his younger days and lower circumstances'.[6] He kept his office until two months before his death, 21 Sept. 1744.

[1] *Genealogist* (n.s.), xxii. 37; PCC 236, 237 Anstis. [2] *Gent. Mag.* 1744, p. 395. [3] J. H. Plumb, *Walpole*, i. 110. [4] E. Hughes, *N. Country Life in 18th Cent.* 164, 271 n. 2, 292-6. [5] Cholmondeley (Houghton) mss. [6] Newcastle (Clumber) mss.

R.S.L.

GIFFORD, John Hoskins (?1693-1744), of Beaminster, Dorset, and Boreham, in Warminster, Wilts.

BRIDPORT 1713-1715
WESTBURY 1727-1734

b. ?1693, 2nd s. of William Gifford of Beaminster, Dorset, and Horsington, Som. by Mary, da. and h. of John Hoskins of Beaminster.[1] *educ.* Wadham, Oxf. 7 Dec. 1710, aged 17; M. Temple 1710. *m.* Dec. 1731, Elizabeth, da. and h. of Nicholas Watts of Cucklington, Som., *s.p. suc.* to Wilts. and Som. estates of bro. Benjamin Gifford, M.P., 1713.

Gifford, a Tory, whose family for some 200 years had held lands at Boreham, a few miles from Westbury, was brought in there on Lord Abingdon's interest in 1727, a petition against the return being unsuccessful. In Parliament he voted against the army estimates in 1732 and the excise bill in 1733. He died in August 1744.

[1] Hoare, *Wilts.* Warminster, 75-76; Hutchins, *Dorset*, ii. 123-24; Collinson, *Som.* ii. 373.

R.S.L.

GILDART, Richard (1671-1770), of Bevington Hill, Liverpool.

LIVERPOOL 1734-1754

b. 1671, s. of James Gildart of Middleham, Yorks. *m.* (contr. 12 Nov. 1707) Anne, da. and coh. of Sir Thomas Johnson (q.v.), 13 ch.
    Mayor, Liverpool 1714, 1731, 1736.

Gildart was partner to his father-in-law, Sir Thomas Johnson, in the shipping, tobacco and rock salt business. By 1717 they were both deeply in debt to the Crown in respect of unpaid duty on tobacco. After Johnson left Liverpool in 1723 Gildart acted as his agent, taking over payments of the interest on his debts. In August 1723 the commissioners of the customs reported that Gildart

has hitherto made due payment of Sir Thos. Johnson's bonds due to the Crown. But on 6 Sept. next another payment is due . . . We have called on Mr. Gildart, but he hath not given another security in the room of Mr. Thos. Ball [Johnson's brother-in-law] lately deceased. Neither has Gildart complied with the condition of his bond to pay £1,000 at last midsummer but says he hath met with disappointment and will certainly pay it at Michaelmas next.

During the following months the collector of the customs at Liverpool reported that Gildart had

not paid '£300 due on account of Johnson's hands on 6 September, nor on his own for £1,000'.[1]

In 1734 Gildart stood for Liverpool, jointly with Thomas Brereton, against Thomas Bootle (qq.v.), who described him as 'a merchant in the town, he is deeply engaged in custom-house bonds to the Crown and who must be in the same measures as [Brereton] and they too are making interest together upon the ministerial foot'.[2] Returned, he supported the Administration, figuring in a list of placemen who voted for the Spanish convention in 1739 with the comment: 'his eldest son receiver general of the land tax for the county of Lancaster, and two of his other sons provided for'.[3] In 1737 he tried to promote a bill for permission to erect a salt refinery in Liverpool, explaining that it would mean 'the saving of a penny per bushel', but failed owing to opposition from the salt department.[4] In 1740, after repeated appeals to the Treasury for relief from his obligations as security to Johnson, a warrant was issued waiving '£381 12s. 8¼d., being the remainder of a debt of £4,503 15s. 0¼d. due to the Crown from Sir Thomas Johnson for tobacco duties and for whom Gildart was surety.'[5] He was returned without opposition in 1741 and 1747. The 2nd Lord Egmont sums him up in his electoral survey (c.1750) as

a very little fellow . . . I believe a merchant and attached to the Minister rather than *Pelham*, and his dealings in trade will keep him always under the lash of the Customs.

By this time he had become one of the leading Liverpool slave traders, sending ships to the Gold Coast to barter tobacco for slaves for the West Indies.

Gildart retired from Parliament in 1754. He obtained a grant of arms from the College of Arms in 1759. His portrait was painted by Joseph Wright of Derby in 1766.[6] He died 25 Jan. 1770, aged 99.

[1] *Trans. Hist. Soc. Lancs. and Cheshire*, lxxxii. 221-3; xc. 186-7. [2] *HMC 15th Rep. VII*, 121. [3] *Gent. Mag.* 1739, p. 305. [4] E. Hughes, *Studies in Admin. and Finance*, 397; *Cal. Treas. Pprs.* 1735-8, pp. 311-12, 365, 367. [5] *Trans. Hist. Soc. Lancs. and Cheshire*, xc. 189. [6] Gomer Williams, *Liverpool Privateers*, 674; *Bd. Trade Jnl.* 1750-53, p. 19; *Trans. Hist. Soc. Lancs. and Cheshire*, lxxxii. 221, 223.

E.C.

GILMOUR, Sir Charles, 2nd Bt. (*d.*1750), of Craigmillar, Edinburgh.

EDINBURGHSHIRE 4 Aug. 1737-9 Aug. 1750

s. of Sir Alexander Gilmour, 1st Bt., M.P. [S], of Craigmillar by Grisel, da. of George Ross, 11th Lord Ross [S]. *m.* Mar. 1733, Jean, da. of Sir Robert Sinclair, 3rd Bt., M.P. [S], of Longformacus, Berwick, 1s. *suc.* fa. 29 Oct. 1731.
    Paymaster of works July 1742-Dec. 1743; ld. of Trade Dec. 1743-Dec. 1744.

Returned for Edinburghshire as an opposition Whig on the recommendation of Robert Dundas (q.v.), Gilmour voted against the Spanish convention in 1739. Receiving through James Erskine (q.v.) a whip from Pulteney asking opposition Members to come to London some time before the next session, which might 'determine the fate of our liberties, if not of our being an independent nation', he voted against the Government on the Spanish convention in 1739 and the place bill in 1740. After Walpole's fall Gilmour followed his friend, Lord Tweeddale, the secretary of state for Scotland, through whom he became attached to Tweeddale's leader and future father-in-law, Carteret,[1] obtaining a place from the new Government. He figured in the court list for the ballot on the second committee set up to inquire into Walpole's Administration, but was not elected to it; was put down as 'Pelham' in the Cockpit list of ministerial supporters in October; and voted with the Government on the Hanoverians, 10 Dec. 1742. Promoted to the board of Trade in December 1743, he was dismissed a year later when the followers of Carteret, now Granville, were turned out with their leader. He did not vote on the Hanoverians in 1746, when he was classed as 'Granville'. Going over to the Government,[2] he was re-elected unopposed in 1747.

He died 9 Aug. 1750.

[1] *HMC Polwarth*, v. 173, 175; Walpole to Mann, 14 July and 9 Oct. 1742; *HMC Egmont Diary*, iii. 253. [2] Gilmour to Pelham, 21 July 1747, Newcastle (Clumber) mss.

R.R.S.

GLANVILLE, William (c. 1686–1766), of St. Clere, nr. Sevenoaks, Kent.

HYTHE   22 Feb. 1728–19 Oct. 1766

b. c.1686, 5th s. of George Evelyn, M.P., of Nutfield, Surr. by his 3rd w. Frances, da. of Andrew Bromehall of Stoke Newington, Mdx.; yr. bro. of George Evelyn (q.v.). *m.* (1) c.1718, Frances (*d.*1719), da. and h. of William Glanville, M.P., 1da.; (2) bef. 1733, Bridget, da. of Hugh Raymond of Langley, Kent, 2s. 3da. Took name of Glanville on his first marriage.

Commr. of revenue [I] 1735–47.

After contesting Bletchingley unsuccessfully on the death of an elder brother in 1724, William Glanville was returned by the Duke of Dorset for Hythe, which he represented for nearly 40 years, despite complaints of his failure to make gifts 'for the public good of the town'.[1] A member of the 1729 gaols committee of the House of Commons, in 1730 he introduced a bill for enabling civil cases to be finally decided at the assizes, 'urging the inconveniences of prolonging suits by bringing them up to Westminster and the opportunities given to

rascally attornies to eat up the substance of poor men'. In the same session he opposed a petition sponsored by Sir John Barnard for terminating the monopoly of the East India Company, describing it as 'a pickpocket petition'. In 1731 he supported a bill for enabling unenumerated goods to come direct from the plantations to Ireland without touching at England. In 1732 he spoke in favour of the bill for voiding the sale of the Derwentwater estates; in 1733 he defended Sir Robert Sutton (q.v.) and opposed a bill for preventing 'the pernicious practice of stock-jobbing'; in 1734 he opposed a bill for enforcing the land qualification for Members; and in 1736 he piloted through the Commons the Quakers' tithe bill, which was thrown out by the Lords.[2] Voting regularly with the Government he was made a commissioner of Irish revenue in 1735, surrendering it to a friend, who paid him half the income,[3] in 1747, when it became inconsistent with a seat in Parliament under the Place Act of 1742. He died 19 Oct. 1766.

[1] Mayor of Hythe to Dorset's secretary, Nov. 1734, Sackville mss, Kent AO. [2] *HMC Egmont Diary*, i. 54, 67, 177, 248, 368; ii. 31; N. C. Hunt, *Two Early Political Assocs.* 86–89; Harley Diary, 17 Mar. and 30 Apr. 1736. [3] Chase Price to Grafton, 19 Oct. 1766, Chase Price mss in the possession of the Marquess of Salisbury.

R.R.S.

GLENORCHY, Lord, *see* **CAMPBELL, John** (*b.* 1696)

GLYNNE, Sir John, 6th Bt. (1713–77), of Hawarden, Flints.

FLINTSHIRE   1741–1747
FLINT BOROUGHS   28 Nov. 1753–1 June 1777

b. 3 Jan. 1712, 4th s. of Sir Stephen Glynne, 3rd Bt., by Sophia, da. and coh. of Sir Edward Evelyn, 1st Bt., M.P., of Long Ditton, Surr. *educ.* Queen's, Oxf. 1730. *m.* (1) 23 Jan. 1732, Honora (*d.*10 Feb. 1769), da. and h. of Henry Conway of Bodrhyddan, Flints., 6s. 8da.; (2) 27 Mar. 1772, Augusta Beaumont, his children's governess, *s.p.* *suc.* bro. as 6th Bt. Aug. 1730; built Hawarden Castle 1752.

Sheriff, Flints. 1751–2.

While still a minor Glynne married the heiress to the estates of two leading Flintshire families, thus acquiring a claim to share the local parliamentary representation with the Mostyns (qq.v.). After contesting Flint Boroughs unsuccessfully in 1734, he was returned unopposed for the county in 1741 as a Tory, voting consistently against the Government and speaking against the Hanoverians in January 1744. A few weeks later he assured Hardwicke, in connexion with the appointment of Flintshire J.P.s that 'no endeavours shall ever be wanting in me to render to his Majesty and to his

Government all the services in my little power';[1] but in 1745 he was arrested for drinking the Pretender's health on a village green, and imprisoned for three months before being released for lack of evidence.[2]

On retiring from the county seat in 1747 Glynne gave it out that he did not intend to stand for Parliament again, but in 1753 he took advantage of an opportunity to be returned for Flint Boroughs without opposition, continuing to represent them at little expense till his death, 1 June 1777.

[1] 10 Mar. 1744, Add. 35587, f. 237.   [2] *Cheshire Sheaf*, i. 141; *Flints. Hist. Soc. Jnl*. iv. 24–5.

P.D.G.T.

GODDARD, John (1682–1736), of Pall Mall, London, and Falmouth, Cornw.

TREGONY   1727–5 July 1736

> *b*. 5 Dec. 1682, 4th s. of Thomas Goddard, director of Bank of England 1694–1700, of Nun's Court, Coleman St., London by Elizabeth, da. of Humphrey Shallcross of Digswell, Herts. *m*. Anne, sis. of Joseph Gulston (q.v.), wid. of one Simondi, Swedish consul at Lisbon, *s.p*.
> Commissary for settling merchants' losses with Spain 1730–*d*.; assistant, R. African Co. 1734–*d*.

Goddard, a Portugal merchant, was returned for Tregony as a Whig in 1727, voting with the Administration on the arrears of the civil list in 1729 and on the Hessians in 1730. During the second reading, 24 Feb. 1730, of a government bill to prevent loans to foreign powers without a licence, he supported Walpole's statement that 'there was a loan from hence for [the Emperor] going on of £400,000', saying that

> he had enquired from the Jews and that there was £40,000 subscribed, and averred it to be true, that the Emperor on this occasion had but 2 shops to go to, the Dutch and us . . . if the powers were too great to the Crown, make the Act yourselves without power of proclamation and make it temporary . . . there were many precedents of it as in the South Sea directors' case.[1]

He left England for Seville on a government mission in June 1731, receiving an allowance of £1,825 p.a. during his negotiations with the Spanish commissioners.[2] In November 1732 he applied for leave to come home to support his interest at Tregony, which Lord Falmouth (Hugh Boscawen, q.v.) had been undermining during his absence.[3] Returning to England, he voted with the Administration in March 1734 against the repeal of the Septennial Act. Re-elected unopposed, with his son-in-law, Henry Penton, he died 5 July 1736, leaving £20,000 to his wife.[4]

[1] *Knatchbull Diary*.   [2] *Cal. Treas. Bks. and Pprs*. 1731–4, p. 214 et passim.   [3] John Goddard to Sir Chas. Wager, 28 Nov. 1732, Cholmondeley (Houghton) mss.   [4] PCC 152 Derby.

E.C.

GODDARD, Richard (c.1676–1732), of Swindon, Wilts.

WOOTTON BASSETT   1710–1713
WILTSHIRE   6 Nov. 1722–1727

> *b*. c.1676, 1st s. of Thomas Goddard of Swindon by Mary, da. of Oliver Pleydell of Shrivenham, Berks. *educ*. M. Temple 1696. *unm. suc*. fa. 1704.
> Sheriff, Wilts. 1713.

Goddard, a Tory, whose family had acquired the manor of Swindon in 1563,[1] was the first of three men of this name to represent the county in the 18th century. Chosen by the county gentry, meeting at Marlborough on 21 Mar 1722, to take the place of Robert Hyde should the latter be too ill to stand, he was again so chosen on election night, 10 Apr., at Wilton.[2] After Hyde's death, 27 Apr. 1722, he was returned at the ensuing by-election but did not stand in 1727. He died 24 Aug. 1732, leaving an estate of nearly £3000 p.a.

[1] A. W. Mabbs, *Docs. rel. to Goddard Fam. of N. Wilts*. nos. 4, 118.   [2] *Wilts. Arch. Mag*. xi. 88, 90, 212.

R.S.L.

GODFREY, Peter (1665–1724), of Woodford, Essex.

LONDON   1715–10 Nov. 1724

> *b*. 1665, 2nd s. of Michael Godfrey of London, merchant, by Anna Maria, da. of Sir Thomas Chamberlain of Woodford, Essex. *m*. (lic. 29 Oct. 1692, aged 27), Catherine (*d*. 1706), da. of Thomas Goddard, merchant, of Nun's Court, Coleman St., London, director of Bank of England 1694–1700, sis. of John Goddard (q.v.), 6s. 1da.; (2) Catherine, da. of Sir Thomas Pennyman, 2nd Bt., of Ormsby, Yorks., *s.p. suc*. bro. Michael 1695.
> Director, Bank of England 1695–8, New E.I. Co. 1698–9, E.I. Co. 1710–14, 1715–18.

Godfrey was the nephew of Sir Edmund Berry Godfrey, the magistrate who was murdered after receiving Titus Oates's depositions concerning the Popish plot. His elder brother, Michael, was one of the founders and the first deputy governor of the Bank of England. Defeated at London in 1713 on the anti-French commercial treaty platform, he was returned there in 1715, classed as a Whig in the list of the Parliament prepared for George I, but as a Tory by Sunderland c.1718–19.[1] He voted against the Government in all recorded divisions. In November 1721 he presented unsuccessfully a petition from the proprietors of the redeemables asking that the 2 millions owing to the Government by the South Sea Company should be used to compensate them for their losses;[2] and in January 1722 he supported a motion for the repeal of the clauses of the Quarantine Act giving emergency powers to the Government.[3] Re-elected in 1722, he died 10 Nov. 1724.

[1] List of Tories, Sunderland (Blenheim) mss. [2] Pol. State, xxii. 511, 513. [3] Hist. Reg. 1722, chron. pp. 105-6.

E.C.

GODOLPHIN, Francis (1706-85), of Baylis, Bucks.

HELSTON   1741-17 Jan. 1766

bap. 2 Nov. 1706, 1st surv. s. of Henry Godolphin, D.D., provost of Eton and dean of St. Paul's (bro. of Sidney Godolphin, M.P., 1st Earl of Godolphin, ld. treasurer), by Mary, da. of Sidney Godolphin (q.v.) of Thames Ditton, Surr., gov. of Scilly Isles. educ. Eton 1718-21; Queen's, Oxf. 1723. m. (1) 18 Feb. 1734, Lady Barbara Bentinck (d. 13 Apr. 1736), da. of William, 1st Earl of Portland, s.p.; (2) 28 May 1747, Lady Anne Fitzwilliam, da. of John Fitzwilliam (q.v.), 2nd Earl Fitzwilliam [I], s.p. suc. fa. 1733; cos. as 2nd Baron Godolphin 17 Jan. 1766.
    Lt. gov. Scilly Isles 1739-66, gov. 1766-d.; recorder, Helston 1766-d.

Godolphin was heir to his cousin Francis, 2nd Earl of Godolphin, and to the barony created in January 1735. George II

did not at all relish the entailing a peerage on Mr. Godolphin, who had married a daughter of Lady Portland, to whom both the King and Queen bore a most irreconcilable hatred for accepting the employment of governess to their daughters in the late reign without their consent, at the time they had been turned out of St. James's and the education of their children, who were kept there, taken from them.[1]

Returned by Lord Godolphin for Helston in 1741, he voted with the Government on the chairman of the elections committee, on 16 Dec., but abstained on the Westminster election petition on the 27th.[2] After the fall of Walpole he steadily supported the Administration. He died 25 May 1785.

[1] Hervey, Mems. 406. [2] Hartington to Devonshire, 27 Dec. 1741, Devonshire mss.

E.C.

GODOLPHIN, Sidney (1652-1732), of Thames Ditton, Surr.

HELSTON	1685-1687
PENRYN	30 Apr. 1690-1695
HELSTON	1698-1713, 1715-1722
ST. MAWES	1722-1727
ST. GERMANS	1727-22 Sept. 1732

bap. 12 Jan. 1652,[1] o. surv. s. of John Godolphin, judge of the Admiralty court, of St. Thomas's, nr. Launceston, Cornw. and St. James's, Clerkenwell, by his 2nd w. Mary Tregos; cos. of Sidney Godolphin, M.P., 1st Earl of Godolphin, ld. treasurer. m. c.1673, Susanna, da. and h. of Rees Tanat of Abertanat, Salop, 1s. 5da. suc. fa. 1678.
    Capt. 10 Ft. 1685, lt.-col. 1694, res. 1696; maj. 2 Ft. 1700, out by 1702; lt. gov. Scilly Isles 1690,

gov. 1700-d.; auditor of crown lands revenues in Wales 1702-d.; auditor of crown revenues Lincs., Notts., Derbys., and Chester 1706-d.; gov. Greenwich Hospital.

At George I's accession Godolphin was re-elected for Helston on his family's interest. Absent from the division on the septennial bill in 1716, he voted against the repeal of the Occasional Conformity and Schism Acts and the peerage bill in 1719. In 1720 and again in 1726 he applied unsuccessfully to Spencer Compton (q.v.), the Prince's treasurer, 'who I am proud to call my patron', to recommend him to the Prince for the post of assay master of the stannaries, observing that

having (beyond expectation) survived the winter, I am not without hopes of living a little longer, in order to which I don't know anything that can contribute more effectually than his Royal Highness's grace and favour.[2]

Brought in by the Administration for Cornish boroughs in 1722 and 1727, he died at the age of 80, 22 Sept. 1732, being then the father of the House.

[1] F. G. Marsh, Godolphins, 22-23, and Additions thereto, 2. [2] HMC Townshend, 208.

E.C.

GODOLPHIN, William, Visct. Rialton (c.1699-1731).

PENRYN	24 June 1720-1722
NEW WOODSTOCK	1727-24 Aug. 1731

b. c.1699, o.s. of Francis Godolphin, M.P., 2nd Earl of Godolphin, by Lady Henrietta Churchill, da. of John, 1st Duke of Marlborough, and suo jure Duchess of Marlborough. educ. Clare Hall, Camb. 1717; Grand Tour (Italy) 1721. m. 25 Apr. 1729, Maria Catherine, da. of Peter S. C. de Jong, burgomaster of Utrecht, s.p. Styled Visct. Rialton 1712-22; Marquess of Blandford 1722-d.

Almost immediately after being returned on the Godolphin interest for Penryn at a by-election in 1720, Lord Rialton left for Italy, reaching Rome in May 1721. In that year there was published in London an anonymous Letter from an English Traveller at Rome to his Father. The letter, which was ascribed to Rialton,[1] described a chance meeting with the Pretender:

I felt in that instant of his approach a strong convulsion of body and mind, such as I was never sensible of before; whether aversion, awe or respect occasioned it, I can't tell. I remarked his eyes fixed upon me, which I confess I could not bear. I was perfectly stunned and not aware of myself when, pursuant of what the standers-by did, I made him a salute. He returned it with a smile, which changed the sedateness of his first aspect into a very graceful countenance; as he passed by, I observed him to be a well sized, clean limbed man.

After relating meetings and discussions with the Pretender on politics and religion, it concludes:

I am not sorry to have contented so far my curiosity and that were he not the Pretender I should like the man very well. We should truly pass much of our time in dullness, had we not the diversion of his house, but I will give you my word I will enter no more upon arguments of this kind with him; for he has too much wit and learning for me: besides that he speaks with such an air of sincerity that I am apprehensive I should become half a Jacobite, if I should continue following these discourses any longer.

On Marlborough's death in 1722 Rialton, who had not stood at the general election and was living abroad, became Marquess of Blandford. Under Marlborough's will he came in for an annual income of £3,000, to be increased to £8,000 when the works at Blenheim were completed. His grandmother, Duchess Sarah, Sir John Vanbrugh observed,

has by this will (for to be sure that was her doings) made my Lord Blandford independent of his father and mother.

In July 1727, the Duchess wrote:

I design to set up the Marquis of Blandford for St. Albans. Not that he will ever sit in the House of Commons, for when he comes into England, which is not expected soon, he will be called up by writ into the House of Lords.[2]

In August 1727 he was in Paris, where an agent of Walpole's, speaking of the activities of the Jacobites there, reported:

I have seen my Lord Blandford very often for a month past and he continues to have his head very confused with all those affairs, and he no longer thinks of returning to England. I supped last evening with the Duke of Beaufort [a prominent English Jacobite] and Lord Blandford, and it seems that those two Lords wish to make a grand intrigue together, for they often enough have secret *teste à teste* conferences, and I find that Lord Blandford is very pleased with the Duke.[3]

He was at Utrecht in October 1727, when he learned of his having been chosen at Woodstock on his grandmother's recommendation. Chesterfield, then ambassador at the Hague, wrote to Lord Townshend on 5 Nov. 1728:

There is one Leigh, who has resided for these last three years chiefly at Utrecht, a notorious Jacobite, and one who has gone to and fro between Amsterdam and Rotterdam, to negotiate with the Jacobites. I am sorry to say that he has been chiefly maintained for these last two years by Lord Blandford, who has likewise sent frequent and considerable sums of money to Hamilton [the Pretender's agent in London] and other Jacobites in this country.[4]

After his marriage he lived in England, where his bride, who brought him a dowry of £30,000, was received coldly by all his family except the dowager Duchess. He does not appear to have spoken or voted in Parliament. In February 1731 the Pretender wrote to Hamilton to let Blandford know

that I hope he will do me and his country what service he can in this conjecture [an attempt at a restoration with French help; see under Hyde, Henry, Viscount Cornbury], and I should be glad if he made my compliments to the Duchess his grandmother, desiring him she would use her influence on her friends that they may join in the same good work.

He died of a 'drinking bout' at Balliol College, Oxford, on 24 Aug. of the same year. His grandmother, who was with him at the end, said 'I would have given half my estate to have saved him', and 'I hope the Devil is picking that man's bones who taught him to drink'.[5]

[1] Bp. Rawlinson, who was in Rome at the time and who knew Rialton, ascribes the letter to Rialton in his own copy of the pamphlet, now in the Bodleian Lib. [2] Coxe, *Marlborough*, iii. 426; *HMC 15th Rep. VI*, 41–42; A. L. Rowse, *Later Churchills*, 14. [3] *HMC 11th Rep. IV*, 199–200. [4] *Letters*, 69. [5] A. L. Rowse, *Early Churchills*, 407; Stuart mss 142/122.

E.C.

GODSCHALL, Sir Robert (c.1692–1742), of College Hill, London, and Weston, in Albury, Surr.

LONDON 1741–26 June 1742

b. c.1692, s. of John Godschall, merchant, of East Sheen, Surr. by his w. Bathia Charleton.[1] *m.* Catherine, da. of William Tryon of Frognal, Kent, *s.p.* Kntd. 31 Oct. 1735.

Director, R. Exchange Assurance 1729–*d.*; ironmonger, master, Ironmongers' Co. 1733; alderman, London 1732, sheriff 1735–6, ld. mayor 1741–*d.* pres. St. Bartholomew's Hospital 1741–*d.*

A Portugal merchant in London, and the brother-in-law of John Barnard (q.v.), Godschall bought the manor of Weston in Surrey in 1729.[2] He served on the committee set up by the common council to prepare the petitions against the excise bill and the Spanish convention, and was a member of the caucus of the corporation in 1738.[3] Defeated for London in 1734, he was returned for it as a Tory in 1741, becoming lord mayor the following September, after being rejected several times by the court of aldermen. Thomas Carte, the Jacobite historian, described him as 'a very honest man, of exceeding good sense, a good writer as well as speaker'.[4] However, when on 20 Jan. 1742 he presented the merchants' petition for adequate protection for their ships, Horace Walpole observed:

This gold-chain came into Parliament cried up for his parts, but proves so dull one would think he chewed opium. Earle [Giles, q.v.] says, 'By God I have heard an oyster speak as well 20 times'.

On 31 Mar. 1742 he brought in a bill for repealing the Septennial Act, which was defeated. He followed

Barnard in voting on 28 Apr. 1742 for replacing the troops sent abroad. He died during his mayoralty 26 June 1742 'of an inflammatory fever'.[5]

[1] Stocken Coll. in Guildhall Lib. [2] Manning & Bray, *Surr.*, ii. 127. [3] 9 Apr. 1733, Jnl. vol. 57; 20 Feb. 1739, Jnl. vol. 58; and see LONDON. [4] Stuart mss 219/191, 227/155. [5] Walpole to Mann, 22 Jan., 1, 29 Apr., 30 June 1742 (n. 31).

E.C.

GOODALL, John (*d.*1725), of Bull Hill, Fowey, Cornw.

FOWEY 1722–19 Feb. 1725

o.s. of William Goodall, mayor of Fowey, by Elizabeth, da. of Sir John Coryton, 1st Bt., M.P., of Newton, Cornw. *m.* Mary, da. of Peter Major, merchant of Fowey. *suc.* fa. 1686.

Goodall, a Fowey merchant, belonged to a prominent local family. He and his father-in-law had an interest of their own in the borough,[1] for which he was returned as a Tory in 1722. Included in a list of supporters sent to the Pretender in 1721, he was in contact with Atterbury's agents during the plot of 1722.[2] He died 19 Feb. 1725.

[1] E. W. Rashleigh, *Hist. Fowey*, 18, 29; C. S. Gilbert, *Hist. Surv. Cornw.* i. 590. [2] Stuart mss 65/16; *Report from the Committee appointed by the House of Commons to examine Christopher Layer and others* (1723), App. F.11.

E.C.

GOODERE, Sir Edward, 1st Bt. (1657–1739), of Burghope, Herefs.

EVESHAM 1708–1715
HEREFORDSHIRE 1722–1727

b. 1657, o.s. of John Goodere of Burghope by Anne, da. of John Morgan of Kent. *m.* (lic. 21 Jan. 1679) Helen, da. and h. of Sir Edward Dineley of Charlton, Worcs., 3s. 1da. *suc.* fa. 1684; *cr.* Bt. 5 Dec. 1707.

Goodere was born in India, the son of a servant of the East India Company, who made a fortune, purchased an estate in Herefordshire and ended as deputy governor of Bombay. He sat for Evesham as a Tory in Queen Anne's last three Parliaments but lost his seat in 1715. Put up by the Herefordshire Tories for the county in 1722, he was returned after a contest. He did not stand again. Before his death, 29 Mar. 1739, one of his three sons was killed in a duel; the younger, a captain in the Royal Navy, was executed for the murder of his elder brother in 1741.[1]

[1] Duncumb, *Herefs.* iv. 173–5.

A.N.N.

GORDON, Alexander (*d.* 1753), of Ardoch (now Poyntzfield), Ross.

INVERNESS BURGHS 13 Apr.–23 Oct. 1722

3rd s. of Sir Adam Gordon, M.P. [S], of Dalpholly, Sutherland by Anne, da. of Alexander Urquhart of

Newhall, Ross;[1] bro. of Sir William Gordon, 1st Bt. (q.v.). *m.* Ann, da. of Sir Robert Munro, 5th Bt., M.P. [S], of Foulis, Ross 1s.

Collector of customs at Inverness 1709–10; muster master gen. [S] June 1716–26; provost, Fortrose 1716.

In 1710, Gordon, a member of the Squadrone, was dismissed as collector of the customs at Inverness for brandy running. On the representations of his brother, Sir William Gordon, and his brother-in-law, Robert Munro (qq.v.), he was to be reinstated in November 1714; but this was successfully opposed by Argyll, who had apparently promised the town council of Inverness that the existing collector should be continued, on the understanding that they should vote for his candidate, William Stewart (q.v.)

During the Fifteen Gordon was sent by his relation, the Earl of Sutherland, to London to apply for assistance, returning with a lieutenant-general's commission for Sutherland, £100 sterling, and a thousand stand of arms. In a duel in 1716 with the son of the 7th Lord Cathcart, who had accused his brother of cowardice, he was badly wounded and Cathcart was killed.[2] Succeeding Henry Cunningham (q.v.) as muster master, he was also elected provost of Fortrose, which he claimed

will enable me to carry on his Majesty's affairs in that country. The doing whereof successfully and faithfully, as I reckon it my greatest honour, so it shall be the greatest study of my life.[3]

Returned for Inverness Burghs in 1722, but unseated on petition, he did not stand again. In his last years he is said to have become 'consecrated to the cause of godliness', through the influence of his wife. He died in March 1753.[4]

[1] *Cal. Treas. Bks.* xxix. 160, 372; *More Culloden Pprs.* ii. 49, 52. [2] Sir Wm. Fraser, *Sutherland Bk.* i. 336; *Cal. Treas. Bks. and Pprs.* 1714–19, p.183; *Stair Annals*, i. 322–3; *HMC Laing*, ii. 186–8. [3] Stowe mss 239, f. 28. [4] D. F. Sage, *Memorabilia Domestica*, 11; J. M. Bulloch, *The House of Gordon* (New Spalding Club), i. App. I, p. 15.

J.M.S.

GORDON, Sir John, 2nd Bt. (c. 1707–83), of Invergordon, Cromarty.

CROMARTYSHIRE 30 Dec. 1742–1747, 1754–1761

b. c.1707, 1st s. of Sir William Gordon (q.v.), 1st Bt., of Invergordon. *m.* (1) Barbara (*d.* 20 Aug. 1729), da. of Henry Raines, LL.D. of East Greenwich, Kent, *s.p.*; (2) 18 Feb. 1739, Mary Weir, ?his cos., wid of Hon. George Ogilvie, *s.p.* *suc.* fa. 9 June 1742.

Sec. for Scotland to Prince of Wales 1745–51; sec. and chamberlain to principality of Scotland 1753–d.

In 1742 Gordon succeeded to his father's seat, attaching himself to the Prince of Wales, who in 1745 made him his secretary for Scotland at a salary of £300 p.a., later increased to £600.[1] With the rest of the Prince's party, he voted with the Government till Frederick went into opposition in 1747. On the outbreak of the Forty-five, he failed in his attempts to prevent his brother-in-law, the 3rd Earl of Cromartie, and his favourite nephew, Lord Macleod, from joining the rebels, but afterwards, through the intercession of the Prince, he saved Cromartie from execution and Macleod from attainder.[2] In 1747, when Cromartyshire was not represented, he stood unsuccessfully, with £1,000 supplied by the Prince,[3] for Tain Burghs, where his brother-in-law controlled Dingwall. After the Prince's death he lost his post but was compensated by the Princess Dowager with a pension.[4] He subsequently attached himself to the Pelhams, who gave him a place of £400 p.a. He died 25 May 1783.

[1] Gordon's diary, J. M. Bulloch, *Gordons of Invergordon*, 86. [2] *Corresp. of Sir John Gordon of Invergordon on the Occasion of the Rebellion, Autumn 1745*, 31–32, et passim; *Gordons of Invergordon*, 46; Walpole to Mann, 21 Aug. 1746. [3] Andrew Fletcher to Pelham, 21 July 1747, Newcastle (Clumber) mss. [4] Gordon's diary, 87.

E.H.-G.

GORDON, Sir Robert, 4th Bt. (1696–1772), of Gordonstown, Moray.

CAITHNESS   1715–1722

b. 1696, 1st s. of Sir Robert Gordon, 3rd Bt., M.P. [S], of Gordonstown by his 2nd w. Elizabeth, da. of Sir William Dunbar, 1st Bt., M.P. [S], of Hempriggs, Caithness. *m.* 26 Apr. 1734, Agnes, 1st da. of Sir William Maxwell, 4th Bt., of Calderwood, Lanark, 4s. 1da. *suc.* fa. Sept. or Oct. 1704.

The Gordons of Gordonstown, the premier baronets of Scotland, were descended from a younger son of the 12th Earl of Sutherland. Sir Robert Gordon's mother married, secondly, James Sutherland, afterwards Dunbar, M.P. Caithness 1710–13, who was created a baronet in 1706 and succeeded to the estate of Hempriggs. Gordon's sister married John Forbes of Culloden, the brother of Duncan Forbes (qq.v.), lord president of the court of session. In spite of being a minor he was brought into Parliament for Caithness in 1715 by John Sinclair of Ulbster, the hereditary sheriff. Though classed as a Whig, he joined the Earl of Mar during the Fifteen, when he was present at Sheriffmuir, described by the Master of Sinclair as 'a young man of 19 years old, of great fire, courage and good sense, and with whom I choosed to take lodging in Perth'. After the battle he made his peace through the Duke of Argyll, by whose good offices he escaped all punishment.[1] In 1719 he was listed as 'against' the peerage bill by Sunderland, and by Craggs as to be approached through Argyll, but no parliamentary votes of his

have been recorded, nor did he stand again. He enjoyed considerable notoriety locally for cruelty to his tenants, it being alleged that on one occasion he imprisoned an old woman 'for taking a head of a ling out of the midden' because 'it was good for curing the gout'.[2] On the death of the 18th Earl of Sutherland in 1766 he claimed that earldom, with the estates, as heir male of the 12th Earl, but his claim was disallowed in 1771 by the House of Lords in favour of the heir of line. He died 8 Jan. 1772.

[1] John, Master of Sinclair, *Mems. of the Insurrection in Scotland in 1715* (Abbotsford Club), 142, 264, 270, 326–8; R. Young, *Annals of the Parish and Burgh of Elgin*, 169 seq. [2] Constance F. Gordon-Cumming, *Memories*, 95–98.

J.M.S.

GORDON, Sir William, 1st Bt. (*d.*1742), of Invergordon, Cromarty, and Dalpholly, Sutherland.

SUTHERLAND   1708–1713, 7 May 1714–1727
CROMARTYSHIRE   1741–9 June 1742

1st s. of Sir Adam Gordon, M.P. [S], of Dalpholly; fa. of Sir John Gordon (q.v.), fa.-in-law of Robert Dundas (q.v.), bro. of Alexander Gordon (q.v.). *m.* (1) a da. of Henderson of Fordell, Fife; (2) 19 Mar. 1704, Isabel, da. and h. of Sir John Hamilton, M.P. [S], of Halcraig, Lanark, Lord Halcraig, S.C.J., 4s. 5da. *suc.* fa. 1700; *cr.* Bt. 3 Feb. 1704.

Commr. for stating army debts 1715–20; sheriff, Ross 1722–7.

The son of a moneylender, Gordon purchased Inverbreakie, which he renamed Invergordon.[1] A member of the Squadrone, he represented Sutherland on the interest of the 16th Earl of Sutherland, to whom he was related. Elected by the House of Commons in 1715 to be one of the commissioners appointed to state the debts due to the army, at a salary of £500 a year, he voted with the Government in every recorded division. During the rebellion that year he and his brother Alexander (q.v.) were active on behalf of the Government under Sutherland, who was commander-in-chief in the north. In February 1716 he asked Robethon, George I's private secretary, that greater recognition should be given to Sutherland for his services in securing the Hanoverian succession.[2] In April 1716 John Forbes wrote to his brother Duncan (qq.v.):

Sir William Gordon is a very busy man, dunning the ministry for his losses sustained by the rebels, which he says amount to no less than £14,000 sterling. I desire you to write north . . . and let us have an account as near as possible of the damage he and his people have really sustained.[3]

In June he accused Lord Lovat of belittling Sutherland's share in the re-capture of Inverness, challenging him to a duel, which was interrupted by the guards. Suggestions that the interruption had been prompted by Gordon himself led to a duel in which his brother Alexander (q.v.) killed his opponent. In the House, he surprised English members by voting in favour of a petition that the wives and widows of English Jacobites should be granted jointures out of their husbands' forfeited estates, but opposing a similar petition on behalf of his compatriots.[4]

A friend of John Law's, Gordon speculated in the French Mississipi scheme, boasting in October 1719 'that having put in £500 in March last, he is now a-selling out for £9,000'.[5] One of the 'chief favourites' of the Duke of Roxburghe, the Squadrone secretary of state for Scotland, he was used by Sunderland for paying Scotch Members.[6] He was one of the Members who were credited by the South Sea Company with stock—in his case £4,000 at 276 on 23 Mar. and a further £3,000 at 300 on 25 Mar.—without paying for it, with the right to 'sell' it back to the Company whenever they chose, taking as 'profit' any increase in the market price.[7] Again returned for Sutherland in 1722, he was active on behalf of the Squadrone, who were so heavily defeated by the Duke of Argyll that George Baillie (q.v.) wrote:

> those of the Scots in the House of Commons that are not Argyll's men act as individuals and but a few by Roxburghe's interest (scarce Sir William Gordon, if anybody else would take him up).

In 1727, when Sutherland returned his grandson for the county, Gordon was put up for Cromartyshire by his son-in-law, the 3rd Earl of Cromartie, but withdrew when Cromartie was offered a pension by the Government for returning Sir Kenneth Mackenzie (q.v.).[8] At the beginning of 1734 financial difficulties obliged him to sell an estate at Deptford.[9] At the general election he stood unsuccessfully for Sutherland against the candidate of the new Earl, who had succeeded Gordon's patron in 1733. In 1741 he was returned for Cromartyshire by the 3rd Earl of Cromartie, voting against the Government on the election of the chairman of the elections committee, 16 Dec. 1741, and on the Westminster election petition, 22 Dec., though the day before Sir Charles Wager (q.v.) had given his son a ship. On a surprise opposition motion to set up a secret committee to inquire into the conduct of the war, 21 Jan. 1742, he was brought in 'from his bed, with a blister on his head, and flannel hanging out from under his wig'. The news of his son's death in a shipwreck off the Suffolk coast had just arrived but

> they concealed it from the father that he might not absent himself. However, as we have good-natured

men too on our side, one of his own countrymen went and told him of it in the House. The old man, who looked like Lazarus at his resuscitation, behaved with great resolution and said he knew why he was told of it, but when he thought his country in danger he would not go away.

He rose again from his bed to vote against the Government on the critical Chippenham election petition, 28 Jan. 1742, which Walpole lost by one vote.[10] He died 9 June 1742.

[1] J. M. Bulloch, *Gordons of Invergordon*, 14. [2] *Culloden Pprs.* 39; Sir W. Fraser, *Sutherland Bk.* ii. 63–64. [3] *More Culloden Pprs.* ii. 111. [4] *HMC Laing*, ii. 186–8; *HMC Stuart*, vi. 106. [5] *Gordons of Invergordon*, 22; *HMC Var.* viii. 281. [6] *HMC Polwarth*, v. 46; see MOODIE, James. [7] *CJ*, xix. 569. [8] *More Culloden Pprs.* ii. 210–21; *CJ*, xx. 37–38; *Knatchbull Diary*, 24 Oct. 1722; *HMC Polwarth*, iii. 282–90; v. 55. [9] Taylor to Chandos, 6 Feb. 1734, Chandos letter bks. [10] Walpole to Mann, 22 Jan. 1742, 21 Aug. 1746.

E.C.

GORE, Charles (?1711–68), of Tring, Herts.

CRICKLADE	21 Nov. 1739–1741
HERTFORDSHIRE	1741–1761
TIVERTON	14 May 1762–1768

b. ?1711, 1st s. of William Gore, and bro. of John Gore (qq.v.). *educ.* Ch. Ch. Oxf. 12 July 1729, aged 18. *m.* 3 Dec. 1741, Ellen, da. of Sir William Humfreys, 1st Bt. (q.v.), of London, sis. and coh. of Sir Orlando Humfreys, 2nd Bt., 3s. 5da. *suc.* fa. 1739.

In 1739 Gore succeeded his father as a Tory at Cricklade, from which he withdrew after a double return in 1741, when he chose to sit for Hertfordshire, where he had been returned unopposed. Like his uncle Thomas (q.v.) he voted against the motion for Walpole's removal in February 1741.[1] In 1742 he was one of the opposition Members included in the court list for the committee of inquiry into Walpole's Administration, but he was not elected to it.[2] He continued to vote with the Opposition till the end of 1744 when, with his uncle, he went over to the Administration, voting for the Hanoverians as a 'new ally' in 1746. He was classed as a government supporter in 1747. The second Lord Egmont wrote in his electoral survey, c.1749–50, that Gore 'ought to be routed by all means if possible, for he is a thorough enemy in his heart, and closely attached to the present system.'

He died 15 Feb. 1768.

[1] Coxe, *Walpole*, iii. 563. [2] Walpole to Mann, 1 Apr. 1742.

R.R.S.

GORE, John (c.1689–1763), of Bush Hill, Mdx.

GREAT GRIMSBY 1747–1761

b. c.1689, 2nd s. of Sir William Gore, gov. Hamburg Co., director of Bank of England and ld. mayor of London, by Elizabeth, da. of Walter Hampton; bro. of William and Thomas Gore (qq.v.). *m.* Hannah, da. of Sir Jeremy Sambrooke of North Mimms,

Herts., 1s. *d.v.p.* 3da. His da. Catherine m. Joseph Mellish, M.P., his da. Anne m. William Mellish (q.v.), his bro.

Director, South Sea Co. 1711–12, 1715–21.

Gore was a Hamburg merchant, trading in partnership with Joseph Mellish, M.P., who became his son-in-law. As a director of the South Sea Company at the time of the Bubble, he was found by the House of Commons to have had 'little or no share in the fraudulent contrivances of the leading directors', and was allowed to retain £20,000 out of a fortune valued at nearly £39,000.[1] He subsequently became a leading government financier, obtaining contracts for remittances for British troops abroad and subsidies to foreign governments amounting to over £5,000,000 between 1741 and 1752, on which he received commission varying from five to fifteen per cent.[2] When in 1743 a rival firm offered to undertake these remittances at a lower rate, Pelham decided for Gore, on the ground of his 'superior advantages in ensuring the regularity of the remittances'.[3]

Gore was returned unopposed for Great Grimsby in 1747. He is described as 'Gore the remittancer' in the 2nd Lord Egmont's electoral survey, c. 1749–50, where he is put down as one of those to be 'routed' on Frederick's accession. Re-elected in 1754, he died 3 Aug. 1763, 'the last surviving director of the South Sea Company in the year 1720'.[4]

[1] *Hist. Reg.* 1721, chron. 211. [2] Namier, *Structure*, 47 n. 1. For details of these contracts see *Cal. Treas. Pprs.* 1739–41 and 1742–5. [3] Coxe, *Pelham*, i. 59–60. [4] *Gent. Mag.* 1763, p. 415.

R.R.S.

GORE, John (*d.*1773), of Charles St., Berkeley Sq., London.

CRICKLADE   1747–1754

b. aft. 1712, 2nd s. of William Gore, and bro. of Charles Gore (qq.v.). *m.* Ann, da. of Sir Emanuel Moore, 3rd Bt., M.P. [I], of Ross Carbery, co. Cork, *s.p.*

Cornet 11 Drags. 1739; capt. 9 Marines 1741; capt. and lt.-col. 3 Ft. Gds. 1750, 1st maj. 1760, lt.-col. 1761–8; col. army 1759; maj.-gen. 1762; col. 61 Ft. 1768–73; lt.-gen. 1772; col. 6 Ft. Feb. 1773–*d.*

Returned on the family interest at Cricklade, Gore was classed as a government supporter in 1747. He voted against the clandestine marriages bill in 1753.[1]

He died 12 Nov. 1773.

[1] Add. 32732, f. 22.

R.R.S.

GORE, Thomas (?1694–1777), of the Inner Temple, London, and Dunstan Park, Berks.

CRICKLADE	1722–1727
AMERSHAM	17 Feb. 1735–Feb. 1746
PORTSMOUTH	3 Mar. 1746–1747
BEDFORD	1747–1754
CRICKLADE	1754–1768

b. ?1694, 3rd s. of Sir William Gore; bro. of John and William Gore (qq.v.). *educ.* I. Temple 1711; Ch. Ch. Oxf. 4 June 1714, aged 19. *m.* 15 Sept. 1748, Mary, da. of Sir William Humfreys, 1st Bt. (q.v.), of London, sis. and coh. of Sir Orlando Humfreys, 2nd Bt., wid. of (i) William Ball Waring, and (ii) John Honywood.

Muster-master gen. 1746–*d.*

After unsuccessfully contesting Cricklade in 1721, Gore was returned for it in 1722 as a Tory on the interest of his elder brother, William (q.v.). Defeated at Cricklade in 1727, he was returned at Amersham on the Drake interest in 1735. Speaking on the gin bill in 1736[1] and on the quartering of troops in 1741, he was among the Tories who voted against the motion for Walpole's removal in February 1741.[2] After Walpole's fall he continued in opposition, signing the opposition whip of November 1743. He went over to the Administration as one of Lord Gower's followers at the end of 1744, spoke in favour of the vote of credit in March 1745, heartily supported the address of thanks on the Hessians in December,[3] and in 1746 was rewarded with a place. At the ensuing by-election his Amersham seat was taken by William Drake, but he was accommodated with a government seat at Portsmouth. He was re-elected in 1747 but chose to sit for Bedford where he had also been returned on the Duke of Bedford's interest.

He died 17 Mar. 1777.

[1] *HMC Egmont Diary*, ii. 257. [2] Coxe, *Walpole*, iii. 563. [3] Owen, *Pelhams*, 198, 291.

E.C.

GORE, William (c.1675–1739), of Tring, Herts.

COLCHESTER	27 Jan. 1711–1713, 6 May 1714–1715
ST. ALBANS	1722–1727
CRICKLADE	1734–22 Oct. 1739

b. c.1675, 1st s. of Sir William Gore; bro. of John and Thomas Gore (qq.v.). *educ.* Queens', Camb. 1691. *m.* Apr. 1709, Lady Mary Compton, da. of George, 4th Earl of Northampton, 5s. 6da. *suc.* fa. 1708.

Director, Bank of England 1709–12, South Sea Co. 1712–15.

Gore was the eldest son of an eminent London merchant, who bought the manor of Tring in 1705. A Tory and a member of the October Club, he sat in Anne's last two Parliaments but did not stand in 1715. In 1718 he bought the manor of Cricklade, carrying with it the appointment of the returning officer.[1] He successfully contested St. Albans in 1722, did not stand in 1727, and in 1734 was returned on his own interest at Cricklade, dying 22 Oct. 1739. His only recorded speech was against a vote of credit in April 1727. One of his daughters married Charles Pelham and another was the mother of William Mellish (qq.v.).

[1] T. R. Thomson, *Materials for a Hist. of Cricklade*, 158.

R.R.S.

GORING, Sir Henry, 4th Bt. (1679–1731), of Highden, and Wappingthorne, nr. Steyning, Suss.

HORSHAM	4 Apr. 1707–1708
STEYNING	1 Feb. 1709–1715
HORSHAM	29 Jan.–16 June 1715

bap. 16 Sept. 1679, 4th s. of Capt. Henry Goring (*d.*1685) of Wappingthorne (s. of Sir Henry Goring, 2nd Bt., M.P. Sussex 1660, Steyning 1661–79, Sussex 1685–7) by his 2nd w. Mary, da. and coh. of Sir John Covert, 1st Bt., of Slaugham, Suss. *m.* (post nupt. settlement 25 Feb. 1714), Elizabeth, da. and coh. of Sir George Matthew of Twickenham, Mdx., 9s. 2da. *suc.* half-bro. Sir Charles Goring, 3rd Bt., 13 Jan. 1714.
Capt. in Col. Edmund Soame's Ft. 1705; transferred to Col. Samuel Masham's Horse 1707; col. 31 Ft. Mar. 1711, half-pay 1713, and June–Sept. 1715.

An officer in the regiment of Colonel Masham, the husband of Queen Anne's favourite, Goring appears to have owed his appointment to the command of a regiment in 1711 to the board set up under the Duke of Ormonde by the new Tory Government to take army promotions out of Marlborough's hands. Returned for Horsham in 1715 but unseated on petition, he was one of the Jacobite officers who were required to sell their commissions on the outbreak of the 1715 rebellion.[1] In the spring of 1716 he was involved in a project to restore the Stuarts, with the help of Swedish troops, to be directed on the English side by his 'intimate friend' General John Richmond Webb (q.v.), he himself engaging 'to join those troops as soon as they land'.[2] Early in 1721, when his name was sent to the Pretender as a probable supporter in the event of a rising, he put forward a new plan for a restoration with the assistance of the Irish troops in Spain under the Duke of Ormonde and those in France under Lt.-Gen. Dillon, writing to Ormonde, 20 Mar.:

I will venture with the utmost deference and respect to tell you that the whole kingdom begs a retrieve, as well the Whigs as the Tories, and if you would come with 1,000 soldiers and 10,000 arms, it is a safe gain. I am told the gentleman in whose hand this

will go through [Dillon] proposes two thousand soldiers and arms. I know these are ready. He will tell you at the same time you receive this what he can do . . .

In a covering note to Dillon he wrote:

I am told you proposed to the Bishop of Rochester [Atterbury] to send 2,000 soldiers and that he thought it too small a number. In this, I can assure you, he is the only person that thinks so who intends to serve the King [the Pretender], and he has sent this information of his own head, without consulting friends in England, for I know they will all go into that number, though probably they would be glad of more. I beg you will not lay this design aside but press the Duke of Ormonde to come, for it cannot fail of success. I will do everything that is to be done in concert with some friends, for the more secrecy the better. We shall not want numbers.

On 22 Apr. Atterbury, who now agreed with the scheme, informed the Pretender:

The time is now come when with a very little assistance from your friends abroad, your way to your friends at home is become safe and easy . . . The worthy Sir Henry Goring will be able to explain things more fully to your friends on the other side, who can with the most dispatch and secrecy convey accounts of them to you.

Goring's zeal was rewarded by a letter from the Pretender of 4 Jan. 1722, saying:

I send to Mr. Dillon for you a warrant for making you a viscount [in the event of a restoration] with the titles in blank for you to fill up as you think fit. The share you have in the present project and that which I hope you will have in my restoration justly deserve the most particular marks of my favour and kindness, and when it pleases God I may see better days, you will find that I shall never forget the part you have acted towards me in my misfortune.[3]

The rising was to have taken place during the general election of 1722 (when he stood unsuccessfully for Steyning), but not enough money had been collected to buy arms in sufficient quantity, on which Lord Mar, one of the Pretender's representatives in France, observed that Goring 'though an honest, stout man, had not showed himself very fit for things of this kind, I mean to have the advising and leading of them'.[4] After the discovery of the plot, he fled to France on 23 Aug., the day before Atterbury's arrest.[5] In the course of the ensuing trials, in which he was referred to as one of the principal managers of the plot, his agent disclosed that Goring had attempted to enlist in the Pretender's service a gang of brandy smugglers said to number a thousand, against whose activities the Government subsequently passed legislation.[6] He remained in exile in France until his death, 12 Nov. 1731.

[1] Dalton, *Geo. I's Army*, i. 358–9. [2] *HMC Stuart*, ii. 67–68. [3] Stuart mss 52/141; 53/48; 57/5; 65/16. [4] 23 Mar. 1722, to the

Pretender, ibid. 58/91. ⁵ *Report from the Committee of the House of Commons appointed to examine Christopher Layer and others*, App. E. 17. ⁶ Howell's *State Trials*, xvi. 336, 374, 397, 449–51; SP Dom. 35/42, pt. i. ff. 225–8; Sir Henry Goring to the Pretender, 6 May 1723, Stuart mss 67/16; *Knatchbull Diary*, 26 Apr. 1723; 9 Geo. I, c. 1.

E.C.

GOUGH, Henry (1681–1751), of Enfield, Mdx.

BRAMBER 1734–13 July 1751

b. 1 or 2 Apr. 1681, 6th s. of Sir Henry Gough, M.P., of Oldfallings and Perry Bar, Staffs. by Mary, da. of Sir Edward Littleton, 2nd Bt., M.P., of Pillaton, Staffs. *m.* 1719, Elizabeth, da. of Morgan Hynde of London, brewer and Dissenter, 1s. 1da.

Director, E.I. Co. 1730–3, 1736–51, chairman 1737, 1741, 1743, 1746, 1747, dep. chairman 1736, 1740, 1742, 1745, 1750.

Gough began his career in the East India trade as the protégé of his uncle Sir Richard Gough (q.v.), with whom he travelled to China when aged only 11, and was brought up to keep his accounts. From 1707 to 1715 he was in command of a merchantman, the *Streatham*, making a 'decent competency' in the service of the Company. From 1730 he was almost continuously a director of the East India Company. It was said that 'if he would take the whole East India Company on him, he must answer for it; for nobody would assist him, though they would contradict him'. Returned for Bramber by his cousin Sir Henry Gough (q.v.), he voted consistently with the Administration, prejudicing his health by his assiduous attendance at debates when afflicted by gout.[1] He died 13 July 1751, leaving a son, Richard Gough, the antiquary.

[1] Shaw, *Staffs.* ii. 192.

S.R.M.

GOUGH, Sir Henry, 1st Bt. (1709–74), of Edgbaston, Warws.

TOTNES 25 Jan. 1732–1734
BRAMBER 1734–1741

b. 9 Mar. 1709, 1st surv. s. of Sir Richard Gough (q.v.). *educ.* Corpus Christi, Camb. 1725; M. Temple 1725. *m.* (1) Catherine (*d.* 22 June 1740), da. of Sir John Harpur, 4th Bt., of Calke, Derbys., *s.p.*; (2) 2 July 1741, Jane Barbara, da. and in her issue h. of Reynolds Calthorpe (q.v.) of Elvetham, Hants, niece of Talbot Yelverton, 1st Earl of Sussex, and gd.-da. of Henry, 1st Visct. de Longueville, 3s. 3da. *suc.* fa. 1728. *cr.* Bt. 6 Apr. 1728.

Director, E.I. Co. 1735–51.

An East India merchant, Gough was first returned to Parliament on the government interest at Totnes, voting for the excise bill. Soon after succeeding his father he bought two more burgages

at Bramber,[1] giving him control of the borough, for which he thenceforth nominated both Members. Returned for Bramber in 1734, he continued to vote with the Government. In 1741 he retired in favour of his neighbour, Thomas Archer (q.v.), to whom he subsequently leased the Bramber seats,[2] retaining the management of the borough in his own hands.

He died 8 June 1774.

[1] 'A State of . . . Bramber', Lowndes mss, West Sussex RO.
[2] Namier, *Structure*, 144.

S.R.M.

GOUGH, Sir Richard (1655–1728), of Edgbaston, Warws. and Gough House, Chelsea, Mdx.

BRAMBER 1715–9 Feb. 1728

b 10 Oct. 1655, 3rd. s. of John Gough of Oldfallings, in Bushbury, Staffs. by his 2nd w. Bridget, da. of John Astley of Wood Eaton, Staffs. *m.* (settlement 5 Sept. 1701) Ann, da. and coh. of Nicholas Crisp of Chiswick, Mdx., 3s. 4da. Kntd. 8 Jan. 1715.

Director, E.I. Co. 1713–20.

The Goughs were of Welsh origin but had been long settled in Staffordshire where they had purchased Oldfallings early in the seventeenth century.[1] Sir Richard Gough, a younger son, made a great fortune in the East India trade, having been 'brought up' under Sir James Houblon, M.P., and as a youth enjoyed the advice and assistance of 'the great Sir Josiah Child'. He 'was reckoned to be well skilled in the knowledge of the British trade and commerce in general, and in that particular branch of it to the East Indies, equal to any in his time.'[2] In 1714 he purchased 18 burgage houses at Bramber giving him control of one of the seats there.[3] Returned in 1715 for Bramber, for which he sat till his death, he voted for the septennial bill, went into opposition with Walpole in 1717, was absent from the division on the repeal of the Occasional Conformity and Schism Acts, and voted against the peerage bill. He died 9 Feb. 1728, directing in his will that he should be buried in the church at Edgbaston, where he had bought an estate in 1717. His will continues:

> I lay my bones and ashes there to reproach them that shall succeed me in the possession of the . . . estate in Edgbaston which I have acquired by the blessing of Almighty God very worthily and honestly through my own application and industry, if ever they should be such ill husbands as to spend or waste the same, as a memorial for them to remember that they will then likewise sell my bones and ashes.[4]

[1] Shaw, *Staffs.* ii. 187–93. [2] H. Gough to T. Wotton, c.1740, Add. 24120, f. 387. [3] State of . . . Bramber', Lowndes mss, West Sussex RO. [4] PCC 43 Brook.

S.R.M.

GOULD, John (c. 1695–1740), of Woodford, Essex, and Bovingdon, Herts.

NEW SHOREHAM 29 Jan. 1729–1734

b. c. 1695, 1st s. of John Gould of Woodford, Essex, director and chairman of E.I. Co., by Rachel, da. of Peter Gelsthorp, apothecary of London. *m.* 21 Aug. 1724, Mary, da. of William Bulkeley of Plaistow, Essex, 2s. *suc.* uncle, Sir Nathaniel Gould (q.v.) 1728, fa. 1736.

Director, E.I. Co. 1724–35; inspector of outport customs accounts 1736–*d.*

John Gould, the son of a wealthy East India merchant, was described in 1715 by the future Sir Dudley Ryder (q.v.) as affecting 'very much an airy, unthinking brisk manner of behaviour, as much of the rake as possible', and as

> waiting for the girls from the school . . . I was ashamed to be seen in his company at church time, lest people, who all take notice of his manner of behaviour in relation to these girls, should take me to be of the same company.[1]

In 1729 he succeeded his uncle, Sir Nathaniel Gould, at Shoreham, voting consistently with the Administration. On 24 Feb. 1730 he spoke in favour of a bill for prohibiting loans to foreign powers. Standing again in 1734 with Walpole's support,[2] he asked the Duke of Newcastle 'to write two or three lines intimating you wish me success at Shoreham. It will be of signal service to my interest',[3] but he came bottom of the poll. He then joined with Sir Thomas Prendergast (q.v.) in a petition which Walpole persuaded them to withdraw. In 1736 he succeeded a younger brother in a place worth £400 a year. He died 25 Aug. 1740.

[1] *Ryder Diary*, 86, 90. [2] Undated memo. by 2nd Duke of Richmond, Richmond mss. [3] 10 Apr. 1734, Add. 32689, f. 190.

P.W.

GOULD, Nathaniel (1661–1728), of Stoke Newington, Mdx. and Bovingdon, Herts.

NEW SHOREHAM 1701–1708, 1710–21 July 1728

b. 3 Dec. 1661, 3rd but 1st surv. s. of John Gould, merchant of London, by his w. Mary. *m.* 1 May 1688, Frances, da. of Sir John Hartopp, 3rd Bt., M.P., of Freathby, Leics., 2da. *suc.* fa. 1695. Kntd. 14 Apr. 1721.

Director, Bank of England 1697–1709, 1713–28 (with statutory intervals), dep. gov. 1709–11, gov. 1711–13; director and sometime gov. Russia Co.

Gould, a leading figure in the City, belonged to a wealthy nonconformist family of London merchants, engaged in the cloth export trade to Turkey and the East. Re-elected as a Whig for Shoreham in 1715, he supported the Government's active policy in the Baltic, seconding a motion on 12 Apr. 1717 that we could not carry on our trade with the Baltic without bringing the King of Sweden to

reason. In 1719 he voted for the repeal of the Occasional Conformity and Schism Acts, but against the peerage bill, on which he was listed as doubtful and to be approached for the Government by Craggs and John Aislabie (qq.v.). During the South Sea crisis he advocated strong measures against the directors;[1] and in November 1721 he spoke in favour of exempting the Turkey Company from the provisions of the quarantine bill. On a bill to prevent frauds in the customs on tobacco (see Perry, Micajah) in February 1723 he proposed

> to have a public warehouse in each port where tobacco was imported to be kept by the King's officers and so the tobacco not to go out till the duty was paid, since the merchants could have no immediate occasion for it but if they had the full duty to be paid there. This broke up the committee . . . [so] that gentlemen might turn their thoughts to this.

Two years later he

> opened a fraud on the drawbacks upon malt . . . alleging that the drawbacks . . . amounted to £62,000 per annum for seven years last past, and that he thought £50,000 of that was clear gains to the county from whence exported, meaning Norfolk . . . but answered by Walpole there was frauds and would be, for it was impossible to prevent them.[2]

In 1726 he published a pamphlet entitled 'An Essay on the Public Debts,' to which a reply, 'A State of the National Debt', reputedly by William Pulteney (q.v.), was published the following year. His last recorded speech was made in February 1728 in reply to Pulteney's pamphlet, on which he observed that if he understood anything, it was numbers, and he dared pawn his credit and reputation to prove that author's calculations and inferences to be false and erroneous. He died six months later, 21 July 1728.

[1] See Gould to Walpole, 18 Apr. 1720, Cholmondeley (Houghton) mss. [2] *Knatchbull Diary*, 8 Feb. 1723, 25 Feb. 1725.

A.N.N.

GOULD, Nathaniel (c. 1697–1738), of Crosby Sq., London.

WAREHAM 12 Feb. 1729–1734

b. c. 1697, 2nd s. of John Gould of Woodford, Essex, and yr. bro. of John Gould (q.v.). *m.* Nov. 1734, Jane, da. of Humphrey Thayer of Hatton Garden, London, *s.p.*

Director, Bank of England 1722–37 (with statutory intervals), dep. gov. 1737–*d.*

Nathaniel Gould was returned at a by-election for Wareham where he was a stranger, consistently supporting the Administration. He was a member of Samuel Holden's (q.v.) dissenting deputies committee and one of the sub-committee of that body who approached Walpole in November 1732 and December 1734 to discuss the repeal of the

Test and Corporation Acts.[1] He lost his seat in 1734, did not stand again and died 30 Mar. 1738.

[1] N. C. Hunt, *Two Early Political Associations*, 134, 145, 169.

R.S.L.

GOUNTER NICOLL, Charles (1704–33), of Racton, Suss.

PETERBOROUGH 29 Jan. 1729–24 Nov. 1733

bap. 7 Oct. 1704, 1st s. of George Gounter of Racton by Judith, da. of Richard Nicoll of Norbiton Place, Surr. *educ.* New Coll. Oxf. 1722. *m.* Elizabeth, da. and h. of William Blundell of Basingstoke, Hants, 1da. *suc.* fa. 1718; K.B. 30 June 1732.

Gounter Nicoll, whose family had been at Racton since the fifteenth century, was the grandson of Col. George Gounter, who assisted the escape of Charles II from England after the battle of Worcester. He took the name of his mother, who became the eventual heir to the Nicoll estates.[1] On the death of the 2nd Earl Fitzwilliam, the Duke of Newcastle wrote to the new Earl's guardian, William Jessop (q.v.), recommending Nicoll, as

a gentleman of a very great estate in Sussex, and who will be, as I am assured, very steady in the interest, and is strongly recommended by the Earl of Scarbrough and Sir Robert Walpole to fill up the late Lord Fitzwilliam's vacancy in that borough. Sir Robert has, or will write to the Dean for that purpose . . . Mr. Banks [Joseph (*d.*1741), q.v.] is the chief person that has put Mr. Nicholl upon standing.[2]

Returned unopposed, in spite of having no connexion with Peterborough, he voted with the Government, who gave him a red ribbon in 1732. Soon after his death, 24 Nov. 1733, his widow prosecuted a news-writer for defaming him for accepting this honour, the cost of the prosecution being met from secret service funds.[3] In 1735 she, with £70,000, married Lord Lindsey, later 3rd Duke of Ancaster. His daughter, with £100,000, married the 2nd Earl of Dartmouth in 1755.

[1] PCC 8 Browning, 317 Price; *VCH Suss.* iv. 114–15. [2] T. Lawson-Tancred, *Recs. of a Yorks. Manor*, 277–8. [3] *CJ*, xxiv. 226.

R.R.S.

GOWER, *see* LEVESON GOWER

GRAEME, David (c.1676–1726), of Orchill and Rohalloch, Perth.

PERTHSHIRE 31 Dec. 1724–14 Mar. 1726

b. c.1676, 2nd s. of James Graeme of Orchill by Lilian, da. of Sir Laurence Oliphant of Gask, Perth. *educ.* Glasgow 1691. *unm.* *suc.* bro. 1712.

Graeme belonged to a cadet branch of the family of the dukes of Montrose, to the first of whom his brother was bailie. Returned as a Whig at a by-election in 1724 for Perthshire, in which the Duke of Montrose had an interest, he died 14 Mar. 1726, leaving debts contracted through the extravagant collection of books and silver.[1]

[1] Louisa Graeme, *Or and Sable*, 432 seq.

J.M.S.

GRAHAM, Lord George (1715–47), of Dundaff, Stirling.

STIRLINGSHIRE 1741–2 Jan. 1747

b. 26 Sept. 1715, 7th s. of James Graham, 1st Duke of Montrose [S], by Lady Christian Carnegie, da. of David, 3rd Earl of Northesk [S]. *unm.*
Midshipman R.N. 1730, lt. 1734, capt. 1740; gov. Newfoundland 1740–1.

Graham, a naval officer, was returned for Stirlingshire as an opposition Whig by his father in 1741. One of the group of Scotch Members known as the Duke of Argyll's gang,[1] he voted against the Administration on the Hanoverians in 1742 and 1744. In the spring of 1745 he opposed the court-martial of Admiral Mathews (q.v.), making a vigorous defence of the admiral in the House.[2] In June, he distinguished himself in a naval action off Ostend, for which he was commended to the Duke of Bedford, the first lord.[3] In the autumn, he was with Admiral Vernon (q.v.), cruising in the Downs against the threatened French invasion.[4] He was absent from the division on the Hanoverians in April 1746, when he was classed as a 'new ally'. He was then cruising off the north of Scotland, watching for French ships coming to rescue the Jacobites.[5] In October, his brother, the 2nd Duke of Montrose, came to fetch him at Bristol, where he had fallen ill.[6] He died at Bath, 2 Jan. 1747.

[1] John Drummond to Ld. Morton, 2 and 4 Dec. 1742, Morton mss, SRO. [2] Yorke's parl. jnl. *Parl Hist.* xiii. 1252, 1268. [3] Sandwich to Bedford, 27 June 1745, Bedford mss. [4] *Vernon Pprs.* (Navy Recs. Soc. xcix,) 471, 475. [5] *Bedford Corresp.* i. 103. [6] *HMC Astley*, 355.

E.C.

GRAHAM, John (d.1755), of Killearn, Stirling.

STIRLINGSHIRE 1722–1727

1st s. of John Graham of Killearn, M.P. [S] Stirlingshire 1703–7, by Catherine Dow. *suc.* fa. aft. 1722.

By 1715 Graham had succeeded his father as chamberlain, i.e. factor, to the Duke of Montrose, his 'near relation',[1] and as deputy-sheriff of Stirlingshire. During the rebellion Lord Mar wrote to him:

I cannot doubt of your good wishes to your rightful King and your oppressed country, and I know the interest you have with my Lord Montrose's men, friends and following; and now, in his absence, what can you do better for the service of all than being instrumental in getting them to join the King's [Pretender's] forces when we come into your neighbourhood . . . I have already sent an order to most of them in his Majesty's name for this effect, but your hearty concurrence and joining with them will, I know, very much forward it, and will be doing what is expected of one of your name and family.

Graham sent this letter to Montrose, who handed it to George I, and subsequently praised Graham's 'good service' to the Government against the rebels.[2] Like his father, he was closely involved in the feud between Montrose and Rob Roy Macgregor, the outlaw. In 1716, as deputy-sheriff of the county, he led a party of soldiers in an attempt to capture Rob Roy, missed him, and burnt down his house. On 21 Nov. of that year Montrose reported to Townshend:

> Mr. Graham of Killearn . . . having the charge of my Highland estate went to Monteith, which is a part of it, on Monday last, to bring in my rents, it being usual for him to be there for two or three nights together at this time of the year, in a country house, for the conveniency of meeting the tenants, upon that account. The same night, about 9 of the clock, Rob Roy, with a party of these ruffians whom he has still kept about him since the late rebellion, surrounded the house where Mr. Graham was with some of my tenants doing his business, ordered his men to present their guns in at the windows of the room where he was sitting, while he himself at the same time with others entered at the door, with cocked pistols, and made Mr. Graham prisoner, carrying him away to the hills with the money he had got, his books and papers, and my tenants' bonds for their fines, amounting to above a thousand pounds sterling, whereof the one-half had been paid last year, and the other was to have been paid now.

At the end of a week Graham was released unharmed, with his books and papers but without the money.[3] In the spring of 1717 he was sent by Montrose to see Rob Roy with 'sweet offers of life, liberty, and treasure' if he would 'bear false witness against . . . Argyll', Montrose's rival, by accusing him of Jacobite intrigues. Rob Roy refused, published the details of the transaction in a letter, and placed himself under Argyll's protection.[4]

In 1722 Graham was returned for Stirlingshire on the Montrose interest, defeating a candidate backed by Argyll, but in 1727 he was defeated by Henry Cunningham, Ilay's most experienced boroughmonger. He died c.1775, when his will was proved.[5]

[1] Scott's *Rob Roy*, ed. A. Lang, 584. [2] *HMC 3rd Rep.* 379, 381–2. [3] *Rob Roy*, pp. cii–iii, cvii. [4] Hamilton Howlett, *Highland Constable*, 213, 226. [5] Indices to services of heirs, Perthshire.

E.C.

GRAHME, James (1650–1730), of Levens, Westmld.

CARLISLE	1685–1687
APPLEBY	1702–1708
WESTMORLAND	1708–1727

b. Mar. 1650, 2nd s. of Sir George Grahme or Graham, 2nd Bt., of Netherby, Cumb. by Lady Mary Johnston, da. of James, 1st Earl of Hartfell [S]; bro. of Richard Graham, M.P., 1st Visct. Preston [S]. *educ.* Westminster; Ch. Ch. Oxf. 1666. *m.* (1) lic 22 Nov. 1675, Dorothy (*d.* 1700), maid of honour, da. of Hon. William Howard, s. of Thomas, 1st Earl of Berkshire, 3s. *d.v.p.* 2da.; (2) lic. 4 Mar. 1702, Elizabeth, da. of Isaac Barton, merchant, of All Hallows, Barking, wid. of George Bromley of the Middle Temple, *s.p.*

Capt in the French service 1671; capt. Earl of Carlisle's regt. of Ft. 1673, Duke of York's regt. of Ft. Jan. 1675, and Coldstream Gds. Oct. 1675; lt.-col. Lord Morpeth's regt. of Ft. 1678–9.

Keeper of the privy purse to the Duchess of York c.1677 and to the Duke of York c.1680; keeper of Pirbright Walk within Windsor forest 1680; ranger and keeper of Bagshot Park within Windsor forest 1682–9; master of the buckhounds and keeper of the privy purse 1685–9; dep. lt. of Windsor castle and forest 1685–9; mayor of Appleby 1717.

A younger brother of the Jacobite leader and conspirator, Lord Preston, Grahme took the oath of allegiance in 1690.[1] In the next reign he was returned for Appleby, subsequently succeeding his brother, Henry, as knight of the shire for Westmorland, where he had bought the estate of Levens from the Bellinghams in 1687, laying out gardens still famous for their topiary work. Classed in 1715 as a Tory who might often vote with the Whigs, he did so on the septennial bill in 1716, making the following short speech:

> Sir, it will be a surprise to some gentlemen, whom I have hitherto had the happiness of agreeing with, to see me disagree with them at present and I am heartily sorry there should be any necessity for it. But two things, I hope, will be my excuse as they are my comfort; I really in my conscience think this bill a good and necessary bill and in the next place that, whatever they think of it now, they themselves will enjoy the advantages of it hereafter; so I am sincerely for it.[2]

He spoke and voted against the repeal of the Occasional Conformity and Schism Acts in 1719, also voting against the peerage bill, though classed as for it by Sunderland to whom he seems to have attached himself.[3] In 1720 he was one of the Members who accepted stock from the South Sea Company—in his case £2,000 at 280 on 22 Mar.—without paying for it, with the right to 'sell' it back to the Company if the price rose, taking the difference as 'profit'.[4] Re-elected unopposed as a Whig in 1722, he was one of the deputy-lieutenants ordered to search the houses of

Roman Catholics and non-jurors for arms during the Atterbury plot.[5] He did not stand in 1727. He died 26 Jan. 1730, leaving his estates to his only surviving child, a daughter, who married Henry Bowes, 4th Earl of Berkshire and later 11th Earl of Suffolk. He was supposed to have been the father of James II's putative daughter Catherine, Duchess of Buckingham, by Catherine Sedley.[6]

[1] J. Bagot, *Col. James Grahme*, 30. [2] A. Corbière to Horace Walpole, 27 Apr. 1716, Cholmondeley (Houghton) mss. [3] Bagot, 31–32. [4] *CJ*, xix. 569. [5] Bagot, 33. [6] Walpole to Mann, 14 Mar. 1743.

R.R.S.

GRANARD, Earl of, *see* FORBES, George

GRANBY, Mq. of, *see* MANNERS, John (*b*.1696), *and* MANNERS, John (*b*.1721)

GRANT, Alexander (c.1674–1719), of Grant, Elgin.

SCOTLAND 1707–1708
INVERNESS-SHIRE 1708–1710
ELGINSHIRE 1710–19 Aug. 1719

b. c. 1674, 1st surv. s. of Ludovick Grant of Freuchie and Grant, M.P. [S], by his 1st w. Janet. da. and h. of Alexander Brodie of Lethen, Nairn; e. bro. of Sir James Grant (q.v.). *educ*. ?Utrecht. *m*. (1) 3 Dec. 1698, Elizabeth (*d*. 22 Apr. 1708), da. of James Stuart, Lord Doune, 1st s. of Alexander, 5th Earl of Moray [S], *s.p.*; (2) contract 7 Apr. 1709, Anne, maid of honour to Queen Anne, da. of John Smith (q.v.), Speaker of the House of Commons 1705–8, *s.p. suc*. fa. 1716.

M.P. [S] Inverness-shire 1703–7.

Commr. of justiciary for northern counties 1702; sheriff, Inverness 1703–17; P.C.[S] 1706; commr. for the union of Scotland with England 1706; ld. lt. Inverness, Banff and Elgin 1715–17.

Col. of a regt. of Ft. [S] 1706, transferred to English establishment Dec. 1707; brig.-gen. 1711; half-pay 1713; gov. Sheerness 1715–17; col. of a new regt. of Ft. 1715–17.

Grant was the head of the leading family of Elginshire, for which he sat as a Whig from 1710 till his death. During the Fifteen rebellion he was active in raising his clan in support of the Government, promising them ample compensation for any losses, which in fact was not forthcoming.[1] Politically he followed the Duke of Argyll, promoting their joint electoral influence by marrying his sister to Lord Lovat in 1716, an alliance described by Argyll's brother, Lord Ilay, as 'a measure settled for the better uniting our interest in the north'. He voted with the Government on the septennial bill but against them on the motion censuring Argyll's rival, Cadogan (q.v.), on 4 June 1717, for which he was dismissed from his military governorship, his

regiment also being disbanded.[2] Later that year he was reported as being 'under the care of the physician of Bedlam and in iron cuffs', railing against Cadogan.[3] He died 19 Aug. 1719.

[1] Sir W. Fraser, *Chiefs of Grant*, i. 358–9; I. F. Grant, *The Grant Clan*, 20–21; *More Culloden Pprs*. ii. 167. [2] *Chiefs of Grant*, i. 352; ii. 34; Sunderland (Blenheim) mss D. II, 16. [3] *HMC Portland*, v. 538.

J.M.S.

GRANT, Archibald (1696–1778), of Monymusk, Aberdeen.

ABERDEENSHIRE 1722–5 May 1732

b. 25 Sept. 1696, 1st s. of Sir Francis Grant, 1st Bt., of Cullen of Buchan, Banff, Lord Cullen, S.C.J., by his 1st w. Jean, da. of Rev. William Meldrum of Meldrum, Aberdeen; bro. of William Grant (q.v.). *educ*. adv. 1714; L. Inn 1725. *m*. (1) 17 Apr. 1717, Anne, da. of James Hamilton of Pencaitland, E. Lothian, 2da.; (2) c.1731, Anne (*d*. bef. 1744), da. of Charles Potts of Castleton, Derbys. 1s.; (3) 18 Aug. 1751, Elizabeth Clark (*d*. 30 Apr. 1759), wid. of Dr. James Callander of Jamaica, *s.p.*; (4) 24 May 1770, Jane, wid. of Andrew Millar of Pall Mall, publisher and bookseller, *s.p. suc*. fa. as 2nd Bt. Mar. 1726.

Keeper of register of hornings 1749–*d*.

Soon after entering Parliament, Grant, who after 1727 voted with the Opposition, became heavily indebted to his stockbroker, George Robinson (q.v.), for losses on dealings in the shares of the York Buildings Company. Being unable to pay his debts, he entered in 1727 into a partnership with Robinson and three others to speculate with the funds of the Charitable Corporation, founded 'for relief of industrious poor by assisting them with small sums upon pledges at legal interest', of which he was a director. By the end of 1731 they had lost the whole of the Corporation's capital, leaving it insolvent with net liabilities of over £450,000.[1]

When exposure had become inevitable, Grant arranged for Robinson to abscond, together with the chief warehouse keeper, Thomson, who had been responsible for issuing the Corporation's money to Robinson for his operations. Their disappearance, together with that of the Corporation's books and accounts, having frustrated an inquiry by the Corporation, the House of Commons, on a petition from the shareholders, appointed a select committee to investigate the affair. On this Grant's two remaining partners disappeared, he himself being taken into custody by the serjeant at arms to prevent him from following suit. On being examined by the committee he denied all knowledge of the defalcations, attempting to throw the blame on his associates. Nevertheless the committee uncovered enough evidence to indict him in the House of Commons on 20 charges of wilful fraud and neglect.

When the case came before the Commons, 5 May 1732,

> so many ladies said to be undone by the managers of the Charitable Corporation induced the Speaker to indulge ladies to be present in the gallery, and witnesses of the justice the Parliament are doing on those vile persons.

Speaking from his place, Grant pleaded guilty to

> most intolerable neglect, but denied he was participant in any fraud, which he pretended was manifest by being himself undone by the bad management of others in the direction, who had stripped him of his fortune as well as the unhappy proprietors.
>
> After a tedious but insufficient defence, he concluded with tears in his eyes that he cast himself on the compassion of the House, and calling God to witness that he had no corrupt intentions, declared his only comfort was that the time was coming when he should clear his innocency to all the world.

On his withdrawal a motion was carried without a dissentient declaring him to have been

> guilty of having been concerned in co-partnerships in which the cash of the . . . Corporation has been employed, and great sums lost and embezzled, and of having been principally concerned in promoting, abetting, and carrying on, many other indirect and fraudulent practices in the management of the affairs of the . . . Corporation.

Expelled from the House, he was prohibited by legislation from leaving the country and from alienating his estates for a year, so that his property might be available to make a just satisfaction to his victims. Next year, further conclusive evidence of his guilt having been provided by the confession of Thomson, the House decided that he should be prosecuted by the attorney-general. A clause continuing the sequestration of his estates was added to a bill for the relief of the Corporation, but was deleted by the House of Lords after hearing counsel representing Grant.[2]

After protracted litigation Grant succeeded in preserving his property, the court holding that Thomson was not a competent witness against his partners.[3] He spent the rest of his long life improving his estate at Monymusk, where he is said to have planted over fifty million trees,[4] and mending his shattered fortune by marrying rich widows. In 1744 the 1st Lord Egmont met him at Buxton paying unsuccessful court to a lady who had gone there 'to be cured of frenzy'.[5] At the general election of 1747 he stood for Aberdeenshire but gave up on learning that the Duke of Argyll was supporting a Pelham candidate. Hearing that Newcastle was proposing to make Grant sheriff of Aberdeenshire as a consolation for not being returned for the county, Argyll wrote to Pelham: 'This requires great consideration, for the blot in his reputation

takes place here as well as in England'.[6] He was not appointed sheriff, but in 1749 he obtained a sinecure, presumably by the influence of his brother, William Grant (q.v.), lord advocate. Two years later he married his third wife, a widow with £30,000. Of his fourth marriage to another widow in 1770 David Hume wrote:

> It will be a curious experiment, whether his sly flattery or her tenacious avarice will get the better . . . I took occasion to mention to her Sir Archibald's extensive and noble plantations; but she told me, that she thought planting was his folly, and that people ought to take care, lest their concern for posterity should hurt themselves. Thus she will check the poor man in the only laudable thing he has ever done.[7]

He died 17 Sept. 1778.

[1] D. Murray, *York Buildings Co.* 69 seq.; *Reports of Committee of the House of Commons on the Charitable Corporation*, 1732 and 1733, passim. [2] *CJ*, xxi. 852, 915; *HMC Egmont Diary*, i. 268–9; *LJ*, xxiv. 307, 309. [3] Add. 35876, f. 210. [4] Boswell's *Johnson*, iii. 486–7. [5] *HMC Egmont Diary*, iii. 297. [6] 12 Aug., Newcastle (Clumber) mss. [7] *Letters of David Hume*, ed. Greig, ii. 225–6.

R.R.S.

GRANT, Sir James, 6th Bt. (1679–1747), of Grant, Elgin.

INVERNESS-SHIRE   1722–1741
ELGIN BURGHS   1741–16 Jan. 1747

b. 28 July 1679, 3rd but 2nd surv. s. of Ludovick Grant of Freuchie and Grant, M.P. [S], and yr. bro. of Alexander Grant (q.v.). *educ.* Elgin. *m.* 29 Jan. 1702, Anne, da. and h. of Sir Humphrey Colquhoun, 5th Bt., of Luss, Dunbarton, 6s. 8da. *suc.* fa.-in-law as 6th Bt. 1718, and bro. Alexander 1719.

James Grant became heir of entail to his father-in-law's estate and baronetcy by a patent executed in 1704. In 1708, upon succeeding to the baronetcy, he became, in accordance with the patent, Sir James Colquhoun of Luss. But in the following year, when he succeeded to the Grant estates, the Colquhoun inheritance passed by the entail to his second son Ludovick (q.v.), whereupon he reverted to his family name of Grant, retaining the title of baronet.

For nearly 20 years Grant was returned for Inverness-shire, on his family's interest, consistently voting with the Administration. His only reported speech was made on 5 May 1732, asking for leniency for his relative, Sir Archibald Grant (q.v.).[1] Described in 1734 as the 'hereditary commoner of Inverness-shire', he denied an allegation that he was 'enslaving the shire' by creating voters, observing: 'I always rely entirely on the gentlemen of the shire for their help and assistance'.[2] In a list of placemen who voted for the Spanish convention in 1739 he is shown as enjoying 'a grant of duties in Scotland', his eldest son, 'a commissioner of police, his second son captain in the army and his brother captain of an independent company'.[3] In 1741, having made over his estates to his son, Ludovick, subject to the payment to him of an allowance of £600 p.a.,[4] he transferred to Elgin Burghs, continuing to vote with the Government. During the 1745 rebellion he remained in London, advising his son 'to stay at home, take care of his country and join no party'. He sent two memorials to Henry Pelham (q.v.), advising the formation of an army on a clan basis from among the loyal clans, and forwarded a letter from the Young Pretender unopened to Lord Tweeddale, the secretary of state for Scotland.[5]

He died in London 16 Jan. 1747.

[1] *HMC Egmont Diary*, i. 269. [2] Sir W. Fraser, *Chiefs of Grant*, i. 378; *Culloden Pprs.* 133-4. [3] *Gent. Mag.* 1739, p. 305. [4] Sir James Grant to Ludovick Grant, 8 Jan. 1736, Seafield Coll. box 48, SRO. [5] *Scots Peerage*, vii. 484; *Chiefs of Grant*, i. 387, 389.

J.M.S.

GRANT, Ludovick (1707–73), of Castle Grant, Elgin.

ELGINSHIRE   1741–1761

b. 13 Jan. 1707, 2nd s. of Sir James Grant, 6th Bt. (q.v.). *educ.* St. Andrews and Edinburgh Univs.; *adv.* 1728. *m.* (1) 6 July 1727, Marion (*d.* 17 Jan 1735), da. of Sir Hew Dalrymple, 1st Bt., of North Berwick, ld. pres. of court of session, 1da.; (2) 31 Oct. 1735, Lady Margaret Ogilvie, da. of James, 5th Earl of Findlater [S], 1s. 7da. *suc.* mother as chief of Colquhoun 1724, and fa. as 7th Bt. 16 Jan. 1747.

Commr. of police [S] Dec. 1737–Apr. 1741.

From 1719 Grant was known as Ludovick or Lewis Colquhoun, laird of Luss, which he inherited when his father, on becoming chief of Grant, was obliged, under the terms of an entail prohibiting the merger of Luss and Grant, to transfer the Colquhoun estates to his second son.[1] While a law student at Edinburgh in 1727, he gave up his intention of standing for Glasgow Burghs after his first marriage, which connected him with a family opposed in politics to Lord Ilay, Walpole's election manager for Scotland. Anxious to placate Ilay, who repeatedly thwarted his hopes of legal preferment, he offered the Campbells his Dunbartonshire interest at the 1734 election, during which, although permanently lamed by a riding accident, he campaigned for Ilay's candidates in the northern counties and burghs. He himself thought of standing for Elginshire but withdrew. On the death of his elder brother in 1732, he became heir to the Grant estates, which his father made over to him in 1735, whereupon he reverted to the name of Grant. His efforts to retain possession of Luss failed when in 1737 the court of session decided the succession in favour of his next brother, James.[2]

Grant's chief object was a seat on the Scotch bench. When, despite his father's appeals to the ministry, this was denied him, his uncle Lord Lovat wrote to Ilay, 21 Jan. 1737:

> I . . . beg that your Lordship may seriously consider what a loss it must be to your Lordship's interest, and what a vast mortification . . . to us all, his relations and friends, if he is disappointed of this gown, since he was a candidate for the two last ones that were disposed of, and that the objection of his having been married to the President's daughter is now entirely out of doors, since she is dead and that he is now married to the Earl of Findlater's daughter, and that the Earl is a friend of your Lordship and to the Administration . . . By preferring him now he will be of vast value to your Lordship both in town and country for he is a man of mettle, forwardness and activity.

Again unsuccessful, he left the bar in disgust, retiring to his estates to devote himself to paying off the debts incurred by his family in government service at the Revolution and in the Fifteen. He wrote to his father, 21 July 1737:

> Observing that former services seem rather to be a drawback upon us in place of recommending us to the favour of the present ministry, I think it highly prudent to live retired . . . Let us never be so ill treated . . . no disappointment shall ever alter my zeal for the present family on the throne, although I shall not regret to see some change of our Scots ministers, if they behave to us no better than they have done.[3]

Unwilling to lose the Grant interest, Ilay at the end of 1737 secured the appointment of Grant to a place worth £400 p.a., which he retained until 1741 when, shortly before standing for Elginshire, he relinquished it to a kinsman, who held it for his benefit until 1761.[4]

Returned for Elginshire after a protracted election campaign, Grant consistently voted with the Administration, but before long was again at odds with Ilay, now Duke of Argyll. At the outbreak of the Forty-five he was ready to abandon a parliamentary career if appointed baron of the court of Exchequer of Scotland, but was warned by his brother-in-law, Lord Deskford, that he must tactfully apply to Argyll in the hope that past differences 'would now be forgot'. 'Making your application at the same time that you profess your zeal appears like making that a condition of the other service'. During the rebellion he gave no assistance to Sir John Cope (q.v.). He reluctantly raised one independent company but did little to prevent his tenants from joining the rebels, declining to raise his clan unless they were paid. Abandoning Castle Grant at the approach of the Highland army, with whom, in his absence, his subordinates made a pact of neutrality, he did not take the field until after Culloden, when he induced his rebel tenants to surrender at discretion, but did little to mitigate the severity of their treatment. Some of the prisoners, indeed, claimed that he had had them arrested for 'his sordid ends', because they were his creditors: 'as Mr. Grant likes money very well, this is a very easy method of paying his debt.'

Criticized by both Whig and Tory, Grant went to London to present a long statement to the Government in justification of his conduct.[5] His arguments were unsuccessful, for at the general election Argyll, at the instance of the Pelhams, foiled his scheme to recover Inverness-shire for the Grants.[6] The 2nd Lord Egmont records in his electoral survey, c.1749–50, 'Sir Ludovick Grant will sooner be with us [Leicester House] than with them [the Pelhams], though with them too.' Retiring from Parliament in 1761 after George III's accession, he died 18 Mar. 1773.

[1] Sir W. Fraser, *Chiefs of Grant*, iii. 487–91; *Chiefs of Colquhoun*, i. 308–13. [2] *Chiefs of Grant*, ii. 112–13, 299–300, 304, 323, 421–2; *Chiefs of Colquhoun*, i. 344, 346–7. [3] *Chiefs of Grant*, ii. 125–6, 135–6, 346. [4] Ibid. 213, 363; *Cal. Treas. Bks. and Pprs. 1739–41*, pp. 141, 145; 1742–5, pp. 159, 162, 180. [5] *Chiefs of Grant*, ii. 146–268; *Origins of the '45* (Sc. Hist. Soc. ser. 2), ii. 269–309, 313–32; *More Culloden Pprs.* iii–v, passim; W. Mackay, *Urquhart and Glenmoriston*. [6] See INVERNESS-SHIRE.

E.H.-G.

GRANT, William (1701–64), of Prestongrange, Haddington.

ELGIN BURGHS   18 Feb. 1747–Nov. 1754

bap. 4 May 1701, 2nd s. of Sir Francis Grant, 1st Bt., of Cullen of Buchan, Banff, and bro. of Archibald Grant of Monymusk (q.v.). *educ.* Edinburgh Univ.; M. Temple 1721; adv. 1722. *m.* Grizell, da. and h. of Rev. John Miller of Neilston, Renfrew, 4da.
Procurator for Church of Scotland and principal clerk of assembly 1731–46; solicitor-gen. [S] 1737–42; commr. for fisheries and manufactures [S] 1738; ld. adv. Feb. 1746–Aug. 1754; ld. of session, Lord Prestongrange, 1754–*d.*; commr. for annexed estates 1754.

William Grant, 'a lawyer in great practice'[1] was appointed solicitor-general for Scotland in succession to Charles Areskine (q.v.), promoted lord advocate in 1737. Dismissed with Areskine when Lord Ilay, Walpole's minister for Scotland, was replaced by Lord Tweeddale in 1742, he was made lord advocate *vice* Robert Craigie (q.v.) on the return of Ilay, now Duke of Argyll, to power in February 1746. Taking his seat a year later for Elgin Burghs, vacated by the death of his kinsman, Sir James Grant, he came to London for consultations on the bill to abolish hereditary jurisdictions in March 1747. He made his first important speech on the introduction of the bill, 7 Apr. 1747, when the Duke of Argyll, with whom the ministry 'had concerted every clause

of the bill, . . . left them in the lurch, all his friends being either absent or voting against the bill'. Grant's speech was described as 'like his situation, every other sentence against the bill, and you will easily imagine how clear he was;' but on the second reading, presumably after Argyll had made it clear that he was not against the bill, he is described as speaking extremely well for it. At a later stage he proposed that the new sheriff provided for by the bill should be appointed by

the great seal, saying it would cost only £30 a piece more, a job of about a thousand pounds to [the Duke of Argyll as keeper of the great seal]. This raised a universal murmur and calling out, 'why that'. Sir W. Yonge got up and spoke against it and so the job was lost.[2]

During the general election of 1747 Grant is said to have used his office to bring pressure on the master of Lovat, then a prisoner in Edinburgh castle for his part in the Forty-five, to give the Fraser interest in Inverness-shire to a Grant candidate, but was foiled by Argyll at the instance of Henry Pelham (see Inverness-shire). Argyll also intervened against Grant's attempt to bring his disreputable brother, Sir Archibald Grant (q.v.), into Parliament for Aberdeenshire against Andrew Mitchell (q.v.), a Pelham candidate. 'He was so much out of humour', Argyll wrote to Pelham, 12 Aug, 1747,

at my opposing his brother . . . that he used this expression to a relation of mine: 'I cannot imagine what the Duke of Argyll means by declaring for Mr. Mitchell,' upon which I bid my friend tell him that I did it at the desire of those who made him King's advocate [the Pelhams].[3]

In the next Parliament Grant defended, 21 Apr. 1749, a payment of £19,000 to Glasgow in compensation for losses incurred in the late rebellion by that city, of whose corporation Argyll was the patron. On 28 Feb. 1752 he introduced a bill for annexing to the Crown estates forfeited in the late rebellion, paying off the encumbrances and devoting the rents to the welfare of the Highlands. Soon after the passing of the Act the murder of one of the crown factors appointed to manage the forfeited estates led to the well-known Appin murder trial, in which Grant acted as prosecutor.[4]

In 1753 Robert Dundas (q.v.), lord president of the court of session, writing to Lord Hardwicke about the shortcomings of the law officers for Scotland, referred to Grant as one who, being 'well employed in private business, loves his money better than public business'.[5] Raised to the bench next year, he died 23 May 1764.

[1] Ramsay of Ochtertyre, *Scotland and Scotsmen in 18th Cent.* i. 121. [2] *HMC Laing*, ii. 386–8; *Culloden Pprs.* 476; *HMC Polwarth*

v. 235, 243; Walpole to Conway, 16 Apr. 1747. ³ Duncan Forbes and Argyll to Pelham, 5, 12 Aug. 1747, Newcastle (Clumber) mss. ⁴ Sir J. Fergusson, *White Hind*, 133 et seq. ⁵ Yorke, *Hardwicke*, i. 621–2.

R.R.S.

GRANTHAM, Richard (*d*.1723), of Goltho Hall, Lincs.

LINCOLN 1710–1713, 1715–1722

1st surv. s. of Vincent Grantham of Goltho by Margaret, da. of Sir Richard Fanshaw of Ware Park, Herts. *educ.* ?Eton 1690. *m.* Elizabeth, *s.p.* Commr. for forfeited estates 1716–*d.*

Grantham, whose family had been seated at Goltho since the 16th century, was returned as a Whig on his own interest for Lincoln in 1715. Heading the ballot of the House of Commons on the appointment of commissioners for the sale of estates forfeited in the late rebellion, at salaries of £1,000 a year, he voted with the Government in every recorded division. In 1719 the Treasury were informed by his colleagues that he and another commissioner, Sir Richard Steele (q.v.), had been absent from duty for two years, which had been 'a great hindrance to the business of the commission and a considerable detriment to the country'. Next year he was similarly reported to the Treasury as having on two occasions been absent for over three weeks without permission, thereby incurring a penalty of £500, which was to be stopped out of his salary.¹ An undated list of payments in the Sunderland papers contains the entry: 'à my Lord Chancellor pour Mons. Grantham £400.'² Defeated at Lincoln in 1722, he died 28 Jan. 1723.

¹ *Cal. Treas. Pprs.* 1714–19, p. 475; 1720–8, p. 23. ² Sunderland (Blenheim) mss. D.II, 4.

P.W.

GRAY, Charles (1696–1782), of Holly Trees, Colchester.

COLCHESTER 26 Feb. 1742–13 Mar. 1755
1761–1780

bap. 20 Sept. 1696, s. of George Gray, alderman of Colchester, by his w. Elizabeth. *educ.* Colchester g.s. 1702; G. Inn 1724, called 1729, bencher 1737. *m.* (1) 1726, Sarah (*d.* 6 June 1751), da. of John Webster, wid. of Ralph, o. surv. s. of Sir Ralph Creffield of Colchester, 2da. *d.v.p.*; (2) 1755, Mary, da. of Randle Wilbraham (q.v.), *s.p.* Alderman, Colchester, 1734; recorder, Ipswich 1761–76; trustee of British Museum.

The son of a prosperous Colchester glazier, Gray acquired by marriage a substantial estate in Colchester, together with Colchester castle; practised successfully as a barrister, becoming the steward of many local manors; and in 1741 stood for Colchester as a Tory against the interest of the Whig corporation. Returned on petition by the anti-Walpole majority of the House of Commons, he instituted legal proceedings against the corporation, which led to its dissolution. His father, a member of the dissolved corporation, voted against him in 1741 and again in 1747, when he died, cutting him out of his will.¹

At this stage of his career Gray seems to have belonged to the extreme wing of the Tory party. In 1743 a French agent, who had been sent over to concert with the English Jacobites plans for a French landing at Maldon in Essex in support of the Pretender early in 1744, reported that he had been informed by Jacobite leaders

ces deux villes de Colchester et Maldon étoient zélées pour leur légitime Roi, et que les Srs. Gray et Savill [Samuel Savill, q.v.], qui résidoient ordinairement dans celle de Colchester étoient d'une fidélité reconnue.²

After the failure of the Forty-five, he was one of the Tories who favoured an alliance with the Prince of Wales's party, writing to the 2nd Lord Egmont in 1749:

It was a glorious expression of your Lordship's that you wanted to regenerate this country, and I most earnestly entreat you not to give over the attempt as impracticable or impossible. The court flood has overspread a great part of the land, but very far from all. There are so many knees left which have not yet nor ever will bow down to Baal, that our state is not to be despaired of . . .

Let but some constitutional terms be first fixed, and let it be a solemn stipulation, that no one concerned shall accept any employment till they are obtained and enacted; I could almost answer for it with my life that success would inevitably follow. What these terms should be is the next question. For my own part it appears to me that the very root of corruption should be struck at, by enabling freeholders of a certain value to vote jointly with the burghers in every corporation in the country. The terms set down sometime ago at Leicester House were extremely good, to which it would rejoice me to see added a bill to take away all informations *ex officio* at the suit of the attorney-general; for this is a way of proceeding very consonant to an inquisition or a star chamber, but quite repugnant to the rest of our constitution.

Any rational terms may certainly be obtained, and beyond, will not be desired by the bulk of disinterested country gentlemen whose views square best with the public good.³

In the 2nd Lord Egmont's electoral survey about this time, Gray is described as

a Tory of tolerable sense, but rather too full of strange reformations, however, I believe I can do a great deal with him.

His reforming zeal is shown by a letter to an Essex friend, 17 Feb. 1750:

Last night was one of the mortifying sort. The constitutional, humane and prudent bill brought in by Mr. Thomas Pitt, to enable the soldiers to demand their discharge after 10 years service upon giving 3 months notice to their officer and paying him £3 for a new recruit, was thrown out at the 3rd reading upon a division 154 against 92. The debate was a very good one and lasted till between 9 and 10 last night. This bill will be offered again next session and so from session to session till sooner or later we get it to pass: and I don't at all despair but that this good time may come.[4]

In 1751 he published a pamphlet entitled *Considerations on Several Proposals lately made for the Better Maintenance of the Poor*, exhorting country gentlemen to interest themselves in the administration of the poor law, which he strongly criticized, and to belie 'the Dutch reproach, that a gentleman and an idleman are synonymous terms'.

Apart from Gray's reforming and humanitarian activities, he was a Hebrew and classical scholar, a numismatist, and an archaeologist, who was responsible for the preservation of Colchester castle. On 19 Mar. 1753 he spoke in support of the bill setting up the British Museum, of which he became an original trustee.[5]

He died 12 Dec. 1782.

[1] L. C. Sier, 'The Ancestry of Charles Gray, M.P.', *Essex Rev.* lxi, 94–96; 'Charles Gray, M.P., of Colchester', ibid. lvii. 18. [2] AEM & D Angl. 82, ff. 149–57. See also BARRY, James. [3] Add. 46577, bdle. 11. [4] Add. 37222, f. 60. [5] *HMC 14th Rep. IX*, 291; J. H. Round, *Hist. Colchester Castle*; Nichols, *Lit. Anecs.* ix. 604; Add. 37222, ff. 91–92.

E.C.

GRAY, Robert.

HINDON   1722–1727

?s. of Elizabeth and bro. of Henry Gray. *m.* Mary, da. of Robert Clayton, *s.p.*

Robert Gray, whose identity has not been determined, was put down by Sunderland in 1721 for the venal borough of Hindon, where he was returned unopposed. No votes of his have been recorded nor did he stand again. He was, however, at Hindon during the 1727 election, after which he gave evidence before the elections committee on behalf of the unsuccessful candidates, George and Henry Fox (qq.v.).[1] A Robert Gray of St. Martin-in-the-Fields, who went out to India in 1730 as factor for the East India Company, died September 1730 at Fort St. George.[2]

[1] *CJ*, xxi. 132. [2] PCC 153 Isham, 122 Ducie; *Gent. Mag.* 1731, p. 266.

R.S.L.

GREATHEAD, Samuel (?1710–65), of Guy's Cliffe, Warws.

COVENTRY   28 Dec. 1747–1761

b. ?1710, 1st surv. s. of John Greathead of St. Mary

Cayon, St. Kitts by his w. Frances. *educ.* Bradford sch.; Trinity, Camb. 4 May 1730, aged 19; L. Inn 1730. *m.* (2) 21 Feb. 1748, Lady Mary Bertie, da. of Peregrine Bertie, M.P., 2nd Duke of Ancaster, 2s.

In 1747 Samuel Greathead (or Greatheed), a wealthy West Indian who had settled near Warwick, was returned for Coventry as a government supporter on the interest of Lord Archer (q.v.). In 1753 he fell foul of Archer, who accused him of attempting to undermine him at Coventry, 'and also to disturb the Whig interest at Warwick, upon which Lord Hillsborough and my brother are chosen'. Through Pelham's mediation, a reconciliation was brought about,[1] as a result of which Greathead headed the poll at Coventry in 1754. He died 2 Aug. 1765.

[1] Ld. Archer to Pelham, 11 June, Greathead to Pelham, 6 Aug. 1753, Newcastle (Clumber) mss.

E.C.

GREGORY, George (1670–1746), of Nottingham.

NOTTINGHAM   29 Jan.–10 June 1701, 1702–1705, 1715–1727
BOROUGHBRIDGE   1727–Apr. 1746

bap. 2 Feb. 1670, 1st s. of George Gregory of Nottingham by Susanna, da. of Martin Lister of Thorpe Arnold, Leics. *educ.* Nottingham (Mr. Cudworth); St. John's, Camb. 1688. *m.* by 1694, Susanna, da. of William Williams of Rempstone Hall, Notts., 2s. *suc.* fa. 1688.

Sheriff, Notts. 1694; commr. for forfeited estates 1716–25; storekeeper of the Ordnance 1722–*d.*

Gregory came of one of the leading families of Nottingham, which he represented as a Whig, with the support of successive Dukes of Newcastle. Obtaining a place after George I's accession, he voted with the Government in all recorded divisions, except on the repeal of the Occasional Conformity and Schism Acts in 1719, when he was absent. In 1727 he reluctantly stood down to facilitate a compromise and was returned by the Duke of Newcastle for Boroughbridge, a proposal to bring him in for Retford having fallen through owing to local opposition.[1] He never again represented Nottingham, where his vote for the excise bill made him unpopular,[2] but continued to correspond with Newcastle about Nottinghamshire affairs.

He was buried at St. Mary's, Nottingham, 10 Apr. 1746.

[1] Geo. Gregory to St. Andrew Thornhaugh, 18 July, Sir Robt. Sutton to Wm. Levinz, 11 Aug. 1727, Foljambe mss. [2] John Plumptre to Newcastle, 21 July 1733, Add. 32688, f. 30.

R.R.S.

GRENVILLE, George (1712–70).

BUCKINGHAM   1741–13 Nov. 1770

b. 14 Oct. 1712, 2nd s. of Richard Grenville of Wotton and bro. of James, Richard and Thomas Grenville (qq.v.). *educ.* Eton 1725–8; Ch. Ch. Oxf. 1730; I. Temple 1729, called 1735, bencher 1763; L. Inn 1734. *m.* May 1749, Elizabeth, da. of Sir William Wyndham, 3rd Bt. (q.v.), 4s. 5da.

Ld. of Admiralty 1744–7; ld. of Treasury 1747–54; treasurer of the navy Mar. 1754–20 Nov. 1755, Nov. 1756–9 Apr. 1757, June 1757–May 1762; P.C. 21 June 1754; sec. of state 28 May–14 Oct. 1762; 1st ld. of Admiralty Oct. 1762–Apr. 1763; 1st ld. of Treasury and chancellor of the Exchequer 15 Apr. 1763–10 July 1765.

George Grenville was brought into Parliament by his uncle, Lord Cobham. Like his elder brother, Richard, he was a member of the political group known as 'Cobham's Cubs'. Making his first reported speech in support of Pulteney's motion for a secret committee to inquire into the conduct of the war, 21 Jan. 1742, he was one of the opposition Members elected by the Commons to a commission of seven appointed to inquire into the public accounts at £1,000 a year each under a bill which was thrown out by the Lords.[1] In the next session he spoke against the Hanoverians, 10 Dec. 1742. One of the signatories of the opposition whip of 10 Nov. 1743,[2] he spoke on the address against the retention of the Hanoverians in British pay, 6 Dec. 1743; introduced a motion against the continental war, 15 Dec.; spoke against the vote for the British forces in Flanders, 11 Jan. 1744; opposed the suspension of the Habeas Corpus Act during the crisis caused by a threatened French invasion, 28 Feb.; attacked an extraordinary payment to the Queen of Hungary, 13 Mar.; and supported a vote of censure, 10 Apr. When the opposition leaders came to terms with the Pelhams at the end of 1744, he obtained a seat on the Admiralty board, which did not prevent him, in his own words, from engaging with Pitt 'in opposing the measures of Government' during the Forty-five rebellion. Going out with the Pelhams in February 1746, he was so aggrieved at being passed over for promotion on their return to office that he tendered his resignation to Pelham, who persuaded him to withdraw it on the understanding that he should be 'the next to go into the Treasury'. The promise was carried out next year, but he was again aggrieved at not succeeding to the post of treasurer of the navy, vacated by Dodington's (q.v.) resignation in 1749. Though externally a docile member of the Cobham group, his 'narrative' shows him to have been seething with suppressed grievances against its other members, especially Pitt, of whom he writes:

> During all this time I still continued giving my support to Mr. Pitt, notwithstanding the many public proofs I received of his indifference, coldness, and slight of every wish and opinion of mine, in the midst of the nearest intercourse and of the strongest professions of friendship.

And again:

> Thus I continued in the same office till Mr. Pelham's death in 1754, giving what support I was able to those who never gave any to me.[3]

Horace Walpole describes him as prolix, pedantic, deceitful, and even less of a gentleman than his elder brother, Richard.[4]

He died 13 Nov. 1770.

[1] Walpole to Mann, 22 Jan., 26 May 1742. [2] Owen, *Pelhams*, 198. [3] *Grenville Pprs.* i. 424–7. [4] *Mems. Geo. II*, i. 136.

R.R.S.

GRENVILLE, James (1715–83).

OLD SARUM	5 Jan. 1742–May 1747
BRIDPORT	25 May 1747–1754
BUCKINGHAM	1754–1768
HORSHAM	1768–Mar. 1770

b. 12 Feb. 1715, 3rd s. of Richard Grenville of Wotton and bro. of George, Richard and Thomas Grenville (qq.v.). *educ.* Eton 1728–32; I. Temple 1734, called 1738. *m.* 1740, Mary, da. and h. of James Smyth of South Elkington, Lincs., 2s.

Ld. of Trade 1746–Dec. 1755; dep. paymaster to forces 1746–55; ld. of Treasury Nov. 1756–Apr. 1757, July 1757–Mar. 1761; cofferer of the Household Mar.–Oct. 1761; P.C. 3 Apr. 1761; jt. vice-treasurer [I] Aug. 1766–Jan. 1770.

James Grenville was originally brought into Parliament by Thomas Pitt (q.v.), subsequently resigning his seat to succeed his brother Thomas at Bridport. Like his elder brothers, a member of the political group led by his uncle, Lord Cobham, he at first acted with the Opposition, voting against the Hanoverians in 1742 and 1746, and signing the opposition whip of 10 Nov. 1743. When Cobham opened negotiations with the Pelhams in January 1746, one of his stipulations was that James should be provided with an employment of £1,000 a year, which was provided in the form of a seat on the board of Trade a month later.[1] In the following April he voted with the Government for the Hanoverians, classed as New Ally. Soon afterwards, according to his brother George, Pitt detached him from his uncle by appointing him deputy paymaster general, which so 'greatly irritated Lord Cobham' that he cut James out of his will.[2] Writing about 1751, Horace Walpole says that James 'had all the defects of his brothers and had turned them to the best account'.[3]

He died 14 Sept. 1783.

[1] Chesterfield to Newcastle, 27 Feb. 1746, Add. 32706, f. 24. [2] *Grenville Pprs.* i. 424–5. [3] *Mems. Geo. II*, i. 136.

R.R.S.

GRENVILLE, Richard (1678–1727), of Wotton, Bucks.

WENDOVER   1715–1722
BUCKINGHAM   1722–17 Feb. 1727

> *b.* 23 Mar. 1678, 1st s. of Richard Grenville of Wotton by Eleanor, da. of Sir Peter Temple of Stantonbury, Bucks. *m.* (lic. 25 Nov. 1710) Hester, 2nd da. of Sir Richard Temple, 3rd Bt., M.P., of Stowe, Bucks., and sis. of Sir Richard Temple, 4th Bt., M.P., afterwards 1st Visct. Cobham, of Stowe, to whose peerage she suc. 1749 when she was cr. Countess Temple, 6s. 1da. *suc. fa.* 1719.

Grenville (pronounced and often spelt 'Greenville'), married the favourite sister of Sir Richard Temple, afterwards Lord Cobham, whose peerage was entailed on her and her sons. At George I's accession he was adopted as the Whig candidate for Buckinghamshire on a compromise with the Tories, but eventually stood down in favour of Richard Hampden (q.v.),[1] by whom he was returned for Wendover, voting with the Government in every recorded division except on Lord Cadogan (q.v.). In the next Parliament he represented Buckingham on the interest of Lord Cobham. On his death, 17 Feb. 1727, Cobham virtually adopted his children, ultimately settling his whole estate on the eldest, Richard (q.v.), thus uniting the estates of Wotton and Stowe.[2]

[1] *Verney Letters of the 18th Cent.* i. 317–20; Earl of Buckinghamshire's mss 40/46, Bucks. RO. [2] *Grenville Pprs.* i. 422 seq.

R.R.S.

GRENVILLE, Richard (1711–79), of Wotton, Bucks.

BUCKINGHAM   1734–1741
BUCKINGHAMSHIRE   1741–1747
BUCKINGHAM   1747–6 Oct. 1752

> *b.* 26 Sept. 1711, 1st s. of Richard Grenville of Wotton and bro. of George, James and Thomas Grenville (qq.v.). *educ.* Eton 1725–9; Grand Tour (Switzerland, Italy and France) 1729–33. *m.* 9 May 1737, Anne, da. and coh. of Thomas Chambers of Hanworth, Mdx. by Lady Mary Berkeley, da. of Charles Berkeley, M.P., 2nd Earl of Berkeley, 1da. *suc. fa.* 1727; styled Lord Cobham from 1749 till 6 Oct. 1752 when he *suc.* his mother as Earl Temple and assumed add. name of Temple.
> P.C. 19 Nov. 1756; 1st ld. of Admiralty Nov. 1756–Apr. 1757; ld. privy seal June 1757–61; ld. lt. Bucks. 1758–63; K.G. 4 Feb. 1760.

When Richard Grenville returned from his grand tour, he found that his wealthy uncle, Lord Cobham, who had married the heiress of Edmund Halsey (q.v.), considered that he too should marry, in view of the distressed state of his affairs. 'To enable him to do so to the highest advantage, Lord Cobham publicly declared that he would settle his whole estate upon him.' On his marriage to a great heiress, whose sister married Lord Vere Beauclerk (q.v.), Cobham settled his estate on his sister, Grenville's mother, and her male issue, on whom his honours were already entailed.[1] He was brought into Parliament by Cobham, under whose direction he, his first cousin George Lyttelton, and their friend William Pitt (qq.v.), went into opposition, forming the nucleus of a political group, variously nicknamed 'the cousinhood', 'the nepotism', 'Cobham's Cubs' or 'the boy patriots'. All three made their maiden speeches on the same day, in support of a place bill, 22 Apr. 1735; signalized the marriage of the Prince of Wales by getting up one after the other to make such disrespectful references to the King that Pitt was cashiered, 29 Apr. 1736; were regarded as the chief stimulators of the Prince's application to Parliament for an increased allowance from the King in 1737; and are described as 'young gentlemen who took great personal liberties' in the debate on the Spanish convention in 1739.[2]

After Walpole's fall the group, reinforced by Richard's brothers, George and James, remained for a time in opposition, Richard himself speaking against the Hanoverians in 1742 and 1744. They came to terms with the Government at the end of 1744, when Lyttelton and George Grenville obtained places, but resumed hostilities a year later owing to Pelham's failure to provide for the other members of the group. On the reconstruction of the Government after the collective resignations in February 1746, Pitt and James Grenville were admitted to office, Richard giving up 'his pretensions to the Treasury'. In the following April, classed as New Allies, 'this ominous band', as Horace Walpole calls them, all voted for the Hanoverians, 'though the eldest Grenville, two years ago had declared in the House that he would seal it with his blood that he never would give his vote for a Hanoverian'. In the next Parliament they were classed as government supporters.

As soon as Cobham died in 1749, Richard Grenville applied successfully for his mother to be made a countess, he himself becoming Lord Cobham. Shortly after this, at a reception given by his wife, he spat for a bet into the hat of one of the guests, who made Lord Gob'em, as he was now called, write him a formal apology, couched in the most humiliating terms.[3] 'The only one of the cousinhood who could not be turned out, having no place' to forfeit, he took an independent line in Parliament, speaking against the Government on the regency bill in 1751. His last speech in the Commons was against the subsidy treaty with Saxony in 1752. Before the next session his mother's death raised him to the Lords, reputedly the richest man in England. Horace Walpole described him at this time as 'the absolute creature of Pitt; vehement in whatever faction he was engaged, and as mischievous as his understanding would let him be.' In 1766 he wrote of him:

> This malignant man worked in the mines of successive factions for nearly thirty years together. To relate them is writing his life.[4]

He died 12 Sept. 1779.

[1] *Grenville Pprs.* i. 423. [2] *Harley Diary*, 23 Apr. 1735; Hervey, *Mems.* 533, 667; Coxe, *Walpole*, iii. 518. [3] Walpole to Mann, 15 Apr. 1746, 26 Feb. 1750. [4] Walpole, *Mems. Geo. II.* i, 134–8, 241.

R.R.S.

GRENVILLE, Thomas (1719–47).

BRIDPORT   12 Dec. 1746–3 May 1747

b. 4 Apr. 1719, s. of Richard Grenville of Wotton and bro. of Richard, George and James Grenville (qq.v.). *unm.*
    Lt. R.N. 1740, capt. 1742.

A distinguished naval officer, Thomas Grenville in 1743 captured a valuable Spanish treasure ship, with a cargo worth about £120,000 or £130,000, of which he estimated his share at £30,000 to £40,000. In 1746 he was brought in for Bridport by the influence of his brother George, then on the Admiralty board. In 1747, though it had been arranged that he should be sent on independent cruise, he was ordered by the Admiralty, in spite of George's opposition, to join Anson's squadron. He died of wounds received in the action off Cape Finisterre, 3 May 1747.[1]

[1] *Grenville Pprs.* i. 20–24, 58–63.

R.R.S.

GRESLEY, Sir Thomas, 5th Bt. (1722–53), of Drakelow, Derbys.

LICHFIELD   30 Nov.–23 Dec. 1753

b. 12 July 1722, 1st surv. s. of Sir Thomas Gresley, 4th Bt., by his 1st w. Dorothy, da. and coh. of Sir William Bowyer, 4th Bt., of Knypersley, Staffs. *educ.* Balliol 1739. *m.* 1749, Wilmot, da. and h. of Mr. Hood of Scraptoft, Leics. *suc.* fa. as 5th Bt. Oct. 1746.
    Sheriff, Derbys. 1750–1.

Gresley, who had inherited large Staffordshire estates from his mother,[1] was one of the heads of the Tory demonstration at Lichfield races in 1747. Chosen to stand for Lichfield at a by-election in 1753 against the ministerial candidate, he was described by Lady Anson as 'the truest country cub I ever saw'.[2] Returned after a contest, he died of smallpox a few weeks later, 23 Dec. 1753. On

29 Jan. 1754 the House of Commons resolved that he had not been duly elected.

[1] F. Madan, 'The Gresleys of Drakelow', *Wm. Salt. Arch. Soc.* n.s. i. 109. [2] *Staffs. Parl. Hist.* (Wm. Salt Arch. Soc.) ii (2), pp. 253, 255.

E.C.

GREVILLE, Hon. Doddington (?1679–1738).

WARWICK   1705–1727

b. ?1679, 3rd s. of Fulke Greville, M.P., 5th Baron Brooke of Beauchamps Court, by Sarah, da. of Francis Dashwood, alderman of London. *educ.* Wadham, Oxf. 18 Apr. 1697, aged 17; All Souls, Oxf. 1699; M. Temple 1697. *unm. suc.* to fa.'s seat at Twickenham 1710.

Doddington Greville, who had considerable personal wealth,[1] represented Warwick on his family's interest in six successive Parliaments. A Tory and member of the October Club, he was absent from the division on the septennial bill in 1716, but voted against the repeal of the Occasional Conformity and Schism Acts and the peerage bill in 1719. He did not stand in 1727, dying 11 Feb. 1738.

[1] PCC 89 Brodrepp.

S.R.M.

GREVILLE, Fulke (1717–c.1805), of Wilbury, Wilts.

MONMOUTH   1747–1754

b. 1717, o.s. of Hon. Algernon Greville, M.P. (s. of Fulke Greville, M.P., 5th Baron Brooke), by Mary, da. and coh. of Lord Arthur Somerset (s. of Henry Somerset, M.P., 1st Duke of Beaufort). *educ.* Winchester 1728–33; B.N.C., Oxf. 1734. *m.* 26 Jan. 1734, Frances, da. and coh. of James Macartney of Ireland, 6s. 1da.
    Envoy extraordinary to Bavaria 1764–70; minister plenip. to the Imperial diet 1765–9.

Greville was returned for Monmouth as a Tory in 1747 by his kinsman, the 4th Duke of Beaufort (q.v. under Somerset, Lord Charles Noel), but did not stand again. In 1756 he published what Horace Walpole (to Conway, 16 Apr. 1756) referred to as

> a wonderful book by a more wonderful author, Greville. It is called *Maxims and Characters*; several of the former are pretty: all the latter so absurd, that one in particular, which at the beginning you take for the character of a man, turns out to be the character of a post-chaise.

Later he was described by Fanny Burney as

> the finest gentleman about town . . . His high birth . . . with a splendid fortune, wholly unfettered, already in his hands, gave to him a consequence in the circles of modish dissipation.[1]

The date of his death has not been ascertained, but

he was living in February 1805 with a fortune much depleted by gambling.[2]

[1] *Mems. of Dr. Burney*, i. 24. [2] *Farington Diary*, iii. 60.

P.W.

GREY, Harry, Lord Grey (1715–68).

LEICESTERSHIRE   16 Feb. 1738–4 Nov. 1739

b. 18 June 1715, 1st surv. s. of Harry Grey, 3rd Earl of Stamford, by Dorothy, da. of Sir Nathan Wrighte of Caldecote Hall, Warws., ld. keeper of the great seal; 1st cos. of George Wrighte (q.v.). *educ.* Rugby 1722–6; Westminster 1726–31. *m.* 18 May 1736, Lady Mary Booth, da. and h. of George, 2nd Earl of Warrington, 3s. 2d. *suc.* fa. as 4th Earl of Stamford 16 Nov. 1739.

Returned for Leicestershire as an opposition Whig at a by-election in 1738, Grey voted against the Government on the Spanish convention on 8 Mar. 1739, succeeding to the peerage eight months later. He died 30 May 1768.

E.C.

GREY, Henry (1683–1740), of Horton, Northumb. and Billingbear, Berks.[1]

WENDOVER	21 Nov. 1709–1713
WALLINGFORD	1 Dec. 1719–1722
BERWICK-UPON-TWEED	11 Mar. 1723–1727
READING	1734–9 Sept. 1740

b. 17 Aug. 1683, 2nd s. of Richard Neville, M.P., of Billingbear; yr. bro. of Grey Neville and uncle of Richard Neville Aldworth (qq.v.). *m.* Elizabeth, 1st da. of James Griffin, M.P., 2nd Baron Griffin of Braybrooke, sis. and coh. of Edward, 3rd Baron, *s.p.* *suc.* to the Northumbrian estates of his maternal uncle Ralph Grey, M.P., 4th Baron Grey of Warke, 1706, and to his e. bro.'s estates at Billingbear 1723.

Henry Neville took the name of Grey by private Act of Parliament in 1707 in accordance with his uncle's will, under which he succeeded to estates charged with £40,000, the price of the 3rd Lord Grey's pardon for his share in Monmouth's rebellion. He was returned as a Whig at a contested by-election for Wallingford in 1719; stood unsuccessfully for Berkshire in 1722; and joined his elder brother, Grey Neville, as Member for Berwick in 1723. Early in 1726, when 'the interest upon the £40,000 amounted to £12,000, . . . the mortgagees foreclosed and entered on his estate', although 'he had coming in £9,700 per annum, in as good rents as in England'. On 18 Feb. Grey

charged his pistols in the morning, taking them with him . . . he sent a letter to his wife and another to Sir Robert Walpole, dated from a tavern, I think in Drury Lane: he told his wife that she would see him no more and Sir Robert, that he desired he would dispose of his borough . . . since then search has been made for him but to no purpose.

Ten days later Grey

has since been heard of from Calais and . . . intends to return when he can reconcile himself to the looking his friends again in the face. Peter Walter [q.v.] proposes to put him in a method of paying his debt and to allow him £2,000 a year out of his estate to live upon, everything else of Grey's to be sold to pay his debts.[2]

In November 1732 he was among several parliamentary candidates considered by the Berwick corporation 'for a third man, to make some sport as they call it'.[3] Successful in 1734 for Reading, he voted with the Government till his death, 9 Sept. 1740.

[1] See Rowland, *Hist. Fam. of Neville*, table v. [2] *HMC Portland*, vii. 426; Dr. Geo. Clarke to Edw. Nicholas (qq.v.), 19 Feb. and 1 Mar. 1726, Egerton mss 2540, ff. 588–9, 596–7. [3] Geo. Liddell to Sir Robt. Walpole, 24 Nov. 1732, Cholmondeley (Houghton) mss.

R.S.L.

GREY, see also DE GREY and GRAY

GRIFFIN, John Griffin (1719–97), of Audley End, Essex.

ANDOVER   28 Nov. 1749–3 Aug. 1784

b. 13 Mar. 1719, 1st s. of William Whitwell of Oundle, Northants. by Anne, da. and eventually sole h. of James Griffin, M.P., 2nd Baron Griffin of Braybrooke. *educ.* Winchester 1734–6. *m.* (1) 9 Mar. 1749, Anna Maria (*d.* 18 Aug. 1764), da. of John, Baron Schutz, *s.p.*; (2) 11 June 1765, Catherine, da. of William Clayton (q.v.) of Harleyford, Bucks., *s.p.* After d. of his uncle Edward, 3rd Baron Griffin (1742), and of his kinsman Henry Howard, 10th Earl of Suffolk (1745), he took name of Griffin 1749, and *suc.* to Audley End; *suc.* fa. 1755; K.B. 3 May 1761; *suc.* mother 1770; the abeyance of the barony of Howard de Walden was terminated in his favour 3 Aug. 1784; *cr.* Baron Braybrooke 5 Sept. 1788, with spec. rem. to his 2nd cos. once removed, Richard Neville Aldworth (q.v.).

Ensign 3 Ft. Gds. 1739, capt. 1743, capt. and lt.-col. 1748, 2nd maj., 1st maj. 1758–9; col. 1756; maj.-gen. 1759; col. 50 Ft. 1759–60, 33 Ft. 1760–6; lt.-gen. 1761; col. 1 tp. Horse Gren. Gds. 1766–88; gen. 1778; col. 4 Drags. 1788–*d.*; f.m. 1796. Ld. lt. Essex 1784–*d.*

After serving in the war of the Austrian succession, Griffin was returned for Andover on the interest of his uncle, John Wallop (q.v.), 1st Earl of Portsmouth, 'almost without opposition, his competitor having but one vote . . . This made the expense light.'[1] In the Seven Years' war he was wounded at Kloster Campen.[2] He continued to represent Andover till he became a peer in 1784, dying 25 May 1797.

[1] Schutz to Lee, 22 Dec. 1749, Lee Pprs. Bucks. RO. [2] R. Griffin, *Hist. Audley End*, 52.

P.W.

GRIFFITH, John (?1687–1739), of Cefnamwlch, Caern.

CAERNARVONSHIRE 27 Apr. 1715–6 June 1739

b. ?1687, 2nd s. of John Griffith by Elizabeth, da. of Robert, 2nd Visct. Bulkeley [I]; bro. of William Griffith (q.v.). *educ.* Ch. Ch. Oxf. 8 June 1703, aged 15. *m.* (settlement 18 June 1718) Ann, da. of Pierce Lloyd of Lligwy and Llanidan, 1s. *suc.* e. bro. Mar. 1715.

John Griffith succeeded to the estate and seat of his elder brother, voting for the septennial bill in 1716. There is no record of his voting during the Sunderland Administration of 1717-20, when like his electoral ally, Thomas Wynn (q.v.), he may have joined the Whig Opposition. During Walpole's Administration he consistently supported the Government. His death on 6 June 1739, when his son was still a minor, ended his family's participation in the representation of the county.

P.D.G.T.

GRIFFITH, William (?1686–1715), of Cefnamwlch, Caern.

CAERNARVON BOROUGHS 1708–1713
CAERNARVONSHIRE 1713–10 Mar. 1715

b. ?1686, 1st s. of John Griffith and bro. of John Griffith (q.v.). *educ.* Ch. Ch. Oxf. 8 June 1703, aged 16; I. Temple 1703. *m.* Mary, da. of Sir Bibye Lake, 1st Bt., *s.p. suc.* fa. c. June 1687.
Sheriff, Caern. 1709-10.

The Griffiths were one of a group of Tory families who controlled the representation of Caernarvonshire at the beginning of the 18th century. William Griffith, who had allied himself with the local Whigs in 1713, was still regarded as a Tory in 1715, when he was again returned for the county, dying a month later, 10 Mar.

P.D.G.T.

GRIMSTON, William (c.1683–1756), of Gorhambury, nr. St. Albans, Herts.

ST. ALBANS 1710–1722, 1727–1734

b. c.1683, 2nd s. of Sir William Luckyn, 3rd Bt., of Little Waltham, Essex by Mary, da. of William Sherington, alderman of London, and gt.-nephew of Sir Samuel Grimston, 3rd Bt., M.P. *m.* 14 Aug. 1706, Jean, da. of James Cooke of London, 10s. 3da. *suc.* gt.-uncle 1700, taking name of Grimston; *cr.* Visct. Grimston [I] 29 May 1719; *suc.* bro. Sir Harbottle Luckyn, 4th Bt., 4 Feb. 1737.

As a minor, William Luckyn inherited the estates of his great-uncle, Sir Samuel Grimston, whose name he assumed. The estates included Gorhambury, formerly the seat of the Bacon family, carrying an important electoral interest at St.

Albans. Returned for St. Albans as a Whig, with the support of the Marlborough interest, he made his first and only reported speech on 4 Apr. 1717, when he was 'one of the courtiers' who opposed a vote of credit for defence measures against Sweden. Otherwise he acted with the Government, securing an Irish peerage in 1719. By this time he had fallen out with Sarah, Duchess of Marlborough, who, rejecting his proposal that they should join interests at the next general election as 'insolent, saucy, and foolish', joined with the corporation to defeat him in 1722. With her acquiescence, he recovered his seat in 1727, but, provoked by his refusal to support her grandson, John Spencer (q.v.), at a by-election for the borough, she once more co-operated with the corporation to oust him at the general election of 1734.[1] Later that year he was pilloried by Pope in the couplet:

> Shades, that to Bacon could retreat afford,
> Become the portion of a booby Lord.[2]

The justification for calling him 'a booby Lord' was a play which he had published in 1705 but subsequently endeavoured to suppress by buying up and destroying all the copies of it. In 1736 it was reprinted with derisive notes and a frontispiece depicting a coroneted ass eating a thistle. The reprint was generally regarded as the Duchess's revenge on Grimston for opposing her at St. Albans.[3]

Grimston's feud with the Duchess continued till her death in 1746. In 1741 he did not stand but thwarted her attempt to secure the return of John Spencer by supporting James West (q.v.). She retorted in 1743 by helping Hans Stanley (q.v.) to defeat Grimston's son at a by-election. He did not put up a candidate in 1747, soon after which the 2nd Lord Egmont in his electoral survey described the Grimstons as 'totally belonging to the Duke of Newcastle'. At last successful in returning his son in 1754, he died 15 Nov. 1756.

[1] *HMC Verulam*, 114-15, 121-2. [2] Pope, *Imitations of Horace* (Twickenham ed.), iv. 68–69. [3] Boswell's *Johnson*, iv. 80, 485-6.

R.R.S.

GROSVENOR, Sir Richard, 4th Bt. (1689–1732), of Eaton Hall, Cheshire.

CHESTER 1715–12 July 1732

b. 26 June 1689, 1st surv. s. of Sir Thomas Grosvenor, 3rd Bt., of Eaton Hall, M.P. Chester 1679-1700, by Mary, da. and h. of Alexander Davies of Ebury, Mdx., scrivener of London; bro. of Robert and Thomas Grosvenor (qq.v.). *educ.* Eton 1698-1704; Grand Tour (Switzerland, Bavaria, Italy and Netherlands) 1704-7. *m.* (1) 1708, Jane (*d.* Feb. 1720), da. of Sir Edward Wyndham, 2nd Bt., M.P., of Orchard Wyndham, Som., sis. of Sir William Wyndham, 3rd Bt. (q.v.), 1da. *d.v.p.*; (2) 1724, Diana, da. of Sir

George Warburton, 3rd Bt. (q.v.), of Arley, Cheshire, *s.p. suc.* fa. June 1700.

Mayor, Chester 1715–16.

The Grosvenors of Eaton, near Chester, were a Cheshire family of great antiquity and substantial fortune, derived mainly from Welsh lead mines. In 1676 Sir Thomas Grosvenor, 3rd Bt., married the heiress to London estates covering a large part of modern Mayfair, Belgravia, and Pimlico, which increased the Grosvenor income from about £4,500 to £22,000 p.a. in 1742. He died in 1700, leaving three minor sons, Richard, Thomas and Robert, and a daughter Anne (*m.* William Leveson Gower, q.v.), who all grew up under the care of Francis Cholmondeley, M.P., uncle of Charles Cholmondeley (q.v.) of Vale Royal, their mother having become mentally deranged.[1] All three sons were returned as Tories on the family interest for Chester, voting consistently against the Government.

Grosvenor was present in September 1715 at a meeting of the Jacobite Cheshire Club, which decided against taking part in the rebellion.[2] His name was included in a list of Jacobite leaders sent to the Pretender in 1721, and in 1730 he was in correspondence with the Stuart court at Rome through the Duchess of Buckingham.[3] He was responsible for the development of the Grosvenor estate in London. On 12 July 1725 the *Daily Post*, a London newspaper, reported:

> The several new streets designed in Grosvenor Buildings in the Parish of St. George, Hanover Square, and lying between New Bond Street and Hyde Park were last week particularly named; upon which occasion Sir Richard Grosvenor, Bart, gave a very splendid entertainment to his tenants and others concerned with those buildings . . . In the centre of those new buildings there is now making a new square called Grosvenor Square [with gardens designed by William Kent], which for its largeness and beauty will far exceed any yet made in or about London.[4]

He died 12 July 1732.

[1] C. T. Gatty, *Mary Davies and the Manor of Ebury*, ii. 185, 197 et passim; AEM & D Angl. 82, ff. 49–57. [2] Ormerod, *Cheshire*, i. 557. [3] Stuart mss 65/16; R. Smith to J. Edgar, 9 Feb. 1730, ibid. 142/146. [4] Quoted in *N. & Q.* (ser. 11), iv. 327, 414–15.

E.C.

GROSVENOR, Robert (1695–1755), of Eaton Hall, Cheshire.

CHESTER   24 Jan. 1733–1 Aug. 1755

b. 7 May 1695, 3rd surv. s. of Sir Thomas Grosvenor, 3rd Bt., M.P., and bro. of Sir Richard and Thomas Grosvenor (qq.v.). *educ.* Eton 1707; B.N.C. Oxf. 1712; I. Temple 1716. *m.* 21 May 1730, Jane, da. and h. of Thomas Warre of Shepton Beauchamp and Swell Court, Som., 2s. (Richard Grosvenor, M.P., 1st Earl Grosvenor, and Thomas Grosvenor, M.P.), 4da. *suc.* bro. as 6th Bt. 31 Jan. 1733.

Mayor, Chester 1737.

During the Forty-five, while supposed by popular rumour to be marching to join the Young Pretender in Lancashire, Grosvenor was presented at court, 'having never been there before, and always counted very high [Tory]'.[1] He was one of the prominent Tories who agreed to support the Prince of Wales's programme in 1747.[2] On 27 Feb. 1748 Thomas Carew (q.v.) reported to Lord Orrery, a leading Jacobite: 'It is said Sir R. Grosvenor is soon to be made a peer, but I hope without foundation'.[3] He died 1 Aug. 1755.

[1] *HMC 15th Rep. VII*, 333; A. Mordaunt to Lady Hertford, 3 Dec. 1745, Northumberland mss. [2] Add. 35870, ff. 129–30. [3] *Orrery Pprs.* ii. 17.

E.C.

GROSVENOR, Thomas (1693–1733), of Eaton Hall, Cheshire.

CHESTER   1727–31 Jan. 1733

b. 7 Dec. 1693, 2nd surv. s. of Sir Thomas Grosvenor, 3rd Bt., M.P., and bro. of Sir Richard and Robert Grosvenor (qq.v.). *educ.* Eton 1706–7; B.N.C. Oxf. 1712. *unm. suc.* bro. as 5th Bt. 12 July 1732.

Grosvenor was returned as a Tory jointly with his brother, Sir Richard Grosvenor, at Chester in 1727. He died of consumption at Naples, 31 Jan. 1733.[1]

[1] C. T. Gatty, *Mary Davies and the Manor of Ebury*, ii. 198.

E.C.

GROVE, Grey James (1682–1742), of Pool Hall, Alveley, Salop.

BEWDLEY   1715–1722
BRIDGNORTH   1734–1741

bap. 10 Nov. 1682, 1st s. of James Grove of Alveley, serjeant-at-law, by Anne, da. of Thomas Grey, M.P., Lord Grey of Groby, sis. of Thomas, 2nd Earl of Stamford. *m.* Penelope, da. and coh. of Thomas Jermyn, M.P., 2nd Baron Jermyn, 2s. *suc.* fa. 1734. Sheriff, Salop 1730–1.

Grove came of an old Shropshire family settled in Alveley by 1562.[1] Returned for Bewdley in 1715 on Lord Herbert of Chirbury's interest, he voted with the Administration except on the peerage bill, on which he abstained. He next stood in 1734, when he successfully contested Bridgnorth on the Whitmore interest, voting for the Spanish convention in 1739 but abstaining on the place bill in 1740. He did not stand in 1741, dying in April 1742.

[1] *Salop Arch. Soc. Trans.* (ser. 4), iv. pp. x–xi.

J.B.L.

GROVE, William (1702–67), of Cross Cheaping, Coventry, and Honiley, Warws.

COVENTRY   1741–1761

b. 14 Dec. 1702, 1st s. of William Grove of Coventry, attorney, by Hannah, da. of Nathaniel Harryman, alderman of Coventry. *educ.* M. Temple 1713. *m.* 2 Oct. 1739, Mary, da. of Thomas Bayley of Madeley, Staffs., wid of John Saunders of Honiley, Warws., 1s. 3da. *suc.* fa. 1734.

Grove, a prominent citizen of Coventry, was returned for it as a Tory in 1741. In March 1742 the freemen of Coventry sent him the following address:

> We take this opportunity to congratulate you, and express the great joy and satisfaction we receive from our happy choice of a person so deserving of us and the public, whose true patriot zeal and behaviour for the honour and service of your country at first setting out, and faithful discharge of that trust during this short but critical period, give us an early and strong confidence of your future good conduct.[1]

Voting against the Administration in all recorded divisions, he was unopposed in 1747. He died 1 May 1767.

[1] *Gent. Mag.* 1742. p. 159.

E.C.

GUERNSEY, Lord, *see* **FINCH, Heneage** (*b.* ?1683), *and* **FINCH, Heneage** (*b.*1715).

GUIDOTT, William (?1671–1745), of Laverstoke and Preston Candover, Hants.

ANDOVER 1708–1727, 20 Jan. 1730–1741

b. ?1671, 1st s. of William Guidott of Wootton St. Lawrence, Hants, bencher of Lincoln's Inn, by his w. Grace. *educ.* New Inn Hall, Oxf. 22 Mar. 1686, aged 14; L. Inn 1686, called 1693, bencher 1719. *m.* (1) lic. 1 July 1706, Jane Hunt, *s.p.*; (2) lic. 4 May 1710, Jane, da. of Sir Francis Child, M.P., ld. mayor of London 1698–9, and sis. of Sir Francis Samuel Child (qq.v.), *s.p.*; (3) 30 Nov. 1739, Patience, da. and h. of John Soper of Preston Candover, Hants, *s.p.* *suc.* fa. 1698.
Steward, Andover 1710, 1713; recorder, Andover by 1727.

Descended from a family of Florentine merchants, settled in Southampton in the sixteenth century, Guidott acted as agent for the Duke of Marlborough. Returned for Andover as a Whig for nearly twenty years on his own interest, he voted with the Administration on the septennial bill in 1716, was absent from the division on the repeal of the Occasional Conformity and Schism Acts, voted for the peerage bill, and was classed by Craggs in 1719 as to be approached through Sarah, Duchess of Marlborough. In 1727 he was sued in Chancery by the Duchess for the recovery of £9,547, which she claimed he had embezzled. The court ordered him to pay £5,494, which on appeal was increased by £754.[1] In the same year he lost his seat at Andover, where he had quarrelled with the corporation. Recovering it at a by-election in 1730 and re-elected unopposed in 1734, he voted with the Opposition

in every recorded division except that on the place bill in 1740, from which he was absent. Defeated in 1741, he died 30 Aug. 1745.

[1] Add. 38056, ff. 121–6; *LJ*, xxiii. 207.

P.W.

GUISE, Sir John, 3rd Bt. (c.1677–1732), of Elmore and Rendcombe, Glos., and Harleyford, in Great Marlow, Bucks.

GLOUCESTERSHIRE 1705–1710
GREAT MARLOW 1722–1727

b. c.1677, o.s. of Sir John Guise, 2nd Bt., M.P., by Elizabeth, da. of John Grubham Howe, M.P., of Compton Abdale, Glos. and Langar, Notts., sis. of Scrope Howe, M.P., 1st Visct. Howe [I], and of John Howe, M.P., of Stowell, Glos., paymaster gen. *m.* (1) lic. 4 June 1696, Elizabeth (*d.*1701), da. of Sir Nathaniel Napier, 2nd Bt., M.P., of Critchell More, Dorset, 1s.; (2) lic. 2 Jan. 1711, Anne, da. and coh. of Sir Francis Russell, 3rd Bt., M.P., of Strensham, Worcs., wid. of (i) Richard Lygon of Madresfield, Worcs., and (ii) Sir Henry Every, 3rd Bt., of Egginton, Derbys., *s.p.* *suc.* fa. 19 Nov. 1695.

Sir John Guise, whose father and grandfather had both represented Gloucestershire, came of an ancient Bedfordshire family, who had held the manor of Elmore since 1274.[1] From his autobiography up to 1720 he appears to have been a cross-grained individual who, though sitting as a Whig under Queen Anne and having 'a great opinion' of George I, described that party as 'bad subjects and worse rulers, unfit either to command or to be commanded.' According to his own account he attempted vainly to effect a reconciliation between the King and the Prince and Princess after their quarrel in November 1717:

> The King, who honoured me with some esteem, supped with me at Kensington and was very merry with me . . . Between this good King and the Princess of Wales I often went, and found 'em extremely animated against each other, nay the King seemed more angry with her than his son . . . Her Royal Highness . . . told me that his Majesty's dislike to her was so much the stronger because he had not always had an aversion for her and had signified so much to her in a manner she did not well understand.

Guise's son commented that his father:

> was too indolent and unhealthy to pursue a court intrigue and of too honest and open a temper to have kept any power there, had he obtained it, which he certainly would, had he brought about the reconciliation he so far advanced; nay, so far had he wrought himself into the old King's favour by his honest and free advice, that the King once asked him what he should do for him. He named something; but when the King mentioned that he would consult his ministry about it, my father told him that he would gladly serve him, but would never be obliged to his ministers.[2]

A somewhat coarse ballad, entitled 'Duke upon Duke' and attributed to Swift, refers to a quarrel and attempted duel about this time between Guise and Nicholas Lechmere (q.v.).

In 1719 Guise bought the manors of Harleyford and Great Marlow from Sir James Etheridge, M.P., thus acquiring a strong political interest there.[3] Before the 1722 election he wrote to Walpole about Buckinghamshire elections, asking him to fulfil 'with speed' a promise which would contribute to the success of Guise's election at Great Marlow.[4] He was returned with Edmund Waller (q.v.) but,

> not liking his brother member, did in all things cross Mr. Waller's interest, which caused not only trouble but expense. For Sir John was of such a spirit of controversy and delighted in it that right or wrong it was all alike to him.[5]

On 21 Feb. 1724 he presented a petition, seconded by John Barnard, from the subscribers to the Bahama Company, claiming 'that they had been bubbled out of their money and could not recover it without help of Parliament'. This was negatived by the House after Walpole had expressed the hope that 'gentlemen would not begin to unravel the misfortunes of the year '20, for then there would be no end'. On 14 March 1727 he moved an amendment to the Address condemning a memorial published by the Austrian ambassador attacking the Government. The motion, which was seconded by a Tory, was rejected without a division.[6] Defeated in 1727 by a government supporter, who, he alleged, had organized a club, or flying squadron, against him, backed by £1,000, he petitioned unsuccessfully.[7] He died 16 Nov. 1732.

[1] *Bristol & Glos. Arch. Soc. Trans.* iii. 49–77. [2] *Mems. of Fam. of Guise* (R. Hist. Soc. Cam. ser. 3, xxviii), 151, 153, 155–7. [3] *VCH Bucks.* iii. 71; Add. 34741, ff. 7–8. [4] 4 Aug. 1722, Cholmondeley (Houghton) mss. [5] See GREAT MARLOW; Probyn mss, Gloucester RO, D.23, E.51. [6] *Knatchbull Diary.* [7] *CJ*, xxi. 480–2.

R.S.L.

GUISE, John (1701–69), of Elmore and Rend-combe, Glos.

AYLESBURY   1722–1727

b. early 1701, o. surv. s. of Sir John Guise, 3rd Bt. q.v.), by his 1st w. *educ.* Marlborough c.1709–11;[1] New Coll. Oxf. 27 June 1720, aged 19. *m.* (settlement 14 June 1732)[2] Jane, o. da. of John Saunders of Mongewell, Oxon., sis. and h. of John Saunders of Mongewell, 2s. 2da. *suc.* fa. as 4th Bt. 16 Nov. 1732.

John Guise was returned as a Whig for Aylesbury in 1722, but no vote of his has been recorded. Defeated there by a follower of Walpole's in 1727, he was again unsuccessful at a by-election for Great Marlow in 1731, despite his father's interest in that borough. He did not stand again, selling the

Marlow estates to Sir William Clayton (q.v.) in 1735.[3] He died in May 1769.

[1] *Mems. of Fam. of Guise* (R. Hist. Soc. Cam. ser. 3, xxviii), 143, 150. [2] *Bristol & Glos. Arch. Soc. Trans.* iii. 72. [3] *VCH Bucks.*, iii. 71.

R.S.L.

GULSTON, Joseph (c.1694–1766), of Walbrook, London, and Kew, Mdx.

TREGONY   2 Mar. 1737–1741
POOLE   1741–May 1765

b. c.1694, 1st s. of Joseph Gulston, merchant of Lisbon. *m.* secretly c.1733, Maricas de Sylva, da. of a Portuguese merchant, 2s. 2da. Director, South Sea Co. 1742–60.

Gulston came of a younger branch of the Gulstons of Wyddial, Herts. (see Gulston, Richard). He was the 'head of the first mercantile house in the British factory at Lisbon,' presumably inherited from his father, who is said never to have been in England. Some time before 1730 he moved to England, accompanied by his widowed sister, who subsequently married John Goddard (q.v.), her daughter, who married Henry Penton (q.v.), and a Portuguese friend of the daughter's, whom he married himself.[1] In 1737 he successfully contested Tregony, for which his brother-in-law, Goddard, had sat 1727–36, and Penton sat 1734–47. In 1741 he transferred himself to Poole, with which borough he was probably connected through his extensive trade with both North and South America. In Parliament he regularly voted with the Administration, from whom he held various contracts: e.g. in 1739 for supplying masts to the Royal Navy, in which connexion his trading interests in New Hampshire are mentioned.[2] In 1742, together with John Gore (q.v.), he obtained a contract for remitting money for paying Danish and Hessian troops, and in January 1743 for remittances to Flanders.[3] These contracts were continued to the end of the war.

Gulston continued to sit for Poole till 1765, when he vacated his seat in favour of his son. He died 16 Aug. 1766.

[1] Nichols, *Lit. Hist.* v. 2–5. [2] *APC Col.* 1720–45, p. 637. [3] *Cal. Treas. Bks. and Pprs.* 1742–45, pp. 37–38, 225–6, 443, 664; T29/30, ff. 258, 285, 378; 29/31, f. 143.

E.C.

GULSTON, Richard (1669–1731), of Wyddial, Herts.

HERTFORD   21 Feb. 1701–6 Dec. 1705
               1710–24 May 1715

bap. 15 Apr. 1669, 1st s. of James Gulston of Wyddial by Mary, da. and coh. of John Rowley of Barkway.

Herts. *educ.* Enfield sch.; Trinity, Camb. 1684; G. Inn 1687. *m.* Margaret, da. and coh. of Dr. Francis Turner of Ely, 2s. *suc.* fa. 1704.

Descended from John Gulston, one of the prothonotaries of the court of common pleas, who bought Wyddial in 1628, Gulston was a high Tory, a member of the October Club, and a follower of Charles Caesar[1] (q.v.) in Hertfordshire politics. Re-elected in 1715, he was unseated on petition the following May, never standing again. He died 11 Mar. 1731.

[1] Cottrell Dormer letter bk. B.13 at Rousham, Oxon., *ex inf.* L. M. Mumby.

E.C.

GUMLEY, John (c. 1670–1728), of Isleworth, Mdx.

STEYNING 1722–1727

b. c.1670, 1st s. of Peter Gumley of St. Clement Danes, cabinet maker, by Elizabeth Davis. *m.* (lic. 28 Apr. 1692, he about 22) Susannah, da. of Samuel White, merchant of London, sis. of Mary, w. of Sir John Wittewrong, 3rd Bt. (q.v.), of Stantonbury, Bucks., 3s. 4da.[1]
Dep. commr. of musters 1716; commr. gen. of musters 1724–*d.*

John Gumley, a wealthy plate-glass manufacturer and army contractor,[2] owed his appointment in 1716 to his son-in-law William Pulteney (q.v.), then secretary-at-war, whose avaricious wife was said to have taken the salary of her father's post, leaving him only the perquisites.[3] In 1722 he contested Bramber unsuccessfully, but was returned for the adjacent borough of Steyning. He did not stand in 1727, dying 19 Dec. 1728.

[1] *Misc. Gen. et Her.* (ser. 4), ii. 11. [2] C. Dalton, *Geo. I's Army*, i. 253; PCC 10 Abbott. [3] Walpole to Mann, 9 Aug. 1742.

J.B.L.

GUMLEY, John (c. 1695–bef. 1749), of Isleworth, Mdx.

BRAMBER 2 Mar.–4 Apr. 1728

b. c.1695, 2nd s. of John Gumley of Isleworth and bro. of Samuel Gumley (qq.v.). *m.* cos. Martha, da. of Sir John Wittewrong, 3rd Bt. (q.v.), *s.p.*

John Gumley was returned for Bramber, where his father was steward of the court leet, but on petition he was unseated for alleged malpractices by the returning officer, who was his father's nominee. When the matter came before the Commons, William Pulteney (q.v.), his brother-in-law, alleged that the reason why it 'was pushed in this manner was because the sitting Member was his relation and Mr. Hoste [q.v.], the petitioner, a relation of another person, viz. Sir R. Walpole'.[1] He inherited his father's share in the Vauxhall glass works.[2] In 1734 he went to Bengal as head merchant,

which was said to be better than going as factor, since it entitled him to be soon a member of Council.[3] He died before 1749.[4]

[1] *CJ*, xxi. 80; *Knatchbull Diary*, 12 Mar. 1728. [2] PCC 10 Abbott. [3] *HMC Egmont Diary*, ii. 14. [4] PCC 46 Busby.

J.B.L.

GUMLEY, Samuel (c.1698–1763), of St. James's, Westminster.

HEDON 29 Nov. 1746–13 Feb. 1747

b. c.1698, 3rd s. of John Gumley sen. of Isleworth and bro. of John Gumley jun. (qq.v.). *m.* 10 Sept. 1751, Martha Colvil, wid., *s.p.*
Lt. 1718; capt. 1720; lt. and capt. Coldstream Gds. 1721; capt. 10 Drags. 1723; capt. 1 Drags. 1724, maj. 1741; capt. and lt.-col. 1 Ft. Gds. 1742, 1st maj. 1749–53; col. army 1749.

Samuel Gumley, a Guards officer of 'good humour and wit', who took part in the battles of Dettingen and Fontenoy, is said to have fought a duel with General Braddock and in later life became a Methodist.[1] He was returned for Hedon at a by-election in 1746 on the interest of his brother-in-law, William Pulteney (q.v.), Earl of Bath, but was unseated on petition for bribery.[2] He again contested it unsuccessfully in 1747 and 1754. He died at Spa in May or June 1763.

[1] Walpole to Montagu, 3 Sept. 1748, to Mann, 28 Aug. 1755. [2] *HMC Polwarth*, v. 202.

J.B.L.

GUNDRY, Nathaniel (1701–54), of Uddens, in Chalbury, Dorset, and Maidenhayne, in Musbury, Devon.

DORCHESTER 1741–May 1750

bap. 2 Apr. 1701,[1] o.s. of Nathaniel Gundry, merchant and twice mayor of Lyme Regis, Dorset by Elizabeth, o. da. and h. of Thomas Warren of Maidenhayne. *educ.* M. Temple 1720; L. Inn 1729. *m.* Mary Kelloway, 1s. 1da. *suc.* fa. 1736.
K.C. 1742; justice of common pleas 1750–*d.*

Nathaniel Gundry, of a Dorset family, was returned unopposed as a Whig for Dorchester in 1741 and 1747 together with the Tory John Browne (q.v.), also a lawyer of Lincoln's Inn. On entering Parliament he sided with the Opposition, voting against Walpole's nominee for chairman of the elections committee in December 1741. Presumably for these services, he was made K.C. after Walpole's fall in 1742;[2] but he continued to vote against the new Administration on the Hanoverians, 1742 and 1744, and was classed as 'against' in 1747. The 2nd Lord Egmont, in a list of future office-holders on Frederick's accession, included him as a possible chancellor to the Queen or the Prince with the comment 'good character but not very able.' In putting forward candidates for vacancies on the bench in 1750, Hardwicke described him to Newcastle (18 May), for the information of the King at Hanover, as having

> sometimes in the House of Commons acted with the Opposition, but I really believe he has never attached himself to them and during this Parliament he has attended very little. To do him justice he is certainly a Whig and thoroughly well affected to the King and his Government.

Pelham also wrote to Newcastle (25 May) that Gundry

> has without a rival the voice of Westminster Hall . . . I talked very frankly to him on his parliamentary behaviour; he said when he first came into Parliament he was without views and very ignorant of the world, that he therefore was led to vote against the then ministry, but he hoped I had observed he had not entered into any opposition of late, that he had a detestation of the Tories, and ever should have, and a thorough contempt for the present Opposition under any other description. I touched him upon the most tender point to that [i.e. the Prince of Wales]; he answered explicitly that he never had anything to do there in his life, nor ever would.[3]

On appointment as a high court judge Gundry vacated his seat, dying of gaol fever on circuit 30 Mar. 1754.

[1] *Som. & Dorset. N. & Q.* xii. 129–31.   [2] Hanbury Williams, *Works*, iii. 37.   [3] Add. 32720, ff. 355, 391.

R.S.L.

GWYN, Edward Prideaux (?1698–1736), of Llansannor, Glam. and Forde Abbey, Dorset.

CHRISTCHURCH	22 Feb. 1724–1727
WELLS	1727–18 Apr. 1729

b. ?1698, 1st s. of Francis Gwyn and bro. of Francis Gwyn (qq.v.). *educ.* Ch. Ch. Oxf. 9 Dec. 1713, aged 15; M. Temple 22 July 1714. *unm. suc. fa.* 1734.

The 'great confident' and correspondent of Hearne, the Oxford antiquary, Gwyn devoted much of his time to antiquarian matters, including the collection of material for a history of Devonshire.[1] He succeeded his father as a Tory at Christchurch in 1724, and again at Wells in 1727, but was unseated on petition two years later. He died c.June 1736.[2]

[1] *HMC Portland*, vii. 234; Hearne, *Colls.* (Oxf. Hist. Soc.), vi. 95; ix. 360 and passim.   [2] PCC Admon. Act Bk. 1736.

E.C.

GWYN, Francis (?1648–1734), of Llansannor, Glam. and Forde Abbey, Dorset.

CHIPPENHAM	1–6 Feb. 1673
	11 Feb. 1673–1679
CARDIFF BOROUGHS	1685–1687
CHRISTCHURCH	1689–1695
CALLINGTON	1695–1698
TOTNES	11 Jan. 1699–1701
CHRISTCHURCH	1701–1710
TOTNES	1710–1715
CHRISTCHURCH	9 Mar. 1717–1722
WELLS	1722–1727

b. ?1648, 1st s. of Edward Gwyn by Eleanor, da. of Sir Francis Popham of Littlecote, Wilts. *educ.* Ch. Ch. Oxf. 1 June 1666, aged 17; M. Temple 1667. *m.* 1690, his cos. Margaret, da. and h. of Edmund Prideaux, M.P., of Forde Abbey, Dorset, 4s. 3da.

Commr. of revenue [I] 1676–81; clerk of P.C. 1679–85; prothonotary and clerk of the Crown for Glam., Brec. and Rad. 1680; under-sec. of state 1680–3, 1688–9; groom of the bedchamber to the King 1683–5; joint sec. to Treasury 1685–7; commr. of accounts 1696–7; sec. to ld. lt. [I] 1701; P.C. [I] 1701; ld. of Trade 1711–3; sec. at war 1713–Sept. 1714; recorder, Totnes and steward, Brecknock.

A prominent Tory, closely attached to Lord Rochester, Francis Gwyn lost both his office and his seat on the accession of George I. Re-elected for Christchurch in 1717, he voted against the Government. In 1722 he was returned for Wells as well as for Christchurch, making his election for the former. He took little active part in politics, spending much of his time in antiquarian studies.[1] In 1727 he stood down in favour of his son, Edward Prideaux Gwyn (q.v.), dying 14 June 1734, aged 86.

[1] Hearne, *Colls.* (Oxf. Hist. Soc.) vi. 194; xi. 359; *HMC Popham*, 254–6.

S.R.M.

GWYN, Francis (?1699–1777), of Llansannor, Glam. and Forde Abbey, Dorset.

WELLS	1741–1754

b. ?1699, 2nd s. of Francis Gwyn and bro. of Edward Prideaux Gwyn (qq.v.). *educ.* Ch. Ch. Oxf. 4 June 1717, aged 18; M. Temple 3 Mar. 1718, called 12 May 1727. *m.* (1) May 1737, Lora (*d.*1734), da. of George Pitt of Strathfieldsaye, *s.p.*; (2) 19 Dec. 1751, Frances, da. of Mathew Combe, M.D., of Winchester, *s.p. suc.* bro. 1736.

Fellow, All Souls 1721–4.[1]

A Tory like the rest of the family, Gwyn reported to his friend, Hearne, the Oxford antiquary, in 1727 that

> the Tories are much nettled at the present proceedings . . . George II continuing things as they were before, and in all probability will act, as we may judge from his beginning, with an higher hand than George I. His late speech in Parliament gives great offence to the Tories, because he commends the last Parliament, and would have such another chosen, speaks well for the Dissenters, etc. But King James may be glad of this since, if matters go on so, his interest must needs be thereby much strengthened.[2]

Returned for Wells in 1741, he voted against the

Administration in every recorded division. Defeated in 1754, he did not stand again, dying 17 Nov. 1777.

[1] *HMC Portland*, vii. 306, 376. [2] *Colls.* (Oxf. Hist. Soc.) ix. 331–2.

E.C.

GYBBON, Phillips (1678–1762), of Hole Park, Rolvenden, Kent.

RYE 2 Dec. 1707–12 Mar. 1762

b. 11 Oct. 1678, 1st surv. s. of Robert Gybbon of Hole Park by Elizabeth, da. and h. of John Phillips. *m.* Catherine, da. of Honor Bier, 1da. *suc.* fa. 1719.
 Commr. of the revenue [I] 1714–26; chairman of committee of privileges and elections 1722–7; surveyor gen. 1726–30; ld. of Treasury 1742–4.

Descended from a wealthy clothier, who bought an estate on the Kent-Sussex border under Henry VIII, Gybbon was returned as a Whig for the neighbouring borough of Rye, which he represented continuously for 55 years. Obtaining a place at George I's accession, he voted with the Government, except on the peerage bill, which he opposed. He was one of the leading ministerial supporters in the Commons who attended private meetings at Walpole's house immediately before and after the opening of the new Parliament in 1722,[1] when he was chosen without a contest to be chairman of the elections committee. As chairman he insisted on committing a rioter to the Gate House for 'having spoke some reflecting words on the Government at Coventry', although both parties to the petition had agreed to the release of all the rioters. On another election petition, he

declared for the ayes and the noes said they had it, and upon going to divide he leaped out of the chair and ran away; his pretence was that a Member had gone out of the House, and so the Committee could not divide after the question, but everyone said it was a partial proceeding, for he as chairman should have taken care the doors had been shut on the question.[2]

He moved unsuccessfully for the special tax on papists to be extended to non-jurors, 6 May 1723, spoke against the restoration of Bolingbroke's estates, and was one of the managers of Lord Chancellor Macclesfield's impeachment in 1725. Going into opposition, he was not re-elected chairman of the elections committee at the opening of the 1727 Parliament, in which he became one of Pulteney's chief followers, closely associated with Samuel Sandys and Sir John Rushout (qq.v.). The most moderate of the three, he spoke against the Government on the civil list arrears in 1729, but objected to a demand by Sandys for the originals of some papers laid before the House by Walpole, 18 Feb. 1730, saying

that he did not speak to discourage the enquiry but he was as far from casting an odium on a minister without just cause as he would be from accusing the meanest servant. But to come to such a motion before the House had read any of those papers to know whether anything was wilfully kept back was not a right thing. So Mr Pulteney declaring he acquiesced, we were freed from the trouble of a division.

Turned out of his office when the ministry was reconstructed on Townshend's resignation in 1730, he moved for the withdrawal of the excise bill, 4 April 1733, but was one of the opposition Members who were against a motion designed to secure its outright rejection, declaring themselves satisfied with its being dropped. His opposition at Westminster did not prevent him from co-operating in Sussex with Newcastle, who in return allowed him to continue to dispose of the Treasury patronage at Rye.[3]

On Walpole's fall Gybbon, Sandys, and Rushout were placed by Pulteney on the new Treasury board on which they combined to outvote and overrule its nominal head, Lord Wilmington (Spencer Cowper, q.v.). When Pelham succeeded Wilmington in 1743, Sandys and Rushout were transferred to other posts but Gybbon, who Walpole prophesied would prove reasonable,[4] was allowed to continue at the board, till they were all turned out with Granville at the end of 1744. In 1746, when he voted for the Hanoverians, he was classed as one of the followers of Pulteney, now Bath.

In the 1747 Parliament Gybbon, classed as Opposition, attached himself to the Prince of Wales,[5] in whose lists of future office holders he figures as a lord of the Treasury. After Frederick's death he made his peace with the Pelhams, with whose support he continued to be returned for Rye till his death, 12 Mar. 1762.

[1] *Knatchbull Diary*, 115. [2] Ibid. 15 Dec. 1722 and 22 Jan. 1723. [3] Ibid. 143–4; *HMC Egmont Diary*, i. 54, 347, 361; Gybbon to Newcastle, 17 and 26 July 1740, Add. 32694, ff. 167, 312. [4] Owen, *Pelhams*, 171. [5] *Dodington Diary*, 16, 86.

R.R.S.

HADDOCK, Nicholas (1686–1746), of Wrotham Place, Kent.

ROCHESTER 1734–26 Sept. 1746

b. 1686, 3rd s. of Adm. Sir Richard Haddock, M.P., of Leigh, Essex by his 2nd w. Elizabeth, da. of Nicholas Hurleston of Rotherhithe, Surr., mariner. *m.* bef. 1717, Frances, 3s. 1da.
 Volunteer, R.N. 1699, midshipman 1702, lt. 1705, capt. 1707, r.-adm. 1734, c.-in-c. Mediterranean 1738–42, v.-adm. 1743, adm. 1744.

Of a well-known naval family, Haddock was brought in by the Administration for Rochester on becoming rear-admiral in 1734. At sea for much of his parliamentary life, he is not recorded as voting. Appointed commander-in-chief in the Mediterranean on the deterioration of relations with Spain in 1738, he blockaded a Spanish squadron in Cadiz, which escaped in October 1740, causing an outcry in England, where the Opposition moved unsuccessfully that his instructions be laid before the House. His failure in the winter of 1741 to prevent a junction of the Spanish and French fleets to escort a Spanish expedition to Italy gave rise to a fresh outburst of indignation at home, in face of which Newcastle, speaking in the Lords, threw the whole blame upon him. Haddock, who had complained bitterly of conflicting instructions and lack of reinforcements, then suffered a complete breakdown, for which his doctor prescribed 'a total recess from business of all kinds'.[1] Returning to England 'melancholy distracted',[2] he did not go to sea again.

Haddock died 26 Sept. 1746, aged 60, leaving Wrotham Place, which he had purchased in 1723, as well as a large fortune from prize money in South Sea and East India stock, to his eldest surviving son Nicholas (q.v.).[3]

[1] H. W. Richmond, *Navy in the War of 1739-48*, pp. 62-68, 151-78; *Parl. Hist.* xi. 768-83, 1000-1; xii. 267. [2] *HMC Egmont Diary*, iii. 258. [3] PCC 297 Edmunds.

E.C.

HADDOCK, Nicholas (1723-81), of Wrotham Place, Kent.

ROCHESTER   26 Jan. 1754-1761

b. 1723, 3rd but 1st surv. s. of Adm. Nicholas Haddock (q.v.). *unm. suc. fa.* 1746.

In 1746 Haddock asked Pelham to support him at Rochester in place of his father. Pelham advised him not to stand,[1] but put him up at a by-election there in 1754. He died 19 July 1781.

[1] Pelham to Bedford, 4 Oct. 1746, Bedford mss.

A.N.N.

HALDANE, George (1722-59), of Bearcrofts, Stirling, and Gleneagles, Perth.

STIRLING BURGHS   1747-Jan. 1758

bap. 10 July 1722, o.s. of Patrick Haldane (q.v.). *unm.*
Ensign 3 Ft. Gds. 1740, capt. and lt.-col. 1749; col. 1758.
Gov. Jamaica, Jan. 1758-*d.*

George Haldane purchased a commission in the Scots Guards, fought at Dettingen (1743), was severely wounded at Fontenoy (1745), returned to Scotland to recuperate, and, after the battle of Falkirk, joined Granby in pursuit of the rebels. In

high favour with Cumberland, he returned to Flanders, distinguishing himself at Roucoux, October 1746, and Lauffeld, July 1747. At the general election of 1747 his father, Patrick, arranged for him to stand for Stirling Burghs, in opposition to a candidate backed by Henry Pelham and the Duke of Argyll. In spite of Pelham's remonstrances Patrick persisted in his campaign for George, who immediately after Lauffeld obtained election leave from Cumberland, omitting to wait upon Pelham on passing through London, where he had an audience with the Prince of Wales, whom he asked for his interest. Apologizing for George's behaviour and ultimate victory, Patrick assured Pelham of his loyalty both to Argyll and himself, promising that George would be 'as zealous to support his Majesty's servants as any Member of the House'.[1] Nonetheless, the Haldanes obtained no favours: in June 1750 Newcastle refused George a military governorship in Ireland or the governorship of Pendennis castle and Patrick, despite the support of his friends, the Breadalbane family, again failed to obtain a judgeship.[2] George himself figures in a Leicester House list of 'particular friends' to be brought into Parliament by the Court on the Prince's accession.[3] At the beginning of 1751, after being 'one of the warmest' of the pro-government speakers during the debates on the Westminster petition at the opening of the session, he co-operated with Leicester House in the attack on General Philip Anstruther (q.v.), talking 'high of enquiries more necessary . . . than prosecutions on elections', till the sudden death of the Prince of Wales, whereupon he moved that the Anstruther affair should be postponed. He remained, however, connected with the Opposition, speaking in January 1752 against the subsidy treaty with Saxony[4] and on 4 June 1753 against the clandestine marriage bill. His search for preferment was ultimately rewarded with the governorship of Jamaica, where he died soon after his arrival, 26 July 1759.

[1] Argyll to Pelham, 23 July 1747, Patrick Haldane to Pelham, 11 July, 4, 18 Aug. 1747, Newcastle (Clumber) mss. [2] J. A. L. Haldane, *Haldanes of Gleneagles*, 153-4, 161-2. [3] Add. 47097. [4] Walpole, *Mems. Geo. II*, i. 57, 59, 81, 243.

E.H.-G.

HALDANE, Mungo (1682-1755), of Gleneagles, Perth.

STIRLINGSHIRE   1715-1722
DUNBARTONSHIRE   1722-23 Jan. 1725
PERTHSHIRE   28 Apr. 1726-1727

b. c.1682, 1st surv. s. of John Haldane of Gleneagles, M.P., by Mary, da. of David Drummond, 3rd Lord Maderty [S], by Lady Beatrix Graham, da. of John,

4th Earl of Montrose [S]; bro. of Patrick Haldane (q.v.). *unm. suc.* fa. 1721.

Commr. of supply for Perthshire 1702; commr. of police [S] Dec. 1730–*d.*

Haldane came of an ancient family, settled at Gleneagles since the fifteenth century. His father, a zealous Whig, had represented Perthshire and Dunbartonshire in the Parliament of Scotland, sitting for Perthshire in the first British Parliament. Through his mother he was connected with the Duke of Montrose, one of the leaders of the Squadrone. Returned as a Whig for Stirlingshire at George I's accession, he voted with the Government in every recorded division of his first Parliament, in which he was put down by Craggs in 1719 to 'Roxburghe and Montrose'. In 1722 he successfully contested Dunbartonshire but was unseated on petition by an Argyll candidate in 1725. He was returned next year at a by-election for Perthshire, where he stood unsuccessfully against the Atholl interest in 1727. In 1730 he was appointed to an office, which he held till his death, 1 June 1755.[1]

[1] J. A. L. Haldane, *Haldanes of Gleneagles*, 100–30.

J.M.S.

HALDANE, Patrick (c.1683–1769), of Bearcrofts, Stirling.

PERTH BURGHS 1715–1722

b. c.1683, 2nd s. of John Haldane of Gleneagles, M.P., and bro. of Mungo Haldane (q.v.). *educ.* St. Andrews 1699; Leyden 1711; adv. 1715. *m.* bef. 1721, Margaret, da. of William, 4th Lord Forrester of Corstorphine [S], 1s. (George, q.v.) 1da. *suc.* bro. Mungo 1755.

Professor of Greek, St. Andrews 1705–7; professor of ecclesiastical history, St. Andrews 1707–18; commr. of the equivalent Nov. 1715–May 1716; provost of St. Andrews 1716–20; commr. for forfeited estates 1716–25; commr. of excise 1724–7; jt. solicitor-gen. [S] 1746–55; sheriff depute Perthshire from 1746.

After ten years as a professor at St. Andrews with a salary of £105 p.a., Haldane was called to the bar, appointed a commissioner of the equivalent with a salary of £500, and returned as a Whig for Perth Burghs in 1715. Next year he exchanged his post for that of a commissioner for the sale of estates forfeited in the late rebellion with a salary of £1,000, carrying out his duties with a severity which earned him the odium not only of the Jacobites but of many other important persons connected with the dispossessed families. He was said to have surprised English members of the Commons by opposing a proposal for allowing the wives and widows of forfeited estate owners in Scotland to be allowed their jointures, after supporting a similar proposal for their English counterparts. He voted with the Government in all recorded divisions, making 'an excellent allegorical speech' in the debate of 24 Apr. 1716 on the septennial bill, 'comparing our times to those of Solon and Pisistratus in the Greek and those of Sulla in the Roman history.' In 1720 he was among the Members of both Houses who were credited by the South Sea Company with stock—in his case £2,000 at 285 on 23 Mar.—without paying for it but with the right to 'sell' it back to the company whenever they chose, taking as 'profit' any increase in the market price.[1]

In December 1721, shortly before the general election of 1722, Haldane was appointed a judge of the court of session, with the support of the Dukes of Roxburghe and Montrose, the leaders of the Squadrone, but against the opposition of their rivals, the Duke of Argyll and Lord Ilay. The appointment gave rise to what he afterwards described as the 'extraordinary persecution' that

> fell on me from some of my countrymen of high rank . . . for no other reason . . . but that of my having, as one of the commissioners of the forfeited estates, executed faithfully the powers given to those commissioners by Act of Parliament.

At the instance of the faculty of advocates, the court of session at first refused to admit him on the ground that he had not served the minimum period of five years as an advocate prescribed by the Act of Union as a necessary qualification for a judgeship. When the decision was overruled on appeal by the House of Lords, his enemies raised objection to him on grounds of character, charging him *inter alia* with Jacobitism, bribery, and extortion by threats. A resolution admitting him was carried by the votes of two extraordinary, that is honorary, lords of session, whose right to vote was challenged by the ordinary lords, themselves seven to six against him. The matter was once more referred to London, where Haldane agreed under pressure to accept a commissionership of excise instead of a judgeship to appease his opponents. At the same time an Act was passed affirming the power of the Crown to appoint to the court of session, the court being limited to the right of remonstrating against an appointment of which they disapproved.[2]

Haldane's excise appointment was not renewed at George II's accession, after which he returned to the bar, acquiring the reputation of being 'not only the best election-monger, but the best election lawyer of his time'. In 1746 he was appointed joint solicitor-general of Scotland, apparently on the recommendation of the Duke of Cumberland, with whom his son, George (q.v.), was a favourite. Next year, with Cumberland's support, he used his electioneering experience to bring in his son for Stirling Burghs against a candidate supported by Pelham. In 1750 he applied unsuccessfully to Lord Chancellor Hardwicke for a judgeship, on the ground that his advancing years made him less able than formerly to sustain the fatigues of the bar. His failing powers are referred to in a letter from Robert Dundas (q.v.), lord president of the court of session, to Hardwicke in 1753, describing Haldane as of little assistance to the lord advocate, being 'quite daised, as we express it.' Further applications on his behalf by George Haldane and the Breadalbane family proving equally fruitless, he retired in 1755 with a pension of £400 p.a.[3]

Haldane's last years were clouded by the death of his son, leaving debts which, together with the cost of his own electioneering activities—in 1754 he is said to have set up candidates in three constituencies[4]—made it necessary for him to sell the family estate of Gleneagles, recently inherited from his brother, Mungo (q.v.), to their half-brother, Robert Haldane, M.P., in 1760.

He died 10 Jan. 1769.

[1] *Cal. Treas. Bks.* xxxii. 520–1; Ramsay of Ochtertyre, *Scotland and Scotsmen in the 18th Cent.*, ii. 479–85; *HMC Stuart*, vi. 106; A. Corbière to H. Walpole, 27 Apr. 1716, Cholmondeley (Houghton) mss; *CJ*, xix. 569. [2] *HMC Portland*, vii. 313; J. A. L. Haldane, *Haldanes of Gleneagles*, 137 seq.; *More Culloden Pprs.* ii. 222–35. [3] Ramsay, 482; Yorke, *Hardwicke*, i. 621–2; Haldane, loc. cit.; Add. 35448, f. 88; 35450, f. 195. [4] Argyll to Newcastle, 19 Nov. 1755, Add. 32737, f. 340.

R.R.S.

HALE, Paggen (c.1715–55), of King's Walden, Herts.

HERTFORDSHIRE   1747–3 Apr. 1755

b. c.1715, 2nd s. of William Hale (q.v.). *educ.* G. Inn 1732, called 1739. *m.* 20 Nov. 1742, Elizabeth, da. of Humphry Morice (*d.*1731, q.v.) by his first w., *s.p. suc.* e. bro. William 1742.

Hale was returned unopposed in 1747 as a supporter of the Administration. In the 2nd Lord Egmont's electoral survey, c.1749–50, he notes against Hale's name: 'We must keep him as he is Dr. Lee's (q.v.) brother-in-law'. He died 3 Apr. 1755.

A.N.N.

HALE, William (?1686–1717), of King's Walden, Herts.

BRAMBER   15 Jan. 1709–1710
ST. ALBANS   1713–27 Apr. 1714
                    1715–2 Oct. 1717

b. ?1686, 1st s. of Richard Hale by Elizabeth, da. and h. of Isaac Meynell of Meynell Langley, Derbys.

educ. B.N.C. Oxf. 30 Sept. 1702, aged 16. *m.* Catherine, da. of Peter Paggen of the Manor House, Wandsworth, Surr., 2s. She later married Humphry Morice (*d.*1731, q.v.). *suc.* fa. 1689.

Descended from on old Hertfordshire family, seated at King's Walden since 1576, Hale was returned for St. Albans as a Whig in 1713 but unseated on petition in favour of a Tory. Re-elected after a contest in 1715, he did not vote on the septennial bill, dying 2 Oct. 1717.

A.N.N.

HALES, Sir Thomas, 2nd Bt. (1666–1748), of Bekesbourne, nr. Canterbury, Kent.

KENT   1701–1705
CANTERBURY   1715–1734, 11 Apr. 1735–1741,
                  23 Jan. 1746–1747

bap. 1 Mar. 1666,[1] 1st surv. s. of Thomas Hales (*d.v.p.*), by Mary, da. and h. of Richard Wood of Abbots Langley, Herts., and gd.-s. of Sir Robert Hales, 1st Bt., M.P. *educ.* I Temple. *m.* (lic. 14 Nov. 1688), Mary, da. of Sir Charles Pym, 1st Bt., M.P., of Brymore, Som. (s. of the famous John Pym, M.P.), sis. and h. of Sir Charles Pym, 2nd Bt., 6s. 4da. *suc.* fa. 1692 and gd.-fa. as 2nd Bt. Dec. 1693.

Commr. for forfeited estates 1716–25.

Hales was the head of the junior branch of a Jacobite family, but he himself was a staunch Whig. After representing his county from 1701–5, he declined an invitation from the Kent Whigs to contest it again in 1715, thenceforth sitting for Canterbury, near which he had an estate. Appointed one of the commissioners for forfeited estates, with a salary of £1,000 a year, he consistently supported the Administration, except in 1719, when he voted against the peerage bill.

In 1732 Hales, as a former commissioner for forfeited estates, became involved in the Derwentwater scandal.[2] His name had been affixed to the contract for a fraudulent sale, under standing instructions which he had left with the secretary to sign for him in his absence when necessary. A motion was introduced that any commissioner empowering the secretary to set his name to contracts was guilty of a violation of the Act under which he had been appointed and of a high breach of trust. As, however, Hales was 'a constant friend to the Revolution and the present Government, and besides this a worthy man in his private character',[3] the ministry opposed the motion and he escaped without even a reprimand.

In 1734 Hales, who had voted for the excise bill despite representations made to him by the Canterbury corporation, was defeated at the poll but was seated on petition. He was again defeated in 1741, remaining out of Parliament till 1746, when he was returned at a by-election, again supporting the Administration. Defeated for the last time in 1747, he died 7 Jan. 1748.

[1] Bekesbourne par. reg. [2] See BOND, Denis. [3] *HMC Egmont Diary*, i. 247.

A.N.N.

HALES, Thomas (?1694–1762), of Bekesbourne, Kent.

MINEHEAD	1722–1727
CAMELFORD	1727–1734
GRAMPOUND	1734–1741
HYTHE	3 Dec. 1744–1761
EAST GRINSTEAD	8 Dec. 1761–6 Oct. 1762

b. ?1694, 1st s. of Sir Thomas Hales, 2nd Bt. (q.v.). *educ.* Oriel, Oxf. 15 Dec. 1711, aged 17; I. Temple. *m.* 22 June 1723, Mary, da. of Sir Robert Marsham, 4th Bt., M.P., sis. of Robert Marsham (q.v.), 1st Baron Romney, 6s. 7da. *suc.* fa. as 3rd Bt. 7 Jan. 1748.
Clerk of the household to the Prince of Wales, 1718–27; clerk of the Green Cloth 1727–60; lt. of Dover castle 1728–50; mayor, Hythe 1747; vice-warden of the Cinque Ports 1750–*d.*

Soon after George I's accession Hales obtained a post in the household of the future George II, where he remained throughout the next reign. In 1722 he was returned for Minehead, near which his father had acquired an estate by marriage. At the next general election he was brought in by the Government for Camelford, after contesting Hythe unsuccessfully on the Duke of Dorset's interest. Before the general election of 1734 he wrote to Dorset in Ireland, 22 Sept. 1733: 'I am often questioned about my standing at Hythe, to which I always give a doubtful answer; when your Grace would have me give any other I hope you'll let me know, and that your Grace did not forget Camelford before you left England, for I hear they are settling these boroughs now'.[1] In the end he was returned by the Administration for Grampound. On his defeat there in 1741, Lord John Sackville (q.v.) wrote to the Duke of Bedford, 11 June: 'I am told a petition will be offered . . . by Mr. Hales . . . There has always been between his family and the Duke of Dorset such a particular friendship that I am afraid I must not vote against him.'[2] The petition was not proceeded with but he was later returned by Dorset for Hythe without opposition.
He died 6 Oct. 1762.

[1] Sackville mss, Kent AO. [2] Bedford mss.

A.N.N.

HALKETT, Peter (1695–1755), of Pitferrane, Fife.

STIRLING BURGHS   1734–1741

b. 21 June 1695, 1st s. of Sir Percy Wedderburn

(afterwards Halkett), 1st Bt., M.P. [S], of Pitferrane, by Janet, da. of Sir Charles Halkett, 1st Bt., M.P. [S], sis. and h. of Sir James Halkett, 2nd Bt., M.P. [S]. *m.* Oct. 1728,[1] Lady Amelia Stuart, da. of Francis, 8th Earl of Moray [S], 3s. *suc.* fa. as 2nd Bt. 20 Mar. 1746.
Capt. R. Scot. Fusiliers June 1717, maj. Nov. 1739; lt.-col. 44 Ft. 1741; col. Feb. 1751.

Halkett, an army officer, whose family had represented Dunfermline before the Union, stood for Stirling Burghs in 1734 on the recommendation of Lord Ilay, Walpole's election manager for Scotland. Returned without making an appearance until the day of the election,[2] he voted with the Administration on the Spanish convention in 1739, and on the place bill in 1740, but did not stand in 1741. Taken prisoner by the rebels at the battle of Prestonpans,[3] he was released on parole by the Young Pretender on condition of not bearing arms for 18 months. In February 1746 he was one of the officers who refused to obey an order by Cumberland to rejoin their regiments, under threat of losing their commissions, saying that the Duke 'was master of their commissions but not of their probity and honour'.[4] He was recommended by Ilay, now Duke of Argyll, as the government candidate for Stirling in 1747,[5] but gave up on being opposed by George Haldane (q.v.), a favourite of Cumberland's. In 1754 he embarked for North America, taking part in the disastrous expedition against Fort Duquesne, where he was killed, 9 July 1755.[6]

[1] *More Culloden Pprs.* iii. 32. [2] Patrick Haldane (q.v.) to Pelham, 18 Aug. 1747, Newcastle (Clumber) mss. [3] *Gent. Mag.* 1745, p. 518. [4] Chevalier de Johnstone, *Mems.* 125–6. [5] Patrick Haldane to Pelham, 4 Aug. 1747, Newcastle (Clumber) mss. [6] *Gent. Mag.* 1755, pp. 378–9.

E.C.

HALL, Charles (1690–1743), of Kettlethorpe, Lincs.

LINCOLN   1727–1734

bap. 6 May 1690, o.s. of Thomas Hall of Kettlethorpe by Amy, da. of Henry Mildmay of Graces, Essex, wid. of Vincent Amcotts of Harrington, Lincs. *unm. suc.* fa. 1698.

Hall, whose grandfather had acquired Kettlethorpe by marriage in the mid-seventeenth century, successfully contested Lincoln as a Tory in 1727, voting consistently against the Administration. He did not stand again, in 1734 supporting his kinsman, Coningsby Sibthorp (q.v.).[1] He died 21 Aug. 1743, leaving all his Lincolnshire estates to his nephew Charles Amcotts.[2]

[1] *Letters and Pprs. Banks Fam.*, ed. Hill (Lincoln Rec. Soc. xlv), 156. [2] R. E. G. Cole, 'The Manor and Rectory of Kettlethorpe', *Associated Architectural Societies Reports*, xxxi. 72–76.

P.W.

HALSEY, Edmund (*d.*1729), of Southwark, Surr. and Stoke Poges, Bucks.

SOUTHWARK   12 Jan.–7 Feb. 1712
BUCKINGHAM   30 Nov. 1717–1722
SOUTHWARK   1722–19 Aug. 1729

Bro. of Anne Halsey, w. of Ralph Thrale of Offley, Herts., fa. of Ralph Thrale (q.v.). *m.* 16 Nov. 1693, Anne, da. and coh. of James Child of Southwark, brewer, 2s. *d.v.p.* 1da. who m. Richard Temple, M.P., 1st Visct. Cobham.
Brewers' Co. 1697, master 1715; director, South Sea Co. 1721–*d.*

Edmund Halsey, who is said to have been a miller's boy at St. Albans, Herts., came to London 'with 4*s.* 6*d.* only in his pocket' and found work at the Anchor Brewery, in Southwark, owned by James Child.[1] Becoming clerk in the counting house, he was taken into partnership in 1693, ten days before his marriage to his employer's daughter, and on Child's death in 1696 became sole owner of the brewery.[2] Unseated at Southwark in 1712, less than four weeks after his election, he was found a seat at Buckingham in 1717 by his son-in-law, Lord Cobham, voting with the Administration. For the 1722 election he went back to Southwark, where he was returned on his own interest after a contest and was unopposed in 1727. In 1724 he bought the Stoke Poges estate from Robert Gayer (q.v.) for £12,000.[3] He died 19 Aug. 1729, leaving the Anchor Brewery to his wife and his daughter, Lady Cobham.

[1] K. C. Balderston, *Thraliana*, i. 299; *N. & Q.* (ser. 3), ii. 133.
[2] *Three Centuries* (Barclay, Perkins & Co. Ltd.), 7–9. [3] *VCH Bucks.* iii. 307.

R.S.L.

HALYBURTON, James (*d.*1765), of Pitcur, Angus, and Firth, Orkney.

ORKNEY AND SHETLAND   1747–1754

o.s. of James Halyburton of Pitcur. *m.* 21 Dec. 1735, Anne, da. and h. of Gilbert Burnet, commr. of excise, *s.p. suc.* fa. 1747.
Ensign 13 Ft. 1735; capt.-lt. 3 Ft. Gds. 1748; capt. and lt.-col. 1750.

Halyburton, whose family had been seated at Pitcur since 1433,[1] was returned as a government supporter for Orkney and Shetland by his brother-in-law, the 14th Earl of Morton. He died 10 May 1765, entailing his estates on his sister.

[1] A. J. Warden, *Angus or Forfarshire*, 23.

P.W.

HAMILTON, Alexander (1684–1763), of Innerwick and of Ballencrieff, Linlithgow.

LINLITHGOWSHIRE   1727–1741

b. 1684, o.s. of James Hamilton of Ballencrieff by Margaret, da. of Sir Thomas Nicholson, 2nd Bt., of Carnock, Stirling. *m.* bef. 1724, Lady Margaret Kerr, da. of William, 2nd Mq. of Lothian [S], 5s. 1da. *suc.* fa. 1687.
Sec. for Scotland to Prince of Wales by 1733–7; postmaster gen. [S] 1746–*d.*

The Hamiltons of Innerwick acquired their lands in the fourteenth century. Alexander Hamilton, whose wardship and marriage were granted to George Baillie (q.v.) in 1692, succeeded his kinsman, Sir Francis Hamilton, 3rd Bt., to the name but not the lands of Innerwick in 1714.[1] Returned unopposed for the county with the backing of Lord Hopetoun in 1727 and again after a contest in 1734, he voted with the Administration in all recorded divisions. He did not stand in 1741 but was given a place in 1746. He died 28 Dec. 1763.

[1] G. Hamilton, *House of Hamilton*, 505.

R.S.L.

HAMILTON, Lord Archibald (1673–1754), of Riccarton, nr. Linlithgow, and Motherwell, Lanark.

LANARKSHIRE   1708–1710
              23 Dec. 1718–1734
QUEENBOROUGH   22 Feb. 1735–1741
DARTMOUTH   27 Mar. 1742–1747

bap. 17 Feb. 1673, 7th s. of William Douglas Hamilton, 3rd Duke of Hamilton [S], by Anne, *suo jure* Duchess of Hamilton, da. and h. of James, 1st Duke of Hamilton [S], niece and h. of William, 2nd Duke of Hamilton [S]. *m.* (1) Anne (*d.*1709), da. of Charles, 2nd Baron Lucas of Shenfield, and wid. of Edward Cary of Caldecote, *s.p.*; (2) 17 Dec. 1718, Anne (*d.*29 Mar. 1719), da. and h. of Claud Hamilton and wid. of Sir Francis Hamilton, 3rd Bt., of Killaugh, co. Down, *s.p.*; (3) 29 Sept. 1719, Lady Jane Hamilton, da. of James, 6th Earl of Abercorn [S], 4s. 4da.
Lt. R.N. July 1690, capt. Sept. 1693; gov. of Jamaica 1710–16; ld. of Admiralty 1729–38; cofferer and surveyor gen. to Prince of Wales 1738–47; ld. of Admiralty 1742–6; gov. of Greenwich Hospital 1746–*d.*

Appointed governor of Jamaica after serving in the navy and sitting for Lanarkshire, Hamilton was brought home in 1716 under arrest on a charge concocted by the local opposition. Acquitted by a board of Trade inquiry,[1] he was re-elected for Lanarkshire in 1718, voted with the Government, and was appointed a lord of the Admiralty in 1729. In 1735 his wife became the mistress of Frederick, Prince of Wales, who gave her a post in his wife's household on his marriage in 1736. According to Hervey, Hamilton was

of so quiet, so secure and contented a temper, that he seemed cut out to play the passive character his wife and the Prince had graciously allotted to him.

He absented himself from the division on the

Prince's allowance in 1737, soon after which he was turned out

> without the least notice given him, or knowing his offence, only [because] his lady is in the service of the Princess of Wales.

Compensated with a post in the Prince's household, he voted with the Opposition till Walpole's fall, except on the motion for the removal of Walpole in February 1741, when he withdrew. He was one of the Prince's servants who obtained office in the new Government, returning to his former post at the Admiralty. In 1746 he was the only member of the Admiralty board not to resign with the Pelhams, on whose return to office he was transferred to the governorship of Greenwich Hospital. Shortly before this his wife, having used her position to such effect that the Prince was told by Carteret that he really 'must not promote nobody but Hamiltons, and have a Scotch colony about him',[2] had been dismissed by Frederick with a pension of £1,200 a year, 'for giving him William Pitt as a rival'. Hamilton himself retained his post under the Prince till 1747, when he was turned out for refusing to follow him into opposition. Offered a pension of £1,200 a year by the Prince, he gratefully accepted

> but returned in an hour with a letter from his wife, to say that, as his Royal Highness was angry with her husband, it was not proper for either of them to take their pensions.[3]

He died 5 Apr. 1754.

[1] CSP Col. 1716-17, pp. 77-90; 1717-18, pp. 47-48, 81-82. [2] Harvey, Mems. 475, 851; Ilchester, Lord Hervey and His Friends, 265 n. 3; HMC Egmont Diary, ii. 468-9. [3] Walpole to Mann, 24 June 1745 and 27 Jan. 1747, to Montagu, 25 June 1745; Mems. Geo. II, i. 76.

R.R.S.

HAMILTON, Basil (1696–1742), of Baldoon, Wigtown.

KIRKCUDBRIGHT STEWARTRY 1741–14 Nov. 1742

b. 8 Sept. 1696, 2nd s. of Lord Basil Hamilton (s. of 3rd Duke of Hamilton), by Mary, da. of David Dunbar and h. to her gd.-fa. Sir David Dunbar, 1st Bt., of Baldoon; 1st cos. of Lord William Hamilton (q.v.). m. bef. 1722, Isabella, da. of Hon. Alexander Mackenzie, M.P. (s. of 4th Earl of Seaforth [S]), 2s. 2da. suc. e. bro. 1703.
Provost, Kirkcudbright.

During the rebellion of 1715, Hamilton commanded a troop of horse, with which he joined the English Jacobites under Thomas Forster (q.v.). Taken prisoner at Preston, he was tried and sentenced to death on 31 May 1716, but was reprieved on the intercession of his uncle, Lord Orkney, with the King and the Duke of Marlborough, though his estates, valued at £1,495 sterling p.a., were forfeited.[1]

In 1722, George Lockhart of Carnwarth, a prominent Jacobite, informed the Pretender that he had given the lord advocate, Robert Dundas (q.v.),

> an assurance that if he would preserve Mr. Basil Hamilton and some honest men's estates from being forfaulted, I would take care so to manage matters that he should be elected to this shire [Edinburghshire].[2]

The estates were successfully claimed by Hamilton's mother, the forfeiture being rescinded by Act of Parliament in 1733. In 1734 he stood unsuccessfully for Dumfries Burghs with the Duke of Queensberry's support against a government candidate. In 1739 he was consulted by an agent of the Pretender's about a scheme for an armed rising in Scotland, but thought 'it was not then a proper time to make an attempt'.[3] Returned in 1741 for Kirkcudbright, where he had a strong interest,[4] he voted against the Government on the chairman of the elections committee in December. He died 14 Nov. 1742.

[1] Scots Peerage, vii. 519-20; HMC Townshend, 170; Forfeited Estates Pprs. (Sc. Hist. Soc. lvii), p. xxxi. [2] Lockhart Pprs. ii. 88-89. [3] Murray of Broughton, Mems. (Sc. Hist. Soc. xxvii), 2-3. [4] HMC Polwarth, v. 87.

E.C.

HAMILTON, Charles, Lord Binning (c.1697–1732).

ST. GERMANS 1722–1727

b. c.1697, 1st s. of Thomas Hamilton, 6th Earl of Haddington [S] (rep. peer 1716-34), by Helen, da. of John Hope of Hopetoun, Linlithgow, sis. of Charles, 1st Earl of Hopetoun [S]. m. 17 Sept. 1715, Rachel, da. of George Baillie (q.v.) by Lady Grisell Hume, da. of Patrick, 1st Earl of Marchmont [S], 4s. 2da.
Knight marischal [S] Feb. 1718–d.

In 1715, Lord Binning accompanied his father, a leader of the Squadrone, as a volunteer to fight the rebels, taking part in the battle of Sheriffmuir. In 1718 he was given the office of knight marischal of Scotland for life with a salary of £400.[1] His father wrote to Grey Neville (q.v.) on 2 Sept. 1720:

> Lord Binning hath had occasion of late to be often at Berwick to wait upon my Lord Marchmont, and some people have pressed him (as he says) to set up for that town to be elected for the next Parliament. He sayeth he owns that he hath a great mind to be in the House of Commons, if it is possible, but that he will not advance one step in this till he knows if you are to stand for that town . . . I thought it was better to write to you plainly how the case stands than that you should hear it by a report and perhaps not so much to my son's advantage, I mean as if he was raising a party in Berwick in opposition to you and your interest, which I dare say you will not easily believe of one who hath always professed a friendship for you, and I swear I never knew him in the least disingenuous. I own I wish it were possible for him to be in the next election of the House of Commons,

but you know he cannot come for any place of Scotland [as the eldest son of a peer of Scotland], so it must be for some place in England.[2]

He was brought in by the Administration for St. Germans, shortly before his return leaving England to accompany Lord Polwarth, his wife's uncle, to the congress of Cambrai.[3] He did not stand again, dying of consumption at Naples 27 Dec. 1732, aged 36.

[1] Sir W. Fraser, *Mems. of the Earls of Haddington*, i. 264. [2] Sunderland (Blenheim) mss. [3] *HMC Polwarth*, iii. 78, 96.

E.C.

HAMILTON, Hon. Charles (1704–86), of Painshill, nr. Cobham, Surr.

TRURO 1741–1747

bap. 13 Nov. 1704, 9th s. of James, 6th Earl of Abercorn [S], by Elizabeth, da. and h. of Sir Robert Reading, 1st Bt., of Dublin; bro. of Hon. George Hamilton (q.v.). *educ.* Westminster 1719; Ch. Ch. Oxf. 1720. *m.* (1) 2da.; (2) Agnes (*d.*1772), da. of David Cockburn, M.D., of Ayr, *s.p.*; (3) Frances, *s.p.*

M.P. [I] 1727–60.

Clerk of the household to Frederick, Prince of Wales 1738–47; receiver gen. of the revenues of Minorca 1743–57.

Hamilton owed his place in the Prince of Wales's household to the influence of his sister, Lady Archibald Hamilton, the Prince's mistress. Returned for a Cornish borough by Lord Falmouth in 1741, he voted with the Opposition till Walpole's fall, after which, with the rest of the Prince's servants, he supported the Government. The only member of the former Opposition to be included in the ministerial list of candidates for a proposed public accounts commission in May 1742, he was put down under 'Winnington', not 'Prince of Wales', in the Cockpit lists drawn up in October by Pelham, who next year appointed him receiver general of Minorca. He spoke against dismissing the Hanoverians on 6 Dec. 1743.[1] He retained his post in the Prince's household till February 1747, when he was dismissed with his brother-in-law, Lord Archibald Hamilton (q.v.), Lady Archibald having received her congé in the previous year. In his old age he supplied Shelburne with a number of discreditable anecdotes about the Prince, declaring that he despised him so heartily that he could not endure to hang up a full length portrait of him, presented to him by Frederick himself, which had ever since been in a store room.[2]

In 1747 Hamilton, not having been re-nominated by Lord Falmouth, made an attempt to get himself returned as a government supporter for Bishop's Castle, resigning his Minorca post, which had been made inconsistent with a seat in the House by the

Place Act of 1742, but resuming it after failing to be elected.[3] When the loss of Minorca in 1756 cost him his receivership, his claim for compensation was vehemently taken up by Henry Fox, who secured a secret service pension of £1,200 a year for 'my old and undone friend, Hamilton'.[4] He spent the rest of his life in retirement, ultimately settling at Bath after financial difficulties had forced him to sell his estate near Cobham, where he had made 'a fine place out of a most cursed hill'.[5] On his death, 11 Sept, 1786, Horace Walpole wrote:

one of my patriarchs of modern gardening has been killed by Anstey, author of *The Bath Guide*. Mr. Hamilton, who has built a house in the Crescent, was also at eighty-three eager in planting a new garden, and wanted some acres, which Anstey, his neighbour, not so ancient, destined to the same use. Hamilton wrote a warm letter on their being refused; and Anstey, who does not hate a squabble in print, as he has more than once shown, discharged shaft upon shaft against the poor veteran [who] . . . died of the volley.[6]

[1] Yorke's parl. jnl. *Parl Hist.* xiii. 140. [2] L. Cust, *Recs. Cust Fam.* (ser. 3), 37; Fitzmaurice, *Shelburne*, i. 48–49. [3] Add. 32711, f. 513; *Gent. Mag.* 1747, p. 343. [4] *Structure*, 446 n.2. [5] Walpole to Montagu, 11 Aug. 1748; Manning & Bray, *Surr.* ii. 768–9. [6] To Lady Upper Ossory, 28 Sept. 1786.

S.R.M.

HAMILTON, Hon. George (c.1697–1775).

WELLS 1734–25 Mar. 1735, 1747–1754

b. c.1697, 6th s. of James, 6th Earl of Abercorn [S], and bro. of Hon. Charles Hamilton (q.v.). *m.* Oct. 1719, Bridget, da. of Col. William Coward, sis. and h. of William Coward (q.v.), 4s. 7da.

M.P. [I] 1727–60.

Ensign 13 Ft. 1727, out by 1740; dep. cofferer to Prince of Wales Oct. 1742–51.

Hamilton acquired by marriage the Coward family's estates in and around Wells, for which he stood unsuccessfully as a Whig in 1722, subsequently petitioning, also unsuccessfully. He attributed his defeat to Walpole, who, he claimed, after promising to be for him, had 'allowed all the Government's servants and his dependants to vote against him'. In 1734 he was returned for Wells as an opposition Whig but was unseated on petition, again owing to Walpole, who actively intervened against him.[1] In 1747 he was once more returned for Wells, this time as a supporter of the Prince of Wales, in whose household he had obtained a place through the influence of his sister, Lady Archibald Hamilton, the Prince's mistress.[2] A petition was presented against him, but its hearing, after being fixed for 10 Mar. 1748 at the bar of the House, was put off till 6 July, which meant till the next session. 'Pray tell Mr. Hamilton that I congratulate him on his reprieve', wrote Henry Bathurst (q.v.) to another Leicester House man, Sir John Cust (q.v.), 'which

I hope the mercy of the ministry will hereafter extend into a pardon'. Apparently it did, for the petition was withdrawn, though Hamilton was classed as Opposition.

After Frederick's death another of his followers, Sir Edmond Thomas, wrote to Cust:

> I told you some time since what Fox would do at Malmesbury—he will get a footing likewise at Wells if poor Hamilton is not a little supported, which I think the Duke of Newcastle might find it in his interest to do.[3]

In fact he never stood again, retiring into private life with bitter feelings towards Wells, which he expressed in his will by the injunction that

> I will on no account be buried at Wells or have any achievement at either the parish church or cathedral church in the said city.[4]

He died at Bath 3 May 1775.

¹ *HMC Egmont Diary*, ii. 115, 161. ² See HAMILTON, Lord Archibald. ³ *L. Cust. Recs. Cust. Fam.* (ser. 3), 128, 143. ⁴ PCC 188 Alexander.

S.R.M.

HAMILTON, Gustavus, 2nd Visct. Boyne [I] (c.1710–46)

NEWPORT I.O.W.   17 Feb. 1736–1741

b. c.1710, o. surv. s. of Hon. Frederick Hamilton of Stackallan, co. Meath by Sophia, da. of James Hamilton of Tollymore. *educ.* Westminster 1719–24; Grand Tour. *unm. suc.* fa. 1715; gd.-fa. Gustavus Hamilton as 2nd Visct. Boyne 16 Sept. 1723.
P.C. [I] 9 Aug. 1736; commr. of revenue [I] 1737–*d.*

Hamilton inherited a large fortune from his grandfather, Gustavus Hamilton, 1st Viscount Boyne, in 1723. Returned for Newport on the government interest in 1736, he was made a commissioner of the revenue in Ireland with a salary of £1,000 a year.[1] He voted with the Administration on the Spanish convention in 1739 and the place bill in 1740 but did not stand again, dying 20 Apr. 1746.

¹ *Gent. Mag.* 1739, p. 304.

P.W.

HAMILTON, Sir James, 2nd Bt. (1682–1750), of Rosehall, Lanark.

LANARKSHIRE   1710–1715, 7 Mar. 1735–15 Mar. 1750

bap. 24 Nov. 1682, 1st surv. s. of Sir Archibald Hamilton, 1st Bt., of Rosehall by his w. Anne Murray of Deuchar, Forfar. *m.* 2 Mar. 1707, his cos. Frances, da. of Alexander Stuart, 5th Lord Blantyre [S], *s.p. suc.* fa. 1709.

Hamilton, whose father had purchased Rosehall in 1691,[1] represented Lanarkshire as a Tory under Queen Anne. At the time of the Swedish plot in 1717 (see Caesar, Charles), he undertook to join Lord Mar, the Pretender's secretary of state, should he land in Scotland.[2] Returned for Lanarkshire in 1735 he voted with the Opposition in every recorded division. In 1741 the Duke of Hamilton, his distant kinsman, advised Murray of Broughton, the Jacobite agent in Scotland, to apply to him for funds towards the preparations for a rising. In 1744 Murray suggested that the Young Pretender should write to him as he seemed well disposed,[3] but he took no active part in the Forty-five. He died 15 Mar. 1750.

¹ *Heraldry of the House of Hamilton*, 56, 79. ² *HMC Stuart*, iv. 556–7. ³ *Mems.* (Sc. Hist. Soc. xxvii), 21, 376.

E.C.

HAMILTON, James, 1st Visct. Limerick [I] (c.1691–1758), of Dundalk, co. Louth.

WENDOVER   1727–1734, 22 Apr. 1735–1741
TAVISTOCK   28 Jan. 1742–1747
MORPETH   1747–1754

b. c.1691, 1st s. of James Hamilton of Tollymore, co. Down by Anne, da. of John Mordaunt, 1st Visct. Mordaunt of Avalon, sis. of Charles, Earl of Peterborough and Monmouth. *m.* 15 Oct. 1728, Lady Henrietta Bentinck, da. of William, 1st Earl of Portland, 1s. 2da. *suc.* fa. May 1700. *cr.* Baron Claneboye and Visct. Limerick [I] 13 May 1719; Earl of Clanbrassil [I] 24 Nov. 1756.
M.P. [I] 1715–19.
P.C. [I] 14 Apr. 1746; gov. co. Louth 1756–*d.*

Described by Horace Walpole as 'a pale ill-looking fellow with a bent brow, a whoreson voice and a dead eye of saffron hue . . . belonging to Lord Bath [William Pulteney]',[1] Limerick was returned on the Hampden interest for Wendover as an opposition Whig. A member of the gaols committee in 1729, he took an active part on the committee appointed to inquire into the affairs of the Charitable Corporation in 1732, seconding a motion that Sir Robert Sutton (q.v.) had been guilty of promoting the fraudulent practices of the Charitable Corporation, introducing a bill to restrain the directors from leaving the country until the end of the next session of Parliament, and in the following session supporting a motion that Sutton was guilty of frauds and breach of trust. He was active in Irish matters and on the council of the Georgia Society.

In 1734 Limerick was defeated at Wendover, but was seated on a petition 'notwithstanding the ministry made it their affair' to oppose him. His petition was supported by the members of the Georgia Society, which he thereafter tried to convert into an instrument of the Opposition. In March 1739 he resigned from the council hoping 'thereby the trustees would be induced to alter their measures,

by which he meant, go over to the minority side.'
On 13 Feb. 1741 he seconded the opposition
motion for Walpole's dismissal.

After Walpole's fall Limerick, having failed to
retain his Wendover seat at the general election, was
returned by the Duke of Bedford at a by-election
for Tavistock. He was one of the opposition Members who were recommended to the King for seats
on the new board of Admiralty but 'demurred to
accept unless more of their party were taken in,
which angered the King.' On 9 Mar. he moved
unsuccessfully in the Commons for a secret committee of inquiry into Walpole's Administration,
with the result that next day the King rejected him
and the other proposed lords of the Admiralty.[2]
On 25 Mar. following he successfully renewed his
motion for an inquiry, becoming chairman of the
secret committee. In July Pulteney rewarded his
services by obtaining for his son the reversion
of the lucrative sinecure of remembrancer of the
Exchequer in Ireland, then held by Lady Limerick's
uncle, Lord Palmerston (q.v.).[3]

Till 1746 Limerick supported the Government,
though in February 1744 he carried a motion
against an increase in the sugar duty proposed by
Pelham.[4] Listed among the followers of Pulteney,
now Lord Bath, he absented himself from the
division on the Hanoverian troops in 1746. Soon
afterwards he joined the Prince's party, figuring in
lists of persons to receive office on Frederick's
accession as paymaster general or a lord of the
Admiralty.

Returned by Lord Carlisle, formerly Lord
Morpeth (q.v.), for Morpeth in 1747, Limerick was
classed as Opposition. He spent the next three years
in Ireland, from which he emerged to move on
4 Feb. 1751, that the army estimates be reduced
from 18,850 men to 15,000. Commenting on his
re-appearance Horace Walpole writes:

> He had preserved a sort of character from the impos-
> sibility of his being dismissed with the rest of his
> friends, as he has secured the reversion of a large
> sinecure for life, and, consequently, had less occasion
> to be intriguing after new preferment. His speeches
> were reckoned severe, and it was not his fault if they
> did not answer the character; he meant to wound but
> his genius did not carry equal edge with his temper.

Except for some speeches on the regency bill of
1751,[5] Limerick took no further active part in
English politics. He died in Ireland, 17 Mar. 1758.

[1] *Corresp. H. Walpole* (Yale ed.), xvii. 364 n.5. [2] *HMC Egmont
Diary*, i. 55, 161–2, 168–70, 174, 243, 267, 271, 368; ii. 46, 155,
166, 343–4; iii. 33, 260. [3] *Corresp. H. Walpole* (Yale ed.), xvii.
492 n.9. [4] Hartington to Devonshire, 21 Feb. 1744, Devonshire
mss; Yorke's parl. jnl. *Parl. Hist.* xiii. 652–5. [5] Walpole, *Mems. Geo.
II*, i. 25–26, 123, 142–3.

R.R.S.

HAMILTON, John (*b.* bef. 1690), of Holm-
patrick, co. Dublin.

WENDOVER   18 Mar. 1728–1734

> *b.* bef. 1690, 2nd s. of Henry Hamilton (*d.*1690) of
> Bailieborough, co. Cavan, by Rebecca Blackwell, and
> yr. bro. of James Hamilton of Carlow, M.P. [I],
> ancestor of the Lords Holmpatrick. *m.* — Ligoe, 1s.
> M.P. [I] 1725–7.

John Hamilton was 3rd cousin to James Hamilton,
1st Viscount Limerick [I] (q.v.), both being descended from the Rev. Hans Hamilton (*d.*1608), a
legitimized son of Alexander Hamilton of Raploch,
co. Stirling.[1] When Richard Hampden (q.v.) chose
to sit for the county in 1728, Hamilton was returned
by a considerable majority for Wendover at the
ensuing election, doubtless through Lord Limerick,
the other sitting Member. He is the 'Mr. Hambleton, of our House', who was consulted by the 1st
Lord Egmont on Irish matters in 1731, when he
drafted a petition and bill for allowing unenumerated commodities to go direct to Ireland from the
colonies, instead of through Great Britain.[2] Unlike
his kinsman, Lord Limerick, he supported the
Government, voting for them on the army in 1732
and the excise bill in 1733. Though put down as a
government candidate for Wendover late in 1733,[3]
he did not stand at the general election of 1734,
after which nothing is known of him.

[1] G. Hamilton, *Hist. House of Hamilton*, 970, 1021. [2] *HMC
Egmont Diary*, i. 169, 170, 354. [3] Cholmondeley (Houghton) mss 68.

R.S.L.

HAMILTON, Lord William (c.1706–34), of Pall
Mall, London.

LANARKSHIRE   16 May–11 July 1734

> *b.* c.1706, 2nd s. of James, 4th Duke of Hamilton, by
> Elizabeth, da. and h. of Digby, 5th Baron Gerard of
> Gerard's Bromley. *m.* 30 Apr. 1733, Frances, da. and
> h. of Francis Hawes of Purley Hall, Berks., *s.p.*

Lord William Hamilton was the brother of the
5th Duke of Hamilton, the head of the Jacobite
interest in Scotland. There were unfounded reports
that he was to be given a troop of horse in 1726,
when George I recalled the Duke of Hamilton from
Rome, where he had been seeing the Pretender.[1]
Made a lord of the bedchamber by George II, the
Duke never performed his duties, continued to
correspond with the Pretender,[2] and was dismissed
in 1733. In that year, without the Duke's knowledge, Lord William eloped with the pretty but
penniless daughter of one of the South Sea directors,
whose estate had been confiscated in 1721.[3]

Returned for Lanarkshire next year on his brother's interest, he died two months later, 11 July.

[1] *Lockhart Pprs.* ii. 62, 267-8, 319-20; *HMC Egmont Diary,* ii. 7. [2] *Stuart mss* 208/124, 215/154. [3] *HMC Carlisle,* 95, 114.

E.C.

HAMILTON, William Gerard (1729-96), of Hampton Court, Mdx.

PETERSFIELD	9 Feb. 1754-1761
PONTEFRACT	1761-1768
OLD SARUM	1768-1774
WAREHAM	1774-1780
WILTON	1780-1790
HASLEMERE	1790-1796

b. 28 Jan. 1729, 1st surv. s. of William Hamilton, barrister, of L. Inn by his 1st w. Helen, da. of David Hay of Woodcockdale, West Lothian. *educ.* Harrow 1742-5; L. Inn 1744; Oriel, Oxf. 1745. *unm. suc.* fa. 1754.
M.P. [I] 1761-8.
Ld. of Trade 1756-61; chief sec. to ld. lt. [I] 1761-4; chancellor of Exchequer [I] 1763-84.

William Gerard ('single speech') Hamilton was returned for Petersfield as a government supporter on the Jolliffe interest a few weeks before the general election of 1754. He died 16 July 1796.

P.W.

HAMMOND, James (1710-42), of Hanover Sq., London.

TRURO 1741-7 June 1742

b. 22 May 1710, 2nd s. of Anthony Hammond, M.P., commr. of the navy, of Somersham Place, Hunts. by Jane, da. of Sir Walter Clarges, 1st Bt., M.P., of St. Martin in the Fields. *educ.* Westminster 1722. *unm. suc.* to estate of uncle at Swaffham, Norf. 1733.
Equerry to Frederick, Prince of Wales 1733-d.

Accompanying Lord Chesterfield (Philip Dormer Stanhope, q.v.) on his embassy to The Hague in 1728, Hammond, the poet, was sent over to London with the act of concurrence of the States General to the Treaty of Vienna in 1732, receiving a gratuity of £200 for his pains. Through Chesterfield he became acquainted with George Lyttelton, William Pitt (qq.v.), and other members of that set, and in 1733 obtained a post in the household of the Prince of Wales. Returned for Truro as an opposition Whig on the recommendation of Chesterfield in 1741, he died 7 June 1742, in Chesterfield's words,

in the beginning of a career which, if he had lived, I think he would have finished with reputation and distinction. But such is the folly, knavery, and futility of the world, and such was his truth, fidelity and attachment to me, that, in my opinion, I have lost more by his death than he has.[1]

Horace Walpole, on the other hand, described

Hammond as 'a man of moderate parts,' who 'attempted to speak in the House of Commons and did not succeed, nor is his poetry at all remarkable'.[2]

[1] Chesterfield, *Letters,* 255, 502; Maty, *Mems. of Lord Chesterfield,* 47-48, 133; *Cal. Treas. Bks. and Pprs.* 1731-4, p. 229. [2] Horace Walpole's ms additions to Maty.

E.C.

HAMPDEN, John (c.1695-1754), of Great Hampden, Bucks.

WENDOVER 1734-4 Feb. 1754

b. c.1695, 2nd s. of John Hampden, M.P., of Great Hampden by his 2nd w. Anne, 2nd da. and coh. of Hon. Frederick Cornwallis (2nd s. of the 1st Baron Cornwallis), and mat. aunt of Anthony Duncombe (q.v.), 1st Lord Feversham. *unm. suc.* e. bro. Richard Hampden (q.v.) at Great Hampden 1728.
Page of honour of the royal stables bef. 1713-c.1715; capt. Col. Sir Robert Rich's regt. of Dragoons c.1715-18; commissary gen. for Gibraltar 1735-47.

John Hampden, 'a very sensible and observing man [who] would have made a figure in the world if his unfortunate brother Richard had not ruined the estate', succeeded in 1728 to an inheritance which was entirely in the hands of government appointed trustees. However, by the sale of outlying properties, arrangements were made for him to retain Great Hampden and Wendover,[1] with its parliamentary interest; and, though he wrote to his steward in 1737 that he had 'been cheated out of a vast sum', his brother's debts to the Crown were cleared or written off by 1739. Returned as a Whig for Wendover in 1734 he was granted a lucrative place, voting with the Administration in all the chief divisions, though he was among the ministerial supporters who voted against them on Pitt's motion of October 1745 to recall all British troops from Flanders. He spoke in support of a Quakers bill in May 1736 but no other speech of his is known for the next 15 years. During this period he sold his Wendover manors and interest to Ralph, Lord Verney (q.v.), with whom, at the cost of six guineas a vote,[2] he was returned in 1741. He took care, apparently, to retain for himself a life interest in one of the seats, for he was again elected in 1747. Horace Walpole relates that when Pitt declared for 10,000 instead of 8,000 seamen in January 1751,

he was attacked by Hampden, who had every attribute of a buffoon but cowardice and none of the qualifications of his renowned ancestor but courage. He drew a burlesque picture of Pitt and Lyttelton under the titles of *Oratory* and *Solemnity*, and painted in the most comic colours what mischief rhetoric had brought upon the nation and what emoluments to Pitt. Pitt flamed into a rage and nodded menaces of highest import to Hampden, who retorted them, undaunted, with a droll voice that was naturally hoarse and inarticulate.

Walpole also wrote that Hampden 'hates the cousinhood [Pitt, Lyttelton, and the Grenvilles] and thinks his name should entitle him to Pitt's office'. In January 1752 he opposed Lord Harley's (q.v.) motion against subsidy treaties in time of peace 'but, with a sneer, said that he approved *bribing electors*, as he saw *by other instances* how it had contributed to quash opposition'. A year later he spoke in favour of Lord Hardwicke's marriage bill.[3] At the time of his death, 4 Feb. 1754, he was receiving a secret service pension of £1,000 a year,[4] presumably in lieu of his office which, in 1747, had become incompatible with a seat in the Commons under the Place Act of 1742.

[1] *Cal. Treas. Bks.* xxvii, p. 511; *Cal. Treas. Bks. and Pprs.*, 1720–28, pp. 401–2; 1729–30, pp. 85, 167; *HMC Egmont Diary*, ii. 508. [2] Hampden to Henry Harding, 1 Jan. 1737, Earl of Buckinghamshire's mss 39/25, 39/31, 40/41, Bucks. RO; *Cal. Treas. Bks. and Pprs.* 1739–41, p. 127; *Malmesbury Letters*, i. 8. [3] Walpole, *Mems. Geo. II*, i. 18, 254, 342; Walpole to Mann, 9 Feb. 1751. [4] Add. 33038, f. 352.

R.S.L.

HAMPDEN, Richard (aft. 1674–1728), of Great Hampden, Bucks.

WENDOVER	1701–1708
BUCKINGHAMSHIRE	1708–1710
BERWICK-UPON-TWEED	22 Dec. 1711–1715
BUCKINGHAMSHIRE	1715–1722
WENDOVER	1722–1727
BUCKINGHAMSHIRE	1727–27 July 1728

b. aft. 1674, 1st s. of John Hampden, M.P., of Great Hampden by his 1st w. Sarah, da. of Thomas Foley of Witley Court, Worcs., wid. of Essex Knightley of Fawsley, Northants; bro. of John Hampden (q.v.). *m.* 1701, his cos. Isabella, da. of Sir William Ellis, 2nd Bt., M.P., of Wyham and Nocton, Lincs., sis. of Sir Richard Ellis, 3rd Bt. (q.v.). *suc. fa.* 1696.

Chairman of committee of privileges and elections 1715–22; teller of the Exchequer 1716–18; treasurer of the navy 1718–20.

Richard Hampden, whose great-grandfather had resisted ship-money, succeeded to the family estates and interest at Wendover on his father's death by his own hand. At George I's accession he insisted on standing for the county, in spite of an appeal from the head of the Buckinghamshire Whigs, Lord Wharton, to

be contented with having been the wilful occasion of this shameful compromise with the Tories . . . without forcing of us to divide amongst ourselves and to tear one another to pieces . . . I am to tell you from Mr. [James] Stanhope [q.v.], that he keeps open for you an employment abroad which is the best the King hath in his gift and which he apprehended would have been agreeable to you, the embassy to Constantinople.[1]

Returned unopposed with a Tory, he was chosen to be chairman of the elections committee of the Commons and to be a member of the secret committee set up to inquire into the late Tory Administration. Next year he moved the impeachment of Lord Winton for his part in the rebellion; supported the septennial bill in a long speech, which he sent to a periodical for publication;[2] and obtained a lucrative sinecure, which did not prevent him from joining the Duke of Argyll in caballing against the Government (see under Lechmere, Nicholas). In 1717, according to auditor Edward Harley (q.v.),

Mr. Hampden, one of the secret committee, nine days before the trial [of the Earl of Oxford in June] told me that there never had been produced to the committee any evidence to prove the articles, that the Lord Oxford's answer had never been read in the secret committee, and that it was a most scandalous proceeding, which he was resolved to expose in the House. Notwithstanding he had said this to me and so many others, yet he becomes the first man that opens the impeachment.[3]

Exchanging his sinecure in 1718 for the still more lucrative office of treasurer of the navy, which he obtained through the King's mistress, the Duchess of Kendal, he spoke in support of the peerage bill in 1719. In the year of the South Sea bubble, 1720, he used naval funds to speculate in the stock of the South Sea Company with a view to making a personal profit, incurring losses later stated in the Commons to be £90,000, of which only £47,941 was secured. Dismissed from his office, he appealed to the Duchess of Kendal, 17 Nov. 1720, admitting that

tant que le saison du profit prodigieux que chacun y faisait a continué, j'ai acheté des terres et des maisons, et j'ai fait d'autres dépenses, n'ayant pas le moindre soupçon que je ne pusse trouver les occasions de me retirer hors de ces actions sans que les affaires du Roy sous mon inspection en reçussent le moindre tort. Mais la chute prompte, inopprimée, et surprennante de ces actions m'a absolument privé du dessein que j'avais formé de replacer l'argent que j'y avois employé, et par ce malheureux baissement du crédit je suis devenu incapable de fournir les sommes qui en peu de semaines seront dues à la marine. Et pour surcroit de malheur, à peine avois-je commencé à travailler par mon crédit à procurer l'argent que j'y devois fournir, que j'ai reçu la nouvelle de ma disgrace, et que le Roy avoit trouvé à propos de mettre un autre en ma place.[4]

After being returned for Wendover in 1722, he applied unsuccessfully to Sunderland for the Constantinople embassy, offering part of the salary and half or two thirds of the annual value of his estates towards the discharge of his debt to the Government.[5] His next move was to petition Parliament for relief in March 1726. The debate on the petition is described as having 'run on the merit and antiquity of the family, and that it was necessary to show some compassion to that, though none to him'.[6] In the end an Act was passed vesting the estates in trustees, provision being made for preserving Great Hampden in the family, while securing the debts to the Crown.

On George II's accession Hampden wrote several begging letters to the new King's mistress, his cousin, Mrs. Howard. Offering through her a seat at Wendover to the Crown, he attributed his position solely to the so-called

> bill for my relief . . . I did hope to find a little more protection from ruin in this reign than in the last, when I was persecuted incessantly by Sir Robert, but on what ground I am yet ignorant of.

At the general election he was 'unresolved till the country [i.e. county] being in distress for a proper person to set up against the compromise, declared for him without his knowledge'. Estimating his prospective expenses at nearly £600, he suggested to Mrs. Howard that if help were not forthcoming he would be obliged to travel abroad 'with any young gentleman at £100 salary . . . and by that means avoid going to gaol'.[7] Returned for both Wendover and the county, he sat for the latter till his death, 27 July 1728.

[1] *Verney Letters of 18th Cent.* i. 317–20; Wharton to Hampden, 9 Oct., 29 Nov. 1714, Glynde mss, E. Suss. RO. [2] *Pol. State* xi. 463; xxxvii. p. vii. [3]*HMC Portland,* v. 668–69. [4] Glynde mss. [5] April 1722, Sunderland (Blenheim) mss. [6] *Knatchbull Diary,* 11 Mar. 1726; *CJ,* xx. 597. [7] Hampden to Mrs. Howard, undated, 30 June, July and Aug. 1727, Add. 22629, ff. 18, 20, 21, 23; *Verney Letters,* ii. 101.

R.S.L.

HANBURY, Capel (1707–65), of Pontypool, Mon.

LEOMINSTER 1741–1747
MONMOUTHSHIRE 1747–7 Dec. 1765

b. 2 Dec. 1707, 3rd s. of John Hanbury (q.v.) of Pontypool, Mon., and bro. of Sir Charles Hanbury Williams (q.v.). *educ.* Ch. Ch. Oxf. 1723. *m.* 7 Oct. 1743, Jane, da. of Thomas Charles, 5th Visct. Tracy [I], 1s. 2da. *suc.* bro. 1739.

Inheriting the family estates and iron works in 1739, Capel Hanbury entered Parliament for Leominster in 1741, voting steadily with the Government. In 1743 he received instructions from Leominster to work for bills to prevent bribery and corruption, to repeal the Septennial Act and to ban placemen and pensioners from Parliament, concluding:

> And, notwithstanding, Mr. Hanbury, your conduct in Parliament hath not hitherto been agreeable to [us] yet we hope you are now convinced that the public treasure has been grossly misapplied, and we doubt not but you will heartily join with our other worthy Member [Robert Harley]. These are our sentiments, and your acting in conformity thereto will be the only means of obtaining the future approbation and esteem of us your constituents.[1]

In 1747 he succeeded his younger brother, Sir Charles Hanbury Williams, as Member for the county. He was described in the 2nd Lord Egmont's electoral survey c.1749–50, as 'a very sour and real enemy of our system, and associates himself chiefly with such'.

He died 7 Dec. 1765.

[1] *Gent. Mag.* 1743, p. 32.

P.D.G.T.

HANBURY, John (?1664–1734), of Pontypool, Mon.

GLOUCESTER 2 Dec. 1701–1702
29 Dec. 1702–1708
MONMOUTHSHIRE 24 Mar. 1720–14 June 1734

b. ?1664, 1st s. of Capel Hanbury of Pontypool by Elizabeth, da. of William Capel. *educ.* Pembroke, Oxf. 26 Mar. 1681, aged 16; M. Temple 1683. *m.* (1) 1701, Albinia (*d.*1702), da. and h. of General William Selwyn, M.P., of Matson, Glos., *s.p.*; (2) July 1703, Bridget, da. and coh. of Sir Edward Ayscough of South Kelsey, Lincs., 9s. 1da. *suc.* fa. 1704.

Director, South Sea Co. 1724–30.

The son of a Worcestershire country gentleman, who bought an estate and ironworks at Pontypool, Hanbury at first had thoughts of a legal career. In his own words:

> I read Coke upon Littleton, as far as tenant in dower; but on the suggestion of a friend, that I should gain more advantage from the iron works at Pontypool than from the profits of the bar, I laid aside tenant in dower, and turned my attention to mines and forges.

He built a house at Pontypool, spending considerable sums on developing the works, where he introduced the method of making iron by furnaces, as well as the art of tinning.[1]

In 1715 Hanbury unsuccessfully contested Gloucester, which he had represented as a Whig under Anne. Returned for Monmouthshire in 1720 'on the independent interest',[2] he voted against the Administration in all recorded divisions. He was one of Marlborough's executors in 1722, after which he became the constant companion of Duchess Sarah.[3]

He died 14 June 1734.

[1] A. A. Locke, *Hanbury Fam.* 152–61. [2] Coxe, *Hist. Tour Mon.* (1801), p. 237. [3] Ilchester & Langford-Brooke, *Sir Charles Hanbury-Williams,* 24–28.

P.D.G.T.

HANBURY WILLIAMS, Charles (1708–59), of Coldbrook, Mon.

MONMOUTHSHIRE 6 Mar. 1735–1747
LEOMINSTER 1754–2 Nov. 1759

b. 8 Dec. 1708, 4th s. of John Hanbury of Pontypool, Mon., and bro. of Capel Hanbury (qq.v.). *educ.* Eton

1720; Grand Tour (Belgium, Switzerland, Italy) 1724-6. *m.* 1 July 1732, Lady Frances Coningsby, da. and coh. of Thomas Coningsby, M.P., 1st Earl of Coningsby, 2da. K.B. 20 Oct. 1744.

Paymaster of marines 1739-46; ld. lt. Herefs. 1742-7; high steward, Leominster 1744-*d.*; envoy, Dresden 1747-9, 1751-5, Berlin 1750-1; ambassador, St. Petersburg 1755-7.

Hanbury Williams came into the fortune of his godfather, Charles Williams, a rich Smyrna merchant, whose name he assumed.[1] Succeeding to his father's seat in March 1735, he made his first reported speech against a place bill, 22 Apr.[2] At the opening of the next session he was chosen to second the Address by Walpole, who in 1737 proposed him for a complimentary mission to the new King of Naples with £4,000 as expenses, but was thwarted by the Duke of Newcastle's telling the King that the British minister at Florence could do the job for £500.[3] In 1739, after moving the address[4] on the Spanish convention, he was again disappointed, this time of the secretaryship to the lord lieutenant of Ireland, which Walpole gave to his own private secretary, Henry Legge (q.v.). 'Where am I to hide myself if Mr. Legge is preferred to me?' he wrote to his friend, Henry Fox (q.v.).

My services in Parliament are of a longer date than his, even in his private capacity to Sir Robert . . . He has had £600 per ann. all this while; I never one shilling for all my expenses of all sorts that attend serving for a county. Thus it stood till this post (as I thought), but now he is removed to £2,000 per annum for the above mentioned services, and I, who had a *promise* of it, am where I was, left to serve on as a volunteer, and in not near so good a way of preferment as I was three years ago, when Mr. Walpole first dragged me out of the character of a country gentleman to make a . . . of me.

Appeased with the office of paymaster of marines, worth £2,000 a year, he is not recorded as speaking again in Parliament, for which he thought he had no talent. Owing to illness he was absent from the divisions on the chairman of the elections committee and the Westminster election in December 1741.

On Walpole's fall Hanbury Williams was in danger of losing his place to one of Pulteney's followers. Asking Fox to

take the matter high, but not too high. Paint the effect of my going out of this office and my interests in the counties of Monmouth, Brecknock, Hereford, Glamorgan, and Carmarthen,

he poured out a stream of vitriolic anonymous lampoons on Pulteney. In spite of his parliamentary inactivity he retained his place till 1746, when he met with a series of misfortunes: his friend Thomas Winnington (q.v.) died; a parliamentary inquiry disclosed that his deputies in the paymaster's office, one of them a former factotum of his, had been speculating with the official balances; and as a result of one of his lampoons he was threatened with a crop of duels, which he avoided by retiring to the country, at the cost of exposing himself to charges of showing the white feather.

He had innumerable enemies [writes Horace Walpole], all the women, for he had poxed his wife, all the Tories, for he was a steady Whig, all fools, for he was a bitter satirist, and many sensible people, for he was immoderately vain.[5]

Deciding to go abroad, he was appointed envoy to Dresden. At the general election next year he exchanged constituencies with his brother, Capel (q.v.), but was defeated, remaining out of Parliament till 1754. He continued to hold diplomatic posts till 1757, when he returned to England in a state of mental derangement, dying insane 2 Nov. 1759.

[1] Ilchester & Langford-Brooke, *Sir Charles Hanbury-Williams*, 25-26. [2] Harley Diary. [3] Hervey, *Mems.* 829-30. [4] Coxe, *Walpole*, ii. 515. [5] Ilchester & Langford-Brooke, 45, 46, 58, 59, 95-101; Coxe, iii. 583, 586; *Corresp. H. Walpole* (Yale ed.), xxx. 312-13.

R.R.S.

HANDASYDE, Roger (c.1684-1763), of Gaines Park, Great Staughton, Hunts.

HUNTINGDON	1722-1741
SCARBOROUGH	1747-1754

b. c.1684, 1st s. of Maj.-Gen. Thomas Handasyde of Gaines Park, gov. of Jamaica, by his 1st w. (*d.* 1704). *educ.* Westminster. *m.* (lic. 21 Jan. 1710) Elizabeth, da. of Sir John Thornycroft, 1st Bt., of Milcombe, Oxon., *s.p. suc.* fa. 1729.

Ensign 28 Ft. 1696; exchanged to 22 Ft. c.1702; capt. 1703; lt.-col. c.1709; col. 22 Ft. 1712-30; col. 16 Ft. 1730-*d.*; brig.-gen. 1735; lt. gov. Fort St. Philip, Minorca, 1737-?47; maj.-gen. 1739; lt.-gen. 1743; gov. Berwick-upon-Tweed 1745; c.-in-c. Scotland Oct.-Dec. 1745.

In an army career of 67 years General Handasyde, of a Northumberland family,[1] appears to have seen little active service. During Marlborough's wars he was in Jamaica with his father, whom he succeeded as colonel of the 22nd Foot in 1712. 'A bitter Whig',[2] he was brought in unopposed by Lord Hinchingbrooke (q.v.) at Huntingdon in 1722, voting with the Administration in all recorded divisions until 1740. His only two known speeches were on army matters: in a debate on the land forces on 14 Feb. 1735 he defended the part played by his regiment in Edinburgh during the recent election of representative peers; and on the mutiny bill of January 1741 he opposed a proposal to cut down the private soldier's daily allowance of beer. He lost his seat in 1741 to the nominees of the young Lord Sandwich, then in opposition.

In the Forty-five, as commander-in-chief in Scotland in succession to Sir John Cope (q.v.), Handasyde occupied Edinburgh on 14 Nov., while Prince Charles Edward was marching into England. In February 1747 he complained to Newcastle that the command in Scotland had once more been given to his inferior in rank.[3] By this time he had joined the Prince of Wales in opposition.[4] Lord Sandwich learned that

> his Royal Highness has persuaded my old antagonist Handasyde to endeavour to give me what trouble he could in Huntingdonshire, and I believe it is as represented because I can no other way account for his forgetting the most formal and public promises he has made me without any kind of condition to support my interest both in town and county. He now talks of opposing me in both, but it is absolutely out of his power to do me the least hurt in either, except hurting my pocket.[5]

At the general election of 1747 Handasyde did not stand for Huntingdonshire but was returned for Scarborough by Lord Carlisle (Lord Morpeth, q.v.) as a Leicester House candidate. On 22 Jan. 1751, described as 'a blundering commander on the Prince's side', he spoke strongly against a libellous attack on the Duke of Cumberland.[6] Though reported in September 1752 to have been nominated for Huntingdonshire 'by a majority of the gentlemen of the greatest property in this county as candidate . . . at the next general election',[7] he did not stand again. His approaches to Newcastle for a 'better regiment' in 1752, and for the colonelcy of a troop of Horse Grenadier Guards in 1760,[8] met with no success. He died 4 Jan. 1763, aged 78.

[1] F. Cundall, *Govs. of Jamaica in first half of the 18th Cent.* 27; *Arch. Aeliana* (ser. 3), iv. 142–5; *VCH Hunts.* ii. 362. [2] Nathaniel Mist to James Edgar, 7 Aug. 1733, Stuart mss 163/183. [3] Newcastle to Handasyde, 28 Nov. 1745, Add. 32705, f. 389; Handasyde to Newcastle, 19 Feb. 1747, Add. 32710, f. 219; W. B. Blaikie, *Origins of the Forty-five* (Sc. Hist. Soc. ser. 2), ii. 345. [4] *HMC Fortescue*, i. 108. [5] Sandwich to Newcastle, 21 Mar. (N.S.) 1747, Add. 32807, f. 209. [6] Walpole, *Mems. Geo II*, i. 10. [7] Manchester to Devonshire, 24 Sept. 1752, Devonshire mss. [8] Handasyde to Newcastle, 5 May 1752, 17 Mar. 1760, Add. 32727, f. 86; 32903, f. 342.

R.S.L.

HANGER, Gabriel (1697–1773), of Cannon Place, Bray, Berks. and Kempsford Hall, Glos.

MAIDSTONE   25 Apr. 1753–1761
BRIDGWATER   21 Nov. 1763–1768

b. 9 Jan. 1697, 1st surv. s. of Sir George Hanger of Driffield Hall, Glos., Turkey merchant, by Anne, da. and coh. of Sir John Beale, 1st Bt., of Farningham, Kent. *m.* 18 Jan. 1736, Elizabeth, da. and h. of Richard Bond of Cobrey Court, Herefs., 3s. 1da. *suc.* fa. 1731, and to Coleraine estates on d. of cos. Anne, wid. of Henry Hare, 3rd Baron Coleraine [I] 1754; *cr.* Baron Coleraine [I] 26 Feb. 1762.
  Entered Bengal establishment of E.I. Co. 1714,

factor 1718, junior merchant 1722, senior merchant 1724.

Hanger resigned from the East India Company on the death of his elder brother in 1725. In 1753 he was returned, probably on Lord Romney's interest, for Maidstone, where he himself had some local connexions. He was classed as a Tory in 1754. He died 24 Jan. 1773.

A.N.N.

HANMER, Sir Thomas, 4th Bt. (1677–1746), of Mildenhall, Suff.

THETFORD   19 Mar. 1701–1702
FLINTSHIRE   1702–1705
THETFORD   1705–1708
SUFFOLK   1708–1727

b. 24 Sept. 1677, s. of William Hanmer of Bettisfield Park, Flints. by Peregrina, da. of Sir Henry North, 1st Bt., of Mildenhall, sis. and coh. of Sir Henry North, 2nd Bt. *educ.* Westminster; Ch. Ch. Oxf. 1693. *m.* (1) lic. 14 Oct. 1698, Lady Isabella Bennet (*d.* 7 Feb. 1723), da. and h. of Henry Bennet, M.P., 1st Earl of Arlington, wid. of Henry Fitzroy, 1st Duke of Grafton, *s.p.*; (2) 1725, Elizabeth, da. and h. of Thomas Folkes of Barton, Suff., *s.p.* *suc.* uncle as 4th Bt. to Flints. estates 1701 and through his mother to Mildenhall.
  Speaker of the House of Commons 1714–15.

At the accession of George I, the French ambassador described Hanmer as the

> chef d'une troupe de 30 à 40 députés qui ont toujours affecté comme lui de se dire Tories, mais fort opposés au Prétendant par zèle pour leur religion et pour les libertés de la nation.

He was offered the post of chancellor of the Exchequer, which he refused. On the breach between the King and the Prince of Wales in 1717 the French ambassador reported:

> Le prince, ayant appelé secrétement le chevalier Hanmer, l'assura qu'il avoit un vif repentir d'avoir sur des perfides conseils regardé les Tories comme ses ennemis, et qu'il veut être dorénavant leur ami, et leur donner toute sa confiance.

He was absent from the debate on Lord Cadogan (q.v.), observing that he was unwilling to lend his shoulders 'to the setting up again of a certain man [Walpole] on horseback'.[1] A year later, Atterbury wrote to the Pretender:

> The most despicable party in England are the Hanoverian Tories, a handful of men without dependants or credit, and whom both sides equally agree in exposing. There has been a meeting of them lately in Yorkshire at the Archbishop's. Hill [Rt. Hon. Richard, see Hill, Sir Rowland] and Sir Thomas Hanmer were there and have laid some new scheme for the winter campaign, and one branch of it is adhering irremovably to the court at Richmond [i.e. to the Prince].[2]

Nothing, however, came of this. For the rest of his

career he was a distinguished but ineffective figure in opposition, whose speeches, Hervey writes,

> were always fine pieces of oratory, but never of any signification . . . With all his sense, what he brought himself to at last, by a wavering odd conduct, was to be neither of use to one party nor a terror to the other, and to be disliked at court without being beloved in the country.[3]

A similar account of him is given by the elder Horace Walpole (q.v.):

> His person, parts, and principles were all of a piece; he had a very handsome mien and appearance, but tis said he could not please the ladies; he could make an eloquent, elaborate, and plausible speech, but never was thought a man of business, or knowledge. He would act and vote with the Tories and yet said he was no Jacobite; he declared himself for the Hanoverian succession, and would never act or vote in support of it; he died at last, poor gentleman, without having much obliged or disobliged any person or party, and rather pitied than either hated or beloved.[4]

The younger Horace Walpole describes him as

> a dainty Speaker, who was first married to the Dowager Duchess of Grafton, and afterwards espousing a young lady, the first night he made some faint efforts towards consummation, and then begged her pardon for her disappointment. See Mr. Thomas Hervey's [q.v.] letter to him on this subject. He lived long, published an edition of Shakespeare, and always wore white gloves. In Othello he made the emendation 'a fellow almost damned in a fair phiz' instead of 'fair wife', because he found no other mention of Cassio's being married.[5]

He died 7 May 1746.

[1] *Hanmer Corresp.* 53, 67; *Pol. State*, vii. 330; xiii. 705; Egmont Diary, 1711–15, Add. 47087. [2] J. H. Glover, *Stuart Pprs.* 32–33; *HMC Portland*, v. 618–19. [3] *Mems.* 78. [4] Coxe, *Walpole*, ii. 48–49. [5] *Corresp. Horace Walpole* (Yale ed.), xxx. 302 n. 48.

R.R.S.

HANMER, Thomas (c.1702–37), of Fenns, Salop.

CASTLE RISING   1734–1 Apr. 1737

b. c.1702, 1st s. of William Hanmer of Fenns by Esther, da. of Humphrey Jennens of Gopsall, Leics. *educ.* St. Catherine's, Camb. 1720. *m.* 9 Apr. 1733 (with £6,000), Lady Catherine Perceval, da. of John Perceval (q.v.), 1st Earl of Egmont, *s.p.*. *suc.* fa. 1724.

The prospective heir of Sir Thomas Hanmer (q.v.), Thomas Hanmer was returned, presumably as a Tory, on the Howard interest for Castle Rising. He died of consumption, 1 Apr. 1737.[1]

[1] Nichols, *Leics.* iv. 859; HMC Egmont Diary, i. 326; ii. 381–2.

R.R.S.

HARBORD, Harbord (?1675–1742), of Gunton and Stanninghall, Norf.

NORFOLK   26 June 1728–1734

b. ?1675, 1st s. of Col. William Cropley of Shelland, Suff. and Thetford, Norf. by Catherine, da. of Sir

Charles Harbord of Stanninghall, wid. of Thomas Wright of Kilverstone, Norf. *educ.* Drinkstone and Bury schools; Caius, Camb. 9 May 1694, aged 18. *m.* (1) Jane, da. and coh. of Sir William Rant of Thorpe Market, Norf., *s.p.*; (2) 17 May 1737, Rebecca, da. of Sir Benjamin Wrench, M.D., of Norwich, wid. of John Marcon of Norwich, *s.p.*

In 1648 Sir Charles Harbord, surveyor general to Charles I, purchased Stanninghall from the Waldegrave family. His only surviving son and heir, John Harbord, who acquired Gunton, dying without heirs in 1710, left the bulk of his estates to his nephew Harbord Cropley, who thereupon assumed the name of Harbord. Returned for the county after a contest at a by-election in 1728 as a government supporter, Harbord voted for the excise bill, but did not stand again. He died 28 Jan. 1742, leaving his Norfolk properties to his nephew William Morden (q.v.) who also took the name of Harbord.[1]

[1] P. Millican, *Hist. Horstead and Stanninghall*, 197–8; Blomefield, *Norf.* viii. 120–1.

S.R.M.

HARBORD, *see also* **MORDEN**

HARDINGE, Nicholas (1699–1758), of Kingston-upon-Thames, Surr.

EYE   15 Feb. 1748–9 Apr. 1758

b. 7 Feb. 1699, 1st s. of Rev. Gideon Hardinge, vicar of Kingston-upon-Thames, by his w. Mary Westbrooke. *educ.* Eton c.1711–18; King's, Camb. 1718, fellow 1722; M. Temple 1721, called 1725. *m.* 19 Dec. 1738, Jane, da. of Sir John Pratt, l.c.j. of the King's bench 1718–25, sis. of Charles, 1st Earl Camden, 9s. 3da. *suc.* fa. 1712.

Clerk of the House of Commons 1731–48; law reader to the Duke of Cumberland 1732; attorney-gen. to the Duke 1733–51; auditor to Princess Emily 1751; jt. sec. to Treasury 1752–d.

Hardinge probably owed his appointment as clerk of the House of Commons to Walpole, like himself an Eton and King's man, who is referred to as his patron in the well-known story of Hardinge's deciding against him on a bet with Pulteney as to the correctness of a Latin quotation. The first clerk of the House to receive a regular salary from the civil list in addition to his fees and to £10 a year granted by his letters patent, he was the author of a report in 1742 on the condition of the journals of the House, which led to their being printed under his direction. 'Though well and promptly paid himself' for the work, 'he was extremely dilatory in paying his debts to Samuel Richardson, the printer and novelist, putting him off with repeated promises to pay and, on the last occasion, only brought to discharge his debt by the firm intervention of Arthur Onslow, the Speaker'.[1] He was said to have persuaded the universities to agree to limit the number of livings held by the colleges to half the number of fellows in return for being excepted from the Mortmain Act of 1736.[2] After 17 years as clerk he was returned by Lord Cornwallis for Eye, selling his office to Jeremiah Dyson, who did not follow this example when he himself resigned the office to enter the House.[3] He is described by Horace Walpole as 'a sensible knowing man, who' as a former clerk of the House was 'not well received as a speaker'. In 1751 he spoke on the Westminster election petition, citing precedents showing that the House had committed offenders to Newgate and made them receive their sentence on their knees; opposed receiving a petition against a Member, as out of order; and supported the restrictions placed on the regent by the regency bill, adding 'that in his opinion even the Duke [of Cumberland] might be removed from the council' of regency, which was 'the more honest as he was actually the Duke's attorney'.[4] Next year he was appointed joint secretary to the Treasury on condition that he paid £800 a year out of his salary to John Jeffreys (q.v.). He died after a short illness 9 Apr. 1758.

[1] O. C. Williams, *Clerical Organization of the House of Commons*, 62–64. [2] Harley Diary, 15 Apr. 1736. [3] Williams, loc. cit. [4] *Mems. Geo. II*, i. 29, 30, 58, 134.

R.R.S.

HARDRES, John (1675–1758), of Canterbury, Kent.

CANTERBURY 1705–1708, 1710–1722

bap. 2 Oct. 1675, 1st s. of Thomas Hardres of Canterbury by Mary, da. and h. of John Short. *educ.* G. Inn 1689; Wadham, Oxf. 1692. *m.* bef. 1704, Anne Thomlinson, 2s. *d.v.p.* 7da. *suc.* fa. 1688.[1]
Capt. of Sandown castle, Kent ?1705–8.

Hardres, a Tory and a member of the October Club, was returned for his native city of Canterbury. From 1715 he voted against the Government, except on the peerage bill, which he unexpectedly supported, receiving through Sunderland £580 from the King's bounty in 1720–1.[2] His name was sent to the Pretender in 1721 as a probable supporter in the event of a rising.[3] Retiring in 1722, he died 14 Jan. 1758.

[1] St. George's, Canterbury, par. reg.; *Arch. Cant.* iv. 56. [2] Sunderland (Blenheim) mss D. II, 4. [3] Stuart mss 65/16.

A.N.N.

HARDRES, Sir William, 4th Bt. (1686–1736), of Hardres Court, nr. Canterbury, Kent.

KENT 1711–1713
DOVER 1713–1715
CANTERBURY 1727–11 Apr. 1735

b. 25 July 1686, o.s. of Sir Thomas Hardres, 3rd Bt., by Ursula, da. of Sir William Rooke of Horton, Kent. *m.* (lic. 26 Mar. 1712) Elizabeth, da. of Richard Thomas of Lamberhurst, Kent, wid. of William Disher of London, merchant, 2s. 2da. *suc.* fa. 23 Feb. 1688.

Hardres, whose family had been settled in Kent since the 13th century, was returned as a Tory under Anne but did not stand in 1715. In 1721 his name was sent to the Pretender as a probable supporter in the event of a rising.[1] Returned for Canterbury in 1727, after unsuccessfully contesting it in 1722, his only recorded vote was against the Government on the Hessians in 1730. He was re-elected in 1734 but when a petition was presented against him he 'dropped his friends and quitted'.[2] He died 8 July 1736.

[1] Stuart mss 65/16. [2] Notebook of William Gray, Canterbury city archives.

A.N.N.

HARDY, Sir Charles (c.1680–1744).

PORTSMOUTH 14 Dec. 1743–27 Nov. 1744

b. c.1680, s. of Philip le Hardy, commr. of garrisons in Guernsey, by Mary, da. of Ezaias Filleul of St. Helier.[1] *m.* Elizabeth, da. of Josiah Burchett (q.v.), sec. of the Admiralty, 3s. 3da. Kntd. 26 Sept. 1732. *suc.* fa. 1705.
Volunteer R.N. 1695, lt. 1701, capt. 1709, r.-adm. 1742, v.-adm. 1743.
Elder Brother of Trinity House, 1722; ld. of Admiralty 1743–*d.*

On the occurrence of two vacancies on the board of Admiralty at the end of 1743, Hardy, who had recently attained flag rank after nearly half a century's service, was appointed to one of them. According to Horace Walpole (to Mann, 30 Nov. 1743), Carteret, whose follower, Lord Winchilsea (Daniel, Lord Finch, q.v.) was then first lord of the Admiralty, filled both vacancies without the knowledge of the Pelhams. Returned for Portsmouth on the Admiralty interest, he voted for the Hanoverians in January 1744, dying 27 Nov. that year.

[1] *Jersey Armorial*, 220.

P.W.

HARE, Henry, 3rd Baron Coleraine [I] (1693–1749).

BOSTON 22 Jan. 1730–1734

b. 10 May 1693, 1st s. of Hon. Hugh Hare, M.P., of East Betchworth, Surr. by Lydia, da. of Mathew Carlton, merchant, of Edmonton, Mdx. *educ.* Enfield; Ch. Ch. Oxf. 1712. *m.* 20 Jan. 1718, Anne, da. and coh. of John Hanger of Holy Trinity, Minories, London merchant, gov. of Bank of England, *s.p.*; she was cos. of Gabriel Hanger (q.v.). *suc.* fa. 1707; gd.-fa. Henry Hare, M.P., as 3rd Baron Coleraine 4 July 1708.
Grand master of freemasons 1727–8.

In 1708 Hare, an antiquary and collector of prints and drawings, inherited an Irish peerage, with large estates in Middlesex, Wiltshire and Norfolk. He married an heiress with a dowry of £100,000, who left him three years later. Returned as a Tory for Boston in 1730 he voted against the Administration on the army in 1732 and the excise bill in 1733. On 17 Jan. 1734 he spoke against the Address, and on 28 and 29 Mar. against authorizing the King to augment his forces in the event of an emergency during the parliamentary recess.[1] He did not stand again. In 1740, having failed to persuade his wife to return to him, he entered into 'a solemn mutual engagement' with Rose Duplessis, the daughter of a French clergyman, 'to take each other for husband and wife, and perform to each other the negative and positive duties of that relationship'. In 1748 he granted her an annuity of £148 p.a. 'in consideration of good services and faithful offices'. He died 10 Aug. 1749, leaving his Middlesex estates to his illegitimate daughter. She being an alien, they escheated to the Crown, but were subsequently granted to her husband James Townsend, M.P., son of Chauncy Townsend (q.v.).[2]

[1] *HMC Egmont Diary*, ii, 8, 71–72. [2] Nichols, *Lit. Anecs.* v. 349–52.

P.W.

HARLEY, Edward (1664–1735), of Eywood, Herefs.

DROITWICH 1695–1698
LEOMINSTER 1698–1700, 3 Apr. 1701–1722

b. 7 June 1664, 2nd s. of Sir Edward Harley, M.P., of Brampton Bryan, Herefs. by Abigail, da. of Nathaniel Stephens of Eastington, Glos. *educ.* Westminster; M. Temple 1681, called 1688. *m.* Sarah, da. of Thomas Foley, M.P., of Witley Court, Worcs., 3s. 1da.
Jt. auditor of the imprest for life 1702; recorder, Leominster 1692–1732.

The Harleys were descended from a long line of Herefordshire squires. In the seventeenth century they were Presbyterians, parliamentarians and Whigs. Sir Edward Harley, M.P. for Herefordshire in ten Parliaments, raised a troop of horse in support of the Prince of Orange in 1688, seized Worcester, and was rewarded by William III with a grant in Radnorshire, carrying extensive electoral influence there. His son, Robert Harley, began as a Dissenter and Whig, but gradually changed his politics, became leader of the Tory party, and was created Earl of Oxford in 1711. Both Robert and his younger brother, Edward, married sisters of the 1st Lord Foley, with whose family the Harleys were closely allied in national and local politics.

Edward Harley, like his elder brother Robert,

began his political career as a Whig but gradually evolved into a Tory. In 1715 he exerted himself with little success to maintain his family's electoral interests in Radnorshire, Bishop's Castle and Leominster. In Radnorshire, he wrote, 'I never met with so much open villainy and secret perfidy as universally prevailed . . . which has brought me to a resolution to dispose of my estate in that county'. The same applied to Bishop's Castle, where 'the baseness and perfidy that I met with in this place has brought me to the like resolution of parting with it, being unwilling to leave the temptation to my son of being drawn into a great expense upon such mercenary rascals'. Only Leominster, 'where I had the least reason to expect success', remained loyal.[1] Re-elected after a contest, he vigorously opposed the motion for the impeachment of his brother, Lord Oxford, successfully refuting charges of financial dishonesty brought against himself as auditor. In February 1718, Lord Mar, the Pretender's secretary of state, suggested that Harley and Lord Harley should be asked for money through Lord Oxford, for a project to restore the Stuarts with the help of Swedish troops (see Caesar, Charles).[2]

At the general election of 1722 Harley at first proposed to decline nomination for Leominster on account of his health, but not wishing to 'refuse the kind invitation'[3] he had received from the borough, he stood, only to be heavily defeated. He lodged a petition but allowed it to drop. Withdrawing into private life, he was responsible for the supervision of the development of the Cavendish-Harley estate in Marylebone, which began in 1717.[4] During his last years he wrote several devotional works. He died 30 Aug. 1735.

[1] *HMC Portland*, v. 663. [2] *HMC Stuart*, v. 456. [3] *HMC Portland*, vii. 315, 318. [4] Summerson, *Georgian London*, 88–93.

A.N.N.

HARLEY, Edward, Lord Harley (1689–1741), of Wimpole, Cambs.

NEW RADNOR 16 July 1711–1715
CAMBRIDGESHIRE 1722–21 May 1724

b. 2 June 1689, 1st s. of Robert Harley, M.P., 1st Earl of Oxford, by Elizabeth, da. of Thomas Foley of Witley Court, Worcs. *educ.* Westminster; Ch. Ch. Oxf. 1707. *m.* 31 Aug. 1713, Lady Henrietta Cavendish Holles, da. and coh. of John Holles, M.P., 1st Duke of Newcastle, 1da. *suc.* fa. as 2nd Earl 21 May 1724.
High steward, Cambridge 1728–*d.*; gov. Foundling Hospital 1739.

The friend of Swift, Pope, and Prior, connoisseur, antiquarian, and collector of books, manuscripts, coins, and pictures, Harley took little interest in politics. In 1715 his uncle, Edward Harley (q.v.), arranged for him to be nominated as a Tory for

New Radnor and Bishop's Castle but he was defeated at both, without, so far as is known, troubling to appear at either. In 1722, after his father had tried unsuccessfully to secure his adoption for Herefordshire, he was returned on his family's interest for Cambridgeshire. There is no record of his having voted or spoken during his two years in the Commons before succeeding to the title. In 1725 the Duke of Wharton included him in a list of Jacobite peers. He and Shippen (q.v.) are mentioned as the only Tories of note who did not go to court on the accession of George II. Lord Cornbury (q.v.) described him to the Pretender in 1735 as 'pretty unfixed, fond of seeming to do what is popular'.[1] He was one of the Tory peers who voted against the motion for Walpole's removal in 1741.

In spite of his wife's great fortune he was always in financial difficulties. As early as 1714 his tutor, Dr. Stratford, warned him of the urgent need for drastic economies:

> You may, without care, be in a worse state than you were before your marriage. Upon your present resolutions the honour, the peace, and the plenty of your future life depends.[2]

The prediction was fulfilled. In 1737 his wife's estates had to be vested in trustees for the payment of debts, including one to the late Dr. Stratford, amounting to nearly £250,000.[3] In 1740 Wimpole was sold to Lord Hardwicke for £86,740.[4] For some time before his death, 16 June 1741, he had

> been so entirely given up to drinking that his life has been no pleasure to him or satisfaction to his friends . . . He had had no enjoyment of the world since the mismanagement of his affairs; it has hurt his body and mind, and has led to his death.[5]

After his death the great Harleian collection was sold, the coins, medals and pictures by public auction, the books to a bookseller, and the manuscripts to the British Museum for £10,000.

[1] Stuart mss 83/89, 108/44, 162/124A. [2] *HMC Portland*, vii. 209. [3] West mss at Alscot Park. [4] Yorke, *Hardwicke*, i. 206. [5] Mrs. Delany, *Autobiog. and Corresp.* (ser. 1), ii. 156–7.

E.C.

HARLEY, Edward (?1699–1755), of Eywood, Herefs.

HEREFORDSHIRE 1727–16 June 1741

b. ?1699, 1st s. of Edward Harley of Eywood, and bro. of Robert Harley (qq.v.). *educ.* Westminster; Ch. Ch. Oxf. 21 Feb. 1717, aged 17; D.C.L. 1737. *m.* 16 Mar. 1725, Martha, da. of John Morgan (q.v.) of Tredegar, Mon., 5s., 2da. *suc.* fa. 1735; cos. as 3rd Earl of Oxford 16 June 1741.

High steward, Hereford 1746–*d.*; Harleian trustee of British Museum 1753–*d.*

Returned for Herefordshire at George II's accession, Edward Harley became a prominent member of the Tory party, speaking against the Hessians and in defence of Queen Anne's Tory administration, 4 and 27 Feb. 1730, and in favour of a reduction of the army in 1732 and 1733.[1] He carried in Mar. 1730 a bill to prevent the packing of juries. In 1736 he voted against the Westminster bridge bill, which was opposed by the city of London, and presented a petition against the mortmain bill on behalf of the trustees of the Charity schools. He states in his parliamentary diary that the motion for Walpole's dismissal, 13 Feb. 1741, was disliked by the Tories, 'whose principles abhor even the shadow of bills of pains and penalties!' In a speech against the motion he reports himself as saying:

> A noble Lord to whom I have the honour to be related [the 1st Earl of Oxford] has been mentioned in this debate. He was impeached and imprisoned, and by that imprisonment his years were shortened, and the prosecution was carried on by the honourable person who is now the subject of your question though he knew at the same time, that there was no evidence to support it. I am now, Sir, glad of this opportunity to return good for evil, and do that honourable gentleman and his family that justice which he denied to mine.

He and his brother Robert then withdrew from the House.[2] Chesterfield in 1745 referred to him and Watkin Williams Wynn (q.v.) as 'the only two people to be regarded' in the Tory party.[3] He was described to the Pretender in 1749 as one of the 'leading men of your Majesty's friends'. About the same time Thomas Carte, the Jacobite historian wrote:

> There cant be two better men nor are they more universally esteemed than the Duke of Beaufort [Lord Noel Somerset, q.v.] and the Earl of Oxford, the chiefs of the Tories. But they are not active enough, the one by his gout and the other by his constitution.[4]

'Much given to books, and a friend to scholars',[5] he maintained a close connexion with Oxford University; was present, as a Radcliffe trustee, at the opening of the Radcliffe Camera in 1749, when Dr. King delivered his celebrated Jacobite oration; and spoke at its aftermath, a meeting at the St. Albans Tavern between the Tories and the Prince of Wales's party[6] to concert measures against a proposed government bill to change the constitution of the University (see Oxford University). He figures as lord privy seal in a Leicester House list of future office holders, dated 29 Apr. 1749.[7] He died 11 Apr. 1755.

[1] *HMC Egmont Diary*, i. 31, 74, 315. [2] Harley Diary. He must have sent the speech to Chandler who printed it *verbatim*. [3] Lodge, *Private Corresp. Chesterfield and Newcastle, 1744–5* (R. Hist. Soc. Cam. 3rd ser. xliv), 44. [4] Stuart mss 301/5 and box I/299. [5] Hearne, *Colls.* (Oxf. Hist. Soc. lxv), ix. 222. [6] Walpole to Mann, 3 May 1749. [7] Add. 47092.

E.C.

HARLEY, Edward, Lord Harley (1726–90).

HEREFORDSHIRE   1747–11 Apr. 1755

b. 2 Sept. 1726, 1st s. of Edward Harley of Eywood, Herefs. (q.v.), 3rd Earl of Oxford. educ. Westminster 1735–44; Ch. Ch. Oxf. 1744; D.C.L. 1749. m. 11 July 1751 (with £50,000), Susanna, da. of William Archer (q.v.) of Welford, Berks., s.p. suc. fa. as 4th Earl 11 Apr. 1755.

Harleian trustee of British Museum 1755–d.; high steward, Hereford 1755–d.; ld. of the bedchamber to George III 1760–d.; ld. lt. Rad. 1766–d.

In 1747 Harley was adopted as one of the Tory candidates for Herefordshire, though not yet 21. Shortly before the election, Lord Foley wrote to Lord Oxford:

As he is under age I am in great fear lest some trick should be played on him on the day of election . . . which if it should happen I think would be of the most evil consequence to your family as well as to the interest of the county.[1]

Returned unopposed, he was put down in the same list as his father for a seat on the Treasury board. After the Prince's death in March 1751 he 'spoke prettily' against a clause of the regency bill for continuing the sitting Parliament till the end of the minority, observing that 'parliaments had originally been annual, then were stretched to triennial, then lengthened out to septennial, and now were going to be made perpetual'; in December 1751 he opposed Pelham's proposal for a land tax at 3s. in the pound; in January 1752 he moved a resolution against subsidy treaties in time of peace; and in December 1753 he moved for the repeal of the Plantation Act, which allowed Jews to become naturalized in the colonies after seven years' residence.[2] He was one of the Tory peers appointed lords of the bedchamber on George III's accession. He died 8 Oct. 1790.

[1] 25 June 1747, Portland mss. [2] Walpole, Mems. Geo. II, i. 144–5, 218, 254, 364.

A.N.N.

HARLEY, Robert (?1706–74).

LEOMINSTER   1734–1741, 29 Mar. 1742–1747
DROITWICH   1754–15 Mar. 1774

b. ?1706, 2nd s. of Edward Harley of Eywood, and bro. of Edward Harley jnr. (qq.v.). educ. Westminster c.1715–19; Ch. Ch. Oxf. 5 Mar. 1723, aged 16; L. Inn 1724, called 1730, bencher 1751. unm.

Recorder, Leominster 1732–d., Tewkesbury 1756–60, 1764–d.

Robert Harley, a practising barrister, succeeded his father as recorder of Leominster in 1732. Returned there as a Tory at the next general election, he voted with the Opposition, except on the motion for Walpole's dismissal in 1741, on which he withdrew with his brother.[1] Defeated in 1741, he re-

covered his seat at a by-election, continuing to vote with the Opposition. He did not stand again till 1750, when he contested Oxford University unsuccessfully. From 1754 he was returned by his cousin, Lord Foley, for Droitwich till his death, 15 Mar. 1774.

[1] Harley Diary.

A.N.N.

HARNAGE, Richard (d.1719) of Norbury, Salop, and Isleworth, Mdx.

BISHOP'S CASTLE   1708–28 Nov. 1719

b. aft. 1641, yr. s. of Edward Harnage of Belswardine Hall, Salop by Mary, da. of William Mynne of Somerton, Oxon. m., 1da.[1]

Richard Harnage, a merchant, was a member of an ancient Shropshire family seated at Belswardine. During the war of the Spanish succession he made a considerable fortune as a government clothing contractor and army agent.[2] His interest at Bishop's Castle was derived from the manors of Norbury and Hardwicke near the borough, which he inherited from his nephew, John Harnage, in 1707.[3] A Whig, he voted for the septennial bill but did not vote on the repeal of the Occasional Conformity and Schism Acts in January 1719, dying in November that year.

[1] PCC 11 Shaller. [2] Cal. Treas. Bks. 1689–1709, passim. [3] Salop Par. Reg. Soc. Hereford Dioc. xix. Norbury, i–ii.

J.B.L.

HARPUR, Sir Henry, 5th Bt. (?1708–48), of Calke Abbey, Derbys.

WORCESTER   10 Jan. 1744–1747
TAMWORTH   1747–7 June 1748

b. ?1708, 1st s. of Sir John Harpur, 4th Bt., of Calke Abbey by Catherine, da. of Thomas Crew, M.P., 2nd Baron Crew of Stene. educ. B.N.C. Oxf. 10 May 1725, aged 16. m. 16 Sept. 1734, Lady Caroline Manners, da. of John Manners, M.P., 2nd Duke of Rutland, 3s. 1da. suc. fa. 24 June 1741.

Harpur contested Derbyshire unsuccessfully in 1734. He did not stand again until 1744 when he was returned for Worcester as a Tory, voting against the Government. Soon after his unopposed return for Tamworth in 1747 he fell ill,[1] dying 7 June 1748.

[1] Hartington to Devonshire, 17 June 1747, Devonshire mss.

R.R.S.

HARRIS, Christopher (c.1687–1718), of Hayne, nr. Crediton, Devon.

OKEHAMPTON   1 Dec. 1709–1718

b. c.1687, 1st s. of Christopher Harris of Hayne by his w. Jane; bro. of John Harris (q.v.). m. bef. 1714,

Mary Ann, da. of John Buller of Morval, Cornw., 1s. 1da.

Descended from an old Devonshire family, Christopher Harris was classed as a Tory in 1715. Returned for Okehampton on the Mohun and his family's interests, he was absent from the division on the septennial bill in 1716. He died 1718 (buried 4 July) *v.p.*, aged 31.

S.R.M.

HARRIS, John (c.1690–1767), of Hayne, nr. Crediton, Devon.

HELSTON 1727–1741
ASHBURTON 1741–5 Oct. 1767

b. c.1690, 1st surv. s. of Christopher Harris of Hayne and bro. of Christopher Harris (q.v.). *educ.* L. Inn 1706, called 1713. *m.* (1) Margaret (*d.* 13 Mar. 1754), da. of Roger Tuckfield of Raddon, Devon, wid. of Samuel Rolle (q.v.) of Heanton Satchville, Devon, *s.p.*; (2) 10 Mar. 1755, Anne, da. of Francis Seymour Conway, 1st Baron Conway, *s.p. suc.* fa. aft. 1718 and bro.-in-law to moiety of manor of Ashburton 1739. Paymaster of the board of Works 1738–40; master of the Household 1741–*d.*

Of a Tory family, Harris was called 'the Hanover Rat' by his neighbour, Samuel Rolle (q.v.), whose widow he married. At George II's accession he was brought in for Helston by the Government, with whom he voted consistently throughout his parliamentary career, moving the Address in 1735. In 1739 his wife succeeded to the estates of her brother, Roger Tuckfield (q.v.), carrying an interest at Ashburton, for which Harris subsequently returned himself and another government supporter without opposition. In 1742 it was incorrectly rumoured that he was to be displaced as master of the Household.[1] He is described in the 2nd Lord Egmont's electoral survey of c.1750 as 'a man who to keep his place I should think would vote and bring in another as directed'. He died 5 Oct. 1767, aged 77.

[1] Walpole to Mann, 7 July 1742.

S.R.M.

HARRIS, John (1703–68) of Pickwell Manor, nr. Barnstaple, Devon, and Wrotham, Kent.

BARNSTAPLE 1741–1747, 1754–1761

bap. 6 Sept. 1703, s. of William Harris of Pickwell Manor by Honor, da. of Arscott Bickford of Dunsland, Devon. *educ.* I. Temple 1724. *m.* 1731, Dorothy, da. of Francis Herbert of Oakley Park, Mont., sis. of Henry Arthur, 1st Earl of Powis (qq.v.), 2s. 2da. *suc.* fa. bef. 1724.

Harris was a country gentleman, with a strong interest at Barnstaple, for which he was returned unopposed in 1741. In October 1742 he was invited

to the Cockpit meeting through H. A. Herbert, later Lord Powis (q.v.). His name does not appear in any extant division list 1741–7, except in that of administration supporters absent from the vote on the Hanoverian troops, 10 Apr. 1746, where he is classed as Old Whig. He did not stand at the general election of 1747. Re-elected in 1754, he died February 1768.

S.R.M.

HARRISON, Edward (1674–1732), of Balls Park, nr. Hertford.

WEYMOUTH AND MELCOMBE REGIS
2 Mar. 1717–1722
HERTFORD 1722–10 Aug. 1726

b. 3 Dec. 1674, 1st surv. s. of Richard Harrison, M.P. Lancaster 1669–79, by Audrey, da. of George Villiers, 4th Visct. Grandison [I]; bro. of George and Thomas Harrison (qq.v.). *m.* bef. 1708, Frances, da. of Reginald Bray of Great Barrington, Glos., sis. of Edmund and William Bray (qq.v.), 1s. 3da. *suc.* fa. 1726.

Capt. of East Indiaman *Gosfright* 1701, *Kent* 1709; gov. and c.-in.-c. Madras 1711–17; director, E.I. Co. 1718–31, dep. chairman 1723, 1728, 1731, chairman 1729; postmaster gen. 1726–*d.*

Under Charles I, Harrison's grandfather, a court official and financier, of a Lancashire family, settled in Hertfordshire, where his son Richard, Harrison's father, became for many years a notable figure in local politics. Going to India as a purser, Harrison became a captain in the China trade. Between 1703 and 1709 he corresponded with Governor Pitt, whose son Robert (qq.v.) married Harrison's cousin, the daughter of Lord Grandison.[1] Appointed governor of Madras, during his period of office he largely rebuilt the settlement, put down a minor revolt, and was presented with a sword of honour by the Company.[2] Returning with a fortune, he entered Parliament for Weymouth, voted for the repeal of the Occasional Conformity and Schism Acts, but did not vote on the peerage bill in 1719, though listed as a supporter. In 1722 he successfully contested Hertford, giving up his seat in 1726 to become postmaster general. A leading figure in the East India Company, he corresponded with Newcastle (4 Sept. 1727, Jan. 1732) on the Company's behalf over the attempts by the Emperor to set up the Ostend and Hamburg Companies.[3] He died 28 Nov. 1732. His daughter, who married the 3rd Viscount Townshend, was the mother of George and Charles Townshend (qq.v.).

[1] Add. 22852, ff. 73–83; *HMC Fortescue*, i. 28–31. [2] H. D. Love, *Vestiges of Old Madras*, ii. 131. [3] Add. 32751, f. 488; 32687, f. 445.

A.N.N.

HARRISON, George (1680-1759), of Balls Park, nr. Hertford.

HERTFORD   23 Jan. 1727-1734, 1741-2 Dec. 1759

> *b.* 10 Feb. 1680, 5th but 2nd surv. s. of Richard Harrison, M.P.; bro. of Edward and Thomas Harrison (qq.v.). *educ.* Charterhouse 1695-7; Wadham, Oxf. 1697. *m.* 12 June 1737, Mary, da. of Edward Feilde of Stanstead Abbots, Herts., *s.p.   suc.* bro. 1732.

George Harrison, who succeeded his brother at Hertford in 1727, did not stand in 1734, but was returned for it without a contest from 1741 till his death, voting with the Administration in every recorded division. Though a wealthy man—the 2nd Lord Egmont in his electoral survey c.1749-50 refers to him as one of the 'money jobbers' and as a representative of the 'monied interest'—he had a secret service pension of £500 p.a.[1] He died 2 Dec. 1759.

> [1] Naimer. *Structure*, 217, 432, 438.

A.N.N.

HARRISON, Thomas (*b.* 1681).

OLD SARUM   30 May 1728-1734

> *bap.* 24 Apr. 1681, 6th s. of Richard Harrison, M.P. of Ball's Park; bro. of Edward and George Harrison (qq.v.). prob. *unm.*
> Cornet 4 Drag. Gds. 1697; a.-d.-c. to Duke of Ormonde, ld. lt. [I], bef. 1705;[1] capt. and lt.-col. 1 Ft. Gds. 1705; brevet col. 1707; col. 6 Ft. 1708-16; adjt.-gen. in Spain 1708, and in Scotland 1715.

Thomas Harrison, a professional soldier, brought back James Stanhope's (q.v.) despatches after the victory at Saragossa in 1710, for which he received £1,000 from the Queen. In the Fifteen he was present at Sheriffmuir and brought the Duke of Argyll's despatches to George I, who gave him £500.[2] He sold his regiment in March 1716. After contesting Steyning unsuccessfully in 1724, he was brought in for Old Sarum at a by-election in 1728 by Thomas Pitt (q.v.), who recruited two voters to defeat the single supporter of Henry Fox (q.v.).[3] In Parliament he voted with the Administration on the Hessians in 1730 but against them on the excise bill in 1733 and the repeal of the Septennial Act in 1734. He was not re-chosen in 1734. On a vacancy at Old Sarum in 1735 he proposed himself for the seat to Thomas Pitt, offering to pay his brother, William (q.v.), to give up his claim to it, a proposal which William regarded as absurd and impertinent.[4] Never standing again, he died before 1755.

> [1] *HMC Ormonde*, n.s. viii. 141-2. [2] *Cal. Treas. Bks.* xxiv. 465; xxx. 129; Dalton, *Geo. I's Army*, i. 334-5. [3] Ilchester, *Ld. Holland*, i. 29-30. [4] Rosebery, *Chatham*, 74-75.

R.S.L.

HARTINGTON, Mq. of, *see* **CAVENDISH, William** (*b.* ?1698), *and* **CAVENDISH, William** (*b.* c.1720)

HARVEY, Daniel (?1664-1732), of Mitcham, Surr.

CLITHEROE   23 Jan. 1707-1708
DUNWICH   5 Feb. 1709-1710
WEYMOUTH AND MELCOMBE REGIS
                1713-3 June 1714, 1715-1722

> *b.* ?1664, 2nd s. of Sir Daniel Harvey of Coombe, Surr., by Elizabeth, da. of Edward Montagu, M.P., 2nd Baron Montagu of Boughton; bro. of Edward Harvey (q.v.). *educ.* Ch. Ch. Oxf. 16 Oct. 1677, aged 13. *m.* 6 May 1707, his cos. Lady Anne Montagu, da. of Ralph, 1st Duke of Montagu, wid. of Alexander Popham of Littlecote, Wilts., *s.p.*
> Cornet and maj. 2 tp. Life Gds. 1693; lt. and lt.-col. 1694; col. of a drag. regt. in Ireland 1695-7; col. 2 Drag. Gds. 1699-1712; brig.-gen. 1703; maj.-gen. 1704; lt.-gen. 1707; lt. gov. Guernsey 1714-*d.*

Having served in Flanders, Spain and Portugal and sat as a Whig in three Parliaments under Anne, Daniel Harvey was made governor of Guernsey on George I's accession. Returned unopposed as a Whig for Weymouth, which for many years his family had represented, he voted with the Government on the septennial bill in 1716. During the split in the Whig party he acted with the opposition Whigs, voting against the Government in the division on Cadogan (q.v.) in 1717, the repeal of the Occasional Conformity Act, and the peerage bill in 1719. He did not stand again for Weymouth but contested Dunwich at a by-election in 1722, coming bottom of the poll with only one vote. He died 6 Sept. 1732.

E.C.

HARVEY, Edward (1658-1736), of Coombe, Surr.

BLETCHINGLEY   1679
CLITHEROE   1705-1713, 30 Mar. 1715-1722

> *b.* 30 Mar. 1658, 1st s. of Sir Daniel Harvey of Coombe and bro. of Daniel Harvey (q.v.). *m.* (1) 8 May 1679, cos. Elizabeth (*d.* 15 Jan. 1696), da. of Sir Eliab Harvey, M.P., of Chigwell, Essex, 3s. 8da.; (2) July 1702, Lady Elizabeth (*d.* 7 Mar. 1724), da. of Francis Newport, M.P., 1st Earl of Bradford, wid. of Sir Henry Lyttelton, 2nd Bt., M.P., of Frankley, Worcs., *s.p.*; (3) 6 July 1725, Mary, da. of Edward Carteret (q.v.), *s.p.   suc.* fa. 1672.
> High steward, Kingston, Surr. 1707-*d.*

Harvey's grandfather, a rich Turkey merchant, was the brother of William Harvey, who discovered the circulation of the blood, and of Eliab Harvey, the grandfather of William Harvey (q.v.). His father, who was ambassador at Constantinople 1668-72, purchased the manor of Coombe in Surrey. He was defeated for Surrey in 1715, but was successful on petition for Clitheroe on the interest of his relation, the 2nd Duke of Montagu. A member of the October Club, he was an ardent supporter of the Stuarts, 'continually talking of designs to bring them back'.[1] The Duke of Berwick wrote to the Pretender, 13 May 1714, that he had been shown some letters from Harvey, who desired 'to be laid at his master's feet, and would give all he is worth, which is considerable, for his service'.[2] In September 1715 the Government received information of a treasonable correspondence between Harvey, the Duc d'Aumont, late French ambassador at London, and the Duke of Ormonde. In the papers of Harvey's agent was found the following letter, dated 9 Jan. 1715, in Harvey's own hand:

> I shall lay out no more money till I am repaid what 22 [the Duc d'Aumont] was pleased to promise me long ago . . . We are now in a hurry on choosing of Parliament men, and how those things will go, God above best does know; but this I will affirm, were those that are to choose left to themselves to choose, no money, court threats, nor any other indirect means used, all would be out of sight on the Tories side; and as it is, I hope all will do well if 6 [the King of France] and 22 stick to their true friends, and on no account forget them and all their good intentions . . . Press 22 to think of his friends, it will be of service I am sure to 6. All looks well for 8 [the Pretender] and in my heart I think better than ever 9 [King George] loses himself.[3]

Harvey was immediately arrested, questioned by the Privy Council, and shown this letter, whereupon he showed the 'utmost consternation', asked to withdraw, and attempted to commit suicide by stabbing himself that night, but, though badly wounded, he recovered. On 3 May 1716 he was re-examined by the committee and committed to Newgate, from which he was released on 10 June, with Lord Barrymore (q.v.) as his bail.[4] While on bail he did not cease from treasonable activities, for in August 1716 a Jacobite agent met Sir William Wyndham (q.v.), Harvey, 'and the rest of the King's friends,' who sent word to the Pretender 'that now was the proper time for him to go about his business, and that he should immediately land in England with 5,000 regulars and 20,000 stand of arms for arming the people'. In 1718 the Stuart papers show him furnishing Lord Mar, the Jacobite secretary of state, with reports of parliamentary proceedings.[5] At the time of the Atterbury plot, his correspondence with a Jacobite agent was intercepted by the Government, including a letter dated 20 July 1722 in which he wrote:

> a cargo of new German ladies of the largest size are coming, and Mahomet Ulrick [the King's Turkish servant] is to be chief over them. . . . In short, only villainy, beggary and Mahomitism is countenanced by those in power.[6]

He was again arrested in August 1722, released on bail for £2,000, but never brought to trial.[7] In his last years he expressed his anti-Hanoverian feelings by shooting pheasants which strayed into his property from Richmond Park.[8] He died at Dunkirk 24 Oct. 1736.

[1] Manning & Bray, *Surr.* i. 402. [2] *HMC Stuart*, i. 322–3. [3] Howell's *State Trials*, xv. 904–18, 925–6, 929–30. [4] *A Full and Authentick Narrative of the intended Horrid Conspiracy and Invasion* (1715), pp. 5–9; *HMC Stuart*, ii. 200, 205, 227. [5] *HMC Stuart*, iv. 57; vii. 592. [6] *Report from the Committee appointed by the House of Commons to examine Christopher Layer and others*, and appendix H.16. [7] S P Dom. 35/32, f. 114. [8] Manning & Bray, loc. cit.

E.C.

HARVEY, John (c.1667–1721), of Ickwell Bury, Beds.

BEDFORDSHIRE   1713–19 July 1715

b. c.1667, 1st s. of John Harvey of Finningley, Notts. and Ickwell Bury by Mary, wid. of John Vassall of Hoxton, London, merchant. *educ.* I. Temple, 1682; St. Catherine's, Camb. 1682; Grand Tour 1688–9.[1] *m.* (lic. 12 May 1696) Sarah, 4th da. of Sir John Robinson, 1st Bt., M.P., of Nuneham Courtnay, Oxon. and Farmingwoods, Northants., ld. mayor of London 1662–3, wid. of John Gore of Gilston, Herts.,[2] 5s. 5da. *suc.* fa. 1692.
Sheriff, Beds. 1711–12.

John Harvey was re-elected for the county as a Tory in 1715 but was unseated on petition. His name was sent to the Pretender in 1721 as a probable supporter in the event of a rising.[3] He died 17 Nov. 1721.

[1] *Beds. Hist. Rec. Soc. Publ.* xl. 6–34. [2] *VCH Northants. Families*, 276. [3] Stuart mss 65/16.

R.S.L.

HARVEY, Michael (1694–1748), of Coombe, Surr. and Clifton Maybank, nr. Milborne Port, Dorset.

MILBORNE PORT   10 June–6 July 1717, 1722–1741,
2 Feb. 1742–1747

b. 10 May 1694, o. surv. s. of Edward Harvey of Coombe (q.v.), by his 1st w. *m.* (settlement 23 Apr. 1715) Rebecca, da. of Sir John Wolstenholme, 3rd Bt., M.P., of Edmonton, Mdx., *s.p. suc.* wid. of cos. Michael Harvey, M.P., at Clifton Maybank 1717 and fa. 1736.

Michael Harvey, a Tory like his father, ruined himself by successive contests at Milborne Port, which he represented for a quarter of a century. His name was sent to the Pretender in 1721 as a probable supporter in the event of a rising.[1] In 1743 a private Act was passed vesting his Leicestershire estates in trustees for the discharge of encumbrances on his Surrey estates. He was also forced to mortgage his Clifton estate and his property at Milborne Port to Peter Walter (q.v.).

In 1747 he was unseated by the House of Commons on a double return at Milborne Port, the merits of the election, as distinct from those of the return, being referred by the House to the elections committee, which had not reported when he died of apoplexy, 3 Oct. 1748. Peter Walter foreclosed on the Clifton and Milborne Port properties shortly before his death, after which his Surrey estates were sold.[2]

[1] Stuart mss 65/16. [2] Hutchins, *Dorset*, iv. 122–3.

R.R.S.

HARVEY, William (1663–1731), of Chigwell, Essex.

OLD SARUM	25 Mar. 1689–1705
APPLEBY	1705–1708
OLD SARUM	1708–1710
WEYMOUTH AND MELCOMBE REGIS	
	18 Apr. 1711–1713, 3 June 1714– 1715
ESSEX	31 May 1715–18 May 1716, 1722– 1727

bap. 18 Dec. 1663, o. surv. s. of Sir Eliab Harvey, M.P., of Chigwell by Dorothy, da. of Sir Thomas Whitmore, 1st Bt., M.P., of Apley, Salop; cos. of Edward Harvey (q.v.). *educ.* St. Paul's; Trinity, Camb. 1680. *m.* 23 Nov. 1680, Dorothy, da. and h. of Sir Robert Dycer, 2nd Bt., of Wrentham, Suff., wid. of his e. bro. Eliab, 3s. 3da. *suc.* fa. 1699.

The grandson of a rich Turkey merchant, whose brother Daniel was the grandfather of Edward Harvey of Coombe (q.v.), William Harvey was a Tory country gentleman and a member of the October Club, with an income of £5,000–£6,000 a year.[1] Returned in 1715 at a by-election for Essex, after contesting Bridport unsuccessfully, he voted against the septennial bill before being unseated on petition. Re-elected for Essex in 1722, he did not stand in 1727, dying 31 Oct. 1731.

[1] Add. 22248, f. 91.

R.R.S.

HARVEY, William (1714–63) of Chigwell, Essex.

ESSEX 1747–11 June 1763

b. 9 June 1714, 1st s. of William Harvey, M.P., of Chigwell by Mary, da. and coh. of Ralph Williamson of Berwick, Northumb.; gd.-s. of William Harvey of Chigwell (q.v.). *m.* 13 Aug. 1750, Emma, da. and coh. of Stephen Skynner of Walthamstow, Essex, 5s. 4da. *suc.* fa. 1742.

Like most of this family a Tory, Harvey was returned unopposed for Essex in 1747. He died 11 June 1763.

E.C.

HARWOOD, *see* **HILL, Thomas**

HARVEY THURSBY, John (?1711–64), of Abington Abbey, Northants.

WOOTTON BASSETT	1741–1747
STAMFORD	1754–1761

b. ?1711, 1st surv. s. of Robert Harvey, barrister, of Stockton, Warws. by Mary, da. and h. of Thomas Thursby of London, merchant. *educ.* Charterhouse; Pembroke, Camb. 9 Nov. 1727, aged 16. *m.* (settlement 12 June 1731) Honor, da. of Robert Pigott (q.v.) of Chetwynd, Salop, 6s. 5da. *suc.* fa. 1726 and to Abington estate of his mother's cos. Richard Thursby 1736, taking add. name of Thursby by Act of Parl. 1736.

John Harvey Thursby's great-grandfather, Robert Harvey, inherited in 1662 the considerable estates of his maternal uncle Hugh Audley, a moneylender. Of these Stockton was devised to John's grandfather, another Robert, and Cole Park, in Malmesbury, Wilts., to his brother Hugh.[1] After succeeding to Abington in 1736 he stood unsuccessfully for Coventry at a by-election in April 1737. Returned for Wootton Bassett as a Tory in 1741, he voted consistently against the Administration. He did not stand in 1747 but was returned for Stamford on Lord Exeter's interest in 1754. He died 1 June 1764.

[1] Baker, *Northants.* i. 11; *VCH Warws.* vi. 227; *Vis. Warws. 1682–3* (Harl. Soc. lxii), 61–62.

R.S.L.

HASKINS STILES, Benjamin (c.1684–1739), of Bowden Park, nr. Chippenham, Wilts. and Moor Park, Herts.

DEVIZES 8 Feb. 1721–1734

b. c.1684, 1st s. of Joseph Haskins Stiles (formerly Haskins), sometime merchant of Amsterdam, by Sarah, 1st da. of Sir John Eyles, M.P., ld. mayor of London 1688, bro. of Sir Francis Eyles, 1st Bt. *m.* (1) by 1708, 1s. 2da. *d.v.p.* young; (?2) by Aug. 1733, Jane.[1] *suc.* fa. 1714; yr. bro. Joseph 1719.

Benjamin Haskins Stiles's father was partner and heir of his maternal uncle Robert Stiles (*d.* 1680), a wealthy Amsterdam merchant and native of Wantage, Berks. His sister married Sir John Eyles, 2nd Bt. (q.v.). On inheriting his younger brother's fortune in 1719, he acquired large estates in north Wiltshire, including Bowden Park, Bishop's Cannings, near Devizes, and the prebend manor of Calne which carried an electoral interest in that borough.[2] He also bought Moor Park and built the existing house there, which was laid out by Leoni under the superintendence of Sir James Thornhill (q.v.).[3] In 1721 he was returned as a Whig on the Eyles interest at Devizes in place of his uncle Francis Eyles (q.v.), who had been expelled from the House as a director of the South Sea

Company. Next year he was returned for both Calne and Devizes, choosing to serve for the latter, probably because a petition was pending at Calne. Re-elected unopposed with Sir Joseph Eyles (q.v.) in 1727, he voted for the Administration on the Hessians, 1730, but absented himself on the report stage of the excise bill, 1733, afterwards voting against it.[4] He did not stand in 1734, dying 4 Apr. 1739.

[1] PCC 90 Henchman. [2] *Wilts. N. & Q.* viii. 146-9, 150-1; *VCH Wilts.* vii. 189; see also CALNE. [3] *VCH Herts.* ii. 377-8. [4] *Gent. Mag.* 1733, p. 580.

R.S.L.

HATTON, see FINCH, Hon. Edward

HAWKE, Sir Edward (1710-81), of Scarthingwell Hall, nr. Tadcaster, Yorks.

PORTSMOUTH 28 Dec. 1747-20 May 1776

b. 21 Feb. 1710, o.s. of Edward Hawke, barrister, of L. Inn, by Elizabeth, da. of Nathaniel Bladen of Hemsworth, Yorks., sis. of Martin Bladen (q.v.) and wid. of Colonel Ruthven. *m.* 3 Oct. 1737, Catherine, da. and h. of Walter Brooke, of Burton Hall, nr. Hull, gd.-da. and coh. of William Hammond of Scarthingwell Hall, 3s. 1da. *suc.* fa. 1718. K.B. 14 Nov. 1747; *cr.* Baron Hawke 20 May 1776.
Entered navy 1720, lt. 1729, cdr. 1733, capt. 1734, r.-adm. 1747, v.-adm. 1748, adm. 1757, adm. of the fleet 1768.
P.C. 10 Dec. 1766; first ld. of the Admiralty Dec. 1766-71.

Hawke first entered the navy as a volunteer, being then the ward of his uncle Martin Bladen (q.v.), whose protection was useful to him in his career. He served successively under Hosier, Sir Charles Wager (q.v.), Thomas Mathews (q.v.) and Peter Warren (q.v.). His first great naval success was in October 1747, when he attacked a French convoy off Belle Isle, capturing seven out of nine ships, for which he was created K.B. a month later. On 18 Dec. of that year, the Duke of Bedford wrote to him:

I have this day wrote to Mr. Mayor of Portsmouth, recommending you to the gentlemen of the corporation to be their representative in Parliament. I most heartily wish you good success.[1]

He was returned unopposed. From 1748 he was serving as commander-in-chief, mainly at Portsmouth, until November 1752 when he struck his flag.

He died 17 Oct. 1781.

[1] Burrows, *Life of Sir Edw. Hawke*, 122, 129, 199.

E.C.

HAWKINS, Philip (?1700-38), of Trewithen, nr. Grampound, Cornw.

GRAMPOUND 1727-6 Sept. 1738

b. ?1700, 4th s. of Philip Hawkins of Pennance, Cornw. by Mary, da. and coh. of Richard Scobell of Menagwins, Cornw. *educ.* Pembroke, Camb. 7 Mar. 1716, aged 15; M. Temple 1717. *m.* Elizabeth Ludlow of London, *s.p.*

The son of an attorney, who 'by his great pains, care and skill in that profession . . . got himself a very great estate', becoming the wealthiest lawyer in Cornwall, Hawkins purchased for £2,700 Trewithen, near Grampound,[1] which he represented from 1727 until his death, voting with the Opposition in every recorded division, though he and his brother John, formerly master of Pembroke, Cambridge, acted in concert with the agents of the Administration at the elections of 1727 and 1734.[2] He died 30 Aug. 1738, leaving Trewithen to his nephew Thomas (q.v.), and bequeathing '£600 to his Majesty in lieu of his tenants having defrauded the Crown of about that sum in the customs'.[3]

[1] *Parochial Hist. Cornw.* i. 257; iv. 103. [2] See GRAMPOUND [3] *Gent. Mag.* 1738, p. 490.

E.C.

HAWKINS, Thomas (?1724-66), of Trewithen, nr. Grampound, Cornw.

GRAMPOUND 1747-1754

b. ?1724, o.s. of Christopher Hawkins of Trewinnard, Cornw., barrister and vice-warden of the stannaries 1742-51, by Mary, da. of Philip Hawkins of Pennance, Cornw. *educ.* Pembroke, Camb. 10 Nov. 1741, aged 17. *m.* June 1756, Anne, da. of James Heywood of Austin Friars, London, 4s. 1da. *suc.* uncle John Hawkins, D.D., master of Pembroke, Cambridge 1736, and uncle Philip (q.v.) at Trewithen 1738.

While still a minor Hawkins inherited from his uncle Philip an electoral interest at Grampound, which was managed by his father, in alliance with Thomas Pitt (q.v.), the Prince of Wales's Cornish election manager. He was returned there in 1747 as a member of the Prince of Wales's party, but did not stand again.[1] He died *v.p.* 1 Dec. 1766 of an inoculation against smallpox, to which he had submitted as an example to his neighbours, many of whom followed his lead, all recovering but himself.[2]

[1] See GRAMPOUND. [2] W. P. Courtney, *Parl. Rep. Cornw.* 192.

E.C.

HAY, Lord Charles (c.1700-60), of Linplum, East Lothian.

HADDINGTONSHIRE 1741-1747

b. c.1700, 3rd s. of Charles Hay, 3rd Mq. of Tweeddale [S], by Lady Susan Hamilton, da. of William,

1st Duke of Hamilton [S], wid. of John Cochrane, 2nd Earl of Dundonald [S]; bro. of John, 4th Mq. of Tweeddale [S]. *unm.* *suc.* kinsman Sir Robert Hay, 2nd Bt., to Linplum 1751.

Ensign 2 Ft. Gds. 1722; capt. 33 Ft. 1727, 9 Drags. 1729; capt. and lt.-col. 1 Ft. Gds. 1743; a.-d.-c. to George II Mar. 1749; col. Aug. 1749; col. 33 Ft. 1753–*d.*; maj.-gen. 1757.

Lord Charles Hay, a professional soldier, with 'more of the parts of an Irishman than of a Scot', was 'so vain of having made a campaign . . . [on the Rhine] in 1734, that he talked of it ever after and went by the name of *Trentquatre*'.[1] Returned unopposed for Haddingtonshire in 1741, he attached himself to Lord Carteret, voting against Walpole's candidate for the chairman of the elections committee. After Walpole's fall he supported the new Administration, in which his brother, Lord Tweeddale, was secretary of state for Scotland, speaking from personal experience on the Hanoverians in December 1743 and January 1744. Next year he was present at Fontenoy, where, in his own words,

> it was our regiment that attacked the French Guards: and when we came to within twenty or thirty paces of them, I advanced before our regiment; drank to them and told them that we were the English Guards, and hoped they would stand till we came quite up to them, and not swim the Scheldt as they did the Main at Dettingen.[2]

He voted for the Hanoverians in April 1746, classed as 'Granville', i.e. Carteret. Reported in November 1746 to be 'confined raving mad' and to have 'been tied in his bed some time',[3] he did not seek election again. Nevertheless he became a.-d.-c. to the King in 1749 and was given a regiment in 1753. Promoted major-general in 1757, he was sent out to America to join the forces of Lord Loudoun, who put him under arrest in July for 'uttering various opprobrious and disrespectful speeches' about the delay in attacking Louisbourg. Remaining under arrest at Halifax and on board ship until he was sent home late in 1758, he demanded a court-martial, which sat from 12 Feb. till 4 Mar. 1760[4], but he died 1 May 1760, before a verdict was announced.

[1] Walpole to Mann, 26 Nov. 1744. [2] Hay to Lord Tweeddale, 20 May (o.s.) 1745, Carlyle, *Frederick the Great* (1869 ed.), vi. 63–64. [3] *HMC Polwarth*, v. 187. [4] Add. 35894, ff. 28–39.

R.S.L.

HAY, Thomas, Visct. Dupplin (1710–87).

SCARBOROUGH   26 Jan.–21 Apr. 1736
CAMBRIDGE   1741–29 July 1758

b. 4 June 1710, 1st s. of George Hay, M.P., 8th Earl of Kinnoull [S], by Abigail, da. of Robert Harley, M.P., 1st Earl of Oxford. *educ.* Westminster 1718; Ch. Ch. Oxf. 1726. *m.* 12 June 1741, Constantia (with £3,000 p.a.), da. and h. of John Kyrle Ernle of

Whetham, Wilts., 1s. *d.v.p.* *suc.* fa. as 9th Earl 29 July 1758.

Commr. of revenue [I] Apr. 1741–6; ld. of Trade 1746–54; chairman of committee of privileges and elections 1747–58; ld. of Treasury 1754–5; jt. paymaster gen. 1755–7; chancellor of duchy of Lancaster 1758–62; recorder, Cambridge 1758–*d.*; P.C. 27 Jan. 1758; ambassador to Portugal 1759–62; chancellor of St. Andrews Univ. 1765–*d.*

Dupplin's father, one of the twelve Tory peers created in 1711, was the brother-in-law of Lord Mar, who headed the Fifteen in Scotland, and the brother of one of the Pretender's chief advisers. Arrested in 1715 with his father, the 7th Earl of Kinnoull, on suspicion of complicity in the rebellion, he was released on bail in 1717. In 1723, having succeeded to the earldom, he made overtures to Walpole,[1] who appears to have accepted them, for when Dupplin went to Oxford he received an allowance from the King, procured by Walpole for his maintenance. By this time Lord Kinnoull was in such financial straits that Dupplin and his brother were unable to go up at the beginning of one term because their father could not provide the money for the journey.[2] In 1728 Lord Kinnoull's needs were relieved by his appointment as ambassador to Constantinople till 1734, when he was recalled under a cloud. On 20 Dec. 1740 Dupplin applied to Newcastle for the governorship of Barbados for his father, who,

> having appropriated his estate in Scotland to the payment of his debts and that in York for the support of his numerous family, has reserved nothing for himself.[3]

The application was unsuccessful, but Lord Kinnoull was granted a secret service pension of £800 a year.[4]

In 1736 Dupplin, after accompanying his father to Constantinople, was put up for a vacancy at Scarborough by his first cousin, the 4th Duke of Leeds, on the recommendation of their common uncle and Leeds's ex-guardian, Edward Harley (q.v.), 2nd Earl of Oxford. Dupplin was a supporter of Walpole's Administration, to which both his patrons were opposed, but Oxford argued that Leeds could not

> expect that you can at present carry one of your own way of thinking without great expense—your interest is now but young. My Lord Dupplin will come in without opposition in all probability and as he is your relation and of your nomination you will put yourself at the head of the corporation and by that means you will establish an interest that you may always with ease maintain.[5]

In fact there was a contest at which Dupplin, by securing the returning officers, was declared elected, only to be unseated by the House of Commons on petition.

In 1741 Dupplin was again defeated at Scarborough but got himself returned unopposed for Cambridge, on the recommendation of Lord Oxford, high steward of the borough. A few days before his return Walpole, who had a high opinion of him, gave him an Irish place with a salary of £1,000 a year, from which he was promoted by Pelham to the board of Trade. Chosen to be chairman of the elections committee of the House at the opening of the next Parliament, he took a leading part in the proceedings on the Westminster petition at the beginning of the 1751 session. A month later, as a member of the board of Trade, he moved a grant-in-aid of the new colony of Nova Scotia in a long speech, of which Horace Walpole observed that Dupplin, 'considering how fond he was of forms and trifles and being busy, was not absolutely a bad speaker'. Behind the scenes Pelham, as Newcastle afterwards (3 Jan. 1757) told Lady Yarmouth,

sachant son honneur, son intégrité, et sa capacité, lui confia toujours, sans réserve, tous les secrets, même les plus importants; et quand le Roy me fit l'honneur de m'appeler à la Trésorerie je fis le même, et je dois principalement à lui le peu de connaissance que j'ai dans les affaires des finances.[6]

In other words, Dupplin assisted Pelham in one of the most important duties of the first lord of the Treasury, the management of parliamentary elections; a matter so secret that Pelham always refused to discuss it even with Newcastle, who on succeeding his brother found himself dependent on Dupplin for information as to the arrangements made for the impending general election.

Though Dupplin earned the confidence of three prime ministers, the world at large, according to Lord Hardwicke, 'opprobriously and injuriously' thought him 'an absolute fool'. Some light on this misconception is thrown by a letter from Hardwicke's daughter-in-law describing

the incessant small talk of my good Lord Dupplin that flows and flows on as smoothly as ever and as uninterrupted in its course. He came here to dinner yesterday . . . fought over the mutiny and sea bills at supper, and has instructed us this morning on the art of colonising and the affairs of Nova Scotia.[7]

Far from a fool, he probably owed his reputation of being one to the fact that the word for a bore had yet to be invented.

Faithful both to his patron and his principles— 'il n'a jamais donné un seul vote pendant près de vingt ans que de la manière le Roy souhaitait', Newcastle told Lady Yarmouth, 'et j'ose dire qu'il ne le fera jamais de sa vie'[8]—Dupplin resigned with Newcastle in 1762 but did not accompany him into opposition. He spent the rest of his life in retirement, planting trees on his estate in Scotland. He died 27 Dec. 1787.

[1] Coxe, *Walpole*, ii. 257. [2] *HMC Portland*, vi. 26; vii. 445, 459. [3] Add. 32695, f. 529. [4] Namier, *Structure*, 222–3. [5] 14 Sept. 1735, Harley mss 29, f. 106. [6] Add. 58141, f. 341; 32870, ff. 9–14; Walpole, *Mems. Geo. II*, i. 16, 27, 63; Add. 32870, ff. 9–14. [7] Newcastle to Hardwicke, 17 Oct. 1753, Add. 32733, f. 781; Hardwicke to Newcastle, 13 Oct. 1755, Add. 32860, ff. 30–34; Add. 35376, ff. 19–20. [8] Add. 32870, ff. 8–14.

R.R.S.

HAY, William (1695–1755), of Glyndebourne, Suss.

SEAFORD 25 Jan. 1734–19 June 1755

b. 21 Aug. 1695, o. surv. s. of William Hay of Glyndebourne by Barbara, da. of Sir John Stapley, 1st Bt., M.P., of Patcham, Suss. *educ.* Lewes g.s. 1710–12; Ch. Ch. Oxf. 1712; M. Temple 1715, called 1723; Grand Tour (France, Germany, Holland) 1720. *m.* 1731, Elizabeth, da. of Thomas Pelham, M.P., of Catsfield Place, Suss., 3s. 2da. *suc.* fa. 1695.

Commr. for victualling the navy 1738–47; keeper of the records in the Tower of London 1754–d.

Hay was returned for Seaford by the Duke of Newcastle, his cousin by marriage, on whose behalf he canvassed energetically at Sussex elections. In spite of physical disabilities—he was a hunchbacked dwarf—he took an active part in the Commons, where he voted with the Government in every recorded division. Making his first reported speech against an opposition place bill in Feb. 1734, he spoke for the Government on the army in 1735, when he published a criticism of the poor law, stating that

every parish is in a state of expensive war with all the rest of the nation, regards the poor of all other places as aliens, and cares not what becomes of them if it can but banish them from its own society. No good therefore is ever to be expected till parochial interest and settlements are destroyed, till the poor are taken out of the hands of the overseers and put under the management of persons wiser and more disinterested, and till they be set to work on a national, or at least a provincial fund, to arise from benefactions and the labour of the poor, as far as they will go, and what more is wanting to be levied by an equal tax.

In 1736 and 1737 he introduced bills for implementing his proposals, but failed to carry them through the House.[1] He also spoke 'with wit' against a bill for preventing clandestine marriages in 1736 and again on the army, 1737 and 1738.[2] Appointed to the victualling board in 1738, he defended himself and his colleagues against charges of neglect in 1740. When in 1747 his office became incompatible with a seat in the Commons under the Place Act, 1742, he gave it up for a secret service pension of £500 a year, which ceased on his appointment to be keeper of the records in the Tower in 1754.[3] In December 1747 he brought in a bill for the better relief of the poor by voluntary charities which passed the Commons but was lost in the Lords. The author of a number of works in verse as well as in prose, including an essay on deformity, he died 22 June 1755.

[1] *Remarks on the Laws relating to the Poor, with proposals for their better Relief and Employment*, 1751; *CJ*, xxii. 607, 746; xxv. 464. [2] *HMC Egmont Diary*, ii. 257, 350. [3] Add. 33038, f. 352.

E.C.

HAYES, James (1715–1800), of Hollyport, Berks.

DOWNTON   12 May 1753–June 1757, 1761–1768, 11 Feb. 1771–1774

bap. 27 Oct. 1715, 1st s. of James Hayes of Hollyport, receiver of the land tax for Berks. 1744–50, by Mary, da. of Richard Aldworth of Stanlake, Berks. *educ.* Eton 1725–34; M. Temple 1732, called 1740, bencher 1768; King's, Camb. 1734, fellow 1737–50. *m.* 20 Mar. 1750, Jane, da. of James Croxton of Chester, 3s. 2da. *suc.* fa. 1750.
2nd justice of Anglesey 1761–78, c.j. 1778–93.

James Hayes, whose father and grandfather had also been barristers of the Middle Temple, was the 'worthy friend and fellow collegiate'[1] of George Proctor (q.v.), M.P. for Downton, who died in 1751. He was brought in for Downton at a by-election as a supporter of the Administration by Anthony Duncombe (q.v.), Lord Feversham, who made him an executor of his will and trustee for his children. He died 9 Sept. 1800.

[1] PCC 154 Busby.

R.S.L.

HAYWARD, Thomas (1706–81), of Quedgeley. Glos.

LUDGERSHALL   1741–1747, 1754–1761

bap. 2 Aug. 1706,[1] 1st surv. s. of William Hayward of Quedgeley by Margaret, da. of Maj.-Gen. William Selwyn, M.P., of Matson, Glos. *educ.* L. Inn 1723, called 1729. *m.* by 1733,[2] Mercy, da. of Charles Parsons of Bredon, Worcs., 3s. 1da. *suc.* fa. 1709.

Thomas Hayward was brought in for Ludgershall in 1741 by his uncle, Colonel John Selwyn (q.v.). Voting with the Administration in all recorded divisions, he was classed as an Old Whig in 1746. He did not stand in 1747 but was again brought in by his cousin George Augustus Selwyn (q.v.) in 1754. He died 14 Mar. 1781.

[1] *Glos. N. & Q.* iii. 91. [2] A daughter was *bap.* at Quedgeley 2 Nov. 1733.

R.S.L.

HEATH, Edmund Pike (aft. 1675–1749), of Sutton, Surr.[1]

CALNE   11 Feb. 1723–1727

b. aft. 1675, 2nd s. of William Heath of Stepney, Mdx., and bro. of Thomas Heath (q.v.). *unm.*

Edmund Pike Heath, presumably a Whig like his brother, was returned for Calne at a by-election in 1723. He did not stand again, dying 4 Jan. 1746.

[1] Manning & Bray, *Surr.* i. 498.

R.S.L.

HEATH (afterwards DUKE), John (c.1717–75), of Gittisham, nr. Honiton, Devon.

HONITON   1747–1754, 1761–1768

b. c.1717, 1st s. of Staplehill Heath of Ottery St. Mary by Anne, da. of Thomas Duke of Otterton, Devon. *m.* (lic. 17 May 1745) Susanna, da. and eventually h. of William Gill of Honiton, attorney, comptroller of the customs at Chester, *s.p. suc.* to Otterton under will of his uncle, Richard Duke, taking the name of Duke by Act of Parliament 1751.

Heath came of an Exeter merchant family, owning some land near the city. His mother's family, also of Exeter origin, held considerable property in south Devonshire, including a moiety of the manor of Ashburton.[1] He was returned as a government supporter for Honiton by the influence of his father-in-law William Gill, formerly port-reeve (i.e. returning officer) of the borough, who 'publicly made interest' for him, by polling paupers and minors, keeping hostile voters drunk and in confinement, and hiring 'a mob of dissolute fellows from all the neighbouring villages under pretence of getting them appointed constables to keep the peace', but in reality to prevent voters coming to the poll.[2] Unsuccessful at Honiton in 1754 and 1768, he died 3 Nov. 1775, aged 58.

[1] Sir W. R. Drake, *Heathiana*; *Trans. Devon Assoc.* l. 499. [2] *CJ*, xxv. 451.

S.R.M.

HEATH, Richard (?1706–52), of Argyle Bldgs., Westminster.

BOSSINEY   1747–5 Feb. 1752

b. ?1706, 1st s. of Sir Thomas Heath of Hatchlands, East Clandon, Surr. by his w. née Hubert of Boys Court, Kent. *educ.* Westminster Apr. 1718, aged 12; Magdalen, Oxf. 1 Nov. 1722, aged 16. *m.* Bridget, da. of John Nicholas of West Horsley, Surr. (bro. of Edward Nicholas, q.v.), 1s. 1da. *suc.* fa. c.1716.

Heath was the grandson of Sir Richard Heath, one of James II's judges, who purchased the manor of East Clandon in 1692. On his father's death the manor was sold under a private act of 1718 to pay the debts encumbering the estate. For some years Heath continued to reside in the family mansion at Hatchlands in Clandon, which, heavily mortgaged by him, was eventually sold to Edward Boscawen (q.v.) in 1749.[1] He was returned for Bossiney in

1747 by Thomas Pitt (q.v.) as a member of the Prince of Wales's party and was classed as Opposition. He died 4 Feb. 1752, leaving the Rev. Thomas Yale Caverley, chaplain to the Princess of Wales, as his executor and guardian of his only son, Nicholas.[2]

[1] *VCH Surr.* iii. 345; Manning & Bray, *Surr.* iii. 47–48; *CJ*, xviii. 578. [2] PCC 187 Bettesworth.

E.C.

HEATH, Thomas (aft. 1674–1741), of Stansted Mountfitchet, Essex.[1]

HASLEMERE 22 Nov. 1704–1705
HARWICH 17 May–29 June 1714
1715–1722

b. after 1674, 1st s. of William Heath of Stepney, Mdx., E.I. capt., by Jane, da. of Edmund Pike of London, grocer; bro. of Edmund Pike Heath (q.v.). *m.* Catherine, da. and coh. of Arthur Bayley of Mile End Green, Virginia merchant, 2s. 1da.
Director, E.I. Co. 1713–15, 1719–21.

After representing Haslemere for a few months, Heath, an East India merchant, stood in 1713 as a Whig for Harwich, where he tied with a Tory, who on a double return was awarded the seat. Next year he was again returned for Harwich at a by-election, with the same result as before. Successful at last in 1715, he voted against the Government on the septennial bill in 1716 and on Lord Cadogan (q.v.) in 1717, with them on the repeal of the Occasional Conformity and Schism Acts, and against them on the peerage bill in 1719. In Feb. 1721 he spoke in favour of Walpole's scheme to ingraft part of the capital stock of the South Sea Company into the Bank of England and part into the East India Company. Put down in Sunderland's plans for the 1722 Parliament to oppose Humphry Parsons (q.v.) at Harwich, he stood in 1722 but was defeated. He 'made interest' at Harwich in 1727, but did not stand. In 1733 he applied unsuccessfully to Walpole for the government interest at Harwich, claiming to have been invited by the corporation to stand at the next general election. He then went down to Harwich 'to offer his service', gaining some support by telling the corporation that Walpole had encouraged him to stand. He had hopes of being adopted by a faction of the corporation, who were said to be prepared to accept anybody, even 'Heath, a lousy fellow', in preference to Lord Perceval (q.v.), but they invited another candidate, with Heath only as a second string.[2] In the end he did not stand. He died 7 Sept. 1741.

[1] Morant, *Essex*, ii, 579. [2] *HMC Egmont Diary*, i. 328, 397; ii. 86, 99–100; iii. 323.

R.R.S.

HEATHCOTE FAMILY

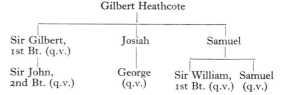

Gilbert Heathcote

Sir Gilbert, 1st Bt. (q.v.) — Josiah — Samuel

Sir John, 2nd Bt. (q.v.) — George (q.v.) — Sir William, 1st Bt. (q.v.) — Samuel (q.v.)

HEATHCOTE, George (1700–68), of Walcot, Som.

HINDON 1727–1734
SOUTHWARK 1734–1741
LONDON 1741–1747

b. 7 Dec. 1700, in Jamaica, o.s. of Josiah Heathcote, a yr. bro. of Sir Gilbert Heathcote (q.v.), West India merchant, of St. Swithin's Lane, London by Catherine, wid. of Thomas Barrett, merchant, of Jamaica. *educ.* Clare, Camb. 1720; L. Inn 1721. *m.* c. 1725, Maria, da. of John Eyles, M.P., of South Broom House, Wilts., 2s. 2da. *suc.* fa. 1706.
Director, S. Sea Co. 1730–3; master, Salters' Co. 1737; alderman of Walbrook ward 1739–49; sheriff of London 1739–40, ld. mayor 1742.

A wealthy West India merchant, Heathcote stood successfully as a Whig for Hindon in 1727, against Henry Fox (q.v.). On petition 'the whole power of the ministry was exerted to give him admittance in the House to the exclusion of Mr. Fox'. At first he supported the Administration, but when the retention of the Hessian troops came before the House on 4 Feb. 1730, he made what Hervey described as

a flaming speech against the Court, which he had collected from a common-place book on tyranny and arbitrary power and extracts of treatises on a free government; and which would have served just as well for any debate that ever was or ever will be in Parliament as that to which it was applied. I took opportunity to wish Sir Robert (with whom I dined) joy of his new friend, and asked him, if he did not think his pains well bestowed.

Thereafter, Heathcote was one of the most frequent and violent speakers for the Opposition. On 4 Mar. 1731 the 1st Lord Egmont reports:

Mr. Heathcote made a motion for a bill to prevent the translation of bishops. His character is that of a republican Whig . . . [He] raised the indignation of the House by prefacing his motion that the bishops clung all together to advance any proposition that had a court air, and were united in all measures that were destructive to their country.

And again on the excise bill in 1733:

Mr. Heathcote spoke violently against the bill . . . [concluding] that if it passed into a law, the people would not submit to it but forcibly repeal it. This was a hot expression and breathed rebellion.

On the other hand, he was one of the opposition Whigs who supported the motion for the Princess

Royal's marriage portion, taking the opportunity 'to express their zeal for the royal family'. He supported the new colony of Georgia, serving as a common councillor and treasurer of the Society till he resigned in 1738, on the ground that some of the trustees were too subservient to Walpole.[1]

Returned for Southwark in 1734, Heathcote moved in March 1736 that his opponent's petition be heard at the bar of the House, to give himself an opportunity of clearing himself publicly of the charges levelled against him. In the same month he spoke in favour of the repeal of the Test Act. In March 1737 he supported Walpole's financial proposals, and opposed Sir John Barnard's scheme for reducing the interest on the national debt. In November 1739 he supported an opposition motion for papers relating to the war with Spain. Next winter he declined an invitation to stand for the lord mayoralty because

> he was just out of an expensive office (that of sheriff) and which had taken up so much of his time that he had not been able to attend to his own affairs and to involve him immediately in those of the mayoralty which would take up more of his time was a step to ruin him and he was resolved not to serve.

Returned for London at the general election of 1741, he voted with the Government on the Bossiney election petition out of friendship for one of the ministerial candidates but two days later, having, it was supposed, 'been schooled on his return into the city' for his vote, 'not only changed sides, but spoke on the contrary side with fury'.

After Walpole's fall, Heathcote's opposition turned to Jacobitism. On 15 Nov. 1745 a report to the Pretender states:

> Alderman Heathcote . . . has been long a vigorous and bold opposer of the measures of the Hanoverian court, by which means he has been reckoned, especially since the base defection of Pulteney, the chief leader of the Patriot Whigs, not in the city of London only but in the nation; he opened himself above two years ago to Sir John Hynde Cotton [q.v.], and did what he could without formally despising the established laws, to force the court to persecute him by which he hoped to drive things to the utmost extremity, but the ministers knew both his abilities and his influence so well that they durst not meddle with him. At the time of the embarkation at Dunkirk [February 1744] he allowed Sir John Cotton to answer for him to Sir Watkin [Williams Wynn, q.v.] and Lord Barrymore [q.v.] and has been ever since in their counsels and confidence.[2]

He was the only one of the London Members who opposed a loyal address upon the threatened French invasion. In February 1745 he warmly supported a bill to abolish the traditional veto of the aldermen of London over the decisions of the common council, which had been confirmed by the London Election Act. In March following he spoke against a grant of £40,000 for the cost of 6,000 Dutch troops sent for during the invasion scare.[3] He opposed the voluntary subscriptions for raising troops and the loyal address of the city on the rebellion,[4] during which the Pretender was informed that

> as many of the King's friends in England as possible would join the Prince when he gave them an opportunity . . . Alderman Heathcote and several more have been with Sir Watkin to assure him that they will rise in the city of London at the same time.

In 1747 a message was sent to the Young Pretender that

> Mr. Alderman Heathcote . . . whose indefatigable zeal and labours in the interest of your royal family, have given a bias to the spirit of that noble metropolis in favour of your royal cause . . . charged me to assure your Royal Highness of his most dutiful attachment, ardent zeal and devotion and that if at any time he has a hint or previous notice of your Royal Highness's designs in attempting anything for the good of the nation, he'll exert himself in conjunction with several others of your faithful subjects to raise a considerable sum of money, which had not been wanting to your Royal Highness in the time you was in Scotland, if his proposals, the most practical of any, had been agreed by the rest of the party.[5]

Heathcote resigned his aldermanic gown in January 1749, giving as his reason 'the frequent detestable instances of apostacy from every principle of honour, integrity and public spirit' of many of his countrymen. He declared his determination to return no more to London but to live in retirement, there to seek 'that small share of happiness, which is to be acquired in this venal country'. He received the thanks of the common council on 26 Jan. 1749

> for his uniform, active and disinterested conduct in every station of public trust, for the many and great services he has done this metropolis, as magistrate and representative in Parliament. For his zealous and laudable endeavours to promote the trade and prosperity of his fellow citizens. For his exemplary public spirit and independence, in making the preservation of the laws and liberties of his country the constant and invariable rule of all his actions.[6]

In 1752 he was 'a principal manager' in a plot to restore the Stuarts with Prussian help.[7] His last public act was the publication of a letter dated 6 Oct. 1762 to the city of London, opposing the proposed peace with France. He died 7 June 1768.

[1] HMC Egmont Diary, i. 27, 153, 274 and passim, 350, 372; ii. 468–9; iii. 20; Ilchester, Ld. Hervey and his Friends, 47. [2] Stuart mss 227/155, 271/3; Coxe, Walpole, iii. 582. [3] Yorke's parl. jnl. Parl. Hist. xiii. 649, 1247–8. [4] Yorke, Hardwicke, i. 478; Marchmont Pprs. ii. 341–8. [5] Stuart mss 269/191, 288/172. [6] E. D. Heathcote, Heathcote Fam. 71; Jnl. vol. 59. [7] Andrew Lang, Pickle the Spy, 178.

E.C.

HEATHCOTE, Sir Gilbert (1652–1733), of Low Leyton, Essex, and Normanton, Rutland.

LONDON	1–22 Feb. 1701, 1701–1710
HELSTON	1715–1722
LYMINGTON	27 Oct. 1722–1727
ST. GERMANS	1727–25 Jan. 1733

b. 2 Jan. 1652, 1st s. of Gilbert Heathcote of Chesterfield, Derbys. by Anne, da. of George Dickons of Chesterfield. *m.* 30 May 1682, Hester, da. and h. of Christopher Rayner, London merchant, 3s. 4da. *suc.* fa. 1690. Kntd. 29 Oct. 1702; *cr.* Bt. 17 Jan. 1733.

Vintner 1681, master of Vintners' Co. 1700; director, E.I. Co. 1698–1704, 1705–9; director, Bank of England 1694–1709, gov. 1709–11, director 1711–23, gov. 1723–5, director 1725–*d.* (with statutory intervals); alderman, London 1702, sheriff 1703–4, ld. mayor 1710–11; col. Blue regt. 1707–10, 1714–*d.*; pres. Hon. Artillery Co. 1720–*d.*; pres. St. Thomas's Hospital 1722–*d.*

Apprenticed to a merchant at 15, Heathcote traded in London as a Spanish wine merchant, having large transactions with the East Indies and with Jamaica, where he handled government remittances. He played an active part in founding the Bank of England of which he was twice governor. A staunch Whig under Queen Anne, in 1710 he was appointed one of the nine trustees of the Silesian loan to the Emperor for carrying on the war against France, to which he contributed £4,000. Shortly afterwards, he headed a deputation from the city against the dismissal of the Whig ministry.[1]

In the list of the 1715 Parliament prepared for George I, Heathcote is classed as a government supporter with the comment:

> Homme fort riche. Il étoit lord maire de Londres du temps de procès de Sacheverell. C'est un homme fameux dans son espèce. Il est fort haï des Tories.

Informations were laid before the Government that in May 1715 Jacobite mobs planned to murder him and the other Whig magistrates and set fire to their houses.[2] A frequent speaker on the government side, principally on trade matters, he said in the debate on the Address of 23 Mar. 1715 that, since the peace, imports from but not exports to France had increased, by which Britain was the loser. On 4 Apr. 1717, he supported Stanhope's request for a vote of credit against Sweden, declaring that the King of Sweden had seized British ships, had refused to make satisfaction, and was now fomenting civil war in England. He supported the Address on 11 Nov. 1718, and on 7 Jan. 1719 he spoke for the repeal of the Occasional Conformity and Schism Acts. In December 1721, while opposing the bill for prohibiting commerce with countries infected with the plague, he declared, in allusion to the Jacobites, that 'he believed the plague has always been more

or less in London; he was very sure it had been always so, since he came to it'. He seconded a motion on 18 Mar. 1725 to recommit the articles of impeachment against Lord Macclesfield, the father-in-law of his nephew William (q.v.).[3] In March 1731 he was given leave to introduce a bill to prevent suits for tithes, which reached a second reading, and in April he opposed a proposal to take off the duty on Irish yarn. He was instrumental in the foundation of the colony of Georgia, speaking in favour of its establishment in May 1732, and obtaining support for the proposal from his fellow directors of the Bank.

One of the richest commoners of his time, with a fortune estimated at £700,000,[4] he purchased large estates in the counties of Lincoln and Rutland, including Normanton, where he built the manor house. He was not 'curious to inquire' into his ancestors, believing it 'more a man's business to look forward and retrieve, than to look backward and repine'.[5] A plain-speaking, self-made man, with a reputation for avarice,[6] he incurred the hatred and ridicule of some of his contemporaries. Pope wrote in his *Moral Essays*:

> The grave Sir Gilbert holds it for a rule
> That every man in want is knave or fool,

and put him into the *Dunciad* as starting

> From dreams of millions; and three groats to pay.

The 1st Lord Egmont (q.v.) remarked that the Ostend Company would never have been set up (in 1722) 'had it not been for the avarice . . . of Sir Gilbert Heathcote and the rest' of the East India Company assistants, who refused the Emperor a reduced rate of interest on the Silesian loan.[7] Made a baronet in January 1733, he died a week later on 25 Jan., 'the father of the City'.

[1] E. D. Heathcote, *Heathcote Fam.* 79–80, 238; *Cal. Treas. Bks.* xxi. 88; *Marlborough Dispatches*, ii. 396; Luttrell, vi. 9, 24, 28, 594; *Wentworth Pprs.* 120. [2] *Cal. Treas. Pprs.* 1714–19, p. 235. [3] Chandler, vi. 14–15, 117–18; Stuart mss 56/32A; *Knatchbull Diary.* [4] *HMC Egmont Diary*, i. 163, 184, 274; *Gent. Mag.* 1732, p. 975; 1733, p. 47. [5] *Heathcote Fam.* 238–9. [6] See Swift, *Corresp.* v. 9; Pope, *A Master Key to Popery.* [7] *HMC Egmont Diary*, iii. 322.

E.C.

HEATHCOTE, John (c. 1689–1759), of Normanton, Rutland.

GRANTHAM	1715–1722
BODMIN	9 Feb. 1733–1741

b. c.1689, 1st surv. s. of Sir Gilbert Heathcote, 1st Bt. (q.v.). *m.* 5 Aug. 1720, Bridget, da. of Thomas White (q.v.) of Wallingwells, Notts., 2s. 6da. *suc.* fa. as 2nd Bt. 25 Jan. 1733.

Director, E.I. Co. 1716–24 and 1728–31; director, Bank of England 1725–35 (with statutory intervals); trustee, British Museum; pres. Foundling Hospital.

Heathcote was returned as a Whig for Grantham in 1715, but did not stand again till 1733 when he was returned unopposed at Bodmin, for which he sat till he was defeated in 1741. He voted with the Administration in every recorded division, except in that on the place bill in 1740 when he was absent. He supported the mortmain bill in 1736.[1] After his defeat at Bodmin in 1741, he spent 'seven months of the year' at Normanton, living the life of a country gentleman. In November 1754 he hoped to be chosen for the county of Rutland, writing to Lord Hardwicke, whose daughter his son had married:

> I haven't heard that I am mentioned, though I would serve them if I was put up. I suppose as I have served the country, they expect I shall go on dealing with the miseries of the people, and doing their drudgery in which they will find themselves mistaken if I have not my country's approbation. I should be glad to be any ways serviceable to the Government and particularly in being chose for this county, if I would be nominated by some of the principals, but hooting for oneself will never answer in my opinion.

But he failed to obtain Lord Exeter's interest,[2] and was not chosen. As the only surviving trustee and one of the commissioners of the Silesian loan, to which his father had contributed in 1710, he made representations to Newcastle on 29 Nov. 1752, and again on 4 Mar. 1755 about the stoppage of the last payment on the loan.[3]

He died 5 Sept. 1759, aged 70.

[1] Harley Diary. [2] Add. 35593, ff. 35–36, 52–53, 60, 360. [3] Add. 32730, f. 317; 32853, f. 109.

E.C.

HEATHCOTE, Samuel (1699–1775), of Hanover Sq., London.

BERE ALSTON   22 Feb. 1740–1747

b. 11 Feb. 1699, 4th s. of Samuel Heathcote of Hackney, and yr. bro. of Sir William Heathcote (q.v.). *m.* (1) 3 May 1720, Elizabeth (*d.* 6 May 1726), da. of Matthew Holworthy of Hackney, *s.p.*; (2) c.1729, Frances, a Frenchwoman, 4s. 3da.

On the death of Sir Francis Drake, 4th Bt. (q.v.), leaving an infant heir, his widow brought in her brother, Samuel Heathcote, for the vacancy at Bere Alston. Before the general election of 1741, Drake's brother, Henry, wrote to Walpole referring to

> the indulgence you showed me last winter on my waiting on you soon after my brother Sir Francis Drake's death, when you was pleased to let me hope your assistance if I found I could retrieve his part of the borough of Bere Alston back into hands that have a natural bent to be entirely devoted to you.
>
> Your momentous affairs may make it necessary, Sir, for me to recall to your remembrance how cruelly I was then made a dupe to the designing and deceitful professions Sir William and Mr. [Samuel] Heathcote [qq.v.] gave me of their faith and friendship. These

two gentlemen, as assiduous in grasping at all they can as any of their family, are now, as I have the most cogent reasons to suspect from Sir William's declining Southampton and from other passages, under-hand endeavouring to engross that borough [Bere Alston] to themselves at the next election. You will find Sir, by casting your eye on the enclosed calculation and the number of votes their sister has the disposal of, if uninterrupted, how easily they may succeed if timely care be not taken by those concerned. You will likewise find by it, what a probability of success my interposing may be attended with if I am honoured with your support.[1]

Heathcote was re-elected unopposed, steadily supporting the Administration. He was replaced in 1747 by his nephew, Sir Francis Henry Drake, 5th Bt., who by that time had come of age. He did not stand again, and died 31 Mar. 1775.

[1] 1 Oct. 1740, Cholmondeley (Houghton) mss.

E.C.

HEATHCOTE, William (1693–1751), of Hursley, Hants.

BUCKINGHAM   22 Oct. 1722–1727
SOUTHAMPTON   29 May 1729–1741

b. 15 Mar. 1693, 2nd s. of Samuel Heathcote of Hackney, Mdx., yr. bro. of Sir Gilbert Heathcote (q.v.), Danzig merchant, director of Bank of England, director of E.I. and Eastland Cos., by Mary, da. and eventually h. of William Dawsonne of Hackney, treasurer of the excise; bro. of Samuel Heathcote (q.v.). *m.* 7 Apr. 1720, Lady Elizabeth Parker, da. of Thomas, 1st Earl of Macclesfield, lord chancellor, 6s. 3da. *suc.* e. bro. Gilbert Heathcote 1710; *cr.* Bt. 16 Aug. 1733.

Sec. and registrar of bankrupts 1723–*d.*

A merchant in early life, Heathcote retired after inheriting a fortune estimated at £90,000, writing in a private notebook:

> I began to draw home that part of my estate that I have abroad in trade, being fully resolved to leave off trade and be content with my present estate.

In November 1718, he purchased Hursley from the heirs of Richard Cromwell for £35,000, building a new mansion at a cost of a further £14,000.[1] In 1737 he bought an estate in Ireland worth £3,000 a year from Lord Burlington. Returned in 1722 for Buckingham on the Denton interest, he subsequently sat for Southampton, near his property at Hursley, voting against the Government in all recorded divisions, except on the 1741 motion for Walpole's removal, which he opposed. He supported the mortmain bill in April 1736. He was on the common council of the Georgia Society till 1739, when he resigned, professedly on the ground that his private business would not allow him to attend board meetings, but actually because, like his first cousin, George Heathcote (q.v.), he considered the board too subservient to Walpole.[2] In spite of his politics, he obtained a baronetcy in 1733, four months after that granted to his uncle Sir Gilbert Heathcote (q.v.). He declined standing at Southampton in 1741,[3] and died 10 May 1751.

[1] E. D. Heathcote, *Heathcote Fam.* 115–19. [2] *HMC Egmont Diary,* ii. 452; iii. 22, 83, 92; Harley Diary. [3] Hen. Drake to Sir Robt. Walpole, 1 Oct. 1740, Cholmondeley (Houghton) mss.

E.C.

HEDGES, John (1688–1737), of Finchley, Mdx.

MITCHELL	1722–1727
BOSSINEY	1727–1734
FOWEY	1734–20 June 1737

b. 26 Feb. 1688, 4th s. of Sir William Hedges of Finchley, Turkey merchant, gov. Bengal 1682–4, and director of Bank of England 1699–1700, by Anne, da. of Paul Nicoll of Hendon Place, Mdx., wid. of John Searle of Finchley. *educ.* Peterhouse, Camb. 1706; I. Temple 1708. *unm.*

Envoy to Sardinia 1726–8; treasurer to Prince of Wales 1729–*d.*

Returned by the Administration for Cornish boroughs, Hedges was one of the managers of Lord Macclesfield's trial in 1725.[1] In March 1726 he went as envoy extraordinary to Turin, where he was concerned in the negotiations on the repartition of the two Sicilies and the Milanese.[2] Put up by the Government to move a motion on Spanish depredations, 13 Mar. 1729, he also moved the Address in January 1735.[3]

In January 1729 Hedges became treasurer to Frederick, Prince of Wales, composing ballads and songs, for which Frederick took the credit. He also lent the Prince £6,000 for the purchase of a house in Pall Mall. Frederick repaid the loan by borrowing the money from Bubb Dodington, boasting, to the indignation of Hedges, 'a man of honour as well as a man of sense', that

> with all his parts I have wheedled him out of a sum of money for the payment of which he has no security if I die, and which, God knows, he may wait long enough for if I live.

In 1737 Hedges tried at Walpole's request to dissuade the Prince from bringing the question of his allowance before Parliament 'by telling him it was impossible he could ever get the money'. When the Prince rejected his advice he and Lord Baltimore (q.v.) 'put his Royal Highness's directions into writing, then asked him if that was what he would have them say, and spoke in the House from that paper'.[4] He said:

> the Prince had all the duty and affection for his Majesty that was possible, and had shown it on all occasions. He put himself to an inconvenient expense to purchase his house at Kew, that he might be near his Majesty

when at Richmond, and he purchased his house in Pall Mall that if it pleased God to enlarge his family by children he might not inconvenience his Majesty in his own palace; that when he came to the duchy of Cornwall he had been at great expense in law to recover the revenue which had been embezzled, and had not yet brought it up to £10,000 a year; that he owes £25,000 and by the best management cannot live upon £60,000 a year, his expenses being £63,000; but neither does he see £60,000 a year, the Duchy income being but £9,500, interest being paid for what he owes, and the fees of his £50,000 coming to £4,000; that the precarious title by which he held the £50,000 allowed him, the same revocable at his Majesty's pleasure, made it impossible for him to settle a scheme for his living, and it was a great uneasiness to him to see her Royal Highness insecure in a jointure in case of his death.[5]

He died four months later, 20 June 1737.

[1] See Howell's *State Trials,* xvi. 929–34. [2] *HMC Portland,* vi. 14; Add. 32748, f. 337. [3] *Knatchbull Diary; HMC Egmont Diary,* ii. 146. [4] Hervey, *Mems.* 309, 311–12, 666–7, 691, 704. [5] *HMC Egmont Diary,* ii. 355–6.

E.C.

HEDWORTH, John (1683–1747), of Chester Deanery, Durham.

| DURHAM CO. | 1713–31 May 1747 |

bap. 10 July 1683, 1st surv. s. of Ralph Hedworth of Chester Deanery by Eleanor, da. of Henry Lambton of Lambton Hall, co. Dur. *educ.* Lincoln, Oxf. 1700; M. Temple 1700. *m.* (1) settlement 28 Aug. 1714, Susanna Sophia, da. of William Pelsant, London merchant, 1da.; (2) 14 Aug. 1729, Margaret, da. and coh. of Samuel Ayton of West Herrington, co. Dur., 1da. *suc.* fa. 1720.

Mayor, Hartlepool 1716, 1728, 1740.

Hedworth, whose family acquired Chester Deanery under James I, was one of the leading Sunderland coal owners, representing them in negotiations for the regulation of competition between them and the Newcastle coal owners.[1] Returned in 1713 for his county, which he continued to represent till his death, he was classed in 1715 as a Whig but voted with the Opposition in all recorded divisions of that Parliament except on Lord Cadogan (q.v.). From 1722 to 1741 his only recorded votes were against the Government on the excise bill in 1733, and the place bill in 1740, but for them on the Spanish convention in 1739. His letters to Walpole, one of which reads, 'I ought to be ashamed of the frequent applications I find myself under the necessity to make to you on the part of my friends', show him to have been an independent supporter of the Government.[2] In his last Parliament he voted for the Government on the chairman of the elections committee on 16 Dec. 1741, was put down as 'Pelham' in the Cockpit list of October 1742, voted for the Hanoverians in 1744, but did not vote in the other two divisions on them, and was classed in 1746 as Old Whig. He died 31 May 1747.

[1] E. Hughes, *North Country Life in 18th Cent.* 159 et passim.
[2] 5 June 1738, Cholmondeley (Houghton) mss.

R.R.S.

HELYAR, William (1662–1742), of East Coker, nr. Ilchester, Som.

ILCHESTER 1689–1690
SOMERSET 1715–1722

b. 10 July 1662, 1st surv. s. of William Helyar of East Coker by Rachel, da. of Sir Hugh Wyndham, 1st Bt., of Pilsdon Court, Dorset. *educ.* Trinity, Oxf. 1680; L. Inn. 1683. *m.* (1) 9 June 1690, Joanna (*d.*11 Oct. 1714), da. and coh. of Robert Hole of South Tawton, Devon, 2s. 3da.; (2) 1719, Anne, da. of William Harbin of Newton Surmaville, Som. *suc.* fa. 1697. Sheriff, Somerset 1701–2.

Helyar was descended from an old Devonshire family, long settled in Somerset, where they had bought the manor of East Coker in 1616. In spite of being heavily fined for royalist activities in the civil war, his father was able to leave him not merely the family property in Somerset and Devonshire, but the lease of a plantation in Jamaica.[1] Returned for Ilchester in the Convention Parliament, Helyar did not sit again till 1715, when he successfully contested his county as a Tory. He voted against the Government in all the recorded divisions except that on the septennial bill in 1716, from which he was absent. He did not stand again, being buried 8 Oct. 1742.

[1] *CSP Col.* 1669–74, pp. 561, 591; PCC 284 Pyne.

S.R.M.

HENLEY, Anthony (?1704–48), of the Grange, nr. Alresford, Hants.

SOUTHAMPTON 1727–1734

b. ?1704, 1st s. of Anthony Henley, M.P., of the Grange, Northington, Hants by Mary, da. and coh. of Hon. Peregrine Bertie of Waldershare, Kent; bro. of Robert Henley (q.v.). *educ.* Ch. Ch. Oxf. 21 Mar. 1720, aged 15. *m.* 11 Feb. 1728, Lady Elizabeth Berkeley, da. of James, 3rd Earl of Berkeley, *s.p. suc.* fa. 1711.

Anthony Henley inherited as a minor the manors of Northington and Swarraton, known as the Grange, which had belonged to his family since 1665. Soon after coming of age he was returned for Southampton in 1727. On his marriage next year Mrs. Delany wrote:

Lady Betty Berkeley, daughter to the Earl of that name, being almost 15 has thought it time to be married and ran away last week with Mr. Henley, a man noted for his impudence and immorality but a good estate and a beau.[1]

No votes of his are recorded till 1733, when the Southampton corporation asked their representatives to oppose the excise bill. Shortly before the bill was introduced the *Weekly Register* of 31 Mar. printed a letter purporting to be the answer returned by Henley to the corporation. The letter ran:

I received yours and am surprised at your insolence in troubling me about the excise. You know what I very well know, that I bought you.
And I know what perhaps you think I don't know, you are now selling yourselves to somebody else.
And I know what you don't know, that I am buying another borough.
May God's curse light on you all.
May your houses be as open and as common to all excise officers as your wives and daughters were to me when I stood for your scoundrel corporation.[2]

The letter appears to have been composed by Henley as a joke; his real letter, which is described as 'short and extremely proper', was immediately published by the mayor of Southampton. He voted against the excise bill, telling John Conduitt (q.v.), a prospective opponent at Southampton, who had voted for the bill, that by so voting he had saved him £1,500 in election expenses.[3] He subsequently voted against the Administration on the repeal of the Septennial Act. At the general election there was a double return for Southampton, on which the House of Commons awarded the seat to Conduitt. Henley did not stand again, dying 24 Dec. 1748.

[1] Mrs. Delany, *Autobiog. and Corresp.* (ser. 1), i. 156–7. [2] *N. & Q.* (ser. 2), xii. 107. [3] *Letters of Jonathan Swift to Charles Ford*, ed. David Nichol Smith, 152.

P.W.

HENLEY, Henry Holt (d.1748), of Leigh, Som., and Colway, Lyme Regis, Dorset.

LYME REGIS 1722–1727, 28 Feb. 1728–8 May 1748

o.s. of Henry Henley, M.P., of Leigh and Colway by Catherine, da. of Richard Holt, M.P., of Nursted, Hants. *educ.* M. Temple 1716, called 1722. *m.* (1) Sarah (*d.* 25 Apr. 1731), da. of Henry Cornish, M.P., of St. Lawrence Jewry, London, and Sherrard St., Westminster, sis. of Anthony Cornish (q.v.), 1s. 3da.; (2) 8 May 1739, Catherine, da. and h. of Rev. Hugh Charles Hare of Docking, Norf. (gd.-s. of Hugh, 1st Baron Coleraine [I]),[1] *s.p. suc.* fa. 1733. Mayor, Lyme Regis 1724–5, 1731–2, 1738–9, 1746–7; recorder, Lyme Regis; clerk of the pipe 1728–d.

Henry Holt Henley, of a Somerset family, was kinsman to the Henleys of the Grange, Hants,[2] two of whom, John and Robert Henley (qq.v.), were also M.P.s for Lyme Regis. Between 1661 and 1715 his father and great-grandfather represented the borough in ten Parliaments, the former being three times mayor. Returned as a Whig for Lyme Regis in

1722, he was unseated in 1727 but was successful on petition against John Burridge (q.v.), who, as mayor, had illegally returned himself. In 1728 he was appointed to a lucrative sinecure which had been held by his brother-in-law, Anthony Cornish (q.v.). He continued to represent the borough, voting for the Administration in all recorded divisions, till his death, 8 May 1748.

[1] Blomefield, *Norf.* x. 364. [2] Hutchins, *Dorset*, iii. 742.

R.S.L.

HENLEY, John (1677–1732), of Wootton Abbots, nr. Lyme Regis, Dorset.

LYME REGIS   1715–1722

b. 1677, 2nd s. of Sir Robert Henley, M.P., of the Grange, Northington, Hants, being 1st s. by his 2nd w. Barbara, da. of John Every of Cothay, in Kittisford, Som., sis. and coh. of John Every of Cothay; bro. of Robert Henley (q.v.). *educ.* Winchester; M. Temple 1695; Trinity, Camb. 17 June 1695, aged 17; Ch. Ch. Oxf. 22 Oct. 1695, aged 18. *m.* Hester, da. of James Bagwell, 3s.

John Henley, who inherited Wootton Abbots from his mother's family, was the grandson of Sir Robert Henley, master of the King's bench, and kinsman to the Henleys of Lyme Regis.[1] His elder brother, the well known Anthony Henley, M.P., was father of another Anthony and of Robert Henley (qq.v.), 1st Earl of Northington. After unsuccessfully contesting Milborne Port in 1702, he was returned unopposed as a Whig on his family's interest at Lyme Regis in 1715. He voted for the Administration in all recorded divisions but did not stand again. On his death on 25 Apr. 1732 he left Wootton Abbots away from his wife and sons to his 'dear and only friend and brother Robert Henley [q.v.] of Glanville Wootton . . . begging him for God's sake not to refuse the care of his unfortunate brother's children.'[2]

[1] Hutchins, *Dorset*, ii. 264; iii. 742–4; *Cal. Treas. Bks.* xiii. 365; *Cal. Treas. Bks. and Pprs.* 1731–4, p. 546. [2] PCC 139 Bedford.

R.S.L.

HENLEY, Robert (c.1708–72), of the Grange, nr. Alresford, Hants.

BATH   1747–30 June 1757

b. c.1708, 2nd s. of Anthony Henley, M.P., and yr. bro. of Anthony Henley (q.v.). *educ.* Westminster 1720; St. John's, Oxf. 1724; fellow of All Souls 1727; I. Temple 1729, called 1732. *m.* 19 Nov. 1743, Jane, da. of Sir John Huband, 2nd Bt., of Ipsley, Warws., sis. and coh. of Sir John Huband, 3rd Bt., 3s. 5da. *suc.* bro. 1748. Kntd. 29 Oct. 1756; *cr.* Baron Henley 27 Mar. 1760; Earl of Northington 19 May 1764.

K.C. 1751; recorder, Bath 1751; solicitor-gen. 1751–4, attorney-gen. 1754–6, to the Prince of Wales; attorney-gen. 1756–7; P.C. 30 June 1757; ld. keeper 1757–61; ld. high steward for trials of Lord Ferrers

1760 and of Lord Byron 1765; ld. chancellor 1761–6; ld. lt. Hants 1764–71; ld. pres. of the council 1766–7.

Though returned for Bath on Ralph Allen's interest (see under Bath constituency) 'as a favourite of the Ministry', Henley spoke against them immediately after taking his seat. Described by Horace Walpole as 'a lawyer in vogue' whose 'abilities did not figure in proportion to the impudence of his ill nature,'[1] he was introduced to Leicester House in 1749 by his friend Bubb Dodington (q.v.), who was authorized by the Prince of Wales to promise him the solicitor-generalship in the next reign.[2] In the list of the future government approved at the Carlton House meeting in April 1750, he figures as attorney-general. In a debate on General Philip Anstruther (q.v.) in April 1751, Horace Walpole reported that 'Henley (the profession out-weighing the faction in him) declared the House could exercise no juridiction in this case'. On Frederick's death, he went over to the Administration, spoke for the regency bill, and was made solicitor-general to the young Prince of Wales.[3] In January 1753 he was offered a puisne judgeship by Hardwicke, but declined on the ground that he had a large family and that it was 'more for their interest for me to continue in my present condition'.[4] In May 1753 he spoke for Hadwicke's bill against clandestine marriages.[5] After representing Bath for ten years he vacated his seat on becoming lord keeper in 1757. He died 14 Jan. 1772.

[1] Walpole, *Mems. Geo. II.* i. 96; Harrowby mss 21 (L. Inn), 20 Dec. 1747. [2] *Dodington Diary*, 6. [3] Walpole, i. 108, 124, 143. [4] Henley to Hardwicke, 11 Jan. 1753, Add. 35592, f. 8. [5] Walpole, i. 345.

R.R.S.

HENLEY, Robert (?1682–1758), of Glanville Wootton, Dorset.

LYME REGIS   24 May 1748–1754

b. ?1682, 3rd s. of Sir Robert Henley, M.P., of the Grange, Northington, Hants, being 2nd s. by his 2nd w.; yr. bro. of John Henley (q.v.). *educ.* Winchester 1696–1701; New Coll. Oxf. 3 Dec. 1701, aged 19. *unm.* *suc.* e. bro. John (q.v.) at Wootton Abbots 1732. Mayor, Lyme Regis 1745–6.

Robert Henley inherited Glanville Wootton from his mother's family. On the death of his kinsman Henry Holt Henley (q.v.) in 1748, he was returned for Lyme Regis, presumably as a stop-gap, by John Scrope (q.v.), 'quite contrary to the inclinations of one so advanced in years.'[1] The last of several members of his family to represent the borough, he did not stand again, dying 2 Sept. 1758.

[1] Ben Hollett and Robt. Henley to Azariah Pinney, 14 and 16 May 1748, Pinney mss.

R.S.L.

HENRY WARBURTON, Philip (1700–60), of Hefferstone Grange, Cheshire.

CHESTER 5 May 1742–1754

> *b.* 3 May 1700, s. of Rev. Matthew Henry of Broadoak, Flints., Presbyterian minister in Chester, by Mary, da. of Robert Warburton of Hefferstone Grange and h. to her bro. Peter Warburton. *educ.* L. Inn 1721, called 1727. *unm. suc.* fa. 1714; mother to Hefferstone Grange 1731 and assumed add. name of Warburton.

Warburton was the son of an 'eminent dissenting teacher' and the maternal great-grandson of Peter Warburton of Hefferstone Grange, chief justice of Chester.[1] Returned unopposed at Chester as a Tory in 1742, he was one of the magistrates who examined the Young Pretender's messenger carrying a letter to Lord Barrymore (q.v.).[2] Voting against the Government in all the recorded divisions, he was classed as Opposition on re-election in 1747, did not stand in 1754, and died 16 Aug. 1760.

> [1] Ormerod, *Cheshire*, ii. 174. [2] SP Dom. 36/73, no. 32 (13).

E.C.

HERBERT, Francis (?1666–1719), of Oakley Park, Mont.

LUDLOW   1689–1690, 1698–1700, 1701–1705,
                    1715–27 Feb. 1719

> *b.* ?1666, 1st s. of Richard Herbert of Bromfield, Salop and Dolgeiog, Mont. by Florence (*d.* Jan. 1706), da. of Richard, 2nd Baron Herbert of Chirbury, sis. and coh. of Henry, 4th Baron Herbert. *educ.* Ch. Ch. Oxf. 26 Mar. 1683, aged 16; G. Inn. 1687. *m.* (lic. 1 Feb. 1702) Dorothy (*d.* Nov. 1717), da. of John Oldbury, London merchant, 5s. 3da. *suc.* fa. 1676.

Francis Herbert, the father of Henry Arthur and Richard Herbert (qq.v.), was a staunch Whig, owning estates in South Shropshire and Montgomeryshire, with a considerable interest in the boroughs of Ludlow and Montgomery. In 1715 he unsuccessfully contested Montgomery Boroughs against an alliance of Tory patrons, but was returned for Ludlow. He is not recorded as voting in the new Parliament but was listed as against the peerage bill by Craggs in 1719. He died 27 Feb. 1719.

J.B.L.

HERBERT, Francis (*b.* 1696), of Ludlow, Salop.

MONTGOMERY   16 Apr. 1748–1754

> *bap.* 3 Nov. 1696, 1st s. of George Herbert, bro. of Francis Herbert (q.v.), by Martha, da. of John Newton of Heighley, Salop, wid. of Richard Owen of Rhiwsaeson; bro of Henry Herbert (q.v.). *m.* Mary (*d.* Nov. 1751), da. of Rowland Baugh of Stonehouse, Onibury, Salop, 3s. 2da.[1]
> Joint comptroller of customs, Chester 15 May 1739–Apr. 1748.

Francis Herbert was brought in for Montgomery after the death of his brother by his 1st cousin Henry Arthur Herbert (q.v.), afterwards 1st Earl of Powis, giving up his post, which was incompatible with a seat in Parliament, to his third son Ffolliot, who held it until his death in 1752.[2] He was frequently one of the bailiffs of the borough of Montgomery which Lord Powis controlled. The date of his death is unknown (alive 1755).

> [1] *Mont. Colls.* vi. 204; viii. 6–7; ix. 400. [2] *Gent. Mag.* 1748, p 245.

J.B.L.

HERBERT, Henry (*d.* 1748), of Ludlow, Salop.

MONTGOMERY   1747–Mar. 1748

> 2nd s. of George Herbert and bro. of Francis Herbert (q.v.) of Ludlow.[1] *unm.*

Herbert was brought in for Montgomery by his cousin Henry Arthur Herbert (q.v.), afterwards 1st Earl of Powis. He died shortly afterwards, March 1748.

> [1] Bradney, *Mon.* iv. 301.

P.D.G.T.

HERBERT, Henry Arthur (c.1703–72), of Oakley Park, Mont.

BLETCHINGLEY   19 Nov. 1724–1727
LUDLOW   1727–21 Dec. 1743

> *b.* c.1703, 1st s. of Francis Herbert of Oakley Park and bro. of Richard Herbert (qq.v.). *m.* 30 Mar. 1751, Barbara, da. and h. of Lord Edward Herbert, bro. of William, 3rd Mq. of Powis, 1s. 1da. *suc.* fa. 1719. *cr.* Baron Herbert of Chirbury 21 Dec. 1743; Baron Powis of Powis Castle, Visct. Ludlow and Earl of Powis 27 May 1748; Baron Herbert of Chirbury and Ludlow with sp. rem. to bro. Richard and cos. Francis Herbert (qq.v.) 16 Oct. 1749.
> Ld. lt. Salop 1734–61, 1764–*d.*; treasurer to Prince of Wales 1737–8; col. of a regt. which he raised in 1745; maj.-gen. 1755; lt.-gen. 1759; gen. 1772; recorder, Ludlow 1745, Shrewsbury 1749–*d.*; comptroller of the Household May–Nov. 1761; P.C. 25 June 1761; ld. lt. Mont. 1761–*d.*; treasurer of the Household 1761–5.

On coming of age Herbert, 'a commoner of a great estate',[1] found himself a temporary seat at Bletchingley. In 1727 he transferred to Ludlow in his native county, Shropshire, establishing complete control over that borough, for which he thenceforth nominated both Members. At the same election he also converted Montgomery into a pocket borough. Appointed lord lieutenant of Shropshire on the death of the last Earl of Bradford in 1734, he became the acknowledged head of the Shropshire Whigs in the Commons, acting as intermediary between them and Walpole, who was said never to have refused any favour he asked. His first reported speech was made at the opening of the 1734 Parliament, proposing Onslow's re-election as Speaker. He spoke against a place bill, 22 Apr. 1735, acting consistently with the Government except in 1737, when he not only spoke and voted for increasing the Prince of Wales's allowance, but used his influence to persuade three other government supporters to vote the same way.[2] Though he made it clear that on other matters he would continue to support the Government, he was rewarded by the Prince with a place in his household, which he resigned when Frederick went into opposition next year.[3] On 11 May 1737 he introduced a bill making it necessary for actions under the anti-bribery Act of 1729 to be brought within two years of the alleged offence, thus in effect, as it was said, legalizing all the bribery and corruption at the last general election, which passed into law.

During the election campaign of 1740–1 Herbert, at Walpole's request, tried to gain control of Bishop's Castle in Shropshire, but was unsuccessful.[4] At the opening of the new Parliament, he was chosen to move the Address. After Walpole's fall he was included in the court list for the secret committee set up to inquire into Walpole's conduct, but was not elected. In the list of ministerial Members to be invited to the Cockpit meeting before the opening of the next session in December 1742, all the Shropshire borough Members, except the Whitmores, are marked with his name (i.e. to be invited through him), as well as John White, M.P. Retford, and John Harris, M.P. Barnstaple,[5] his brother-in-law. 'I have all the reason in the world to be satisfied with his services', Pelham wrote of him in 1743 when Herbert was to be created Lord Herbert of Chirbury, a title which had become extinct in 1738. In 1748 his distant cousin, the last Marquess of Powis, a Roman Catholic and Jacobite duke, died, leaving his estates to Herbert, who promptly wrote to Newcastle:

As the late Marquis of Powis by giving me his estate, has done so much for a Protestant family, I should be very sorry to find that his Majesty with the interposition of my friends, should not be prevailed upon to honour me with his approbation of it by granting me his titles. . . .
P.S.—Let me add further that my disappointment in the point above mentioned, would make a very unfavourable impression upon the minds of those in the country that are the friends of the Government and are my friends; and have expressed very greatly their joy and satisfaction with my good fortune; to which they hope for the addition of the title.[6]

Created Earl of Powis, he continued to lead the Shropshire Whigs till the next reign.

He died 11 Sept. 1772.

[1] Hervey, *Mems.* 805. [2] *HMC Egmont Diary*, ii. 352–3; *Dodington Diary*, 450; Harley Diary. [3] Hervey, *Mems.* 851. [4] To Sir R. Walpole, 9 Sept. 1740, Cholmondeley (Houghton) mss. [5] Add. 32699, ff. 467–8. [6] Namier, *Structure*, 279, 298.

R.R.S.

HERBERT, James (*d.* 1721), of Tythrop, Bucks.

QUEENBOROUGH	1710–1713
AMERSHAM	19 Mar. 1714–1715
OXFORDSHIRE	25 May 1715–25 Apr. 1721

1st s. of James Herbert, M.P., of Tythrop, by Lady Catherine Osborne, da. of Thomas, 1st Duke of Leeds. *m.* 15 Sept. 1710, Maria, da. of James Hallet of Edgware, Mdx., 3s. 2da. *suc.* fa. 1709.

The great-grandson of the 4th Earl of Pembroke, Herbert, who had estates on the Oxfordshire border of Buckinghamshire, was returned as a Tory at a by-election in 1715, voting against the Administration in all recorded divisions. He died 25 Apr. 1721, 'drowned . . . by a slip off a footbridge betwixt his own house and Thame', supposed to have been caused by 'an apoplexy', while

he was walking out alone into his grounds, as he used to do, about ten in the morning. There had indeed about five days before been a very hard bout, which might have helped, at a meeting Duke Wharton had with the Tory gentlemen.[1]

[1] *HMC Portland*, vii. 296.

E.C.

HERBERT, James (c.1713–40), of Tythrop, Bucks.

OXFORD	8 Feb. 1739–21 Nov. 1740

b. c.1713, 1st s. of James Herbert and bro. of Philip Herbert (qq.v.). *unm. suc.* fa. 1721.

Returned unopposed as a Tory at a by-election for Oxford in 1739, Herbert voted against the Government on the Spanish convention and the place bill in 1740. He died 21 Nov. 1740.

E.C.

HERBERT, Hon. Nicholas (?1706–75), of Great Glemham, Suff.

NEWPORT	22 Jan. 1740–1754
WILTON	17 Apr. 1757–1 Feb. 1775

b. ?1706, 7th s. of Thomas Herbert, M.P., 8th Earl of Pembroke, by his 1st w. Margaret, da. and h. of Sir Robert Sawyer, M.P., of Highclere, Hants; bro. of Hon. Robert Sawyer, Thomas and William Herbert (qq.v.). *educ.* ?Eton 1725; Ch. Ch. Oxf. 2 Dec. 1726, aged 20. *m.* 19 July 1737, Anne, da. of Dudley North (q.v.), of Little Glemham, Suff., 2da.
Cashier and accountant to the treasurer of the navy 1742–5; treasurer to Princess Amelia 1757–60; sec. of Jamaica 1765–*d.*

Nicholas Herbert was born at Werrington, Devon, at the house of his brother-in-law Sir Nicholas Morice (q.v.). Returned for Newport in 1740 on the Morice interest in succession to his brother Thomas (q.v.), he was absent from the divisions on the place bill in 1740 and the chairman of the elections committee 1741, was summoned to the Cockpit meeting in October 1742 through

John Scrope (q.v.), and voted with the Administration on the Hanoverians in 1742, 1744 and 1746. He was classed as a government supporter in 1747. He died 1 Feb. 1775.

E.C.

HERBERT, Philip (1716–49), of Tythrop, Bucks.

OXFORD   3 Dec. 1740–1749

> b. c.1716, 2nd s. of James Herbert (d. 1721) and bro. of James Herbert (qq.v.). educ. L. Inn 1735, called 1740. m. 7 Mar. 1747, Mary, da. and h. of Edward Butler (q.v.), s.p. suc. bro. James 1740.

Herbert succeeded his brother James in representing Oxford as a Tory in 1740, voting against the Administration in all recorded divisions. He died 22 July 1749, aged 32.

E.C.

HERBERT, Richard (1704–54).

LUDLOW   11 Feb. 1727–1741, 30 Dec. 1743–17 May 1754

> bap. 13 Dec. 1704, 2nd s. of Francis Herbert of Oakley Park, Mont., and bro. of Henry Arthur Herbert (qq.v.). unm.
> Entered army as lt.-col. 4 Oct. 1745; warden of the mint Apr. 1754–d.

Herbert, who was returned on the interest of his brother, voted for the Administration on the civil list in 1729, but his name does not appear on the other six extant division lists of that and the succeeding Parliament. He was not put up in 1741, but was brought in again in 1743, voting for the Hanoverian troops in 1744 and 1746, and was classed as a government supporter in 1747. In 1752 his brother Lord Powis, who had been urging his preferment for ten years, applied on his behalf to Henry Pelham for the post of clerk comptroller of the King's Household. Pelham replied (7 Oct.):

> I have a true regard for him . . . and a sincere affection for your Lordship. Nobody could therefore have stood, in my good wishes in competition with Mr. Herbert, but you may remember I told you the difficulty that would arise, in Mr. Herbert's having retired from the world so long, and of consequence never having appeared in Parliament, or even in London, I believe from almost the time this Parliament was first chosen. I took the liberty to say to you that I even doubted whether in these circumstances, it was right for your Lordship to ask for an employment of attendance for your brother . . . I was in hopes Mr. Herbert would have passed one winter in London, mixed with his friends, and attended public business as others do. Had that been the case I should not have hesitated one moment in recommending him to the King. But as the King knows everything that your Lordship or I do, and perhaps is told much more than is true, how can I propose one in these circumstances to an office, that has a monthly attendance

upon his Majesty at court, and into which I know the King is every day more and more inquisitive.[1]

To Newcastle, then in Hanover with the King, Pelham wrote (19 Oct.):

> I should have been for Mr. Herbert . . . had not his misfortune been such ever since his duel with Lord Belfield, that sometimes, as I am told, he does not know what he does. This I have hinted to Lord Powis several times, when he has recommended his brother, but he says it is not so, and that he is perfectly well in health, but uneasy to see he is not taken notice of. You may imagine this is a very tender point to talk upon.[2]

When Powis insisted, Pelham played for time by suggesting that the matter should rest until the King's return in November; though he had to admit that the names of several persons seeking the office had already been sent over to Hanover. This enabled him to postpone forwarding Herbert's name until the very day that word of Sir Francis Drake's (q.v.) appointment to the office reached him. To Powis's further remonstrance, he replied:

> Notwithstanding this, I let my letter go, hoping that your brother being mentioned on this occasion, may the more easily succeed upon another, if your Lordship continues your resolution of bringing him into business, and his attending the House.[3]

Apparently Powis did continue his resolution, for immediately after Pelham's death Newcastle was trying to satisfy Herbert by the offer of the wardenship of the mint. But as a second vacancy among the clerk comptrollers of the Household had been simultaneously set aside for John Grey (q.v.), who was not even in Parliament at that time, Herbert considered it beneath his dignity to accept the wardenship unless the salary was made equal to Grey's. On 2 Apr. a private addition of £400 p.a. was arranged,[4] but one month after the general election Herbert died, 17 May 1754.[5]

[1] Powis mss.   [2] Add. 32730, f. 142.   [3] 14, 26 Oct. 1752, Powis mss.
[4] Add. 32995, ff. 110, 126, 130, 180.   [5] Mont. Coll. viii. 6.

J.B.L.

HERBERT, Hon. Robert Sawyer (1693–1769), of Highclere, Hants.

WILTON   1722–1768

> b. 28 Jan. 1693,[1] 2nd s. of Thomas Herbert, M.P., 8th Earl of Pembroke; bro. of Hon. Nicholas, Thomas and William Herbert (qq.v.). educ. Ch. Ch. Oxf. 1709. m. bef. 1723, Mary, da. of John Smith (q.v.), Speaker of the House of Commons, s.p. suc. to mother's estates 1706.
> Groom of the bedchamber to George I 1723–7; commr. of revenue [I] 1727–37; ld. of Trade 1737–51; ld. lt. Wilts. 1750–2; surveyor of crown lands 1751–d.

Robert Herbert inherited Highclere under the will of his maternal grandfather, Sir Robert Sawyer (d. 1692), who entailed his estates on his daughter's younger sons, then unborn.[2] Returned on his father's interest at Wilton in 1722, he held minor government posts for over 30 years, voting for successive Administrations in all recorded divisions. A founder member of White's, he appears to have fancied himself as a man of fashion. Nicknamed 'Amoretto', he was satirized by Chesterfield, in letters to Lady Suffolk, for his attempts at gallantry and wit during visits to Bath.[3] His wife was bed-chamber woman to Queen Caroline. Although she had long been 'a personal and warm enemy' of Sir Robert Walpole, she was 'so sensible, so well-bred, so handy, so cheerful and so agreeable' that the Queen showed special preference for her.[4] In 1751 he was appointed surveyor general by Pelham, who wrote to Robert Nugent (q.v.):

> He has been of the Board of Trade upwards of 20 years, tho' *in it* I believe not as many times. You know the connexions I have had, and now have with that family, how many years they have served the King, and what access almost every branch of it has at court. In this situation, could I refuse my good offices for such a change of employment?[5]

He died 25 Apr. 1769, leaving Highclere to his nephew Henry Herbert, M.P., afterwards 1st Earl of Carnarvon.

[1] *Top. and Gen.* iii. 408. [2] PCC 175 Fane. [3] *Chesterfield Letters*, 290-3, 310. [4] Hervey, *Mems.* 882. [5] Claud Nugent, *Mem. of Robert, Earl Nugent*, 253.

E.C.

HERBERT, Hon. Thomas (c.1695–1739), of Gerard St., Soho.

NEWPORT 18 Feb. 1726–25 Dec. 1739

b. c.1695, 4th s. of Thomas Herbert, M.P., 8th Earl of Pembroke; bro. of Hon. Nicholas, Robert Sawyer and William Herbert (qq.v.). *unm.*
  Lt. and capt. 1 Ft. Gds. 1719, capt. and lt.-col. 1730; mayor, Wilton, 1732; paymaster to the Gibraltar garrison 1735–*d.*; equerry to the King 1735–*d.*; commr. of revenue [I] 1737–*d.*

Thomas Herbert was returned for Newport on the interest of his first cousin, Sir William Morice (q.v.), voting with the Administration on the civil list arrears in 1729 and on the army in 1732, but absent from the division on the Hessians in 1730 and the excise in 1733. In the next Parliament he voted with the Government on the repeal of the Septennial Act in 1734 and the Spanish convention in 1739. Either he or his brother William supported an opposition motion for an inquiry into the state of the navy on 24 Feb. 1735.[1]

He died 25 Dec. 1739.

[1] *HMC Egmont Diary*, ii. 153-4.

E.C.

HERBERT, Hon. William (c.1696–1757).

WILTON 1734–31 Mar. 1757

b. c.1696, 5th s. of Thomas Herbert, M.P., 8th Earl of Pembroke; bro. of Hon. Nicholas, Robert Sawyer and Thomas Herbert (qq.v.). *m.* bef. 1741, Catherine Elizabeth Tewes of Aix-la-Chapelle, 3s. 2da.; fa. of Henry Herbert, M.P., 1st Earl of Carnarvon.
  Lt. 1 Life Gds. 1722; capt. and lt.-col. 1 Ft. Gds. 1738; brevet-col. and a.-d.-c. to George II 1745; col. 6 Marines Feb.–Dec. 1747, 14 Ft. 1747–53 and 2nd Drag. Gds. 1753–*d.*; maj.-gen. 1755.
  Groom of the bedchamber 1740–*d.*; paymaster to the Gibraltar garrison 1740–*d.*

William Herbert, a professional soldier, was returned on his family's interest for Wilton, voting with the Administration in all recorded divisions. He died 31 Mar. 1757.

E.C.

HERLE, Edward (1682–1721), of Landrew and Prideaux, Cornw.

LAUNCESTON 1713–14 Apr. 1721

bap. 12 Apr. 1682, 1st s. of Nicholas Herle, M.P., of Landrew by his w. Elizabeth Reed of Upton, Devon. *educ.* Exeter, Oxf. 1699. *m.* 1714, Elizabeth, da. and h. of William Northmore, of Thornleigh, Devon, 1s. 1da. *suc.* uncle at Prideaux 1697.
  Sheriff, Cornw. 1713.

Returned as a Tory for Launceston in 1715 on the recommendation of George Granville, M.P., 1st Lord Lansdowne,[1] Herle is not recorded as voting. Described as 'a gentleman of bright parts, a lovely aspect, and admired and esteemed by all', but 'miserably tormented by the gout, so as to be a perfect cripple with it',[2] he died 14 Apr. 1721.

[1] John Bewes to John Anstis (q.v.), 22 Feb. 1715, *N. & Q.* (ser. 8), xii. 442-4. [2] C. S. Gilbert, *Cornwall*, iii. 41.

E.C.

HERNE, Joseph (aft. 1682–1723), of the Inner Temple, London.

DARTMOUTH 1715–1722

b. aft. 1682, 2nd s. of of Sir Joseph Herne, M.P., merchant and alderman of London, by Elizabeth, da. of Sir John Frederick, M.P., of St. Peter-le-Poor, London. *educ.* ?Eton; L. Inn 1696; King's, Camb. 1697; I. Temple Oct. 1701, called June 1707. *m.* Penelope, da. of Sir John Mordaunt, 5th Bt., M.P., of Walton, Warws., sis. of Sir Charles Mordaunt, 6th Bt. (q.v.), 2da. *suc.* e. bro. Frederick in March 1723.
  Director, E.I. Co. 1710–22.

The Hernes, wealthy London merchants and financiers trading to the East Indies and North America from Dartmouth,[1] frequently represented the borough in the early eighteenth century. Joseph Herne, related through his mother to another wealthy London family, also formerly Members for Dartmouth,[2] was returned on his family's interest after a contest. Classed in 1715 as a Tory who might often vote with the Whigs, he voted consistently against the Government, moving the motion against Lord Cadogan (4 June 1717), and speaking against the vote for measures against Sweden (8, 9, 13 Apr. 1717), the Address in three successive sessions (7 May 1717, 11 Nov. 1718, 23 Nov. 1719), the Quadruple Alliance (15 Nov. 1718),[3] and the peerage bill (7 Dec. 1719). He did not stand in 1722, dying 19 Dec. 1723.

[1] *CSP Col.* 1689–92, pp. 500, 509. [2] S. Young, *Annals of the Barber-Surgeons*, 551–5; E. H. Fellowes, *Fam. of Frederick*, 19–27. [3] Thos. Brodrick to Lady Midleton, 15 Nov. 1718, Brodrick mss.

S.R.M.

HERON, Henry (c.1675–1730), of Cressy Hall, Lincs.

BOSTON   1713–1722
LINCOLNSHIRE   1722–1727

> *b.* c.1675, 1st surv. s. of Sir Henry Heron of Cressy Hall by Dorothy, da. of Sir Thomas Long, 2nd Bt., of Draycot Cerne, Wilts. *m.* Abigail, da. and h. of Sir William Heveningham of Ketteringham, Norf., 1s. 1da. *suc.* fa. 1695.
> Recorder, Boston 1723–*d.*

Heron, whose great-grandfather acquired Cressy Hall in 1600, was returned as a Tory for Boston, voting consistently against the Administration after George I's accession. In 1721 his name was sent to the Pretender as a probable supporter in the event of a rising.[1] Returned for the county in 1722, he did not stand again. He died 10 Sept. 1730, aged 55.

[1] Stuart mss 65/10.

P.W.

HERON, Patrick (c.1672–1761), of Heron, Kirroughtrie, Kirkcudbright.

KIRKCUDBRIGHT STEWARTRY   1727–1741

> *b.* c.1672, s. of Andrew Heron of Kirroughtrie by Jean, da. of John Dunbar of Machermore. *m.* (1) Margaret, da. of — Stewart, provost of Wigtown; (2) Jane, da. of — Graham of Ingliston, provost of Dumfries, 2s. 1da.; (3) 1721, Isabel, da. of — Neilson of Dumfries, merchant, wid. of Thomas Maxwell of Cuil, Buittle, Kirkcudbright, *s.p.*

Patrick Heron's family had been at Kirroughtrie since the early fifteenth century. A well-known cattle breeder and agriculturalist, he made money in the cattle trade, considerably enlarging the family estates.[1] During the 1715 rising he joined Lord Lovat to fight the rebels in Galloway, but ran away at the first encounter.[2] Returned for Kirkcudbright Stewartry in 1727, he voted consistently

with the Administration He died 22 Oct. 1761, three weeks after his only surviving son.

[1] P. H. M'Kerlie, *Hist. Lands and Owners in Galloway*, 425–6. [2] Murray of Broughton, *Memorials* (Sc. Hist. Soc. xxvii), 317–18.

P.W.

HERTFORD, Earl of, *see* SEYMOUR, Algernon

HERVEY, Carr, Lord Hervey (1691–1723), of Ickworth, Suff.

BURY ST. EDMUNDS   1713–1722

> *b.* 17 Sept. 1691, o.s. of John Hervey, M.P., 1st Earl of Bristol, by his 1st w. Isabella, da. of Sir Robert Carr, 3rd Bt., M.P., of Sleaford, Lincs., sis. and h. to Sir Edward Carr, 4th Bt.; half-bro. of John, Lord Hervey, and Hon. Felton and Thomas Hervey (qq.v.). *educ.* Clare, Camb. 1708; Grand Tour (France, Flanders, Holland, Germany, Italy) 1711–13. *unm.*
> Gentleman of the bedchamber to the Prince of Wales 1714–*d.*

Carr, Lord Hervey, was the son and heir of a wealthy Suffolk country gentleman who, having served for nine years as a Whig Member of Parliament, was raised to the peerage in 1703 and created Earl of Bristol at the coronation of George I. During his grand tour he visited Hanover to pay his court to the future George I and George II. Returned on his family's interest for Bury St. Edmunds in 1713, he entered the service of the Prince of Wales in 1714, following him into opposition from 1717 to 1720. He lost his seat by neglect in 1722, when his stepmother describes him as 'utterly ruined both in reputation and fortune', adding: 'the life he leads must soon put an end to his trouble'. He died, 'drowned in drink',[1] 14 Nov. 1723. The apocryphal story that he was the father of Horace Walpole is probably a garbled version of contemporary gossip about the paternity of the 3rd Earl of Orford.[2]

[1] *Letter Bks. of John Hervey, 1st Earl of Bristol*, ii. 171, 249. [2] Hervey, *Mems.* 741–2.

R.R.S.

HERVEY, Hon. Felton (1712–73), of Bury St. Edmunds, Suff.

BURY ST. EDMUNDS   1747–1754, 9 Dec. 1754–1761

> *b.* 12 Feb. 1712, 10th s. of John Hervey, M.P., 1st Earl of Bristol, by his 2nd w. Elizabeth, da. and h. of Sir Thomas Felton, 4th Bt., M.P., of Playford Hall, Suff.; half-bro. of Carr, Lord Hervey, and bro. of John, Lord Hervey, and Hon. Thomas Hervey (qq.v.). *educ.* Bury St. Edmunds g.s.; Eton 1727–30. *m.* 25 Dec. 1740, Dorothy, da. of Solomon Ashley (q.v.), wid. of Charles Pitfield of Brixton, 1s. 3da.
> Equerry to the Queen 1736–7; groom of the bedchamber to the Duke of Cumberland Dec. 1737–56.

Felton Hervey was unjustly dismissed as a boy from his post of page to the Princess of Wales, but was subsequently vindicated. After succeeding his brother, Thomas (q.v.), as equerry to the Queen, he was appointed to the Duke of Cumberland's household at a salary of £400 p.a. In 1746 his father chose him to succeed his elder brother, Thomas, as Member for Bury St. Edmunds, because, though 'a known courtier', he was 'the only son of all those it pleased God to give me who never yet had disobeyed me, and therefore I UNASKED nominated him'.[1] He died 16 Aug. 1773.

[1] Letter Bks. of John Hervey, 1st Earl of Bristol, iii. 141–2, 147–8, 312.

R.R.S.

HERVEY, John, Lord Hervey (1696–1743), of Ickworth, Suff.

BURY ST. EDMUNDS 2 Apr. 1725–11 June 1733

b. 15 Oct. 1696, 1st s. of John Hervey, M.P., 1st Earl of Bristol, by his 2nd w.; half-bro. of Carr, Lord Hervey, and bro. of Hon. Felton and Thomas Hervey (qq.v.). educ. Westminster 1712–13; Clare, Camb. 1713–15; visited France and Hanover 1716–17. m. 21 Apr. 1720, Mary (maid of honour to the Princess of Wales c.1717–20), da. of Brig.-Gen. Nicholas Lepell, 4s. 4da. summ. to Lords in his fa.'s barony as Lord Hervey of Ickworth 1733.
Vice-chamberlain 1730–40; P.C. 8 May 1730; ld. privy seal 1740–2.

Hervey was returned on his family's interest for Bury St. Edmunds in 1725, at the opening of Pulteney's seventeen year political opposition to Walpole. He states that 'he lived in long intimacy and personal friendship with the former, and in his public and political conduct he always attached himself to the latter' (103).[1] At George II's accession in 1727, when most people expected Walpole to be replaced by Sir Spencer Compton (q.v.),

> there were none among the many his power had obliged (excepting General Churchill [q.v.] and Lord Hervey), who did not in public as notoriously decline and fear his notice as they used industriously to seek and covet it. These two men constantly attended him, and never paid so much as the compliment to Sir Spencer Compton, who had already opened a levee (28).

Chosen to move the Address at the opening of George II's first Parliament, he went abroad for his health in July 1728, with a pension of £1,000 a year procured for him by Walpole. Returning in September 1729, he was pressed by Pulteney to join him in opposition, but refused to do so, at the cost of a breach, leading to a duel, with Pulteney. Simultaneously he resigned his pension in a letter to Walpole, expressing the hope that the King would 'consider me in some manner which I shall not

be ashamed to own' (103–10). At the end of the next session, during which he spoke and wrote for the Government, he was appointed vice-chamberlain to the King, in succession to Lord Harrington (William Stanhope, q.v.). 'Lodged all the year round in the court' (1), he became the chief friend and mentor of Frederick, Prince of Wales, till the end of 1731, when he discovered that he had been supplanted by Bubb Dodington (q.v.) (xxxvi–ix). In April 1732, 'perceiving the Prince to show more coolness than usual towards him, [he] took it into his head' that this was due to Frederick's mistress, Miss Vane, then six months gone with a child, to whose paternity the Prince, Harrington, and Hervey were supposed to have co-equal claims (290). On this he sent her a letter by his brother-in-law, Bussy Mansel (q.v.),

> wherein he upbraided her with the ill services she did him with the Prince, and if she did not repair them would discover what he knew of her and use her as she deserved. Upon reading of this letter she fell into a fit, which surprised Mansel, who asked her what was in the letter. She threw it him. He swore he would be my Lord Hervey's death, for making him the messenger of so great an affront, and for deceiving him, for that my Lord told him his letter was only to recommend a midwife. To prevent murder, Miss Vane was obliged to acquaint the Prince with what happened, who made the matter up, but much resented the ill-treatment of his mistress, as did the King and Sir Robert Walpole, when they heard it.[2]

In January 1733 he is described as having 'tried the humblest and meanest ways possible to be reconciled to the Prince, but to no purpose; he attends his levy every day and has not for some months been spoken to'.[3] The Prince never forgave him, but he soon made his peace with the King and Queen, bringing them accounts of parliamentary debates, particularly those on the excise bill, which they were so impatient to hear that when he returned to St. James's after the second reading had been carried at one o'clock in the morning, 'the King took him into the Queen's bedchamber, and there kept him without dinner till near three in the morning, asking him ten thousand questions, relating not only to people's words and actions, but even to their looks' (143, 149). Raised to the Lords at the end of the session to strengthen ministerial debating power there, he devoted the summer to attending on the Queen, who mounted him on days when the King was hunting

> so that he might ride constantly by the side of her chaise, and entertain her, whilst other people were entertaining themselves with hearing dogs bark and seeing crowds gallop.
> Sunday and Monday Lord Hervey lay constantly in London; every other morning he used to walk with the Queen and her daughters at Hampton Court. His real

business in London was pleasure; but as he always told the King it was to pick up news, to hear what people said, to see how they looked, and to inform their Majesties what was thought by all parties of the present posture of affairs, he by these means made his pleasure in town and his interest at court reciprocally conducive to each other (221–2).

At the beginning of 1734 the Prince complained

that it was extremely hard that a man whom the whole world knew had been so impertinent to him and whom he never spoke to should be picked out by the Queen for her constant companion and her most distinguished favourite.

He told his sisters that the reason of his coming so seldom to the Queen was Lord Hervey's always being there; that they knew he had as lief see the devil as Lord Hervey; that the Queen knew it too, and consequently he supposed kept Lord Hervey there to keep him away.

His sisters . . . owned that Lord Hervey had been in the wrong to him once . . . but that he had behaved with great penitence ever since. . . . They said, too, that this crime was committed two years ago; that the Queen had resented it at first; but when Lord Hervey had done all he could to atone for his fault, and was so assiduous a servant in private and so useful to the court in public, that it would neither be prudent in the Queen with regard to herself, nor just in her with regard to Lord Hervey, still to behave to him as if he was never to be forgiven, and that all his attachment, submission, and services should for ever for the future be to no purpose.

Besides this they said that the King liked to have Lord Hervey with him and made him come to give an account of the proceedings of one House of Parliament or the other every day; in short that he was useful and agreeable both to the King and Queen, and though his crime had been of such a nature that the Prince might expect the Queen not to protect him at first, yet it was not the sort that no repentance could wipe away the remembrance of it; and that if Lord Hervey's past conduct had deserved the Queen's anger, it must be owned too that by his behaviour ever since he had merited her forgiveness (274–5).

In the summer he describes himself as

in greater favour with the Queen, and consequently with the King, than ever; they told him everything, and talked of everything before him. The Queen sent for him every morning as soon as the King went from her, and kept him, while she breakfasted, till the King returned, which was generally an hour and a half at least. By her interest, too, she got the King to add a thousand pounds to his salary, which was a new subject of complaint to the Prince. She gave him a hunter, and on hunting days he never stirred from her chaise. She called him always her 'child, her pupil, and her charge'; used to tell him perpetually that his being so impertinent, and daring to contradict her so continually, was owing to his knowing she could not live without him; and often said 'it is well I am so old, or I should be talked of for this creature'.

Lord Hervey made prodigious court to her, and really loved and admired her. He gave up his sole time to her disposal; and always told her he devoted it in winter to her business, and in summer to her amusement (398–9).

By 1737 his favour had begun to excite the jealousy of Walpole, a man 'apt to conceive jealousies and suspicions and . . . to annoy and depress those against whom these jealousies and suspicions were conceived' (809, 924).

On the Queen's death that year,

several of Sir Robert Walpole's enemies, as well as some of Lord Hervey's injudicious friends, tried to stimulate and persuade Lord Hervey at this time to endeavour to ruin Sir Robert Walpole in the palace, to make use of his perpetual access to the King for this purpose, . . . telling him how capable he was of stepping into Sir Robert's place, and how glad the at present broken Whig party would be to unite under his banner, if he would set up his standard. But these people knew little of the true situation of things.

Instead he raised the question of his future with Walpole, who promised to look after him; but 'he now began to know Sir Robert Walpole too well to depend much on the most lavish professions of kindness and esteem' (921–4). In 1739 according to Horace Walpole, Hervey and his friends forced Stephen Fox (q.v.) 'into the secretaryship of the Treasury, against the inclination of the minister [Walpole]; an instance then unparalleled'.[4] When in the same year Newcastle learned that Hervey was to be appointed lord privy seal he protested so violently that Walpole advised against it, 'but nevertheless he obtained it, having much the King's ear and favour'.[5] He retained his office for five months after Walpole's fall, though the new chief ministers, his personal enemies, at odds with one another on many points, were agreed on one, 'which is to get me from the King's ear, and not to suffer the traversing power to all their schemes, which they have felt in so many instances I have there, to maintain its hold'. In Pulteney's words, he 'stuck like a burr and there was no brushing him off'.[6] It was not till 'they told the King that the whole machine of government at present was at a stop merely on my account' that George II gave way, saying to Hervey:

My Lord, you know I have resisted this measure as long as ever I could; I am now forced to bring it into immediate execution. I hope in time to do something you may like and in the meantime am very ready to give you a pension of £3,000 a year (942–59).

Refusing 'to be rolled in the dirt of that pensionary gutter', he went into opposition, though his appearance was such that most people were 'thinking my natural death not far off and my political demise already over' (944, lv). In the short time left to him he published two anti-ministerial pamphlets, as well as a lampoon on the King and Carteret, which 'made a great noise'; made 'three remarkably fine orations' against the repeal of the Gin Act by the new chancellor of the Exchequer; and spoke 'an hour and a half, with the greatest applause, *against the Hanoverians'.*[7] He died 5 Aug. 1743, aged 46, leaving a historical masterpiece, his *Memoirs* of the first ten years of the reign of George II, based on his experiences at court.

[1] The references in brackets in the text are to the pages of the 1931 ed. of Hervey's *Memoirs*. [2] *HMC Egmont Diary*, i. 264-5. [2] *HMC Carlisle*, 6. [4] *Mems. Geo. II*, i. 205. [5] *HMC Egmont Diary*, iii. 140. [6] L. Twells, *Lives of Pocock etc.* ii. 62. [7] Walpole to Mann 16 Oct. 1742, 2 Feb. 1743; *Mems. Geo. II*, i. 67.

R.R.S.

HERVEY, John (1696–1764), of East Betchworth, Reigate, Surr.

REIGATE	16 Feb. 1739–1741
WALLINGFORD	1754–30 July 1764

bap. 25 June 1696, 1st s. of Stephen Hervey, M.P., justice of Anglesey, by his cos. Anne, da. of John Hervey, of St. Mary-at-Hill, London, Turkey merchant and treasurer of the Turkey Co.[1] *educ.* M. Temple 1709, called 1723; bencher 1745. *m.* c.1731, Anne, da. of Sir Christopher Des Bouverie by Elizabeth, da. of Ralph Freeman of East Betchworth, 2s. *suc.* fa. 1707.

Justice of Brecon 1745–d.

Hervey, the son of a former M.P. for Reigate, was put up for the borough in 1739 by his friend, Lord Hardwicke, to hold the seat for Hardwicke's son, Philip Yorke (q.v.), who was still under age. Returned unopposed, he voted with the Government, standing down in favour of Yorke in 1741. In 1747, when Yorke was standing for both Cambridgeshire and Reigate, Hervey was invited by Hardwicke to represent Yorke at Reigate, making the speech proposing him and his cousin, Charles Cocks (q.v.), for the borough.[2] He died 30 July 1764.

[1] *N. & Q.* (ser. 9), iv. 51. [2] Hardwicke to Philip Yorke, 16, 20 and 26 June 1747, Add. 35351, ff. 103-5, 108, 114-15.

R.R.S.

HERVEY, Hon. Thomas (1699–1775), of Bond St., London.

BURY ST. EDMUNDS	29 June 1733–1747

b. 20 Jan. 1699, 2nd s. of John Hervey, M.P., 1st Earl of Bristol, by his 2nd w.; half-bro. of Carr, Lord Hervey, and bro. of Hon. Felton and John, Lord Hervey (qq.v.). *educ.* Westminster 1712–17; Ch. Ch. Oxf. 1717–19. *m.* Aug. 1745, Anne, da. of Francis Coghlan, counsellor at law in Ireland, 1s.

Equerry to Queen Caroline 1728–37; surveyor of the King's gardens 1738–60.

Thomas Hervey was returned in 1733 for the family seat at Bury St. Edmunds, in succession to his brother, John, Lord Hervey, who procured him a present of money from Walpole in 1737 and a post of £500 p.a. in the royal Household next year.[1] Throughout his parliamentary career he supported

the Government, except in the crucial division on the chairman of the elections committee, 16 Dec. 1741, when he voted with the Opposition, saying on being asked why he had done so, 'Jesus knows my thoughts, one day I blaspheme and pray the next.' 'Tom Hervey is quite mad', Horace Walpole wrote, referring not only to this incident, but to Hervey's having recently been in an asylum.[2] Hervey himself attributed his 'madness' to the effects on 'a distressed mind in a distempered body' of a dispute with Sir Thomas Hanmer (q.v.), whose wife, a considerable heiress, had left him to put herself under Hervey's protection in 1737.[3] In 1739 she had made a will bequeathing to Hervey the reversion of her estates in Cambridgeshire, Middlesex, Anglesey and Caernarvonshire, which had been settled 'after death of me and my husband and failure of issue of my body to the use of such person or persons as I should appoint'.[4] At the same time she appealed to Hanmer to leave to Hervey her principal estate of Barton, Suffolk, which he had acquired absolutely under their marriage settlement.[5]

> I am [she wrote] perhaps the only woman who, in my situation, would not either have exposed you to the world, or have wronged your family; though what would have been an injury to yours would have been but justice to my own: for, supposing me capable of having a child, your giving my estate to your heir, or my giving an heir to your estate, are but one and the same injustice.

After her death in 1741, Hanmer not only ignored her request but as life tenant proceeded to cut down the timber on one of Hervey's reversionary estates. On this Hervey published an open letter to Hanmer accusing him of being an impotent fortune hunter:

> You once made some little feint towards joining of your person on the wedding night and the next morning begged pardon for her disappointment.

Alleging that she had agreed to marry Hanmer only under pressure from her parents, the letter continues:

> In my opinion the man that takes a woman, who has not made that man her choice is in fact committing but a lawful sort of rape; to which indeed your guilt is analogous in sound only; for it must be confessed that your enormity was not a rape but rapine.

On Hanmer's death in 1746, Barton went to his nephew, but Hervey succeeded to the other estates.[6]

Before the general election of 1747 Hervey decided not to stand again, to the relief of his father, who wrote:

> If I should sum up all the articles wherein he has been guilty towards me and if possible much more so towards my dearest and most valuable friend, Sir Thomas Hanmer, the black list would so terrify his already affrighted soul that it must cast him into

irrecoverable madness, a consequence I have long and carefully avoided.

But on learning that his brother, Felton, was being put up for the seat by Lord Bristol, he threatened to 'split the family interest' by 'offering himself . . . to serve a body of men whom he had for six years so shamefully neglected as never to come near them either before, at, or after his last election'.

> He wrote a long letter to the mayor and corporation, in which he recounted the bead roll of his distresses, and concluded: 'to add to my misfortune, I have married a woman without a shilling, to prevent her running distracted or making away with herself'.

In the end he thought better of it. He never stood again but continued to air his grievance in open letters 'full of madness and wit'.[7] He died 18 Jan. 1775, commemorated by Dr. Johnson: 'Tom Hervey, though a vicious man, was one of the genteelest men that ever lived.'

[1] Hervey, *Mems.* 740–1. [2] To Mann, 16 Dec.; *Corresp. H. Walpole* (Yale ed.), xxx. 23. [3] *Letter from Hon. Thos. Hervey to Sir Thos. Hanmer* (1742). [4] PCC 92 Spurway. [5] *Hanmer Corresp.* 74. [6] PCC 54 Alexander; *Letter from Hervey to Hanmer.* [7] *Letter Bks. of John Hervey, 1st Earl of Bristol*, iii. 308, 328; *Corresp. H. Walpole* (Yale ed.), xxx. 115–16; Walpole to Conway, 6 May 1763.

R.R.S.

HESKETH, Thomas (?1699–1735), of Rufford, Lancs.

PRESTON 1722–1727

b. ?1699, 1st s. of Thomas Hesketh of Rufford, Lancs. by Anne, da. of Sir Richard Graham, 1st Bt., of Norton Conyers, Yorks. *educ.* B.N.C. Oxf. 17 May 1715, aged 16. *m.* 10 July 1722, Martha, da. and coh. of James St. Amand, apothecary, of St. Paul's, Covent Garden by Elizabeth, da. of Sir William Juxton, 1st Bt., of Little Compton, Glos., 4s. *suc.* fa. 1721.

The head of an ancient Lancashire family, with an income of 'near £2,000 per annum',[1] Hesketh was returned for Preston in 1722 in succession to, and with the support of, Henry Fleetwood (q.v.). 'Very much a Tory',[2] he was a member of the local Jacobite club.[3] He did not stand again, dying 18 Apr. 1735.

[1] *Gent. Mag.* 1735, p. 219. [2] E. Hamilton to Sunderland, undated, Sunderland (Blenheim) mss. [3] C. Hardwick, *Preston*, 252.

E.C.

HEWETT, *see* THORNHAGH

HEYSHAM, Robert (1663–1723), of Stagenhoe, Herts.

LANCASTER 1698–1715
LONDON 1715–1722

bap. 16 Aug. 1663, 2nd s. of Giles Heysham of Lancaster by Elizabeth, da. of Robert Thornton of Oxcliffe, nr. Lancaster; bro. of William Heysham (q.v.). *m.* (1) Mary, da. and coh. of Edmund Thornton (q.v.), draper, of London and Stagenhoe, Herts., *s.p.*; (2) her sis. Jane, da. and coh. of Edmund Thornton, 1s. 1da.

Alderman, London 1720; draper 1720–*d.*; master, Drapers' Co. 1720–1; pres. Christ's Hospital 1721–*d.*

Born in Lancaster, Heysham came to London, where he became an eminent Barbados merchant, trading in partnership with his brother William (q.v.). From 1700 to 1704 he acted as agent for the colony, on which he was frequently consulted by the board of Trade. Originally a Hanoverian Tory, he was returned for London as a Whig in 1715, but voted consistently with the Opposition. He was chairman of a committee of the House of Commons on woollen manufactures in 1715; spoke against the septennial bill in 1716; moved an address to the King against the embargo on trade with Sweden on 27 Feb. 1718; and opposed the Address on 11 Nov. 1718. In that year he was chairman of a committee on the continuance of expiring laws, and in 1719 of one to bring in a bill for preventing frauds by bankrupts.[1] On 1 June 1721 he carried a motion for allowing Col. Raymond, one of the South Sea directors, £30,000 out of his estate, and on 13 Dec. following he spoke in favour of a petition for a Quaker affirmation bill. Unsuccessful in 1722, he died 25 Feb. 1723, described as 'a very great benefactor' to his native town and 'generous to all without partiality in respect to religious profession'.[2]

[1] *CJ*, xviii. 72; xix. 22, 55. [2] Wm. Stout, *Autobiog.* 102.

E.C.

HEYSHAM, William (1666–1716), of Lancaster.

LANCASTER 1705–13 June 1716

bap. 27 Jan. 1666, 3rd s. of Giles Heysham of Lancaster and bro. of Robert Heysham (q.v.). *m.* 3 Sept. 1687, Elizabeth, da. and coh. of Humphry Brockden of Barbados, 2s. 1da.

Heysham was a Barbados merchant, trading in London in partnership with his brother Robert, whom he succeeded as agent for the colony in 1704. Next year he joined his brother as Member for Lancaster, for which he was re-elected in 1715 as a Whig, voting against the Septennial bill. He died June 1716.

E.C.

HEYSHAM, William (1691–1727), of East Greenwich, Kent.

LANCASTER 16 July 1716–14 Apr. 1727

b. 10 Dec. 1691, 1st surv. s. of William Heysham (q.v.). *educ.* Ch. Ch. Oxf. 1709, M. Temple 1709. *m.* 1 Oct. 1719, Sarah, da. of Richard Perry, London merchant, sis. of Micajah Perry (q.v.). *suc.* fa. 1716.

Heysham succeeded his father at Lancaster, voting against the Government in all recorded divisions. His only reported speech was against the army, 28 Jan. 1726. He died at Bath 14 Apr. 1727, described by a Lancaster Quaker as 'an indolent man and of no service'.[1]

[1] W. Stout, *Autobiog.* 109.

E.C.

HICKMAN, Sir Willoughby, 3rd Bt. (1659–1720), of Gainsborough, Lincs.

KINGSTON-UPON-HULL 1685–1687
EAST RETFORD 1698–1700
 15 Apr.–11 Nov. 1701
 28 Nov. 1702–17 Jan. 1706
LINCOLNSHIRE 1713–28 Oct. 1720

bap. 29 Aug. 1659, 1st surv. s. of Sir William Hickman, 2nd Bt., M.P., of Gainsborough by Elizabeth, da. and h. of John Neville of Mattersey, Notts. *m.* (lic. 8 Sept. 1683) Anne, da. of Sir Stephen Anderson, 1st Bt., of Eyworth, Beds., 4s. 6da. *suc.* fa. 10 Feb. 1682.
Steward of Kirton 1682–9.

Descended from London merchants, who had settled in Lincolnshire at the end of the 16th century, Hickman had sat in five Parliaments before being returned for his county. A Tory and a member of the October Club, he was absent from the division on the septennial bill but voted against the repeal of the Occasional Conformity and Schism Acts and the peerage bill in 1719. He died 28 Oct. 1720.

P.W.

HILL, Andrew (*d.* 1755), of Walthamstow, Essex, and Whitton Court, Salop.

BISHOP'S CASTLE 1741–1747

Yr. s. of Andrew Hill of Court of Hill, Salop by Anne, da. of Serjt. Thomas Powys of Henley, in Bitterley, Salop. *unm.*

Andrew Hill owned estates in Bitterley adjacent to those of the Walcot family, on whose interest he was returned as a Tory after a sharp and expensive contest. Voting consistently with the Opposition, he did not stand again. He died 31 May 1755.

J.B.L.

HILL, John (c.1690–1753), of Thornton Hall, nr. Malton, Yorks.

HIGHAM FERRERS 1747–3 July 1753

b. c.1690, 1st s. of John Hill of Thornton. *educ.* M. Temple 1706. *unm.*
 Commr. of customs 1723–47; gov. Scarborough castle 1744–*d.*

John Hill, whose family bought the manor of Thornton in 1669, was appointed a commissioner of customs when the number of commissioners was doubled on the extension of their functions in Scotland in 1723. During the debates on the excise bill in 1733 he gave evidence to the House of Commons on the frauds in the customs. Speaking for the rest of the board, he 'gave it as his opinion that, exclusive of running, he believed the frauds amounted to as much as the duty paid the public'. It was thought that 'considering the number of questions asked a man in such an assembly, and many in order to puzzle, . . . [he] acquitted himself very well'.[1] Though his office disqualified him from a seat in Parliament, some of its duties were highly political. On the eve of the general election of 1734, the 1st Lord Egmont (Lord Perceval, q.v.)

visited Mr. Hill of the Custom House to desire him to influence the officers under them at Harwich in favour of my son's election. He told me he was last Thursday at Sir Robert Walpole's, who gave him a letter I wrote him for that purpose, and bade him take care of my son: whereupon when he went to the board that morning he advised with the clerk in what proper and safe manner to signify the Government's pleasure to these officers; that the clerk told him the two Philipses [Harwich customs officers] were such rogues that they would betray him if a letter were writ down to them; wherefore he ordered a letter that night to the Collector Davis to come up and receive orders by word of mouth.

When the collector arrived, Hill told him in Egmont's presence that Walpole 'would have the officers of the customs to vote for Lord Perceval and Mr. Leathes' (qq.v.), adding that if they refused Davis should notify this by express.

He cautioned that his name should not be used if possible as directing anything, for what he did now was more, by G——, than he could do for anyone beside.

Some of the officials still proving recalcitrant, Egmont wrote to Hill asking that they should 'be sent for up to be out of the way during the election.' After consulting some of the other customs commissioners Hill replied that

we must beg your Lordship's pardon for not complying with your request, since we think we cannot be justified in it.[2]

Next year Hill was reported to be standing himself for Scarborough, not far from his estate. 'If Mr. Hill should stand', wrote the Duke of Leeds, who was putting up Lord Dupplin (q.v.), 'nothing can be done for Lord Dupplin at all . . . but by a vast expense, and I doubt if even that would do'. In the event, it appeared that Hill had been keeping the town in suspense to serve the real government candidate, William Osbaldeston, who was related to him. Later the Duke complained of threats to turn out the customs officers if either they or their relations voted for Dupplin.[3]

After Walpole's fall Pulteney, now a member of the new Government,

> went in to the King to ask him to turn out Mr. Hill for opposing him at Hedon, 'Sir' said the King, 'was it not when you was opposing me? I wont turn him out: I will part with no more of my friends'. Lord Wilmington [Spencer Compton, q.v.] was waiting to receive orders accordingly, but the King gave him none.[4]

In 1747 Hill gave up his customs post on being returned for Higham Ferrers by Lord Rockingham (Sir Thomas Wentworth, q.v.), with whose family he had long been closely connected. When Rockingham died in 1750 he left Hill £1,000, which Hill left back to the dowager Marchioness on his own death, 3 July 1753. He also left her sister, Lady Isabella Finch, £1,000 with all his plate and china, making the new Marquess of Rockingham his executor and trustee.[5]

[1] *HMC Carlisle*, 103-4. [2] *HMC Egmont Diary*, ii. 82, 85, 93. [3] To Ld. Oxford, 17 Sept. and 17 Oct. 1753; James Trymmer to Ld. Oxford, 21 Sept. 1753, Harley mss. [4] Walpole to Mann, 9 Aug. 1742. [5] PCC 42 Penfold.

R.R.S.

HILL, Sir Roger (c.1642–1729), of Denham, Bucks.

AMERSHAM   1679–1681
WENDOVER   15 July.–21 Nov. 1702, 1705–1722

b. c.1642, 2nd s. of Roger Hill, M.P., of Poundisford, Som., baron of the Exchequer, by his 2nd w. Abigail, da. of Brampton Gurdon of Assington Hall, Suff. *educ.* Jesus, Camb. 1658; I. Temple 1658, called 1666. *m.* 11 July 1667, Abigail, da. of John Lockey of Holmes Hill, Herts., 3s. 2da. Kntd. 18 July 1668.
  Sheriff, Bucks. 1672–3.

Sir Roger Hill, whose father came from an old Somerset family and was M.P. for Bridport in the Long Parliament, bought the manor of Denham from the Bowyers in 1670.[1] Described by Judge Jeffreys in 1685 as 'a horrid Whig' and 'a fierce exclusionist',[2] he was returned for the sixth time on the Hampden interest at Wendover in 1715, voting for the Administration in all recorded divisions. Standing again in 1722, at the age of 80, he apparently lost the Hampden interest to Sir Richard Steele (q.v.), who beat him by 71 votes. He died 29 Dec. 1729, aged 87.

[1] Lipscomb, *Bucks*. iv. 445, 456. [2] *CSP Dom*. 1685, pp. 122–3.

R.S.L.

HILL, Sir Rowland, 1st Bt. (1705–83), of Hawkstone, Salop.

LICHFIELD   1734–1741

bap. 28 Sept. 1705, 1st s. of John Hill of Wem, Salop, apothecary, afterwards of Lutwyche, Salop by Sarah,

da. of John Stubbs of Saw, in Kingsley, Staffs.; 1st cos. of Samuel and Thomas Hill (qq.v.). *m.* (1) 2 June 1732, Jane (bur. 22 Dec. 1773), da. of Sir Bryan Broughton, 3rd Bt. (q.v.), of Broughton, Staffs., 6s. 4da.; (2) 23 Sept. 1776, Mary, da. and coh. of German Pole of Radbourne, Derbys., wid. of Thomas Powys of Berwick, Salop, *s.p.* *suc.* fa. 1713; uncle Rev. Richard Hill to Hawkstone 1727; cos. Samuel Hill (q.v.) to Whitmore Park, Staffs., and Willenhall, Warws. 1758. *cr.* Bt. 20 Jan. 1727.
  Sheriff, Salop 1731–2.

Sir Rowland Hill, lord mayor of London 1549–50, one of the richest merchants of his time, bought considerable estates in Shropshire, including the manor of Hawkstone, where he was born. He settled the manor on a brother, from whom it descended to the Rev. Richard Hill, an able and important official, deputy paymaster of the forces in Flanders, envoy to Brussels, a lord of the Treasury under William III, and a member of the council of the lord high admiral and envoy to Turin under Anne. A moderate Tory, 'of the sort who were in earnest for the succession of the House of Hanover,' Richard Hill remained influential in high circles under George I, though holding no office. He died unmarried in 1727, having settled his estates on his nephews, Rowland, Samuel and Thomas (qq.v.).[1]

Rowland Hill was made a baronet by George I, presumably by the influence of his uncle, from whom he inherited an estate of £8,000 p.a., together with stock in the Bank of England worth £30,998.[2] Returned unopposed as a Tory at Lichfield in 1734 with the support of his cousin Samuel Hill (q.v.),[3] he voted with the Opposition but did not stand again. He spent the later years of his life trying to moderate the religious propensities of his eldest son, Richard Hill, M.P., and of his sixth son, the Rev. Rowland Hill, both of whom were ardent Methodists.[4]

He died 7 Aug. 1783.

[1] *Salop Arch. Soc. Trans*. lv. 143–57. [2] Richard Hill's will, PCC 141 Farrant. [3] H. Sanders, 'Hist. Shenstone', printed by J. Nichols in *Biblio. Topog. Britannica* (1793), ix. 63. [4] Rev. Edwin Sidney, *Life of Sir Richard Hill* and *Life of Rowland Hill*.

E.C.

HILL, Samuel (?1691–1758), of Shenstone Park, nr. Lichfield, Staffs.

LICHFIELD   1715–1722

b. ?1691, 1st s. of Samuel Barbour of Prees, Salop by Elizabeth, da. of Rowland Hill of Hawkstone, Salop; 1st cos. of Sir Rowland and Thomas Hill (qq.v.). *educ.* Eton; St. John's, Camb. 29 Apr. 1707, aged 16; M. Temple 1708; Grand Tour (Italy, France) c.1709–15. *m.* 1722 (with £10,000), Lady Elizabeth Stanhope, da. of Philip, 3rd Earl of Chesterfield, sis. of Hon. Charles, John, Philip Dormer and Sir William Stanhope (qq.v.), *s.p.* *suc.* fa. between

1710 and 1715; uncle Rev. Richard Hill to Shenstone and other estates 1727.

King's Latin sec. 1714–18; registrar of courts of Admiralty, Delegates and Prizes 1714–*d*.

Samuel Barbour was brought up by and assumed the name of his uncle, Richard Hill (see Hill, Sir Rowland), who sent him to Cambridge and then 'abroad to visit the most polite courts of Europe, under the powerful recommendation of his great friend, who had lived there in a public character much esteemed, especially among the Italian princes.' At George I's accession he succeeded his uncle as King's Latin secretary, a small sinecure, and was also made registrar of several courts.[1] Returned on his uncle's interest for Lichfield in 1715, classed as a Tory who might often vote Whig, he voted against the Government in every recorded division. He either resigned or was dismissed from the Latin secretaryship in 1718,[2] but remained registrar of the Admiralty etc., which he may have held under a life patent. In 1722 he retired from Parliament, having found it 'not agreeable to his natural temper which could not away with [conform to] the manner of speaking and transacting business in that honourable House'. Beyond supporting Tory candidates at Lichfield he appears to have taken no further active part in politics.[3]

He died 21 Feb. 1758, said to be worth £300,000.[4]

[1] H. Sanders, 'Hist. Shenstone', printed by J. Nichols in *Biblio. Topog. Britannica* (1793), ix. 61–63. [2] *Cal. Treas. Bks.* xxxii. 680. [3] Sanders, op. cit. [4] *Gent. Mag.* 1758, p. 146.

E.C.

HILL, Thomas (1693–1782), of Tern, Salop.

SHREWSBURY   9 Mar. 1749–1768

b. 1693, 1st s. of Thomas Harwood, a Shrewsbury draper, by Margaret, da. of Rowland Hill of Hawkstone, Salop; 1st cos. of Sir Rowland and Samuel Hill (qq.v.). *m.* (1) 14 Feb. 1723, Anne (*d.* 21 Dec. 1739), da. of Richard Powys of Hintlesham, Suff., 1s. 2da.; (2) 3 May 1740, Susan Maria, da. and coh. of William Noel (q.v.), 2s. 2da. *suc.* uncle Rev. Richard Hill to Tern 1727, and cos. Samuel Hill (q.v.) to Shenstone, Salop 1758.

Thomas Harwood assumed the name of Hill in 1712, when his uncle, Richard Hill, settled on him the estate of Tern.[1] About this time he was sent abroad by his uncle, who wrote to him at Hamburg in October regretting his being 'so perfectly idle . . . so long', and advising him to employ himself 'in reading, writing and arithmetic', and in learning German; and in 1714 directed him to proceed from Saxony to Amsterdam, where he tried to place him 'in any good house where you may be bred a merchant'. Finally he was articled to Clifford, 'one of the greatest and richest bankers living'. He

remained on the continent till 1721, when (he wrote to his father on 4 Apr.) his uncle gave him

> leave to go to make a tour to Cambrai, or Paris, or any other part of France, and so to return home before winter . . . I perceive my uncle would gladly have me see what passes there [at Cambrai] if the Congress meets and for that end I believe he will endeavour to place me with some of the King's ambassadors, perhaps as one of the secretaries, but if there be no Congress then I verily believe he will order me to return before winter.

He does not seem to have set up as a merchant, but his correpondence 1740–59 shows him engaged in extensive financial transactions, lending nearly £8,000 to George Crowle (q.v.), and considerable sums to Lord Lincoln, Velters Cornewall (q.v.), etc. On 1 Dec. 1753 he sent a message to Sir Edward Leighton: 'I have not such a sum as £9,000 but if he pleases I will do my endeavours to procure it for him'; and on 17 Aug. 1754 wrote to his cousin Samuel Hill (q.v.) advising him to lend £20,000 to 'a very honest gentleman', Sir Thomas Mostyn (q.v.). In October 1753, after consulting Bartholomew Burton, M.P., Hill invested £14,000 in Bank of England stock;[2] and there is further correspondence, all carried on from Shrewsbury, about other English stocks and even French 'actions'.

On 27 Nov. 1740 Hill wrote to Lord Weymouth, who controlled Tamworth in conjunction with Lord Middleton: 'Lord Middleton is ready to acquiesce hoping your Lordship will be pleased to nominate me for Tamworth'; but nothing came of it. At a by-election in 1749 he was returned unopposed for Shrewsbury with the support of both Lord Powis (Henry Arthur Herbert, q.v.), and the local Tories. Though classed as a Tory, he became a regular member of the Powis group, receiving Newcastle's whip as long as Powis adhered to him. He died 11 June 1782.

[1] *Salop Arch. Soc. Trans.* lv. 152; Richard Hill's will, PCC 141 Farrant. All docs. subsequently cited without references are from the Attingham mss, Salop RO. [2] Bank of England recs.

E.C.

HILL, Trevor (1693–1742), of Hillsborough, co. Down, and Turweston, Bucks.

AYLESBURY   30 Apr. 1715–1722
MALMESBURY   1722–13 Dec. 1722

b. 1693, 1st s. of Rt. Hon. Michael Hill, M.P., of Hillsborough by Anne, da. and h. of Sir John Trevor, M.P., of Brynkinalt, Denb., master of the rolls and Speaker of the House of Commons. *m.* bef. 1717, Mary, da. and coh. of Anthony Rowe, M.P., of Muswell Hill, Mdx., clerk of the Green Cloth, wid. of Sir Edmund Denton, 1st Bt., M.P., of Hillesden. Bucks, 4s. 1da. *suc.* fa. 1699; *cr.* Baron Hill of Kilwarlin and Visct. Hillsborough [I] 21 Aug. 1717.

M.P. [I] 1713–17.

P.C. [I] 20 Sept. 1717; gov. co. Down 1729.

Hill was descended from Moyses Hill who went to northern Ireland with the Earl of Essex in the reign of Elizabeth I. His mother became the 3rd wife of Alan Brodrick, 1st Visct. Midleton [I] (q.v.). At the general election of 1715 he stood unsuccessfully as a Whig for Saltash, which his father had represented 1692–5. Returned three months later for Aylesbury at a by-election, he voted for the septennial bill and the repeal of the Occasional Conformity and Schism Acts, but against the peerage bill December 1719. In September 1720, when owing Walpole some £9,000 for South Sea stock, he refused to pay and 'already bankrupt . . . fled to Newmarket in the hope of recuperating on horses what he had lost on the shares.' He is described by Horace Walpole as 'one of the most profligate and worthless men of the age, with good parts and a friend of the Duke of Wharton', by whom he was returned for Malmesbury in 1722, only to be unseated on petition.[1] Defeated at Appleby in 1723, he did not stand again.[2]

Hearne refers to him in July 1725 as

a very handsome man [who] had two hundred graces in his lips. [He] . . . is one of those wanton, immodest gentlemen that, a year or two ago, used to ride naked and make strange work with young women . . . till at last a carter happened to whip some of them, as they were thus naked, at a place in Buckinghamshire, after which we heard no more of their pranks.[3]

He died 5 May 1742.

[1] Plumb, *Walpole*, i. 318–19; Corresp. H. Walpole (Yale ed.), xxxiv. 260. [2] *HMC 10th Rep. IV*, 345. [3] Hearne, *Colls*. (Oxf. Hist. Soc.), viii. 405.

R.S.L.

HILL, Hon. Wills (1718–93), of North Aston, Oxon.

WARWICK 1741–17 Nov. 1756

b. 30 May 1718, 1st surv. s. of Trevor, 1st Visct. Hillsborough [I] (q.v.). *m.* (1) 1 Mar. 1748 (with £20,000), Lady Margaret FitzGerald (*d.* 25 Jan. 1766), da. of Robert, 19th Earl of Kildare [I], sis. of James, 1st Duke of Leinster [I], 2s. 3da.; (2) 11 Oct. 1768, Mary, *suo jure* Baroness Stawell, da. of Edward, 4th Baron Stawell, wid. of H. B. Legge (q.v.), *s.p. suc.* fa. as 2nd Visct. 5 May 1742; *cr.* Earl of Hillsborough [I] 3 Oct. 1751; Baron Harwich 17 Nov. 1756; Earl of Hillsborough 28 Aug. 1772; Mq. of Downshire [I] 20 Aug. 1789.

Gov. co. Down 1742–*d.*; P.C. [I] 25 Aug. 1746; comptroller of the Household May 1754–Dec. 1755; P.C. 21 June 1754; treasurer of the chamber Dec. 1755–Nov. 1756; first ld. of Trade 1763–5, Aug.–Dec. 1766; joint postmaster gen. 1766–Jan. 1768; conjointly sec. of state for the American dept. and first ld. of Trade Jan. 1768–Aug. 1772; sec. of state for the southern dept. Nov. 1779–Mar. 1782.

Shortly before succeeding to the title Hillsborough was returned for both Warwick and Huntingdon as an opposition Whig, choosing to sit for Warwick. Taking the lead in the agitation against the Lords' rejection of the bill indemnifying witnesses against Walpole, he supported a motion declaring this to have been an obstruction to justice, which might prove fatal to the liberties of the country.[1] During the next two sessions he spoke and voted against the Hanoverians, attaching himself to Dodington, who summoned him from Ireland in September 1744 to 'help to soften the misfortunes that you cannot prevent and disdain to contribute to'. After Dodington entered the Government in December 1744 Hillsborough continued to adhere to him, writing to him from Ireland on the outbreak of the rebellion that he only awaited his summons 'to do my little endeavours towards making things better' and inquiring 'whether our friends gain or lose ground, and whether they are more united in court than in opposition'.[2] Moving an address against the Government's proposal to give permanent commissions to officers in privately raised regiments on 4 Nov. 1745,[3] he voted against the Hanoverians in 1746, when he was regarded by the ministry as a doubtful supporter.

At the beginning of the next Parliament Hillsborough was classed as Opposition. However, when Dodington joined the Prince of Wales in 1749 he made no attempt to recruit him. The 2nd Lord Egmont wrote in his electoral survey, c.1749–50:

Lord Hillsborough has strangely and fulsomely declared himself in commendation of this Administration. He seems a man not to be depended upon at all, if to be avoided.

Thenceforth he became a regular government spokesman. In 1751 he moved the address of condolence on the death of the Prince of Wales, spoke on the Regency bill in support of the clause prolonging the sitting Parliament in the event of a demise, and drew up the heads of a bill for a similar prolongation of the Irish Parliament. Writing about that time Horace Walpole describes him as

a young man of great honour and merit, remarkably nice in weighing whatever cause he was to vote in, and excellent at setting off his reasons, if the affair was at all tragic, by a solemnity in his voice and manner that made much impression on his hearers.

In 1752 he is said by Newcastle to have 'distinguished himself extremely' on the subsidy treaty with Saxony, speaking 'very strongly for us and upon right principles'. During the same session he also spoke in support of a bill for granting forfeited estates in Scotland to foreign Protestants, grounding himself on the 'mountains of Papists settled by Protestants in Ireland'.[4] In 1753 he spoke for Lord

Hardwicke's clandestine marriage bill and for a bill for an annual census. He received his reward on the formation of the Newcastle Government in 1754, when he was given a household appointment.

Hillsborough defined his political principles in a pamphlet published in 1751, advocating a union between Great Britain and Ireland, in which he suggests that what he calls the 'unnecessary spirit of opposition' might be mitigated by the importation into the British Parliament of an element of disengaged and unbiased Irish representatives who

> are yet untainted with that unhappy distinction between court and country. I had almost said, that unmeaning distinction. A prince, who knows our constitution, if not irritated by an unnecessary malignant opposition to his measures, and the people, if not inflamed by the bad arts of a few designing ambitious, turbulent spirits, will easily distinguish, and naturally pursue the public good. Their interests are truly inseparable. They should not be supposed capable of being divided, and ought not to be distinguished away by party or by factions. At least it is a contradiction to the principles of patriotism, certainly to those of liberty, to enlist in a party against the court; to think it a breach of engagements ever to imagine it right in its measures, or give a vote in its favour. As if his Majesty were the only person in his dominions, incapable of knowing his own interests, and his ministers were almost infallibly either weak or wicked.[5]

Under George III these principles were to carry him to high political office.

He died 7 Oct. 1793.

[1] Walpole to Mann, 26 May 1742. [2] *HMC Var.* vi. 18, 19. [3] Owen, *Pelhams*, 289. [4] Walpole, *Mems. Geo. II*, i. 80, 145, 260; *HMC Stopford-Sackville*, i. 177, 180. [5] *A proposal for uniting the Kingdoms of Great Britain and Ireland* (London and Dublin 1751, 2nd ed.), 37–38.

R.R.S.

HILLERSDEN, William (1676–1725), of Elstow, Beds.

BEDFORD	15 Dec. 1707–1710
BEDFORDSHIRE	1715–1722

bap. 24 Apr. 1676, 1st s. of Thomas Hillersden, M.P., of Elstow by Mary, da. of John Forth of Hackney, Mdx. *educ.* Wadham, Oxf. 1693; I. Temple 1693. *m.* by 1705, Elizabeth, da. of William Farrer (q.v.) of Biddenham, Beds., 1s. 3da. *suc.* fa. 1698.
Sheriff, Beds. 1700–2.

William Hillersden, whose father had represented Bedford in three Parliaments under William III, was descended from Sir Thomas Hillersden, who bought the site of Elstow abbey in 1616.[1] Returned for the county in 1715, he voted with the Administration in all recorded divisions, receiving the whip through his father-in-law, the chairman of ways and means. Defeated by a Tory in 1722, he died 6 Apr. 1725.

[1] *Beds. Hist. Rec. Soc. Publ.* v. 75–93.   R.S.L.

HILLSBOROUGH, Earl of, *see* HILL, Hon. Wills

HILLSBOROUGH, Visct., *see* HILL, Trevor, *and* HILL, Hon. Wills

HINCHINGBROOKE, Visct., *see* MONTAGU, Edward Richard

HINXMAN, Joseph (?1701–40), of the New Forest, Hants.

CHRISTCHURCH	1727–21 Mar. 1740

b. ?1701, e.s. of Joseph Hinxman of North Hinton, Hants. *educ.* Winchester 1715–19; Trinity, Oxf. 28 Feb. 1721, aged 19; L. Inn 1720, called 1727. *m.* Beata, 3s. 2da.
Woodward and keeper of New Forest.

Hinxman owned the manor of North Hinton, near Christchurch, for which he stood unsuccessfully in 1724. Returned in 1727 after a contest, he voted regularly with the Administration in every recorded division till his death, 21 Mar. 1740.

P.W.

HITCH, Robert (?1670–1723), of Leathley, Yorks.

KNARESBOROUGH	1715–1722

b. ?1670, s. of Henry Hitch of Leathley by Alathea, da. and coh. of Col. Robert Brandling. *educ.* Wakefield sch.; Trinity, Camb. 11 June 1687, aged 16; G. Inn 1690. *m.* Alice, da. of Richard Aldburgh,[1] 2s. 3da.
Commr. for stating army debts 1720–2.

Hitch was returned after a contest for Knaresborough, not far from his estate. Except on the peerage bill, when he was absent, he voted with the Government. Rewarded with a commissionership for stating the army debts in 1720, he did not stand in 1722, dying 6 Nov. 1723. One of his sons was receiver general for the West Riding.

[1] Thoresby, *Ducatus Leodiensis*, 188.

R.R.S.

HOARE, Henry (1705–85), of Stourhead, Wilts.

SALISBURY	1734–1741

b. 7 July 1705, 1st s. of Henry Hoare of Stourton, banker, by Jane, da. of Sir William Benson of Bromley, Mdx. and sis. of William Benson (q.v.). *educ.* Westminster c.1715; Grand Tour. *m.* (1) 11 Apr. 1726, Anne (*d.* 4 Mar. 1727), da. of Samuel Masham, M.P., 1st Baron Masham, 1da. *d.v.p.*; (2) 6 July 1728, Susan, da. of Stephen Colt, 3s. *d.v.p.*, 2da. *suc.* fa. 1725.

Henry Hoare, an eminent banker known as 'the magnificent',[1] was a grandson of Sir Richard Hoare, M.P., the founder of Hoare's bank in Fleet Street, of which Henry himself became a partner in 1726.

After succeeding to his estates he began to lay out and plant a fine landscape garden at Stourhead, which had been bought by his father from the Stourtons in 1720. Returned as a Tory for Salisbury, he did not vote in any recorded division and did not stand again. In June 1766 he put up £13,000 in cash to enable his son-in-law, Lord Bruce, to buy out Earl Verney's (q.v.) interest in Great Bedwyn.[2] He died 8 Sept. 1785.

[1] H. P. R. Hoare, *Hoare's Bank*, 35. [2] Lord Cardigan, *Wardens of Savernake*, 278.

R.S.L.

HOBART, Sir John, 5th Bt. (1693–1756), of Blickling, nr. Norwich, Norf.

ST. IVES 1715–1727
NORFOLK 1727–28 May 1728

b. 11 Oct. 1693, 1st s. of Sir Henry Hobart, 4th Bt., M.P., of Blickling by Elizabeth, da. and coh. of Joseph Maynard of Clifton Reynes, Bucks. *educ.* Clare, Camb. 1710. *m.* (1) 8 Nov. 1717, Judith (*d.* 7 Feb. 1727), da. and coh. of Robert Britiffe (q.v.), 3s. (2 *d.v.p.*), 5da.; (2) 10 Feb. 1728, Elizabeth, da. of Robert Bristow (q.v.), 2s. *suc.* fa. 21 Aug. 1698; uncle Thomas Grey, 2nd Earl of Stamford, to Bere Alston estate 1720 under will of Sir John Maynard, M.P. K.B. 27 May 1725. *cr.* Baron Hobart of Blickling 28 May 1728; Earl of Buckinghamshire 5 Sept. 1746.
    V.-adm. Norf. 1719–*d.*; ld. of Trade 1721–7; treasurer of the chamber 1727–44; assay master of the stannaries 1727–38; ld. lt. Norf. 1739–*d.*; capt. of gent. pensioners 1744–*d.*; P.C. 3 Jan. 1745.

Hobart's family, settled at Blickling since 1616, had represented the county and boroughs of Norfolk since the seventeenth century. His father strenuously supported the revolution in 1688, became a gentleman of the horse to William III, and fought at the battle of the Boyne. Besides his electoral influence in Norfolk, he controlled one, and from 1741 two, seats at St. Ives, and from 1721 one seat at Bere Alston, for all of which he returned government supporters, mostly his own relatives and friends. His sister, Henrietta Howard, later Lady Suffolk, was George II's mistress.

Returned for St. Ives in 1715, Hobart voted for the septennial bill and the repeal of the Occasional Conformity and Schism Acts, but against the peerage bill. On 23 Mar. 1726 he seconded a motion for bringing in a bill making some provision for the family of Richard Hampden (q.v.). At the accession of George II he was returned for both Bere Alston and Norfolk, choosing to sit for the county. No doubt through his sister's influence, he was appointed treasurer of the chamber and assay master of the stannaries, and was created a peer at the coronation.

He died 22 Sept. 1756, aged 61.

E.C.

HOBART, John, Lord Hobart (1723–93), of Blickling, nr. Norwich, Norf.

NORWICH 1747–22 Sept. 1756

b. 17 Aug. 1723, 1st surv. s. of John Hobart (q.v.), afterwards 1st Earl of Buckinghamshire, by his 1st w. *educ.* Westminster 1732–9; Christ's, Camb. 1739; Grand Tour (Italy 1746–7).[1] *m.* (1) 14 July 1761, Mary Ann (*d.* 30 Dec. 1769), da. and coh. of Sir Thomas Drury, 1st Bt. (q.v.), 4da.; (2) 24 Sept. 1770, Caroline, da. of William Conolly (q.v.), 3s. *d.v.p.* 1da. *suc.* fa. 22 Sept. 1756.
    Comptroller of the Household Dec. 1755–6; P.C. 27 Jan. 1756; ld. of the bedchamber to George II and George III Nov. 1757–Nov. 1767; envoy to St. Petersburg 1762–5; ld. lt. [I] 1777–80.

Hobart was returned as a Whig for St. Ives and Norwich on his family's interest in 1747, choosing to sit for Norwich. He died 3 Sept. 1793.

[1] *Corresp. H. Walpole* (Yale ed.), xix. 60, 421.

E.C.

HOBLYN, Robert (1710–56), of Nanswhyden, Cornw. and Bristol, Glos.

BRISTOL 24 Nov. 1742–1754

bap. 5 May 1710, 1st s. of Francis Hoblyn of Nanswhyden by Penelope, da. of Col. Sidney Godolphin (q.v.) of Shropshire. *educ.* Eton 1725; C.C.C. Oxf. 1727; Grand Tour. *m.* Jane, da. and h. of Thomas Coster (q.v.), *s.p.*[1] *suc.* fa. 1711.
    Speaker of the stannators assembled in the parliament of tinners for the county of Cornwall 1750.

Robert Hoblyn, a well-known book collector, of an old Cornish family,[2] made his fortune by tin mining, supplying the brass working industry at Bristol, in association with his father-in-law, Thomas Coster (q.v.). Returned as a Tory for Bristol, he voted regularly against the Government and was classed as Opposition in 1747. But on 21 Jan. 1749 he wrote to his friend, Edward Southwell, the other Member for Bristol, about a recent debate on the army estimates:

Had I been well last Wednesday we should not have parted on the division, though arguments against standing armies in time of peace make as strong an impression on me as they can on anyone—but surely though we have a peace, we are not yet come to that absolute state of peace that should put us quite off our guard . . . If an opposition is to come from a certain quarter I am glad a man of Dr. Lee's sense is at the head of it; if conducted by some others it might be of less consequence as to weight in the House, but do more real mischief and widen breaches that all honest men must wish to see healed—too strict a union between two brothers [the Pelhams] cant be so fatal as a division between two greater brothers [the Prince of Wales and the Duke of Cumberland].[3]

About the same time the 2nd Lord Egmont in his electoral survey described Hoblyn as 'an insignificant man, obedient to the dictates of the people'.

Shortly before the next general election it was reported that he 'was to be set up for the Whig interest and would act agreeably to the ministry',[4] but he did not stand again. He died 17 Nov. 1756, by his will appointing Southwell one of the trustees of his property.[5]

[1] PCC 334 Glazier. [2] Maclean, *Trigg Minor*, i. 473. [3] Add. 11759, f. 230. [4] Ld. Edgcumbe to Enys, 7 Oct. 1753, autograph coll. R. Inst. Cornw. [5] PCC 87 Paul.

R.R.S.

HOBY, Sir Thomas, 4th Bt. (aft. 1706–44), of Bisham, Berks.

GREAT MARLOW   8 Apr. 1732–1 June 1744

b. aft. 1706, 1st s. of Sir Thomas Hoby, 3rd Bt., by Elizabeth, da. of Sir John Mill, 3rd Bt., sis. of Sir Richard Mill, 5th Bt. (q.v.). *unm. suc.* fa. 25 July 1730.

During the seventeenth century several members of the Hoby family represented Great Marlow, where their estates across the Thames at Bisham gave them an interest. At a by-election in 1732 Sir Thomas Hoby was narrowly returned for the borough against Lord Sydney Beauclerk (q.v.), whose petition to be heard at the bar of the House was rejected through Walpole's influence.[1] Though voting against the Government on the excise bill, 1733, and on the attempt to repeal the Septennial Act, 1734, he was supported by the Buckinghamshire gentry as a government candidate for the 1734 election,[2] thereafter voting with the Administration. He died 1 June 1744.

[1] *HMC Egmont Diary*, i. 257. [2] Cholmondeley (Houghton) mss 68.

R.S.L.

HODGKINSON, Robert (?1721–92), of Overton, Derbys.

WAREHAM   26 Jan. 1748–1754

b. ?1721, 3rd s. of Joseph Banks (*d.*1741, q.v.) of Revesby Abbey by his 1st w.; bro. of William Banks (q.v.). *educ.* Ch. Ch. Oxf. 8 June 1741, aged 19. *m.* 1757, Bridget, da. of Thomas Williams of Edwinsford, Carm., *s.p. suc.* to Overton estate and assumed name and arms of Hodgkinson in 1743.

Sheriff, Carm. 1784–5.

As a younger son Robert Banks was indentured to a Bristol merchant in October 1739. Following the deaths of his eldest brother Joseph in 1740 and his father in 1741, he succeeded his next brother William, as second surviving son under entail, to the Overton estate of his maternal grandfather William Hodgkinson.[1] Though a stranger to Wareham, he was seated there on petition in 1748, presumably as a government supporter, since he and John Pitt (q.v.) replaced two of the Prince's

followers. He did not stand again. Shortly after his wife's death he died by his own hand, 11 Nov. 1792.[2]

[1] *Letters and Pprs. Banks Fam.* (Lincoln Rec. Soc. xlv), pp. xxx, 181. [2] *Gent. Mag.* 1792, p. 1060.

R.S.L.

HODGKINSON, *see also* **BANKS, William**

HOGHTON, Sir Henry, 5th Bt. (c.1679–1768), of Hoghton Tower, nr. Preston, Lancs.

PRESTON	1710–1713, 1715–1722
EAST LOOE	17 Feb. 1724–1727
PRESTON	1727–1741

b. c.1679, 1st surv. s. of Sir Charles Hoghton, 4th Bt., M.P., by Mary, da. of John Skeffington, 2nd Visct. Masserene [I]. *educ.* M. Temple 1695. *m.* (1) Oct. 1710, Mary (*d.* 23 Feb. 1720), da. of Sir William Boughton, 6th Bt., of Lawford, Warws., *s.p.*; (2) 14 Apr. 1721, Elizabeth Lloyd (*d.* 1 Dec. 1736), wid. of Lord James Russell, yr. s. of William, 1st Duke of Bedford; (3) Susanna (with £8,000), da. of Thomas Butterworth of Manchester, *s.p. suc.* fa. 10 June 1710.

Commr. for forfeited estates 1716–25; judge advocate gen. 1734–41.

The Hoghtons, one of the oldest families in Lancashire, were Presbyterians. Hoghton's grandfather, the 3rd Bt., fought for Parliament in the civil war, was returned for the county in 1656, and after the Restoration made Hoghton Tower an asylum for nonconformist ministers. His father, M.P. for Lancashire in 1679–81, 1681 and 1689–90, carried on the tradition. Under Hoghton the house became a regular Presbyterian chapel, with a congregation of 180. He also founded several nonconformist chapels in Preston and the neighbourhood.

On succeeding to the baronetcy, Hoghton successfully contested Preston as a Whig in 1710 but lost his seat in 1713. Returned unopposed in 1715, he steadily supported the Government. As a deputy lieutenant of Lancashire and colonel of militia he took an active part in putting his county 'in a posture of defence' during the rebellion. In the fighting at Preston his town house was occupied alternately by the King's and the rebel forces as a strong point.[1] In 1716 he was chosen by the House of Commons to be one of the commissioners for the sale of estates forfeited for high treason in the rebellion, with a tax-free salary of £1,000 a year.

In 1722 Hoghton gave up his seat at Preston to stand for the county. On the declaration of the poll a local supporter wrote to Lord Sunderland:

> After a vast expense and fatigue Sir Harry Hoghton as the poll now stands has lost his election . . . Your Lordship knows that Sir Harry gave up his interest to Mr. Pulteney [Daniel, q.v.] at Preston where he

might have succeeded himself, so hope your Lordship will not let so true a friend to the Government be turned out of the House.[2]

After unsuccessfully contesting Kingston-upon-Hull at a by-election in January 1724, he was brought in by the Government for East Looe in the following February.

In 1727 Hoghton was returned unopposed for Preston. At the dissolution in 1734 Walpole appointed him judge advocate general. Though his support of the excise bill and other unpopular votes had antagonized Lord Derby, his opponents were unable to find a candidate to stand against him and he was once more allowed a walk-over.[3] In 1741 he was defeated and resigned his post.

During the rebellion of 1745 Hoghton corresponded direct with Pelham about internal security in Lancashire. In reply to a letter from Pelham notifying him of the landing of the Young Pretender and of the military position, he observed that if the friends of the Government in Lancashire had

> nothing to depend on but our own zeal and courage we are in a bad case. We have some friends but few in comparison to those against us . . .
> I can't end this without asking pardon for differing in opinion that the dispositions of the people and the strength of the enemy is far different from what it was in the year 1715. As to our own county, our enemies are as strong as then, and I know of no converts to be depended on.
> You are kind in remembering the part I acted then. I am the same now, only 30 years older, and am ready still to venture my life and fortune for my king and country.

On the approach of the rebel army he wrote to Pelham:

> Our militia have answered as to keeping the peace of the county, but can't be of any service in stopping the progress of the rebels and as our first 14 days have expired and I fear in the general confusion we are in no condition to collect the money for the other 14 days and the men must disperse if they have not their pay.

He and his family took refuge in Yorkshire till the rebellion was over, when his insistence, as a justice of the peace, on enforcing the full rigour of the law against Roman Catholics brought him into collision with the Government. The proceedings instituted by him and his fellow justices were stayed by Order-in-Council, and it was intimated that if there were any further trouble they would 'be left out of the commission of the peace, for the lords of the Privy Council are very angry with them'. 'As I'm reduced to the station of only a country justice', Hoghton commented, 'I shan't meddle, and notwithstanding these discouragements I'll never alter, but do the best service I can, which can't be much upon the footing we are at present'.[4]

Hoghton died on 23 Feb. 1768 at the age of 91, after a life exemplifying his 'family's steadiness at all times to support the honest interest in this disaffected country'.[5]

[1] G. C. Miller, *Hoghton Tower*, 112-14, 123-4, 179-80, 187, 198.
[2] E. Hamilton to Sunderland, n.d., Sunderland (Blenheim) mss.
[3] Hoghton to Walpole, 2 Apr. 1734, Cholmondeley (Houghton) mss.
[4] Miller, op. cit. 116, 119, 120-22. [5] Hoghton to Walpole, 2 Apr. 1734, loc. cit.

E.C.

HOLDEN, Samuel (c.1675-1740), of Roehampton, Surr.

EAST LOOE   20 Feb. 1735-12 June 1740

b. 1675, s. of Joseph Holden (yr. s. of Henry Holden of Aston, Derbys.), merchant of St. Bride's, London by his 2nd w. Priscilla Watt; father-in-law of John Jolliffe (q.v.). *m.* Jane Whitehalgh of the Whitehaugh, Instones, Staffs., 1s. 3da.
Director, Bank of England 1720-7, 1731-40 (with statutory intervals); dep. gov. 1727-9, gov. 1729-31; gov. Russia Co. 1728-40.

Holden belonged to a junior branch of a good Derbyshire family. Losing his father when he was five, he was sent while young to the Russia Company's factory at Riga on the Baltic, where he remained several years. He then returned to London, where he had a counting-house in Winchester St., trading mainly with Russia, but also with Smyrna, Leghorn and Lisbon. Having acquired a large fortune, he became a Bank director and a leading man in the city of London. In 1723 Peter the Great entrusted him with the care of Russian apprentices sent to England for training.[1]

In 1732 Holden was chosen chairman of a committee set up by the Dissenters to consider the question of applying to Parliament for the repeal of the Test and Corporation Acts. According to Hervey, Walpole, to whom such an application would have been politically embarrassing, contrived to pack the committee with 'moneyed men in the City' all 'absolutely dependent' on him, and speaking and acting as he prompted. At any rate, after consultation with ministers, Holden and his committee reported to the general assembly of the Dissenters, and with some difficulty eventually got them to agree, that in present circumstances an application to Parliament was unlikely to succeed and was inadvisable.[2]

In 1732-4 Holden, in his capacity of governor of the Russia Company, advised the board of Trade at all stages of the negotiations for the commercial treaty with Russia of December 1734.[3] In February 1735 he was returned for East Looe by the Administration, with whom he voted in all recorded divisions. In the spring of that year, he and John Bance (q.v.) handled the remittances for the Danish subsidy.[4] In June he was chosen agent for Massachusetts, as an 'eminent friend and benefactor' of that province and as one

> whom God has set in the chair among your brethren the Dissenters, and honoured you before the greatest men at court as well as in the city for wisdom, modesty and integrity.

But he refused the post on the ground that

> the various affairs I am engaged in, besides my private concerns, make it impossible for me to go through that trust in the manner I ought. But I do assure you and the rest of the gentlemen I will do 'em all the services in my power, and I do really think what I may say will have more weight and be better attended to without than under the character of agent.[5]

In 1735, having kept the Dissenters politically quiet during the excise crisis and secured their continued support of the Administration at the general election of 1734, Holden obtained from Walpole a statement that, although the ministry regarded the moment as unpropitious, they would not ask the Dissenters to defer their application any longer, but left it to them to decide whether to make an application at the next session. On this he and the rest of the committee set about organizing an agitation for the repeal of the Acts. But on 14 Jan. 1736, after seeing Walpole again, Holden reported that there was no hope of government backing, and that, without it, there was no prospect of success. In spite of this, and of a further appeal by Holden for reconsideration of the matter, the general assembly decided to proceed with an application to Parliament. On 12 Mar. 1736 he spoke in favour of a motion for the repeal, which was defeated. On the next day he resigned as chairman of the committee:

> Neither my strength nor leisure will allow my continuing in this station, yet I do assure you I shall not only contribute what in me lies for removing the grievances we still lament so far as the circumstances of the times and common prudence shall render it fit to be pushed, but likewise on all occasions use my best endeavours for promoting your interest in particular and the common welfare of all.[6]

In March 1737 he supported Walpole's plan for reducing the national debt against Sir John Barnard's. In the summer of that year he became one of the five trustees of a loan to the Emperor on the copper mines of Silesia.[7] On 30 Mar. 1739 he spoke for a new motion for the repeal of the Test Act.[8] He died 12 June 1740, leaving £60,000 of his fortune to be shared among his wife and two surviving daughters, and the excess to be distributed to charity.[9] Holden chapel at Harvard University was a result of this bequest.[10]

[1] See 'A City man two hundred years ago', *National Rev.* lxxviii. 539-47, by Lord Hylton, a descendant of Holden's; *N. & Q.* clix.

443. [2] N. C. Hunt, *Two Early Political Associations*, 130, 134-7; Hervey, *Mems.* 130. [3] *Bd. Trade Jnl.* 1728-34, pp. 300, 351, 379-80, 395-6; N. C. Hunt 'The Russia Company and the Government 1730-42', *Oxford Slavonic Pprs.* vii. 29-53. [4] *Cal. Treas. Bks. and Pprs.* 1735-8, p. 20. [5] *Jnl. of House of Representatives of Massachusetts* 1735-6, pp. 87, 112; 1740-1, p. 115, *National Rev.* loc. cit. [6] Hunt, pp. 146-52, 201. [7] Add. 23800, f. 327. [8] *HMC Egmont Diary*, iii. 47. [9] PCC Browne 172. [10] *Publs. Col. Soc. Mass.* xv. 125.

E.C.

HOLLAND, Rogers (c.1701–61), of Chippenham, Wilts.

CHIPPENHAM   1727–June 1737

b. c.1701, 1st s. of John Holland of Chippenham by Dorothy, da. (or gd.-da.) of Jonathan Rogers of Chippenham.[1] *educ.* G. Inn. 1720, called 1724. *m.* (1) 1 Mar. 1731, Mary (*d.* 27 Mar. 1733), da. of William Mayo (q.v.) of Hope under Dinmore, Herefs., 1s.; (2) 14 Feb. 1735, Mildred Martin, wid.[2] *suc.* fa. 1723.

C.j. Anglesey, Caern. and Merion. 1737–*d.*

Holland was called to the bar in 1724 'at the request of' Sir Robert Raymond (q.v.), then justice of the King's bench.[3] He was a native of Chippenham, for which he was returned unopposed in 1727 and in 1734 after a hard contest. In Parliament he voted with the Administration in all recorded divisions, except that on the excise bill, which he opposed. After serving on the gaols committee, he became for many years a keen member of the governing board of the Georgia Society.[4] On his appointment as a Welsh judge in 1737 he had to stand for re-election and was easily beaten by Edward Bayntun Rolt (q.v.). He did not stand again but as a member of the corporation he remained a factor in Chippenham politics. In July 1740 the Duke of Newcastle was informed that there were

> hopes of turning out two Tories at Chippenham and bringing in two Whigs. In order to do it Mr. Holland the Welsh judge's attendance [at the corporation] is absolutely necessary. It is near the time that the Welsh judges go their circuit . . . Sir Robert Walpole promised Holland to get him excused but I believe forgot it.[5]

In 1754 Bayntun Rolt, now a government supporter, pressed Newcastle for £100 a year which had been promised to Holland 'for the support and better education of his son' at Cambridge.[6] He died 17 July 1761.

[1] Phillipps, *M.I. of N. Wilts.* 1-2; *Wilts. Arch. Mag.* xliii. 133. [2] *Gent. Mag.* 1735, p. 107; PCC 393 Cheslyn. [3] *Pension Bk. of G. Inn*, ii. 193. [4] *HMC Egmont Diary*, i. 45, 297. [5] John Selwyn to Newcastle, 23 July 1740, Add. 32694, f. 236. [6] Add. 32995, f. 114.

R.S.L.

HOLMES, Henry (*d.* 1738), of Thorley, Yarmouth, I.o.W.

YARMOUTH I.o.W.   2 Apr. 1695–12 Apr. 1717

s. of Thomas Holmes of Kilmallock, co. Limerick.
m. c.1693, Mary, illeg. da. of Sir Robert Holmes,
M.P., of Thorley, 8s. 8da.

Lt. 8 Ft. 1687, capt. 1689, maj. 1692; capt. of
Hurst castle, I.o.W. 1683–1714; lt.-gov. I.o.W.
1710–14.

Of an Irish family, Sir Robert Holmes was
appointed governor of the Isle of Wight by Charles
II in 1667 and was granted lands by the Crown
near Yarmouth, where he built a magnificent
house.[1] He represented Newport 1678–9 and 1685–7
and Yarmouth 1689–90, while his brother, Sir John
Holmes, sat for Newtown 1677–81. On his death in
1692 he left the Isle of Wight property to his
nephew, Henry Holmes, on condition that he
should marry Sir Robert's illegitimate daughter,
Mary.[2] From 1695 Henry Holmes represented
Yarmouth, where he had an electoral interest for
one seat. Re-elected as a Tory in 1715, he voted
against the septennial bill in 1716, but in 1717 the
House of Commons awarded the seat to his opponent. His name was sent to the Pretender in 1721 as
a probable supporter in the event of a rising.[3]
He did not stand again, dying 23 June 1738.

[1] Sir R. Worsley, *Isle of Wight* (1781), p. 140.   [2] PCC 203 Fane.
[3] Stuart mss 65/16.

P.W.

HOLMES, Henry (1703–62).

NEWTOWN I.O.W.   1741–1747
YARMOUTH I.O.W.   1747–11 Aug. 1762

bap. 28 Feb. 1703, 2nd s. of Henry and bro. of
Thomas Holmes (qq.v.). *m.* cos. Anne, da. of Nicholas
Lysaght of Mountnorth, co. Cork by Grace, yst. da.
of Col. Thomas Holmes, *s.p.*

Ensign 28 Ft. 1721, lt. 1723, capt. 1727, maj. 1740,
lt.-col. 1743, col. 1746; col. 31 Ft. 1749–*d.*; maj.-gen.
1756; lt.-gen. 1759; lt.-gov. I.o.W. 1754–*d.*

Henry Holmes was returned for Newtown by his
brother Thomas Holmes (q.v.) in 1741, voting with
the Administration in all recorded divisions. The
second Lord Egmont wrote of him in his electoral
survey, 1749–50:

He . . . is cordially against us and intimate with the
most malignant of their people—but he has a regiment.

He died 11 Aug. 1762.

P.W.

HOLMES, Thomas (1699–1764), of Yarmouth, I.o.W.

NEWTOWN I.O.W.   1727–25 Apr. 1729, 1734–1741
YARMOUTH I.O.W.   1747–21 July 1764

bap. 2 Nov. 1699, 1st s. of Henry, and bro. of Henry
Holmes (qq.v.). *m.* (1) Anne (*bur.* 29 Sept. 1743), da.
of Henry Player of Alverstone, Hants, wid. of Colby
Apsley, 1s. *d.v.p.*; (2) Catherine, da. of John Leigh

of Shorwell, I.o.W., *s.p.* *suc.* fa. 1738. *cr.* Baron
Holmes [I] 11 Sept. 1760.

Gov. I.o.W. Apr. 1763–*d.*

In 1727 Holmes was returned as a Tory for
Newtown, where his family shared the electoral
influence with the Worsleys (qq.v.). He voted
against the Administration on the civil list on 23 Apr.
1729 but on 25 Apr. the House of Commons
awarded the seat to his opponent. Re-elected
unopposed in 1734, he voted against the Administration on the Spanish convention in 1739 and
was absent from the division on the place bill in
1740. He did not stand in 1741, when he made an
agreement with Sir Robert Walpole to support the
Government on condition he should become the
Government's manager for the three Isle of Wight
boroughs. After Walpole's fall he renewed the
agreement with Pelham.[1] Returned with his
brother, Henry, for Yarmouth in 1747, he was
classed as a government supporter. He died in 1764
(buried 21 July).

[1] Add. 38333, f. 95.

P.W.

HOLTE, Sir Lister, 5th Bt. (1720–70), of Aston, Warws.

LICHFIELD   1741–1747

b. 26 Apr. 1720, 1st s. of Sir Clobery Holte, 4th Bt., by
Barbara, da. and h. of Thomas Lister of Whitfield,
Northants. *educ.* Hartlebury sch. Salop; Magdalen,
Oxf. 1737. *m.* (1) 5 Oct. 1739 (with £12,000 and
jointure of £1,000 p.a.), Lady Anne Legge (*d.* June
1740), da. of William Legge, M.P., 1st Earl of
Dartmouth, *s.p.*; (2) 18 July 1742 (with £10,000),
Mary (*d.* 16 July 1752), da. of Sir John Harpur, 4th
Bt., sis. of Sir Henry Harpur (q.v.) of Calke, Derbys.,
s.p.; (3) 5 July 1755 (with £2,000), Sarah, da. of
Samuel Newton of King's Bromley, Staffs., *s.p.*
suc. fa. 25 July 1729.

Sheriff, Cheshire 1767.

Descended from an ancient and royalist Warwickshire family, Holte inherited an estate of 'not less
than £4,000 per annum'. On coming of age he stood
as a Tory for Lichfield, where he had cultivated an
interest by purchasing the market tolls for £400 for
the benefit of the city and contributing £100 to a
new market house.[1] Returned unopposed, he consistently voted against the Government. In 1747 he
was defeated, subsequently leading a Birmingham
contingent to the Tory demonstration at Lichfield
races.[2] He never stood again, dying 8 Apr. 1770.

[1] A. Davidson, *Holtes of Aston*, 42–43.   [2] *Staffs. Parl Hist.* (Wm.
Salt Arch. Soc.), ii (2), p. 253.

E.C.

HOME, see HUME

HONYWOOD, Robert (*d.* 1735), of Markshall, Essex.

ESSEX 18 May 1716–1727

b. bef. 1676.[1] s. of Charles Ludovic Honywood of Charing, Kent by Mary, da. of Mr. Clement of Portsmouth. *m.* Mary, da. and eventually h. of Sir Richard Sandford, 2nd Bt., of Howgill Castle, Westmld., 5s. 1da. *suc.* his distant cos. John Lamotte Honywood (M.P. Essex 1679–81, 1693) to Markshall and other Essex estates 1693.

Descended from Sir Robert Honywood of Charing, who purchased Markshall in 1605, Honywood and his younger brother Philip, the general, who was deprived of his regiment in 1710 for drinking 'damnation and confusion' to the Harley ministry,[2] were strong Whigs. Defeated at the general election of 1715, he was unsuccessful at a by-election in May 1715 but was seated on petition a year later. He voted against the Government on Lord Cadogan (q.v.) in 1717, with them on the repeal of the Occasional Conformity and Schism Acts but against them on the peerage bill in 1719. He did not stand in 1727, dying in January 1735.

[1] His yr. bro. Philip, who was first commissioned in 1694, must have been born c.1677. [2] Dalton, *English Army Lists*, iv. 30.

E.C.

HOOPER, Edward (?1701–95), of Worthy Park, Hants.

CHRISTCHURCH 1734–Dec. 1748

b. ?1701, 1st s. of Edward Hooper of Heron Court, Christchurch, Hants by Lady Dorothy Ashley Cooper, da. of Anthony Ashley Cooper, 2nd Earl of Shaftesbury. *educ.* Trinity, Oxf. 5 May 1720, aged 18; M. Temple 1717, called 1724. *unm. suc.* fa. 1759.

Paymaster of pensions 13 July 1742–22 Dec. 1744; commr. of customs 1748.

The Hoopers acquired the lease of Heron Court, near Christchurch, in 1661, and bought the fee simple in 1700.[1] After standing unsuccessfully for Christchurch in 1727, Edward Hooper was returned for it as a Whig in 1734. In Parliament he attached himself to Pulteney, speaking on 16 Nov. 1739 in support of Pulteney's bill to encourage seamen by giving up to them the Government's share in the prize money. Through his cousin, the 4th Earl of Shaftesbury, a common councillor of the Georgia Society, he became associated with the affairs of that colony, seconding a motion for an inquiry into its advantages on 28 Jan. 1740, presenting the Society's petition for further support on 21 Jan. 1741, and on the 28th moving that £10,000 might be given for this purpose.[2] After Walpole's fall Hooper was elected to the secret committee set up by the House of Commons in

April 1742 to inquire into the last ten years of Walpole's Administration; and in July he was rewarded by Pulteney, now Lord Bath, with a place of £900 a year, according to Horace Walpole, 'for one day saying his Lordship had spoke with the tongue not of a man but an angel'.[3] Losing his place when most of the Bath-Granville squadron were turned out on Granville's fall in 1744, he was classed among Bath's followers in 1746, but in the next Parliament he was put down as a government supporter. In 1748 he was appointed a commissioner of customs to vacate his seat for Sir Thomas Robinson (q.v.). Although no longer in Parliament, he continued active in Christchurch elections, where from 1754 he controlled both seats, returning his cousin James Harris, later 1st Earl of Malmesbury, for one, and generally placing the other at the disposal of the Government.[4] He died 6 Sept. 1795, leaving all his property to Lord Malmesbury.

[1] *VCH Hants*, v. 97. [2] *HMC Egmont Diary*, iii. 104, 181, 184. [3] *Corresp. H. Walpole* (Yale ed.), xvii. 384, n. 19. [4] Add. 32873, f. 486; *Malmesbury Letters*, i. 83.

P.W.

HOPE, John (c.1684–1766), of Culdraines.

KINROSS-SHIRE 1727–1734, 1741–1747

b. c.1684, 3rd s. of Sir Thomas Hope, 4th Bt., of Craighall, Fife by Anne, da. and h. of Sir William Bruce, 1st Bt., of Kinross. *m.* (1) Charlotte, da. of Sir Charles Halkett, 1st Bt., sis. of Sir Peter Halkett, 2nd Bt. (q.v.), of Pitfirrane, *s.p.*; (2) 1706, Marianne, da. of Rev. William Denune of Pencaitland, East Lothian, 1da. *suc.* e. bro. as 7th Bt. 5 Apr. 1729, and to his mother's Kinross estates, taking add. name of Bruce.

Lt. and capt. 2 tp. Horse Gren. Gds. 1708; capt. and lt.-col. 3 Ft. Gds. 1708; lt.-col. 26 Ft. 1716–18; col. of a regt. of Ft. 1743–8; maj.-gen. 1754; lt.-gen. 1758; gov. Bermuda 1721–7; hereditary sheriff of Kinross-shire by 1715–47.

A younger son, Hope entered the army but sold his lieutenant-colonelcy in 1718. Next year, after unsuccessfully applying to Craggs for employment,[1] he went to Sweden with a recommendation from his kinsman, Lord Polwarth, to the British ambassador, Lord Carteret, who promised to 'do all the service I can to Colonel Hope, who deserves everyone's esteem'.[2] When Carteret became secretary of state in 1721, Hope was made governor of Bermuda, which enabled him to pay off his debts.[3] Returned for Kinross-shire in 1727, he voted with the Administration on the civil list arrears in 1729. Following Carteret into opposition in 1730, he spoke, 21 Feb. 1733, against two motions for raising the duty on rum and molasses imported into the colonies,[4] and, 13 Feb. 1734, in favour of a motion to prevent the dismissal of any officer not over the rank of colonel, except by court martial. Again returned for his county, which was represented only in alternate Parliaments, in 1741, he voted with the Opposition on the chairman of the elections committee, but supported the Government after his patron, Carteret, joined the ministry in 1742, and obtained a regiment in 1743. On 10 Apr. 1745 he seconded a motion in favour of Admiral Mathews.[5] He did not stand again, dying 5 June 1766.

[1] Hope to Craggs, 17 Mar. 1719, Stowe 247, f. 110. [2] *HMC Polwarth*, ii. 422. [3] *CSP Col.* 1722-3, p. 249. [4] Stuart mss 160/164A. [5] Yorke's parl. jnl. *Parl. Hist.* xiii. 1268.

P.W.

HOPE, Thomas, of Maidstone, Kent.

MAIDSTONE 1727-1734

m. Sept. 1734, Mrs. Saunderson, wid., of Hammersmith, Mdx.

Nothing is known of Thomas Hope's origins except that he was a local man. He is described in 1727 by Lady Hervey, in a list of imaginary portraits, as 'A gentleman; three quarters',[1] and in 1735 as 'a butcher, who at his election gave the butchers who voted for him silver handles to their steels'.[2] Returned for Maidstone in 1727 with government support, he voted consistently with the Administration, but was defeated in 1734, after which he did not stand again. In October 1734, when he was helping to oppose the Duchess of Marlborough's interest at New Woodstock, he is called 'a creature of Sir Robert Walpole's and is said to have a very great interest in him (as appears from his having helped five or six persons to places in the Government by Sir Robert's means)'.[3]

[1] *Letters of Lady Suffolk*, i. 345. [2] *Arch. Cant.* xliii. 274. [3] Thos. Major to Duchess of Marlborough, 20 Oct. 1734, Blenheim mss.

A.N.N.

HOPE BRUCE, see HOPE, John

HOPE WEIR, Hon. Charles (1710-91) of Craigiehall, Linlithgow, and Blackwood, Lanark.

LINLITHGOWSHIRE 13 May 1743-1768

b. 8 May 1710, 2nd surv. s. of Charles Hope, M.P. [S], 1st Earl of Hopetoun [S], by Lady Henrietta Johnstone, da. of William, 1st Mq. of Annandale [S]. *educ.* Glasgow Univ. 1724; Leyden 1728; Grand Tour. *m.* (1) 26 July 1733, Catherine (*d.* 5 Dec. 1743), da. and h. of Sir William Weir, 2nd Bt., of Blackwood, Lanarks, 6s. 2da.; (2) 20 Mar. 1746, Anne Vane (div. May 1757), da. of Hon. Henry Vane (q.v.), 2s.; (3) 2 Apr. 1766, Helen, da. of George Dunbar of Leuchold, Linlithgow, 1s. 3da. *suc.* uncle 2nd Mq. of Annandale to Craigiehall estate 1730; acquired Blackwood estate on marriage and assumed add. name of Weir.

Gov. of Blackness castle 1744-*d.*; muster-master

gen. [S] 1744-59; trustee for fisheries and manufactures 1755-84; commr. for forfeited estates 1755; chamberlain of Ettrick forest 1768-*d.*

Just before the 1734 election Charles Hope Weir, the son of a representative peer who controlled Linlithgowshire, was granted a pension of £400 p.a., which he relinquished shortly before his return in 1743.[1] Though he then defeated a placeman seeking re-election, he supported the Government, voting for the Hanoverians in 1744 and 1746, when he was classed as an Old Whig. On the formation of the Broad-bottom Administration in December 1744 he received two lucrative appointments. After his elopement with Anne Vane in 1746, he asked Newcastle, as a family friend, to intercede with her father, Henry Vane (q.v.).[2] Re-elected without opposition in 1747, he was consulted by Pelham on a Lanarkshire by-election in 1750.[3] Unlike most of his compatriots, he voted with the ministry on the case of General Philip Anstruther (q.v.).[4] In 1753 he applied to Newcastle to be appointed to the board of manufacturers,[5] which he was two years later. Again returned unopposed in 1754, he died 30 Dec. 1791.

[1] *HMC Polwarth*, v. 112; *Cal. Treas. Bks. and Pprs.* 1742-5, p. 360. [2] Hope Weir to Newcastle, 25 Mar. 1746, Add. 32706, f. 334. [3] Omond, *Arniston Mems.* 146. [4] Walpole, *Mems. Geo. II*, i. 60. [5] Hope Weir to Newcastle, 18 Apr. 1753, Add. 32731, f. 383.

E.H.-G.

HOPKINS, Edward (?1675-1736), of Coventry.

COVENTRY 1701-1702, 25 Feb. 1707-1710
EYE 1713-1727

b. ?1675, s. of Richard Hopkins, M.P., of Coventry by Mary, da. of Alderman Johnson. *educ.* Eton; Trinity, Oxf. 2 July 1692, aged 17; Grand Tour (Flanders, France, Italy) 1696-1700. *m.* 1 Mar. 1725, Anna Maria, da. and coh. of Dr. Hugh Chamberlayne[1] of Alderton Manor and Hinton Hall, Suff., 3s. 2da. *suc.* fa. 1707.
M.P. [I] 1721-7.
Commr. of revenue [I] 1716-22; sec. to ld. lt. [I] 1722-4; master of the revels [I] 1722-*d.*; P.C. [I] 1722.

Hopkins belonged to a prominent Coventry family who represented the city in most Parliaments from 1660 to 1710, when he transferred to Lord Cornwallis's borough of Eye. A staunch Whig, connected with Lord Sunderland through his uncle, Thomas Hopkins, M.P. Coventry 1701, who had been Sunderland's secretary,[2] he voted with the Government in all recorded divisions after George I's accession. Rewarded with an Irish place, he exchanged it to become secretary to the Duke of Grafton as lord lieutenant, from whom he obtained the post of master of the revels, or censor of plays, in Ireland at £300 p.a.[3] On 26 Apr. 1723 he supported the bill for a special tax on Roman Catholics, but declared that the second reading should be postponed to give the House more time to consider it, in which Walpole acquiesced.[4] He did not stand in 1727, dying 17 Jan. 1736.

[1] Nichols, *Atterbury Corresp.* v. 48. [2] M. D. Harris, 'Mems. of Edward Hopkins', *EHR*, xxxiv. 491–504. [3] Chas. Maddox to Edw. Hopkins, 3 Oct. 1722, Hopkins mss. [4] *Knatchbull Diary*.

R.R.S.

HOPKINS, John (c.1663–1732), of Broad St., London.

ST. IVES   1710–1715
ILCHESTER   1715–1722

b. c.1663. *unm.*

'Vulture Hopkins', so called from his rapacity, was a London merchant, who made a great fortune by speculation, especially in the South Sea bubble. Returned as a Whig for a venal borough in 1715, he supported the Government, except on the peerage bill, which he voted against. His only recorded speech was made on 20 Apr. 1717, in support of the proposals voluntarily submitted by the Bank of England and the South Sea Company for reducing the interest payable on loans made to the Government, and against a proposal that the interest on the debt should be compulsorily reduced by Act of Parliament, as a breach of parliamentary faith, giving a dangerous blow to public credit. Defeated at Great Bedwyn in 1722, he died 25 Apr. 1732, aged 69, worth £300,000. Under his will, the bulk of his fortune, consisting of estates in London, Middlesex, Surrey, Kent, Wiltshire, Northamptonshire etc., passed to the male issue, according to priority of birth, of the four daughters of a distant kinsman, whose only son, on whom the estates had been entailed, had recently died.[1] Pope refers to this will in his epistle to Bathurst on the use of riches in the line asking:

What can they give? to dying Hopkins heirs?

[1] *Pol. State*, xliii. 419; *Gent. Mag.* 1732, p. 832.

S.R.M.

HOPKINS, Sir Richard (d. 1736), of St. Botolph's, Bishopsgate, London.

LONDON   11 Dec. 1724–1727

b. aft. 1676, s. of Richard Hopkins of St. Botolph's by Rose, da. of George Sherard of Bushby, Leics.[1] *m.* Ann, da. of William Lethieullier, London merchant, *s.p.* Kntd. 26 July 1722.

Director, R. Exchange Assurance 1720, S. Sea Co. 1721–*d.*; sub-gov. S. Sea. Co. 1733–*d.*; gov. London Assurance; Cutlers' Co., transferred to Fishmongers' 1730, prime warden, Fishmongers' Co. 1730–2; sheriff, London 1723–4, alderman 1724.

Hopkins, a Turkey merchant,[2] stood as a Whig in the fiercely contested sheriffs' election of 1723.[3] Returned for London at a by-election in 1724, he was unsuccessful in 1727. He died 2 Jan. 1736, the senior alderman below the chair, said to be worth £100,000.[4]

[1] Chester *London Marriage Licences*; Nichols, *Illus. of Lit. Hist.* i. 411–12; PCC 34 Derby. [2] *Pol. State*, xxviii. 526–7. [3] A. J. Henderson, *London and the National Government*, 84–93. [4] *Hist. Reg.* 1736, chron. p. 13.

E.C.

HOPTON, Edward Cope (1708–54), of Canon Frome, nr. Hereford.

HEREFORD   1741–1747

bap. 9 Feb. 1708, o.s. of Richard Hopton (q.v.). *educ.* Ch. Ch. Oxf. 1725. *m.* 29 Feb. 1733, Mary, da. and h. of Timothy Briggenshaw of St. John's Bredwardine, Herefs., 1s. 1da.
High steward, Worcester 1751.

Returned as a Tory for Hereford in 1741, Hopton voted consistently against the Government. On the opposition motion of 21 Jan. 1742 to set up a secret committee to inquire into the war, he was 'carried in with crutches'.[1] He did not stand again, dying 24 Apr. 1754.

[1] Sir Robt. Wilmot to Devonshire, 23 Jan. 1742, Devonshire mss.

A.N.N.

HOPTON, Richard (1685–1764), of Canon Frome, nr. Hereford.

HEREFORDSHIRE   1715–1722

b. 1685, s. of Edward Hopton of Canon Frome, Herefs. by his 1st w. Hannah, da. of Robert Clarkson, draper and alderman of London. *educ.* Ch. Ch. Oxf. 11 Oct. 1700, aged 15; I. Temple 1704. *m.* 29 Dec. 1705, Elizabeth, da. of Thomas Geers, M.P., of Bridge Sellers, Herefs., wid. of William Gregory of How Caple, Herefs., 8s. 6da. *suc.* fa. 1692.

Richard Hopton came of an old Herefordshire family. Immediately on Queen Anne's death he notified Robert Harley, Earl of Oxford, that 'upon the . . . assurances my Lord Scudamore (q.v.) has given me of his desisting I design to offer my service to the county.'[1] Returned unopposed as a Tory, he spoke against the repeal of the Occasional Conformity and Schism Acts in 1719, voting against the Government except on the peerage bill, when he was absent. He did not stand again, but in 1722 took a leading part in the agitation against the attempt to compromise the Hereford borough election. He died 21 Feb. 1764.

[1] 21 Aug. 1714, Portland mss.

A.N.N.

HORNER, Thomas (1688–1741), of Mells, Som. and Melbury, Dorset.

SOMERSET   1713–1715
WELLS   1715–30 May 1716, 27 June 1716–
                                  12 Apr. 1717
SOMERSET   1727–1741

bap. 1688, 1st s. of George Horner, M.P., by Elizabeth, da. and coh. of Col. Robert Fortescue of Filleigh, Devon, *educ.* Trinity, Oxf. 14 May 1705, aged 17. *m.* 1713, Susanna, da. of Thomas Strangways, sis. and coh. of Thomas Strangways jun. of Melbury, Dorset, 2s. *d.v.p.* 1da. *suc.* fa. 1708; assumed add. name of Strangways on his w.'s succeeding to Melbury 1726. Sheriff, Som. 1711–12.

A Somerset squire, whose family had acquired Mells at the dissolution of the monasteries, Horner sat as a Tory for his county with Sir William Wyndham in Anne's last Parliament. In 1715 he successfully contested Wells, afterwards narrowly escaping arrest on the discovery of Wyndham's plans for a western rising.[1] Retaining his seat just long enough to vote against the septennial bill before being unseated on petition, he was re-elected, only to meet the same fate. He did not stand for Wells again, but from 1727 represented the county once more, voting against the Government.

In 1729 Horner's wife, who had already inherited Melbury as the co-heir of her brother, succeeded on the death of her sister, the Duchess of Hamilton, to the rest of the Strangways estates. Seven years later she arranged a clandestine marriage between their only surviving child, a 13 year-old daughter, and Stephen Fox (q.v.), the brother of her paramour, Henry Fox (q.v.), though her husband strongly objected to the match on the ground not only of the age of the bride but of the politics of the bridegroom. She attempted to appease him by representing that the marriage had taken place without her knowledge, also procuring a written undertaking from Fox not to interfere in county politics.[2] Horner seems never to have forgiven his daughter, to whom he refers in his will only as 'the person who shall under my marriage settlement be entitled to receive the sum of seven thousand and five hundred pounds, the provision made for a daughter of the said marriage settlement'. On his death 19 Nov. 1741, without surviving male issue, Mells passed to his younger brother, the Strangways estates devolving ultimately on his daughter.

[1] Harbin, *Som. M.P.s*, 189.   [2] Ilchester, *Lord Holland*, i. 31–32, 44–46.

S.R.M.

HORSEMONDEN TURNER, William (1678–1753), of Maidstone and Stede Hill, in Harrietsham, Kent.

MAIDSTONE   1734–1741, 1747–14 Apr. 1753

b. 23 Apr. 1678, o.s. of Anthony Horsemonden of Maidstone, sometime clerk to the Skinners Co., by his 2nd w. Jane, da. of Sir William Turner of Richmond, Surr. *m.* (1) 25 May 1725,[1] Elizabeth (*d.* 27 Oct. 1730), da. of John Kenward of Yalding, Kent, wid. of Thomas Bliss, M.P., of Maidstone, and bef. that of Ambrose Ward of Yalding, *s.p.*; (2) 19 Dec. 1745, Elizabeth, da. of Richard Read of Lenham and Gravesend, Kent, *s.p.* *suc.* fa. aft. 1689 and mat. uncle John Turner 1721, when he took add. name of Turner.

A Maidstone attorney, Turner, after succeeding his uncle and marrying the 76 year-old widow of a rich brewer, formerly Member for the borough, acquired the estate of Stede Hill from the Stedes in 1726.[2] He became the leader of the Whigs in Maidstone, where he was returned as a government supporter in 1734. Defeated in 1741, he took advantage of the dissolution of the Maidstone corporation[3] to secure from the lord chancellor a new charter favourable to the popular party; returned with it to Maidstone immediately before the general election of 1747; and was elected, bringing in with him Robert Fairfax. Next day he wrote to Hardwicke:[4]

> The concern which your Lordship was so good as to express for the issue of an election, obliges me . . . to acknowledge the share you have had in it by despatching and facilitating of everything that might conduce so lucky an event, as I am in hopes will fully answer the expectations of all our friends, having been so fortunate to bring in with me Mr. Fairfax . . . whose sentiments are perfectly the same with our own, and as we have also a corporation (through your Lordship's assistance) entirely founded upon the same principles.

According to a note by Frederick, Prince of Wales, in the 2nd Lord Egmont's electoral survey c.1749–50, Turner was governed by John Scrope (q.v.), of the Treasury. Although then dead, he may have been the Mr. Turner who in 1754 was included in a list of secret service pensions at £200 a year.[5] He died 14 Apr. 1753.

[1] Russell, *Maidstone*, 205 n.   [2] R. H. Goodsall, *Stede Hill*, 144–53.   [3] See MAIDSTONE.   [4] 28 June 1747, Add. 35692, f. 309.   [5] Add. 33038, f. 415.

A.N.N.

HOSKYNS, Sir Hungerford, 4th Bt. (c.1677–1767), of Harewood, Herefs.

HEREFORDSHIRE   6 Mar. 1717–1722

b. c.1677, 2nd s. of Sir John Hoskyns, 2nd Bt., M.P., of Harewood, Herefs. by Jane, da. of Sir Gabriel Lowe of Newark, Glos. *educ.* M. Temple 1701.

m. 1716, Mary, da. of Theophilus Leigh of Adlestrop, Glos., niece of James Brydges, 1st Duke of Chandos, 2s. 2da. *suc.* bro. as 4th Bt. 17 Dec. 1711.

Cornet 7 Drag. Gds. 1705, lt. 1708; lt. 3 Hussars 1709.

The younger son of a Herefordshire baronet, M.P. for the county 1685–7, Hoskyns entered the army during the war of the Spanish succession, but resigned on succeeding to the title and estates. Returned without opposition for the county at a by-election in 1717, he supported the Administration, voting for the repeal of the Occasional Conformity and Schism Acts and for the peerage bill. He was defeated in 1722, when his Tory opponents made great play with his vote against the Occasional Conformity Act. It was also alleged that he, though the representative of a cider county, had moved for a duty on cider, a story which the Duke of Chandos, whose niece he had married, described as 'so impossible and ridiculous it requires no answer.' He also antagonized Lord Oxford by canvassing his tenants and even his butler without permission. After his defeat he applied for financial assistance to Chandos, who replied:

I am truly sorry for your ill-success in the county election, I can hardly call it a disappointment, it having been no other than what by the accounts I have for some time received I did expect to be . . . It is not in my power to assist you in what you desire, my own affairs are really so embarrassed by my losses in the South Sea and African companies that notwithstanding the great retrenchments I have made in my way of living I find I must come to a much greater still.

Nor was Chandos in favour of an election petition:

As to the ground you say there is of petitioning the Parliament all I can say to it is, that if you can clearly disprove his qualification it will certainly vacate his election but as it is an invidious charge, you must be sure you can make it good before you bring it to a trial, also the attempting it will do you still more prejudice I doubt in the county.[1]

Hoskyns never stood again, dying at the age of 90, 21 Dec. 1767.

[1] Chandos to Wodehouse, 14 Apr. 1722, to Hoskyns, 8 Mar., 3 Apr., 3 May 1722, Chandos letter bks.

A.N.N.

HOSTE, James (1705–44), of Sandringham, Norf.

BRAMBER   4 Apr. 1728–1734

bap. 15 Oct. 1705, s. of James Hoste by his 2nd w. Anne Bresley. *educ.* Corpus Christi, Camb. 1722. *m.* Susan, da. of Anthony Hammond of South Wootton, Norf., uncle of James Hammond (q.v.), 1da.

Hoste was descended from Jacques Hooste of Middleburgh, Zealand, who fled to England in 1569; his grandfather, a wealthy merchant, bought

the estate of Sandringham; and his father's first wife, Elizabeth Walpole, was Sir Robert Walpole's aunt. Put up for Bramber on the Gough interest in 1727, he obtained 19 votes against 11 for John Gumley (q.v.), William Pulteney's brother-in-law, who however was awarded the seat by the returning officer, nine of Hoste's votes being disallowed.[1] When his petition came before the Commons, Pulteney suggested that the reason why it

was pushed in this manner was because the sitting Member was his relation and Mr. Hoste, the petitioner, a relation of another person's, viz. Sir R. Walpole, upon which Sir George Oxenden [q.v.] said that gentleman was always flinging out reflections and this was one on the whole House, and a scandal as if every Member acted under an attachment to one man or the other, and that whenever he did reflect so he neither could nor would not sit still. Mr. Pulteney replied that what he spoke in the House he always thought right and would justify it either in or out of the House; and then the debate went on, but some time after . . . Mr. Pelham took notice that by something he had heard behind he apprehended that matter was not yet at an end and said it was usual for the gentlemen to give their words on the like occasion; so Sir George Oxenden said he had nothing to say, for what fell on justifying in the House or out did not fall from him, and then Pulteney explained himself in a little softer manner and both said they meant nothing farther in it and so it ended.[2]

Seated by the Commons, Hoste voted with the Government in every recorded division. He did not stand again, dying 20 Aug. 1744.

[1] 'State of . . . Bramber', Lowndes mss, W. Sussex RO. [2] *Knatchbull Diary*, 12 Mar. 1728.

R.R.S.

HOTHAM, Sir Charles, 4th Bt. (1663–1723), of Scorborough, nr. Beverley, Yorks.

SCARBOROUGH   15 Apr. 1695–1702
BEVERLEY   1702–8 Jan. 1723

b. 1663, o.s. of Rev. Charles Hotham, rector of Wigan, by Elizabeth, da. of Stephen Thompson of Hambleton, Yorks. *educ.* Sedbergh; St. John's, Camb. 1681. *m.* (1) 9 Sept. 1690, Bridget (*d.* 4 Aug. 1707), da. of William Gee of Bishop's Burton, Yorks., 2s. 3da.; (2) Lady Mildred, da. of James Cecil, M.P., 3rd Earl of Salisbury, wid. of Sir Uvedale Corbet, 3rd Bt., of Longnor, Salop, and sis. of Sir Richard Corbet, 4th Bt. (q.v.), *s.p.s. suc.* fa. 1672; and 1st cos. as 4th Bt. Aug. 1691.

Raised infantry corps in Yorks. and appointed col. 1705; brig.-gen. 1710; half-pay 1713; raised new regt. and appointed col. 1715; col. 16 Drag. Gds. 1717–18, 36 Ft. 1719; trans. 8 Ft. 1720, R. Drag. Gds. 1721–*d.*

The Hothams were an ancient Yorkshire family, seated since the beginning of the 13th century at Scorborough, near Beverley, which they represented in most Parliaments in the 17th century. Returned first for Scarborough and then for the family seat at Beverley, Hotham served in Spain during the war of the Spanish succession and in the north of England during the rebellion of 1715.[1] A staunch Whig, he voted with the Government in all recorded divisions after George I's accession. On 4 Dec. 1717 he supported a vote of censure on Shippen (q.v.) for reflecting on the King's speech, and on 22 Jan. 1718 spoke against an opposition motion for the retention of half-pay officers. He seconded the peerage bill on 7 Dec. 1719, and on 10 June 1721 spoke in favour of allowing John Aislabie (q.v.) to retain his estate as it was at the end of 1719. He died 8 Jan. 1723, aged 60.

[1] A. M. W. Stirling, *The Hothams*, i. 120-41.

R.R.S.

HOTHAM, Sir Charles, 5th Bt. (1693-1738), of Scorborough, Yorks.

BEVERLEY 31 Jan. 1723-1727, 8 Mar. 1729-15 Jan. 1738

b. 25 Apr. 1693, 1st s. of Sir Charles Hotham, 4th Bt., (q.v.). *m.* Apr. 1724, Lady Gertrude Stanhope, da. of Philip, 3rd Earl of Chesterfield, sis. of Hon. Charles, John, Philip Dormer, and Sir William Stanhope (qq.v.), 1 surv. s. 3da. *suc.* fa. 8 Jan. 1723.
Capt. in his fa.'s regt. 1715; lt.-col. 7 Drag. Gds. 1720; groom of the bedchamber to George II 1727-*d.*; col. 18 Ft. 1732-5, 1st tp. Horse Gren. Gds. 1735-*d.*

As a youth Hotham visited Hanover, where he made friends with the electoral prince, afterwards George II. Succeeding his father to the family seat at Beverley, he voted with the Administration in every recorded division. He was made a groom of the bedchamber on the accession of George II, who sent him to Berlin in 1730 on a confidential mission to arrange a double marriage between the heirs apparent and the Princesses Royal of England and Prussia.[1] The mission was unsuccessful but Hotham acquitted himself to the satisfaction of George II, who rewarded him with a regiment in 1732 and a better one in 1735. He died prematurely, 15 Jan. 1738.

[1] A. M. W. Stirling, *The Hothams*, i. 142-238.

R.R.S.

HOUBLON, Jacob (1710-70), of Hallingbury, Essex.

COLCHESTER 20 Mar. 1735-1741
HERTFORDSHIRE 1741-1747, 1761-1768

b. 31 July 1710, o. surv. s. of Charles Houblon, Portugal merchant, of Bubbingworth Hall, Essex by Mary, da. and h. of Daniel Bate, London merchant, of Barton Court, Abingdon, Berks. *educ.* Corpus Christi, Camb. 1725; migr. to Emmanuel 1730. *m.* 31 July 1735, Mary, da. of Sir John Hynde Cotton, 3rd Bt. (q.v.), of Madingley, Cambs., 3s. 2da. *suc.*

fa. 1711; and his fa.'s 1st cos. Sir Richard Houblon 1724.
Sheriff, Herts. 1757-8.

Coming over from Flanders as Protestant refugees in the sixteenth century, the Houblons in the seventeenth attained great eminence in the city of London. Three Houblon brothers were founding directors of the Bank of England, one of whom was its first governor, and another M.P. for London 1698-1700. The governor's son, Sir Richard Houblon, himself a director of the Bank, left his real and personal property in trust to his cousin, Jacob Houblon, then a minor, in tail male, ordering that the personal estate should be laid out in the purchase of further lands to be similarly entailed. The estate of Hallingbury on the confines of Essex and Hertfordshire, was bought in 1729 by the trustees.[1]

Jacob Houblon completely severed his family's Whig and city of London ties to become a Tory squire. Returned for Colchester and then for Hertfordshire as a Tory, he joined the Cocoa Tree Club, becoming connected with the extreme Tories by his marriage to Sir John Hynde Cotton's daughter. During his first 12 years in Parliament he regularly voted against the Government, except on the motion for Walpole's removal in 1741, when he was among the Tories who walked out. His father-in-law and Sir Robert Abdy (q.v.), another extreme Tory, stood sponsors for his eldest son. The baptism was celebrated 'with the greatest magnificence imaginable'.

> Most of the gentlemen within 15 or 20 miles of Mr. Houblon's seat in Essex were present, and most of the common people within 4 or 5 miles were made so welcome that they lay in heaps round his house dead drunk . . . There were 20 knights and baronets and 150 gentlemen.[2]

He did not stand in 1747. Re-elected in 1761, he died 15 Feb. 1770.

[1] Lady A. Archer Houblon, *Houblon Fam.* ii. 1-58. [2] *Daily Gazetteer*, 14 Sept. 1736.

E.C.

HOWARD, Hon. Charles (c.1696-1765).

CARLISLE 1727-1761

b. c.1696, 2nd s. of Charles Howard, M.P., 3rd Earl of Carlisle, by Lady Anne Capell, da. of Arthur, 1st Earl of Essex; bro. of Henry, Lord Morpeth (q.v.). *unm.* K.B. 2 May 1749.
Ensign 2 Ft. Gds. 1715, capt. 1717, capt. and lt.-col. 1719; col. and a.-d.-c. to George II 1734; col. 19 Ft. 1 Nov. 1738-48;[1] brig.-gen. 1742; maj.-gen. 1743; commanded a brigade at Dettingen and Fontenoy, where he was wounded four times; lt.-gen. 1747; col. 3 Drag. Gds. 1748-*d.*; gen. 1765.
Lt. gov. Carlisle 1725-49, gov. 1749-52; gov. Inverness and Fort Augustus 1752-*d.*

Howard was returned on his family's interest. Unlike his elder brother, Lord Morpeth, he invariably supported the Administration. When instructed by his constituents to oppose the excise bill before its details had been made known, he replied that 'as I was ignorant what the proposal would be, I believed they, at a greater distance, could not be much less so', and asked them if they wished him to vote against it whatever he thought of it. He was authorized to vote as he thought fit. He is not reported as speaking but sent his father long reports of parliamentary proceedings. In 1734, after repeated applications, he was offered the choice between becoming a groom of the bedchamber and being appointed a.-d.-c. to the King with the rank of colonel, choosing the latter, because 'though the aide-de-camp was but ten shillings a day, yet for the sake of getting the rank of colonel I preferred it to the other, which was much a better income'.[2]

During the rebellion of 1745, after Carlisle had been recaptured from the rebels, Howard was put in command of the city. As commandant he did not show towards his constituents 'that complaisance' which his local political supporters regarded as 'necessary, or at least convenient for his interest'. When told 'that it was not only his own personal interest that would be lost, but that of the family also for ever, he replied he would not do dirty work upon any consideration'. His last act as commandant of Carlisle was to commit two of its aldermen to gaol on a charge of having carried the keys of the city to the Young Pretender. However, though thought by his friends to have 'rather hurt, than augmented, his interest',[3] he retained his seat unopposed till he retired in 1761.

He died 26 Aug. 1765.

[1] From him the regt. received the title of the 'Green Howards'. [2] *HMC Carlisle*, 102–31, 138. [3] G. G. Mounsey, *Carlisle in 1745*, 178, 196, 201, 205.

R.R.S.

HOWARD, Charles, Visct. Morpeth (1719–1741).

YORKSHIRE   6 May–9 Aug. 1741

bap. 22 May 1719, 1st s. of Henry Howard (q.v.), 4th Earl of Carlisle, by his 1st w. *educ.* Grand Tour. *unm.*

Returned unopposed as an opposition Whig in 1741, standing jointly with Sir Miles Stapylton (q.v.), a Tory,[1] Morpeth died 9 Aug. 1741 before Parliament met, of a 'venereal distemper which he caught in Italy and kept secret so long that it proved at last incurable'.[2]

[1] *HMC Hastings*, iii. 30; *HMC Carlisle*, 195–7. [2] *HMC 12th Rep IX*, 204.

E.C.

HOWARD, Henry, Visct, Morpeth (?1693–1758).

MORPETH   1715–1 May 1738

b. ?1693, 1st s. of Charles Howard, M.P., 3rd Earl of Carlisle; bro. of Hon. Charles Howard (q.v.). *educ.* Eton; Trinity, Camb. 2 May 1711, aged 17. *m.* (1) 27 Nov. 1717, Lady Frances Spencer (*d.* 27 July 1742), da. of Charles Spencer, M.P., 3rd Earl of Sunderland, 3s. 2da.; (2) 8 June 1743, Isabella, da. of William, 4th Baron Byron, 1s. 4da. *suc.* fa. as 4th Earl 1 May 1738. K.G. 18 Nov. 1756.

Entering Parliament for the family seat at Morpeth, Lord Morpeth supported the Government of his father-in-law, Lord Sunderland, except in the division on Lord Cadogan (q.v.) when he voted against them. Soon afterwards he went into opposition, speaking, 16 Feb. 1722, against Walpole's proposal that the South Sea Company should be allowed to dispose of part of their capital to pay their debts, and, 26 Oct. 1722, against the augmentation of the army. In 1725 he joined Pulteney in opposing a motion for Lord Macclesfield's impeachment,[1] of which he became a manager. On 7 Feb. 1727 he moved unsuccessfully for papers relating to the recent sending of the fleet into the Baltic.

In the next reign Morpeth continued active in opposition, advocating the reduction of the army year after year on the annual estimates. On 4 Feb. 1730 he is described as speaking 'in his usual manner' against the retention of the Hessians on British pay. On 13 Feb. 1734 he moved for a bill to make all army officers not above the rank of colonel irremovable except by a court-martial or by an address of both Houses, which was rejected without a division. His last recorded speech in the Commons was made in 1737 on his almost annual motion for reducing the army to 12,000, the Prince of Wales being in the gallery of the House.[2] On succeeding to the peerage he took the Howard influence in Yorkshire over to the Opposition, securing the return of his son joined to a Tory for Yorkshire at the general election of 1741. After Walpole's fall he adhered to Pulteney, who tried unsuccessfully to have him made lord privy seal at the end of 1743.[3] He was to have had that office in the abortive Bath-Granville Administration in February 1746, when Bath gave up the attempt to form a Government and 'slipped down the back stairs, leaving Lord Carlisle in the outward rooms, expecting to be called in to kiss hands for the Privy Seal'.[4] He figured as first lord of the Treasury in Frederick's shadow cabinet, but died without having ever attained office, 3 Sept. 1758.

[1] *Knatchbull Diary*, 12 Feb. 1725. [2] *HMC Egmont Diary*, i. 28; ii. 350. [3] Owen, *Pelhams*, 203. [4] Walpole, *Mems. Geo. II*, i. 174.

R.R.S.

HOWARD, Henry, Lord Walden (1707–45), of Audley End, Essex.

BERE ALSTON 2 Mar. 1728–28 Sept. 1733

b. 1 Jan. 1707, o.s. of Charles Howard, 9th Earl of Suffolk, by Henrietta, da. of Sir Henry Hobart, 4th Bt., sis. of Sir John Hobart, 5th Bt. (q.v.). *educ.* Magdalene, Camb. *m.* 13 May 1735 (with £25,000), Sarah, da. of Thomas Inwen (q.v.), brewer, of St. Saviour's, Southwark, *s.p. suc.* fa. as 10th Earl 28 Sept. 1733.

Recorder, Saffron Walden 1735–*d.*

Lord Walden was brought up by his father and had little contact with his mother after she became mistress to the Prince of Wales, later George II.[1] Returned for Bere Alston by his uncle, Sir John Hobart, he voted consistently against the Government until he succeeded to the peerage in 1733. By his subsequent marriage to an heiress he was able to discharge the existing mortgages at Audley End.[2] On his death intestate, 22 Apr. 1745, his title, but not his estates, passed to Henry Bowes Howard, 4th Earl of Berkshire, father of Thomas Howard and William Howard, Lord Andover (qq.v.).

[1] Lewis Melville, *Lady Suffolk and her Circle*, 263. [2] W. Addison, *Audley End*, 63.

S.R.M.

HOWARD, Hon. Thomas (1721–83), of Ashtead Park, Surr.

CASTLE RISING	1747–1768
MALMESBURY	1768–1774
MITCHELL	29 Dec. 1774–10 Aug. 1779

b. 11 June 1721, 5th s. of Henry Bowes, 11th Earl of Suffolk and 4th Earl of Berkshire, by Catherine, da. and h. of James Grahme of Levens (q.v.); bro. of William Howard, Lord Andover (q.v.). *educ.* Eton 1732; St. John's, Oxf. 1738; I. Temple 1742, called 1744, bencher 1779. *m.* 13 Apr. 1747, Elizabeth, da. of William Kingscote of Kingscote, Glos., 1da. *suc.* fa. at Ashtead 1757; his. gt.-nephew as 14th Earl of Suffolk and 7th Earl of Berkshire 10 Aug. 1779.

Returned for Castle Rising on the family interest, Howard is described in the 2nd Lord Egmont's electoral survey, c.1749–50, as 'a thorough Jacobite —but will be with us in the manner of [Richard] Shuttleworth and [Thomas] Lister [qq.v.]'.

R.R.S.

HOWARD, William, Visct. Andover (1714–56), of Elford Hall, Staffs.

CASTLE RISING 16 Apr. 1737–1747

b. 23 Dec. 1714, 1st surv. s. of Henry Bowes Howard, 11th Earl of Suffolk and 4th Earl of Berkshire; bro. of Hon. Thomas Howard (q.v.). *educ.* Eton 1725–8. *m.* 6 Nov. 1736, Lady Mary Finch, da. of Henry Finch (q.v.), 2nd Earl of Aylesford, 1s. 3da.

Returned as a Tory on the family interest at Castle Rising, Andover voted against the Government on the Spanish convention in 1739 and the place bill of 1740. He was one of the Tories who withdrew on the motion for Walpole's dismissal in 1741, though his father in the Lords voted for it. His father planned to put him up for Westmorland in 1741 but in the end withdrew him in favour of Sir Philip Musgrave (q.v.).[1] Re-elected for Castle Rising, he did not stand again, dying *v.p.* 15 July 1756.

[1] Geo. Crowle to Sir Robt. Walpole, 7 May 1737, Cholmondeley (Houghton) mss; see WESTMORLAND.

R.R.S.

HOWE, Emanuel Scrope, 2nd Visct. Howe [I] (c.1699–1735), of Langar, Notts.

NOTTINGHAMSHIRE 1722–15 May 1732

b. c.1699, 1st surv. s. of Scrope Howe, M.P., 1st Visct. Howe [I], by Juliana, da. of William Alington, 3rd Baron Alington [I]. *m.* 8 Apr. 1719 (with £5,000 and £1,500 p.a.), Maria Sophia Charlotte, da. of Charlotte Sophia, Countess of Darlington, mistress of George I and w. of John Adolph, Baron von Kielmansegge, 6s. 4da. *suc.* fa. 26 Jan. 1713.

Gov. Barbados 1732–*d.*

Howe was the son of a former Whig M.P. for Nottinghamshire, for which he himself was returned in 1722, after an expensive contest, and again in 1727, this time unopposed. He appears to have acted with the opposition Whigs, voting against the Administration on the Hessians in 1730 and the army in 1732. In the latter year, to repair his finances, which had not recovered from the contest of 1722, he gave up his seat and on Newcastle's recommendation[1] was appointed governor of Barbados worth 'a good £7,000 a year',[2] where he died 29 Mar. 1735.

[1] Howe to Newcastle, 14 May and 7 Aug. 1732, Add. 32687, ff. 451, 462. [2] Sir Robt. Worsley to Sir Rich. Worsley, 24 Nov. 1721, Worsley mss.

R.R.S.

HOWE, George Augustus, 3rd Visct. Howe [I] (?1724–58), of Langar, Notts.

NOTTINGHAM 1747–6 July 1758

b. ?1724, 1st surv. s. of Emanuel Scrope Howe, 2nd Visct. Howe [I] (q.v.). *educ.* Westminster Nov. 1732, aged 8; Eton c.1734. *suc.* fa. 29 Mar. 1735. *unm.*

Ensign 1 Ft. Gds. 1745, lt. and capt. 1746; a.-d.-c. to Duke of Cumberland 1747; capt. and lt.-col. 1 Ft. Gds. 1749; col. 1757; col. commandant 3 btn. 60 Ft. Feb.–Sept. 1757; col. 55 Ft. Sept. 1757–*d.*; brig.-gen. 1757.

During Howe's minority and for some years afterwards his aunt, Lady Pembroke, managed the family's political interests in Nottinghamshire.[1] At a by-election for Nottingham in May 1747, when Howe himself was serving in Flanders, she allowed the corporation to set him up against an opposition candidate. Newcastle refused his support and none of the Howes appeared at the election, though it was reported locally that 'the women of the Howe family', i.e. Lady Pembroke and her sister-in-law, the Dowager Lady Howe, 'were perpetually teazing Lady Yarmouth to intermeddle in his favour'. The corporation spent a good deal of money, but Howe was heavily defeated.

At the dissolution in June it was given out that Howe would be standing for the county as well as for the borough. In the county, however, he received so little support that at a meeting called to choose the Whig candidates his name was withdrawn.[2] In a three-cornered contest for the borough, in which his opponents were supported by Newcastle, Lady Pembroke secured the powerful influence of the local banker, Abel Smith, by arranging for a marriage between his eldest son and her ward and cousin, Miss Howe.[3] In Howe's absence she made a public entry into Nottingham, playing a conspicuous part in the election, at which Howe was returned unopposed.[4] He was classed as a government supporter in 1747.

Howe was again returned for Nottingham in 1754, this time with Newcastle's support. On the outbreak of war with France he served with great distinction in North America, where he was killed in a skirmish at Ticonderoga on 6 July 1758.

[1] See MORDAUNT, Hon. John. [2] John Sherwin and J. S. Charlton to Newcastle, 25 May 1747, John Thornhaugh and John White to Newcastle, 9 and 24 June 1747, Add. 32711, ff. 126, 130, 277, 503. [3] John Plumptre to Newcastle, 12 Aug. 1747, Add. 32712, f. 372. [4] John Plumptre and John Sherwin to Newcastle, 17 June 1747, Add. 32711, ff. 391 and 393.

R.R.S.

HOWE, John (bef. 1690–1742), of Stowell, Glos. and Great Wishford, Wilts.

GLOUCESTER   6 Feb.–5 Aug. 1727
WILTSHIRE   12 Apr. 1729–1741

b. bef. 1690,[1] o.s. of Rt. Hon. John Grubham Howe, M.P., paymaster gen., of Stowell by Mary, da. and coh. of Humphrey Baskerville of Pontrilas, Herefs., wid. of Sir Edward Morgan, 3rd Bt., of Llantarnam, Mon.; cos. of Sir Richard Grubham Howe, 3rd Bt., and Emanuel Scrope, 2nd Visct. Howe (qq.v.). m. Jan. 1712,[2] Dorothy, 1st da. of Henry Frederick Thynne of Remnan's, Old Windsor and Sunbury, Mdx., yr. bro. of Thomas, M.P., 1st Visct. Weymouth, 8s. 5da. suc. fa. 1722; to Wilts. and Glos. estates of cos. Sir Richard Grubham Howe, 3rd Bt. 1730; cr. Baron Chedworth 12 May 1741.

Recorder, Warwick 1737.

Returned as a Tory at by-elections for Gloucester and Wiltshire, Howe voted against the Government till 1734, speaking against the Address, 13 Jan. 1732, and against a government motion to provide funds for fulfilling treaty engagements with Denmark, 3 Apr. following.

On 14 Feb. 1735, on a government proposal for increasing the army, a ministerial supporter wrote:

> Mr. John Howe, who has always been a strong opposer, made a speech which surprised most people; he argued for the merits of the question and the necessity of the augmentation, but concluded with differing from gentlemen in the manner of raising them; he was for taking foreigners into pay . . . so voted against us.

A fortnight later he both spoke and voted for the first time with the Administration on a treaty with Denmark.[3] Thenceforth he can be regarded as a follower of Walpole, whose 'confidential friend' he became. This did not prevent him from preserving a certain independence: e.g. on 19 Mar. 1735 he was one of six Members ordered to prepare and bring in a place bill, which was strongly opposed by the Government; or from supporting, on three occasions and 'in the warmest terms of approbation', Sir John Barnard's (q.v.) proposals, made in 1737, for the further reduction of interest on the national debt, arguing that the country gentlemen would benefit by it.[4] In March 1739 he spoke for the convention with Spain, as 'a plain country gentleman, who lives upon his rents, and being satisfied his rents depend on the trade of the nation, will be careful no way to injure that trade'. After the outbreak of war he spoke in favour of postponing Pulteney's proposal of 16 Nov. 1739 to bring in a bill for securing the trade with America and encouraging seamen to join the navy, on the ground that such a bill should emanate from the Crown. His speech in support of the secretary at war's motion in December 1740 to provide funds for eleven new regiments, was cut short as

> I find myself unable to pursue my design because I can't read my notes, which, being written by another hand, are difficult to make out as 'tis the dusk of the evening.[5]

Two months later he spoke against the motion for the removal of Walpole from office, 'warmly' opposing the suggestion that Walpole should withdraw from the House during the debate. Shortly after this he was raised to the peerage for 'the uniform support which he gave to [the] Administration'.[6] He died 3 Apr. 1742.

[1] HMC Portland, vii. 17. [2] Wentworth Pprs. 244. [3] HMC Egmont Diary, i. 215, 253; ii. 156; HMC Carlisle, 152. [4] Coxe, Walpole, i. 503. [5] Chandler, xi. 27; xiii. add. 149. [6] Coxe, i. 503, 652.

R.S.L.

HOWE, Sir Richard Grubham, 3rd Bt. (?1651–1730), of Great Wishford, Wilts.

HINDON	1679–1681
TAMWORTH	1685–1687
CIRENCESTER	1690–1698
WILTSHIRE	1701, 1702–1727

b. ?1651, o. surv. s. of Sir Richard Grubham Howe, 2nd Bt., M.P., by his 1st w. Lucy,[1] da. of Sir John St. John, 1st Bt., of Lydiard Tregoze, Wilts. *educ.* Ch. Ch. Oxf. 13 July 1667, aged 16. *m.* 12 Aug. 1673, Mary, da. of Sir Henry Frederick Thynne, 1st Bt., of Kempsford, Glos., sis. of Thomas Thynne, M.P., 1st Visct. Weymouth, *s.p. suc.* fa. 1 May 1703.

Howe, a High Church Tory, whose father had represented Wiltshire, was himself returned eight times for the county, sitting altogether in thirteen Parliaments. Re-elected unopposed in 1715 and 1722, he voted against the Administration in every recorded division. In 1721 his name was sent to the Pretender as a probable supporter in the event of a rising.[2] He died 3 July 1730, leaving his estates to his cousin John Howe (q.v.).

[1] Hoare, *Wilts.* Hundred of Branch and Dole, 49, add. 39.
[2] Stuart mss 65/16.

R.S.L.

HOWORTH, Sir Humphrey (c.1684–1755), of Maesllwch, Rad.

RADNORSHIRE	1722–4 Feb. 1755

b. c.1684, s. of Humphrey Howorth of Maesllwch. *m.* (1) Sibel (*d.* 4 Mar. 1742), da. of Roger Mainwaring, 1s. 1da.; (2) Mary, da. of John Walbeoffe of Llanhamlach, Brec., wid. of Henry Williams of Gwernyfed, Brec. Kntd. 21 Aug. 1715.
Receiver of crown rents in Cheshire 1714–30.

Howorth represented Radnorshire for 33 years, voting regularly with the Administration. His ownership of Maesllwch gave him considerable electoral influence but for his first 20 years he had to face continual contests, usually followed by petitions, involving him in great expense. For this he blamed the Duke of Chandos, lord lieutenant of the county, who had unsuccessfully attempted to set up his son, Lord Carnarvon (q.v.), against him in 1727. On 10 Sept. 1740 he wrote to Walpole:

> The power of the Crown in the hands of the Duke of Chandos has constantly been, and is now with great warmth given against us, and nothing omitted in his Grace's power to support the enemy, who make it their business to rail at everything that is done by the Administration, to inflame the people. His Grace has I am assured offered his interest against me, and proposed that the party should join him in opposing Mr. Lewis [Thomas, *b.* 1690, q.v.], neither of which could be attempted were the King's interest in other hands. This, Sir, obliged us all to be your petitioners, that the above power for the sake of this county might be put into other hands, as the only

means to establish the King's interest here, and give quiet to it.

On 24 Jan, 1741 he reported that Lewis too had turned against him.

> When I came out of that country hither, there was not the least talk of an opposition, and I had, as I thought, secured my interest so well, that it was not possible for the Tories to have raised their head; this has been my chief aim for many years, which has from time to time cost me at least £10,000, and nothing left to be thought of, but to wait for any breach in the Whig interest. This it seems, has now happened, and from Mr. Lewis's own letters to me, and from his behaviour since he came to town, I can make no doubt, but he had been one of the chief instruments of the opposition intended to be given me, and indeed now declared to be so, which is acted by him in an underhand, poor, low manner, and I doubt, is so base, as to inform Sir Robert and you, that the general bent of the country is against me, that they had rather choose any body, than myself, and that therefore he could think of no way to save the county, but by putting up a Whig.[1]

Once again he was faced with a contest, making further inroads into his resources; nor was his position improved when he was ordered to pay into the Treasury £3,000 arrears from the crown rents collected by him in Cheshire between 1714 and 1730. He was forced to sell much of his estate to his tenants, thus increasing its political value; for, as was subsequently pointed out,

> the political power of the estate [lies] entirely in a number of cottagers upon an extensive manor, who from the necessity and distress of their late landlord, Sir Humphrey Howorth, became freeholders, the commissioners of the land tax, in those times being his friends and assessing these his cottagers to give them a right of voting and a freehold forever in the county.
>   Cottagers . . . are always subject to the command of their lord: the word *trespass* in the law perpetually overhauls them; and with these cottagers and the friends of his neighbourhood Howorth frequently disappointed the united efforts of every other part of Radnorshire.

About 1749–50 the 2nd Lord Egmont describes him as 'miserably poor' and necessarily 'dependent on any Administration as his affairs stand'. He died 4 Feb. 1755, leaving Maesllwch encumbered by a mortgage of £26,000, and by the Treasury claim against it, which with interest, amounted in 1765 to £8,000.[2]

[1] Cholmondeley (Houghton) mss. [2] Chase Price to Portland, 12 Sept. 1765, Portland mss.

R.R.S.

HUCKS, Robert (1699–1745), of Clifton Hampden, nr. Abingdon, and Aldenham, Herts.[1]

ABINGDON	1722–1741

bap. 5 Mar. 1699, 1st surv. s. of William Hucks (q.v.). *educ.* Trinity, Camb. 1717; I. Temple 1720. *m.*

22 Dec. 1730, Sarah, da. of Henry Coghill of Pennes Place, in Aldenham, sis. and h. of Henry Coghill of Pennes Place, niece and h. of Thomas Coghill of Wigbournes, in Aldenham, 2s. 6da. *suc.* fa. 1740.

Recorder, Wallingford 1733; King's brewer 1740–d.; treasurer of the Foundling Hospital 1744.

Robert Hucks was returned for Abingdon, his mother's town, at three contested elections, consistently voting with the Government. An 'enemy of religious establishments', he spoke in 1736 against a grant to repair Henry VII's chapel and promoted the mortmain bill to restrain the alienation of land to religious and charitable institutions. Next year he was one of the common councillors of the Georgia trust who resigned owing to their objection to the appropriation of land in Georgia to the endowment of the Church of England there. Though remaining a trustee, he took little further interest in the colony, observing in 1739 that 'if we may have peace with Spain by giving up Georgia it were a good thing'.[2] He did not stand in 1741. In 1743, having succeeded his father as King's brewer and the owner of 'several thousand butts', he presented a petition to the Treasury from London victuallers, praying for the repeal of the Pot Act, a levy on publicans.[3]

He died 21 Dec. 1745.

[1] See J. A. Gibbs, *Hist. Antony and Dorothea Gibbs*, 37–40.
[2] *HMC Egmont Diary*, ii. 236, 372–3, 479; iii. 28, 36, 109; Harley Diary; see also WHITE, John, and MORE, Robert. [3] Mathias, *Brewing Industry in England*, 22, 116; *Cal. Treas. Pprs.* 1742–5, pp. 230, 232.

R.S.L.

HUCKS, William (bef. 1678–1740), of Great Russell St., Bloomsbury, and Wallingford, Berks.

ABINGDON   20 Jan. 1709–1710
WALLINGFORD   1715–28 Nov. 1740

b. bef. 1678, 1st s. of William Hucks of St. Giles's-in-the-Fields, Bloomsbury, brewer, by his w. Lydia Head; bro.-in-law of Thomas Inwen (q.v.). *m.* (lic. 1 Sept. 1696) Elizabeth, da. of Robert Selwood of Abingdon, 2s. 1da. *suc.* fa. 1691.

King's brewer 1715–d.

Hucks inherited his father's share in the Horn Brewery, Duke Street, Bloomsbury, later holding five-sevenths of the family brewing interests in London. Returned as a Whig for Wallingford in four contested elections, he voted consistently with the Government. In 1727 he had a crown lease of Wallingford Castle, which included Ewelme, Oxon.[1] He was responsible for the erection of the statue of George I on the steeple of St. George's, Bloomsbury.[2] He died 28 Nov. 1740.

[1] See J. A. Gibbs, *Hist. Antony and Dorothea Gibbs*, 37–39, further additions and corrections, xvi (4); Cussans, *Herts.* i(1), 246; *Cal. Treas. Bks. and Pprs.* 1720–8, pp. 359, 365. [2] *N. & Q.* (ser. 11), ii. 50–51, 135, 199.

R.S.L.

HUGHES, Edward (*d.* 1734), of Hertingfordbury, Herts.

SALTASH   1722–26 Jan. 1734

Prob. s. of John Hughes of Hertingfordbury, sheriff of Herts. 1718. *m.* 26 Nov. 1713 (with £2,000), Elizabeth, da. of Richard Harrison of Balls Park, Herts., 2s. 1da.; bro.-in-law of Edward and George Harrison (qq.v.).[1]

Judge advocate gen. of the army 1714–d.

Hughes's family seems to have been well-established in Hertfordshire, where he himself was J.P.[2] Marrying into an influential and wealthy local family he was returned for Saltash on the Admiralty interest in 1722, and again in 1727, though Richard Edgcumbe (q.v.) reported to Newcastle that 'at Saltash they don't relish Mr. Hughes, but make no difficulty of choosing a better man'.[3] He voted with the Administration except in the divisions on the excise bill and on the repeal of the Septennial Act, from which he was absent, speaking for them in the debate of 12 Feb. 1730 on Dunkirk, and on 18 Feb. supporting the petition from the African Company for a subsidy towards the maintenance of its forts and settlements. A member of the gaols committee in 1728–9, he told the 1st Lord Egmont (q.v.) in February 1730 that:

there was great occasion to revise the committee, to keep the judges in order, who had behaved strangely, and used us so contemptuously . . . Mr. Hughes added he could tell me something that would make me stare, and reached even to the judges. I did not encourage him to impart it to me, knowing his warmth against the judges, and great freeness in these affairs . . . However, I commended his zeal, and that deservedly, for he seemed a very honest and conscientious man.

He was referring to a charge against the lord chief justice of the common pleas, which was found by the committee on investigation to be groundless. In 1732, when a bill enabling the Charitable Corporation to raise new capital was before Parliament, Egmont learned that Hughes had complained to the directors of the corporation of being 'ill used by them', in having 'no shares given him for being for the bill'.[4]

He died in debt 26 Jan. 1734, his widow renouncing the executorship of his will to his principal creditor.[5]

[1] PCC 35 Ockham; Clutterbuck, *Herts.* ii. 186, 206. [2] *Hertford County Recs., Sessions Rolls 1699–1850*, pp. 65, 70. [3] 14 Aug. 1727, SP Dom. Cal. Geo. II. [4] *HMC Egmont Diary*, i. 42, 45, 46, 51, 243; O. C. Williams, *Clerical Organization of the House of Commons*, 325 seq. [5] PCC 35 Ockham.

E.C.

HUME, Abraham (1703–72), of Goldings, Essex.

STEYNING   1747–1754
TREGONY   1761–1768

b. 1703, 4th s. of Robert Home (later Hume) of Ayton, Berwick, by Hannah Curtis of Mile End, Mdx.; bro. of Alexander Hume (q.v.). *m.* 2 Oct. 1746, Hannah, da. of Sir Thomas Frederick, gov. of Fort St. David, India, sis. of Thomas Frederick, Sir John Frederick, 4th Bt., and Sir Charles Frederick (qq.v.), 2s. 1da. *suc.* bro. 1765. *cr.* Bt. 4 Apr. 1769.

Director, South Sea Co. 1742–5; director, R. Exchange Assurance 1748; commissary to the forces abroad 7 Dec. 1742[1]–6; commissary gen. of stores at home and abroad 25 Dec. 1746–7,[2] and from 13 Mar. 1756.[3]

Abraham Hume, a merchant, who had been employed as an army commissary during the war of the Austrian succession, was returned for Steyning at the end of the war. In 1754 he gave up his seat to his brother Alexander, standing himself for Maidstone, where he was defeated. After the election he sent Newcastle a statement of his claims for services rendered to the Government, viz.:

> Abraham Hume in July of the year 1742 contracted with the Treasury for furnishing bread to the British troops in Flanders . . . No bread was furnished that campaign, the troops not taking the field; by which Mr. Hume was a considerable sufferer. In the campaign of 1747 he had an accident in his knee, which has lamed him for the remainder of his life. In the same year he was at a great expense chosen for Steyning . . . and served for that place during the whole time of the last Parliament.
>
> The war being at an end, when it was settled who were entitled to half-pay, Mr. Hume put in his claim, but was persuaded not to insist upon it by the chancellor of the Exchequer [Henry Pelham], who told him, he thought it not worth his while and that something better might offer, telling him at the same time, as he was in Parliament, it was not decent to have half-pay.
>
> When Mr. Revell [q.v.] died Mr. Hume thought it a good opportunity to put the chancellor of the Exchequer in mind of what he had formerly said to him, as he was sensible no objection could be made to his abilities for the undertaking, but to his mortification he found that the present undertakers had got so far the preference that unless he would lower the price two or three thousands a year, he did not succeed. This Mr. Hume thought too hazardous to himself, but made a proposal to undertake the contracts at £500 a year less than they had been done for till that time, but this was not thought an object sufficient to induce him to alter the intended measures,—Mr. Hume very readily gave up all thought of this affair trusting that something else might soon offer.[4]

The statement concludes by asking for some reward for his zeal and attention, as well as for his election expenses at Steyning and Maidstone, amounting to £3,650.[5] Newcastle's reply has not been preserved, but on the outbreak of the seven years' war Hume was re-appointed to his former post of army commissary. He died 10 Oct. 1772.

[1] *Cal. Treas. Pprs.* 1742–5, p. 421. [2] T29/30, p. 449. [3] Add. 33039, 149; T29/33, p. 46. [4] Add. 33054, f. 372. [5] Add. 32995, f. 173.

R.R.S.

HUME, Alexander (c.1693–1765), of Wormleybury, Herts.

SOUTHWARK   30 June 1743–1754
STEYNING   1754–1761
SOUTHWARK   1761–15 Sept. 1765

b. c.1693, 1st s. of Robert Home (later Hume) of Ayton, Berwick; bro. of Abraham Hume (q.v.). *m.* 5 Apr. 1733, Mary, da. of Sir Thomas Frederick, gov. of Fort St. David, India, sis. of Thomas Frederick, Sir John Frederick, 4th Bt., and Sir Charles Frederick (qq.v.), 1da. *d.v.p.* Her sis. Hannah m. Abraham Hume. *suc.* fa. 1742. Bought Wormleybury 1739.

Director, E.I. Co. 1737–40, 1742–5, 1747–8.

The son of a navy victualler,[1] Hume stood for Chippenham with his brother-in-law, John Frederick, but was defeated by a narrow majority. He prepared a petition, writing to Walpole in January 1741:[2]

> enclosed is the state of the case I mentioned to you yesterday as a thing of great consequence to Mr. Frederick's and my interest at Chippenham. The benefit we expect from it depends entirely on despatch.

He spent £4,057 on the election, including the petition, which was lost in the critical division on which Walpole resigned. Successful at Southwark as a government supporter in 1743, spending £3,500 on his election,[3] and again in 1747, he voted for the Administration in all recorded divisions. In a memorandum to Newcastle, he claimed to have steadily supported the Administration except over the proposals for the reduction in the navy from 10,000 to 8,000 men (in January 1751), and in two other minor cases, adding:

> Mr. Hume's general conduct in Parliament . . . has always (except for the foregoing instances) been conformable to the wishes of the Government. He has indeed sometimes taken upon him to introduce bills of a public nature and conducted them through the House, particularly in the year 1744 he formed the plan for the prolongation of the East India Company's charter on their lending a million at 3% whereby the interest paid by the public for that, and for every subsequent year, was kept down to a more moderate price than it would have been if that plan had not taken place. Mr. Hume had so great a share in this, that Mr. Pelham with Mr. Scrope [John, q.v.] designed to come to Mr. Hume's house to settle the agreement with him and Mr. Gough [Henry, q.v.]. In the year 1746 he brought in a bill to regulate insurances on ships, whereby many ships have been saved and frauds prevented. In 1747 he brought in a bill for the relief and support of seamen maimed and disabled and of the widows of seamen killed or drowned in the merchant service, whereby many who would otherwise have been reduced to beggary find wherewith to subsist. And in 1750 he brought in a bill, laying a duty on Irish sail cloth equal to the bounty given by the Irish which had almost, and would soon have completely ruined that necessary and valuable manufacture in Great Britain.

Out of Parliament he has always used his best endeavours to support the prudent views of the Administration. In the great scheme for reducing the interest on the public funds he was particularly active, as he was in concerting the scheme for the alteration of the duties on tea, which have produced such a great increase to the revenue [see Barnard, Sir John]. And in a more private way, assisted considerably in a loan to the Dutch at Mr. Pelham's desire, to make good his Grace's agreement for the retreat of the Russians out of Germany at the latter end of the last war [of the Austrian succession].

He supported the bill for the naturalization of the Jews in April 1753.[4] He died 15 Sept. 1765.

[1] PCC 298 Trenley. [2] Cholmondeley (Houghton) mss. [3] Add. 32995, f. 172. [4] Add. 33055, ff. 265-7.

E.C.

HUME CAMPBELL, Hon. Alexander (1708–60), of Birghamsheil, Berwickshire.

BERWICKSHIRE   1734–1741, 19 Jan. 1742–19 July 1760

b. 15 Feb. 1708, 2nd surv. s. of Alexander Hume, M.P. [S], 2nd Earl of Marchmont [S], lord clerk register, by Margaret, da. and h. of Sir George Campbell of Cessnock, lord justice clerk; twin bro. of Hugh, Lord Polwarth (q.v.). educ. private sch. London 1716–?21; Holland (Utrecht and Franeker) 1721–?5; Edinburgh Univ.; adv. 1929; I. Temple, called 1731. m. 16 July 1717, Elizabeth Pettis of Savile Row, London, s.p.
Solicitor-gen. to Prince of Wales Dec. 1741–Jan. 1746; lord clerk register Jan. 1756–d.

'A very masterly speaker and able lawyer', Hume Campbell was returned for his native county of Berwickshire in 1734 as an anti-Walpole Whig. In his first Parliament he 'trod the same paths of invectives' against Walpole as his twin brother, Lord Polwarth, and his friend, William Pitt (qq.v.). At the opening of the next Parliament, from which Polwarth, now Earl of Marchmont, was excluded, the Berwickshire election, a double return, was treated as a trial of strength between Walpole and the Opposition.

> Their man [Horace Walpole writes] was Hume Campbell, Lord Marchmont's brother, lately made solicitor to the Prince for being as troublesome, as violent, and almost as able as his brother. They made a great point of it, and gained so many of our votes that at ten at night we were forced to give it up without dividing.

Two days later he spoke in support of the first of the opposition attempts to set up a secret committee to bring charges against Walpole, whom he called a 'tympany of corruption'. He was included in the opposition list for the secret committee, narrowly failing to be elected to it.[1] After Walpole's fall he at first acted with the Duke of Argyll's adherents, voting for the revival of the secret committee,

1 Dec. 1742; then with the new Government, which the Prince of Wales supported, voting for the Hanoverians, 10 Dec. 1742. But in 1744, on 18 Jan. and again on 1 Feb., following Pitt, he spoke and voted with the Opposition, in defiance of the Prince's orders, each time making one of the best speeches in the debate.[2] In November 1745 he fell out with Pitt, who,

> having been engaged to make up a quarrel between his friend, Hume Campbell, and Lord Home, in which the former had kissed the rod . . . within a very few days treated the House with bullying the Scotch declaimer.[3]

Two months later he was dismissed by the Prince for attacking Lord Tweeddale, the secretary of state for Scotland, 'on the Scotch affairs'.[4] During the next session, encouraged by his friend, Lord Chesterfield (Philip Dormer Stanhope, q.v.), who had recently been appointed secretary of state, he made overtures to the ministry, speaking for them on a vote for the forthcoming campaign in Flanders, 26 Jan. 1747; an election petition, 11 Feb.; and in support of the bill for abolishing hereditary jurisdictions in Scotland, 14 Apr.[5] On this Pelham, faced with a new Opposition launched by the Prince, opened negotiations with Hume Campbell, the upshot of which is described in a letter from the Duke of Newcastle to Lord Lothian, lord clerk register:

> Your Lordship is sensible that Mr. Hume Campbell is very considerable in the House of Commons and of much more weight than any one in the Opposition can be. He is very well disposed to act entirely with us: the only thing he insists on is that a proper regard should be shown, and that immediately, to my Lord Marchmont, his brother, and upon this Mr. Hume Campbell's concurrence with us will absolutely depend . . . Mr. Hume Campbell desired that he [Lord Marchmont] should be of the sixteen peers and have an employment of credit. The only employment likely to be vacant is the first commissioner of police, which Mr. Hume Campbell thought my Lord Marchmont would very readily accept if he could be of the sixteen. But as that is not practicable Mr. Hume Campbell has left it with his brother that if my Lord Marchmont cannot come into Parliament he shall have some employment of more value than the first commissioner of police. The only expedient that has occured to my brother and me is if your Lordship would have the goodness to exchange the register's office for that of first commissioner of police, in which case care would be taken to have the salary made up to the value of the register's office.[6]

As Lothian 'peremptorily' refused the exchange, Marchmont had to content himself with 'receiving by my brother the price Mr. Pelham thought fit to offer him', that is the police office, with its salary made up to that of the register's office, £1,500 a year.[7] Hume Campbell himself was supposed to have received 'a considerable pension, on which he neglected the House of Commons, giving himself up entirely to his profession'. After three years 'in a state of neutrality', he began 'to frequent the House again' in 1750.[8] About the same time the 2nd Lord Egmont wrote in his electoral survey for a new Parliament on the Prince's accession:

> Hume Campbell—it will be right to have him in such a way as not to appear against us, and I suppose it easy to be done.

In Egmont's lists of persons to receive offices etc. in the next reign, Hume Campbell is put down on 29 Apr. 1749 for a pension of £1,000 a year but in a later list, dated April 1750, he figures as 'chancellor to the Prince'.

He died 19 July 1760.

[1] Walpole to Mann, 22 Jan., 1 Apr. 1742; *Mems. Geo. II*, i. 19; ii. 113. [2] John Drummond to Ld. Morton, 4 Dec. 1742, Morton mss. SRO; Yorke's parl. jnl. *Parl. Hist.* xiii. 466, 636-7. [3] Walpole, *Mems. Geo. II*, i. 19; *Marchmont Pprs.* i. 147. [4] Ibid. i. 166; Walpole to Mann, 3 Jan. 1746. [5] *HMC Polwarth*, v. 183 seq., 194, 202, 236-42. [6] 23 June 1747, Add. 32711, f. 493. [7] *HMC Polwarth*, v. 252; *Marchmont Pprs.* i. 177. [8] Walpole to Mann, 2 Dec. 1748, 10 Jan. 1750; *Mems. Geo. II*. i. 19 n.

R.R.S.

HUME CAMPBELL, Hugh, Lord Polwarth (1708-94).

BERWICK-ON-TWEED   1734-27 Feb. 1740

b. 15 Feb. 1708, 1st surv. s. of Alexander Hume, M.P. [S], 2nd Earl of Marchmont [S]; twin. bro. of Hon. Alexander Hume Campbell (q.v.), *educ.* private sch. London 1716-?21; Holland (Utrecht and Franeker) 1721-?5; Edinburgh Univ. *m.* (1) 1 May 1731, Anne, da. and coh. of Robert Western of St. Peter's, Cornhill, 1s. 3da.; (2) 30 Jan. 1748, Elizabeth, da. of Windmill Crompton, linen draper, of Cheapside, 1s. *suc.* fa. as 3rd Earl 27 Feb. 1740.

First commr. of police [S] 1747-64; rep. peer [S] 1750-84; P.C. 22 Nov. 1762; gov. of bank of Scotland 1763-90; keeper of the great seal [S] 1764-*d.*

Sir Robert Walpole said that 'of all the men he ever knew', Lord Polwarth and his twin brother, Hume Campbell,

> were the most abandoned in their professions to him on their coming into the world: he was hindered from accepting their services by the present Duke of Argyll [then Lord Ilay] of whose faction they were not.

On this the whole family went into opposition, with the result that its head, the 2nd Earl of Marchmont, was dismissed from his office of lord clerk register in 1733.[1] At the general election of 1734 Lord Marchmont was not re-elected to the Lords as a representative peer of Scotland, but both his sons were returned to the House of Commons, where 'they made a great figure'. In a debate on an opposition place bill, 22 Apr. 1735,

> several young Members, who never spoke before,

distinguished themselves . . . as Mr. William Pitt, Mr. Lyttelton, Lord Polwarth and Mr. Hume, Lord Marchmont's sons . . . all for the bill.

On 16 Feb. 1737 Polwarth spoke against the bill imposing penalties on Edinburgh for the Porteous riots. Two days later he attacked Walpole for his 'base treatment of his father', to which Walpole replied that the reason why Lord Marchmont and his friends 'were turned out was that they were endeavouring to be at the head of affairs', and that a minister who put up with such behaviour 'would be a pitiful minister'.[2] In a debate on the army, 3 Feb. 1738, a government speaker having said that an army was necessary to support the Whig interest and that without it the Tory interest would prevail, Polwarth retorted that this showed that the ministerial party, who called themselves Whigs, acted in contradiction of Whig principles and were really Tories, while those whom they called Tories were the true Whigs. Excluded from the Commons by his accession to the peerage on the death of his father in 1740 and excluded from the Lords by Lord Ilay, who controlled the election of the representative peers of Scotland, he remained connected with the Opposition till 1747, when he and his brother came to terms with the Pelhams, Marchmont accepting an office of £1,500 a year.[3] Soon after his appointment, Ilay, now Duke of Argyll, reported to Pelham from Scotland that Marchmont was giving out that 'I was near a political demise', and that 'he was to be minister in this country'.[4] In fact, though he re-entered Parliament as a representative peer in 1750, he never again played a significant part in public life.

He died 10 Jan. 1794.

[1] Walpole to Mann, 2 Dec. 1748; *HMC Polwarth*, v. 295. [2] *HMC Egmont Diary*, ii. 150-2, 171. [3] See HUME CAMPBELL, Hon. Alexander. [4] 1 Aug. 1747, Newcastle (Clumber) mss.

R.R.S.

HUMFREYS, Sir William, 1st Bt. (c.1651-1735), of Barking, Essex.

MARLBOROUGH   1715-1722

b. c.1651, 2nd s. of Nathaniel Humfreys of Candlewick Street, London, citizen and ironmonger, by his w. Mary. *m.* (1) bef. 1682,[1] Margaret (*d.* 19 Aug. 1704), da. of William Wintone of Dymock, Glos., 1s. 1da.; (2) 6 Jan. 1705, Ellen, wid. of Robert Lancashire, London merchant, *s.p.* Kntd. 26 Oct. 1704; *cr.* Bt. 30 Nov. 1714.

Sheriff, London 1704-5, alderman 1707, ld. mayor 1714-15; master, Ironmongers' Co. 1705; director, E.I. Co. 1711-14, Bank of England 1719-30 (with statutory intervals).

Col. Green regt. 1714-*d.*

Sir William Humfreys, whose father was of Welsh extraction from Montgomeryshire,[2] was by trade an oilman, or drysalter, in the Poultry. He owed his baronetcy to his entertainment as lord mayor of George I, on his accession, at Guildhall on 29 Oct. 1714. Returned as a Whig on the Duke of Somerset's interest at Marlborough in 1715, he voted for the Administration in all recorded divisions. He did not stand again, dying 26 Oct. 1735.

[1] PCC 72 Cottle. [2] Add. 24120, f. 449.

R.S.L.

HUMPHREY, Paul (c.1687–1751), of Chipstead, Surr.

GATTON 25 Oct. 1745–18 Apr. 1751

b. c.1687, s. of Toby Humphrey of Gray's Inn by Anne, da. of Paul Docminique (q.v.). m., 1da. d.v.p. suc. cos. Charles Docminique (q.v.) 1745.

Succeeding to the Docminique estates and electoral interest at Gatton, Humphrey voted against the Administration in 1746 and was listed as Opposition in 1747. In 1749 the 2nd Lord Egmont considered him a possible supporter, adding that he was 'a very low odd man'. He died 18 Apr. 1751, aged 64.[1]

[1] Manning & Bray, Surr. ii. 237, 248.

R.R.S.

HUNGERFORD, John (c.1658–1729), of Lincoln's Inn.

SCARBOROUGH 28 Apr. 1692–26 Mar. 1695
1702–1705
22 Nov. 1707–8 June 1729

b. c.1658, 1st s. of Richard Hungerford of Wilts. educ. L. Inn 1677, called 1687, bencher 1707. m. (lic. 5 Aug. 1687) Mary, da. of Abraham Spooner, vintner, of London, s.p.
Commr. of the alienation office 1711–14; cursitor of Yorks. and Westmld. for life.

Hungerford, who bought the manor of Hungerford in 1721, is described in his memorial in its church as 'descended from the Hungerfords of the Lea and Down Ampney' in Gloucestershire.[1] A successful barrister, he was standing counsel to the East India Company and to King's College, Cambridge. First returned for Scarborough in 1692, he was expelled from the House of Commons in 1695 for taking a bribe, but was re-elected in 1702 again for Scarborough, which he represented as a Tory in every Parliament till his death.

In 1715 Hungerford spoke against the Address, and vigorously defended Bolingbroke, Ormonde, Strafford and Oxford against the charge of high treason. He spoke and voted against the septennial bill in 1716. Next year, he opposed a vote of credit

against Sweden in April, but in June he separated himself from his party by speaking for Lord Cadogan (q.v.) though he voted against him. Later he spoke against a standing army in time of peace, saying that 'when there is occasion for an army, the officers with a drum, a guinea, and a barrel of ale, can bring one together'.[2] He opposed the Address in November 1718, and voted against the repeal of the Occasional Conformity and Schism Acts in 1719. In a list drawn up by Sunderland before the division on the peerage bill, for which he spoke and voted, he is put down to 'Craggs sen.', whom he seconded at a meeting of the general court of proprietors of the South Sea Company, 8 Sep. 1720, in a vote of confidence in the directors, saying that in all his experience he had never known such wonderful results to be produced in so short a time. In February 1721 he became chairman of a committee set up by the House of Commons to investigate the numerous flotations of joint-stock companies. The committee's report presented in April, led to the passing of the so-called Bubble Act, whose object was to protect the South Sea Company against its rivals. He was also chairman of a similar committee set up in 1722 to inquire into the Harburg lottery, whose report led to the expulsion from the Commons of the 1st Lord Barrington (q.v.).[3]

At the time of the Atterbury plot, Hungerford opposed the suspension of the Habeas Corpus Act in October, the special tax on the Roman Catholics in November 1722, and the bill of pains and penalties against Atterbury in March 1723, also acting as counsel for Christopher Layer, one of the agents in the plot.[4] In a debate on extending the malt tax to Scotland on 10 Feb. 1724,

Mr. Walpole said he had done no more than errare cum patribus, and that those who had presided in the Treasury before could not find out any way to get it, and yet that gentleman [Hungerford] never thought fit to differ with them so much as with those now. Upon which Hungerford fell upon him and vindicated Lord Oxford, that he went out of the Treasury without an acre of land more than when he came in, and if it was a fault, that gentleman that impeached him should have made it so that it shewed plainly by his not doing it he thought it part of his duty to make the Scotch pay, and in very foul language went on without the least provocation.[5]

He spoke against the army in November 1724, against the Address in March 1726 and against the supply in April 1727. He was one of the most frequent non-ministerial speakers of his time, rivalling William Shippen and surpassing Archibald Hutcheson (qq.v.) in the number of his reported speeches. He proposed and promoted a number of bills against betting and gambling, but his chief claim to fame was

> his easy and popular eloquence, intermixing his speeches in matters of the greatest weight and importance with quick facetious turns, which put the House in a good humour and seldom failed of having the intended effect.[6]

An example of this was his last recorded speech, 23 Feb. 1728, when on a dispute between Walpole and Pulteney, in which warm expressions had passed on both sides, Hungerford 'interposed in a jocular speech, that put the House in a good humour and so the dispute ended'.[7]

Hungerford died 8 June 1729, leaving his property in trust for his wife during her life time, after which it was to be sold, two-thirds of the proceeds to go to King's College, Cambridge, and the remaining third to his friend, Dr. Mangey, canon of Durham, who was said to have taken advantage of Hungerford's last moments 'to make him give his estate, or great part of it, away to uses he never intended.'[8] The will bitterly attacks Lord Chancellor King for refusing to allow Hungerford to sell his office of cursitor of Yorkshire, 'upon pretence that the punishment inflicted on the Earl of Macclesfield doth debar him from so doing'; but, really, according to Hungerford, because Lord King proposed to give the office when it became vacant to his son,

> the first person of his rank and station that ever acted so meanly as to make his children cursitors, but however I forgive him.[9]

[1] Add. 33412, ff. 145–7; *Berks. N. & Q.* i. 26–27. [2] *HMC Stuart*, v. 301. [3] *Pol. State*, xx. 180–2; *CJ*, xix. 392, 418; xx. 75, 88; J. Carswell, *South Sea Bubble*, 116–17, 138–40. [4] Howell's *State Trials*, xv. 233–7. [5] *Knatchbull Diary*. [6] *Pol. State*, xxxvii. 620–1. [7] Chandler, vii. 23. [8] *HMC Egmont Diary*, ii. 250. [9] PCC 167 Abbott.

R.R.S.

HUNGERFORD, Walter (1675–1754), of Studley House, nr. Calne, Wilts.

CALNE 1701, 1734–1747

b. 9 July 1675,[1] 1st surv. s. of Sir George Hungerford, M.P., of Cadenham, Wilts. by Frances, da. of Charles Seymour, M.P., 2nd Baron Seymour of Trowbridge, sis. of the 5th and 6th Dukes of Somerset. *m.* 22 Nov. 1703, Elizabeth Dodson of St. Clement Danes,[2] *s.p. suc.* fa. 1714.

Commr. of appeals in the excise 1708–14; sheriff, Wilts. 1727–8.

Walter Hungerford was descended from the 1st Lord Hungerford whose grandson acquired the manors of Studley and Cadenham in 1468.[3] His father had represented both Calne and the county and his elder brother George was M.P. for the borough at his death in 1698. As a young man he

went to sea with a loan of £500 from his father, against whom he later raised an 'unchristian' and lengthy suit in Chancery.[4] Returned for Calne in 1701, he did not stand again till 1715 when he was defeated. Successful in 1734 and 1741, he voted against the Spanish convention in 1739 but thenceforth supported the Administration. His only known speeches were on 16 Mar. 1739, when he opposed a motion to take the duty off Irish yarn, and on 6 Dec. 1743, when he spoke against an opposition motion to discontinue the Hanoverians in English pay.[5] On the reconstruction of the ministry in December 1744, he wrote to Walpole, now Lord Orford,

> During my long service in Parliament, I have seen many vacancies filled and places given to gentlemen of much later sitting there, and not more zealous in the support of the Administration, without once experiencing any of their favours . . . My Lord, the late incident must occasion many alterations and gives an opportunity to my friends to move for me. I earnestly therefore entreat your Lordship's early application and recommendation of me to be provided for at this juncture in some post or other.[6]

Classed as an Old Whig in 1746, he did not stand again, dying 31 May 1754.

[1] Hoare, *Hungerfordiana*, 58. [2] Add. 33412, f. 135. [3] *Wilts. Arch. Mag.* xxxiv. 388, 404. [4] PCC 82 Aston. [5] *HMC Egmont Diary*, iii. 36; Yorke's parl. jnl. *Part. Hist.* xiii. 140. [6] 22 Dec. 1744, Cholmondeley (Houghton) mss.

R.S.L.

HUNT, George (?1720–98) of Lanhydrock, nr. Bodmin, Cornw.

BODMIN 19 Jan. 1753–1784

b. ?1720, 2nd s. of Thomas Hunt of Mollington, Cheshire by Mary Vere, da. of Russell Robartes, M.P., sis. of Henry, 3rd Earl of Radnor. *educ.* Queen's, Oxf. 10 Mar. 1738, aged 17. *unm. suc.* uncle, the 3rd Earl of Radnor, at Lanhydrock 1741.

Hunt's estate at Lanhydrock carried an important interest at Bodmin, for which he was returned in 1753, after contesting it unsuccessfully in 1747. He died 8 Nov. 1798.

E.C.

HUNTER, Thomas Orby (c.1716–69), of Crowland, Lincs. and Waverley Abbey, Surr.

WINCHELSEA 1741–Jan. 1759, 5 Apr. 1760–20 Oct. 1769

b. c.1716, o.s. of Maj.-Gen. Robert Hunter, gov. of New York 1710–19 and of Jamaica 1729–34, by Elizabeth, da. and h. of Sir Thomas Orby, 1st Bt., of Crowland, wid. of Lord John Hay. *m.* 4 Apr. 1749, Jacomina Caroline, da. of Hon. William Bellenden, gd.-da. of John, 2nd Lord Bellenden [S], 4s. 3da. *suc.* fa. 1734.

Dep. paymaster of forces in Flanders 1742–8; commissary to treat with France 1748; ld. of Admiralty Nov. 1756–Apr. 1757 and July 1757–Apr. 1763; superintendent of supplies to the allied armies in Germany Dec. 1758–Apr. 1760; ld. of Treasury Apr. 1763–1765.

Hunter was returned on the Treasury interest in 1741, when Walpole evicted Bubb Dodington and Robert Bristow (qq.v.) from Winchelsea. He owed his appointment as deputy paymaster in 1742 to Lord Stair.[1] In Parliament he voted regularly with the Administration. The 2nd Lord Egmont wrote of him in his electoral survey of c.1749–50:

Hunter is one of the oldest acquaintances I have and was bred up from a boy with me. I am persuaded he would be glad to act with me, but his engagements and obligations are very strong to Pelham.

He died 20 Oct. 1769.

[1] Pelham to Stair, 24 June 1742, Add. 35453, ff. 160–4.

R.R.S.

HUTCHESON, Archibald (c.1659–1740), of the Middle Temple and Golden Sq., Westminster.

HASTINGS 1713–1727

b. c.1659, 1st s. of Archibald Hutcheson of Stracum, co. Antrim. educ. M. Temple 1680, called 1683, bencher 1726. m. (2) lic. 18 Aug. 1715, Mary Gayer, wid. (d. 19 Feb. 1727), of Stepney; (3) Rebecca; (4) 1731, Elizabeth, wid. of Col. Robert Stewart of Montserrat, s.p.s.[1]
Attorney-gen. Leeward Is. 1688–1702; ld. of Trade Dec. 1714–Jan. 1716; dep. steward of Westminster Aug. 1726–Jan. 1727.

Hutcheson, lawyer and economist, was the man of business of the Duke of Ormonde, 'from whom he had received signal obligations'. Returned for Hastings as a Whig who would often vote with the Tories, he was given a place on the board of Trade on George I's accession. After Ormonde's flight in 1715, he made a long and spirited defence of his patron in the House, taking over the administration of Ormonde's affairs in England and visiting him in Paris.[2] Early in 1716 he resigned his place, speaking against the septennial bill in April following. In the summer of that year, he was described as one of the principal Tory advisers of the Prince of Wales, later George II,[3] and as having been 'a mighty man for the Government, but is at present a malcontent, for he was not enough considered, and so sides highly with the Prince'.[4] He opposed the vote of credit against Sweden in April 1717, and a month later spoke against the South Sea Company's proposals for taking over the national debt. In January 1718 he and Walpole led for the Opposition in the debate on the retention of half-pay officers, having 'already prepared the minds of the assembly by causing his

book of abstracts and observations to be distributed gratis to most of the Members', 'to show that the lists of half-pay were charged with many officers who had no right to it'. He wrote several treatises on the national debt, claiming to be 'the first who set the debts of the nation in a fair and full light . . . which, till then had been kept as a mystery from the people'. During the South Sea crisis he proposed that all transactions made during the boom should 'be esteemed of no more force or validity, than the bargains of children, lunatics and madmen'.[5] An opponent of Walpole's 'ingraftment' scheme, he proposed

a scheme of his own in a committee for retrieving of credit, etc., the method . . . was to bring down the prices of stocks of all our companies to the sums paid in by the first proprietors, that is £100 South Sea stock would be at seventy pounds, that being the sum originally paid by the proprietors at the founding of the Company. He also proposed that all the money and effects that should arise out of the late directors' estates and others, with other sums etc. should be applied to appeasing of the annuitants, the subscribers of the many subscriptions and such who bought the South Sea stock at the high prices. Though many think this the most equitable way of relieving the unhappy sufferers, yet the committee would not hear of it, which put Mr. Hutcheson somewhat out of humour, being a gentleman not a little attached to his own thoughts. He was so far provoked as to say loudly that he would never appear in that committee again, and so walked out of the House, on which some were so indecent as to hiss.[6]

Nevertheless he was elected to the secret committee set up by the House of Commons to investigate the South Sea scandal.

In 1721–2 Hutcheson had several conversations and some correspondence with Sutherland, in which he pressed for an early dissolution of Parliament and for triennial and even annual Parliaments.[7] Early in 1722 he introduced a bill, which passed the Commons but was rejected by the Lords, for correcting abuses in despatching writs to sheriffs and enforcing the penalties against returning officers who made false returns. He also took part in the successful agitation for the repeal of the clauses of the Quarantine Act giving emergency powers to the Government. Put up for Westminster in 1722 with the support of Atterbury and the Tories, he was returned with a huge majority, but was unseated on petition in December, having already taken his seat for Hastings, for which he had also been elected against a government candidate. At the opening of the new Parliament he moved that the elections committee should be a select one, instead of open to anyone who wished to join it, but nobody else supporting him, the motion dropped. He opposed the suspension of the Habeas Corpus Act in October

1722, and in March 1723 spoke in Atterbury's defence and against the bill of pains and penalties against Plunkett.[8] In a debate on the tobacco frauds that year, he proposed successfully that a single commission of customs for both England and Scotland should be set up.[9] He spoke against the army in 1724 and against the supply in 1726. He remained on close terms with the Jacobites, one of whose leaders, Lord Orrery, wrote to the Pretender 10 May 1724: 'Mr. Hutcheson is a very honest man, and to be depended upon. I think he is a good friend of yours, but he is of a peculiar turn, and will serve the cause in his own way'.[10] And in 1728 Atterbury wrote to his daughter:

I should be glad to know how Mr. Hutcheson does, who is, I think, several years older than I, and therefore in danger of going sooner. Whenever he goes, we shall loose a worthy, honest, incorruptible man, which is, at this time of day, a great rarity . . . The Duke of Ormonde's affairs will never find one, after he is gone, I fear, that will manage them with so disinterested a zeal, and so much to his service . . . Give him many thanks from me . . . for the many instances of his friendship, and assure him that, wherever I am, I carry about me the same grateful heart towards him, and am in all respects just the same as I was when I left England, except in point of health.[11]

Hutcheson did not stand again, dying 12 Aug. 1740.

[1] Nichols's *Atterbury Corresp.* iv. 226; v. 109; PCC 227 Browne; Add. 18683, f. 3. [2] *HMC Stuart*, v. 524; vii. 299–300; Stuart mss 156/75, 157/138. [3] Coxe, *Walpole*, ii. 73. [4] *HMC Stuart*, vii. 314. [5] *Pol. State*, xv. 88; xxiii. 367; *Abstracts of the number and yearly pay of the Land Forces . . . for the year 1718.* [6] Stuart mss 52/157. [7] *Copies of some letters from Mr. Hutcheson to the late Earl of Sunderland* (1722). [8] *Pol. State*, xxiii. 361–6; Stuart mss 57/125 (see LONDON); *Knatchbull Diary*, 29 Mar. 1723. [9] See PERRY, Micajah. [10] Stuart mss 74/58A. [11] *Atterbury Corresp.* iv. 152–3.

E.C.

HUXLEY, George (c.1687–1744), of Stoke, Bucks.

BEDFORD   1722–28 May 1725
NEWPORT I.o.W.   1 Feb. 1726–1741

b. c.1687, 1st s. of Thomas Huxley of Bow, Mdx. by Arabella, da. of Sir William Becher of Howbury, Beds. *educ.* Clare, Camb.; M. Temple 1704. *m.*, 1s. Commr. of victualling 1725–9; muster-master gen. 1729–42.

Returned for Bedford in 1722, Huxley was made a commissioner of victualling in 1725. He lost his seat at the by-election but was brought in by the Government for Newport, voting with the Administration in all recorded divisions. In 1729 he became muster-master general with a salary of £800.[1] He died 19 July 1744.

[1] *Gent. Mag.* 1739, p. 306.

P.W.

HYDE, Henry, Visct. Cornbury (1710–53).

OXFORD UNIVERSITY   26 Feb. 1732–23 Jan. 1751

b. 28 Nov. 1710, 1st surv. s. of Henry Hyde, M.P., 4th Earl of Clarendon and 2nd Earl of Rochester, high steward of Oxf. Univ., by Jane, da. of Sir William Leveson Gower, 4th Bt., of Stittenham, sis. of John, 1st Baron Gower. *educ.* Ch. Ch. Oxf. 1725, D.C.L. 1728. *unm. summ.* to Lords in his fa.'s barony as Baron Hyde of Hindon 23 Jan. 1751.

The great-grandson of Lord Chancellor Clarendon, and the grandson of James II's brother-in-law, Lord Rochester, Cornbury as a young man was inducted into the Jacobite councils by James II's daughter, the Duchess of Buckingham, with whom he went to Rome to meet the Pretender secretly in January 1731. There he submitted to the Pretender a plan for gaining both the Whig and the Tory chiefs of the Opposition by promising them places and honours in the event of a restoration. The proposals were approved by the Pretender, who appointed him a lord of his bedchamber before his departure in April.[1]

On returning to England Cornbury, who was badly off, refused a pension of £400 a year which had been obtained for him from the King by his brother-in-law, Lord Essex,[2] entering Parliament for Oxford University, with which his family had long been connected. During the next few years he became involved in the negotiations opened by the English Jacobites with the French government for the restoration of the Stuarts with French help. In 1733 he went over to Paris to communicate to the French authorities the plans which had been prepared for seizing the Tower, with the names of the leaders of the rising in the various counties, and of the military officers who were thought could be relied on. Louis XV promised that an attempt should be made, but on examination the French were dissatisfied with the arrangements for an English rising and with Cornbury's demand for 14,000 French troops. The outbreak of the war of the Polish succession finally led to the abandonment of the project. Disheartened by what he regarded as the French breach of faith, and by accusations brought against him by the English Jacobites of having disclosed the negotiations to his friend Bolingbroke, he wrote in 1735 to the Stuart court announcing his intention henceforth of severing his connexion with the Jacobites.[3] Turning to his parliamentary duties, he took an active part in his university's campaign against the mortmain bill of 1736, which aimed at restricting bequests of lands to and the number of livings owned by charitable bodies. In 1737 and 1738 he spoke against the army.[4] Under the influence of his cousin, Sir

William Wyndham (q.v.), he engaged in a flirtation with the Prince of Wale's party and was incorrectly reported to have been appointed a gentleman of the Prince's bedchamber.[5] In fact he was beginning to drift away from the Opposition, refusing to join in their secession from Parliament in 1739.[6] He spoke against the motion for Walpole's removal in 1741.

In the next Parliament Cornbury generally supported the Government. Before Walpole's fall he voted against the opposition motion of 18 Dec. 1741 for papers on foreign affairs.[7] He was included in both the government and the opposition lists for the secret committee, to which he was elected, subsequently opposing an opposition motion for the indemnification of witnesses against Walpole. In April 1742 he refused an offer of a peerage, made on Pulteney's recommendation.[8] He was absent on the Hanoverian troops in November 1742, spoke for the Address in December 1743 and for the Hanoverians in January 1744, and supported the loyal address on the threatened French invasion in February. During the Forty-five he was one of the 'friends' of the Government who voted against them on the question of recalling British troops from Flanders. He also opposed the sending of Hessians to Scotland, 'the national being the only constitutional troops'.[9] In the division on the Hanoverians in 1746 he voted against the Government and was classed among the 'doubtfuls'. In 1747 he was reclassified as Opposition.

In 1748, disgusted with the state of public affairs and despairing of doing any good, Cornbury applied to George II for leave to go abroad for the recovery of his impaired health. He wrote to the King:

> Family attachments, the habits and prejudices of first connections, and the consequences of these in several parts of my life, have deprived me of all the satisfaction I could have felt, and of all the advantages I must have found, in being more particularly attached to your Majesty's service.[10]

Abroad he occupied himself with arranging to pay off the family debts by selling his estate of Cornbury. In December 1750 he returned to England to apply to the King for a peerage, which was readily granted, on the ground that

> I felt . . . the impossibility of my ever taking my seat again in the House of Commons with any satisfaction. I had seen too much of opposition, and knew too well the materials of which it was made, to put to sea again in that rotten vessel. I knew the inefficiency, and had long enough felt the difficulty of standing single and unconnected in that assembly. I believed too, that my health would not allow my attendance there, even if I could have attended with any satisfaction, and to any purpose.

On Cornbury's elevation to the Lords he wrote to Arthur Onslow, the Speaker, to explain his reasons for leaving the Commons. He told Onslow that he regarded the Pelhams as the best available ministers and that if he had been beginning his career he would have connected himself with them, but that his previous political affiliations made it impossible for him to do so consistently with self-respect. He considered 'party divisions and distinction the greatest national misfortune' and deplored the lack of 'authority in Government', which, he told George II, was 'felt in every corner of the country' but could be remedied 'without much difficulty. There belongs enough . . . to the crown of England'.[11] This letter, or something like it, seems to have been read and approved by George III soon after he came to the throne.[12]

Cornbury died of a fall from his horse in Paris, 26 Apr. 1753.

[1] Stuart mss 142/99; 143/176; 144/49. [2] Cal. Treas. Bks. and Pprs., 1731-3, pp. 102, 146, 184. [3] Stuart mss 162/124, 165; 163/156; 164/194; 183/131. [4] HMC Egmont Diary, ii. 255, 350; HMC Carlisle, 193. [5] Stuart mss 224/122; Gent. Mag. 1738, p. 222. [6] Coxe, Walpole, iii. 519. [7] Owen, Pelhams, 25. [8] Letter to Speaker Onslow, 27 Jan. 1751, Royal archives. [9] Yorke's parl. jnl. Parl. Hist. xiii. 135, 463, 648; Owen, op. cit. 285; Walpole to Mann, 20 Dec. 1745. [10] Add. 32715, f. 163. [11] Add. 32723, f. 422; letter to Onslow. [12] Sedgwick, Letters from Geo. III to Bute, 82-83.

E.C.

HYDE, Robert (1650–1722), of Hatch, nr. Hindon, and Heale, Wilts.

HINDON	23 Feb. 1677–24 Jan. 1679, 1685–1687, 1689–1698
WILTSHIRE	1702–20 Apr. 1722

b. 10 Oct. 1650, 2nd but o. surv. s. of Alexander Hyde, bp. of Salisbury, by Mary, da. of Robert Townson, bp. of Salisbury. educ. Magdalen Hall, Oxf. 1666; M. Temple 1667, called 1673. m. (1) 4 May 1674, Lady Finetta Pope (d. 16 Oct. 1700), da. of Thomas, 3rd Earl, sis. and coh. of Thomas, 4th Earl of Downe [I], 1da. d.v.p.; (2) 26 Jan. 1704, Arundell, da. of Thomas Penruddock, M.P., of Compton Chamberlayne, Wilts., s.p. suc. under entail to Wilts. estates of uncle Sir Robert Hyde, M.P., c.j. of King's bench 1665;[1] and fa. 1667.

Hyde, whose father was first cousin to Lord Chancellor Clarendon, was a High Church Tory and member of the October Club. In 1721 his name was sent to the Pretender as a probable supporter in the event of a rising.[2] He was returned five times for Hindon, where he had an interest, and seven times for the county, though on the last occasion too 'ancient and infirm' to appear at the election,[3] dying ten days later, 20 Apr. 1722.[4]

[1] Wilts. N. & Q. vi. 344, 389; Baker, Northants. i. 708; Wilts. Arch. Mag. xxiv. 93-94. [2] Stuart mss 65/16. [3] Wilts. Arch. Mag. xi. 88, 90. [4] Pol. State, xxiii. 454.

R.S.L.

HYETT, Charles (1677–1738), of Painswick House, nr. Gloucester, Glos.

Gloucester   1722–1727

b. 10 Apr. 1677, 1st s. of Benjamin Hyett, clerk of the peace for Gloucestershire. *m.* 11 Mar. 1707, Anna, da. of Nicholas Webb, alderman of Gloucester, 2s. Constable of Gloucester castle bef. 1714.

Hyett, who came of an old Gloucestershire family, purchased considerable properties near Gloucester in the early eighteenth century,[1] building Painswick House, five miles from the city, in 1725.[2] Returned in 1722 for Gloucester unopposed as a Tory, he did not stand again, dying 17 Feb. 1738. His sons, Nicholas and Benjamin Hyett, contested Gloucester unsuccessfully on the extreme Tory interest in 1734 and 1741.

[1] Rudder, *Glos.* 251, 317. [2] W. R. Williams, *Parl. Hist. Glos.* 208.

S.R.M.

HYLTON, John (1699–1746), of Hylton Castle, co. Dur.

Carlisle   1727–1741, 26 Jan. 1742–25 Sept. 1746

bap. 27 Apr. 1699, 2nd s. of John Hylton of Hylton Castle by Dorothy, da. of Sir Richard Musgrave, 2nd Bt., of Hayton, Cumb. *unm. suc.* e. bro. 1722.

The Hyltons belonged to a small group of ancient families holding feudal baronies, who for some generations had the designation of baron.[1] Known himself as 'the Baron', Hylton is said to have been of a 'mild and generous disposition, though of reserved habits' and to have been one of the last to keep a domestic fool.[2] For nearly 20 years he represented Carlisle as a Tory on the interest of his relations, the Musgraves, co-operating in elections with his Whig fellow-Member, Charles Howard, who stood separately from him on the interest of the Earls of Carlisle. In Parliament he normally voted against the Government, but allowed Howard to persuade him, though he did not 'much relish it', to abstain in 1736 from the division on a Quakers' relief bill, in compliment to Lord Carlisle.[3] He also was one of the Tories who abstained from the division on the motion for Walpole's removal in February 1741. Defeated at the general election that year, he regained his seat on petition, voting against the Government in all three divisions on the Hanoverians. He died 25 Sept. 1746, the last male representative of his line, leaving his estates to his nephew, Sir Richard Musgrave, 4th Bt., on condition that he took the name of Hylton.

[1] *CP,* vii. 19. [2] Surtees, *Durham,* ii. 22–23, 36. [3] *HMC Carlisle,* 101, 164, 165.

R.R.S.

INCHIQUIN, Earl of, *see* **O'BRIEN, William**

INGE, William (1669–1731), of Thorpe Constantine, nr. Tamworth, Staffs.

Tamworth   1715–1722

bap. 28 Sept. 1669, 1st s. of William Inge of Thorpe Constantine by Frances, da. of Sir Thomas Gresley, 2nd Bt., of Drakelow, Derbys. *educ.* Queen's, Oxf. 1686; I. Temple 1687. *m.* Elizabeth, da. and coh. of Robert Phillips of Newton Regis, Warws., 2s. 1da. *suc.* fa. 1690.

Inge's great-grandfather married the heiress of a London alderman, who bought Thorpe Constantine in 1631. Returned unopposed as a Tory for the neighbouring borough of Tamworth in 1715, he voted against the Government. In 1721 his name was sent to the Pretender in a list of probable supporters in the event of a Jacobite rising. He did not stand again. Said to have been 'a considerable scholar and an industrious antiquary',[1] he died in 1731 (buried 3 July).

[1] Stuart mss 65/16; S. Shaw, *Staffs.* i. 406.

R.R.S.

INGOLDSBY, Thomas (1689–1768), of Waldridge, nr. Aylesbury, Bucks.

Aylesbury   13 Feb. 1730–1734

b. 3 Mar. 1689, 1st surv. s. of Richard Ingoldsby of Waldridge by Mary, da. of William Colmore of Warwick. *educ.* ?Winchester 1704; ?St. John's, Oxf. 1706. *m.* Anne, da. of John Limbrey of Tangier Park, Hants, 1 surv. da. *suc.* fa. 1703.
Sheriff, Bucks. 1721.

Thomas Ingoldsby, of an old Buckinghamshire family,[1] was grandson of Sir Richard Ingoldsby, K.B., M.P., the regicide and cousin of Oliver Cromwell, who sat in the Protector's 'other House' as Lord Ingoldsby and represented Aylesbury from 1661 to 1681. Returned for Aylesbury at a by-election in 1730, when he defeated the sitting Member, one of Walpole's followers, Ingoldsby voted with the Government on the excise bill 1733 and on the repeal of the Septennial Act 1734. He was listed in 1733 as a supporter of administration candidates throughout Buckinghamshire[2] for the general election of 1734, at which he did not stand. He died late in 1768.

[1] Lipscomb, *Bucks.* ii. 169. [2] Cholmondeley (Houghton) mss 68.

R.S.L.

INGRAM, Hon. Arthur (1689–1736), of Temple Newsam, Yorks.

Horsham   16 June 1715–10 Apr. 1721

bap. 21 Dec. 1689, 3rd s. of Arthur Ingram, M.P., 3rd Visct. Irwin [S], by Isabella, 1st da. and coh. of

John Machell of Hills, Suss., M.P. Horsham 1681–1700; bro. of Hon. Charles and Henry Ingram (qq.v.). *educ.* Oriel, Oxf. 1706; L. Inn 1706. *unm.* *suc.* bro. as 6th Visct. 10 Apr. 1721.

Ld. lt. Yorks. E. Riding 1728–36.

Descended from Sir Arthur Ingram, M.P. (*d.* 1642), a merchant and official who bought the manor of Temple Newsam and other estates in Yorkshire, the Ingrams acquired by marriage the estate of Hills, near Horsham, at the beginning of the eighteenth century. Returned for Horsham on petition in 1715, Arthur Ingram voted with the Government, except on the septennial bill, which he opposed, possibly because his constituents had petitioned against it.[1] He vacated his seat on succeeding to the peerage in 1721. In 1723 he contracted to buy out his chief opponent at Horsham, Charles Eversfield (q.v.), but was unable to raise sufficient capital to complete the purchase.[2] He is described by Lady Mary Wortley Montagu as 'a quite new man, that has a great deal of wit, joined to a diabolical person'.[3] He died 26 May 1736.

[1] *CJ*, xviii. 430. [2] W. Albery, *Parl. Hist. Horsham*, 74–75. [3] *Works* (1893), i. 483.

J.B.L.

INGRAM, Arthur (*d.* 1742), of Borrowby, Yorks.

HORSHAM 16 June 1715–1722

1st surv. s. of Arthur Ingram of Borrowby by Jane, da. of Sir John Mallory of Studley, Yorks. *m.* Elizabeth Barns, 1da. *suc.* nephew Arthur Ingram 1708; *fa.* 1713.

Commr. for forfeited estates 1716–25.

Ingram was related to the Ingrams, Viscounts Irwin (qq.v.), on whose interest he was brought in on petition for Horsham, giving all his recorded votes for the Government. He was not put up again, dying 17 June 1742.[1]

[1] Temple Newsam mss, Leeds Central Lib. TN/F 15.

J.B.L.

INGRAM, Hon. Charles (1696–1748), of Hills, nr. Horsham, Suss.

HORSHAM 7 Feb. 1737–28 Nov. 1748

b. 27 Mar. 1696, 7th s. of Arthur Ingram, M.P., 3rd Visct. Irwin [S]; bro. of Hon. Arthur and Henry Ingram (qq.v.). *educ.* Oriel, Oxf. 1714. *m.* 9 Mar. 1726, Elizabeth, da. and coh. of Charles Scarborough of Windsor, clerk of the Green Cloth, wid. of Francis Brace of Biddenham, Beds., 1s. 3da.

Ensign 3 Ft. Gds. 1718, lt. 1720; capt. 16 Ft. 1724; capt. and lt.-col. 3 Ft. Gds. 1737; maj. and col. 1743; adjutant-gen. 1743; res. 1748.

Returned for Horsham on the family interest, Ingram regularly voted with the Government. Nevertheless his military promotion was so slow

II—M

that in 1742 his brother, Henry Ingram (q.v.), 7th Viscount Irwin, wrote to the Duke of Newcastle (15 June) asking on his behalf for a regiment:

He has now been four and twenty years in the service, sat one Parliament, is in this, and brought in the man you wished for [Sir Richard Mill, q.v.], which I would flatter myself may entitle him to this mark of his Majesty's favour.

In 1747, still without a regiment, Charles wrote to his brother pointing out that he was now the oldest colonel in the army without a regiment, as well as being

in actual service and venturing my life . . . If these will not entitle me to a regiment I must get out, for it will be impossible to continue with any credit or reputation to myself after such a slight being put upon me.

Lord Irwin took the matter up with the Duke of Newcastle,[1] who replied four months later that he had written to the Duke of Cumberland in Germany strongly recommending Ingram's claim but that 'his Royal Highness's answer was not so favourable as I wished it' and in short that 'to my great concern, I see no prospect of success'.[2] On this Ingram resigned his commission. He died 28 Nov. 1748.

[1] Add. 32699, f. 280; 17 and 25 July 1747, Add. 32712, ff. 213, 215. [2] W. Albery, *Parl. Hist. Horsham*, 89.

J.B.L.

INGRAM, Charles (1727–78), of Temple Newsam, Yorks.

HORSHAM 1747–14 Apr. 1763

b. 19 Mar. 1727, 1st s. of Hon. Charles Ingram (q.v.). *educ.* Westminster 1737–43. *m.* (lic. 28 June 1758) Frances Gibson, illegit. da. of Samuel Shepheard (q.v.), 5da. *suc.* uncle as 9th Visct. Irwin [S] 14 Apr. 1763.

Groom of the bedchamber to George III as Prince of Wales and King 1756–63; rep. peer [S] 1768–*d.*

Before Charles Ingram was returned as a minor on his family's interest, his uncle, Henry Ingram (q.v.), 7th Viscount Irwin, had applied on his behalf to Newcastle for a commission in the Guards.[1] Dropping this scheme because Charles 'was the only son in the family',[2] he next applied unsuccessfully for an equerryship to the King.[3] In 1751 he was too late with an application for Charles to be given a post in the new Prince of Wales's household,[4] but obtained a promise from the King to 'provide for him upon a proper occasion'. He was most indignant when Charles was passed over for a vacant post of groom of the bedchamber to the Prince in 1752 in favour of a connexion of Pelham's,[5] but achieved his object in 1756. Two years later Charles married a great heiress, by whom he became the father of George IV's mistress, Lady Hertford. He died 19 June 1778.

[1] 10 Apr. 1746, 25 May 1747, Add. 32707, ff. 45, 251. [2] 19 Jan. 1748, Add. 32714, f. 71. [3] 29 Jan. 1747, Add. 32710, f. 289; 11 June 1747, Add. 32711, f. 256. [4] *HMC Var.* viii. 174. [5] 14 Jan. 1753, Newcastle (Clumber) mss.

J.B.L.

INGRAM, Hon. Henry (1691–1761).

HORSHAM   1722–26 May 1736

b. 30 Apr. 1691, 4th s. of Arthur Ingram, M.P., 3rd Visct. Irwin [S]; bro. of Hon. Arthur and Charles Ingram (qq.v.). *educ*. Oriel, Oxf. 1708–12. *m*. bef. June 1737, Anne, da. and coh. of Charles Scarborough of Windsor, Berks., clerk of the Green Cloth, *s.p. suc.* bro. as 7th Visct. 26 May 1736.
Commissary gen. of stores, Gibraltar 1727–30, Minorca 1735–56; ld. lt. Yorks. E. Riding 1736–*d.*

Brought in for Horsham on the family interest, Ingram gave all his recorded votes for the Government. On succeeding to the peerage he completed the contract made by his brother Arthur to buy burgages at Horsham from Charles Eversfield (q.v.), thereby gaining complete control of the borough.[1] He died 4 Apr. 1761.

[1] W. Albery, *Parl. Hist. Horsham*, 74–76.

J.B.L.

INWEN, Thomas (*d.* 1743), of St. Saviour's, Southwark.

SOUTHWARK   23 Jan. 1730–19 Apr. 1743

m. Sarah, da. of William Hucks (q.v.) of St. Giles's-in-the-Fields, brewer, 1da.

Returned for Southwark at a by-election in 1730 and at the general election of 1734, Inwen, a brewer, voted against the Administration in all recorded divisions. On 10 Mar. 1732 he supported a bill to prevent the importation of hops from America into Ireland.[1] Re-elected in 1741, he was absent from the divisions on the election of the chairman of the elections committee in December 1741 and the Hanoverians in December 1742. He died 19 Apr. 1743, leaving his property in trust to his only daughter, Sarah, who had married Henry Howard, 10th Earl of Suffolk, and appointing Robert Hucks (q.v.) one of his executors.[2]

[1] *HMC Egmont Diary*, i. 234–5. [2] PCC 167 Boycott.

E.C.

IRBY, Sir William, 2nd Bt. (1707–75), of Whaplode, Lincs.

LAUNCESTON   24 Mar. 1735–1747
BODMIN   1747–1761

b. 8 Mar. 1707, o.s. of Sir Edward Irby, 1st Bt., M.P., of Whaplode, Lincs. by Dorothy, da. of Hon. Henry Paget of Dublin, yr. s. of William, 7th Lord Paget.

educ. Westminster 1719–22. *m*. 26 Aug. 1746, Albinia, da. of Henry Selwyn of Matson, Glos., 2s. 1da. *suc*. fa. 11 Nov. 1718; and to unsettled estates of his cos. Henry Paget, M.P., 1st Earl of Uxbridge, 1743; *cr*. Baron Boston 10 Apr. 1761.
Page of honour to the King 1724–8; equerry to Prince of Wales 1728–36; vice-chamberlain to Princess of Wales 1736–51, chamberlain 1751–72; chairman of committees in the House of Lords 1770–*d*.

A lifelong courtier, Irby served for nearly 50 years in the households of George I, Frederick, Prince of Wales, and the Princess Dowager, of whom Horace Walpole calls him 'the Polonius.'[1] Returned on petition for Launceston in 1735, he followed his master, the Prince of Wales, into opposition in 1738, voting against the Government except on the motion for Walpole's dismissal in February 1741, when he withdrew. After Walpole's fall he supported the Government, reverting to opposition with Frederick in 1747. In that year he was included among the followers of the Prince who were to be brought by him into Parliament, not being able to bring in themselves. After rejecting an invitation to stand for Queenborough,[2] he was brought in by Thomas Pitt (q.v.) for both Old Sarum and Bodmin, opting to sit for Bodmin, where he eventually established a strong personal interest. In the 2nd Lord Egmont's lists of promotions on Frederick's accession he is put down for a peerage, which he secured on George III's accession.
He died 30 Mar. 1775.

[1] Walpole, *Mems. Geo. II*, i. 87. [2] *HMC Fortescue*, i. 108, 109.

R.R.S.

ISHAM, Sir Edmund, 6th Bt. (1690–1772), of Lamport Hall, Northants.

NORTHAMPTONSHIRE   31 Mar. 1737–15 Dec. 1772

b. 18 Dec. 1690, 4th s. of Sir Justinian Isham, 4th Bt., and bro. of Sir Justinian Isham, 5th Bt. (qq.v.). *educ*. Rugby 1699–1707; Wadham, Oxf. 1707. *m*. (1) 17 Feb. 1735, Elizabeth (*d*. 19 July 1748), da. of Edward Wood of Littleton, Mdx., *s.p.*; (2) 4 May 1751, Philippa, da. of Richard Gee of Orpington, Kent, *s.p. suc*. bro. as 6th Bt. 5 Mar. 1737.
Fellow of Magdalen, Oxf. 1720–36; adv. Doctors' Commons 1724; judge adv. court of Admiralty 1731–41.

A younger son, expected to earn a living, Edmund Isham embarked on an academic and legal career. On succeeding to the title and estates he took it for granted that he would be adopted as the Tory candidate for the county. Within a week of his mother's death he wrote to his wife to apply to a Northamptonshire landowner, Lady Betty Germain, for her interest, explaining:

I dare not apply to Lady Betty personally by letter, which I know would be proper, because the gentlemen as yet have not met, and I am not publicly to presume they will nominate me.

Always a dandy—at Oxford his laundress had complained that he wore 'four, many times five, shirts a week'—he wrote again to his wife about his dress for the election:

My dear—They tell me I must proceed to the election on horseback, and ought to make something of a figure, and should have a scarlet coat, therefore desire you would send to my tailor to order him to make me a scarlet cloth riding coat trimmed black and lined with a black alepine, the sleeves the same as my grey coat, faced with black and scarlet cloth breeches . . . You may send it next Thursday by the Northampton coach, or at farthest the Monday after, for I believe the election will be on Thursday se' ennight.[1]

Returned unopposed for the rest of his life, he voted against the Government in every recorded division under Walpole and Pelham, speaking against the Spanish convention in 1739. He opposed the bill for the naturalization of the Jews in May 1753, arguing that the Scriptures and history showed that unconverted Jews could never become true Englishmen.[2]

He died 15 Dec. 1772.

[1] E. G. Forrester, *Northants. County Elections, 1695–1832*, pp. 58, 59. [2] *Parl. Hist.* xiv. 1379–83.

R.R.S.

ISHAM, Sir Justinian, 4th Bt. (1658–1730), of Lamport Hall, Northants.

NORTHAMPTON   1685–1687, 1689–1690
                   9 Mar. 1694–1698
NORTHAMPTONSHIRE   1698–13 May 1730

b. 11 Aug. 1658, 3rd *s.* of Sir Justinian Isham, 2nd Bt., M.P., of Lamport Hall, Northants, being 2nd *s.* by his second *w.* Vere, da. of Thomas Leigh, M.P., 1st Baron Leigh. *educ.* Ch. Ch. Oxf. 1674; L. Inn. 1677. *m.* 16 July 1783, Elizabeth, da. of Sir Edmund Turner of Stoke Rochford, Lincs., 6s. 5da. *suc.* bro. 26 July 1681.

Sir Justinian Isham was the head of the Tories in Northamptonshire, which he and his descendants represented continuously from 1698 to 1772. He supported the Revolution, forming part of the guard for the Princess Anne at Nottingham in 1688, but voted against making William of Orange King, and refused to sign the association in 1696.

At George I's accession, Isham proposed to retire but allowed himself to be persuaded to stand again 'for the sake of preserving peace and good neighbourhood', and because 'if he should not . . . the Whigs will undoubtedly get in'. His chief concern was for a place which he had secured for his eldest son (q.v.) after the Tory triumph in 1710. Writing

from the country on 15 Nov. 1714, he advised his son to seek the good offices of the new first lord of the Treasury, Lord Halifax, a Northamptonshire neighbour, with whom the Ishams were on friendly terms.

It is what he may expect, and I think what I ought to do, and if you can be continued in your post upon so safe terms, both I and you should be wanting in ourselves in not doing it. I find everybody of the other side is not turned out . . . and maybe they will not care to disoblige many Parliament men. I can rejoice in nothing so much as in doing, honestly and fairly, what can conduce to your advantage.

On 7 Dec. his son reported:

Lord Halifax sent for me to come to him yesterday morning and told me that he had a piece of news to tell me as disagreeable to him as it could be to me, for when he and the rest of the commissioners [of the Treasury] had agreed to continue me in commission, and my name laid before the King for a warrant, a certain person [Walpole] whom my Lord said it was not then proper to name insisted I should be struck out, and get one put in my room.

Isham was bitterly disappointed:

If you had not been put into such hopes, [he replied] but had been turned out by the lords of the Treasury it had been no more than what might have been expected, and I believe would not much have troubled either of us: but to be struck out by the King himself is a thousand times worse, it showing a particular mark of his disfavour.

On 18 Dec. 1714, Halifax wrote apologetically to him:

The King . . . was very touched and concerned at your manner of taking the putting out of Mr. Isham. He has commanded me to assure you that the first opportunity he has to prefer Mr. Isham he will allow me to put him in mind of him, and he will convince you and all the world that he shall be glad to oblige you.[1]

Thereafter Isham voted consistently with the Opposition. His name was sent to the Pretender in 1721 as a probable supporter in the event of a rising.[2] He died 13 May 1730.

[1] E. G. Forrester, *Northants. County Elections 1695–1832*, 37–40; *Letters of Lady Mary Wortley Montagu*, i. 122–3. [2] Stuart mss 65/16.

R.R.S.

ISHAM, Sir Justinian, 5th Bt. (1687–1737), of Lamport Hall, Northants.

NORTHAMPTONSHIRE   21 May 1730–5 Mar. 1737

b. 20 July 1687, 1st *s.* of Sir Justinian Isham, 4th Bt., and bro. of Sir Edmund Isham, 6th Bt. (qq.v.). *m.* 11 Sept. 1725, Mary, da. of Lisle Hacket of Moxhull, Warws., *s.p. suc.* fa. 13 May 1730.
    Commr. of leather duties and land taxes 1711–14.

After the Tory victory in 1710, Isham was given a place worth £500 a year, which he lost when the Whigs returned to power in 1714. In 1719 he went to Italy, where his father wrote to him at Genoa:

I am glad to find your travels prove so pleasant to you, and I don't question but your stay at Rome will be no less diverting, though I am sorry there is a person there that must make it pretty difficult how you manage in that respect.

And again:

The Pretender being now at Rome 'twill require a good deal of caution how you behave yourself in that respect, for this court have their spies in all parts.

He was presumably the Mr. Isham whose name was sent to the Pretender in 1721 as a probable supporter in the event of a rising. On his father's death he was assured that

all agree in desiring you to supply the place of your father: the interest is entirely settled in your family, and we hope it will be best if not the only expedient to prevent any disturbance in the county.

After 'a dear bought victory',[1] against a Whig opponent, he was re-elected unopposed in 1734, voting with the Opposition. He died suddenly on 5 Mar. 1737, 'a hale, strong man, not fifty years old. His servant was up with him in the morning, when he was very well, but before he could return to him found him dead.'[2]

[1] E. G. Forrester, *Northants. County Elections 1695–1832*, pp. 40, 41, 48, 52; Stuart mss 65/16. [2] *HMC Egmont Diary*, ii. 363.

R.R.S.

IVORY TALBOT, John (?1691–1772), of Lacock Abbey, Wilts.

LUDGERSHALL   1715–1722
WILTSHIRE   1727–1741

b. ?1691, 1st s. of Sir John Ivory of New Ross, co. Wexford by Anne, 1st da. and coh. of Sir John Talbot, M.P., of Lacock Abbey. *educ.* Ch. Ch. Oxf. 23 Apr. 1707, aged 15. *m.* by 1717, Mary, da. of Thomas Mansel, M.P., 1st Baron Mansel of Margam, 2s. 1da. *suc.* fa. 1695,[1] and to Wiltshire estates of gd.-fa. Sir John Talbot under will in 1714, when he assumed add. name of Talbot.

Ivory Talbot's maternal ancestor, Sir William Sharington, acquired Lacock from the Crown in 1540 at the dissolution of the monasteries.[2] Returned as a Tory for Ludgershall a year after succeeding to his estates, and later twice unopposed for the county, he voted consistently against the Government. His only recorded speech was against the Quakers tithe bill, 3 May 1736. In 1721 his name was sent to the Pretender as a probable supporter in the event of a rising.[3] In 1735 the mother of his nephew, Thomas, 2nd Lord Mansel, then aged 14, objected successfully to his being made sole guardian of her son because she 'did not care that Mr. Talbot, whose wife is mad . . . and is himself driven to drink, should have the sole

management of her son's education'.[4] He did not stand again, dying October 1772.

[1] *N. & Q.* (ser. 7), ix. 447; x. 214–15; *CSP Dom. 1694–5*, p. 402. [2] *VCH Wilts.* iii. 314. [3] Stuart mss 65/16. [4] *HMC Egmont Diary*, ii. 143.

R.S.L.

JACKSON, Richard (1688–1768), of Crutched Friars, London.

SUDBURY   31 Jan.–27 Apr. 1734

b. 1688. *m.* Elizabeth, da. of Edward Clarke, 1s. 2da. Director, S. Sea Co. 1730–63, dep. gov. 1764–d.

A wealthy Italian merchant, Jackson was elected a director of the South Sea Company in 1730; figured in both the lists submitted by outgoing directors and the shareholders of the Company at the election of new directors in 1733; and remained a director till he became deputy governor in 1764. After contesting Sudbury unsuccessfully in 1726, he was returned for it at the end of the 1734 Parliament as a Government supporter. He was defeated in 1734, petitioning but withdrawing his petition. He did not stand again, dying 11 Jan. 1768. His only son was Richard Jackson, M.P., who corresponded with Benjamin Franklin.[1]

[1] C. Van Doren, *Letters and Pprs. Benjamin Franklin and Richard Jackson, 1753–85*, pp. 2–3.

R.R.S.

JACOMB, Robert (*d.* 1732), of Feltwell, Norf. and Whitehall, London.

THETFORD   1722–14 Dec. 1732

b. 6 Dec. 1680, 3rd s. of William Jacomb of St. Mary Aldermary, London, by Mary, da. of Robert Blayney of London. *m.* (1) Francis Eyre (*d.*1716), 1s.; (2) Lucy Pemberton, 1s. Inspector gen. of accounts of the out ports 1716–20; dep. paymaster gen. 1720–d.

The son of 'a quiet country gentleman',[1] Robert Jacomb was a partner in the firm of Gibson, Jacob & Jacomb, scriveners and bankers. He started as a clerk to Thomas Gibson (q.v.),

who recommended him to Sir Robert Walpole as a man well skilled in funds and government's accounts, and so Sir Robert finds him, depending on him more than on any other in matters of this nature.[2]

When Walpole returned to the pay office in 1720, Jacomb became his deputy there, handling his private and official investments during the South Sea crisis. He was the author of the 'ingraftment scheme', a proposal to transfer part of the inflated capital of the South Sea Company to the Bank of England and the East India Company, which was adopted by Walpole, passed into law, but never put into operation.[3] Brought into Parliament by Walpole's influence in 1722, he frequently served on the committees appointed each session to prepare the finance bills (see under Kelsall, Henry).[4] He died 14 Dec. 1732.

¹ H. H. Drake, *Hundred of Blackheath*, 14. ² *HMC Egmont Diary*, i. 118. ³ J. H. Plumb, *Walpole*, i. 306, 325–6, 338. ⁴ *CJ*, xx. 242 et passim.

R.R.S.

JANSSEN, Abraham (c.1699–1765), of Wimbledon, Surr.

DORCHESTER   18 May 1720–1722

> *b.* c.1699, 1st s. of Sir Theodore Janssen, 1st Bt., and bro. of Stephen Theodore Janssen (qq.v.). *unm. suc.* fa. as 2nd Bt. 22 Sept. 1748.
> Director, E.I. Co. 1725–8.

Abraham Janssen was returned on petition at a by-election for Dorchester after a Tory had defeated him by one vote. In Parliament no vote of his has been recorded and he did not stand again. He died 19 Feb. 1765.

R.S.L.

JANSSEN, Stephen Theodore (d. 1777), of St. Paul's Churchyard, London.

LONDON   1747–1754

> 4th s. of Sir Theodore Janssen, 1st Bt., and bro. of Abraham Janssen (qq.v.). *m.* 13 Dec. 1750, Catherine, da. of Col. Peter Soulegre of Antigua, 1da. *suc.* bro. Sir Henry Janssen as 4th Bt. 21 Feb. 1766.
> Stationer 1745–65; master, Stationers' Co. 1749–51; alderman of London 1748–65, sheriff 1749–50, ld. mayor 1754–5, chamberlain 1765–76; director, French Hospital 1769.

Janssen was a leading London merchant and the owner of the French enamel works at Battersea. In a memorandum to Newcastle of 10 Jan. 1756 he claimed to have

> formed the plan for reducing the excise upon tea, and prosecuted it, till it was brought into the House by Sir John Barnard [q.v.], where it passed into a law in 1745, by which reduction the revenue has benefited £1,970,180. He was principally instrumental in establishing that seasonable association in the City, for the taking bank notes in payment immediately after the fight of Preston Pans in 1745, by which public credit was revived from the lowest ebb, and for which he had the then chancellor of the Exchequer's letter of thanks . . . He was the means of bringing in the bill for prohibiting cambrics during the late war with France, which has preserved a great quantity of our wealth from going into that kingdom.[1]

When he was returned for London as an opposition Whig in 1747, Pelham observed: 'I could have wished the merchants had chosen a better subject than Janssen, but forward fellows fare best in this world'.[2] On 18 Dec. 1747 he supported a bill to prohibit insurance of French ships in war time, and in the debates of 25 Nov. 1751 on Alexander

Murray he 'defended the city'.[3] Associated with Admiral Vernon (q.v.) in the foundation of the British Herring Fishery Company in 1750, of which he was vice-president,[4] he used to send Newcastle unsolicited advice on commercial matters, including 'several important papers regarding the trade of this nation' which had come into his possession.[5] During his mayoralty he incurred heavy debts, which he was unable to settle owing to business difficulties. On going bankrupt in January 1756, he applied for a place to Newcastle, as

> a man who has never had any selfish views, but who has devoted twenty years of his life to the service of the King and his Government, at great expense and labour, and neglect of his private concerns.

He continued:

> And now, my Lord, indulge me to say that I have had twenty-five years experience in with close application to all commercial affairs, as well as to all branches of the revenue, so that, if at this most critical conjuncture, I should be thought qualified to serve the King and his Government, your Grace might rely upon my fulfilling my duty in every particular.[6]

He was given no job, but by living on 'eighteen shillings a week' he was able to repay all his debts. Elected chamberlain of London in 1765, he stood unsuccessfully for the Isle of Wight borough of Yarmouth in 1768. He resigned his post of chamberlain on account of his age 6 Feb. 1776, receiving the thanks of the livery 'for his uniform zeal and activity in promoting, on every occasion, the true interest of this metropolis' in the various capacities in which he had served it.[7] He died a year later, 7 Apr. 1777.

¹ Manning & Bray, *Surr.* iii. 270; Walpole, *Mems. Geo. II*, ii. 177; Add. 32862, f. 71. ² To Horace Walpole sen. 4 July 1747, Add. 9186, f. 105. ³ Walpole, i. 30, 212. ⁴ Add. 32721, f. 105; *Gent. Mag.* 1750, p. 474. ⁵ 24 May 1751, Add. 34724, f. 308. ⁶ Add. 32862, f. 69. ⁷ Nichols, *Lit. Anecs.* iii. 408–11.

E.C.

JANSSEN, Sir Theodore, 1st Bt. (c.1654–1748), of Wimbledon, Surr.

YARMOUTH I.o.W.   12 Apr. 1717–31 Jan. 1721

> *b.* c.1654, 1st s. of Abraham Janssen of Angoulême, France by Henrietta Manigaut. *m.* 26 Jan. 1698, Williamsa (with £12,000), da. of Sir Robert Henley, M.P., of the Grange, Hants, 5s. 3da. Kntd. 26 Feb. 1698; *cr.* Bt. 11 Mar. 1715.
> Director, Bank of England, with statutory intervals, 1694–9, 1700–1, 1707–11, 1718–19; director, South Sea Co. 1711–18, 1719–21.

Theodore Janssen, of a Flemish Protestant family settled in France, came to England in 1680, and was naturalized in 1684. He became one of the most eminent merchants and financiers of his time, a founding director of both the Bank of England and its rival, the South Sea Company, as well as a founder of the new East India Company. From 1695 he was among the chief contractors for remittances to the army abroad.

Janssen was over 60 when he entered the House of Commons as a Whig in 1717, voting for the Government on the repeal of the Occasional Conformity and Schism Acts but against them on the peerage bill in 1719. He was defeated at the election of South Sea directors in 1718, but unfortunately for himself was reinstated on the board in 1719. When the frauds began to come out in 1721 he and the other directors with seats were expelled from the House, committed to the custody of the serjeant-at-arms, and examined by the committee set up to investigate the affair. Questioned as to an account showing that £574,000 South Sea stock had been disposed of to unnamed persons, he said that when the account in question had been laid before the Company's committee of treasury, of which he was a member,

> an objection being made that blanks were left for the names of the buyers of this stock, the late sub-governor and Mr. Knight [the cashier] said there were reasons for passing the account in that manner; and that the stock was disposed of to persons whose names were not proper to be known to a great many; but at a fit time a perfect account thereof should be made up; and that, if the bill did pass, the stock would be well sold.

On the introduction of the bill confiscating the property of the directors and other guilty parties for the relief of their victims, Janssen petitioned the House for lenient treatment on the ground that

> he had by his industry acquired an estate of near £300,000 before the late scheme was thought of; that he had no hand in the contriving or carrying on the said scheme; but often opposed the methods of proceeding in the execution thereof; that he knew nothing of taking in or holding any stock for any person, without a valuable consideration paid, or secured, or of any difference paid upon such stock.[1]

He also applied to Walpole, asking for his 'kind and powerful assistance', and to Humphry Morice (q.v.):

> I little expected to give trouble to my friends upon so doleful an occasion as I now find myself involved in, but my case is so very hard, even beyond that of any other of the directors, having a numerous family unprovided for, and given an account of my whole estate without concealing any part of it, hoping thereby to have better quarter, that I am under a necessity to implore my friends' kind assistance and to beg the favour of them to be next Thursday at the House of Commons when my case is like to come under consideration. You'll oblige me, therefore, to be there and to concur with those who shall endeavour to procure me a subsistence something answerable to the number of my children and to the estate I was possessed of before this unhappy undertaking.[2]

When his case came up on 2 June 1721, Walpole's brother, Horace, seconded by Sir Richard Steele, proposed that he should be allowed to keep £50,000 out of an estate valued at £243,000, which was carried after some debate by 134 to 118. In fact he appears to have kept £100,000 out of an estate worth £300,000.[3]

Besides losing most of his fortune Janssen, with the other directors, was statutorily disqualified from sitting in Parliament or holding public office. He died 22 Sept. 1748, aged 94.

[1] CJ, xix. 425–6, 524. [2] J. H. Plumb, Walpole, i. 352n.; 30 May 1721, Morice mss. [3] CJ, xxi. 170, 245.

R.R.S.

JEAFFRESON, Christopher (1699–1749), of Dullingham, Cambs.

CAMBRIDGE 28 Dec. 1744–1747, 6 May 1748–18 Jan. 1749

b. 12 July 1699, 1st s. of John Jeaffreson of Roushall, Suff. by his w. Anne Stott of Kettleburgh, Suff. educ. Histon, Cambs.; Magdalene, Camb. 1717. m. Elizabeth, da. of Sir John Shuckburgh, 3rd Bt., of Shuckburgh, Warws., 2s. 1da. suc. fa. 1746.

Christopher Jeaffreson succeeded to estates in the West Indies and Suffolk, acquired by his great-uncle, John Jeaffreson, who migrated to Antigua in 1624.[1] At a by-election in 1744 he was returned unopposed for Cambridge on the interest of his friend, Samuel Shepheard (q.v.), voted for the Hanoverians in 1746, and was classed as Old Whig. At the general election of 1747 he was replaced by Shepheard, who was anxious to substitute him in the second seat for Lord Dupplin, but was dissuaded by Henry Bromley, Lord Montfort (q.v.).[2] On Shepheard's death next year he was again returned. He died 18 Jan. 1749, according to William Cole, the Cambridge antiquary, 'from too much drinking, which brought him into a consumption. He was one of the tallest men I ever saw'.[3]

[1] Oliver, Antigua, ii. 106–9. [2] See SHEPHEARD, Samuel. [3] Add. 5808, f. 47.

R.R.S.

JEFFERIES (formerly **WINNINGTON**), **Edward** (c.1670–1725), of Ham Castle, nr. Droitwich, Worcs.

DROITWICH 1708–20 July 1725

b. c.1670, 3rd s. of Sir Francis Winnington, M.P., by his 2nd w. Elizabeth, da. and coh. of Edward Salwey of Stanford, Worcs.; uncle of Thomas Winnington (q.v.). educ. M. Temple 1687, called 1694, bencher 1720. m. c.1708, Jane, da. of William Bloome of Altofts, Yorks., niece and h. of Henry Jefferies of Ham Castle, Worcs., 3s. d.v.p.

Q.C. 1710; puisne justice of Carm., Card. and Pemb. 1711–12; 2nd justice of Chester, 1714–*d*.

Edward Winnington, who took the name of Jefferies when his wife succeeded to her uncle's property in 1709, was described by a contemporary as 'the most pleasing as well as most powerful advocate at the bar he had ever known upon the Oxford circuit'.

> He . . . might have attained the highest honours in his profession, had not his ambition been restrained by his love of country sports, particularly by the pleasures of the chase, for he kept his foxhounds to the last, amidst the fullness of business, as his father, Sir Francis, had done before.[1]

A distinguished speaker in Parliament and a Tory, he supported the Harley Administration, under which he was made a Welsh judge. After George I's accession he became a leading member of the Opposition, speaking against the Government on the septennial bill in 1716, the army in 1717, and the repeal of the Occasional Conformity and Schism Acts and the peerage bill in 1719. In 1721 he was elected to the South Sea committee. Hitherto he had not received an increase of salary granted to all the other Welsh judges but in 1721 his salary was

> ordered to be augmented as well as the others, and the arrears to be paid him from the time the others were augmented. This is said to be procured without his privity, by his friend the Viscount [Harcourt]; he seems very uneasy at it, but it is thought he will take it.[2]

In 1722 he seconded an unsuccessful motion by Archibald Hutcheson (q.v.) for election petitions to be heard by a select committee, pointing out

> that this had been the constant usage and practice . . . and that it had never been otherwise, till the long Parliament in 1641, when all things were in confusion.

In 1725 he fell ill

> of a mortification in his foot, occasioned by the cutting of a corn which, in pursuit of the pleasures of the chase, had been hurt and bruised to a great degree, and, to stop the mortification, his leg was cut off, an operation which he bore with incredible fortitude, but died in two or three days after,[3]

20 July 1725, leaving his estate to his elder brother, Salwey Winnington, M.P.

[1] Nash, *Worcs.* ii. 20. [2] *HMC Portland*, iv. 693; vii. 307. [3] Nash, oc. cit.

R.R.S.

JEFFREYS, John (1706–66), of the Priory, Brecon, and Sheen, Surr.

BRECONSHIRE 1734–1747
DARTMOUTH 1747–Jan. 1766

b. 1706, 1st surv. s. of John Jeffreys, M.P., by Elizabeth, da. of Anthony Sturt, M.P., of London. *unm. suc.* fa. 1715.

Jt. sec. to Treasury 1742–46; sec. to chancellor of the Exchequer 1752–4; warden of the mint 1754–*d*.; dep. ranger of St. James's and Hyde Parks 1757–*d*.

Jeffreys came of a leading Breconshire family. His father and his uncle, Sir Jeffrey Jeffreys, were wealthy tobacco merchants who sat for Brecon county and borough respectively. A gamester, and a popular member of White's, he soon ran through his private fortune.

After unsuccessfully contesting Brecon borough on coming of age, Jeffreys was returned for the county by a small majority in 1734, representing it till 1747, when he was brought in on the government interest at Dartmouth. He began his career in opposition, attaching himself to Pulteney, who after Walpole's fall made him joint secretary of the Treasury, worth about £5,000 p.a. in wartime, an appointment described by Horace Walpole as White's contribution to the Government.[1] Though notoriously inefficient and quite incapable of carrying on the business of the Treasury should anything happen to John Scrope (q.v.), the octogenarian senior secretary, he was the only one of Pulteney's friends who was not turned out at the end of 1744. 'I have known the man long', Pelham, a fellow member of White's, replied, when told that almost everybody in the House of Commons was asking 'what public reason could be given for keeping in' Jeffreys. 'I think him a good retired inoffensive creature, and as such had no desire to show resentment to him on the account of others; nor did I imagine the public would think itself at all interested in his situation one way or the other'.

In 1746 Pelham told James West (q.v.), his secretary as chancellor of the Exchequer, that 'as Mr. Scrope was very old' he desired West to replace Jeffreys; but that 'he was so pressed by Mr. Jeffreys' friends that he could not remove him without some provision', and that West would have to allow him £1,000 p.a. till other arrangements could be made, meanwhile retaining the office of secretary to Pelham. When West became senior secretary on Scrope's death in 1752, Jeffreys was quartered on the new joint secretary, Nicholas Hardinge (q.v.).[2] Announcing these changes to Newcastle, Pelham remarked that they would enable him 'to show some mark of regard to little Jeffreys, by naming him secretary to me as chancellor, with the same advantages he had before. You know Arundell [q.v.], Lord Lincoln, etc. press me much upon this and it suits with my own inclination also'.[3] He continued to be financially supported by successive Administrations till his death 30 Jan. 1766.

[1] Walpole to Mann, 26 Dec. 1743. [2] See under WEST, James. [3] Pelham to Newcastle, 10 Apr. 1752, Add. 32726, f. 393.

R.R.S.

JEKYLL, Sir Joseph (c.1662–1738), of Bell Bar, Herts.

EYE	14 Dec. 1697–1713
LYMINGTON	1713–1722
REIGATE	1722–19 Aug. 1738

b. c.1662, 4th s. of John Jekyll of London by Tryphena, wid. of Richard Hill. *educ.* M. Temple 1680, called 1687, bencher 1697. *m.* Elizabeth, da. of John Somers of Clifton, Worcs., sis. and coh. of Lord Chancellor Somers, *s.p.* Kntd. 12 Dec. 1700.
C.j. Chester 1697–1717; King's serjeant 1700; master of the rolls 1717–*d.*; P.C. 31 July 1717; 1st commr. of the great seal 7 Jan.–1 June 1725.

Jekyll entered Parliament in 1697 under the aegis of his brother-in-law, Lord Chancellor Somers, on whose death in 1716 he acquired through his wife, Somers's sister, an interest at Reigate, which he subsequently represented. Under Anne he supported the Whig junto and was one of the managers of Sacheverell's impeachment.

In 1715 Jekyll was elected to the secret committee set up by the House of Commons to prepare the impeachment of the leaders of the late Tory Government. When the articles charging Lord Oxford with high treason and other high crimes and misdemeanours were moved in the Commons, he took exception to those relating to high treason, for which he considered there was insufficient evidence. He spoke to the same effect on the charges against Ormonde, saying that they did not amount to more than high crimes and misdemeanours and that though he had voted with the Whigs for many years, 'yet now their proceedings were so slightly founded and straining the law, that he could not nor would not vote with them'. In a further debate on Oxford's impeachment he reiterated his reasons for differing from the rest of the committee observing 'that it was the duty of an honest man never to act by a spirit of party'. His speech, Oxford's brother wrote, 'threw the whole party into confusion and raised so great a storm upon Sir Joseph, that the Speaker desired to know whether they were impeaching the Lord Oxford or Sir Joseph Jekyll'. Years later a Tory friend told the 2nd Lord Oxford that Jekyll, though

he was brother-in-law and owed his fortune to your father's implacable enemy, old Summers, and he himself was a Whig virulent enough in all conscience ... acted the fairest part to your father of any of that set of men; not out of the least personal regard ... but out of regard only to the justice of the cause.

During the split in the Whig party from 1717 to 1720, Jekyll at first adhered to the Government, speaking (4 June 1717) against an opposition motion accusing Lord Cadogan (q.v.) of peculation, which was defeated by only 10 votes. Rewarded

with the office of master of the rolls, he was attacked by Shippen (12 June 1717) as a timeserver who had sacrified his principles for a place. In the following session (4 Dec. 1717) he spoke against an opposition motion reducing the army to 12,000; but a few days later he supported another opposition motion for breaking certain regiments, which was only defeated by 14 votes. 'Most people were surprised at Sir Joseph Jekyll's leaving the Court', wrote a Jacobite observer, adding ironically, 'but he is a man of honour and is provided for during life as master of the rolls'. At the opening of the next session he was regarded as one of the 'chief managers against the Court', joining the Opposition in attacking the war with Spain (11 Nov. 1718), only to change his mind and support the war a month later (17 Dec.). In 1719 he supported the Government on the repeal of the Occasional Conformity Act, but opposed them on the peerage bill. In the debate on the South Sea Company's proposals in January 1720 he severely rebuked the chancellor of the Exchequer, Aislabie, for saying that 'things of this nature must be carried on with spirit'.

This spirit, says he, is what had undone the nation; our business is to consider thoroughly, deliberate calmly, and judge of the whole upon reason, not with the spirit mentioned. Mr. Aislable desired to explain; said he only meant that credit was to be so supported; which caused some smiling.[1]

On the collapse of the Bubble he took the lead in forcing the Government to agree to an inquiry by another secret committee of the Commons, to which he was elected. When the committee brought charges of corrupt practices against ministers, directors and others, he again surprised the House by speaking for the acquittal of Sir George Caswall (q.v.), on the ground that the case against him had not been made out, and by abstaining from voting on the charges against Charles Stanhope (q.v.), in response, it was reported, to a personal appeal from the King. No one, however, 'was so warm and inveterate' as he against Lord Sunderland; he moved the resolution for consolidating the bill against Aislabie with that providing for the confiscation of the estates of the guilty directors; and he strenuously resisted Walpole's attempts to reduce the extent of confiscation. He also attacked Walpole's scheme for setting the South Sea Company on its feet. Later in the session he supported the Government on a subsidy to Sweden, which was hotly attacked by the Opposition. On a government proposal for discharging the civil list debt by a special tax of 6*d.* in the pound on official salaries, he moved and carried in committee a motion for increasing the tax to 1*s.*, which was reversed next day by the full House.

During Walpole's Administration, Speaker Onslow writes, Jekyll was

> not in a set opposition to the Ministry and was sometimes for them . . . yet . . . he usually differed in the House of Commons from those who were in power and had much dislike of Sir Robert Walpole in many things and bore no great reverence to his character in general.[2]

According to Walpole this animosity arose from Jekyll's failure to obtain the lord chancellorship on Lord Macclesfield's resignation in January 1725, when he 'pressed to be made chancellor, and his not being so made him Sir Robert's enemy ever after'. At the end of that year Walpole refers to 'righteous Sir Joseph' as the only man gained by Pulteney; but at the beginning of 1726 'the master of the rolls and the anti-courtiers as they call themselves', i.e. the opposition Whigs, voted with the Government on the army, Jekyll's speech having 'so great weight' that without further debate it was resolved to maintain the existing strength. In the same session he supported the Government on the treaty of Hanover but opposed them on a vote of credit.

In George II's first Parliament Jekyll's recorded votes and speeches were consistently anti-Government till the excise bill when

> Sir Joseph Jekyll, who is not used to vote with the Court, said he could not see one argument against it, and they who were against it had their own private advantage in their thoughts, not the good of the public.

In the same speech he declared that it was his invariable rule to come to the House

> undetermined, and resolved so to remain, till I am fully informed by other gentlemen, in the course of the debate, of all the facts which ought to be known.[3]

At the opening of the next Parliament

> the master of the rolls got up and before he sat down changed his opinion seven times, and as often the party which thought they had got him roared out the *Hear him* . . . but at last he differed from both sides.

A few weeks later the Government were defeated on the Marlborough election petition as a result of a speech by Jekyll, 'who spoke against the Court at twelve o'clock at night, after a hearing and debate of two days'. Writing of this affair, Hervey states that the Queen was greatly displeased by Jekyll, 'whom she was always cajoling, always abusing, always hoping to manage, and always finding she was deceived in'. He describes Jekyll as

> an impracticable old fellow of four score, with no great natural perspicuity of understanding, and had, instead of enlightening that natural cloud, only gilded it with knowledge, reading, and learning, and made it more shining, not less thick . . . He was always puzzled and confused in his apprehension of things, more so in forming an opinion upon them, and most

of all in his expression and manner of delivering that opinion when it was formed . . . His principal topics for declamation in the House were generally economy and liberty.

Nevertheless,

> though no individual in the House ever spoke of him with esteem or respect, but rather with a degree of contempt and ridicule, yet, from his age, and the constant profession of having the public good at heart beyond any other point of view, he had worked himself into such a degree of credit with the accumulated body that he certainly spoke with more general weight, though with less particular approbation, than any other single man in that assembly . . . The balance of the Marlborough election was turned, as well as many other points, merely by his weight being thrown into the anti-court scale.

In 1736 Jekyll was the author of the Mortmain and Gin Acts, designed respectively to check the alienation of land to religious and charitable institutions, and to reduce drunkenness by putting a duty of 20s. a gallon on gin. The first is described as 'drove on by the intemperate zeal of Sir Joseph Jekyll,' a strong anti-clerical. The Gin Act was so unpopular that, according to Hervey, Walpole

> rather, I believe, to mark out who was the author of this Act than in favour to the master of the rolls (for he hated him heartily), got a particular guard of thirty men to be set round the master's house, under the pretence and show of protecting it from the attacks of the mob.

On the opposition motion in 1737 for an increase of the Prince of Wales's allowance Jekyll, after being spoken to by the Queen, 'spoke and acted . . . in his usual double, balancing character, for he argued on both sides and voted for neither'. His last recorded speech was made on 3 Feb. 1738, when he argued that the emergence of Russia as a great military power had made a standing army in England unnecessary, saying 'he thought he saw a northern star arising, which if properly managed might preserve the liberties of Europe'.[4]

On Jekyll's death, 19 Aug. 1738, the 1st Lord Egmont wrote of him:

> A noted Parliament man, and head of the flying squadron, he had the character in general of a man of probity, though some doubted it, because he sometimes gave into the court measures when least expected. Many good public bills were moved for and prepared by him, and some that were otherwise, particularly that against bequeathing lands in fee by will for charitable uses, or even money to be laid out in land for that end. He had a hatchet face and surly look, always looking grave and speaking sententiously, and was reckoned a great patron of the freethinkers . . . He was a generous man to his relations, but left his next immediate heir, Mr. Jekyll, out of his will because he returned from his travels through France and not through Holland, as Sir Joseph had directed him.[5]

His will left £20,000 East India stock to be applied after his wife's death to the reduction of the national debt. In 1747 an Act was passed authorizing the sale of £13,582 of this stock for the benefit of his residuary legatees, who had been reduced to want. Sir James Thornhill's (q.v.) picture of the House of Commons, c.1730, contains a portrait of him by Thornhill's son-in-law, Hogarth.

[1] *HMC Portland*, v. 512, 570, 665; vii. 447; *HMC Stuart*, v. 301-2; Chandler, vi. 33; Coxe, *Walpole*, ii. 182-3. [2] Stuart mss 52/137, 53/14, 55/15; *HMC Portland*, v. 612; *HMC 14th Rep. IX*, 470. [3] Sir Dudley Ryder's Diary, 18 Oct. 1739, Harrowby mss; Coxe, *Walpole*, ii. 492-3; *Knatchbull Diary*, 28 Jan. 1726; Chandler, vi. 357; vii. 339-40; *HMC Egmont Diary*, i. 343. [4] *HMC Carlisle*, 147; Hervey, *Mems.* 419-20, 570, 691; Harley Diary, 15 Apr. 1736; Walpole, *Mems. Geo. II*, ii. 134; Cobbett, x. 446. [5] *HMC Egmont Diary*, ii. 507.

R.R.S.

JENISON, Ralph (1696–1758), of Elswick Hall, nr. Newcastle, Northumb. and Walworth Castle, co. Dur.

NORTHUMBERLAND   16 Apr. 1724–1741
NEWPORT I.o.W.   20 June 1749–15 May 1758

bap. 23 Dec. 1696, 1st surv. s. of Ralph Jenison of Elswick and Walworth by Elizabeth, da. and h. of Cuthbert Heron of Chipchase, Northumb. *educ.* Christ's, Camb. 1719–20. *m.* 10 Dec. 1751, Susan, da. of Thomas Allan of the Flatts, co. Dur., 1s. *d.v.p. suc.* fa. 1704; gd.-fa. Robert Jenison 1714.
Sheriff, Northumb. 1716; freeman of Newcastle-upon-Tyne 1718; master of the buckhounds 1737–44, 1746–57.

Jenison, who came of an old family of Newcastle merchants, was returned for Northumberland on petition in 1724. He usually supported the Government, but was absent from the division on the excise bill in 1733 and voted for the repeal of the Septennial Act in 1734. Re-elected in 1734 after an expensive contest, he was made master of the buckhounds in succession to Lord Tankerville, with whom he was politically connected, in 1737. Probably owing to the cost of the contest of 1734, which seriously impaired his fortune, he did not stand for Northumberland in 1741, when a promise of a seat obtained for him by Tankerville from Walpole in 1740 came to nothing.[1] Forced to sell Elswick Hall in 1742 he gave up the mastership of the buckhounds in 1744, receiving as compensation a pension of £1,200,[2] till he recovered the post two years later when Tankerville refers to him as Newcastle's 'constant slave'. In the Northumberland by-election of February 1748 he acted as agent to Tankerville's son, Lord Ossulston (q.v.).[3] He probably owed his return for Newport, Isle of Wight, in 1749 to Tankerville, whose brother-in-law, Lord Portsmouth, was governor of the island.

He died 15 May 1758.

[1] Tankerville to Newcastle, 4 Feb. 1740, Add. 32696, f. 72; Jenison to Jacob Tonson, n.d., Add. 28275, f. 487. [2] Walpole to Mann, 24 Dec. 1744. [3] Tankerville to Newcastle, 17 Jan. 1747, and Jenison to Lady Tankerville, 1 Jan. 1748, Add. 32714, ff. 27, 63.

E.C.

JENKINS, Tobias (1660–1730), of Grimston, York.

YORK   1695–1700, 1701–1705, 1715–1722

bap. 16 June 1660, o. surv. s. of Tobias Jenkins of Grimston by Antonyna, da. of Rev. Henry Wickham, D.D. *m.* (1) Lady Mary Powlett, da. of Charles Powlett, 1st Duke of Bolton, 2da.; (2) 2s. 1da. *suc.* fa. 1697.
Alderman and ld. mayor of York 1701, 1720.

Jenkins, a York alderman, who had represented the city as a Whig under William III and Anne, was returned for it again on George I's accession after a contest, voting with the Government. From the beginning of the session of 1719–20 he was drawing a secret service pension. Before the next general election he wrote to Lord Sunderland that

the last election cost near £1500, so that my great expense for the public service at that time will not allow me in prudence to lay out more of my own fortune, besides that the difficulty and expense now brought upon me seems to arise from my firm adherence to the present Administration.

He was prepared to stand again if 'well supported' or alternatively to use his

interest to sway that election for the service I have always directed it, and I am sure your Lordship is too considerate not to allow my own interests to have some share in designing that in this latter case if I be out of Parliament the provisions which I have most by your favour may be put into a condition more for my ease and in my own name.

A further letter, pressing for a decision, begs 'that £300 of the salary which I had by your Lordship's favour, now due at Lady Day next, might be forthwith paid'.[1] He did not stand again and died intestate in 1730.

[1] Sunderland (Blenheim) mss.

R.R.S.

JENKINSON, Sir Robert, 3rd Bt. (1685–1717), of Walcot, Oxon. and Hawkesbury, Glos.

OXFORDSHIRE   1710–29 Oct. 1717

bap. 23 Nov. 1685, 1st s. of Sir Robert Jenkinson, 2nd Bt., M.P., by Sarah, da. and h. of Thomas Tomlins of Bromley, Mdx.; bro. of Sir Robert Bankes Jenkinson (q.v.). *educ.* Trinity, Oxf. 1703; L. Inn 1705. *m.* (lic. 4 Feb. 1712) Henrietta Maria, da. of Charles Scarborough, clerk of the Green Cloth, *s.p. suc.* fa. 30 Jan. 1710.

A Tory and a member of the October Club, Jenkinson succeeded his father as knight of the shire, voting against the septennial bill in 1716. He died 29 Oct. 1717, 'much lamented, being a very honest, worthy gentleman'.[1] His widow subsequently married Charles Eversfield (q.v.) and his younger brother, Colonel Charles Jenkinson, was the father of Charles Jenkinson, 1st Earl of Liverpool.

[1] Hearne, *Colls.* (Oxf. Hist. Soc.) vi. 102.

E.C.

JENKINSON, Sir Robert Bankes, 4th Bt. (1687–1738), of Walcot, Oxon. and Hawkesbury, Glos.

OXFORDSHIRE   4 Dec. 1717–1727

bap. 24 Jan. 1687, 2nd s. of Sir Robert Jenkinson, 2nd Bt., M.P., and bro. of Sir Robert Jenkinson, 3rd Bt. (q.v.). *educ.* Trinity, Oxf. 1703; L. Inn 1705, called 1713. *m.* 12 June 1718, Catherine, da. of Sir Robert Dashwood, 1st Bt., M.P., of Northbrook, Oxon., 2s. 2da. *suc.* bro. 29 Oct. 1717.

The grandson of Sir John Bankes of Corfe Castle and Kingston Lacy, Dorset, chief justice of the common pleas, Jenkinson succeeded his brother for Oxfordshire, voting as a Tory, against the Administration. He was put up unsuccessfully by the 2nd Earl of Abingdon for the recordership of Oxford in 1721,[1] in which year his name was sent to the Pretender as a probable supporter in the event of a rising.[2] Returned unopposed in 1722 he did not stand in 1727. He died 2 July 1738 at Oxford, 'of a consumption'.[3]

[1] *HMC Portland*, vii. 293. [2] *Stuart mss* 65/16. [3] *Hist. Reg.* 1738, chron. p. 27.

E.C.

JENNINGS, James (?1670–1739), of Shiplake, Oxon.

ABINGDON   13 Dec. 1710–1713, 1715–1722

b. ?1670, 1st s. of Robert Jennings of Shiplake, headmaster of Abingdon school 1657–83, by Mary, da. of James Jennens of Long Wittenham, Berks. *educ.* Wadham, Oxf. 5 July 1686, aged 16. *m.* 1698, Frances, da. of Harry Constantine of Merley and Lake, Dorset, 6s., 4da. *suc.* fa. 1704.[1]

Sheriff, Oxon. 1694

James Jennings, whose father is said to have 'got a plentiful estate' as an Abingdon schoolmaster,[2] buying Shiplake from the Plowdens in 1689, was returned for Abingdon against a Tory. In a list of the new Parliament prepared for George I he is classed as a Tory, with a note stating that 'quoyque Tory, il s'est opposé cette fois au fils de my lord Harcourt et l'a emporté'.[3] In fact he voted against the Government in all recorded divisions. He stood unsuccessfully in 1722, splitting the Tory vote, and was again defeated in 1734, though in the latter

year he had the support of the majority of the corporation.[4]

He died 9 Mar. 1739.

[1] Climenson, *Hist. Shiplake*, app. p. 335, 296–7; A. E. Preston, *St. Nicholas, Abingdon*, 345–7. [2] Wood, *Fasti Oxon.* ii. 103. [3] 1 June 1715, Worsley mss. [4] Mrs. Elizabeth Pevvy to Walpole, 10 Apr. 1734, Cholmondeley (Houghton) mss.

R.S.L.

JENNINGS, Sir John (1664–1743), of Newsells, in Barkway, Herts.

QUEENBOROUGH   1705–1710
PORTSMOUTH   1710–3 Feb. 1711
ROCHESTER   1715–1734

b. 1664, 15th child of Philip Jennings of Dudleston, Salop by Christiana, da. of Sir Gerard Eyton of Eyton, Salop. *m.* Alice, da. of Francis Breton of Wallington, Herts., 1s. Kntd. 24 Oct. 1704.

Lt. R.N. 1687, capt. 1689, r.-adm. 1705, v.-adm. 1708, adm. 1708; c.-in-c. Mediterranean 1711–13; ld. of Admiralty 1714–27; gov. Greenwich Hospital 1720–*d.*; r.-adm. of England 1733–4.

A distinguished admiral, Jennings was returned as a Whig by the Administration under Queen Anne, but was defeated at Queenborough in 1710, when he was also returned for Portsmouth, only to be unseated on petition. Appointed a lord of the Admiralty at George I's accession he was returned for Rochester on the Admiralty interest in 1715, voting with the Administration, except on the peerage bill, which he opposed. He commanded a squadron off the coast of Scotland against the Pretender early in 1716, and, for the last time, off the coast of Spain in 1726. Shortly afterwards he resigned from the Admiralty, 'not so much upon the account of my indisposition as upon the objection I made to serve there with Lord Berkeley', the first lord. On George I's death Berkeley was dismissed but Jennings was 'not at all solicitous to return to that board again', desiring only 'if my Lord Torrington is to be vice-admiral of England, that I may in my turn be rear-admiral of the same, till the proper time comes that you can prevail for my being created an English baron'.[1] Though appointed rear-admiral of England in January 1733, he 'quitted his flag' a year later, when his junior, Sir John Norris (q.v.), was made admiral of the fleet and commander-in-chief. He did not stand at the 1734 election, and died 23 Dec. 1743.

[1] Jennings to Walpole, 26 July 1727, Cholmondeley (Houghton) mss.

A.N.N.

JENNINGS, Philip (?1679–1740), of Dudleston, Salop.

QUEENBOROUGH   1715–1722

b. ?1679, 1st s. of Edward Jennings, Q.C., M.P., of the I. Temple by Elizabeth, da. of John Horne of Foster

Lane, Cheapside, girdler; gd.-s. of Philip Jennings of Dudleston. *educ.* Eton c.1693–97; St. John's, Camb. 2 Jan. 1698, aged 18; I. Temple 1698, called 1704, bencher 1735. *m.* (1) 23 Dec. 1705, Diana (*d.* 12 Oct. 1708), da. of Sir William Bowyer, 2nd Bt., of Denham, Bucks., 1s. *d.v.p.* 1da.; (2) 1721, Dorothy, da. of George Clerke of Launde Abbey, Leics., sis. and h. of Sir Talbot Clerke, 6th Bt., 3s. 6da. *suc.* fa. 1725.

Philip Jennings, a lawyer and nephew of Sir John Jennings (q.v.), to whom he presumably owed his return, voted for the septennial bill in 1716, against the repeal of the Occasional Conformity and Schism Acts in 1719, but for the peerage bill in that year. He did not stand again, dying on 10 Feb. 1740.

A.N.N.

JENYNS, John (1659–1717), of Hayes, Mdx.

CAMBRIDGESHIRE 1710–1 Feb. 1717

b. 1659, 1st s. of Roger Jenyns of Hayes by Sarah, da. of Joseph Latch. *m.* (lic. 16 Feb. 1682) Jane, da. of James Clitherow of Boston House, Mdx., 3s. *suc.* fa. 1693.

Jenyns's father, who bought the manor of Hayes in 1677[1] and also owned an estate in the Isle of Ely,[2] was the grandson of Sir John Jenyns, or Jennings, of Sandridge, Hertfordshire, and the first cousin of the Jennings sisters, Frances, Duchess of Tyrconnel, and Sarah, Duchess of Marlborough. He was an original member of the corporation set up by Act of Parliament in 1663 to drain the fens, serving successively as conservator, bailiff, and surveyor general of fens till his death in 1693.

Jenyns himself was elected to the Fen Corporation as conservator at the age of 25, succeeding on his father's death to the surveyor generalship, which he held for twenty years.[3] Though returned as a Tory for Cambridgeshire, he voted against the French commercial treaty in 1713 and Steele's expulsion in 1714. Classed at George I's accession as a Tory who might often vote Whig, he voted against the septennial bill in 1716, dying 1 Feb. 1717.

[1] Lysons, *Environs of London*, ii. 590. [2] Lysons, *Cambs.* 29, which confuses Roger Jenyns with his son and namesake. [3] W. M. Palmer, 'Fen Office Docs.', *Camb. Antiq. Soc. Proc.* xxxviii. 96.

R.R.S.

JENYNS, Soame (1704–87), of Bottisham, Cambs.

CAMBRIDGESHIRE   1741–1754
DUNWICH   1754–Nov. 1758
CAMBRIDGE   29 Nov. 1758–1780

b. 1 Jan. 1704, o.s. of Sir Roger Jenyns (yr. bro. of John Jenyns, q.v.) of Bottisham by Elizabeth, da. of Sir Peter Soame, 2nd Bt., of Haydon, Essex. *educ.* St. John's, Camb. 1722. *m.* (1) his cos. Mary (*d.* 30 July 1753), da. of Col. Soame of Dereham Grange, Norf., *s.p.*; (2) 26 Feb. 1754, his cos. Eliza-

beth, da. of Henry Grey of Hackney, *s.p.* *suc.* fa. 1740.

Ld. of Trade 1755–80.

William Cole, the Cambridge antiquary, gives the following account of Soame Jenyns:

He was son to Sir Roger Jenyns, knt., of Bottisham in Cambridgeshire, who being an artful, cunning, and intriguing man, raised from a small beginning in fortune, for he was of a good family of Hayes, a very considerable state by his management in the Fen Corporation.

He was married very young by his father to a young lady of between £20 and £30,000, to whom he [i.e. Sir Roger] was left guardian, and without much consulting the inclinations of the young couple, who were first cousins in blood, she being a natural daughter to Colonel Soame of Dereham Grange, Norfolk; so that it was generally supposed there never was any great affection between them . . . On the death of Sir Roger, Mrs. Jenyns, under the pretence of a journey to Bath for her health, made an elopement with one Mr. Levyns [William Levinz, q.v.], whom I remember at Eton school, and was a Leicestershire gentleman, with whom it was supposed that she had lived very familiarly, even while that gentleman used to be at Mr. Jenyns's house at Bottisham on the footing of a friend and acquaintance; and what made it more extraordinary, Mrs. Jenyns was neither young nor handsome, a very bad complexion, lean scraggy arms, and noways inviting. Since which elopement about the year 1742 they never cohabited together, a separate maintenance being allowed to the lady, who lived altogether in or about London.

Cole adds that on her death Jenyns married another first cousin, 'who had lived in the house with him long before his wife's elopement and even after; and has been said to have occasioned early differences between them'.

In 1741 Jenyns was returned unopposed for Cambridgeshire. He had, Cole writes,

no other interest in the county than what my Lord Montfort [Henry Bromley, q.v.] procures him and indeed would not have been chosen at all had it not been for the same gentleman and Mr. Sam. Shepheard [q.v.], who were distressed whom to apply to in the county for a proper representative, many of the principal gentry of the county, to whom it was offered, refusing it. And indeed Sir Roger and Mr. Jenyns himself had always been on the contrary interest to these gentlemen; but they were thoroughly satisfied with their choice.

He voted regularly with the Government, except on Pelham's proposal in 1744 for an additional tax on sugar, against which he made his only recorded speech in this Parliament, possibly at the instance of Montfort, whose fortune was derived from plantations in Barbados.[1]

In 1747 Jenyns, standing with Philip Yorke (q.v.), was again returned unopposed for the county, at a joint cost of £2,000, towards which he contributed £500, the balance being paid by Lord

Hardwicke. Thenceforth he attached himself to that family, celebrating their doings in verse with such assiduity that Horace Walpole dubbed him 'the poet laureate of the Yorkes'. When in spite of this he was required to give up his seat to Lord Granby at the next general election, he became 'uneasy' though, as Hardwicke observed,

> he has no reason to be so in respect of a seat for himself in Parliament, for he will certainly be taken care of . . . Part of his uneasiness has arisen from a dislike of being laid aside for the county, and a dissatisfaction with my Lord Montfort . . . He cannot argue or suppose that it is reasonable that things should go on upon the unequal foot they were upon.[2]

In the event Montfort arranged for him to be brought in by Sir Jacob Downing (q.v.) at Dunwich. A list of secret service pensions in March 1754 shows him as receiving one of £600 a year.[3] He died 18 Dec. 1787.

[1] Add. 5873, f. 51; Owen, *Pelhams*, 217. [2] Philip Yorke to Hardwicke, 4 Aug. 1747, Hardwicke to P. Yorke, 30 June 1753, Add. 35351, ff. 124, 288; Walpole, *Mems. Geo. II*, ii. 140. [3] Add. 33038, f. 415.

R.R.S.

JESSOP, William (1665–1734), of Broomhall, Yorks.

ALDBOROUGH 1702–1713, 1715–8 Nov. 1734

b. 1665, s. of Francis Jessop of Broomhall by Barbara, da. of Robert Eyre of Highlow, Derbys. *educ.* G. Inn 1683, called 1690, bencher 1715. *m.* (lic. 15 Jan. 1697) Mary, da. and h. of James Darcy, M.P., 1st Baron Darcy [I], of Sedbury Park, Yorks., 1s. *d.v.p.* 4da. *suc.* fa. 1691.
Justice of the Anglesey circuit 1707–12, c.j. 1712–29; commr. and receiver of the alienation office 1717–*d.*; puisne justice of Chester 1729–*d.*

Jessop was legal adviser to John Holles, Duke of Newcastle, who brought him into Parliament. In 1709 he fought a duel with William Levinz (q.v.), the Duke's chief opponent in Nottinghamshire.[1] After the Duke's death in 1711, when his widow disputed the will leaving his estates to his nephew, Thomas Pelham, created Duke of Newcastle 1715, Jessop sided with Pelham. He stood on Pelham's interest for Aldborough in 1713 but was defeated by the Duchess,[2] regaining his seat in 1715, after the dispute had been determined in Pelham's favour. During the debates on the South Sea directors he was referred to as (25 May 1721) as having lost money in another of Sir John Blunt's fraudulent companies. He subsequently spoke warmly (3 July 1721) against allowing the directors to retain 15% of their estates in return for prompt payment.[3] As a placeman he voted with the Government in all recorded divisions, except on the army in 1732 and the excise bill in 1733, when he was absent. He

died 8 Nov. 1734. One of his daughters married Andrew Wilkinson (q.v.).

[1] Luttrell, vi. 396. [2] T. Lawson-Tancred, *Recs. of a Yorks. Manor*, 234–66. [3] Chandler, vi. 248, 257.

R.R.S.

JEWKES, John (1683–1743), of Petworth, Suss.

BRIDPORT 20 Feb. 1730–1734
ALDBOROUGH 19 Feb. 1735–25 Sept. 1743

bap. 28 Apr. 1683,[1] 1st s. of Humphrey Jewkes of Petworth by Sarah, da. of John Whitehead of Clandon, Surr. *educ.* Eton; Peterhouse, Camb. 1702; I. Temple 1702; L. Inn. 1713. *unm. suc.* fa. 1710.

John Jewkes, a lawyer, of a Petworth family, was returned as a Whig for Bridport in 1730 at a by-election caused by James Pelham's (q.v.) opting to sit for Newark. In Parliament he voted consistently with the Administration in all recorded divisions. From 1733 onwards he acted as the Duke of Newcastle's informant and agent in the Petworth neighbourhood for matters relating to the election of the county Members for Sussex.[2] For these services, presumably,[3] he was given a seat at the Duke's pocket borough of Aldborough in 1735, when Henry Pelham (q.v.) opted to sit for Sussex. He died 25 Sept. 1743.

[1] Petworth par. reg., Add. 5699, f. 96. [2] Jewkes to Newcastle, Add. 32688–32698, passim. [3] Jewkes to Newcastle, 4 May 1734, Add. 32689, f. 218.

R.S.L.

JODRELL, Paul (?1715–51), of Duffield, Derbys.

OLD SARUM 25 Jan–30 June 1751

b. ?1715, 1st s. of Paul Jodrell of Duffield, barrister-at-law, by Judith, da. and coh. of Gilbert Sheldon. *educ.* L. Inn 1723, called 1735, bencher 1751; Trinity, Oxf. 7 Nov. 1730, aged 15. *m.* July 1744, Elizabeth, da. of Richard Warner of North Elmham, Norf., 3s. 1da. *suc.* fa. 1744.
K.C. 1747; solicitor-gen. to Prince of Wales 1748–*d.*

Paul Jodrell's mother was of the family of Archbishop Sheldon and his paternal grandfather was clerk to the House of Commons. 'A very rising man'[1] at the bar, he was appointed solicitor-general to Frederick, Prince of Wales, who brought him in for Old Sarum in January 1751. Going over with most of the Prince's party to the Pelhams on Frederick's death, he was continued in his post but soon afterwards died, 30 June 1751. John Willey (q.v.) 'had a very high opinion of his integrity as well as his abilities'; and Sir Edmund Thomas (q.v.) considered his death 'a most mortifying one to his friends, to whom it is almost irreparable, and a great one to his country at this juncture'.[2]

[1] Walpole, *Mems. Geo. II*, i. 96. [2] *Recs. Cust. Fam.* iii. 144.

R.S.L.

JOHNSON, Sir Henry (c.1661–1719), of Braden-ham, Bucks.

ALDEBURGH 1689–29 Sept. 1719

b. c.1661, 1st s. of Sir Henry Johnson, M.P., of Friston Hall, Suff. by Mary, da. and h. of William Lord of Melton, Kent; bro. of William Johnson (q.v.).[1] *m.* (1) lic. 14 May 1686, Anne, da. and h. of Hugh Smithson, 3rd s. of Sir Hugh Smithson, 1st Bt., of Stanwick, Yorks., 1da.; (2) 11 Mar. 1693, Martha, *suo jure* Baroness Wentworth, da. and h. of John Lovelace, M.P., 3rd Baron Lovelace of Hurley, Berks., *s.p. suc.* fa. 1683. Kntd. 13 or 18 Mar. 1685.

Sir Henry Johnson, a Blackwall shipbuilder, owned the manor of Aldeburgh and other property near that borough,[2] for which he and his brother sat continuously from 1689. On their re-election as Tories in 1715 after a contest, their Whig opponents petitioned; the petition was referred to the elections committee of the House of Commons, who found in favour of the petitioners; but the committee's recommendation was overruled by the House, who awarded the seats to the sitting Members, the only success scored by the Tories on an election petition in 1715.[3] He voted against the Government in all recorded divisions till his death, 29 Sept. 1719, leaving his estates to his grand-daughters, one of whom married William Conolly (q.v.).

[1] Lysons, *Environs of London*, iii. 465. [2] W. A. Copinger, *Manors of Suff.* v. 97, 131. [3] *CJ*, xviii. 176.

R.R.S.

JOHNSON, Sir Thomas (1664–1728), of Castle St., Liverpool.

LIVERPOOL 1701–2 Feb. 1723

bap. 27 Oct. 1664, s. of Thomas Johnson of Bedford Leigh, Lancs., mayor of Liverpool 1670, by his w. Elizabeth (née Sweeting). *m.* (1) Lidia Holt (bur. 9 Sept. 1696), 1da. who m. Richard Gildart (q.v.); (2) 7 Apr. 1697, Elizabeth Barrow. *suc.* fa. 1700. Kntd. 20 Mar. 1708.

Mayor, Liverpool 1695; collector of customs on Rappahannock River, Virginia 1723–5.

Thomas Johnson was one of the leading citizens of Liverpool, which he represented as a Whig for over 20 years, the last ten without opposition. A shipper and tobacco merchant, he was also a pioneer of the new rock salt industry, acting as its mouth-piece in Parliament. In 1711 he introduced a bill for making the river Weaver navigable from the Mersey to the rock salt works in Cheshire, which was rejected owing to the opposition of the brine salt and other interests but ultimately passed in 1721. He was largely responsible for providing Liverpool with a floating dock, engaging Thomas Steers to draw up plans and introducing a bill for the con-struction of the dock, which received the royal assent

in 1710.[1] Other municipal improvements and deve-lopments to which he contributed were the consti-tution of Liverpool as a separate parish, distinct from Walton; the building of St. Peter's and St. George's churches; and the establishment of the market in Derby Street. He was knighted in 1708, when he presented a loyal address from Liverpool on a threatened Jacobite invasion.[2]

After the accession of George I, Johnson sup-ported the Government. In 1716, when some of the Jacobite prisoners taken at Preston pleaded guilty and begged for transportation, he submitted pro-posals to the Treasury for transporting them at 40s. per head, the prisoners to serve Johnson or his assigns for seven years. The offer was accepted, and in March the Treasury paid Johnson £1,000 in part payment of his contract. When some of the better class prisoners argued that they had pleaded for simple transportation and would not 'consent to be slaves', Johnson had them 'turned into a dungeon . . . and fed only with bread and water'. In the end, all the prisoners, numbering 639, were transported by Johnson. In 1717 he made an unsuccessful bid of £61,000 for the whole of the French part of St. Kitts in the West Indies, which had been advertised for sale by the commissioners for trade and plantations.[3]

Johnson was frequently in financial difficulties over the redemption of the bonds which tobacco importers were allowed to deposit as security for the duty payable on tobacco stored in customs ware-houses if not re-exported. In 1717 he and his partner and son-in-law, Richard Gildart, were in debt to the Crown in respect of unpaid duty on tobacco to the extent of £7,825 3s. 1d. On 18 Jan. 1719 the collector of the customs at Liver-pool reported to the commissioners of customs at London:

> Sir Thomas Johnson and Mr. Richard Gildart are both in London raising money to pay off their debts to the Crown. But neither has yet paid any of the old bonds for long due but have sent ships and effects to London to raise money there for there is a great scarcity of it here and trading almost at a stand.

At the general election of 1722, his property qualification was called into question by his opponent. In 1723 he resigned his seat to take up the post of collector of customs in Virginia, leaving Gildart to cope with his debts. He seems to have remained in Virginia until 1725, when he was given a pension of £350 p.a. in lieu of his office. He died in London 'at his lodgings in Charing Cross' on 28 Dec. 1728.[4]

[1] *Hist. Soc. Lancs. and Cheshire*, lxxxii. 167–9, 234; E. Hughes, *Studies in Admin. and Finance*, 233, 255, 395; T. S. Willan, *Naviga-tion of River Weaver* (Chetham Soc. ser. 3, iii), 1–21. [2] J. Picton,

Liverpool Municipal Recs. ii. 12; *Norris Pprs.* (Chetham Soc. old ser. ix), 170–1. ³ *Cal. Treas. Bks. and Pprs.* 1714–19, pp. 196, 200, 327; A. C. Wardle, 'Sir Thomas Johnson and the Jacobite Rebels', *Hist. Soc. Lancs. and Cheshire,* xci. 125–43; Oliver, *Antigua,* i. p. xc. ⁴ *Norris Pprs.* 90, 96, 99–100, 110, 149, 161, 163; A. C. Wardle, *Hist. Soc. Lancs. and Cheshire,* xc. 181–97.

E.C.

JOHNSON, William (aft. 1661–1718), of Blackwall, Mdx.

ALDEBURGH   1689–14 Nov. 1718

b. aft. 1661, 2nd s. of Sir Henry Johnson, M.P., and bro. of Sir Henry Johnson of Bradenham, Bucks. (q.v.). *m.,* at least 1s. 6da.

William Johnson was returned for Aldeburgh on the interest of his brother, Sir Henry Johnson (q.v.). A Tory, he voted against the septennial bill. He died 14 Nov. 1718.

R.R.S.

JOHNSTONE, Sir James, 3rd Bt. (1697–1772), of Westerhall, Dumfries.

DUMFRIES BURGHS   20 Jan. 1743–1754

b. 9 Feb. 1697, 1st s. of Sir William Johnstone, 2nd Bt. (q.v.), of Westerhall. *educ.* ?Leyden 1713; adv. 1720. *m.* 1 Sept. 1719, Barbara, da. of Alexander Murray, 4th Lord Elibank [S], 8s. 6da. *suc.* fa. 8 Oct. 1727.
Provost of Lochmaben; sheriff of Dumfries 1743.

In 1732 Johnstone, whose brother had married the dowager Marchioness of Annandale, mother of the 3rd Marquess, then a minor, began

bestirring himself to set up in the [Dumfries] boroughs for himself and endeavouring to twist them out of Mr. [Charles] Areskine's [q.v.] hands, in which he availed himself of my Lord [Annandale]'s name and interest.

He was also supporting a candidate for the shire against Areskine. The Annandales at this time were engaged in a family lawsuit against Lord Hope, whose lawyer was Areskine. It was represented to Lady Annandale by Duncan Forbes (q.v.) that Johnstone's conduct was 'extremely offensive to the personal friends of Mr. Areskine', some of whom were judges in the court of session, where the Annandale case was depending, and had 'hitherto in the Marquess's cause been of opinion with his Lordship'. He went on:

I hardly know how to express what I am next to say to your Ladyship. I ought not surely to insinuate that passions or disobligations may pervert judgment, but our judges are no more than men, and I leave it to your Ladyship to consider from what you have formerly heard or experienced, whether it is prudent, without any necessity, to give occasions for raising or playing with their passions to your prejudice.

He accordingly suggested that she should write to Johnstone, asking him to 'lay aside his design for

this time', and to let him, Forbes, have such a letter as he could show to Areskine's friends 'to convince them that your Ladyship will have no hand in the opposition that Mr. Areskine . . . may meet'.[1] She followed his advice, with the result that Johnstone did not stand till 1743, when he was returned unopposed at a by-election caused by the death of his nephew by marriage, Lord John Johnstone (q.v.). He voted against the Hanoverians in 1744 and was absent from the division on them in 1746, when he was classed as 'doubtful'. Meanwhile Lady Annandale had given him the joint charge of the 3rd Marquess, who had developed symptoms of insanity after the death of his younger brother, Lord John Johnstone in 1742.[2] Again returned unopposed in 1747, he lost his control of the Annandale estates and interest in 1748, when the Marquess was declared insane and Lord Hopetoun, as his nearest heir, became his tutor-at-law. He did not stand again, dying 10 Dec. 1772.

¹ *More Culloden Pprs.* iii. 66–69. ² Greig, *Letters of David Hume,* i. 60–89, 337–41.

R.S.L.

JOHNSTONE, Lord John (1721–42), of Johnstone, Dumfries.

DUMFRIES BURGHS   1741–13 Nov. 1742

b. 8 June 1721, 5th and posth. s. of William Johnstone, 1st Mq. of Annandale [S], being 2nd s. by his 2nd w. Charlotte van Lore, da. and h. of John van den Bempdé of Hackness Hall, Yorks. and Pall Mall, Westminster. *educ.* under Edward Johnstone of Galabank;[1] Glasgow Univ. 1737; France 1739. *unm.*

Lord John Johnstone, whose mother was remarried to a brother of Sir James Johnstone (q.v.), came back from France in November 1739 with instructions from his brother, the 3rd Marquess of Annandale, to enlist the family interest in support of the Government.[2] Nevertheless, on being returned for Dumfries Burghs in 1741, though under age, he voted against Walpole's candidate for the chairman of the elections committee but was included in the Cockpit list of ministerial supporters drawn up by Pelham in October 1742. He died of consumption 13 Nov. 1742.

¹ C. L. Johnstone, *Hist. Johnstones,* 167. ² Marchioness of Annandale to Geo. II, 21 Nov. 1739, Add. 32692, f. 464.

R.S.L.

JOHNSTONE, Sir William, 2nd Bt. (d. 1727), of Westerhall, Dumfries.

DUMFRIES BURGHS   1708–1710, 9 May 1713–1715
DUMFRIESSHIRE   1713–1722

2nd s. of Sir James Johnstone, M.P. [S], of Westerhall by Margaret, da. of John Bannatyne of Corehouse, Lanark. *m.* bef. Mar. 1701, Henrietta, da. and coh. of James Johnston of Sheens, Edinburgh, 2s. *suc.* bro. as 2nd Bt. 30 Sept. 1711.

M.P. [S] Annan 1698–1702, 1703–7.

Johnstone was related to the 1st Marquess of Annandale, on whose interest he was returned for Dumfriesshire. His only recorded vote was for the peerage bill in 1719, when he was classed as a government supporter. He did not stand again, dying 8 Oct. 1727.

R.R.S.

JOLLIFFE, John (?1697–1771), of Petersfield, Hants.

PETERSFIELD   1741–1754, 1761–1768

b. ?1697, 3rd s. of Benjamin Jolliffe of Cofton Hall, Worcs. by Mary, da. of John Jolliffe, M.P., of London, merchant, sis. of Sir William Jolliffe (q.v.). *educ.* Westminster; Univ. Coll. Oxf. 21 Oct. 1712, aged 15; M. Temple 1714, I. Temple 1720. *m.* (1) 30 Mar. 1731, Catherine (*d.* 24 June 1731), da. and h. of Robert Michell, M.P., of Petersfield, *s.p.*; (2) June 1744, Mary, da. and coh. of Samuel Holden (q.v.), 3s. 1da.

Commr. for wine licences 1720–41; receiver gen. of duchy of Lancaster 1738 for life, but res. 1751.

Jolliffe inherited from his first wife property in Petersfield, carrying an electoral interest there, on which he returned his uncle Sir William Jolliffe (q.v.) in 1734. In 1738 he was appointed receiver general of the duchy of Lancaster, paying the previous holder a large sum of money to resign. Next year he bought the manor of Petersfield from Edward Gibbon (q.v.) for £5,693,[1] thereby gaining control of the second seat. Returned in 1741, on the retirement of his uncle, he voted consistently with the Administration and was classed as a government supporter in 1747. His fortune was further increased by a second marriage and by the death of his uncle, who left him a considerable share of his estate. In the 2nd Lord Egmont's electoral survey, c.1749–50, Petersfield is described as 'in Jolliffe, entirely with us'. He died 31 Jan. 1771.

[1] H. G. H. Jolliffe, *Jolliffes of Staffs.* 32, 34, 45; Jolliffe mss at Ammerdown Park, Som. in possession of Ld. Hylton.

P.W.

JOLLIFFE, Sir William (1660–1750), of Ewell, Surr. and Pleshey, Essex.

PETERSFIELD   1734–1741

b. 1660, 1st s. of John Jolliffe, M.P., of London, merchant, by Rebecca, da. of Walter Boothby of Tottenham. *unm. suc.* fa. 1679. Kntd. 8 Jan. 1715.

Director, Bank of England 1714–42 (with statutory intervals); director, R. African Co. 1699–1706.

Descended from the Jolliffes of Staffordshire and Worcestershire, William Jolliffe, a rich Turkey merchant and moneylender, bought estates in Surrey, Essex and Yorkshire.[1] After unsuccessfully contesting Maldon in 1715, with his nephew, Samuel Tufnell (q.v.), he was returned as a Whig for Petersfield in 1734 on the interest of another nephew, John Jolliffe (q.v.). No votes of his have been recorded, but in 1740 he presented a petition of the Levant Company against the import of raw silk from Russia. The 1st Lord Egmont cites him as an example of coveteousness, observing that, though supposed 'to be worth a hundred thousand pound, if not two', he 'brags that in his whole life he never bought a book, picture or print.'

> One night, being at a public house in company, he would needs cook a plate of meat with his own hand, and . . . happened to burn a hole in the plate, upon which the landlord told him he expected to be paid for it. 'Why yes', said Sir William, 'I think it just, but then I will have the plate', and accordingly when the company broke up took it away with him.[2]

In his will he left provision for the erection of an equestrian statue of William III, which stood in the courtyard of Petersfield House, until it was removed, some years later, to the square, where it still stands.[3]

He died 7 Mar, 1750.

[1] *Tufnell Pprs.* 50–51. [2] *HMC Egmont Diary*, iii. 311. [3] H. G. H. Jolliffe, *Jolliffes of Staffs.* 38.

P.W.

JONES, Robert (?1682–1715), of Fonmon Castle, Glam.

GLAMORGAN   30 Jan. 1712–19 Dec. 1715

b. ?1682, 2nd s. of Oliver Jones of Fonmon Castle by Mary, da. of Martin Button of Duffryn. *educ.* Jesus, Oxf. 7 Apr. 1698, aged 15. *m.* 1703, Mary, da. of Sir Humphrey Edwin of Llanvihangel, Glam. 2s. 4da. *suc.* e. bro. 1686.

Sheriff, Glam. 1703–4.

Robert Jones was the grandson of Col. Philip Jones, M.P., a member of Cromwell's 'other House' and comptroller of his household. His aunt, the widow of his father's elder brother, Sir John Jones of Fonmon, married the notorious Judge Jeffreys.[1] A Tory under Queen Anne, Jones was again returned for Glamorgan as a Tory in 1715. He died 19 Dec. 1715.

[1] G. T. Clark, *Limbus Patrum Morganiae et Glamorganiae*, 215.

P.D.G.T.

JONES, Roger (?1691–1741), of Buckland, Brec.

BRECON   1713–1722

b. ?1691, o. surv. s. of Edward Jones, M.P., of Buckland by Margaret, da. of Roger Otis of Keventilly, Mon. *educ.* Balliol, Oxf. 16 May 1707, aged 15; I. Temple 1707. *m.* (1) Dorothy (*d.* 16 Mar. 1735), da. of Henry Cornish of London, merchant, *s.p.*; (2) Eleanor, *s.p. suc.* fa. 1696.

Roger Jones was one of the leading squires of Breconshire, but he owed his election for the borough to the support of the Morgans of Tredegar (qq.v.). The son of a Jacobite, he was reckoned a Tory in 1713 and a Whig in 1715, with this explanatory note in the list of the new Parliament prepared for George I:

> Il étoit Tory dans le dernier Parlement. Il vient d'épouser une jeune femme Whig et promet de se mettre du parti de madame.[1]

Absent from the division on the septennial bill, he voted against the repeal of the Occasional Conformity and Schism Acts, and was absent from the division on the peerage bill, though expected to support it.[2] Resigning the borough to a Morgan in 1722, he unsuccessfully fought the county with Tredegar support. Afterwards, although his interest was computed at 400 of the 1,200 freeholders in Breconshire, he declined to stand again, 'being unwilling as 'tis thought to put himself to any expense'.[3] He died in 1741.

[1] Worsley mss. [2] Stowe mss 247, ff. 184-99. [3] R. Eliot to Walpole, 20 Dec. 1733, Cholmondeley (Houghton) mss.

P.D.G.T.

JONES, Thomas (c.1667-1715), of Shrewsbury, Salop.

SHREWSBURY   3 Jan.-21 Sept. 1710
1713-27 May 1714
1 Feb.-31 July 1715

> *b.* c.1667, 1st s. of William Jones of Caneghora, Denb. by Grace, da. of Sir Peter Pinder, 1st Bt., of Iddinshall, Cheshire. *educ.* Emmanuel, Camb. 1685. *m.* (1) Mary (*d.* 1 Nov. 1712), da. and coh. of Sir Francis Russell, 2nd Bt., of Strensham, Worcs., *s.p.*; (2) Jane, da. of Sir Edward Leighton, 1st Bt., M.P., of Wattlesburgh, Salop, *s.p.*, who *m.* after 1715 Sir Charles Lloyd, 3rd Bt. *suc.* fa. 1694.[1]
> Sheriff, Denb. 1698-9, Salop 1699-1700.

Jones's great-grandfather was steward of Shrewsbury; his great-uncle William was M.P. Shrewsbury 1659, and his grandfather, Sir Thomas Jones, chief justice of the common pleas 1683-6, was town clerk of the borough and M.P. Shrewsbury 1660-79. He contested Shrewsbury unsuccessfully as a Whig in 1702; was returned for it at a by-election in 1710, but lost his seat at the general election; was returned again in 1713 but was unseated on petition, and was re-elected in 1715. He died 31 July 1715, aged 48, soon after the opening of Parliament.[2]

[1] PCC 128 Box. [2] Owen & Blakeway, *Hist. Shrewsbury*, ii. 293.

J.B.L.

JORDAN, Thomas (?1689-1750), of Gatwick, nr. Reigate, Surr.

REIGATE   21 Apr. 1720-1722

> *b.* ?1689, 1st surv. s. of William Jordan (q.v.).[1] *educ.* Trinity, Oxf. 7 May 1706, aged 16; M. Temple 1709, called 1719. *unm. suc.* fa. 1720.

Thomas Jordan, the last male representative of his family, was returned unopposed as a Whig in succession to his father, William Jordan (q.v.). He did not stand again, dying 20 July 1750.

[1] Manning & Bray, *Surrey*, ii. 189.

R.R.S.

JORDAN, William (c.1665-1720), of Gatwick, nr. Reigate, Surr.

REIGATE   15 Mar. 1717-1720

> *b.* c.1665, s. of Thomas Jordan of Gatwick. *educ.* M. Temple 1681. *m.* (lic. 1 Feb. 1689, aged 24) Philippa, sis. and h. of John Brown of Buckland, Surr., 4s. 3da. *suc.* fa. 1694.

The Jordans were country gentlemen, settled at Gatwick since the fourteenth century. On the death of Sir John Parsons (q.v.) in 1717, William Jordan successfully contested the resulting vacancy at Reigate as a Whig on the interest of Sir Joseph Jekyll (q.v.), voting for the repeal of the Occasional Conformity and Schism Acts but against the peerage bill. He died 7 Apr. 1720.

R.R.S.

KAYE, Sir Arthur, 3rd Bt. (?1670-1726), of Woodsome, Yorks.

YORKSHIRE   1710-10 July 1726

> *b.* ?1670, 1st surv. s. of Sir John Kaye, 2nd Bt., M.P. Yorks. 1685-98, 1701, 1702-6, by Anne, da. of William Lister of Thornton in Craven, Yorks. *educ.* Ch. Ch. Oxf. 2 Mar. 1686, aged 15. *m.* (lic. 22 July 1690) Anne, da. and coh. of Sir Samuel Marow, 1st Bt., of Berkswell, Warws., 1da. *suc.* fa. 8 Aug. 1706.

The Kayes owned very extensive estates in the west of Yorkshire,[1] which Kaye and his father represented in most Parliaments for over 40 years. A Tory and a member of the October Club, he voted against the Government in every recorded division after 1715. During the election campaign in 1715 Lord Carlisle reported that Kaye was said to have been concerned in the distribution of a Jacobite pamphlet, adding: 'If it can be fixed upon Sir Arthur, I hope it may be thought at least a sufficient cause to expel him from the House'.[2] He died 10 July 1726.

[1] Stuart mss 248/151. [2] *HMC Portland*, v. 507-8.

R.R.S.

KAYE, Sir John, 4th Bt. (1697–1752), of Woodsome, Yorks.

YORK 1734–1741

bap. 4 Sept. 1697, 1st s. of George Kaye of Denby Grange, Kirkheaton, Yorks. by Dorothy, da. and h. of Robert Savile of Bryan Royd, nr. Elland, Yorks. *educ.* Ch. Ch. Oxf. 1715. *m.* (1) Ellen (*d.* 29 Jan. 1729), da. of John Wilkinson of Greenhead, nr. Huddersfield, 1s.; (2) 29 July 1730, Dorothy, da. of Richard Richardson, M.D., of North Bierley, Yorks., 4s. *suc.* uncle Sir Arthur Kaye, 3rd Bt. (q.v.), 10 July 1726; to estates of his uncle Thomas Lister (formerly Kaye) of Thornton-in-Craven, Yorks., 1745, taking add. name of Lister before Kaye.
Alderman, York 1735, ld. mayor 1737.

In 1727 Kaye stood unsuccessfully for Yorkshire as a Tory at a by-election caused by the death of his uncle, whose title and estates he had inherited. Invited by the local Tories to stand for York city in 1734, he replied

> that if they would choose him, he would do the city all the service he could; but at the same time he gave them to understand that he would spend no money, which did not at all please, for the great love they have for Sir John was for the money they were in hopes he would spend amongst them.[1]

However, he was returned without a contest, voting against the Government. Defeated in 1741, he was invited to stand again at a by-election in 1742, but declined on grounds of ill-health, recommending George Fox (q.v.), who was duly elected.[2] His name appears in a list of leading Jacobite sympathizers prepared for the French foreign office in 1743.[3] He died 5 Apr. 1752.

[1] Sir W. Wentworth to Ld. Malton, 22 Dec. 1733, Rockingham mss. [2] W. W. Bean, *Parl. Rep. of Six Northern Counties*, 1113. [3] Stuart mss 248/151.

R.R.S.

KECK, Anthony (1708–67), of Great Tew, Oxon.

NEW WOODSTOCK 31 Mar. 1753–30 May 1767

b. 1708, 2nd s. of John Tracy of Stanway (gd.-s. of John, 3rd Visct. Tracy) by Anne, da. of Sir Robert Atkyns, M.P., chief baron of the Exchequer; his paternal gd.-mother was Katherine, da. of Sir Anthony Keck, M.P. *m.* 3 Aug 1736, Lady Susan Hamilton, da. of James, 4th Duke of Hamilton [S], whose 1st w. (not the mother of Lady Susan) was a da. of Robert, 2nd Earl of Sunderland, 2da. *suc.* to Keck estates in Oxon. 1729 and assumed name of Keck.

Keck was returned for New Woodstock on the Marlborough interest, throughout his parliamentary career remaining the Duke's dependant and protégé.
He died 29 May 1767.

E.C.

KEENE, Benjamin (c.1697–1757).

MALDON 14 Jan. 1740–1741
WEST LOOE 1741–1747

b. c.1697, 1st s. of Charles Keene, mercer, alderman and mayor of King's Lynn, Norf., by Susan, da. of Edmund Rolfe of Heacham, Norf. *educ.* Lynn g.s.; Pembroke, Camb. 1713; Leyden. K.B. 1754.
Consul, Madrid 1724; minister, Madrid 1727–39; ld. of Trade 1741–4; paymaster of pensions Jan.–Aug. 1745; envoy, Lisbon 1745–50; ambassador, Madrid 1749–*d*.

According to the second Lord Hardwicke, 'Keene's father and mother were of families which had exercised the principal magistracies of Lynn, and were strongly attached to the Walpole interest . . . Lord Townshend, secretary of state, took early notice of his talents'.[1] Under these auspices he was sent to Madrid, first as agent for the South Sea Company and then as consul and minister, remaining there till the outbreak of the war with Spain in 1739. On his return he was brought into Parliament and made a commissioner of Trade. Walpole, who had the highest opinion of his abilities, wrote shortly before his fall to the Duke of Devonshire: 'Mr. Keene is truly so deserving a man, of so precarious a future, and so liable to be made a sacrifice for the sake of his friends upon any change, that I know nothing that I wish more than to see him in some way established'.[2] One of his last official acts was to provide for Keene by giving him and Henry Legge (q.v.) for their joint lives equal shares in a reversion of a place in the customs worth £1,200 p.a. Eventually Keene bought out Legge's interest for £3,500, Legge retaining the reversion.

After Walpole's fall there was some talk of impeaching Keene for his share in the negotiations for the Spanish convention of 1739. In the event he retained his place till the beginning of 1745 when he was made paymaster of pensions. But as he wrote to his life-long friend, Abraham Castres, the consul-general at Lisbon: 'While [the House] is sitting agreeable thoughts never enter into my imagination. If this country were quiet and friendly no spot upon earth would please me so much, but I was not formed for party squabbles'. He was therefore delighted to exchange appointments with the British minister in Lisbon, leaving to take up his post in 1746.

Keene never returned to England, although he remained a Member of Parliament until 1747. In 1749 he was appointed ambassador to Spain, where he remained for the rest of his life. He died at Madrid on 15 Dec. 1757, leaving behind him so high a reputation as a diplomat that it was said that 'being compared with him carries along with it the éloge of any public minister'.

[1] This biography is based on *The Private Correspondence of Sir Benjamin Keene*, ed. Richard Lodge. [2] 25 Aug. 1741, Devonshire mss.

A.N.N.

KELSALL, Henry (?1692–1762), of Colkirk, Norf.

CHICHESTER	3 Dec. 1719–1722
BOSSINEY	1722–1727
MITCHELL	1727–1734

b. ?1692, s. of Henry Kelsall of Chester. *educ.* Westminster under Knipe; Trinity, Camb. 7 Feb. 1708, aged 15, fellow 1714. *m.*, 1da.

Senior clerk, Treasury c.Nov. 1714–*d.*; commr. of land tax 1735–*d.*

Kelsall was at school with the Duke of Newcastle,[1] to whom he presumably owed his Treasury post and his return for Chichester in 1719, after which he was brought in by the Government for Cornish boroughs. From the death of William Lowndes (q.v.) in 1724, he was second in command to John Scrope (q.v.) at the Treasury, serving on the committees of the Commons who drew up the finance bills each session.[2] He also sent out the letters inviting the principal men on the government side in the Commons to Walpole's house to hear the King's speech read before the meeting of Parliament in January 1734, when he was falsely reported to have 'broke and run away'.[3] He did not stand in 1734, and was appointed a commissioner of taxes a year later, still retaining his Treasury post. In June 1761 he attempted 'to *sell* his place of commissioner of taxes' to a relation of Sir Francis Dashwood's (q.v.), but Newcastle 'absolutely refused' to allow it. On 1 Feb. 1762, feeling himself about to pass 'into the only more benevolent hands than your Grace's', he applied to Newcastle for a 'small pension' for his daughter, which was subsequently granted.[4] He died a few days later, 10 Feb. 1762.

[1] Add. 32934, f. 139. [2] *CJ*, xx. 261 et passim. [3] *HMC Egmont Diary*, ii. 6. [4] Add. 32924, ff. 50–51; 32934, f. 139; 32935, f. 344.

E.C.

KEMP, Sir Robert, 3rd Bt. (1667–1734), of Ubbeston, Suff.

DUNWICH	1701–1705, 1708–5 Feb. 1709, 1713–1715
SUFFOLK	9 Feb. 1732–18 Dec. 1734

bap. 25 June 1667, 1st s. of Sir Robert Kemp, 2nd Bt., M.P., of Gissing, Norf. by Mary, da. and h. of John Sone of Ubbeston. *educ.* St. Catharine's, Camb. 1685. *m.* (1) Letitia, da. of Robert King of Great Thurlow, Suff., 1da.; (2) c.1699, Elizabeth (*d.* 1709), da. and h. of John Brand of Edwardstone, Suff., 5s. 2da.; (3) Martha (*d.* 1727), da. of William Blackwell of Mortlake, Surr., 3ch.; (4) 9 July 1728, Amy, da. of Richard Phillips, wid. of John Burrough of Ipswich, *s.p. suc.* fa. 26 Sept. 1710.

Kemp, whose father acquired Ubbeston manor by marriage, stood unsuccessfully as a Tory for Dunwich in 1715. In 1721 his name was sent to the Pretender as a probable supporter.[1] Returned for Suffolk in 1732, he voted against the Government on the excise bill in 1733 and for the repeal of the Septennial Act in 1734. He died shortly after being re-elected, 18 Dec. 1734.

[1] Stuart mss 65/16.

R.R.S.

KEMP, Robert (1699–1752), of Ubbeston, Suff.

ORFORD	23 Feb. 1730–1734

b. 9 Nov. 1699, s. of Sir Robert Kemp, 3rd Bt. (q.v.), by his 2nd w. *educ.* Pembroke, Camb. 1718; M. Temple 1721. *unm. suc.* fa. as 4th Bt. 18 Dec. 1734.

Returned as a Tory, voting against the Government in all recorded divisions, Kemp did not stand again. He died 15 Feb. 1752.

R.R.S.

KEMYS, Sir Charles, 4th Bt. (1688–1735), of Cefn Mably, Glam.

MONMOUTHSHIRE	1713–1715
GLAMORGAN	22 Feb. 1716–1734

b. 23 Nov. 1688, o.s. of Sir Charles Kemys, 3rd Bt., M.P., of Cefn Mably by his 1st w. Mary, da. and coh. of Philip Wharton, 4th Baron Wharton, sis. of Thomas Wharton, M.P., 1st Mq. of Wharton, wid. of William Thomas of Wenvoe, Glam. *educ.* Trinity, Camb. 1706. *unm. suc.* fa. Dec. 1702.

Sheriff, Glam. 1712–13.

Although Kemys was nephew to the Whig leader, Lord Wharton, and a personal friend of George I's before his accession, he was an avowed Jacobite, who was reputed to have declined the new King's invitation to attend him at court, saying; 'I should be happy to smoke a pipe with him as Elector of Hanover, but I cannot think of it as King of England'.[1] He did not stand in 1715, but was returned unopposed for Glamorgan at a by-election early in 1716, voting against the Administration in all recorded divisions of that Parliament. He was again unopposed in 1722 and 1727. No further votes of his are known. Continuing to support the Stuart cause in Glamorgan,[2] he was listed in 1730 along with Lord Gower, Lord Barrymore, and Watkin Williams Wynn (qq.v.) as one of the Jacobite leaders in the north-west.[3] Before the general election of 1734 he made known his 'intention of giving myself ease, being of late years deprived of health'.[4] He died soon afterwards, 29 Jan. 1735.

[1] D. Williams, *Hist. Mon.* 321. [2] *Cymmrodorion Soc. Trans.* 1920-1, pp. 19-20. [3] Stuart mss 133/151. [4] Kemys Tynte mss 1/10, Glam. RO.

P.D.G.T.

KEMYS, Edward (c.1693-1736), of Pertholey, Mon.

MONMOUTH 1722-1734

b. c.1693, 1st s. of Edward Kemys of Pertholey and Maesgenwith by Anne, da. of Reginald Bray of Barrington, Glos.,[1] sis. of William and Edmund Bray (qq.v.). *educ.* Eton 1705-11; King's, Camb. 1712-19, fellow 1715. *unm. suc. fa.* 1710.

Distantly related to Sir Charles Kemys, 4th Bt. (q.v.), Kemys came of a family seated at Pertholey since the end of the sixteenth century. Returned as a Tory for Monmouth by the Duke of Beaufort in 1722 and 1727, his only recorded vote was against the Administration on the Hessians in 1730. He did not stand again, dying in 1736.

[1] J. A. Bradney, *Hist. Mon.* iii. 154-5.

P.W.

KEMYS TYNTE, Sir Charles, 5th Bt. (1710-85), of Halswell, nr. Bridgwater, Som. and Cefn Mably, Glam.

MONMOUTH 14 Mar. 1745-1747
SOMERSET 1747-1774

b. 19 May 1710, 3rd s. of Sir John Tynte, 2nd Bt., M.P., by Jane, da. of Sir Charles Kemys, 3rd Bt., M.P., of Cefn Mably; bro. of Sir Halswell Tynte (q.v.). *m.* 9 Mar. 1738, Anne, da. of Rev. Thomas Busby of Addington, Bucks., *s.p. suc.* uncle Sir Charles Kemys, 4th Bt. (q.v.), 1735 and took name of Kemys before Tynte; bro. as 5th Bt. 15 Aug. 1740.
Steward of anniversary dinner of independent electors of Westminster 1748.

After contesting Glamorgan unsuccessfully in the Tory interest in January 1745, Tynte was brought in for Monmouth in March by the Duke of Beaufort (Lord Charles Noel Somerset, q.v.). From 1747 he was returned for Somerset till he retired in 1774. The 2nd Lord Egmont in his electoral survey c.1749-50 describes him as having 'a very good interest at Bridgwater and (without management) will expect to be suffered to exert it for one Tory'. He died 25 Apr. 1785.

R.R.S.

KENNEDY, Thomas (1673-1754), of Dunure, Ayr.

AYR BURGHS 9 Jan 1720-2 Sept. 1721

b. 1673, 1st s. of Sir Thomas Kennedy of Kirkhill and Dunure, ld. provost of Edinburgh 1685-7 by Agnes Halden. *educ.* Edinburgh 1688; Utrecht 1692; adv. 1698. *m.* 19 Aug. 1714, Grizel, da. of Patrick Kynynmont of Kynynmont, Fife, wid. of Sir Alexander Murray, 1st Bt., of Melgund, Forfar, *s.p. suc. fa.* 1715.
Jt. solicitor-gen. [S] 1709-14; ld. adv. 30 Mar.-9 Oct. 1714; baron of the Exchequer [S] 1721-*d.*

Kennedy, who came of a junior branch of the earls of Cassilis [S], was made lord advocate by the Tory Government in 1714, after acting unofficially in this capacity.[1] Commenting on the appointment, a Jacobite M.P. observed: 'Though not perhaps so tight a Tory as could have been wished, [he] was much preferable to any of his predecessors, and there was little reason to doubt his concurring with the Queen's measures'.[2] He lost his post on George I's accession, notwithstanding applications to Argyll and Ilay, as well as to their opponents, the Squadrone, and to Walpole. He also sought arrears of salary for himself and one of his brothers, promotion for two more brothers, and a pardon for another, who had been employed at the Jacobite court. In the last he was supported by Duncan Forbes and James St. Clair (qq.v.). He ended as the client of the Duke of Argyll, to whom he owed his return for Ayr Burghs, and probably the appointment which terminated his brief parliamentary career. In 1736 one of his brothers was made deputy governor of Inverness by the influence of Argyll's brother, Lord Ilay.[3] He died 19 May 1754.

[1] G. W. T. Omond, *Lord Advocates of Scotland,* i. 300. [2] *Lockhart Pprs.* i. 458-9. [3] H. Tayler, *Seven Sons of the Provost,* 49-50 51-52, 53, 130-1, 177-8.

J.M.S.

KENSINGTON, Baron, *see* **EDWARDES, William**

KENT, Clement (?1682-1746), of Crookham, Berks.

WALLINGFORD 1705-1708
READING 1722-1727

b. ?1682, 1st s. of Clement Kent of Goring, Oxon. by Sarah, da. of Sebastian Lyford of Crookham and Reading. *educ.* Balliol, Oxf. 12 June 1700, aged 17; I. Temple 1700. *m.* 8 Jan. 1704, Barsheba Marsh of Stepney, Mdx., 2s. *suc. fa.* 1701; maternal gd.-fa. at Crookham 1703.
Capt.-lt. Ld. Henry Scott's Ft. 1704; capt. Sir Daniel Carroll's Drags. 1711-12; sheriff, Berks. 1714-15; capt. 11 Drags. 1726-c.1730.

Clement Kent, related to Samuel Kent (q.v.), came of an old Reading family, his grandfather being a clothier in that town. On succeeding to his estates he joined the army, served in Portugal, and went on half-pay when his regiment was disbanded in 1712. After representing Wallingford in the 1705 Parliament he did not stand again until 1722, when he was returned, apparently as a Tory, for Reading. No vote of his has been recorded and he did not stand again. In 1726, having informed an army board that he was aged 41 with 16 years service, he obtained a troop in the 11th Dragoons, then stationed at Reading,[1] going on half-pay about 1730. He died 25 Dec. 1746.

[1] *N. & Q.* (ser. 12), v. 52, 106–7, 184; Williams, *Hist. Rec. 11th Hussars*, 20.

R.S.L.

KENT, Samuel (c.1683–1759), of Vauxhall, Surr. and Fornham St. Genevieve, Suff.

IPSWICH 1734–8 Oct. 1759

b. c.1683, 5th s. of Thomas Kent of Christchurch, Southwark, Norway merchant, by Sarah, da. of Daniel Wight of Southwark, distiller. *m.* Sarah, da. of Richard Dean, skinner, of London, 2s. 1da.

Sheriff, Surr. 1729–30; distiller to the Court 1739; purveyor of Chelsea Hospital 1740.

Kent, a wealthy wholesale malt distiller with interests in the South Sea Company and the Sun Fire Office, was invited to stand for Ipswich in January 1730, but declined.[1] He appears to have had no estates in Suffolk until he purchased Fornham St. Genevieve in 1731. He topped the poll in 1734, was successful in 1741 and was returned unopposed in 1747. Kent, wrote Egmont in 1750, 'always votes dead with the Court and has done so as long as I can remember'.

He died 8 Oct. 1759.

[1] *Suff. Notes from 1729*, reprinted from *Ipswich Jnl.* 24 Jan. 1730, p. 74.

E.C.

KENTON, Francis (?1689–1755), of Castle St., Salisbury, Wilts.

SALISBURY 1722–1727

b. ?1689, s. of Thomas Kenton of Salisbury by Susanna,[1] da. of Herbert Salladin of Salisbury. *educ.* Queen's, Oxf. 15 Dec. 1705, aged 16; I. Temple 1706. *m.* (settlement 7 Dec. 1743)[2] Henrietta, sis. of Robert Eyre, formerly of Bengal, *s.p.*

Francis Kenton, who became an alderman of Salisbury, was returned there in 1722, presumably as a Whig, but did not stand again. He died 5 Mar. 1755.

[1] Lic. Salisbury 20 Oct. 1686. [2] PCC 106 Paul.

R.S.L.

KEPPEL, George, Visct. Bury (1724–72).

CHICHESTER 19 Aug. 1746–22 Dec. 1754

b. 5 Apr. 1724, 1st s. of William Anne, 2nd Earl of Albemarle, by Lady Anne Lennox, da. of Charles,

1st Duke of Richmond. *educ.* Westminster 1732–40. *m.* 20 Apr. 1770, Anne, da. of Sir John Miller, 4th Bt., of Lavant, Suss., 1s. *suc.* fa. as 3rd Earl 22 Dec. 1754; K.G. 26 Dec. 1765.

Ensign 2 Ft. Gds. 1738; capt.-lt. 1 Drags. 1741; capt.-lt. 2 Ft. Gds. 1743, capt. and lt.-col. 1745; brevet col. 1746; col. 20 Ft. 1749–55, 3 Drags. 1755–*d.*; maj.-gen. 1756; lt.-gen. 1759; gov. Jersey 1761–*d.*; c.-in-c. at capture of Havana 1762; gen. 1772.

Ld. of the bedchamber to the Duke of Cumberland 1746–65; equerry to the Princess of Wales 1751; P.C. 28 Jan. 1761.

The son and grandson of successful courtiers, Lord Bury became the 'chief favourite'[1] of the Duke of Cumberland, whom he served as aide-de-camp at Dettingen, Fontenoy and Culloden. He was chosen by Cumberland to bring the news of Culloden to the King, who gave him a present of £1,000 and made him his own aide-de-camp.[2] When he was returned for Chichester by his uncle, the Duke of Richmond, in 1746 Newcastle wrote to Lord Albemarle:

I must congratulate you upon the justice, which all the world does to dear Bury. He is now Member for Chichester, and consequently a Sussex man, which is an additional reason for me to love him.[3]

According to the Duke of Richmond there was no officer in the army 'under forty years old that knows more than Bury';[4] but Wolfe, who served under him, had a different opinion:

Lord Bury professes fairly, and means nothing; in that he resembles his father, and a million of other showy men that are seen in palaces and in the courts of Kings. He desires never to see his regiment, and wishes that no officer would ever leave it.[5]

Re-elected in 1747 while serving in Flanders, he was classed as a government supporter. His only known vote was against Lord Hardwicke's clandestine marriage bill, 4 June 1753.[6] He died 13 Oct. 1772.

[1] Walpole, *Mems. Geo. II*, i. 82. [2] Walpole to Mann, 25 Apr. 1746; C. S. Terry, *Albemarle Pprs.* i. 2, 4. [3] Add. 32708, f. 128. [4] Add. 32707, f. 98. [5] R. Wright, *Life of Wolfe*, 185–6. [6] Add. 32732, f. 22.

P.W.

KER, James (*d.* 1768), of Bughtrig, Roxburgh.

EDINBURGH 1747–1754

s. of Thomas Ker of Edinburgh, deacon of the corporation and a magistrate of the city, by Margaret, da. and coh. of John Kerr of the Canongate. *m.* 8 July 1725, Jean (*d.* 1 Oct. 1746), da. of Gavin Thompson of Edinburgh, 3s. 11da.; (2) 6 Aug. 1756, Elizabeth, da. of Lord Charles Kerr, s. of the 1st Mq. of Lothian [S], 5s. 2da.

'Mr. Ker, the jeweller', the Duke of Argyll wrote to Pelham, 23 July 1747, discussing candidates at the Edinburgh election, is certainly a Whig, but he was too much a patriot at a certain time to be a favourite of mine, and I am told that he is weak and whimsical, though his professions of zeal for the present Administration are strong enough.[1]

Returned on the interest of the incorporated trades of Edinburgh, of which he was convenor, against a candidate supported by Argyll and Pelham, Ker called on Argyll and wrote to Pelham the day after his election, to apologise for standing against their candidate, promising to support the Government.[2] On receipt of a reply from Pelham, he wrote (20 Aug.):

> To speak honestly my sentiments, am sorry the town should be so poorly represented. Its indeed a sphere of life am quite unequal to . . . but since it has fallen on me, its no small encouragement . . . that you are pleased to allow me to hope for your countenance and friendship, which will endeavour to prove by such uniform conduct as not to give the lie to the character which my friends have been so good as to give you of me, a man zealous for the King and our happy constitution and sincere well-wisher to the administration in your hands, as the head of the honest Whig interest.[3]

He was rewarded with a secret service pension of £300 p.a.[4]

By the next general election Ker's vanity, Argyll reported to Pelham, had 'gradually made him the object of the hatred and contempt of his fellow citizens'. He had highly disobliged many members of the city council; had 'made the merchants his enemies by opposing a scheme they had of improving the harbour of Leith'; 'the several traders also complain of him for treating them with haughtiness and contempt'; in short, 'the town will not bear Mr. Ker'.[5] He was not put up in 1754, consequently losing his secret service pension.[6] He died 24 Jan. 1768.

[1] Newcastle (Clumber) mss. [2] Argyll and Ker to Pelham, 30 July 1747, ibid. [3] Ibid. [4] Add. 33038, f. 352. [5] Argyll to Pelham, 15, 19, 28 Oct. 1747, Newcastle (Clumber) mss. [6] Add 33038, f. 352.

R.R.S.

KERR, Hon. William (bef. 1682–1741).

BERWICK-UPON-TWEED	1710–1713
DYSART BURGHS	1715–1722
ABERDEEN BURGHS	13 Apr.–25 Oct. 1722
BERWICK-UPON-TWEED	7 May 1723–1727

b. bef. 1682, 3rd s. of Robert, 3rd Earl of Roxburghe [S], by Lady Margaret Hay, da. of John Hay, M.P. [S], 1st Mq. of Tweeddale [S]. *unm.*

Col. 7 Drags. 1709–*d.*; groom of the bedchamber to the King 1714–27; brig.-gen. 1727; gov. Blackness 1723–*d.*; maj.-gen. 1735; lt.-gen. 1739.

Kerr, a professional soldier, who served under Marlborough and was wounded at Sheriffmuir, was the brother of the Duke of Roxburghe, the head of the Squadrone, secretary of state for Scotland 1716–25. Returned in 1715 for Dysart Burghs on the interest of Lord Rothes, also a Squadrone leader, he voted consistently with the Government. In 1721, his Dysart seat being no longer available, he accepted an invitation to contest Berwick,[1] which he had represented under Anne, but withdrew to stand for Aberdeen Burghs where he was returned against an Argyll Whig, Colonel John Middleton (q.v.), who was awarded the seat on petition, though 'such was the number of friends Kerr personally had that he came within one vote'. Describing the decision as 'a blow to the Duke of Roxburghe and . . . a great victory to the Duke of Argyll', but of no consequence to the Government, since both candidates were supporters of the ministry, Lord Finch (q.v.), continued:

> When Kerr desired me to help him I knew not the name of his boroughs and when I asked him that he could name me but three out of five, so I was forced to spend 1/– for the list of the Parliament, so that I might know at least that.[2]

Returned next year at a by-election for Berwick, he did not stand again, dying 17 Jan. 1741.

[1] Rich. How and others to Kerr, 20 June 1721, Sunderland (Blenheim) mss. [2] To Ld. Nottingham, 29 Oct. 1722, Finch mss.

J.M.S.

KERR, William Henry, Earl of Ancram (c.1710–75).

RICHMOND   11 Dec. 1747–Mar. 1763

b. c.1710, 1st s. of William, 3rd Mq. of Lothian [S], by Margaret, da. and coh. of Sir Thomas Nicholson, 1st Bt., of Kemnay, Aberdeen. *m.* 6 Nov. 1735, Lady Caroline Darcy (with £20,000), da. of Robert, 3rd Earl of Holderness, 1s. 2da. *suc.* fa. as 4th Mq. 28 July 1767.

Cornet 11 Drags. 20 June 1735; capt. 11 Ft. 1739; capt. 1 Ft. Gds. 1741; lt.-col. 11 Drags. 1745; col. 1745; a.-d.-c. 1745–6 and groom of the bedchamber 1746 to Duke of Cumberland; col. 24 Ft. 1747–52; col. 11 Drags. 1752–*d.*; maj.-gen. 1755; lt.-gen. 1758; gen. 1770.

Ancram was wounded at Fontenoy, commanded the cavalry on the left wing at Culloden, and became a member of the Duke of Cumberland's personal staff. On learning that Sir Conyers Darcy (q.v.) had been adopted as a candidate for Yorkshire, Henry Pelham observed that this gave 'great satisfaction at court, as it would be a means of bringing in Lord Ancram for Richmond'.[1] Ancram was duly returned for Richmond in succession to Darcy by his brother-in-law, the 4th Earl of Holderness. In Parliament he followed the lead of the Duke of Cumberland. He died 12 Apr. 1775.

[1] To Hartington, July 1747, Devonshire mss.

R.R.S.

KETELBY, Abel (?1676–1744), of Bitterley, nr. Ludlow, Salop.

LUDLOW 1722–1727

b. ?1676, 1st surv. s. of Edward Ketelby of Bitterley, Salop and Wolverley, Worcs. by Anne, da. of Abel Gower of Boughton St. John, Worcs. and Napton-on-the-Hill, Warws. *educ.* Balliol, Oxf. 1 July 1691, aged 15; M. Temple 1693, called 1699, bencher 1724. *m.* Mary Williams of London, 1da. *suc.* fa. 1725.

Landgrave of S. Carolina 1709; agent and attorney-gen. for S. Carolina 1712–16; recorder, Ludlow 1719–43.

Abel Ketelby, a successful Tory lawyer, came of an ancient Shropshire family, seated near Ludlow, of which he became recorder. After the 1715 rebellion he was one of the principal counsel engaged to defend the Jacobites imprisoned at Carlisle, later defending the Jacobite agent John Matthews.[1] In 1720 he appeared for the Crown against Lord Coningsby (q.v.), who afterwards wrote in a pamphlet that Lord Chancellor Macclesfield had irregularly confirmed Ketelby as recorder.[2] Returned for Ludlow on his own and the Tory interest, he defended Layer at his trial for complicity in the Atterbury plot, spoke against the bill of pains and penalties on John Plunket, and moved an amendment to an Act relating to the registration of Papists.[3] As a former agent for South Carolina he served on a committee of the House set up to consider a petition from that colony asking for the removal of rice from the list of 'enumerated' commodities, i.e. goods which could not be exported to foreign countries without first being sent to England.[4] In 1727 he stood unsuccessfully for Great Bedwyn, drawing a disapproving comment from an old Tory:

> The lawyer, although each must plead for their fee, had shewed himself too partial besides; for his name hath been so often in print in relation to trials on the Crown side.[5]

He did not stand again, and died 5 Dec. 1744.

[1] *HMC Stuart*, iii. 377; Howell's *State Trials*, xv. 1364. [2] *LJ*, xxi. 417, 450. [3] *State Trials*, xvi. 94–114; *Knatchbull Diary*, 7 Mar. 1724. [4] *CJ*, xx. 62. [5] Earl of Ailesbury to Jas. Bruce, 6 Sept. 1727, Savernake mss.

J.B.L.

KEYT, Sir William, 3rd Bt. (1688–1741), of Ebrington, Glos. and Stratford-on-Avon, Warws.

WARWICK 22 Nov. 1722–25 Feb. 1735

b. 8 July 1688, 1st s. of William Keyt of Ebrington, Glos. by Agnes, da. of Sir John Clopton of Clopton, Warws. *educ.* privately. *m.* 23 Nov. 1710, Anne, da. of William, 4th Visct. Tracy, of Rathcoole [I], 3s. 2da. *suc.* gd.-fa. as 3rd Bt. 30 Nov. 1702.

Recorder, Stratford-on-Avon 1709–*d.*

Keyt was descended from an old Gloucestershire family, who acquired their Warwickshire estates by purchase in the seventeenth century. In 1715 he was turned out of the commission of the peace for proclaiming the Pretender, to whom his name was sent in 1721 as one of the chief Warwickshire Jacobites.[1] On his election for Warwick in 1722 a local Whig wrote:

> There has been above £3,000 spent on both sides at Warwick. Sir William Keyt, who is returned, is a Tory indeed; barring that, I hear a mighty good character of him in all respects.[2]

He sat for Warwick, voting against the Government, till 1735, when he was unseated on petition.

Keyt subsequently left his wife to live with her maid on his Gloucestershire estate, where he impaired his fortune by extravagant expenditure on building. When his mistress, viewing his house, asked 'what is a kite without wings', he added two large side extensions to it. Deserted by her, he took to the bottle. Setting fire to his house after a prolonged drinking bout in September 1741, he perished in the flames, resisting attempts to rescue him.[3]

[1] *VCH Warws.* iii. 253 n. 49; Stuart mss 65/16. [2] *HMC Portland*, vii. 368–9. [3] *London Mag.* 1741, p. 464; R. Graves, *The Spiritual Quixote* (2nd ed. London 1774), iii. 168–9, 172–3.

S.R.M.

KINASTON, William (?1682–1749), of Ruyton Hall, Salop.

SHREWSBURY 1734–24 Feb. 1749

b. ?1682, 2nd s. of William Kinaston of Lee, Salop by Jane, da. and h. of Thomas Kinaston of Ruyton of the Eleven Towns, Salop. *educ.* Shrewsbury; St. John's, Camb. 16 July 1699, aged 17; I. Temple 1699, called 1706. *m.* Dorothy Taylor of Essex, 4da. *suc.* fa. 1723.

Master in Chancery 1721–*d.*; recorder, Shrewsbury 1733–*d.*

William Kinaston was a member of a junior branch of the Shropshire Kynastons, who had been seated at Ruyton since the sixteenth century. A Whig and an active member of the Shrewsbury corporation, he is said by a political opponent to have

> come in to be mayor by a writ of mandamus though he was neither rightly elected nor the senior alderman; he acted partially during his time and used such indirect means to compass his designs that his name became odious . . . the corporation lost their grandeur; honour, honesty, and justice were expelled the house; tyranny and oppression ruled in their stead for many years,[1]

a reference to the new bye-laws concerning the admission of freemen passed in his mayoralty, which eventually gave the Whigs control of the franchise.

On becoming a master in Chancery Kinaston gave Lord Chancellor Macclesfield a present of 1,500 guineas. When the state of the chancery suitors funds was investigated in 1724 he was found to have a deficit of over £26,900, but retained his office after giving security for the debts.[2] In 1734, shortly after becoming recorder of the borough, he was returned for Shrewsbury, voting with the Government. He had a reputation for meanness; after the 1747 election his fellow-member, Sir Richard Corbet, complained that he paid no part of its cost; and he was known as 'heavy Billy, not from the weight of his purse, but the unwieldiness of his body'.[3] He died 24 Feb. 1749.

[1] *Salop Arch. Soc. Trans.* (ser. 3), i. 219–221; (ser. 4), iv. 64.
[2] Howell's *State Trials*, xvi. 771, 1055, 1067, 1094, 1184. [3] *Salop Arch. Soc. Trans.* (ser. 4), iv. 64.

J.B.L.

KING, John (1706–40).

LAUNCESTON   1727–22 July 1734

bap. 13 Jan 1706, 1st s. of Peter King, M.P., 1st Baron King, ld. chancellor 1725–33, by Anne, da. of Richard Seys of Boverton Court, Glam. *educ.* Clare, Camb. 1723. *m.* May 1726, Elizabeth, da. of John Fry of Yarty, Devon. *suc.* fa. as 2nd Baron 22 July 1734.
Outranger, Windsor forest 1726–40.

Returned as a government candidate for Launceston in 1727, King voted with the Administration, but was absent from the division on the excise bill. In 1734 he was returned for Exeter as well as Launceston but succeeded to the peerage before taking his seat.

King's wife, to whom his father, the lord chancellor, was guardian, had a great fortune, but was only 15 at the time of their marriage, which was not consummated, for, according to the 1st Lord Egmont,

> Sir Peter caused them to separate, though he detains her fortune. The young man lately writ his wife that he was willing to live with her, but her parents would not suffer him. My Lady King is charged by the world with influencing her husband to act in this scandalous manner. She says to everybody that her daughter-in-law is ugly, and a fool, to which the young woman replies that they knew she was ugly before they made the marriage, and as much a fool as she is, she never showed it more than marrying Mr. King.[1]

He died at sea on his way to Portugal, 10 Feb. 1740.

[1] *HMC Egmont Diary*, i. 121.

E.C.

KING, Thomas (?bef. 1660–1725), of St. Margaret's, Westminster, and Sheerness, Kent.

QUEENBOROUGH   31 Oct. 1696–1708, 1710–1722

b. prob. bef. 1660, 1st s. of Thomas King, M.P.,

of Harwich and bro. of Dr. John King, master of Charterhouse. *m.*, 2da.[1]

Ensign 3 Ft. 1678, 2nd lt. 1687; capt. 13 Ft. 1688; dep. gov. Tower of London 1688–9; capt. and lt.-col. 2 Ft. Gds. 1688; capt. and lt.-col. 1 Ft. Gds. 1689; lt.-gov. Sheerness 1690–d.; brevet col. 1706; ret. bef. 1715.

Thomas King, a professional soldier, was described in his old age by the 1st Lord Egmont as being 'full of anecdotes of King Charles the Second's reign'.[2] Though a Tory under Anne, he was continued as lieutenant governor of Sheerness, near Queenborough, where he was returned for the ninth time in 1715. Classed as a Whig who would often vote Tory, he voted against the septennial bill in 1716, was absent on the repeal of the Occasional Conformity and Schism Acts, and voted for the peerage bill in 1719. He was defeated by two government nominees in 1722, and died 17 July 1725.

[1] PCC 157 Romney. [2] *HMC Egmont Diary*, i. 209.

A.N.N.

KING, *see also* **DASHWOOD KING**

KIRKPATRICK, William (c.1705–78), of Lochmaben, Dumfries.

DUMFRIES BURGHS   13 Feb. 1736–June 1738

b. c.1705, 3rd s. of Sir Thomas Kirkpatrick, 2nd Bt., of Closeburn, Dumfries by his 2nd w. Isabel, da. of Sir William Lockhart, 1st Bt., of Carstairs, Lanark. *educ.* Leyden 1726; adv. 1728. *m.* 21 Dec. 1746, Jean, da. of Charles Areskine (q.v.) of Alva, Clackmannan, and Tinwald, Dumfries, Lord Tinwald S.C.J., and lord justice clerk, 1s.
Professor of public law, Edinburgh 1734–5; principal clerk of court of session 1738–d.; sheriff, Dumfries 1747.

William Kirkpatrick, a lawyer, whose grandfather had represented the county under William III, contested a by-election for Dumfries Burghs in May 1735 on the interest of Charles Areskine (q.v.), his future father-in-law, who had been elected in 1734 but chose to sit for Dumfriesshire. Awarded the seat on petition after a double return, he vacated it in June 1738 on appointment as clerk of session. He died 22 May 1778.

R.S.L.

KNATCHBULL, Sir Edward, 4th Bt. (c.1674–1730), of Mersham Hatch, nr. Ashford, Kent.[1]

ROCHESTER   1702–1705
KENT   1713–1715, 1722–1727
LOSTWITHIEL   29 Feb. 1728–3 Apr. 1730

b. c.1674, 1st s. of Sir Thomas Knatchbull, 3rd Bt., by Mary, da. of Sir Edward Dering, 2nd Bt., M.P.

m. 22 Dec. 1698, Alice. da. of John Wyndham of Norrington, Wilts., 5s. 3da. *suc.* fa. c.1712.

Sub-commr. of prizes 1702–4; muster master gen. of marines 1704–9.

Knatchbull came of one of the leading parliamentary families of Kent, which his grandfather and his uncle, the 1st and 2nd Bts., had represented. 'In the Queen's time', his first cousin, the 1st Lord Egmont, writes, 'he was a pretty warm Tory, but gradually came off from violence'.[2] Returned for his county under Anne, he lost his seat in 1715 but recovered it in 1722, when he resumed the parliamentary diary which he had started in the late reign. By this time he had become a moderate Tory, keenly interested in parliamentary business and procedure, prepared on occasion to vote against his own party. During his first session he was the author of an Act empowering separate parishes to set up workhouses; in a debate on frauds on the collection of the tobacco duty in Scotland, he proposed a helpful amendment which Walpole accepted; and shortly afterwards he with a number of other Tories voted with the Government against an opposition motion on the same subject, because it would have broken the Act of Union (16, 21, 29 Jan. and 8 Feb. 1723). As time went on the diary shows an increasing admiration for Walpole's ability, coupled, after 1725, when Pulteney and his friends went into opposition, with a corresponding dislike of the personal attacks made on Walpole by the discontented Whigs. Nevertheless he adhered to his party till the last session, when he voted against them on the Address; abstained on two subsequent opposition motions; and finally voted with 'a few other Tories' against a motion personally attacking Walpole, 'for I saw plainly there was nothing warranted by the evidence to justify the personal question' (17 Jan., 14 and 21 Feb., 7 Mar. 1727).

When Knatchbull came to make his preparations for the general election of 1727, he found that in Kent 'his old friends were shy of his inclination to side with the Government and the Whigs declared they would choose men that had always been staunch to the party and, as they said, no turn-coats'.[3] Shortly before the dissolution he wrote to Walpole through the Duke of Dorset, one of the heads of the Whig interest in Kent, explaining that he was meeting with great opposition and that 'the ground of this opposition is pretty well known to be my zeal for the public service, and my particular attachment to you'. He went on to say that the Duke of Dorset had promised, if he would stand down for Kent, to bring him in for Hythe should a vacancy occur there; but that as that

eventuality was problematical he was writing to ask Walpole 'to speak in such a plain manner to the Duke of Dorset and my Lord Leicester [lord lieutenant of Kent] that they may openly act for me in this election'. He concluded:

> I will . . . detain you no longer but to desire you would remember if I am deprived of a seat in Parliament this one who without any other motive but the public good and a true love for you has ended his days in Parliament for your service, which although it may be a crime with some, sure I am with me it is such for which I shall die an impenitent sinner.[4]

In the end it was decided that he should not stand for Kent but that he should be brought in by the Government for Lostwithiel, which he says 'was directed to be done by the King on the Duke of Dorset mentioning to him the hardship I had in Kent . . . Sir R. Walpole concurred in this, and executed the King's commands in my behalf with great willingness' (8 Mar. 1728).

In the new Parliament Knatchbull consistently supported the Administration, except on an opposition motion to make the holding of a pension incompatible with a seat in the House, when he abstained, feeling that 'they should not have divided on such a popular point' (16 Feb. 1730). He was also an active member of the gaols committee. He died 3 Apr. 1730, having, Egmont writes,

> caught his illness the long night that the House sat upon the Dunkirk inquiry, for he then went away fainting about twelve, and though the fever did not show itself immediately, so that he went abroad the very next day, and continued so to do and to attend the House, yet he was not right well, and at last fell down about 10 days since . . . He was coming into a good post when he died, for the Court had an esteem for him, and he latterly attached himself to Sir Robert Walpole. The King told my wife this night at the drawing room he was very sorry to hear of his death.[5]

His parliamentary diary is an important source of information on the proceedings and procedure of the House of Commons 1722–30.

[1] The references in the text are to *The Parliamentary Diary of Sir Edward Knatchbull*, ed. A. N. Newman (R. Hist. Soc. Cam. 3rd ser. xciv). [2] *HMC Egmont Diary*, i. 90–91. [3] Ibid. [4] 21 July 1727, Cholmondeley (Houghton) mss. [5] *HMC Egmont Diary*, loc. cit.

R.R.S.

KNIGHT, John (?1686–1733), of Gosfield Hall, Essex.

ST. GERMANS	1710–1722
SUDBURY	1722–2 Oct. 1733

b. ?1686, 1st s. of John Knight, M.P., of St. Clement's Dane, treasurer of the customs 1694–7, director of Bank of England 1694–7. *educ.* Wadham, Oxf. 26 Mar. 1703, aged 16; M. Temple 1702. *m.* (1) Elizabeth Slaughter of Cheyne Court, Herefs., *s.p.*; (2) 1724, Ann, da. and coh. of James Craggs, jt. postmaster gen., sis. and coh. of James Craggs (q.v.), wid. of John Newsham (q.v.) and afterwards wife of Robert Nugent (q.v.), 1s. 1da. *d.v.p.*

Assistant, R. African Co. 1716–22; sec. Leeward Is. 1718–22.

Knight, whose father was expelled from the House in 1698 for false endorsing of exchequer bills, acquired by purchase and foreclosure the Cornish estates of John Tredenham, M.P. (*d.* 1710), carrying an interest for one seat at St. Mawes.[1] He bought Gosfield Hall in 1715,[2] when he was returned as an administration candidate for St. Germans, voting with the Government. Returned for Sudbury in 1722, and again in 1727, when he **was also** returned for St. Mawes, he voted against the Government on the civil list arrears, 1729, for them on the Hessians, 1730, against them on the army, 1732, but for them on the excise bill, 1733, seconding the Address, 16 Jan. 1733.[3] He died 2 Oct. 1733. His widow and heir erected a splendid monument by Rysbrack with an inscription by Pope[4] to his memory in Gosfield church, but, marrying Robert Nugent (q.v.) soon afterwards, she 'ordered it to be enclosed . . . with a wainscot screen to shut it off from her sight when she went to church, which, however, she seldom did'.[5]

[1] W. P. Courtney, *Parl. Rep. Cornw.* 92. [2] Morant, *Essex*, ii. 382. [3] *HMC Egmont Diary*, i. 307. [4] Pope, *Works* (ed. Elwin & Courthope), ix. 455–6, 475. [5] *HMC Portland*, vi. 70.

E.C.

KNIGHT, Robert (1702–72), of Barrells, Warws. and Luxborough, Essex.

GREAT GRIMSBY	1734–1747
CASTLE RISING	1747–1754
GREAT GRIMSBY	3 Dec. 1762–1768
MILBORNE PORT	25 May 1770–30 Mar. 1772

b. 17 Dec. 1702, 1st s. of Robert Knight of Barrells by Martha, da. of Jeremiah Powell of Edenhope, Salop.[1] *educ.* I. Temple 1719. *m.* (1) 10 June 1727, Henrietta (*d.* 26 Mar. 1756), da. of Henry St. John, 1st Visct. St. John, 1s. *d.v.p.* 1da.; (2) 18 June 1756, Mary, wid. of Sir John Le Quesne, alderman of London, *s.p.* *suc.* fa. 1744; *cr.* Baron Luxborough [I] 8 Aug. 1745; Earl of Catherlough [I] 14 May 1763; K.B. 18 May 1770.

Recorder, Grimsby 1761.

Knight was the son of the South Sea Company's cashier, who fled to France in 1721 and became a banker in Paris. In 1727 he married Bolingbroke's half-sister, from whom he separated in 1736 on finding her in bed with her doctor.[2] Returned in 1734 for Great Grimsby, he was one of several new Whig Members who voted against the Government on the Address, 29 Jan. 1735, but subsequently returned to his allegiance, speaking against Sir John Barnard's (q.v.) scheme for the conversion

of the national debt in 1737 and for the convention with Spain in 1739.[3] After Walpole's fall he procured a pardon for his exiled father, on the ground that the ex-cashier had been sufficiently punished by the forfeiture of all his available assets in England, amounting to over £200,000.[4] Continuing to support the Government, he spoke in favour of sending for the Hessians during the rebellion of 1745 and for the Hanoverian troops in 1746,[5] when he was created an Irish peer. In 1747 he was returned for Castle Rising by the 2nd Earl of Orford, to whom he was said to have also owed his Irish peerage, their link, according to Orford's brother, Horace Walpole, being the manager of the actresses whom they were respectively keeping.[6] He died 30 Mar. 1772.

[1] W. Cooper, *Wootton Wawen*, 114–15. [2] *HMC Egmont Diary*, ii. 294. [3] *HMC Carlisle*, 147; Coxe, *Walpole*, iii. 517–18. [4] *Gent. Mag.* 1742, p. 442; *HMC Egmont Diary*, iii. 269. [5] Owen, *Pelhams*, 291, 306 n.3. [6] Walpole to Mann, 26 June 1747.

R.R.S.

KNIGHT, Thomas, *see* **MAY**

KNIGHT, William (?1668–1721), of West Dean, nr. Midhurst, Suss.

MIDHURST 1713–26 Oct. 1721

b. ?1668, s. of Edward Woodward of Fosters, Surr. by Elizabeth, da. of Sir Christopher Lewknor of West Dean. *educ.* Ch. Ch. Oxf. 20 Nov. 1685, aged 17. *m.* 1st cos. Elizabeth Knight (formerly Martin), da. and h. of Michael Martin of Eynsham, Oxon. by Francis, da. and coh. of Sir Christopher Lewknor of West Dean; cos. and eventually h. of Sir Richard Knight of Chawton, Hants, assuming name of Knight. She was h. of her 1st cos. once removed, John Lewknor, M.P., of West Dean. He took the name of Knight on his marriage, which was *s.p.* *suc.* fa. 1702. Sheriff, Surr. 1702–3, Suss. 1709–10.

William Knight married the heiress of the Lewknors, who owned the manor of West Dean, carrying an interest at Midhurst, for which he was returned as a Tory. He was absent from the vote on the septennial bill in 1716, but voted against the repeal of the Occasional Conformity and Schism Acts and the peerage bill in 1719. He died 26 Oct. 1721, leaving all his estates to his wife, who later married Bulstrode Peachey (q.v.).

J.B.L.

KNIGHT, *see also* **PEACHEY, Bulstrode**

KNIGHTLEY, Valentine (1718–54), of Fawsley, Northants.

NORTHAMPTONSHIRE 14 Apr. 1748–2 May 1754

b. 1 Sept. 1718, 1st surv. s. of Lucy Knightley of

Fawsley by his 1st w. Jane Grey, da. and coh. of Henry Benson of Dodford, Northants. by Elizabeth, da. and coh. of Thomas Grey, Lord Grey of Groby. *educ.* ? Eton 1732; St. John's, Oxf. 1735. *m.* 21 Dec. 1740, Elizabeth, da. of Edward Dummer of Swaythling, Hants, coh. of her bro. John Dummer, 6s. 3da. *suc.* fa. 1738.

Sheriff, Northants. 1743–4.

Of an old Northamptonshire family, who frequently represented the county and the town, Knightley was elected as knight of the shire in succession to Thomas Cartwright, after a hot contest, during which he issued a denial of charges of disaffection brought against him by his opponent, threatening legal proceedings.[1] A year later the 2nd Lord Egmont in his electoral survey wrote of Knightley:

> Reputed a Jacobite but a very gentlemanlike man and I believe not what he is supposed, I have met him often, and have so good an opinion of him as to think if he engages with us that he will not deceive us. Sir Cordell Firebrace [q.v.] has a friendship and influence with him, and I can depend upon him in the assurances he will give me. Knightley is of a very ancient family, and has a very good estate, £4,000 a year.

In 1753 Horace Walpole, after a visit to Northamptonshire, described Knightley as

> entertaining all the parishes round with a turtle-feast, which, so far from succeeding, has almost made him suspected for a *Jew*, as the country parsons have not yet learned to wade into green fat.[2]

He was re-elected unopposed but died shortly after, 2 May 1754.

[1] E. G. Forrester, *Northants. County Elections 1695–1832*, p. 64.
[2] To John Chute, 4 Aug. 1753. The reference is to the agitation against the Jewish Naturalization Act.

R.R.S.

KNOLLYS, Francis (?1697–1754), of Thame, Oxon. and Lower Winchendon, Bucks.

OXFORD   24 Oct. 1722–1734

b. ?1697, 1st s. of Francis Knollys, M.P., of Lower Winchendon by Elizabeth, da. and coh. of John Striblehill of Thame, Oxon. *educ.* Thame g.s.;[1] Hart Hall, Oxf. 7 Apr. 1714, aged 16. *unm. suc.* fa. 1701.

Descended from Sir Francis Knollys, treasurer of the Household to Queen Elizabeth, Knollys was returned as a Tory for Oxford in 1722.

> Our Member for the town [an Oxford don wrote] was chosen yesterday, without opposition, a young gentleman, unmarried, of £1,700 *per annum*, and money in his pocket. His name Knollys, a relation of Tom Rowney's [q.v.] and brought in by his interest.[2]

Re-elected in 1727, he was one of the defaulters on the call of the House on 13 Mar. 1733 when, his excuse not being allowed, he was taken into custody

by the serjeant-at-arms. He was thus prevented from taking part in the division of 15 Mar. on the excise bill, but having been discharged on the 16th he voted against the bill on the report stage.[3] No other vote of his is recorded. He did not stand in 1734, and died 24 June 1754.

[1] F. G. Lee, *Hist. Thame*, 598. [2] *HMC Portland*, vii. 337. [3] *CJ*, xxii. 87, 92; *Gent. Mag.* 1733, p. 580.

E.C.

KNOLLYS, Henry (?1689–1747), of Grove Place, Nursling, Hants.

ST. IVES   1722–1734

b. ?1689, 1st s. of Francis Knollys of Grove Place by Margaret, da. of Edward Fleming of North Stoneham, Hants. *educ.* Trinity, Oxf. 17 Oct. 1704, aged 15; M. Temple 1705. *m.*, 1s. *suc.* fa. 1701.

Sheriff, Hants 1716–17.

Descended from Sir Henry Knollys, comptroller of the Household to Charles I, who granted him the manor of Nursling, Knollys came into a good estate while still a minor. Sent down from Oxford in 1707 for 'being disobedient, and insulting, and very abusive to the society', he was re-admitted the next year after much controversy among the college authorities.[1] In 1719 his friend, Lord William Powlett (q.v.), having made him a freeman of Lymington in 1717,[2] tried unsuccessfully to put him up for that borough. Returned in 1722 for St. Ives on the Powlett interest,[3] he voted with the Administration in every recorded division. In 1731 he failed to get elected as verderer of the New Forest by 1,195 votes to 2,163.[4] He did not stand in 1734, and died at the beginning of 1747. On the death of his son, Thomas, in 1751, Grove Place passed to his brother-in-law Sir Richard Mill, 5th Bt. (q.v.).[5]

[1] Hearne, *Colls.* (Oxf. Hist. Soc.), ii. 82–83, 91. [2] Edw. King, *Old Times Revisited, Lymington, Hants*, 193. [3] S. Burrard, *Annals of Walhampton*, 29–30, 34. [4] *Gent. Mag.* 1731, p. 217. [5] *VCH Hants*, iii. 434–5.

E.C.

KNOLLYS, William, Visct. Wallingford (1694–1740), of St. George's, Hanover Sq., Westminster.

BANBURY   9 Apr. 1733–6 June 1740

b. 15 Oct. 1694, 1st surv. s. of Charles Knollys, titular 4th Earl of Banbury, by Elizabeth, da. of Michael Lister of Burwell, Lincs. *m.* 1st cos, Mary Catherine, da. of John Law, director gen. of the French finances, by Catherine, da. of Nicholas Knollys, titular 3rd Earl of Banbury.

Ensign Col. Pocock's regt. 1715; cornet 2 Drag. Gds. 1718, lt. 1727; 2nd maj. 1st tp. Life Gds. 1737–d.

Knollys claimed to be descended from William Knollys, M.P., 1st Earl of Banbury, comptroller of the Household to Queen Elizabeth. His father, who had repeatedly petitioned in vain for a writ of summons to the House of Lords, called himself and was known as the Earl of Banbury, Knollys assuming the courtesy title of Viscount Wallingford.[1] Unsuccessful at a by-election for Banbury in January 1730 created by the succession to the peerage of his friend Francis North (q.v.),[2] he was returned at a by-election in 1733, but no votes of his are recorded in that Parliament. Re-elected in 1734, he voted with the Administration on the Spanish convention in 1739 and on the place bill in 1740. He died *v.p.* 6 June 1740.

[1] See *CP* for the Banbury peerage case [2] He named North in his will and appointed him his executor, PCC 190 Browne.

E.C.

KNOWLES, Charles (c.1704–77), of Lovelhill, nr. Windsor, Berks.

GATTON 28 Nov. 1749–Mar. 1752

b. c.1704, reputedly illegit. s. of Charles Knollys, titular 4th Earl of Banbury, the fa. of William Knollys (q.v.). *m.* (1) 22 Dec. 1740, Mary (bur. 16 Mar. 1742), da. of John Alleyne of Barbados, 1s. *d.v.p.*; (2) 29 July 1750, Maria Magdalena Theresa, da. of Henry Frances, Comte de Bouget, 1s. 1da. *cr.* Bt. 31 Oct. 1765.

Entered navy 1718, lt. 1730, cdr. 1731, capt. 1739, r.-adm. 1747, v.-adm. 1755, adm. 1760, r.-adm. of Great Britain 1765–70.

Surveyor and engineer of the fleet on the Cartagena expedition 1741; gov. Louisburg 1746–8; c.-in-c. Jamaica 1747–8; gov. Jamaica 1752–6; pres. of the Russian Admiralty 1770–4.

Knowles, who entered the navy as a captain's servant, spent much of his naval career in the West Indies, where he married the daughter of a leading Barbados planter. After serving in the expeditions against Portobello and Cartagena, on which he published several pamphlets, he was appointed governor of Louisburg, but soon applied for a transfer to the West Indies, explaining to Anson that he had 'more the glory of his Majesty's arms at heart than views after private lucre'.[1] Appointed commander-in-chief in Jamaica, he co-operated with Edward Trelawny (q.v.), the governor of the colony, in using their posts to secure personal privileges in trading with the captured French colonies, to the exclusion of other local merchants.[2] Ordered to be court-martialled in 1749 on charges of negligence in an action of 1748, he took steps to have himself returned for Gatton on the nomination of Paul Humphrey (q.v.). A letter to one of his brother officers on 5 Dec. 1749 mentions that 'the cunning admiral has got a seat in the House of Commons last week, and it is supposed he will have art enough to acquit himself at his

trial'.[3] In the event he was reprimanded. He gave up his seat in 1752 on being appointed governor of Jamaica.

He died 9 Dec. 1777.

[1] Add. 15956, f. 136. [2] R. Pares, *War and Trade in W. Indies*, 183–4. [3] *HMC Du Cane*, 203.

A.N.N.

KYNASTON, Corbet (1690–1740), of Hordley, Salop.

SHREWSBURY 27 May 1714–9 Apr. 1723
SHROPSHIRE 1734–17 June 1740

bap. 2 Feb. 1690, 1st s. of John Kynaston by his 1st w. and half-bro. of Edward Kynaston (qq.v.). *educ.* I. Temple 1719–20. *unm. suc.* fa. 1733.

Corbet Kynaston was one of the six M.P.s whose arrest was ordered in September 1715 on a charge of being 'engaged in a design to support the intended invasion of the kingdom'.[1] He made his escape, leaving 12 pictures of the Duke of Ormonde at his seat in the county, having already dispersed a large number of them 'to spirit up the mob to revenge their idol'.[2] He surrendered himself on 9 Jan. 1716 but was soon released, voting against the Government in all extant divisions of that Parliament. His name was sent to the Pretender in 1721 as a probable supporter in the event of a rising.[3] Re-elected in 1722 but unseated on petition, he stood for Shrewsbury again in 1727. He was defeated by a fellow Tory, Sir John Astley (q.v.), who had been awarded £24,000 damages against him in a lawsuit over transactions in South Sea stock.[4] To avoid paying, he went abroad to France, where he remained till his father's death, when he came to terms with Astley, with whom he was returned for the county in 1734, again voting against the Government. On his death, 17 June 1740, his friend, Thomas Carte, the Jacobite historian, wrote to the Pretender's secretary:

The King hath had a great loss in the death of Corbet Kynaston, who was a man of the honestest principles in nature and would have ventured his life and fortune for him in any circumstances whatever. No man in England could have carried his county with him more entirely than he could on any occasion for his Majesty's service; and I do not know how the loss can be supplied.[5]

[1] *Pol. State*, x. 416. [2] *A Full and Authentick Narrative of the intended Horrid Conspiracy* (1715), p. 75. [3] *Hist. Reg.* 1716, p. 111; Stuart mss 65/16. [4] *Salop Arch. Soc. Trans.* (ser. 2), vi. 217. [5] 7 Aug. 1740, Stuart mss 224/117.

R.R.S.

KYNASTON, Edward (1709–72), of Garth and Bryngwyn, Mont. and Hardwick, Salop.

BISHOP'S CASTLE 1734–1741
MONTGOMERYSHIRE 1747–18 May 1772

b. 6 Oct. 1709, 1st s. of John Kynaston by his 2nd w. and half-bro. of Corbet Kynaston (qq.v.). *educ.* Eton 1725; St. John's, Camb. 1726; L. Inn 1726. *m.* Victoria, da. and h. of Sir Charles Lloyd, 3rd Bt., of Garth, Mont., *s.p. suc.* bro. Corbet Kynaston at Bryngwyn and Hardwick 1740; fa.-in-law at Garth 1743.

Recorder, Welshpool 1750–62.

Edward Kynaston was the favourite son of his father, on whose death in 1733 he inherited the greater part of the personal property at the expense of his half-brother, Corbet Kynaston.[1] In 1734 he was returned as a Tory for Bishop's Castle on the interest of John Walcot (q.v.), voting with the Opposition. He did not stand in 1741 but in 1747 he was brought in for Montgomeryshire by Sir Watkin Williams Wynn (q.v.), on whose death in 1749 he became trustee for his estate. He was put down as clerk of the Green Cloth in a list of future office holders drawn up by the 2nd Lord Egmont, who wrote of him in his electoral survey, c.1749–50:

> This man is reckoned a Jacobite but he talks now in a very different strain from what he did formerly, and declares himself for us [i.e. for Leicester House]—at least for a time.

Nevertheless Lord Powis, on succeeding in 1748 to the estates of the Marquess of Powis, carrying the greatest electoral influence in Montgomeryshire, made no attempt to dislodge Kynaston, who was a nephew of Powis's follower, Thomas Hill (q.v.), and was used by both Powis and Hill in negotiations with the Shropshire Tories.

He died 18 May 1772.

[1] PCC 113 Ockham.

J.B.L.

KYNASTON, John (1664–1733), of Hardwick, Salop.

SHREWSBURY   1695–20 Dec. 1709
SHROPSHIRE   1710–1715, 1722–1727

b. Aug. 1664, 1st surv. s. of Edward Kynaston, M.P. Shrewsbury, of Hordley, Salop by Amy, da. and h. of Thomas Barker of Albrightlee, Salop. *educ.* Eton 1679–83; St. John's, Camb. 1683. *m.* 22 Sept. 1686, Beatrice (bur. 7 Dec. 1703), da. of Sir Vincent Corbet, 2nd Bt., of Moreton Corbet, Salop, sis. and h. of Sir Vincent Corbet, 3rd Bt., 2s. 1da.; (2) 27 Oct. 1708, Anne, da. of Thomas Harwood of Tern, Salop, sis. of Thomas Hill (q.v.), 2s. 2da. *suc.* fa. 1693. Sheriff, Salop 1689–90; mayor of Shrewsbury 1696.

The head of an ancient Shropshire family, with a rent roll of about £8,000 a year,[1] Kynaston was the leader of the Shropshire Tories under Queen Anne. His second wife is said to have carried the contributions of the local Jacobites to St. Germain.[2] In 1715 he lost his county seat, recovering it in 1722, after which he did not stand again. In 1731 he

preferred an unsuccessful claim to the barony of Powys. He died 10 Sept. 1733, disinheriting his eldest son Corbet (q.v.) of all except his entailed estates, in favour of his younger son Edward (q.v.).[3]

[1] *Gent. Mag.* 1733, p. 495.   [2] Owen & Blakeway, *Hist. Shrewsbury*, i. 508 n.4.   [3] *Salop Arch. Soc. Trans.* (ser. 2), vi. 217.

J.B.L.

LADE, John (c.1662–1740), of Warbleton, Suss. and St. Saviour's, Southwark.

SOUTHWARK   1713–20 Apr. 1714, 3 May 1714–1722,
17 Jan. 1724–1727

b. c.1662, 1st surv. s. of Thomas Lade of Warbleton by Mary, da. of John Nutt, D.D., of Mayer's, Selmeston, Suss. *unm. suc.* fa. 1668; *cr.* Bt. 11 Mar. 1730.

Director, S. Sea Co. 1721–4, 1733–9.

Lade, a rich brewer in Southwark and a South Sea Company director, was returned unopposed in 1715, classed as a Whig who would often vote with the Tories. He voted for the septennial bill in 1716, but went into opposition with Walpole in 1717, voting against the Government in the division on Lord Cadogan (q.v.) in June that year. In 1719 he was absent from the division on the repeal of the Occasional Conformity and Schism Acts, and voted against the peerage bill. He was defeated in 1722, but was returned at the top of the poll at a by-election two years later. He never stood again. In 1730 he was made a baronet, with remainder to his great nephew, John Whithorne, who took the name of Lade. He died 30 July 1740.

E.C.

LAMB, Matthew (?1705–68), of Brocket Hall, Herts. and Melbourne Hall, Derbys.

STOCKBRIDGE   1741–1747
PETERBOROUGH   1747–6 Nov. 1768

b. ?1705, 2nd s. of Matthew Lamb of Southwell, Notts. *educ.* L. Inn 1726, called 1733. *m.* c.1740, Charlotte, da. of Thomas Coke of Melbourne Hall, vice-chamberlain to Queen Anne, sis. and h. of George Lewis Coke (*d.* 1751), 1s. 2da. *suc.* uncle Peniston Lamb 1735, *cr.* Bt. 17 Jan. 1755.

Solicitor to the Post Office 1738–*d.*; counsel for board of Trade 1746–*d.*; K.C. 1754.

The son of a Southwell attorney, who was legal adviser to the Cokes of Melbourne Hall,[1] Lamb was trained in the law by his uncle, Peniston Lamb, a successful barrister, versed in 'pleading and demurring, weaving settlements and ravelling threads of adverse wills', who left him a fortune estimated at £100,000, together with his chambers in Lincoln's Inn. Through his uncle, the executor of the will and guardian of the children of John, 2nd Earl Fitzwilliam (q.v.), he became land agent, legal adviser and moneylender to many members of the aristocracy, including the Fitzwilliams, the 3rd Duke of Marlborough who, at one time, was paying him £9,000 p.a. in interest on loans, Lord Thanet, and Lord Ashburnham.[2] He was one of the executors of the will of Edward Wortley Montagu (q.v.), his fellow Member at Peterborough. As land agent to the Salisburys, he was entrusted with the negotiation for the marriage of Lady Catherine Cecil with Lord Perceval, later the 2nd Lord Egmont (q.v.),[3] who wrote in his electoral survey: 'Lamb is very rich and is necessary to and consequently intimate with a great number of the nobility . . . He can do most of any man with Lord Salisbury'. In 1746 he bought Brocket Hall, around which, according to his grandson, the 2nd Lord Melbourne, he 'did the Salisburys out of some land'.[4] The widow of the first Marquess of Salisbury used to declare that the rise of the Lamb family was from the plunder of the earls of Salisbury.[5]

In 1741, thinking 'he could afford himself the luxury of a seat in Parliament', he 'agreed for one that stood waiting to be hired at Stockbridge',[6] showing himself a faithful government supporter. His appointment to be counsel to the board of Trade in 1746, and a report that he was to be made a K.C., though he 'never was an hour in Westminster Hall as a counsel in his life', excited great indignation in the legal profession.[7] Transferring in 1747 to Peterborough, where he managed the Fitzwilliam interest, he attained the dignity of K.C. in 1754. He died 6 Nov. 1768, leaving a fortune estimated at over £1,000,000.

[1] *Ld. Melbourne's Pprs.* (ed. Sanders) 1–2; W. Torrens, *Mems. William, 2nd Visct. Melbourne,* 11; *Lond. Mag.* 1735, p. 99. [2] *Banks Pprs.* (Lincoln Rec. Soc. xlv), 90; A. L. Rowse, *Later Churchills,* 53; Yorke, *Hardwicke,* i. 219–20; *HMC Egmont Diary,* i. 157, 172; ii. 367; iii. 131. [3] *HMC Egmont Diary,* ii. 323–4, 327, 334, 337–8, 347, 353. [4] A. Hayward, *Sketches of Eminent Statesmen,* i. 331–2. [5] *GEC Baronetage,* v. 100 n. [6] Torrens, i. 12. [7] *HMC Polwarth,* v. 186.

E.C.

LAMBERT, Daniel (1685–1750), of Savage Gardens, Tower Hill, and Perrotts, Banstead, Surr.

LONDON 1741–1747

b. 7 Sept. 1685, 3rd s. of Daniel Lambert of Perrotts by Elizabeth, da. of Rev. Thomas Emmes, rector of East Tisted, Hants. *m.* (lic. 9 May 1709) Mary, da. and coh. of John Wilmot, London merchant, of Well House, Banstead, *s.p.* Kntd. 18 Feb. 1744.
    Common councillor, London 1732–7; vintner 1737–50; master, Vintners' Co. 1741; sheriff 1733–4, alderman 1737–50, ld. mayor Mar.–Oct. 1741; auditor of Irish Society 1735–7, gov. 1741–4.

Lambert, whose family had been settled at Perrotts since the sixteenth century, purchased

the manor from an elder brother.[1] A Portugal merchant, he was active in London politics, serving on committees set up by the common council to prepare the petitions against the excise bill, and the Spanish convention, and to press the merchants' complaints against Spanish depredations.[2] On the death of Humphry Parsons (q.v.) in March 1741 he served as lord mayor for the remainder of the year, receiving the thanks of the common council

> for his constant attendance, his judicious and faithful discharge and great dispatch of the duties of that high station, for the easy access given his fellow citizens, and for the frequent opportunities he gave this court of meeting together for the dispatch of the public business in this City.[3]

Returned for London as a Tory that year, he voted against the Administration in all three Hanoverian divisions, but with them in February 1744 on an opposition motion to tack a demand for an inquiry into the state and disposition of the naval forces to the loyal address upon a threatened French invasion.[4] He was knighted by George II on presenting the city's address upon the same occasion.[5] On 6 Feb. 1745 he spoke against Pelham's additional duty on wines, fearing, as a merchant engaged in the Portuguese trade, that

> the King of Portugal would, in return for the new duty on his wines, lay a further impostion on our English manufactures, from which our commerce would receive a notable prejudice, and that of our rivals, the French, as much benefit.[6]

He lost his seat in 1747. Next year, meeting Frederick, Prince of Wales, who denounced the peace,

> Sir Daniel, in the spirit of an old Tory, made no scruple of declaring his sentiments against a war on the continent, and added that we were incapable of prosecuting it for want of money.[7]

He died 13 May 1750 of gaol fever caught from the prisoners as he sat on the bench at the Old Bailey.[8]

[1] Manning & Bray, *Surr.* ii. 589. [2] 9 Apr. 1733, 20 Feb. 1739, Jnl. vols. 57, 58; Stuart mss 204/144. [3] 12 Nov. 1741, Jnl. vol. 58. [4] Yorke's parl. jnl. *Parl. Hist.* xiii. 649. [5] *HMC Egmont Diary,* iii. 286. [6] Yorke's parl. jnl. *Parl. Hist.* xiii. 1127. [7] Yorke, *Hardwicke,* i. 666–7. [8] Griffiths, *Chrons. of Newgate,* i. 438.

E.C.

LAMBERT, Edmund (?1665–1734), of Boyton, Wilts.

HINDON 1708–1713
SALISBURY 1715–1722

b. ?1665, 1st s. of Thomas Lambert, M.P., of Boyton by Eleanor, da. of Edward Topp. *educ.* Ch. Ch. Oxf. 3 Feb. 1682, aged 16; M. Temple 1683, called 1689. *m.* bef. June 1689,[1] Sarah, da. of Peter Blake of Andover, Hants, sis. and h. of Peter Blake, 4da. *suc.* fa. 1692.

Lambert's family had been seated at Boyton since the time of Elizabeth.[2] A member of the October Club, he sat as a Tory for Hindon under Queen Anne until he was defeated there in 1713. Returned for Salisbury at the accession of George I, he voted against the Government in all recorded divisions but did not stand again. In 1722 his name was sent to the Pretender as a probable supporter in the event of a rising.[3] He died 29 Jan. 1734.

[1] PCC 23 Fane. [2] Hoare, *Wilts*. Hundred of Heytesbury, 203. [3] Stuart mss 65/16.

R.S.L.

LAMBTON, Henry (1697–1761), of Lambton Hall, co. Dur.

DURHAM   25 Jan. 1734–26 June 1761

bap. 9 Nov. 1697, 1st s. of Ralph Lambton of Barnes, co. Dur. by Dorothy, da. and coh. of John Hedworth of Harraton, co. Dur.; bro. of Gen. John Lambton, M.P. *educ.* Queen's, Oxf. 1715; L. Inn 1719. *unm. suc.* fa. 1717; uncle William Lambton, M.P., at Lambton 1724.
   Mayor, Hartlepool 1729, 1741, 1753.

On the death in 1724 of William Lambton, who had represented the county in six Parliaments between 1685 and 1702, his nephew, Henry Lambton, succeeded to an estate which had been held by his ancestors since before the thirteenth century.[1] Having also inherited extensive colliery interests, he became active in the coal lobby as the head of the Sunderland coal owners, in which capacity he was described in 1731 as one who 'will be drawn but not led'.[2] After a narrow defeat at a by-election for Durham in 1730, he was returned there unopposed as a Whig at another by-election in January 1734, continuing to represent it till his death. Voting with the Administration in all recorded divisions under Walpole, but absent on the Hanoverians in 1742, 1744 and 1746, he was classed as Old Whig in 1746 and as 'for' in 1747. He died 26 June 1761.

[1] Surtees, *Durham*, ii. 175. [2] E. Hughes, *N. Country Life in 18th Cent.* 241.

R.S.L.

LANE, Sir Richard (c.1667–1756), of Worcester.

MINEHEAD   18 Dec. 1721–9 Jan. 1722
WORCESTER   1727–1734

b. c.1667, 1st s. of Richard Lane of St. Augustine's, Bristol, sugar baker, merchant and mayor of that city, by his w. Susanna. *m.* (lic. Chester 3 Jan. ?1692) Sarah Davie of Salford, Lancs., 4s. 5da. *suc.* fa. 1705.[1] Kntd. 21 Oct. 1714.
   Mayor, Worcester 1709–10; sheriff, Worcs. 1714–15.

Richard Lane, who came of an old Bristol family of merchants, moved to Worcester, where he was established as a merchant and sugar baker by 1699,[2] later becoming a prominent figure in the salt trade. According to his own account he,

being in July 1710 mayor of the city of Worcester, put a stop to the insolent progress of Dr. Sacheverel and his deluded followers, who came here with ensigns of war, inciting the Queen's subjects to sedition and rebellion against her and legal successors in the Protestant line in favour of an abjured Popish pretender; and in the first year of King George the First (being then sheriff of the county of Worcester) raised the posse comitatus and (thro' God's blessing) defeated great numbers who came in tumults there with arms, to the same illegal purpose.[3]

In 1721 at a by-election for Minehead, he

took the writ from the person ordered to convey it to the returning officer, and kept it in his pocket till the very day of the election; and yet he escaped unpunished, though the messenger directed to carry the writ was taken into custody of the serjeant-at-arms.[4]

He was later unseated on petition. In 1725,

being informed by some persons concerned in the salt works of Cheshire that the strongest brine there lay lower than the pits in Droitwich were commonly sunk [he] ordered the talc which was at the bottom of the pits to be sunk through. Upon this the strong brine broke out with such violence, and in such abundance, that two men who were at work in the pit were thrown to the surface and killed. Soon after everyone sunk his pit through the talc and obtained such a profusion of strong brine that not one tenth part of it has ever been used; but ran to waste. From henceforth the old pit became of no value at all, which some years before was worth near £5,000 p.a. and esteemed the surest property a man could enjoy.[5]

Returned for Worcester after a contest in 1727, he consistently supported the Administration. He was rewarded with the receiver generalship of the land tax for Worcestershire for his eldest son, while his second son was appointed a commissioner for licensing hawkers and pedlars. In March 1732 he is reported as speaking in favour of the free export of wool and yarn from Ireland, 'for Ireland having more than it can consume will still find ways to get rid of it'.[6] As a salt exporter—during these years he was engaged in a protracted lawsuit with the salt commissioners on a claim for nearly £23,000 in respect of allowances on shipments of salt to Ireland over a period of six months—he protested against the export of rock salt to Ireland because, as there was no restriction on refining it there, it would undercut his own salt.[7] In the course of a speech in February 1733, opposing a reduction of the army, he made a facetious allusion to Walpole, saying

It was the case of the prophet Daniel who because he was premier minister had many that envied his place, who pushed him even into the den of lions, but he came off with honour, and continued in the favour of Nebuchadnezzar and his successor.

On the excise bill, after an opposition Member had made 'a bantering speech against the bill', Lane 'answered him the same way, which though it diverted the House was by serious gentlemen disapproved'.[8] He did not stand in 1741. In 1747 he printed a leaflet outlining a scheme for paying off the national debt.[9] He died, aged 89, 29 Mar. 1756.

[1] PCC 119 Gee. [2] Bristol & Glos. Arch. Soc. Trans. lxxvi, ped. opp. 132; Nash, *Worcs*. i. p. xxx; ii. p. cxx; *Westm. Abbey Reg.* (Harl. Soc. x), 389. [3] *Address to Honourable Commons of Great Britain in Parliament assembled* (1747). [4] *A complete History of the late Septennial Parliament* (1722) p. 77. [5] Nash, i. 299. [6] *HMC Egmont Diary*, i. 239. [7] E. Hughes, *Studies in Admin. and Finance*, 244, 397 and n.; *HMC Egmont Diary*, i. 240. [8] *HMC Egmont Diary*, i. 317, 350. [9] *Address*.

R.S.L.

LANE, *see also* **FOX** (afterwards **FOX LANE**), **George**

LANSDELL, John (*d.* 1739), of Halsted, Kent.

LISKEARD   1722–1727

m., 2s.
Dep. treasurer of the Ordnance 1709–22; assistant, R. African Co. 1716–22.

Lansdell, who bought the manor of Chamberhouse, in Crookham, Berks. in 1716[1] and the manor of Halsted in Kent from Edward Ashe (q.v.)[2] before 1726, served under the elder Craggs at the Ordnance office. Returned for Liskeard by Craggs's son-in-law, Edward Eliot (q.v.), in 1722, he did not stand again. In 1738 he sold Halsted to Lord Vere Beauclerk (q.v.) for £22,989.[3] He died 4 July 1739, leaving two-thirds of his fortune to his eldest son, John, and the remaining third to his second son, Chrysostom.[4]

[1] VCH Berks. iii. 317. [2] PCC 157 Henchman. [3] Hasted, *Kent*, i. 320-1. [4] PCC 157 Henchman.

E.C.

LAROCHE, John (c.1700–52), of Pall Mall, and Englefield Green, Surr.

BODMIN   31 Jan. 1727–20 Apr. 1752

b. c.1700, 1st s. of Peter Crothaire (afterwards Laroche) of Bordeaux, barber to Prince George of Denmark. *educ.* Queens', Camb. 1717; M. Temple 1717. *m.* bef. 1731, Elizabeth, da. of Isaac Garnier of St. James's, Westminster, apothecary to the army, 3s. 4da. *suc.* fa. 1745.
Assistant, R. African Co. 1732–46.

Laroche, a merchant of Huguenot extraction, seems to have begun life as steward of the Robartes family,[1] who had the chief interest at Bodmin.

Henry Robartes, 3rd Earl of Radnor, left him £1,000 in his will in 1741, and John Robartes, 4th Earl of Radnor, left his Cornish estates to Laroche's children in 1757.[2] After standing unsuccessfully for Bodmin in June 1725 he was returned for it as a Whig in 1727, subsequently building up a strong interest of his own in the corporation. His only recorded speeches were made on 15 April 1736 in favour of a bill designed to check the alienation of lands to charities and on 4 Feb. 1740 and 21 Jan 1741 in defence of the board of Georgia trustees, of whom he was an original member.[3] He voted against the Hessians in 1730 but otherwise regularly voted with the Administration till the critical divisions before the fall of Walpole, when he was absent, owing to illness, from those on the chairman of the elections committee and on the Westminster election petition in December 1741.[4] After Walpole's fall he supported successive Administrations till his death, 20 Apr. 1752.

[1] MacLean, *Trigg Minor*, i. 153 n. [2] PCC 49 Spurway; PCC 231 Hering. [3] Harley Diary, 15 Apr. 1736; *HMC Egmont Diary*, iii. 108, 180. [4] Coxe, *Walpole*, iii. 583, 586.

E.C.

LASCELLES, Daniel (1714–84), of Goldsborough, nr. Knaresborough, Yorks.

NORTHALLERTON   3 Apr. 1752–Dec. 1780

bap. 20 May 1714, 2nd s. of Henry Lascelles by his 1st w. and bro. of Edwin Lascelles (qq.v.). *educ.* I. Temple 1731. *m.* Elizabeth Southwick, whom he div. in 1751, *s.p.*

A partner in the family business, Daniel Lascelles succeeded his father at Northallerton, which he represented till he stood down to make room for his elder brother, Edwin, in 1780. He died 24 May 1784.

R.R.S.

LASCELLES, Edwin (1713–95), of Harewood, nr. Leeds, Yorks.

SCARBOROUGH	8 Dec. 1744–1754
NORTHALLERTON	1754–1761
YORKSHIRE	1761–1780
NORTHALLERTON	9 Dec. 1780–1790

bap. 5 Feb. 1713, 1st s. of Henry Lascelles by his 1st w. and bro. of Daniel Lascelles (qq.v.). *educ.* Trinity, Camb. 1732; I. Temple 1731. *m.* (1) 5 Jan. 1747, Elizabeth (*d.* 31 Aug. 1764), da. and h. of Sir Darcy Dawes, 4th Bt., of Lyons, Essex, *s.p.*; (2) 31 Mar. 1770, Jane, da. of William Coleman of Garney, Devon, wid. of Sir John Fleming, 1st Bt., of Brompton Park, Mdx., *s.p.* *suc.* fa. 1753; *cr.* Baron Harewood 9 July 1790.

Edwin Lascelles, who took no part in the family business, was returned for Scarborough on his own interest. He voted for the Hanoverians in 1746 and was classed as a government supporter in the next Parliament. He died 25 Jan. 1795.

R.R.S.

LASCELLES, Henry (1690–1753), of Harewood and Northallerton, Yorks.

NORTHALLERTON   16 May 1745–Mar. 1752

b. 20 Dec. 1690, 2nd surv. s. of Daniel Lascelles, M.P., of Stank and Northallerton by Margaret, da. of George Metcalfe of Northallerton. *m.* (1) 8 Apr. 1712, Mary, da. and coh. of Edward Carter of Barbados, 5s.; (2) 1731, Janet, da. of John Whetston of Barbados, *s.p.*
    Collector of customs, Barbados 1715–30; director, E.I. Co. 1737–45.

Henry Lascelles came of an old Yorkshire family, who had recently become connected with Barbados. As a youth he went to Barbados, where from 1715 he combined the business of a merchant with the post of collector of customs. In 1730 he turned over his customs post to his brother, Edward, getting his accounts passed by the commissioners of customs in 1733. Soon afterwards he settled in England, buying the estate of Harewood in 1739 and founding the firm of Lascelles and Son, sugar factors, of Mark Lane, London. By 1740 he had secured a contract for supplying the forces in the Leeward Islands and was able, by speaking to Walpole, to obtain the privilege of transhipping some prize Spanish sugar, contrary to the customs regulations.[1] He was included in the Treasury list of underwriters of a loan in 1744, taking £90,000.[2]

About this time Lascelles ran into trouble. As collector of customs he had been repeatedly accused of frauds in connexion with the administration of the $4\frac{1}{2}$ per cent export duty on sugar, notably by Walpole's brother, Horace (q.v.), the auditor general for the plantations, in a memorial to the Treasury in 1730. All these attacks were warded off till Robert Dinwiddie, surveyor general of the customs for the southern part of America, reported to the commissioners of customs the results of investigations which they had ordered him to make into the conduct of the local collectors of customs. The substance of his report, so far as the Lascelles brothers were concerned, was that they had been systematically defrauding the Government, in Henry's case by pocketing about one-third and in Edward's over a half of the proceeds of the $4\frac{1}{2}$ per cent duty. It also emerged that the commissioners of customs had been induced to pass Henry's accounts on the recommendation of a surveyor general of customs, who was disclosed by Dinwiddie's investigations to have been a party to the

frauds. In these circumstances Dinwiddie himself dismissed Edward, while the commissioners, with the approval of the attorney general, filed a bill against Henry Lascelles in the court of Exchequer for surcharging his accounts.[3] On 4 July 1744 Henry Lascelles's partner, Maxwell, wrote to Edward Lascelles in Barbados:

> This matter has been brewing ever since the fall of the Earl of Orford, and your brother became obnoxious to the new ministry, I believe from some public declarations in favour of the old to which he was obliged. Not only the Treasury was put into other hands, but some new commissioners of the customs were made . . . Lord Wilmington [Spencer Compton, q.v.] who was at the head of the former was old and disregarded, and therefore the latter board exerted a greater power than belonged to them, especially in the instance of Mr. Dinwiddie, and although at the old man's [Wilmington's] death the Treasury underwent a second change and came again into the hands of those that had been of the old ministry, yet these did not care to intermeddle or discourage an inspection proposed and countenanced before their time for the great clamour of the necessity of it and for the same reason I fear the present lords of the Treasury will not now interpose in the matter.[4]

At the end of the year Henry Lascelles took an opportunity of bringing his eldest son, Edwin, into Parliament for Scarborough. He followed this up in May 1745 by entering the Commons himself for his native town, Northallerton, where he bought control of one seat from William Smelt (q.v.), who vacated the seat by accepting a Barbados post, no doubt procured for him by Lascelles.[5] On 19 Sept. he petitioned the Treasury for a discharge from the prosecution, on the ground that his accounts had been formally passed by the commissioners of customs in 1733. Before reaching a decision the Treasury ordered the commissioners 'to report . . . forthwith what new matter has been laid before them to induce them to open an account which has been for so many years closed and passed'. On receipt of the commissioners' reply setting out the grounds for their action, the Treasury ordered process against Lascelles to be stayed, 'it not appearing . . . that the commissioners have laid before them any new matter'.[6] Commenting on this transaction, the 2nd Lord Egmont wrote in his electoral survey, 1749–51:

> Lascelles may be easily compelled by terror of an enquiry into his West Indian affairs. But query whether for the sake of a great example, and in particular on account of one very obnoxious man who may be come at by such an enquiry, it may not be necessary to waive the advantage of his vote and influence.

On which the Prince of Wales minuted: 'This must be talked over'. No further action was in fact taken against Lascelles, who gave up his seat to his second son, Daniel, in 1752 by accepting the chief stewardship of the honour of Berkhampstead, the first M.P. to use a stewardship to get out of Parliament.[7] He died 16 Oct. 1753, leaving a fortune of £284,000.[8]

[1] R. Pares, 'A London West India Merchant House 1740–69', *Essays presented to Sir Lewis Namier*, ed. Pares and Taylor, 76–78; R. Pares, *War and Trade in the West Indies*, 492. [2] *Gent. Mag.* 1744, p. 225. [3] Pares, 'A London West India Merchant House', loc. cit.; *Cal. Treas. Bks. and Pprs.* 1720–28, pp. 97–98; 1742–5, pp. 269–71, 527–8; T1/318. [4] Pares, loc. cit. [5] J. H. Parry, 'The Patent Places in the British West Indies', *EHR*, lxix. 213. [6] *Cal. Treas. Bks. and Pprs.* 1742–5, pp. 716, 731, 784. [7] B. Kemp, 'The Stewardship of the Chiltern Hundreds', *Essays presented to Sir Lewis Namier*, 208. [8] Pares, 'A London West India Merchant House', 107.

R.R.S.

LAUGHARNE, John (?1665–1715), of Boulston, Pemb.

HAVERFORDWEST 1702–15 Feb. 1715

b. ?1665, 1st s. of Rowland Laugharne of St. Bride's, Pemb. by Theodosia, da. of Sir Christopher Wray of Ashby, Lincs. *educ.* Jesus, Oxf. 15 Feb. 1682, aged 16. *m.* 26 Dec. 1698, Anne, da. and h. of Lewis Wogan, M.P., of Boulston.

Descended from a distinguished parliamentary soldier in the civil war, Laugharne was a Tory under Anne. Re-elected for Haverfordwest in 1715, he died 15 Feb. 1715, the night after his election.

P.W.

LAURIE, Sir Robert, 4th Bt. (aft. 1708–79), of Maxwelton, Dumfries.

DUMFRIES BURGHS 19 June 1738–1741

b. aft. 1708, 1st s. of Sir Walter Laurie, 3rd Bt., of Maxwelton by his 1st w. Jean, da. of one Nisbet of Dean, Midlothian. *m.* 4 Feb. 1733, Christian, 1st da. of Charles Areskine (q.v.), of Alva, Clackmannan, and Tinwald, Dumfries, Lord Tinwald, S.C.J., and lord justice clerk, 1s. 2da. *suc.* fa. 23 Nov. 1731.

Sir Robert Laurie was nephew (through 'Annie Laurie') of Alexander Fergusson (q.v.) of Craigdarroch. Brought in for Dumfries Burghs by his father-in-law, Charles Areskine, at a by-election in 1738, he voted with the Administration on the Spanish convention in 1739 and the place bill of 1740, but did not stand again. He died 28 Apr. 1779.

R.S.L.

LAWSON, Gilfrid (?1657–1749), of Brayton, Cumb.

CUMBERLAND 1701, 1702–1705, 1708–1734

b. ?1657, 1st s. of Wilfred Lawson, M.P., of Brayton by Sarah, da. and coh. of William James of Washington, co. Dur.; nephew of Sir Wilfred Lawson, 3rd Bt. (q.v.). *educ.* Queen's, Oxf. 19 Oct. 1675, aged 18. *unm. suc.* cos. as 6th Bt. and to Isel estate 8 Aug. 1743.

Gilfrid Lawson was the grandson of Sir Wilfred Lawson, 1st Bt., M.P. Cumberland 1660, who left Isel to his eldest son, the father of Sir Wilfred Lawson (q.v.), and Brayton to his second son, Gilfrid's father. A moderate Tory, though a member of the October Club, he voted after 1715 consistently against the Government. On 4 Apr. 1717 he rebuked James Stanhope (q.v.) for declaring that no one but 'such as . . . were not the King's friends' could refuse to support the vote of credit for measures against Sweden. He said that if a Member

must be accounted an enemy to the King when he happens not to fall in with his ministers . . . they had nothing else to do but to retire to their country seats.[1]

On 15 Dec. 1720 he attacked the South Sea directors and on the 19th seconded Sir Joseph Jekyll's motion for a select committee of the Commons to inquire into the affairs of the Company. On 6 Apr. 1723 he opposed the bill of pains and penalties against Atterbury.

No further speeches by Lawson are reported till 1730, when he spoke in favour of removing the duty on salt, as most affecting the poor. In the same and the succeeding session he is referred to in the 1st Lord Egmont's diary as 'an ancient Member', giving his opinion on points of parliamentary procedure. He also spoke against the removal of the duty on Irish yarn, and against the wool bill in 1731.[2] In 1734 he retired, giving his interest to his first cousin once removed, Sir Joseph Pennington (q.v.), having 'broke with all other considerable people in the county'.[3]

He died 23 Aug. 1749.

[1] Chandler, vi. 117. [2] *HMC Egmont Diary*, i. 62, 72–73, 147, 177, 186. [3] B. Bonsall, *Sir Jas. Lowther and Cumb. and Westmld. Elections 1754–75*, p. 7.

R.R.S.

LAWSON, Sir Wilfred, 3rd Bt. (1697–1737), of Isel, Cumb.

BOROUGHBRIDGE 31 Jan. 1718–1722
COCKERMOUTH 1722–13 July 1737

b. 1697, 1st s. of Sir Wilfred Lawson, 2nd Bt., M.P., by Elizabeth, da. and h. of George Preston of Holker, Lancs. *educ.* Queen's, Oxf. 1713; I. Temple 1715. *m.* 14 Mar. 1724, Elizabeth Lucy, da. of Henry Mordaunt, M.P., bro. of Charles, 3rd Earl of Peterborough, 3s. 2da. *suc.* fa. 1705.

Groom of the bedchamber to George I 1720–c.1725.

Early in the seventeenth century the Lawsons, a Yorkshire family, acquired by marriage the estate of Isel, near Cockermouth, which they represented under Charles II and William and Mary. When Lawson himself first stood for the borough at a by-election in 1717 there was a double return, on which the seat was awarded by the Commons to his opponent, Lawson admitting himself to be under age. Soon afterwards he was brought in by Newcastle for Boroughbridge, making his maiden speech in support of the Government on the Address, 11 Nov. 1718, voting for the repeal of the Occasional Conformity and Schism Acts, but against the peerage bill. Appointed to a place in the royal household in June 1720, he figured next year in the report of the South Sea committee of the House of Commons as one of the Members who had accepted bribes from the Company—in his case £1,000 stock at 320—on the usual terms (see Chaplin, Sir Robert).[1]

In 1722 Lawson was returned on his own interest for Cockermouth, which he represented till his death. He continued to speak in support of the Government till January 1724, when he supported an opposition motion for disbanding some additional troops taken on in 1723; in February 1725 he supported Pulteney's motion for referring the report on Lord Macclesfield to a select committee instead of proceeding to impeach him; in March 1726 he again supported Pulteney in opposing a vote of credit; and in January 1727 he moved for papers relating to the accession of Sweden to the treaty of Hanover, the motion being rejected without a division.

In the next Parliament Lawson became one of the leading opposition Whigs, speaking against the Government on a vote of credit in 1728 and the civil list arrears in 1729, when he led for the Opposition on the Address.[2] He again spoke first for them in January 1732 against the treaty of Seville, and in February 1733 on the army estimates; carried a motion for papers on Spanish depredations in February 1733; seconded an opposition motion for the repeal of the Test Act in 1736; and spoke in favour of an increase in the Prince of Wales's allowance in 1737. He died 13 July that year.

[1] CJ, xix. 569; see FORESTER, William. [2] Knatchbull Diary, 23 Jan. 1727, 21 Jan. 1729, app. 125, 136.

R.R.S.

LAWTON, John (c.1700–40), of Lawton, Cheshire.

NEWCASTLE-UNDER-LYME   1734–7 June 1740

b. c.1700, 1st surv. s. of John Lawton, M.P., of Lawton by Lady Anne Montagu, da. of Hon. George Montagu, M.P., yr. s. of Henry Montagu, M.P., 1st Earl of Manchester. m. July 1733, Jane Cooper, wid.,[1] s.p. suc. fa. 1736.

Chief clerk of the sureties of the excise 1723–34.

Lawton, whose father had represented Newcastle-under-Lyme almost continuously between 1689 and 1710, gave up a post in the excise at a salary of £170 p.a. to stand for it in 1734. Returned after a contest, he consistently voted with the Administration till his death on 7 June 1740, leaving an estate said to be worth £1,800 p.a.[2]

[1] Gent. Mag. 1733, p. 382. [2] Staffs. Parl. Hist. (Wm. Salt Arch. Soc.), ii (2), pp. 169, 240.

E.C.

LEATHES, Carteret (1698–1780), of Oakley House, nr. Harwich, Essex.

SUDBURY   1727–1734
HARWICH   1734–1741
SUDBURY   1741–1747

b. July 1698, 1st s. of John Mussenden of Hillsborough, co. Down by Jane, da. of Adam Leathes; bro. of Hill Mussenden (q.v.). educ. Wadham, Oxf. 1717. m. Loveday, da. of S. Garrod of Lincs., 3s. 1da. suc. uncle William Leathes (resident at Brussels c.1718–24) and assumed name of Leathes 1727. Recorder, Harwich 1734.

In 1727 Leathes, on succeeding to his uncle's fortune, which included an estate near Harwich, 'made interest . . . to be chose' there, but in the end was returned for Sudbury. 'A man of . . . good parts', with 'a very plausible way of telling his story', he was described in 1733 as 'a friend to the Government, a sure one, and has not given a vote against us'.[1]

In 1733, learning that the sitting Members for Harwich, Lord Egmont and Sir Philip Parker, intended to retire at the forthcoming general election, Leathes applied to Walpole for the government interest there. After consulting Egmont and Parker, who raised no objection, Walpole agreed that the government interest should go to Leathes and Egmont's son, Lord Perceval (q.v.), standing jointly, i.e. on the understanding that each should do his best to secure that his supporters gave their second votes to the other. But at the last moment Leathes, declaring himself unable to persuade his supporters to carry out this compact, joined with a third candidate, Charles Stanhope (q.v.), against Perceval, who was defeated, leaving Leathes in control of the borough.[2]

In 1741 Leathes nominated his brother, Hill Mussenden, to succeed him at Harwich, reverting himself to Sudbury. He supported the Administration till the end of 1743, when he and his brother voted with the Opposition on a motion to discontinue the service of the Hanoverians from British pay,[3] abstaining from both the two subsequent divisions on them in 1744 and 1746. He lost control of Harwich in 1747, when his brother was replaced there by a government nominee. He himself never stood again, but continued to play a part in Harwich politics. In 1763 his name appears in a list of the corporation drawn up by the chief government agent there, with the note:

> He has for many years been trying to take this borough from the Crown, and once had it, viz. from year 1734 to year 1742. He will not have it again if I live.[4]

He died in 1780.[5]

[1] *HMC Egmont Diary*, i. 380–1, 457; ii. 82; iii. 323. [2] See HAR-WICH. [3] Owen, *Pelhams*, 202, 208. [4] Namier, *Structure*, 368, 379. [5] Add. 19139, ff. 144–51.

R.R.S.

LECHMERE, Anthony (1674–1720), of Hanley Castle, Worcs.

BEWDLEY	11 Oct.–20 Dec. 1710
TEWKESBURY	18 June 1714–June 1717

b. 17 June 1674,[1] 1st s. of Edmund Lechmere of Hanley Castle, Worcs. by Lucy, da. of Anthony Hungerford of Farleigh Castle, Som.; bro. of Nicholas Lechmere (q.v.). *educ.* Eton 1690; M. Temple 1693. *m.* by 1709, Anne, da. of Thomas Foley of Stoke Edith, Herefs., 1s. 1da. *suc.* fa. 1703.
Receiver gen. and cashier of the customs 1717–*d.*[2]

The Lechmeres had been settled at Hanley Castle on the Severn, north of Tewkesbury, since before the time of Edward I.[3] 'Honest ingenious' Anthony Lechmere was classed as a Whig in 1715, when he was re-elected unopposed on his family's interest, but his only recorded vote was against the septennial bill. In June 1717 he was appointed to office to vacate a seat for his younger brother Nicholas Lechmere (q.v.). He died of apoplexy 8 Feb. 1720.[4]

[1] E. P. Shirley, *Hanley and the House of Lechmere*, 46. [2] *Cal. Treas. Bks.* xxxi. 375. [3] Nash, *Worcs.* i. 560; Fosbrooke, *Glos.* ii. 254. [4] Shirley, 54.

S.R.M.

LECHMERE, Edmund (1710–1805), of Hanley Castle, Worcs.

WORCESTERSHIRE	1734–1747

b. 4 Apr. 1710,[1] o. s. of Anthony Lechmere (q.v.) of Hanley Castle. *educ.* Fulham under Mr. Lewis Vaslet; Trinity, Camb. 1728. *m.* (1) 12 Oct. 1732, Elizabeth (*d.* 13 Sept. 1762), da. and (in her issue) h. of Sir Blunden Charlton, 3rd Bt., of Ludford, Herefs., 2s.; (2) 4 June 1765, Elizabeth, da. of Rev. John Whitmore, vicar of Lechlade, Glos., 1s. *suc.* fa. 1720.
Sheriff, Worcs. 1732–3.

Described by Horace Walpole as 'a great grazier and a mere country squire', Edmund Lechmere, unlike his father and his better known uncle (Nicholas, q.v.), was a Tory. Returned unopposed for the county in 1734, he voted against successive Administrations in all recorded divisions. At the 1741 election he and another Tory defeated two

opposition Whigs, he himself heading the poll. The contest was the subject of some verses by Sir Charles Hanbury Williams (q.v.), who represents Lechmere as replying to a question put to him by one of his opponents, George Lyttelton (q.v.), asking why he was standing against men whose political aims appeared to be the same as his own:

> Because, Sir, you're a Whig, and I'm a Tory.
> Howe'er with us you the same schemes pursue,
> You follow those who ne'er will follow you;
> My principles to you I'll freely state,
> I love the church, and Whiggism I hate;
> And tho', with you, Sir Robert I abhor,
> His Whiggish heart is what I hate him for;
> And if a Whig the minister must be,
> Pult'ney and Walpole are alike to me.[2]

On 15 Feb. 1744, however, he voted with the Government on an amendment to the Address, moved by Edmund Waller (q.v.), calling for an inquiry into the state of the navy.[3] He did not stand in 1747, when the Whig candidate, Lord Deerhurst (q.v.), wrote to him shortly before the election:

> I am extremely concerned, my dear Lechmere, that any measures should have been taken in the county disagreeable to you, though you do not go so far as to intimate by whom. My declarations and wishes have been too public to make me suspected of meaning you personally any ill, and I must frankly assure you that whatever part in this contest the necessity of the times may oblige you to take, my friendship shall not in the least be abated towards you.

Four years later Deerhurst, who had vacated his seat on succeeding to the peerage as Earl of Coventry, wrote again:

> The real esteem I have for you as well as the remembrance of some past conversation with you will not allow me to take any measures in regard to the county till I am informed of your disposition in that respect. If your inclinations are to be in Parliament, my brother [John Bulkeley Coventry, q.v.] I know would drop all thought of it . . .

Lechmere's 'rural passion', however, prevailed, despite a further invitation from Lord Coventry in November 1753.[4] He died at a great age 29 Mar. 1805.

[1] E. P. Shirley, *Hanley and the House of Lechmere*, 57–59. [2] Sir C. Hanbury Williams, *Works*, i. 62 n., 66. [3] Hartington to Devonshire, 16 Feb. 1744, Devonshire mss. [4] Deerhurst to Lechmere, 18 June 1747, 18 Mar. 1751, 24, 30 Nov., 13 Dec. 1753, Lechmere Pprs., Worcs. RO.

R.S.L.

LECHMERE, Nicholas (1675–1727), of the Middle Temple, London.

APPLEBY	1708–1710
COCKERMOUTH	1710–12 June 1717
TEWKESBURY	25 June 1717–4 Sept. 1721

b. 5 Aug. 1675, 2nd s. of Edmund Lechmere of Hanley Castle, Worcs. and bro. of Anthony Lechmere (q.v.). *educ.* M. Temple 1693, called 1698, bencher 1714. *m.* 1719, Lady Elizabeth Howard, da. of Charles, 3rd Earl of Carlisle, *s.p.* *cr.* Baron Lechmere 4 Sept. 1721.

Q.C. 1708; solicitor-gen. 1714–15; chancellor of duchy of Lancaster for life June 1717; attorney-gen. 1718–20; P.C. 1 July 1718.

'A good lawyer, a quick and distinguished orator, much courted by the Whig party, but of a temper violent, proud, and impracticable',[1] Lechmere was appointed solicitor-general at George I's accession. Elected to the secret committee set up by the Commons to inquire into the conduct of the late Tory Government, he spoke in favour of Ormonde's impeachment and collaborated with Walpole in drawing up the articles for Bolingbroke's. In December 1715 he was forced to resign in consequence of a quarrel with the attorney-general, Sir Edward Northey (q.v.), who accused him of misleading him on a point of law, or, according to another account, was turned out by Lord Chancellor Cowper

> for an encomium made at the trial of one of the rebels upon the good behaviour of the University of Oxford during the rebellion, and that only to contradict Sir Joseph Jekyll [q.v.] who had spoke before him and had found fault with them for their ill conduct.

On the opening of the new session in January 1716, he successfully called for the impeachment of the captured rebel lords, in a speech which he sent to a periodical for publication, becoming chairman of the committee appointed to conduct the impeachments, he himself undertaking Lord Derwentwater's. He was also chiefly responsible for the suspension of the Habeas Corpus Act and an Act attainting the heads of the rebels in Scotland; but when the Government brought in a bill for expediting the trial of rebels he joined with the Tories in obstructing it. He next proposed a general amnesty for rebels who laid down their arms, to which Walpole replied that he would not inquire into the reasons or motives for it, but that he himself had been offered £60,000 for the life of one single person, whereupon Lechmere withdrew his proposal. He and Lord Coningsby (q.v.) then nearly caused a quarrel between the two Houses by inserting an attack on the late Tory ministers in the preamble of a money bill, which the Lords could not amend, though they strongly objected to the passage as prejudging matters due to come before them in their judicial capacity.[2] He and Coningsby also introduced a bill for strengthening the Protestant interest by enforcing the laws against Papists. When the septennial bill came on, Lechmere, 'who

always damns everything which does not originally come from himself', attacked it on the second reading; and on the report stage 'struck at the Scotch nation' in the persons of their elected peers, by moving for the insertion of a clause that no elected Member having a pension should sit in either House.[3] During the summer recess he joined the Duke of Argyll in caballing against the Government; supplied Argyll with precedents to show that the Prince's powers as Regent were not as ample or honourable as in previous cases; and promoted congratulatory addresses to the Prince on his appointment to be Regent, with a view to making mischief between him and his father. At the end of 1716 it was reported that he was to be the head of Argyll's party in the House of Commons.[4]

On the split in the Whig party in April 1717 Lechmere adhered to Sunderland, becoming one of his chief spokesmen in the House of Commons, where he repeatedly clashed with Walpole. Rewarded with the duchy of Lancaster for life, but with no prospect of being re-elected at Cockermouth, he was returned for his elder brother's seat at Tewkesbury. In 1718 he succeeded Northey as attorney-general. In 1719 he was put down by Craggs as 'doubtful', to be spoken to by the King on the peerage bill, on which he took the line that though as it stood it contained nothing for the 'benefit of the Commons', there was nothing to prevent them from taking 'care of themselves by adding what was necessary, and then put us in mind of the many sugar plums we were to hope for, concluding on his word of honour to be against the whole if every part of what he had mentioned were not agreed to by the Lords'.[5] During the debate of 22 Jan. 1720 on the South Sea scheme, which was said to have been agreed at his chambers, he answered Walpole's criticisms by 'invectives against Walpole's former scheme, giving great preference to this'. After a further speech by Walpole answering him, he rose to reply,

> but this was prevented by the whole committee rising at once and going into the floor; the chairman tore his throat with 'To order, hear your member', but all to no purpose other than to mortify Lechmere, by the members crying out 'We have heard him long enough'.[6]

In the following March he was accused by the solicitor-general, Sir William Thompson (q.v.), of corrupt practices as attorney-general, but was completely vindicated by an inquiry.[7] However, a little over a month later, following the reunion of the Whig party and the reconciliation of the King with the Prince of Wales, he was dismissed. The Princess of Wales was told that he had been turned out because it was he who had proposed that her children should be taken away from their parents during the breach in the royal family. Congratulating Stanhope on Lechmere's dismissal, Lord Cowper observed that everybody who had anything to do with him 'must be glad to be rid of him'.[8]

After the collapse of the South Sea bubble, Lechmere was elected to the secret committee set up by the Commons to investigate the Company's affairs, but on the ground of illness took little part in its proceedings. According to his sister-in-law:

> The town will have it his illness is political; he has very seldom attended the secret committee and spoke very seldom in the House, but talks very high out of it . . . He is so little beloved that I believe he has many undeserved reflections cast on him. 'Tis said Mr. Knight's going off [i.e. the absconding of the South Sea Company's cashier] is very serviceable to him since there would have been some discoveries made not much to his honour had Knight stayed.

After the committee had reported he taunted Walpole with acting as counsel for the South Sea directors and with the failure of his scheme for restoring public credit. In September he was raised to the Lords 'to convince the world of his innocence' of the charges brought against him by Thompson, though, as his wife remarked, 'the disposition at that time was not to favour him and if anything could have been found against him, it would have been carried as far as possible'.[9] He played no further significant part in politics, dying of apoplexy 18 June 1727.

[1] Nash, *Worcs.* i. 561. [2] *Lady Cowper Diary*, 73, 119-20; *Pol. State*, x. 588-96; xi. 108, 187-8, 189-90, 212-15, 475; xxxvii. p. vii; *Dudley Ryder Diary*, 1715-6, p. 184. [3] A. Corbière to Horace Walpole, 27 Apr. 1716, Cholmondeley (Houghton) mss. [4] Coxe, *Walpole*, ii. 76, 78; *Dudley Ryder Diary*, 373. [5] T. Brodrick to Ld. Midleton, 10 Dec. 1719, Brodrick mss. [6] Coxe, 182-3. [7] *Pol. State*, xix. 319-21, 403-24. [8] *Lady Cowper Diary*, 165. [9] *HMC Carlisle*, 30, 35.

R.R.S.

LEE, George (?1700–58).

BRACKLEY	25 Jan. 1733–Mar. 1742
DEVIZES	23 July 1742-1747
LISKEARD	1747-1754
LAUNCESTON	1754-18 Dec. 1758

b. ?1700, 5th s. of Sir Thomas Lee, 2nd Bt., M.P., of Hartwell House, Bucks. by Alice, da. and h. of Thomas Hopkins, London merchant; bro. of John, Sir Thomas, 3rd Bt., and William Lee (qq.v.). *educ.* Clare, Camb. 1716; Ch. Ch. Oxf. 4 Apr. 1720, aged 19; D.C.L. 1729; M. Temple 1719, Doctors' Commons 1729. *m.* 5 June 1742, Judith, da. of Humphry Morice (q.v.) of Werrington Park, Devon, *s.p.* Kntd. 12 Feb. 1752.

Chairman of the committee of elections and privileges 1741-7; ld. of Admiralty 1742-4; treasurer of the household to the Princess of Wales 1751-7;

dean of Arches and judge of the P.C.C. Dec. 1751-8; P.C. 13 Feb. 1752.

Lee, a lawyer like his elder brother William, specialized as a 'civilian', rising to be head of his profession. Returned as a Whig for Brackley by the Duke of Bridgwater, with whom the Lees were politically connected in Buckinghamshire, he acted with the Opposition. His election as chairman of the elections committee in December 1741, when he defeated the government candidate by four votes, was the beginning of the end of Walpole's Government.

In the new Government Lee accepted a seat on the Admiralty board, though the Duke of Bridgwater warned him that if he did so 'he would never choose him again into Parliament'.[1] After the Prince of Wales had tried unsuccessfully to secure a nomination for him at Truro from Lord Falmouth, arrangements were made for Francis Eyles (q.v.) to vacate a seat for him at Devizes. He remained in the Government till December 1744, when he went out with Granville. On 18 Feb. 1745 he attacked the ministry for masking their retention of the Hanoverian troops by transferring them to the Queen of Hungary, paying her an increased subsidy.[2] In April 1746 he spoke for the Hanoverians, attacking Pitt for his volte-face on them in a speech of which Horace Walpole wrote that 'no criminal at the Place de Grève was ever so racked as he by Dr. Lee, a friend of Lord Granville, who gave him the question both ordinary and extraordinary'.[3]

At the beginning of 1747 Lee joined the Prince of Wales's new opposition. He approved Frederick's invitation to the Tories to 'coalesce and unite with him' on the eve of the general election.[4] Returned for a Cornish borough on the Prince's recommendation, he became one of the leaders of the Leicester House party. He was destined by Frederick to be his first chancellor of the Exchequer, a post for which Horace Walpole thought

> he was little qualified; for though he was a speaker of great weight in Parliament, which was set off with a solemn harmonious voice, and something severe in his style, his business of civilian had confined him to too narrow a sphere for the extensive knowledge of men that is requisite to a Prime Minister.[5]

On Frederick's death in 1751 Lee advised the Princess to place herself unconditionally in the hands of the King.[6] He conducted the negotiations with the Pelhams as to the composition of her new household, in which he was appointed treasurer. Thereafter, like most of the Leicester House party, he supported the Administration till 1755, when he followed the Princess back into opposition. He resigned his appointment with her in 1757, 'finding himself a cypher at that court'.[7]

He died 18 Dec. 1758.

[1] *HMC Egmont Diary*, iii. 261. [2] Owen, *Pelhams*, 254. [3] To Mann, 15 Apr. 1746. [4] Owen, 312. [5] *Mems. Geo. II*, i. 91. [6] See PERCEVAL, John, Lord Perceval, later 2nd Ld. Egmont. [7] *Mems. Geo. II*, iii. 28.

R.R.S.

LEE, George Henry, Visct. Quarendon (1718–72), of Quarrendon, Bucks., Ditchley Park and Spelsbury, Oxon.

OXFORDSHIRE   27 Feb. 1740–15 Feb. 1743

b. 21 May 1718, 1st s. of George Henry Lee, 2nd Earl of Lichfield, by Frances, da. of Sir John Hales, 4th Bt., of Hackington, Kent. *educ.* Westminster 1728; St. John's, Oxf. 1736. *m.* 16 Jan. 1745, Dinah, da. and coh. of Sir Thomas Frankland, 3rd Bt. (q.v.), *s.p. suc.* fa. as 3rd Earl of Lichfield 15 Feb. 1743.

Custos brevium of the common pleas 1743–72; ld. of the bedchamber to the King 1760–2; high steward, Oxf. Univ. 1760–2, chancellor 1762–*d.*; capt. of gent. pensioners 1762–*d.*; P.C. 14 July 1762; dep. ranger of Hampton Court Park 1762–72.

Returned unopposed for the county as a Tory at a by-election in February 1740, Quarendon made his first recorded speech in December that year against the army estimates. In February 1741 he was among the Tories who abstained from voting on the motion for the dismissal of Walpole, which his father supported in the Lords. At the opening of the next Parliament he is described as speaking 'often and well' against the Government.[1] He supported the motion for a committee of inquiry into Walpole's Administration, to which he was elected, figuring on both the government and the opposition lists.[2] He also spoke for Lord Strange's motion of censure on the Lords for rejecting a bill indemnifying those giving evidence against Walpole. His last reported speech in the Commons was made in December 1742 against the Hanoverians. After his accession to the House of Lords in 1743, he gradually faded out of political life; but he was one of the prominent Tories who agreed to support the Prince's programme in 1747.[3] In the next reign Horace Walpole wrote of him: 'If he did not make the figure that his youth had promised, the Jacobites could not reproach him, as he had drowned his parts in the jovial promotion of their cause'.[4] He died 19 Sept. 1772.

[1] Walpole to Mann, 17 Dec. 1741. [2] Same to same, 1 Apr. 1742. [3] Add. 35870, ff. 129–30. [4] *Mems. Geo. II*, iii. 166–7

E.C.

LEE, John (1695–1761), of Riseley, Beds.

MALMESBURY   1747–1754
NEWPORT   1754–Nov. 1761

b. 8 May 1695, 3rd s. of Sir Thomas Lee, 2nd Bt., M.P.; bro. of George, Sir Thomas, 3rd Bt., and William Lee (qq.v.). *m.* (1) 5 July 1739, Constance (or Charlotte) (*d.* 12 July 1740), da. of Adm. Sir Thomas Hardy, *s.p.*; (2) Mary, da. of John Browne of Riseley, Beds., 2s.

Ensign 1 Ft. Gds. 1717, lt. and capt. by 1727, capt.-lt. 1735, capt. and lt.-col. 1736; res. c.1745.

Seeing no prospect of advancement after over 30 years in the army,[1] John Lee resigned his commission and was brought into Parliament in 1747 by the Prince of Wales, no doubt on the recommendation of his brother, George Lee. On the Prince's death in 1751 he went over to the Government with his brother, who in 1752 asked Pelham to give John a post vacated by the death of Sir Thomas Reade (q.v.), but was told that

there were several gentlemen who had served the King well in Parliament that were candidates for those kind of employments, and that since the late Act of Parliament [the Place Act 1742] passed, there were not many left for the King to oblige his old friends.[2]

In 1753 he was on Pelham's list for a seat, which was ultimately provided by Humphry Morice (q.v.), George Lee's father-in-law. In 1754 George Lee attempted unsuccessfully to obtain a place for him from Newcastle, writing 9 Apr. 1754: 'It would be an additional favour if it could be done before the election, because it will save him trouble and expense of a second election'. Following George back into opposition in 1755, he died c. Nov. 1761.

[1] Geo. Lee to Newcastle, 9 Apr. 1754, Add. 32735, f. 68. [2] Pelham to Newcastle, 3 Oct. 1752, Add. 32730, f. 30.

R.R.S.

LEE, Sir Thomas, 3rd Bt. (1687–1749), of Hartwell, nr. Aylesbury, Bucks.

CHIPPING WYCOMBE   1710–1722
BUCKINGHAMSHIRE   1722–1727, 29 Jan. 1729–
                                                        1741

b. 31 Mar. 1687, 1st s. of Sir Thomas Lee, 2nd Bt., M.P.; bro. of George, John and William Lee (qq.v.). *m.* 13 Sept. 1720, Elizabeth, da. and h. of Thomas Sandys of London, 2s. 1da. *suc.* fa. Aug. 1702.

In 1619 the Lees, an old Buckinghamshire family, inherited Hartwell, sitting for the neighbouring borough of Aylesbury throughout the reigns of Charles II and William III. Lee himself represented Wycombe on his own and the Wharton interest until 1722, when he was returned for the county with the support of Sunderland and the ministry.[1] He was not a candidate in 1727, but was returned in 1729 and in 1734, after which he did not stand again. Though a Whig, all his recorded votes were against the Administration after 1715, except on the repeal of the Occasional Conformity and Schism Acts, 1719.

He died 17 Dec. 1749.

[1] Francis Sheldon to Sir John Pakington, 1721, Pakington mss 111/23.

R.R.S.

LEE, William (1688–1754), of Totteridge, Herts.

CHIPPING WYCOMBE   1727–6 June 1730

b. 2 Aug. 1688, 2nd s. of Sir Thomas Lee, 2nd Bt., M.P., bro. of George, John and Sir Thomas Lee, 3rd Bt. (qq.v.). educ. Wadham, Oxf. 1704; M. Temple 1703, called 1710; I. Temple 1717, bencher 1725. m. (1) Anne (d. 1729), da. of John Goodwin of Bury St. Edmund's, 1s.; (2) May 1733, Margaret, da. of Roger Drake, wid. of Francis Melmoth, merchant, s.p. Kntd. 8 June 1737.

Recorder, Wycombe, 1718; Latin sec. to the King 1718–30; recorder, Buckingham 1722; K.C. 1728; serjeant-at-law 1730; attorney-gen. to Prince of Wales 1728–30; justice of King's bench 1730, c.j. 1737; P.C. 21 July 1737; chancellor of the Exchequer 'ad interim' 1754.

William Lee was returned on his family's interest but, unlike his brothers, supported the Administration during his short period in the House. He died 8 Apr. 1754.

R.R.S.

LEEVES, Robert (c.1685–1743), of Steyning, Suss.

STEYNING   24 Apr.–8 Aug. 1713, 1715–12 Apr. 1717

b. c.1685, s. of William Leeves of Tortington Place, Suss. by Anne Seymour of Halford, Dorset. m. Elizabeth, 4s.

Robert Leeves was a native of Steyning, for which he was re-elected as a Tory in 1715, voting against the septennial bill before he was unseated on petition for bribery in 1717. He did not stand again, but continued to take part in local politics.[1] He died 15 May 1743, aged 58.[2]

[1] Chandos to Leeves, 22 June 1727, Chandos letter bks. [2] J. Dallaway, Hist. Western Division of Suss. ii (2), p. 169.

J.B.L.

LEGGE, Hon. Edward (c.1710–47).

PORTSMOUTH   15–19 Dec. 1747

b. c.1710, 5th s. of William Legge, 1st Earl of Dartmouth, by Lady Anne Finch, da. of Heneage Finch, M.P., 1st Earl of Aylesford; bro. of George Legge, Visct. Lewisham, and Hon. Henry Legge (qq.v.). unm. Entered navy 1726, lt. 1734, capt. 1738.

In 1747 Edward Legge's brother Henry wrote to his patron, the Duke of Beford, who as 1st lord of the Admiralty had recently appointed Edward to the command of a squadron in the West Indies, and now was proposing to bring him into Parliament on the Admiralty interest at Portsmouth:

> The least return the Legges can make for the many instances of partiality they have received from your Grace, is to do all in their power to make the effects of that favour as little troublesome to their benefactor as possible; and for my own part I can see no objection to the declaring Ned a candidate for Portsmouth since your Grace is so kind as to see none to accepting of him in that light yourself.[1]

Edward was duly returned on 15 Dec. but a few days later news arrived from the West Indies that he had died on 19 Sept.

[1] 4 Aug. 1747, Bedford mss.

P.W.

LEGGE, George, Visct. Lewisham (?1704–32).

GREAT BEDWYN   1727–26 Mar. 1729

b. ?1704, 1st s. of William Legge, 1st Earl of Dartmouth; bro. of Hon. Edward and Henry Legge (qq.v.). educ. Magdalen, Oxf. 22 Jan. 1720, aged 15. m. 22 Mar. 1722,[1] Elizabeth, da. and h. of Sir Arthur Kaye, M.P., 3rd Bt., of Woodsome, Yorks., 2s. 2da.

Lord Lewisham was returned as a Tory for Great Bedwyn on the Bruce interest[2] but was unseated on petition. He died v.p. of smallpox 29 Sept. 1732.

[1] Hist. Reg. 1722, chron. 18; HMC Dartmouth, v. 326. [2] Ld. Ailesbury to Jas. Bruce, 6 Sept. 1727, Savernake mss.

R.S.L.

LEGGE, Hon. Henry (1706–64), of Mapledurham, Hants.

EAST LOOE   27 Nov. 1740–1741
ORFORD   1741–29 Aug. 1759
HAMPSHIRE   3 Dec. 1759–23 Aug. 1764

b. 29 May 1708, 4th s. of William Legge, 1st Earl of Dartmouth; bro. of Hon. Edward Legge and George Legge, Visct. Lewisham (qq.v.). educ. Ch. Ch. Oxf. 1726. m. 29 Aug. 1750, Mary Stawell, cr. Baroness Stawell 21 May 1760, da. and h. of Edward, 4th Baron Stawell, 1s. suc. to Mapledurham under the will of Leonard Bilson (q.v.) taking the name of Bilson before Legge 1754.

Sec. to Sir Robert Walpole c.1735–9, to the ld. lt. [I] 1739–41, to Treasury 1741–2; surveyor of woods and forests north and south of the Trent 1742–5; ld. of Admiralty 1745–6, of Treasury 1746–9; envoy to Prussia Feb.–Nov. 1748; P.C. 28 June 1749; treasurer of the navy 1749–54; chancellor of the Exchequer Apr. 1754–Nov. 1755, Nov. 1756–Apr. 1757, July 1757–Mar. 1761.

A younger son, with a living to earn, Legge was intended for the navy but gave it up after one or two voyages to become secretary to Sir Robert Walpole, to whom he had been introduced by Edward Walpole (q.v.). In 1739 he was appointed secretary to the Duke of Devonshire as lord lieutenant of Ireland on the understanding that the post would not involve residence in Ireland or interfere with his attendance on Walpole, and that he should retain it till a secretaryship to the Treasury fell vacant: 'in the meanwhile', he told his father, 'my income is very much increased, and if Sir Robert should die I shall still have a very good place in present, and I dare say find a most kind and generous patron in the Duke of Devonshire'. Brought into Parliament by Walpole in 1740, he became joint secretary to the Treasury in 1741. Walpole remained 'fond of him to the greatest degree of partiality' till Legge tried to marry his daughter, after which, according to Horace Walpole, he 'could never bear his name'. Nevertheless, one of Walpole's last acts as minister was to provide for Legge by procuring for him and Benjamin Keene (q.v.) jointly the reversion to a place in the customs worth £1,200 p.a.[1]

After Walpole's fall Legge appealed to the Duke of Bedford, his 'intimate friend and companion', to save him from being turned out of the Treasury to make room for a friend of Pulteney's. 'This', he wrote, 'is the crisis of my fortune, upon which the whole success of my future life depends . . . Not only my whole income is taken away, but that which was my study and profession, and by which I hoped, one day or other, to have been serviceable to the public'. In reply to Bedford's representations, Pulteney pointed out that 'Lord Orford [Walpole] himself thought a step of this kind so natural (I mean that whoever was to be in the Treasury should bring a friend of their own into Mr. Legge's place), that he provided for Mr. Legge with a reversion which he imagined likely to happen soon'. However, in deference to Bedford, Legge was compensated with the office of surveyor of woods and forests, observing, 'to be sure, it is a fall, but . . . they have laid the boughs of trees under me to break it'.[2] He spoke for the Hanoverians in 1744 and for Admiral Mathews (q.v.) in 1745, when Bedford, now 1st lord of the Admiralty, gave him a seat on that board. He moved the Address at the opening of the next session, also speaking very well for an address thanking the King for sending for 6,000 Hessians during the rebellion.[3] Promoted next year by Pelham to the Treasury board, he was sent by Newcastle in 1748 on a goodwill mission to Berlin, where he offended George II and Newcastle by saying, or being reported as saying, that the King's arrival in Hanover had spoilt a promising negotiation with Prussia, and that Newcastle was 'under the tutelle of the Hanoverian ministers'. The King was for

dismissing Legge, calling him 'fool every day' and abusing Newcastle 'for sending a man purely because he can make a speech in the House of Commons'; while Newcastle, though not prepared to go so far, thought it 'cruel of my friend Legge', who, he wrote to Pelham, had showed himself not 'the simple, plain, disinterested man we all thought him'. Pelham replied that he had never supposed Legge to be a simple, plain, disinterested man;

nor do I think so of any others, whose professions are the following of a Court and raising themselves in the world by that means. I think him full as good a man as his neighbours; more able and as willing to serve those that serve him as any one I have been acquainted with, in that way, for a great while. I hope, therefore, he has not, in the most absurd instance, made that impracticable, which his other qualities made eligible.[4]

As it happened, Legge's diplomatic gaffes led to his promotion in 1749 to the post of treasurer of the navy, vacated by Bubb Dodington. In the ordinary course this lucrative office would have been filled by his senior, Henry Fox, whom he would have succeeded at the War Office. But the duties of the secretary at war brought him into personal relations with the King, who since the Prussian affair had taken such a dislike to Legge that he would not have him in his closet.[5]

When the Pelhams broke with Bedford by turning out his friend Sandwich in 1751, Legge

submitted to break his connections with the two latter by being the indecent messenger of Lord Sandwich's disgrace. The Duke met him on the steps of Bedford House . . . and would scarce give him audience; but even that short interview could not save Legge from the confusion he felt at his own policy; and, with the awkwardness that conscience will give even to an ambassador, he said, he had happened, as he was just going out of town, to visit the Duke of Newcastle, where he had not been in two months before, and had been requested by him to be the bearer of this notification.[6]

Continuing to change from patron to patron, he died 23 Aug. 1764.

[1] *Some Account of the Character of the Rt. Hon. H. B. Legge*; *HMC Dartmouth*, 328; Walpole, *Mems. Geo. II*, i. 190-2 seq.; Walpole to Mann, 26 Jan. 1748; Sir R. Wilmot to Devonshire 12 Jan., 4 Feb. 1742, Devonshire mss. [2] *Bedford Corresp.* i. 1-9. [3] Yorke's parl. jnl. *Parl. Hist.* xiii. 463, 1268; Owen, *Pelhams*, 291. [4] Coxe, *Pelham*, i. 446, 447-8. [5] Walpole to Mann, 23 Mar. 1749. [6] Walpole, *Mems. Geo. II*, i. 191-2.

R.R.S.

LEGH, John (1668-1739), of Adlington, Cheshire.

BODMIN 1715-1722

bap. 8 Dec. 1668, 1st surv. s. of Thomas Legh of Adlington by Joanna, da. and h. of Sir John Maynard, M.P. *educ.* B.N.C. Oxf. 1687. *m.* 17 July 1693, Isabella, da. of Robert Robartes, M.P., Visct. Bodmin, 1s. 2da. *suc.* fa. 1691.

Sheriff, Cheshire 1704–5; gov. Yarmouth I.o.W. 1715.

Legh, a Whig, was returned for Bodmin in 1715 by his brother-in-law, Charles Bodvile Robartes, 2nd Earl of Radnor. He served as colonel of a regiment of Cheshire militia during the rebellion[1] and voted with the Government. In 1722 he stood down in favour of his son, Charles Legh, who was defeated. He died in 1739 (buried 12 Dec.).

[1] J. Croston, *Nooks and Corners of Lancs. and Cheshire*, 341–2; Ormerod, *Cheshire*, iii. 660.

E.C.

LEGH, Peter (1707–92), of Lyme Hall, Cheshire.

NEWTON   15 Dec. 1743–1774

bap. 7 Jan. 1707, 1st surv. s. of Thomas Legh (M.P. Newton 1701–13, yr. bro. of Peter Legh of Lyme, M.P. Newton 1685) by Henrietta, da. and h. of Thomas Fleetwood of Bank Hall, Lancs. *educ.* Westminster 1721–7; St. John's, Camb. 1727. *m.* 20 Dec. 1737, Martha, da. and h. of Thomas Bennett of Salthrop, Wilts., 2s. *d.v.p.* 3da. *suc.* fa. 1717; his niece at Bank Hall 1740; his uncle Peter Legh at Lyme 1744.

Legh was the nephew of Peter Legh of Lyme, the non-juring proprietor of the borough of Newton. After his father's death he was brought up by his uncle, who on his own son's death made him his heir[1] and returned him for Newton in succession to William Shippen (q.v.). In 1745 he and some other Cheshire Tories are said to have met at Lyme to consider joining the rebels but at his suggestion decided against it.[2] In 1746 he voted against the Hanoverians. He died 20 May 1792.

[1] E. Legh, Baroness Newton, *House of Lyme*, 386–7. [2] Ibid. 388–9; W. Beamont, *House of Lyme*, 185–6.

E.C.

LE HEUP, Isaac (c.1686–1747), of Gunthorpe, Norf.

BODMIN   1722–1727
GRAMPOUND   31 Jan. 1732–1734
CALLINGTON   1734–1741

b. c.1686, 1st s. of Thomas Le Heup of St. Lo, Normandy, and St. Anne's, Westminster by Jeanne, da. of Pierre Harmon of Caen, Normandy. *m.* 10 Aug. 1720, Elizabeth, da. and coh. of Peter Lombard of Burnham Thorpe, Norf., tailor to Queen Anne, 1s. 2da.; bro.-in-law to Horatio Walpole (q.v.), 1st Baron Walpole. *suc.* fa. 1736.
    Envoy to the Diet at Ratisbon 1726–7; envoy to Sweden 1727; commr. of customs 1741–2.

The son of a Huguenot who had emigrated to England on the revocation of the Edict of Nantes, Le Heup was connected by his marriage with Horace Walpole, who describes him as 'a man of great wit and greater brutality'.[1] Returned for

Bodmin as a government supporter in 1722, he purchased Gunthorpe from the trustees of the South Sea Company in 1726, when he was appointed British representative at the Diet of Ratisbon, only to be expelled in April 1727 as a reprisal for the expulsion of the Imperial minister from London.[2] In July 1727 he was sent as envoy to Stockholm, from which he was immediately recalled 'for very indecent behaviour' to the Prince of Wales at Hanover[3] on his way to take up his appointment. He was said to have told the Prince

> amongst other insolent and rude expressions . . . that he and his family had kept his father and grandfather upon the throne, which was more than all the German princes could do, and that if they did not please him (for he was independent, had £10,000 a year, and did not care a straw for all of them), he would turn Jacobite.[4]

On learning of his recall, he wrote to Townshend (22 Sept.):

> The heavy concern I labour under and my ignorance of the particulars with which I am charged hindered me from writing to your Lordship on this unfortunate behaviour of mine . . . I shall not now undertake to say anything to excuse what I have done nor palliate facts of which I do not know the least little but what I have been informed of since I came to Sweden, and which I thought to have been an invention of some enemy's, when I heard the first report of my having committed any fault against the respect due to his Royal Highness . . . I have received the mortifying news, that his Highness hath complained of me himself which convinces that I have been guilty of some most unpardonable fault, though I hope still to find the heinous circumstances with which it is told not to be true, and whatsoever my offence is, his goodness is so great, that I conceive hopes that he will grant me his pardon, which I have begged in the humblest manner upon the first apprehension I had of it, and hope that it will be imputed to a phrenzy caused by my want of rest and excess of heat and wine for which last I beg forgiveness heartily, and hope his Highness will become my mediator to the King that he will most graciously please to bear no farther resentment of the guilt of my tongue which on this occasion most certainly held no correspondence with my heart.[5]

He never received another diplomatic appointment. Unsuccessful for Wallingford in 1727, he was returned for Grampound in 1732 and for Callington, a Walpole borough, in 1734, voting with the Administration in every recorded division. He did not stand in 1741, was made a commissioner of customs the following August, but was dismissed a year later, following the fall of Walpole.

He died 25 Apr. 1747, aged 61.

[1] *Corresp. H. Walpole* (Yale ed.), xix. 111 n.53. [2] C. F. Chance, *Alliance of Hanover*, 506–631. [3] Walpole to Mann, loc. cit. [4] Chandos to Westfaling, 14 Sept. 1727, Chandos letter bks. [5] SP For. 95/48, ff. 15, 17, 27–28.

E.C.

LEICESTER, Sir Francis, 3rd Bt. (1674–1742), of Tabley, Cheshire.

NEWTON 1715–1727

b. 30 July 1674, 1st surv. s. of Sir Robert Leicester, 2nd Bt., of Tabley by Meriell, da. and h. of Francis Watson of Church Aston, nr. Newport, Salop. *educ.* Eton 1686–92; St. John's, Camb. 1692; M. Temple 1694. *m.* bet. 1701 and 1705, Frances, da. and h. of Joshua Wilson of Pontefract and Colton, Yorks., wid. of Byrom Thornhill of Fixby, Yorks., 1da. *suc.* fa. 7 July 1684.

Sheriff, Cheshire 1705–6.

Leicester, a Tory country gentleman, was returned for Newton by his lifelong friend, Peter Legh of Lyme, the proprietor of the borough. Soon after his return he wrote to Legh:

In a little time I shall be of Sir [Michael] Warton's mind, that one may hear more in 2 hours out of the House than in a whole session within doors.

When Legh's brothers joined the rebels in the Fifteen, Leicester assured him:

You may depend upon one thing, if it should happen —as I hope in God it will not . . . that the Government should take your estates, you shall enjoy one half God blesses me with with the same faith, freedom and cheerfulness and candour as myself the other half, and that as long as I have sixpence in the world.[1]

Leicester did not stand again. He died 5 Aug. 1742, leaving an estate of £10,000 p.a.[2]

[1] E. Legh, Baroness Newton, *Lyme Letters*, 232, 265. [2] *Gent. Mag.* 1742, p. 443.

E.C.

LEIGH, Hon. Charles (?1685–1749), of Leighton Buzzard, Beds.

WARWICK	13 Dec. 1710–1713
HIGHAM FERRERS	12 Mar. 1714–1722
BEDFORDSHIRE	1722–1727, 16 Feb. 1733–1734

bap. 28 Mar. 1686, 3rd but 2nd surv. s. of Thomas Leigh, 2nd Baron Leigh of Stoneleigh, by his 2nd w. Eleanor, da. of Edward Watson, 2nd Baron Rockingham. *educ.* I. Temple 1701; Balliol, Oxf. 1702. *m.* Lady Barbara Lumley, da. of Richard, 1st Earl of Scarbrough, sis. of Hon. Charles, John and James Lumley and Sir Thomas Lumley Saunderson (qq.v.), 3rd Earl of Scarbrough, *s.p. suc.* to Leighton Buzzard estates of his gt.-uncle Hon. Charles Leigh 1704.

Charles Leigh, who had sat as a Tory under Queen Anne, was again returned on the Wentworth interest for Higham Ferrers in 1715. Described as a Tory who might often vote Whig, he voted against the Government in all recorded divisions of that Parliament. Transferring to Bedfordshire in 1722, he was one of five Tories who voted against the restoration of Bolingbroke's estates in 1725.[1] He did not stand in 1727, though he had been mentioned earlier as a 'good Tory', who might be put up by the young Duke of Bedford.[2] Returned again at a by-election early in 1733, he voted against the Administration on the excise bill, 1733, and the repeal of the Septennial Act, 1734. Defeated at the general election of 1734, he did not stand again. He died 28 July 1749.

[1] *Knatchbull Diary*, 20 Apr. 1725. [2] E. F. D. Osborn, *Pol. and Social Letters of a Lady of 18th Cent.* 39.

R.S.L.

LEIGHTON, Daniel (1694–1765), of Boreham, nr. Chelmsford, Essex.

HEREFORD 1747–1754

bap. 21 June 1694, 4th s. of Sir Edward Leighton, 1st Bt., M.P., of Wattlesborough, Salop being 1st s. by his 2nd w. Jane, da. of Daniel Nichol, alderman of London. *educ.* Wadham, Oxf. 1710; I. Temple 1711. *m.* 8 June 1717, Jane, da. of Nathaniel Thorold of Lincoln, wid. of Capt. Michael Barkham, 2s. 2da.

Exempt and capt. 1 Life Gds. 1716, guidon and maj. 1717, cornet and maj. 1720–37; lt.-col. 4 Drags. 1737; res. 1749.

Declining a rich family living in Shropshire, Leighton entered the army, serving at Fontenoy in 1745 and in Scotland in 1746. In 1747 he was invited to stand for Hereford by a group of townsmen, who were 'unable to secure the services of a resident squire'.[1] Returned after a contest, he was classed as Opposition. Two years later he sold out of the army 'as belonging to the Prince', who made his son an equerry and his wife a bedchamber woman to the Princess of Wales. After the Prince's death he went over to the Government, speaking for them on the army, 28 Nov. 1751. In 1752 he applied to Pelham for the post of governor of Tilbury, but did not secure it, though Pelham commented on his application: 'He does and will do well in Parliament'.[2]

Leighton did not stand again. He died January 1765.

[1] Duncomb, *Herefs.* iii. 169–70. [2] Pelham to Newcastle, 8 May 1752, Add. 32727, f. 130.

A.N.N.

LENNARD, Sir Samuel, 3rd Bt. (1672–1727), of West Wickham, Kent.

HYTHE 1715–8 Oct. 1727

b. 2 Oct. 1672, o.s. of Sir Stephen Lennard, 2nd Bt., M.P., by Elizabeth, da. of Delalynd Hussey of Shapwick, Dorset, wid. of John Roy of Woodlands, Dorset. *educ.* M. Temple 1689; Trinity, Oxf. 1690. *unm.*, 2s. illegit. *suc.* fa. 15 Dec. 1709. Kntd. Apr. 1718.

Capt. Earl of Denbigh's Drags. 1696–7; half-pay 1698; capt. Visct. Shannon's regt. of Marines 1702; exempt and capt. 2 tp. Life Gds. 1704; a.-d.-c. to Prince George of Denmark; guidon and maj. 1709, cornet and maj. 1709, lt. and lt.-col. 1713; groom of the bedchamber to the Prince of Wales 1714–17; capt. of Sandgate castle 1718–d.[1]

A Whig, whose father had represented the county, Lennard was appointed to the Prince of Wales's household when this was first set up in November 1714. Returned on the Lord Warden's interest for Hythe from 1715, he voted with the Government except on Lord Cadogan (q.v.), resigning his place after the Prince's breach with the King. He owed his knighthood to standing proxy for Prince Frederick when he was installed as Knight of the Garter in April 1718.[2] He died 8 Oct. 1727.

[1] *Arch. Cant.* xxi. 254. [2] *Cal. Treas. Bks.* xxxii. 468.

A.N.N.

LENNOX, Charles, Earl of March (1701–50), of Goodwood, Suss.

CHICHESTER   1722–27 May 1723

b. 18 Mar. 1701, o.s. of Charles, 1st Duke of Richmond, by Anne, da. of Francis, Lord Brudenell, wid. of Henry, 2nd Baron Belasyse of Worlaby. *educ.* Grand Tour (Holland, France, Vienna, Italy) 1719–20. *m.* 4 Dec. 1719, Lady Sarah Cadogan, da. and coh. of William Cadogan (q.v.), 1st Earl Cadogan, 4s. 8da. *suc.* fa. as 2nd Duke 27 May 1723; gd.-m. Duchess of Portsmouth as Duke of Aubigny 14 Nov. 1734; K.B. 27 May 1725; K.G. 26 May 1726.

Guidon 1 tp. Life Gds. 1721; capt. 1 Horse Gds. 1722; a.-d.-c. to the King 1724–32; col. 1724; brig.-gen. 1739; maj.-gen. 1742; lt.-gen. 1745; gen. 1745; col. 1 Horse Gds. 1750–d.

Ld. of the bedchamber to the King 1726–35; ld. high constable 1727; master of the horse 1735–d.; P.C. 9 Jan. 1735; mayor, Chichester 1735; e. bro Trinity House 1737–d., master 1741–5; ambassador to France 1748–9; high steward, Chichester 1749.

At the age of 18 Lord March was married to the 13 year old daughter of the 1st Earl Cadogan to cancel a gambling debt between their parents. Leaving immediately after the marriage for his grand tour, he did not meet his bride again until he returned in 1722, when, seeing her at the theatre without recognising her, he at once fell in love with her.[1] Returned on the Goodwood interest in 1722, he succeeded to the dukedom a year later. As Duke of Richmond he took an active part in Sussex elections, always recommending one of the Members for Chichester, of which he was the patron; unsuccessfully attempting to develop an interest at Arundel and New Shoreham; and vigorously supporting his friend the Duke of Newcastle in the county. His frequent letters to Newcastle bear out Hervey's description of him:[2]

> Friendly, benevolent, generous, honourable and thoroughly noble in his way of acting, talking and

thinking; he had constant spirits, was very entertaining, and had a great deal of knowledge.

He died 8 Aug. 1750.

[1] C. Lennox, *A Duke and his Friends*, i. 34–35, 58. [2] *Mems.* 252.

P.W.

LESLIE, Hon. Thomas (*c*.1701–72), of Stenton, Fife.

DYSART BURGHS   1734–1741
PERTH BURGHS   20 Jan. 1743–1761

b. c.1701, 3rd s. of John, 9th Earl of Rothes [S], by Lady Jean Hay, da. of John, 2nd Mq. of Tweeddale [S]. *educ.* privately. *m.* ?1753, 1da.

Ensign 26 Ft. 1717; lt. 2 Drags. 1726; half-pay 1729; capt. 46 Ft. 1741; equerry to Prince of Wales Oct. 1742; barrack master [S] (with rank of col.) 1748–68.

The impecunious younger son of one of the leaders of the Squadrone, and the cousin of another, Lord Tweeddale, Leslie was returned in 1722 for Dysart Burghs by his father, as sheriff, but on a double return the seat was awarded by the Commons to his opponent.[1] Successful in 1734, he voted with the Opposition on the Spanish convention in 1739 and on the place bill in 1740. He did not stand in 1741 but was returned on his family's interest for Perth Burghs at a by-election in 1743. Following Tweeddale, he voted with the Government on the Hanoverians in 1744 and 1746, when he was classed as a follower of Tweeddale's friend, Granville. Serving against the rebels in the Forty-five, he was wounded and captured at Prestonpans.[2]

By 1747 Leslie had transferred his allegiance to Pelham, who helped to secure his re-election for Perth.[3] Later that year he applied to Newcastle for the post of barrack master.

> I . . . formerly gave you in a memorial of 30 years service in the army . . . yet I am still a captain in a young regiment . . . I am a Whig, and of a Whig family, ready to serve your Grace and therefore ought to be taken care of and this employment will make up in some measure my disappointments in the army.[4]

He obtained the post but chronic financial troubles led to a stream of further appeals to Newcastle for assistance and finally to the loss of his seat.

He died 17 Mar. 1772.

[1] *CJ*, xx. 33, 48–49. [2] *Whitefoord Pprs.* 36, 66–67; *HMC Laing*, ii. 359. [3] Patrick Haldane to Pelham, 11 July 1747, Newcastle (Clumber) mss. [4] 15 Oct. 1747, Add. 32713, f. 265.

E.H.-G.

LEVESON GOWER, Hon. Baptist (?1703–82).

NEWCASTLE-UNDER-LYME   1727–1761

b. ?1703, 4th s. of John Leveson Gower, M.P., 1st Baron Gower, by Lady Catherine Manners, da. of

John, 1st Duke of Rutland; bro. of Hon. Thomas and William Leveson Gower (qq.v.). *educ.* Westminster, May 1717, aged 13; St. John's, Camb. 22 Apr. 1720, aged 16. *unm.*

Ld. of Trade, 1745–9.

Baptist Leveson Gower was returned as a Tory for Newcastle-under-Lyme on his family's interest. He consistently voted against the Government till his brother, Lord Gower, joined the Administration in December 1744, when he was appointed a lord of Trade, resigning in June 1749. He became a member of the Duke of Bedford's circle, joined White's, and in 1751 went into opposition with Bedford, parting company with Lord Gower. He absented himself from the division on the Saxon subsidy, which Bedford opposed, in January 1752.[1]

He died 4 Aug. 1782.

[1] Add. 32726, f. 84.   E.C.

LEVESON GOWER, Granville, Visct. Trentham (1721–1803).

BISHOP'S CASTLE   6 Dec. 1744–1747
WESTMINSTER   1747–1754
LICHFIELD   15 Apr.–25 Dec. 1754

b. 4 Aug. 1721, 1st surv. s. of John Leveson Gower, 1st Earl Gower, by Lady Evelyn Pierrepont, da. of Evelyn, 1st Duke of Kingston; bro. of Hon. Richard Leveson Gower (qq.v.). *educ.* Westminster 1731–40; Ch. Ch. Oxf. 1740. *m.* (1) 23 Dec. 1744, Elizabeth (*d.* 19 May 1746), da. and h. of Nicholas Fazakerley (q.v.) of Prescot, Lancs., 1s. *d.v.p.*; (2) 28 Mar. 1748, Lady Louisa Egerton (*d.* 14 Mar. 1761), da. of Scroop, 1st Duke of Bridgwater, 1s. (George Granville, 1st Duke of Sutherland), 3da.; (3) 25 May 1768, Lady Susanna Stewart, da. of Alexander, 6th Earl of Galloway [S], 1s. (Granville, 1st Earl Granville), 3da. *suc.* fa. as 2nd Earl Gower 25 Dec. 1754. K.G. 11 Feb. 1771; *cr.* Mq. of Stafford, 1 Mar. 1786.

Ld. of Admiralty 1749–51; P.C. 22 Dec. 1755; ld. privy seal 1755–7; master of the horse 1757–60; master of the wardrobe 1760–3; ld. chamberlain 1763–5; ld. pres. of the Council 1767–79, 1783–4; ld. privy seal 1784–94.

Ld. lt. Staffs. 1755–1800; high steward, Stafford 1769.

Lord Trentham entered Parliament for Bishop's Castle at a by-election in December 1744, when his father went over to the Administration. In 1747 he was returned for Westminster, in spite of stiff opposition from the Jacobite dominated Association of Independent Electors, on the interest of his brother-in-law, the Duke of Bedford. On his appointment as a lord of the Admiralty in 1749 he was re-elected after scenes of unprecedented violence. He made his maiden speech on 28 Jan. 1751, when George Cooke (q.v.) presented a petition from several of the electors of Westminster against his election, alleging partiality on the part of the high bailiff and demanding a scrutiny. According to Horace Walpole he

replied with great manliness and sense, and spirit, reflecting on the rancour shown to him and his family, and asserting that the opposition to him had been supported by perjury and by subscriptions, so much condemned and discountenanced by the Opposition, when raised to maintain the King on the throne during the last rebellion. In answer to the censure on the high bailiff, he produced and read a letter from Mr. Cooke to the high bailiff, while he was believed in their interest, couched in the strongest terms of approbation of his conduct and integrity. This was received with a loud and continued shout.[1]

In June 1751, after Lord Sandwich's dismissal and the Duke of Bedford's ensuing resignation, when Lord Gower refused to resign with Bedford, Trentham wrote to Pelham, 14 June 1751:

I am informed that it is properly to you that I should address myself to desire leave to quit H.M. service; I am very sorry as you may well imagine to find myself under the necessity to act thus, as it is seemingly deviating from that filial duty, which till now I have made the rule by which I have steered my conduct in life, and which nothing but an absolute conviction that my honour is concerned should make me in appearance even depart from. I would have it understood, that my resignation does not arise from Lord Sandwich's dismissal from the King's service, but from a sense of injuries done to me, and to those with whom I am more intimately connected. The serving H.M. and his royal family as a private man shall be my future ambition, no usage, or ill-treatment shall make me depart from that.

Pelham replied, 14 June:

I don't know who has informed your Lordship that I am the proper person to address yourself to for leave to quit H.M. service: but whoever they are, they are ignorant of all forms, for I have nothing to do in your department. I know not of any injuries done to your Lordship, and I only know, I have myself acted a different part towards you ever since I knew you. I am very sorry for what you are doing.[2]

In 1752 he absented himself from the division on the subsidy treaty with Saxony and voted against the bill for resettling the Highlands, both of which were attacked by Bedford in the Lords.[3] His political standing may be inferred from the French ambassador's description of him as 'jeune homme et sans aucune sorte de considération', who would prove no great source of strength to Bedford,[4] and his tastes from Richard Rigby's (q.v.) remark to the Duke of Bedford that 'politics have been at a stand ever since you last came out of the House of Lords; and gaming ever since Trentham went to Newmarket'.[5] Soon after succeeding his father he went over to the Administration, thenceforth holding high court and political offices almost continuously till his death, 26 Oct. 1803.

[1] Walpole, *Mems. Geo. II*, i. 14–15.   [2] Newcastle (Clumber) mss.
[3] Add. 32726, ff. 84, 221.   [4] Mirepoix to Puysieux, 5 July 1751, AECP Angl. 432, ff. 70–72.   [5] *Bedford Corresp.* ii. 108.

E.C.

LEVESON GOWER, Hon. Richard (1726–53).

Lichfield   1747–19 Oct. 1753

> b. 30 Apr. 1726, 4th s. of John Leveson Gower, 1st Earl Gower; bro. of Granville Leveson Gower, Lord Trentham (q.v.). *educ.* Westminster 1735–43; Ch. Ch. Oxf. 1744. *unm.*
>
> Under-sec. of state 1749–51.

The Duke of Bedford wrote, 13 July 1746, that his father-in-law, Lord Gower, finding his son Richard

> very averse to the profession of the law, has, upon consideration and our entreaties, given up the design of forcing him into a profession he dislikes, and in which, consequently, he must have miscarried; and I wish my opinion could have prevailed so far with my Lord, as to have induced him to have given him leave to have taken a captain's commission in my regiment when it was first raised, a profession to which he was naturally inclined, and in which consequently (knowing the good parts he has), I think he would have succeeded. But Lord Gower's old dislike to an army life got the better of all these reasonings, and there is now (considering his age) no other system of life for him to pursue, but an idle one, or *le métier d'un ministre aux cours étrangères*, which, though I look upon it as a kind of banishment, is yet much preferable to the former.

Shortly afterwards Richard Leveson Gower went to The Hague as secretary to Lord Sandwich, who assured Bedford that

> no care or pains shall be wanting that can in any shape contribute to the giving my friend Dick a proper insight into business and at the same time an advantageous introduction into the world.

In the summer of 1747 he was returned for Tavistock by the Duke of Bedford, but made his election for Lichfield, for which he had also been returned after a contest. In the autumn Lord Sandwich asked Bedford to

> prevail on my Lord Gower to send Leveson back to me before I go to Aix-la-Chapelle. I believe it is his inclination, and I assure your Grace it is mine, because I have all the reason in the world to be satisfied with his behaviour, both public and private, and have a most sincere satisfaction in the hopes of being serviceable in the education of a person so nearly allied to your Grace.

Bedford replied:

> The Duchess and I are both infinitely obliged to you for your goodness to Mr. Leveson. We think him very much improved, and are very happy to find you are satisfied with him. I hope he will make a good figure in life. If he does, it will be wholly owing to your Lordship, for in the way he was before he went abroad with you, he must inevitably have been spoiled. I wish you would talk to him about economy for he has drawn another note on Lord Gower for £50, which makes him very uneasy.

In reply Sandwich suggested that Leveson Gower should go to the Congress of Aix-la-Chapelle as joint secretary to the plenipotentiaries at a salary of £300 a year,

> which would be an addition to Leveson's income that would render the drafts upon my Lord Gower . . . less frequent; though, without my friend has some addition of this sort, I cannot possibly take his Lordship's part in the discussion about the two great frequency of the demands from hence . . . I may possibly be persuaded to tell my friend he does wrong if he draws on my Lord for more than a thousand pounds a year; but otherwise, I must stick by my companion, and rather desire your Grace to represent to my Lord the great expense of a congress, and the impossibility for a man of spirit to make a proper figure without unlimited credit at home.

He went in this capacity to Aix-la-Chapelle, carrying back to England news of 'the signature of the definitive treaty of peace', for which he was granted £1,000 by the lords justices. Appointed under-secretary of state in the Duke of Bedford's department at a salary of £1,000 p.a., he became the boon companion of Richard Rigby (q.v.), won cricket matches for Bedford at Woburn, and spent much of his time at White's, which he joined in 1747. In June 1751 he resigned with the Duke of Bedford, who obtained for him from the King the reversion to a post in the secretary of state's office.[1] In 1752 he followed the same political course as his brother, Lord Trentham (q.v.). He was to have been put up at Brackley on the Duke of Bridgwater's interest at Bedford's recommendation in 1754,[2] but died before the general election, 19 Oct. 1753.

[1] *Bedford Corresp.* i. 127–8, 45, 295, 317, 331–2, 558; ii. 97, 193–4.
[2] Bedford to Bridgwater, 19 Oct. 1753, Bedford mss.

E.C.

LEVESON GOWER, Hon. Thomas (?1699–1727).

Newcastle-under-Lyme   1722–1727

> b. ?1699, 3rd s. of John Leveson Gower, M.P., 1st Baron Gower; bro. of Hon. Baptist and William Leveson Gower (qq.v.). *educ.* Ch. Ch. Oxf. 15 Mar. 1716, aged. 16. *unm.*

Thomas Leveson Gower was returned unopposed as a Tory on his family's interest. In May 1725 he was chosen a member of the committee 'to manage the evidence against Thomas, Earl of Macclesfield',[1] the former lord chancellor, who was being impeached for corruption.

He died 12 Aug. 1727.

[1] Chandler, vi. 345.

E.C.

LEVESON GOWER, Hon. William (c.1696–1756).

Staffordshire   29 Dec. 1720–13 Dec. 1756

> b. c.1696, 2nd s. of John Leveson Gower, M.P., 1st Baron Gower; bro. of Hon. Baptist and Thomas Leveson Gower (qq.v.). *m.* 26 May 1730, Anne, da.

of Sir Thomas Grosvenor, 3rd Bt., M.P., of Eaton Hall, Cheshire. 1da.

William Leveson Gower was returned unopposed for Staffordshire as a Tory at a by-election in 1720 and at the next four general elections. He consistently voted against the Government, signing the opposition whip on 10 Nov. 1743,[1] till the end of 1744, when he went over to the Administration with his brother Lord Gower. Re-elected in 1747 after a bitterly contested election, he followed the Duke of Bedford into opposition in 1751, severing his political connexion with his brother. When in December of that year the Princess Emily wished him to be made treasurer to the Prince of Wales and auditor to herself, he 'applied to Mr. Pelham, who insisted on his asking Lord Gower's interest, which he refused to do'.[2] He voted in January 1752 with the Administration on the Saxon subsidy treaty, which the Duke of Bedford had attacked in the House of Lords,[3] but subsequently reverted to opposition.[4]

He died 13 Dec. 1756.

[1] Newdigate mss 2550. [2] Walpole, *Mems. Geo II*, i. 226. [3] Newcastle to Dorset, 25 Jan. 1752, Add. 32726, f. 84. [4] Add. 33034, 173-6.

E.C.

LEVINZ, William (?1671–1747), of Grove and Bilby, Notts.

EAST RETFORD 28 Nov. 1702–17 Jan. 1706
1708–1710
NOTTINGHAMSHIRE 1710–1722
30 May 1732–1734

b. ?1671, 1st s. of Sir Creswell Levinz of Evenley, Northants. by Elizabeth, da. of William Livesay of Lancs. *educ.* St. John's, Oxf., 26 Aug. 1688, aged 17; G. Inn 1681, transferred to I. Temple 1689, called 1693. *m.* 4 June 1693, Ann, da. of Samuel Buck of Gray's Inn, 1s. 2da. *suc.* fa. 1701.

Towards the end of the seventeenth century Sir Creswell Levinz, a distinguished lawyer and judge, bought estates in Nottinghamshire, one of which carried with it an interest at Retford. His eldest son, William, became one of the leaders of the Nottinghamshire Tories; was returned for Retford in 1702 and again in 1705, when he was unseated on petition; and sat for the county during the last two Parliaments of Anne.

On George I's accession Levinz learned that the agents of Lord Pelham, who had just been confirmed in possession of the Holles estates in Nottinghamshire, were boasting 'of the great sums they had at their disposal and of how they would bear all before them'.[1] In a conciliatory letter he wrote to Pelham to say that, though they were strangers, he thought it a respect due to one 'possessed of so

great a fortune in the county' to inform him that he proposed to stand again at the impending general election.[2] Returned unopposed, he subscribed £100 towards the cost of raising a Nottinghamshire regiment in the rebellion of 1715, showing himself 'as zealous to put the laws in operation against Roman Catholics as anybody'. However, in 1721 his name was sent to the Pretender as a probable supporter in the event of a rising.[3]

In 1722 Levinz lost his seat after a close contest, of which he wrote:

It has been my fortune to see a good deal of election affairs in my time, but I never yet saw anything come near this, where the methods of menaces and promises have been so extravagant and the corruption so open and avowed.[4]

In 1727 he threatened to join Sir Robert Clifton (q.v.) in contesting both Retford and the county, with influential Whig support; but in the end, though 'the whole body of Tories importuned him most earnestly to stand', he concluded an agreement with the local Whig leaders not to stand himself for the county on condition that they would not oppose his nominee at Retford.[5] In 1732, when both the Whig Members for the county simultaneously vacated their seats, the Tories 'had a good chance of bringing in two of their own people', but Levinz agreed to a compromise, under which a Whig candidate was returned for one of the vacancies and Levinz himself for the other.[6] Finally in 1734, when it was expected that his 'game' would be 'to compromise in both the county and Retford for himself and his son', who came of age that year, his 'backwardness to expense and trouble' led him to consent 'not to meddle at Retford', provided that his son was allowed to succeed to his seat for the county without opposition.[7] The bargain was carried out, Levinz being considered by the Whigs to have performed his side of it 'very handsomely'.[8] He died in May 1747.

[1] A. S. Turberville, *Welbeck Abbey*, i. 330. [2] Levinz to Ld. Pelham, 27 Sept. 1714, Add. 32686, f. 22. [3] A. C. Wood, *Hist. Notts.* 236; Sir. F. Molyneux to Newcastle, 22 Aug. 1715, Add. 32686, f. 46; Stuart mss 65/16. [4] Turberville, loc. cit. [5] Sir Robt. Sutton to Newcastle, 4 Sept. 1727, SP Dom. 36/3. [6] Ld. Howe to Newcastle, 13, 16 May 1732, Add. 32687, ff. 451, 455. [7] John Plumptre to Newcastle, 21 July 1733, and Thos. Bennett to Newcastle, 22 Oct. 1733, Add 32688, ff. 30, 554. [8] Thos. Bennett to Newcastle, 8 June 1734, Add 32689, f. 264.

R.R.S.

LEVINZ, William, jun. (c.1713–65), of Grove and Bilby, Notts.

NOTTINGHAMSHIRE 1734–1747

b. c.1713, o.s. of William Levinz (q.v.). *educ.* Eton 1728; Trinity, Camb. 1731. *unm. suc.* fa. 1747.
   Commr. of customs 1747–63; receiver gen. of customs 1763–5.

Soon after Levinz's return (see under his father, Levinz, William), he engaged in an affair with the wife of Sir George Savile (q.v.), who complained that he could not venture on divorce proceedings because 'Mr. Levinz was a Tory, and the lawyers of the spiritual courts were all such, and he had experience how far party governed their judgments.'[1] At a by-election in 1738 he helped to secure Tory support for John Mordaunt (q.v.), with whom he was returned unopposed in 1741. He was one of the Tories who withdrew on the motion for the removal of Walpole in February 1741. Next year he eloped with the wife of another Whig M.P., Soame Jenyns (q.v.), though she was 'neither young nor handsome, a very bad complexion, lean scraggy arms, and no ways inviting'.[2] In Parliament he consistently voted with the Opposition till 1746 when he went over to the Administration, voting with them on the Hanoverians.

In 1747, owing to financial difficulties, Levinz entered into an agreement with Newcastle not to stand but to place his interest at Newcastle's disposal, in return for a commissionship of customs, (£1,000 p.a.).[3] By this arrangement Newcastle secured the unopposed return of two Whigs for the county, while Levinz was able to save his estate at Grove, though not his other estate at Bilby, which he sold in 1748 for £5,500.

After Newcastle's fall in 1762 Levinz appears to have come to terms with Bute, not only escaping the proscription of Newcastle's friends, but being promoted to the post held by one of them, William Mellish (q.v.), worth nearly twice as much as his own.[4] Levinz sold Grove in the same year.[5] He died 17 Aug. 1765, aged 52.

[1] *HMC Egmont Diary*, ii. 224–5. [2] R. F. Scott, *St. John's Coll., Cambridge*, iii. 353–4. [3] Levinz to Newcastle, 5, 8 June 1747, Add. 32711, ff. 217, 258. [4] Add. 32800, ff. 140, 211. [5] Piercy, *Hist Retford*, 229.

R.R.S.

LEWEN, George (*d.* 1743), of Ewell, Surr.

WALLINGFORD   1727–1734

1st s. of George Lewen of Poole, Dorset, merchant, by his w. Catharine. *m.* (1) Susan, da. of John Godschall, Turkey merchant, sis. of Sir Robert Godschall (q.v.), 1da.; (2) Nov. 1732, Elizabeth, da. of Thomas Shatterden, afterwards Drax, sis. of Henry Drax (q.v.), *s.p.* *suc* fa. 1718; to Ewell estates of his uncle, Sir William Lewen (q.v.) 1722.[1]

Lewen, according to the petition against him, 'by most notorious bribery', menaces and promises, 'procured himself to be returned' head of the poll at Wallingford, 'although he was altogether a stranger to the electors till a very few days before the election'.[2] As a Tory he voted consistently

against the Administration. He lost his seat in 1734, lodging a petition which he subsequently withdrew. He died 1 Apr. 1743.

[1] Hutchins, *Dorset*, iii. 246; Manning & Bray, *Surr.* i. 470. [2] *CJ*, xxi. 50.

R.S.L.

LEWEN, Sir William (c.1657–1722), of Ewell, Surr.

POOLE   1708–1710, 7 Mar. 1711–1722

b. c.1657, 2nd s. of Robert Lewen of Wimborne Minster, Dorset, and yr. bro. of George Lewen, merchant and mayor of Poole. *m.* 30 July 1685, Susannah, da. of Richard Taylor of Turnham Green, Mdx., *s.p.* Kntd. 17 Dec. 1712.
Alderman of London 1708, sheriff 1712–13, ld. mayor 1717–18; master, Haberdashers' Co. 1709–10; col. Blue regt. 1711–14.

Sir William Lewen, a London merchant, who was first returned for Poole during his brother's mayoralty, represented the borough in four Parliaments. A Hanoverian Tory under Queen Anne, he voted against the Government in all recorded divisions of the 1715 Parliament. He died 16 Mar. 1722, making his nephew George Lewen (q.v.) his heir.

R.S.L.

LEWIS, Thomas (?1661–1732), of St. Pierre, Mon.

MONMOUTHSHIRE   30 Apr.–8 Aug. 1713
                           1715–1722

b. ?1661, 1st s. of Thomas Lewis of St. Pierre by Delarivière, da. of Sir Thomas Morgan, 1st Bt., of Chenston, Herefs. *educ.* Ch. Ch. Oxf. 15 Feb. 1678, aged 16. *m.* (1) Jane Rachael Beecher of Hawberry, Beds., 2s. 1da.; (2) Catherine, da. of Hugh Calverley Cotton of Combermere, Cheshire. *suc.* fa. 1682.

Thomas Lewis was distantly related to John Morgan of Tredegar (q.v.), to whom he owed his return. Though a Whig, all his recorded votes were against the Government. During the split in the Whig party James Craggs (q.v.) asked Morgan to secure his attendance, especially on the bill for the repeal of the Occasional Conformity and Schism Acts;[1] but he voted against the Government both on this measure and on the peerage bill. He did not stand in 1722, dying 29 May 1732.

[1] NLW, Tredegar mss 53/108, 121–2.

P.D.G.T.

LEWIS, Thomas (1690–1777), of Harpton Court, nr. Radnor.

NEW RADNOR BOROUGHS   1715–1761

b. 18 Oct. 1690, 1st s. of Col. Thomas Lewis of Harpton Court by Margaret, da. and coh. of William Howes of Greenham, Berks. *educ.* Wadham, Oxf.

1709. *m.* 12 Feb. 1743, Ann, da. and coh. of Sir Nathan Wright, 3rd Bt., of Cranham Hall, Essex, *s.p. suc. fa.* 1724.

Recorder, New Radnor 1731, 1766, bailiff 1740, 1750, 1752.

Lewis was the son of a Radnorshire landowner, whose estate was one and a half miles from New Radnor, the political preserve of the Harleys under William III and Anne. In 1693, when he was three, his father and uncle were involved in an affray in the streets of New Radnor with Robert Harley, then M.P. for the borough and later Earl of Oxford, swords being drawn on both sides. By 1714 relations between the two families had so improved that he was chosen to accompany Thomas Harley, M.P. for the county, on a mission to Hanover in the last months of Anne's reign.

> Carry yourself respectfully to Mr. Harley, and always speak honourably of him . . . [his father wrote] Take leave of my Lord Treasurer [the Earl of Oxford], and thank him for all favours. Wish him all imaginable prosperity, and the like to the Auditor [Edward Harley, q.v.], to whom I will write a letter of thanks if you think fit.

When, however, the Harleys fell from power on George I's accession a few months later, Lewis stood sucessfully against Lord Harley (q.v.) for New Radnor, which he represented continuously for 46 years. His action, ascribed by tradition to a slight received by him from Thomas Harley during his mission, gave rise to a feud between the two families which continued till his death. The feud was deplored by his mother, who on learning that Lewis was supporting the impeachment of Lord Oxford, wrote to him

> You cannot imagine the concern I am under. I can't eat, drink, or sleep, for fear you have a hand in [the] blood of these men. My Lord of Oxon is our neighbour and friend; be tender of his life, and do not, for any advantage in this world, give your vote against him or the Duke [of Ormonde]; and give me the satisfaction that you are not ungrateful to him, which will very much quiet the mind of your uneasy mother.[1]

In his first Parliament he voted against the septennial bill in 1716, but thereafter he became a most reliable government supporter, appearing on the ministerial side in all the other division lists extant during his long political career. His support was not unrewarded. On 5 Aug. 1727 John Verney (q.v.), who was standing against him at New Radnor, wrote to Walpole:

> I am already sure of a majority of legal votes. But the returning officer, who is Mr. Lewis's brother, has declared he will return him right or wrong; they have made two hundred new burgesses within this fortnight, and I dare say will make a thousand if they are necessary . . . Mr. Lewis is now in town, and

probably will wait upon you, and I am persuaded that the least word from you, will make him desist, for he has a place in the custom house, which was granted to his father for two and thirty years, and since his death he has enjoyed the profits of it, and I am sure it is either in his own name or held in trust for him.[2]

In 1739 Walpole agreed to finance from secret service funds the cost of legal and other proceedings resulting in the issue of a new charter to Radnor, which enabled Lewis to replace the Harleys as the dominant influence in that corporation.[3] On 26 Oct. 1740 he applied to Walpole for the electorally important post of steward of the King's manors in Radnorshire, whose then holder, the 1st Duke of Chandos, had allied himself with the Harleys:

> The reason which obliges my now pressing it, [is] to prevent their making new burgesses in November, having till then adjourned their court leets for that purpose, as they made 140 at the last, the Duke's agents being absolutely in the hands of our greatest opposers. As this will be taking the very means of opposition either for town or county out of their hands and thereby save many hundred pounds as well as trouble, I shall humbly submit it to you.[4]

So intent was he on gaining his objective that the mere rumour that the county Member, Sir Humphrey Howorth (q.v.), coveted the same office, was enough to make Lewis support Howorth's opponent in the 1741 election, although the two men had hitherto been firm friends and allies. He secured the office for his brother, Henry Lewis, in 1746,[5] after which he was left in undisturbed possession of the seat till the end of the reign.

He died 5 Apr. 1777.

[1] G. Cornwall Lewis, *Ped. of Lewis of Harpton*, 6–7, 9–10, 11. [2] Cholmondeley (Houghton) mss. [3] *CJ*, xxiv. 226; Chase Price to Duke of Portland, 15 Sept. 1765, Portland mss. [4] Cholmondeley (Houghton) mss. [5] *Gent. Mag.* 1746, p. 384.

R.R.S.

LEWIS, Thomas (c.1679–1736), of Soberton, Hants.

WHITCHURCH	5 May–21 Dec. 1708
WINCHESTER	1710–1713
HAMPSHIRE	1713–1715
SOUTHAMPTON	1715–1727
SALISBURY	1727–1734
PORTSMOUTH	1734–22 Nov. 1736

b. c.1679, 3rd but 1st surv. s. of Richard Lewis, M.P., of Edington and Corsham, Wilts. and the Van and St. Fagan's, Glam. by his w. Mary James. *educ.* Salisbury sch. *m.* (1) Anna Maria (*d.* 1709), da. and h. of Sir Walter Curll, 1st Bt., of Soberton, *s.p.*; (2) settlement 8 Feb. 1710, Elizabeth Turnour of St. Martin-in-the-Fields, London, 1da. *suc. fa.* 1706.

Lewis, whose father had represented Westbury in nine Parliaments, came of an old Welsh family with large estates in Glamorgan. A member of the October Club under Queen Anne, he was returned as a Tory for Southampton in 1715, voting against the Administration in all recorded divisions of that Parliament. His name was sent to the Pretender in 1721 as a probable supporter in the event of a rising.[1] However, during a debate in February 1726 on the treaties with Hanover and Spain, he 'left his friends' and declared himself 'an humble servant of the great man', Walpole. In return, it was alleged, he was 'to be a peer and the honour to be entailed on his daughter and her issue and she is to be married to Sir Robert's second son'. Next month he spoke in support of the Administration on increasing the number of seamen, and in February 1727 he opposed Pulteney's motion on the right of the House to be informed about the disposition of public money. Returned in 1727 as a Whig for both Salisbury and Buckingham, he chose to sit for the former, voting for the Government in all recorded divisions. He made a 'set' speech, i.e. one learned by heart, in support of Pelham's motion for maintaining the land forces in January 1729, when the 1st Lord Egmont described him as 'a country gentleman, without place or pension, and one of the richest commoners in England'. He also spoke in February 1731 for the Hessians and in February 1733 for keeping the army up to 18,000 men, saying that 'in 1715 he was warm for reducing the army but has since seen the ill consequences of it. It was our weakness that encouraged the rebellious plots in the late reign.' In April 1734 he complained successfully for a breach of privilege on one of his servants, who was carrying out an order of the House. At the election in 1734 he was beaten at Salisbury but was returned for an Admiralty seat at Portsmouth, Sir Charles Wager (q.v.) having written to Walpole in 1733:

> I forgot to mention to-day . . . whether you remembered to speak to Mr. Lewis about Portsmouth in case he is not like to be chose at Sarum.[2]

His last recorded speech was against a place bill in April 1735.

Lewis died 22 Nov. 1736. In his will he left his estates, which were heavily encumbered, to his only grandchild, the 4th Earl of Plymouth, then 'a sickly minor of about 4 years old', with remainder successively to Sir Robert and Horace Walpole, and their issue, both of whom received substantial legacies and were appointed executors.[3]

[1] Stuart mss 65/16. [2] G. T. Clark, *Genealogies of Morgan and Glamorgan*, 42-44, 52-53; *HMC Portland*, vii, 425, 428; *HMC Egmont Diary*, i. 126, 315; ii. 78; iii. 337; *CJ*, xxii. 308; Wager to Walpole, 14 June 1733, Cholmondeley (Houghton) mss. [3] PCC 33 Ware; *HMC Carlisle*, 175.

R.S.L.

LEWISHAM, Visct., *see* **LEGGE, George**

LIDDELL, George (1678-1740), of Eslington, Northumb.

BERWICK-UPON-TWEED   1727-9 Oct. 1740

bap. 1 Aug. 1678, 4th s. of Sir Henry Liddell, 3rd Bt., M.P., of Ravensworth by Catherine, da. and h. of Sir John Bright, 1st Bt., of Badsworth, Yorks.; cos. of Thomas and uncle of Sir Henry Liddell, 4th Bt. (qq.v.). *unm.*

The Liddells of Ravensworth were descended from a Newcastle merchant, who bought the Durham estates of the Gascoines, including a rich coal-field, in 1607.[1] Like the rest of the family, a coal-owner, George Liddell was one of the founders of the 'Grand Alliance', a cartel which dominated the north country coal trade for the rest of the century. From 1727 he was returned for Berwick with the support of the government interest there. On excellent terms with Walpole, who called him 'the wise man of the north', he voted with the Government on every recorded division.[2] On 14 Apr. 1738 Edward Harley's parliamentary diary refers to a bill relating to the forfeited Derwentwater estate, the proceeds of which went to Greenwich Hospital.

> The outward pretence for this bill was to sell part of the estate to clear off the mortgage upon it. The private interest was a job for Colonel Liddell, for it was intended to sell that part of the estate upon which were mines and woods and lands capable of great improvement, and not that part which was fully improved.

In a list of the division on the Spanish convention in 1739, Liddell is shown as 'director for Greenwich Hospital of Lord Derwentwater's estates'.[3] He died 9 Oct. 1740.

[1] Surtees, *Durham*, ii. 209. [2] E. Hughes, *North Country Life in 18th Cent.* 235, 271 n. 2, 274. [3] *Gent. Mag.* 1739, p. 306.

R.R.S.

LIDDELL, Sir Henry, 4th Bt. (1708-84), of Ravensworth Castle, co. Dur.

MORPETH   1734-1747

bap. 1 Aug. 1708, 1st s. of Thomas Liddell by Jane, da. of James Clavering of Greencroft, co. Dur.; gd.-s. of Sir Henry Liddell, 3rd Bt., M.P., and nephew of George Liddell (q.v.). *educ.* Peterhouse, Camb. 1725; Grand Tour c.1730. *m.* 27 Apr. 1735, Anne, da. of Sir Peter Delmé, ld. mayor of London, 1da. who m. (1) Augustus Henry Fitzroy, M.P., 3rd Duke of Grafton, from whom she was div.; (2) John Fitzpatrick, M.P., 2nd Earl of Upper Ossory. *suc.* gd.-fa. as 4th Bt. 1 Sept. 1723; *cr.* Baron Ravensworth 29 June 1747.

Mayor, Hartlepool 1739.

One of the chief north country coal-owners, Liddell was returned in 1734 for Morpeth, where he established an interest by offering £10 a man.[1] Next year it was reported that two cooks had been imported from Paris at 100 guineas a year, one for the Duke of Newcastle and the other for Liddell, who was living at great expense.[2] A government supporter, he spoke for the Spanish convention in 1739[3] and was one of the five members of the court list elected to the secret committee set up to inquire into Walpole's Administration in 1742.[4] He voted against the Government on the Address and abstained from the division on the Hanoverians in December of that year, but spoke for them in January 1744, declaring that he had come to the House undetermined and had been convinced by the debate. Next month he opposed Pelham's proposal to increase the duty on sugar. In 1745 he was so incensed by Pitt's statement that the British and Hanoverian troops could not act together that he threatened to put the question to the vote, but was appeased by a conciliatory reply from Pitt.[5] He again spoke for the Hanoverians in 1746. His elevation to the peerage in 1747 did not go down well with the old corps of Whigs, who thought that he had been 'but a wavering friend'.[6] In 1753 he brought charges of Jacobitism against Andrew Stone and William Murray (qq.v.) on evidence so unsubstantial that the most charitable explanation of his conduct was 'honest wrong-headed Whig zeal'.[7] He died 30 Jan. 1784, the father of Horace Walpole's correspondent, Lady Ossory.

[1] J. M. Fewster, 'Pol. and Admin. of Morpeth in the later 18th Cent.' (Durham Univ. Ph.D. thesis), 83. [2] HMC Carlisle, 159. [3] Coxe, Walpole, iii. 517. [4] Walpole to Mann, 1 Apr. 1742. [5] Owen, Pelhams, 208, 217, 254-5. [6] Duke of Richmond to Newcastle, 7 June 1747, Add. 32711, f. 254. [7] Chesterfield Letters, 2014.

R.R.S.

LIDDELL, Richard (?1694–1746), of Wakehurst Place, Suss.

BOSSINEY 12 May–11 Dec. 1741, 18 Mar. 1742–22 June 1746

b. ?1694, 1st s. of Dennis Liddell, M.P., of Wakehurst Place by Martha, da. of Sir Richard Haddock, M.P., comptroller of the navy. educ. Ch. Ch. Oxf. 3 June 1712, aged 17; I. Temple 1712. unm. suc. fa. 1717.
Sec. to ld. lt. [I] 1745–d.; P.C. [I] 1745.

Liddell's father, a commissioner of the navy and a friend of Pepys, bought Wakehurst for £9,000 in 1694.[1] Liddell himself gained notoriety in November 1729 when he was surprised in adultery with Lady Abergavenny by her husband, who was awarded £10,000 damages against him.[2] In order to avoid paying the damages, he appears to have made over his estates to his younger brother Charles.[3] In December 1733 Lord Ailesbury reported from Brussels:

Mr. Liddell here is a very pretty gentleman and well bred . . . No doubt he has a good estate, as one may judge by appearance in going to all countries to divert himself, and as he told me Lord Abergavenny should never have a shilling of his money.[4]

Returned for Bossiney as an opposition Whig in 1741, he was unseated on petition by 7 votes, including that of another wronged husband, Sir William Morice, gained by his kinsman, Lord Abergavenny, 'for what reason is obvious enough'.[5] Re-seated on a further petition after Walpole's fall, he voted against the Hanoverians in 1742 and 1744, signing the opposition whip of 10 Nov. 1743.[6] Lord Chesterfield (Philip Dormer Stanhope, q.v.), states that 'everybody was much surprised' when he appointed Liddell his secretary on becoming lord lieutenant of Ireland in 1745,

and some of my friends represented to me, that he was no man of business, but only a very genteel, pretty young fellow. I assured them, and with truth, that that was the very reason why I chose him,[7]

telling Liddell:

Sir, you will receive the emoluments of your place, but I will do the business myself, being determined to have no first minister.[8]

He died shortly afterwards, 22 June 1746.

[1] G. W. E. Loder, Wakehurst Place, 69–71. [2] HMC Egmont Diary, i. 50; Pol. State, xxxix. 217-20. [3] Loder, 77–78, 125. [4] HMC 15th Rep. VII, 235. [5] Stuart mss 216/111; Coxe, Walpole, iii. 582. [6] Owen, Pelhams, 198. [7] Chesterfield Letters, 2090. [8] M. Maty, Mems. of Chesterfield (1777 ed.), 151.

E.C.

LIDDELL, Thomas (d. 1718), of Bedford Row, London.

LOSTWITHIEL 1715–14 May 1718

o.s. of Robert Liddell (bro. of Sir Henry Liddell, 3rd Bt., M.P., of Ravensworth Castle, co. Dur.) by Priscilla, da. of William Kiffin, London merchant;[1] educ. ?L. Inn 1699. m. Mary, and had issue.[2]

Returned as a Whig for Lostwithiel in 1715, Liddell spoke in favour of Ormonde's impeachment in 1715 and for the septennial bill in 1716. A coal-owner, like his cousins, George and Sir Henry Liddell, 4th Bt. (qq.v.), he was a member of the Tyneside coal lobby in the House.[3]

He died 14 May 1718.

[1] Hist. Reg. 1718, chron. p. 22; Surtees, Durham, ii. 213. [2] PCC 120 Tenison. [3] E. Hughes, North Country Life in 18th Cent. 293, 297.

E.C.

LIGONIER, John Louis (1680–1770), of Cobham Place, Surr.

BATH   25 Mar. 1748–27 Apr. 1763

b. 17 Oct. 1680, 2nd s. of Louis de Ligonier of Monteuquet, France by Louise, da. of Louis de Poncet. *unm.* K.B. 12 July 1743; *cr.* Visct. Ligonier [I] 31 Dec. 1757; Baron Ligonier 27 Apr. 1763; Earl Ligonier 10 Sept. 1766.

Capt. 10 Ft. 1703; brevet maj. 1706; brevet col. 1711; lt.-col. 12 Ft. 1712; lt. gov. Minorca 1713–16; lt.-col. 3 Drag. Gds. 1716–20; col. 7 Drag. Gds. 1720–49; a.-d.-c. to George II 1729–43; ranger of Phoenix Park 1735–51; brig.-gen. 1735; maj.-gen. 1739; gov. Kinsale 1739–40; lt.-gen. 1743; gen. 1746; lt.-gen. of Ordnance 1749–57; P.C. 1 Feb. 1749; col. 2 Drag. Gds. 1749–53; gov. Guernsey 1750–2, of Plymouth 1752–9; col. R. Horse Gds. 1753–7, 1 Ft. Gds. 1757–*d.*; f.m. 1757; c.-in.-c. 1757–66; master gen. of the Ordnance 1759–63.

A naturalized Huguenot refugee, Ligonier joined the English army in 1702 as a volunteer, acquired a commission in 1703, and served throughout the war of the Spanish succession. At the age of 40 he bought the colonelcy of a cavalry regiment stationed in Ireland, where he remained for the next 20 years. During the war of the Austrian succession he was taken prisoner at Lauffeld, but was released with an offer of peace from Louis XV, which led to the ending of the war.

On the conclusion of peace Ligonier, now 67, succeeded Field Marshal Wade as Member for Bath, for which he sat without opposition till he received an English peerage in 1763. He died 28 Apr. 1770, in his ninetieth year.

R.R.S.

LIMERICK, Visct., *see* **HAMILTON, James**

LINDSAY, Patrick (1686–1753).

EDINBURGH   1734–1741

bap. 10 Mar. 1686, o. surv. s. of Patrick Lindsay, rector of St. Andrews g.s., by Janet, da. of John Lindsay of Newton. *m.* (1) contr. 22 June 1715, Margaret, da. of David Monteir of Edinburgh, merchant, 3s. 2da.; (2) Janet (*d.* Nov. 1739), da. of James Murray of Polton, Midlothian, *s.p.*; (3) 7 May 1741, Lady Catherine Lindsay, da. of William, 18th Earl of Crawford, *s.p.*

Ensign Sir Robert Rich's Ft. 1711; half pay 1713. Ld. provost of Edinburgh 1729–31, 1733–5; gov. I.o.M. 1747–*d.*

An Edinburgh upholsterer, who had served in Spain during the war of the Spanish succession, Lindsay was brought into Parliament by Lord Ilay, with whom he appears to have been associated in procuring the election of the Duke of Atholl as a representative peer of Scotland in 1733, and of the court list in 1734.[1] He made his first reported speech in support of the army estimates, 14 Feb. 1735. On the outbreak of the Porteous riots next year he was sent by the Edinburgh magistrates to the commander of the troops stationed in the vicinity, General Moyle, who, not being anxious to incur the fate of Captain Porteous, refused to act without written instructions from the competent authorities, which were not forthcoming. In a letter to Walpole about this affair, Ilay wrote:

> I have had great difficulty to prevent mischief between General Moyle and Mr. Lindsay. Moyle says that Lindsay was drunk and never asked his assistance, Lindsay says that he told him he came from the magistrates to ask his assistance.[2]

He was subsequently examined by both Houses on the matter. On 16 May 1737 he spoke against the bill inflicting penalties on the provost and city of Edinburgh, but his condemnation of the local clergy, who openly condoned the lynching, exposed him to charges of doing more damage to Edinburgh than all the evidence for the bill.[3] He spoke[4] and voted with the Government on the Spanish convention in 1739, also voting with them against the place bill in 1740, but was not put up in 1741. Appointed governor of the Isle of Man by the Duke of Atholl in 1747, he died 20 Feb. 1753.

[1] *HMC Polwarth*, v. 110. [2] Coxe, *Walpole*, i. 491–4; iii. 367.
[3] *Parl. Hist.* x. 263–6. [4] Coxe, iii. 517.

R.R.S.

LISBURNE, Visct., *see* **VAUGHAN, John** (*d.* 1741)

LISLE, Edward (1692–1753), of Moyles Court, Hants.

MARLBOROUGH   1727–1734
HAMPSHIRE   1734–1741

b. 17 May 1692,[1] 1st s. of Edward Lisle, barrister-at-law, of Crux Easton and Moyles Court by Mary, da. of Sir Ambrose Phillipps of Garendon, Leics. *educ.* M. Temple 1710; Magdalen, Oxf. 1711. *m.* 8 Nov. 1726, a da. (with '£60,000 and upwards')[2] of John Carter of Weston Colville, Cambs., wid. of one Bush, *s.p. suc.* fa. 1722.

Edward Lisle, whose family had held lands in the Isle of Wight since the twelfth century, was the heir male of John de Lisle who was summoned to Parliament in person in 1299. His father's uncle, John Lisle, M.P., the regicide, was a member of Cromwell's 'other House', as Lord Lisle, and married the well-known Lady Alice Lisle, the heiress of Moyles Court, who was judicially murdered by Judge Jeffreys in 1685. Returned as a Tory on the Bruce interest at Marlborough in 1727, he was again successful there with Frances Seymour (q.v.) in 1734, but decided to sit for Hampshire, in which his estates lay. In Parliament he voted against the Administration in all recorded divisions. His only reported speeches were on 26 Feb. 1735, when he supported the appointment of a committee to enquire into the postmaster general's power to open letters, and on 21 Jan. 1736 in connexion with a petition against his return for Hampshire, which was delayed till April that year and then not heard. At Michaelmas 1739 one Caecilius Calvert exhibited a bill in the court of Chancery, claiming Lisle's estates, on the ground that an annuity to him of £400, which was charged on them, had not been paid. Lisle fled to Montpellier, in France, telling his servants that he 'did not know whether he should ever return to the kingdom again'. On 28 Feb. 1740 Calvert petitioned the House, stating that he could not proceed with his bill because of Lisle's parliamentary privilege. Lisle was ordered to attend the House on 13 March, when, in his absence, it was resolved that he 'be suspended from the benefit of the privilege of this House (except as to his person) until he shall attend this House in his place'.[3] He died 15 June 1753.

[1] *Genealogist*, vii. 267–8. [2] *Pol. State*, xxxii. 510. [3] *CJ*, xxiii. 481, 499.

R.S.L.

LISTER, Thomas (1688–1745), of Gisburn Park, nr. Clitheroe, Yorks.

CLITHEROE 23 Apr. 1713–15 May 1745

b. 8 Oct. 1688, 1st s. of Thomas Lister of Arnoldsbigging, and Westby, Yorks. by Elizabeth, da. of John Parker of Extwisle, Lancs. *educ.* Eton 1698–1706;[1] Balliol, Oxf. 1706; M. Temple 1709. *m.* 27 Nov. 1716, Catherine, da. and coh. of Sir Ralph Assheton, 2nd Bt., M.P., of Middleton and Whalley, Lancs., 2s. 3da.; bro.-in-law of Sir Nathaniel Curzon, 4th Bt. (q.v.). *suc.* fa. 1706.

Lister's family had long been settled in the neighbourhood of Clitheroe, where they had acquired an interest, which he was able to turn after the 1722 election into control of one seat. A Tory, he consistently voted against the Government, speaking on 7 May 1728 against a vote of credit.[2] He transferred the family seat from Arnoldsbigging to Lower Hall in Gisburn, which his father had acquired from Sir John Assheton in 1697, and which he rebuilt on a grand scale in 1724.[3]

He died 15 May 1745.

[1] H. L. Lyster-Denny, *Memorials of an Ancient House*, 134. [2] *Knatchbull Diary*, app. 124, 128. [3] Lyster-Denny, loc. cit.

E.C.

LISTER, Thomas (1723–61), of Gisburn Park, nr. Clitheroe, Yorks.

CLITHEROE 29 Oct. 1745–29 Nov. 1761

b. 19 Jan. 1723, 1st s. of Thomas Lister (q.v.). *educ.*

Westminster 1736; Emmanuel, Camb. 1742. *m.* 3 Sept. 1748, Beatrix, da. of Jessop Hulton of Hulton Park, Lancs., 1s. 2da. *suc.* fa. 1745.

Lister, a Tory like his father, voted against the Government on the Hanoverians in 1746. The 2nd Lord Egmont in his electoral survey c.1749–50, wrote of him: 'Though reputed a strong and sour Jacobite, he has talked otherwise of late, and that if it were not for proscription there would not be a Jacobite in England'.

He died 29 Nov. 1761.

E.C.

LISTER KAYE, *see* **KAYE, Sir John**

LITTLETON, James (1668–1723), of North Ockendon, Essex.

WEYMOUTH AND MELCOMBE REGIS 1710–17 Mar. 1711, 18 Apr.–22 May 1711, 1713–1715

QUEENBOROUGH 1722–3 Feb. 1723

bap. 29 Oct. 1668,[1] 4th s. of James Littleton of Lingfield, Surr., being o.s. by his 3rd w. Susan,[2] née Medlicot, of London, wid. of one White, attorney-at-law. *m.* Jane, da. of Richard Bunch, M.D., 1s. 2da. *suc.* Ann, wid. of cos. Sir Thomas Littleton, 3rd Bt., M.P., to North Ockendon estate 1714.

Lt. R.N. bef. 1690,[3] capt. 1693; commodore and c.-in-c. West Indies 1710–12; commr. and c.-in-c. Chatham 1714–22; r.-adm. 1717; 2nd in command to Adm. Sir George Byng (q.v.) in the Baltic 1717; v.-adm. 1718.

James Littleton's grandfather, Thomas, was a younger brother of Edward Littleton, M.P., 1st Baron Lyttleton of Mounslow,[4] whose daughter and heir, Anne, married her kinsman Sir Thomas Littleton, 2nd Bt. Their son Sir Thomas Littleton, 3rd Bt., Speaker of the House of Commons and treasurer of the navy, died without issue in 1710, making James his eventual heir. After a successful career in the navy, Littleton was returned three times as a Whig for Weymouth, for which he sat in Anne's last Parliament, after being twice unseated on petition. He did not stand in 1715, when his son succeeded him at Weymouth, but, after further service afloat in 1717, he was brought in on the Admiralty interest for Queenborough in 1722. He died shortly afterwards, on 3 Feb. 1723, and was buried at North Ockendon, six admirals supporting the pall.[5]

[1] *Misc. Gen. et Her.* (ser. 3), i. 37, 72–73. [2] Lic. (Vic. Gen.) to marry 31 Oct. 1667. [3] *CSP Dom.* 1689–90, p. 396. [4] *Vis. Surr.* 1662–68 (Harl. Soc. lv), 74; *Salop Arch. Soc. Trans.* (ser. 4), iii. 302–32. [5] Morant, *Essex*, i. 103.

R.R.S.

LITTLETON, Thomas (*d.* 1722), of North Ockendon, Essex.

WEYMOUTH AND MELCOMBE REGIS 1715–1722

o.s. of Adm. James Littleton (q.v.). *unm.*
Capt. 14 Ft. 1720–*d.*

Littleton, who was returned unopposed for Weymouth in succession to his father, voted with the Government in all recorded divisions. He died *v.p.* in 1722.[1]

[1] Morant, *Essex,* i. 103.

R.R.S

LIVINGSTONE, *see* **CAMPBELL, James**

LLOYD, John (?1717–55), of Peterwell, Card.

CARDIGANSHIRE 1747–3 June 1755

b. ?1717, 1st surv. s. of Walter Lloyd (q.v.). *educ.* Jesus, Oxf. 16 Apr. 1735, aged 17; I. Temple 1735, called 1739. *m.* 24 Mar. 1750, Elizabeth, da. of Isaac Le Heup (q.v.) of Gunthorpe, Norf., *s.p. suc.* fa. 1747; bro.-in-law Sir Lucius C. Lloyd, 3rd Bt., at Maesyfelin, Card. 1750.
Attorney-gen. for S. Wales 1747–*d.*

Lloyd succeeded to his father's post and seat in 1747 and was re-elected on the Whig interest in 1754. He died 3 June 1755.

P.D.G.T.

LLOYD, Philip (*d.* 1735), of Grosvenor St., Westminster, and Bardwin, Northumb.

SALTASH	5 Feb. 1723–1727
AYLESBURY	1727–6 Feb. 1730
CHRISTCHURCH	22 Jan. 1732–1734
LOSTWITHIEL	1734–18 Mar. 1735

m. Catherine.[1]
Capt. Col. Lucas's Ft. 1715, 7 Drags. 1726, half-pay 1729; equerry to George II 1730–*d.*

Connected with Philip, Duke of Wharton, Lloyd was probably the man of that name present at the drinking bout between Sir Christopher Musgrave (q.v.) and Wharton in 1723.[2] In that year he was put up by Wharton for Saltash, where he was successful after lavish entertainments, the bills for which were never paid.[3] Though elected as an opposition candidate, he attached himself to Walpole, for which Wharton revenged himself by writing:

Dear Lloyd, they say, you're Walpole's ferret,
To hunt him out poor Molly Skerrett,
And thus are grown by vices sinister,
A pimp to such a scrub minister;
Stick to your usual voting trade,
Nor Chetwynd's rights presume to invade,
To purchase Molly to his bed.[4]

In 1724 he eloped with a Miss Cade, who had '£5,000 while he had nothing, but they have set up coach and chariot and make a great flutter.'[5] In 1727 he applied to Walpole for financial assistance towards the cost of his election for Aylesbury:

As I would not detain you the last time I had the honour of waiting upon you at Chelsea, to give you a true account of my affairs at Aylesbury I hope you will pardon the liberty I now take of doing it. I have been at £500 expense there, and though I am assured my interest there is so strong that no opposition can hurt, yet my agents let me know I must provide £400 more in case of necessity; now Sir, what I would humbly beg of you is, to lend me £300, which I will most faithfully repay in a short time. The reason that obliges me to apply to you is, Mr. Manning's being at Honiton (where he stays till the election is over) who is the trustee for my wife, and consequently without his being in town, I have it not in my power to raise one shilling from the rent and judgement due to me from the Duke of Wharton and which is my all. I hope Sir Robert Walpole knows me so well, as to be assured I don't mean to deceive him, and not repay him again with the utmost gratitude.[6]

Losing his seat when he had to seek re-election on being appointed equerry to the King in 1730, but returned by the Administration for Christchurch in 1732 and for Lostwithiel in 1734, he voted with them in every recorded division.
He died 18 Mar. 1735.

[1] His admon. 1735. [2] Lewis Melville, *Philip, Duke of Wharton,* 90. [3] W. P. Courtney, *Parl. Rep. Cornw.* 155. [4] Melville, 117. 'Chetwynd' refers to Walter, 1st Visct. Chetwynd (q.v.). [5] *HMC Hastings,* iii. 1–2. [6] Aug. 1727, Cholmondeley (Houghton) mss.

E.C.

LLOYD, Richard (c.1703–57), of Mabws, Card.

CARDIGAN BOROUGHS 7 May 1730–1741

b. c.1703, 1st s. of Erasmus Lloyd of Mabws, Card. by Jane, da. of Thomas Pryse of Glanfraed, nephew of Lewis Pryse (q.v.). *educ.* L. Inn. 1720. *m.* a da. of Edward Games of Tregaer, Brec., 1da.

Returned on petition as a Whig in 1730, Lloyd was re-elected in 1734, when he exerted himself both in the boroughs and the county on behalf of the Government.[1] He voted with the Administration in every recorded division except that on the repeal of the Septennial Act, when he voted against them. Defeated in 1741, he petitioned repeatedly, his petition being finally dismissed by the House on 23 Jan. 1746. He died 16 July 1757.

[1] Rich. Lloyd to Sir Robt. Walpole, 12 June 1734, Cholmondeley (Houghton) mss.

P.D.G.T.

LLOYD, Richard (?1696–1761), of Hintlesham Hall, Suff.

MITCHELL	14 May 1745–1747
MALDON	1747–1754
TOTNES	13 Dec. 1754–Sept. 1759

b. ?1696, s. of Talbot Lloyd of Lichfield. *educ.* Lichfield sch.; St. John's, Camb. 12 June 1713, aged 16; fellow 1718–23; M. Temple 1720, called 1723, bencher 1738. *m.* Elizabeth, da. of William Field of Crustwic, Essex, 2s. 1da. *suc.* fa. bef. 1713, and bro.-in-law to Crustwic. Kntd. 23 Nov. 1745. K.C. 1738; solicitor-gen. 1754–6; serjeant-at-law 1759; baron of the Exchequer 1759–61; recorder, Harwich, Orford and Ipswich.

Little is known of Lloyd's parentage or early career except that he was deputy recorder and legal adviser to the 1st Lord Egmont (q.v.) at Harwich between 1727 and 1734. By 1741 he was sufficiently eminent in his profession to be briefed as counsel for the government candidates when the Westminster election petition was heard at the bar of the House of Commons, acquitting himself extremely well, though eclipsed by his opponent, William Murray (q.v.).[1] In 1744 he is mentioned in a legal skit as aspiring to become solicitor-general.[2]

In 1745 the widow of the 3rd Earl of Winchilsea died at the age of 90, leaving Lloyd the whole of her estate and appointing him her sole executor; the will throws no light on her reasons for making him her heir. A month later he entered Parliament for a Cornish borough as a government supporter. At the end of the year he was knighted as one of a deputation from the bench and bar presenting a loyal address to the King. He was chosen to open the trial of Lord Balmerino and was one of the managers of Lord Lovat's trial in 1746.

At the general election of 1747 Lloyd was returned for Maldon, where he had built up a strong interest.[3] In 1748 he was suspected of trying to 'steal' the borough of Orford from the Treasury.[4] In the House he spoke as one of the leading government lawyers on the Westminster election petition, the Anstruther case, the regency bill, and the repeal of the Jewish naturalization bill. He is reported to have spoken against Lord Hardwicke's marriage bill in committee but to have afterwards voted for it, without assigning any reason for his change of opinion.[5] He succeeded Murray as solicitor-general in 1754 but was not considered fit to succeed him as attorney-general in 1756, in the end having to content himself with a judgeship.

He died 6 Sept. 1761.

[1] *HMC Egmont Diary*, iii. 352; Walpole to Mann, 24 Dec. 1741, 25 Feb. 1742. [2] Foss, *English Judges*, viii. 327–8. [3] *HMC Lothian*, 162. [5] See ORFORD. [4] Walpole, *Mems. Geo. II*, i. 108–9, 152, 344, 364.

E.C.

LLOYD, Robert (?1688–1734), of Aston Hall, nr. Oswestry, Salop.

SHROPSHIRE 1710–1713, 1722–1727

b. ?1688, 1st s. of Robert Lloyd, M.P., of Aston Hall by Mary, da. of Sir John Bridgeman, 2nd Bt., of Castle Bromwich, Warws. *educ.* Magdalen, Oxf.

5 Apr. 1707, aged 18; I. Temple 1708. *unm. suc.* fa. 1709.

On coming of age Lloyd was returned for the county as a Tory after a contest. Soon after his election he presented the rectory of Selattyn, nr. Oswestry, to Dr. Sacheverell, whose induction was made the occasion of a tumultuous progress through the country. He did not stand again till 1722, when he was again returned after an expensive contest. He died 7 June 1734, leaving his estates crippled by his and his father's election expenses.[1]

[1] *Salop Arch. Soc. Trans.* (ser. 4), xii. 11.

J.B.L.

LLOYD, Salusbury (d. 1734), of Leadbrook, Flints.

FLINT BOROUGHS 21 May 1728–1734

m. (lic. 9 May 1695) Letitia Salusbury, h. to the Salusburys of Leadbrook, Flints.,[1] 1s. *d.v.p.* 1da.

Lloyd, christened John, took the name of Salusbury on his marriage, when he acquired an estate carrying a considerable interest in Flint. Having rented another estate in the neighbourhood, he stood for the Boroughs with government support in 1727. Though his opponent secured a large majority, there was a double return, the head bailiff being Lloyd's tenant and threatened with eviction if he did not return his landlord.[2] Awarded the seat by a party vote of the House of Commons in defiance of the evidence, he voted with the Government in all recorded divisions, except on the excise bill, which he opposed. He did not seek re-election, and died 26 Dec. 1734, leaving his property to his son-in-law, Thomas Brereton (q.v.).

[1] *Chester Marriage Lic.* 1691–1700 (Lancs. & Cheshire Rec. Soc. lxxvii), 96. [2] *CJ*, xxi. 175.

P.D.G.T.

LLOYD, Walter (?1678–1747), of Peterwell, Card.

CARDIGANSHIRE 1734–22 Mar. 1742

b. ?1678, s. of David Lloyd of Voelallt, Card. *educ.* B.N.C. Oxf. 6 July 1697, aged 19; I. Temple 1695, called 1700, bencher 1725. *m.* ?1713, Elizabeth, da. and h. of Daniel Evans of Peterwell, 5s. 4da. Attorney-gen. S. Wales 1715–d.

Walter Lloyd established his family as a political power in Cardiganshire by his marriage to the heiress of Peterwell, an estate which gave him control of Lampeter, one of the Cardigan boroughs, and an important interest in the county. As an active Whig partisan, he was appointed local law officer of the Crown immediately after the Hanoverian succession. Returned for the county without opposition in 1734, he supported Walpole's

Administration. Unseated by the Opposition after Walpole's fall in 1742, he stood unsuccessfully for Cardigan Boroughs in 1746, dying in February 1747.

P.D.G.T.

LOCK, William (?1687–1761) of Richmond, Surr.

GREAT GRIMSBY 1741–1761

b. ?1687. *unm.*, 1 s.

Returned for Grimsby in 1741, Lock, a wealthy London merchant, voted consistently with the Administration. The 2nd Lord Egmont in his electoral survey c.1749–50, wrote under Grimsby:

> Lock is a particular acquaintance of mine and though a broker's son and particular, yet a man of honour that I can depend upon. A little civility and some kindness in subscriptions, will do a great deal with him. By his means I hope to get the clue to the proper management of this borough.

He died 21 Oct. 1761.

P.W.

LOCKHART, James (?1675–1718), of Lee, Lanark.

LANARKSHIRE 1715–19 Oct. 1718

b. ?1675, 7th s. of Sir William Lockhart of Lee, M.P. [S], by his 2nd w. Robina, da. of John Sewster of Wistow, Hunts., niece of Oliver Cromwell. *educ.* ?Edinburgh, M.A. 1693. *m.* Dorothy, da. and coh. of Sir William Luckyn, 1st Bt., of Little Waltham, Essex, 3s. 4da. *suc.* bro. John 1707.
    Commr. of the equivalent 1717–*d.*[1]

Lockhart's family had been at Lee since the thirteenth century. Six members of it, including two of his brothers, had represented Lanarkshire in the Parliament of Scotland. His father, Sir William Lockhart, was a distinguished soldier and diplomat, lord justice clerk, and ambassador to France under Cromwell, to whom he was related by marriage. Returned for Lanarkshire as a Whig in 1715, he voted with the Administration on the septennial bill in 1716, dying 19 Oct. 1718.

[1] See BOTELER, John.

J.M.S.

LOCKWOOD, Richard (1676–1756), of College Hill, London, and Dews Hall, nr. Maldon, Essex.

HINDON 1713–1715
LONDON 1722–1727
WORCESTER 1734–1741

b. 1676, o. surv. s. of Richard Lockwood of Gayton, Northants., sheriff of Northants. 1695, by Susanna, da. and h. of Edward Cutts of Maldon, Essex. *educ.* ?Westminster 1684. *m.* Matilda, da. of George Vernon of Sudbury, Derbys., sis. of Henry Vernon, M.P., 5s. *suc.* fa. 1696 or 1697.
    Assistant, R. African Co. 1720–5; director, R. Exchange Assurance 1720, dep. gov. 1732.

Lockwood, a wealthy Turkey merchant,[1] sat as a Tory in Anne's last Parliament, but lost his seat at Hindon in 1715, when he also stood unsuccessfully for Worcester. In 1722 he stood for London, as a second string getting the Duke of Chandos, with whom he was associated on the board of the African Company and to whom he also acted as banker, to recommend him to Mrs. Luttrell for a seat at Minehead. Mrs. Luttrell was willing but the arrangement fell through because Lockwood found that his campaign in London would not permit him to appear in person at Minehead, as was considered desirable.[2] Returned at the head of the poll, he was classed by the Pretender's agent in London as a Jacobite supporter.[3] In 1725 he received the thanks of common council for his 'pains and applications' in opposing the city of London elections bill.[4] Before the next session, when the affairs of the African Company were about to come before Parliament, he and other M.P.s connected with it divested themselves of their stock, 'so that when the dispute comes before the House they may stand clear of being impeached as interested persons or speaking with a design to promote their own private fortunes'.[5] In 1727 he lost his London seat. Returned for Worcester after a contest in 1734, he voted against the Government on the Spanish convention in 1739 and the place bill in 1740, speaking on the gin bill in 1736[6] and against a bill to regulate and check frauds in marine insurance, 27 Mar. 1740. In 1735 he bought the estate of Dews Hall in Essex, making considerable additions to the house.[7]

He did not seek re-election, dying 30 Aug. 1756, aged 80.

[1] Chandos to Mrs. Luttrell, 23 Jan. 1722, Chandos letter bks. [2] Chandos to Mrs. Luttrell, 23 Jan., 18 Feb. 1722, to Lockwood, 12 Jan. 1722, Chandos letter bks. [3] Stuart mss 60/144. [4] Jnl. vol. 57; see LONDON. [5] 22 Oct. 1725, Wood to Humphry Morice, Morice mss. [6] *HMC Egmont Diary*, ii. 257. [7] *VCH Essex*, iv. 80.

E.C.

LOCKYER, Charles (*d.* 1752), of Ilchester, Som. and Ealing, Mdx.

ILCHESTER 1727–1747

1st s. of Thomas Lockyer of Ilchester, Som. by his w. Elizabeth; bro. of Thomas Lockyer (q.v.). *unm.*

Charles Lockyer belonged to a leading Ilchester dissenting family, owning property in and around the town.[1] He was for some time in the service of the South Sea Company as chief accountant, giving evidence to the secret committee set up in the House of Commons to inquire into the South Sea bubble. Returned unopposed for his native town in 1727, after a contest in 1734, and unopposed again in 1741, he voted consistently with the Government.

He stood down in favour of his younger brother Thomas in 1747, and died 'of a paralytic disorder',[2] 13 Feb. 1752.

[1] Basil Williams, 'Family Memoir', 5 seq. (communicated by W. B. Williams). [2] PCC 42 Bettesworth.

S.R.M.

LOCKYER, Thomas (1699–1785), of Mapperton, nr. Ilchester, Som. and New Buildings, Coleman St., London.

ILCHESTER 1747–1761

bap. 19 Sept. 1699, 4th s. of Thomas Lockyer of Ilchester, Som.; bro. of Charles Lockyer (q.v.). *m.* (1) 1728, Elizabeth (*d.* bef. 1751), da. of Joseph Tolson, E.I. Co. capt., 2s. *d.v.p.* 2da.; (2) c. 1780, Mary, da. of Thomas Handcock of Fore St., London, *s.p. suc.* to trusteeship of his e. bro. John Lockyer's properties nr. Ilchester 1734.

Thomas Lockyer, a Dissenter,[1] 'from small beginnings as a broker, a banker, an East India trader, and a dealer in the funds, acquired a great fortune'.[2] In 1746 he bought the manor of Mapperton,[3] near Ilchester, where he succeeded his elder brother Charles, in 1747, as a government supporter. The 2nd Lord Egmont states in his electoral survey, c.1749–50, that 'Lockyer may absolutely have the command of this borough and will give it wholly to us'. He retained control of the borough till his death, 9 July 1785.

[1] *Gent. Mag.* 1785, p. 574. [2] Egmont to Bute, 3 June 1762, Bute mss. [3] Basil Williams, 'Family Memoir', 19 (communicated by W. B. Williams).

S.R.M.

LOMAX, Caleb (c.1695–1730), of Childwick Bury, nr. St. Albans, Herts.

ST. ALBANS 1727–7 Mar. 1730

b. c.1695, 1st surv. s. of Joshua Lomax (q.v.). *educ.* L. Inn 1713. *m.* Mary Rose, 2s. *suc.* fa. 1724.

When in 1727 Lord Grimston (q.v.) suggested to Sarah, Duchess of Marlborough, that he and her grandson, John Spencer (q.v.), should stand jointly against Lomax for St. Albans, she declined on the ground that 'Mr. Lomax's interest is so strong that your Lordship and my grandson cannot be chosen without spending and bribing to the amount of a thousand pounds'.[1] Returned after a contest, he voted for the Government on the civil list arrears in 1729, and died 7 Mar. 1730.

[1] *HMC Verulam*, 121.

A.N.N.

LOMAX, Joshua (c.1652–1724), of Childwick Bury, nr. St. Albans, Herts.

ST. ALBANS 15 Jan.–10 Mar. 1701, 1708–1710, 3 Dec. 1717–1722

b. c.1652, o.s. of Joshua Lomax of Bolton, Lancs. by his w. Anne. *educ.* L. Inn 1670. *m.* (lic. 29 Mar. 1683) Ruth, da. and coh. of John Lee of Plaistow, Suss., 2s. 5da. *suc.* fa. 1685.

Joshua Lomax was the son of a successful Lancashire attorney, who bought Childwick Bury in 1666. Both he and his father were Dissenters. After standing unsuccessfully for St. Albans in 1715, he was returned for it at a by-election in 1717, defeating the Duchess of Marlborough's candidate. In Parliament he voted for the repeal of the Occasional Conformity and Schism Acts and for the peerage bill. Defeated in 1722, he died 11 Dec. 1724.

A.N.N.

LONDON, John (1671–1734), of Colne Engaine, Essex, and Stoke Newington, Mdx.

WILTON 1710–17 Mar. 1711, 1713–1722

b. 9 Jan. 1671,[1] 3rd s. of Samuel London of Colne Engaine by Mary, da. of Richard Bridge of Wakes Colne, Essex. *m.*, 1s. 1da.

John London, a Dissenter,[2] was descended from Roger London, who bought the manor of Overhall, in Colne Engaine, in 1551. As a factor of Blackwell Hall,[3] the centre of the London cloth trade, he held valuable army clothing contracts under Anne and George I.[4] Returned unopposed as a Whig for Wilton in 1715, he voted with the Administration in all recorded divisions. He did not stand again, dying 25 Nov. 1734.

[1] Morant, *Essex*, ii. 219. [2] *CJ*, xvi. 559. [3] Luttrell, vi. 696, [4] *Cal. Treas. Bks.* xx. 265; xxvi passim; *Cal. Treas. Pprs.* 1714–19, p. 252.

R.S.L.

LONDONDERRY, Earl of, *see* **PITT, Ridgeway, and PITT, Thomas** (*d.* 1729)

LONG, Charles (1679–1723), of Hurts Hall, Saxmundham, Suff.

DUNWICH 1715–1722

bap. 21 Sept. 1679, o. surv. s. of Samuel Long of Longville, Jamaica, chief justice and speaker of house of assembly, Jamaica, by his w. Elizabeth. *m.* (1) 26 July 1699, Amy. da. of Sir Nicholas Lawes, gov. of Jamaica, 1s. 1da.; (2) 27 May 1703, Jane, da. and h. of Sir William Beeston, lt.-gov. Jamaica, wid. of Sir Thomas Modyford, 5th Bt., 3s. 3da. *suc.* fa. 1683.

Commr. for forfeited estates Mar. 1719–*d.*

Succeeding as an infant to the largest property in Jamaica, Charles Long bought an estate in Suffolk, not far from Dunwich, for which he was returned in 1715, voting with the Government. In 1718 he petitioned unsuccessfully for a 31 years crown lease of Dunwich, pleading that he had been 'at great expense to preserve H.M.'s interest in the borough'.[1] In 1720 he and a number of other persons obtained a patent granting them all gold and silver mines in Jamaica for 31 years. Long and his associates put up £150,000, a large part of which he, as treasurer, invested in South Sea stock at the height of the boom, with disastrous results. As a result, his grandson writes, he became 'involved in a labyrinth of intricate accounts and lawsuits, besides which the powers of his mind entirely sank'.[2] Nevertheless he stood again in 1722 for Dunwich, declaring, it was said locally, 'that he would spend £5,000 rather than lose it'.[3] Defeated, he died 8 May 1723.

[1] *Cal. Treas. Bks.* xxxii. 417; see DUNWICH. [2] R. M. Howard, *Longs of Jamaica*, i. 67–71. [3] A. Bence to Ld. Strafford, 5 Dec. 1721, Add. 22248, f. 131.

R.R.S.

LONG, Sir James, 5th Bt. (?1681–1729), of Draycot Cerne, nr. Chippenham, Wilts.

CHIPPENHAM 1705–1713
WOOTTON BASSETT 1715–1722
WILTSHIRE 1727–16 Mar. 1729

b. ?1681, 3rd s. of James Long (who *d.v.p.*, o.s. of Sir James Long, 2nd Bt., M.P.) by his 1st w. Susan, da. of Col. Giles Strangways, M.P., of Melbury, Dorset. *educ.* Balliol, Oxf. 1 Feb. 1699, aged 17. *m.* 9 June 1702, Henrietta, da. of Fulke Greville, M.P., 5th Baron Brooke, of Beauchamps Court, 2s. 4da. *suc.* bro. Sir Giles Long, 4th Bt., 1697.

The Longs of Drayton were a branch of the ancient Wiltshire family of Long of Wraxall, a line of squires most of whom had, since the fifteenth century, represented either the county or one of the Wiltshire boroughs. Sir James Long, a Tory and member of the October Club, after sitting for Chippenham under Anne, was returned unopposed for Wootton Bassett, the other neighbouring borough, in 1715, voting against the Government in all recorded divisions. In 1721 his name was sent to the Pretender as a probable supporter in the event of a rising.[1] Returned unopposed for his county in 1727, he died 16 Mar. 1729.

[1] Stuart mss 65/16.

R.S.L.

LONG, Richard (?1689–1760), of Rood Ashton, Wilts.

CHIPPENHAM 1734–1741

b. ?1689,[1] 1st s. of Richard Long of Rood Ashton by his 1st w. Elizabeth, da. of Thomas Long of Rowden, Chippenham. *educ.* ?M. Temple 1706. *m.* Anne, da. and h. of John Martyn of Hinton, Steeple Ashton, Wilts., 2s. 3da. *suc.* fa. 1730; to the Chippenham estate of his mat. uncle Thomas Long 1730.

Richard Long was descended from Thomas Long (*d.* 1509) of Semington, in Steeple Ashton, who was almost certainly of the ancient Wiltshire family of Long of Wraxall.[2] In 1730 he inherited an estate near Chippenham, for which he was returned as a Tory after a hot contest. His only recorded vote was against the Spanish convention in 1739. He did not stand again and died 6 May 1760.

[1] M.I. at Chippenham. [2] *Misc. Gen. et Her.* n.s. iii. 46, 70.

R.S.L.

LONG, Sir Robert, 6th Bt. (?1705–67), of Draycot Cerne, nr. Chippenham, Wilts.

WOOTTON BASSETT 1734–1741
WILTSHIRE 1741–10 Feb. 1767

b. ?1705, o. surv. s. of Sir James Long, 5th Bt. (q.v.). *educ.* Westminster, Jan. 1718, aged 12; Balliol, Oxf. 17 Mar. 1722, aged 16. *m.* 29 May 1735, Lady Emma Child, da. of Richard Tylney (formerly Child) (q.v.), 1st Earl Tylney [I], 4s. 2da. *suc.* fa. 16 Mar. 1729.

After sitting for the borough of Wootton Bassett, Long, a Tory, was returned four times unopposed for his county, voting consistently against the Walpole and Pelham Administrations. The 2nd Lord Egmont, in his electoral survey, c.1749–50, describes him as 'a weak Tory, conceited, sour, but will be for us if the rest are'. He died 10 Feb. 1767.

R.S.L.

LONG, *see also* **PARKER, Sir Philip**

LONGUEVILLE, Charles (c. 1678–1750) of Inner Temple, London.

DOWNTON 1715–1722
GREAT BEDWYN 1722–1727
EAST LOOE 1727–1741

b. c.1678, 1st s. of William Longueville, barrister, of Inner Temple by Elizabeth, da. and coh. of Sir Thomas Peyton, 2nd Bt., of Knowlton, Kent. *educ.* Clare, Camb. 1695; I. Temple 1693, called 1702, bencher 1728. *unm. suc.* fa. 1721.
Auditor to Queen Caroline ?1727–37, auditor to Princesses Amelia and Caroline 1738.

Charles Longueville was grandson of Sir Thomas Longueville of Bradwell, Bucks., who had been forced to sell the family estates in 1650 as a result of the Civil War.[1] His father, William, an eminent lawyer, became 'standing chamber counsel'[2] to Thomas Bruce, 2nd Earl of Ailesbury, and his family. Returned as a Tory in 1715, he voted against the Government in all recorded divisions. In 1721 the report of the secret committee of enquiry into the South Sea bubble disclosed that he was one of the Members who had accepted stock from the Company without paying for it.[3] In the next Parliament he sat for Great Bedwyn on the Bruce interest. At George II's accession he obtained a court place, thereafter supporting Walpole's Administration. He died 22 or 25 Aug. 1750.

[1] *VCH Bucks.* iv. 286. [2] *Mem. of Thomas Bruce, 2nd Earl of Ailesbury* (Roxburgh Club), 408, 615. [3] *CJ*, xix. 570.

R.S.L.

LORNE, Mq. of, *see* CAMPBELL, John (*b* 1723)

LOWE, Samuel (?1693–1731), of Goadby Marwood, Leics.

ALDEBURGH 24 Nov. 1718–19 July 1731

b. ?1693, s. of Henry Lowe of Goadby Marwood by Elizabeth, da. of Samuel Long of Jamaica, nephew of Charles Long (q.v.). *educ.* Ch. Ch. Oxf. 21 Apr. 1710, aged 16; M. Temple 1711. *unm. suc.* fa. 1714. Comptroller of the Ordnance [I] 1718–30.

Lowe, who inherited considerable sugar plantations in Jamaica,[1] was reported to have £7,000 a year. When he stood for Aldeburgh in 1718, he was said to be proposing to buy all the herrings in the town at a cost of £2,000.[2] Lord Strafford, against whose interest he was standing, afterwards described him as a gamester.[3] Returned after a contest, he voted for the repeal of the Occasional Conformity and Schism Acts and for the peerage bill in 1719, but subsequently went over to the Opposition, voting with them on the civil list arrears in 1729 and the Hessians in 1730. He died 19 July 1731, leaving his fortune to his two sisters, one of whom married Theobald Taaffe (q.v.).

[1] R. M. Howard, *Longs of Jamaica*, i. 58–59. [2] John Ward to Sir Hen. Johnson (q.v.), 19 Nov. 1718, Add. 22248, f. 60. [3] 22 Nov. 1719, Add. 22248, f. 90.

R.R.S.

LOWNDES, Richard (?1707–75), of Winslow, Bucks.

BUCKINGHAMSHIRE 1741–1774

b. ?1707, 1st s. of Robert Lowndes of Winslow by his w. Margaret; gd.-s. of William Lowndes (q.v.). *educ.* Eton; Worcester, Oxf. 13 July 1724, aged 17. *m.* Essex, da. and coh. of Charles Shales, banker, of London, 1s. 2da. *suc.* fa. 1727.
Sheriff, Bucks. 1738.

Lowndes, who had inherited considerable estates in Buckinghamshire, stood unsuccessfully for the county in 1734. Returned for it unopposed in 1741 and 1747 as a Tory, he voted consistently against the Pelham Administration.

He died 6 Oct. 1775.

E.C.

LOWNDES, William (1652–1724), of Chesham, Bucks.

SEAFORD 1695–1715
ST. MAWES 1715–1722
EAST LOOE 27 Oct. 1722–20 Jan. 1724

b. 1 Nov. 1652, 1st s. of Robert Lowndes of Winslow by Elizabeth, da. of Peter FitzWilliam. *educ.* free school, Buckingham. *m.* (1) Elizabeth (*d.* 1680), da. of Sir Robert Harsnett, Treasury serjeant, 1s.; (2) 1683, Jane Hopper (*d.* 1685), 1da.; (3) Elizabeth (*d.* 1689), da. of Richard Martyn, D.D., 1s. 1da.; (4) 1691, Rebecca, da. of John Shales, 7s. 7da. *suc.* fa. 1683.
Clerk, Treasury c.1675, senior clerk 1690, sec. 1695–*d.*

For nearly thirty years secretary to the Treasury, Lowndes is described, in the survey of the 1713 and 1715 Parliaments drawn up for George I, as having

toujours été du parti le plus fort et il s'est trouvé toujours si nécessaire dans la Chambre pour dresser tous les actes touchant le revenu et les subsides qu'on ne l'a jamais fait sortir de son employ.

Returned by the Administration for a Cornish borough, he laid before the House, 10 May 1715, a detailed statement of civil list revenue and expenditure during the last two reigns, concluding with the statement that

there have been no payments out of secret service monies at the Treasury since his Majesty's accession to the throne, as was usual in former reigns.

On 20 Aug. these payments that year were resumed with an issue of £10,000 for secret service to Lowndes.[1] He was *ex officio* a member of the select committees who drafted the finance bills each session.

During the split in the Whig party, 1717–20, Lowndes spoke in support of Walpole's proposals for consolidating the national debt and establishing a sinking fund, which were introduced by the new head of the Treasury, James Stanhope (q.v.), 20 May 1717; submitted to the House Sir Isaac Newton's plan for checking the outflow of silver by devaluing the gold guinea from 21s. 6d. to 20s., 21 Dec. 1717; and defended a vote for half-pay officers, which was attacked by Walpole, now in opposition, 22 Jan. 1718. After Walpole's return to the Treasury in 1721, Lowndes proposed unsuccessfully that the late directors of the South Sea Company should be allowed to keep one-eighth of their confiscated estates, 23 May 1721, subsequently supporting Walpole in securing comparatively lenient treatment for Aislabie and Sawbridge (qq.v.). On 12 July he seconded Walpole's proposal to discharge the civil list debt by a deduction of 6d. in the pound from all salaries, wages and pensions paid by the Crown.

In 1722 Lowndes stood unsuccessfully for Westminster, where he owned about 4 acres on a crown lease for 99 years, originally forming part of the Pulteney estate. On his petition the election was declared void by the House of Commons on the ground that there had been great riots and tumults in violation of the right of election, but by this time Lowndes had been brought in by the Administration for another Cornish borough. At the beginning of 1723 he secured authority to purchase the fee simple of his Westminster property and of two fields in Knightsbridge, which now bear his name, and that of his Buckingham estate, by a private Act of Parliament. In the same session, 29 Mar. 1723, he introduced a bill for repairing gaols, which was rejected *nem. con.*, as he had made it a public bill to save the cost of a private one, though it was really concerned with Buckinghamshire only. On 26 Apr. he introduced a bill for laying a special tax on Papists, which passed into law. At the opening of the next session he moved, 16 Jan. 1724, for an account of the produce of the customs duties on tea, coffee, chocolate etc. during the past seven years, with a view to reducing the losses caused by smuggling by converting the duties into an excise.[2] Four days later he died, 20 Jan., after signing some accounts asked for by the House of Commons. In laying these accounts before the Commons, 22 Jan., Walpole paid a tribute to Lowndes, in whom 'this House has lost a very useful Member, and the public as able and honest a servant as ever the Crown had.'[3] According to Lord Chesterfield he was the author of 'take care of the pence, for the pounds will take care of themselves'.[4]

[1] *CJ*, xviii. 118; *Cal. Treas. Pprs.* xxix. 693. [2] *Knatchbull Diary*, 29 Mar., 26 Apr. 1723, 26 Jan. 1724. [3] *CJ*, xx. 242. [4] *Chesterfield Letters*, 1051.

R.R.S.

LOWTHER, Hon. Anthony (aft. 1694–1741), of Lowther, Westmld.

COCKERMOUTH 20 July 1721–1722
WESTMORLAND 1722–1741

b. aft. 1694, 3rd s. of John Lowther, M.P., 1st Visct. Lonsdale, by Katherine, da. of Sir Henry Frederick Thynne, 1st Bt., sis. of Thomas Thynne, M.P., 1st Visct. Weymouth. *unm.*
Commr. of revenue [I] 1726–34.

Anthony Lowther, one of the handsomest men of his time,[1] was brought in on the Lawson interest for Cockermouth at a by-election in 1721. Returned unopposed for Westmorland on his family's interest at the general election of 1722, he obtained an Irish place, which he resigned in 1734. Next year his

brother, Lord Lonsdale, resigned the privy seal, not on any specific grievance but owing to his general dislike of the management of public affairs. According to Hervey, Lowther,

who very unreasonably thought his merit superior to an employment of £1,000 a year in Ireland, and for that reason quitted it, contributed to strengthen these opinions, hoping that his brother's dislike of things would grow into a dislike of persons, and that he should blow him up to be an enemy to those whom his own vanity had induced him to think had not been enough his friends.[2]

He voted against the Spanish convention in 1739, absented himself from the division on the place bill in 1740, and died 24 Nov. 1741.

[1] Mrs. Delany, *Autobiog. and Corresp.* vi. 163. [2] Hervey, *Mems.* 451; *HMC Egmont Diary*, ii. 175.

R.R.S.

LOWTHER, James (?1673–1755), of Whitehaven, Cumb.

CARLISLE 26 Nov. 1694–1702
CUMBERLAND 1708–1722
APPLEBY 2 May 1723–1727
CUMBERLAND 1727–2 Jan. 1755

b. ?1673, 2nd s. of Sir John Lowther, 2nd Bt., M.P., of Whitehaven by Jane, da. of Woolley Leigh of Addington, Surr. *educ.* Queen's, Oxf. 17 Dec. 1688, aged 15; M. Temple 1682, called 1712, bencher 1714. *unm. suc.* fa. to family estates 1706; e. bro. as 4th Bt. 2 Oct. 1731.
Principal storekeeper of the Ordnance 1696–1712; director, South Sea Co. 1733–6; v.-adm. of Cumb. and Westmld.; alderman, Carlisle 1739–*d.*; vice-pres. Foundling Hospital 1753.

Though a younger son, Lowther succeeded on his father's death to the family property in and around Whitehaven, his elder brother having been disinherited. At the next general election he was returned for Cumberland, which he represented in every Parliament but one till his death. An independent Whig, he voted in the first Hanoverian Parliament against the septennial bill, for the repeal of the Occasional Conformity and Schism Acts, and against the peerage bill.

Lowther lost his Cumberland seat in 1722, but was brought in by the head of his family, Lord Lonsdale, for Appleby. Recovering his county seat in 1727, he either abstained or voted against the Government, except on the motion of 21 Jan. 1742 to set up a secret committee of the Commons to inquire into the conduct of the war, on which he was persuaded by Lord Hartington to vote for Walpole.[1] After Walpole's fall he voted against the Hanoverians in December 1742, was absent from the division on them in January 1744, but voted for them in April 1746, when he was classed as Old Whig. When Frederick, Prince of Wales, launched his new Opposition in June 1747 Lowther promised him to support it,[2] and in the next Parliament he was classed as Opposition.

Apart from seconding the Address in 1724, Lowther's only reported speeches were made in 1732, one supporting a petition from the South Sea Company for permission to fund three-quarters of their capital at 4%; the other supporting a bill for relieving the sufferers from the Charitable Corporation frauds, in which he made it clear that he was concerned not for the sufferers but for the interests of the subscribers to a new loan designed to put the Corporation on its feet.[3] Next year he was elected a director of the South Sea Company on the list put up by the shareholders against that sponsored by the outgoing directors.[4]

Lowther, who did much to develop his collieries and the harbour at Whitehaven, seems to have had scientific interests. He was a fellow of the Royal Society, before whom he performed an experiment showing that mine damp, brought from Whitehaven in a bladder, could be ignited by a candle.[5] He had the reputation of being excessively parsimonious. According to Shelburne, Sunderland, on becoming first Lord of the Treasury, made an appointment for Lowther to call on him, with a view to offering him a seat on the Treasury board on account of his great property.

> The morning was bad; nobody came in to Lord Sunderland, who at last rang his bell to know whether Sir James Lowther had been there. The servants answered that nobody had called; upon his repeating the enquiry the servants said that there was an old man, somewhat wet, sitting by the fireside in the hall, whom they supposed had some petition to deliver to his Lordship. When he went out it proved to be Sir James Lowther. Lord Sunderland desired him to be sent about his business, saying that no such mean fellow should sit at his Treasury.[6]

According to another story Lowther,

> after changing a piece of silver in George's coffee house, and paying 2d. for his dish of coffee, was helped into his chariot (for he was then very lame and infirm), and went home; some little time after he returned to the same coffee house on purpose to acquaint the woman who kept it that she had given him a bad halfpenny, and demanded another in exchange for it.[7]

He died 2 Jan. 1755, one of the richest commoners in the kingdom, reputed to be 'worth above a million'.

[1] Coxe, *Walpole*, iii. 587. [2] Add. 32808, f. 281. [3] *HMC Egmont Diary*, i. 263, 275. [4] *Knatchbull Diary*, 9 Jan. 1724; *Gent. Mag.* 1733, p. 97. [5] *HMC Egmont Diary*, ii. 262. [6] E. Fitzmaurice, *Shelburne* (1912 ed.), i. 26–27. [7] W. King, *Anecdotes*, 102–3.

R.R.S.

LOWTHER, John (?1684–1729), of Ackworth, Yorks.

PONTEFRACT   1722–1 July 1729

> *b.* ?1684, s. of Ralph Lowther of Ackworth, uncle of John Lowther, 1st Visct. Lonsdale. *educ.* Univ. Coll. Oxf. 27 Feb. 1701, aged 16. *unm.*

Lowther was brought into Parliament by his kinsman, Sir William Lowther, 1st Bt. (q.v.). No votes of his are recorded. He died at Bath 1 July 1729.

R.R.S.

LOWTHER, Sir Thomas, 2nd Bt. (c. 1699–1745), of Holker Hall, nr. Lancaster, and Marske, Yorks.

LANCASTER   1722–23 Mar. 1745

> *b.* c.1699, 1st s. of Sir William Lowther, 1st Bt., of Marske, Yorks. by Catherine, da. and h. of Thomas Preston, M.P. Lancaster 1688–97, of Holker Hall. *m.* July 1723, Lady Elizabeth Cavendish, da. of William Cavendish, M.P., 2nd Duke of Devonshire, 1s. *suc.* fa. Apr. 1705.

Lowther inherited through his mother an estate carrying an interest at Lancaster, for which he was returned unopposed in 1722. On 4 Mar. 1726 he presented a petition for a bill to grant him the freehold of this estate, which he held on a crown lease with 22 years still to run. The petition was granted but the House passed a resolution that they would accept no more petitions of this kind, though in fact they subsequently allowed other grants of crown lands.[1] Like his relative, Sir James Lowther (q.v.), he was noted for political independence, voting against the Government on the excise bill in 1733 and the repeal of the Septennial Act in 1734. He was absent from the divisions on the Spanish convention in 1739 and the place bill in 1740. Ministerial lists of absent Members class him as a government supporter on 21 Nov. 1739 but as Opposition on 18 Nov. 1740. In the crucial divisions before the fall of Walpole, his nephew, Lord Hartington (q.v.), wrote that on the election of a chairman of the elections committee

> Sir Thomas Lowther also went against us. Sir Robert sent me to him but he told me immediately that he was obliged to vote for Lee [George, q.v.] because he was his particular friend.

And a few days later:

> I did all I could to get Sir Thomas Lowther down at the Westminster election. I wrote to him a very civil letter but it would not do.[2]

On 21 Jan. 1742 Hartington persuaded him to vote against an opposition motion to set up a secret committee to inquire into the conduct of the war,[3] but ten days later he reported:

As for Sir Thomas Lowther I cannot say much for him. He seems a great deal biased by Sir James, and he has declared that he thinks they are pushing matters too far . . . I have spoke to Sir Thomas to attend when the army comes on, and I think he seems to think that it would be improper to diminish our forces at this time, so I hope we shall have him with us.[4]

Absent from the divisions on the Hanoverians in 1742 and 1744, he died 23 Mar. 1745.

[1] *Knatchbull Diary*, 7 Mar. 1726; C. Strateman, *Liverpool Tractate*, 32. [2] Cholmondeley (Houghton) mss 66; Hartington to Devonshire 17, 27 Dec. 1741, Devonshire mss. [3] Sir Robt. Wilmot to Devonshire, 23 Jan. 1742, ibid. [4] To Devonshire, 2 Feb. 1742, ibid.

E.C.

LOWTHER, Sir William, 1st Bt. (c.1665–1729), of Swillington, Yorks.

PONTEFRACT 1701–1710, 22 Mar. 1716–6 Mar. 1729

b. c.1665, 1st s. of Sir William Lowther, M.P. Pontefract 1660–79, 1695–8, of Swillington by Catherine, da. of Thomas Harrison of Dancer's Hill, Mdx. *educ.* Barwick-in-Elmet sch., Yorks.; Christ's, Camb, 1681; G. Inn. 1682. *m.* Anabella, da. of Banastre Maynard, M.P., 3rd Baron Maynard, 3s. 2da. *suc.* fa. 1705; *cr.* Bt. 6 Jan. 1715.
Sheriff, Yorks. 1697–8.

Lowther was the largest single burgage holder at Pontefract, where he owned 60 burgages.[1] Returned for it on petition in 1715, he voted with the Administration, speaking for the repeal of the Occasional Conformity and Schism Acts. In 1717, though he claimed to be able to choose the mayor and Members of Parliament, he complained that two of the Pontefract aldermen were disaffected and suggested that the Government should send down a mandamus ordering the mayor to replace them by Lowther himself and his son. Later in the year he got the late mayor and some other members of the corporation to sign a document surrendering their charter,[2] with the result that in 1718 the corporation received an order from the attorney-general to show cause against the issue of a new charter.[3] Though the threat does not appear to have been carried into execution, Lowther was able thenceforth to nominate both Members without opposition till his death, 6 Mar. 1729.

[1] C. Bradley, 'Parl. Rep. Pontefract, Newark and East Retford 1754–68' (Manchester Univ. M.A. thesis), 21. [2] SP Dom. 35/9, ff. 36, 188. [3] R. Holmes, *Pontefract*, ii. 342.

R.R.S.

LOWTHER, Sir William, 2nd Bt. (c.1694–1763), of Swillington, Yorks.

PONTEFRACT 8 Apr. 1729–1741

b. c.1694, 1st s. of Sir William Lowther, 1st Bt. (q.v.). *educ.* Sidney Sussex, Camb. 1713. *m.* (1) 1719, Diana (*d.* 1 Jan. 1736), da. of Thomas Condon of

Yorks., *s.p.*; (2) 17 Aug. 1736, Catherine, da. of Sir William Ramsden, 2nd Bt., *s.p. suc.* fa. 6 Mar. 1729.

Lowther's first recorded vote after succeeding his father at Pontefract, was against the Government on the Hessians in 1730. His maiden speech, 4 Mar. 1731, was against a bill for preventing the translation of bishops, on the ground that

at present . . . there was a nobler set of bishops than had been seen since the Reformation; that to take away the only reward of their merit, in writing against infidelity and setting a bright example, which is preferring them by translation to a better bishopric, would be destroying all learning.

On 18 Mar. next he spoke in favour of giving a second reading to a bill for preventing suits on tithes.[1] He supported the excise bill, speaking 'short but close to the purpose and had loud heerums from the ministerial bench'; but he was one of the Whigs who defected on the city of London's petition against the bill, for which he was called 'a whimsical fellow' by George II.[2] Later he spoke against Sir William Wyndham's attempt to move the previous question on Walpole's motion for dropping the bill.[3] At a general meeting at York in November 1733 to choose the candidates for the county, he proposed two Whigs, Sir Rowland Winn and Cholmley Turner (q.v.), thus provoking the great Yorkshire election contest next year.[4] On 13 Mar. 1734 he spoke against the repeal of the Septennial Act on the ground that there had been an increase in the number of Papists. In the published list of the division on the Spanish convention, for which he voted, he is shown as having a brother with a post in the customs.[5] Falling into financial difficulties, he sold his Pontefract burgages to George Morton Pitt (q.v.) for £9,600 in 1740 and did not stand again. He died 22 Dec. 1763.

[1] *HMC Egmont Diary*, i. 153, 163. [2] *HMC Carlisle*, 105; Hervey, *Mems.* 162. [3] *HMC Egmont Diary*, i. 361. [4] Ld. Carlisle to Walpole, 8 Nov. 1733, Cholmondeley (Houghton) mss. [5] *Gent. Mag.* 1739, p. 306.

R.R.S.

LUCKYN, *see* GRIMSTON

LUMLEY, Hon. Charles (c.1693–1728).

CHICHESTER 1727–11 Aug. 1728

b. c.1693, 5th s. of Richard Lumley, 1st Earl of Scarbrough, of Lumley Castle, co. Dur. and Stanstead, nr. Chichester, Suss. by Frances, da. and h. of Sir Henry Jones of Aston, Oxon.; bro. of Hon. James, John and Thomas Lumley (qq.v.) *unm.*
Equerry to Prince of Wales 1718–c.1726; groom of the bedchamber to George II as Prince of Wales and King c.1726–*d.*

Richard Lumley, 1st Earl of Scarbrough, was descended from an ancient Durham family, who in the sixteenth century acquired by marriage the Sussex estates of the earls of Arundel. A signatory of the invitation to William of Orange, he obtained from Queen Anne the grant of the office of surveyor of petty customs and subsidies at the port of London, a sinecure worth £1,200 a year, for the lives of his sons Richard and Thomas (q.v.), later 2nd and 3rd Earls of Scarbrough, which he bequeathed in equal shares to his three younger sons, Charles, John, and James. Returned unopposed for Chichester in 1727, on the joint interests of the 2nd Lord Scarbrough and the Duke of Richmond (Charles Lennox, Lord March, q.v.), Charles Lumley died 11 Aug. 1728.

A.N.N.

LUMLEY, Henry (c.1660–1722).

SUSSEX	1701, 1702–1705
ARUNDEL	1715–1722

b. c.1660, 2nd s. of Hon. John Lumley by Mary, da. and coh. of Sir Henry Compton, K.B., of Bambridge, Suss.; bro. of Richard Lumley, 1st Earl of Scarbrough, one of the signatories of the invitation to William of Orange. *m.* (1) Elizabeth Thimbleby of Lincs., *s.p.*; (2) Anne, da. of Sir William Wiseman, 2nd Bt., of Canfield, Essex, 1da.

Capt. 1 Drag. Gds. 1685, lt.-col. 1688; brevet col. 1689; col. 1 Drag. Gds. 1692–1717; brig.-gen. 1693; maj.-gen. 1697; lt.-gen. 1703; gen. of Horse 1711; gov. Jersey 1703–*d.* (for life from 1710).

After a distinguished military career under William III and Marlborough, Lumley was returned in 1715 for Arundel on the interest of his brother. Though a Whig, he opposed the impeachment of Ormonde, 21 June 1715, but he voted for the septennial bill in 1716, and spoke for the Government on the army, 4 Mar. 1717. About this time he was passed over for a military appointment in favour of Lord Cadogan (q.v.), against whom he and other senior army officers voted in the division of 4 June 1717.[1] He spoke again for the Government on the army next December but a few days later, on the public breach in the royal family, he sold his regiment for about £9,000 when his nephew, Lord Lumley, was forced to sell his own for adhering to the Prince of Wales.[2] On 4 Feb. 1718 he spoke in favour of an opposition motion to make offences committed by soldiers triable by civil magistrates instead of by court martial. He did not stand again, dying 18 Oct. 1722.

[1] *HMC Stuart*, iv. 144. [2] *HMC Portland*, v. 545; *Pol. State*, xiv. 507, 620.

R.R.S.

LUMLEY, Hon. James (c.1706–66).

CHICHESTER	31 Jan. 1729–1734
ARUNDEL	1741–1747

b. c.1706, 7th s. of Richard Lumley, 1st Earl of Scarbrough; bro. of Hon. Charles, John and Thomas Lumley (qq.v.). *educ.* Eton 1718; King's, Camb. 1723. *unm.*

Groom of the bedchamber to Prince of Wales 1728–34; commr. for office of master of the horse 1734–5; avener and clerk-marshal to the King 1735–41.

Jemmy Lumley, as he was known, was the reverse of his eldest brother, Lord Scarbrough, who was said to have all the gallantry of the camp and the politeness of the court. Uncouth and illiterate, on giving a party 'he would write all the cards himself and every one of them was to desire *he's* company and *she's* company, with other curious pieces of orthography'—a story borne out by his surviving letters. Late in life he made himself a public laughing-stock by prosecuting a lady who had horsewhipped him for refusing to pay a sum which she had won from him at whist.[1]

Appointed to the household formed by Frederick, Prince of Wales, in 1728, Lumley was brought in for Chichester on his family's interest in succession to his elder brother, Charles, voting consistently with the Government. He did not stand at the next general election, giving up his post to his brother, John (q.v.), to become a commissioner for the office of master of the horse on Lord Scarbrough's resignation of that post in 1734 till it was filled by the Duke of Richmond in 1735, when he was appointed avener and clerk-marshal.

In 1739 the death of John Lumley gave James the whole income of the sinecure bequeathed by his father to his three younger sons.[2] Next year Lord Scarbrough died, leaving him the Lumley estates, worth £6,000 a year, with an important electoral influence in Arundel and the county.[3] At the general election of 1741 he stood for Arundel, where he came into collision with Newcastle's brother-in-law, Sir John Shelley (q.v.). Suspecting Newcastle of intriguing against him, he threatened to declare for the opposition candidate in the county.[4] With some difficulty he was pacified, but shortly before the election the Duke of Richmond reported to Newcastle that Lumley had

insisted upon giving up his place . . . and then says he very ingeniously, *I shall be at liberty when I have no place to vote as I please* . . . He said that he did not give it up upon any pique, and would let all his acquaintance in Sussex know that he continued firm in the true Whig interest there.

Richmond advised Newcastle to see Lumley:

For you may depend upon it, it will hurt our affairs

in Sussex. Let the fool say what he will, they will insist upon it he is disobliged and his people will not be so staunch as I could wish, and ten to one (if this thing should happen) he may openly turn against us himself. 'Tis a strange cur, you have more influence over him, but I am sure I have none.[5]

A month later Lumley sent a message to Sir Robert Walpole by Sir John Shelley, saying that 'he desired to be made an English peer, or to have his name added to the patent of the place he now enjoys in the Customs House'; i.e. that he should be given it for his own life, instead of for that of his only surviving elder brother, Thomas.

> If Sir Robert Walpole did this immediately before the election he will be entirely attached to him, and be directed by Sir John Shelley in relation to the elections at Arundel, and will concert measures with him to throw out Mr. Orme (q.v.). If neither of these things are done before the election, he says he will be Sir Robert's bitter enemy, and never forgive him.[6]

A few days later, the 'lying inconstant creature', as Lady Shelley called him, denied sending any such message. Returned for Arundel, he supported Walpole till his fall, after which he deserted him on Lord Limerick's motion for an enquiry into his conduct.[7] He then went into opposition till he retired in 1747. He died 14 Mar. 1766, heavily in debt,[8] leaving his Durham estates to his nephew, the 4th Earl of Scarbrough, and his Sussex estates to another nephew, the 2nd Earl of Halifax.

[1] Walpole to Montagu, 25 June 1745, 14 May 1761. [2] See LUMLEY, Charles. [3] *HMC Egmont Diary*, iii. 107; Add. 32697, f. 78. [4] Add. 32695, ff. 294, 298, 334, 336, 343. [5] 3 Mar. 1741, Add. 32696, f. 178. [6] Add. 32690, ff. 280-2. [7] Newcastle to the Duchess, 23 Jan. 1741, Add. 33073, f. 205; Coxe, *Walpole*, iii. 596. [8] Montagu to Walpole, 7 Mar. 1766.

R.R.S.

LUMLEY, Hon. John (c.1703–39).

ARUNDEL 23 Feb. 1728–16 Oct. 1739

b. c.1703, 6th s. of Richard Lumley, 1st Earl of Scarbrough; bro. of Hon. Charles, James and Thomas Lumley (qq.v.). *unm.*

Cornet 7 Drags. 1721, capt. 1723; capt. and lt.-col. 2 Ft. Gds. 1732; equerry to the King 1727–34; groom of the bedchamber to Prince of Wales 1734–*d.*

John Lumley, who shared the sinecure bequeathed by his father to his three younger sons,[1] stood for Arundel on his family's interest, coming out bottom of the poll but securing the seat on petition. Holding court appointments, he consistently voted with the Government till the breach in the royal family, when George II complained that one of the 'boobies and fools' whom the Prince of Wales listened to was 'that stuttering puppy, Johnny Lumley'.[2] He abstained from voting on the Spanish convention, dying shortly afterwards, 16 Oct. 1739.

[1] See LUMLEY, Charles. [2] Hervey, *Mems.* 817.

R.R.S.

LUMLEY (afterwards SAUNDERSON), Hon. Thomas (c.1691–1752), of Sandbeck, Yorks.

ARUNDEL 1722–1727
LINCOLNSHIRE 1727–29 Jan. 1740

b. c.1691, 4th s. of Richard Lumley, 1st Earl of Scarbrough; bro. of Hon. Charles, James and John Lumley (qq.v.). *educ.* Eton 1706–7. *m.* 27 June 1724, Lady Frances Hamilton, da. of George Hamilton, 1st Earl of Orkney [S], 2s. *suc.* to estates of cos. James Saunderson, M.P., 1st Earl of Castleton [I], taking the name of Saunderson 1723; bro. as 3rd Earl of Scarbrough 29 Jan. 1740; K.B. 27 May 1725.

Capt. Col. Tyrrel's Drags. 1715; lt.-col. 37 Ft. 1717–18; lt.-col. Duke of Ancaster's Ft. 1745; clerk to the council of the duchy of Lancaster 1716–31; envoy to Portugal 1722–5; treasurer to Prince of Wales 1738–51.

Thomas Lumley bought a troop in one of the new regiments raised during the 1715 rebellion but left the army in 1718 at the wish of Lord Castleton, who had made him his heir. Returned in 1722 for Arundel on his family's interest, he was appointed envoy to Portugal, where he remained till 1723, when he succeeded on Lord Castleton's death to estates in Lincolnshire and Yorkshire, worth £8,000 a year, assuming the name of Saunderson. After coming to an arrangement with his creditors, a list of whom in 1724 shows liabilities of nearly £24,000, including over £10,000 to his elder brother, Lord Scarbrough,[1] he came home for good at the beginning of 1725, when he was one of the rich commoners chosen to inaugurate the revival of the order of the Bath that year.

Elected for Lincolnshire without opposition in 1727, Saunderson applied for a peerage as Lord Castleton's heir. Owing to George II's aversion to granting peerages the request was unsuccessful 'notwithstanding the most pressing solicitations of my Lord Scarbrough, who, upon his application to her Majesty to use her good offices in favour of his brother, was answered, that she durst say no more to the King upon this head'.[2] Going into opposition, he voted against the Government on the civil list debate in 1729 and in all subsequent recorded divisions of that Parliament. He spoke frequently, chiefly in debates connected with the army and foreign affairs. In 1734 he made a speech against the excise bill, arguing that 'supposing that no tobacco be run, then it must be sold dearer . . . ; but if the tobacco be dearer, then the Dutch will run more upon you'.[3]

Re-elected unopposed for Lincolnshire without a contest in 1734, Saunderson continued to speak and vote with the Opposition. In 1737 he was among the Members of the House of Commons who were sounded by the Prince of Wales about an application to Parliament for an increase in his allowance.[4] Expressing hearty approval, he spoke for an increase in the ensuing debate and was rewarded with the post of treasurer to the Prince in 1738. In the debate on the convention in 1739 he spoke first for the Opposition, 'with a great deal of pompous nonsense' about Captain Jenkins and his ear.[5]

In 1740 Saunderson succeeded to the earldom of Scarbrough on the suicide of his elder brother, who left a will remitting 'to my brother Sir Thomas Saunderson any sum or sums of money he shall owe me at the time of my death and any annuity for his own or my own life which he may be engaged to pay me'; giving him £20,000 for the payment of his debts; and, subject to various other legacies, bequeathing all his real and personal estate to James Lumley. The new Earl did not conceal his disappointment at not succeeding to the family estates, taking the line that it was 'an ill return for the confidence he put in his brother when, being in the entail, so that without his consent the late earl could not dispose of it, he generously consented the cutting it off'.[6]

After Walpole's fall Scarbrough, along with the rest of the Prince's servants, supported the new Government, attending the Prince when he went to court on 17 Feb. 1742 and moving an address approving the Hanoverians on 1 Feb. 1743. He lost his post on Frederick's death, dying a year later, 15 Mar. 1752.

[1] E. Milner, *Recs. of the Lumleys*, 181, 188. [2] Coxe, *Walpole*, ii. 631. [3] *HMC Egmont Diary*, i. 126, 143, 171, 318, 349. [4] *Dodington Diary*, 444. [5] Coxe, iii. 519. [6] *HMC Egmont Diary*, iii. 107.

R.R.S.

LUTTRELL, Alexander (1705–37), of Dunster Castle and East Quantoxhead, nr. Minehead, Som.

MINEHEAD   1727–4 June 1737

b. 10 May 1705, 1st s. of Alexander Luttrell, M.P., by Dorothy, da. of Edward Yard of Churston Ferrers, Devon. *educ.* Ch. Ch. Oxf. 1722. *m.* 1726, Margaret, da. of Sir John Trevelyan, 2nd Bt. (q.v.), of Nettlecombe, Som., 1da. *suc.* fa. 1711.

The last male representative of a line which had been seated at Dunster Castle since 1375, Alexander Luttrell was returned as a Tory on his family's interest for Minehead at the first opportunity after coming of age, voting regularly against the Government. He died 4 June 1737, aged 32, leaving to his only child, a daughter, an estate so heavily indebted that it was put into Chancery. According to his daughter's husband, Henry Fownes Luttrell, the borough of Minehead was 'the rock which my father Luttrell foundered upon'.[1]

[1] H. C. Maxwell-Lyte, *Hist. Dunster*, i. 225–6, 233.

S.R.M.

II—Q

LUTWYCHE, Thomas (1674–1734), of the Inner Temple and Lutwyche Hall, Salop.

APPLEBY	1710–1722
CALLINGTON	1722–1727
AMERSHAM	23 Feb. 1728–13 Nov. 1734

bap. 21 Sept. 1674, 1st surv. s. of Edward Lutwyche, justice of common pleas, of Lutwyche Hall by Anne, da. of Sir Timothy Tourneur of Bold, Salop. *educ.* Westminster, K.S. 1688; Ch. Ch. Oxf. 1692; I. Temple, called 1697. *m.* Elizabeth, da. of William Bagnall of Bretforton, Worcs., 2s. 3da. *suc.* fa. 1709. Q.C. 1710.

An able Tory lawyer and a member of the October Club, returned for Appleby by Lord Thanet, Lutwyche voted against the Government in all recorded divisions after George I's accession, speaking against the peerage bill in 1719. In February 1721 he seconded a motion that the report of the secret committee inquiring into the South Sea Company should be printed. Returned for Callington in 1722, probably with the support of Sir John Coryton (q.v.), he opposed the bill of pains and penalties against George Kelly in March 1723, and in May attacked the bill for laying a tax on papist estates as an odious form of religious persecution. He was one of the managers of the trial of Lord Chancellor Macclesfield in 1725, when he was reported to have refused the attorney-general's place in succession to Sir Robert Raymond (q.v.).[1] He did not stand in 1727, but was returned next year for Amersham on the Drake interest, opposing the Address in January 1729, and speaking against the Hessians in February following. In the spring of 1732 he supported a bill to declare void the sale of the Derwentwater estates (see Bond, Denis) on the ground

that the fraud both of commissioners and purchasers appears so gross, that unless we would condemn all the bills that ever passed in this House from former times till now, reverse all forfeitures and attainders by Act of Parliament heretofore and never exercise the like power for the future, we ought to commit this bill.

In April 1733 he spoke in favour of rendering the Qualification Act more effective.[2] He died 13 Nov. 1734.

[1] *HMC Portland*, v. 614–15; vii. 407. [2] *HMC Egmont Diary*, . 261, 346.

E.C.

LUXBOROUGH, Baron, *see* KNIGHT, Robert.

LYMINGTON, Visct., *see* WALLOP, Hon. John

LYON, Hon. Thomas (1704–53).

FORFARSHIRE   1734–4 Jan. 1735

bap. 6 July 1704, 7th s. of John Lyon, 4th Earl of Strathmore [S], by Lady Elizabeth Stanhope, da. of Philip Stanhope, 2nd Earl of Chesterfield. *m.* 20 July 1736, Jean, da. and coh. of James Nicholson of West Rainton, co. Dur., 3s. 4da. *suc.* bro. as 8th Earl of Strathmore [S] 4 Jan. 1735.

Returned as a Tory on the Strathmore interest in 1734, Lyon vacated his seat next year on succeeding to the peerage. He died 18 Jan. 1753.

R.R.S.

LYSTER, Richard (?1692–1766), of Rowton Castle, Salop.

SHREWSBURY   1722–9 Apr. 1723, 1727–1734
SHROPSHIRE   11 Dec. 1740–13 Apr. 1766

b. ?1692, 1st s. of Thomas Lyster of Rowton Castle by Elizabeth, da. of Dr. William Beaw, bp. of Llandaff. *educ.* Shrewsbury; Ch. Ch. Oxf. 3 July 1708, aged 16; I. Temple 1708. *m.* Anne, da. of Robert Pigot of Chetwynd, Salop, 2s. 2da., all *d.v.p. suc.* fa. 1702.

A strong Tory and reputed Jacobite, Lyster was unseated for Shrewsbury on a party vote in 1723. On being called to order for a discourtesy to the House, he said: 'When you learn justice, I will learn manners'; but when it was proposed to bring him to the bar of the House Robert Walpole said 'Let him go, he has been hardly enough used'.[1] He was successful in 1727, but was defeated in 1734, after being the only Member to say 'No' to the motion for a grant to the Princess Royal on her marriage in 1733.[2] In 1740 he was returned unopposed for the county, the first Lyster to represent it although the family had been seated at Rowton since the end of the fifteenth century. Every known vote given by him in the House before 1754, was against the Government. He died 13 Apr. 1766.

[1] J. B. Blakeway, *Sheriffs of Shropshire*, 144–5. [2] *HMC Egmont Diary*, i. 371–2.

J.B.L.

LYTTELTON, George (1709–73), of Hagley Hall, Worcs.

OKEHAMPTON   28 Mar. 1735–18 Nov. 1756

b. 17 Jan. 1709, 1st s. of Sir Thomas Lyttelton, 4th Bt., and bro. of Richard and William Henry Lyttelton (qq.v.). *educ.* Eton 1725; Ch. Ch. Oxf. 1726; Grand Tour (Germany, France, Italy) 1728–30. *m.* (1) June 1742, Lucy (*d.* 19 Jan. 1747), da. of Hugh Fortescue, M.P., of Filleigh, Devon, 1s. 1da.; (2) 10 Aug. 1749, Elizabeth, da. of Sir Robert Rich, 4th Bt. (q.v.), of Ross Hall, Suff., *s.p. suc.* fa. as 5th Bt. 14 Sept. 1751; *cr.* Baron Lyttelton of Frankley 18 Nov. 1756.

Sec. to Frederick, Prince of Wales 1737–44; ld. of Treasury 1744–54; cofferer of the Household Mar. 1754–Nov. 1755; P.C. 21 June 1754; chancellor of the Exchequer Nov. 1755–Nov. 1756.

On Lyttelton's return from the grand tour he was introduced by Bubb Dodington (q.v.) to Frederick, Prince of Wales, with whom he became a great favourite. In 1734, at the instance of his uncle, Lord Cobham, who had broken with Walpole, he persuaded the Prince to replace Dodington, a member of the Government, by Chesterfield, one of the leaders of the Opposition, as his political adviser. Next year he was brought into Parliament by his brother-in-law, Thomas Pitt (q.v.), with whose brother, William, and his own cousin, Richard Grenville (qq.v.), he acted under Cobham's direction, forming a family group known as 'Cobham's Cubs'. With them he delivered a series of speeches against the Government, including a personal attack on Walpole for turning Cobham and William Pitt out of the army 'merely for voting as their consciences directed them in Parliament'. His appointment to be the Prince's secretary in 1737 was interpreted as a sign that Frederick intended to go into open opposition, for 'there was nobody more violent in the Opposition, nor anybody a more declared enemy to Sir Robert Walpole'. He is described about this time as

extremely tall and thin. His face was so ugly, his person so ill made and his carriage so awkward, that every feature was a blemish, every limb an incumbrance, and every motion a disgrace. But, as disagreeable as his figure was, his voice was still more so, and his address more disagreeable than either. He had a great flow of words that were always uttered in a lulling monotony, and the little meaning they had to boast of was generally borrowed from the commonplace maxims and sentiments of moralists, philosophers, patriots, and poets, crudely imbibed, half digested, ill put together, and confusedly refunded.[1]

After Walpole's fall, the Cobham group parted company with the Prince, who supported the new ministry, while they continued in active opposition. Nevertheless, Lyttelton retained his post with the Prince till the leaders of the Opposition came to terms with the Pelhams at the end of 1744, when he was appointed a lord of the Treasury. On this the Prince dismissed him, explaining, when Lyttelton pointed out that two of the Prince's servants, Lord Baltimore and Lord Archibald Hamilton, had been allowed to hold seats on the Admiralty board without forfeiting their places under him, that they 'had obtained their employments under the King *through him*, but that we had obtained ours *through others*, of whom he did not approve'. With the rest of the group he joined Pitt, who was still out of place, in harassing the Government at the end of 1745, but after Pitt's admission to office in February 1746 he returned to his allegiance, speaking so well in support of the bill abolishing hereditary jurisdictions in Scotland that Pelham 'begged him to recollect it and . . . have it printed that it might be sent down to Scotland: . . . to reconcile the minds of the Scotch to the bill'.[2]

In 1747 Lyttelton was re-elected for Okehampton, at the cost of a quarrel with the Prince, who had intended to nominate one of his servants for the seat.[3] In 1750 a negotiation for a reconciliation, involving Pitt, was begun but came to nothing owing to the Prince's death in 1751. Soon after this the negotiation leaked out through an insufficiently addressed letter from Lyttelton to his father, which was opened in the post office.[4]

Lyttelton continued a member of the family group till 1755, when he severed his connexion with it by refusing to follow Pitt into opposition. Left out of the Pitt–Newcastle ministry in 1757, he never again held office.

He died 22 Aug. 1773.

[1] Hervey, *Mems.* 386–8, 850–1; *HMC Egmont Diary*, ii. 351.
[2] M. Wyndham, *Chrons. of 18th Cent.* i. 193, 210. [3] See under OKEHAMPTON. [4] See ante, i. 59–60.

R.R.S.

LYTTELTON, Richard (1718–70), of Little Ealing, Mdx.

BRACKLEY 1747–1754
POOLE 1754–1761

b. 1718, 5th s. of Sir Thomas Lyttelton, 4th Bt., of Hagley Hall, Worcs. and bro. of George and William Henry Lyttelton (qq.v.). *educ.* prob. Marylebone sch.; at Besançon 1737–8. *m.* 23 Dec. 1745, Rachel, da. of Wriothesley Russell, 2nd Duke of Bedford, wid. of Scroop Egerton, 1st Duke of Bridgwater, *s.p.* K.B. 27 Aug. 1753.

Page of honour to Queen Caroline 1734–7; ensign 3 Ft. Gds. 1737; capt. 10 Marines 1741; lt.-col. 1744; col. 1747; master of the jewel office 1756–62; maj.-gen. 1757; lt.-gen. 1759; gov. Minorca 1762–6, Guernsey 1766–*d.*

Lyttelton served as a volunteer in the war of the Austrian succession, acting as aide-de-camp to Lord Stair at Dettingen and attending the Duke of Cumberland at Fontenoy. Failing to get the advancement he expected, he wrote home in July 1745: 'I am so discontented that if I could possibly live without the army I would not continue in it longer than this campaign'.[1] A few months later his whole position was changed by his marriage to the dowager Duchess of Bridgwater: 'she forty, plain, very rich, and with five children; he six and twenty, handsome, poor, and proper to get her five more'.[2] On the eve of his marriage, which proved a very happy one, he wrote to his father:

I have lived long enough in the world to think the bloom of youth an unnecessary ingredient in an agreeable woman . . . As to her circumstances, they are such as give me a fortune in the present beyond the utmost of my ambition, and secure me an independency hereafter to put an honest man above the frowns of a minister; whilst on the other hand the weight of her fortune and the interest of her brother and son, the Dukes of Bedford and Bridgwater, must contribute greatly to my advancement in the army if I choose to continue in it.

In 1746, seeing the Duke of Cumberland's favourites 'being put over his head,' he threatened to resign;[3] his wife appealed to her brother, the Duke of Bedford, to use his influence for her husband; and at last in April 1747 he was promoted colonel, a favour for which, he wrote to Bedford, 'I am solely indebted to your goodness'.[4]

At the general election of 1747 Lyttelton was returned for Brackley, which he controlled through his step-son, the young Duke of Bridgwater, still a schoolboy at Eton, living in the holidays with his mother. On 4 Mar. 1749 Horace Walpole wrote to Mann:

a great storm . . . was stirred up by Colonel Lyttelton, who, having been ill-treated by the Duke, has been dealing with the Prince. He discovered to the House some innovations in the mutiny bill, of which, though he could not make much, the Opposition have, and fought the bill for a whole fortnight; during the course of which the world has got much light into many very arbitrary proceedings of the commander-in-chief.

He renewed his vendetta against Cumberland in January 1751, on a government motion condemning a treasonable leaflet, in which the commander-in-chief was accused of planning to establish military government. Supporting a previous speaker, who had maintained that some of the charges made in the leaflet were not ungrounded, Lyttelton, 'with a greater command of absurdity',

told a long story of Colonel George Townshend's (q.v.) having been refused leave to stay in Norfolk, though he was cultivating the Whig interest, and an alarming history of the Duke's having placed two sentinels to guard the ruins of Haddocks Bagnio and the Rummer tavern at Charing Cross, which had been burnt down.[5]

On the Prince of Wales's death two months later Horace Walpole wrote (to Mann 1 Apr. 1751),

Dick Lyttelton, one of the patriot officers, had collected depositions on oath against the Duke for his behaviour in Scotland, but I suppose he will now throw the papers into Hamlet's grave.

Lyttelton now became involved in a bitter quarrel with his brother-in-law, the Duke of Bedford, over the custody of the young Duke of Bridgwater. On 13 Apr. 1751 he wrote to Bedford complaining that the young Duke's 'good disposition has been perverted . . . and estranged from us' and that there had been 'caballing' and 'wicked practices to set him against his mother'.[6] Rejecting these 'groundless imaginations', Bedford warned Lyttelton (14 Apr. 1751) that if he saw his nephew

> improperly used or treated at your house, I would as his next relation apply to Mr. Egerton, his guardian, to interpose the authority the late Duke of Bridgwater gave him and me to apply to the court of Chancery.

The upshot was that the custody of the young Duke was transferred from his mother to his uncle, who thereby gained control of the borough of Brackley.[7] Soon afterwards Lyttelton made his peace with Pelham, who found him another seat at Poole in 1754.

He died 1 Oct. 1770.

[1] M. Wyndham, *Chrons. of 18th Cent.* i. 112–135, 136. [2] Walpole to Mann, 20 Dec. 1745. [3] Wyndham, i. 137, 205. [4] *Bedford Corresp.* i. 112, 208. [5] Walpole, *Mems. Geo. II*, i. 10–11. [6] Bedford mss. [7] Ld. Camelford, 'Family Characters and Anecdotes', Boconnoc mss.

R.R.S.

LYTTELTON, Sir Thomas, 4th Bt. (1686–1751), of Hagley Hall, Worcs.

WORCESTERSHIRE   6 Mar. 1721–1734
CAMELFORD   1734–1741

> *b.* 1686, 1st surv. s. of Sir Charles Lyttelton, 3rd Bt., M.P., by Anne, da. of Thomas Temple of Frankton, Warws. *m.* 8 May 1708, Christian, da. of Sir Richard Temple, 3rd Bt., M.P., 6s. 6da. *suc.* fa. 1716.
> Ld. of Admiralty 1727–41.

Lyttelton was returned in the Whig interest for his county, which he represented without opposition during the next two Parliaments. His political career was epitomized by his cousin, Sarah Duchess of Marlborough, who wrote in 1733: 'Sir Thomas Lyttelton has always voted as he is directed; and 'twas for that reason, I imagine, he has an employment he can know nothing about'. His vote for the excise bill cost him his seat for the county in 1734, when he gave up before the poll, but he was brought in for Camelford by his son-in-law, Thomas Pitt (q.v.).[1] He remained in office till 1741 when, having agreed to support his eldest son, George (q.v.), a prominent member of the Opposition, in standing for the county, he retired with a pension of £1,000 p.a.[2]

Lyttelton's wife was the sister of Sir Richard Temple, 4th Bt., M.P., afterwards 1st Viscount Cobham, and of Hester, wife of Richard Grenville (q.v.). His eldest daughter, Christian, married Thomas Pitt (q.v.), elder brother of William Pitt (q.v.). His children, of whom George, Richard, and William Henry became M.P.s, were thus first cousins of Richard, George, James, Henry and

Thomas Grenville (qq.v.) and connected by marriage with Thomas and William Pitt.

He died 14 Sept. 1751.

[1] M. Wyndham, *Chrons. of 18th Cent.* i. xx, 35, 39. [2] Ibid. 83 seq.; Walpole, *Mems. Geo. II*, i. 201 n.3.

R.R.S.

LYTTELTON, William Henry (1724–1808).

BEWDLEY   9 Dec. 1748–23 Jan. 1755, 1774–1790

> *b.* 24 Dec. 1724, 6th s. of Sir Thomas Lyttelton, 4th Bt., and bro. of George and Richard Lyttelton (qq.v.). *educ.* Eton c.1740; St. Mary Hall Oxf. 1742; Grand Tour; M. Temple 1743, called 1748. *m.* (1) 2 June 1761, Mary (*d.* 28 May 1765), da. and coh. of James Macartney of Longford, Ireland, 2s. 1da.; (2) 19 Feb. 1774, Caroline, da. of John Bristowe (q.v.) of Quidenham, Norf., 5s. 1da. *cr.* Baron Westcote [I] 29 July 1776; *suc.* nephew, Thomas Lyttelton, M.P., 2nd Baron Lyttelton, as 7th Bt. 27 Nov. 1779; *cr.* Baron Lyttelton 13 Aug. 1794.
> Sub-cofferer of the Household 1754–5; gov. S. Carolina 1755–60, Jamaica 1760–66; envoy to Lisbon 1766–71; ld. of Treasury 1777–82.

William Lyttelton was said by Dr. Johnson to have more chaff than grain in him, as everything had that grew to such a prodigious length. After a foreign tour with Henry Thrale, the brewer, whose father paid all expenses,[1] he persuaded his father, with the eloquent support of William Pitt, to allow him to give up the bar and to bring him in for an impending vacancy at Bewdley, not far from Hagley.

> I have long seen in his mind [Pitt wrote to Sir Thomas Lyttelton] the promise of very particular talents for the business of the world, accompanied with a sound judgement; and particularly have always marked and loved in him the strong seeds of honour and virtue in his heart. All these, Sir Thomas, are now ripening, or rather ripened for action, and it would be ten thousand pities should they be stifled, for a long time at least, and perhaps entirely lost, in the inglorious and unprofitable labours of Westminster Hall.

He added

> Nothing can be kinder and more flattering to me than your thinking of putting him under, as you are pleased to call it, my protection. If I can be of any little use to him at his beginning in our parliamentary warfare, be assured it will be a most sensible pleasure to me. Should he on any occasion want direction, he will always find the surest and best in his brother Lyttelton. The director and pupil are most worthy of each other, and you, dear Sir Thomas, of the comfort of both.[2]

Lyttelton's only recorded speech in his first Parliament was in answer to Sir John Hynde Cotton's motion on 27 Nov. 1751 to reduce the army to 15,000.[3] He died 14 Sept. 1808.

[1] *Thraliana*, i. 200, 300. [2] M. Wyndham, *Chrons. of 18th Cent.* ii. 1–3. [3] Walpole, *Mems. Geo. II*, i. 213.

R.R.S.

LYTTON, John Robinson (1724–62), of Knebworth, Herts.

BISHOP'S CASTLE 1747–1754

bap. 30 Sept. 1724, 1st surv. s. of William Robinson Lytton of Knebworth by Elizabeth, da. and h. of Giles Heysham of Stagenhoe, Herts. *educ.* Jesus, Oxf. 1741, D.C.L. 1746. *m.* 12 Apr. 1744, Leonora, da. and h. of Humphrey Brereton of Borras, Denb., 1da. *d.v.p.* *suc.* fa. 1732.

Sheriff, Herts. 1758–9.

Lytton, who does not appear to have had any Shropshire connexions, was returned for Bishop's Castle soon after marrying a wife said to have a fortune of £50,000.[1] His D.C.L. Oxford shows him to have been a Tory and in the 1747 Parliament he was classed as Opposition. He died April 1762.

[1] *Gent. Mag.* 1744, p. 227.

J.B.L.

MACKAY, Hon. George (c.1715–82), of Skibo, Sutherland.

SUTHERLAND 1747–1761

b. c.1715, 3rd s. of George Mackay, 3rd Lord Reay [S], by his 3rd w. Mary, da. of John Doull (or Dowell) of Thuster, Caithness. *educ.* ?Aberdeen Univ. M.A. 1730; *adv.* 1737. *m.* 13 Dec. 1766, Anne, da. of Eric Sutherland, o.s. of the attainted 3rd Lord Duffus [S], 5s. 4da. (his 2nd and 3rd sons suc. as 7th and 8th Lord Reay[S]).

Capt. independent co. of Ft. 1745; capt. Lord Loudoun's Ft. 1746; ret. 1748.

Master of the mint [S] 1756.

In 1741 Mackay stood unsuccessfully for Sutherland against General James St. Clair (q.v.), who was supported by his nephew, the Earl of Sutherland. In 1745, under the threat of rebellion, his father made proposals to the Earl of Sutherland for a bond of friendship. In formal documents signed at Tongue and Dunrobin in July 1745 they pledged themselves to bury all differences 'in everlasting oblivion', to unite in the King's cause, and to act 'in mutual concert' in all future parliamentary elections.[1]

During the rebellion Mackay, as captain of an independent company raised by his father, distinguished himself in March 1746 in the action near Tongue, resulting in the capture of recently landed French money, for which he obtained a regular commission[2] with Pelham's assistance. In 1747, prompted by his father, he obtained 'the ministry's approbation' of his candidature for Sutherland. St. Clair agreed to withdraw, but subsequently, joined by Sir John Gordon (q.v.) and supported by the Sutherland interest, 'contrary to concert' stood against Mackay, who complained to Pelham: 'I submit to you if it was fair'. When, however, Mackay was returned, Argyll wrote to Pelham: 'I fear in point of right he has the wrong end of the string'.[3] In Newcastle's secret service accounts for 1754–6 he is shown as receiving a secret service pension of £300 a year which may have been a continuation of his father's pension.[4]

He died 25 June 1782.

[1] Angus Mackay, *Bk. of Mackay*, 186–7, 450–3. [2] *More Culloden Pprs.* iv. 66, 91; *Bk. of Mackay*, 190; Reay to Pelham, 1 Aug. 1747, Newcastle (Clumber) mss. [3] Reay to Pelham, 17 June, 1 Aug. 1747; Argyll to Pelham, 23 July, 6 Aug. 1747; G. Mackay to Pelham, 31 July 1747, ibid. [4] Namier, *Structure*, 217, 220; *HMC Polwarth*, v. 110–12.

E.H.-G.

MACKENZIE, Sir George, 4th Bt. (c.1702–48), of Cromarty and Grandvale.

CROMARTYSHIRE 25 Mar. 1729–1734

b. c.1702, 1st s. of Hon. Sir Kenneth Mackenzie, 3rd Bt. (q.v.), of Cromarty by his 2nd w. *m.* c.1747, Elizabeth Reid, sis. of Capt. John Reid of Greenwich, *s.p.* *suc.* fa. 13 Sept. 1728.

Mackenzie succeeded his father as Member for Cromartyshire in 1729, voting with the Administration on the army in 1732, but against them on the excise bill in 1733 and the repeal of the Septennial Act in 1734. He did not stand again. Becoming bankrupt, he sold the estate of Cromarty in 1741. During the Forty-five he remained loyal to the Government, although his cousin, the 3rd Earl of Cromartie, joined the rising. He died 20 May 1748.

[1] Sir W. Fraser, *Earls of Cromartie*, ii. 415, 417.

P.W.

MACKENZIE, Hon. Sir Kenneth, 3rd Bt. (c.1658–1728), of Cromarty and Grandvale.

SCOTLAND 1707–1708
CROMARTYSHIRE 1710–1713, 1727–13 Sept. 1728

b. c.1658, 2nd s. of George Mackenzie, 1st Earl of Cromartie [S], by Anna, da. of Sir James Sinclair, 1st Bt., of Canisbay and Mey, Caithness. *educ.* Aberdeen Univ. 1679. *m.* (1) Mary, sis. of David Kinnear of Kinnear, *s.p.*; (2) 1701, Anne Campbell, 6s. 2da.; (3) contract 14 Jan. 1726, Elizabeth Edwards of Monmouth, wid. of Alexander Sutherland of Kinminitie, Banff., and bef. that of Charles Graydon, *s.p.*[1] *cr.* Bt. [S] with precedency of the original patent of 1628 on his fa.'s resignation of the baronetcy 29 Apr. 1704.

M.P. [S] Cromartyshire 1693–1707.

Mackenzie's father gave him the estate of Cromarty soon after 1685 and resigned the baronetcy to him in 1704. Returned in 1727 as a government supporter[2] for Cromartyshire, which he had represented under Anne, he died shortly afterwards, 13 Sept. 1728.

[1] *Scots Peerage*, iii. 76, 204; ix. 63, 69. [2] *HMC Polwarth*, v. 54–55.

P.W.

MACKENZIE, Kenneth (1717–61), of Seaforth.

INVERNESS BURGHS   1741–1747
ROSS-SHIRE   1747–1761

b. Nov. 1717, 1st s. of William, 5th Earl of Seaforth [S] (attainted 1716), by Mary, da. and h. of Nicholas Kennett of Coxhoe, co. Dur. *educ.* partly in France under Jesuits. *m.* 11 Sept. 1741, Lady Mary Stewart (*d.* 1751), da. of Alexander, 6th Earl of Galloway [S], niece of George, 9th Earl Marischal [S], 1s. 6da. *suc.* fa. 8 Jan. 1740.

Mackenzie, commonly known as Lord Fortrose, was the son of a Roman Catholic Jacobite, who had forfeited his estates and title for taking part in the Fifteen rebellion, was pardoned in 1726, and died in 1740. In 1741 a kinswoman wrote:

> Lord Fortrose has given up his religion, his king, and country at once and is a great courtier, as no doubt you'll know by his election affairs; what Ross folks may think of this I know not.[1]

Placing his considerable influence in Ross-shire, Inverness-shire and Inverness Burghs at the disposal of the Government, he was brought into Parliament with the support of Lord Ilay, Walpole's electoral manager in Scotland,[2] and allowed to buy back the forfeited Seaforth estates for £25,000.[3]

Put down as 'Pelham' in the Cockpit list of October 1742, he voted with the Government on the Hanoverians in December of that year and in 1744, but was absent from the division on them in 1746, when he was classed as Old Whig. During the Forty-five he took an active part against the rebels, raising two independent companies from his clan, though his cousin, George Mackenzie, 3rd Earl of Cromartie, joined the rising.[4] From 1747 he was returned for his county, attaching himself to the Pelhams rather than Ilay, now Duke of Argyll, as more likely to secure the restoration of the title. He died without having achieved this, 18 Oct. 1761.

[1] Add. 39190, f. 27. [2] See MUNRO, Robert. [3] A. Mackenzie, *Hist. Mackenzies*, 316. [4] *More Culloden Pprs.* iv. 68, 117, 126, 153, 193; v. 12.

P.W.

MACKENZIE, *see also* STUART MACKENZIE

MACKWORTH, Herbert (1687–1765), of Gnoll, Glam.

CARDIFF BOROUGHS   16 Feb. 1739–20 Aug. 1765

b. 7 Sept. 1687, 1st s. of Sir Humphrey Mackworth, M.P., of Gnoll by Mary, da. and h. of Sir Herbert Evans of Gnoll; bro. of William Mackworth Praed (q.v.). *educ.* Westminster; Magdalen Oxf. 1704; I. Temple 1708. *m.* 24 Apr. 1730,[1] Juliana, da. of William Digby, M.P., 5th Baron Digby of Geashill [I], 1s. 6da. *suc.* fa. 1727.

Herbert Mackworth, of an old Derbyshire and Shropshire family, inherited through his mother large estates in Glamorgan and Monmouthshire. These included coalmines and several industrial enterprises together with the Gnoll copper works at Neath, which he himself further developed.[2] He owed his election for Cardiff to the Windsor interest and his own control of Neath and Aberavon, two boroughs within the constituency. Returned unopposed as a Tory, he voted consistently against the Administration, except on the motion for Walpole's removal, 13 Feb. 1741, when he was one of the Tories who voted against the motion. He died 20 Aug. 1765.

[1] *Hist. Reg.* 1730, chron. p. 33. [2] D. Rhys Phillips, *Hist. Vale of Neath*, 227, 238, 268–80, 310.

P.D.G.T.

MACKWORTH, Sir Thomas, 4th Bt. (*d.* 1745), of Normanton, Rutland.

RUTLAND   17 Dec. 1694–1695, 1701–1708
PORTSMOUTH   1713–1715
RUTLAND   5 Apr. 1721–1727

o. surv. s. of Sir Thomas Mackworth, 3rd Bt., M.P., by his 2nd w. Anne, da. of Col. Humphrey Mackworth, M.P., of Betton, Salop. *unm. suc.* fa. Nov. 1694.

Sheriff, Rutland 1696–7.

Of an ancient Rutland family, Mackworth's father fought on the King's side in the civil war, went into exile in the Netherlands, and represented his county from 1679 until his death. Returned for Rutland unopposed as a Tory at a by-election in 1721, Mackworth headed the poll in 1722, but was ruined by the expense of the contest. Next year his estates were sold by order of the court of Chancery to pay his debts, Normanton being bought subsequently by Sir Gilbert Heathcote (q.v.).[1] In the winter of 1729 he was in Paris, where he told a Jacobite that

> if the King [the Pretender] were Protestant or dissembled to be one, or brought up his son one, his restoration would be secure . . . the present government will entirely ruin them in all things and . . . if the King had 5,000 or 6,000 good troops, they'd beat the 18,000 they have now in England, if they would not all desert over to him.[2]

He died at Kentish Town in February 1745, leaving his London property in trust to his illegitimate son, Thomas Mackworth.[3]

[1] Blore, *Rutland*, 132–3. [2] Stuart mss 132/59. [3] PCC 51 Seymer.

E.C.

MACKWORTH PRAED, William (1694–1752), of Trevethoe, nr. St. Ives, Cornw.

ST. IVES   1734–1741

b. 3 Nov. 1694, 3rd s. of Sir Humphrey Mackworth, M.P., and bro. of Herbert Mackworth (q.v.). *educ.* M. Temple 1709. *m.* 19 Jan. 1715 (with £4,000), Ann, da. and h. of Robert Slaney of Rudge, Salop, 4s. 2da.

In 1714 John Praed, M.P. St. Ives 1708-13, finding himself in financial difficulties, came to an agreement with Sir Humphrey Mackworth, M.P., a successful lawyer, under which Mackworth was to pay Praed's debts, on condition that Praed, who was unmarried, arranged a match between his great-niece, Bridget Penrose, the heiress-at-law to the Praed estates, and Mackworth's son, William. When the scheme fell through, owing to the objection of the Penrose family, Praed arranged for young Mackworth to marry the daughter of a Bristol merchant, half of whose dowry went to pay off Praed's debts, in return for which Praed on the marriage day executed an indenture adopting William Mackworth as his son and heir, subject to his assuming the name of Praed. On Praed's death in 1717 both Mackworth Praed and the Penroses laid claim to the estates. After prolonged legal proceedings an agreement was reached in 1733, under which Mackworth Praed secured the Trevethoe estate, carrying an interest at St. Ives.[1] Returned next year for St. Ives as a Tory, he voted against the Spanish convention in 1739, was absent from the division on the place bill in 1740, and was one of the Tories who voted against the motion for Walpole's removal in 1741. He did not stand again, dying before May 1752.

[1] *Parochial Hist. of Cornw.* iii. 101; G. C. Boase, *Collectanea Cornubiensia*, 756-8; Add. 36178, ff. 285-95.

E.C.

MACKYE, John (1707-97), of Palgowan, Kirkcudbright.

LINLITHGOW BURGHS   25 Jan. 1742-1747
KIRKCUDBRIGHT STEWARTRY   1747-1768

b. 23 Apr. 1707, o.s. of Alexander Mackye, or McKie, M.P. [S], of Larg and Palgowan by Christian, 2nd da. of Sir James Dunbar, 1st Bt., of Mochrum, wid. of Maj. Thomas Young of Leny, Wigtown. *educ.* ?Edinburgh Univ.; Leyden 1728; adv. 1731. *m.* 28 July 1755, Jane, 1st da. of George Ross, 13th Lord Ross [S], sis. and h. of William, 14th Lord Ross [S] (whom she suc. 1754), *s.p.* suc. fa. 1733; assumed add. name of Ross before Mackye 1755.
Treasurer of the Ordnance 1763-80; receiver gen. of stamp duties 1780-94.

One of the group known as the Duke of Argyll's gang,[1] Mackye voted with the Opposition in all recorded divisions. At the 1747 election he moved to the county where, with the backing of the Duke of Queensberry and Lord Selkirk and, surprisingly, with that of the lord justice clerk, Andrew Fletcher

(Lord Milton), he ousted a government candidate, who was supported by Fletcher's master, the former Lord Ilay, now 3rd Duke of Argyll.[2] Continuing in opposition throughout this Parliament,[3] he subsequently attached himself to Lord Bute, to whom he acted as private secretary. He died in October 1797.

[1] John Drummond to Ld. Morton, 2 and 4 Dec. 1742, Morton mss, SRO. [2] Argyll to Pelham, 23, 26 July, 1 Aug. 1747; John Maxwell to Pelham, 4 Aug. 1747, Newcastle (Clumber) mss, [3] List of 21 Mar. 1754, ibid.

R.S.L.

MACLEOD, Norman (1706-72), of Dunvegan, Skye.

INVERNESS-SHIRE   1741-1754

b. 1706, 1st surv. s. of Norman Macleod of Macleod by Anne, da. of Hugh Fraser, 9th Lord Lovat [S]. *m.* (1) c.1726, Janet (*d.* 1741), da. of Sir Donald Macdonald, 4th Bt. [S], of Sleat, Skye, 1s. 2da.; (2) post nupt. contract 1748, Anne, da. of William Martin of Inchture, Perth, 1s. 3da. *suc.* fa. 1706.
Gentleman of the police [S] 1754-64.

A posthumous son, Macleod succeeded his father as head of one of the most powerful of the Highland clans. During his minority the estates were managed by his tutor, John Macleod of Contullich, an active Jacobite agent, in recognition of whose service young Macleod was created a baron in the Jacobite peerage in 1716.[1]

In 1739, Macleod and his neighbour and kinsman, Sir Alexander Macdonald of Sleat, who had devised a scheme of deporting some of their tenants to be sold in the American plantations, were threatened with prosecution when it was found that these unfortunates, many of them women and small children, had not been convicted of any crimes punishable by transportation. Macleod appealed to his friend Duncan Forbes (q.v.), the lord president:

> You know better than I that were we never so innocent, a prosecution would be attended with a multitude of inconveniences, and ought in my weak judgment to be shunned if possible. You not only know best if it can be shunned but likewise the proper means how to shun it and are the only person in earth we would mostly, nay entirely, rely on, do therefore in God's name what you think best for us.[2]

No proceedings were brought against them. In 1741 Macleod was elected for Inverness-shire with the support of his cousin, Lord Lovat, and that of Duncan Forbes, voting consistently against the Administration with the group of Scotch Members known as the Duke of Argyll's gang.

In 1740 Lord Lovat, who was negotiating for French support in bringing about a restoration of the Stuarts (see Erskine, James), sent Macleod's name to the French as one of the chiefs whom he thought would join a rising. After the fiasco of the French expedition of February 1744 (see Barry, James), the Young Pretender began to consider the possibility of a rising without foreign help. In November 1744 the leading Jacobites of Scotland held consultations, at which Macleod was said to have been among those undertaking to raise their clans even if the Prince came without regular troops. According to Murray of Broughton, the Jacobite agent in Scotland, Macleod was given a letter from the Young Pretender, with power to treat with others in support of the cause, and was informed of the Prince's impending arrival in May 1745, arranging to post his people on the island of Uist to watch and answer signals.[3] On 25 June he reported to Duncan Forbes an 'extra-ordinary rumour . . . that the Pretender's eldest son was to land somewhere in the Highlands', adding in a subsequent letter that he was having spies posted, though he himself thought the project 'entirely defeated and blown into air'.[4] Shortly after landing in July, the Young Pretender sent for Macleod, from whom a few days later he received a messenger asking 'if the Prince had a power signed by the King his father'. Having given satisfaction on this point, the Prince expected Macleod to join him shortly.[5] On 3 Aug. Macleod wrote to Forbes:

> To my no small surprise, it is certain that the pre-tended Prince of Wales is come on the coast of South Uist . . . The Duke of Atholl's brother is the only man of any sort of note . . . that I can hear of that's alongst with him . . . Sir Alexander Macdonald and I, not only gave no sort of countenance to these people, but we used all the interest we had with our neighbours to follow the same prudent method; and I am persuaded we have done it with that success that not one man of any consequence benorth the Grampians will give any sort of assistance to this mad rebellious attempt . . . As it can be of no use to the public to know whence you have this information, it is, I fancy, needless to mention either of us but this we leave in your own breast, as you are a much better judge of what is or is not proper to be done.

Eight days later, Macdonald informed Forbes that many chiefs were now joining the rebellion, adding:

> You may believe, my Lord, our spirits are in a good deal of agitation and that we are much at a loss how to behave in so extraordinary an occurrence. That we will have no connection with these madmen is certain, but are bewildered in every other respect till we hear from you . . . I pledge Macleod in writing for him and myself.[6]

After Prestonpans the Young Pretender sent again to Macleod,[7] and to Lovat, who was preparing to send the Frasers under his son, the Master of Lovat, to join the rebels. Forbes then devised with Macleod a subterfuge to delay, and if possible to prevent, the Frasers from coming out. Macleod met Lovat, who reported after the interview:

> He swore to me that he should answer to God, and wished that God might never have mercy on him, and that he might never enter into the kingdom of heaven but that his bones might rot on earth, be burnt and his ashes blown up in the air, if he did not come with all speed imaginable, and with all his men that was already prepared, and come and join my son, and the clan Fraser, and march south with them to the Prince's service, wherever he was.[8]

In return, Lovat promised that the Frasers would not march without the Macleods. After waiting and reminding Macleod of his engagements, Lovat sent the Frasers out at the end of November. Macleod was then given commissions by Forbes to raise four independent companies of 100 men each from his clan on behalf of the Government. Sent to expel the rebels from Aberdeenshire, he was defeated by them at Inverury on 23 Dec. Early in the new year, hearing that the Prince's followers had vowed to capture him, he fled to Skye. After their defeat at Culloden, he took part in driving the cattle and burning the houses of their leaders, writing to Skye that if the Prince were found, he should be given up in order to claim the reward on his head. At Lovat's trial in 1747, evidence was given relating to Macleod's activities in the rebellion. Though expected to take up the accusations, he did not do so.[9]

Macleod was absent from the division on the Hanoverians in 1746, when he was classed as 'doubtful'. He was opposed to the bill banning Highland dress, and voted against the bill abolishing hereditary jurisdictions in Scotland. Re-elected in 1747 with the support of the Administration, he was one of the few of his compatriots who voted for the rejection of the petition against General Anstruther (q.v.) on 5 Mar. 1751. He retired in 1754 with a sinecure worth £400 p.a., of which he was deprived by Bute in 1764. He lived away from the 'implacable illwill and malice' of his Jacobite clansmen, who believed 'that he had not only deserted but betrayed their cause'. A gambler and a drunkard, he died deep in debt 21 Feb. 1772.[10]

[1] R. C. Macleod, *Macleods*, 25; *HMC Stuart*, iii. 370, and vols, v, vi, vii. [2] W. C. Mackenzie, *Western Isles*, 45–48; I. F. Grant, *Macleods*, 404–9; *More Culloden Pprs.* iii. 141. [3] Murray of Broughton, *Memorials* (Sc. Hist. Soc. xxvii), 108–9, 112, 143–5, 423, 428, 466; Lord Elcho, *Affairs of Scotland*, 1744–6, p. 63. [4] *More Culloden Pprs.* iv. 10, 12. [5] Butler to Duke of Ormonde, Aug. 1745; A. and H. Tayler, *Stuart Pprs. at Windsor*, 138–9. [6] *Culloden Pprs.* 203–4, 207. [7] W. B. Blaikie, *Itinerary of Prince Charles Edward Stuart* (Sc. Hist. Soc. xxiii), 18. [8] Howell's *State Trials*, xviii. 754–5. [9] *More Culloden Pprs.* iv. 80–87; v. 45–47, 83; Grant, 461; *HMC Polwarth*, v. 213. [10] *More Culloden Pprs.* v. 112–13; Grant, 64, 463, 494–8; Walpole, *Mems. Geo. II*, i. 60; *The Highlands of Scotland in 1750*, p. 48.

E.C.

MADAN, Martin (1700–56), of New Bond St., London.

WOOTTON BASSETT 1747–1754

b. 1 July 1700,[1] 1st s. of Martin Madan of Nevis, West Indies by Penelope, da and coh. of Col. Sir James Russell, member of the council of Nevis. *educ.* perhaps Westminster 1714 and in London under Dr. Samuel Dunster; Trinity, Camb. 1716. *m.* 14 Dec. 1723, Judith, the poetess, da. of Spencer Cowper (q.v.) of Hertingfordbury, Herts., 7s. 2da. *suc.* fa. 1704.

Lt. and capt. Coldstream Gds. 1717; capt. 1 Drag. Gds. 1721, maj. 1734, lt.-col. 1742–6; equerry to Frederick, Prince of Wales 1736–49; groom of the bedchamber to the Prince 1749–51.

Martin Madan's father, of an old Waterford family, emigrated from Ireland to the West Indies about 1682 and acquired plantations in Nevis and St. Kitts. His sister Penelope married Augustus Schutz, master of the robes and keeper of the privy purse to George II, whose brother Col. John Schutz was groom of the bedchamber to Frederick, Prince of Wales. His wife was niece to Lord Chancellor Cowper.

For 29 years Madan was a professional soldier, commanding his regiment at Dettingen (1743) and Fontenoy (1745). On his appointment to the Prince's household he wrote to his wife, 6 May 1736:

> The noble manner the Prince has conferred this honour on me very much enhances its value. His Royal Highness did not know Sir William Irby [q.v.] was to be appointed chamberlain till the King sent him a message as he was dressing. He . . . immediately turned to [James] Lumley [q.v.] and said 'Now I have an opportunity to provide for Madan: write to him and let him know I have not forgot him'.[1]

On retiring from the army Madan was defeated at Bridport in 1746 but was returned at the general election of 1747 for Wootton Bassett as a supporter of the Prince of Wales.[2] While doing a tour of duty with the Prince, he wrote from Cliveden, 17 Sept. 1747:

> Do but imagine my poor lame feet trudging after my master from eight in the morning till 4 or 5 in the afternoon. And then . . . dinner is ready, his R.H. sets himself down with us, we eat heartily, drink in proportion and are very merry till about nine, when we adjourn to dress, and play at cards with their R. Highnesses till between 12 and one, then supper is served up, and about two we repair to our beds to recover our spirits.

A martyr to gout, he had a fit on 15 July 1753 and did not stand again for Parliament.[3] He died 4 Mar. 1756.

[1] F. Madan, *Madan Fam.* 73, 80, 82, 94–96. [2] *HMC Fortescue*, i. 117–18. [3] Madan, 83, 93.

R.S.L.

MAISTER, Henry (1699–1744), of Hull and Winestead, Yorks.

KINGSTON-UPON-HULL 6 Feb. 1734–1741

bap. 1 Feb. 1699, 1st s. of William Maister (q.v.). *m.* (1) 25 Aug. 1724, Mary (*d.* 1725), da. of Rev. Henry Tymperon of Carnaby, Yorks., *s.p.*; (2) 19 Jan. 1727, Mary, da. of Sir Arthur Cayley, 3rd Bt., of Brompton, Yorks., 3s. 1da. *suc.* fa. 1716.

Sheriff, Hull 1727.

Returned for Hull at a by-election in 1734 and re-elected at the ensuing general election, Henry Maister voted regularly with the Government. He did not stand in 1741. In 1743 he lost his wife and two children in a fire which destroyed his house at Hull.[1] He died 15 Dec. 1744.

[1] *Gent. Mag.* 1743, p. 217.

R.R.S.

MAISTER, William (aft.1660–1716), of Hull, Yorks.

KINGSTON-UPON-HULL 1701–28 Oct. 1716

b. aft. 1660, 1st s. of Henry Maister, alderman, chamberlain and mayor of Hull, dep. gov. of E.I. and Hamburg companies, by Anne, da. of William Raikes, alderman and chamberlain of Hull and warden of Trinity House.[1] *m.* aft. Feb. 1696, Lucy, da. of Alderman John Rogers of Hull, sis. of Nathaniel Rogers (q.v.) and wid. of George Dickinson, collector of customs, Hull, 4s. 1da.[2] *suc.* fa. 1699.

Sheriff, Hull, 1699.

William Maister belonged to a leading merchant family of Hull, which he represented as a Whig in eight successive Parliaments till his death, 28 Oct. 1716.

[1] *Paver's Marriage Licences* (Yorks. Arch. Soc xliii), ii.2; J. Foster, *Ped. of Raikes*. [2] *Cal. Treas. Bks.* x. 253, 1300; Poulson, *Holderness*, ii. 445.

R.R.S.

MAITLAND, Charles (c.1708–51), of Pittrichie, Aberdeen.

ABERDEEN BURGHS 30 Apr. 1748–16 Feb. 1751

b. c.1704, o.s. of Hon. Alexander Arbuthnott, afterwards Maitland, M.P. [S], baron of the Exchequer [S] (3rd s. of the 2nd Visct. Arbuthnott [S]), by Jean, da. of Sir Charles Maitland, 3rd Bt., M.P. [S], sis. and h. of Sir Charles Maitland, 4th Bt., of Pittrichie. *educ.* adv. 1727. *unm.* *suc.* fa. June 1721.

Sheriff, Edinburgh 1747–8.

On 23 July 1747 the Duke of Argyll reported to Henry Pelham that at the election for Aberdeen Burghs

> Mr. Maitland, the great favourite, appeared there as delegate from the town [Inverbervie] of Lord Arbuthnott, a non-juror. I am informed that this Mr. Maitland did lately give most false account of the late poll election at Brechin to the Earl of Morton, which his Lordship was to send you.[1]

At a by-election for Aberdeen Burghs in 1748 Maitland was returned on the interest of his first cousin, Lord Arbuthnott, defeating David Scott (q.v.), the ministerial candidate. In 1750 Lord Morton told Newcastle that some time ago Maitland had been talked of for the next vacancy in the court of session but that now he seemed to have been dropped.[2] He died a year later, 13 Nov. 1751.

[1] Newcastle (Clumber) mss. [2] Add. 32723, f. 322.

R.R.S.

MALPAS, Visct., see CHOLMONDELEY, Hon. George

MANESTY, Sprig (d. 1728), of Woodford, Essex.

QUEENBOROUGH 1727–29 Sept. 1728

m. (1) 25 Apr. 1703, Agnes (bur. 19 Mar. 1718), da. of Andrew Crawley of Clapham, 1s. 2da. all d.v.p.;[1] (2) Anne Miller, 2s. 1da.

Sec. board of victualling 1705–27; commr. of victualling 1727–d.; manager, Sun Fire Office 1725–d.; assistant, R. African Co. 1727–d.

Brought in on the government interest at Queenborough in 1727, Manesty died 29 Sept. 1728, and was buried in his father-in-law's vault at Clapham.

[1] Ex. inf. Eric E. F. Smith, hon. sec. London and Mdx. Arch. Soc.

R.R.S.

MANNERS, John, Mq. of Granby (1696–1779).

RUTLAND 21 Jan. 1719–22 Feb. 1721

b. 21 Oct. 1696, 1st s. of John Manners, M.P., 2nd Duke of Rutland, by his 1st w. Catherine, da. of William Russell, M.P., Lord Russell, and sis. of Wriothesley, 2nd Duke of Bedford; bro. of Lord Robert, Lord Sherard and Lord William Manners (qq.v.). educ. perhaps Eton c.1707. m. 27 Aug. 1717, Bridget, da. and eventually h. of Robert Sutton, 2nd Baron Lexinton of Aram, 5s. 6da. suc. fa. as 3rd Duke 22 Feb. 1721. K.G. 13 Nov. 1722.

Ld. lt. Leics. 1721–d.; ld. of the bedchamber 1721–7; P.C. 17 July 1727; chancellor of duchy of Lancaster 1727–36; ld. steward of the Household 1754–61; one of lords justices Apr.–Sept. 1755; master of the horse 1761–6.

Returned for Rutland in 1719, Granby voted for the peerage bill. In 1721 he succeeded to the dukedom, carrying an extensive electoral interest in Rutland and Leicestershire, as well as the control of one seat at Grantham. The death of his father-in-law, Lord Lexinton, in 1723, brought him further electoral influence in Nottinghamshire, where he controlled one seat at Newark. A lord of the bedchamber under George I, he was promoted on George II's accession to the chancellorship of the duchy of Lancaster, which he resigned in 1736 on

being rebuked by the King for disposing of a duchy office without obtaining royal approval.[1] Going into opposition, he voted in the Lords against the Government, eventually attaching himself to the Prince of Wales, in whose shadow cabinet he figures as lord chamberlain. After Frederick's death in 1751 Henry Pelham, who had married Rutland's sister, tried to persuade the King to win over the Manners family by giving the Blue Regiment, later the Royal Horse Guards, to the Marquess of Granby (q.v.). Writing to Newcastle at Hanover about the next general election, Pelham observed that 'if this affair were once settled as we wish, the King's interest in the north would be almost without a negative, our own family connection easy, and your elections without expense there'.[2] George II, however, flatly refused to give the regiment to Granby, commenting unfavourably on his character and those of the other members of the Manners family: 'I love none of them'.[3] When the Duke of Rutland was at last brought into the Cabinet as lord steward in the summer of 1754, Newcastle wrote to him:

the support and countenance which your Grace and your family are so good as to give us are the greatest honour and strength that any Administration can have.[4]

He died 29 May 1779.

[1] HMC Egmont Diary, ii. 272. [2] 8 May 1752, Add. 32727, f. 132. [3] Newcastle to Pelham, 3/14 Aug. 1752, 'Most private', Add. 32729, f. 9. [4] Add. 32736. f. 95.

E.C.

MANNERS, John, Mq. of Granby (1721–70).

GRANTHAM 1741–1754
CAMBRIDGESHIRE 1754–18 Oct. 1770

b. 2 Jan. 1721, 1st s. of John Manners (q.v.), 3rd Duke of Rutland; bro. of Lord Robert Manners Sutton (q.v.). educ. Eton 1732; Trinity, Camb. 1738; Grand Tour, extending to European and Asiatic Turkey, 1740–2. m. 3 Sept. 1750, Lady Frances Seymour, da. of Charles, 6th Duke of Somerset, 4s. 3da.

Col. 1745; maj.-gen. 1755; col. R. Horse Gds. 1758–d.; lt.-gen. 1759; lt.-gen. of the Ordnance 1759–63, master gen. 1763–Jan. 1770; col. 21 Drags. 1760–3; c.-in-c. 1766–Jan. 1770.

P.C. 2 May 1760; ld. lt. Derbys. 1764–6.

Returned for Grantham on the Rutland interest in 1741 while still in Turkey,[1] Granby was absent from all the recorded divisions of his first Parliament, except that of 18 Jan. 1744 on the Hanoverians, in which he voted against the Government. During the Forty-five he served in Scotland as colonel of a regiment raised by his brother, the Duke of Rutland, retaining his rank when the regiment was disbanded. He was classed as 'doubtful' in 1746 but as 'opposition' at the opening of the 1747 Parliament. At this time his reputation was that of a racing man and a gambler already deep in debt.[2] When pressed by the Pelhams in 1752 to gain 'the great and extensive interest of the Rutland family' by giving Granby the Blue Regiment (the Royal Horse Guards), George II flatly refused, referring to him as 'a sot, a bully, that does nothing but drink and quarrel, a brute'.[3]

He died 18 Oct. 1770.

[1] W. E. Manners, *Life of Granby*, 10. [2] Walpole to Mann, 1 Sept. 1750. [3] Newcastle to Pelham, 3/14 Aug. 1752, Add. 32729, f. 9.

R.R.S.

MANNERS, Lord Robert (c.1717–82), of Bloxholm, Lincs.

KINGSTON-UPON-HULL 1747–31 May 1782

b. c.1717, 8th s. of John Manners, M.P., 2nd Duke of Rutland, being 3rd s. by his 2nd w. Lucy, da. of Bennet Sherard, M.P., 2nd Baron Sherard [I], sis. of Bennet Sherard, M.P., 1st Earl of Harborough; bro. of John Manners, Mq. of Granby (*b.* 1696), Lord Sherard and Lord William Manners (qq.v.). *m.* 1 Jan. 1756, Mary Digges of Roehampton, Surr., 3s. 2da. Ensign 2 Ft. Gds. 1735, lt. 1740; capt. and lt.-col. 1 Ft. Gds. 1742; col. and a.-d.-c. to George II 1747; col. 36 Ft. 1751–65; maj.-gen. 1757; lt.-gen. 1759; col. 3 Drag. Gds. 1765–*d.*; gen. 1771.

Lt.-gov. Hull 1749–*d.*

Lord Robert Manners, an army officer who served in Flanders during the war of the Austrian succession, was the brother-in-law of Henry Pelham, to whose recommendation he presumably owed his return in 1747 for Hull, where he was a stranger. Appointed lieutenant-governor of Hull in 1749, he retained his seat, with the support of the Government, for 35 years. He died 31 May 1782, aged 64.

R.R.S.

MANNERS, Lord Sherard (c.1713–42).

TAVISTOCK 1741–13 Jan. 1742

b. c.1713, 6th s. of John Manners, M.P., 2nd Duke of Rutland, being 1st s. by his 2nd w.; bro. of John Manners, Mq. of Granby (*b.* 1696), Lord Robert and Lord William Manners (qq.v.). *unm.*

In 1741 Thomas Pitt (q.v.), the Prince of Wales's manager for the Cornish boroughs, offered to find Manners a seat for £800, which he declined to pay. Brought in for Tavistock by the Duke of Bedford,[1] he was absent from the division on the chairman of the elections committee in December 1741 and died 13 Jan. 1742.

[1] Add. 47091, ff. 1–9.

E.C.

MANNERS, Lord William (1697–1772), of Croxton Park, Lincs.

LEICESTERSHIRE 17 Dec. 1719–1734
NEWARK 31 Jan. 1738–1754

b. 13 Nov. 1697, 2nd s. of John Manners, M.P., 2nd Duke of Rutland, by his 1st w.; bro. of John, Mq. of Granby (*b.*1696), Lord Robert and Lord Sherard Manners (qq.v.). *unm.*

Gent. of the bedchamber to Prince of Wales ?1722–7; ld. of the bedchamber to the King 1727–38.

Manners sat for Leicestershire, which his father had represented, voting with the Administration in all recorded divisions, till 1734, when he declined to stand again for the county 'to the great annoyance of his friends'.[1] Throwing up his post in 1738,[2] he was returned for Newark by his brother, the 3rd Duke of Rutland, whom he followed into opposition, voting against the Government on the Spanish convention in 1739 and the place bill in 1740, but with them on the motion for the dismissal of Walpole in February 1741. In the next Parliament he was absent from the division on the chairman of the elections committee, 16 Dec. 1741, but voted with the Administration on the Hanoverians in December 1742. In 1743 Henry Pelham, his brother-in-law, offered him a post on the Treasury board, which he refused.[3] He voted against the Hanoverians in 1744, but for them in 1746, when he was classed as 'doubtful'. Listed as Opposition in 1747, he attached himself to Frederick, Prince of Wales, figuring as comptroller of the Household in the 2nd Lord Egmont's lists of office-holders in the next reign. In 1751 Pelham suspected him of restraining his brother the Duke, over whom he had great influence, from joining the Administration.[4]

Portrayed by Hogarth in the gambling scene of 'The Rake's Progress',[5] Manners was reputed to have been the only nobleman to have made a considerable private fortune as a professional gamester. Horace Walpole describes him as 'better known in the groom-porter's annals than in those of Europe', in which resort of court gamblers he won 1,200 guineas in one evening during the New Year festivities in 1728. He spent much of his time looking after the Belvoir foxhounds and his extensive racing studs.[6] By the daughter of a Shrewsbury apothecary he had seven illegitimate children, four sons and three daughters, to whom he left over £100,000 in cash, as well as other property.[7] The eldest of them, John Manners, succeeded him in his seat at Newark in 1754.

He died of a fall from his horse 23 Apr. 1772.

[1] *HMC Hastings*, iii. 19. [2] Stuart mss 207/68. [3] Pelham to Devonshire, 1 Dec., and Hartington to Devonshire, 13 Dec. 1743,

Devonshire mss. ⁵ Walpole, *Mems. Geo II*, ii. 2; Pelham to Devonshire, 4 July 1751, Devonshire mss. ⁴ F. G. Stephens, *Cat. Prints and Drawings in the Brit. Mus.* iii (1), p. 162. ⁶ To Mann, 28 Mar. 1754; W. E. Manners, *Life of Granby*, 7, 39. ⁷ PCC 186 Taverner; *Recs. Cust Fam.* (ser. 3), 4–5.

E.C.

MANNERS SUTTON, Lord Robert (1722–62), of Kelham, Notts.

NOTTINGHAMSHIRE   1747–19 Nov. 1762

b. 21 Feb. 1722, 2nd s. of John Manners (q.v.), 3rd Duke of Rutland; bro. of John Manners, Mq. of Granby (*b.* 1721, q.v.). *unm.* *suc.* on d. of mother to estates of mat. gd.-fa. Lord Lexinton, and took add. name of Sutton 16 June 1734.
    Capt. Duke of Kingston's Lt. Horse 1745–6; lt.-col. Duke of Cumberland's Drags. 1746–8; col. comdt. 21 Drags. 1760–*d.*
    Gent. of the bedchamber to Prince of Wales 1749–51; master of the harriers and foxhounds 1754–*d.*

During the 1745 rebellion Lord Robert Sutton (as he was usually styled) commanded a troop of the newly-formed Duke of Kingston's Light Horse at Culloden. After Kingston's Horse was disbanded in 1746, he joined the Duke of Cumberland's Dragoons, was taken prisoner at the battle of Lauffeld in 1747, supped the same evening with Marshal de Saxe, and was exchanged next day.[1] Returned unopposed for his county in 1747 as a government supporter, he went over to the Prince of Wales's party in 1749, deserting the Duke of Cumberland, who used to say 'that he was never hurt but by the ingratitude of Mr. Townshend [George, q.v.] and Lord Robert Sutton, whom he had made the greatest efforts to oblige'.[2] He died 19 Nov. 1762.

¹ W. E. Manners, *Life of Granby*, 17–32; HMC Astley, 373, 378. ² Walpole, *Mems. Geo. II*, i. 40.

R.R.S.

MANSEL, Hon. Bussy (?1701–50), of Briton Ferry, Glam.

CARDIFF BOROUGHS   31 Jan. 1727–1734
GLAMORGAN   9 Mar. 1737–26 Nov. 1744

b. ?1701, 3rd s. of Thomas Mansel, M.P., 1st Baron Mansel of Margam, Glam. by Martha, da. and h. of Francis Millington of Newick Place, Suss.; bro. of Hon. Robert Mansel (q.v.). *educ.* Ch. Ch. Oxf. 6 July 1717, aged 16. *m.* (1) 17 May 1724, Lady Elizabeth Hervey (*d.* 3 Sept. 1727), 1st da. of John Hervey, M.P., 1st Earl of Bristol, sis. of Carr and John, Lords Hervey (qq.v.), *s.p.*; (2) 13 Mar. 1729, Lady Barbara Blackett, o. da. of William Villiers, M.P., 2nd Earl of Jersey, wid. of Sir William Blackett, 2nd Bt. (q.v.), 1da. *suc.* to Briton Ferry on d. of kinsman, Thomas Mansel, M.P., 1706; bro. Christopher as 4th Baron 26 Nov. 1744.

The Mansel family had represented Glamorgan uninterruptedly from 1670 to 1712, when Bussy's father, Sir Thomas Mansel, was one of the twelve

peers created to give a Tory majority in the House of Lords. After Lord Mansel's death in 1723, Bussy himself became a leading political figure in the county. In addition to his own estate of Briton Ferry, he managed the interest of his nephew, the 2nd Lord Mansel, until the latter came of age in 1740; and in 1738 he inherited a tenure for life of the Stradling estate of St. Donat's. Returned as a Tory on the family interest at a by-election for Cardiff in January 1727, he was again successful at the general election in that year, voting always with the Opposition. According to the 1st Lord Egmont he was the bearer, in April 1732, of a letter from his brother-in-law, Lord Hervey, to Anne Vane, the Prince of Wales's (and Hervey's) mistress, 'upbraid[ing] her with the ill services she did him with the Prince.' Miss Vane fell into a fit and threw the letter back to Mansel, who

swore to her he would be my Lord Hervey's death for making him the messenger of so great an affront, and for deceiving him, for that my Lord told him his letter was only to recommend a midwife. To prevent murder Miss Vane was obliged to acquaint the Prince with what happened, who made the matter up.[1]

In 1734 Mansel stood for the county but was narrowly defeated by William Talbot (q.v.). On Talbot's succession to the peerage Mansel was not opposed at the ensuing by-election, retaining his seat until 1744 when he too became a peer. He continued to vote with the Opposition both before and after Walpole's fall but was one of those Tories who, on 13 Feb. 1741, voted for the Administration on the motion to dismiss Walpole. A man of miserly disposition, he was reputed to have left a large fortune at his death on 29 Nov. 1750.

¹ HMC Egmont Diary, i. 264–5; Hervey, *Mems.* 482.

P.D.G.T./R.S.L.

MANSEL, Hon. Robert (1695–1723), of Margam, Glam. and Crayford, Kent.

MINEHEAD   18 Dec. 1721–29 Apr. 1723

b. 2 Nov. 1695, 1st s. of Thomas Mansel, M.P., 1st Baron Mansel of Margam, and bro. of Bussy Mansel (q.v.). *m.* Apr. 1718, Anne, da. and coh. of Adm. Sir Clowdisley Shovell, M.P., of May Place, Crayford, Kent, 2s. 1da.

Robert Mansel, the heir to an ancient Welsh family, was an active Jacobite, whose name was sent to the Pretender in 1721 as one of the leaders of Glamorgan in the event of a rising.[1] Returned for Minehead on the Luttrell interest at a by-election in December 1721, he died a few months before his father, 29 Apr. 1723.

¹ C. A. Maunsell & E. P. Statham, *Maunsell Fam.* ii. 21–26; Stuart mss 65/16.

S.R.M.

MARCH, Earl of, *see* LENNOX, Charles

MARSHALL, Henry (1688–1754), of St. Mary at Hill, London, and Theddlethorpe, Lincs.

AMERSHAM 1734–2 Feb. 1754

bap. 25 Mar. 1688, 1st surv. s. of Charles Marshall, grocer, of St. Mary at Hill, London by Margaret, da. of Henry Loades, chamberlain of London. *unm. suc.* fa. 1708. Kntd. 5 Sept. 1745.

Master, Drapers' Co. 1738–9; alderman, London 1737–d., sheriff 1740–1, ld. mayor 1744–5; pres. St. Bartholomew's Hospital 1745–d.

Marshall was returned for Amersham as a Tory on the interest of the Drake family, to whom he was related,[1] voting consistently against the Administration. On 31 Mar. 1736 he voted against the Westminster bridge bill, which was opposed by the common council of the city of London.[2] In 1738 he was made a member of a committee of aldermen formed to bring complaints against Spanish depredations before Parliament, of several committees of the common council, and of the caucus of the corporation.[3] He was one of the Tories who voted against the motion for Walpole's dismissal in February 1741.[4] In 1745, according to George Heathcote (q.v.), he and Sir John Barnard (q.v.) 'industriously and artfully surprised the City' into voting a loyal address on the rebellion.[5] At the end of his mayoralty he received the thanks of the common council for

his faithful discharge of and constant attendance to the duties of that high office, his steady attachment to the true interest of this corporation, for his frequent calling us together in common council, and his readiness on all occasions to promote the welfare of his fellow citizens.[6]

In 1747 he was classed as Opposition. He died 2 Feb. 1754.

[1] See *Yorks. Arch. Jnl.* vii. 94–96. [2] *Harley Diary.* [3] *Stuart mss* 204/144; see under LONDON. [4] *HMC Egmont Diary,* iii. 192. [5] *Marchmont Pprs.* ii. 345–7. [6] *Jnl.* vol. 58, 3 Oct. 1745.

E.C.

MARSHAM, Sir Robert, 5th Bt. (1685–1724), of the Mote, Maidstone.

MAIDSTONE 1708–22 June 1716

b. 17 Sept. 1685, o.s. of Sir Robert Marsham, 4th Bt., M.P., by Margaret, da. and h. of Thomas Bosville of Eynsford, Kent. *educ.* St. John's, Oxf. 1701. *m.* 19 Aug. 1708, Elizabeth, 1st da. and coh. of Adm. Sir Clowdisley Shovell, M.P. ('dowry £15,000 and £20,000 more at her mother's death'), 4s. (3 *d.v.p.*) 4da. *suc.* fa. 26 July 1703; *cr.* Baron Romney 22 June 1716.

Lt.-gov. Dover castle 1717–d.

Marsham, whose father had represented Maidstone in four Parliaments, was himself returned

there on his family's interest for the fourth time in 1715. A staunch Whig, he was appointed in April 1715 to the second committee set up by the Commons to inquire into the late peace and the conduct of the late Tory ministry. One of the earliest peers created by George I, he is said to have paid £5,000 for his title.[1] He died 28 Nov. 1724.

[1] *HMC Egmont Diary,* iii. 260.

A.N.N.

MARTIN, James (c.1694–1744) of Quy, Cambs.

CAMBRIDGE 1741–15 Dec. 1744

b. c.1694, 4th s. of William Martin of Evesham, Worcs. by Elizabeth, da. of John Knight of Barrells, Warws.; bro. of John and Thomas Martin (qq.v.). *unm.*

James Martin, a banker, at the sign of 'the Grasshopper', in Lombard Street, was taken into partnership by his brother Thomas (q.v.) in 1714, becoming senior partner about 1727.[1] Buying the manor of Quy from Sir Francis Whichcote (q.v.), he was returned unopposed for Cambridge in 1741, voting with the Government on the chairman of the elections committee in 1741 and on the Hanoverians in 1742 and 1744. He was much afflicted with the stone, which brought him to the grave 'in the middle of life',[2] 15 Dec. 1744.

[1] J. B. Martin, *'The Grasshopper' in Lombard St.* 45. [2] Add. 5808, f. 46.

R.R.S.

MARTIN, John (1692–1767), of Overbury Court, Worcs.

TEWKESBURY 1741–1747

bap. 8 July 1692, 3rd s. of William Martin of Evesham, Worcs.; bro. of James and Thomas Martin (qq.v.). *m.* (1) by 1724, Catherine, da. of Joseph Jackson of Sneed Park, Glos., 3s. 4da.; (2) 21 July 1763, his kinswoman Anna Kinloch, wid.,[1] of Chipping Norton, Oxon., *s.p.*

John Martin, though not a partner, was connected with the family bank in Lombard Street by 1731. He succeeded his younger brother James (q.v.) as senior partner in 1744, retiring in 1761.[2] Defeated at Tewkesbury in 1734, he was returned there unopposed as a Whig in 1741, voting with the Administration in all recorded divisions, but did not stand again. He died 7 Mar. 1767.

[1] PCC 143 Legard. [2] J. B. Martin, *'The Grasshopper' in Lombard St.* 88–90.

R.S.L.

MARTIN, Matthew (d. 1749), of Alresford Hall, Essex.

COLCHESTER 1722–1727, 1734–26 Feb. 1742

m. Sarah, da. of Samuel Jones, commander of an East Indiaman, 5s. 3da.

Elder bro. of Trinity House 1720; director, E.I. Co. 1722–29, 1732–40; mayor, Colchester 1726, high steward 1746.

Martin, who claimed to be descended from the Martins of Saffron Walden, served as a captain in the East India Company's service. He distinguished himself as commander of the *Marlborough* Indiaman, which he defended against three French ships of war, bringing her safely into Fort St. George with a cargo valued at £200,000. For this he received from the Company a reward of £1,000 and a gold medal set with 24 large diamonds. He purchased Alresford Hall, near Colchester, in 1720 and was granted a patent of arms on 18 Sept. 1722.[1] He successfully contested Colchester as a Whig in 1722, did not stand in 1727, and was unopposed in 1734. He voted with the Administration on the Spanish convention in 1739, and was absent from the division on the place bill in 1740. Re-elected after a contest in 1741, he voted for Walpole's candidate for the chairman of the elections committee before being unseated on petition. He died 20 July 1749.

[1] Morant, *Essex*, ii. 188–9; *Essex Rev.* vi. 184; xi. 158–62.

E.C.

MARTIN, Samuel (1714–88), of Abingdon Bldgs., London.

CAMELFORD   1747–1768
HASTINGS   1768–1774

b. 1 Sept. 1714 in Antigua, 1st s. of Samuel Martin of Greencastle, Antigua, speaker of the assembly 1753–63, by his 1st w. Frances, da. of John Yeamans, attorney-gen. of Antigua; half-bro. of Josiah Martin, gov. of N. Carolina 1771–5. *educ.* Westminster; Trinity, Camb. 1729; I. Temple 1730, called 1736, bencher 1766. *unm.*, 1s.[1] *suc.* fa. 1776.

Dep. agent for Antigua 1742–4; agent for Monserrat 1742–9; for Nevis 1744–50; sec. to chancellor of the Exchequer Apr. 1754–Nov. 1755; sec. of the Treasury Nov. 1756–Apr. 1757, Apr. 1758–Apr. 1763, when given reversion of usher of the Exchequer (to which he never succeeded); treasurer to the Princess of Wales Oct. 1757–8 Feb. 1772. Granted 1 May 1772, pension of £1,200 for life.[2]

Martin came of one of the oldest and most respected West Indian families.[3] In 1747 he was included in the Prince of Wales's list of persons 'not able to bring in themselves' for whom safe seats had been provided.[4] Returned by Thomas Pitt (q.v.) for Camelford, in February 1748 he opposed a bill of poundage on all imported goods and merchandises, enlarging on the ruinous effects of existing duties on English trade; on 4 Feb. 1751 he 'made a speech of great wit against standing armies, with very new arguments'; and a few days later spoke ably against the Bavarian subsidy.[5] The second Lord Egmont (q.v.) wrote of him as 'a fellow whom I had supported with the Prince . . . and who slighted me in the House, warping into Nugent's [Robert, q.v.] set', and who, on the Prince's death 'had insolently answered me the first day that his attachments were now at an end'.[6] Going over to the Government, he supported the regency bill in May 1751, but in November of that year he voted against the army, with Lords Egmont and Middlesex, the only members of the late Prince's faction to do so.[7]

He died 20 Nov. 1788.

[1] Add. 41347, f. 51b. [2] T52/62/11–12. [3] *Caribbeana*, i. 184. [4] *HMC Fortescue*, i. 108. [5] *Parl. Hist.* xiv. 178–9; Walpole, *Mems. Geo. II*, i. 26, 48. [6] Occasional memoranda, Add. 47091. [7] *Mems. Geo. II*, i. 136, 216.

E.C.

MARTIN, Thomas (c.1679–1765), of Cheshunt, Herts. and Clapham, Surr.

WILTON   1727–1734

b. c.1679, 1st s. of William Martin of Evesham, Worcs., bro. of James and John Martin (qq.v.). *m.* Elizabeth, da. of Richard Lowe of Cheshunt, *s.p.*

Thomas Martin's grandfather and great-grandfather had both been mayors of Evesham. Entering the firm of Smith and Stone, bankers, at the sign of 'the Grasshopper', in Lombard Street, before 1699, he became a partner in 1703 and sole partner in 1711. Three years later he took his brother James Martin (q.v.) into partnership. He retired about the time he entered Parliament as a Whig for Wilton in 1727.[1] Voting with the Administration in all recorded divisions, he did not stand again. He died 21 Apr. 1765.

[1] J. B. Martin, '*The Grasshopper' in Lombard St.* 40, 43–46.

R.S.L.

MARTON, Edward (c.1714–58), of Capernwray, nr. Lancaster, Lancs.

LANCASTER   1747–4 Dec. 1758

b. c.1714, 1st s. of Oliver Marton of Capernwray, barrister, recorder of Lancaster, by his 2nd w. Jane, da. of Roger Wilson of Casterton, Westmld. *educ.* Harrow c.1731; Trinity Hall, Camb. 1732; G. Inn 1728, called 1737, bencher 1749. *unm. suc.* fa. 1744. Recorder, Lancaster 1748–*d.*

Marton's family came from Yorkshire, but in the early eighteenth century his father purchased property in Lancashire, including Capernwray and the advowson of Lancaster. After contesting Lancaster unsuccessfully at a by-election in 1745, he was returned for it unopposed in 1747 as a government supporter. In December 1748 it was reported that he and a friend at the Newton races were 'stoned at . . . and urged to drink the Pretender's health, but, drew their pistols and made their way through the Jacobite mob.'[1] He died 4 Dec. 1758.

[1] *Remains of John Byrom* (Chetham Soc. xliv), ii (2), p. 474.

E.C.

MARTYN, Thomas (?1689–1750), of the Middle Temple, London.

DARTMOUTH 1722–1727

b. ?1689, 1st s. of Thomas Martyn, merchant, of Plymouth, Devon by his w. née Addis of Egg Buckland, Devon. *educ.* Pemb. Oxf. 29 Mar. 1707, aged 17; M. Temple 1710, called 1714. *m.* 6 Oct. 1719, Elizabeth, da. of Sir Francis Drake, 3rd Bt., M.P., of Buckland, Devon, sis. of Sir Francis Drake, 4th Bt. (q.v.), 2da. *suc.* fa. bef. 1716.

Sec. of the commissions of the peace to the ld. chancellor, Lord King 1725; justice for Caernarvon, Merioneth and Anglesey 1726–*d.*

In 1722 Martyn's brother-in-law, Sir Francis Drake (q.v.), recommended him for Dartmouth to Lord Chief Justice King, one of the government managers in the west of England, with whom he had travelled on the western circuit. Returned unopposed for Dartmouth, as a government supporter,[1] he did not stand again, devoting himself to his duties on the Welsh circuit. In 1741 he applied unsuccessfully for a judicial office to Lord Hardwicke (Philip Yorke, q.v.) on the ground that

I have long faithfully served the Crown in Wales, and I hope my conduct there or elsewhere hath not been unserviceable to the common interest. The gout makes travelling in the mountains very fatiguing, and there being a vacancy in Ireland by the death of Mr. Baron Wainwright I humbly beg your Lordship for a remove thither. Such a promotion will make me perfectly happy and another gentleman may choose to continue here with my present commission rather than go abroad.[2]

He died 17 May 1750, leaving his wife and her 'unhappy daughters' in extreme poverty.[3]

[1] Lady E. F. Eliott-Drake, *Fam. and Heirs of Sir Francis Drake*, ii. 202–3, 222; *HMC Townshend*, 137. [2] 16 May 1741, Add. 35586, f. 358. [3] Eliott-Drake, ii. 261.

S.R.M.

MASON, Charles (*d.* 1739), of Rockley, Salop.

BISHOP'S CASTLE 1695–13 May 1701, 1701–1705
MONTGOMERY BOROUGHS 1705–1708
BISHOP'S CASTLE 1708–1710, 1715–1722,
26 Apr. 1726–1727

2nd s. of Thomas Mason of Rockley and Church Stoke, Salop. *m.* Mary Harnage, 1s. *suc.* fa. 1705.

Ensign, Lord Herbert of Cherbury's regt. of Ft.

1689; jt. comptroller of the mint 1696–1701; receiver gen. and paymaster of transports 1707–8.

Charles Mason belonged to one of the leading families of Bishop's Castle. His uncle, Sir Richard Mason, his cousin Sir William Brownlow, and his elder brother Richard Mason, had all served for it and he himself represented it in eight Parliaments. A staunch but disreputable Whig, he left his first post under a cloud and the second owing the Crown nearly £6,000. When a writ of extent on his estates was issued to compel him to pay, he turned it to his own advantage by using it to prevent a private creditor foreclosing on mortgages of £7,700, whilst by successive stays of Exchequer process he enjoyed the rents of his estates.[1] In 1715 Mason particularly aroused the animosity of the Harleys (qq.v.), who complained of his 'villainous roguery', alleging him to be unqualified because his lands were under extent, and suggesting that Lord Coningsby (q.v.), their arch-enemy, had paid his election expenses.[2] Re-elected after a contest, he voted with the Government. In 1722 the Duke of Chandos, who had bought the Harleys' Shropshire property, would do nothing to prejudice Mason's election, but would not join interests with him, writing:

By what I hear he'll have a difficult task, for I fear he is not much prepared with 'unum necessarium',[3]

which was money. He was defeated, but on petition it was stated, four years after the election, that

most of these [voters] thus bribed were tenants to the petitioner and always in his interest, and that in general, they declared, they would have voted for the petitioner but for the sitting Member's money.[4]

He was awarded the seat, but lost it in 1727, after which he did not stand again. In 1728, when a double return from Montgomery was before the elections committee, he gave evidence to the committee against the right of the freemen of the outboroughs to vote at parliamentary elections, from his experience as a Member for the borough, 1705–8. In his evidence he

said nobody would be for their right of voting but who was for a popish prince, because those boroughs were under the influence of the Duke of Powys, a papist; this was resented and a debate on censuring him and Mr. Earle, the chairman, ordered to reprimand him, which he did and said the committee did not proceed with so much severity as he deserved in commiseration of his miserable circumstances.[5]

He died in 1739.

[1] *Cal. Treas. Bks.* xvi. 7, 135–6; xxiv. 51, 54; *Cal. Treas. Pprs. 1697–1702*, p. 424; *1720–8*, p. 417; *Cal. Treas. Bks. and Pprs. 1729–30*, p. 411. [2] *HMC Portland*, v. 505, 663. [3] To Capt. Oakely, 8 Mar., to Mr. Wollaston, 22 Mar. 1722, Chandos letter bks. [4] *CJ*, xx. 682. [5] *Knatchbull Diary*, 18 Mar. 1728.

J.B.L.

MASSINGBERD, Sir William, 3rd Bt. (1677–1723), of Bratoft Hall, Lincs.

LINCOLNSHIRE 3 Jan. 1721–1 Dec. 1723

bap. 25 Sept. 1677, o.s. of Sir William Massingberd, 2nd Bt., of Bratoft Hall by Elizabeth, da. of Richard Wynn of Cateaton St., London. *educ.* Merchant Taylors' 1690–1; St. Catherine's, Camb. 1694. *unm. suc.* fa. 1719.

A member of an old Lincolnshire family, seated at Bratoft since 1538, Massingberd stood unsuccessfully as a Tory for Boston in 1719. On his return for the county at a contested election in 1721 a Tory wrote:

> Sir William Massingberd, indefatigable in the service of his country, has got such a majority in the county election that the Whigs tremble at his name and the measures he has taken in several boroughs in this county to rout that party out of Parliament.[1]

Re-elected unopposed in 1722, he died 1 Dec. 1723.

[1] Massingberd Mundy deposit 2/10/19, Lincs. Archives Office.

P.W.

MASTER, Legh (c.1694–1750), of New Hall, Ashton in Makerfield, Lancs. and Codnor Castle, Derbys.

NEWTON 1727–1747

b. c. 1694, 1st s. of Sir Streynsham Master, gov. of Madras 1677–81, and director of the E.I. Co. 1698, of Codnor Castle, Derbys. by his 2nd w. Elizabeth, da. of Richard Legh, M.P., of Lyme, Cheshire. *educ.* Isleworth sch. Mdx.; St. John's, Camb. 1711. *m.* 26 Apr. 1716, Margaret (*d.* 25 July 1733), da. and coh. of Thomas Launder of New Hall, Ashton in Makerfield, 3s.; (2) 10 July 1739 (with £15,000), Anne, da. and coh. of Charles Smith of Isleworth, Mdx. *suc.* fa. at Codnor Castle and Stanley Grange, Derbys. 1724.

Mayor, Wigan 1726.

Master, a Tory, was returned for Newton by his uncle, Peter Legh of Lyme, the proprietor of the borough. After regularly voting against the Government he was absent from the division on the place bill in 1740 and again from that on the chairman of committees on 16 Dec. 1741. On 29 Dec. Sir Watkin Williams Wynn (q.v.) wrote:

> I think Mr. Legh of Lyme and others should insist on Legh Master's attending his duty. In all our late divisions our opponents have forced the lame, the halt, and the blind to attend. A small fit of illness, and slight fit of the gout cannot be a plea where there is an honest heart at this time, when the fate of the country may very possibly turn upon a single vote.[1]

However, he continued to be absent from all subsequent recorded divisions. He was not put up in 1747, and died 2 Apr. 1750.

[1] HMC 15th Rep. VII, 324.

E.C.

MASTER, Thomas (1690–1770), of the Abbey, Cirencester, Glos.

CIRENCESTER 23 Jan. 1712–1747

bap. 12 July 1690, 1st s. of Thomas Master, M.P. Cirencester 1685–7, 1689–90, of the Abbey, Cirencester by Elizabeth, da. and h. of John Driver of Aston, Glos. *educ.* Ch. Ch. Oxf. 1706. *m.* Apr. 1709, Joanna, da. and h. of Jasper Chapman of Stratton, Glos., 1s. *suc.* fa. 1710.

Thomas Master was descended from one of Queen Elizabeth's physicians, who obtained a grant of the site of the abbey of Cirencester in 1565, since when each generation of the family had represented the borough. A life-long Tory, he himself was returned there without opposition for thirty-five years, sharing its representation with the Bathursts (qq.v.). Included in 1721 in a list of those likely to support an uprising in favour of the Stuarts,[1] he consistently voted against the Government after George I's accession. In his only recorded speech on 3 May 1736 he opposed the Quaker tithe bill. He retired in 1747 in favour of his son, on whose death in 1749, leaving an infant heir, he put up a cousin, John Coxe (q.v.). In 1753 he emerged from his retirement to join with Coxe in standing once again for the borough, but ultimately withdrew.[2] He died 5 Feb. 1770.

[1] Stuart mss 65/16. [2] Add. 32733, f. 610.

A.N.N.

MASTER, Thomas, jun. (1717–49).

CIRENCESTER 1747–29 May 1749

bap. 31 May 1717, o.s. of Thomas Master (q.v.). *educ.* Westminster 1729; Balliol, Oxf. 1735. *m.* 26 Dec. 1742, his father's ward Elizabeth Chester, da. and h. of Sir William Cann, 3rd Bt., of Compton Greenfield, Glos., 2s.

Master, a Tory, was returned unopposed on his father's interest for Cirencester in 1747. Classed as Opposition, he died 29 May 1749.

A.N.N.

MATHEWS, Thomas (1676–1751), of Llandaff Court, Glam.

GLAMORGAN 2 Jan. 1745–1747
CARMARTHEN 1747–2 Oct. 1751

b. Oct. 1676, 1st s. of Brig.-Gen. Edward Mathews of Llandaff by Jane, da. of Sir Thomas Armstrong, M.P. *m.* (1) post nupt. settlement 9 Jan. 1707, Henrietta (*d.* Sept. 1737), da. of Isaiah Burgeois (or Burges) of Antigua and Shoreditch, London, dr. of physic,[1] 1s.; (2) 9 Nov. 1738 ('with £40,000'), Millicent, da. and coh. of John Fuller of Red Lion Sq., Holborn, sheriff of London, *s.p. suc.* fa. 1697.[2]

Entered navy 1690, lt. 1699, capt. 1703; commr. of the navy at Chatham 1736–42; v.-adm. 1742; c.-in-c. Mediterranean and minister to Sardinia and the

Italian States Mar. 1742–Aug. 1744; adm. 1743; r.-adm. of Great Britain 1744–7; dismissed the service 1747.

Thomas Mathews was the senior representative of an old Welsh family seated at Llandaff since the time of Richard II.[3] After a not undistinguished naval career, including good service under Sir George Byng (q.v.) in 1718 off Cape Passaro, he retired to his Glamorgan estate in 1724. Here he was prominent in the Whig interest, unsuccessfully contesting Cardiff Boroughs in 1727 and 1734. Returning in 1736 to what was virtually civilian employment in the Chatham dockyard, he claimed his seniority in 1742 and was sent to command the fleet in the Mediterranean. There, in February 1744, his numerically superior force fought an indecisive action off Toulon with a Franco-Spanish fleet, the result of which was the breaking of the British blockade. Whatever his deficiencies as an admiral in handling the fleet on this occasion, Mathews brought the Spanish admiral to close action, having to fight his own ship as well as the battle after his flag captain was severely wounded at the first broadside. He was not well served by some of the other captains, who did but little to support him; and Lestock, the vice-admiral, with whom he was on bad terms, avoided action altogether by obeying the letter, but not the intentions, of Mathews's signals.[4] The outcry in England at this apparent failure caused Mathews to resign his command in August. Four months later he was narrowly successful over a Tory opponent at a contested by-election for Glamorgan and was thus in his place when the Toulon affair came before the House in March 1745. Mathews himself gave an account of the battle and was closely questioned by Members during the subsequent parliamentary inquiry, which lasted for a month. 'Some questions . . . were asked Mr. Mathews while Mr. Lestock was at the bar, which were not so well answered; but of this one would be very tender'.[5] When the evidence was closed on 4 Apr. he spoke several times in his own defence, observing that 'for an impartial speech . . . Fox's [was] the severest he ever heard'. Later,

he assured the committee he did not mean to offer any affront to Mr. Lestock, when he came aboard him the 10th of February [1744], that what he said of its being very cold proceeded out of a pure regard to the vice-admiral's ill state of health . . . [He] did not doubt that upon his trial it would appear he had acted with skill and judgment, and not with that ignorance and incapacity which had been objected to him.[6]

As a result of the inquiry the House recommended on 11 Apr. 1745 that courts martial be held on both

admirals, six named captains and several lieutenants. An attempt made on the previous day by Mathews's friends to have his name omitted from the address was defeated by 218 to 75. The amendment in his favour was moved by a Tory, seconded by a follower of Carteret's and supported by Pelham. It was opposed by Fox, George Grenville and Admiral Vernon.[7] According to Horace Walpole the inquiry

was carried on with more decency and impartiality than ever was known in so tumultuous, popular and partial a court . . . the Tories, all but one single man, voted against Mathews, whom they have not forgiven for lately opposing one of their friends in Monmouthshire [recte Glamorgan] and for carrying his election. The greater part of the Whigs were for Lestock . . . Mathews remains in the light of a hot, brave, imperious, dull, confused fellow.[8]

Another observer wrote:

This great majority, as it shewed the general sense of the House, was no small mortification to [Mathews] and his friends, who certainly did not know their strength or else they had never made this unlucky attempt; and so far Mr. Pelham had forgot to copy his predecessor [Walpole], who always counted noses before he embarked on any motion. It was certainly a wrong step for . . . had Mr. Mathews and his friends cheerfully concurred with the House, he would have appeared in a much better light . . . but no man is at all times wise.[9]

Acquitted on all charges at the ensuing courts martial in the face of the strongest evidence, Lestock was promoted and re-employed. The gravamen of the many charges against Mathews was that he prepared insufficiently for the battle, did not fight his hardest, and failed to take every possible step to destroy the enemy. On 22 Oct. 1746, after a four months' hearing, he was found guilty by the court and sentenced to 'be cashiered and rendered incapable of any employ in his Majesty's service'.[10]

Mathews, now an old man with a rich wife, bore his disgrace with equanimity; in December 1746 'never man appeared to the world so insensible as he doth after such a sentence passed on him . . . he frequents the Court and all public places and gives himself very little concern, which aggravates some. He's very happy to be of such a temper.'[11] No votes of his have been recorded, but in 1746 he was classed among the followers of Lord Bath. For the 1747 election he moved to Carmarthen, where he was brought in by Griffith Philipps (q.v.), classed as Opposition. He died 2 Oct. 1751.

[1] PCC 158 Poley. [2] CSP Dom. 1697, p. 166. [3] G. T. Clark, Limbus Patrum Morganiae et Glamorganiae, 7–9. [4] H. W. Richmond, Navy in War of 1739–48, ii. 1–58. [5] HMC Du Cane, 51. [6] Yorke's parl. jnl. Parl. Hist. xiii. 1261, 1263–4, 1270. [7] Owen, Pelhams, 265. [8] To Mann, 15 Apr. 1745. [9] HMC Du Cane, 54. [10] Richmond, ii. 55, 260–7. [11] HMC Du Cane, 156.

P.D.G.T./R.S.L.

MAULE, John (1706–81), of Inverkeilor, Forfar.

ABERDEEN BURGHS   8 June 1739–Aug. 1748

> b. 1706, 2nd surv. s. of Hon. Harry Maule, M.P. [S], of Kellie, Forfar by his 2nd w. Anne, da. of Patrick Lindsay of Kilbirnie, Ayr; half-bro. of William Maule, Earl of Panmure [I] (q.v.). educ. adv. 1725. unm.
>
> Keeper of register of sasines 1737; baron of the Exchequer [S] 1748–d.

John Maule was the secretary[1] of Lord Ilay, later Duke of Argyll, who managed elections in Scotland under Walpole and the Pelhams. Returned on the interest of his half-brother, Lord Panmure, he voted consistently with the Administration, which however did not protect him from suspicion on account of his Jacobite ancestry. During the Forty-five,

> when the magistrates of Edinburgh were searching houses for arms, they came to Mr. Maule's, brother of Lord Panmure and a great friend of the Duke of Argyll. The maid would not let them go into one room, which was locked, and, she said, full of arms. They now thought that they had found what they looked for and had the door broke open—where they found an ample collection of coats of arms.[2]

About this time he and Lord Panmure sent a memorandum to Henry Pelham denying charges of their having been brought into Parliament by, and of favouring, the Jacobite interest.[3] Classed as 'Old Whig' in 1746, he was re-elected unanimously in 1747, vacating his seat next year on being appointed to a sinecure 'as a douceur to the Duke of Argyll' for failing to get Charles Areskine (q.v.) made lord president of the court of session.[4] He died 2 July 1781.

[1] HMC Polwarth, v. 235. [2] Horace Walpole to Mann, 13 Sept. 1745. Maule's father was a great antiquarian. [3] Newcastle (Clumber) mss. [4] HMC Polwarth, v. 261, 266; Horace Walpole to Geo. Montagu, 18 May 1748.

R.R.S.

MAULE, William (1700–82), of Brechin Castle, Forfar.

FORFARSHIRE   1 May 1735–4 Jan. 1782

> b. 1700, 3rd but 1st surv. s. of Hon. Harry Maule, M.P. [S], of Kellie, Forfar by his 1st w. Lady Mary Fleming, da. of William, 5th Earl of Wigtown [S]; half-bro. of John Maule (q.v.). educ. Leyden 1718; Scots Coll. in Paris 1719. unm. suc. e. bro. James as titular Lord Maule 1729; fa. as titular Earl of Panmure [S] 23 June 1734; cr. Earl of Panmure of Forth [I] 6 Apr. 1743.
>
> Ensign 1 Ft. Oct. 1727; capt. 25 Ft. 1737; capt. and lt.-col. 3 Ft. Gds. 1741, maj. 1745; col. army 1745; col. 25 Ft. 1747; col. 21 Ft. 1752; maj.-gen. 1755; lt.-gen. 1758; gen. Apr. 1770; col. 2 Drags. Nov. 1770–d.

Maule's father, with his brother, the Earl of Panmure, took a prominent part in the rebellion of 1715, after which he fled to Holland, returning to Scotland in 1719 under the general indemnity.

In 1723 the death in exile of Lord Panmure, attainted of high treason, made him head of the family, whose chief object became the recovery of their forfeited estates and honours. His sons, James and William, were presented at court on George II's accession, when James was disappointed of his hopes of entering Parliament but William obtained a commission in the army. The family then placed themselves under the protection of Lord Ilay, from whom Maule's father, now titular Earl of Panmure, received through Lord Lovat a message during the political crisis caused by the excise bill in 1733:

> He bid me acquaint your Lordship that the present dispute in Scotland is not between Whig and Tory, but is plainly a design of my Lord Aberdeen and my Lord Stair, joined with the Squadrone [the anti-Argyll party in Scotland], to turn his brother [the Duke of Argyll] and him out, that they might govern Scotland themselves . . . He told me frankly that if your Lordship would bring off your friends from joining the Squadrone, that he, having now the north administration in his hands, would use his endeavour to restore your Lordship's family, and did not doubt of success if you give him a handle for it.[1]

Ilay did not procure the restoration of the Panmure estates, but with his support William Maule, having become head of the family by the deaths of his elder brother and his father, was returned for Forfarshire, which he represented till his death. Voting with the Government, both before and after Walpole's fall, he was put down under 'Winnington' (q.v.) in the Cockpit list of government supporters in October 1742, and obtained an Irish peerage in 1743. During the war of the Austrian succession he served at Dettingen and Fontenoy. Though charged by the Duke of Cumberland in February 1746 with being 'brought into Parliament by the Jacobite interest',[2] he was listed that year by Newcastle as 'Old Whig'. It was not, however, until 1764 that he recovered his family's estates. He died 4 Jan. 1782.

[1] Registrum de Panmure, ed. J. Stuart, i. pp. lxxxii–v, cxxxix–cxli. [2] More Culloden Pprs. v. 36.

R.R.S.

MAXWELL, John (c.1700–54), of Cardoness, Kirkcudbright.

KIRKCUDBRIGHT STEWARTRY   31 Dec. 1742–1747

> b. c.1700, 1st surv. s. of Col. William Maxwell of Cardoness by Nicholas, o. da. of Hon. William Stewart, M.P. [S] (4th s. of James, 2nd Earl of Galloway [S]). educ. Glasgow 1717. m. Agnes, da. of Thomas Irving of Dublin, surgeon, 3s. suc. fa. 1752.
>
> Ensign 21 Ft. 1729, lt. 1740; capt. 15 Ft. 1743, maj. 1751.

Maxwell, an army officer, whose family were

cadets of the Maxwells of Calderwood,[1] was related through his mother to James, John and William Stewart (qq.v.). Returned unopposed for Kirkcudbright in 1742 at a by-election caused by the death of Basil Hamilton, he voted with the Administration on the Hanoverians in 1744. Classed in 1746 as 'Old Whig', he stood again in 1747, supported by Argyll, Pelham and the Earl of Galloway, but withdrew before the contest when his canvass showed that he would be beaten 27 to 24. He alleged that Andrew Fletcher (Lord Milton), Argyll's deputy in Scotland, intervened personally in favour of his opponent, who had full opposition support. 'I dare say', commented Argyll, 'some of the gentlemen thought they supported the Court, at least the winning side'.[2] Maxwell died before the next election, in February 1754.

[1] Fraser, *Book of Carlaverock*, i. 604: P. H. M'Kerlie, *Lands and their Owners in Galloway*, iii. 28–29. [2] Maxwell to Pelham, 4 Aug. 1747, Argyll to Pelham, 23 July, 1 Aug. 1747, Newcastle (Clumber) mss.

R.S.L.

MAY (formerly **BRODNAX**, afterwards **KNIGHT**), Thomas (?1701–81), of Godmersham Park, nr. Canterbury, Kent.

CANTERBURY   1734–1741

b. ?1701, 1st surv. s. of Col William Brodnax of Godmersham, being o.s. by his 2nd w. Anne, da. of Christopher May of Greenwich. *educ.* Balliol, Oxf. 2 June 1720, aged 18. *m.* 11 July 1729, Jane, 1st da. and coh. of William Monke of Buckingham House, Shoreham, Suss., 5s. 5da. *suc.* fa. 1726; cos. Dame Anne May to Rawmere, Suss. 1726; cos. Elizabeth Knight to Chawton, Hants 1738.
    Sheriff, Kent 1729–30.

This Member twice changed his name by private Act of Parliament: in 1727 from Brodnax to May, under the will of his mother's cousin, Sir Thomas May, M.P. (d.1718), on succeeding to the May estates; and in 1738 to Knight on inheriting the estates of his father's cousin, Elizabeth Knight, widow of William Woodward Knight and Bulstrode Peachey (qq.v.). On the second occasion one Member is alleged to have proposed 'a general bill to enable that gentleman to take what name he pleased'.[1] Returned, apparently as a Tory, for Canterbury in 1734, voting with the Opposition, he did not stand again. He died 26 Feb. 1781.

[1] *Gent. Mag.* 1781, p. 147.

A.N.N.

MAYNARD, Thomas (?1685–1742), of Hoxne Hall, nr. Eye, Suff. and Passenham, Northants.

EYE   1710–1715
WEST LOOE   1715–1722

b. ?1685, 1st s. of Hon. William Maynard (yr. s. of William, 2nd Baron Maynard) of Hoxne Hall and Passenham by Susan, da. and h. of Thomas Eyans, merchant, of Bow, Mdx. *educ.* Bury sch. under Mr. Leeds; Christ's, Camb. 2 June 1702, aged 16. *unm. suc.* fa. 1704.
    Commr. for stores in Minorca July 1717–23; commr. of customs in Scotland 1723–Sept. 1730.

Maynard had an estate in the vicinity of Eye which he represented as a Whig under Queen Anne. In 1715 he was returned for West Looe, voting with the Administration in all recorded divisions. Appointed commissioner for stores in Minorca in 1717, he did not stand in 1722, and a year later he was given a place in the customs, which he retained till 1730. He died 8 Sept. 1742, leaving his estates to his cousin Charles, 1st Viscount Maynard.[1]

[1] PCC 278 Trenley.

E.C.

MAYO, William (aft. 1665–1723), of Hope under Dinmore, nr. Hereford.

HEREFORD   1722–14 Mar. 1723

b. aft. 1665, 2nd s. of Humphrey Mayo of St. Peter's, Hereford, and Hope under Dinmore by Mary, da. of William Jarrett of Aldington, Worcs. *m.* Anne ?Smith, 9s. 4da. *suc.* bro. Thomas, 1719, to an estate worth £600 a year.[1]

Mayo, whose family had for several generations been prominent in local politics, owed his return to a revolt by the local gentry against the domination of Lord Chandos and the Foleys.[2] Described as the 'creature' of Lord Coningsby (q.v.), to whom he owed his appointment as a j.p.,[3] he died 14 Mar. 1723.

[1] Lord Coningsby, *Additional Case relating to the Parish of Leominster*, 17. [2] See under HEREFORD. [3] *HMC Portland*, vii. 318–19; Coningsby, loc. cit.

A.N.N.

MEAD, Nathaniel (d.1760), of Goosehays, nr. Romford, Essex.

AYLESBURY   1715–1722

s. of William Mead of Goosehays. *educ.* M. Temple 1700, called 1704. *m.* (1), 2s. *d.v.p.*;[1] (2) Martha,[2] da. of Sir Thomas Scawen of Carshalton, Surr., sis. of Thomas Scawen (qq.v.), 1s. 1da. Kntd. 17 Feb. 1715.
    Serjeant-at-law 1715; under-steward of Havering-atte-Bower by 1715.[3]

Sir Nathaniel Mead, who was one of 13 serjeants appointed on the same day in January 1715, was related to the Aylesbury families of Mead and Phillips.[4] Defeated for that borough by one vote in 1713, he was returned there as a Whig in 1715, voting for the septennial bill, 1716, and the repeal of the Occasional Conformity and Schism Acts, 1719, but against the peerage bill in December

1719. In April 1715 he applied to Walpole unsuccessfully for a commissionership of forfeited estates.[5] His only recorded speech was in support of the Government on the Address, November 1718.[6] He did not stand again. 'Under the disgrace of a supersedeas' he was removed from the commission of the peace for Essex in 1747 by Lord Hardwicke, to whom he wrote: 'I hope that my behaviour in Parliament during the seven years that your Lordship well remembers I sat there hath not rendered me disagreeable to the present ministry'.[7] He died 15 Apr. 1760.

[1] Lysons, *Environs of London*, iv. 200. [2] PCC 421 Warburton; *N. & Q.* (ser. 2), xi. 215. [3] *Cal. Treas. Pprs.* 1714-19, p. 127. [4] Lipscomb, *Bucks.* ii. 63-4. [5] Mead to Walpole, 27 Apr. 1715, Cholmondeley (Houghton) mss. [6] Thos. Brodrick to Lady Midleton, 15 Nov. 1718, Brodrick mss. [7] Mead to Hardwicke, 2 Nov. 1747, Add. 35589, f. 331.

R.S.L.

MEADOWS, Sidney (c.1699–1792), of Conholt, nr. Andover, Hants.

PENRYN	1722–1727
TRURO	1727–1734
TAVISTOCK	1734–1741

b. c.1699, 1st s. of Sir Philip Meadows, M.P., of St. Martin-in-the-Fields by Dorothy, da. of Edward Boscawen, M.P., sis. of Hugh Boscawen (q.v.), 1st Visct. Falmouth. *m.* 2 June 1742, Jemima, da. of Hon. Charles Montagu of Durham (yst. s. of Edward Montagu, M.P., 1st Earl of Sandwich), *s.p. suc.* fa. 1757.
  Knight marshal Jan. 1758–*d.*

Meadows's grandfather, Sir Philip Meadows, was Latin secretary to Cromwell, who sent him as ambassador to Portugal and Denmark; his father, M.P. Truro 1698–1700 and Tregony 1705–8, went as envoy to Vienna in 1707. Returned for Penryn and Truro on the Boscawen interest, he voted against the Administration in all recorded divisions, except that on the civil list arrears in 1729, from which he was absent. Chosen for Tavistock by the Duke of Bedford in 1734, he voted with the Opposition on the Spanish convention in 1739 and on the place bill in 1740. He never stood again.

In 1758 Meadows became knight marshal of the Marshalsea court in Southwark, a post which his father and grandfather had held, he and the lord steward of the Household acting as judges in this court. He died 15 Nov. 1792 'extremely rich in personal property as well as in land. It was said of him that he had not been on the east side of Bond Street more than twice a year for the last 30 years, and that was on his way to receive dividends at the bank'.[1]

[1] *Gent. Mag.* 1792, pp. 1060–1.

E.C.

MEDLYCOTT, James (c.1658–1731), of Ven House, nr. Milborne Port, Som.

MILBORNE PORT	1710–1722

b. c.1658, 1st s. of Thomas Medlycott, M.P., of Abingdon, Berks. by ?Sarah Webster, wid.;[1] bro. of Thomas Medlycott (q.v.). *educ.* M. Temple 1679, called 1685. *m.* (lic. 21 June 1695) Anne Howard of St. Clement Danes, 4s. (3 *d.v.p.*) 6da. *suc.* fa. 1716.
  Master in Chancery 1706–17.

Descended from an ancient Somerset family, James Medlycott was a successful lawyer, who in 1706 became a master in Chancery, an extremely lucrative office which he eventually sold for £3,000.[2] About the same time he also purchased the manor of Ven,[3] carrying a major interest at Milborne Port, which he represented as a Whig in three Parliaments. Under George I he followed Walpole into opposition, voting against the repeal of the Occasional Conformity and Schism Acts and against the peerage bill in 1719. Retiring from Parliament in 1722, he seems to have run into financial trouble, probably due to his expenditure on Milborne Port, combined with the cost of building Ven House, which was completed about 1730. His name appears in the bankruptcy list of April 1731,[4] just before his death on 2 May the same year.

[1] St. Botolph Aldersgate reg. [2] Luttrell, vi. 74; Howell, *State Trials*, xvi. 1154. [3] Phelips, *Som.* i. 291. [4] *Gent. Mag.* 1731, p. 177.

S.R.M.

MEDLYCOTT, Thomas (1662–1738), of Binfield, Berks. and Dublin.

MILBORNE PORT	1705–1708
WESTMINSTER	1708–1715
MILBORNE PORT	1727–1734

bap. 22 May 1662, 2nd s. of Thomas Medlycott, M.P., of Abingdon, Berks.; bro. of James Medlycott (q.v.). *educ.* M. Temple 1680, called 1687, bencher 1712; Irish bar 1691. *m.* (lic. 1 Jan. 1687) Sarah,[1] da. of Mrs. Ursula Goddard, wid., of Mugwell (Monkwell) St., Cripplegate, 2s. 1da.
  M.P. [I] 1692–9, 1703–*d.*
  Attorney-gen. of the Palatinate temp. William III; dep. steward of Westminster 1708; chairman of committee of privileges and elections 1714; commr. of revenue [I] Feb. 1714–July 1727, Feb. 1728–Oct. 1733.[2]

Thomas Medlycott began his career in Ireland as secretary and estate manager to the 2nd Duke of Ormonde, from whom he obtained in 1698–9 lands in Kilkenny, Tipperary and Waterford, and from whose brother, Lord Arran, he purchased land in Mayo in 1701.[3] In 1705 he was returned on his family's interest at Milborne Port, from which he transferred to Westminster in 1708. A Hanoverian Tory,[4] he was appointed a commissioner of revenue in Ireland early in 1714, retaining his post on

George I's accession, after which he went over to the Whigs. He did not stand in 1715, remaining in Ireland occupied with his official duties and his private affairs. In the summer of 1721 he began to look for an English seat at the next general election, writing to his friend Edward Southwell (q.v.), 29 July:

Did you make my compliments to my Lord Nottingham and make me agreeable too, to Colonel [John] Hanbury [q.v.] our knight of Monmouthshire, to whose conduct and disposal I would have my new purchased rents payable by Monmouth town, to be distributed to the poor townsmen of Monmouth, if it could by his friendship and management make me an interest in that borough. If you see Mr. Hanbury I wish you could sound him about this . . .

On 16 Jan. 1722 he wrote asking to be remembered to Lords Sunderland, Cadogan (q.v.) and Carteret; and on 13 Feb. about his intention to come to England to look after his election. There seem to have been some doubts in England as to his politics, for he wrote to Southwell, 22 Feb.:

Pray at your leisure introduce to that great man [?Sunderland] a discourse of me and my services and votes in Parliament against the Pretender, which his Lordship and Baron Bothmar remember, and pray find out the bottom of this . . . But make no great public question of [it] . . . that may invite competitors . . .[5]

He did not secure a seat in 1722 but was returned by his brother for Milborne Port at George II's accession, when he either gave up or was turned out of his Irish place. In the new year he was reinstated, apparently on the understanding that he remained at his post in Ireland, for on 27 Dec. 1730 he wrote to Dodington (George Bubb, q.v.) who also held an Irish place:

I have desired to attend this sessions in England to do my duty in Parliament for his Majesty's service, as I am bound, and, indeed, my own corporation take it ill that I have so long neglected them (having been absent almost three years). Besides, my own private affairs in Monmouthshire require my being there. Forgive me, Sir, therefore, if I humbly beg you to intercede with Sir Robert Walpole to procure me leave. Nobody is more dutifully his servant.

On 2 Dec. 1731 he wrote again to Dodington:

Some few months ago I took the liberty to acquaint you of the indispensable necessity that was upon me to be in England this winter to settle my [late] brother's affairs . . . I could not think it became me (a servant of the Crown) to be absent from the Irish Parliament on the arrival of a new lord lieutenant, so have struggled against all the importunities of my sister and her children, till his Majesty's affairs here were pretty well over. They being now so, I hope you, Sir, will be so good as to interest yourself on my behalf, and please to be my advocate to Sir Robert Walpole for his leave that I may take the first opportunity to come over. I need not tell you, Sir, that I have been near four years without stirring from the

board, and persuade myself that that will be some excuse for an indulgence upon this pressing occasion . . . besides the ambition I have to attend his Majesty's service to your Parliament there.[6]

In June 1732 he was given leave of absence and in October 1733 his son-in-law was appointed his successor, on the ground that Medlycott was 'obliged to remain in England as a Member of Parliament'.[7] In the House he voted with the Government for the excise bill and against the repeal of the Septennial Act. His only recorded speech was made on 21 Feb. 1733 against the clause in the bill for the relief of the sugar colonies providing that no sugar, molasses, or rum should be imported into Ireland except from Great Britain.[8] Ousted from Milborne Port in 1734 by his nephew, Thomas, he died shortly before September 1738, leaving the bulk of his estate in trust for Thomas John Medlycott, apparently an illegitimate son.[9]

[1] PCC 218 Brodrepp. [2] Cal. Treas. Pprs. 1708–14, p. 611. [3] H. E. Medlicott, Medlicott Fam. 51. [4] HMC Egmont Diary, iii. 334–5. [5] Add. 34778, ff. 81, 110, 114, 118. [6] HMC Var. vi. 56. [7] Cal. Treas. Bks. and Pprs. 1731–4, pp. 238, 251, 289, 406, 593. [8] HMC Egmont Diary, i. 329, 333. [9] PCC 218 Brodrepp.

S.R.M.

MEDLYCOTT, Thomas (1697–1763), of Ven House, nr. Milborne Port, Som.

MILBORNE PORT 1734–Jan. 1742, 2 Dec. 1747–21 July 1763

bap. 22 Oct. 1697, 1st s. of James Medlycott (q.v.). educ. ?Eton 1707; Balliol, Oxf. 1711; M. Temple 1720. m. bef. 1730, Elizabeth (d. 15 June 1741), da. of Anthony Ettrick of High Barnes, co. Dur., wid. of Musgrave Davison,[1] 1s. d.v.p.; (2) betw. 3 Sept. 1742 and 26 Mar. 1743, Elizabeth, wid. of Gilbert Dawson,[2] s.p. suc. fa. 1731.

Commr. of hawkers and pedlars Jan.–Sept. 1742; commr. of taxes Sept. 1742–1744.

Returned for the family seat at Milborne Port in 1734, Thomas Medlycott voted regularly with the Government. In 1741 he and another government supporter, whom he had put up for the second Milborne Port seat, were returned after a contest; but when faced with a petition, which in the state of the House might have led to the loss of both seats, he agreed to vacate his own seat by temporarily taking an office of profit, leaving one of his opponents to be returned unopposed.[3] He was re-elected for the next Parliament, towards the end of which he was drawing a secret service pension of £600 a year. The rest of his political career is that of a parliamentary beggar, perpetually in financial difficulties, partly due to the cost of maintaining his interest at Milborne Port.[4] On his death, 21 July 1763, his estate passed to his nephew, Thomas Hutchings, who assumed the name and arms of

Medlycott and succeeded him as Member for the borough.

[1] PCC 159 Spurway. [2] PCC 26 Caesar. [3] *Gent. Mag.* 1742, pp. 44, 50. [4] Namier, *Structure*, 217, 406-9.

S.R.M.

MEGGOTT, George (1669-1723), of Stoney Lane, St. Olave's, Southwark.

SOUTHWARK   1722-12 Nov. 1723

bap. 10 May 1669, 1st s. of Sir George Meggott, brewer, of St. Olave's by his 2nd w. Elizabeth. *m.* (lic. 15 Oct. 1690) Mary, da. of William Smith, coal merchant, of St. Saviour's, Southwark, 2s. 4da. *suc.* fa. 1702.[1]

In Sunderland's lists for the 1722 Parliament Meggott is put down for Southwark, which his father, a rich brewer in St. Olave's, had contested unsuccessfully in 1695. Returned at the top of the poll, he became 'ill of a fever' during the election.[2] He died 12 Nov. 1723, leaving a half share in his two brewhouses to his wife, and the other to his son Smith Meggott,[3] who subsequently traded in partnership with Robert Hucks (q.v.).

[1] Ex. inf. W. H. Challen. [2] *The Post Boy*, 22-24 Mar. 1722. [3] PCC 173 Bolton.

E.C.

MELLISH, William (c.1710-91), of Blyth, Notts.

EAST RETFORD   1741-18 Dec. 1751

b. c.1710, 2nd s. of Joseph Mellish of Doncaster and Blyth by Dorothy, da. of Sir William Gore, ld. mayor of London. *educ.* Eton 1725; Peterhouse, Camb. 1726; L. Inn 1725; I. Temple 1734. *m.* (1) 27 Feb. 1735, Catherine (*d.* 19 Mar. 1747), da. of Joseph da Costa, wid. of Joseph da Costa Villareal of Edwinstowe, Notts., 2s.; (2) 22 July 1762, Anne, da. of John Gore (q.v.) of Bush Hill, Mdx., s. of above mentioned Sir W. Gore, 5s. 1da. *suc.* to Blyth on d. of e. bro. 1757.
Ld. treasurer's remembrancer in the Exchequer 1733-54; commr. of excise 1751-60; receiver gen. of customs 1760-Jan. 1763, 1765-86; jt. sec. to the Treasury July 1765.

In 1635 John Mellish, merchant tailor of London, bought the estate of Blyth in Nottinghamshire for £3,900.[1] His son, a wealthy Oporto merchant, dying unmarried, left Blyth in 1703 to a cousin, Joseph Mellish, who became one of Newcastle's earliest and most important political supporters in the county. Joseph Mellish died in 1733, leaving three sons, of whom the eldest, Edward, inherited Blyth, and the youngest, Joseph, was M.P. for Grimsby from 1761 to 1774.

The second son, William, was intended for the bar. When his father died he was a fellow of Peterhouse and had been provided by Newcastle with the small sinecure of lord treasurer's remembrancer

in the Exchequer.[2] A few months later he refers to his 'having received so many obligations from your Grace' as his 'only excuse' for asking Newcastle to recommend him to Walpole for another Exchequer sinecure, that of clerk of the estreats, 'worth rather better than £100 per annum', which he did not obtain because Walpole was keeping it for his son Horace.[3]

In 1735 Mellish married the widow of a wealthy Portuguese Jew, who had probably become acquainted with his family through the Portuguese business.[4] In 1741 he stood for East Retford without Newcastle's support or approval,[5] spending his wife's money like water, paying first £50, then £100, and finally £150 a vote.[6] When Parliament met he voted with the Opposition in return for a promise that if he did so a petition which had been brought against his return should be dropped.[7] He was not invited to the Cockpit meeting of ministerial supporters in the Commons before the opening of the next session. In December 1742 he voted for the Hanoverians, but in January 1744 he spoke and voted against them, though opposing any inquiry into their conduct. During the rebellion of 1745 he informed the House that the city of London 'were most heartily for' bringing over 'Hessians and Hanoverians too, as necessary to our security'.[8] He voted for the Hanoverians in 1746, when he was classed as 'Old Whig'.

Returned unopposed for Retford in 1747, this time with Newcastle's support, Mellish is described in the 2nd Lord Egmont's electoral survey, c. 1749-50, as

a low thorough paced creature of Pelham connected with Gore [John (q.v.)], the remittancer. A great dealer in subscriptions, of which he has had more benefit from this ministry than almost anybody not directly employed in the money affairs. He is not at all inclined to us.

In an appended list of 'the most obnoxious men of an inferior degree', he is put by Egmont among the 12 'worst cast for us in the whole House'.

In 1751 Mellish gave up his seat for a commissionership of excise, with a salary of £1,000 per annum, co-operating in the return of one of Newcastle's nephews for the vacancy at this and subsequent elections. In 1760 Newcastle gave him the post of receiver general of customs, with a salary of £1,500 per annum, which he held till the beginning of 1763, when he was turned out in the proscription of Newcastle's friends. Under the Rockingham Administration in 1765 he was compensated with the appointment of joint secretary to the Treasury but returned to his old place when it fell vacant a few weeks later, preferring it 'to all the emoluments he could propose from Treasury favour'.[9]

He died 16 Dec. 1791.

[1] J. Raine, *Hist. Blyth*, 79–88. [2] *Cal. Treas. Bks. and Pprs.* 1731–4, p. 235. [3] Mellish to Newcastle, 2 Nov. 1733, Add 32689, f. 46; Horace Walpole's 'Short Notes' of his life, *Corresp.* (Yale ed.), xiii. 8. [4] M. J. Landa, 'Kitty Villareal, the Da Costas and Samson Gideon' (Jewish Hist. Soc. of England, xiii), 271–91. [5] Mellish to Newcastle, 22 Nov. 1741, and Newcastle's draft reply, Add 32695, ff. 423, 425; Newcastle's instructions to his agent at Retford, 5 Mar. 1741, Add. 32696, f. 194. [6] John Bristow to Newcastle, 13 Apr. 1741, and J. White to Newcastle, 15 and 22 Apr. and 9 May 1741, Add. 32696, ff. 307, 322, 345, 494. [7] Coxe, *Walpole*, iii. 583; Hartington to Devonshire, 22 Dec. 1741, Devonshire mss. [8] Edward Mellish to Newcastle, 27 Apr. 1747, Add. 32710, f. 469; Yorke's parl. jnl. *Parl. Hist.* xiii. 472. [9] Newcastle to White, 3 Dec. 1765, Add. 33003, f. 32.

R.R.S.

MEREDITH, Sir Roger, 5th Bt. (?1677–1739), of Leeds Abbey, Kent.

KENT 1727–1734

b. ?1677, 6th s. of Sir Richard Meredith, 2nd Bt., M.P., by Susanna, da. of General Philip Skippon, M.P., of Foulsham, Norf. *educ.* Lincoln, Oxf. 19 Oct. 1693, aged 16; M. Temple 1694, called 1703. *m.* 22 Sept. 1728, Mary, da. of Francis Tyssen of Shacklewell, Hackney, wid. of Samuel Gott, *s.p. suc.* bro. Aug. 1723.

Fellow, All Souls 1701–9; recorder, Maidstone 1715–d.

Meredith, whose family, of Welsh origin, had been seated at Leeds Abbey since the time of James I, was on 9 May 1709 'struck off the book from being fellow of [All Souls] for his not going into orders at the time appointed by the statutes'.[1] On succeeding his brother, an idiot for 44 years,[2] at Leeds Abbey in 1723 he was reported not to 'thrive with this estate, notwithstanding he is a worthy man'.[3] After a contested election he was returned for the county with the support of the Administration, together with Sir Robert Furnese (q.v.), with whom he went over to opposition shortly afterwards. He voted consistently against the Government except on the introduction of the excise bill, which he supported, though he later voted against it. Not standing in 1734, he died 3 Jan. 1739.

[1] Hearne, *Colls.* (Oxf. Hist. Soc.), ii. 197. [2] *Cal. Treas. Bks.* xix. 177. [3] Hearne, viii. 259.

A.N.N.

MERRILL, John (d.1734), of Lainston, Hants.

TREGONY 7 Nov. 1721–1727

ST. ALBANS 23 Jan. 1733–1734

m. Susanna, da. of Hugh Chudleigh of Westminster (yr. bro. of Sir George Chudleigh, 3rd Bt., of Atherington, Devon), 1s.[1]

Chief clerk to William Pulteney as sec. at war 1715–17; dep. to Pulteney as cofferer of the Household 1723–5; director, S. Sea Co. 1724–7.

Merrill was probably the clerk in the pay office who became deputy to John Howe, M.P., the paymaster general, by 1710.[2] After the Hanoverian succession he was attached to William Pulteney, to whom he presumably owed his return for Tregony in succession to Daniel Pulteney (q.v.). In 1725 Walpole received an anonymous letter alleging that Pulteney, who had recently gone into opposition, had been getting accounts of Treasury transactions 'as to application of money. Mr. [William] Clayton [q.v.] and Mr. Merrill are the machines that he works by'.[3] Losing both his place and his seat, he did not re-enter Parliament till 1733, when he was returned for St. Albans by the Duchess of Marlborough on Pulteney's recommendation.[4] On his death, of gout, 19 Dec. 1734, Pulteney wrote:

> I have lost . . . the truest friend, I may almost say servant, that ever man had in Mr. Merrill. He understood the . . . revenues . . . as well, perhaps better than any man in it. It is utterly impossible for me to go through the drudgery by myself, which I used to do easily with his assistance, and herein it is that opposition galls the most.[5]

[1] Vivian, *Vis. Devon*, 190; PCC 11 Ducie. [2] *Cal. Treas. Bks.* xix. 46; xxiv. 44. [3] Plumb, *Walpole*, ii. 128. [4] Wm. Pulteney to Duchess of Marlborough, 24 Nov. 1732, Blenheim mss. [5] Jonathan Swift's *Corresp.* ed. F. Elrington Ball, v. 281.

E.C.

METCALFE, James (d.1730), of Roxton, Beds.

BEDFORD 16 Apr. 1728–Nov. 1730

bro. of William Metcalfe, afterwards of Roxton, and cos. of William Metcalfe, B. Med. of Trinity, Oxf. (s. of James Metcalfe of St. Andrew's, Holborn).[1] *m.*, 1 surv. da.

James Metcalfe, whose parentage has not been ascertained, acquired his Bedfordshire property after 1715.[2] In 1727 he stood unsuccessfully for Bedford, but on petition a compromise was arranged, under which he was declared duly elected.[3] Although he stood on the Tory interest, he supported the Administration in Parliament, voting with them on the civil list arrears, April 1729, and the Hessians, February 1730. Taken seriously ill by 26 Nov.,[4] he was buried 4 Dec. 1730 at Roxton.

[1] PCC 366 Auber; Foster, *Al. Ox. 1715–86*, p. 948. [2] *VCH Beds.* iii. 219. [3] See BEDFORD. [4] F. St. J. Orlebar, *Orlebar Chron.* 297.

R.S.L.

METCALFE, Lascelles (d.1781), of St. James's St., Westminster.

GREAT BEDWYN 1741–47, 15 Dec. 1747–1754

s. of Lascelles (or Lewis) Metcalfe of Stockton-on-Tees, co. Dur. *unm.*

Lascelles Metcalfe, a London merchant, who owned property in Stockton at his death,[1] was descended from John Metcalfe, a Stockton mill-owner in 1660.[2] Shortly before 1741 he bought the manor of Stokke, in Great Bedwyn,[3] thus acquiring a considerable interest in the borough, for which he was returned unopposed at the general election. In Parliament he supported the Administration in all recorded divisions, being classed as 'Old Whig' in 1746. At the 1747 election on a double return, he and William Sloper jun. were seated by the House of Commons, largely owing to the efforts of Henry Fox on their behalf.[4] In 1752 he sold Stokke to Lord Verney (q.v.), who at first undertook to support him at the next election but later chose another man.[5] He stood with Verney against Bruce nominees in 1761, when they were heavily defeated, Metcalfe not standing again. He died 13 Aug. 1781.

[1] PCC 399 Webster. [2] *Top. and Gen.* ii. 117. [3] State of the borough of Bedwyn, Ailesbury mss. [4] Ilchester, *Lord Holland*, i. 144. [5] Add. 32995, ff. 81, 193.

R.S.L.

METHUEN, Paul (c.1672–1757), of Bishops Cannings, Wilts.

DEVIZES   1708–1710
BRACKLEY   1713–20 Apr. 1714, 1715–1747

b. c.1672, 1st s. of John Methuen, M.P., ld. chancellor of Ireland, by Mary, da. of Seacole Chivers of Quemerford, Wilts. *unm. suc.* fa. 1706; K.B. 27 May 1725.
  Dep. to his fa. as envoy to Portugal 1694–5 and 1696–7; envoy to Portugal 1697–1706, to Spain 1705–6, to Turin 1706; ambassador, Portugal 1706–8; ld. of Admiralty 1709–10; ld. of Treasury 1714–17; P.C. 29 Oct. 1714; ambassador, Spain 1715; sec. of state 1716–17; comptroller of the Household 1720–5; treasurer of the Household 1725–30.

The grandson of a wealthy Wiltshire clothier and the son of the eponymous negotiator of the famous treaty with Portugal, Methuen followed his father's profession till 1708, when he entered Parliament for Devizes, subsequently representing Brackley on the 1st Duke of Bridgwater's interest. Appointed to the Treasury at George I's accession, he was sent to Spain to negotiate a new commercial treaty, but soon returned on grounds of health, leaving negotiations to be completed by George Bubb (q.v.), better known as Dodington. In 1716 he became acting secretary of state during the absence of James Stanhope (q.v.) with the King in Hanover, succeeding to the southern department on Townshend's dismissal in December. In April 1717 he followed Townshend and Walpole into opposition, speaking against the Government in a foreign affairs debate, 17 Dec. 1718, and on the peerage bill in 1719. Returning to office with Townshend and Walpole in 1720, first as comptroller and then as treasurer of the Household, with the duty of laying royal messages before the Commons, he was one of the leading Administration spokesmen. This did not prevent him from opposing Bolingbroke's government-sponsored petition for a pardon in 1725, in what Knatchbull describes as a 'long, heavy, dull, ill-natured speech'.[1] He resigned with Townshend in 1730, according to Hervey on the pretence of

disliking the conduct of the Court in general; but his true reason was his disapprobation, not of any actual sin, but their sin of omission in not making him secretary of state

for which Townshend had recommended him in place of the Duke of Newcastle. Hervey continues:

The character of this man was a very singular one. It was a mixture of Spanish formality and English roughness, strongly seasoned with pride, and not untinctured with honour. He was romantic . . . to the highest degree of absurdity; odd, impracticable, passionate, and obstinate; a thorough coxcomb and a little mad. As to the affair of party, he called himself always a Whig. After he had quitted he went too often to court to be well with the Opposition, and too seldom to Parliament to be well with either side, a conduct which procured him the agreeable mixed character of courtier without profit, and a country gentleman without popularity.[2]

Methuen emerged from his retirement in 1732 to make a 'very handsome speech' in defence of his friend, Sir Robert Sutton (q.v.), accused of complicity in the frauds on the Charitable Corporation.[3] Next year he spoke and voted against the excise bill, urging that it should be deferred to another session. In 1737, after consulting Bubb Dodington, he refused to vote for an increase in the Prince of Wales's allowance, despite heavy pressure from Frederick;

but, at the importunate and repeated request of his Royal Highness, and reflecting that he had not attended the House so as to give one single vote since the excise bill, he was prevailed on to promise his Royal Highness to be absent, as he used to be.[4]

He voted against the Spanish Convention in 1739 but did not vote on the place bill in 1740, when he was included in a ministerial list of opposition Members absent on the Address, 18 Nov. In the next Parliament he moved the appointment of Dr. Lee (q.v.) as chairman of the elections committee, 16 Dec. 1741, did not vote in the subsequent recorded divisions, and was classed by the Government in 1746 as doubtful.[5] As a result of the Duke of Bridgwater's death he lost his Brackley seat in 1747, not standing again. He died 11 Apr. 1757, leaving a fine collection of pictures and a fortune estimated at a quarter of a million, of which £50,000 in guineas was deposited in his house.

[1] *Knatchbull Diary*, 20 Apr. 1725. [2] Hervey, *Mems.* 101–2. [3] *HMC Egmont Diary*, i. 267, 368. [4] *Dodington Diary*, 448. [5] Cholmondeley (Houghton) mss 66; Walpole to Mann, 16 Dec. 1741.

R.R.S.

METHUEN, Paul (1723–95), of Corsham and Bradford-on-Avon, Wilts.

WESTBURY   1747–16 Mar. 1748
WARWICK   13 Dec. 1762–1768, 20 May 1768–1774
GREAT BEDWYN   1774–Feb. 1781

b. 16 May 1723, 1st s. of Thomas Methuen of Bradford-on-Avon by Anne, da. of Isaac Selfe of Beanacre, Wilts. *educ.* Oriel, Oxf. 1741. *m.* 25 June 1749, Christian, da. and coh. of Sir George Cobb, 3rd Bt., of Adderbury, Oxon., 2s. 1da. *suc.* fa. 1738 and to the estate of his fa.'s cousin, Sir Paul Methuen (q.v.), 1757.

Paul Methuen was returned as a Tory on Lord Abingdon's interest for Westbury, but was unseated on petition. He did not stand again till the next reign.

He died 22 Jan. 1795.

R.S.L.

MEWS, Sir Peter (?1672–1726), of Hinton Admiral, nr. Christchurch, Hants.

CHRISTCHURCH   1710–19 Mar. 1726

b. ?1672, s. of Col. John Mews of London by Sarah, da. of John Mellish of London, merchant. *educ.* St. John's, Oxf. 31 May 1688, aged 15; All Souls, Oxf. *m.* 3 Sept. 1719, Lydia, da. and coh. of George Jarvis of Islington, Mdx., *s.p.* Kntd. 13 July 1712.
Chancellor, Winchester diocese 1698–*d.*

The nephew and heir of Dr. Peter Mews, bishop of Winchester (*d.*1706), Mews in 1708 bought the manor of Christchurch, carrying control of the borough. Returned for Christchurch as a Tory, he voted regularly against the Administration after 1715. His name was sent to the Pretender in 1721 as a probable supporter in the event of a rising.[1] He died 19 Mar. 1726.

[1] Stuart mss 65/16.

P.W.

MEWS, *see also* **ST. JOHN, Paulet**

MEXBOROUGH, Earl of, *see* **SAVILE, John**

MEYRICK, Owen (1682–1759), of Bodorgan, Anglesey.

ANGLESEY   1715–1722

b. 1682, 2nd but 1st surv. s. of William Meyrick of Bodorgan by Jane, da. of William Bold of Trerddol. *m.* 1704, Anne, da. of Piers Lloyd of Lligwy, 7s. 1da. *suc.* fa. 1717.
Sheriff, Anglesey 1705–6; custos rot. Anglesey 1715–*d.*

One of the largest Anglesey landowners, Meyrick was a Whig and the leader of the opposition to the influence of the Bulkeley family in the county.[1]

After unsuccessfully contesting the county seat in 1708 and 1710, he was returned for it without opposition in 1715 under an agreement with Lord Bulkeley, steadily supporting the Government. In a list of payments made by Lord Sunderland c.1721, Meyrick is shown as sharing £300 with Stephen Parry (q.v.).[2] He lost his seat in 1722, never standing again, but continued to organize the opposition to the Bulkeley family, putting up first his nephew and then his son for the county, without success in his own lifetime.

He died 8 Apr. 1759.

[1] See under ANGLESEY. [2] Sunderland (Blenheim) mss D.II,4.

P.D.G.T.

MICHELL, John (1710–66), of Boston, Lincs.

BOSTON   1741–1754, 1761–30 Nov. 1766

b. 20 Jan. 1710, 2nd s. of Simon Michell of St. John's, Clerkenwell by Charity, sis. and h. of Richard Hutton of Lincoln's Inn. *educ.* Charterhouse; King's, Camb. 1727–30; L. Inn 1727. *m.* (1) Hannah (*d.* 28 Oct. 1749), da. of Mrs. Anne Hall,[1] *s.p.*; (2) 20 May 1754, Frances, da. of Jacob Preston of Beeston St. Laurence, Norf., wid. of William Jermy, 2s. 1da.
Mayor, Boston 1744, 1758; recorder 1759.

Michell was a wine merchant at Boston, for which he was returned as a Tory in succession to his partner and brother-in-law, Richard Fydell (q.v.). He voted against the Administration in all three divisions on the Hanoverians in the 1741 Parliament and was classed as Opposition in 1747. He died 30 Nov. 1766.

[1] PCC 301 Greenly; Malcolm, *Londinium Redivivum*, iii. 268.

P.W.

MICHELL, Matthew (?1705–52), of Chitterne, Wilts.

WESTBURY   16 Mar. 1748–29 Apr. 1752

b. ?1705, 1st s. of Christopher Michell of Chitterne by Anne, 1st da. of William Willys of London, merchant (3rd s. of Sir Thomas Willys, 1st Bt., of Fen Ditton, Cambs.), sis. and coh. of Sir William Willys, 6th Bt. *m.* 4 Mar. 1749, Frances (with £20,000[1]), da. of John Ashfordby of Cheshunt, Herts., 1s. 1da. *suc.* fa. 1728.
Lt. R.N. 1729, capt. 1740.

Matthew Michell's family had been settled at Chitterne, some ten miles from Westbury, for several generations. He went to sea in 1713 at the age of 8,[2] received his first command in 1738, and, as captain of the *Gloucester*, circumnavigated the world with Anson (q.v.), 1740–2. Later he was made commodore of a squadron in the Downs during the Jacobite rebellion 1745–6, and of a fleet stationed off the Scheldt to assist the Dutch, 1747–8.

At the 1747 election Pelham arranged for Michell

to stand with Chauncy Townsend (q.v.) against the Bertie interest at Westbury. According to Townsend:

> He [Pelham] named Admiral Michell to me but he would go only £1,000. The election and petition cost my part £2,850 and I paid on account Michell's £1,350 and Mr. Pelham paid Michell £500, he having advanced that sum above his £1,000 agreed.[3]

Michell himself, who remained at sea for a further 9 months and was in his absence represented at Westbury by his brother, wrote to Anson from Flushing Roads, 19 June 1747:

> I have received a letter from my brother Robert who has gone down to Westbury to try what interest the family of the Michells has that way in regard to me. I am to return you my hearty thanks for your kind recommendation to Mr. Pelham.[4]

After his defeat he wrote again to Anson:

> I suppose my brother has waited on you to acquaint you with the bad success I met with at Westbury. I have directed him to follow your advice . . . By my brother's account I have had a great deal of injustice done me by the returning officer.

Later he complained that 'I have been at a very great expense about my election, as well as giving my friends a great deal of trouble'.[5] After the success of his petition in March 1748, he retired from the navy, supporting the Administration until his death, 29 Apr. 1752.

[1] *Gent. Mag.* 1749, p. 141. [2] M.I. at Chitterne (Hoare, *Wilts.* Hundred of Heytesbury, 174). [3] To James West, 26 June 1754, Add. 32735, f. 573. [4] Add. 15956, f. 244; see *CJ*, xxv. 574, 576. [5] 14 July 1747 and 11 Jan. 1748, Add. 15956, ff. 250, 260.

R.S.L.

MICKLETHWAIT, Joseph (c.1680–1734), of Swine, nr. Hull, Yorks.

ARUNDEL 29 Mar. 1718–1727
KINGSTON-UPON-HULL 1727–16 Jan. 1734

b. c.1680, 2nd s. of Joseph Micklethwait of Swine by Constantine, da. of Sir Thomas Middleton, M.P., of Stansted Mountfitchet, Essex; bro. of Thomas Micklethwait (q.v.). *unm. suc.* bro. 28 Mar. 1718; *cr.* Baron Micklethwaite [I] 14 Aug. 1724; Visct. Micklethwaite [I] 6 June 1727.

Sec. Barbados 1715–18; sec. to Stanhope as chancellor of the Exchequer 1717–18.

Joseph Micklethwait, like his brother, Thomas, was taken up by the 3rd Earl of Shaftesbury and Sir John Cropley. On 16 June 1709, Cropley gave him a letter of recommendation to Stanhope in Spain, stating that

> he was placed in Holland by my Lord Shaftesbury and indeed was little from [him] when he was there. My Lord answers for his capacity and good graces . . . He has served a full time with great credit to a considerable merchant in Holland, and speaks Dutch as well as English, . . . and I am confident will Spanish ere he waits on you with this. He also understands

the theory of navigation extremely well. His own fortune is £1,500, and the time being come to choose a place to settle in, my Lord Shaftesbury and I have thought Spain under your protection the best settlement for him, especially now we think a peace must be near at hand, and let me assure you that if you have yourself any thoughts of meddling in trade either whilst you are in Spain or afterwards you will never meet any person more capable to give you satisfaction in any such concern . . . His aim and design is to follow trade and be a merchant in whatever part you can best countenance him in.[1]

He served in Spain as secretary to Stanhope, on whose return to England he became his principal man of business. Succeeding to his brother's fortune and seat at Arundel in 1718, he voted with the Government. Created an Irish peer in 1724, he was raised to an Irish viscountcy at George II's accession, when he transferred from Arundel to Hull, five miles from his family estate, continuing to vote with the Government. He died 16 January 1734, leaving his estate to his mistress, Anne Ewer, sister to the wife of the 3rd Earl of Shaftesbury. She died in 1738, desiring 'to be buried in the same private manner Lord Micklethwaite was buried and to lay me in the same vault with him in Hadley churchyard'. She left her property to her own family, whence it eventually passed to the Shaftesbury family.[2]

[1] Chevening mss by permission of the 7th Earl Stanhope. [2] Poulson, *Holderness*, ii. 201; PCC 148 Ockham, 233 Henchman.

A.N.N.

MICKLETHWAIT, Thomas (1678–1718), of Swine, nr. Hull, Yorks.

ARUNDEL 1715–18 Mar. 1718

bap. 19 July 1678, 1st s. of Joseph Micklethwait of Swine and bro. of Joseph Micklethwait (q.v.). *educ.* Jesus, Camb. 1695. *unm. suc.* to London and other estates of Sir John Cropley, 2nd Bt., M.P., 1713.

Treasurer to commrs. of transport 1708–15; ld. of Treasury 1717–18; lt.-gen. of the Ordnance 18 Mar. 1718–*d.*

The grandson of an eminent physician, who bought the manor of Swine from the Darcys in the middle of the seventeenth century, Thomas Micklethwait was introduced by his relation, the 3rd Earl of Shaftesbury, and his friend, Sir John Cropley, to James Stanhope (q.v.), on whose recommendation he was given a place by Lord Treasurer Godolphin in 1708. While Stanhope was in Spain his London interests were looked after by Micklethwait, who wrote to him, 11 Mar. 1712: 'The greatest ambition I ever had was to be known to you and engaged in your service'.[1] In 1713 Cropley died, leaving his estates in Cambridgeshire, Leicestershire, Durham, and London to 'my very dear friend, Thomas Micklethwait'.[2] Returned for the venal borough of Arundel in 1715, he was appointed to the Treasury board when Stanhope succeeded Walpole as first lord and chancellor of the Exchequer in 1717. When a year later Stanhope gave up the Treasury to become once more secretary of state, Micklethwait was transferred to a post in the Ordnance. He died a few days later, 28 Mar. 1718, leaving his estates to his brother, Joseph, and his heirs, on condition that they took the surname of Cropley, 'in gratitude to the memory of my dear friend, Sir John Cropley, who gave me much the greatest part of what I now have in the world',[3] a condition which was not observed.

¹ Cropley to Harley, 17 May [1711], Portland mss, box 132, bdle 9, item 1; Cropley to Stanhope, 18 May 1708, Chevening mss by permission of the 7th Earl Stanhope. ² PCC 252 Leeds. ³ PCC 130 Tenison.

A.N.N.

MIDDLESEX, Earl of, *see* **SACKVILLE, Charles**

MIDDLETON, John (1678–1739), of Seaton and Fettercairn, Aberdeen.

ABERDEEN BURGHS 1713–1715, 22 July 1715–1722, 25 Oct. 1722–4 May 1739

b. 27 Sept. 1678, 6th but 2nd surv. s. of George Middleton, D.D., principal of King's College, Aberdeen, by Jane, da. of James Gordon of Seaton. *m.* c.1712, Elizabeth, da. of William Cunningham of Enterkin, Ayr, 2s. 5da.

Capt. 3 Ft. 1709; lt.-col. 25 Ft. 1711–17; brevet col. 1711; lt.-gov. Tynemouth castle 1715–17; col. 25 Ft. 1721–32, 13 Ft. 1732–*d.*; brig.-gen. 1735; gov. Holy Is. bef. 1739; purveyor of coal and candle for Edinburgh garrison by 1739.

Middleton belonged to an Aberdeen family, related to the earls of Middleton, whose forfeited peerage he hoped to have revived in his favour.[1] One of the signatories of George I's accession proclamation at St. James's on 1 Aug. 1714, he served during the Fifteen on the staff of the Duke of Argyll.[2] Returned as a Whig for Aberdeen Burghs on petition against a Jacobite, he voted for the septennial bill in 1716, but followed Argyll into opposition in 1717, when he voted for the motion against Lord Cadogan (q.v.), at the cost of being turned out of his military appointments. He also voted against the Government on the repeal of the Occasional Conformity and Schism Acts in 1719, after which he followed Argyll back to the Government, voting for the peerage bill later that year. Appointed colonel of his regiment in 1721, he was once more returned on petition in 1722, this time against the brother of the Duke of Roxburghe, the head of the anti-Argyll faction in Scotland, known as the Squadrone, which was regarded as 'a great victory for the Duke of Argyll'.[3] Thenceforth he

was re-elected without opposition, voting with the Government in all recorded divisions. He was said to have secured the interest of Lord Arbuthnott, a non-juror, who controlled one of the constituent burghs, 'by drinking the Pretender's health, and used to ask a dispensation from Sir Robert Walpole to preserve an interest so dishonourably procured'.[4] In 1733 he and Andrew Fletcher (Lord Milton) were described as the 'great favourites' of Argyll's brother, Lord Ilay, who relied on them for managing elections in Scotland.[5] He died 4 May 1739.

¹ Anna C. Biscoe, *Earls of Middleton*, 383. ² P. Rae, *Hist. Rebellion of 1715*, pp. 60, 219. ³ Ld. Finch to Ld. Nottingham, 29 Oct. 1722, Finch mss. ⁴ NLS, gen. col. 4, 34. 1. 7. ⁵ Spalding Club, *Misc.* iii. 48.

J.M.S.

MIDDLETON, Thomas (1676–1715), of Stansted Mountfitchet, Essex.

ESSEX 21 Jan. 1707–1713, 8 Feb.–29 Apr. 1715

bap. 12 Sept. 1676, 1st s. of Sir Thomas Middleton (M.P. Harwich 1679–81, 1688–1700) of Stansted Mountfitchet by Mary, da. of Sir Stephen Langham of Quinton, Northants., wid. of Thomas Styles of Lincs. *educ.* St. Catharine's, Camb. 1692. *m.* 14 July 1696, Elizabeth, da. of Sir Richard Onslow (q.v.) of Clandon, Surr., 5da. *suc.* fa. 1702.

Descended from Sir Thomas Myddelton, M.P., lord mayor of London (1613), of Chirk Castle, Denbigh, Middleton was returned as a Whig in 1715, dying 29 Apr. the same year.

E.C.

MIDDLETON, Sir William, 3rd Bt. (c.1700–57), of Belsay Castle, Bolam, Northumb.

NORTHUMBERLAND 1722–28 Sept. 1757

b. c.1700, 1st s. of Sir John Middleton, 2nd Bt., by Frances, da. of John Lambert of Calton, Yorks., gd.-da. of the Cromwellian general. *m.* May 1725, Anne, da. and coh. of William Ettrick of Silksworth, co. Dur., 1da. *suc.* fa. 17 Oct. 1717.

Middleton's family, who had been settled at Belsay in Northumberland since the thirteenth century, had represented the county since early in the fifteenth. After the Restoration they were one of the few big landowning families to remain Presbyterians. During Middleton's minority his chief trustee was the Presbyterian minister at Belsay and his mainstay at elections was the Presbyterian vote, which was especially strong among the farmers.[1] In spite of this he became a member of the Jockey Club and the owner of a first-rate stud, bred from newly imported Arabians.

On coming of age Middleton was returned as a Whig for the county, which he continued to represent for the rest of his life. He usually supported the Government but voted against them on the excise bill in 1733 and the place bill of 1740. In May 1742 he was one of the members on the court list who were chosen as commissioners of public accounts under an opposition bill which was thrown out in the Lords.[2] When the Duke of Cumberland passed through Northumberland in January 1746 to assume command of the army in Scotland, he took Middleton with him, 'making him, though a civilian, a colonel and placing him on his staff'.

According to family tradition Middleton 'was always borrowing money and always in debt',[3] probably owing to the enormous cost of the county election of 1734, which also crippled Ralph Jenison (q.v.). From 1754 he appears in Newcastle's secret service accounts as receiving a pension of £800 p.a., but when it started is not known.[4] He died 28 Sept. 1757.

[1] 'Account of Fam. of Middleton of Belsay' by Sir Arthur Middleton, 7th Bt., in possession of Sir Stephen Middleton, 9th Bt. [2] Walpole to Mann, 26 May 1742. [3] 'Account of Fam. of Middleton.' [4] Namier, *Structure*, 217–18.

L.B.N.

MIDLETON, Visct., *see* BRODRICK, Alan

MILL, Sir Richard, 5th Bt. (?1689–1760), of Woolbeding, nr. Midhurst, Suss.

MIDHURST   6 Nov. 1721–1722, 1 Feb. 1729–1734
PENRYN   1734–1741
HORSHAM   1741–1747

b. ?1689, 2nd s. of Sir John Mill, 3rd Bt., of Woolbeding, Suss. by Margaret, da. and h. of Thomas Grey of Woolbeding. *educ.* St. John's, Oxf. 12 Mar. 1708, aged 18. *m.* 12 Mar. 1713, Mary, da. of Robert Knollys of Grove Place, Nursling, Hants, 4s. 5da. *suc.* bro. John 1706; Thomas Knollys (s. of Henry Knollys, q.v.) at Grove Place 1751.
    Sheriff, Hants 1723–4.

Brought in successively for Midhurst by the Duke of Somerset, for Penryn by Richard Edgcumbe (q.v.), and for Horsham by the 7th Viscount Irwin (q.v.) at the request of the Duke of Newcastle,[1] Mill voted consistently with the Administration. Retiring in 1747, he died 16 May 1760.

[1] Irwin to Newcastle, 15 June 1742, Add. 32699, f. 280.

J.B.L.

MILLER, Edmund (?1669–1730), of Petersfield, Hants.

PETERSFIELD   1722–28 June 1726, 9 May–
                                         17 July 1727

b. ?1669, 1st s. of John Miller of Marsworth, Bucks. by Bridget, da. of Edmund West, M.P., of Marsworth. *educ.* Eton 1682–6; Trinity, Camb. 9 June

1686, aged 16, fellow 1692; L. Inn 1693; M. Temple 1699, called 1699. *unm. suc.* fa. 1709.
    Serjeant-at-law 1715; baron of the Exchequer [S] 1726–*d.*

Miller acted as counsel for the fellows of Trinity in their proceedings against their master, Richard Bentley, till 1720, when he is said to have sold them to Bentley in return for a sum of £528.[1] Returned as a Whig on his own interest for Petersfield, where he had purchased property, he spoke on 22 Jan. 1724 in support of the army estimates; on 12 Feb. 1725 moved the bill of pains and penalties against Lord Chancellor Macclesfield; and on 17 Mar. seconded a motion designed to restrain the universities of Oxford and Cambridge from purchasing new advowsons and presentations to benefices. On 20 Mar. 1724 he described Bolingbroke's pardon as 'the melancholiest news that ever came to England',[2] and on 20 Apr. 1725 he spoke against the return of Bolingbroke's estates. At the by-election in 1727, caused by his appointment to office as a baron of the Exchequer in Scotland, he succeeded on petition, but did not stand at the ensuing general election. He died 21 May 1730, leaving 5s. to every Petersfield voter for each vote cast for him and describing the high church clergy as the 'vermin of the nation'.[3]

[1] J. H. Monk, *Bentley*, ii. 82; R. C. Jebb, *Bentley*, 84. [2] *Knatchbull Diary*. [3] PCC 169 Auber.

P.W.

MILLER, Thomas (?1688–1733), of Lavant, nr. Chichester, Suss.

CHICHESTER   1715–1727

b. ?1688, o.s. of Sir John Miller, 2nd Bt., M.P., by his 1st w. Margaret, da. of John Peachey of Chichester. *educ.* New Coll. Oxf. 29 Jan. 1707, aged 18. *m.* Jane, da. of Francis Gother, or Goater, alderman of Chichester, 3s. 1da. *suc.* fa. 29 Nov. 1721.

Miller belonged to one of the leading families of Chichester. Both his grandfather and his father, the 1st and 2nd Bts., were mayors of Chichester, which they represented in Parliament under William III and Anne. His mother also belonged to a prominent local family, and after her death his father married the daughter and heiress of another leading townsman, William Elson, M.P. Chichester 1713–15. Classed as a Whig who would often vote with the Tories, he was returned for Chichester after a contest in 1715, voting against the Government except in the division on the septennial bill, when he was absent. After his re-election unopposed in 1722, Newcastle wrote of him as one who 'though inclined to be a Tory, may, I believe, by good management, be brought off'.[1] He and his family duly became Newcastle's staunch supporters in Sussex. On his death, 6 Nov. 1733, his youngest son wrote to Newcastle: 'He to the last expressed the same value as he always had for your Grace, and desired us all to promote your interest as far as lay in our power'.[2]

¹ Newcastle to Sunderland, 31 Mar. 1722, Sunderland (Blenheim) mss. ² Thos. Miller to Newcastle, 15 Nov. 1733, Add. 32689, f. 30.

A.N.N.

MILLES, Samuel (c.1669–1727), of Herne and Canterbury, Kent.

CANTERBURY 1722–1727

b. c.1669, o. surv. s. of Christopher Milles of Herne by his 2nd w. Sarah, da. of Samuel Desborough, M.P., of Elsworth, Cambs. *educ.* I. Temple 1686, called 1693; St. Catherine's, Camb. 1687. *m.* (lic. 14 Dec. 1692) Anne, da. of Thomas Hales of Bekesbourne, Kent, sis. of Sir Thomas Hales, 2nd Bt. (q.v.), 6s. 6da. *suc.* fa. 1701.
Chief steward of the liberties of St. Augustine and of the court of record at Canterbury 1703–*d.*[1]

Samuel Milles, of an old Kent family, who held a legal post under the dean and chapter of Canterbury, was returned for the city as a Tory in 1722, together with his brother-in-law, Sir Thomas Hales, a Whig. He was one of the few Tories who voted with the Government on a personal attack made by Pulteney and his friends on Walpole in 1727.[2] Defeated at the general election that year, he died 10 Dec. 1727.

¹ *CSP Dom.* 1703–4, p. 461. ² *Knatchbull Diary*, 7 Mar. 1727.

A.N.N.

MILNER, James (aft.1658–1721), of Weston Green, Thames Ditton, Surr.

MINEHEAD 23 May 1717–24 Nov. 1721

b. aft. 1658, 2nd s. of Tempest Milner, alderman of London, by his w. Ann, da. of James Houblon, London merchant.[1] *unm.*

James Milner was a Portugal merchant, who under Anne was concerned in the business of remitting money to H.M. ships at Lisbon and other Mediterranean ports, and for the payment of troops in Spain and Portugal.[2] In September 1710 Harley was advised that

Mr. James Milner understands the Portuguese exchange best, and he has a cabal under him who are concerned in what he undertakes, and they are men of substance.[3]

On the controversy over the trade treaty with France in 1713 he published a paper on the importance of British trade with Portugal. The paper was republished in 1743 in *The British Merchant*, a collection of papers relating to the treaty by some of the most eminent merchants of the time.

Unsuccessful for Minehead in 1715 but returned on petition in 1717, Milner voted for the repeal of the Occasional Conformity and Schism Acts and the peerage bill. Shortly after the collapse of the South Sea bubble he published *Three Letters relating to the South Sea Company and the Bank*, in which he strongly criticized the acceptance of the Company's offer to take over the national debt:

I confess [he wrote] when the two proposals were before the House of Commons, I . . . was most inclined to the bank, because they said plainly what they would give the annuitants in stock; and I thought that body of men not addicted to the scandalous tricks of stock-jobbing; neither, in my opinion, would their stock have advanced above 200, or 250 per cent. Had the South Sea been limited in such a manner, the nation had been safe.

He concluded:

As I early foresaw the ruin of my country from this project, so I have opposed it in all places, public and private. I was ridiculed by a great man for standing in my own light. I answered, I was discharging my duty to my country; among the directors, I had no intimacy, but with two. One of 'em I saw often and did all I could to persuade him to sell, and disqualify himself, that he might not have the destructive consequences of such wild schemes to answer for. The other avoided me, but yet I followed him with letters to the same purpose, as will appear by his answers which follow . . .
My honest freedom in opposing their iniquity is called passion, and ungentleman-like language; and my telling him November would be the fatal month, is ridiculed; and my foresight of this evil has only met with the fate of that prophetess to whom, 'tis said, the gods granted the gift of prophecy, yet told her she should not be believed. Though this has been my fate, yet I thank God when the Parliament shall meet, I hope to come into the House with the peace of a good conscience, for having honestly endeavoured to save my dear country from this foreseen, but dreadful ruin.

When Parliament met on 8 Dec., Milner is reported to have

reflected in his speech on three or four of the directors, whom he said he could name, but named only Mr. Gibbon, who he said gave money for refusals of stock in order to raise the price, and sold his own.[4]

On 15 Dec., when the sub-governor and deputy-governor of the company presented their accounts to the House, Milner was among those who 'made several exceptions to the conduct of the South Sea directors, and, in particular, to their lending out vast sums of money belonging to the company, without being duly authorized for that purpose'.[5] On 7 Feb. he opposed Walpole's scheme for ingrafting part of the capital stock and fund of the South Sea Company into the stock and fund of the Bank of England. On 2 May he spoke second in a debate on public credit, urging that, as the principal cause of the crisis had been the fraudulent dealing of the South Sea directors, some relief should be given to subscribers, and carrying a motion that the seven millions due from the South Sea Company to the Government be remitted. In the debates on the allowances to be made to the directors from their confiscated estates, he opposed the more generous of those suggested for Sir John Blunt. He also opposed a proposal to allow the directors 15 per cent out of their estates for prompt payment.

On 23 Nov. 1721 Milner 'shot himself in the head, and died the next day'.[6] In his will drawn up in September 1721 he left his fortune to his nephew and his nieces, the children of his elder brother, John Milner, M.P., who had been consul-general at Lisbon.[7]

[1] Thoresby, *Ducatus Leodiensis*, 176–7; PCC 16 Leeds and 11 Marlbro.; Lady A. Houblon, *Houblon Fam.* i. 358. [2] *Cal. Treas. Bks.* xxii–xxvii, passim. [3] *HMC Portland*, iv. 573. [4] Ibid. v. 609. [5] Chandler, vi. 224. [6] *Hist. Reg.* 1721, chron. p. 44. [7] PCC 11 Marlbro.

E.C.

MILNER, Sir William, 1st Bt. (c.1696–1745), of Nun Appleton, Yorks.

YORK 1722–1734

b. c.1696, 1st s. of William Milner of Nun Appleton, alderman and mayor of Leeds, by Mary, da. of Joshua Ibbetson, also mayor of Leeds. *educ.* Eton; Jesus, Camb. 1713; M. Temple 1713. *m.* 5 Dec. 1716, Elizabeth, da. of Sir William Dawes, 3rd Bt., abp. of York 1714–24, 1s. 1da. *cr.* Bt. 26 Feb. 1717. *suc.* fa. 1740.

The son of a Leeds clothing merchant, Milner was returned in 1722 for York as a Tory on the interest of his father-in-law, the archbishop, who was said to aim at making it 'a church borough'.[1] In 1725 he was one of the Tories who voted against the restoration of Bolingbroke's estates.[2] In the next Parliament he went over to the Government, voting with them on the Hessians 1730, the army 1732, and the repeal of the Septennial Act 1734, but against them on the civil list arrears 1729, and the excise bill 1733. His only recorded speech was made, 19 Feb. 1732, on a complaint of breach of privilege by a clergyman who had accused him publicly of having a pension of £500 a year. He denied the charge, adding that while serving in Parliament he would never accept a place or pension, from this or any other ministry, to keep his opinion unbiased. He stood again in 1734 but withdrew before the poll. Defeated in 1741, he died 23 Nov. 1745.

[1] T. Jenkins to Sunderland, undated, Sunderland (Blenheim) mss. [2] *Knatchbull Diary*, 20 Apr. 1725.

R.R.S.

MILSINGTON, Visct., *see* **COLYEAR, Charles**

MILTON, Baron, *see* **DAMER, Joseph** (*b.*1718)

MILTON, Visct., *see* **FITZWILLIAM, John**

MINSHULL, Edward (*b.* ?1685), of Stoke, Cheshire.

BRAMBER 1 June 1715–1722

b. ?1685, s. of Edward Minshull of Stoke by his w. Anne. *educ.* Shrewsbury; St. John's, Camb. 2 Apr. 1702, aged 16. *suc.* fa. 1698.

Minshull belonged to a branch of one of the most ancient Cheshire families. Defeated at Bramber in 1715 by a Tory but returned on petition by the Whig majority of the House of Commons, he voted with the Government in all recorded divisions. His only reported speech was a 'very slender' defence of John Aislabie (q.v.), 8 Mar. 1721.[1] Convicted next February of cheating a banker of bank bills to the value of £350,[2] he did not stand again. The date of his death is unknown.

[1] Coxe, *Walpole*, ii. 210. [2] *Hist. Reg.* 1722, chron. p. 14.

R.R.S.

MISSING, Thomas (*d.*1733), of Stubbington, in Titchfield, Hants.

SOUTHAMPTON 1722–1727

m. Rebecca, 1s. 5da.
Mayor, Portsmouth 1720–1.

Thomas Missing, a Portsmouth merchant whose parentage has not been ascertained, was made a freeman and alderman there in January 1711. In March 1715 he obtained a lucrative contract for victualling the garrison at Gibraltar, which he held till his death.[1] Five years later he was given similar contracts for troops in Nova Scotia and Newfoundland.[2] Returned, presumably as a Whig, for Southampton in 1722, he was defeated in 1727. In September 1728 he proposed to the board of Trade that 'as he hath a correspondence that way and hath with reputation carried over a great many to America', he should be engaged to transport yearly a number of Protestant Palatines to Carolina 'and victual them till they can support themselves'.[3] He died 6 July 1733.

[1] *Cal. Treas. Bks.* xxix. 412. [2] *Cal. Treas. Pprs.* 1720–28, p. 26. [3] *CSP Col. 1728–9*, pp. 191–2.

R.S.L.

MISSING, Thomas (aft.1710–88), of Stubbington, in Titchfield, Hants.

POOLE 1741–1747

b. aft. 1710,[1] o.s. of Thomas Missing (q.v.) of Stubbington. *m.* (1) 13 Nov. 1739, Anne, da. of George

Streatfield of Stoke Newington, Mdx., *s.p.*; (2) 2 Nov. 1744, Miss Champneys of Combe, *s.p.* *suc.* fa. 1733. Sheriff, Hants 1739–40; mayor, Portsmouth 1750–1, 1756–7.

Thomas Missing built a workhouse at Poole in 1739 at a cost of £500.[2] Returned there in 1741, presumably in view of his trading connexions with America, he voted with the Administration in all recorded divisions. Falling out with his fellow Member, Joseph Gulston,[3] before the 1747 election, he did not stand again. He died 25 Sept. 1788.

[1] PCC 204 Price. [2] Hutchins, *Dorset*, i. 32. [3] See POOLE.

R.S.L.

MITCHELL, Andrew (1708–71), of Thainston, Aberdeen.

ABERDEENSHIRE 1747–1754
ELGIN BURGHS 1 Jan. 1755–28 Jan. 1771

b. 15 Apr. 1708, o. s. of Rev. William Mitchell, minister of St. Giles and King's chaplain, by his 1st w. Margaret, da. of Sir Hugh Cunningham, provost of Edinburgh, wid. of James Steuart, town clerk of Edinburgh. *educ.* Edinburgh Univ.; Leyden 1730–1; Paris 1731–2; Italy 1732–5; M. Temple 1734, called 1738; adv. 1736. *m.* 22 July 1722, his 2nd cos. Barbara, da. and h. of Thomas Mitchell of Thainston, 1da. (*d.* 1729). *suc.* fa. 1727; served h. to Thainston in right of his da. 1741. K.B. 13 Dec. 1765.

Under-sec. for Scotland 1742–6; commissary in Brussels for negotiating a commercial agreement with Austria and the Netherlands 1752–5; envoy to Prussia 1756–June 1765, Dec. 1765–d.

Mitchell's father, a rich and eminent divine, five times moderator of the General Assembly, married him at the age of 14 to an heiress aged 10. After the deaths of his wife, sister, father, and infant daughter, he left Scotland in 1730, possessed of a substantial fortune, to continue his studies abroad. Returning home in 1735, he was made private secretary to Lord Tweeddale, on whose appointment to be secretary of state for Scotland in 1742 Mitchell became under-secretary till Tweeddale's resignation in 1746.

In 1747 Mitchell accepted an offer by his relation, Sir Arthur Forbes, M.P. for Aberdeenshire, to stand down in his favour.

I have seen [he wrote] so much of the management of parties and known too many Members to think of the House of Commons as I once did . . . The promises of great men are lighter than air . . . I have hopes of the Duke of Newcastle and his brother's concurrence but . . . everything is to be feared from a certain eminent personage [the Duke of Argyll] who does not choose that his countrymen should be known to or connected with anybody but himself . . . I am resolved to act a fair and honourable part if ever I shall be in Parliament; but I do propose a reward for myself— that of being employed either at home or abroad in a station agreeable to me and in which I may be useful;

for my ambition at present is stronger than my avarice.[1]

He was returned, with the support of the Pelhams, at whose instance Argyll also declared for him.[2] Pressed to declare that he owed his election to Argyll, he refused,[3] thus incurring the Duke's displeasure. He also made himself unpopular with his compatriots by defending General Philip Anstruther (q.v.).[4] But his real crime, he was told, was

in having some share of the Duke of Newcastle's and Mr. Pelham's favour, without depending upon those who call themselves the Scotch ministry.[5]

Owing to Argyll's hostility he was forced to give up his seat in 1754, but in 1755 Newcastle persuaded Argyll to let him in for Elgin Burghs. Next year he was appointed envoy to Berlin, where he died 28 Jan. 1771.

[1] *Culloden Pprs.* 475–7. [2] Argyll to Pelham, 12 Aug. 1747, Newcastle (Clumber) mss. [3] Mitchell to Newcastle, 15 July 1747, Add. 32712, f. 121. [4] Walpole, *Mems. Geo. II*, i. 95. [5] HMC 5th Rep. 627.

E.H.-G.

MITCHELL, William (c.1703–45), of Carshalton, Surr., Fowlmere, Cambs. and Hemingford Grey, Hunts.

HUNTINGDONSHIRE 1741–15 Sept. 1745

b. c.1703, o. surv. s. of James Mitchell of Fowlmere and Hemingford Grey by Jane, da. of Sir Levinus Bennet, 2nd Bt., M.P., of Babraham, Cambs., sis. and eventually coh. of Sir Richard Bennet, 3rd Bt. *educ.* Eton; Corpus Christi, Camb. 1723. *m.* 4 Feb. 1730, Elizabeth, da. of Bryan Gunning of Castle Coote, co. Roscommon, 3s. 1da. *suc.* fa. 1728.

Sheriff, Cambs. and Hunts. 1737–8.

William Mitchell's father was one of two brothers 'both Scotchmen [who] at their first coming into England came with packs at their backs: but by a most unheard of niggardliness and parsimony so raised their condition that they both died extremely rich'. 'A short black man, rather inclinable to be fat and . . . thick set', Mitchell usually lived at Carshalton but 'had a house at Hemingford Grey . . . where he was obliged sometimes to reside to keep up his interest in' Huntingdonshire.[1] His wife's nieces, the three celebrated Gunning sisters, were born at the manor there, which he leased for some years to his brother-in-law, John Gunning.[2] When Lord Robert Montagu (q.v.) succeeded to the dukedom of Manchester in 1739, Mitchell stood for the ensuing vacancy for Huntingdonshire but was defeated, though supported by the Duke of Newcastle, 'firmly attached to the present Administration,' and recommended to the new Duke of Manchester 'by much the greatest part of the gentlemen as a proper person to succeed me as member for the county'.[3]

He was returned with the Duke of Manchester's support at the top of the poll at the general election of 1741, which 'cost him a vast sum, . . . on the Whig interest'. In Parliament he voted for Walpole's nominee for chairman of the elections committee in December 1741 but absented himself from the divisions on the Westminster petition a few days later.[4] Under the new Administration he voted for the Hanoverians in 1742 and 1744. He died intestate on 15 Sept. 1745, the Duke of Manchester later becoming a guardian for his three sons.[5]

[1] Cole mss 5808, ff. 166–8. [2] H. Bleackley, *The Beautiful Duchess*, 5. [3] Newcastle to the Duke of Devonshire, 30 Oct. 1739, Devonshire mss; Manchester to Newcastle, 26 Oct. 1739, Add. 32692, f. 423. [4] Cole mss 5808, f. 167; Coxe, *Walpole*, iii. 586. [5] Cole mss 5842, p. 107; 5808, f. 167.

R.S.L.

MOLESWORTH, Sir John, 4th Bt. (1705–66), of Pencarrow, Cornw.

NEWPORT   1734–1741
CORNWALL   12 Dec. 1744–1761

bap. 28 Feb. 1705, 1st s. of Sir John Molesworth, 3rd Bt., by Jane, da. of John Arscott of Tetcott, Devon. *m.* 1728, Barbara, da. of Sir Nicholas Morice, 2nd Bt. (q.v.), 2s. 1da. *suc.* fa. June 1723.

Molesworth was returned as a Tory for Newport on the interest of his brother-in-law, Sir William Morice (q.v.). He did not stand in 1741 but in 1744 he succeeded his wife's brother-in-law, Sir John St. Aubyn, 3rd Bt., as knight of the shire for Cornwall, voting consistently against the Walpole-Pelham Governments.

He died on 4 Apr. 1766.

E.C.

MOLESWORTH, Robert (1656–1725), of Brackenstown, nr. Swords, co. Dublin, and Edlington, nr. Doncaster, Yorks.

CAMELFORD   1695–1698
LOSTWITHIEL   1705–17 Jan. 1706
EAST RETFORD   17 Jan. 1706–1708
MITCHELL   1715–1722

b. 7 Sept. 1656, posth. and o.s. of Robert Molesworth, an eminent Dublin merchant, by Judith, da. and coh. of John Bysse, recorder of Dublin during the Protectorate, and baron of the Exchequer [I] at the Restoration. *educ.* Trinity Coll. Dublin 1672. *m.* (1) 16 Aug. 1676, Letitia, da. of Richard, 1st Baron Coote of Coloony [I], sis. of Richard Coote, M.P., 1st Earl of Bellomont [I], 17 ch. of whom 7s. and 2da. surv.[1] *suc.* fa. at birth; *cr.* Baron Molesworth of Philipstown and Visct. Molesworth of Swords [I] 16 July 1716.
    M.P. [I] 1695–9 and 1703–14.
    Envoy to Denmark 1689–92; P.C. [I] Aug. 1697–Jan. 1713 and 9 Oct. 1714–*d.*; ld. of Trade Nov. 1714–Dec. 1715.

Molesworth's father had been in great favour

with Cromwell, who granted him Irish estates. Molesworth himself had been an active supporter of William III in 1689. Noted for his skill as a political pamphleteer and the vigour of his speeches in debates, he was returned for Mitchell in 1715, having been appointed a lord of Trade for his 'small share of the King's accession to the Crown', but he resigned that office in favour of his eldest son, John, at the end of the year.[2] He was made an Irish peer in 1716, when he spoke for the septennial bill. In 1717 he supported the vote of credit against Sweden, publishing a pamphlet in which he used his knowledge of Scandinavia to attack Swedish institutions and the character of Charles XII.[3] In the same year he led an agitation for the repeal of the Occasional Conformity and Schism Acts, declaring at a meeting at the Rose Tavern that since the laws against the Dissenters had only been made because they supported the Protestant succession, the King must be willing to revoke them.[4] On 11 Nov. 1718 in the debate on the Address he 'spoke against the question, though he voted neither way'.[5] In 1719 he voted for the repeal of the Occasional Conformity and Schism Acts, but did not vote on the peerage bill, though he wrote a pamphlet in defence of it.[6] Having long opposed the policy of subjecting the English settlers in Ireland to officials sent from London, on Mar. 1720 he spoke against a bill further subjecting the Irish judicature to the English House of Lords.[7]

Molesworth became one of the fiercest critics of the Administration on the collapse of the South Sea bubble, in which he had lost £2,000 of borrowed money. In December 1720 he insisted that the South Sea directors should be called to account, and a month later he declared that, like Roman parricides, they should be sewn up in sacks and thrown into the river. Elected a member of the secret committee set up by the Commons to inquire into the scheme, he became 'the favourite of the afflicted', who sought redress through his means. Having urged that the Government should take steps to secure the person and papers of Knight, the South Sea Company cashier, he later denounced as a frivolous pretext their offer to place before the House an exchange of letters with the Emperor, showing it was impossible because of the special privileges of Brabant, where Knight had taken refuge. But he absented himself from the division on Charles Stanhope on 28 Feb. after receiving a message from the King asking him as a personal favour not to vote in that division. On 25 May 1721 he spoke unsuccessfully in favour of allowing Sir John Blunt £10,000, since Blunt had provided the committee with more information than any other director, and on 1 June he carried a proposal allowing the like sum to Sir Robert Chaplin (q.v.).[8]

On 19 May 1721 Molesworth wrote to his eldest son

> I continue steadfast in my purpose, notwithstanding the opposition given by the Court, old and new ministry, the majority of the Parliament (who are dipped) and the relations, bribed and interested, of all concerned . . . Every day opens fresh scenes of misery and robbery . . . The gentlemen at the helm were not only content to plunder, but connived at all that did so. The land tax which is the clearest of all the branches of the revenue, has had the collecting of it put into such hands, that the proper officers upon our requiring have made a return of about £690,000 in arrear for the last year 1720. This proceeds from appointing collectors such as were their friends, relations (staunch Whigs all), beggars themselves, their securities little better, who run away with the public money, or have laid it out in purchasing South Sea stock for themselves, the Treasury not calling them to account in time . . . all the methods and course of the Exchequer being broken.[9]

He was not, as was generally supposed, the author of the attacks on the Sunderland government printed in *Cato's Letters*, which were written by John Trenchard (q.v.). His last recorded speech, attacking the treaty with Sweden, 19 June 1721, was 'very much warmer . . . than any of the Tories' and was said to have been particularly resented by Carteret.

At the general election of 1722, Molesworth agreed to stand as an opposition candidate for Westminster, but withdrew before the poll.[10] Defeated at Bodmin, he retired to Ireland, where he died 22 May 1725.

[1] *HMC Var.* viii. 319. [2] Ibid. 287. [3] *A Short Narrative of the life and death of John Rhinholdt, Count Patkul.* [4] Report of Bonet, 5/16 Apr. 1717, quoted in W. Michael, *Quadruple Alliance*, 50. [5] Thos. Brodrick to Lady Midleton, 15 Nov. 1718, Brodrick mss. [6] *A Letter from a Member of the House of Commons to a Gentleman without doors relating to the Bill of Peerage*; *HMC 7th Rep.* 683. [7] *HMC Var.* viii. 283-5. [8] Ibid. 296-7, 350; *HMC Portland*, v. 608; Chandler, vi. 220-1, 232, 238-40, 247-8; Stuart mss 52/137. [9] *HMC Var.* viii. 312-13. [10] Ibid. 326, 334.

E.C.

MOLYNEUX, Samuel (1689-1728), of Dublin, and St. Martin-in-the-Fields, London.

BOSSINEY   1715-1722
ST. MAWES   1 Feb. 1726-1727
EXETER   1727-13 Apr. 1728

b. 16 July 1689, o. surv. s. of William Molyneux of Dublin by Lucy, da. of Sir William Domvile, attorney-gen. [I]. *educ.* Trinity Coll. Dublin 1708. *m.* 5 Apr. 1717, Lady Elizabeth Capel, da. of Algernon, 2nd Earl of Essex, and coh. of her gt.-aunt Lady Dorothy Capel of Tewkesbury, *s.p.* suc. fa. 1698.
M.P. [I] 1727-*d.*
Sec. to the Prince of Wales 1715-27; P.C. [I] ?1715; ld. of Admiralty July 1727-*d.*

Molyneux was descended from Sir Thomas Molyneux, chancellor of the Exchequer in Ireland under Queen Elizabeth. His father, a distinguished mathematician with substantial estates in Armagh, Kildare, and Roscommon, died when he was young, leaving him to the care of his uncle, Dr. Thomas Molyneux, a physician. While at Trinity College he began to devote himself to astronomy, which became his life-long study. In 1712 he visited the Duke of Marlborough at Antwerp, whence he proceeded with the Duke's recommendation to Hanover, where he was received with great favour. A few months before the death of Queen Anne he was sent by that court over to England on a secret mission.[1] Appointed secretary to the Prince of Wales at the accession of George I, he was returned for Bossiney, speaking for the septennial bill in 1716. On the breach between the King and the Prince in 1717, Pope wrote to Lady Mary Wortley Montagu:

> I must tell you a story of Molyneux: the other day at the Prince's levée, he took Mr. Edgcumbe [Richard, q.v.] aside, and asked, with an air of seriousness 'what did the Czar of Muscovy, when he disinherited his son, do with his secretary?' To which Edgcumbe answered 'he was sewed up in a football, and tossed over the water'.[2]

At this time Molyneux told his kinsman, the first Lord Egmont (q.v.), that when everyone was forced to choose between the King's and the Prince's courts 'he had computed what every person concerned lost or gained by the party they chose, and that he found for £20 advantage the Prince's court abandoned or stayed with him'.[3] He himself adhered to the Prince, voting with the Opposition on the motion on Lord Cadogan (q.v.) in June 1717, the repeal of the Occasional Conformity and Schism Acts, and the peerage bill. In February 1722, after the reconciliation in the royal family, he supported Walpole's proposal for a bridge across the Thames at Lambeth, declaring that 'the building of the bridge would be agreeable to his highness and be convenient for his family's passing and re-passing to his country house'.[4]

At George II's accession Molyneux, having failed to secure a seat in the previous Parliament till 1726, was appointed to the Admiralty board. Returned for Exeter, which he had unsuccessfully contested in 1722, he was seized with a fit in the House of Commons, dying a few days later, 13 Apr. 1728, aged 38. Soon after his death his widow married a Swiss surgeon, who won an action for defamation on a charge of having killed him by administering opium to him in his last illness with her connivance.[5]

[1] Sir Capel Molyneux, *Account of Fam. of Sir Thos. Molyneux*, 35-38. [2] *Works*, ed. Elrington Ball, ix. 395. [3] *HMC Egmont Diary.*

i. 375. ⁴ Stuart mss 58/38. ⁵ Chandos letter bks. 20, 21 Dec. 1721,
1 Feb. 1722; Molyneux, 38–39; *A Letter from the Rev. Mr. Middleton
to the Hon. Lady Molineux on the occasion of the death of the Rt. Hon.
Samuel Molineux*, Dublin, 1730; see *Gent. Mag.* 1781, pp. 320–1.

E.C.

MONCKTON, John, 1st Visct. Galway [I] (1695–1751), of Serlby, Notts.

CLITHEROE   1727–1734
PONTEFRACT   1734–1747, 5 Jan. 1749–15 July 1751

b. 1695, o. surv. s. of Robert Monckton, M.P., of
Cavil and Hodroyd, Yorks., ld. of Trade 1706–13, by
Theodosia, da. and coh. of John Fountaine of Melton-
on-the-Hill, Yorks. *educ.* Trinity Hall, Camb. 1713.
m. (1) Lady Elizabeth Manners (*d.*22 Mar. 1730), da.
of John Manners, M.P., 2nd Duke of Rutland, 3s.
1da.; (2) Nov. 1734, Jane, da. of Henry Warner
Westenra of Rathleagh, co. Dublin, 3s. 1da. *suc.* fa.
1722; *cr.* Visct. Galway [I] 17 July 1727.
Commr. revenue [I] 1734–48; surveyor gen. of lands,
woods and forests in England and Wales 1748–*d.*

The Moncktons were an old Yorkshire family,
whose ancestral estates were in the East and West
Ridings, but the 1st Lord Galway, an original
member of the Dilettanti Society, established
himself at Serlby in Nottinghamshire, where he
built a new family seat, in which he housed his fine
collection of old masters.[1] After contesting Clitheroe
unsuccessfully in 1722, he was returned for it unopposed by agreement with Sir Nathaniel Curzon
(q.v.) in 1727, probably in return for selling him
some burgages in that borough.[2] Turned out of
Clitheroe in 1734, he brought himself in for
Pontefract, where in 1729 he had purchased 77
burgages for £6,000, giving him control of one seat.
Connected by marriage with Henry Pelham, who
like him had married one of the daughters of the 2nd
Duke of Rutland, he voted regularly with the
Government till he gave up his seat to his eldest son
in 1747. When in 1748 the post of surveyor general
of crown lands fell vacant by the death of Thomas
Walker (q.v.), Pelham wrote to Newcastle, recommending Galway to the King for the post, on the
ground that his

> unalterable behaviour in Parliament for near thirty
> years [actually not quite twenty], the great expense he
> has been at in bringing himself in, and, at last, his
> purchasing a borough are merits we dont meet with
> every day.[3]

Newcastle reported that the King

> seemed mightily to approve it, only said, he was not
> in Parliament and that so many places were now
> excluded [by the Place Act, 1742] that we should give
> those that were not to Parliament men. I told the
> King that I concluded Lord Galway's design was to
> come into Parliament, that he had a borough of his
> own.[4]

His son made way for him at Pontefract, which he
represented till his death, 15 July 1751.

[1] D. H. Monckton, *Gen. Hist. Fam. Monckton*, 106. [2] See
CLITHEROE. [3] 7 Oct. 1748, Add. 32717, f. 36. [4] 2/13 Nov. 1748,
Add. 32717, f. 253.

R.R.S.

MONCKTON, Hon. Robert (1726–82).

PONTEFRACT   26 Nov. 1751–1754, 24 Mar.–
                               30 Sept. 1774
PORTSMOUTH   10 Aug. 1778–21 May 1782

b. 24 June 1726, 2nd surv. s. of John, 1st Visct.
Galway [I], and bro. of William, 2nd Visct. [I]
(qq.v.). *educ.* Westminster 1737. *unm.*, 3s. 1da. illegit.
Ensign 3 Ft. Gds. 1741; capt. 34 Ft. 1744, maj.
1747; lt.-col. 47 Ft. 1751; col. 1757; col. commandant
60 Ft. 1757–9; col. 17 Ft. 1759–*d.*; maj.-gen. 1761;
lt.-gen. 1770.
Lt.-gov. Nova Scotia 1755–61; gov. New York
1761–5, Berwick-on-Tweed 1765–78, Portsmouth
1778–*d.*

Monckton was returned on his father's death for
the family borough of Pontefract as a stop-gap. He
died 21 May 1782.

R.R.S.

MONCKTON, Hon. William (?1725–72), of Serlby, Notts.

PONTEFRACT   1747–Dec. 1748
THIRSK   1 Apr. 1749–1754
PONTEFRACT   1754–18 Nov. 1772

b. ?1725, 1st surv. s. of John Monckton, 1st Visct.
Galway [I], and bro. of Hon. Robert Monckton
(qq.v.). *educ.* Westminster Sept. 1737, aged 12. *m.* 12
Aug. 1747, Elizabeth (formerly Sarah), da. of Joseph
da Costa Villareal of College Hill, London,[1] 3s. 2da.
suc. fa. as 2nd Visct. Galway [I] 15 July 1751; to
estates of his maternal aunt, Lady Frances Arundell
of Allerton Mauleverer 1769, and took add. name of
Arundell.
Receiver gen. of crown rents, Yorks. and co. Dur.
1748; master of the staghounds 1765–70.

Succeeding to the family seat at Pontefract in
1747, Monckton was classed as a government supporter. Vacating his seat in favour of his father by
temporarily accepting an office in 1748, he was
returned next year for Thirsk on the Frankland
interest.

He died 18 Nov. 1772.

[1] 'Kitty Villareal, the Da Costas and Samson Gideon', *Jewish
Hist. Soc. Trans.* xiii. 273–4, 280, 282.

R.R.S.

MONOUX, Sir Humphrey, 4th Bt. (?1702–57), of Wootton, Beds.

TAVISTOCK   24 Feb. 1728–1734
STOCKBRIDGE   1734–1741

b. ?1702, o.s. of Sir Philip Monoux, 3rd Bt., M.P., by
Dorothy, da. of William Harvey (q.v.) of Chigwell,

Essex. *educ.* Trinity, Oxf. 19 Feb. 1720, aged 17. *m.* 11 Dec. 1742, Jane Elizabeth, wid. of Charles Wake Jones of Waltham Abbey, Essex, da. of Sir Samuel Vanacker Sambrooke, 3rd Bt., sis. of Sir Jeremy Vanacker Sambrooke, 4th Bt. (q.v.), *s.p.* *suc.* fa. 25 Nov. 1707.

Monoux, whose family since 1514[1] had been seated at Wootton, not far from Woburn, contested the county unsuccessfully as a Tory in 1727. Brought in next year by his neighbour, the 3rd Duke of Bedford, for Tavistock, where he succeeded his uncle, Sir John Cope, he voted against the Government. In 1734 he was returned by the Duke of Marlborough for Stockbridge, according to Sarah, Duchess of Marlborough, 'to buy . . . his interest' for Marlborough's brother, John Spencer (q.v.), who was standing as the 4th Duke of Bedford's candidate for Bedfordshire. After observing that he had 'picked the late Duke of Bedford's pocket and was a confederate in all the mischiefs that happened to him', i.e. in the Duke's ruinous gambling proclivities, she went on to say that 'though I believe he will be a sure vote against the ministers from his being a Jacobite, yet I think it is mighty disagreeable to choose so scandalous a man when one might have put in one of reputation, and without adding to the numbers of what all people who love their country wished to do'.[2]

Monoux, who duly voted against the Government, did not stand again. He died 3 Dec. 1757.

[1] *Walthamstow Antiq. Soc. Publ.* xvii. 1; *VCH Beds.* iii. 329.
[2] G. Scott Thomson, *Letters of a Grandmother*, 114.

S.R.M.

MONSON, Charles (?1695–1764), of Spring Gardens, London.

LINCOLN   1734–1754

b. ?1695, 3rd s. of George Monson of Broxbourne, Herts. by Anne, da. of Charles Wren of the Isle of Ely; bro. of George and John Monson, 1st Baron Monson (qq.v.). *educ.* Pembroke, Camb. 11 Feb. 1713, aged 17; G. Inn 1713, called 1720, bencher 1742. *unm.*
Dep. paymaster of the army 1737–46; recorder, Lincoln 1742.

Monson, a practising lawyer, unsuccessfully contested Lincoln in 1728, when his brother Lord Monson gave up to him an estate of £600 p.a. to enable him to stand.[1] Returned on his brother's interest in 1734, he voted consistently with the Administration. In 1737 he was appointed deputy paymaster of the army with a salary of £1,000 p.a. He resigned this post in 1746,[2] as it had become inconsistent with a seat in the House of Commons under the Place Act of 1742. He died 26 Aug. 1764.

[1] Monson mss 7/10/31, Lincs. Archives Office. [2] *Gent. Mag.* 1739, p. 306; 1746, p. 45.

P.W.

MONSON, George (c.1693–1739), of Gray's Inn, London.

GREAT GRIMSBY   1727–1734

b. c.1693, 2nd s. of George Monson of Broxbourne, Herts.; bro. of Charles and John Monson, 1st Baron Monson (qq.v.). *educ.* Corpus Christi, Camb. 1708; G. Inn 1708, called 1720, bencher 1736. *unm.*

Returned for Grimsby in 1727, Monson, a practising lawyer, voted consistently with the Administration. He did not stand again, dying 7 July 1739.

P.W.

MONSON, John (?1692–1748), of Burton, Lincs.

LINCOLN   1722–28 May 1728

b. ?1692, 1st s. of George Monson of Broxbourne, Herts.; bro. of Charles and George Monson (qq.v.). *educ.* Ch. Ch. Oxf. 26 Jan. 1708, aged 15. *m.* 8 Apr. 1725, Lady Margaret Watson, da. of Lewis Watson, M.P., 1st Earl of Rockingham, 3s. K.B. 27 May 1725. *suc.* fa. 1726; uncle Sir William Monson, 4th Bt. (q.v.), as 5th Bt. 7 Mar. 1727; *cr.* Baron Monson 28 May 1728.
Capt. of gent. pensioners 1733–4; P.C. 21 July 1737; ld. of Trade 1737–*d.*

Monson, whose family had been settled in Lincolnshire since the fourteenth century, was returned for Lincoln on his family's interest in 1722. He was among the first to be made a knight of the Bath when that order was revived in 1725. In 1727 he inherited the title and Lincolnshire estates of his uncle, carrying an interest for one seat at Lincoln. Created a peer in 1728, he was appointed to the board of Trade, which under his administration was noted for its inactivity.[1] On his death, 20 July 1748, the Duke of Newcastle, wrote to Henry Pelham:

> The King has lost a most honest and useful servant, his country a most disinterested Member, and all that knew him intimately a most valuable friend, and we in particular, a most affectionate one. My own loss is greater than anybody's.[2]

[1] O. M. Dickerson, *American Colonial Govt.* 35, n. 51. [2] Add. 32715, f. 490.

P.W.

MONSON, Hon. Lewis, *see* WATSON, Hon. Lewis

MONSON, William (c.1655–1727), of Broxbourne, Herts. and Burton, Lincs.

LINCOLN	1695–1698
HEYTESBURY	1702–1708
HERTFORD	1708–1710
ALDBOROUGH	16 Apr. 1715–1722

b. c.1655, 2nd s. of Sir John Monson, K.B., of Burton,

Lincs. by Judith, da. of Sir Thomas Pelham, 2nd Bt., M.P., of Halland, Suss. *m.* 12 Apr. 1688, Laetitia, da. of John Poulett, M.P., 3rd Baron Poulett, *s.p.* suc. bro. Sir Henry Monson, 3rd Bt., M.P., as 4th Bt. 6 Apr. 1718.

Monson, a Whig with an estate of £1,200–£1,500 p.a., was one of the guardians of the future Duke of Newcastle, by whom he was returned for Aldborough in 1715. He voted with the Administration on the septennial bill in 1716 and the repeal of the Occasional Conformity and Schism Acts in 1719, but against them on Lord Cadogan (q.v.) and on the peerage bill. In Sunderland's plans for the 1722 Parliament he was to be replaced by Charles Stanhope (q.v.) at Aldborough.[2] He died 7 Mar. 1727, his title and property passing to his nephew, John Monson (q.v.).

[1] T. Lawson-Tancred, *Recs. of a Yorkshire Manor*, 254, 256. [2] Sunderland (Blenheim) mss.

P.W.

MONTAGU, Charles (aft.1695–1759), of Papplewick, Notts.

WESTMINSTER	3 Dec. 1722–1727
ST. GERMANS	1734–1741
CAMELFORD	1741–1747
NORTHAMPTON	1754–29 May 1759

b. aft. 1695, o.s. of Sir James Montagu, M.P., chief baron of the Exchequer (bro. of Charles Montagu, M.P., 1st Earl of Halifax), by his 1st w. Tufton, da. of Sir William Wray, 1st Bt., of Ashby, Lincs.[1] *educ.* L. Inn 1712. *m.* (settlement 10 Apr. 1725) Ann, da. and h. of Sir Theodore Colladon of Chelsea,[2] subgoverness to the Princesses, 2s. 1da. *suc.* fa. 1723.
Auditor gen. of duchy of Cornwall 1735–51; auditor of the household to Prince of Wales 1738–51, and to Princess 1751–d.

Returned as a government supporter in 1722, Montagu did not stand again till 1734, when he was brought in by Richard Eliot (q.v.) for St. Germans. Attaching himself to Frederick, Prince of Wales, who appointed him first to a duchy of Cornwall office, and later also to a household post, he is mentioned by Hervey in 1737 as one of those who were against the Prince's going into opposition.[3] He did not vote in the divisions on the Spanish convention in 1739 and the place bill in 1740; and was among those who withdrew on the motion for the removal of Walpole in February 1741. Returned for Camelford by Thomas Pitt (q.v.), Frederick's election manager, he voted with the Prince's party, of which he was classed as a member in 1746. In 1747 he was put up by Thomas Pitt for Okehampton, where he was opposed by George Lyttelton (q.v.). His election had been regarded as 'fixed and sure', but Pitt soon began to speak 'very uncertainly' about his prospects, while

he himself complained of 'agitation of mind', which hindered him 'from sleeping a wink', and looked on Okehampton 'as entirely lost'. Though professing himself 'ready on all occasions to obey his Royal Highness's commands', he never appeared at Okehampton, on the ground that he 'was so much out of order that he was not able to undertake the journey', pleading 'his infirmities so strongly that it could no longer be insisted on'.[4]

He died 29 May 1759.

[1] PCC 240 Richmond. [2] Agnew, *Protestant Exiles*, i. 143–4. [3] Hervey, *Mems.* 851. [4] *HMC Fortescue*, i. 108, 117, 122–6.

E.C.

MONTAGU, Edward (aft.1684–1738).

NORTHAMPTON 1722–1734

b. aft.1684, 2nd s. of Edward Montagu of Horton, Northants. by Elizabeth, da. of Sir John Pelham, 3rd Bt., M.P., of Halland, Suss.; bro. of George Montagu (*b.* c.1684, q.v.), 1st Earl of Halifax. *m.* (lic. 9 Mar. 1709) Arabella, da. of John Trevor of Trevalyn, Denb. and Plas Teg, Flints., wid. of Robert Heath of Lewes, Suss., 5s. 2da.
Ensign 1 Ft. Gds. 1702; capt. 2 Drag. Gds.; lt.-col. R. Drags. 1709; brevet col. Drags. 1711; col. 11 Ft. 1715–*d.*; lt.-gov. Fort St. Philip, Minorca 1725; gov. Kingston-upon-Hull 1733–*d.*; brig.-gen. 1735.

Edward Montagu, an army officer, who had been taken prisoner at Brihuega in 1710, commanded his regiment at Sheriffmuir in 1715. Returned on his family's interest at Northampton, he supported the Government, voting for the excise bill in 1733, contrary to the instruction of the Northampton corporation, with the result that he was defeated at the next general election.[1] He died 2 Aug. 1738.

[1] E. C. Forrester, *Northants. County Elections 1691–1832*, p. 57.

R.R.S.

MONTAGU, Edward (1692–1775), of Sandleford, Berks. and Allerthorpe, Yorks.

HUNTINGDON 1734–1768

bap. 13 Nov. 1692, 2nd s. of Hon. Charles Montagu, M.P., of Durham (5th s. of Edward Montagu, M.P., 1st Earl of Sandwich), being 1st s. by his 2nd w. Sarah, da. of John Rogers of Newcastle-upon-Tyne; bro. of James and John Montagu (qq.v.). *educ.* ?Eton 1706; Clare, Camb. 1710; L. Inn 1710. *m.* 5 Aug. 1742, Elizabeth, da. of Matthew Robinson of Edgeley and West Layton, Yorks., sis. of Matthew Robinson Morris, 2nd Baron Rokeby [I] (q.v.), 1s. *d.v.p.*

Edward Montagu, the husband of Elizabeth Montagu, the blue stocking, was a mathematician, interested in scientific pursuits, agriculture and estate management, but does not seem to have mixed much with his wife's literary coterie. During the minority of his cousin, the 4th Earl of Sandwich, he stood as a Whig for the family borough of

Huntingdon, ousting his relation, Edward Wortley.[1] In Parliament he voted consistently against successive Administrations in all recorded divisions. At the 1741 election he was again returned after a contested election in which the young Earl of Sandwich, then in opposition, 'exerted himself' on his behalf 'with great vigour and success'.[2] He continued in opposition after Walpole's fall, expressing the opinion that the proposal, in 1742, to take Hanoverian troops into British pay was to him 'a worse thing than any . . . attempted' by Walpole and that 'England is become a province to Hanover'. In a letter of 3 Dec. 1743 he describes himself as 'one who loves Great Britain and is more concerned for his country than the fatal Elector of Hanover'.[3] Before the general election of 1747 Sandwich, now a member of the Government, wrote to the Duke of Newcastle from The Hague:

> I have obligations to Mr. Montagu, the present Member for Huntingdon, that will put me under great difficulties how to set him aside without subjecting myself to his reproach . . . However, if I am upon the spot, I don't at all doubt but that I can make him easy, and name anyone I please in his room that will cut the same part in public matters that I shall, which he never can be brought to do, since, though he is a very honest man, he will always be an opposer of all Administrations.[4]

Sandwich also wrote to Pelham and to the Duke of Bedford in the same strain.[5] In the end Montagu was again returned by Sandwich, who even paid £500 of his election expenses, but he continued to be classed as 'against' by Newcastle. From a letter to his wife on 30 June 1747, the day after the poll, it is clear that he had no idea of Sandwich's real feelings towards him.[6]

He died 20 May 1775.

[1] Wm. Hewett to Duke of Devonshire, 6 Sept. 1733, Devonshire mss. [2] HMC 12th Rep. IX, 204. [3] E. J. Climenson, Elizabeth Montagu, i. 130, 135, 171. [4] 3 May 1747, Add. 32808, f. 116. [5] To Pelham, 11 Apr. 1747, Newcastle (Clumber) mss; to Bedford, 19 May 1747, Bedford mss. [6] Climenson, i. 240.

R.S.L.

MONTAGU, Edward Richard, Visct. Hinchingbrooke (1692–1722), of Hinchingbrooke, Hunts.

HUNTINGDON   1713–1722
HUNTINGDONSHIRE   13 Apr.–3 Oct. 1722

b. 7 July 1692, o.s. and h. ap. of Edward Montagu, 3rd Earl of Sandwich, by Elizabeth, 2nd da. of John Wilmot, 2nd Earl of Rochester, sis. and coh. of Charles, 3rd Earl of Rochester. educ. Trinity, Camb. 1706; Grand Tour (Italy) c.1708. m. 12 Apr. 1707, Elizabeth, da. of Alexander Popham, M.P., of Littlecote, Wilts. by Anne, da. of Ralph Montagu, 1st Duke of Montagu, 3s. 2da.
Capt.-lt. 4 Drags. 1709, capt. 1712; capt. and

lt.-col. Coldstream Gds. 1715; a.-d.-c. to George I 1715; lt.-col. 12 Ft. 1716–17; col. Richard Lucas's regt. of Ft. Sept.–Dec. 1717; col. 37 Ft. 1717–d.
Ld. lt. Hunts. Feb. 1722–d.

Lord Sandwich, being of weak intellect, was kept under restraint in his own house till his death in 1729, the administration of the estates devolving on Lord Hinchingbrooke, whose Jacobite mother lived in France. Re-elected as a Whig for the family borough in 1715, he usually supported the Government, seconding the Address, moved by Walpole, 23 Mar. 1715, voting for the septennial bill in 1716, and moving the Address 11 Nov. 1718. In January 1719 he unexpectedly joined Walpole in opposing the repeal of the Occasional Conformity and Schism Acts.[1] He did not vote on the peerage bill in December that year. After the South Sea crash he spoke with Walpole against the motion, which was carried 12 Dec. 1720, that the directors of the South Sea Company should lay an account of their proceedings before the House.[2] On 4 Jan. 1721 he moved unsuccessfully that all the directors should be taken into custody. Later, however, he pleaded for leniency on behalf of two of them. Transferring to the county in 1722, he died 3 Oct. that year, leaving two young sons.

[1] HMC Portland, v. 576. [2] Coxe, Walpole, i. 142.

R.S.L.

MONTAGU, George (c.1684–1739), of Horton, Northants.

NORTHAMPTON   1705–19 May 1715

b. c.1684, 1st s. of Edward Montagu of Horton and bro. of Edward Montagu (b. aft.1684, q.v.). m. (1) 8 Apr. 1706, Ricarda Posthuma (d.Apr. 1711), da. and h. of Richard Saltonstall of Chipping Warden, Northants., 1da.; (2) Lady Mary Lumley, da. of Richard, 1st Earl of Scarbrough, sis. of Hon. Charles, James, John and Thomas Lumley (qq.v.), 1s. 6da. suc. uncle, Charles Montagu, M.P., 1st Earl of Halifax, as 2nd Baron Halifax, 19 May 1715; cr. Earl of Halifax 14 June 1715; K.B. 27 May 1725.
Auditor of the Exchequer 1714–d.; ranger of Bushey Park 1715–d.; P.C. 27 Nov. 1717.

On coming of age Montagu was returned as a Whig on his family's interest for Northampton. At George I's accession he was appointed to the greatest sinecure in England, the auditorship of the Exchequer, worth £7,000 a year, by his uncle, Charles Montagu, Earl of Halifax, then 1st lord of the Treasury, to whose barony he succeeded in 1715, the earldom of Halifax being at the same time revived in his favour. He died 9 May 1739.

R.R.S.

MONTAGU, George (c.1713–80), of Windsor, Berks.

NORTHAMPTON 13 Apr. 1744–1754

> b. c.1713, 1st s. of Brig.-Gen. Edward Montagu (b. aft.1684, q.v.). educ. Eton 1725–8; I. Temple 1729; Trinity, Camb. 1731; Grand Tour with George Selwyn (q.v.) 1739–44. unm.
> Usher of the black rod [I] 1761–3; dep. ranger of Rockingham forest 1766–d.; private sec. to Lord North as chancellor of the Exchequer 1767–d.

George Montagu, Horace Walpole's friend and correspondent, was returned for Northampton on the interest of his first cousin, the 2nd Earl of Halifax, then in opposition. He followed Halifax over to the Government at the end of 1744, voting for the Hanoverians in 1746, when he was classed by Newcastle as 'New Ally'. Re-elected unopposed in 1747, he was classed as a government supporter, but gave up his seat in 1754. Thereafter, except for an interlude in Ireland during the vice-royalty of Lord Halifax, and a few excursions to town,

> he remained 'buried in squireland' at the three houses he successively occupied, Roel, Greatworth, and Adderley, drinking port, nursing the gout and dozing over his fire in the company of his brother John, who, according to Sir Walter Scott, was still a midshipman at the age of 60. [1]

His attachment to Lord North, who as chancellor of the Exchequer made him his private secretary, an absolute sinecure, worth about £400 a year, eventually led to his estrangement from Horace Walpole. He died 9 May 1780.

> [1] H. Walpole Corresp. (Yale ed.), ix. p. xxiv.

R.R.S.

MONTAGU, James (?1687–1748), of Belford, Northumb. and Newbold Verdon, Leics.

CHIPPENHAM 1708–1710
CAMELFORD 1715–1722

> b. ?1687, 1st s. of Hon. Charles Montagu, M.P., of Durham by his 1st w. Elizabeth, da and coh. of Francis Forster of Belford;[1] bro. of Edward (b.1692 q.v.) and John Montagu (q.v.). educ. Trinity, Camb. 28 June 1702, aged 14. m. (1) Mary, s.p.; (2) lic. 5 Apr. 1736,[2] Penelope, da. of George Hewett of Stretton and Great Glen, Leics., wid. of Sir William Chester, 5th Bt., of Chicheley, Bucks., s.p. suc. fa. 1721; gt.-uncle Nathaniel, Baron Crew of Stene, bp. of Durham, at Newbold Verdon 1721.

A Whig under Queen Anne, Montagu was associated with his uncle Sidney Wortley (q.v.) in the cartel controlling the Tyneside coal trade in the early eighteenth century.[3] Returned for Camelford in 1715, he voted with the Administration except on the peerage bill in 1719, which he opposed. Unsuccessful for Durham in 1722, and growing deaf, he spent the major part of his time at Newbold

Verdon, where he made great improvements to the house and grounds. In 1726 he sold the Belford estate, inherited from his mother, for £12,000. He died during a visit to London 30 Oct. 1748,[4] leaving Newbold Verdon to his cousin, Edward Wortley (q.v.).[5]

> [1] New Hist. Northumb. i. 229. [2] Foster, London Marriage Licences. [3] E. Hughes, N. Country Life in 18th Cent. 167–8, 233. [4] New Hist. Northumb. i. 392; E. J. Climenson, Elizabeth Montagu, i. 262; Letters of Mrs. Elizabeth Montagu (1809), ii. 303–4. [5] PCC 336 Strahan.

E.C.

MONTAGU, John (aft. 1692–1734), of Westminster.

STOCKBRIDGE 24 Apr.–2 Sept. 1734

> b. aft.1692, 3rd s. of Hon. Charles Montagu, M.P., of Durham, being 2nd s. by his 2nd w.; bro. of Edward (b.1692, q.v.) and James Montagu (q.v.). unm.
> Capt., Brig.-Gen. Vesey's Ft. 1716; capt. and lt.-col. 1 Ft. Gds. 1718; lt.-col. 18 Ft. 1719.

The grandson of the first Earl of Sandwich, Montagu was returned as a Whig for Stockbridge in 1734 but died a few months later on 2 Sept.

P.W.

MONTAGU, John (1719–95), of Lackham, Wilts.

HUNTINGDON 10 Mar. 1748–1754

> b. 1719, 4th s. of James Montagu of Lackham by Elizabeth, da. of Sir John Eyles of Southbroom, in Bishop's Cannings, Wilts. educ. R. Acad. Portsmouth 1733. m. 2 Dec. 1748, Sophia, da. of James Wroughton of Wilcot, Wilts., 4s. 1da.
> Lt. R.N. 1740, capt. 1746, r.-adm. 1770, v.-adm. 1776, adm. 1782; c.-in-c. N. American station 1771–4; gov. and c.-in-c. Newfoundland 1776–9; c.-in-c. Portsmouth 1783–6.

John Montagu was the great-great-grandson of Henry, 1st Earl of Manchester, whose third son James acquired Lackham by marriage in 1636.[1] A distinguished naval officer, he was present in the actions off Toulon, 11 Feb. 1744, and Cape Finisterre, 3 May 1747, having obtained his first command in 1745. In June 1747 he deputized for Kelland Courtenay (q.v.), Lord Sandwich's brother-in-law, at his election for Huntingdon.[2] Some months later he wrote to Lord Anson (q.v.), asking to be removed from his ship because it was under orders for the West Indies:

> My patron, Lord Sandwich, would not have objected to my going to the East [sic] Indies, if he did not desire something better for me by being near home. Your Lordship is not unacquainted with the view I have of being in Parliament. Mr. Courtenay, the present Member, is now very ill and it's thought can't live long and to be absent at such a time may be of great detriment to me.[3]

On Courtenay's death early in March 1748 Montagu

was at once brought in by Lord Sandwich as a government supporter. However, in 1753 Sandwich, again in opposition and wishing to be rid of his kinsman, drafted a letter to Montagu:

> I cannot say that I see things there in such a situation as would make it an advisable thing either for your sake or for mine that you should offer yourself a candidate at this time. In the first place the coming in for Huntingdon would be attended with much more expense now I am out of employment than it formerly was, and the recommending two persons of my own family [the other was Edward Montagu, q.v.] would give a handle to those who are desirous of acting against me, to urge how unreasonable I am to the people of the town, in never letting them have the least share in the choice of their representatives or even of one of them and this language supported by many, and backed with the weight of Administration who would certainly exert themselves against me [might create considerable expense. Further, it might be disadvantageous to Montagu now to have to be in opposition; on the other hand] it would discredit me among people I may hereafter choose to connect myself with, dare I to recommend the Members of Parliament that could not act in general as I should myself.[4]

Montagu was accordingly dropped for the 1754 election and did not stand again. In 1757, when captain of the *Monarque*, he had the unpleasing task of arranging for Admiral Byng's (q.v.) confinement and execution in his own ship. After holding several important appointments he died in September 1795, 'a man possessing the strictest integrity and a most benevolent heart, unhappily alloyed by some intemperance'.[5]

[1] *Wilts. Arch. Mag.* iii. 87; *Wilts. N. & Q.* iii. 172. [2] E. J. Climenson, *Elizabeth Montagu*, i. 240. [3] 18 Jan. 1748, Add. 15956, f. 262. [4] 31 May 1753, Sandwich mss. [5] Charnock, *Biog. Navalis*, v. 483.

R.S.L.

MONTAGU, Lord Robert (c.1710–62), of Kimbolton, Hunts.

HUNTINGDONSHIRE 1734–21 Oct. 1739

b. c.1710, 2nd and yst. s. of Charles Montagu, 1st Duke of Manchester, by Dodington, 2nd and yst. da. of Robert Greville, 4th Baron Brooke of Beauchamps Court. *m.* 3 Apr. 1735, Harriet, da. and coh. of Edmund Dunch (q.v.) of Little Wittenham, Berks., gt.-niece of John Churchill, 1st Duke of Marlborough, 2s. 2da. *suc.* bro. as 3rd Duke of Manchester 21 Oct. 1739.
V.-chamberlain to Queen Caroline 1735–7; ld. lt. Hunts. 1739–*d.*; ld. of the bedchamber 1739–61; ld. chamberlain to Queen Charlotte 1761–*d.*

Lord Robert Montagu was brought in as a Whig for the county by his brother, the Duke of Manchester, in 1734, though Sarah, Duchess of Marlborough, refused her support because 'I know what your Grace has been obliged to vote and likewise what my Lord Robert Montagu must vote

for the same reason'.[1] His only recorded vote was in favour of the Administration on the Spanish convention in 1739. At the time of his marriage Lord Hervey, his 'brother vice-chamberlain', wrote to Henry Fox (qq.v.):

> What will Miss Harriet make Ld. Robert besides a husband, a father and a penitent? There are few improvements his head will allow of; but I dare say she knows his wants as well as her own so well that all the improvement in her power will be amply bestowed.[2]

He succeeded to the dukedom in October 1739, but lost his family's electoral pre-eminence in the county to his kinsman, the 4th Earl of Sandwich, and was unable to nominate candidates for the 1747 and 1754 Parliaments.[3] He died 10 May 1762.

[1] *HMC 8th Rep.* pt. 2 (1881), p. 110. [2] Lord Ilchester, *Lord Hervey and his Friends*, 225. [3] See HUNTINGDONSHIRE.

R.S.L.

MONTAGU, Hon. William (c.1720–57), of Waresley Park, Hunts.

HUNTINGDONSHIRE 9 Nov. 1745–1747
BOSSINEY 22 Feb. 1752–1754

b. c.1720, yr. s. of Edward Richard Montagu, Visct. Hinchingbrooke (q.v.), and grandson of Edward, 3rd Earl of Sandwich. *educ.* ?Westminster Apr. 1728, aged 7. *m.* 13 Nov. 1749, Charlotte, da. of Francis Naylor, formerly Blundell, of Offord Darcy, Hunts., *s.p.*
Lt. R.N. 1740, capt. 1745.

William Montagu, a naval officer of some distinction, received his first command in the West Indies in May 1744 but was soon unjustly put under arrest for seven months by Commodore Charles Knowles (q.v.), from whom he obtained damages in a civil suit in 1752. On his release he was made a post captain, 23 May, carrying home the news of the capture of Louisbourg, 27 June 1745, for which he received a grant of £500 in August.[1] Three months later he was brought in by his brother, Lord Sandwich, at a by-election for Huntingdonshire, being classed as a 'New Ally' in 1746. On 3 May 1747 he took a prominent part in Anson's victory off Finisterre. Before the general election of July 1747, Sandwich 'upon some quarrel he has with his brother Capt. Montagu . . . determined to drop him, though the gentlemen had agreed to choose him for the county'.[2] Consequently he could not stand again, though Sandwich later 'intended to propose [him] at Huntingdon in case of early vacancy' and asked his cousin Edward Wortley (q.v.) to bear him in mind for the forthcoming by-election at Bossiney in December 1747. Wortley, however, after offering Montagu the vacancy, thought 'it would not be proper for me to do as I had designed',[3] but he did provide him with a stop-gap seat there four years later. Meanwhile by December 1751, Montagu had once more been nominated by Sandwich as candidate for the county at the next general election, but he eventually stood down in favour of Coulson Fellowes (q.v.)[4] and did not stand again. He died 10 Feb. 1757.

[1] *Cal. Treas. Bks. and Pprs.* 1742–5, p. 820. [2] *HMC 10th Rep. I,* 296; Sandwich to Newcastle, 3 May 1747, Add. 32808, ff. 116–17. [3] Sandwich to Pelham, 4 Nov. 1747, Newcastle (Clumber) mss; Wortley to Sandwich, 6 Nov. 1747, Wortley mss, R. Inst. Cornwall. [4] Sandwich to Ld. Trentham and the Duke of Bedford, 15 Dec. 1751, circular letter from Fellowes, 18 Apr. 1753, Bedford mss.

R.S.L.

MONTAGUE, *see* **MONTAGU** *and also* **WORTLEY MONTAGU**

MONTGOMERIE, John (1680–1731), of Giffen, Ayr.

AYRSHIRE   1710–1727

bap. 11 Sept. 1680,[1] 1st s. of Hon. Francis Montgomerie, M.P., P.C. [S], of Giffen (2nd s. of Hugh, 7th Earl of Eglintoun [S]) by his 2nd w. Elizabeth, da. of Sir Robert Sinclair, 1st Bt., M.P. [S], of Longformacus, Berwick, and wid. of Sir James Primrose of Barnbougle, Linlithgow. *educ.* Glasgow 1694. *m.* (contract 28 Sept. 1704) Lady Mary Carmichael, da. of John, 1st Earl of Hyndford [S], 1da. *suc.* fa. bef. Jan. 1729.
    Master of the mint [S] 1710–d.; groom of the bedchamber to the Prince of Wales 1714–27; gov. New York and New Jersey 1727–d.
    Capt.-lt. 3 Ft. Gds. 1715–17, capt. and lt.-col. 1723; left army by 1727.

Returned as a Whig on the interest of a first cousin, the 9th Earl of Eglintoun, Montgomerie entered the service of the Prince of Wales at George I's accession. In 1715 he obtained a company in the guards, which he lost in 1717 for voting against the Government in the debate on the charges of corruption against Lord Cadogan (q.v.).[2] He voted for the repeal of the Occasional Conformity and Schism Acts but against the peerage bill in 1719, when he was put down as to be spoken to by the Duke of Argyll. He figures in the list of Members found by the secret committee on the South Sea bubble in 1721 to have accepted stock from the Company while the South Sea bill was before Parliament but he was able to show that the transaction was a bona fide one, for which he had given security.[3] He owed his promotion in 1723 to the Prince of Wales, who 'sent for Cadogan and spoke for John Montgomery, whereupon he altered a whole scheme of promotions he had before settled'.[4] About 1725 financial difficulties forced him to sell his estate to Sir John Anstruther (q.v.). In 1727 he gave up his seat to

become governor of New York, where he died 1 July 1731.

[1] *Scots Peerage,* ix. 81. [2] *Pol. State,* xiv. 80; Sunderland (Blenheim) mss D. II, 16. [3] *CJ,* xix. 569, 572. [4] Coxe, *Walpole,* ii. 291.

J.M.S.

MOODIE, James (*d.* 1724).

ORKNEY AND SHETLAND   1715–1722

2nd s. of James Moodie of Melsetter, Orkney by his 1st w., ?a da. of James Douglas, 11th Earl of Morton [S]. *unm.*
    Sec. to commrs. for stating army debts, 1715–22.

Returned for Orkney and Shetland in 1715, Moodie, the son of a naval captain, voted with the Administration in all recorded divisions except on the septennial bill, when he was absent. On 17 July 1721 he wrote to Sunderland that at the beginning of the 1719 session,

Sir William Gordon [q.v.] came to me, as he said from your Lordship, and assured me in your name that four hundred pounds should be paid me at the end of that session, this sum being in place of the original sum promised to me annually by the Duke of Roxburgh; by this means the difference was that the Earl of Sunderland was to be my paymaster.

Gordon had then advanced part of the sum, since when Moodie had 'received nothing but promises and delays'. Sunderland had referred him to Walpole and George Baillie (q.v.)

for the despatch of my affair. It is fit I acquaint you that if it came to either of their hands I shall still be delayed, and the reasons are, the first I have still opposed, and the latter opposes me and has all along delayed the performances of the Duke of Roxburgh's promises.

On 29 Aug. 1721 Moodie gave a receipt for £200 from Gordon, completing the £400.[1] He lost his seat in 1722 and died in his father's lifetime 4 Feb. 1724.

[1] Sunderland (Blenheim) mss D. II, 4.

J.M.S.

MOORE, Arthur (c.1666–1730), of Fetcham Park, Surr.

GREAT GRIMSBY   1695–1700, 1701–1715,
                           11 Feb. 1721–1722

b. c.1666. *m.* (1) 17 Mar. 1692, Susannah (*d.* 23 Feb. 1695), da. of Dr. Edward Browne of Crane Court, London, 2da.; (2) 4 Nov. 1696, Theophila, da. and h. of William Smythe of the I. Temple, London, paymaster of the gent. pensioners, 3s. 3da.
    Comptroller of army accounts 1704–7; director, E.I. Co. 1706–9; ld. of Trade 1710–14; director, R. African Co. 1710, S. Sea Co. 1711–14; high steward, Great Grimsby 1715–d.

An Irish adventurer, Moore was said to have

begun life as a footman, which gave rise to the story that the elder Craggs,

> who had worn livery too and who was getting into a coach with him, turned about and said 'God! Arthur, I am always going to get up behind; are not you?'[1]

Speaker Onslow describes him as

> of very extraordinary parts, with great experience and knowledge of the world, very able in parliament, and capable in the highest parts of business . . . His acquisitions had been very great by trade and afterwards by every method, as it has been said, that his interest and power and opportunities opened to him; but his profusion consumed all.[2]

He figured prominently in the financial scandals of the last days of Anne's reign, when he was accused in the House of Lords of corruptly helping Bolingbroke and Lady Masham to fill their pockets at the public expense and was simultaneously expelled from his directorship of the South Sea Company for attempting to use one of their ships for his private trade. Defeated at Grimsby in 1715, he was among the Members and agents of the late Tory Government who were expressly excepted from the Indemnity Act of 1717. He seems to have made his peace with the Government in 1718, when his two younger sons were jointly granted the reversion of their grandfather's place of paymaster of the gentlemen pensioners.[3] He re-appeared in 1720, the year of the South Sea bubble, as the promoter of a joint stock company, which failed to obtain the necessary patent of incorporation.[4] Re-elected next year for Grimsby, in succession to another corrupt South Sea director, Sir Robert Chaplin, he defended his former protégés in the South Sea company when the confiscation of their estates came before the House of Commons, also speaking on behalf of John Aislabie (q.v.).[5] Losing his seat in 1722, he died 4 May 1730, 'broken in all respects but in his parts and spirits.'[6]

[1] Walpole to Mann, 1 Sept. 1750. [2] Onslow's note to Burnet's *Hist. of his own Time*, vi. 162–3. [3] *N. & Q.* (ser. 2), vi. 13–14. [4] J. Carswell, *South Sea Bubble*, 67, 155, 166. [5] Stuart mss 52/157. [6] Onslow, ut supra.

P.W.

MOORE, Daniel, of Tarriers, Bucks.

ILCHESTER   1722–1727

Moore was elected for Ilchester as a government supporter[1] with William Burroughs, who in 1732 included money owing by Moore among 'debts due to me, which I look upon to be desperate, or at least doubtful'.[2] He did not stand again.

[1] Sunderland (Blenheim) mss. [2] *A True and Exact Particular and Inventory of all . . . the lands . . . of William Burroughs* (London 1732), p. 69.

S.R.M.

MOORE, Henry, 4th Earl of Drogheda [I] (1700–27).

CAMELFORD   1722–29 May 1727

b. 7 Oct. 1700, 1st s. of Charles, Visct. Moore (1st s. of Henry Hamilton Moore, 3rd Earl of Drogheda [I]) by Jane, da. and h. of Arthur Loftus, 3rd Visct. Loftus of Ely [I]. m. 11 Feb. 1720, Charlotte, da. of Hugh Boscawen (q.v.), 1st Visct. Falmouth, 1da. d.v.p. suc. fa. 21 May 1714 and gd.-fa. as 4th Earl of Drogheda 7 June 1714.

Succeeding to the family estates at the age of 13, Drogheda promptly took to drink. His grandmother and guardian, Lady Drogheda, then sent him on the grand tour, accompanied by a French Huguenot refugee as governor. At Brussels, in June 1717, he gave his companion the slip and set off alone for Paris, informing his grandmother that he could no longer bear the man's 'peevish humours'. Running short of money in Paris, he returned home, where, in 1719, his grandmother obtained from the lord chancellor of Ireland a release from responsibility for him, writing 'sure he exceeds all the youth that ever went before him for wickedness'. An allowance of £1,500 p.a. was granted him, which he invariably exceeded. A year later, he married a daughter of Hugh Boscawen, the government manager for the Cornish boroughs, who brought him in for Camelford at the next general election. Having dissipated his fortune in racing and every kind of extravagance, he died at Dublin 29 May 1727, aged 26, leaving debts exceeding £180,000, which forced his successor to sell a large portion of the family's estates in co. Louth.[1]

[1] Anne, Countess of Drogheda, *Hist. Moore Fam.* 112–16, 145.

E.C.

MOORE, William (1699–1746), of Polesden Lacey, Surr.

BANBURY   25 Nov. 1740–26 Oct. 1746

bap. 4 June 1699,[1] 1st s. of Arthur Moore (q.v.) by his 2nd w. m. — (d. 25 Dec. 1740) of Linton, Glos.,[2] s.p. suc. fa. at Fetcham Park, Surr. 1730; uncle Col. Thomas Moore at Polesden Lacey 1735.

In February 1735 Moore sold Fetcham Park to pay his father's debts,[3] succeeding his uncle at Polesden Lacey shortly afterwards. Returned for Banbury by his friend Francis, Lord North (q.v.),[4] he voted against the Administration in every recorded division except that on the motion for the removal of Walpole in February 1741. He was one of the Whigs who signed the opposition whip of 10 Mar. 1743.[5] He died 26 Oct. 1746, bequeathing his estates to North's son, George III's prime minister, whose trustees sold Polesden Lacey a year later for £5,500 to pay the debts encumbering the estate.[6]

[1] Chester, *Westm. Abbey Reg.* 34. [2] Bodl. North mss, b. 14, f. 78. [3] Wm. Moore to Thos. Moore, 25 Feb. 1735, ibid. c. 11, f. 109. [4] See Ld. North to Wm. Moore, 10 July 1743 and 3 Aug. 1745, ibid. ff. 122, 124. [5] Owen, *Pelhams*, 198. [6] Bodl. North mss, c. 11, f.135.

E.C.

MORDAUNT, Sir Charles, 6th Bt. (?1697–1778), of Walton D'Eiville, nr. Kineton, Warws. and Little Massingham, nr. King's Lynn, Norf.

WARWICKSHIRE 6 Feb. 1734–1774

b. ?1697, 1st s. of Sir John Mordaunt, 5th Bt., M.P., of Walton D'Eiville and Little Massingham by his 2nd w. Penelope, da. of Sir George Warburton, 1st Bt., of Arley, Cheshire. *educ.* New, Oxf. 8 June 1714, aged 16; L. Inn 1718. *m.* (1) 1 Dec. 1720, Dorothy (*d.* Mar. 1726), da. of John Conyers, M.P., of Walthamstow, Essex, aunt of John Conyers (q.v.), 2da.; (2) 7 July 1730, Sophia, da. of Sir John Wodehouse, 4th Bt., of Kimberley, Norf., sis. of Sir Armine Wodehouse, 5th Bt. (q.v.), 2s. *suc.* fa. 6 Sept. 1721.

A wealthy and influential Tory, the head of a family settled in Warwickshire since the sixteenth century, Sir Charles Mordaunt was returned for the county without a contest for 40 years. Presumably he was the Mr. Mordaunt of Warwickshire whose name was sent to the Pretender early in 1721 as a probable supporter in the event of a rising.[1] He was one of the Tories who withdrew on the motion for the removal of Walpole in February 1741. In May 1742 he was included in the opposition list for a proposed committee on the public accounts.[2] In the 2nd Lord Egmont's electoral survey, c.1749–50, he is described as being 'well inclined to us. He has a great weight among the Tories. An estate of £2,500 p.a.' In the same Lord Egmont's lists for a new government on the Prince's accession he is put down for a place on the Treasury or Admiralty boards. He was one of the 'heads of the Tories' who came to consult Egmont after the death of the Prince.[3]

He died 11 Mar. 1778.

[1] Stuart mss 65/16. [2] Walpole to Mann, 26 May 1742. [3] Egmont mss, Add. 49097–8.

S.R.M.

MORDAUNT, Hon. Harry (?1663–1720).

BRACKLEY 2 Jan. 1692–1698, 1701–1702,
26 Nov. 1705–1708
RICHMOND 1708–4 Jan. 1720

b. ?1663, 3rd s. of John Mordaunt, 1st Visct. Mordaunt, by Elizabeth, da. and h. of Hon. Thomas Carey; bro. of Charles, 3rd Earl of Peterborough. *educ.* Westminster (K.S.); Ch. Ch. Oxf. 17 Dec. 1680, aged 17. *m.* (1) Margaret (*d.* 22 July 1706), nat. da. of Sir Thomas Spencer, 3rd Bt., of Yarnton, Oxon., 5s.

2da.; (2) Penelope, da. and h. of William Tipping of Ewelme, Oxon., 1da.

Col. of a regt. of Ft. 1694, of Marines 1702, and of Ft. 1703–13; c.-in-c. Guernsey 1697; treasurer of Ordnance 1699–*d.*; brig.-gen. 1704; maj.-gen. 1706; lt.-gen. 1709.

Mordaunt was returned as a Whig for Richmond by his cousin, Lord Wharton. He did not vote after 1715, but spoke for the Government, 8 Apr. 1717, on a motion for a vote of credit against Sweden. He died 4 Jan. 1720.

R.R.S.

MORDAUNT, John (1697–1780), of Freefolk, Hants.

PONTEFRACT 7 Feb. 1730–1734
WHITCHURCH 19 Apr. 1735–1741
COCKERMOUTH 1741–1768

b. 1697, 1st s. of Hon. Harry Mordaunt (q.v.), by his 1st w. *unm.* K.B. 26 June 1749.

Page of honour to Queen Anne 1711, to George I 1714; equerry to the Princesses 1720; entered army 1721; capt. 1724; capt. 3 Drags. 1726; capt. and lt.-col. 3 Ft. Gds. 1731; equerry to the King 1737–60; col. army 1741; col. 58 Ft. 1741–2, 18 Ft. 1742–7; brig.-gen. 1745; maj.-gen. 1747; col. 12 Drags. 1747–9, 7 Drag. Gds. July–Nov. 1749, 10 Drags. 1749–*d.*; gov. Sheerness 1752–78; lt.-gen. 1754; gen. 1770; gov. Berwick 1778–*d.*

Mordaunt, 'an officer of gallantry, with some wit,'[1] was returned in 1730 for Pontefract on the interest of Lord Galway (q.v.); for Whitchurch in 1735 by John Wallop (q.v.); and for Cockermouth in 1741 on the Lawson interest. His sister had married Sir Wilfred Lawson (q.v.), on whose death in 1737, leaving two infant sons, she and Mordaunt took charge of the estate. Building up a strong personal interest, he repelled an attempt by Sir James Lowther (q.v.) to oust him in 1747,[2] thereafter retaining the seat without opposition.

A Whig, Mordaunt consistently supported Walpole, speaking as well as voting for the Government, especially in army debates. In one of these, on 3 Feb. 1738, he embarrassed his leaders by declaring he was in favour of a standing army because it 'was absolutely necessary for supporting the Whig interest', and if it 'should be disbanded, or very much reduced, the Tory interest would prevail.' He also spoke on 6 Mar. 1739 for the Spanish convention and on 8 Mar. 1742 against the motion for an inquiry into Walpole's Administration.

After Walpole's fall Mordaunt, in the interval of campaigning in Flanders and Scotland, where he commanded a brigade at Culloden, continued to vote with the Government and was classed in 1746 as 'Old Whig'. But on 4 Mar. 1752 he spoke and voted against a government bill for purchasing forfeited estates in Scotland with a view to settling foreign Protestants on them. He was supposed to be speaking on the orders of the Duke of Cumberland, who disapproved of the policy of appeasing the Highlands.[3]

In 1757 Mordaunt commanded the unsuccessful expedition against Rochefort, but was acquitted of all blame by a court martial. He declined to stand in 1768 and died 23 Oct. 1780.

[1] Walpole, *Mems. Geo. II*, i. 220. [2] B. Bonsall, *Sir Wm. Lowther and Cumb. and Westmld. Elections*, 12 n. 3, 13. [3] Walpole, op. cit. i. 257-8; Walpole to Mann, 23 Mar. 1752.

R.R.S.

MORDAUNT, Hon. John (?1709–67).

NOTTINGHAMSHIRE	14 Feb. 1739–1747
WINCHELSEA	1747–1754
CHRISTCHURCH	1754–1761

b. ?1709, yr. s. of John Mordaunt, M.P., Visct. Mordaunt (s. of Charles, 3rd Earl of Peterborough), by Lady Frances Powlett, da. of Charles Powlett, M.P., 2nd Duke of Bolton. *educ.* Westminster Sept. 1719, aged 10. *m.* (1) 9 Oct. 1735, Mary (*d.* 12 Sept. 1749), da. of Scrope Howe, M.P., 1st Visct. Howe [I], wid. of Thomas Herbert, M.P., 8th Earl of Pembroke, *s.p.*; (2) Elizabeth, da. of Samuel Hamilton, *s.p.*

Cornet, R. Horse Gds. 1726–36; ranger of Alice Holt and Walmer Forest by 1741; lt.-col. Duke of Kingston's Horse, Oct. 1745–Sept. 1746.

Soon after marrying the dowager Countess of Pembroke[1] Mordaunt resigned his commission in the army and began to look for a parliamentary seat in Nottinghamshire, where his wife's family, the Howes, had an hereditary interest. In 1737, on the news that one of the Members for the county was dying, Lady Pembroke, without consulting the local Whig leaders, announced that her husband would stand for the vacancy to keep up the Howe interest till her nephew, the 3rd Lord Howe (q.v.), came of age.[2] Having previously come to a mutual assistance agreement with the local Tory leaders, Mordaunt, though a Whig, was unanimously adopted by a meeting of 'the country interest', while a corresponding meeting of 'Lords and gentlemen in the Whig interest', indignant at his tactics, passed resolutions declaring him not a proper person to represent the county and undertaking to support any suitable gentleman who might offer himself as a candidate.[3] No one being prepared to face the cost of a contest, he was returned unopposed. He continued to represent the county, voting with the Government, till 1747, when he withdrew to make way for Lord Howe and was accommodated by Newcastle with a government seat at Winchelsea.

Mordaunt rejoined the army in 1745 as lieutenant-colonel of the Duke of Kingston's Horse,

one of the temporary regiments raised by noblemen at their own expense during the rebellion. Next year he was turned out of his command to make room for the Duke of Rutland's son, Lord Robert Sutton (q.v.), thus losing the prospect of acquiring permanent rank as lieutenant-colonel when the regiment was subsequently placed on the establishment as the Duke of Cumberland's Dragoons. When the sinecure of clerk of the pipe fell vacant in 1748 he besieged Pelham in London with applications for the place in compensation for the loss of his commission. 'I am plagued out of my life for this place', Pelham complained to Newcastle, 'Jack Mordaunt follows me everywhere . . . ' Having failed to extract a promise from Pelham, Mordaunt sent two 'most pressing letters' to Newcastle begging for his support. 'There is one thing', he wrote, that 'has given me great pain, that Mr. Levinz [William Levinz, jun., q.v.] should have so good a place, who voted against the royal family for three Parliaments together, and this is my third Parliament, and never gave one vote against them'.[4] He did not get the place but in consideration of his 'bad luck' he was given a secret service pension of £800 p.a., which was increased to £1,200 on compassionate grounds when he retired from Parliament in 1761.[5] He died 1 July 1767.

[1] See Hervey, *Mems.* 589–90. [2] Lady Pembroke to Newcastle, 28 Sept. 1737, Add. 32690, f. 374. [3] John Plumptre to Newcastle 29 Oct. 1737, 3 July 1738, George Gregory to Newcastle, 2 Sept. 1738, Add. 32690, f. 406; 32691, ff. 226, 309, 311. [4] Pelham to Newcastle, 16 Sept. 1748, Mordaunt to Newcastle, 7 and 16 Sept. 1748, Add. 32716, ff. 192, 231, 233. [5] Namier, *Structure*, 217, 473; Mordaunt to Newcastle, 26 Jan. 1761, Add. 32918, f. 74.

R.R.S.

MORDEN, William (?1696–1770), of Suffield and Gunton, Norf.

BERE ALSTON	5 Feb.–17 Apr. 1734
DUNWICH	21 Feb. 1738–1741
BERE ALSTON	1741–1754

b. ?1696, 1st s. of John Morden of Suffield by Judith, da. of William Cropley of Shelland, Suff., sis. and coh. of Harbord Harbord (q.v.). *educ.* Thurlow and Bury sch.; Caius, Camb. 4 Feb. 1713, aged 16; M. Temple 1716. *m.* 25 Apr. 1732, Elizabeth, da. and coh. of Robert Britiffe (q.v.) of Baconsthorpe, Norf., half-sis. of Judith, 1st w. of Sir John Hobart, 5th Bt. (q.v.), afterwards 1st Earl of Buckinghamshire, 2s. *suc.* fa. 1726; uncle Harbord Harbord 1742, when he took the name of Harbord. K.B. 20 Oct. 1744; *cr.* Bt. 22 Mar. 1746.

Towards the end of the 1727 Parliament, Morden, a Norfolk country gentleman, was returned for Bere Alston by his neighbour and brother-in-law, Sir John Hobart. In 1734 he contested Norfolk unsuccessfully at great personal expense to Walpole,[1] but later in the Parliament he was returned un-opposed for Dunwich, near his Suffolk estate. For the rest of his parliamentary career he sat for Bere Alston on the Hobart interest, voting consistently with the Government until he retired in 1754. He died 17 Feb. 1770.

[1] Coxe, *Walpole*, i. 456.

S.R.M.

MORE, Robert (1703–80), of Linley Hall, nr. Bishop's Castle, Salop.

BISHOP'S CASTLE   1727–1741
SHREWSBURY   1754–1761

b. May 1703, o.s. of Robert More of Linley (formerly a London merchant), by his 2nd w. Sarah, da. of John Walcot of Walcot, Salop. *educ.* Queens', Camb. 1723–5. *m.* (1) 1750, Ellen, da. of Thomas Wilson of Trevallyn, Denb., 2s.; (2) 8 Feb. 1768, Catherine, da. of Thomas More of Millichope, Salop. *suc.* fa. 1719.

In 1727 More was returned on his own interest for Bishop's Castle, which his great-grandfather had represented in the Short and Long Parliaments and his uncle 1681, 1689 and 1695–8. In Parliament he voted with the Administration, while his nephew, John Walcot, a Tory, who had recently acquired the manor of Bishop's Castle, voted with the Opposition. During the last session he abstained from a division on a bill for limiting the number of placemen in the House of Commons, on the ground that,

> though he liked the bill, he did not know if the passing it at this time might not embarrass the King's affairs, as we are going into a war, when it will be necessary the next Parliament should consist of Members that will concur in the court measures, as placemen will be sure to do.[1]

At the opening of More's election campaign in 1733 he applied to Walpole for a place for the son of Edward Morris, an influential constituent, without whose support he would

> sink under Mr. Walcot's opposition. And to give you a proof that I have no other view than to prevent the Tory interest, whoever you please shall have the benefit of what you do for Mr. Morris. Whoever you will put up upon that interest, I will freely resign my pretentions to, and assist with my vote interest, and purse.[2]

On 1 Feb. 1734 Morris reported that three of Walcot's servants had gone about Bishop's Castle with a drunken mob (though few of them burgesses) crying 'down with the roundheads, damn More, down with him'; that Corbet Kynaston (q.v.), Mytton, and Lyster (q.v.), all three leading Tories, had persuaded Walcot to give More this opposition —'your relations take it ill you did not vote some-times along with Mr. Walcot'; and that 'Mr.

Walcot's servants give out, they'll double what any body else do. I am more than £20 out of pocket, I want a bill. I can do nothing without money'.[3] More was re-elected, but did not contest the seat in 1741.

More's only recorded speeches were made in 1736 on the mortmain bill, when he spoke with 'warmth and bitterness' against the universities,[4] and on a bill, which he helped to prepare and bring in, for explaining the Bribery Act of 1729. He was a member of the parliamentary gaols committee of 1729, revived in 1730; and of the common council of the Georgia Society, set up by royal charter in 1732, from which in 1736 he and John White (q.v.) jointly resigned, continuing however to act as trustees. Their ostensible reason for resigning was 'their absence from town the greatest part of the year and their parliamentary business when in town'. It was thought, however, that White, 'a professed Dissenter', resigned because the council would not 'leave room for public encouragement to set up dissenting congregations in Georgia' but did appropriate land for endowing the church of England, and that he had persuaded More to resign with him.[5]

While out of Parliament More spent a good deal of his time on foreign travel. Two of his journeys can be traced in a passport and through corres-pondence preserved at Linley Hall, which he started building in 1742 from designs by Henry Joynes, long employed at Blenheim Palace as clerk of the works to Vanbrugh. In 1749 he set out for Portugal, and in October was at Madrid; most of 1750 he spent in Italy, returning about the end of the year by way of Vienna and Leipzig to England. In 1751 he visited Scandinavia, Russia, and northern Germany, returning to Hull in September. On 3 Aug. 1749 Benjamin Keene (q.v.), minister at Madrid, wrote to the British consul at Lisbon:

> I forgot to mention Mr. More to you. I knew him in Parliament; a great friend of Mr. White's, your cousin Laroche, and the Heathcotes [qq.v.]. I have made him speak. I have heard him speak well in the House. This will be strange to you who have seen his invincible modesty in Lisbon. He has been on the top of the mountain at St. Ildefonso to see where the water came from, without opening his eyes to see it squirt out of the fine fountains below. And he has found out what neither you nor I ever did, that the snow that braves out the summer, lies on the south, not the north side of the mountain. *D'ailleurs* great knowledge, good sense and probity.[6]

More was returned unopposed for Shrewsbury in 1754 but declined standing again in 1761. He died 5 Jan. 1786.

[1] *HMC Egmont Diary*, ii. 37. [2] 15 Oct. 1733, Cholmondeley (Houghton) mss. [3] More mss at Linley Hall. [4] Harley Diary,

15 Apr. 1736; Chandler, ix. 234-5. ⁵ *HMC Egmont Diary*, i. 55, 285; ii. 233-5, 239, 268-9, 373. ⁶ Sir R. Lodge, *Private Corresp. of Sir Benjamin Keene*, 152.

J.B.L.

MORETON, Matthew Ducie (c.1662–1735), of Moreton, Staffs. and Tortworth, Glos.

GLOUCESTERSHIRE 1708–1713, 1715–9 June 1720

b. c.1662, 1st s. of Edward Moreton of Moreton and Engleton, Staffs. by Elizabeth, da. and h. of Robert Ducie of Little Aston, Staffs., niece and h. of William Ducie, 1st Visct. Downe [I], of Tortworth, Glos. *m.* 11 Jan. 1690, Arabella, da. and coh. of Sir Thomas Prestwich, 2nd Bt., of Hulme, Lancs., 3s. 4da. *suc.* fa. 1687; *cr.* Lord Ducie, Baron of Moreton, 9 June 1720.

Cornet, Lord Grey's independent tp. of Horse 1685; cornet, 3 Drag. Gds. 1687, capt. by Sept. 1689, maj. 1690, lt.-col. 1694, out by 1702.

Sheriff, Staffs. 1704–5, Glos. 1705–6.

Vice-treasurer [I] Apr.–May 1717; jt. vice-treasurer [I] May 1717–June 1720; P.C. [I] Sept. 1717.

Moreton's father acquired by marriage the estates of the Ducies, descended from Sir Robert Ducie, 1st Bt., lord mayor of London, who purchased Tortworth and other Gloucestershire property early in the seventeenth century. Returned for Gloucestershire as a Whig, Moreton voted from 1715 consistently with the Government, speaking for the peerage bill in 1719. On the reunion of the Whig party in 1720 he was raised to the peerage in compensation for the loss of his place, which was required for Sir William St. Quintin.[1] He died 2 May 1735, aged 72.

¹ *HMC Polwarth*, ii. 567.

S.R.M.

MORETON, Hon. Matthew Ducie (bef. 1700–1770), of Tortworth, Glos.

CRICKLADE   1 Feb. 1721–1722
CALNE   28 Feb. 1723–1727
TREGONY   6 Feb. 1729–1734
LOSTWITHIEL   31 Mar.–2 May 1735

b. bef. 1700, 1st s. of Matthew Ducie Moreton (q.v.), 1st Lord Ducie, Baron of Moreton. *educ.* poss. Harrow 1709. *unm. suc.* fa. as 2nd Lord Ducie 2 May 1735; *cr.* Baron Ducie of Tortworth, with a sp. rem. 27 Apr. 1763.

Constable of St. Briavels, warden, forest of Dean and ld. lt. Glos. 1755–8; high steward, Gloucester 1755–66.

Moreton entered Parliament for the venal borough of Cricklade at a contested by-election in 1721, despite a petition alleging that he had 'used such menaces and threats to the . . . bailiff that, if he had returned . . . Thomas Gore [q.v.], he would have been in danger of losing his life'.[1] Defeated in 1722 by one vote, he was returned for Calne at another

contested by-election, perhaps on the interest of his kinsman, Walter Hungerford (q.v.).[2] After contesting Gloucester unsuccessfully in 1727, he was brought in by the Administration for Tregony at a by-election in 1729 and for Lostwithiel at a further by-election in 1735, a month before he succeeded to the peerage. He voted consistently for the Administration in all recorded divisions. On Walpole's fall he agreed to hold the office of surveyor of the petty customs in London in trust for H. B. Legge and Benjamin Keene (qq.v.), as the office was not consistent with a seat in Parliament; but in 1752 he asked to be relieved of the trust, 'not relishing the appearance of a place without the reality'.[3] He died 25 or 27 Dec. 1770.

¹ *CJ*, xix. 423. ² The connexion was through the Lords Seymour of Trowbridge. See *CP*, iv. 451, *sub* Downe, and 474, *sub* Ducie. ³ Legge to Pelham, 22 Sept., to Newcastle, 28 Sept. 1752, Add. 32729, ff. 334, 360.

R.S.L.

MORGAN, Anthony (d. 1729), of Freshwater, I.o.W.

YARMOUTH I.o.W.   1695–1710
NEWPORT I.o.W.   1715–12 Apr. 1717
YARMOUTH I.o.W.   12 Apr. 1717–1727
LYMINGTON   1727–19 Apr. 1729

m. by 1691, Catherine, da. and h. of Thomas Urry of Freshwater, 6s. 1da.

Brig. and lt. 1 Life Gds. by 1691, exempt and capt. 1692, guidon and maj. 1694, cornet and eld. maj. 1697; lt.-gov. I.o.W. 1702–10, 1715–d.; gov. Cowes castle 1715–d.

Anthony Morgan acquired the manor of Freshwater by his marriage.[1] As lieutenant-governor of the Isle of Wight under Anne he built up an interest at Newport and at Yarmouth, which he appears to have managed for the Government after George I's accession. In December 1714 the governor of the Isle of Wight, General Webb (q.v.), complained that 'Colonel Morgan has more credit with the great people than I have'.[2] He was returned for Newport in 1715 on the government interest but in 1717, when his petition succeeded, he chose to sit for Yarmouth, voting consistently with the Administration. Transferring to Lymington in 1727, he died 19 Apr. 1729, cutting off his eldest son with a shilling and leaving his property to be divided among his five younger sons.[3]

¹ *VCH Hants*, v. 241; PCC 23 Lort. ² T. Stephens, *The Castle Builders*, 41. ³ PCC 171 Abbott.

P.W.

MORGAN, John (1671–1720), of Tredegar, Mon.

MONMOUTHSHIRE 1701–7 Mar. 1720

b. 4 Jan. 1671, 4th s. of William Morgan, M.P., of

Tredegar and Machen, Mon. by his 1st w. Blanche, da. and h. of William Morgan of Dderw, Brec. *m.* 9 Jan. 1700, Martha, o. da. of Gwyn Vaughan of Trebarried, Brec., 7s. 2da. *suc.* e. bro. Thomas Morgan, M.P., at Tredegar, Machen and Dderw (then worth £7,000 p.a.) 1700; uncle, John Morgan, M.P., at Ruperra, Glam. 1715.

Custos rot. Mon. from 1700; ld. lt. Mon. and Brec. 1715–*d.*

The Morgans of Tredegar were the leading Whig family in South Wales, with estates in Monmouthshire, which they represented in every Parliament from the Revolution to the beginning of the nineteenth century; in Breconshire, where they controlled the county and borough seats; and in Glamorganshire, where they had a strong interest. Returned for Monmouthshire in 1701, John Morgan established the reputation of a great supporter of the Whig interest in the county.[1] After George I's accession he voted for the septennial bill in 1716 but was absent from the division on the Occasional Conformity and Schism Acts, though he had been obliged in matters of patronage by the Government and pressed to attend.[2] He did not vote on the peerage bill, on which he was classed as doubtful and to be spoken to by Sunderland. He died 7 Mar. 1720.

[1] W. Coxe, *Hist. Tour through Mon.* i. 68. [2] Tredegar mss 53/120/2, NLW.

P.D.G.T.

MORGAN, Sir John, 4th Bt. (1710–67), of Kinnersley Castle, Herefs.

HEREFORD   1734–1741
HEREFORDSHIRE   5 May 1755–29 Apr. 1767

b. 11 July 1710, o.s. of Sir Thomas Morgan, 3rd Bt. (q.v.). *educ.* Westminster 1721; Queen's, Oxf. 1726. *m.* 17 Dec. 1750, Anne, da. and coh. of Sir Jacob Jackobson, director of South Sea Co., of Walthamstow, Essex, *s.p. suc.* fa. 14 Dec. 1716.

Sheriff, Herefs. 1752–3.

Returned for Hereford as a Tory, Morgan voted with the Opposition. He did not stand in 1741 but came in later for the county. He died 29 Apr. 1767.

A.N.N.

MORGAN, Maurice (1692–1733).

YARMOUTH I.o.W.   10 Apr. 1725–24 Apr. 1733

bap. 27 Sept. 1692, 2nd s. of Anthony Morgan (q.v.) of Freshwater, I.o.W. *unm. suc.* fa. 1729.

Ensign, Ld. Paston's regt. of Ft. 1704; 3 Ft. Gds. 1709; lt. 1 Drag. Gds. 1712; capt. 4 Drags. 1719; capt. and lt.-col 3 Ft. Gds. 1722; lt.-gov. I.o.W. 1731–*d.*

Returned for Yarmouth in 1725 on the government interest, Morgan voted with the Administration in all recorded divisions, except on the excise bill when he was absent. Succeeding his father as lieutenant-governor of the Isle of Wight in January 1731, he died 24 Apr. 1733.

P.W.

MORGAN, Sir Thomas, 3rd Bt. (c.1685–1716), of Kinnersley Castle, Herefs.

HEREFORDSHIRE   30 July 1712–14 Dec. 1716

b. c.1685, o.s. of Sir John Morgan, 2nd Bt., M.P., by Hester, da. and coh. of James Price of Pilleth, Rad. *m.* c.1709, Anne, da. and h. of John Roydhouse of London, 1s. *suc.* fa. Feb. 1693.

Morgan's grandfather was general of horse under Monk; his father sat in 1681 for New Radnor, where he had acquired estates through his wife, and for Herefordshire 1685–7 and from 1689 till his death in 1693. Re-elected for the county as a Tory in 1715, Morgan voted against the septennial bill. He died 4 Dec. 1716.

A.N.N.

MORGAN, Thomas (1702–69), of Ruperra, Glam.

BRECON   24 May 1723–1734
MONMOUTHSHIRE   1734–1747
BRECONSHIRE   1747–12 Apr. 1769

b. 20 May 1702, 2nd s. of John Morgan of Tredegar and bro. of William Morgan (qq.v.). *m.* c.1725, Jane, da. and coh. of Maynard Colchester, M.P., of Westbury-on-Severn, Glos., 4s. 2da. *suc.* nephew William Morgan (q.v.) 1763.

Ld. lt. Mon. and Brec. 1731–*d.*; judge advocate-gen. 1741–68.

Morgan sat successively for the three seats controlled by his family, voting with the Walpole and Pelham Governments and being classed as a government supporter in 1747. He died 12 Apr. 1769.

P.D.G.T.

MORGAN, William (1700–31), of Tredegar, Mon.

MONMOUTHSHIRE   1722–24 Apr. 1731

b. 8 Mar. 1701, 1st s. of John Morgan of Tredegar and bro. of Thomas Morgan (qq.v.). *m.* c.1724, Lady Rachel Cavendish, da. of William Cavendish, M.P., 2nd Duke of Devonshire, 2s. 2da. *suc.* fa. 1720. K.B. 27 May 1725.

Ld. lt. Mon. and Brec. 1720–*d.*

Succeeding as a minor, William Morgan was returned on his family's interest for Monmouthshire on coming of age, married a daughter of the Duke of Devonshire, and was one of the wealthy government supporters who were created knights of the Bath when Walpole revived that order in 1725. He voted with the Government on the civil list arrears in 1729, but was absent from the division on the Hessians in 1730, dying 24 Apr. 1731.

P.D.G.T.

MORGAN, William (1725–63), of Tredegar, Mon.

MONMOUTHSHIRE   1747–16 July 1763

b. 28 Mar. 1725, 1st s. of Sir William Morgan of Tredegar and nephew of Thomas Morgan (qq.v.). *educ*. Westminster 1738; Ch. Ch. Oxf. 1743. *unm. suc*. fa. 1731.

Returned unopposed as a Whig on the Tredegar interest, Morgan followed the politics of his cousin, Lord Hartington (q.v.).

He died 16 July 1763.

P.D.G.T.

MORICE, Humphry (c.1671–1731), of the Grove, Chiswick, Mdx.

NEWPORT   1713–1722
GRAMPOUND   1722–16 Nov. 1731

b. c.1671, o.s. of Humphry Morice, London merchant (a yr. bro. of Sir William Morice, 1st Bt., M.P.), by Alice, da. of Sir Thomas Trollope, 1st Bt., of Casewick, Lincs. *m*. (1) 1704, Judith (*d*. 1720), da. of Thomas Sandes, London merchant, 3da.; (2) 2 June 1722, Catherine, da. of Peter Paggen of the Manor House, Wandsworth, Surr., wid. of William Hale (q.v.), 2s. *suc*. fa. 1689.
Director, Bank of England 1716–31 (with statutory intervals), dep. gov. 1725–6, gov. 1727–9.

Humphry Morice lost his mother while still a boy and was brought up at Werrington with his cousin, Sir Nicholas Morice (q.v.). At about the age of 18 he succeeded to his father's business, carrying on an extensive trade with Africa, America, Holland and Russia.

In 1710 Humphry asked Nicholas to bring him into Parliament but was told that all the seats for Newport and Launceston were already bespoke. Returned for Newport in 1713, on 6 Mar. 1714 he voted with the Whigs against Sir Robert Steele's (q.v.) expulsion. On the Prince of Wales's birthday later in the year Nicholas was displeased to learn that Humphry had 'appeared in a most splendid manner at court, being the finest there, drawing . . . all the killing eyes of the ladies and the admiration of the men'. Worse still, he 'heartily voted for' the septennial bill after giving Nicholas the impression at breakfast that morning that he was 'zealous against' it.[1]

The politics of the cousins were temporarily reconciled when Humphry followed his friend Walpole into opposition, voting against the bill repealing the Occasional Conformity and Schism Acts in 1719. But they diverged again when Walpole,

after rejoining the Government in 1720, used Humphry as a whip for the London Members, writing to him on 14 Dec. 1720:

> The question of the forces comes on this morning, and I am certainly informed the Tories are resolved to give a direct opposition. Pray go to the Bank and speak to all our friends there, and send to all our Members that live in the city to beg they will be in the House before one o'clock.

On 10 Oct. 1721 Nicholas gave Humphry notice that he did not propose to bring him in again for Newport:

> I perceive you are very solicitous and seem to rely on me to be elected again, which I can scarce believe considering when you gave up the right and privileges of your borough in voting for the septennial bill on no pretence that induced you to it but to please the ambition of Mr. Walpole who, no doubt, will take care of you at the ensuing election for so signal a piece of service.

And again, on 3 Mar. 1722, beginning his letter with 'Dear Sir' instead of the usual 'Dear Brother':

> I . . . assure you that my love and affection for you is as great as ever, and were you my own brother I could not love you with more sincerity, but you very well know when you voted for the septennial bill I then told you that was not the way to Cornwall, nor can I imagine that you will lose your seat in Parliament if I don't recommend you, for it stands with reason that the great Mr. Walpole cannot in justice desert you for whom you have done so much.[2]

In the end Humphry was brought in for Grampound by the Administration.

Humphry Morice died suddenly on 16 Nov. 1731. He was said to have taken poison[3] to forestall the discovery that he had used his position as director of the Bank of England to defraud the Bank of more than £29,000 by getting them to discount fictitious bills of exchange. He had also embezzled trust funds left to his own daughters by an uncle, leaving debts amounting to nearly £150,000. As the widow refused to admit liability for the £29,000, the Bank brought an action against her, which after 43 years of litigation resulted in their recovering £12,000 and writing off the balance.[4]

[1] Sir Nich. Morice to Humphry Morice, 30 Oct. 1710, 14 Dec. 1714, 16 Mar. 1722; Rich. Blighe to Humphry Morice, 17 Aug. 1713, Morice mss in Bank of England. [2] Ibid. [3] Thos. Carte to Corbet Kynaston, 20 Jan. 1732, Add. 21500, f. 62. [4] W. Marston Acres, *The Bank of England from within*, i. 154–5.

E.C.

MORICE, Humphry (1723–85), of Werrington, Devon.

LAUNCESTON   2 Feb. 1750–1780

b. 1723, 1st s. of Humphry Morice (q.v.) by his 2nd w. *unm. suc*. fa. 1731 and cos. Sir William Morice, 3rd Bt. (q.v.), to Werrington 1750.

Clerk comptroller of the Green Cloth 1757–61;

comptroller of the Household Dec. 1762–Apr. 1763; P.C. 10 Jan. 1763; warden of the stannaries 1763–83; recorder, Launceston 1771–82.

As the heir of Sir William Morice, Humphry Morice acquired not only considerable wealth but the control of the boroughs of Launceston and Newport. He also inherited Sir William Morice's feud with the Duke of Bedford, who offered, 'if he would have nothing to do' with Henry Pelham, to 'withdraw all opposition and leave his towns absolutely to himself'.[1] Morice reported this to Henry Pelham, informing him that he had rejected the Duke's offer and would 'choose none but what are agreeable to his Majesty, and particularly that the two Tories now chosen there he had no thoughts of electing again'.[2] He was as good as his word, but in spite of his steady adherence to successive governments, he never attained more than minor office. He died at Naples, 18 Oct. 1785.

[1] Pelham to Newcastle, 21 May 1752, Add. 32727, f. 230. [2] Same to same, same date (ostensible letter to be shown to the King), ibid. f. 242.

E.C.

MORICE, John (aft. 1661–1735), of Walthamstow and Newmanhall, Quendon, Essex.

NEWPORT 11 Dec. 1722–1727

b. aft. 1661, o.s. of John Morice, M.P., Turkey merchant, gov. R. African Company (a yr. bro. of Sir William Morice, 1st Bt., M.P.), by Mary,[1] da. of Robert Lowther, alderman of London. *m.* Ann, da. of Sir Jeffrey Jeffreys, alderman of London, 1s. 2da. *suc.* fa. 1705.

John Morice was returned by his cousin, Sir Nicholas Morice, because, unlike Humphry Morice (q.v.), who sat for Newport in the previous Parliament, he held Tory principles.[2] He died 13 Feb. 1735.

[1] Lic. 16 Feb. 1661, *Faculty Office Marriage Lic.* (Brit. Rec. Soc. xxxiii), 13. [2] Sir Nich. Morice to Humphry Morice, 16 Mar. 1722, Morice mss in Bank of England.

E.C.

MORICE, Sir Nicholas, 2nd Bt. (1681–1726), of Werrington, Devon.

NEWPORT 1702–27 Jan. 1726

b. 1681, 1st surv. s. of Sir William Morice, 1st Bt., M.P., of Werrington by his 2nd w. Elizabeth, da. of Richard Reynell of Ogwell, Devon. *educ.* Exeter, Oxf. 1698. *m.* (lic. 21 Mar. 1704) Lady Catherine Herbert, da. of Thomas Herbert, M.P., 8th Earl of Pembroke, 1s. 2da. *suc.* fa. as 2nd Bt. 7 Feb. 1690.

Sir Nicholas Morice was the grandson of Sir William Morice, secretary of state under Charles II, who purchased in 1651 the estate of Werrington, carrying with it an important interest in the neighbouring Cornish boroughs of Newport and Laun-

ceston. As a Tory and a member of the October Club, he consistently opposed the Administration under George I. Though complaining of being 'recalled to ride four hundred miles to be baffled and laughed at, for . . . it has been evident that this Parliament never denied the Court any one individual thing they have asked', he came up from Cornwall to vote against that 'godly bill to root out the best established church in the world', as he sarcastically called the bill for repealing the Occasional Conformity and Schism Acts; but next year he was committed to the custody of the serjeant at arms for defaulting on the call of the House for the peerage bill. He strongly disapproved of Walpole, refusing, in his own words, 'to stoop and submit, cap in hand, to a man whom I fear not and value much less, and who in every respect since [sic] this King's reign was my inferior'.[1] His name was included in a list of Jacobite supporters sent to the Pretender in 1721.[2] He died 27 Jan. 1726.

[1] *CJ*, xix. 188; to Humphry Morice, 20 Dec. 1718, 10 Mar. 1719, 4 Oct. 1724, Morice mss in Bank of England. [2] Stuart mss 65/16.

E.C.

MORICE, Sir William, 3rd Bt. (?1707–50), of Werrington, Devon.

NEWPORT 1727–1734
LAUNCESTON 1734–17 Jan. 1750

b. ?1707, o.s. of Sir Nicholas Morice, 2nd Bt. (q.v.). *educ.* Salisbury sch.;[1] C.C.C. Oxf. 24 Aug. 1724, aged 17. *m.* (1) Sept. 1731, Lady Lucy Wharton (div. 1738), da. of Thomas Wharton, M.P., 1st Mq. of Wharton, 1 da. *d.v.p.*; (2) 9 Sept. 1741, Anna, da. of Thomas Bury of Berrynarbor, Devon, sis. of Thomas Bury (q.v.), *s.p. suc.* fa. 27 Jan. 1726. Recorder, Launceston.

A Tory, if not a Jacobite, Morice contributed to the election fund raised by the Cornish Tories in 1741.[2] Nevertheless in December that year he voted with the Government on the Bossiney election petition, having been won over by his kinsman, Lord Abergavenny (like himself an injured husband),[3] whose wife had been seduced by one of the opposition candidates, Richard Liddell (q.v.).[4] Otherwise he regularly voted with the Opposition.

In 1744 Morice came into collision with the Duke of Bedford over hunting rights near Werrington. He wrote to the Duke: 'You seem to treat me rather like one of your meanest vassals and dependants than a gentleman', but 'though I am not adorned with those gawdy titles you are nor master of such large possessions yet I have as quick a sense of an injury offered to me as you can have and have as much spirit and inclination to resent it'.[5] In 1748 Bedford, having purchased an estate at Newport, opened an unsuccessful attack on Morice in his boroughs.[6] He died 17 Jan. 1750.

[1] Joseph Moyle to Humphry Morice, 22 Sept. 1722, Morice mss in Bank of England. [2] Stuart mss 219/91, 220/81. [3] See under FITZROY, Lord Augustus. [4] Coxe, *Walpole*, iii. 581–2. [5] 11 and 18 May 1744, Bedford mss. [6] *HMC Fortescue*, i. 132.

E.C.

MORLEY LONG, *see* PARKER, Sir Philip

MORPETH, Visct., *see* HOWARD, Charles, *and* HOWARD, Henry (*b.* ?1693)

MORRIS, Edmund (?1686–1759), of Loddington, Leics.

LEICESTERSHIRE   1722–1727

b. ?1686, 1st s. of Charles Morris of Loddington by Susanna, da. and coh. of Sir Edmund Bacon, 4th Bt., M.P., of Redgrave, Suff. *educ.* Rugby 1696; Magdalen, Oxf. 14 Dec. 1702, aged 16; M. Temple 1703. *m.* 2 Aug. 1720, Anne, da. of Sir Alexander Campbell, M.P. [S], of Calder, Nairn., 1s. 4da. *suc.* fa. 1710.
Sheriff, Leics. 1746–7.

Morris was the grandson of John Morris, a London upholsterer, who purchased Loddington in 1670.[1] In 1721 his name was sent to the Pretender as a probable supporter in the event of a rising.[2] He was returned for Leicestershire as a Tory in 1722 but did not stand again. He was buried at Loddington 30 July 1759.

[1] Nichols, *Leics.* iii. 330; iv. 401. [2] Stuart mss 65/16.

E.C.

MORRIS, *see also* ROBINSON (afterwards ROBINSON MORRIS)

MORTON, John (?1714–80), of Tackley, nr. Woodstock, Oxon. and Danesfield, Medmenham, Bucks.

ABINGDON	1747–8 Feb. 1770
NEW ROMNEY	5 Mar. 1770–1774
WIGAN	23 May 1775–25 July 1780

b. ?1714, 1st s. of John Morton of Tackley. *educ.* Abingdon sch.; Trinity, Oxf. 28 May 1730, aged 15; I. Temple 1732, called 1740, bencher 1758. *m.* by June 1751, Elizabeth, da. of Paul Jodrell of Duffield, Derbys., sis. of Paul Jodrell (q.v.).
Recorder, Woodstock 1743; K.C. 1758; c.j. Chester 1762–*d.*; attorney-gen. to the Queen Mar. 1770–*d.*; dep. high steward, Oxf. Univ. 1770–*d.*

A successful Tory lawyer, who was counsel and became deputy high steward of Oxford University, Morton was on friendly terms with several members of the Leicester House set, including Jodrell, the Prince's solicitor-general, whose sister he married,[1]

II—T

and the 2nd Lord Egmont, who put him down c.1750 as counsel for the board of Trade in a list of office holders in Frederick's reign. On 23 Jan. 1750 he spoke in support of an amendment to the mutiny bill moved by Egmont, following this up with an exceptionally fully reported speech moving an amendment of his own, which was opposed by the secretary at war, Henry Fox. Next year he spoke on the regency bill, and in 1752 he was one of a number of leading Tories who spoke for a motion by Lord Harley against subsidy treaties in peace time.[2]
He died 25 July 1780.

[1] W. R. Ward, *Georgian Oxford*, 263; *Recs. Cust. Fam.* iii. 128, 133, 137. [2] Walpole, *Mems. Geo. II*, i. 144, 254.

R.S.L.

MOSTYN, John (?1709–79).

MALTON   30 Dec. 1741–1768

b. ?1709, 2nd s. of Sir Roger Mostyn, 3rd Bt., and bro. of Savage and Sir Thomas Mostyn (qq.v.). *educ.* Westminster June 1722, aged 13; Ch. Ch. Oxf. 25 June 1728, aged 18. *unm.*
Ensign 1733; capt. 16 Ft. 1736; capt.-lt. 2 Ft. Gds. 1742, capt. and lt.-col. 1743; groom of the bedchamber 1746–*d.*; col. army 1747; col. 7 Ft. 1751–4, 13 Drags. 1754–8; maj.-gen. 1757; col. 5 Drags. 1758–60; lt.-gen. 1759; col. 7 Drags. 1760–3, 1 Drag. Gds. 1763–*d.*; gov. Minorca 1768–*d.*; gen. 1772.

Mostyn was returned by his uncle and his cousin, the 1st and 2nd Marquesses of Rockingham. Voting with the Government, he was classed about 1749–50 by the 2nd Lord Egmont as one of the 12 'most obnoxious men of an inferior degree' in the House of Commons, with the comment: 'Jack Mostyn, very ill inclined to us and forward'.
He died 16 Feb. 1779.

R.R.S.

MOSTYN, Sir Roger, 3rd Bt. (1673–1739), of Mostyn, Flints.

FLINTSHIRE	1701–1702
CHESHIRE	1702–1705
FLINT BOROUGHS	1705–1708
FLINTSHIRE	1708–1713
FLINT BOROUGHS	1713–1715
FLINTSHIRE	1715–1734

b. 31 July 1673, 1st s. of Sir Thomas Mostyn, 2nd Bt., M.P., by Bridget, da. and h. of Darcy Savage of Leighton, Cheshire. *educ.* Jesus, Oxf. 1690. *m.* 20 July 1703, Lady Essex Finch, da. of Daniel Finch, M.P., 7th Earl of Winchilsea and 2nd Earl of Nottingham, 6s. 6da. *suc.* fa. 1700.
Constable, Flint castle 1702–5; paymaster of marines 1711; teller of the Exchequer Dec. 1714–June 1716; ld. lt. Flints. 1727–*d.*

A leader of the Flintshire Tories and a supporter of the Hanoverian succession, Mostyn followed his father-in-law, Lord Nottingham. Made a teller of the Exchequer when Nottingham joined the Whig Government on George I's accession, he was dismissed with Nottingham in 1716, thereafter consistently voting against the Government, till he retired from Parliament in 1734.

He died 8 May 1739.

P.D.G.T.

MOSTYN, Savage (?1713–57).

WEOBLEY   1747–16 Sept. 1757

> b. ?1713, 3rd s. of Sir Roger Mostyn, 3rd Bt., and bro. of John and Sir Thomas Mostyn (qq.v.). educ. Westminster June 1725, aged 11. unm.
>
> Lt. R.N. 1734, capt. 1739; comptroller of the navy 1749–55; r.-adm. 1755; ld. of Admiralty 6 Apr.–2 July 1757; v.-adm. 1757.

Promoted captain on the outbreak of war with Spain in 1739, Mostyn took part in the operations against Cartagena in 1741. In 1745 his failure to engage two French ships off Ushant gave rise to a public outcry and service criticism, not allayed by his acquittal by a court martial ordered at his own request. Two years later he incurred further criticism for failing to attack a weakly escorted French convoy, mistaking the East Indiamen for ships of the line.[1] After contesting Scarborough unsuccessfully in 1744, he was returned in 1747 as a government supporter for Weobley on Lord Weymouth's interest, which he owed to his cousin, Lord Winchilsea. In 1749 he was one of a number of admirals and captains summoned to the Admiralty to discuss an unpopular government proposal to subject half-pay officers to courts martial; the only officer to speak in favour of the proposal, he was rewarded a month later with the comptrollership of the navy.[2]

Mostyn died 16 Sept. 1757, leaving £60,000 to his nephew, afterwards Sir Roger Mostyn, M.P.[3]

[1] Richmond, Navy in the War of 1739–48, ii. 114–15; iii. 78–80. [2] Augustus Hervey's Jnl. 81. [3] UCNW Baron Hill mss.

R.R.S.

MOSTYN, Thomas (1704–58), of Mostyn, Flints.

FLINTSHIRE   1734–1741, 1747–24 Mar. 1758

> b. 26 Apr. 1704, 1st s. of Sir Roger Mostyn, 3rd Bt., and bro. of John and Savage Mostyn (qq.v.). educ. Westminster 1716; Ch. Ch. Oxf. 1720. m. c.1733, Sarah, da. and coh. of Robert Western of London, 4s. 5da. suc. fa. as 4th Bt. 8 May 1739.

Mostyn, a Hanoverian Tory, forced a Jacobite sheriff of Flintshire to proclaim George II.[1] Though more interested in literature than in politics, he took a leading part in the Tory preparations for the Flintshire elections in 1734[2] when he succeeded his

father as knight of the shire, consistently voting against the Administration. In 1741 he stood down by agreement, declining pressing invitations to stand for Flint Boroughs in view of the heavy cost of the previous election there, towards which he had contributed over £2,000. Resuming the county seat in 1747, he continued to sit for it unopposed as a Tory till his death, 24 Mar. 1758.

[1] Cheshire Sheaf (n. s.), i. 18–19. [2] Add. 32688, f. 332.

P.D.G.T.

MOUNTRATH, Earl of, see COOTE, Algernon, and COOTE, Hon. Henry

MUNDY, Wrightson (?1712–62), of Osbaston, Leics. and Markeaton, Derbys.

LEICESTERSHIRE   1747–1754

> b. ?1712, 1st s. of Francis Mundy of Osbaston by Anne, da. of Sir John Noel, 4th Bt., of Kirkby Mallory, Leics.; nephew of Sir Clobery and William Noel (qq.v.). educ. Winchester 1728–30; Pembroke, Camb. 1 July 1731, aged 19. m. 1 Apr. 1736, Anne, da. of Robert Burdett of Bramcote, Warws., sis. of Sir Robert Burdett (q.v.), 2s. 4da. suc. fa. 1720.
>
> Sheriff, Derbys. 1737–8.

Mundy was descended from Sir John Mundy, lord mayor of London 1522–3, who purchased Markeaton in Derbyshire. His grandfather, Francis Mundy, acquired Osbaston by his marriage to the heiress of the Wrightson estates. His father, a zealous Jacobite, had impaired his health and fortune by contesting Leicestershire in 1719.[1] Thomas Carte, the Jacobite historian, in a memorandum to the Pretender, speaks of him as 'zealous in his father's principles'.[2] Before the county election of 1741 he wrote, 23 Sept. 1740, to his friend, Sir Thomas Cave, who was standing for Leicestershire with Edward Smith but was unable to canvass owing to an attack of gout:

> Mr. Ashby's [the Whig candidate] continual application to the freeholders and our inactivity I much fear gives him great advantage. It was not thought improper by the same friends who accidentally met last night to ride the county immediately, and as you cannot do it yourself, we thought it advisable you should by proxy. I trouble you with this to inform you that I will attend Mr. Smith as your deputy, if you think proper and will make your excuse to the freeholders in the best manner I can. My attending Smith can do no harm and if it should be of any service to you, I shall think myself sufficiently requited for my trouble,

adding, 6 Oct.:

> I pretend not to arrogate to myself an interest superior to any other gentleman. What I have is owing to my father's name.

Smith reported to Cave, 23 Feb. 1741, that

our good and faithful friend Mr. Mundy sent hither last night a particular detail of his proceedings, which are very numerous and I think full of success, the pains he has taken are prodigious.

In 1747 Cave stood down in favour of Mundy, who was returned unopposed.[3] The 2nd Lord Egmont, in his electoral survey c.1749–50, wrote of him as

a young man reputed a thorough Jacobite. He is talked up among the Tories as the most promising man of the whole party but has never spoken yet. He has talked of late in the same style with Lister [Thomas, q.v.], that nothing but ill usage and despair had made men Jacobites.

He did not stand in 1754 because of ill health.[4] He died 18 June 1762.

[1] Nichols, *Leics.* iv. 523. [2] Stuart mss 216/111. [3] Braye mss at City of Leicester mus. 23D57/3027, 3028, 3126. [4] Nichols, ii. 542.

E.C.

MUNRO, Sir Harry, 7th Bt. (c.1720–81), of Foulis, Ross.

ROSS-SHIRE   11 Dec. 1746–1747

TAIN BURGHS   1747–1761

b. c.1720, o. surv. s. of Col. Sir Robert Munro, 6th Bt. (q.v.). *educ.* Westminster 1734–6; Leyden 1736; Doddridge's acad. at Northampton 1737–?9. *m.* 13 Jan. 1753, Anne, da. of Hugh Rose, M.P., of Kilravock, Nairn, 3s. 2da. *suc.* fa. 17 Jan. 1746.

Capt. Loudoun's regt. of Ft. 1745, half-pay 1748; chamberlain of Ross 1747–*d.*

Munro, a staunch Presbyterian and Hanoverian, like the rest of his family, was educated at a nonconformist school in Northampton, kept by his father's friend, Dr. Doddridge, who subsequently published an account of the family. In May 1745 he wrote from London to Duncan Forbes (q.v.), asking him to support his father, then commanding the Black Watch in Flanders, for the county seat, vacated by the death of Charles Ross (q.v.) at Fontenoy in April. 'By a seat in Parliament my father may be able . . . to procure me a civil post'.[1] On the outbreak of the Forty-five, in which his father was killed at Falkirk and his uncle assassinated by the rebels, Munro, having obtained a captain's commission in a newly raised regiment, joined Sir John Cope (q.v.) with his company. Captured at Prestonpans, he returned after Culloden to Ross-shire, where he was active in rounding up rebel Mackenzies and supplying lists of the disaffected. Elected for Ross-shire in December 1746, he was rewarded for his services in reporting on rebel activities in the county[2] by a local office worth £S1,000 or £83.6s.8d. sterling p.a. His anti-Jacobite zeal did not prevent him from paying a visit, accompanied by Sir Ludovick Grant (q.v.), to Lord Lovat on the eve of his execution, when 'they advised him

to beware of giving offence by his last words lest it should hinder the mercy towards his son', for whose pardon they subsequently interceded with Newcastle, offering to stand bail for him, if released.[3]

Under Pelham's plan for the 1747 Parliament Munro exchanged Ross-shire for Tain Burghs, where Sir John Gordon (q.v.) raised an unexpected but unsuccessful opposition.[4] In the debate of 17 Mar. 1752, on the forfeited estates bill, Hardwicke suggested that any surplus money might be used to compensate loyalists: 'Could a nobler use be made of it than in rewarding Sir Harry Munro, who and whose family had done and had suffered so much for the service of the Crown?' In February 1754 the Exchequer of Scotland was ordered to issue £5,000 out of Lord Elcho's forfeited estates to pay off the debts encumbering the Munro estates, any surplus being allocated to Munro personally.[5] Re-elected at the general election that year, he retired in 1761. He died 12 June 1781.

[1] *More Culloden Pprs.* iii. 235–7. [2] Yorke, *Hardwicke*, i. 449; Munro to Loudoun, 4 Aug. 1746, Loudoun mss; see *More Culloden Pprs.* v. 159. [3] *HMC Laing*, ii. 392; Munro to ? Stone, 2 July 1747, Add. 32712, f. 11. [4] Andrew Fletcher to Pelham, 21 July 1747, Newcastle (Clumber) mss. [5] Walpole, *Mems. Geo. II*, i. 271; T17/16, 159.

E.H.-G.

MUNRO, John (c.1712–49), of Newmore, Ross.

ROSS-SHIRE   15 Feb. 1733–1734

b. c.1712, 1st s. of George Munro of Newmore by Margaret, da. of Duncan Forbes, M.P. [S], of Culloden, sis. of John and Duncan Forbes (qq.v.). *unm. suc.* fa. 1737.

Ensign 14 Ft. 1731; lt. 32 Ft. 1735;[1] capt. 42 Ft. 1740, lt.-col. 1747.

Descended from a collateral branch of the Munros of Foulis, John Munro obtained 'a pair of colours' through the influence of his uncle, Duncan Forbes. Next year he decided to stand at a by-election for Ross-shire, though the head of his house, Sir Robert Munro of Foulis (q.v.), had set up his brother for the county. His uncle disapproved,

as the period of this Parliament is so short, and as living in London might draw the young fellow into a course of complications and expense that do not suit his purpose, or his fortune.

However,

by his calculation he had a dead majority amongst the Whigs, so that he was secure, unless the Mackenzies cast the balance, and as he had been informed that Sir Robert Munro had very early wrote to the late [i.e. attainted] Lord Seaforth for his interest with the freeholders of his name he . . . mounted his steed, rode post to Paris, where Lord Seaforth then was, outran Sir Robert's letter upon the road, and had a favourable answer from my Lord before Sir Robert's letter reached him.[2]

Though Sir Robert Munro gained the support of Lord Ilay, Walpole's election manager for Scotland, John Munro carried his election, his opponent giving up. In Parliament he supported the Government, voting for the excise bill in 1733, but he did not stand in 1741. Exchanging into Sir Robert Munro's regiment in 1740, he served at Fontenoy. He died in 1749.[3]

[1] See Duncan Forbes to Walpole, 29 July 1735, Cholmondeley (Houghton) mss. [2] *More Culloden Pprs.* iii. 61–64; *Gent. Mag.* 1731, p. 85. [3] A. Mackenzie, *Munros of Foulis*, 199.

R.R.S.

MUNRO, Robert (1684–1746), of Foulis, Ross.

TAIN BURGHS   1710–1741

b. 24 Aug. 1684, 1st s. of Sir Robert Munro, 5th Bt., M.P. [S], of Foulis by Jean, da. of John Forbes, M.P. [S], of Culloden. *educ.* ?Edinburgh. *m.* ?1713, Mary, da. of Henry Seymour, M.P., of Woodlands, Dorset, 3s. 1da. *suc.* fa. as 6th Bt. 11 Sept. 1729.
Capt. 1 Ft. 1710; lt.-col. and capt. of an independent co. 1714–16; gov. Inverness 1715–16; lt.-col. 42 Ft. 1739–45; col. 37 Ft. 1745–*d.*
Commr. for forfeited estates 1716–25.

Munro, an army officer, came of a Presbyterian family, at bitter feud with the Jacobite Mackenzies of Ross-shire. Re-elected unopposed in 1715 for Tain Burghs, which he had represented as a Whig since 1710, he was appointed a commissioner for the sale of estates forfeited in the late rebellion, voting with the Government in all recorded divisions. He was one of the Members who were credited with fictitious stock by the South Sea Company, in his case £6,000 at 275 on 23 Mar. which he 'sold' back to the Company a month later at 330.[1] In spite of having been convicted and fined £200 for kidnapping some opponents at the Dingwall town council elections in 1721,[2] he was re-elected in 1722, after a contest. On 24 Oct. 1722 he made his only reported intervention in debate, moving unsuccessfully that an election petition by General Charles Ross (q.v.) should be heard at an early date.[3] He retained his seat, without further opposition, voting regularly with the Government, till 1741, when he was defeated by Charles Areskine, the lord advocate, with the support of Lord Ilay, Walpole's election manager for Scotland. On this Munro wrote to Walpole, 24 June 1741:

I hope you have a true account of the manner in which the elections in this kingdom have been carried on. My Lord Ilay's conduct towards me makes it improper for me to trouble you with particulars, because I may be thought prejudiced, for the power of the Government has not in any instance since the Union been so much exerted as at this time to bring in Lord Fortrose [Kenneth MacKenzie, q.v.], and keep me out of Parliament.

He sent a copy of this letter to Pelham, stating that Ilay could have made

at least ten Members in room of as many of our Members now declared patriots, but it was not consistent with his scheme of aggrandising his family, so that a person to depend on the Duke of Argyll, was more agreeable to the Earl than one absolutely attached to Sir Robert Walpole and the Administration, and the opposition given by the Earl to any who was to act in concert with the Duke, was faint without intention to prevail.
There was a design to try if the 16 peers could be more modelled to the Duke's list than the list which my Lord Ilay concerted at London, but this was found impracticable without acting too openly and could not be coloured over, because all the world here knew that Lord Oliphant, the person of least weight among the Scots peers, could carry any list for the Court, being enabled in the same manner as the Earl of Ilay was.[4]

Munro petitioned, with the result that after Walpole's fall Areskine was unseated by the Commons, but a motion for declaring Munro duly elected failed. At the ensuing by-election Munro, though said to be prepared to spend £8,000,[5] was defeated by Robert Craigie, Areskine's successor as lord advocate, put up by Ilay's successor as minister for Scotland, Lord Tweeddale.

During the war of the Austrian succession Munro, in command of a newly formed Highland regiment, the Black Watch, distinguished himself at Fontenoy, where he remained standing under heavy fire 'because (as he said), though he could easily lie down, his great bulk would not suffer him to rise so quickly'.[6] He was killed at Falkirk, 17 Jan. 1746.

[1] *CJ*, xix. 569, 571, 578. [2] A. Mackenzie, *Munros of Foulis*, 121–7. [3] *Knatchbull Diary*. [4] Newcastle (Clumber) mss. [5] NLS mss 1337, ff. 21–22. [6] P. Doddridge, *Life of Col. Gardiner* (1763), app. iii. 253.

R.R.S.

MURE, William (1718–76), of Caldwell, Renfrew.

RENFREWSHIRE   23 Dec. 1742–1761

b. late 1718, 1st s. of William Mure of Caldwell by Anne, da. of Sir James Stewart of Goodtrees and Coltness, ld. advocate, wid. of James Maxwell of Blawarthill. *educ.* Glasgow Univ. 1730; adv. 1739; Leyden 1740; France 1741–2. *m.* 25 Feb. 1752, Katherine, da. of James Graham, Lord Easdale, S.C.J., 2s. 4da. *suc.* fa. 1722.
Baron of Exchequer [S] 1761–*d.*

A serious young Presbyterian, who cut short his grand tour to pursue further studies in France, Mure came home in spring 1742. Returned in the following December for his county, he voted with the Opposition on the Hanoverians, 6 Dec. 1743[1] and 18 Jan. 1744, but was absent from the division on them in 1746. Re-elected in 1747, he was at first regarded as an opponent by Pelham, who on

8 May 1752 had a scheme 'for choosing a good man for the shire of Renfrew in the room of one Mure, who has never given us a vote in the two Parliaments in which he has represented that county'.[2] On 6 Aug. Argyll reported to Pelham that Mure had been rechosen, adding: 'He has never yet given us a vote but I have had hopes given me that he may'.[3] He had come over by October 1753, when Pelham sent him a letter asking him to attend at the opening of Parliament, to which he replied:

> My attendance there is entirely at your command and my voice determined in your service . . . but . . . I might perhaps be as usefully employed were I to continue here in the country to look after some disputed elections in the neighbouring counties.[4]

Returned as a government supporter in 1754, he retired from Parliament in 1761 on becoming a baron of the Exchequer of Scotland.

He died 25 Mar. 1776.

[1] *Caldwell Pprs.* ii(1), p. 58. [2] To Newcastle, 8 May 1752, Add. 32727, f. 130. [3] Newcastle (Clumber) mss. [4] *Caldwell Pprs.* ii(1), pp. 108–9.

E.H.-G.

MURRAY, Alexander (c.1680–1750), of Broughton, Wigtown, and Cally, Kirkcudbright.

KIRKCUDBRIGHT STEWARTRY 1715–1727

b. c.1680, 2nd s. of Richard Murray, M.P. [S], of Broughton by Anna, da. and de facto h. of Alexander Lennox of Cally; bro. of John Murray, M.P. [S]. *educ.* Glasgow 1696. *m.* 1726, Lady Euphemia Stewart, da. of James, 5th Earl of Galloway [S], 1s. James, M.P. *suc.* bro. 1704.

Of a family seated in Wigtownshire since the sixteenth century, sharing a common ancestry with the earls of Annandale, Murray inherited extensive estates in Kirkcudbright from his mother, the heiress of the Lennoxes of Cally. Returned for Kirkcudbright in 1715, he voted with the Administration except on the peerage bill in 1719, when he was absent. Re-elected unopposed in 1722, he lost the support of many of the freeholders by advocating leniency towards those who in 1724 rioted in protest against land enclosures in Kirkcudbright and Wigtownshire.[1] Defeated in 1727, he considered petitioning, but desisted when advised that the petition would fail.[2] He did not stand again himself but in 1740 he drafted a memorandum for a prospective Member, providing for safeguards against a Member who accepted a place or pursued a course of action without first informing his constituents.[3] He died 1 May 1750.

[1] R. Wodrow, *Analecta* (Maitland Club lx), iii. 159. [2] David Lidderdail to Murray, 2 Oct. 1727, SRO Murray of Broughton and Cally Pprs., letter 68. [3] *Ibid.* ms 1396.

J.M.S.

MURRAY, Alexander (c.1686–1755), of Cringletie, Peebles.

PEEBLESSHIRE 1715–1722, 1741–1747

b. c.1686, 1st s. of Alexander Murray by Susan, da. of John Douglas of Mains, Dunbarton. *m.* (contract 3 Apr. 1718) Katherine, da. of Sir Robert Stewart, 1st Bt., M.P. [S], of Tillicoultry, Clackmannan, Lord Tillicoultry, S.C.J., 7s. 4da. *suc.* fa. c.1711 and uncle John Murray to Cringletie 1719.

Of a junior branch of the Murrays of Blackbarony,[1] who had represented Peeblesshire in the pre-Union Parliament of Scotland, Alexander Murray was returned unopposed as a Whig for the county in 1715 and again in 1741. Voting with the Government in all recorded divisions of both Parliaments, he was classed as 'Granville' in 1746. He died in September 1755.

[1] J. W. Buchan, *Peeblesshire*, ii. 494–5.

R.S.L.

MURRAY, Hon. James (c.1690–1770).

DUMFRIESSHIRE 22 Feb. 1711–1713
ELGIN BURGHS 1713–7 Apr. 1715

b. c.1690, 2nd s. of David Murray, 5th Visct. Stormont [S], by Margery, da. and h. of David Scott of Scotstarvet, Fife.; bro. of Hon. William Murray (q.v.), 1st Earl of Mansfield. *educ.* adv. 1710. *unm.*

Commr. for settling trade with France 1713.

Re-elected for Elgin Burghs in 1715 but unseated on petition, Murray was active as a Jacobite agent in England and Scotland during the Fifteen, when he was sent by the Pretender in September with a commission of commander-in-chief for Lord Mar. Arrested and put in Newgate in April 1716 on suspicion of high treason, but discharged the following month,[1] he concerted measures between the Jacobite leaders in England and Scotland during the Swedish plot of 1717[2] (see Caesar, Charles). In 1718–19 he negotiated the marriage of the Pretender with Princess Clementina Sobieska, acting as proxy at the wedding. In 1720, during Mar's imprisonment in Switzerland, he performed the functions of secretary of state to the Pretender without the title.[3] Leaving Rome at the end of the year, he lived in France with a pension from the Pretender until 1725, when he was appointed governor to Charles Edward Stuart. Created Earl of Dunbar in the Jacobite peerage, he became secretary of state to the Pretender in 1727, resigning in 1747. He spent the rest of his life at Avignon, where he died in August 1770.

[1] *HMC Stuart*, i. 415–16, 430, 439; ii. 69; *Secret Hist. of Rebels in Newgate* (1717), p. 69. [2] *HMC Stuart*, iv. 453–4 et passim. [3] A. & H. Tayler, *Jacobite Court at Rome in 1719* (Sc. Hist. Soc. ser. 3, xxxi), 202.

E.C.

MURRAY, Lord James (1690–1764), of Garth, Perth.

PERTHSHIRE 1715–14 Nov. 1724

b. 28 Aug. 1690, 3rd but 2nd surv. s. of John, 1st Duke of Atholl [S], by his 1st w. Lady Katherine Hamilton, da. of William, 3rd Duke of Hamilton [S]; half-bro. of Lord John Murray (q.v.). *educ.* St. Andrews 1705. *m.* (1) 28 Apr. 1726, Jane (deed of separation 23 July 1745, *d.* 13 June 1748), da. of Thomas Frederick of Downing St., Westminster, sis. and h. of Sir John Frederick, 1st Bt., wid. of James Lannoy of Hammersmith, Mdx., 2s. 2da.; (2) 11 May 1749, Jean, da. of John Drummond of Megginch, Perth, *s.p. suc.* fa. as 2nd Duke 14 Nov. 1724; cos. James Stanley, M.P., 10th Earl of Derby, both in the sovereignty of the I.o.M. and as Lord Strange in the peerage of England, 7 Mar. 1737; K.T. 11 Feb. 1734.
Capt.-lt. 1 Ft. Gds. 1712, capt. and lt.-col. 1714; 2nd lt.-col. 1 Ft. 1718–24.
Hereditary sheriff, Perth 1724–48; rep. peer [S] 1733–41; ld. privy seal [S] 1733–63; keeper of great seal [S] 1733–*d.*; P.C. 31 Jan. 1734.

Returned on the Atholl interest for Perthshire, Murray adhered to the Government in the Fifteen, in which three of his brothers joined the rebels, two of them, the Marquess of Tullibardine and Lord George Murray, surviving to hold high command in the rebel army during the Forty-five. On Tullibardine's attainder the family honour and estates were settled by Act of Parliament on Murray who, though classed at his election as a Tory, voted in all recorded divisions with the Government, applying unsuccessfully for a place and a pension for his father.[1] Succeeding to the dukedom in 1724, he attached himself to Lord Ilay, from 1725 the head of affairs in Scotland, to whom he owed his appointment to office and election as a representative peer in 1733. On the outbreak of the rebellion of 1745 he fled to London, leaving his family and property in charge of his pardoned brother, Lord George Murray, whom he had appointed as his deputy in Perthshire to deal with the crisis, but who promptly went over to the rebels.[2] After the rebellion he refused to intervene on behalf of Jacobite prisoners, 'having during the whole period of the late rebellion been determined to have nothing to do with the cases of those whose wickedness and folly should bring themselves into distress on that account, farther than to take shame to myself for the disgrace some of my relations have brought upon them and their family'.[3]

He died 8 Jan. 1764.

[1] *Atholl Chron.* ii. 325. [2] K. Tomasson, *The Jacobite General*, 16–21. [3] *Atholl Chron.* iii. 339.

J.M.S.

MURRAY, John (*d.* 1753), of Philiphaugh, Selkirk.

LINLITHGOW BURGHS 16 Apr. 1725–1734
SELKIRKSHIRE 1734–2 July 1753

1st s. of Sir James Murray, M.P. [S], of Philiphaugh, Lord Philiphaugh, S.C.J., and ld. clerk register [S], by his 2nd w. Margaret, da. of Sir Alexander Don, 1st Bt., of Newton, Berwick. *m.* 31 Dec. 1711, Eleanor, 1st da. of Lord Basil Hamilton (6th s. of William, 3rd Duke of Hamilton [S]), 4s. 2da.; bro.-in-law of John Pringle (q.v.). *suc.* fa. 1708.
Hereditary sheriff, Selkirk 1708–c.34.

Unable as hereditary sheriff to stand for the county, John Murray, whose family acquired their Philiphaugh estates in the fifteenth century, entered Parliament for Linlithgow Burghs, which included the burgh of Selkirk, at a contested by-election in 1725. Re-elected unopposed in 1727, he voted with the Administration till 1734, when he went into opposition, voting against Walpole on the repeal of the Septennial Act. Resigning the sheriffdom in favour of one of his sons, he was returned in 1734 for the county, where he was unopposed till his death. Continuing to vote with the Opposition, he received a circular letter in September 1737 from Lord Marchmont, urging the attendance of opposition Members at the opening of the new session.[1] He remained in opposition till Walpole's fall, after which he obtained a place for his eldest son as chamberlain of Ettrick forest.[2] In the list of Members to be invited to the meeting of ministerial supporters at the Cockpit before the opening of the next session, he was put down to Lord Tweeddale, the secretary of state for Scotland, thereafter voting with the Government in all recorded divisions. He returned to opposition in 1747 when he was said to have 'carried his election by one vote gained by Lord Marchmont'.[3] (q.v. under Hume Campbell, Hugh, Lord Polwarth.) He died 2 July 1753.

[1] *HMC Polwarth*, v. 142. [2] *Cal. Treas. Bks. and Pprs. 1742–5*, p. 218. [3] Argyll to Pelham, 1 Aug. 1747, Newcastle (Clumber) mss.

R.S.L.

MURRAY, Lord John (1711–87), of Pitnacree, Perth, and Banner Cross, Yorks.

PERTHSHIRE 1734–1761

b. 14 Apr. 1711, 4th surv. s. of John, 1st Duke of Atholl [S], by his 2nd w. Mary, da. of William Ross, 12th Lord Ross of Halkhead [S]; half-bro. of Lord James Murray (q.v.). *educ.* private sch. Chelsea 1720; ?St. Andrews Univ.; Leyden 1728. *m.* 13 Sept. 1758, Mary, da. of Richard Dalton. Sheffield merchant, 1da.
Ensign 3 Ft. Gds. 1727, lt. 1733, capt.-lt. and capt. 1737, capt. and lt.-col. 1738; col. army 1743; col. 42 Ft. 1745–*d.*; maj.-gen. 1755; lt.-gen. 1758; gen. 1770; raised 2nd bn. 42 Ft. 1780.

Returned on the Atholl interest for Perthshire

on coming of age, Murray, Queen Anne's godson, voted with the Government in every recorded division. After serving in Germany as a.-d.-c. to the King in 1743, he obtained in 1745 the colonelcy of the Black Watch, to which the Rev. (later Professor) Adam Ferguson was appointed Gaelic speaking chaplain, 'to be a kind of tutor or guardian to Lord John . . . to gain his confidence and keep him in peace with his officers, which it was difficult to do'.[1] Recalled from Flanders at the outbreak of the '45, during which his half-brothers, the attainted 'Duke William' and Lord George, held high command in the rebel army, he served in 1746 with his regiment under General St. Clair (q.v.) at L'Orient, and thereafter in Ireland. After the peace he resumed his assiduous attendance in Parliament, unsuccessfully applying to Newcastle for preferment either to a regiment of dragoons or the government of Kinsale in 1753.[2]

He died 26 May 1787.

[1] *Atholl Chron.* ii. 318–19, 460–3, 465; *Autobiog. of Dr. Alexander Carlyle*, 295. [2] Murray to Newcastle, 23 June 1753, Add. 32732, ff. 93–95.

E.H.-G.

MURRAY, Hon. Robert (1689–1738), of Stanwell, Mdx.

WOOTTON BASSETT   1722–1727
GREAT BEDWYN   1734–25 Mar. 1738

b. 7 Jan. 1689, 3rd s. of Charles Murray, 1st Earl of Dunmore [S], by Katherine, da. and h. of Richard Watts of Great Munden, Herts. *m.* c.1708, Mary, da. of Sir Charles Halkett, 1st Bt., of Pitfirrane, Fife, 1da.[1]
Ensign 3 Ft. Gds. 1705, lt. and capt. 1709, capt. and lt.-col. 1710, 2nd maj. 1717; col. 37 Ft. 1722–35, 38 Ft. 1735–*d.*; brig.-gen. 1735.

Robert Murray, a professional soldier, was younger brother of John, 2nd Earl of Dunmore, a representative peer and lord of the bedchamber to George II. He was returned as a government supporter at Wootton Bassett in 1722, did not stand in 1727, but was later returned for Great Bedwyn. He died 25 Mar. 1738.

[1] *Scots Peerage*, iii. 385; ix. 78.

R.S.L.

MURRAY, Hon. William (1705–93), of Ken Wood, Mdx.

BOROUGHBRIDGE   29 Nov. 1742–8 Nov. 1756

b. 2 Mar. 1705, 4th s. of David Murray, 5th Visct. Stormont [S], and bro. of Hon. James Murray (q.v.). *educ.* Perth g.s.; Westminster 1718–23; Ch. Ch. Oxf. 1723–7; L. Inn 1724, called 1730. *m.* 20 Sept. 1738, Lady Elizabeth Finch, da. of Daniel Finch, M.P., 7th Earl of Winchilsea and 2nd Earl of Nottingham. *cr.* Lord Mansfield 8 Nov. 1756; Earl of Mansfield, Notts. with sp. rem. to Louisa, Viscountess Stormont,

31 Oct. 1776; Earl of Mansfield, Mdx. with sp. rem. to his nephew, Visct. Stormont, 1 Aug. 1792.
K.C. 1742; solicitor-gen. 1742–54; attorney-gen. 1754–6; P.C. 19 Nov. 1756; l. c. j. of King's bench 1756–88.

Murray came of a well-known Jacobite family; in the 1715 rebellion both his father and his eldest brother were taken up on suspicion of high treason; another brother, James (q.v.), went into exile, eventually becoming secretary of state to the Pretender. According to his own account, as a schoolboy

I saw very soon the blessings of a free government, and I did not, even then, argue so weakly as to think that a free government could be preserved but by allowing such a resistance as was necessary at the Revolution . . .
When I went to the university, as I was upon a foundation, I took all the oaths to the Government. When I took them I well knew the force of those engagements. I was not ignorant of the nature of the question, if it can be called a question, for I never could see the doubt. That a Protestant should reason himself into a Jacobite is as incomprehensible in politics as it is in religion that a man should reason himself into an atheist.[1]

He seems to have antedated his conversion, for during a visit to his Jacobite brother in Paris at the end of his second year at Oxford he wrote to his brother-in-law, John Hay, titular Earl of Inverness and secretary of state to the Pretender:

I flatter myself you will excuse the ambition of a young man, if I make use of the freedom I at present have, to desire you to make a tender of my duty and loyalty to the King; a very small present, but all I have to offer. Twill in some measure excuse my presumption for offering my service, though in so private a station as not to be able to render any considerable, that I do it at a time when so many are wanting to their duty, that 'tis some merit to protest against it . . . The chief end I would propose from my studies and education, and the greatest glory I can aim at is to be able to serve his Majesty in any way that he pleases to command me.[2]

Choosing the law as the most independent profession, Murray quickly made his name at the parliamentary bar. In 1736, as counsel for the bishops against the Quakers bill, he gained such 'credit with the clergy' that at a by-election for Oxford University in 1737 he was considered by the Whigs as a candidate to oppose William Bromley jun.; but, in his own words, 'the great business I was then coming in to at the bar of the House of Commons made it imprudent for me to think of coming into Parliament; and this idea was dropped'.[3]

During the next five years Murray rose to the top of his profession, appearing before the House of Commons for the city of Edinburgh on the Porteous riots bill in 1737, for the merchants' petition against the Spanish depredations in 1738, and for the opposition candidates in the Westminster election in 1741, when Horace Walpole describes him as speaking 'divinely', 'beyond what was ever heard at the bar'[4] of the House. He received many offers of a seat but determined that when he came into Parliament it 'should be in connection with the Whigs, and in office, so that there might be no possibility of doubt concerning the conduct I meant to hold'.[5] These conditions were fulfilled in 1742, when the Duke of Newcastle decided that it was essential to strengthen himself in the House of Commons and that in Murray, who had recently acted for him in a private matter, he had found 'a sure way of doing it. I know (and my brother is now fully convinced of it) that I can absolutely depend upon Mr. Murray. He will beat them all . . . I mean Pitt, Lyttelton, etc.'. Newcastle's friends agreed, the Duke of Richmond observing that 'the only objection that can be made to him is what he can't help, which is that he is a Scotchman, which (as I have a great regard for him) I am extremely sorry for'.[6] One of the Members for Boroughbridge died opportunely; Sir John Strange (q.v.), the solicitor-general, was ready to resign his office; and at the end of November Murray entered Parliament as solicitor-general. Within a fortnight of taking his seat, he made his maiden speech, as Horace Walpole reports,

> with the greatest applause; Pitt answered him with all his force and art of language, but on an ill-founded argument. In all appearance they will be great rivals.

In the next session,

> Murray shines as bright as ever he did at the bar, which he seems to decline to push his fortune in the House of Commons under Mr. Pelham.[7]

In 1751 Chesterfield describes Murray and Pitt as

> beyond comparison the best speakers [in the House of Commons] . . . They alone can inflame or quiet the House; they alone are so attended to in that numerous and noisy assembly that you might hear a pin fall while either of them is speaking.[8]

But his Jacobite connexions were a serious liability, especially after the Forty-five rebellion. Many years later, when he had become Lord Mansfield, the Duke of Newcastle wrote:

> Men of my Lord Mansfield's parts and abilities generally can make their own way in this country; but in his Lordship's case it was impossible. He had the misfortune to be so nearly allied to the most declared enemies of the Protestant succession; his own character not known in that respect; his first appearance in the world marked with the most intimate connection with the late Lord Bolingbroke and Mr. Pope; and his public appearances as counsel and his private friendships and acquaintances with those at the head of the opposition, Sir Wm. Wyndham, Lord Bath, Lord Granville, etc.; that nothing but the most determined resolution and support from me,

not tainted with those principles or those acquaintances, could have forced his way to the great stations he has been in.[9]

At the end of 1752 the younger Horace Walpole (q.v.), prosecuting a secret personal vendetta against the Pelhams, circulated an anonymous leaflet suggesting that they were under the influence of a 'dangerous faction, who intend to overthrow the Government and restore the exiled and arbitrary House of Stuart'; that 'a Scotchman of a most disaffected family and allied in the nearest manner to the Pretender's first minister' had been 'consulted on the education of the Prince of Wales and entrusted with the most important secrets of Government'; in short, that two Jacobites, Murray and his friend, Andrew Stone (q.v.), the Duke of Newcastle's confidential advisers, governed the country. The leaflet started a witch-hunt against Murray and Stone, culminating in formal charges of Jacobitism, which were found by a cabinet inquiry to be absolutely baseless.[10] Nevertheless the affair put an end to Murray's political career. As Chesterfield (Stanhope, Philip Dormer, q.v.) wrote at the time:

> The evidence against them was really nothing; but, upon the whole, the affair has affected them both, and they will feel the weight of it as long as they live. No reasonable man, I believe, thinks them Jacobites now, whatever they may have been formerly. But parties do not reason, and every Whig party man, which is nine in ten of the Whig party, is fully convinced that they are at this time determined and dangerous Jacobites.[11]

On Pelham's death a year later, one of the chief objections to Murray as his successor was that he had 'too lately been the object of clamour on the worst species of Scotch principles'. When the chief justiceship of the King's bench fell vacant in 1756, he claimed it, 'agreeably to his constant asseverations that he meant to rise by his profession, not by the House of Commons'.[12]

He died 20 Mar. 1793, the founder of English commercial law.

[1] Murray's speech before the Committee of Council, 23 Feb. 1753, Add. 33050, f. 331. [2] 6 Aug. 1725, Stuart mss 85/21. The letter appears to be a copy. [3] Murray's speech, loc .cit. [4] To Mann, 24 Dec. 1741. [5] Murray's speech, loc. cit. [6] P. Yorke, *Hardwicke*, i. 307. [7] To Mann, 9 Dec. 1742, 24 Jan. 1744. [8] To his son, 11 Feb. 1751. [9] To Stone, 15 Oct. 1762, Add. 32943, f. 224. [10] Walpole, *Mems. Geo. II*, i. 298–332. [11] To Dayrolles, 6 Apr. 1753. [12] *Mems. Geo. II*, i. 380; ii. 223–4.

R.R.S.

MUSGRAVE, Sir Christopher, 5th Bt. (1688–1736), of Edenhall, Cumb.

CARLISLE	1713–1715
CUMBERLAND	1722–1734

b. 25 Dec. 1688, o.s. of Philip Musgrave, M.P., by Mary, da. of George Legge, M.P., 1st Baron Dartmouth. *educ.* Ch. Ch. Oxf. 1706. *m.* 21 June 1711, Julia, da. of Sir John Chardin of Kempton Park, Mdx., 11 ch. *suc.* fa. 1689, gd.-fa. as 5th Bt. 29 July 1704.

Clerk of Privy Council 1710–16.

Musgrave belonged to one of the chief Cumberland families. His grandfather, Sir Christopher Musgrave, a leading Tory politician, sat in Parliament for 43 years till ·his death in 1704. Under James II his father, Philip, M.P. Appleby 1685–7, obtained the post of clerk of the Privy Council, which descended to Musgrave via an uncle. In 1713 he was returned for Carlisle, where his family had a strong interest, though it was thought that if he had chosen to stand on the high Tory interest for the county he could easily have thrown out Gilfrid Lawson (q.v.).[1] He did not stand in 1715 on learning that he would be opposed by Lord Carlisle,[2] but in 1722 he was returned for Cumberland, in the last contested election for that county for 46 years. In 1723 he and the Duke of Wharton are said to have taken

> an occasion of treating about three score of the country people and, after they had drunk a good deal, the Duke and Sir Christopher Musgrave pulled off their coats and waistcoats, fell down upon their knees, and drank the Pretender's health.[3]

Knatchbull describes him as 'a hot headed fellow', who by his 'heat' was apt to play into the hands of the Government in the House of Commons and 'spoil a fair game'. In 1725 he was one of five Tories who voted against the restoration of Bolingbroke's estates.[4] He did not stand again, and died 3 Jan. 1736.

[1] *HMC Portland*, v. 343. [2] R. S. Ferguson, *Cumb. and Westmld. M.P.s*, 101–4. [3] *HMC Lonsdale*, 123. [4] *Knatchbull Diary*, 23 Jan., 20 Apr. 1725.

R.R.S.

MUSGRAVE, Sir Philip, 6th Bt. (?1712–95), of Edenhall, Cumb.

WESTMORLAND 1741–1747

b. ?1712, 1st s. of Sir Christopher Musgrave, 5th Bt. (q.v.). *educ.* Eton 1725–8; Oriel, Oxf. 8 Jan. 1733, aged 20. *m.* 24 June 1742, Anne, da. of John Turton of Orgreave, Staffs., 2s. 8da. *suc.* fa. 3 Jan. 1736.

Returned as a Tory for Westmorland after a contest, Musgrave voted against the Government. He did not stand again but took an active part in supporting the Duke of Portland at the county election of 1768.[1] He died 5 July 1795.

[1] B. Bonsall, *Cumb. and Westmld. Elections*, 75–76, 96.

R.R.S.

MUSSENDEN, Hill (1699–1772), of Herringfleet, Suff.

HARWICH 1741–1747

b. 1699, 2nd s. of John Mussenden of Hillsborough, co. Down by Jane da. of Adam Leathes; yr. bro. of Carteret Leathes (q.v.). *m.* (settlement 30 June 1736)[1] Martha, da. of Sir Henry Johnson, M.P., of Friston Hall, Suff., sis. of Sir Henry Johnson (q.v.), *s.p.*

Commr. of alienation office 1738–44.

Mussenden was returned for Harwich on the interest of his brother, Carteret Leathes. Like his brother he supported the Administration till the end of 1743, when they both voted with the Opposition on the Hanoverians. He again voted against the Hanoverians in 1744,[2] losing his place on the formation of the Broad-bottom Government in December. He abstained from voting on them in 1746. Never standing again, he died 23 Nov. 1772, leaving his property to his brother.

[1] Copinger, *Suff. Manors*, v. 44–45. [2] Owen, *Pelhams*, 202, 208.

R.R.S.

MUSSENDEN, *see also* **LEATHES**

MYDDELTON, John (1685–1747), of Chirk Castle, Denb.

DENBIGH BOROUGHS 27 Apr. 1733–1741
DENBIGHSHIRE 1741–23 Feb. 1742

bap. 21 Oct. 1685, yr. s. of Richard Myddelton of Shrewsbury and Crutched Friars, London by Elizabeth, da. of Sir William Ryder of Bethnal Green, Mdx.; bro. of Robert Myddelton (q.v.). *m.* (settlement 26 Feb. 1724) Mary da., of Thomas Liddell of Bedford Row, London, 2s. 2da. *suc.* e. bro. to Chirk Castle 1733.

John Myddelton succeeded his brother as a Tory at Denbigh Boroughs in 1733, concluding an agreement with Watkin Williams Wynn (q.v.), under which they undertook to support one another in Denbighshire at the impending general election. Re-elected without a contest, he voted with the Opposition on the convention in 1739 and the place bill of 1740, although early in 1739, with a view to recovering the county seat, he had formed an electoral alliance with the Government as a result of which his kinsman, William Myddelton of Gwaynynog, was appointed receiver general of revenue in North Wales. Standing for the county seat against Wynn in 1741, he was heavily defeated at the poll but was returned by William Myddelton, who had been appointed sheriff of Denbighshire in the previous year. At the opening of the new Parliament he voted with the Government on the chairman of the elections committee. After Walpole's fall he was unseated by the House of Commons, who committed

William Myddelton to Newgate, also having him turned out of his receivership and the commission of the peace.[1]

John Myddelton died 9 Apr. 1747.

[1] NLW Chirk Castle mss E.903, 3201, 4650, 4795, 5296, 5423; *CJ*, xxiv. 18–19, 89–92.

P.D.G.T.

MYDDELTON, Sir Richard, 3rd Bt. (1655–1716), of Chirk Castle, Denb.

DENBIGHSHIRE 1685–9 Apr. 1716

b. 23 Mar. 1655, 4th s. of Sir Thomas Myddelton, 1st Bt., M.P., by his 1st w. Mary, da. of Thomas Cholmondeley of Vale Royal, Cheshire. *educ.* B.N.C. Oxf. 1670. *m.* 19 Apr. 1686, Frances, da. and coh. of Sir Thomas Whitmore of Buildwas, Salop, wid. of William Whitmore of Hackney, Mdx., 1s. 2da. *suc.* e. bro. Sir Thomas Myddelton, 2nd Bt., 5 Feb. 1684.
Recorder, Denbigh and custos. rot. Denb. 1684–*d.*; sheriff, Denb. 1688.

Sir Richard Myddelton considerably increased the Chirk Castle estates, marrying a Shropshire heiress and buying the lordship of Ruthin. A moderate Tory, who did not oppose the Hanoverian succession, he died 9 Apr. 1716.

P.D.G.T.

MYDDELTON, Richard (1726–95), of Chirk Castle, Denb.

DENBIGH BOROUGHS 1747–May 1788

b. 26 Mar. 1726, 1st s. of John Myddelton (q.v.). *educ.* Eton 1739–43;[1] St. John's, Oxf. 1744. *m.* (1) 14 Mar. 1761, Elizabeth (*d.* 7 Nov. 1772), da. of Sir John Rushout, 4th Bt. (q.v.), of Northwick Park, Worcs., 1s. 3da.; (2) 1778, Mary Lloyd (*d.* 14 Mar. 1788), 1da.; (3) Euphemia Crawford of Pall Mall, *s.p. suc.* fa. 1747.
Ld. lt. Denb. 1748–*d.*, custos. rot. 1749–*d.*; steward of the lordship of Denbigh 1748–*d.*, of Bromfield and Yale 1749–*d.*; recorder, Denbigh 1749–*d.*

Richard Myddelton was barely 21 when he succeeded his father but Henry Pelham gave him the most important offices in Denbighshire, pressing him to take the opportunity of Sir Watkin Williams Wynn's death

to push for the county, and then you may bring in . . . any good man you think proper for the town of Denbigh. A minority, the divisions and distresses of the Williams family, will probably open a door for your easy entrance.[2]

Myddelton, whose only ambition was an English peerage, preferred to leave the county to Sir Lynch Salusbury Cotton (q.v.) and to hold the boroughs uncontested. Though his applications for a peerage were unsuccessful,[3] he steadily adhered to Newcastle, who treated him as one of Lord Powis's

group. During his last twenty years in the House he hardly ever attended.

He died 2 Apr. 1795.

[1] W. M. Myddelton, *Chirk Castle Accounts*, 467, 503. [2] NLW Chirk Castle mss E.613. [3] Add. 32995, f. 260; 32917, ff. 387–8.

P.D.G.T.

MYDDELTON, Robert (1678–1733), of Chirk Castle, Denb.

DENBIGH BOROUGHS 1722–5 Apr. 1733

bap. 14 June 1678, 1st surv. s. of Richard Myddelton of Shrewsbury and Crutched Friars, London; bro. of John Myddelton (q.v.). *educ.* B.N.C. Oxf. 1694–7; M. Temple 1695, called 1702. *m.* 5 May 1720, Ann, da. of Sir James Reade, 2nd Bt., of Brocket Hall, Herts., sis. and coh. of Sir John Reade, 3rd Bt., *s.p. suc.* fa. 1700 and cos. Sir William Myddelton, 4th Bt., to Chirk Castle, 5 Jan. 1718.
Recorder, Shrewsbury 1710, Denbigh 1718–*d.*

On the death of Sir Richard Myddelton (q.v.), whose son had no desire to enter Parliament, his cousin, Robert Myddelton, stood for the county on the Chirk Castle interest at the ensuing by-election, but was defeated by Watkin Williams (Wynn). In 1722, having succeeded to the Chirk Castle estate, he stood again, with the support of the Administration, whom he requested to arrange for the shire election to precede that for the boroughs so that if he were defeated for the former he could be returned for the latter.[1] Defeated for the county but returned for the boroughs, he voted with the Tories against the Government, even joining his opponent, Watkin Williams Wynn, in opposing a loyal address from the county on the Atterbury plot.[2] He continued to oppose the Administration till his death, 5 Apr. 1733.

[1] NLW Chirk Castle mss E.401, 3983–4, 4109; Add. 35584, f. 247. [2] Yorke, *Hardwicke*, i. 76.

P.D.G.T.

NAPIER, Sir Nathaniel, 3rd Bt. (?1668–1728), of Middlemarsh Hall, and Critchell More, Dorset.

DORCHESTER 1695–1708, 1710–1722

b. ?1668, o. surv. s. of Sir Nathaniel Napier, 2nd Bt., M.P., by Blanche, da. and coh. of Sir Hugh Wyndham of Silton, Dorset, justice of the common pleas. *educ.* L. Inn 1683; Trinity, Oxf. 10 Apr. 1685, aged 16. *m.* (1) July 1691, Jane (*d.* 1692), da. of Sir Robert Worsley, 3rd Bt., M.P., of Appuldurcombe, I.o.W., *s.p.*; (2) 28 Aug. 1694, Catherine, da. of William Alington, M.P., 1st Baron Alington of Wymondley, sis. and coh. of Giles, 2nd Baron, 5s. 3da. *suc.* fa. Jan. 1709.

Sir Nathaniel Napier was descended from Sir Robert Napper or Napier, M.P., chief baron of the Irish Exchequer, who acquired Middlemarsh about 1592 and built and endowed the almshouse in Dorchester, known as Napper's Mite, in 1615.[1] Four generations of his family had represented Dorset boroughs or the county since 1586; and he himself sat for Dorchester in nine Parliaments, for two of which, 1702–5, he was joined by his father. A Tory under Queen Anne, no votes of his in the 1715 Parliament have been recorded. His name was sent to the Pretender in 1721 as a probable supporter in the event of a rising.[2] He did not stand again, dying 24 Feb. 1728.

[1] Hutchins, *Dorset*, ii. 370; iii. 125; iv. 481, 483–4. [2] Stuart mss 65/16.

R.S.L.

NASMYTH, Sir James, 2nd Bt. (c.1704–79), of Dawyck and Posso, Peebles.

PEEBLESSHIRE 28 Apr. 1732–1734
7 Feb. 1735–1741

b. c.1704, 1st s. of Sir James Nasmyth, 1st Bt., of Dawyck and Posso by Barbara, da. of Andrew Pringle of Clifton, Roxburgh. *m.* Jean, da. of Thomas Keith, 2s. *suc.* fa. 20 July 1720.

Sir James Nasmyth was the son of a successful lawyer whose family had been granted lands in Posso in 1554.[1] He first contested the county unsuccessfully in 1727 against John Douglas (q.v.), a brother of the hereditary sheriff, the Earl of March, who died, leaving an infant son, in 1731. When Douglas died a year later, Nasmyth, with the support of the deputy sheriff, defeated a former Member for the shire, Sir Alexander Murray, 3rd Bt., of Stanhope, whose petition was rejected by the House of Commons. At the 1734 election, when another deputy sheriff was apparently neutral, Nasmyth and Murray were involved in a double return; on petition Murray withdrew, leaving the seat to Nasmyth. He voted with the Administration in all recorded divisions till he retired in 1741. A botanist of some repute, he died 4 Feb. 1779.

[1] J. W. Buchan & H. Paton, *Peeblesshire*, iii. 442–3, 562–9.

R.S.L.

NASSAU, Richard Savage (1723–80), of Easton, Suff.

COLCHESTER 1747–1754
MALDON 1774–17 May 1780

b. 1 June 1723, 2nd s. of Frederick Nassau de Zuylesteyn, 3rd Earl of Rochford, by Bessy, illegit. da. of Richard Savage, M.P., 4th Earl Rivers. *educ.* Westminster 1734–9. *m.* 24 Dec. 1751, Anne (*d.* 9 Mar. 1771), da. and h. of Edward Spencer of Rendlesham, Suff., wid. of James, 5th Duke of Hamilton [S], 2s. 1da.; (2) name unknown (*d.* 18 Oct. 1773).[1] Groom of the bedchamber Jan.–Oct. 1760; clerk of the Green Cloth (£1,018 p.a.) Jan. 1771–*d.*

Nassau was returned for Colchester as a government supporter in 1747 on the interest of his brother, the 4th Earl of Rochford, who had inherited the Essex estates of the Rivers family through his mother.[2] He did not stand in 1754 but reluctantly allowed himself to be returned as a stop-gap in 1774. He died 17 May 1780.

[1] *Gent. Mag.* 1773, p. 526. [2] *Essex Rev.* li. 75–76.

E.C.

NAYLOR, George (?1671–1730), of Hurstmonceaux, Suss.

SEAFORD 12 Dec. 1706–1710, 1713–1722

b. ?1671, 1st s. of Francis Naylor of Staple Inn by Bethia (lic. 1 July 1665), da. of George Beadnall of Newcastle-upon-Tyne. *educ.* St. John's, Oxf. 5 June 1684, aged 13; L. Inn 1685, called 1694. *m.* 4 July 1704, Grace, da. of Thomas Pelham, M.P., 1st Baron Pelham of Laughton, 1da. *d.v.p.*

In 1704 George Naylor, 'a gentleman of £4,000 p.a.',[1] married the eldest daughter of the 1st Lord Pelham. Returned for Seaford in 1706 on the Pelham interest, he bought Hurstmonceaux from the Earl of Sussex in 1708 for £38,215.[2] In 1711 Lord Pelham died, appointing Naylor one of his executors and guardian of his heir, the future Duke of Newcastle, then a minor. Re-elected for Seaford in 1715, he voted for the septennial bill, but parted political company with Newcastle during the split in the Whig party by voting with Walpole on the charges against Cadogan (q.v.) in 1717 and on the peerage bill in 1719. Not put up again, he died 29 June 1730.

[1] *Suss. N. & Q.* x. 165. [2] *Suss. Arch. Colls.* iv. 162; *VCH Suss.* ix. 134.

R.R.S.

NEALE, John (1687–1746), of Allesley Park, Warws. and Cherington, Glos.

CHIPPING WYCOMBE 8 Feb.–10 Mar. 1722
COVENTRY 3 Apr.–20 Nov. 1722
11 Dec. 1722–1734, 15 Feb.–22 Mar. 1737
12 Apr. 1737–1741

bap. 11 July 1687, 1st s. of Henry Neale, M.P., of Allesley Park by Anna Maria, da. and h. of John Hanbury of Freckenham, Suff. *educ.* Pembroke, Oxf. 1705, M. Temple 1705. *m.* Frances, da. of Roger Pope of Oswestry, Salop, 3da. *suc.* fa. 1730.

Neale's grandfather, John Neale, M.P., of Dean in Bedfordshire, distinguished himself in the parliamentary cause during the civil war and married the cousin and ward of Oliver Cromwell. His father bought Allesley, two miles from Coventry, in 1692 and contested the city in 1701. Returned as a Whig for Chipping Wycombe at a by-election in 1722, he was elected for Coventry at the general election of that year, standing jointly with Sir Adolphus Oughton (q.v.) on the corporation interest. On petition the election was declared void, but he was returned at a new election a month later, and was unopposed in 1727. Absent from the divisions on the Hessians in 1730 and on the army in 1732, he voted for the excise bill on 14 Mar. 1733, when he was described as 'husband to one of the Queen's bedchamber women'.[1] He made his maiden speech on the committee stage of the bill two days later, declaring that his constituents supported the bill, but when, on 11 Apr. a petition from Coventry against the bill was presented by William Bromley (q.v.), it was

> seconded by Mr. Neale, who had voted against the London one the day before, and who at the same time he seconded it assured the House it did not import the sense of the city.[2]

On 8 May he supported an address of thanks on the Princess Royal's marriage to the Prince of Orange. On 12 Feb. 1734, in a debate on how 'to prevent the running of wool both from England and Ireland', he said that there was 'a sure method' of doing this 'namely, for the Parliament to buy all the wool and yarn of both kingdoms and sell it again at a proper price'. Seven days later he opposed a new bill to oblige Members to produce their qualification to the House of Commons and to swear to it.[3]

Before the 1734 election Neale wrote to Walpole:

> I have no ways agreed to join with anybody at Coventry yet, but my friends tell me I may bring in whomsoever I have a mind to, if I have a mind to, if I insist on it, and I can say I think my interest as good there as ever, but if you are sure of Sir Adolphus [Oughton] for the future I should be loth to turn him out, but if not, I will be ready to obey your commands.

Defeated by John Bird, a local merchant who stood on the anti-excise platform, he recovered his seat when Walpole gave Bird an office incompatible with a seat in the House, Neale being returned for the vacancy at a by-election in April 1737. He wrote to Walpole, 27 Dec. 1737:

> I am honoured with your letter, and if able, will be at the meeting of the Parliament, though I must beg leave to consult my friends at Coventry upon all occasions, having spent too much money and stood too much fire in supporting your cause, to be not only opposed by my friends, but in conjunction with your enemies to support a tool of theirs for one [Oughton] and for the other, one [Bird] founded his popularity upon his virulence against the excise and opposition to the bulwark of the Whig interest at Coventry, being almost totally supported by the Tories. If I should do anything to incur the displeasure of my friends at Coventry, can I any more expect the support of your friends next time than last?[4]

He was absent from the division on the Spanish convention in 1739 and voted for the place bill in 1740. Defeated in 1741, he sold the advowson of Allesley to pay for his electioneering debts.[5] He died 19 Dec. 1746.

[1] *Gent. Mag.* 1733, p. 577. [2] Oughton to Edw. Hopkins, Saturday 17th [Mar. 1733] and Saturday 14th [Apr. 1733], Stuart mss Box I/125. [3] *HMC Egmont Diary,* i. 371; ii. 28, 31. [4] 24 Sept. 1733, Cholmondeley (Houghton) mss. [5] Whitley, *Parl. Rep. Coventry,* 148; *VCH Warws.* vi. 7.

E.C.

NEALE, Robert (1706–76), of Corsham, Wilts.

WOOTTON BASSETT   1741–1754

b. 27 May 1706, 1st s. of Robert Neale of Yate, Glos. and Corsham, clothier, by Sarah, da. of William Arnold of Corsham. *m.* 3 Nov. 1735, Elizabeth, da. of Thomas Smith of Shaw House, Melksham, Wilts., sis. and h. of John Smith of Shaw House. *suc.* fa. 1733.

Robert Neale, the son and heir of a wealthy Wiltshire clothier, acquired further estates in north Wiltshire both by marriage and purchase.[1] In 1741 he stood on his own interest at Wootton Bassett as a government supporter, heading the poll. Consistently supporting the Administration, he was classed as 'Old Whig' in 1746. He was re-elected in 1747 but, despite heavy expenditure and much bribery, he was defeated in 1754, never standing again. He wrote to Newcastle on 15 Feb. 1755, ascribing the loss of his seat, interest, and £1,800 to having complied with Pelham's wish that he should contest both seats.[2] Nevertheless a secret service pension of £500 a year which he had been receiving from Pelham[3] was discontinued. He died 3 July 1776.

[1] J. A. Neale, *Charters and Recs. Neales of Berkeley.* [2] Namier, *Structure,* 431 n.11. [3] Ibid. 437; Add. 33038, f. 415.

R.S.L.

NEDHAM, Robert (?1703–62), of Howbery Park, Oxon. and Mourne Park, co Down.

OLD SARUM   1734–1741

b.? 1703, 1st s. of Robert Nedham of St. Thomas in the Vale and St. Catherine's, Jamaica by Elizabeth, da. of William Shirley of Jamaica. *educ.* Trinity, Oxf. 30 May 1723, aged 19; I. Temple 1725. *m.* 21 May 1733, Catherine, da. of Robert Pitt (q.v.), of Stratford sub Castle, Wilts., sis. of Thomas Pitt of Boconnoc and William Pitt, Earl of Chatham (qq.v.), 3s. 1da. *suc.* fa. 1738.

Robert Nedham, whose grandfather had gone to Jamaica after the civil war, was descended from a younger son of the 1st Viscount Kilmorey [I]. Having settled in England, he did not inherit his father's Jamaica estates.[1] Brought in at Old Sarum in 1734 by his brother-in-law, Thomas Pitt (q.v.), he voted against the Government on the Spanish convention, 8 Mar. 1739, but thereafter he seems to have gone over to the Administration, as he is included in two lists of ministerial supporters who were absent from divisions on the right of search, 21 Nov. 1739, and the Address, 18 Nov. 1740.[2] Presumably for this reason he was not put up by Pitt in 1741 and 1747. When Pitt proposed to bring him into Parliament in 1754, Newcastle noted that it was 'utterly impossible'.[3] He died August 1762.

[1] M. C. Owen, *Sewells of the Isle of Wight*, 104–5. [2] Cholmondeley (Houghton) mss. [3] Add. 32995, f. 120.

R.S.L.

NEGUS, Francis (1670–1732), of Dillinghoo, Suff.

IPSWICH 13 Nov. 1717–9 Sept. 1732

bap. 3 May 1670, 1st s. of Francis Negus of St. Paul's, Covent Garden, sec. to Henry, Duke of Norfolk, and surveyor of the mews, by his w. Elianore Boone. *m.* (lic. 14 Feb. 1704) Elizabeth, da. and h. of William Churchill (q.v.),[1] 1s. 1da. *suc.* fa. 1712.

Ensign 3 Ft. 1687, capt. 1691, maj. 1694; commn. renewed 1702; brevet lt.-col. 1703; ranger of Bagshot Rails and Sandhurst Walks, Windsor forest; jt. cmmr. for executing the office of master of the horse 1715–17, sole 1717–27; avener and clerk marshal 1717–*d.*; master of the buckhounds, ranger of Swinley Chase, lt. and dep. ranger of Windsor forest 1727–*d.*; assistant, R. African Co. 1728–*d.*; gov. Chelsea waterworks.

Negus, an army officer, served under Marlborough in the war of the Spanish succession. Succeeding his father-in-law, William Churchill, at Ipswich in 1717, he voted regularly with the Government. He is described by the first Lord Egmont as knowing 'many modern anecdotes' and as having 'a good interest at court', though he complained that the ministry 'gave him no assistance at Ipswich'.[2] He died 9 Sept. 1732, commemorated in the *Ipswich Gazette* by a poem beginning: 'Is Negus gone? ah! Ipswich weep and mourn'.[3]

[1] PCC 126 Price. [2] *HMC Egmont Diary*, i. 90, 292; iii. 334. [3] Copinger, *Suff. Manors*, iv. 248.

R.R.S.

NELTHORPE, James (c.1675–1734), of Lynford Hall, Norf.

TIVERTON 1 Mar. 1728–1734

?*bap.* 17 Nov. 1675, s. of Edward Nelthorpe of St. Mary Abchurch, London by his w. Mary. *educ.* ?Merchant Taylors' 1687. *unm.*, 1s.

'Rugged Nelthorpe', so called, 'not from any rigid virtue, but from his pride and ill-nature', acquired the manor of Lynford from Sir Charles Turner (q.v.) in 1717, building Lynford Hall, where Sir Robert Walpole often spent a night on his way to Houghton.[1] Returned for Tiverton, no doubt on Walpole's recommendation, he voted consistently with the Administration, except on the

excise bill, when he was absent. He died 20 Apr. 1734 leaving his natural son, James Nelthorpe, to Walpole's guardianship.[2]

[1] *HMC Portland*, vi. 164–5; Blomefield, *Norfolk*, ii. 263, 264. [2] PCC 139 Ockham.

S.R.M.

NESBITT, Albert (*d.*1753), of Coleman St., London and Putney, Mdx.

HUNTINGDON 29 Dec. 1741–1747
MITCHELL 1747–12 Jan. 1753

2nd s. of Andrew Nesbitt of Brentner and Malmusoy, co. Donegal by Anne Lindsay. *m.* 1729, Elizabeth, da. of John Gould of Woodford, Essex, director, E.I. Co., 1da.

Nesbitt came over from Ireland and set up in business in London as a Baltic merchant c.1717. After his marriage, he went into partnership with his brother-in-law Nathaniel Gould (q.v.), trading in Coleman Street under the name of Gould and Nesbitt. After Gould's death in 1738, Nesbitt took his nephew, Arnold Nesbitt (q.v.) into partnership, trading under the style of Nesbitt and Arnold. He appears to have been concerned in the wine trade with France. The wealth he acquired as a merchant enabled him to purchase his family's estates in Ireland from his elder brother Thomas c.1737.[1] Returned unopposed for Huntingdon at a by-election in 1741, after standing unsuccessfully for it at the general election that year against Lord Sandwich's candidates, he voted consistently with the Administration. In 1747 Sandwich, now a member of the Government, wrote to Pelham: 'As for Mr. Nesbitt, my only objection to him is that I can't choose him for Huntingdon without hurting if not endangering, my interest in that borough',[2] so he nominated him for Mitchell instead. He died suddenly on 12 Jan. 1753, leaving his Irish estates to his daughter, and his business, together with the property he had purchased in and around Winchelsea, to his nephew.[3]

[1] *Bd. Trade Jnl.* 1722–8, pp. 78, 319–20; A. & C. Nesbitt, *Nesbitt Fam.* 37, 39, 41; *Cal. Treas. Bks. and Pprs.* 1742–5, pp. 505, 579, 702. [2] 25 May 1747 (N.S.), Newcastle (Clumber) mss. [3] PCC 24 Searle.

E.C.

NESBITT, Arnold (?1721–79), of West Wickham, Kent and Icklesham, nr. Winchelsea, Suss.

MITCHELL 27 Jan. 1753–1754
WINCHELSEA 1754–1761
CRICKLADE 1761–1768
WINCHELSEA 15 Jan. 1770–1774
CRICKLADE 1774–7 Apr. 1779

b. ?1721, 3rd s. of Thomas Nesbitt of Grangemore, co. Westmeath by Jane, da., and h. of Arnold Crosby of Lismore, co. Cavan. *m.* 28 Nov. 1758, Susannah, da. of Ralph Thrale (q.v.), sis. of Henry Thrale, M.P., *s.p.*; at least 2s. illegit.

Arnold Nesbitt was apprenticed to his uncle, Albert Nesbitt (q.v.), an eminent London merchant, became his partner, and succeeded to his business, his Winchelsea property and his seat in 1753. He was classed as a government supporter in 1754. He died 7 Apr. 1779.

E.C.

NEVILLE, Grey (1681–1723), of Billingbear, Berks.

ABINGDON	1705–1708
WALLINGFORD	1708–1710
BERWICK-UPON-TWEED	1715–24 Nov. 1723

b. 23 Sept. 1681, 1st s. of Richard Neville, M.P., of Billingbear by Catherine, da. of Richard Grey, 2nd Baron Grey of Warke; bro. of Henry Grey and uncle of Richard Neville Aldworth (qq.v.). *m.* Elizabeth, da. of Sir John Boteler, 1da. *d.v.p.* *suc.* fa. 1717.
Commr. for stating the army debts 1715–22.

Grey, known as 'Bishop', Neville was returned as a Whig for Berwick on the interest of his brother, Henry Grey (q.v.), who had inherited the Northumberland estates of the Greys of Warke. In 1715 he collaborated with his fellow Member for Berwick, John Shute, later Lord Barrington, in preparing a statement for the Government setting out the grounds for repealing the Occasional Conformity and Schism Acts,[1] for which he spoke and voted in 1719. He also voted for the septennial bill but opposed the peerage bill, commenting ironically on the Government's attempt to rush it through a thin House.[2] After the collapse of the South Sea bubble he spoke, 8 Dec. 1720, in support of a motion, which was lost, calling for an inquiry into the responsibility of ministers for the affair, four days later carrying another requiring the South Sea directors to lay an account of their proceedings before the Commons. He subsequently defended Lord Sunderland against the charges brought against him in the House of Commons, saying that 'though he hated all that had promoted the South Sea scheme, yet on such trivial evidence he would be for even one that was accused of murdering his father'.[3] He also opposed the proposal that John Aislabie should be included in the bill for confiscating the estates of the South Sea directors.[4] Three days before the election at Berwick in 1722 his brother, at his instance, wrote to Sunderland stating that Neville had been given to understand that Sunderland had offered 'to procure him £1000 towards his expenses at Berwick'.

> If your Lordship has any such kind intentions to assist a gentleman who (as well as myself) has personally served your Lordship, the sooner you are pleased

> to do it, the greater the obligation will be. I beg your Lordship will either give me leave to wait on you at your own hour, or that you vouchsafe to order your secretary to give me an explicit answer, that in case my poor brother cannot have any favour from his Majesty we may have time to raise the money to support him.[5]

Re-elected, he died next year, 24 Nov. 1723.

[1] *Dudley Ryder Diary*, 154. [2] Thos. Brodrick to Ld. Midleton, 8 Dec. 1719, Brodrick mss. [3] Geo. Tilson to Ld. Whitworth, 15 Mar. 1721, Add. 37324, f. 90. [4] Coxe, *Walpole*, ii. 215. [5] Hen. Grey to Sunderland, 28 Mar. 1722, Sunderland (Blenheim) mss.

R.R.S.

NEVILLE, *see also* ALDWORTH, Richard Neville *and* GREY, Henry

NEWDIGATE, Sir Roger, 5th Bt. (1719–1806), of Arbury, Warws. and Harefield, Mdx.

MIDDLESEX	5 Aug. 1742–1747
OXFORD UNIVERSITY	31 Jan. 1751–1780

b. 20 May 1719, 7th s. of Sir Richard Newdigate, 3rd Bt., by his 2nd w. Elizabeth, da. of Sir Roger Twisden, 2nd Bt., M.P., of Bradbourne, Kent. *educ.* Westminster 1727; Univ. Coll. Oxf. 1736; Grand Tour 1738–40 (France, Italy, Netherlands). *m.* (1) 31 May 1743, Sophia (*d.* 9 July 1774), da. of Edward Conyers of Copt Hall, Essex, sis. of John Conyers (qq.v.), *s.p.*; (2) 3 June 1776, Hester, da. of Edward Mundy of Shipley, Derbys., sis. of Edward Miller Mundy, M.P., *s.p.* *suc.* bro. 14 Apr. 1734.
Steward of the anniversary dinner of the independent electors of Westminster 1748.

A large landowner in Warwickshire and Middlesex, Newdigate was returned as a Tory for the latter county in 1742. In a debate on 23 Jan. 1745, he denounced Pelham's proposal to maintain 28,000 men in Flanders in the coming year as 'an old measure from a new ministry'. Pitt retorted

> that if they completed their last augmentation of 12,000 men, they would have a more numerous army on foot than they kept during King William's wars. In the heat of his argument, he turned once or twice to Sir R. Newdigate, and asked with an air of disdain 'if this could be called an old measure from a new ministry'? . . . Mr. Pitt's fulminating eloquence silenced all opposition. Sir R. Newdigate professed an acquiescence, though till he had further lights he could not give a thorough approbation to the question.[1]

During the rebellion he refused to join the county association in defence of the Hanoverian succession.[2] Defeated for Middlesex in 1747, he was returned for Oxford University in 1751, in time to oppose a bill for the naturalization of foreign Protestants and the regency bill.[3] Next year he spoke for Lord Harley's (q.v.) motion against subsidies in peacetime. In 1753 he opposed every stage of the bill for the naturalization of the Jews and supported the repeal of the Plantation Act under which foreigners could be naturalized after seven years' residence in the Colonies.[4] He died 23 Nov. 1806.

[1] Yorke's parl. jnl. *Parl Hist.* xiii. 1054-6. [2] R. J. Robson, *Oxfordshire Election of 1754*, p. 2. [3] Newdigate Diary, Warws. RO. [4] Walpole, *Mems. Geo. II*, i. 254, 365.

E.C.

NEWLAND, George (?1692-1749), of Gatton, Surr.

GATTON 16 May 1738-22 Oct. 1749

b. ?1692, 4th s. of Sir George Newland, M.P., of Smithfield, London by Rebecca, da. of Edward Turgis, London merchant; bro. of William Newland (q.v.). *educ.* St. John's, Oxf. 26 July 1709, aged 17, demy, Magdalen 1711-20, fellow 1720-38, reader in moral philosophy 1727-31, D.C.L. 1729, vice-pres. 1733. *unm. suc.* bro. 1738.

Professor of geometry, Gresham Coll. London 1732-d.; gov. St. Bartholomew's, Bridewell, and Bethlehem Hospitals 1738-d.

On Newland's appointment to the professorship of geometry at Gresham College, Hearne, the Oxford antiquary, commented:

I think his being a citizen's son gave him some title preferable to others, *ceteris paribus.* It is a genteel sinecure, and no wonder a learned man did not get it, the citizens of London being friends to little else but trade.[1]

Succeeding to his brother's estates, he was returned for Gatton, voting consistently with the Opposition. Shortly before his death the 2nd Lord Egmont in his electoral survey described him as 'a strong Jacobite'. After his death intestate, 22 Oct. 1749, his heirs procured a private Act in 1751, under which the manor of Gatton was sold to Sir James Colebrooke (q.v.) for £23,000.[2]

[1] *Colls.* (Oxf. Hist. Soc.), xi. 30. [2] Manning & Bray, *Surr.* ii. 232.

R.R.S.

NEWLAND, William (?1685-1738), of Gatton, Surr.

GATTON 1710-4 May 1738

b. ?1685, 1st s. of Sir George Newland, M.P. London 1710-14; bro. of George Newland (q.v.). *educ.* St. John's, Oxf. 13 May 1703, aged 17; I. Temple, called 1711. *m.* Martha, da. of Edmund Shepherd, painter-stainer of London, 3da.

The son of a wealthy scrivener, William Newland inherited in 1703 from his kinsman, Thomas Turgis, M.P., the manor of Gatton, carrying control of one of the seats there. Returned for Gatton as a Tory at the first opportunity after coming of age, he voted against the Government in all recorded divisions till his death 4 May 1738.

R.R.S.

NEWNHAM, Nathaniel (c.1699-1778), of Basinghall St., London, and Newtimber Place, Suss.

ALDBOROUGH 9 Dec. 1743-1754
BRAMBER 1754-1761

b. c.1699, 2nd s. of Nathaniel Newnham of Streatham, Surr. by Honoria, da. and coh. of Thomas Kett of St. Mary Axe, London merchant; bro. of Thomas Newnham (q.v.). *m.* Sarah Adams, 5s. 1da.

Director, E.I. Co. 1738-40, 1743-6, 1748-51, 1753-d.; South Sea Co. 1761.

A merchant of 'great authority in the court of directors of the India Company', Newnham, after purchasing Newtimber in Sussex in 1741, was brought into Parliament by Newcastle as a Dissenter, whose return might help to secure the nonconformist vote at Lewes. In Parliament he acted as a dependant of Newcastle's, but made 'no progress' with the Duke, as 'his modesty . . . made him afraid of being troublesome in too frequent waiting on him'. In 1754 Newcastle turned him out to make way for Pitt at Aldborough, observing, when Newnham's brother-in-law, Sir Dudley Ryder, interceded for him, that he was 'of no consequence in himself', Eventually he was brought in by the Government free of charge for Bramber, 'within seven miles of his house', which did not please him, as proximity to one's constituents was well-known to lead to endless trouble and expense.[1]

He died 17 Sept. 1778.

[1] Dudley Ryder Diary, 1, 9 Nov. 1753, 23 Mar. 1754, Harrowby mss.

R.R.S.

NEWNHAM, Thomas (1697-1761), of Winchester, Hants.

QUEENBOROUGH 1741-1754

b. 1 May 1697, 1st s. of Nathaniel Newnham of Streatham, Surr. and bro. of Nathaniel Newnham (q.v.). *m.* Penelope, da. of B. R. Shelley of Brockhampton, Salop.[1]

Thomas Newnham was the son of a wealthy nonconformist London merchant. The family were old acquaintances of the Pelhams in Sussex,[2] where a senior branch had acquired an estate at Maresfield. Defeated at Marlborough in 1734, he petitioned unsuccessfully, 'notwithstanding the utmost efforts of Sir Robert Walpole' on his behalf in the House of Commons.[3] In 1740 he was believed by his family to be drinking himself to death at Winchester, but a year later he was returned on the Admiralty interest for Queenborough, voting with the Government. In 1753 he decided not to stand again for Queenborough, as the corporation were 'much dissatisfied with him' and his health would not stand a contested election. Though Pelham was prepared to find him another borough, Newnham could not afford to pay the current price of £1,500-£2,000, his father, who complained of his extravagance, refusing to advance more than £1,000. So informed by Newnham's brother-in-law, Sir Dudley Ryder (q.v.), Pelham replied that

> he could not disburse the King's money [i.e. the secret service money] for him without the King's knowing it, and that the King did not understand that the Newnham family are on such terms with him.[4]

He died 18 Sept. 1761.

[1] H. W. L. Way, *Way Fam.* 33. [2] Sir Dudley Ryder's diary, 9 Nov. 1753, Harrowby mss. [3] *HMC Egmont Diary*, ii. 167. [4] Sir Dudley Ryder's diary, 23 Dec. 1740, 15 Aug. 1753, 27 Feb., 18 and 20 Mar. 1754.

R.R.S.

NEWPORT, Henry, Lord Newport (1683–1734).

BISHOP'S CASTLE   5 Mar. 1706–1708
SHROPSHIRE   1708–1710, 1713–1722

b. 8 Aug. 1683,[1] 1st s. of Richard Newport, 2nd Earl of Bradford (M.P. Shropshire 1670–81, 1689–98), by Mary, da. and coh. of Sir Thomas Wilbraham, 3rd Bt., M.P., of Woodhey, Cheshire; nephew of Hon. Thomas Newport (q.v.). *educ.* Ch. Ch. Oxf. 4 May 1699, aged 15. *unm. suc.* fa. as 3rd Earl 14 June 1723. Ld. lt. Staffs. 1715–25, Salop and Mont. 1724–*d.*

Newport, a staunch Whig, came of an ancient Shropshire family with a long record of parliamentary service, possessing a dominant political interest in the county. His grandfather, the 1st Earl, who sat in the Long Parliament and fought for Charles I, was comptroller of the Household and later treasurer to Charles II, James II, William III, and Anne. His father, the 2nd Earl, was the leader of the Shropshire Whigs. The family had wide connexions, with the Foresters of Dothill Park, near Wenlock, where the Newports had an interest; with the Bridgemans, and through them with the Corbets of Moreton Corbet and the Toyn Lloyds; and with Sir Humphrey Briggs, a distant cousin through the Wilbrahams (qq.v.).

In the county Newport fought every election between 1708 and 1722, heading the poll in 1715, but was defeated in 1722. During the rebellion of 1715 he raised a regiment of militia at Shrewsbury, serving as its colonel.[2] In Parliament he voted for the septennial bill and for the repeal of the Schism and Occasional Conformity Acts, but did not vote on the peerage bill.

In 1723 Newport succeeded his father as leader of the Shropshire Whigs. As Earl of Bradford he did his utmost to exclude his family from the succession to his estates by cutting off entails and leaving all his unentailed property in trust for his natural son John Newport, by his mistress Anne

Smyth, with reversion to her if her son, a lunatic, died without children. On her death she left the reversion to William Pulteney (q.v.), her former lover, who in 1742, when he was at the height of his power, made sure of inheriting the estate by causing an Act to be passed for preventing the marriage of lunatics.[3] After Bradford's death, 25 Dec. 1734, the family interest fell into abeyance, for his brother and heir was an imbecile.

[1] *Wm. Salt Arch. Soc.* n.s. ii. 188. [2] H. Owen & J. B. Blakeway, *Shrewsbury*, i. 505. [3] PCC 4 Ducie; Horace Walpole's note, *Works of Sir Charles Hanbury Williams*, 52–57; *Westminster Abbey Reg.* 343, 361.

J.B.L.

NEWPORT, Hon. Thomas (?1655–1719), of Brigstock Park, Northants.

LUDLOW   1695–1698, 1 Mar. 1699–1700
WINCHELSEA   7 Jan.–27 Feb. 1701
WENLOCK   1715–20 June 1716

b. ?1655, 5th s. of Francis Newport, M.P., 1st Earl of Bradford, by Diana, da. of Francis Russell, M.P., 4th Earl of Bedford; uncle of Henry, Lord Newport (q.v.). *educ.* Ch. Ch. Oxf. 21 May 1672, aged 17; I. Temple, called 1678. *m.* (1) Lucy (*d.* 1696), da. of Sir Edward Atkyns, ld. chief baron of the Exchequer, *s.p.*; (2) 22 July 1700, Penelope (*d.* 1705), da. of Sir Orlando Bridgeman, 1st Bt., of Ridley, Cheshire, *s.p.*; (3) Anne, da. of Sir Robert Pierrepont of Nottingham, *s.p. suc.* uncle Andrew Newport, M.P., of Shrewsbury 1699; *cr.* Baron Torrington 20 June 1716. Commr. of customs Nov. 1699–Jan. 1712; ld. of Treasury 1715–18; P.C. 30 Mar. 1717; teller of the Exchequer Mar. 1718–*d.*

Thomas Newport was brought in for Much Wenlock in 1715 on the interest of his brother, Lord Bradford, in succession to another brother. Appointed a lord of the Treasury, he spoke and voted for the septennial bill.[1] Raised to the peerage in 1716, he was mentioned as a possible successor to James Stanhope (q.v.) as first lord of the Treasury,[2] but in the end he was appointed a teller of the Exchequer. He died 27 May 1719, leaving a fine collection of paintings to his brother, Lord Bradford.

[1] Ant. Corbière to Horace Walpole, 27 Apr. 1716, Cholmondeley (Houghton) mss. [2] *HMC Stuart*, iv. 472.

J.B.L.

NEWSHAM, James (1715–69), of Chadshunt, Warws.

ST. GERMANS   1741–1747
ST. MAWES   10 Dec. 1754–1761

b. 7 Oct. 1715, o.s. of John Newsham (q.v.) of Chadshunt by his 2nd w. *educ.* privately under David Mallet;[1] Grand Tour 1735.[2] *unm. suc.* to Chadshunt 1724; to Kentish property of his mother and assumed name of Craggs 1756; and to property of his aunt Elizabeth Eliot 1765.[3]

Newsham hoped to add to his paternal estates the Essex properties of his step-father and his mother's share of the Craggs fortune, but his hopes were disappointed by her marriage to Robert Nugent (q.v.). He did everything in his power to prevent the match, but to no avail. 'Le mariage s'est fait', wrote one of his friends, 'et mon ami se trouve assez petit gentilhomme'.[4] Some consolation was provided by the £50,000 settled on him by his mother at this time.[5]

Returned for St. Germans in 1741 on the interest of his uncle by marriage, Richard Eliot (q.v.), he voted against the Government on the chairman of the elections committee, but no other vote of his is recorded.

He died at Lille, France, November 1769.

[1] Pope's *Works* ed. Elwin & Courthope, ix. 438–9. [2] Jas. Newsham to Thos. Robinson, 12 June 1735, Add. 23794, f. 62. [3] Hasted, *Kent*, i. 439. [4] W. Bristow to the Countess of Denbigh, 10 June 1737, *HMC Denbigh*, v. 216. [5] *HMC Carlisle*, 183.

E.C.

NEWSHAM, John (1673–1724), of Chadshunt, Warws.

LOSTWITHIEL   25 June 1720–1722

b. 15 Apr. 1673, 1st surv. s. of Charles Newsham of Chadshunt by Elizabeth, da. and h. of John Hide of East Greenwich, Kent. *educ.* New Coll. Oxf. 1690; M. Temple 1693. *m.* (1) Anna Maria (*d.* Jan. 1705), da. of William Bridges, London merchant, *s.p.*; (2) July 1712,[1] Anne, da. and coh. of James Craggs sen., postmaster gen., sis. of James Craggs (q.v.) and afterwards w. of John Knight of Gosfield Hall, Essex, and Robert Nugent (qq.v.), 1s. *suc.* fa. 1705.

Of an ancient Warwickshire family, Newsham was returned for Lostwithiel by the Administration in 1720, presumably through the influence of his brother-in-law, James Craggs (q.v.). On 25 Apr. 1721, when the part of the report of the committee of secrecy relating to the elder Craggs's estate came before the House, his brother-in-law Samuel Trefusis (q.v.) asked for counsel to speak for them, adding 'he [Trefusis] never had been used to speak in the House, or but very rarely, and Mr. Newsham ... not at all.'[2]

He died 21 Nov. 1724.

[1] PCC 279 Bolton. [2] Chandler, vi. 243–4.

E.C.

NEWTON, Michael (c.1695–1743), of Barr's Court, Glos. and Culverthorpe, Lincs.

BEVERLEY   1722–1727
GRANTHAM   1727–6 Apr. 1743

b. c.1695, o.s. of Sir John Newton, 3rd Bt., by Susanna, da. of Michael Warton of Beverley, sis. and coh. of Sir Michael Warton (q.v.). *m.* 14 Apr. 1730, Margaret, Countess of Coningsby, da. of Thomas

II—U

Coningsby, 1st Earl of Coningsby (q.v.), 1s. *d.v.p.* 1da. *suc.* as coh. to real and as sole h. to personal estates of his uncle Sir Michael Warton 1725; fa. as 4th Bt. 12 Feb. 1734. K.B. 27 May 1725.

The Newtons of Haydon derived their fortune from a Grantham usurer, whose money was used to acquire the reversion of the estates and baronetcy of an unrelated insolvent namesake, Sir John Newton, 1st Bt., of Barr's Court, Gloucestershire, the last of his line.[1] In 1725 Michael Newton inherited another fortune from his maternal uncle, Sir Michael Warton (q.v.), on whose interest he was returned for Beverley in 1722, before transferring in 1727 to Grantham, which he represented for the rest of his life. Though one of the wealthy commoners invested with the order of the Bath when Walpole revived that order in 1725, he voted against the Government in every recorded division till his death, 6 Apr. 1743, when the baronetcy became extinct.

[1] *N. & Q.* (3 ser.), i. 190.

R.R.S.

NICHOLAS, Edward (?1662–1726), of West Horsley, Surr.

SHAFTESBURY   1689–3 May 1715
                           19 May 1715–20 Apr. 1726

b. ?1662, 1st s. of Sir John Nicholas, M.P., of West Horsley, clerk of the Privy Council, by Penelope, da. of Spencer Compton, M.P., 2nd Earl of Northampton. *educ.* New Coll. Oxf. 15 Jan. 1679, aged 16. *m.* Rachel, da. of Thomas Wyndham, M.P., of Witham Friary, Som., sis. and coh. of Hopton Wyndham, M.P., *s.p. suc.* fa. 1705.

Paymaster and receiver gen. to Queen Mary 1693–1702; paymaster of Queen Anne's private pensions and bounties 1702–7, 1713–14; treasurer to Prince George of Denmark c.1703–7; commr. of the privy seal 1711–13.

Edward Nicholas was the grandson of Sir Edward Nicholas, M.P., secretary of state to Charles I and Charles II, who came from Winterbourne Earle, Wiltshire, acquiring further estates at West Horsley and at Gillingham, near Shaftesbury. Returned for Shaftesbury in 1689, he represented the borough for 37 years in 13 successive Parliaments, holding minor offices under the Crown for 17 years. A Tory and member of the October Club, he lost his office on the Hanoverian succession. Unseated on petition after the 1715 election, but again returned a fortnight later at the ensuing by-election, he voted against the Government in all recorded divisions of that Parliament. In 1721 his name was sent to the Pretender as a probable supporter in the event of a rising.[1] Nevertheless, on 25 Sept. 1722 he wrote to his Whig nephew, Spencer Compton (q.v.), the Speaker, that there might be something like an opposition when the House meets on the choice of a Speaker . . . and if such a thing is suspected I should be glad you would let me know it, that I might use my little interest with some of my western acquaintance to prevail with them to do as I am sure I will.[2]

He did not attend the opening of the second session of this Parliament, when his friend and correspondent George Clarke (q.v.) wrote to him:

I had several enquiries after you in the House of Commons . . . my answer was that you wrote me word there was so much water in the roads that you could not come up. The next question was how did his letter come? and to that I had not an answer ready.

He was also absent from the opening of the third session in November 1724. Suffering from ill-health, he spent much time at Bath. He died 20 Apr. 1726.[3]

[1] Stuart mss 65/16. [2] HMC Townshend, 344. [3] Egerton 2540, ff. 254, 351, et passim.

R.S.L.

NICOLL, see **GOUNTER NICOLL**

NIGHTINGALE, see **GASCOIGNE NIGHTINGALE**

NOBLE, Thomas (c.1656–1730), of Leicester, and Rearsby, nr. Leicester.

LEICESTER 3 Feb. 1719–1722

b. c.1656, 1st s. of Thomas Noble of Rearsby, alderman of Leicester. m. (1) bef. 1693, Mary Harvey, wid., of Lincs., 1s. 1da.; (2) 13 Oct. 1702, Mary, da. of Sir William Keyt, 2nd Bt., of Ebrington, Glos., sis. of Sir William Keyt, 3rd Bt. (q.v.), s.p.

Noble, whose family had settled at Rearsby in the sixteenth century, was returned, presumably as a Tory, for Leicester at a by-election in 1719 in time to vote against the peerage bill. In Sunderland's plans for the 1722 Parliament he is put down as to be replaced by Lawrence Carter (q.v.) at Leicester, but he did not stand again, dying 3 May 1730.

E.C.

NOEL, Sir Clobery, 5th Bt. (?1695–1733), of Kirkby Mallory, Leics.

LEICESTERSHIRE 1727–30 July 1733

b. ?1695, 1st s. of Sir John Noel, 4th Bt., by Mary, da. and coh. of Sir John Clobery of Winchester, Hants; bro. of William Noel and 1st cos. of Wrightson Mundy (qq.v.). educ. Magdalen, Oxf. 30 Dec. 1710, aged 15. m. 24 Aug. 1714, Elizabeth, da. of Thomas Rowney (q.v.) of Oxford, 6s. 1da. suc. fa. 1 July 1697. Sheriff, Leics. 1717–18.

Noel, whose family had acquired Kirkby Mallory by marriage in the sixteenth century, was a Jacobite. In 1718 he and Francis Mundy,

his brother-in-law, 'undertook to bring 2,000 men well mounted into the field in the county' in the event of a rising to restore the Stuarts.[1] Returned unopposed for the county in 1727, he was absent from the division on the civil list arrears in 1729, but voted against the Administration in subsequent divisions. He died 30 July 1733.

[1] Stuart mss 216/111.

E.C.

NOEL, Hon. James (1711–52), of Exton, Rutland.

RUTLAND 1734–17 June 1752

b. 22 July 1711, 3rd s. of Baptist Noel, 3rd Earl of Gainsborough, by Lady Dorothy Manners, da. of John, 1st Duke of Rutland; 2nd cos. of John and Thomas Noel (qq.v.). educ. Westminster 1724–8. unm.

The son of the leading Tory peer in Rutland, Noel was returned unopposed for the county, voting against the Administration in every recorded division except on the motion for Walpole's dismissal in 1741, which he opposed. He died 17 June 1752.

E.C.

NOEL, Hon. John (1659–1718), of North Luffenham, Rutland, and Walcot, Northants.

RUTLAND 1710–23 Jan. 1711, 1715–26 Dec. 1718

b. 7 Nov. 1659, 7th s. of Baptist Noel, 3rd Visct. Campden (M.P. Rutland 1640–3), but 3rd by 4th w. Elizabeth, da. of Montagu Bertie, M.P., 2nd Earl of Lindsey; half-bro. of Edward Noel (M.P. Rutland 1661–78), 1st Earl of Gainsborough. educ. M. Temple 1676. m. 11 June 1696, Elizabeth, da. of Bennet Sherard, M.P., 2nd Baron Sherard [I], sis. and coh. of Bennet Sherard (M.P. Rutland 1713–15), 1st Earl of Harborough, wid. of Edward Ingram, 2nd Visct. Irwin [S], 4s. 3da.

Noel, whose family had represented Rutland since the sixteenth century, was returned unopposed as a Whig in 1715, voting for the septennial bill in 1716. He died 26 Dec. 1718.

E.C.

NOEL, John (1702–28), of North Luffenham, Rutland, and Walcot, Northants.

RUTLAND 1727–6 Jan. 1728

b. 15 Dec. 1702, 1st surv. s. of Hon. John Noel, and bro. of Thomas Noel (qq.v.). unm. suc. fa. 1718.

Soon after coming of age Noel was returned unopposed for his county at the general election of 1727, dying four months later, 6 Jan. 1728.

E.C.

NOEL, Thomas (c.1704–88), of Exton, Rutland, and Walcot, Northants.

RUTLAND   4 Mar. 1728–1741, 31 Jan. 1753–1788

b. c.1704, 2nd surv. s. of Hon. John Noel (q.v.). *m.* 6 Nov. 1756, Elizabeth, da. of William Chapman, gamekeeper at Exton, wid. of Baptist Noel, 4th Earl of Gainsborough, *s.p. suc.* bro. John (q.v.) at Walcot 1728.

Noel was returned for Rutland as a Whig in 1728 at a by-election caused by the death of his brother John, voting with the Administration on the civil list arrears in 1729 and the repeal of the Septennial Act in 1734, but against them on the excise bill in 1733. Re-elected unopposed with his cousin James Noel (q.v.) in 1734, he voted against the Administration, except on the motion for the dismissal of Walpole in February 1741, which he opposed. He did not stand at the general election of that year on being faced with the candidature of John Finch (q.v.), whose family had previously supported him,[1] but he was again returned in 1753 after the death of James Noel. The first master of the Cottesmore Hunt, and an authority on hound breeding, publishing the first book on the subject in 1732,[2] he died 18 June 1788, aged 83.

[1] Ld. Gainsborough to Ld. Winchilsea, 24 Apr. 1741, Finch mss at HMC. [2] *VCH Rutland*, i. 301, 305.

E.C.

NOEL, William (1695–1762), of Bloomsbury Sq., London.

STAMFORD   24 Oct. 1722–1747
WEST LOOE   1747–May 1757

b. 19 Mar. 1695, 2nd s. of Sir John Noel, 4th Bt., and bro. of Sir Clobery Noel, 5th Bt. (q.v.). *educ.* Lichfield g.s.; Pembroke, Camb. 1713; I. Temple 1717, called 1721, bencher 1738. *m.* Elizabeth, da. of Sir Thomas Trollope, 3rd Bt., of Casewick, Lincs., 4da.
Dep. recorder, Stamford 1736; K.C. 1738; c.j. Chester 1749–*d.*; justice of common pleas 1757–*d.*

Noel, a practising lawyer, was descended from a Leicestershire family, seated at Kirkby Mallory. He was returned for Stamford in 1722, on the interest of the 8th Earl of Exeter (Brownlow Cecil, q.v.), from whom he received a yearly pension for dealing with his accounts.[1] He acted with the Opposition till Walpole's fall, speaking against the Hessians in 1731, against the army in 1732, and for the allowance to the Prince of Wales in 1737;[2] but he withdrew on the motion for the removal of Walpole in February 1741. In March 1742 his name appears in both the court and the opposition lists for the secret committee on Walpole, to which he was elected.[3] At the opening of the next session he went over to the Government, voting for the Hanoverians, 10 Dec. 1742; but on 6 Dec. 1743 he spoke in favour of an address for disbanding them, saying that though he was in general for them, he thought that the 'national discontent must be given way to' and that he was 'afraid of acting with a discontented army', which would be 'not an addition of strength but of weakness'.[4] He voted against the Hanoverians on 18 Jan. 1744 but spoke next day against an opposition motion for an inquiry into them,[5] and voted for them in 1746, when he was classed as 'Old Whig', One of the managers of the House of Commons at the trial of Lord Lovat, he sat for West Looe on the government interest from 1747, till he was made chief justice of Chester in 1749. He died 8 Dec. 1762.

[1] 'The Historical Part of Stamford Election 1734', Cholmondeley (Houghton) mss. [2] *HMC Egmont Diary*, i. 125–6; Harley Diary. [3] Walpole to Mann, 1 Apr. 1742. [4] Yorke's parl. jnl. *Parl. Hist.* xiii. 146. [5] Owen, *Pelhams*, 212.

P.W.

NORRIS, Edward (1663–1726), of Utkinton, Cheshire.

LIVERPOOL   1715–1722

b. 1663, 5th s. of Thomas Norris, M.P. Liverpool 1688–95, of Speke, Lancs. by Catherine, da. of Sir Henry Garraway, ld. mayor of London 1640. *educ.* B.N.C. Oxf. 1683, M.B. 1691, M.D. 1695. *m.* 12 July 1705, Anne, da. and h. of Peter Gerard of Crewood, Cheshire, 1s. 2da. (da. Susannah m. Hugh Williams, q.v.).[1]
F.R.S. 1698; F.R.C.P. 1716.

Norris was descended from a distinguished family, who had represented Liverpool almost continuously since the Revolution. He practised medicine at Chester until 1698, when he was chosen by the new East India Company as secretary to the embassy of his brother, Sir William Norris, M.P., to the Mogul emperor. On 28 Apr. 1701, he entered the Mogul's camp at Parnella 'in a rich palanquin, bearing his Majesty's letters to the Emperor'. He sailed for England in September 1702 with a cargo valued at 147,000 rupees, 60,000 rupees of which belonged to the Company and 87,000 to Sir William Norris. After an illness caused by the hardships of the journey, he resumed the profession of medicine at Utkinton, near Chester.[2] Returned unopposed as a Whig for Liverpool in 1715, he voted with the Government on the septennial bill, but against them on the repeal of the Occasional Conformity and Schism Acts and the peerage bill. He did not stand in 1722, and died 22 July 1726.

[1] *The Moore Rental* (Chetham Soc. xii), 142–3. [2] *Norris Pprs.* (Chetham Soc. ix), pp. xix–xx.

E.C.

NORRIS, Sir John (c.1670–1749), of Hemsted, Kent.

RYE	1708–1722
PORTSMOUTH	1722–1734
RYE	1734–13 May 1749

b. c.1670. *m.* 30 May 1699, Elizabeth, da. of Matthew Aylmer, 1st Lord Aylmer [I] (q.v.), wid. of Capt. Chester Moore R.N. (*d.s.p.* 1696), 9s. 3da. Kntd. 25 Nov. 1705.

Lt. R.N. 1689, capt. 1690, r.-adm. 1707, v.-adm. 1708, adm. 1709; c.-in-c. Mediterranean 1710–11; c.-in-c. Baltic squadron 1715–27; ld. of the Admiralty 1718–30; adm. of the fleet and c.-in-c. 20 Feb. 1734–*d.*

Of unknown parentage, but said to come 'of a respectable Irish family', Norris entered the navy as a boy in 1680, rising to the rank of admiral in 1709, when his father-in-law, another distinguished Irish naval officer, became commander-in-chief of the fleet. In the previous year he was returned for Rye, of which he became joint patron with Phillips Gybbon (q.v.), buying in or about 1718 the neighbouring manor of Hemsted and the other Kent and Sussex properties of the Guldeford family.[1] Employed on naval and diplomatic missions to the Baltic under George I, he succeeded his father-in-law on the Admiralty board in 1718. Nevertheless he voted against the peerage bill, observing that it would have been better for him

> to have continued in tempest of sea till it had been over, for to the fault of my judgment and I fear my fortune I am unable to think on it in the way that would do me most good in my private affairs.[2]

However, he retained his place till 1730, when he and his son, John (q.v.), spoke against the Government in the critical Dunkirk debate of 27 Feb. Turned out at the end of the session, and superseded in his command by Sir Charles Wager (q.v.) in 1731,[3] he voted against the Government on the army in 1732 and on the excise bill in 1733. Coming to terms with the Government at the beginning of 1734, he was appointed admiral of the fleet and commander-in-chief. In a letter of thanks to Walpole, shortly before the general election that year, he wrote:

> I have received by a messenger from the mayor of the city of Rochester their offer to choose me without any expense one of their representatives, which I have excused myself from accepting, that I may not oppose the person you approve should stand there; and that I may make things as agreeable to you as is in me to do, I will decline standing for Portsmouth and with pleasure see myself succeeded there by any body you shall appoint; and only stand at Rye in the room of Captain Norris.[4]

In 1739 he attended meetings of the cabinet committee set up to prepare for war against Spain, on whose outbreak he was appointed to command the Channel fleet. He was also called into the Cabinet when matters relating to the naval side of the war came up.[5] In 1740 he and Wager, the first lord of the Admiralty, introduced a seamen's registration bill, which was so severely criticized that it was withdrawn. He then proposed to the Cabinet to find the additional men required for the fleet by putting some troops and marines on board, replying to Walpole's objections that the King would not like the scheme for using the army to man the fleet that their business was 'to give the King the best advice . . . and not consider what advice he would like best'. In 1741 he created a scene in the House of Commons by offering to fight Pulteney for saying that his fleet had done nothing, but was 'pulled down' by Walpole.[6]

When Wager resigned with Walpole in 1742, Norris refused an offer of the second seat on the new Admiralty board under Lord Winchilsea, formerly Lord Finch (q.v.), expressing surprise that his old friend Gybbon, through whom Pulteney had conveyed the offer, 'should bring me such a message, having been so long the first officer of the fleet'. He also refused the command of the Mediterranean fleet, writing to the King:

> Ever since you have been in this kingdom the chief direction of sea affairs has been in the hands of a seaman. I once flattered myself your Majesty did me the honour to think me capable of it, and I am sure all those who now have the principal part in your Majesty's business did formerly think, and have often declared I was. Since it is now thought otherwise, I must look upon it as a strong admonition that I am grown too old for my business, and therefore I come to beg your Majesty's permission to retire.[7]

His resignation was not accepted but he was allowed to give up his command, also ceasing to attend the meetings of the war committee. Recalled to take command of the fleet assembled to deal with a threatened French invasion in February 1744, he quarrelled with the Admiralty, resigning his command as soon as all danger was over. On 24 Feb. 1749 he presented to the House of Commons a petition signed by five admirals and fifty-two captains against a bill making half-pay naval officers subject to trial by court martial. He died 13 June 1749.

[1] D. D. Aldridge, in *The Mariner's Mirror*, li. 173–83, ex inf. Julian M. Gwyn; J. Charnock, *Biog. Navalis*, ii. 341; Hasted, *Kent*, iii. 82–83. [2] *HMC Polwarth*, ii. 404. [3] *HMC Egmont Diary*, i. 73, 195. [4] 9 Apr. 1734, Cholmondeley (Houghton) mss. [5] *EHR*, xxxiv. 296 et seq.; Hervey, *Mems.* 925, 938. [6] *HMC Egmont Diary*, iii. 183–4. [7] H. W. Richmond, *The Navy and the War of 1739–48*, i, 180–1.

R.R.S.

NORRIS, John (1702–67).

RYE	1727–Sept. 1732

bap. 31 July 1702,[1] 3rd but 1st surv.s. of Sir John Norris and bro. of Matthew Norris (qq.v.). *m.* 13 Jan. 1729, Judith da. and coh. of Robert Western, 1s. 1da. *suc.* fa. 1749.

Usher of the customs house in the port of London 1732–*d.*

At George II's accession Norris was returned for Rye on his father's interest. Voting regularly with the Opposition, he spoke against the Government on the Address, 21 Jan. 1729, the Hessians, 4 Feb. 1730, and Dunkirk, 27 Feb. 1730. On 21 Apr. 1730 he initiated a four hours' debate by moving for an address to lay before the House any secret articles to the treaty of Seville, which took the ministry by surprise. His last reported speech was made against the Government on the payment of a debt to Denmark, 31 Mar. 1732.[2] Six months later he vacated his seat on succeeding, under a reversionary grant,[3] presumably obtained for him by his father, to a customs post which disqualified its holder from sitting in Parliament. He died 12 Nov. 1767.

[1] *Reg. St. Paul's, Covent Gdn.* (Harl. Soc.), i. 120. [2] *HMC Egmont Diary,* i. 73, 95, 250; iii. 330–1. [3] *Gent. Mag.* 1732, p. 980.

R.R.S.

NORRIS, Matthew (1705–38).

RYE 21 Jan. 1733–1734

bap. 12 July 1705,[1] 5th s. of Sir John Norris and bro. of John Norris (qq.v.). *m.* by 1734, Euphemia, da. of Lewis Morris sen. of Morrisania, New York, member of the New York assembly and gov. New Jersey, *s.p.*[2]

Capt. R.N. 1724; freeman, New York 1734; commr. of navy at Plymouth 1737–*d.*

Matthew Norris succeeded his brother John at Rye, where he was replaced by their father at the next general election. Appointed to the New York station, he became a freeman there on the grounds of his marriage and his strenuous opposition to the bill in favour of the sugar colonies.[3] Three years later he was appointed naval commissioner at a salary of £500 p.a. He died 27 Dec. 1738.[4]

[1] *Reg. St. Paul's, Covent Gdn.* (Harl. Soc. xxxiii), 131. [2] PCC 17 Henchman; New Jersey Hist. Soc. *Coll.* iv. 40, 57. [3] New York Hist. Soc. *Coll.* (1885), 493. [4] *Hist. Reg.* 1738.

R.R.S.

NORTH, Dudley (?1686–1730), of Little Glemham, Suff.

THETFORD 1710–1722
ORFORD 1722–4 Feb. 1730

b. ?1686, 1st s. of Hon. Sir Dudley North, M.P., by Anne, da. of Sir Robert Cann, 1st Bt., M.P., of Compton Greenfield, Glos. *educ.* in Kensington (privately, Mr. 'Agier'); St. John's, Camb. 12 May 1701, aged 15. *m.* bef. 1708, Catherine (with £20,000), da. and (in her issue) coh. of Elihu Yale (who gave

his name to Yale Univ.) of Plas Grono, nr. Wrexham, gov. of Fort St. George, Madras 1687–92, 3s. 2da.;[1] fa.-in-law of Hon. Nicholas Herbert (q.v.). *suc.* fa. 1691.

The son of the well known merchant, economist, and Tory politician, North was the uncle of the 6th Lord North and Grey, one of the Jacobite leaders implicated in the Atterbury plot in 1722. Himself one of the leading Suffolk Tories, he was returned by Sir Thomas Hanmer (q.v.) for Thetford till 1722, when he transferred to Orford on the Price Devereux interest. From 1715 he voted against the Government in all recorded divisions except on the civil list arrears in 1729, when he was absent. He died 4 Feb. 1730.

[1] Bingham, *Elihu Yale,* 306–7.

R.R.S.

NORTH, Hon. Francis (1704–90), of Wroxton Abbey, Oxon.

BANBURY 1727–17 Oct. 1729

b. 13 Apr. 1704, 1st s. of Francis North, 2nd Baron Guilford, ld. of Trade 1712–14, by Alice, da. and coh. of Sir John Brownlow, 3rd Bt., of Humby, Lincs. *educ.* Eton 1718; Trinity, Oxf. 1721; Grand Tour c.1722. *m.* (1) 17 June 1728, Lady Lucy Montagu (*d.* 7 May 1734), da. of George, 1st Earl of Halifax, 1s. 1da.; (2) 24 Jan. 1736, Elizabeth (*d.* 21 Sept. 1745), da. of Sir Arthur Kaye, 3rd Bt. (q.v.), of Woodsome, Yorks., wid. of George Legge, Visct. Lewisham (q.v.), 2s. 3da.; (3) 13 June 1751, Catherine, da. and eventually h. of Sir Robert Furnese, 2nd Bt. (q.v.), wid. of Lewis Watson, 2nd Earl of Rockingham, *s.p. suc.* fa. as 3rd Baron Guilford, 17 Oct. 1729; cos. William as 7th Baron North 31 Oct. 1734; *cr.* Earl of Guilford 8 Apr. 1752.

Gent. of the bedchamber to Frederick, Prince of Wales Oct. 1730–51; gov. to Prince George, later George III, Sept. 1750–Apr. 1751; treasurer to Queen Consort Dec. 1773–*d.*

High steward, Banbury 1766–*d.*

North's family acquired Wroxton, three miles from Banbury, in the reign of Charles II, by the marriage of Lord Keeper Guilford to Lady Frances Pope, the daughter and heir of Thomas, 3rd Earl of Downe. His father, a Tory, was dismissed from office on the accession of George I, but went over to 'the court interest for some trifling pension' in 1725.[1] After coming of age, he was returned for Banbury as a Whig on his family's interest, succeeding to the peerage two years later. He then entered the household of Frederick, Prince of Wales, eventually becoming for a short time governor to the future George III, whose resemblance to his own son, the future prime minister, was so striking that Frederick is said to have remarked that 'one of their wives had played her husband false'.[2] George II called him 'a very good poor creature, but a very weak man',[3] and Horace Walpole 'an amiable worthy man, of no great genius'.[4] He died 4 Aug. 1790, only two years before the death of his son, the great Lord North.

[1] Stuart mss 80/84. [2] Wraxall, *Mems.* i. 310. [3] Hervey, *Mems.* 817. [4] *Mems. Geo. II*, i. 86.

E.C.

NORTHCOTE, Sir Henry, 5th Bt. (1710–43), of Hayne and the Pynes, nr. Exeter, Devon.

EXETER 11 Mar. 1735–24 May 1743

bap. 1710, 1st s. of Sir Henry Northcote, 4th Bt., of Hayne and Corfe, Devon by Penelope, da. and coh. of Robert Lovett of Liscombe, Bucks. and Corfe. *educ.* Trinity, Oxf. 1729. *m.* 16 Aug. 1732, Bridget Maria, da. and h. of Hugh Stafford of the Pynes, 4s. *suc.* fa. Feb. 1730.

The Northcotes made a fortune from the clothing trade in the sixteenth century, acquiring Hayne by marriage in the time of Elizabeth.[1] Returned unopposed as a Tory for Exeter in 1735 and 1741, Northcote was absent from the division on the Spanish convention, voted against the Government on the place bill, and abstained from the division on the motion for the removal of Walpole in February 1741. In November 1742, unlike his fellow Member for Exeter, Humphrey Sydenham, he accepted instructions from the city chamber to promote a bill for restoring triennial Parliaments and a place bill.[2] He died 24 May 1743.

[1] Lysons, *Devon* i, pp. cx–cxi; ii. 361, 478; W. G. Hoskins, *Devon*, 125–6, 443. [2] Sir H. Northcote to the town clerk of Exeter, 27 and 30 Nov. 1742, *HMC Exeter*, 245–6.

S.R.M.

NORTHEY, Sir Edward (1652–1723), of Epsom, Surr.

TIVERTON 16 Dec. 1710–1722

b. 7 May 1652, 2nd s. of William Northey, barrister, of the Middle Temple and Old Ford, Mdx. by his 2nd w. Elizabeth Garrett. *educ.* Queen's, Oxf. 1668; M. Temple 1668, called 1674, bencher 1696. *m.* lic. 1 Dec. 1687 Anne, da. of John Jolliffe of St. Martin Outwich, London and Woodcote Green, Surr., alderman of London, sis. of Sir William Jolliffe (q.v.), 2s. 3da. Kntd. 1 June 1702.

Attorney-gen. June 1701–Apr. 1707, Oct. 1710–Dec. 1717; commr. for building 50 new churches in and about London and Westminster 1715.

The son of a bencher of the Middle Temple, Northey was appointed attorney-general, without a seat in Parliament, in the last year of the reign of William III. He was continued in this office under Anne till 1707, when he was removed as a result of changes made by the Whig Junto.[1] Re-appointed

and brought into Parliament by the Tory Government in 1710, he continued in office at George I's accession, being classed in 1715 as a Whig who would often vote Tory. He spoke in the debate of 21 June on Ormonde's impeachment, admitting that there were some matters in the secret committee's report upon which an impeachment might be grounded but declining to explain himself further at that time. In the autumn he replaced Sir Richard Onslow on the secret committee. He voted for the septennial bill in 1716 and spoke in support of the vote of credit for measures against Sweden 8 Apr. 1717. In December 1717 he retired with a pension of £1,500 a year for the joint lives of the King and himself, subject to the condition that it should be forfeited upon his accepting any office of at least equal value to the annuity.[2] In 1719 he voted against the Government on the repeal of the Occasional Conformity and Schism Acts and the peerage bill. He did not stand in 1722, having been put down in Sunderland's plans for that Parliament as to be replaced by Arthur Arscott (q.v.) at Tiverton. For the last three years of his life he was 'afflicted with a paralytic distemper whereby he was deprived of the use of his right hand and became unable to write'.[3] He died 16 Aug. 1723.

[1] Luttrell, vi. 169. [2] *Cal. Treas. Bks.* xxxii. 240. [3] PCC 170 Richmond.

S.R.M.

NORTHEY, William (c.1690–1738), of Compton Bassett, nr. Calne, Wilts.

CALNE   1713–1715
WOOTTON BASSETT 1715–1722

b. c.1690, 1st s. of Sir Edward Northey (q.v.). *educ.* Eton;[1] King's, Camb. 1705; M. Temple 1700, called 1712; Grand Tour. *m.* 19 Sept. 1721, Abigail, da. of Sir Thomas Webster, 1st Bt. (q.v.), of Battle Abbey, Suss., 3s. 1da. *suc.* fa. 1723.

William Northey, who had sat as a Tory for Calne in the 1713 Parliament, was returned for Wootton Bassett, another neighbouring borough, in 1715. In the same year he bought the Compton Bassett estate from the heir of Sir Charles Hedges, M.P.[2] Classed in 1715 as a Whig who would often vote with the Tories, he supported the septennial bill in 1716 but followed his father in opposing the repeal of the Occasional Conformity and Schism Acts and the peerage bill in 1719. Defeated at Wootton Bassett in 1722 and 1727, he did not stand again, dying 11 Nov. 1738, aged 48.

[1] Manning & Bray, *Surr.* ii. 621. [2] Marsh, *Hist. Calne*, 304.

R.S.L.

NORTHEY, William (c.1721–70), of Compton Bassett, nr. Calne, Wilts.

CALNE	1747–1761
MAIDSTONE	1761–1768
GREAT BEDWYN	13 Nov. 1768–24 Dec. 1770

b. c.1721, 1st s. of William Northey (q.v.). *educ.* Corpus Christi, Camb. 1739; M. Temple 1739. *m.* (1) 20 June 1742 Harriet (*d.* 25 Oct. 1750), da. of Robert Vyner (q.v.) of Gautby, Lincs., *s.p.*; (2) 4 May 1751, Anne, da. of Edward Hopkins (q.v.) of Coventry, 3s. 4da. *suc.* fa. 1738.

Groom of the bedchamber 1760–d.; ld. of Trade Apr. 1770–d.

In 1747 William Northey bought the prebend manor of Calne,[1] carrying with it one of the Calne seats, for which he was returned that year. In Parliament he was one of the Tories who consorted with Leicester House. About 1750 the 2nd Lord Egmont wrote of him in his electoral survey:

> He wishes us well and is likely to take a part in employment with us. He is one of the best of the young men as to the hopes of parliamentary abilities. He has pretty good parts and a good deal of application and some turn this way. But he is still a little affected with projects of wild reformation though not desperately.

Egmont put him down for a seat at the board of Trade in Frederick's reign.

In November 1751 Northey spoke in favour of a proposal to reduce the army to 15,000 men. In January 1752 he seconded a motion against subsidy treaties in time of peace, and on 28 Feb. and 4 Mar. he spoke against the bill for purchasing forfeited estates in Scotland.[2] After again proposing the reduction of the army to 15,000 men in January 1753,[3] he warmly opposed the bill for the naturalization of the Jews in May, and on its repeal in the next session twitted ministers for their lack of 'deep penetration or great foresight'.[4] In the next reign he was one of the Tories who accepted office. He died 24 Dec. 1770, aged 49.[5]

[1] *Wilts. Arch. Mag.* xliii. 28; *Wilts. N. & Q.* viii. 150–51. [2] Walpole, *Mems. Geo. II*, i. 213, 254, 257, 260. [3] Coxe, *Pelham*, ii. 241. [4] *Parl. Hist.* xv. 145. [5] *Genealogist*, n.s. x. 178.

R.S.L.

NORTHLEIGH, Stephen (?1692–?1731), of Peamore, in Exminster, Devon.

TOTNES	1713–1722

b. ?1692, s. of Henry Northleigh of Peamore. *educ.* Exeter, Oxf. 17 Apr. 1711, aged 18. *m.* 2 Dec. 1714, Margaret, da. of Sir William Davie, 4th Bt., of Creedy, in Sandford, Devon,[1] 2da.

Descended from an old Devonshire family, Northleigh was returned in 1713 as a Tory for Totnes. Re-elected unopposed in 1715, his only recorded vote was against the septennial bill. His name was amongst those sent to the Pretender in 1721 as a probable supporter in the event of a rising.[2] He did not stand again, dying probably in 1731.[3]

[1] Vivian, *Vis. Devon*, 270. [2] Stuart mss 65/16. [3] Admon. Exeter 1731, 1733.

S.R.M.

NORTHMORE, William (1690–1735), of Northmore House, Okehampton, and Cleve, nr. Exeter, Devon.

OKEHAMPTON	1713–1722, 1727–17 Mar. 1735

bap. 1 July 1690, o.s. of William Northmore of Throwleigh, nr. Okehampton, by Anne, da. of Rev. Thomas Hutton of St. Kew, Cornw., sometime rector of Northlew, nr. Okehampton. *m.* (1) settlement 25 Aug. 1711, his cos. Anne (bur. 7 Mar. 1717), da. and h. of Thomas Northmore, attorney, of Cleve, M.P. Okehampton 1695–8, *s.p.*; (2) May 1720, Florence (bur. 1 Jan. 1726), da. of Sir Arthur Chichester, 3rd Bt. (q.v.), of Raleigh, Devon, *s.p.*; (3) 11 Sept. 1734, Elizabeth, da. of William Oxenham of Oxenham, Devon, *s.p.* *suc.* uncle 1713; fa. 1716.

The Northmores, an old Devonshire family, settled at Welle, near South Tawton, since 1332, acquired Throwleigh and a large estate at Okehampton in the seventeenth century, subsequently holding civic office in the borough and building Northmore House, the present town hall, in 1685.[1] In 1713 William Northmore inherited Cleve from his uncle Thomas Northmore, who held many of the Monck estates in mortgage, in his will ordering their sale for the benefit of his nephew and his wife.[2] In the same year he was returned as a Tory on his own interest for Okehampton. Re-elected in 1715, he voted against the Government in all recorded divisions. In 1721 his name was sent to the Pretender as a probable supporter in the event of a rising.[3] He did not stand in 1722 but resumed his seat in 1727, voting with the Opposition against the Hessians in 1730 and the excise bill in 1733. He died 17 Mar. 1735.

[1] C. Worthy, *Devonshire Wills*, 335–8; Lysons, *Devon*, ii. 371–2; W. G. Hoskins, *Devon*, 447. [2] PCC 122 Aston. [3] Stuart mss 65/16.

S.R.M.

NORTON, Thomas (1684–1748), of Ixworth Abbey, nr. Bury St. Edmunds, Suff.

BURY ST. EDMUNDS	1727–1747

b. 1684, s. of Col. William Norton of Wellow, Hants by Elizabeth, da. of Sir Thomas Norton, 1st Bt., of Coventry. *educ.* Bury g.s. *m.* Frances, da. of Sir Compton Felton, 5th Bt., M.P., of Playford Hall, Suff., uncle of Elizabeth Felton, w. of John Hervey, 1st Earl of Bristol, *s.p.* *suc.* fa. 1696; uncle Maj. Richard Norton to Ixworth Abbey 1708.[1]

Capt. and brevet-col. 1 Ft. Gds. 1710, res. Mar. 1714; dep. gov. Chelsea Hospital 1730–d.

Norton was the grandson of Col. Richard Norton, M.P., an intimate friend of Oliver Cromwell's, governor of Southampton and later of Portsmouth. Returned on his own interest with the support of the 1st Earl of Bristol, with whom he was connected by marriage, he was described by Walpole in 1733 as having 'been ever a steady Whig, and never swerved from his principles, or given a vote against us'.[2] Continuing to vote with the Government in every recorded division till he retired in 1747, he died 28 Apr. 1748.

[1] *N. & Q.* (ser. 10) vii. 330–2; Copinger, *Suff. Manors*, i. 337.
[2] *Letter Bks. of John Hervey, 1st Earl of Bristol*, iii. 103–4.

R.R.S.

NUGENT, Robert (1709–88), of Gosfield, Essex.

ST. MAWES   1741–1754
BRISTOL   1754–1774
ST. MAWES   1774–June 1784

b. 1709, o. surv. s. of Michael Nugent of Carlanstown, co. Meath by Mary, da. of Robert Barnewall, 9th Baron Trimlestown [I]. *educ.* Fagan's acad. Dublin. *m.* (1) 14 July 1730, Lady Emilia Plunkett (*d.*16 Aug. 1731), da. of Peter, 4th Earl of Fingall [I], 1s. *d.v.p.*; (2) 23 Mar. 1737, Anne (*d.* 22 Nov. 1756), da. and coh. of James Craggs, postmaster gen., sis. and coh. of Rt. Hon. James Craggs (q.v.), wid. of (i) John Newsham and (ii) John Knight (qq.v.), *s.p.*, assuming add. name of Craggs before Nugent; (3) 2 Jan. 1757, Elizabeth, da. of Henry Drax (q.v.) of Ellerton Abbey, Yorks., wid. of Augustus, 4th Earl of Berkeley, 1da. *suc.* fa. 1739; *cr.* Visct. Clare [I] 19 Jan. 1767; Earl Nugent [I] 21 July 1776.

Comptroller of the household to Prince of Wales Nov. 1747–51; ld. of Treasury Apr. 1754–Dec. 1759; P.C. 15 Dec. 1759; jt. vice-treasurer [I] Jan. 1760–July 1765; first ld. of Trade Dec. 1766–Jan. 1768; jt. vice-treasurer [I] July 1768–Mar. 1782.

Nugent came of an old-established Irish Roman Catholic family, kinsmen to the Earls of Westmeath. In 1730 he fled to London to avoid marrying his cousin, Clare Nugent, by whom he had a son whom he never recognized. He is then said to have become a tutor in the family of the Earl of Fingall, whose sister he married.[1] After the death of his first wife, he renounced Roman Catholicism and joined the Church of England. His second marriage, to a wealthy widow, brought him £50,000,[2] a country estate in Essex and control over one seat at St. Mawes. She was fat and ugly, and he was notoriously unfaithful to her.[3] Through her, he became a friend of Pope, and was introduced to Lord Chesterfield. He was soon deep in the counsels of the leaders of the Opposition, who consulted him in the winter of 1740 on the tactics to be followed in the next session of Parliament.[4] He addressed verses to Frederick, Prince of Wales,[5] and wrote a momentarily famous

Ode to Pulteney (1739), describing his own conversion from 'error's poison'd springs' to the principles of the glorious Revolution. When he was returned for St. Mawes in 1741, Chesterfield wrote to him:

I heartily congratulate you as a member of Parliament, and would congratulate my country upon it, if you could propagate your principles in that House as effectually as you have your likeness in many others.[6]

An able and witty speaker with a strong Irish brogue, he soon came to the fore in debates. Horace Walpole wrote to Mann on 24 Dec. 1741: 'This modest Irish converted Catholic stallion does talk a prodigious deal of nonsense in behalf of English liberty.' Nugent had just carried several former government supporters off to the country to prevent their voting in the critical division on the Westminster election petition.[7] He spoke against the Hanoverians in December 1742; supported the Address on 1 Dec. 1743; on 6 Dec. 1743 spoke in favour of a motion to disband the Hanoverians; and on 11 Jan. 1744 supported the continuing of British troops on the Continent. He 'said a few words' in favour of a Tory bill for ascertaining the qualifications of justices of the peace in March 1745, and talked of 'impeachments and bills of penalties' in a debate on an address for the courts martial of Mathews and Lestock the following April.[8] He spoke for the Hanoverians in April 1746, when he was classed by Newcastle as a 'doubtful' ally, and supported the bill to abolish hereditary jurisdictions in Scotland a year later.[9]

Re-elected for St. Mawes in 1747, Nugent was given office in the Prince of Wales's household, speaking against the Address in November 1748. Horace Walpole wrote to Mann on 4 Mar. 1749:

there is a faction in the Prince's family, headed by Nugent, who are for moderate measures. Nugent is most affectedly an humble servant of Mr. Pelham and seems only to have attached himself to the Prince, in order to make the better bargain with the ministry; he has great parts, but they never know how to disentangle themselves from bombast and absurdities.

In 1751 Walpole writes:

Nugent's attachments were to Lord Granville; but all his flattery addressed to Mr. Pelham, whom he mimicked in candour, as often as he resembled Lord Granville in ranting.

In February of that year he revived a bill for the naturalization of foreign Protestants, which he had unsuccessfully presented in December 1747, but it was thrown out on the third reading.[10] At Leicester House Nugent acted in opposition to the 2nd Lord Egmont (q.v.), who noted in March 1751 that the Prince had talked 'angrily to Nugent . . . for his conduct in the House in opposing me and continually to be with the other side and to form a party'. Shortly after the death of the Prince, Egmont reported,

> Nugent . . . gave a dinner to Lord Granville and Henry Fox etc., where they were very merry, laughing at Nugent for having lent money to the Prince, which he had lost—but Nugent denied it.[11]

He then rallied to the Pelhams, commending the regency bill 'extravagantly' in May 1751. In June, he acted as intermediary in the reconciliation between Granville and Pelham.[12] Granville asked Pelham for the post of surveyor general of the land revenue for him, but this had already been promised to another. Pelham then offered him the post of treasurer to the board of Ordnance, writing (24 Sept. 1751):

> If you like it, I will certainly engage to no other person, but most zealously support your interest with his Majesty. If you do not, there is no hurt done . . . Believe me, dear Nugent, it will be a great pleasure to me to have you cheerfully as well as zealously with us, and if at any time you have thought me cold towards you, you have mistook me, and so far done me wrong . . . As *your* friend, and *my* neighbour [Granville] is not in town, I have spoke of this to no one, but I hear my brother's thoughts and disposition are the same as mine.

Nugent declined as the salary was lower than had been supposed by Pelham, who replied:

> I am exceedingly mortified that things turn out as I now find it. I was in hopes we should have opened this session not only friends but fellow servants, and that upon such a foot as you and your best friends would have thought honourable for us both.[13]

He supported the subsidy treaty with Saxony in January 1752;[14] spoke in favour of the bill for the naturalization of the Jews in April 1753; and in May of that year strenuously opposed Hardwicke's marriage bill, asking:

> Will you confine the great people to marry merely among one another and prevent them from getting a little wholesome blood which they so much want? Will you marry disease to distemper?[15]

Horace Walpole commented: 'Nugent shone extremely in opposition to the bill, and, though every now and then on the precipice of absurdity, kept clear of it.'[16]

On Pelham's death Nugent was given office by Newcastle. He died in Dublin 14 Oct. 1788, having returned to the Roman Catholic faith.

[1] Claud Nugent, *Memoir of Robert, Earl Nugent*, pp. 1-9. See also *The unnatural father or the persecuted son. A candid narrative of the most unparalleled sufferings of Robert Nugent jnr. by the means and procurement of his own father*, London, 1755. [2] *HMC Carlisle*, 183. [3] Walpole to Mann, 7 Jan. 1742; to Geo. Montagu, 25 July 1748 and 15 May 1750. [4] Chesterfield to Geo. Lyttelton, 5 Nov. 1740, Chesterfield, *Letters*, 433-4. [5] *An Ode to his Royal Highness on his Birthday* (1739) and *An Ode to Mankind: addressed to the Prince of Wales* (1741). [6] Quoted Claud Nugent, 245. [7] Sir Robt. Wilmot to Devonshire, 12 Jan. 1742, Devonshire mss. [8] Yorke's parl. jnl. *Parl. Hist.* xiii. 138-40, 393, 1245, 1268. [9] *HMC Polwarth*, v. 236. [10] *Mems. Geo. II*, i. 46, 54, 92. [11] 'Occasional Memoranda', Add.

47073; Nugent also told his cousin Lord Westmeath he had not lent money to the Prince, see Claud Nugent, 232. [12] *Mems. Geo. II*, i. 123, 197; *Parl. Hist.* xxiv. 634. [13] Pelham to Nugent, 3 Aug. and 27 Sept. 1751, Claud Nugent, pp. 253-6. [14] Walpole, *Mems. Geo II*, i. 243. [15] *HMC 14th Rep. IX*, 314. [16] To Hen. Seymour Conway, 24 May 1753.

E.C.

O'BRIEN, Sir Edward, 2nd Bt. (1705–65), of Dromoland, co. Clare.

PETERBOROUGH 1727–9 Apr. 1728

b. 7 Apr. 1705, o.s. of Lucius O'Brien, M.P. [I], by Catherine, da. of Thomas Keightley, ld. treasurer of Ireland, by Lady Frances Hyde, da. of 1st Earl of Clarendon. *educ.* Balliol, Oxf. 1721. *m.* c.1730, Mary, da. of Hugh Hickman, of Fenloe, co. Clare, 3s. 6da. *suc.* gd.-fa. Sir Donough O'Brien, 1st Bt., M.P. [I], 17 Nov. 1717.
M.P. [I] 1727–*d.*

O'Brien, whose mother was Queen Anne's cousin, appears to have had no connexion with North-amptonshire, except through his kinsman, the 8th Earl of Thomond, who owned estates in the county. Nevertheless in 1727 he was returned as a Tory for Peterborough by the partiality of the sheriff, only to be unseated on petition.[1] At a by-election in 1728 it was reported that the Tories intended to put him up again,[2] but in the event he did not stand. He died 26 Nov. 1765.

[1] *CJ*, xxi. 26. [2] *Letters and Pprs. Banks Fam.* (Lincoln Rec. Soc. xlv), 88–89.

R.R.S.

O'BRIEN, William, 4th Earl of Inchiquin [I] (c.1700–77).

NEW WINDSOR 1722–1727
TAMWORTH 1727–1734
CAMELFORD 1741–1747
AYLESBURY 1747–1754

b. c.1700, 1st s. of William O'Brien, 3rd Earl of Inchiquin [I], by Mary, da. of Sir Edward Villiers, knight-marshal, sis. of Edward Villiers, 1st Earl of Jersey. *m.* (1) 28 Mar. 1720, his 1st cos. Lady Anne Hamilton (*d.*6 Dec. 1756), da. and h. of George Hamilton, 1st Earl of Orkney [S], and *suo jure* Countess of Orkney, 4s. 4da.; (2) 12 Oct. 1761, Mary, da. of Stephen Moore, 1st Visct. Mount Cashell [I], *s.p. suc.* fa. 24 Dec. 1719; K.B. 28 May 1725.
Grand master of freemasons 1740–1; gov. co. Clare 1741 and custos rot. 1762–*d.*; gent. of the bedchamber to Frederick, Prince of Wales Dec. 1744–51; P.C. [I] 15 Nov. 1753.

Succeeding to an estate of £9,000 p.a.,[1] Inchiquin took his seat in the Irish House of Lords in September 1721. Returned on the government interest for Windsor in 1722 and on the interest of his first cousin, the 2nd Viscount Weymouth, for Tamworth in 1727, he voted with the Administration on the civil list in 1729, but went into opposition the following year. At a meeting of Irish gentlemen to consider matters before Parliament relating to Ireland in April 1731, he is mentioned as always voting against the ministry.[2] In 1734 he was not put up for Tamworth, where he stood unsuccessfully at a by-election in 1735. Returned for Camelford in 1741 on the recommendation of Frederick, Prince of Wales, whose household he entered in 1744,[3] he voted against the Administration on the chairman of the elections committee in 1741, but for them on the Hanoverians in 1742, 1744 and 1746, reverting to opposition with his master in 1747, when he was returned for Aylesbury. Affected with an impediment in his speech which caused him to stutter,[4] he is not known to have spoken in the House. Losing his place on Frederick's death, he did not stand again. He died 18 July 1777.

[1] *HMC Carlisle*, 232. [2] *HMC Egmont Diary*, i. 169–70. [3] *HMC Fortescue*, i. 108. [4] Walpole, *Mems. Geo. II*, iii. 241.

E.C.

O'BRIEN, *see also* **WYNDHAM O'BRIEN**

OCKENDEN, William (*d.*1761), of Temple Mills, Bisham, Berks. and Weybridge, Surr.

GREAT MARLOW 3 Dec. 1744–1754

1st s. of William Ockenden of St. Bennet Gracechurch, London by Mary, da. of Elias Simes of St. Clement Danes, London. *unm. suc.* fa. 1721.[1]
Clerk of the Council to the Prince of Wales 1749–51.

William Ockenden, who had lived in Ireland,[2] inherited property in 1739 and 1741 from his maternal uncles Elias Simes of Hurley, Berks. and John Simes of Chiswick.[3] A maker of copper and brass utensils at Temple Mills,[4] across the river from Marlow, he acquired a political interest in that borough through his workmen, who were customers of the Marlow tradesmen.[5] He was returned on this interest, by two votes only, in December 1744 at a by-election caused by the death of his neighbour in Bisham, Sir Thomas Hoby (q.v.), a petition against him being abandoned after a hearing of three days. Voting against the Administration on the Hanoverians in 1746, he was classed as Opposition in 1747, when he was re-elected without a contest. Joining the Prince of Wales's party, he received an appointment in his household in 1749. Put down for 'some place' in the Ordnance in the next reign, he was one of the 2nd Lord Egmont's associates at the time of Frederick's death in 1751.[6] He did not stand in 1754, when he was approached by Newcastle to give his support to the administration candidates.[7] At his death, 2 July 1761, he was the owner of mills in Weybridge.

[1] PCC Admons. Dec. 1721 and Dec. 1752. [2] PCC 261 Cheslyn. [3] PCC 202 Henchman and 107 Spurway; *CJ*, xxiv. 709–10. [4] *VCH Berks*. i. 382. [5] See GREAT MARLOW. [6] Add. 47073. [7] Add. 32995, f. 126.

R.S.L.

OFFLEY, Crewe (c.1683–1739), of Wichnor, Staffs.

NEWCASTLE-UNDER-LYME	27 Feb. 1706–1708
	1 Feb. 1709–1710
	2 June 1715–1722
BEWDLEY	1722–1734

b. c.1683, 2nd s. of John Offley of Madeley by Anne, da. and h. of John Crewe of Crewe Hall, Cheshire; bro. of John Crewe (q.v.). *m.* Margaret, da. and h. of Sir Thomas Lawrence of Chelsea, 2s. *suc.* mother to Wichnor 1708; and to certain of the estates of his uncle, Sir John Crewe of Utkinton 1711.

Returned on petition as a Whig for Newcastle-under-Lyme in 1715, Crewe Offley voted for the septennial bill in 1716. In a list of Members who voted against the Government on Lord Cadogan (q.v.) in June 1717, he is shown as having been granted a reversion. He also voted against them on the repeal of the Occasional Conformity and Schism Acts in 1719, but for them on the peerage bill, on which he was put down by Craggs as to be approached by John Wallop (q.v.). Returned in 1722 for Bewdley by Lord Herbert of Chirbury, he voted with the Administration till 1734, when he was defeated.

He died 28 June 1739.

A.N.N.

OFFLEY, John (c.1717–84), of St. James's, Westminster.

BEDFORD	1747–1754
ORFORD	1754–1768
EAST RETFORD	1768–1774

b. c.1717, 1st s. of Crewe Offley (q.v.). *educ.* Grand Tour 1739. *unm. suc.* fa. 1739.
Surveyor of the King's private roads 1756–7; groom of the bedchamber 1757–62.

John Offley, described by Lord Hardwicke as 'a gentleman of a considerable estate'[1] was returned for Bedford in 1747 on the Duke of Bedford's interest, classed as a government supporter. A well-known gamester, he joined White's in 1749, losing £1,300 in one night at play.[2]

He died 3 Apr. 1784, aged 66.

[1] Hardwicke to Philip Yorke, 20 June 1747, Add. 35351, f. 108. [2] Walpole to Rich. Bentley, 9 Jan. 1755.

R.S.L.

OFFLEY, *see also* **CREWE** (formerly **OFFLEY**), **John**

OGLE, Sir Chaloner (c.1680–1750), of Twickenham, Mdx. and Kirkley, Northumb.

ROCHESTER 24 Nov. 1746–11 Apr. 1750

b. c.1680, o.s. of John Ogle of Newcastle-upon-Tyne by Mary, da. of Richard Braithwaite of Warcop, Westmld. *m.* (1) c.1726, Henrietta (*d.*18 Sept. 1737), da. of Anthony Isaacson of Newcastle-upon-Tyne, *s.p.*; (2) 30 Oct. 1737, his 1st cos. Isabella, da. of Nathaniel Ogle of Newcastle-upon-Tyne and Kirkley, *s.p.* Kntd. May 1723. *suc.* fa. 1740.

Entered R.N. 1697, lt. 1702, capt. 1708; c.-in-c. Jamaica 1732–5; r.-adm. 1739; c.-in-c. W. Indies 1742–5; v.-adm. 1743, adm. 1744, adm. of the fleet 1749.

A distinguished naval officer, of a Northumberland family descended from a younger son of Ralph, 3rd Lord Ogle, who died in 1513,[1] Ogle received his knighthood for capturing two notorious pirate ships off the West African coast in February 1722. While in Jamaica under Admiral Edward Vernon (q.v.) in 1742, he was tried and found guilty of an assault upon the governor, Edward Trelawny (q.v.), in that during a quarrel between them he had laid his hand on the hilt of his sword, but at Trelawny's request no judgment was given.[2] On returning to England from the West Indies in 1745, he was president of the court martial which tried certain officers for misconduct during the action off Toulon, 11 Feb. 1744. In the following year he was brought in by the Administration for Rochester on the death of Admiral Nicholas Haddock (q.v.). Pelham would have preferred Admiral John Byng (q.v.), but acquiesced in the Duke of Bedford's choice of Ogle— 'he won't be so much employed abroad, and of consequence a better attender in Parliament'.[3] In a news-letter of 24 Dec. 1746 Ogle is described as 'snug [at Rochester] and will hardly care to go to sea any more'.[4] Re-elected in 1747 he died 11 Apr. 1750, being succeeded at Rochester by Byng.

[1] *New Hist. Northumb.* xii. 501–3. [2] *Vernon Pprs.* (Navy Recs. Soc. xcix), 254–5, 260–1. [3] Pelham to Bedford, 4 Oct. 1746, Bedford mss. [4] *HMC Du Cane*, 157.

A.N.N.

OGLETHORPE, James Edward (1696–1785), of Westbrook, nr. Haslemere, Surr.

HASLEMERE 1722–1754

b. 22 Dec. 1696, 3rd surv. s. of Sir Theophilus Oglethorpe, M.P. Haslemere 1698–1701, brig-gen. and gent. of the horse to James II, by Eleanor, maid to the Duchess of Portsmouth and laundress to Charles II, da. of Richard Wall of Tipperary. *educ.* Eton; C.C.C. Oxf. 1714; travelled France, Austria (serving under Prince Eugene at the siege of Belgrade) and Italy 1716–18. *m.* 15 Sept. 1744, Elizabeth, da. of Sir Nathan Wright, 2nd Bt., of Cranham Hall, Essex, *s.p.* *suc.* bro. to Westbrook c.1728.[1]

Ensign 1 Ft. Gds. bef. 1709, lt. and capt. 1713,

res. 23 Nov. 1715; assistant R. African Co. 1731, dep. gov. 1732; trustee for Georgia 1732–52; c.-in-c. S. Carolina and Georgia, and col. of a regt. of Ft. 1737–48; brig.-gen. 1743; maj.-gen. 1745; lt.-gen. 1747; gen. 1765.

Oglethorpe was born into a strong Jacobite family. His father took an active part in Jacobite conspiracies against William III. His sisters, one of whom was created a countess by the Pretender in 1722, were brought up in the Stuart court at St. Germain. His only surviving elder brother, after inheriting the family property, went into voluntary expatriation, entered the Pretender's service, was made a Jacobite baron in 1717, and is said to have died at St. Germain. He himself resigned his army commission during the Fifteen rebellion and went abroad, paying his duty to the Pretender at Urbino in 1718. Returning to England at the end of that year to look after his expatriated brother's affairs, he was elected in 1722 on his family's interest for Haslemere, which he represented for the next 32 years. On the eve of the poll he became involved in a fight, wounding Captain Richard Onslow (q.v.). A month later he killed a linkman in a drunken brawl in a London brothel, apparently in self-defence.[2] His first recorded speech, 8 Apr. 1723, shows why, to the end of his career, people were 'uncertain whether he was a Whig or a Jacobite'.[3] Speaking against the bill for banishing Atterbury, he said:

> The Pretender has none but a company of silly fellows about him; and it was to be feared that if the Bishop, who was allowed to be a man of great parts, should be banished, he might be solicited and tempted to go to Rome, and there be in a capacity to do more mischief by his advice, than if he were suffered to stay in England under the watchful eye of those in power.[4]

On 17 Apr. 1725 he spoke against the payment of the civil list arrears.

In the next Parliament Oglethorpe became a frequent speaker, acting with the Opposition up to the beginning of 1732, except in the debate of 28 Jan. 1730 on the army, when, though 'a very obstinate Tory', he spoke and voted with the Government. At the opening of the 1732 session he spoke for the Address; on 23 Mar. he disagreed with Pulteney on the question whether Members should be required to swear to their qualifications; and in May he again clashed with the leaders of the Opposition by opposing their motion for the punishment of his relation, Sir Robert Sutton (q.v.), for complicity in the frauds on the Charitable Corporation.[5] On the first of these occasions Henry Pelham, defending Lord Tyrconnel (q.v.) for leaving his party, observed that he believed his example would be followed, a prediction verified by Oglethorpe, who after consulting his friend, Lord Ilay, wrote to Walpole:

> Though it never was in my power to do you any service, yet my only shewing that I had an inclination towards it, has had an ill effect upon the interest in the borough of Haslemere for which I serve.
>
> The majority of the people signed an address, approved my manner of acting in Parliament, and desired Mr. Burrell [Peter, q.v.] and me to be candidates at the next election.
>
> Some of the warmest of the Tories were of another opinion and angry at my manner of voting of late, and at my not joining with one whom they proposed, they set up Sir Harry Peachey [q.v.] and Mr. Foulks, resolving to be revenged on me. Though I have a great majority, yet this division of my friends occasions an opposition and expense where there otherwise would have been none. Therefore, Sir, as I have lost some friends, I hope you will assist me in gaining of others.

After specifying his requirements for supporting his interest at Haslemere, he concluded:

> Were these things done it would save us a great deal of expense, secure our election and put Mr. Burrell and me in a capacity of expressing how much he as well as I am, Sir, Your most obedient humble servant.[6]

Oglethorpe's change of party was cloaked by his impending departure on the great enterprise of his life. In 1729, moved by the death of a friend in a debtors' prison, he had secured the appointment of a House of Commons committee, of which he was chairman, to inquire into the state of the gaols. The reports of the committee led to the release of a considerable number of debtors with no means of subsistence. To meet this situation Oglethorpe, in association with the 1st Lord Egmont (q.v.), persuaded the Government to grant a royal charter and financial assistance to a body of trustees, who were empowered to settle poor persons from this country in a new colony carved out of South Carolina, to be called Georgia. In November 1732 he sailed with a party of migrants to Georgia, where he remained, except for short visits to England on the colony's business, till he came home for good in the autumn of 1743. Now a government supporter, he voted with the Hanoverians and was classed by Newcastle in 1746 as 'Old Whig.' Having been made colonel in 1737 of a regiment raised for the defence of Georgia, he was commissioned in March 1744 to raise a regiment of Hussars to defend the coast against a prospective French invasion.[7] At the same time his great friend and housemate, Colonel Cecil, the Pretender's chief agent in England, was sent to the Tower on a charge of high treason. When during the rebellion next year Oglethorpe, in command of a cavalry force, allowed the rearguard of the retreating rebel army to escape, his failure was alternatively attributed to Jacobitism or cowardice. 'He is an unfortunate man', his friend, the 1st Lord Egmont, wrote,

> his vanity and quarrelsomeness rendering him incapable to preserve the friendship of his acquaintance or make new friends, and every mouth is now open against him with a kind of satisfaction.[8]

Court martialled on a charge of having disobeyed or neglected his orders, he was honourably acquitted, but when his regiment was disbanded in 1748 he was not given a new one. Classed as a government supporter on his return in 1747, he is described in 1751 by Horace Walpole as a 'troublesome and tiresome speaker', voting with 'the sad refuse of all the last Oppositions' against a 3s. land tax.[9] At the general election of 1754 he stood for Westminster as well as for Haslemere, but was defeated at both. Except for an unsuccessful attempt to recover his Haslemere seat in 1768, he spent the last thirty years of his long life in retirement, dying 1 July 1785, aged 88.

[1] VCH Surr. iii. 37; HMC Egmont Diary, i. 186. [2] A. A. Ettinger, Oglethorpe, 14–83. [3] Walpole, Mems. Geo. II, i. 113. [4] Chandler, vi. 308. [5] HMC Egmont Diary, i. 12, 215, 244, 261, 271. [6] Undated, Cholmondeley (Houghton) mss 2396d. [7] Ettinger, 258–9. [8] HMC Egmont Diary, iii. 142, 244, 289, 313. [9] Mems. Geo. II, i. 113, 218.

R.R.S.

OKEDEN, William (?1662–1718), of Little Critchell, Dorset.

CORFE CASTLE	1689–1690
WAREHAM	1690–1695
CORFE CASTLE	1715–26 Sept. 1718

b. ?1662, 1st s. of William Okeden of Little Critchell by Mary, da. of John Wyndham of Orchard Wyndham, Som., sis. of Sir William Wyndham, 1st Bt., M.P. educ. Trinity, Oxf. 4 July 1677, aged 15. m. Magdalen (d.1688), da. of Bartholomew Lane of Wimborne Minster, Dorset, 2s. illegit. 1da. suc. fa. 1694.
Sheriff, Dorset 1699.

William Okeden's grandfather Edmund, whose family had been seated at Ellingham, Hants, since the time of Henry VII, succeeded to Little Critchell and properties in Corfe and the Isle of Purbeck, on the death of his maternal grandfather George Uvedale in 1629.[1] Returned for Corfe Castle as a Whig in 1715, he is not recorded as voting. He died 26 Sept. 1718, leaving his estates to his two natural sons by his housekeeper, Mary Morgan, to the exclusion of his legitimate descendants.[2]

[1] Hutchins, Dorset, iii. 128, 469. [2] PCC 94 Browning.

R.S.L.

OLIPHANT, Charles (c.1665–1719).

AYR BURGHS	1710–9 Dec. 1719

b. c.1665, 2nd s. of Charles Oliphant of Langton, ?Edinburgh, a principal clerk of the court of session, by Barbara, da. of Patrick Kinloch of Alderston, Haddington. *educ.* Edinburgh Univ., M.A. 1684, M.D. by 1713, F.R.S. 1713. *m.* a da. of Sir John Young of Leny, Edinburgh, 1da.

Descended from the 3rd Lord Oliphant, Charles Oliphant was a physician and the author of a treatise on the treatment of fevers published in 1699. Returned by the Duke of Argyll for Ayr Burghs, classed in 1715 as a Whig who would often vote with the Tories, he voted with the Government on the septennial bill in 1716 and the repeal of the Occasional Conformity and Schism Acts in 1719. His eldest brother, James, was in 1713 appointed first underkeeper of the Queen's wardrobe in Scotland, retaining the office after George I's accession. His younger brother, William, voted as Lord Oliphant in an election of representative peers in 1750 but did not assume the title. He died 9 Dec. 1719.

J.M.S.

OLMIUS, John (1711–62), of New Hall, Boreham, Essex.

WEYMOUTH AND MELCOMBE REGIS
10 Mar. 1737–1741
COLCHESTER 1741–26 Feb. 1742, 1754–1761
WEYMOUTH AND MELCOMBE REGIS
1761–5 Oct. 1762

b. 18 July 1711, o.s. of John Olmius of Braintree, Essex, dep. gov. of Bank of England, by Elizabeth, da. and h. of Thomas Clarke, London merchant. *m.* 8 Sept. 1741, Anne, da. and h. of Sir William Billers of Thorley, Herts., ld. mayor of London 1733–4, 1s. 1da. *suc.* fa. 1731; *cr.* Baron Waltham [I] 22 June 1762.
Sheriff, Essex 1746–7.

Olmius was the grandson of a wealthy Dutch merchant, who bought the Essex estates of the Earl of Scarsdale at the beginning of the eighteenth century.[1] After unsuccessfully contesting Weymouth in 1735, he was returned there by Bubb Dodington in 1737, in which year he bought New Hall in Essex, formerly the seat of the dukes of Buckingham and Albemarle. With Walpole's backing he made an unsuccessful attempt to wrest Weymouth from Dodington in 1741, when he was returned for Colchester, voting with the Government till he was unseated in February. In 1742 the secret committee on Walpole, before which he gave evidence, stigmatised the Weymouth and Essex elections as examples of Walpole's 'notorious attacks upon the freedom of elections'.[2]

In 1743 Olmius lent Frederick, Prince of Wales, £2,800 at 5 per cent.[3] After unsuccessfully contesting Colchester again in 1747, he was put down 'for Colchester or anywhere' in the 2nd Lord Egmont's list of persons to be brought in by the Court in the next reign.

In 1754 Olmius succeeded in a third attempt at Colchester. In 1757 he presented a memorial to Newcastle, 'to be laid before the King when there was any design to create Knights of the Bath':

In the year 1733 soon after I came of age I offered myself as a candidate to the borough of Maldon, which Sir Robert Walpole hearing, he desired me to decline standing there and he would bring me in for Orford, but he not succeeding at that place (at that time) I was left to take care of myself, which I did at Weymouth since which time I have purchased so many burgage tenures there that I stand in fear of none and as its a borough that chooses four Members by the same electors I leave any one to judge its value. I served for the said borough in the Parliament which was chose 1734 and I flatter myself I behaved well, Sir Robert offering me (though unasked) a Red Ribbon, which I told him I would accept being a distinguished mark of H.M.'s favour. He likewise twice offered me an Irish peerage which I then declined, telling him I should be extremely happy if I could obtain an English one, believing neither my family, fortune or principles could be objected to. I remember his answer, I was very young, it might be got in time, and the other would be a good step towards it.

In the year 1741 I was returned on a large legal majority for Colchester (for which place I now serve and think I may without vanity say no man has a better interest than myself). I lost my seat next sessions for my steady adherence to Sir Robert Walpole, although I might have kept it had I temporised, having had many offers to that purpose.

But I am now coming to the most material point viz. very early in the last rebellion I went to Kensington with the following proposal—

Hoping H.M. will be graciously pleased to accept this small mark of my zeal for his sacred person and royal family it is most humbly proposed by Mr. Olmius of New Hall in Essex to enlist with all expedition 500 men to be mustered at a week's notice from H.M. and upon such notice to have arms sent down for the said corps, the expense of the whole (arms and officers excepted) to be borne by me and also their subsistence and pay for two months, I myself attending wherever they went as a volunteer.

The return I met with for this offer which was so well intended was the loss of Lord Fitzwalter's [ld. lt. of Essex] friendship. His Lordship put me on a pocket sheriff[4] for the county of Essex and when I spoke to him, he told me in a rage, such offers did not become any private gentleman, but only lords lieutenant and the very prime of the nobility and he insisting upon my serving that office, I did it and believe to the satisfaction of everybody.[5]

In the next reign he applied to Bute for an English peerage in the Coronation honours.[6] He was given an Irish one three months before his death, 5 Oct. 1762.

[1] Morant, *Essex*, ii. 84. [2] *CJ*, xxiv. 293–5. [3] Daniel Avery to Prince of Wales, 20 Feb. 1749, Newcastle (Clumber) mss. [4] i.e. put him up for the office though he was not one of the three nominated in the Exchequer from whom sheriffs were normally selected. [5] Add. 32874, f. 209. [6] Bute mss.

R.R.S.

ONGLEY, Samuel (1697–1747), of Old Warden, Beds.

NEW SHOREHAM 29 Jan. 1729–1734
BEDFORD 1734–15 June 1747

bap. prob. 2 Nov. 1697, o. surv. s. of Samuel Ongley of St. Michael's, Cornhill, London, draper, by Elizabeth, da. of Edward Falkingham of St. Michael's, Cornhill.[1] *educ.* ?Merchant Taylors' 1709–12; St. John's, Oxf. 13 Dec. 1716, aged 19. *m.* 19 Sept. 1726, Anne, da. of John Harvey (q.v.) of Northill, Beds., *s.p. suc.* uncle Sir Samuel Ongley, M.P., at Old Warden 1726.

Sea coal meter in the customs house 1721–c.1728.

Although there are discrepancies in accounts of Ongley's birth and parentage, he was certainly the heir of Sir Samuel Ongley, M.P. for Maidstone, a linen draper in Cornhill and director of the South Sea Company, who died unmarried on 25 Aug. 1726, 'very rich, said £10,000 p.a., £5,000 to be sure'.[2] Immediately after succeeding to Old Warden he married his neighbour's sister at Northill. A month later, on 25 Oct. 1726, Lady Elizabeth Osborn wrote:[3]

> It was agreed [by the Whig country gentlemen of Bedfordshire] that Ongley has hardly any principles, at least not violent if he is a Tory, and that 'tis necessary to court him and bring him over if they can to the Whig interest. My brother [Pattee] Byng [q.v.] carries him . . . in his coach to Bedford, and then is to carry him to the Whig inn where they will meet . . . all the Whigs who are to propose . . . to him

that he should stand for the county against the young 3rd Duke of Bedford's Tory nominees. In the end he stood unsuccessfully as a ducal candidate for the borough in 1727, and on petition was declared to be incapable of claiming to sit in Parliament because of his customs house office.[4] This he must soon have resigned, for in January 1729 he was returned unopposed at a double by-election for the notoriously venal borough of New Shoreham. The following month he was appointed to the gaols committee of the House of Commons. In 1734 he moved back to Bedford where he was returned unopposed and again in 1741, voting against the Administration in all recorded divisions. Shortly before the next general election he died on 15 June 1747, his estates passing to his cousin Robert Henley, afterwards Ongley, M.P.

[1] *Lics. Vic. Gen.* (Harl. Soc. xxxi), 244. [2] Le Neve, *Knights* (Harl. Soc. viii), 508; PCC 189 Plymouth. [3] E. F. D. Osborn, *Pol. and Soc. Letters of a lady of the 18th century*, 39. [4] *CJ*, xxi. 139.

R.S.L.

ONSLOW, Arthur (1691–1768), of Imber Court, Surr.

GUILDFORD 15 Feb. 1720–1727
SURREY 1727–1761

b. 3 Sept. 1691, 1st s. of Foot Onslow, M.P., by Susanna, da. and h. of Thomas Anlaby of Etton, Yorks., wid. of Arnold Coldwall of Guildford. *educ.* Guildford g.s. 1698; Winchester 1706; Wadham, Oxf. 1708; M. Temple 1707, called 1713, bencher 1728. *m.* 8 Oct. 1720, Anne, da. and coh. of John Bridges, niece and coh. of Henry Bridges, of Imber Court, 1s. 1da. *suc.* fa. 1710.

Sec. to chancellor of the Exchequer 1714–15; receiver gen. of Post Office 1715–20; recorder, Guildford 1719; Speaker of the House of Commons 1728–61; P.C. 25 June 1728; chancellor to Queen Caroline 1729–37; treasurer of the navy 1734–42.

At George I's accession Onslow, then an unsuccessful barrister, was appointed secretary to his uncle, Sir Richard Onslow (q.v.), the new Whig chancellor of the Exchequer. Returned in 1720 on the Onslow interest for Guildford, which he exchanged for the county in 1727, he quickly made his mark in Parliament. At the opening of the Parliament of 1722 he was one of the leading ministerial supporters in the Commons who were invited to Walpole's house to discuss the bill for suspending the Habeas Corpus Act on the discovery of the Atterbury conspiracy, subsequently taking a leading part in the passing of a bill of pains and penalties against one of the conspirators.[1] He was one of the managers of Lord Macclesfield's impeachment in 1725, when he also spoke against the reversal of Bolingbroke's attainder. 'I endeavoured', he wrote,

> to found my character rather upon the rectitude of my actings than upon any other fame, and therefore often voted with both parties as I thought them to be in the right. I loved independency and pursued it. I kept firm to my original Whig principles, upon conscience, and never deviated from them to serve any party cause whatsoever: and all this I hope and am persuaded, was what chiefly laid the foundation of my rise to the chair of the House of Commons without any the least opposition, although Sir Robert Walpole sometimes said to me, that the road to that station lay through the gates of St. James's.

On 17 Jan. 1727 he was chosen to move the Address.

Soon after George II's accession, when most people were expecting that Walpole would be displaced by Sir Spencer Compton (q.v.), the then Speaker, Onslow

> went to wait upon him at Chelsea, a place he had for retreat, as much as a first minister can enjoy, so near the town. I found him at that time, alone, and he kept me a great while with him. At first he seemed a little shy of talking, and I imagine he thought I came by direction . . . to report what he should say in our conversation; but I had no such base view, nor ever was an instrument of that sort for any person, and he soon perceived I had no such motive, and came only out of pure respect and affection for him, as was the truth, I really believing that all power was to be in other hands. Upon this he took me into his arms with a flood of tears that came immediately from him, crying out, that this kindness of his friends had drawn

a weakness from him, which his enemies never could do. He then made me sit down by him, for I was going away, and entered into a long discourse of his ministry . . . and in this conversation, or some other not long after, I found he would not dislike my being the next Speaker; but of that nothing was ever said by him to me till he was in the full return of his former power, and which soon came about, with very ample increase of it.[2]

Walpole's reasons for preferring Onslow to Compton as Speaker were that Compton, as a defeated rival, might be dangerous in the chair of the new House of Commons, whereas Onslow,

> as he had no great pretensions to it from his age, his character, his weight in the House, or his particular knowledge of the business . . . must look upon his promotion entirely as an act of his favour, and consequently think himself obliged, in honour, interest, and gratitude, to show all the complaisance in his power to his patron and benefactor.

Onslow, however, had other ideas.

> No man [Hervey writes] courted popularity more, and to no man popularity was ever more coy. He cajoled both parties and obliged neither; he disobliged his patron by seeming to favour his opponents, and gained no credit with them because it was only seeming.[3]

By 1731 it was known that Walpole 'was not well with the Speaker, and consequently the Speaker not well at court'. Horace Walpole relates that Onslow

> one day judiciously bragged to the Queen of some compliments that had been made him on his impartiality by Sir J. Rushout and Mr. Gybbon, then in the Opposition; and added, 'These, Madam, are the honours I carry with me to Ember Court'. She replied, 'Oh, you are in the right . . . There was Sir Spencer Compton [who had combined the post of Speaker with that of paymaster of the forces], who was so simple as to prefer carrying a hundred thousand pound to his Ember Court'.[4]

In 1732 Onslow, who was entitled to speak and vote when the House was in committee, voted with the Opposition on the army estimates. Next year he made amends by voting for the excise bill and supporting Walpole at the ensuing party meeting at the Cockpit; on 6 Feb. 1734 he spoke for the Government in a debate on an increase in the army; and at the dissolution in April he followed the example of his predecessor by accepting a lucrative sinecure.

In the next Parliament Onslow, having been unanimously re-elected Speaker, voted with Walpole on the Spanish convention in 1739, subsequently denouncing the secession of the Opposition.[5] When the opposition leaders were considering their plan of campaign against the ministry at the opening of the Parliament of 1741, Chesterfield expressed the opinion that, 'as for opposition to their Speaker, if it be Onslow, we shall be but weak, he having, by a certain decency of behaviour made himself many

personal friends in the minority'.[6] After his unanimous re-election, the Opposition, 'to flatter his pretence to popularity and impartiality, call him their own Speaker'. On a tie for the last two places on the secret committee set up by the Commons to inquire into Walpole's Administration, it was agreed that the choice should be left to Onslow. He, 'with a resolution not supposed to be in him, as he has been the most notorious affecter of popularity', chose the court candidates. Accused of having done so because of his sinecure, he at once resigned it, 'to show his disinterestedness'. Nevertheless, Walpole is said to have 'always thought the Speaker not enough attached to him and treated him very roughly on his first visit after his disgrace'.[7]

Onslow voted with the Government on the Hanoverians in 1742 and 1744. In 1747 he attended the meeting of the leading ministerial Members of the Commons at Pelham's house two nights before the opening of the new Parliament.[8] He spoke against the regency bill in 1751 and the clandestine marriage bill in 1753. Shortly before his re-election as Speaker in 1754, he told Pelham

> that if I was to be Speaker again, he must not expect that I would act otherwise than I had always done, and which he knew was not always pleasing to ministers, his answer was, 'Sir, I shall as little like, as any one else in my station, to have a Speaker in a set opposition to me and the measures I carry on; but I shall as little like to have a Speaker over-complaisant, either to me or to them'.[9]

The first career Speaker, he died 17 Feb. 1768.

[1] *Knatchbull Diary*, 15–16, 115. [2] *HMC 14th Rep. IX*, 516–17. [3] Hervey, *Mems.* 39, 74–75. [4] *HMC Egmont Diary*, i. 205–6; *Corresp. H. Walpole*, xxx. 292, n. 25. [5] *HMC Egmont Diary*, i. 366; ii. 24; iii. 43. [6] Coxe, *Walpole*, iii. 580. [7] Walpole to Mann, 3 Dec. 1741, 1 and 8 Apr. 1742; *Mems. Geo. II*, i. 129 n. [8] Owen, *Pelhams*, 143, n. 4. [9] *HMC 14th Rep. IX*, 516–17.

R.R.S.

ONSLOW, Denzil (c.1642–1721), of Pyrford, Surr.

HASLEMERE   1679–1681, 1689–1695
SURREY   1695–1698
GUILDFORD   1701–1713, 12 Mar. 1714–10 Dec. 1717
SURREY   25 Dec 1717–27 June 1721

b. c.1642, 6th s. of Sir Richard Onslow, M.P., by Elizabeth, da. and h. of Arthur Strangways of London. *m.* (1) c.1671, Sarah, da. and coh. of Sir Thomas Foote, 1st Bt., wid. of Sir John Lewis, 1st Bt., of Ledston, Yorks, *s.p.*; (2) Jane Yard, wid., da. of Henry Weston of Oakham, Surr. and sis. of John Weston, M.P., *s.p.*
  Commr. of victualling 1706–11, 1714–*d.*; outranger of Windsor forest 1717–*d.*

A younger brother, with a scanty provision, bred to no business, having soon left that he was designed for, with very moderate abilities of any kind,

Denzil Onslow, according to his great-nephew, the Speaker,

> came to make as reputable a figure and to be in as much consideration in his country as any gentleman in it.

He achieved this by marrying a wealthy widow, with whose money he purchased the estate of Pyrford, where 'he lived in a fashion equal almost to any man in the county'. Though 'above forty years with very little interruptions a Member of the House of Commons', he is said by the Speaker to have known 'no more of the business there than one who had been of the standing of a session'. Deprived of his office by the Tory Government in 1711, he was reinstated by the Whigs in 1714, securing a second office from the 2nd Lord Onslow (q.v.) in 1717 so that he might vacate his seat at Guildford in order to contest the county, 'for the sake of keeping up the interest of the family'.[1] He died 27 June 1721, leaving his property to the children of his nephew, the 1st Lord Onslow (q.v.), whose peerage, failing male issue, had been entailed on him by a special remainder.

[1] *HMC 14th Rep. IX*, 495–6, 503.

R.R.S.

ONSLOW, Denzil (c.1698–1765), of Mickleham, Surr.

GUILDFORD   24 Nov. 1740–1747

b. c.1698, s. of Richard Onslow of Drungewick, Suss. by Sarah, da. of Thomas Calvert, M.P., and gt.gd. s. of Sir Richard Onslow, M.P. *m.* cos. Anne, da. and coh. of Thomas Middleton, M.P., of Stansted Mountfitchet, Essex by Anne, da. of Sir Richard Onslow, 3rd Bt. (q.v.), 2s. *suc.* fa. 1712.
    Receiver gen. of the Post Office 1727–40; paymaster of the board of Works 1743–55; commr. of stamp duties 1755–7; commr. of the salt office 1757–65.

Denzil Onslow succeeded his cousin Richard Onslow (q.v.) at the Post Office, which he in turn had to resign as incompatible with a seat in the House of Commons when he was returned on his family's interest for Guildford in 1740. Voting with the Administration in every recorded division, he spoke for the Hanoverians on 18 Jan. 1744.[1] He resigned his seat in 1747 in preference to giving up his place at the board of Works, which had become incompatible with a seat in the House under the Place Act of 1742. In 1748 he was called upon to explain why there were errors in his Post Office accounts, and in 1764 the Treasury inquired why there had been no proceedings taken on his arrears as paymaster of the board of Works. On his death, 15 Nov. 1765, he owed the sum of £1,648 16s. 7d., which was still outstanding in 1783.[2]

[1] Yorke's parl. jnl. *Parl. Hist*. xiii. 463.   [2] Treasury minute bks. T29/31, f. 88, 29/36, f. 69, 29/53, f. 255.

R.R.S.

ONSLOW, Sir Richard, 3rd Bt. (1654–1717), of Clandon, Surr.

GUILDFORD   1679–1681, 1685–1687
SURREY   1689–1710
ST. MAWES   1710–1713
SURREY   1713–Nov. 1715

b. 23 June 1654, 1st s. of Sir Arthur Onslow, 2nd Bt., M.P., by Mary, da. and coh. of Sir Thomas Foote, 1st Bt., ld. mayor of London 1649–50. *educ.* St. Edmund Hall, Oxf. 1671; I. Temple 1674. *m.* 31 Aug. 1676, Elizabeth, da. and h. of Sir Henry Tulse, ld. mayor of London 1683–4, 2s. 2da. *suc.* fa. 21 July 1688; *cr.* Baron Onslow 19 June 1716.
    Lt.-col. of Marines 1690; ld. of the Admiralty 1690–3; high steward, Guildford 1701–*d.*; Speaker of the House of Commons 1708–10; gov. Levant Co. 1709–*d.*; P.C. 15 June 1710 and 1714; chancellor of the Exchequer 1714–15; teller of the Exchequer 1715–*d.*; ld. lt., Surr. 1716–*d.*

Sir Richard Onslow, known as 'Stiff Dick', was the grandson of Sir Richard Onslow (1601–64), who, in the words of his descendant, Speaker Onslow,

> laid the foundations of that interest both in the county and in the town of Guildford that our family have ever since kept up to a height that has been scarcely equalled in any county by one family, having been chosen for the county to all Parliaments, except five, from 1627; and for Guildford to every Parliament since 1660, except for two years upon a vacancy for a friend by our family interest, and sometimes for Haslemere, Gatton and Bletchingley, in the same county, once two of our family together for the county, and several times two of them for Guildford.[1]

The second of the three Speakers produced by the family, he played a prominent part under Anne, particularly in connexion with the Act of Succession, which he conducted through the Commons. Appointed chancellor of the Exchequer at George I's accession, but soon displaced by Walpole, he wrote to the King representing that after his 'unwearied and successful endeavours' to promote 'those laws which have so happily settled the Crown of Great Britain on your Majesty', it was hard 'to be with contempt dismissed your service, without the least cause of misdemeanour assigned'.[2] He was compensated with a tellership of the Exchequer for life and a peerage, but having been a member of the House of Commons committee whose report had led to the impeachment of the heads of the late Tory Government, he was reluctant to take out his patent until the impeachments were out of the way, so that 'they who had been accusers might not sit as judges in the same cause'. After some months, owing to the delay in trying Lord Oxford, he compromised by taking out his patent and abstaining from voting on anything relating to the impeachments.[3] He died 5 Dec. 1717.

[1] *HMC 14th Rep. IX*, 476, 491. [2] 29 Oct. 1715, Cholmondeley (Houghton) mss. [3] *HMC 14th Rep. IX*, 493.

R.R.S.

ONSLOW, Richard (c.1697–1760).

GUILDFORD 1727–16 Mar. 1760

b. c.1697, 2nd s. of Foot Onslow M.P. and yr. bro. of Arthur Onslow (q.v.). *m.* (1) 9 Dec. 1726, Rose (*d.* Feb. 1728), da. and coh. of John Bridges, sis.-in-law of Arthur Onslow, *s.p.*; (2) Pooley, da. of Charles Walton of Little Bursted, Essex, niece and h. of Admiral Sir George Walton, 3s. 1da.

Receiver gen. of the Post Office 1720–7; accomptant to his bro. as treasurer of the navy 1734–42.

Capt. 11 Ft. 1716, 30 Ft. 1719, 15 Ft. 1721; capt.-lt. and lt.-col. 1 Ft. Gds. 1724, capt. 1727; col. 39 Ft. 1731, 8 Ft. 1739, 1 tp. Horse Gren. Gds. 1745; brig.-gen. 1742; maj.-gen. 1743; lt.-gen. 1747.

Gov. Fort William 1752–9; Plymouth 1759–*d.*

Richard Onslow was left by his parents' deaths in the charge of his elder brother, Arthur, the future Speaker, who, thinking him cut out for the army by 'a courage and firmness in him', combined with 'a large and fine make in his person, and . . . a very handsome and manly countenance', gave him a start in life by raising the money to buy him a company in the Guards.[1] In 1720 Arthur, on entering Parliament, turned over to Richard a £400 a year place in the Post Office, which was incompatible with a seat in the Commons. In 1722 Richard figured in an election brawl with James Oglethorpe at Haslemere, where the Onslows had an interest.[2] Returned on his family's interest at Guildford in 1727, he had to resign his Post Office place, obtaining another in 1734 under his brother as treasurer of the navy, which he held till Arthur Onslow resigned that place in 1742. Voting steadily with the Government, marrying two heiresses, and backed by the Onslow influence, he rose steadily to a high rank in the army. He died 16 Mar. 1760. Presumably as a compliment to his brother, the Speaker, Sir James Thornhill's (q.v.) picture of the House of Commons, c.1730, contains a portrait of him by Thornhill's son-in-law, Hogarth.

[1] *HMC 14th Rep. IX*, 501–2. [2] A. A. Ettinger, *Oglethorpe*, 81–82.

R.R.S.

ONSLOW, Hon. Richard (1713–76).

GUILDFORD 1734–5 June 1740

b. 1713, o.s. of Thomas, 2nd Baron Onslow (q.v.). *educ.* Eton 1725–8; Sidney Sussex, Camb. 1730. *m.* 16 May 1741, Mary, da. of Sir Edmund Elwill, 3rd

Bt., sis. of Sir John Elwill, 4th Bt. (q.v.), *s.p.*. *suc.* fa. as 3rd Baron 5 June 1740; K.B. 13 Mar. 1752.

Ld. lt. Surr. and high steward, Guildford 1740–*d.*

On coming of age Onslow was returned on his family's interest at Guildford, voting with the Administration. After succeeding to the peerage in 1740 he devoted himself to racing and hunting. Towards the end of his life it was stated that owing to his extravagance he had agreed to be placed by his heirs on a small allowance.[1] But when he died, 8 Oct. 1776, he is said to have left a fortune of £18,000 a year.[2]

[1] Barlow, *Complete English Peerage* (1775), p. 277. [2] *Gent. Mag.* 1776, p. 483.

R.R.S.

ONSLOW, Thomas (1679–1740), of Clandon, Surr.

GATTON 1702–1705
CHICHESTER 26 Nov. 1705–1708
BLETCHINGLEY 1708–Nov. 1715
SURREY 30 Nov. 1715–5 Dec. 1717

bap. 27 Nov. 1679, o. surv. s. of Richard Onslow (q.v.), 1st Baron Onslow. *m.* (1) 17 Nov. 1708 (with about £70,000), Elizabeth, da. and h. of John Knight, merchant of Jamaica, niece and h. of Col. Charles Knight, also of Jamaica, 1s. *suc.* fa. as 2nd Baron Onslow 5 Dec. 1717.

Outranger of Windsor Great Park 1715–17; ld. lt. Surr. and high steward, Guildford 1717–*d.*; teller of the Exchequer 1718–*d.*

At George I's accession Thomas Onslow spoke on the address to the new King, observing that in this case the occasion was one for congratulation rather than condolence. Re-elected in 1715, he spoke on 21 June in defence of the Duke of Ormonde. In November he succeeded his father as knight of the shire for Surrey, vacating his Bletchingley seat by taking an office of £600 p.a.[1] On 20 Feb. 1717 he moved the Address, his last recorded speech before being called to the Lords by his father's death. He continued to play a leading part in Surrey elections, complaining in 1720 to Sunderland of the expense to which he was being put

in promoting his Majesty's service in the county of Surrey, which I fear must fall without his Majesty's kind support and your Lordship's assistance.

And again in 1722:

I am now going to another election . . . but now depend on your Lordship's goodness and promise, or will never more engage, for 'tis ruin to my family, and the fatigue of so many elections intolerable.[2]

A figure in the City, he presided in 1720 over the insurance company known at the time as 'Onslow's Bubble', which survives today as the Royal Exchange Assurance. He married a West Indian heiress, with whose money he rebuilt Clandon by Leoni. According to his cousin, the Speaker, he was not without parts and spirit and some knowledge of the world, and had a notion of magnificence suited to his rank and fortune, but had such a mixture of what was wrong in everything he thought, said and did, and had so much of pride and covetousness too, that his behaviour, conversation, and dealings with people were generally distasteful and sometimes shocking, and had many bitter enemies but with very few friends.[3]

He died 5 June 1740.

[1] *HMC 14th Rep. IX*, 494–5. [2] Sunderland (Blenheim) mss. [3] *HMC 14th Rep. IX*, 494–5.

R.R.S.

ORD, John (1710–45), of Newcastle-upon-Tyne, Fenham and Newminster Abbey, Northumb.

MITCHELL   1741–1 July 1745

bap. 27 Dec. 1710, 1st s. of Thomas Ord, attorney, of Newcastle-upon-Tyne, Fenham and Newminster Abbey (bro. of Robert Ord, q.v.) by Anne, da. of John Bacon of Staward, Northumb.; bro. of William Ord (q.v.). *educ.* Kensington sch.; Trinity, Camb. 1727; L. Inn 1730. *suc. fa.* 1737.
Gov. of Hostmen's Co. in Newcastle-upon-Tyne 1740; mayor 1744–*d.*

Ord's grandfather, a wealthy Newcastle attorney, who had purchased large estates in his county, was connected with Sidney Wortley (q.v.) as a coal owner and a member of the cartel which dominated the coal trade in the eighteenth century.[1] Returned for Mitchell as an opposition Whig in 1741 on the nomination of Lord Sandwich, the head of Wortley's family, he voted against the Administration in all recorded divisions. He died 1 July 1745.

[1] E. Hughes, *N. Country Life in 18th Cent.*, 168–95, 209–14.

E.C.

ORD, Robert (1700–78), of Petersham, Surr. and Hunstanworth,   Bingfield   and   Newbiggin, Northumb.

MITCHELL   1734–1741
MORPETH   1741–Sept. 1755

b. 1700, 9th s. of John Ord, attorney in Newcastle-upon-Tyne, of Newbiggin, Fenham and Newminster, Northumb. being 5th by his 2nd w. Anne, da. of Michael Hutchinson of Loft House, nr. Leeds; uncle of John and William Ord (qq.v.). *educ.* L. Inn 1718; called 1724. *m.* Oct. 1727, Mary, da. of Sir John Darnell, 1s. 5da. *suc.* bro. Ralph to Hunstanworth and Newbiggin estates 1724; bought Bingfield 1733.
Sec. to chancellor of the Exchequer Feb. 1742–Dec. 1743; dep. cofferer of the Household Dec. 1743–Dec. 1744; chief baron of the Exchequer [S] 1755–75; chancellor of Durham dioc. 1753–64.

A 'most intimate and particular friend'[1] and legal adviser[2] of Pulteney's, Ord was returned for Mitchell by Lord Falmouth (Hugh Boscawen, q.v.) in 1734.

He spoke for the mortmain bill on 15 Apr. 1736,[3] voted against the Administration on the Spanish convention in 1739 and the place bill in 1740; spoke for the Opposition in a debate on the embargo on the provision of victuals on 1 Dec. 1740, and ten days later spoke against the army estimates, extolling the achievements of the Duke of Argyll, who had been recently dismissed from his posts. In 1741 he was returned by Lord Carlisle, to whom he wrote on 14 May:

> I had an account . . . yesterday that they have done me the honour at Morpeth to choose me one of their representatives. As this is entirely owing to your Lordship's favour, I hope you will excuse my troubling you with my thanks for it, as the only return in my power to make to your Lordship, and at the same time permit me, like other beggars (I don't say sturdy ones) because I have already received favours of your Lordship which I do not deserve, to desire the continuance of them.[4]

After the fall of Walpole, he was one of Pulteney's friends who were given office, becoming secretary to the new chancellor of the Exchequer, Sandys, whom he followed to the Household in December 1743 as deputy cofferer, both being turned out on the formation of the Broadbottom Administration in December 1744. He voted for the Hanoverians in 1742, 1744 and 1746, but was classed as Opposition in 1747 when he was again returned for Morpeth. By the next Parliament he had rallied to the Administration, vacating his seat on obtaining a judicial office in 1755.

He died 12 Feb. 1778.

[1] Wm. Pulteney to Vernon, 16 June 1741, *Vernon Pprs.* (Navy Recs. Soc. xcix), 241. [2] C. Hanbury Williams, *Works*, i. 59. [3] Harley Diary. [4] Carlisle mss.

E.C.

ORD, William (*d.*1768), of Fenham, Newminster Abbey and Whitfield, nr. Morpeth, Northumb.

BOSSINEY   12 Dec. 1747–1754

b. aft. 1711, 2nd s. of Thomas Ord, attorney, of Newcastle-upon-Tyne, Fenham and Newminster Abbey; bro. of John Ord (q.v.). *m.* 18 Mar. 1746 (with £20,000), Anne, da. of William Dillingham of Red Lion Sq., London, 3s. 5da.[1] *suc.* bro. to Fenham and Newminster 1745; bought Whitfield 1750.
Sheriff, Northumb. 1747–8.

Ord, who succeeded to his family's estates in 1745, was returned for Bossiney, presumably as an opposition Whig, by Edward Wortley (q.v.), with whom his family were closely connected.[2] He did not stand again. As one of the owners of the Walker colliery, then the most important in the north of England, he made mining history with the sinking of the first deep mining shaft in 1762.[3] In later life he was afflicted with an obsession for hanging himself. On his first attempt he was cut down by his servant, the second time the rope broke, but the third time he succeeded,[4] 24 Jan. 1768.

[1] Nichols, *Leics.* i. 615. [2] Sandwich to Pelham, 4 Oct. 1747, Newcastle (Clumber) mss. See also ORD, John. [3] *New Hist. Northumb.* xiii. 44. [4] R. Welford, *Men of Mark 'twixt Tyne and Tweed*, iii. 236.

E.C.

ORLEBAR, John (1697–1765), of Hinwick, Beds.

BEDFORD 1727–1734

b. 1697, o.s. of John Orlebar of Red Lion Sq., London, master in Chancery, by Elizabeth, da. of John Whitfield of Ives Place, Maidenhead, Berks. *educ.* Eton 1707–15; M. Temple 1707, called 1720; King's, Camb. 1715. *m.* 29 Dec. 1729, Mary, da. of Samuel Rolt of Milton Ernest, Beds., M.P. Bedford 1701, 1713–15, 1s. 4da. *suc.* fa. 1721; cos. Richard Orlebar at Hinwick 1733.
Commr. of excise 1738–*d.*; bencher, M. Temple 1742.

John Orlebar, like his father and grandfather a bencher of the Middle Temple, was descended from George Orlebar, who acquired Hinwick with Podington, Bedfordshire, through his wife in 1647.[1] Returned as a Whig for Bedford in 1727, he voted with the Administration in all recorded divisions. When in 1728 an attempt was made by the Whig members of the Bedford corporation to turn out their Tory recorder, Lord Bruce, by legal proceedings,[2] the prospective vacancy was offered to Orlebar who replied to the mayor that 'in case you succeed . . . I shall very willingly accept the favour you offer me and cheerfully defray the expense of it,'[3] but nothing came of it. He did not stand again, was given a place in the excise in 1738, and died 19 Dec. 1765. A number of his letters, describing parliamentary proceedings 1739–42, are printed in vol. iii of Coxe's *Walpole*.

[1] F. St. J. Orlebar, *Orlebar Chron.* 310. [2] John Bardolph to John Orlebar, 1728, Orlebar mss 1776, Beds. RO. [3] Members of Bedford Corp. to John Orlebar, 22 Nov. 1728, and John Orlebar to the mayor, Nov. 1728, ibid. 1779, 1780.

R.S.L.

ORME, Garton (1696–1758), of Woolavington, nr. Midhurst, Suss.

ARUNDEL 23 Nov. 1739–1754

b. c.1696, 1st surv. s. of Robert Orme, M.P. Midhurst 1705–9, 1710–11, of Woolavington, Suss. by Dorothea, da. of John Dawnay, 1st Visct. Downe [I]. *m.* (1) 1715, Charlotte (*d.* Jan. 1727), da. of Capt. Jonas Hanway, R.N., 1da.; (2) 4 Mar. 1727, Anne Lafitte, da. of Rev. Daniel Lafitte of Bordeaux, vicar of Woolavington 1691–1731. *suc.* fa. 1711.
Gent. usher to Princess of Wales 1736–58; gent. in waiting to the Prince 1750–1.

Garton Orme's grandfather acquired by marriage the estates of the Garton family, including the manors of Woolavington and East Dean, near the boroughs of Arundel and Midhurst. Succeeding as a minor, he was taken up by his neighbour, the Duke of Richmond, who in 1734 applied on his behalf for the Duke of Somerset's interest at Midhurst in the event of a future vacancy there.[1] It was probably to Richmond's recommendation that he owed the post of gentleman usher to the Princess of Wales on her marriage in 1736. Returned unopposed on his own interest for Arundel in 1738, he voted with the Opposition as a servant of the Prince of Wales. He was re-elected in 1741 after an expensive contest, spending money so freely that it was assumed that he was being financed by the Prince.[2] Till Frederick's death he consistently voted with the Leicester House party, in which he was never more than a minor figure. His name does not appear in any of the lists of proposed appointments in a future reign.

In 1747 Orme was again returned for Arundel, this time in conjunction with Theobald Taaffe (q.v.), defeating candidates supported by his old patron, the Duke of Richmond, who unsuccessfully tried to induce them to petition 'against the bribery of Orme and Taaffe'. Learning of moves to turn him out at the next election, he wrote in 1748 to the Duke, suggesting that there was no reason why they should not reach a mutually satisfactory arrangement relating to the borough, since 'I have no further design there than to secure myself' and 'shall be glad to come into any measures that will not prejudice my own interest'.[3] Nothing seems to have come of this overture. Soon afterwards he fell into financial difficulties. In 1750 a private Act was passed enabling him to sell or mortgage his estates and his daughter's portion for the payment of his debts. In 1752 he sold his East Dean estate for £12,000. He did not stand in 1754.

Orme died 20 Oct. 1758, leaving a lurid local reputation. According to tradition, he got rid of his first wife by pushing her down a well, a story which received some support in 1845, when one of the Orme coffins on being opened was found to be full of stones. He was also supposed to have hired a highwayman to waylay his daughter on her way to London to protest against his alienation of her patrimony. For many years it was the tradition for owners and heirs of Lavington to commemorate him by spitting when they came to the boundary of the East Dean estate.[4]

[1] Somerset to Richmond, 25 Nov. 1734, Richmond mss. [2] Lady Shelley to Newcastle, 20 July 1740, Add. 32694, f. 207. [3] Pelham to Richmond, 2 July 1747, Orme to Richmond, 1 Oct. 1748, Richmond mss. [4] A. M. Wilberforce, *Lavington*, 33–6.

R.R.S.

OSBALDESTON, William (1688–1766), of Hunmanby, nr. Scarborough, Yorks.

SCARBOROUGH 21 Apr. 1736–1747
1754–5 Sept. 1766

b. 20 July 1688, 1st s. of Sir Richard Osbaldeston, M.P., of Hunmanby by Elizabeth, da. and coh. of John Fountayne of Melton; bro. of Fountayne Wentworth Osbaldeston, M.P. *educ.* Beverley; St. John's, Camb. 1706. *unm. suc.* fa. 1728.

Osbaldeston, a Yorkshire country gentleman, was related to John Hill (q.v.), commissioner of customs, who had considerable influence at Scarborough.[1] When he stood with government backing for Scarborough at a by-election in 1735 his opponents complained of threats to turn out the local customs house officials if they or their relations voted for his opponents.[2] Defeated but seated by the House of Commons on petition, he was re-elected in 1741, voting regularly with the Government. He lost his seat in 1747, having, according to Pelham, 'starved the cause',[3] but recovered it in 1754, continuing to represent Scarborough till his death, 5 Sept. 1766.

[1] James Trymmer to Ld. Oxford, 21 Sept. 1735, Harley mss. Duke of Leeds to Ld. Oxford, 17 Oct. 1735, ibid. [3] 4 July 1747, Add. 9186, f. 105.

R.R.S.

OSBORN, Sir Danvers, 3rd Bt. (1715–53), of Chicksands, nr. Biggleswade, Beds.

BEDFORDSHIRE 1747–June 1753

b. 17 Nov. 1715, 3rd but 1st surv. s. of John Osborn of Chicksands (who *d.v.p.*, 1st s. of Sir John Osborn, 2nd Bt.), by Sarah, da. of George Byng, 1st Visct. Torrington, sis. of Pattee Byng (qq.v.). *educ.* Westminster 1723; Trinity Hall, Camb. 1732–5. *m.* 25 Sept. 1740, Lady Mary Montagu, da. of George Montagu, M.P., 1st Earl of Halifax, sis. of the 2nd Earl and sis.-in-law of Sir Roger Burgoyne, 6th Bt. (q.v.), 2s. *suc.* fa. 1719 and gd.-fa. as 3rd Bt. 28 Apr. 1720.

Gov. New York June 1753–*d.*

The Osborns acquired the manor and site of the dissolved priory of Chicksands in 1587.[1] Sir Danvers Osborn, who succeeded to the baronetcy as a child, was returned unopposed as a government supporter for the county in 1747 in succession to his brother-in-law, Sir Roger Burgoyne. The 2nd Lord Egmont in his electoral survey c.1749–50 marked him as 'to continue—not an improper man'. When he applied for a vacant place at the board of Green Cloth in 1752, Pelham described him as a 'very good man but I am afraid the Duke of Bedford would give him trouble in his re-election',[2] but the King 'knew nothing' of him,[3] so he was not appointed. Next year he vacated his seat on being made governor of New York, where he died by his own hand on 12 Oct. 1753,[4] a few days after his arrival.

[1] *VCH Beds.* ii. 271. [2] Pelham to Newcastle, 29 Sept. 1752, Add. 32729, f. 396. [3] Newcastle to Pelham, 12 Oct. 1752, Add. 32730, f. 74. [4] *Collectanea Top. et Gen.* iii. 127; *Bd. Trade Jnl.* 1750–3, p. 467.

R.S.L.

OSSULSTON, Lord, *see* BENNET, Charles

OSWALD, James (1715–69), of Dunnikier, Fife.

DYSART BURGHS 1741–1747
FIFESHIRE 1747–1754
DYSART BURGHS 1754–1768

b. 1715, 1st s. of Capt. James Oswald, M.P., of Dunnikier, provost of Kirkcaldy. *educ.* Kirkcaldy burgh sch.; Edinburgh Univ.; L. Inn 1733; Leyden 1733; Grand Tour; adv. 1738. *m.* 19 Jan. 1747, Elizabeth, da. of Joseph Townsend (q.v.), London brewer, wid. of Abraham Reynardson, cos. of Chauncy Townsend (q.v.), 1s. *suc.* fa. c.1725.

Burgess of Edinburgh 1742; commr. of the navy Dec. 1744–June 1747; ld. of Trade Dec. 1751–9, of Treasury 1759–63; P.C. 20 Apr. 1763; jt. vice-treasurer [I] 1763–7.

Oswald's father, a wealthy merchant, who purchased Dunnikier in 1703, established an independent interest in Dysart Burghs, for which Oswald himself was returned unopposed in 1741. He was expected to support Walpole but joined the Opposition, voting against the Government on the election of the chairman of the elections committee on 16 Dec. 1741. According to Horace Walpole:

> Sir R. [Walpole] sent a friend to reproach him; the moment the gentleman, who had engaged for him, came into the room, Oswald said, 'You had like to have led me into a fine error! Did you not tell me, that Sir Robert would have the majority?'[1]

'The surest way of becoming remarkable here', Oswald wrote on 7 Jan. 1742, 'is certainly application to business, for whoever understands it must make a figure.'[2] One of the group of Scotch Members known as the Duke of Argyll's gang, 'the flower of Kirkcaldy' became one of the principal opposition speakers on economic and naval affairs, signing the opposition appeal to supporters to be in town for the opening of the session 1743–4. He spoke for a motion to discontinue the Hanoverians in British pay, 6 Dec. 1743; against continuing British troops in Flanders for the next campaign, 11 Jan. 1744; for Lord Limerick's (q.v.) proposed duty on foreign linens instead of Pelham's proposal for a duty on sugar, 20 Feb. 1744; against the arrest of Lord Barrymore (q.v.) without the previous consent of the House, 28 Feb.; against the Austrian subsidy, 10 Apr. 1744, and for the amendments made by the Lords to the bill to make it high treason to correspond with the sons of the Pretender, 3 May.[3] His friend David Hume wrote, 4 Aug. 1744: 'He has shown me the whole economy of the navy, the source of the navy debt, with many other branches of public business. He seems to have a great genius for these affairs, and I fancy will go far in that way if he perseveres.'[4]

On the formation of the Broad-bottom Administration at the end of 1744 Oswald secured a commissionership of the navy. 'The office named for me is one of trouble and business', he wrote. 'It is a sort of apprenticeship indeed to the greatest scene of business in the country.'[5] It did not prevent him from attacking the Government's handling of the rebellion in a speech on 28 Aug. 1745, and the bill for abolishing hereditary jurisdictions in Scotland, 14 Apr. 1747.

In June 1747 Oswald resigned his office which, under the Place Act of 1742, was about to become incompatible with a seat in the Commons.

> I fear much he will not have a seat in the next Parliament [David Hume wrote] though it were a thousand pities. He sets out for Scotland in a few days with his wife, who seems to be a sensible woman but old and also dry and reserved . . . She keeps, as they say, all in her own power; so that, to tell truth, I am not excessively fond of this marriage, though he is. But if it were not for the advantage of its enabling him to throw up his office and continue in Parliament I wish him rather a bachelor.[6]

Contrary to expectations he was returned for Fife, though the Government's interest went to his opponent. At first he 'attended no court', devoting himself to the study of trade, finance and colonial affairs;[7] but in 1750 he connected himself with Bubb Dodington (q.v.), who found him 'entirely disposed to assist us', i.e. Dodington's party at Leicester House. In January 1751 he spoke against the Government on the question of a reduction in the number of seamen. In February Dodington, with Frederick's authority, sounded him as to his terms for entering the Prince's service. Oswald explained that he had just been approached by Pelham and

> offered to be made comptroller of the navy, with a promise of all Mr. Pelham's power to reform the abuses of it, and full liberty to follow his own opinion in Parliament . . . But as he saw no reform could be thoroughly and effectually brought about, but by the concurrence of the Crown, which was not to be hoped for in our present situation, he had much rather attach himself to his Royal Highness from whom only he could hope for that concurrence; but as he was no courtier and had no connexions of that kind, he must be contented to do his best in that station that was offered him.

He authorized Dodington to say 'that he would refuse all offers of the Court' if the Prince was willing to admit him into his service. This led to an audience with Frederick at which Oswald agreed to accept the office of clerk of the Green Cloth and 'to kiss hands on Lady day'.[8] In the 2nd Lord Egmont's

list of office holders in the next reign he is put down as secretary to the Admiralty or secretary to Prince George as lord high admiral. Meanwhile he took a prominent part in the opposition attacks on General Philip Anstruther (q.v.), in the course of which he showed himself

> a master of a quickness and strength of argument, not inferior to Fox or any speaker in the House. The rapidity of his eloquence was astonishing; not adorned but confined to business.

After the Prince's death Oswald re-opened negotiations with Pelham, who gave him a seat on the board of Trade. On 28 Feb. 1752 he spoke 'with fine warmth' for a bill empowering the Government to purchase forfeited estates in Scotland.[9]

He died 24 Mar. 1769.

[1] Walpole to Mann, 22 Jan. 1742. [2] Mems. of Jas. Oswald of Dunnikier, 13–15. [3] John Drummond to Ld. Morton, 2, 4, and 11 Dec. 1742, Morton mss, SRO; Yorke's parl. jnl. Parl. Hist. xiii. 140, 393, 654, 670, 702, 857. [4] Letters of David Hume (ed. J. Y. T. Greig), i. 58. [5] Mems. 39. [6] New Letters of David Hume, 28. [7] Caldwell Pprs. ii(1), pp. 93–107; Letters of David Hume, i. 142–4. [8] Dodington Diary, 80–88, 89, 90–93. [9] Walpole, Mems. Geo. II, i. 59, 226–7, 257.

E.H.-G./E.C.

OUGHTON, Adolphus (?1684–1736), of Fillongley and Tachbrook, Warws.

COVENTRY   1715–20 Nov. 1722
                11 Dec. 1722–4 Sept. 1736

b. ?1684, 1st s. of Adolphus Oughton of Fillongley by Mary, da. of Richard Samwell of Upton, Northants., aunt of Sir Thomas Samwell (q.v.). educ. Trinity, Oxf. 19 Mar. 1702, aged 17; M. Temple 1703. m. (1) c.1712, his cos. Frances (d.June 1714), da. of Sir Thomas Wagstaffe of Tachbrook by Frances, da. of Richard Samwell, wid. of Sir Edward Bagot, 4th Bt., M.P., of Blithfield, Staffs., s.p.; (2) Elizabeth, da. of John Baber by Mary, da. and coh. of Sir Thomas Draper, 1st Bt., of Sunninghill, Berks., s.p. suc. fa. 1684; cr. Bt. 27 Aug. 1718.

Capt. and lt.-col. 1 Ft. Gds. 1706; 1st maj. and col. Coldstream Gds. 1715, lt.-col. 1717; col. 8 Drag. Gds. 1733; brig.-gen. 1735.

Groom of the bedchamber to Prince of Wales Sept. 1714–Dec. 1717.

Oughton's family settled at Fillongley, near Coventry, soon after the Restoration. He served under Marlborough at Blenheim, Oudenarde and Menin,[1] accompanying him into exile as his aide de camp in 1712.[2] In 1714 he inherited from his first wife £5,000 and a lease of 25 years of Tachbrook,[3] where he generally resided. At the accession of George I he was given a place in the Prince's household. Returned as a Whig for Coventry in 1715 with his cousin Sir Thomas Samwell (q.v.), he voted for the septennial bill in 1716. The only member of the Prince's household who did not vote against Lord Cadogan (q.v.), he resigned his post, receiving a secret service payment of £500 from Sunderland in 1718.[4] He voted with the Administration on the repeal of the Occasional Conformity and Schism Acts but was absent from the division on the peerage bill in 1719. On 3 June 1721 he opposed a motion for allowing Jacob Sawbridge (q.v.) £10,000 out of his estates.

Oughton was again returned for Coventry in 1722, after a violent contest, leading to a duel in which he was wounded by Lord Craven, brother of Fulwar Craven, his Tory opponent. He was at this time said to be one of the chief advisers of General Cadogan (q.v.), who had succeeded Marlborough as head of the army.[5] Unseated on petition but re-elected, he was unopposed in 1727. He was absent from the divisions on the civil list in 1729, on the Hessians in 1730, and on the army in 1732, possibly because he was serving with his regiment in Ireland. The agitation against the excise bill in Coventry caused him to abstain from the division on the bill on 14 Mar. 1733, but on the committee stage of the bill two days later he was embarrassed by his fellow Member, John Neale, who declared that their constituents supported the bill. On 17 Mar. he wrote to Edward Hopkins (q.v.):

> This unexpected incident is very likely to lose me my Minorcan government, which by the way is near £2,000 p.a. and which I believe by this time I had been in possession of, had not this cursed excise affair intervened and made the usual court artifices be put upon me of keeping it open *in terrorem*. However, whilst I lay well intrenched behind the instructions of my constituents and kept myself in a state of neutrality I was pretty sure, by the assistance of my friends to have weathered the point; but this behaviour of my worthy coadjutor having beat me out of that fastness, that behaviour which before was in my behalf softened with the terms of prudence and circumspection, is now deemed the result of obstinacy and perverseness.

And on 3 Apr.

> on m'a mis le marché en mains, and if I do not vote for the wine bill at least . . . I must renounce all hopes and thoughts of any present or future recompense for all my life spent in the service, a hard lesson this.[6]

He did not get the post, though he voted with the Government on the repeal of the Septennial Act in 1734. Re-elected in 1734 he died 4 Sept. 1736, leaving an illegitimate son, James Adolphus Dickenson Oughton, who became a general in the army.

[1] *Verney Letters of 18th Cent.* i. 264, 267; *HMC 10th Rep. VI*, 186. [2] *Marlborough, Dispatches*, v. 579–80. [3] *Verney Letters*, i. 275. [4] Bonet's disp. 7/18 June 1717, Deutsches Zentral-archiv.; Sunderland (Blenheim) mss D.II, 4. [5] *HMC Portland*, v. 543; vii. 329. [6] Hopkins mss.

OWEN, Sir Arthur, 3rd Bt. (c.1674–1753), of Orielton, Pemb.

PEMBROKESHIRE	1695–1705
PEMBROKE BOROUGHS	1708–23 Feb. 1712
PEMBROKESHIRE	1715–1727

b. c.1674, 1st surv. s. of Sir Hugh Owen, 2nd Bt., M.P., of Orielton by Anne, da. and h. of Henry Owen of Bodeon, Anglesey. *m.* Emma, da. of Sir William Williams, 1st Bt., M.P., Speaker of the House of Commons 1678–81, 6s. 6da. *suc.* fa. 13 Jan. 1699.
Mayor, Pembroke 1705, 1706, 1707; ld. lt. Pembrokeshire and Haverfordwest 1715–*d.*; v.-adm. of N. Wales 1716.

Owen, whose family controlled Pembroke Boroughs, had a strong interest in the county, of which he was made lord lieutenant in 1715. Returned for Pembrokeshire as a Whig that year, he voted for the septennial bill in 1716, but against the repeal of the Occasional Conformity and Schism Acts in 1719, when he was absent from the division on the peerage bill. Losing his seat in 1727, he did not stand again. He died 6 June 1753.

P.D.G.T.

OWEN, John (?1698–1775), of Bath, Som.

WEST LOOE	20 Feb. 1735–1741

b. ?1698, 2nd s. of Sir Arthur Owen, 3rd Bt., and bro. of Sir William Owen, 4th Bt. (qq.v.). *educ.* Oriel, Oxf. 10 Nov. 1715, aged 17. *m.* 5 Nov. 1736, his cos. Anne, da. of Charles Owen of Nash, Pemb., 4s. 2da.
Ensign 3 Ft. 1725; lt. 1 Drags. 1726; capt. 12 Ft. 1730; capt. 7 Drags. 1738; lt. col. 12 Drags. 1748–60; col. 59 Ft. 1760–*d.*; maj.-gen. 1762; lt.-gen. 1772.[1]

Owen, an army officer, had been promised a seat by Walpole, to whom his elder brother wrote, 8 June 1734:

> I doubt not you have heard that Mr. Campbell [John, q.v.] had as quiet an election as could desire for the county of Pembroke, in which I think he'll not disown my endeavours to make it so, agreeable to your desire and proposal, by which you were to bring in my brother for East or West Looe, in which you were at present disappointed, but as I did not doubt but you would set the matter right in my brother's favour, I fully performed my promise. Had I acted otherwise he should have been chosen in Pembrokeshire, but I don't doubt your completing your proposal.[2]

Brought in for West Looe at the next by-election, he voted with the Administration on the Spanish convention, was absent from the division on the place bill, and did not stand again. He died 29 Dec. 1775.

[1] *N. & Q.* (ser. 12), ii. 392. [2] Cholmondeley (Houghton) mss.

E.C.   E.C.

OWEN, John (?1702–54), of Presaddfed, Anglesey.

ANGLESEY 1741–1747
BEAUMARIS 29 Jan. 1753–20 Feb. 1754

b. ?1702, 2nd s. of John Owen of Presaddfed by his 2nd w. Lettice, da. of David Williams of Glanalaw. *educ.* Jesus, Oxf. 16 Nov. 1719, aged 17. *unm. suc.* e. bro. William Owen at Presaddfed 1721.

The son of a successful lawyer, who bought an estate in Anglesey, Owen was returned in 1741 by an alliance between a group of Tory families and the local Whigs under his leadership against the Bulkeley interest.[1] In Parliament he voted consistently with the Opposition. Quarrelling with his Whig allies in 1747, he went over to the Bulkeleys, who in 1753 rewarded him with the Beaumaris seat vacated by the death of the 6th Lord Bulkeley (q.v.). He died 20 Feb. 1754, having been forced to sell most of his estate to meet his expenditure on the 1741 contest.

[1] See ANGLESEY.

P.D.G.T.

OWEN, William (?1697–1781), of Orielton, Pemb.

PEMBROKE BOROUGHS 13 Nov. 1722–1747
PEMBROKESHIRE 1747–1761
PEMBROKE BOROUGHS 1761–1774

b. ?1697, 1st s. of Sir Arthur Owen, 3rd Bt., and bro. of John Owen of Bath (qq.v.). *educ.* New Coll. Oxf. 16 June 1713, aged 16. *m.* (1) 12 Dec. 1725, Elizabeth, da. of Thomas Lloyd of Grove, Pemb., 1da.; (2) 26 July 1728, his cos. Anne (*d.*21 Dec. 1764), da. of John Williams of Chester, 2s. 2da. *suc.* fa. as 4th Bt. 6 June 1753.[1]
Ld. lt. Pemb. 1753–78.

Returned for Pembroke on the Orielton interest in 1722, Owen voted with the Administration in every recorded division. In a published list of the placemen who voted for the Spanish convention in 1739, he is shown as having 'two brothers captains of Dragoons and his third brother lieutenant in the Guards'.[2] He continued to represent Pembroke till 1747, when he was returned for both the boroughs and the county, choosing to sit for the latter. In 1753 he succeeded his father as lord lieutenant of Pembrokeshire, after writing to Newcastle:

I have received an account of my father's death who was . . . lieutenant and custos of the county of Pembroke and Haverfordwest and had some other grants . . . which obligeth me to trouble your Grace to beg your application to his Majesty for me to succeed my father . . . in which trusts no man can have his Majesty's interest and his administration more at heart.[3]

He died 7 May 1781.

[1] Ex inf. Cdr. C. H. H. Owen. [2] *Gent. Mag.* 1739, p. 306. [3] Add. 32732, f. 26.

P.W.

OXENDEN, Sir George, 5th Bt. (1694–1775), of Deane Court, Kent.

SANDWICH 9 May 1720–1754

b. 26 Oct. 1694, 2nd s. of George Oxenden, M.P., and bro. of Sir Henry Oxenden, 4th Bt. (q.v.). *educ.* Trinity Hall, Camb. 1710, fellow 1716–20. *m.* May 1720, Elizabeth, da. and coh. of Edmund Dunch (q.v.), 3s. 3da. *suc.* bro. 21 Apr. 1720.
Ld. of Admiralty 1725–7, of Treasury 1727–June 1737.

In 1720 Oxenden, on the death of his brother, succeeded to the baronetcy, married an heiress and was returned to Parliament for Sandwich on his family's interest. He moved the Address on 20 Oct. 1721. On 12 Feb. 1725 he moved for the impeachment of Lord Chancellor Macclesfield, of whose trial he was chosen one of the managers, opening it 'with many flowers and some sharpness'.[1] Appointed a lord of the Admiralty at the end of the same session, he became a lord of the Treasury at George II's accession. On 7 May 1728 a debate on the King's message for a special supply to meet foreign engagements was

opened by Sir George Oxenden, who did it very awkwardly, by calling for an opposition, and saying that gentlemen who were for supplying his Majesty were usually treated as if they were giving up the constitution of Parliament by giving up the undoubted right of giving money.

When he moved the Address on 21 Jan. 1729

he was out once or twice, and would have been more but that [Edward] Thompson [q.v.] had his speech wrote out in his hat, and sat next him and prompted him.[2]

Horace Walpole describes him at this stage of his career as

the fine gentleman of the age, extremely handsome, a speaker in Parliament, a lord of the Treasury, very ambitious, and a particular favourite of my father—till he became so of my sister-in-law. That, and a worse story, blasted all his prospects and buried him in retirement.[3]

The first of these scandals is referred to by the 1st Lord Egmont (q.v.), commenting on a report at the beginning of 1732 that Oxenden's town and country houses and their contents had been seized for debt:

Sir George Oxenden is a proud, conceited, lewd man but one would think an estate of £2,500 a year, and the post of lord of the Treasury, would have kept men out of gaol, from whence now it is only his being a Member of Parliament that does it. Sir Robert Walpole was his patron, and gave him the great employment he has, and in return he got the lady of my Lord Walpole, Sir Robert's son, with child, and this unlawful issue will inherit the estate.

In 1734 Oxenden joined Lord Middlesex (q.v.) in contesting Kent; both were defeated, but Oxenden was returned for Sandwich.[4] Later in the year he became involved in a further scandal. According to Hervey:

> He had had two children by his wife's sister, who was married to his most intimate friend, Mr. Thompson, from whom, upon Sir George Oxenden's account, she was separated, and died in childbed not without Sir George's being suspected of having a greater share in her catastrophe than merely having got the child.

He continued in office till 1737, when he was dismissed for voting against the Government on the Prince of Wales's allowance, after learning that he was in any case going to be turned out for neglect of his duties. 'Nobody was sorry for him', Hervey writes, 'for he was a very vicious, ungrateful, good-for-nothing fellow. He passed his whole life in all manner of debauchery and with low company'.[5] He spoke against the Government on the navy estimates, 1 Feb. 1740, but voted against the motion for Walpole's dismissal in February 1741. Though opposed by the Government at Sandwich in 1741, he not only retained his seat but brought in a friend for the other. Attaching himself to the Prince of Wales, who gave his eldest son a place in his household, he voted with the rest of the Leicester House party for the Hanoverian troops in 1742 and 1744. Speaking on Pitt's promotion to be paymaster general in May 1746 he said that the ministry had

> made more fuss and racket with one repenting sinner in the House of Commons than with the ninety-nine honest Members whose actions are so just to the Crown as not to call for repentance, unless it be when they see a notorious sinner exalted above them.[6]

In 1747, when Oxenden was re-elected unopposed on a compromise with the Government, the Prince offered to pay young Oxenden's election expenses at Ludgershall,[7] but in 1749 he turned him out. Next year Oxenden made overtures to Pelham, intimating that 'a place for his son would be very convenient', to which Pelham replied that he would do what he could, but that 'the King like other men', had his 'prejudices' and it was 'not easy to wipe them off'.[8] In 1754 Oxenden told Newcastle that he would be willing to resign his seat to any person whom Newcastle recommended in return for a place in the revenue for his son of about £500 a year. Newcastle 'would give no promise but encouraged him to hope for such an employment for his son, he having been turned out by the late Prince of Wales'. A commissionership of excise or customs appears to have been contemplated.[9] Oxenden duly gave up his seat at Sandwich but his son never received a place, a year later marrying the daughter and heiress of Sir George Chudleigh 'with £50,000'.[10]

After retiring from Parliament Oxenden continued to take an active interest in East Kent politics, about which he corresponded with Newcastle during the general election of 1761.[11]

He died 20 Jan. 1775.

[1] *HMC Portland*, vi. 4. [2] *Knatchbull Diary*. [3] To Lady Upper Ossory, 1 Sept. 1780. [4] *HMC Egmont Diary*, i. 213; ii. 101-2. [5] Hervey, *Mems.* 741-2; *HMC Egmont Diary*, ii. 360. [6] *HMC 8th Rep.* pt. 2, p. 111. [7] *HMC Fortescue*, i. 118. [8] Pelham to Newcastle, 3 Aug. 1750, Add. 32722, f. 26. [9] Add. 32995, ff. 98, 186, 258. [10] *HMC Hastings*, iii. 105. [11] Namier, *Structure*, 67 n. 1, 101, 114, 414.

R.R.S.

OXENDEN, Sir Henry, 4th Bt. (c.1690–1720), of Deane Court, Kent.

SANDWICH 1713–21 Apr. 1720

b. c.1690, 1st s. of George Oxenden, M.P., master of Trinity Hall, Camb., by Elizabeth, da. of Sir Basil Dixwell, 1st Bt., M.P., of Broome, Kent; gd.-s. of Sir Henry Oxenden, 1st Bt., M.P. *educ.* Trinity Hall, Camb. 1705. *m.* 27 July 1712, Anne, da. of John Holloway of Oxford, barrister, *s.p. suc.* fa. 1703; uncle, Sir Henry Oxenden, 3rd Bt., Feb. 1709.

During the seventeenth century the Oxendens, an old Kent family, had provided Members for Sandwich. Returned as a Whig for Sandwich on the family interest, Oxenden voted with the Administration on the septennial bill in 1716 but was absent from the division on the repeal of the Occasional Conformity and Schism Acts in 1719. In a list drawn up by Craggs before the peerage bill in 1719 he is put down as to be approached on behalf of the Government by Josiah Burchett (q.v.), but he did not vote in the division on the bill. He died 21 Apr. 1720.

P.W.

PACEY, Henry (c.1669–1729), of Boston, Lincs.

BOSTON 1722–10 Dec. 1729

b. c.1669, 1st s. of Richard Pacey of Bolingbroke and West Keal, Lincs., yeoman, by Catherine, da. of Col. John Butler of Hundelby, Lincs. *m.* (1) Elizabeth (*d.* 3 Apr. 1716), da. and h. of William Packharness of Freston, Lincs., 6s. 3da.; (2) Cassandra Pindar of Kempley, Glos., 1s. *suc.* fa. 1691.
Receiver of land tax for part of Lincs. 1711; mayor, Boston 1708, 1720, dep. recorder 1709-15, 1724-7; judge of Admiralty, Boston 1711.[1]

Descended from a family of Lincolnshire yeomen, Pacey owned property in Boston, which he successfully contested in 1722 as a Tory. In the county election of 1723 he 'made all the interest he could' for the Tory candidate, Sir Neville Hickman.[2] He voted against the Administration on the civil list arrears in April, and died 10 Dec. 1729.

[1] P. Thompson, *Hist. Boston*, 456, 459. [2] Letter from W. Johnson, 15 Dec. 1724, Spalding Gentlemen's Soc. mss.

P.W.

PACKER, Robert (aft. 1675–1731), of Shellingford and Donnington, Berks.

BERKSHIRE   23 July 1712–4 Apr. 1731

> b. aft. 1675, o.s. of John Packer of Shellingford by Elizabeth,[1] da. of Richard Stephens of Eastington, Glos. m. 27 Feb. 1700, Mary, da. and coh. of Sir Henry Winchcombe, 2nd Bt., M.P., of Bucklebury, Berks., sis. of Frances, Viscountess Bolingbroke, 4s. 1da. suc. fa. 1687.
> Sheriff, Berks. 1708–9.

Packer was the great-grandson of John Packer, M.P., who bought the manor of Shellingford in 1620 and later that of Donnington.[2] Entering Parliament at a by-election in 1712 on the elevation of his brother-in-law, Henry St. John, to the peerage, he was returned unopposed in 1715 and after contests in 1722 and 1727, voting consistently against the Government. His name was sent to the Pretender in 1721 as a Jacobite supporter.[3] A letter to Lord Harley (q.v.), 14 Dec. 1725, describes him and his son (q.v.) as 'helpless creatures' for not standing up to Bolingbroke, who had cut down all the hedges and trees at Bucklebury, which his son had inherited as a minor. 'A man of sense and spirit would make him fly his country once more'. The letter also refers to 'poor Packer's weakness and inactivity'.[4] He died 4 Apr. 1731.

[1] Marriage Lics. Vic. Gen. (Harl. Soc. xxiii), 248. [2] A. L. Humphreys, Bucklebury, ped. facing p. 322; VCH Berks. iv. 92, 476. [3] Stuart mss 65/16. [4] HMC Portland, vii, 409–11.

R.S.L.

PACKER, Winchcomb Howard (1702–46), of Donnington and Shellingford, Berks.

BERKSHIRE   5 May 1731–21 Aug. 1746

> b. 20 Nov. 1702, 1st s. of Robert Packer (q.v.) of Shellingford and Donnington. educ. Westminster c.1715–17. unm. suc. to Bucklebury estate of his aunt Frances, Viscountess Bolingbroke 1718; fa. 1731.

Although Lady Bolingbroke made Winchcomb Packer, then a minor, her heir, he and his father had to face much opposition at Bucklebury both from the Crown, owing to Bolingbroke's attainder, and from Bolingbroke himself, claiming as life tenant thereof, after his restoration and return to England in 1725.[1] Entering Parliament as a Tory at a by-election in 1731 on his father's death, he voted consistently against the Government. In 1738 he obtained an Act of Parliament under which he sold Shellingford to Sarah, Duchess of Marlborough, who had engaged support for the bill from her grandson, John Spencer (q.v.), the ultimate beneficiary.[2] He died 21 Aug. 1746.

[1] VCH Berks. iii. 292; A. L. Humphreys, Bucklebury, 322; see PACKER, Robert. [2] VCH Berks. iv. 476; Duchess of Marlborough to Packer, 19 Apr. 1738, Berks. RO, D/EHy.

R.S.L.

PAGE, Sir Gregory, 1st Bt. (c.1668–1720), of Greenwich.

NEW SHOREHAM   18 Dec. 1708–1713
                1715–25 May 1720

> b. c.1668, 1st s. of Gregory Page of Wapping, Mdx. by his 2nd w. Elizabeth Burton of Stepney, wid. m. (lic. 21 Jan. 1690, aged 21) Mary, da. of Thomas Trotman of London, 2s. 2da. suc. fa. 1693; cr. Bt. 3 Dec. 1714.
> Director, E.I. Co. 1709–d., chairman, 1716.

According to the 1st Lord Egmont, Page 'had been a drayman [?dragoman] to Sir Charles Ayres of Kew Green, but being a man of parts rose to be a director of the East India Company and knight baronet.'[1] Sir Charles Ayres, i.e. Sir Charles Eyre, was an officer of the East India Company, who ended his career as the first president of Bengal, 1699–1700, while Page's father was a shipwright and shipowner, with a brewhouse in Wapping, of sufficient standing to be one of the aldermen nominated by the Crown to the corporation of London in 1687.[2] Page, who is described in his marriage licence as a brewer, made a great fortune as a shipowner, trading with China and the East Indies.[3] Re-elected in 1715 as a Whig for Shoreham, where the chief industry was shipbuilding, he voted with the Government, except on the peerage bill in 1719, when he was absent from the division. In that year he was one of the directors of the East India Company who attended a meeting of the Treasury board to consider a report by the board of Trade supporting demands from the woollen industry for protection against the importation of stained calicoes from India. Giving evidence, he said that

> if a prohibition upon the stained calicoes takes place, all the Company's settlements on the coast of Coromandel, which depend upon the fabric of calico, must be ruined, and instead of such prohibition being an advantage to the weavers, it will let in all the stained and striped linens from Hamburg and Holland, which are more expensive and less lasting than those made here, as was the case upon the prohibition in 1701.[4]

In the end an Act prohibiting the wearing of stained calicoes was passed in 1721.

Page died 25 May 1720, leaving his elder son an 'immense fortune . . . which some made to amount to £5, 6, or 700,000', besides legacies totalling nearly £100,000 to his wife and other children. In an unprinted marginal note to an account of an alleged attempt by this son to commit suicide in 1736, Egmont states that the story was 'a scandalous lie, as afterwards appeared'.[5]

[1] HMC Egmont Diary, ii. 251. [2] Marriage Lics. Vic. Gen. 1660–8 (Harl .Soc. xxxiii), 197; Cal. Treas. Bks. ii. 176; v. 1117; viii. 1998;

Beaven, *Aldermen of London*, i. 164; PCC 61 Box. ³ *Marriage Lics. Vic. Gen.* 1687–94 (Harl. Soc. xxxi), 131; *CSP Dom.* 1702–3, p. 428; *Cal. Treas. Bks.* xxi. 85. ⁴ *Cal. Treas. Pprs.* 1714–19, p. 487. ⁵ *HMC Egmont Diary*, loc. cit.; PCC 52 Shaller.

R.R.S.

PAGE, John (?1696–1779), of Watergate House, nr. Chichester, Suss.

GREAT GRIMSBY   1727–1734
CHICHESTER   1741–1768

b. ?1696, s. of Edward Page of Chichester by his w. Mary. *m.* (1) Catherine (*d.*1736), da. of Robert Knight, cashier of the South Sea Co., sis. of Robert Knight (q.v.), 1st Earl of Catherlough [I], 1da.; (2) 25 June 1741, Anne, da. and h. of Francis Soane of Stockbridge, nr. Chichester, 1da. who m. George White Thomas, M.P.

Director, E.I. Co. 1730–2; dep. paymaster gen. 1755–7; searcher of customs, Chester and Liverpool 1761–*d.*

Page came of an old Sussex family, resident at Donnington, near Chichester.[1] He began life as an employee in the South Sea Company,[2] marrying the daughter of its cashier, Robert Knight, who absconded in the 1720 crisis. About 1726 he retired and bought the manor of Donnington,[3] settling down as a country gentleman.

At the 1727 general election Page was returned on the Knight interest for Great Grimsby, which he had contested unsuccessfully in 1722. In Parliament he took an independent line, voting with the Administration on the civil list arrears in 1729 but against them on the Hessians in 1730; abstaining on the army in 1732 and the excise bill in 1733; and voting with the Opposition for the repeal of the Septennial Act in 1734. He was one of '20 friends of the Court' who did not vote on a place bill, which was warmly opposed by the Administration in 1734, leaving the House before the question was put 'because he could not oppose so reasonable and popular a bill'.[4] He became a member of the gaols committee and of the council of the Georgia Society, of which he was also an original trustee.[5]

In 1734 Page gave up his Grimsby seat to his brother-in-law, Robert Knight (q.v.), to stand on his own interest for Chichester, where he came out bottom of the poll. By 1741 however, his interest was so strong that he was returned for Chichester against the wishes of the Duke of Richmond,[6] who wrote to Newcastle, referring to Page's protestations of loyalty to Walpole: 'I am convinced Page must either deceive Sir Robert or be the vilest of men for it is notorious how publicly he abuses Sir Robert every day', adding later, 'I am sure we won't have Page without buying him'.[7] A few months later he married as his second wife the daughter of an

influential Chichester alderman, after which he was invariably re-elected without opposition.

At the beginning of the new Parliament Page was regarded as a doubtful supporter of the Government. He did not vote on the chairman of the elections committee nor was he included in the Cockpit list of ministerial supporters in October 1742, but thereafter he voted with the Administration in all recorded divisions. Classed in the next Parliament as a government supporter, he remained faithful to Newcastle till the Duke's death in 1768, when he himself retired from Parliament. He died 26 Jan. 1779.

¹ *VCH Suss.* iv. 150. ² Namier, *England in the Age of the American Rev.* 34. ³ *VCH Suss.* ⁴ *HMC Egmont Diary*, ii. 37. ⁵ Ibid. i. 55, 344; ii. 471; iii. 34. ⁶ See CHICHESTER. ⁷ Add. 32696, ff. 6, 20.

A.N.N.

PAGET, Thomas (c.1685–1741).

ILCHESTER   11 Dec. 1722–1727

b. c.1685, o. surv. s. of Hon. Henry Paget (2nd s. of William, 6th Lord Paget) by his 2nd w. Mary, da. of Col. Hugh O'Rorke, sheriff of co. Leitrim, Ireland. *m.* Mary, da. and coh. of Peter Whitcombe of Great Braxted, Essex, 1da.

Capt. and lt.-col. 1 Ft. Gds. 1711; lt.-col. 1 tp. Horse Gren. Gds. 1715; col. 32 Ft. 1732–8, 22 Ft. 1738–*d.*; brig.-gen. 1739; groom of the bedchamber to George II as Prince of Wales and King 1714–*d.*; dep. gov. Minorca 1741–*d.*

Paget contested Ilchester unsuccessfully as a Government supporter in 1722, but was returned for it shortly afterwards on petition.[1] He did not stand again. He died in Minorca,[2] 28 May 1741.

¹ See ILCHESTER. ² PCC Admon. Mar. 1742.

S.R.M.

PAGET, Thomas Catesby, Lord Paget (1689–1742).

STAFFORDSHIRE   1715–1727

b. 1689, 1st surv. s. of Henry Paget, M.P., 1st Earl of Uxbridge, by Mary, da. and coh. of Thomas Catesby of Whiston, Northants. *educ.* Trinity, Oxf. 1707. *m.* 6 May 1718, Lady Elizabeth Egerton, da. of John Egerton, M.P., 3rd Earl of Bridgwater, 2s.

Gent. of the bedchamber to Prince of Wales, 1719–27; ld. of the bedchamber 1727–36.

At George I's accession Paget's father, a Hanoverian Tory, who had represented Staffordshire 1695–1712, adhered to the Whig government. Rewarded with an earldom at the coronation, he put up Paget for Staffordshire, asking Lord Gower, the leading local Tory, to 'be merciful to the young man at first setting out, and not exert his interest to the utmost'.[1] Returned unopposed, Paget voted with the Opposition, except on Lord Cadogan (q.v.), speaking against the septennial bill. Appointed to the Prince of Wales's household in 1719, he was again returned without a contest in 1722. In 1727 he gave up Staffordshire to contest Middlesex as a Whig but was defeated and never stood again. He resigned his post at court in 1736 owing to ill-health, which prevented him from performing his duties.[2]

Horace Walpole records that 'in the intervals of bad weather in hunting seasons', Paget 'published some pieces, particularly *An Essay on Human Life* in verse 1734, quarto; *Some reflections upon the Administration of Government*, a pamphlet in 1740', adding: 'in both these pieces there is much good sense, the former is written in imitation of Pope's Ethic Epistles, and has good lines, but not much poetry'.[3]

Paget died 4 Feb. 1742, and was buried in Westminster Abbey.

[1] *HMC 5th Rep.* 188. [2] *Cal. Treas. Bks. and Pprs.* 1735–8, p. 220; *HMC Bath*, ii. 182. [3] *Catalogue of Royal and Noble Authors* (1758), ii. 131.

E.C.

PAKINGTON, Sir Herbert Perrott, 5th Bt. (c.1701–48), of Westwood, nr. Droitwich, Worcs.

WORCESTERSHIRE 1727–1741

b c.1701, o. surv. s. of Sir John Pakington, 4th Bt. (q.v.), being o.s. by his 2nd w. *m.* 22 June 1721, Elizabeth, da. of John Conyers, K.C., of Walthamstow, Essex, 2s. 2da. *suc.* fa. 13 Aug. 1727.

Pakington succeeded his father as a Tory for Worcestershire in 1727. Re-elected unopposed in 1734, he voted against the Administration in all recorded divisions except on the motion for the removal of Walpole in February 1741. He did not stand again and died 24 Sept. 1748.

R.S.L.

PAKINGTON, Sir John, 4th Bt. (1671–1727), of Westwood, nr. Droitwich, Worcs.

WORCESTERSHIRE 1690–1695, 1698–1727

b. 16 Mar. 1671, o.s. of Sir John Pakington, 3rd Bt., M.P., by Margaret, da. of Sir John Keyt, 1st Bt., of Ebrington, Glos. *educ.* St. John's, Oxf. 1688. *m.* (1) lic. 28 Aug. 1691, Frances, da. of Sir Henry Parker, 2nd Bt., M.P., of Honington, Warws., 4s. *d.v.p.* 3da.; (2) lic. 26 Aug. 1700, Hester, da. and h. of Sir Herbert Perrott, M.P., of Haroldston, Pemb., 1s. *suc.* fa. Mar. 1688.
Recorder, Worcester 1726–d.

Sir John Pakington, a well-known Tory and member of the October Club, whose father and grandfather had both represented Worcestershire, was himself returned for the county for the tenth time in 1715, voting against the Administration in all recorded divisions of that Parliament. Although the greater part of his estates lay in Worcestershire,

he was also lord of the manor of Aylesbury, where he had been returned in 1702, but in later life he does not seem to have exercised electoral influence in that borough. On 21 Sept. 1715 the House of Commons agreed to his arrest, with Sir William Wyndham (q.v.) and other Tories, on the ground that he was engaged in a design to support the Pretender's intended invasion;[1] but though forewarned, he made no attempt to escape and was able to prove his innocence before the Privy Council.[2] A year later James Stanhope (q.v.) learned from Lord Townshend that Pakington was promoting a complimentary address from his county to the Prince of Wales during the King's absence.[3] Speaking against the peerage bill in December 1719 Pakington

> enumerated what had been done in every session for the Crown, and at the end of each sentence concluded, who was this done by? Why surely by the House of Commons against whom the door of the House of Peers is to be now shut, and why? Why truly to screen two noble dukes and advance half-a-dozen of our members; when that was done, all would be safe.[4]

In 1721 his name was sent as a probable supporter in the event of a rising to the Pretender, who, the following year, thanked him for his 'zeal and readiness to serve me'.[5] Returned for the last time in 1722, he alone opposed the re-election of the Speaker, Spencer Compton (q.v.), in

> a very reflecting speech upon him without any provocation, complaining he was never invited to dinner by him or the Green Cloth all the last Parliament, took notice of his great places and that he might possibly pass his accounts [as paymaster of the forces abroad] by privy seal as his predecessor, meaning Lord Chandos, had done, took notice there was no necessity of having men of great parts in the Chair, provided they had nothing in view but the service of the House, and that it was preposterous to go to plough with a razor.[6]

He died soon after the dissolution of Parliament, 13 Aug. 1727.

[1] *CJ*, xviii. 325. [2] *A Full and Authentick Narrative of the intended horrid Conspiracy and Invasion* (1715), pp. 19–21. [3] Coxe, *Walpole*, ii. 75. [4] Thos. Brodrick to Ld. Midleton, 10 Dec. 1719, Brodrick mss. [5] Stuart mss 65/16, 63/151. [6] *Knatchbull Diary*, 9 Oct. 1722.

R.S.L.

PALMER, Sir Geoffry, 3rd Bt. (1655–1732), of Carlton Curlieu, Leics.

LEICESTERSHIRE 1708–1713, 5 Aug. 1714–1722

b. 12 June 1655, 1st s. of Sir Lewis Palmer, 2nd Bt., M.P., by Jane, da. and coh. of Robert Palmer of Carlton Scroop, Lincs. *educ.* Trinity, Camb. 1672. *m.* Elizabeth, da. and coh. of Thomas Grantham of Goltho, Lincs., and Rievaulx Abbey, Yorks., *s.p. suc.* fa. 1714.

Palmer was the grandson of Sir Geoffry Palmer,

a staunch royalist, who was made attorney-general, and created a baronet at the Restoration. Re-elected as a Tory for Leicestershire in 1715 after two expensive contests,[1] he voted against the Administration in all recorded divisions, but did not stand again. He died 29 Dec. 1732.

[1] *Verney Letters of 18th Cent.* i. 329, 332–3.

E.C.

PALMER, Peregrine (?1703–62), of Fairfield, Stoke Courcy, Som.

OXFORD UNIVERSITY   12 Nov. 1745–30 Nov. 1762

b. ?1703, 2nd s. of Nathaniel Palmer, M.P., and bro. of Thomas Palmer (q.v.). *educ.* Balliol, Oxf. 3 July 1719, aged 16; All Souls 1727. *m.* da and h. of one Longman, *s.p. suc.* to Fairfield estates on d. of his sis.-in-law 1737.

In 1737 Palmer inherited Fairfield from his sister-in-law, who expressed in her will the hope that he would live there, marry, and have children 'to enjoy what little is left'.[1] At a by-election for Oxford University in the same year he and Edward Butler (q.v.) were the rival Tory candidates for the vacancy; but when on canvassing the Tory vote it was found that Butler had a great majority, 'Palmer went at the head of his own friends and voted for the doctor.'[2] On Butler's death in 1745 he was returned for the university, which he represented unopposed for the rest of his life. The 2nd Lord Egmont in his electoral survey c.1749–50 describes him as 'an honest plain man, much affected with the gout, and wont attend often, a Tory but I believe will be with us'. His only recorded vote was against the Hanoverians in 1746. He died 30 Nov. 1762, leaving £500 to All Souls.[3]

[1] *Somerset Wills*, iii. 89. [2] *HMC 10th Rep. I*, 490. [3] W. R. Ward, *Georgian Oxford*, 224.

R.R.S.

PALMER, Sir Thomas, 4th Bt. (1682–1723), of Wingham, Kent.

KENT   1708–1710
ROCHESTER   1715–8 Nov. 1723

bap. 5 July 1682, 1st s. of Herbert Palmer by Dorothy, da. of John Pincheon of Writtle, Essex; gd.-s. of Sir Thomas Palmer, 2nd Bt. *educ.* Canterbury and Sutton sch. in Kent; Caius, Camb. 1699. *m.* (1) 18 Nov. 1700, Elizabeth (*bur.* 29 July 1714), da. of Sir Robert Marsham, 4th Bt., M.P., sis. of Robert Marsham (q.v.), 1st Baron Romney, 3s. 4da., of whom 3s. and 1da. *d.v.p.* and *s.p.*; (2) Susanna Cox (?wid.) (*bur.* 15 Jan. 1721), 1 illegit. s.; (3) Elizabeth, wid. of (i) one Jolly, (ii) George Markham of Nettleham, Lincs.,[1] 1da. *suc.* fa. 1700; uncle Sir Henry Palmer, 3rd Bt., 19 Sept. 1706.

Commr. for stating army debts 1715–?20.

Returned on the Admiralty interest for Roches-

ter, Palmer consistently supported the Administration, speaking for the repeal of the Occasional Conformity and Schism Acts 7 Jan. 1719. 'A man of pleasure and very extravagant in all things', he died 8 Nov. 1723, leaving 'his estate, which was not settled on his daughters, to Herbert Palmer his [illegitimate] son'.[2]

[1] *Canterbury Marriage Lics.* (ser. 5) 1701–25, p. 311. [2] *Misc. Gen. et Her.* i. 118.

A.N.N.

PALMER, Thomas (?1685–1735), of Fairfield, Stoke Courcy, nr. Bridgwater, Som.

BRIDGWATER   1715–1727
                    5 Feb. 1731–16 Mar. 1735

b. ?1685, 1st s. of Nathaniel Palmer, M.P., of Fairfield by Frances, da. of Sir William Wyndham, 2nd Bt., M.P.; bro. of Peregrine Palmer (q.v.). *educ.* New Coll. Oxf. 10 Oct. 1700, aged 15; M. Temple 1702, *m.* Elizabeth, da. and coh. of Sir Thomas Wroth, 3rd Bt., M.P., of Petherton Park, nr. Bridgwater Som., *s.p. suc.* fa. 1717.

Recorder, Bridgwater, c.1720–34.

Palmer, whose family had been settled in Somerset since the sixteenth century,[1] was returned for Bridgwater in succession to his father, who had represented the county, Minehead, and Bridgwater on the Tory interest in most Parliaments between James II's and George I's accessions. Himself a Tory, his name was included in a list of supposed sympathizers sent to the Pretender in 1721.[2] His only recorded speech in his first Parliament was made on 10 June 1721 in favour of allowing John Aislabie (q.v.) to keep as much of his fortune as he possessed before the South Sea bill was introduced.

In 1722 Palmer was at first reported to be putting up for the county[3] but in the end he stood again for Bridgwater, where he was returned after a contest. In this Parliament he spoke against an augmentation of the army, 26 Oct. 1722, and in support of a petition from one of the Atterbury conspirators for the postponement of the second reading of a bill of pains and penalties against him, 27 Mar. 1723. He was one of the managers of Lord Chancellor Macclesfield's impeachment in 1725. In 1727 he supported amendments to an address condemning a memorial published by the imperial minister against the Government,[4] and spoke against a vote of credit, 12 Apr., and against diverting the surplus of certain duties from the sinking fund to fund a new loan, 26 Apr.

Palmer did not stand in 1727, but was returned at a by-election in 1731, when he spoke against taking off the duty on Irish yarn and against a bill for naturalizing children born abroad of British fathers. In a debate on 3 Apr. 1732, when many of the opposition expressed the hope that Hanover would one day be under some other power, he said that

> the provinces of Bremen and Verden must one day
> . . . be annexed to the crown of Great Britain . . .
> They are not to be esteemed accessions to Hanover
> . . . but accessions to Britain. Till this be done, the
> crown of England will be at eternal charges to defend
> those provinces, all our treaties and motions will have
> a tendency and direction to their preservation, and
> the mind of English subjects never easy to their
> Prince.

As a member of the select committee of inquiry into the frauds of the Charitable Corporation, he made a 'very eloquent and moving speech' condemning Sir Robert Sutton (q.v.), one of the directors of the Corporation. In the next session he repeated his attack on Sutton, opposed a lottery for the relief of the victims of the frauds, and proposed instead a grant confined to hard cases, belonging to 'the fair sex'. In the same session he also spoke in favour of a reduction in the army, against the diversion of £500,000 from the sinking fund to current services, and against the excise bill.[5] In 1734 he opposed a small increase in the army and 'spoke himself sick' against an address authorizing an increase in the forces during the recess if necessary.[6]

Palmer did not stand in 1734 but at a pre-election meeting of Somerset country gentlemen he 'distinguished himself so remarkably' by extolling the merits of the family of Lord Hinton (afterwards Earl Poulett), a Whig, who had offered himself to the meeting as a candidate, 'that it has lost him some of the esteem many of the gentlemen had for him'. In the end he 'found it necessary to send to those manors where he had an interest to secure them' for a Tory candidate.[7]

Palmer died 16 Mar. 1735, leaving a projected history of Somerset unfinished.[8] After making provision for various members of his family, he left the residue of his estate to his wife, thinking himself 'in conscience obliged to make her the best return I can, which is to give her the entire possession of an estate redeemed by her own generosity'. In his will he further left directions that his body should be opened in the presence of his medical advisers so 'that the calamitous illness which I have been so long afflicted with, and to which all the persons I have applied to have neither been able to find the cause or the cure, may after my death be of use to some other unhappy persons who may be in the same condition, and may be helped by the knowledge.'[9]

[1] Collinson, *Som.* i. 254. [2] Stuart mss 65/16. [3] *HMC Portland* vii. 300. [4] *Knatchbull Diary*, 67–68 [5] *HMC Egmont Diary*, i. 177, 187,

253, 267, 368; Stuart mss 160/46; *HMC Carlisle*, 105. [6] *HMC Egmont Diary*, ii. 24, 72, 74. [7] *HMC Portland*, vi. 47–48. [8] *HMC 6th Rep.* 346. [9] *Som. Wills*, ii. 88.

S.R.M.

PALMERSTON, Visct., *see* **TEMPLE, Henry**

PANMURE, Earl of, *see* **MAULE, William**

PAPILLON, David (1691–1762), of Acrise, Kent.

NEW ROMNEY	1722–29 Apr. 1728
	13 May 1728–1734
DOVER	1734–1741

b. 1691, 1st s. of Philip Papillon (q.v.) by his 1st w. *educ.* Morland's sch. Bethnal Green, London; I. Temple 1706, called 1715, bencher 1744; Utrecht 1707–9; Grand Tour (Germany) 1709. *m.* 1717, Mary, da. of Timothy Keyser, merchant, of London, 3s. 6da. *suc.* fa. 1736.

Commr. of excise 1742–54.

David Papillon, a practising lawyer, was brought in for New Romney as part of the arrangement under which his father surrendered his seat in 1720. During the contested election of 1727, when he was opposed by Sir Robert Austen and John Essington (qq.v.), he wrote:

> It is truly an unhappy circumstance to be thus treated
> as a common nuisance to two such powers and could
> I think how to avoid it and at the same time not be
> sunk into the lowest degree of being despised, I would
> most willingly . . and though I should like being in
> Parliament yet too many enemies is not to be wished.[1]

He was unseated on petition but one of the successful candidates made his election elsewhere and Papillon filled this vacancy. In Parliament he voted consistently with the Administration except on the civil list arrears in 1729. He spoke 17 Feb. 1731 for the place bill; 10 Mar 1732 for a bill to prevent the export of New England hops to Ireland duty free; and 13 Apr. 1732 on a bill to prevent the manufacture of hats in the colonies.[2]

In 1734 Papillon successfully contested both New Romney and Dover on the government interest against the Furneses (qq.v.), choosing to sit for Dover. He gave up his seat to the Sackville family in 1741, in return for a commissionership of excise, which he retained till 1754 when, through the good offices of his schoolfellow and lifelong friend, Lord Hardwicke,[3] he arranged for it to be transferred to his son. He died 26 Feb. 1762.

[1] David Papillon to Sir Philip Yorke, 1 Aug. 1727, Add. 35585, f. 71. [2] *HMC Egmont Diary*, i. 134, 235, 256. [3] Yorke, *Hardwicke*, i. 51, 57; ii. 563.

P.W.

PAPILLON, Philip (1660–1736), of Fenchurch St., London, and Acrise, nr. Dover, Kent.

DOVER   1701–Aug. 1720

b. 26 Nov. 1660, 1st surv. s. of Thomas Papillon, M.P., of Dover and London by Jane, da. of Thomas Brodnax of Godmersham, Kent. *m.* (1) 10 Sept. 1689, Anne (*d.* 1693), da. of William Jolliffe of Caverswall Castle, Staffs., 1s. 2da.; (2) 1695, Susannah, da. of George Henshaw, 2s. 3da. *suc.* fa. 1702.
    Cashier of victualling 1689–99; receiver of the stamp duties 1720–?1723.

The son of Thomas Papillon, exclusionist, East India merchant, and commissioner for victualling the navy, who represented Dover in every Parliament but one from 1673 to 1695, Philip Papillon was returned as a Whig for Dover on his family's interest for nearly twenty years, from 1715 consistently supporting the Government. He resigned his seat in 1720 for a receivership of the stamp duties,[1] but in 1727 stood again for Dover to 'prove that it was a reality which he [had] sacrificed'[2] in 1720. He was defeated and did not stand again.

He died 12 Sept. 1736.

[1] See DOVER. [2] David Papillon to Sir Philip Yorke, 1 Aug. 1727, Add. 35585, f. 71.

A.N.N.

PARGITER FULLER, Samuel (c.1690–1722), of Westminster, and Stedham, Suss.

PETERSFIELD   7 Nov. 1715–1722

b. c.1690, 1st s. of Samuel Pargiter of St. Andrew, Holborn, merchant, and consul at Nice, by his w. Frances. *m.* c.1713, Margaret, da. and h. of Douse Fuller of Chamberhouse, Berks. and Stedham, Suss. and assumed add. name of Fuller, 1s. *suc.* fa. 1709.

Returned as a Whig for Petersfield at a by-election in 1715, Fuller voted against the septennial bill in 1716, for the repeal of the Occasional Conformity and Schism Acts and against the peerage bill in 1719.

He tried unsuccessfully to present a petition from Lady Derwentwater, 1716; to provoke a debate on Gibraltar, 1719; and to divide the House on Aislabie's expulsion, 1721.[1] He died 21 Nov. 1722.

[1] *Dudley Ryder Diary*, 186; W. Michael, *England under Geo. I*, ii. 130; Coxe, *Walpole*, ii. 210.

P.W.

PARKER, Armstead (c.1699–1777), of Burghberry Manor, Peterborough, Northants.

PETERBOROUGH   29 Jan. 1734–1741
                3 May 1742–1747, 1761–1768

b. c.1699, o.s. of Charles Parker (q.v.). *m.* 28 Jan. 1738, Elizabeth, da. of Francis Rogers, keeper of the wardrobe to James II, and h. of her uncle, Humphrey Rogers of Munden, Herts., 1s. 2da. *suc.* fa. 1730.

Parker was returned in 1734 for Peterborough as a Tory on his family interest, voting against the Government. He did not stand in 1741 but was re-elected unopposed in succession to the 3rd Lord Fitzwilliam in 1742, voting against the Government till 1746, when he supported them on the Hanoverians.[1] He died 5 Feb. 1777.

[1] Owen, *Pelhams*, 307, n. 3.

R.R.S.

PARKER, Charles (c.1663–1730), of Burghberry Manor, Peterborough, Northants.

PETERBOROUGH   1710–1722

b. c.1663, 2nd s. of Samuel Parker of Paxton, Northants. by Mary, da. of Thomas Armstead of Obthorpe, Lincs. *m.* bef. 1698, Katharine Wilson, 1s. 1da. *suc.* maternal uncle, Thomas Armstead to part of Thurlby estate in Lincs. 1672.
    Sheriff, Northants. 1726–7.

Parker, who held property in Peterborough on a lease from the bishop,[1] was returned for the city as a Tory, voting against the Government on the septennial bill in 1716, but absenting himself from later divisions, at the cost of being twice committed to the charge of the serjeant at arms for defaulting on calls of the House.[2] Defeated in 1722, he could not stand in 1727, when he was sheriff, using his office to send the election precept to a Tory bailiff, who returned a Tory, Sir Edward O'Brien (q.v.), instead of the Whig, Sidney Wortley (q.v.), who had polled more votes. At a by-election next year he was reported to have declared his intention of standing[3] but he did not do so. He died in 1730.

[1] J. Bridges, *Northants.* ii. 543. [2] *CJ*, xviii. 281; xix. 493. [3] *Letters and Pprs. Banks Fam.* ed. Hill (Lincoln Rec. Soc. xlv), 88–89.

R.R.S.

PARKER, George, Visct. Parker (c.1697–1764), of Shirburn Castle, Oxon.

WALLINGFORD   1722–1727

b. c.1697, 1st s. of Thomas Parker, M.P., 1st Earl of Macclesfield, by Janet, da. and h. of Robert Carrier of Wirksworth, Derbys. *educ.* I. Temple 1706; Clare, Camb. 1715; Corpus Christi, Camb. 1718; Grand Tour (Italy) 1720–2. *m.* (1) 18 Sept. 1722, Mary (*d.* 4 June 1753), da. and coh. of Ralph Lane, a Turkey merchant, of Woodbury, Cambs., 2s.; (2) 20 Dec. 1757, Dorothy Nesbitt, *s.p. suc.* fa. as 2nd Earl of Macclesfield 28 Apr. 1732.
    Teller of the Exchequer 1719–*d.*; high steward, Henley-on-Thames.

Parker, who was endowed with a lucrative sinecure obtained for him by his father on becoming lord chancellor, entered Parliament as a Whig at a contested election in 1722. His only recorded speech was made on Sir William Yonge's (q.v.) divorce bill, 5 Dec. 1724, when he spoke from personal knowledge of the lady.[1] He did not stand again. A distinguished astronomer, he built an observatory at Shirburn and was largely responsible for the adoption of the 'New Style' calendar in 1752. He died 17 Mar. 1764.

[1] *Knatchbull Diary.*

R.S.L.

PARKER, Sir Philip, 3rd Bt. (1682–1741), of Erwarton, Suff.

HARWICH 1715–1734

b. 23 Mar. 1682, o.s. of Sir Philip Parker, 2nd Bt., by Mary, da. of Samuel Fortrey of Kew, Surr. and Byall Fen, Cambs. *educ.* C.C.C. Oxf. 1698. *m.* 11 July 1715, Martha, da. of William East of the M. Temple, 2da. *suc.* fa. as 3rd Bt. c.1700; to Wilts. estate of his uncle, Calthorpe Long 1729, assuming the name of Parker-a-Morley Long.

For nearly 20 years Parker sat as a Whig for Harwich, where his estate of Erwarton, only two miles away, gave him a natural interest. In 1716 he obtained the reversion of a lease of the duty on sixpenny writs in the court of Chancery for 41 years and in 1717 he and his fellow Member, Thomas Heath, were granted a 31 year lease of the crown property in Harwich.[1] In 1730 his political career and grievances were outlined by his brother-in-law, Lord Egmont (John Perceval, Visct. Perceval (I), q.v.), who complained that

no man in England had deserved better of this Government, and no man was treated worse. That his merit even exceeded that of any other man's. That in Queen Anne's time, while yet a young man, and not come to his fortune, he stood for the county of Suffolk against two Tories, Sir Thomas Hanmer and Sir Robert Davers [qq.v.] and though he lost it, yet showed so great interest in his county that he polled two thousand single votes. That when the first plot against the late King broke out, he presented an association in the defence of the Hanover succession, signed by the well affected of his county, which their representatives in Parliament, nor even their lord lieutenant of the county, my Lord Cornwallis, through fear of the times, durst not do; that he presented also an association from the town of Harwich, even while my Lord Bolingbroke was recorder there; that afterwards he got that lord turned out, and my Lord Orford chosen recorder in his room; that ever since he was in Parliament he stuck to his principle, and never opposed the Court in anything except in the peerage bill, which he voted against for this King's sake, against whom it was levelled, the Act for repealing my Lord Bolingbroke's attainder, which he believes the Court now thinks he was right in doing, and in the late bill to prevent bribery and corruption, which as a lover of his country he was obliged to do; that his zeal in all was so remarkable that he has been accused of being a pensioner, for people could not imagine how otherwise a gentleman could be so zealous and steady for a Government under whom he never enjoyed nor sought for a place. That all the reward for his zeal and incredible expense for the service of his country, and the Hanover suc-

cession, and in modelling Harwich, a Jacobite town, to become honest and loyal, has been a constant endeavour of the Government to undermine his natural interest in his own borough.

Parker himself was so disgruntled by his treatment that in 1730 he supported an opposition bill excluding pensioners from the House, voted with the Opposition on the army in 1732, and absented himself from the divisions on the excise bill. However, he attended the meeting of ministerial supporters called by Walpole to rally his party after the withdrawal of the bill.[2] Next year he voted with the Government on the repeal of the Septennial Act. Retiring from Parliament in 1734 owing to declining health, he died 20 Jan. 1741.

[1] *Cal. Treas. Bks.* xxx. 88; xxxi. 315. [2] *HMC Egmont Diary*, i. 15–16, 56, 365, 447. He also voted against the Government on Lord Cadogan (q.v.) in 1717.

R.R.S.

PARKER, Thomas, Visct. Parker (1723–95).

NEWCASTLE-UNDER-LYME 1747–1754
OXFORDSHIRE   23 Apr.1755–1761
ROCHESTER   1761–17 Mar. 1764

b. 12 Oct. 1723, 1st s. of George Parker (q.v.), 2nd Earl of Macclesfield, by his 1st w. *educ.* Hertford, Oxf. 1740. *m.* 12 Dec. 1749, Mary, da. of Sir William Heathcote, 1st Bt. (q.v.), of Hursley, Hants, 2s. 3da. *suc.* fa. as 3rd Earl 17 Mar. 1764.

Returned unopposed for Newcastle-under-Lyme on Lord Gower's interest, Parker was classed as a government supporter. On 15 Nov. 1753 he seconded Sir James Dashwood's (q.v.) motion for a call of the House to discuss the necessity for the repeal of the Act for the naturalization of the Jews.[1]

He died 9 Feb. 1795.

[1] Coxe, *Pelham*, ii. 291–3.

E.C.

PARRY, Stephen (1675–1724), of Neuadd Trefawr, Card.

CARDIGAN BOROUGHS 1715–15 Dec. 1724

b. c.1675, o.s. of John Parry of Panteynon by Margaret Bulbell of Dublin. *m.* Anne, da. and h. of David Parry of Neuadd Trefawr, *s.p.* *suc.* fa. 1722.

Parry was returned as a Tory on the interest of Lewis Pryse (q.v.) in 1715. Absent from all recorded divisions in this Parliament, he was twice committed to the custody of the serjeant at arms for failing to attend calls of the House. In 1721 his name was sent to the Pretender as a probable supporter in the event of a rising.[1] Nevertheless a list of Members and their relations to whom Sunderland distributed £2,000 about this time contains the entry: 'à M. Parry et M. Meyrick [Owen, q.v.], deux Membres du pays de Galles £300'.[2] Again unopposed in 1722, he died 15 Dec. 1724, aged 49.[3]

[1] *CJ*, xix. 61, 188; Stuart mss 65/16. [2] Sunderland (Blenheim) mss D. II, 4. [3] S. Meyrick, *Card.* 128.

E.C.

PARSONS, Henry (1687–1739), of Wickham Bishops,[1] nr. Maldon, Essex.

LOSTWITHIEL   25 Feb. 1724–17 Jan. 1727
MALDON   25 Jan. 1727–29 Dec. 1739

bap. 24 July 1687,[2] 3rd s. of Sir John Parsons but 1st by his 2nd w.; half-bro. of Humphry Parsons (qq.v.). *unm.*
    Purveyor, Chelsea Hospital 1714–*d.*; commr. of victualling 1727–*d.*; assistant, R. African Co. 1728–*d.*

Parsons, a London merchant, was appointed by his friend, Walpole, to be master baker at Chelsea Hospital, where 'he became known as the purveyor, an unofficial position . . . reputed to be worth £500 p.a.'.[3] He secured from Walpole the contracts for meat, butter and cheese, as well as bread, and sold him the hospital's victualling bills at five per cent discount.[4] In 1717 he was heavily in debt, having borrowed from his father £4,000 as his share of his family's estate, as well as owing 'several great sums as yet unpaid'.[5] After contesting Maldon unsuccessfully in 1722, he petitioned but withdrew his petition at Walpole's instance.[6] Brought in for Lostwithiel in 1724, he vacated his seat on being appointed commissioner of the victualling office, which, together with the purveyorship, was said to have brought his emoluments to £2,000 p.a.[7] In 1727, instead of standing for re-election at Lostwithiel, he was returned unopposed at Maldon, where he managed the government interest.[8] He steadily supported the Administration till his death, 29 Dec. 1739.

[1] PCC 19 Browne. [2] *Registers of Christ Church, Newgate* (Harl. Soc. Regs. xxi), 66. [3] C. G. T. Dean, *Royal Hospital, Chelsea*, 194. [4] Ibid.; J. H. Plumb, *Walpole*, i. 205. [5] PCC 42 Whitfield. [6] See COMYNS, John. [7] *Gent. Mag.* 1739, p. 306. [8] See MALDON.

E.C.

PARSONS, Humphry (c.1676–1741), of the Red Lion Brewery, Aldgate, and the Priory, Reigate, Surr.

HARWICH   1722–1727
LONDON   1727–1741

b. c.1676, 1st surv. s. of Sir John Parsons by his 1st w.; half-bro. of Henry Parsons (qq.v.). *m.* 16 Apr. 1719, Sarah, da. of Sir Ambrose Crowley, M.P., alderman of London and dep. gov. of South Sea Co., sis. of John Crowley (q.v.), 1s. 2da., one of whom m. Sir John Hynde Cotton, 4th Bt. (q.v.). *suc.* fa. 1717.
    Alderman, London 1721, sheriff 1722–3, ld. mayor 1730, 1740; Waxchandlers' Co. 1721, translated to

Grocers' Co. 1725, master 1726–31; president, Bethlehem and Bridewell Hospitals 1725–*d.*

Parsons, a wealthy brewer, stood unsuccessfully on his family's interest at Reigate in 1717, and again in 1722, when he was returned at Harwich. An extreme Tory, he received literature from the Jacobites overseas for distribution in the city of London. In March 1726 the Jacobite Duke of Wharton wrote to him, asking him to explain the differences between the Pretender and his wife to their friends in the city, adding:

> The personal knowledge I have of your fidelity and capacity encourages me to write freely to you from this place, and I am sure I can give no greater proof of my dependence on your friendship than in trusting you with my life and fortune.
> Your zeal for the King and the unwearied application with which you have through the whole course of your life studied his Majesty's service and the good of your country have induced me to apply to you at this juncture . . . The loyalty and affection of the city of London for the royal family are formidable to the King's enemies, and therefore it is not to be doubted but that great pains have been taken to show this circumstance to them in such light as would alarm and surprise them.[1]

In 1727 he was returned for London, where he is described as being 'universally beloved for his good nature and open behaviour, and very popular amongst the common people for his great affability and condescension'.[2] Just before becoming lord mayor, he is reported to have declared that he would never 'come near the person of their King for fear he should knight him, as he surprised others, and says that if he should be caught that way, he is sure his wife would never bed him afterwards'.[3]

The owner of a 'brilliant stable',[4] Parsons distinguished himself by being first at the kill in a royal hunt at Versailles in 1729 and, on being asked the price of his horse by Louis XV, by answering that it was beyond any price other than his Majesty's acceptance. Louis XV shortly afterwards granted him a patent allowing him to export his beer to France duty-free, and sent him his portrait set in diamonds.[5] Thereafter he paid frequent visits to Versailles, where 'the King of France distinguished him more than . . . any prince or ambassador, inviting him every day to hunt with him or ordering his hunting equipages for him'.[6]

Parsons took an active part in the opposition to Walpole's excise bill both in the city and in Parliament, where he explained in a speech

> some of the hardships which the brewers laboured under by being subject to the excise laws. He said his brother [Henry Parsons, q.v.] and Mr. Hucks [William or Robert, qq.v.] knew what he said to be true and called upon them to declare what they knew, but they did not think proper to do it.[7]

He moved that the city's petition, praying to be heard by counsel against the bill, should be received and read.[8] Re-elected for London at the top of the poll in 1734, he was chosen lord mayor a second time on 22 Oct. 1740, telling the common hall that he would serve, 'let the expense be what it would'. He was the first lord mayor to ride in a coach and six in his procession, and the only man to serve that office twice in the 18th century.[9] On 18 June 1740 he received the thanks of the common council for his strenuous support of the place bill.[10] He died 21 Mar. 1741, aged 65.

[1] Stuart mss 68/118; 91/63. [2] *Jnl. of the shrievalty of Richard Hoare*, 63. [3] Stuart mss 131/40. [4] T. A. Cook, *Hist. of the Turf* (1901), i. 131. [5] D. Hughson, *Hist. London*, ii. 195; *A Hymn to Alderman Parsons, our Lord Mayor* (1741). [6] Stuart mss 131/40; Walpole to Mann, 2 Nov. 1741. [7] Stuart mss Box 1/125. [8] *HMC Egmont Diary*, i. 358. [9] J. Entick, *A new and accurate Hist. and Survey of London* (1766), ii. 472–3. [10] Jnl. vol. 58.

E.C.

PARSONS, Sir John (d.1717), of the Priory, Reigate, Surr.

REIGATE 1685–1687, 11 Jan.–1 Mar. 1689, 1690–1698, 1701–25 Jan. 1717

s. of Richard Parsons, brewer, of St. Botolph, Aldgate. *m.* (1) Jane, da. of Richard Milward, London merchant, 2s. 2da.; (2) 1678, Elizabeth, da. of Humphrey Beane of Epsom, Surr., alderman of London, 1s. 6da.[1] Kntd. 15 Aug. 1687.
Commr. of victualling 1683–90; alderman, London 1687, sheriff 1687–8, ld. mayor 1703–4; Brewers' Co. 1688, master 1689–90, translated to Fishmongers' Co. 1703, prime warden 1706–8.

Parsons was the owner of the Red Lion Brewery in Aldgate, famous for its porter, known as 'Parsons' black champagne'.[2] In 1681 he bought a property, with a number of vote-carrying houses, at Reigate, which he represented with two brief intervals from 1685 till his death, 25 Jan. 1717. He also stood unsuccessfully for London in 1701 and 1705. A Tory with Jacobite leanings,[3] he is not recorded as speaking or voting during the short time for which he sat under George I.

[1] P. Boyd's units, citizens of London 15796, 49881 in Lib. of Soc. of Genealogists; Brewers' Co. records; PCC 42 Whitfield. [2] Beaven, *Aldermen of London*, ii. 196. [3] W. Hooper, *Reigate*, 119, 121.

R.R.S.

PASKE, Thomas (c.1675–1720), of Much Hadham, Herts.

CAMBRIDGE UNIVERSITY 1710–18 Sept. 1720

b. c.1675, 3rd s. of Thomas Paske of Much Hadham, fellow of Clare, Camb. *educ.* Clare, Camb. 1692, fellow 1698, LL.D. 1707. *unm.*
Advocate of court of arches, chancellor of the diocese of Exeter, and official of the archdeaconry of Lincoln.

II—Y

Paske, an ecclesiastical lawyer, is described as 'the favourite of the church party, by his great acquaintance as agent to Mr. Annesley and Mr. Windsor'[1] (q.v.), who jointly represented Cambridge University 1705–10. Succeeding Annesley as a moderate Tory, under George I he voted against the Government. He died 18 Sept. 1720, having been for some time in declining health.

[1] *HMC Portland*, iv. 605; v. 94.

R.R.S.

PEACHEY, Bulstrode (c.1681–1736), of West Dean, Suss. and Chawton, Hants.

MIDHURST 1722–14 Jan. 1736

b. 1681, 5th s. of William Peachey, London merchant, by Mary, da. and h. of John Hall of Newgrove, Petworth, Suss.;[1] bro. of Sir Henry, James and Sir John Peachey, 2nd Bt. (qq.v.). *m.* 8 June 1725, Elizabeth, da. and h. of Michael Martin of Eynsham, Oxon., wid. of William Woodward Knight (q.v.), taking the add. name of Knight, *s.p.*
Cornet R. Horse Gds. 1704; exempt 3 Life Gds. 1705.

In 1722 Bulstrode Peachey was returned unopposed for Midhurst, where he had bought burgages from the 6th Lord Montagu, the Roman Catholic lord of the manor, subsequently increasing his holding to 49 by further purchases from Montagu.[2] In 1725 he consolidated his interest at Midhurst by marrying the widow of William Woodward Knight (q.v.). His only recorded vote was for the Hessians in 1730. He died 14 Jan. 1736.

[1] PCC 214 Brent. [2] A. A. Dibben, *Cowdray Archives*, pt. 1, p. xxii.

J.B.L.

PEACHEY, Sir Henry (? 1671–1737), of Newgrove, Petworth, Suss.

SUSSEX 1701–1702, 1708–1710
MIDHURST 2 Feb. 1736–23 Aug. 1737

b. ?1671, 1st s. of William Peachey of Newgrove and bro. of Bulstrode, James and Sir John Peachey, 2nd Bt. (qq.v.). *educ.* ?Eton 1685; Trinity, Oxf. 22 Nov. 1689, aged 18. *m.* 16 May 1693, Jane, da. of William Garrett of St. Dionis Backchurch, London, 2s. *d.v.p.* 2da. *suc.* fa. 1685. Kntd. 22 Mar. 1696; *cr.*Bt. 21 Mar. 1736, with a sp. rem. to bros. John and James.

The son of a London merchant with an estate at Petworth, Peachey sat for the county as a Whig under Queen Anne, losing his seat in 1710. He applied to Newcastle for support as a prospective candidate for Sussex on the elevation of Spencer Compton (q.v.) to the peerage in 1728, but was not adopted.[1] He stood for Haslemere in 1734, withdrawing before the poll.[2] Returned for Midhurst in succession to his brother, Bulstrode Peachey

Knight, he died soon afterwards, 23 Aug. 1737, aged 66.

¹ Peachey to Newcastle, 10 Jan. 1728, SP 36/5, ff. 11-12. ² E. Oglethorpe to Sir. Robt. Walpole, n.d. 1734, Cholmondeley (Houghton) mss.

J.B.L.

PEACHEY, James (1683–1771), of Fitleworth, Suss. and Burghope nr. Leominster, Herefs.

LEOMINSTER 1747–1754

b. 5 Nov. 1683, 8th s. of William Peachey and bro. of Bulstrode, Sir Henry and Sir John Peachey, 2nd Bt. (qq.v.). *unm.*, 1s.
　Gov. of Gombroon.

Having made a fortune in India, Peachey returned to England about 1739, buying in 1743 an estate near Leominster for which he was returned in 1747, classed as Opposition. The second Lord Egmont wrote in his electoral survey c.1749–50:

James Peachey, if he lives, may probably be chose again, though he loves money and may decline a very hard contest. But I know him particularly well and should think him no bad man, though something will be expected to be done for one or both of his nephews, and a share of any subscriptions going forward for himself. And though he is naturally a republican Whig of levelling and wild notions of government yet this will not hinder him in the least from acting with us for reasons such as I have mentioned. I suspect that he designs if he can to try for his second nephew at this borough.

Defeated for Hereford in 1754, he did not stand again, dying 16 Feb. 1771.

A.N.N.

PEACHEY, Sir John, 2nd Bt. (c.1680–1744), of West Dean, Suss.

MIDHURST 3 Feb. 1738–9 Apr. 1744

b. c.1680, 4th but 2nd surv. s. of William Peachey and bro. of Bulstrode, James and Sir Henry Peachey (qq.v.). *m.* (2) lic. 15 Mar. 1706, Henrietta, da. of George London, principal gardener to Queen Anne, 2s. 3da. *suc.* bro. Henry Peachey as 2nd Bt. 23 Aug. 1737.
　Capt. 7 Ft. 1719.

Peachey was returned for Midhurst in succession to his brother, Sir Henry Peachey, voting with the Opposition. In 1741 he was invited by the Tories to stand for Sussex but declined.¹ In the next Parliament his only vote was with the Opposition on the chairman of the elections committee, 16 Dec. 1741. He died 9 Apr. 1744, aged 64.²

¹ John Whitfield to Newcastle, 25 Apr. 1741, Add. 32696, f. 373. ² M. I. at West Dean, Add. 5699, f. 203.

J.B.L.

PEACHEY, Sir John, 3rd Bt.(?1720–65), of West Dean, Suss.

MIDHURST 23 Apr. 1744–1761

b. ?1720, 1st s. of Sir John Peachey, 2nd Bt. (q.v.), by his 2nd w. *educ.* Westminster June 1729, aged 9; M. Temple 1736; Ch. Ch. Oxf. 17 Nov. 1737, aged 17. *m.* 18 Aug. 1752, Elizabeth, da. and h. of John Meeres Fagg of Glynley, Suss., *s.p. suc.* fa. 9 Apr. 1744.

Peachey was returned in succession to his father, voting against the Hanoverians in 1746. Classed as Opposition in 1747, he seems to have gone over to the Government by 1751, when his brother, James Peachey, later created Lord Selsey, was appointed a groom of the bedchamber to the new Prince of Wales. He died 30 June 1765.

J.B.L.

PEACHEY KNIGHT, *see* **PEACHEY, Bulstrode**

PEARSE, Thomas (*d.*1743), of Tower Hill, London, and Witchampton, Dorset.

WEYMOUTH AND MELCOMBE REGIS
　　　1722–11 Oct. 1726, 1727–1741

?s. of James Pearse of Weymouth. *m.* (1), 1s. 3da.; (2) bef. 1730, da. of Thomas Best of Chatham, 2s.²
　Chief clerk, navy office to 1726; commr. of the navy 1726–*d.*; director, South Sea Co. 1721–24.

Pearse appears to have been a business man who, like John Phillipson (q.v.), for some time combined the position of a clerk in the navy office with that of a South Sea director. Returned unopposed for Weymouth, his native town, he vacated his seat on being appointed a commissioner of the navy in 1726 but did not stand at the ensuing by-election. Re-elected in 1727 after a contest, he was unopposed in 1734, voting with the Government in every recorded division.

When in 1740 George Bubb Dodington set up four opposition candidates at Weymouth, Walpole gave Pearse and John Olmius (q.v.) 'the strongest assurance of my friendship and support against everybody that shall think fit to oppose those gentlemen that deserve so very well of all the King's servants'.³ During the election campaign he approved a scheme drawn up by Pearse's friends at Weymouth for the removal of several local revenue officers to enable the Government to carry all four Members. After losing the election, Pearse gave evidence to the secret committee set up by the House of Commons to enquire into Walpole's Administration. He admitted that the mayor of Weymouth had been offered the post of collector of customs if he would pack the corporation, in order to choose a returning officer for the forthcoming election. Another inducement was a promise to procure the mayor's brother-in-law, a clergyman, 'any living that became vacant in the gift of the Crown or the Lord Chancellor.' Asked whether, when the mayor refused, he, Pearse, had said that 'if fair means would not do, foul must,' meaning that their charter would be attacked, he replied that 'he did not know but he may have said "have at your charter" '.[4]

Pearse died, still in possession of his place, 3 Apr. 1743.

[1] Hutchins, *Dorset*, iii. 477. [2] PCC 129 Boycott; Berry, *Kent Fams.* 382. [3] Coxe, *Walpole*, iii. 557. [4] *CJ*, xxiv. 293-5.

R.R.S.

PEIRSE, Henry (1692-1759), of Bedale, nr. North-allerton, Yorks.

NORTHALLERTON 1713-1715, 1722-1754

bap. 25 Feb. 1692, 1st s. of John Peirse of Lazenby, Yorks. by Elizabeth, da. of Sir Henry Marwood, 2nd Bt., M.P., of Little Busby, Yorks. *m.* 15 Feb. 1754, Anne Johnson, or Masters, 1s. *suc.* fa. 1726.

Henry Peirse inherited from his grandfather the manor of Bedale, which his family had bought early in the seventeenth century. On coming of age in 1713 he was returned for the neighbouring borough of Northallerton, where he controlled one seat. He did not stand in 1715 but was re-elected in 1722, voting steadily with the Government except on the place bill of 1740, which he supported, and on the chairman of the elections committee in 1741, when he was absent. Though he never received a place, the 2nd Lord Egmont in his plans for a new Parliament puts him down as a man who 'may be had as I take it by any Government'. Retiring in 1754, he died 2 Oct. 1759.

R.R.S.

PELHAM, Charles (c.1679-1763), of Brocklesby, Lincs.

GREAT GRIMSBY 1722-1727
BEVERLEY 1727-1734, 2 Feb. 1738-1754

b. c.1679, 1st s. of Charles Pelham of Brocklesby, by Elizabeth, da. of Michael Warton, M.P., of Beverley, Yorks., sis. of Sir Michael Warton (q.v.). *m.* (1) 29 June 1714, Anne (*d.* 8 Mar. 1739), da. of Sir William Gore, ld. mayor of London, sis. of William, John and Thomas Gore (qq.v.), *s.p.*; (2) Mary, da. of Robert Vyner of Gautby, Lincs. (q.v.), *s.p. suc.* fa. 1692; as coh. to Beverley estates of his uncle, Sir Michael Warton 1725.

Descended from a junior branch of the Pelhams of Sussex, Charles Pelham was returned as a Tory for Grimsby in 1722, transferring in 1727 to Beverley, where he had inherited property from his uncle. In Parliament he voted against the Govern-

ment, except on the motion for Walpole's dismissal in February 1741, when he was one of the Tories who withdrew before the division. Retiring in 1754, he died 6 Feb. 1763.

R.R.S.

PELHAM, Henry (c.1694-1725), of Stanmer, nr. Lewes, Suss.

HASTINGS 1715-1722
LEWES 1722-2 June 1725

b. c.1694, 1st s. of Henry Pelham, M.P., of Stanmer, uncle of the Duke of Newcastle, by Frances, da. and coh. of John Bine of Rowdell, Suss.; bro. of Thomas Pelham of Stanmer (q.v.). *unm. suc.* fa. 1721.

Pelham was brought into Parliament by his first cousin, the Duke of Newcastle, soon after coming of age. He supported the Government except in the case of the peerage bill, on which he was absent. Returned by Newcastle for Lewes in 1722, he died of consumption 2 June 1725.

R.R.S.

PELHAM, Hon. Henry (1695-1754), of Esher Place, Surr.

SEAFORD 28 Feb. 1717-1722
SUSSEX 1722-6 Mar. 1754

b. c. Jan. 1695,[1] 2nd s. of Thomas Pelham, M.P., 1st Baron Pelham, of Halland, Suss. by Lady Grace Holles, da. of Gilbert Holles, M.P., 3rd Earl of Clare. *educ.* Westminster; Hart Hall, Oxf. 6 Sept. 1710, aged 15. *m.* 29 Oct. 1726, Lady Katherine Manners, da. of John, 2nd Duke of Rutland, 2s. *d.v.p.* 6da. (2 *d.v.p.*).
Served as volunteer in 1715 rebellion; treasurer of the chamber 1720-22; ld. of the Treasury 1721-4; sec. at war 1724-30; P.C. 1 June 1725; paymaster gen. 1730-43; first ld. of the Treasury 25 Aug. 1743-*d.*; chancellor of the Exchequer 12 Dec. 1743-*d.*

Soon after coming of age Pelham was returned for Seaford by his brother, the Duke of Newcastle, voting against the Government on Lord Cadogan (q.v.) in 1717[2] but with them on the repeal of the Occasional Conformity and Schism Acts and the peerage bill in 1719. He made his first reported speech 6 May 1720, when the reunion of the Whig party was marked by an address for discharging the civil list debt, which was moved by Pelham and seconded by Walpole. On 15 Mar. 1721 he helped Walpole to secure Sunderland's acquittal by the House of Commons on a charge of taking bribes from the South Sea Company. When Walpole succeeded Sunderland as head of the Treasury in April, Pelham exchanged his court post under his brother, then lord chamberlain, for a seat on the Treasury board.

After Sunderland's death in 1722 the Pelham brothers sided with Walpole against Carteret, who was replaced as secretary of state by Newcastle in 1724, Pelham becoming secretary at war. Promoted to the post of paymaster of the forces in 1730, he refrained from taking the perquisites, out of which others made great fortunes. Hervey describes him at this time as

> strongly attached to Sir Robert Walpole, and more personally beloved by him than any man in England. He was a gentlemanlike sort of man, of very good character, with moderate parts, in the secret of every transaction, which, added to long practice, made him at last, though not a bright speaker, often a useful one; and by the means of a general affability he had fewer enemies than commonly fall to the share of one in so high a rank.[3]

In the House of Commons he acted as deputy to Walpole, who eventually adopted him as his political heir-apparent.

On Walpole's fall Pelham automatically succeeded to the leadership of the old corps of Whigs in the Commons, whom he represented in the negotiations with Pulteney and Carteret. In the new Government he retained the paymastership, refusing the chancellorship of the Exchequer, though urged by Walpole to take it. When Pulteney elected to follow Walpole to the Lords as Earl of Bath, the leadership of the Commons devolved on Pelham, who thus found himself as paymaster at the head of the House of Commons, like Walpole before him, in each case for a short time.[4]

As head of the House of Commons, Pelham presided at the Cockpit meeting of government supporters before the opening of the next session, during which he did so well that it was settled that he should replace Wilmington (Spencer Compton, q.v.) at the Treasury before Parliament re-assembled in December 1743. On Wilmington's death in July Bath applied for the post, but Pelham obtained it, much to the satisfaction of Walpole, now Orford, though he warned Pelham that Bath would try to secure a continuance of the existing Treasury board, containing a majority of his nominees, to 'make, if he can, an arrant Wilmington of you'. However, the day after Pelham assumed office, John Scrope (q.v.), secretary of the Treasury, reported that 'he was as much at home there as if he had been at the head of that board for seven years'. When the King returned from Hanover in November, Pelham had no difficulty in arranging for the reconstitution of the Treasury board with himself as chancellor of the Exchequer as well as first lord, as Walpole had been before him.[5]

Though head of the Treasury and minister for the House of Commons, Pelham was still without the indispensable attribute of an eighteenth century prime minister, a superior interest in the Closet.

This was possessed by Carteret, who had gained it by giving in to the King's foreign views, at the cost of making himself and his ally Bath more unpopular in a year than Walpole had been after twenty.[6] Relying on the royal favour, Carteret rode rough-shod over his colleagues, saying of Pelham

> he was only a chief clerk to Sir Robert Walpole, and why he should expect to be more under me I cant imagine. He did his drudgery and he shall do mine.

But Carteret had failed to take into account the effects of the precedent created in 1742, when the House of Commons had forced the King to give up Walpole. It was to avoid a repetition of 1742 that George II reluctantly agreed to part with Carteret, now Granville, in 1744. And when in 1746 Pelham with most of his colleagues resigned as a protest against their opponents' continued influence in the Closet, they had to be recalled after a two days' interregnum had shown that a Bath-Granville ministry could count on no more than 80 votes in the Commons, compared with 192 Members who went to Pelham's levee to compliment him on his resignation. Though in appearance the King's defeat had been effected by the resignation of ministers, its real cause in 1744-6, as in 1742, was that his chosen minister could not command a majority in the House of Commons. As Speaker Onslow said with satisfaction: 'This Parliament has torn two favourite ministers from the throne'.[7]

On returning to office, Pelham set himself to preventing as far as possible a recurrence of what he called 'the long Opposition which was permitted to go on for so many years that at length they were become the masters. I pray I may never see the like again'. Completing the operation begun when he brought the heads of the Opposition into the Government after Granville's fall in 1744, he won over Pitt with a lucrative sinecure, Sir John Barnard by admitting him to the ring of underwriters of government loans, and Hume Campbell by a place for his brother and a pension for himself. Having thus taken the brains out of the Opposition, he caught them unprepared by a snap general election, which gave him a comfortable majority in 1747. The conclusion of peace in 1748 cleared the way to what he described as 'my one selfish ambition',

> to have been the author of such a plan as might, in time to come, have released this nation from the vast load of debt they now labour under; and even in my own time to have had the satisfaction of demonstrating to the knowing part of the world that the thing was not impossible.

Next year he successfully introduced a scheme for reducing the interest on the national debt from 4 to 3 per cent, weathering a storm in the city of London, from which Walpole had flinched when a similar opportunity had presented itself in 1737. In 1750, depressed by defections to the Prince of Wales's opposition, he wrote:

> The House of Commons is a great unwieldy body, which requires great art and some cordials to keep it together; we have not many of the latter in our power; the Opposition is headed by the Prince, who has as much to give in present as we have, and more in reversion. This makes my task a hard one, and if it were not for that I should sleep in quiet.

This threat was removed by the Prince's death in 1751, after which 'opposition . . . and even the distinctions of party . . . in a manner ceased'.[8] By this time Pelham had made his peace with George II, promising him

> that I would never enter into any cabal *again* to prevent H.M. from either removing or bringing into his service any person he had either a prejudice against or a predilection for.

When in 1751 he offered to retire with the post of auditor of the Exchequer, a life sinecure worth £8,000 a year, which had fallen vacant, the King told him, instead of retiring, to hold it in the name of his nephew and son-in-law, Lord Lincoln. His favour excited the jealousy of Newcastle, who reported to Hardwicke, 6 Sept. 1751:

> The King is very gracious, civil, and indeed familiar, both at the levee and in the Closet. His Majesty talks very confidentially upon foreign affairs, but is totally silent upon everything at home, and upon all employments that become vacant, upon which H.M. talks to nobody but Mr. Pelham, who sees him but once or at most twice a week, but then he has long audiences . . . The truth is, that in fact everything passes through my brother's hands, and I am with regard to the King as much a stranger as if I was not in the ministry . . . Mr. Pelham is much embarrassed, inwardly pleased with his great situation at home and great affluence of fortune, got singly by the Court whenever he leaves it.

George II even came to compare him favourably to Walpole, who, he told Newcastle in 1752, 'managed the money matters very ill; he did not indeed give money abroad, but he gave it away liberally at home'; adding 'he was a great man, he understood the country; but that with regard to money matters, your brother does that, understands that, much better,' no doubt referring to the fall of secret service expenditure from nearly £80,000 a year under Walpole to about £30,000 under Pelham.[9]

Though recognised as 'the premier', Pelham made no attempt to acquire Walpole's position of 'sole minister'. The ministry for practical purposes consisted of himself, his brother, and Hardwicke: as George II remarked in 1750, 'they are the only ministers; the others are for show'. In this triumvirate, Pelham confined himself as far as possible

to domestic matters, leaving foreign affairs to Newcastle, with Hardwicke as the receptacle of each brother's complaints about the other. Thus Pelham complained to Hardwicke that Newcastle

> always had a partiality and regard for the late Lord Stanhope [q.v. under Stanhope, James]. I know he thinks no minister has made a great figure but him in the two reigns. He will therefore imitate him as far as he can, and, I doubt, if he is not checked by somebody, will bring himself, if not his country, into the same distress that fertile but well-intentioned lord did before him.

Similarly Newcastle complained to Hardwicke that

> Of all subjects my brother is the most uneasy when I talk to him upon that of elections. He will do everything himself—he consults none of his friends—he neither has time or patience to give it all the attention, *alone*, that such a great undertaking does require, and things arise which he did not expect. He is conscious that, nobody being consulted, nobody but himself can be blamed and that is what makes him sore when anything happens.

But on neither side was there any serious question of a rupture. As Pelham said:

> The bottom of his politics and his brother's too, for they must in the end be the same, . . . was to choose a new Parliament, that should be a thorough Whig Parliament, all of a piece, such a one as might serve the King if he lived, and be steady to put the young King in the right way, if the old one died.[10]

Felix opportunitate mortis, Henry Pelham, 'that often underrated minister', died unexpectedly 6 Mar. 1754, on the eve of the general election for which he had been preparing, the first prime minister who 'had the honour of dying a commoner'. To his contemporaries his chief virtue was that of setting an example of integrity in public life. 'Let it be remembered', Horace Walpole, no friend of his, wrote of him, that he 'died poor'. And Chesterfield:

> He wished well to the public and managed the finances with great care and personal purity. He was *par negotiis neque supra*, had many domestic virtues and no vices . . . Upon the whole, he was an honourable man and a well-wishing minister.[11]

[1] T. Lawson-Tancred, *Recs. of a Yorkshire Manor*, 241. [2] AECP Angl. 226, f. 186. [3] 'Family Characters and Ancedotes', by Ld. Camelford, 1781, Fortescue mss at Boconnoc; Hervey, *Mems.* 120; Yorke, *Hardwicke*, i. 629–30. [4] Hervey, 945, 949; Coxe, *Pelham*, i. 83; Yorke, iii. 331. [5] Owen, *Pelhams*, 160, 190; Coxe, i. 82–85. [6] Coxe, i. 103; Stuart mss 249/6. [7] *HMC Egmont Diary*, iii. 281, 315; Owen, 211, 272–3, 295; Walpole to Mann, 26 Nov. 1744. [8] To Newcastle, 29 Sept. 1752, Add. 32729, f. 396; 4 Aug. 1748, Add. 32716, f. 13; 18 May 1750, Add. 32720, f. 348; Walpole, *Mems. Geo. II*, i. 228. [9] To Newcastle, 9 Sept. 1750, Add. 32722, f. 343; *Mems. Geo. II*, i. 84–85; Yorke, ii. 116–17; Owen, 319–20; Namier, *Structure*, 195–6. [10] Owen, 319; Coxe, *Pelham*, ii. 73; Yorke, ii. 12; 17 Oct. 1753, Add. 32733, f. 81; *Dodington Diary*, 141, 150–1. [11] L. S. Sutherland, 'The City of London and the Devonshire-Pitt Administration, 1756–7', *Proc. Brit. Acad.* 1960, p. 148; *Mems. Geo. II*, i. 371; *Mems. Geo. III*, i. 40; *Chesterfield Letters*, ed. Bradshaw, iii. 1419.

R.R.S.

PELHAM, Henry (?1729–1803), of Lee, Kent.

BRAMBER   22 Nov. 1751–1754
TIVERTON   1754–June 1758

b. ?1729, 3rd surv. s. of Thomas Pelham of Lewes, Suss. and bro. of Thomas Pelham jun. (qq.v.). *educ.* Corpus Christi, Camb. 1746; fellow of Peterhouse 1751. *m.* 1 Sept. 1767, Jane, da. of Nicholas Hardinge (q.v.), 1s. 1da. *suc.* bro. John to Catsfield and Crowhurst 1786;[1] to estates of his niece Miss Cressett, taking add. name of Cressett 1792.

     Commr. of customs 1758–88.

Henry Pelham was returned in 1751 as a government supporter. He died early in 1803.

[1] *VCH Suss.* ix. 79–80, 241.

R.R.S.

PELHAM, James (c.1683–1761), of Crowhurst, Suss.

NEWARK   1722–1741
HASTINGS   1741–1761

b. c.1683, 2nd s. of Sir Nicholas Pelham of Catsfield and Crowhurst, and bro. of Thomas Pelham of Lewes (qq.v.). *unm.*
     Capt. 8 Drags. 1711; capt. and lt. col. 1 Ft. Gds. 1716; sec. to ld. chamberlain c.1720–d., to Prince of Wales 1728–37; dep. cofferer of the Household 1749–54.

Having seen active service in the war of the Spanish succession, James Pelham was promoted under George I but, as second cousin of the great Pelhams and a friend of the Walpoles, exchanged his military for a political career. In 1710 he had written to Walpole's brother, Horace (q.v.): 'I am convinced you intend to keep your promise of making me a great man'.[1] In the Hastings elections of 1715 and 1722 he acted as the agent of the Duke of Newcastle,[2] who about 1720 appointed him his secretary and in 1722 returned him for Newark. At the 1727 election he was returned both for Bridport and Newark, opting to serve for the latter.

On the formation of the Prince of Wales's household in 1728, Pelham was appointed secretary to the Prince. He resigned the post in 1737 when he voted with the Administration and against his master on the Prince's allowance. In 1741 he was transferred to Hastings, with a view to relieving him of the expense of the Newark elections. Discontented with his financial position, he complained to Newcastle (22 April), reminding him of the loss which he had suffered by Newcastle's buying South Sea stock for him, and of £2,000 which he had lent the Duke.

     I must observe [he wrote] that I am the only one your Grace has ever suffered to spend scarce any of their

own money at any of your towns and add that my small estate is now mortgaged for six thousand pounds and if I was to be out of all employment I should not have fifty pounds a year to live upon at the later end of my days.

Newcastle replied 26 Apr.: 'I have ever taken it extreme kindly that you have not pressed me for it when it might have been inconvenient to me to pay it'.[3] In the course of the next ten years he was made deputy cofferer of the Household under Newcastle's nephew Lord Lincoln; given a sinecure in the customs of about £700, held for him by his nephew John Pelham;[4] and granted a secret service pension of £500 p.a. Still discontented, he wrote to Newcastle, 5 July 1750:

     The King is so gracious as to allow me five hundred a year . . . but as I have nothing to shew for it 'tis most likely any alteration in the Ministry would put it out of my power to ask a favour of this sort. What I propose is a pension upon Ireland of six hundred for 21 years, the exchange etc. would bring it lower than what I now receive . . . I mentioned this to Mr. Pelham who approves of my trying it at this time; both my offices are less than anybody has for near thirty years constant expensive attendance, the cofferer to be sure is a very precarious tenure.

However, on meeting with a refusal from Newcastle, he declared himself 'entirely satisfied'.[5] Needless to say, he voted with the Government in every recorded division.

     Throughout these years James Pelham looked after Newcastle's electoral interests in Sussex, particularly in Hastings, Seaford and Rye. He was also on occasion used as a whip for Newcastle's private party in the House. On 30 Jan. 1751, when Pitt was in hot water for speaking and voting with the Opposition on the navy estimates, Newcastle sent a letter to 'dear Jemmy' desiring that, in view of the 'able and affectionate manner' in which Pitt had defended him against attacks in recent debates,

     neither you, nor any of my friends would give into any clamour . . . that may be made against him from any of the party on account of his differing as to the number of seamen.[6]

He was to show this letter to seven of the Members owing their election to Newcastle, who presumably dealt with the others himself.

     About 1754 James Pelham's health began to decline. He did not stand in 1761 and died 27 Dec. 1761, still in possession of his pension and sinecure.

[1] *HMC Townshend*, 337. [2] S. H. Nulle, *Thomas Pelham Holles, Duke of Newcastle*, 47, 140. [3] Add. 32696, ff. 343, 383. [4] Ibid. 32946, f. 47; 38334, ff. 211–12. [5] Ibid. 33066, ff. 146, 158. [6] Coxe, *Pelham*, ii. 144.

L.B.N.

PELHAM, Sir Nicholas (?1650–1739), of Catsfield and Crowhurst, Suss.

SEAFORD 23 Feb. 1671–1679
SUSSEX 1679–1681
SEAFORD 1689–1690
LEWES 24 Nov. 1702–1705, 27 Jan. 1726–1727

b. ?1650, 3rd s. of Sir Thomas Pelham, 2nd Bt., M.P., of Halland, Suss. but 1st by his 3rd w. Margaret, da. of Sir Henry Vane, M.P., of Fairlawn, Kent. *educ.* Ch. Ch. Oxf. 13 May 1665, aged 14. *m.* Jane, da. and coh. of James Huxley of Dornford, Oxon., 2s. 1da. Kntd. 20 Apr. 1661.

Sir Nicholas Pelham was brought back to Parliament at the age of 75 by his great-nephew, the Duke of Newcastle, as a stop-gap to fill the vacancy created by the death of another great-nephew, Henry Pelham of Stanmer (q.v.). Replaced at the next general election, he died 8 Nov. 1739 in his ninetieth year. An obituary notice writes of him:

He was upwards of sixty years in the commission of the peace, a gentleman of the most exemplary life, having spent all his days in the continued exercise of piety and charity.[1]

[1] *Gent. Mag.* 1739, p. 605.

R.R.S.

PELHAM, Thomas (?1678–c.1760), of Lewes, Suss.

LEWES 1705–1741

b. ?1678, 1st s. of Sir Nicholas Pelham and bro. of James Pelham (qq.v.). *educ.* St. Edmund Hall, Oxf. 3 July 1693, aged 15; G. Inn 1696. *m.* (settlement 22 Sept. 1704) his cos. Elizabeth, da. of Henry Pelham, M.P., of Stanmer, clerk of the pells 1698–1721, sis. of Henry Pelham of Stanmer (q.v.), 8s. 4da. *suc.* fa. 1739.
Commr. for stating army debts 1715–17; ld. of Trade 1717–41.

Pelham succeeded his father at Lewes, which he represented as a Whig on the family interest for 36 years. At George I's accession he obtained a place of £500 a year, which he exchanged for one of £1,000 a year, no doubt through the influence of his kinsman and patron, the Duke of Newcastle, when the board of Trade was reconstituted after the split in the Whig party in 1717. On 23 Mar. 1720 he made his first and last reported speech, against Walpole's motion for fixing the rate of conversion of government securities into South Sea stock. An occasional rather than a constant attender at board of Trade meetings, but a regular voter for the Government, he nearly lost his seat at the general election of 1734. 'Old Tom Pelham', Newcastle wrote to his wife during a pre-election visit to Sussex in the summer of 1733, 'is as unpopular as possible and has personally disobliged the whole town'.[1] If

the election were lost, his son-in-law, William Hay (q.v.), reported to the Duke in November,

the loss of it must be imputed to Mr. Pelham's inactivity, who will not stir for all the frequent and earnest solicitations of myself and all his friends. He knows little of his affairs; nothing but by report, though he has opportunities every hour of the day to satisfy himself of the truth. He has not been round the town since he went with your Grace, nor I believe asked a single man for his vote; and I am fairly persuaded that half the votes that have been lost have been lost by this unpardonable negligence.

A few days later Hay wrote that his father-in-law had been so upset at learning of these defections that he had taken to his bed for a week.[2] He just scraped home by eight votes, but at the next election he was retired with a pension of £800 a year.[3] He was succeeded both at Lewes and at the board of Trade by his eldest son, Thomas (q.v.), whom he survived by sixteen years, dying c.January 1760.[4]

[1] Add. 33073, f. 80. [2] Add. 32689, ff. 7, 24. [3] *Cal. Treas. Bks. and Pprs.* 1739–41, p. 579. [4] PCC 31 Lynch.

R.R.S.

PELHAM, Thomas (c.1705–37), of Stanmer, nr. Lewes, Suss.

LEWES 1727–21 Dec. 1737

b. c.1705, 3rd s. of Henry Pelham, M.P., of Stanmer, and bro. of Henry Pelham of Stanmer (q.v.). *m.* 5 Feb. 1725, Annetta, da. of Thomas Bridges of Constantinople, 1s. 1da. *suc.* bro. to family estates 1725.

At a very early age Thomas Pelham, commonly known as Turk Pelham, was sent to Constantinople as apprentice to John Lethieullier, a Turkey merchant, whose step-daughter he married, despite the disapproval of his family. Shortly after his marriage he succeeded on the death of his elder brother to the family estates, worth over £2,000 a year. He declined a proposal by Newcastle to nominate him at once for his brother's seat,[1] but after returning to England he was brought in by Newcastle at the general election of 1727, voting with the Government in all recorded divisions. At the next general election Newcastle complained that he 'never comes to Lewes but he gets drunk and then talks in so imprudent and extravagant a manner that he makes his friends very uneasy'.[2] He died of drink 21 Dec. 1737.[3]

[1] Add. 33085, ff. 110, 138. [2] Add. 32688, f. 526. [3] *HMC 14th Rep. IX*, 238.

R.R.S.

PELHAM, Thomas, jun. (c.1705–43).

HASTINGS 22 Feb. 1728–1741
LEWES 1741–1 Aug. 1743

b. c.1705, 1st s. of Thomas Pelham of Lewes, Suss. and bro. of Henry Pelham of Lee (qq.v.). *educ.* Corpus Christi, Camb. 1722. *m.* 10 May 1738, Sarah, da. of John Gould of Hackney, sis. of John and Nathaniel Gould (qq.v.), 2s.

Sec. to British ambassadors, congress of Soissons 1728–30, to Paris embassy 1730–41; ld. of Trade 1741–*d.*

Soon after coming of age Thomas Pelham was brought into Parliament and given a diplomatic appointment by his second cousin, the Duke of Newcastle, then secretary of state. His duties did not prevent him from voting in all the recorded divisions of his first two Parliaments, except that on the place bill in 1740. In 1741 he succeeded to his father's seat at Lewes and place at the board of Trade. Soon afterwards he fell dangerously ill of consumption,[1] dying in his father's lifetime, 1 Aug. 1743.

[1] James Pelham to Newcastle, 25 May 1742, Add. 32699, f. 256.

R.R.S.

PELHAM, Thomas, jun. (1728–1805), of Stanmer, nr. Lewes, Suss.

RYE   13 Dec. 1749–1754
SUSSEX   1754–17 Nov. 1768

b. 28 Feb. 1728, s. of Thomas Pelham of Stanmer (q.v.). *educ.* Westminster 1740; Clare, Camb. 1745; Grand Tour (France, Switzerland, Italy, Germany) 1746–50. *m.* 15 June 1754, Anne, da. and h. of Frederick Meinhardt Frankland (q.v.), 4s. 4da. *suc.* fa. 1737; 1st Duke of Newcastle as Baron Pelham of Stanmer 17 Nov. 1768; *cr.* Earl of Chichester 23 June 1801.

Ld. of Trade 1754–61, of Admiralty 1761–2; P.C. 6 Sept. 1765; comptroller of the Household 1765–74; surveyor gen. of the customs of London 1773–*d.*; c.j. in eyre north of Trent 1774–5; keeper of the great wardrobe 1775–82.

Thomas Pelham was returned for Rye by the Duke of Newcastle while absent on the grand tour. Next year Henry Pelham wrote to Newcastle:

The people of Rye complain a little of hearing nothing of their Member. Thomas Pelham must make 'em a visit before Christmas or else I fear we shall lose all our credit in that town, which I think at present is as well set as any of your boroughs in Sussex.[1]

On Henry Pelham's death Thomas succeeded him as knight of the shire. He followed Newcastle into opposition in the next reign, inheriting his Sussex estates.

He died 8 Jan. 1805.

[1] 12 Oct. 1750, Add. 32723, f. 142.

R.R.S.

PENDARVES, Alexander (?1665–1725), of Roskrow, Cornw.

PENRYN   1689–1698, 16 Jan. 1699–1705
SALTASH   1708–1710
PENRYN   1710–22 Jan. 1714
HELSTON   12 Apr. 1714–1715
LAUNCESTON 11 Jan. 1721–8 Mar. 1725

b. ?1665, 3rd s. of John Pendarves of Roskrow by Bridget, da. of Sir Alexander Carew, 2nd Bt., M.P., of Antony, Cornw. *educ.* Exeter, Oxf. 14 July 1682, aged 17; G. Inn 1682. *m.* (1) Lady Dorothy Bourke, da. of Richard, 8th Earl of Clanricarde [I]; (2) 17 Feb. 1718, Mary, da. of Bernard Granville, bro. of George Granville, M.P., 1st Baron Lansdowne; she later m. Dr. Patrick Delany.

Commr. of prizes 1703–5; surveyor gen. of crown lands 1714.

A Tory, Pendarves was brought in for Launceston by his intimate friend George Granville, later Lord Lansdowne.[1] Like Lansdowne, he was arrested in 1715 and was brought prisoner to Plymouth, in company with several other Cornish gentlemen suspected of being favourable to the Pretender.[2] After his release, he visited Lansdowne at Longleat, where he met and married Mary Granville, the future Mrs. Delany. According to her he was 'excessively fat, of a brown complexion, negligent in his dress, and took a vast quantity of snuff, which gave him a dirty look; his eyes were black, small, lively and sensible; he had an honest countenance, but altogether a person rather disgusting than engaging. He was good-natured and friendly, but so strong a *party man* that he made himself many enemies'.[3] His name was sent to the Pretender as a Jacobite supporter in 1721, and he was in contact with Atterbury's agents during the plot of 1722.[4] He died of a fit on 8 Mar. 1725, leaving his widow, who had unfortunately dissuaded him from signing his will the day before, with nothing but her jointure.[5]

[1] Mrs. Delany, *Autobiog. and Corresp.* i. 22–4. [2] Walter Moyle to Humphry Morice, 26 Sept. 1715, Morice mss in Bank of England. [3] Mrs. Delany, 34. [4] Stuart mss 65/16; *Report from the Committee appointed by the House of Commons to examine Christopher Layer and others*, app. F. 11. [5] Mrs. Delany, 107.

E.C.

PENGELLY, Thomas (1675–1730), of Cheshunt, Herts.

COCKERMOUTH   29 Apr. 1717–16 Oct. 1726

bap. 16 May 1675, s. of Thomas Pengelly of Moorfields, London, and Cheshunt, Turkey merchant, by Rachel, da. of Lt.-Col. Jeremy Baines. *educ.* I. Temple 1692, called 1700, bencher 1710. *unm.* Kntd. 1 May 1719.

Serjeant-at-law 1710; King's prime serjeant 1719; chief baron of the Exchequer 1726–*d.*

Pengelly was legal adviser to the 6th Duke of Somerset, who returned him for Cockermouth.[1] At first he supported the Government, voting for the repeal of the Occasional Conformity and Schism Acts and speaking violently for the peerage bill, because it would have kept men of property in the Commons.[2] On the collapse of the South Sea bubble he spoke in favour of the bill restraining the directors from leaving the country. Elected to the secret committee set up by the Commons to inquire into the affair, he was the first to inform the House of the flight of the company's cashier. In spite of his legal and political claims he was passed in the race for legal promotion by a much junior barrister, Philip Yorke (q.v.), for whom Lord Chancellor Macclesfield was supposed to have an undue partiality. It is said that he

> was so disgusted at frequently hearing the chancellor declare that Mr. Yorke had not been answered that he one day threw up his brief and declared he would no more attend a court where he found that Mr. Yorke was not to be answered.[3]

On Macclesfield's fall in 1725 Pengelly played a leading part in promoting and conducting his impeachment. Having unsuccessfully applied for the chief justiceship of the King's bench,[4] he went into opposition, speaking in support of Pulteney's motion of 9 Feb. 1726 for an inquiry into the public debt, and on 16 Feb. against the treaty of Hanover. Soon afterwards he was appointed chief baron of the Exchequer, thus terminating his parliamentary career.

He died of gaol fever 14 Apr. 1730.

[1] *HMC 7th Rep.* 681, 683. [2] *HMC Egmont Diary*, i. 113. [3] R. Cooksey, *Lord Somers*, 72. [4] *Knatchbull Diary*, 36, 38, 42; Pengelly to Newcastle, 24 Feb. 1725, Add. 32687, f. 65.

R.R.S.

PENNINGTON, Sir John, 3rd Bt. (c.1710–68), of Muncaster, Cumb.

CUMBERLAND 8 Jan. 1745–1768

b. c.1710, 1st surv. s. of Sir Joseph Pennington, 2nd Bt. (q.v.). *unm. suc.* fa. 3 Dec. 1744.
Comptroller of cash in the excise 1734–8; ld. lt. Westmld. 1756–8.

In 1745 Pennington, as colonel of the Cumberland and Westmorland militia, took part in the defence of Carlisle against the rebels, doing his best, but without success, to prevent his men from surrendering the town as soon as it was invested.[1] In the same year he had succeeded his father as Member for Cumberland, which he represented unopposed in four Parliaments. He voted against the Administration on the grant for Hanoverian troops in 1746,

but in 1747 he was classed as a government supporter. In the next reign he adhered to Bute.

He died 26 Mar. 1768.

[1] G. C. Mounsey, *Carlisle in 1745*, p. 65.

R.R.S.

PENNINGTON, Sir Joseph, 2nd Bt. (1677–1744), of Muncaster, Cumb.

CUMBERLAND 1734–3 Dec. 1744

b. 4 Oct. 1677, 1st s. of Sir William Pennington, 1st Bt., of Muncaster by Isabella, da. and coh. of John Stapleton of Warter, Yorks. *educ.* Queen's, Oxf. 1695. *m.* 20 Mar. 1706, Margaret, da. of John Lowther, M.P., 1st Visct. Lonsdale, 4s. 1da. who was mother of Robert Lowther, M.P., and Sir James Lowther, 5th Bt., M.P. *suc.* fa. 12 July 1730.
Comptroller of cash in the excise 1723–34.

Pennington came of an old Cumberland family, whose natural interest in the county was strengthened by alliances with the Lowthers. He was also connected with the Lawsons through his mother, who was first cousin to Gilfrid Lawson (q.v.). In 1720 he was recommended by his brother-in-law, Lord Lonsdale, for a place to Walpole, who replied that he had 'always understood that a sinecure of about £300 or £400 per annum was his only view, and that no employment of business or personal attendancy was at all agreeable to his life or circumstances'.[1] In 1723 he obtained a place, which he surrendered in 1734 to his son in order to be returned for the county on the recommendation of his brother-in-law in succession to Gilfrid Lawson, who gave him his interest.[2] Re-elected in 1741, he voted with the Government in all recorded divisions till his death, 3 Dec. 1744.

[1] *HMC Lonsdale*, 122. [2] B. Bonsall, *Sir James Lowther and Cumb. and Westmld. Elections*, 7.

R.R.S.

PENTON, Henry (?1705–62), of Eastgate House, Winchester, Hants.

TREGONY 1734–1747
WINCHESTER 1747–1761

b. ?1705, 1st s. of John Penton of St. Laurence, Winchester. *educ.* New Coll. Oxf. 31 Jan. 1722, aged 16. *m.* Feb. 1733 (with £10,000), Miss Simondi, da. of Swedish consul at Lisbon by his w. Anne, sis. of Joseph Gulston (q.v.) and afterwards w. of John Goddard (q.v.),[1] at least 1s. *suc.* fa. 1724.[2]
King's letter carrier 1747–61; recorder, Winchester.

Of an old Winchester family, Penton was returned for Tregony on the interest of his wife's step-father, John Goddard (q.v.), voting with the Administration in every recorded division. In April 1743 he was granted the reversion of the office of King's letter carrier, which fell in four years later.[3] At the general election of 1747 he transferred to his native Winchester, retaining the seat until 1761, when he stood down in favour of his son. His only recorded speech was made on 19 Mar. 1748 in support of a petition from London traders for suppressing hawkers and pedlars. The 2nd Lord Egmont wrote of him in his electoral survey of c.1749–50:

> I believe he will be with us. He is either a spy for the Ministry or not cordial with them, for I have heard him more than once express dissatisfaction. And he has strained opportunities to do it to me, yet I know but little of him.

He died 1 Sept. 1762.

¹ Nichols, *Lit. Hist.* v. 4–5. ² *General Hist. Hants* (1861), i. 80. ³ *Gent. Mag.* 1743, p. 275; 1747, p. 103.

E.C.

PEPPER, John (*d.*1725), of Enfield Chase, Mdx.

STEYNING   1715–22 Oct. 1725

3rd s. of Capt. George Pepper of Ballygarth, co. Meath by his w. Hannah. *m.* Johannah, 1da.
    M.P. [I] 1715–22 Oct. 1725.
    Capt. Earl of Roscommon's Ft. 1689, Erle's Ft. 1690, 8 Drags. 1693; maj. 1695; adjt.-gen. in Ireland 1706; lt.-col. bef. 1707; col. 8 Drags. 1707–19; brig.-gen. 1707; maj.-gen. 1710; res. 1719; ranger of Epping forest and Enfield Chase 1714–25.

After serving in Spain and Portugal during the war of the Spanish succession, Pepper in 1714 bought the office of ranger of Enfield Chase, overbidding the future Duke of Chandos.[1] In the 1715 rebellion he was sent with his regiment to hold down Oxford, where he made several arrests.[2] Returned as a Whig for Steyning, he voted with the Government on the septennial bill and the repeal of the Occasional Conformity and Schism Acts, but was absent on the peerage bill. While the South Sea scheme was before Parliament he accepted a bribe of £4,000 stock at 180 from the Company on the usual terms (see Chaplin, Sir Robert); but when he came to receive his 'profit' on the stock, complained that it had been sold too soon, the price having since continued to rise.[3] Accusing of pocketing the proceeds of selling timber from Epping forest, he sold his office to William Pultency (q.v.), dying 'unlamented' a few days later, 22 Oct. 1725, at Dover on his way to France 'to take the air at Montpellier for the recovery of his broken constitution'.[4]

¹ C. H. C. & M. Baker, *James Brydges, 1st Duke of Chandos*, 386–7. ² Hearne, *Colls.* (Oxf. Hist. Soc.), v. 125; *Pol. State*, x. 336–8. ³ *CJ*, xix. 569. ⁴ *HMC Var.* viii. 395; Baker, 394–7; *Pol. State*, xxx. 418.

J.B.L.

PERCEVAL, John, Visct. Perceval [I] (1683–1748).[1]

HARWICH   1727–1734

b. 12 July 1683, 1st surv. s. of Sir John Perceval, 3rd Bt., of Burton, Kanturk, co. Cork by Catherine, da. of Sir Edward Dering, 2nd Bt., M.P. *educ.* Westminster 1698; Magdalen, Oxf. 1699; Grand Tour 1705–7. *m.* 10 June 1710, Catherine, da. of Sir Philip Parker, 2nd Bt., of Erwarton, Suff., 3s. 4da. *suc.* bro. as 5th Bt. 9 Nov. 1691; *cr.* Baron Perceval [I] 21 Apr. 1715; Visct. Perceval [I] 25 Feb. 1723; Earl of Egmont [I] 6 Nov. 1733.
    M.P. [I] 1703–14.
    P.C. [I] Oct. 1704; recorder, Harwich 1728–34.

Perceval was descended from an ancient Somerset family, who in the early seventeenth century had settled in Ireland, where they had acquired large grants of forfeited lands. Succeeding to an estate of about £6,000 a year (ii. 185), he was created an Irish peer on George I's accession, but took little part in public life till the opening of the next reign, when, in his own words,

> I waited on the King, and told him that though loving my ease, I never yet would be in Parliament, yet having observed in all reigns that the first that was summoned was always most troublesome to the Prince, I was resolved to stand, that I might contribute my poor services to the settlement of his affairs. The King took it extremely kind and thanked me; asked me where it was? I replied at Harwich, where my brother [-in-law, Sir Philip Parker, 3rd Bt., q.v.] had a natural interest, and would give me his to join my own; that his Majesty had servants there that had votes, and if his Majesty would not suffer them to be against me, I should meet with no opposition, and be at no expense. The King replied, they should be at my service, and said he would speak to Sir Robert Walpole to order . . . that the Post Office should be for me. Upon this security I went down, but how were the King's orders obeyed? I was kept there two months and a half under a constant declaration that the government servants were to be against me, and Phillipson, the commissary of the packets [father of John Phillipson, q.v.], averred that I had not the Government's interest, and even named another person who was to come and oppose me on the Government's account . . . It was not till the very day before the election that, when I could be worried no longer, the Post Office thought fit to give their directions to Phillipson, and then the Government's servants declared themselves.

Nor were his troubles at an end, for

> ever since our friends are treated in the hardest manner imaginable. The town is poor, and the people subsist by serving the packets with beer, bread, candles, and working for the packet boats. In these matters none of our friends are suffered to do anything till they forsake us to range themselves on Phillipson's side; then they may be employed, but otherwise are left to starve. What is this but ruining my brother's interest and mine there, and who can we attribute this to but the ministry? (i.20).

When he and Parker complained of Phillipson, charging him with being a Jacobite, Walpole promised that 'he should be out . . . but nothing came of it' till 17 Feb. 1730, when Walpole told Perceval that

> he had spoke to the King, and received his orders to turn him out; he said he had done it before, but he

was not able; that a great many things were laid to his charge that he was not to blame in, and that he could not do everything expected of him (iii. 347–8; i. 15–19, 50).

Perceval at the time attributed his treatment to the resentment of the ministers at his having applied to the King instead of to them for the government interest at Harwich, and to their suspicion that he and Parker were trying to convert it from a government borough into a private one (i. 22). Connecting the decision to comply with his and Parker's repeated requests for Phillipson's dismissal with Parker's voting against the Government on a bill for excluding pensioners from the House of Commons, on which they had been defeated on 16 Feb., he thought that the fear that Parker, with both his brothers-in-law, Perceval and William East, might vote against them in the impending critical debate on Dunkirk, had 'cast the ministry into so great apprehensions of their friends deserting them, that they think it necessary to use us in a more decent manner than before' (i. 56). He also believed that his troubles at Harwich were due to Edward Carteret (q.v.), joint postmaster general, whom he supposed to have protected Phillipson, while being himself protected by his nephew, Lord Carteret (i. 23). In fact, as he learned four years later, the chief author of his troubles at Harwich was not Carteret but the other joint postmaster general, Edward Harrison (q.v.), whose daughter and heiress had married Lord Townshend's eldest son, Charles (q.v.), Lord Lynn, 'for Harrison designed to have brought in a son of my Lord Townshend's' for the seat taken by Perceval (ii. 82). As had been hinted to him at the time, Walpole, as minister for the House of Commons, had been ready to placate the Parker-Perceval-East group by dismissing Phillipson, but had been prevented from doing so by Townshend (i. 47). Had Phillipson's retention or dismissal not been connected with the struggle for power between Walpole and Townshend, which was about to end in Townshend's resignation, such a parish pump affair would not have been referred to the King; for when, on the death of Phillipson's successor as agent of the packets in 1734, Perceval, having obtained a promise in favour of his own nominee for the post from Walpole, expressed a fear that 'the King's promise in favour of another might be surreptitiously obtained, unknown to Sir Robert', he was told by Walpole that the 'matter was of too small a nature ever to reach the King's ear' (ii. 5).

For the rest of the Parliament Perceval was usually on excellent terms with Walpole, whom he regarded as 'the ablest minister in the kingdom', though he deplored 'the neglect the ministry show

of the ancient gentry and men of fortune in the disposal of employments and favours, which they choose to bestow on little and unknown persons' (i. 18, 41). Not that he had much to complain of in this respect for, besides an Irish earldom for himself, he obtained a place in the Prince of Wales's household for his brother-in-law, whose widow at his instance was granted a pension when, in the words of the epitaph which he composed for him, 'God removed him . . . from the land of the living and undoubtedly preferred him to a higher place' (i. 23, 203). An independent supporter of the Government, he voted with them in all the five recorded divisions of this Parliament, but sometimes voted against them 'out of conscience and not from a spirit of opposition' (i. 297). In the debate on Dunkirk in 1730, he was among the government supporters who secured an amendment to the proposed ministerial motion by making it clear that otherwise 'the Court would lose . . . all the independent Members of the House' (i. 73). When pressed in 1731 by an emissary from Walpole to vote against a bill for excluding pensioners from the House of Commons he 'flatly refused to be against it, telling him that my honour and conscience obliged me to be for it' (i. 125). In 1734 he was one of 'twenty friends of the Court who left the House', in order not to have to vote against the Government on a place bill, for which he must have voted had he been present,

for otherwise having no employment, my opposing so reasonable a thing might be interpreted as if I were a secret pensioner, yet I apprehended some danger might arise from passing it, because parties are now so high and envenomed against each other, that were the new Parliament almost entirely independent of the Crown, I know not how violently they may behave against the public measures next year, when we shall be perhaps engaged in war (ii. 37–38).

He went to court and to Walpole's levees, but not to the meetings of ministerial supporters in the Commons which were held the evening before the opening of a new session, to hear the King's speech and the heads of the proposed Address, looking on them 'as a precluding the judgment which for honour sake at least ought to have the appearance of being determined by the debates of the House' (i. 2). A member of the gaols committee and of the Georgia Society, he was also active on Irish affairs, serving on the drafting committee of the bill allowing unenumerated goods to come direct from the plantations to Ireland,[2] which he carried to the Lords in 1731 (i. 187). In 1733 he spoke on Irish and Georgian matters (i. 334–5, 373). In the same year he published anonymously a pro-government pamphlet, of which Walpole ordered the Post Office to reprint 3,000 copies for distribution before the elections (i. 488, ii. 86). His parliamentary status and relations with the ministry are shown by his being invited to the select meeting of leading ministerial Members of the Commons held at Walpole's house the night before the Cockpit meeting in January 1734, though he did not attend either for the reason already given (ii. 7).

At the general election of 1734 Perceval, now Earl of Egmont, stood down in favour of his son, Lord Perceval (q.v.), for whom he had obtained a promise of the government interest at Harwich from Walpole. About a fortnight before the election, due on 27 Apr., the Customs and the Post Office, on Walpole's instructions, sent word orally to those of their officers, numbering twelve out of the thirty-two members of the Harwich corporation who elected the parliamentary representatives of the borough, that they should vote for Perceval and the other government candidate, Carteret Leathes (q.v.), it being considered too dangerous to put into writing orders which, if they fell into the hands of the Opposition, could be produced in Parliament as a proof that the Government were interfering with the freedom of elections (ii. 82–3, 91–2). Up to that time no third candidate had made an appearance, though there was a strong anti-Perceval party in the corporation, headed by Egmont's old enemy, Phillipson. Egmont fancied that this party would be cowed by the appointment of his nominee to the agency of the packets, whose holder, as he himself had found when Phillipson held it, could bring pressure to bear on opponents by depriving them of the orders for the packets, on which they depended for their livelihood (ii. 9–10). In fact it seems to have goaded them into looking for an alternative to Perceval, on the ground that his father 'had put a person into the agency of the packets, who was odious to them all', besides having 'represented several there [e.g. Phillipson] to be Jacobites' (ii. 100). On 16 Apr. Walpole told Egmont that they had sent to Lord Harrington (William Stanhope, q.v.), offering 'him the choice of a Member if he will send one down, but I told my Lord he should not accept it, for I desired your son to be chosen' (ii. 85). On 19 and 21 Apr. Leathes showed Walpole letters to him signed by 20 of the 32 voters, inviting him or Walpole to recommend some other candidate than Perceval, 'for they were determined not to choose' him, his father, his uncle, 'or any of the family, who had used them ill, broke promises etc., and were odious to them' (ii. 87, 90). By this time Harrington had accepted the offer on behalf of his brother, Charles Stanhope (q.v.). On this Walpole told Egmont, who had been pressing the King 'to order his servants to vote for my son':

I have done all I can, except to write under my own hand, which I dare not, nor should the King's name be used, but your son may freely use my name and tell all the government servants that if they will in anything oblige me, they will vote for him (ii. 90).

On 24 Apr., three days before polling day, Egmont, in response to a last minute appeal from his son, asked Walpole to order the Post Office and the Customs to send for six of their Harwich officials, who had stated their intention of voting against Perceval, so that they might 'be out of the way during the election'. Walpole replied:

My Lord, I think it impossible for me to do what you desire, and those to whom I was to give my orders would think it too great a hardship to be put on them, to send for a number of officers the day before the election. In my station, where what I do or do not do everything is imputed to me, makes this too dangerous to venture upon [sic.]. I have with great honour and truth kept my engagements to your Lordship, and declared so to all persons concerned, and must beg you will excuse me taking this step (ii. 92–93).

At the election 19 electors voted for Leathes and Stanhope, the remaining 13 voting for Perceval, two of whom also voted for Leathes, the official vote, despite statements to the contrary by both sides, being equally divided. Writing from Harwich, Parker told Egmont that it was 'impossible to describe the malice of the other side, so that some of them seem as if they would sacrifice their employments'. When the result was announced, Phillipson exclaimed: 'Lord, now let thy servant depart in peace, for my eyes have seen thy salvation', several of the voters crying out: 'Liberty! we are free from the tyranny we were under' (ii. 93, 95–98, 100). Nevertheless Egmont blamed his defeat on Walpole, who, he suggested, had never 'meant at the bottom my son should be chose' (ii. 106), while his son regarded himself as having lost the election 'by the treachery of Sir Robert Walpole', though admitting that this view was not shared by the King, who took 'his minister's part in some measure against my father and me, which appeared by his withdrawing much of the civility and particular respect which he had before showed to him'.[3]

After this setback Egmont took no further part in politics, but he continued active on the council of the Georgia Society till 1742, when he resigned, 'partly by reason of my ill health and partly from observing the ill behaviour of the ministry and Parliament with respect to the colony' (iii. 265). He died 1 May 1748, leaving a diary which is one of the chief sources of information on the House of Commons from 1730 to 1734.

[1] The references in the text are to *HMC Egmont Diary*. [2] *CJ*, xxi. 727. [3] Add. 47091, f. 3.

R.R.S.

PERCEVAL, John, Visct. Perceval (1711–70).

WESTMINSTER   31 Dec. 1741–1747
WEOBLEY   9 Dec. 1747–1754
BRIDGWATER   1754–7 May 1762

b. 24 Feb. 1711, o.surv. s. of John Perceval (q.v.), 1st Earl of Egmont [I]. *m.* (1) 15 Feb. 1737, Lady Catherine Cecil (*d.*16 Aug. 1752), da. of James Cecil, 5th Earl of Salisbury, 2s. 1da.; (2) 26 Jan. 1756, Catherine, da. of Hon. Charles Compton, 4th s. of George, 4th Earl of Northampton, 4s. 4da. *suc.* fa. as 2nd Earl 1 May 1748; *cr.* Baron Lovel and Holland 7 May 1762.
  M.P. [I] 1731–48.
  Lord of the bedchamber to the Prince of Wales 1748–51; P.C. 9 Jan. 1755; jt. postmaster gen. 1762–3; first ld. of Admiralty 1763–6.

Perceval's strength, according to Horace Walpole, was 'indefatigable application'. By the age of twenty he had published several anonymous political pamphlets and acquired a seat in the Irish Parliament, where his attacks on local abuses gave offence in government circles.[1] On coming of age he was put up as a government candidate for his father's seat at Harwich, promising Walpole 'that if he would be his friend he would be his', though he had recently published an anonymous attack on the excise bill. Defeated at Harwich in 1734 he went over to the Opposition, offering his house in Pall Mall to the Prince of Wales on his expulsion from St. James's in 1737.[2] The offer was refused, but led to an invitation from the Prince in 1740 to stand at the forthcoming general election for a Cornish seat, which at the last moment proved to have been allocated to someone else.[3] Perceval then joined Daniel Boone (q.v.) in standing for Haslemere but gave up on payment of their expenses by their opponents.[4] He next intrigued his way into a committee formed by 'a body of the lower kind of tradesmen' at Westminster to organize a petition against the return of two government candidates, at once finding himself 'master of the committee and consequently of the whole opposition in the city of Westminster'.[5] On the annulment of the election, he was unanimously adopted as one of the opposition candidates. Returned unopposed, three days after taking his seat he made his maiden speech on Pulteney's motion for a secret committee on the conduct of the war. In his speech he 'blundered out what they had been cloaking with so much art, by declaring that he should vote for it as a committee of accusation' against Walpole, who paid him the compliment of immediately rising to reply.[6] After Walpole's fall he spoke and voted with the Government, also publishing an able defence of Pulteney's political conduct which made him very unpopular with the Opposition and his constituents. He also incurred much ridicule by producing, it was said at

a cost of £3,000, a genealogical history of his family, 'deducing the Percevals from ancient houses with which they were in fact unconnected'.[7]

In 1747 Perceval, 'rejected by Westminster and countenanced nowhere', stood for Weobley, having obtained an assurance from Pelham that he would be 'taken care of and assisted',[8] with the result that though defeated at the poll he was returned on petition. No sooner had he secured his seat than he went over to the Opposition, attaching himself to the Prince of Wales, who appointed him to his bedchamber. At the opening of the next session he published a pamphlet attacking the Pelhams as 'treacherous servants, who have taken [their Sovereign] captive in his closet and still detain him prisoner on his throne'. In the House he took the lead in the Opposition, making, according to Horace Walpole, who was at that time connected with Leicester House,

as great a figure as perhaps was ever made in so short a time. He is very bold and resolved, master of vast knowledge, and speaks at once with fire and method. His words are not picked and chosen like Pitt's, but his language is useful, clear and strong. He has already by his parts and resolution mastered his great unpopularity, so far as to be heard with the utmost attention, though I believe nobody had ever more various difficulties to combat. All the old corps hate him, on my father's and Mr. Pelham's account; the new part of the ministry on their own. The Tories have not quite forgiven his having left them in the last Parliament . . . and besides all this, there is a faction in the Prince's family . . . who are for moderate measures.[9]

During the remaining two years of Frederick's life Egmont, as he had become on the death of his father, was the Prince's chief political adviser, drawing up for him detailed plans for the opening fortnight of the next reign, including drafts of the new King's speeches to the Privy Council and Parliament, an analysis of the composition of the sitting House of Commons, with a view to the choice of its successor, and lists of dismissals and appointments, in the latter of which he himself figures as a future secretary of state. It was to him that Frederick wrote:

Let us remember both Henry IV and Sully, in all times these are our models, let us follow 'em in most all, except in their extravagances.[10]

On the night of Frederick's death the Princess sent Egmont to Carlton House to collect the Prince's political papers, those relating to his accession plans being burnt in her presence at Leicester House by George Lee (q.v.) and Egmont, who, however, kept his own copies. Next morning he held a meeting of twenty-three members of the Opposition at his house, urging them 'to remain united, to listen to no applications, not to discover any opinions of what was best to be done till we could see further; but determine to wait to see events [and] to stand by the Princess and her children'. He learned that his action was not approved by the Princess who, when told that he was 'keeping our friends together for her as much as I could', only said 'if the Prince could not keep them together how shall I', and suspected him of 'making a faction'. She repeatedly excused herself from seeing him, though she had long conferences with Lee, who was in favour 'of throwing ourselves disinterestedly into the hands of the Pelhams without conditions if the Princess was made Regent'. It became plain to him that she 'thought it necessary for her own purpose to abandon all the Prince's friends', which he recognized was 'not impolitic in her circumstances'.[11] The bulk of the party followed the Princess and Lee, but Egmont himself continued in opposition till the end of the Parliament.

Egmont died 20 Dec. 1770, having, in the words of the 2nd Lord Hardwicke, 'made very little of his ambition. He did not draw well with others and could not abide Mr. Pitt',[12] whose career he attacked in an unpublished pamphlet, preserved in his papers, along with a mass of valuable information on Leicester House in the last years of Frederick, Prince of Wales.

[1] Walpole, *Mems. Geo. II*, i. 35; *HMC Egmont Diary*, i. 92, 172, 447; ii. 117. [2] Ibid. i. 259, 376–8, 327; ii. 51, 435. [3] Add. 47091, p. 3. [4] *HMC Egmont Diary*, iii. 188, 219, 244. [5] Add. 47091, pp. 5–9. [6] Walpole to Mann, 22 Jan. 1742. [7] Walpole, *Mems. Geo. II*, i. 36–38; Walpole to Mann, 4 Mar. 1749; A. R. Wagner, *English Genealogy*, 350. [8] *Mems. Geo. II*, i. 37–38; Cary to Egmont, undated, Add. 46977. [9] To Mann, 4 Mar. 1749. [10] Add. 46977. [11] Add. 47097–8, passim. [12] Add. 3514, f. 237.

R.R.S.

PERIAM, John (?1701–88), of Milverton, Som.

MINEHEAD 19 Mar. 1742–1747

b. ?1701, 1st s. of John Periam of Milverton, Som. by Elizabeth, da. of John Southey of Fitzhead, Som.[1] *educ.* St. John's, Oxf. 6 Mar. 1719, aged 17. *m.* 1761, Martha Dare, *s.p. suc.* mother-in-law to various properties in Taunton after 1761.[2]

By the early sixteenth century the Periams had established themselves as well-to-do merchants in Exeter, holding civic and high legal offices.[3] A Somerset squire of comparatively small estate, John Periam was in 1742 returned as a Tory for Minehead at an uncontested by-election, voting regularly against the Government. In 1747 he prepared to stand again, this time as the candidate of Henry Fownes Luttrell, who wrote:

the civilities I have received from my friend, Mr. Periam, and the many solicitations I have received from other gentlemen in his favour, lays me under an obligation to serve him to the utmost of my power.

But Luttrell's 'utmost' did not extend beyond issuing an address on Periam's behalf and the election, which was contested, promised to be very expensive. In these circumstances Periam withdrew after consulting his supporters, then changed his mind after a further meeting, only to withdraw finally on finding that some of his voters had transferred their promises to an opponent after his first withdrawal.[4] Never standing again, he died in 1788.

[1] *Illustrated Western Weekly News* (Plymouth), 30 Oct. 1915, p. 7. [2] PCC 90 Calvert. [3] W. H. Hamilton Rogers, *West-Country Stories & Sketches*, 159; *Illustrated Western Weekly News*, 30 Oct. 1915, p. 6. [4] Sir H. C. Maxwell Lyte, *Dunster*, i. 230, 235, 236.

S.R.M.

PERROT, Henry (1689–1740), of Northleigh, Oxon.

OXFORDSHIRE 17 May 1721–6 Jan. 1740

b. 29 Sept. 1689, 1st s. of James Perrot of Northleigh, by his w. Anne. *m.* (2) 2 Apr. 1719, Martha, da. and h. of Brereton Bouchier of Barnsley, Glos., niece of James Brydges, 1st Duke of Chandos,[1] 2da. *suc.* fa. 1725.

Perrot, whose father was nicknamed 'Golden Perrot' on account of his wealth,[2] came of a staunchly royalist family, long connected with the University of Oxford.[3] Returned unopposed for the county as a Tory, he voted against the Administration in every recorded division of the Parliament of 1727–34. In 1737–8 he went to the south of France, where he met the Duke of Ormonde, whose secretary wrote from Avignon, 17 Mar. 1738:

I am just going to meet . . . Mr. Perrot at Nîmes. He has been so roughly treated by the gout at Montpellier, that he is not able to come thus far to take his leave of his Grace [Ormonde], and wrote to me to meet him there this night. He returns by Bordeaux to Paris, and so directly to old England, where I believe he will enjoy but little of the session, which we hear will be a short one.[4]

In 1739 he told Carte, the Jacobite historian, that

at the meeting of the High Borlase Society [the Tory club] in August last at Oxford, he proposed to the gentlemen to give a power to the Duke of Ormonde to represent their sense to any foreign court, in order to procure the assistance they thought necessary to effect a restoration, engaging themselves to make good whatever he should represent or undertake for in their names. They indeed expressed themselves ready to give such a power at the same time that they did not care to enter into the consideration of the particular measures proper to make the enterprize and landing of foreign troops successful. But when they met in greater numbers at London last winter at the opening of the session of Parliament, they declined giving that power.[5]

He died near Paris 6 Jan. 1740, leaving Northleigh

to his brother, Thomas, and the rest of his property to his daughters.[6]

[1] *HMC Portland*, vii. 296–7. [2] Hearne, *Colls.* (Oxf. Hist. Soc.), viii. 327. [3] E. L. Barnwell, *Perrot Fam.* 79–106. [4] *HMC 10th Rep.* I, 503–4, 508, 512, 516. [5] Stuart mss 216/111. [6] PCC 86 Browne.

E.C.

PERRY, Micajah (*d.*1753), of St. Mary Axe, London, and Epsom, Surr.

LONDON   1727–1741

s. of Richard Perry, merchant, of Leadenhall St., London, director of Bank of England 1699–1701, by his w. Sarah;[1] bro.-in-law of William Heysham (q.v.). *m.* Elizabeth, da. of Richard Cocke, linen-draper, of London,[2] *s.p. suc.* fa. 1720; gd.-fa. Micajah Perry 1721.

Haberdashers' Co., master 1727–8; alderman of London 1728, sheriff 1734–5, ld. mayor 1738–9; col. Orange Regt. 1738–45.

Perry's grandfather was the greatest tobacco merchant in England and agent for Virginia.[3] Inheriting the family business in 1721, Perry handled the affairs of the Virginia planters in London, and was frequently consulted by the board of Trade about the colony.[4] In 1723 he told a House of Commons committee investigating customs frauds in Scotland

> that his father . . . paid upon the importation of tobacco, to the Crown, for duties, from £80,000 to £100,000 p.a., and that he does not now pay above £30,000 p.a. because the North Britons give greater prices in Virginia to the correspondents there than he is capable of rendering them here. That he sent out five ships the last year, none of which came home above half laden, although the last crop but one was greater than had been for these two seven years, and that he lost £1,500 by that voyage; that, the same year, the North Britons sent out above 51 sail, all which returned home full-freighted.[5]

As a result an Act was passed, putting the customs administration of England and Scotland under one commission.[6]

Returned for London as a government candidate in 1727, Perry soon went over to the Opposition, speaking against the Address in January 1729 and taking a prominent part in the debates on Spanish depredations. In February 1729 he presented a petition from Virginia against a clause in the Act unifying the customs of England and Scotland which prohibited the import of tobacco stripped from the stalk and in 1730 one on behalf of New York for allowing salt to be imported into it from Europe, securing the passing of bills for those purposes. He supported John Barnard's (q.v.) petition in 1730 to end the monopoly of the East India Company, and in 1732 he moved unsuccessfully that a qualification in the funds be as good as a qualification in land for Members of Parliament. In March 1732 he presented

a petition designed to encourage the growing of coffee in Jamaica, as a result of which an Act was passed to promote the growing of coffee in the Plantations.[7] He opposed the Molasses Act of 1733, which aimed at giving the West Indian sugar colonies a monopoly of the North American market for their products, writing to the governor of New York:

> Last year when the sugar islands presented their petition it was a good deal of surprise to me to find no advocate in the House of Commons for the continent but myself, and I very unequal to such a task, however, I ventured to deliver my sentiments as well as I was able, and had the good fortune to bring over to me one Mr. Barnard, a colleague of mine . . . It was laid down as a fundamental that the islands were the only useful colonies we had and that the continent was rather a nuisance. It happened a little unluckily that I had at that time in my hands an account from the custom house of the amount of the duty on sugars imported from all the islands, and I made it appear that I paid more duty on tobacco singly, than they all did upon their importation. I had also an account of their exports and it appeared that my family have exported more of the manufactures of this country to the continent than the island of Barbados ever took off in one year.[8]

But, as he told the same correspondent,

> it is my misfortune at present to be so much out of favour . . . that my appearance at the Council board would rather do you hurt than good.[9]

Perry and Barnard, described as 'the two tribunes of the London plebeians',[10] led the opposition to the excise bill. On its first reading he

> undertook . . . to make it appear that the utmost which can possibly be recovered by this bill is £20,000; the frauds (said he) can be but upon 800 hogsheads of tobacco, the duty of which is not £12,000. The pretence of loss to the government by the method of bonding for the duty is made one great argument for this bill, but this very morning the chief tobacco merchants of London were with me to give me an account of the bonds they are under, and they assured me they have now actually in their cellars 12,000 hogsheads of tobacco ready to answer their bonds, the value of which is exceeding more than the £140,000 due from them by those bonds; they are gentlemen of such character and credit, that I can so far depend on their veracity, as to offer for a bottle of claret to answer for all they owe the government.
> . . . If this bill passes, if I continue in the same mind I am, I will quit my trade, as every honest man will do, for if I should offer at a seat in Parliament, is it possible I can act an independent part? No, sir, this bill will subject me to arbitrary power, and my vote must be at the will of the Minister . . . It is pretended this bill will ease the fair trader, but on the contrary it will distress them. For the tobacco trade cannot be carried on without the credit of long time given the merchant by taking his bond for the duty. To expect ready money for his duty because he shall not pay it till the retailer pays him, is impossible, the retailer cannot himself pay ready money to the merchants,

but is commonly allowed twelve or fifteen months' time.

I own there may be men found who are of overgrown fortunes, and able to pay down the duty, and when you have turned out of the trades a number of fair and reputable merchants, who have less wealth but more regard to their fellow subjects, these richer men may take it up, but then the trade will be monopolized into a very few hands, and the planter will be enslaved to them. Sir, I speak against my own interest in urging this; for though I have not a very great fortune, because my grandfather and father, who with me have followed this trade for 70 years, left me their own example to content myself with a fair and honest gain, rather than to make haste to be rich, yet my fortune is perhaps good enough for me to commence one of these monopolizers; but I scorn the thought, and shall choose to sit down and leave off business rather than increase what I have by extortion and the oppression of my fellow traders.[11]

When Walpole was insulted by the anti-excise mob, Perry joined in the general disavowal of these proceedings so vehemently that his tears 'flowed down his cheek'. Next year he supported a petition of the tea merchants to be relieved from the excise. In 1736 he voted against the Westminster bridge bill to which the common council were opposed, and in March 1737 he supported Barnard's scheme for a reduction of the interest on the national debt. In 1738 he presented the merchants' petition on Spanish depredations, taking the chair of the committee of the whole House to consider the petition, 30 Mar., resulting in a motion for an address to the King 'to use his royal endeavours with his Catholic Majesty to obtain effectual relief for his injured subjects'. On 23 Feb. 1739 he moved unsuccessfully that the city of London's petition against the Spanish convention should be heard by counsel; in September he received the public thanks of the livery of the city of London for his 'endeavours to preserve us from the ruinous consequences we then too justly apprehended from the convention with Spain'; and on 18 June 1740 he was thanked by the common council for his support of the place bill. In February 1741 he voted unexpectedly against the motion for Walpole's dismissal.[12]

In 1741 Perry was defeated for London. In the spring of 1743 he went to Bath 'in a condition which made his friends despair for his life', suffering from 'a dropsy and not able ever to attend' the meetings of the corporation.[13] In November 1746 he resigned his aldermancy owing to ill-health. Having apparently fallen into financial difficulties, he was granted a pension of £200 p.a. by the court of aldermen, to whom he returned 'his most humble and hearty thanks for their generous and kind concern for him and for the seasonable support they have given him in his present necessity'.[14] He died 22 Jan. 1753.

[1] N. & Q. clxxxix, 59. [2] W. P. Treloar, A Ld. Mayor's Diary, pp. x–xii; Oliver, Antigua, iii. 20. [3] Pol. State, xxii. 332; CSP Col. xxix. 10. [4] E. Donnan, 'Micajah Perry', Jnl. of Econ. & Business Hist. iv. 70–98. [5] CJ, xx. 102. [6] 9 Geo. I, cap. 21. [7] HMC Egmont Diary, i. 68, 240; iii. 330; Winnington to Fox, 25 Jan. 1729, Fox mss; CJ, xxi. 232–3, 829, 845–6; 2 Geo II, cap. 9; 5 Geo. II, cap. 24. [8] Jnl. of Econ. & Business Hist. iv. 96. [9] Cadwaller Colden Pprs. ii. 105–6. [10] Hervey, Mems. 168. [11] HMC Egmont Diary, i. 351–2. [12] Hervey, Mems. 168; Egmont Diary, ii. 19; iii. 192; Harley Diary, 31 Mar. 1736; Chandler, x. 182, 257; Proceedings of the Court of Hustings and Common Hall of the Liverymen of the City of London at the late election for Ld. Mayor, 1739; Jnl. of Common Council, vol. 58, 18 June 1740. [13] Stuart mss 249/113; 254/154. [14] A Ld. Mayor's Diary, p. x.

E.C.

PETERSHAM, Visct., see **STANHOPE, Hon. William**

PETTY, Henry, 1st Baron Shelburne [I] (1675–1751), of Wycombe, Bucks.

GREAT MARLOW 1715–1722
CHIPPING WYCOMBE 1722–1727

b. 22 Oct. 1675, yst. s. of Sir William Petty, acting surveyor gen. [I], by Elizabeth, da. of Sir Hardress Waller of Castletown, co. Limerick, wid. of Sir Maurice Fenton, 1st Bt., M.P., who was cr. Baroness Shelburne for life 31 Dec. 1688. m. 1699, Arabella, da. of Charles Boyle, M.P., Visct. Dungannon [I], sis. of Charles Boyle, M.P., 3rd Earl of Cork [I], 3s. 1da. d.v.p. suc. bro. to family estates Apr. 1696; cr. Baron Shelburne [I] 16 June 1699; Earl of Shelburne 29 Apr. 1719.
Jt. prothonotary of common pleas [I] 1692–1700; jt. ranger of Phoenix park 1698–d.

Soon after succeeding to the family estates, Shelburne bought the manors of Temple Wycombe, Loakes and Windsor, near Wycombe, which he contested unsuccessfully in 1702. Returned as a Whig for Great Marlow in 1715, he was absent from the division on the septennial bill, voted for the repeal of the Occasional Conformity and Schism Acts, but did not vote on the peerage bill. In 1722 he was returned for Wycombe but did not stand again. He died 17 Apr. 1751, leaving estates in England and Ireland said to be worth £16,000 a year, besides £250,000 in the funds.[1] The bulk of his fortune devolved on his nephew, John Fitzmaurice, created Earl of Shelburne [I] 1753, the father of the 1st Marquess of Lansdowne.

[1] Gent. Mag. 1751, p. 187.

R.R.S.

PEYTO, William (bef. 1698–1734), of Chesterton, Warws.

WARWICKSHIRE 1715–11 Jan. 1734

b. bef. 1698, 1st s. of William Peyto of Chesterton, sheriff of Warws. 1695, by his w. Elizabeth.[1] unm.[2] suc. fa. 1699.

The Peytos had been prominent in Warwickshire since the thirteenth century and had acquired the

Chesterton estate by marriage in 1341. Peyto's soundness as a Tory was vouched for in 1715 by his kinsman, the Jacobite Lord Willoughby de Broke, in the same way as that of Andrew Archer (q.v.) had been by William Bromley (q.v.).[3] He voted steadily against the Government. His name was sent to the Pretender in 1721 as a probable supporter in the event of a rising.[4] He died 11 Jan. 1734.

[1] PCC Admon. Apr. 1699. [2] Ibid. Jan. 1734. [3] HMC Portland. vii. 211. [4] Stuart mss 65/16.

S.R.M.

PHELIPS, Edward (?1677–1734), of Montacute, Som.

ILCHESTER   1708–1715
SOMERSET   1722–1727

b. ?1677, s. of Capt. John Phelips of Kilpatrick, Ireland, and London by Alice Molyneux. educ. Trinity, Oxf. 23 Apr. 1695, aged 17; L. Inn 1695. m. (1) c.1702, his cos. Ann, da. and coh. of Sir Edward Phelips, M.P., of Montacute, 1s. 2da; (2) c.1720, her sis. Elizabeth, da. and coh. of Sir Edward Phelips, 3s. 1da. suc. uncle Sir Edward Phelips to Montacute 1699, and to fa.'s properties in England 1701.[1]
Comptroller of the mint June 1711–Dec. 1714.

Edward Phelips was descended from Sir Edward Phelips, speaker of the House of Commons and master of the rolls, who built Montacute at the end of the sixteenth century. After representing Ilchester under Anne as a Tory, he stood unsuccessfully for it in 1715, subsequently bringing an action against the bailiff for refusing him a copy of the poll.[2] In 1721 his name was sent to the Pretender as a probable supporter in the event of a rising.[3] He was returned unopposed for the county in 1722 but did not stand in 1727. He was buried at Montacute, 13 May 1734.

[1] PCC 143 Dyer. John Phelips's Irish properties went to his wife. [2] The Case of the Defendant in the Writ of Error. Thomas Smith, bailiff of the borough of Ilchester . . . plaintiff. Edward Phelipps defendant. [3] Stuart mss 65/16.

S.R.M.

PHILIPPS, Erasmus (1699–1743), of Picton Castle, Pemb.

HAVERFORDWEST   8 Feb. 1726–15 Oct. 1743

b. 8 Nov. 1699, 1st s. of Sir John Philipps, 4th Bt., and bro. of John Philipps (qq.v.). educ. Pembroke, Oxf. 1720; L. Inn 1721. unm. suc. fa. as 5th Bt. 5 Jan. 1737.

Philipps published An Appeal to Common Sense, or some considerations offered to restore public credit in 1721 and The State of the Nation in respect of her commerce, debts and money in 1725, putting forward various proposals for the encouragement of trade and for settling the national debt.[1] Returned apparently as a Whig on his family's interest for Haverfordwest he voted against the Administration in

every recorded division. He became a trustee of the Georgia Society in 1732.[2] On 7 June 1734 he wrote to Walpole:[3]

> I should not have presumed to give you the trouble of this letter, if justice to an injured character did not oblige me. My brother John [q.v.] acquaints me, that when he took the liberty to wait on you last Tuesday with regard to the late election for Haverfordwest, you were pleased, on mention of my name, to say, that you had been informed I made a common practice of railing at you, had declared I would use my endeavours to ruin you, and had called you a wretch. The hearing of these things surprise me to the last degree, and indeed fill me with concern: my answer, Sir, to the shocking charge is plainly this, that from whomsoever you may have received these informations concerning me, they are all of them, upon my word of honour, utterly false and entirely groundless, and I can appeal to God the searcher of hearts that I never in my life uttered the least disrespectful word of you, Sir, of your brother, Mr. Horace Walpole [q.v.], or of any of your family. Not knowing what other gross falsities may have been reported of me to you, permit me, Sir, before I conclude, to satisfy you as to one thing, (whereof however I believe you have no doubt) I mean my real affection to King George and his family; and on this occasion I do with the greatest truth aver, that his Majesty has not a more loyal and dutiful subject than myself, indeed I have always detested the thought of being otherwise.

He was absent in Italy for the recovery of his health at the time of the Spanish convention in 1739, and voted against the Administration on the chairman of the elections committee in December 1741. On 15 Oct. 1743, when he was 'returning to Bath, some pigs frightened his horse, which ran back and threw him into the river [Avon], just below the bridge, and he was drowned'.[4]

[1] Pol. State. xx. 420–6, 438–49; xxx. 1–45. [2] HMC Egmont Diary, i. 344. [3] Cholmondeley (Houghton) mss. [4] Nichols, Lit. Hist. iii. 585.

E.C.

PHILIPPS, Griffith (c.1715–81), of Cwmgwili, Carm.

CARMARTHEN   22 Nov. 1751–1761, 1768–1774

b. c.1715, 1st surv. s. of Grismond Philipps of Cwmgwili by Jane, da. of Miles Stedman of Dolygaer, Brec. educ. L. Inn 1741, called 1744. m. (1) Avis (d. 15 Sept. 1755), da. of Gen. Brockhurst, 1s. 3da.; (2) Jan. 1757, Lucretia Elizabeth, da. of Henry Folkes of London, 1s. 3 other ch. suc. fa. 1740.

After standing unsuccessfully for Carmarthen in 1741, Griffith Philipps in 1746 gained control of the borough, for which he was returned with the support of the Government in 1751, ending his life as its patron. In 1742 a local opponent wrote of him:

> Even Griffith Philipps had so much the sincerity of a courtier as to say he was glad of the minister's fall. The boy was a liar when at school, and now he continues the same and excellent person.[1]

When in 1754 he was opposed by Sir Thomas Stepney, Newcastle was told that

> Mr. Philipps, the present Member, has done such things in his family and which are of such a nature, that I find his being supported is the only reason for the step Sir Thomas is taking. He tells me that if any other person had been named, he should never have thought of an opposition.[2]

In his only known application for patronage, he wrote to Newcastle:

> I hope your Grace will on this occasion be so good as to consider the persecutions I have for several years sustained on account of my attachment to the Government and in particular to your Grace and your brother Mr. Pelham.[3]

He died 27 Feb. 1781.

[1] John Adams to Thos. Pryse, M.P., 11 Feb. 1742, Gogerddan mss, NLW box 17B. [2] Add. 32734, ff. 365–6. [3] Add. 32873, f. 506.

P.D.G.T.

PHILIPPS, Sir John, 4th Bt. (c.1666–1737), of Picton Castle, Pemb.

PEMBROKE BOROUGHS 1695–1702
HAVERFORDWEST 4 Mar. 1718–1722

b. c.1666, 1st surv. s. of Sir Erasmus Philipps, 3rd Bt., M.P. Pembroke 1654, by Catherine, da. and coh. of Hon. Edward Darcy by Elizabeth, da. of Philip Stanhope, 1st Earl of Chesterfield; uncle by marriage to Sir Robert Walpole. *educ.* Westminster 1679; Trinity, Camb. 1682; L. Inn 1684. *m.* 12 Dec. 1697, Mary, da. and h. of Anthony Smith, E.I. merchant, 3s. 4da. *suc.* fa. 18 Jan. 1697.

Philipps, who owned large estates in Pembrokeshire and Carmarthenshire, was returned for Haverfordwest on his family's interest in 1718, voting with the Administration. Poor eyesight caused him to retire from Parliament in 1722, when he wrote to his wife, 4 Jan.,

> it is become painful to me to sit in the House of Commons where, for want of reading the bills and other matters that are laid before them, I am by no means master of their business and often times at a loss to know which way to give my vote.[1]

An active member of the societies for the propagation of the Gospel in foreign parts and for promoting Christian knowledge, he was also a patron of George Whitfield and a friend of John Wesley.[2] In 1730 he took up the cause of the persecuted Protestants in Poland, collecting several hundred pounds for their relief among his acquaintances, including £50 from Walpole.[3] He died 5 Jan. 1737, aged 70, leaving in his will a legacy for the relief of the Salzburgers and other persecuted Protestants.[4]

[1] NLW, Picton Castle mss. [2] T. Shankland, 'Sir John Philipps', *Trans. Cymmrod. Soc.* 1804–5, pp. 74–79. [3] HMC Hastings, iii. 5. [4] HMC Egmont Diary, ii. 376.

P.D.G.T.

PHILIPPS, John (1700–64), of Picton Castle, Pemb.

CARMARTHEN 1741–1747
PETERSFIELD 9 Dec. 1754–1761
PEMBROKESHIRE 1761–23 June 1764

b. 8 Nov. 1700, 2nd s. of Sir John Philipps, 4th Bt., and bro. of Erasmus Philipps (qq.v.). *educ.* Pembroke, Oxf. 1720; L. Inn 1721, called 1727. *m.* 22 Sept. 1725, Elizabeth, da. of Henry Shepherd of London, 1s. 3da. *suc.* bro. as 6th Bt. 15 Oct. 1743.

Ld. of Trade Dec. 1744–Mar. 1745; custos rot. Haverfordwest 1761–*d.*; P.C. 10 Jan. 1763.

In early life Philipps was on good terms with his cousins, the Walpoles, whom he presented with a genealogical table showing their joint descent from Cadwalader. Perhaps because, as Horace Walpole hints, he was given no place, he turned to opposition, becoming 'a very zealous and active Jacobite'[1] and president of the Society of Sea Serjeants, a Jacobite organization in South Wales. Returned for Carmarthen by the Tory corporation in 1741, he soon became one of the principal Tory speakers in Parliament. On 19 Feb. 1742 he attempted to defer the granting of supply pending redress of existing grievances; on 9 Mar. he supported a motion for a secret committee of inquiry into the last twenty years of Walpole's Administration; and on 29 Apr. he led the attack against the transfer of 4,000 troops from Ireland into England to replace those sent to Flanders. At the end of the year he supported a place bill. He spoke against the Hanoverians in 1742 and 1744, and was one of the 'anti-ministerial cabinet' formed in December 1743 to co-ordinate the actions of the Opposition in the following session.[2] On 24 Feb. 1744 he opposed an increase in land and naval forces against a threatened French invasion to restore the Stuarts. Four days later he opposed the arrest of Lord Barrymore (q.v.) before the suspension of the Habeas Corpus Act, attempting the next day to defer its suspension.

On the formation of the Broad-bottom Administration in December 1744 Philipps was made a lord of Trade. But, 'resolved to give us an early specimen that he would be as troublesome a placeman as a patriot', on 23 Jan. 1745 he supported an amendment delaying the supply for the Ordnance. Next month he again opposed the supply and spoke against the grant of two short months' pay to the Hanoverians. On 20 Mar. he opposed a grant for the transport of the Dutch troops sent over during the invasion scare of 1744 and spoke against the Saxon subsidy.[3] At the end of the month he resigned his place on the board of Trade. In June he spoke in favour of annual parliaments. When Parliament was re-called during the Forty-five, he attempted to attach to the Address a clause demanding shorter parliaments and a diminution of governmental influence in elections,[4] and made strenuous attempts 'to get the subscriptions and associations for the King declared illegal'. He spoke against the Hanoverians in 1746, deriding Pitt's *volte face*.

Philipps did not stand in 1747, leaving Parliament 'on the desperate situation of the Jacobite cause'.[5] In 1747–8 he supported the agitation against a bill to naturalize foreign Protestants, a measure to which the pro-Jacobite common council of the city of London were bitterly opposed.[6] At this time he lived in Oxford, 'the sanctuary of disaffection', becoming a considerable benefactor of Pembroke College.[7] Created a D.C.L. at the great Jacobite demonstration on the opening of the Radcliffe Camera in 1749 (see under Oxford University), he sent assurances of continued loyalty to the Pretender.[8] The idol of the Jacobite-dominated association of the independent electors of Westminster (see under Westminster),[9] he moved for a habeas corpus for Alexander Murray,[10] a Jacobite agent, who was imprisoned in Newgate on the orders of the House of Commons after the violent election of 1749–50. Returning to Parliament after the death of Pelham he remained in opposition till the new reign. He died 23 June 1764.

[1] Walpole to Montagu, 11 Aug. 1748; to Countess of Upper Ossory, 9 Dec. 1784. [2] Owen, *Pelhams*, 199. [3] Yorke's parl. jnl. *Parl. Hist.* xiii. 665, 670, 673, 1051, 1124–5, 1202, 1246–7. [4] John Maule (q.v.) to Etough, 18 Oct. 1745, ibid. 1328. [5] Walpole, *Mems. Geo. II*, i. 114; Owen 306. [6] *A letter to Sir John Philips Bt. occasioned by a bill brought into Parliament to naturalize foreign Protestants*. [7] *Mems. Geo. II*, i. 114; *VCH Oxon.*, iii. 294, 297. [8] Stuart mss 301/5. [9] See *Cry aloud and Spare not. Addressed to the Worthy Independent Electors of Westminster* (1747), and *Westminster Elections 1741–50*. [10] *Mems. Geo. II*, i. 114.

E.C.

PHILLIPPS, Ambrose (?1707–37), of Garendon Park, Leics.

LEICESTERSHIRE   5 Feb. 1734–6 Nov. 1737

b. ?1707, 1st s. of William Phillipps of Garendon by Jane, da. of Sir Samuel Dashwood, M.P., ld. mayor of London 1703. *educ.* Magdalen, Oxf. 18 July 1724, aged 16. *unm. suc. fa.* 1729.

Phillipps's grandfather, Sir Ambrose Phillipps, an eminent lawyer, purchased Garendon in 1683 for £28,000. His own father, a Turkey merchant as well as a country gentleman, who further increased the family fortune,[1] was included in a list of leading Jacobites sent to the Pretender in 1721.[2] After leaving the university, Phillipps travelled extensively in France and Italy, where he acquired a taste for and knowledge of architecture, which he applied in designing the gardens and extensions of the house at Garendon.[3] Returned as a Tory for

Leicestershire at a by-election in 1734, he voted against the Government on the repeal of the Septennial Act. He died 6 Nov. 1737, aged 30.

[1] Nichols, *Leics.* iii. 802–4. [2] Stuart mss 65/16. [3] Nichols, 802.

E.C.

PHILLIPS, James (1672–1730), of Carmarthen.

CARMARTHEN   4 Jan. 1725–1727

bap. 11 July 1672, 1st s. of John Phillips, alderman of Carmarthen, by Anne, da. of Thomas Newsham. *m.* by 1700, Jane, da. of John Scurlock of Pibwr, 1s. 2da. *suc. fa.* 11 Aug. 1730.

Mayor, Carmarthen 1709.

Phillips was the son of 'a strenuous asserter of the rights and privileges of the inhabitants of the ancient borough of Carmarthen',[1] for which he was returned, apparently as a Tory, at a by-election in 1725. Defeated by a Whig in 1727, he petitioned, but gave up after the House of Commons had rejected a motion declaring that the franchise was in the inhabitants as well as in the freemen.[2]

He died 28 Nov. 1730.

[1] *Carmarthenshire Mon. Inscriptions*, p. v. [2] *CJ*, xxi. 96.

R.R.S.

PHILLIPSON, John (1698–1756), of Park Hall, nr. Harwich, Essex.

NEW SHOREHAM   1734–1741
HARWICH   1741–27 Nov. 1756

b. 28 Apr. 1698, o.s. of John Phillipson, agent of the Harwich packet boats, who m. (1) Rachel, da. of Robert Lane, and (2) Grace, da. of Kendrick Edisbury, M.P., of Harwich. [1] *m.* 29 Aug. 1717, da. of Richard Burton, commr. of the navy, 1da. *suc. fa.* 1742.

Clerk in the navy office; chief clerk of the navy ticket office to 1739; commr. of the navy 1739–43; ld. of Admiralty 1743–4; surveyor gen. of woods and forests north and south of Trent 1745–*d.*; director, South Sea Co. 1733–55, dep. gov. 1756.

Phillipson's father started life as an ordinary seaman on a Harwich packet boat at the end of the seventeenth century, rose to command a packet in the wars with France, and, having married the daughter of a previous agent of the Harwich packet boats, was appointed to that post by Bolingbroke, then recorder of Harwich. As agent he managed the influence exercised by the Post Office in Harwich through the packet service, claiming that during his twenty years' tenure of the post he had

> always endeavoured to get the majority of the electors in the interest of the Government and on every vacancy of a capital burgess . . . espoused such as had any dependance on it.

A capital burgess, alderman, and several times mayor of Harwich, he amassed a considerable fortune, building up a strong interest, which he strengthened by marrying his son to the daughter of a commissioner of the navy.

Young Phillipson, like his father-in-law, began as a clerk in the navy office, which he combined with outside business interests. In 1727 he stood as a candidate for Harwich, but was withdrawn by his father at the request of Walpole, who was committed to Lord Perceval and Sir Philip Parker (qq.v.).[2] At the beginning of 1733 he was elected a director of the South Sea Company on the proprietors' list, which defeated the house list, i.e. the old directors, by a great majority.[3] Later in the year it was learned at Shoreham that

> Mr. Phillipson, a merchant and director of the South Sea Company, is coming in about a fortnight to offer his services for the said borough, who will be strongly assisted by the shipbuilders and corporation.[4]

Discussing this development with the Duke of Richmond, who was setting up a candidate of his own for Shoreham, Walpole told Sir Charles Wager, the first lord of the Admiralty, that 'of all men in the world he must desire he would not espouse' Phillipson as 'being the reputed author of the South Sea calculation against him,'[5] i.e. behind the recent agitation which had led to the overthrow of the old directors and to a demand in the House of Lords for a parliamentary inquiry into the alleged mismanagement of the Company's affairs. Returned by a large majority, he voted with the Government on the Spanish convention in 1739, when he was made a commissioner of the navy.

In 1741 Phillipson transferred himself to Harwich, where he had been elected a capital burgess in 1736.[6] Retaining his place after Walpole's fall, he was made a lord of the Admiralty by Carteret in 1743.[7] When in 1744 the Duke of Bedford, on becoming first lord of the Admiralty, refused to have him on the board on the ground that as a former clerk he was 'not of quality enough', he was compensated with the post of surveyor of woods and forests.[8]

In 1746 Phillipson married his only daughter to Robert Bristow (q.v.), who was returned next year for Shoreham. He himself was again returned at Harwich where, the 2nd Lord Egmont states in his electoral survey, c.1749–50,

> Phillipson has now got so great a footing . . . that he can carry two Members. But for a good employment he must always bring in one for the Court. Though he is a bold kind of man, and gives himself great airs to the Ministers about this borough on all occasions, yet he cannot afford to lose an employment, or to contend at great expense against power.

According to his own account, he was sent for in 1754 by Newcastle, who 'after *kissing* and *hugging* him, and that sort of stuff, *as he termed it*, begged he would take Shoreham in hand, which to oblige him

he had undertaken, and had cost him near £5,000'. In fact he received £1,000 from the secret service money for his son-in-law's election at Shoreham.[9]

Phillipson died 27 Nov. 1756, leaving his fortune to his daughter. On his death the Phillipson interest at Harwich became extinct.

[1] J. H. Bloom, *Heraldry and Mon. Inscriptions in Harwich*, 27 and ped. of Phillipson at end. [2] *Structure*, 359 et seq.; HMC Egmont Diary, i. 78, 423; ii. 60, 168; iii. 325, 327. [3] *Gent. Mag.* 1733, p. 97. [4] R. Masters to Newcastle, 1 Oct. 1733, Add. 32688, f. 437. [5] M. E. Matcham, *A Forgotten Russell*, 46. [6] *HMC Egmont Diary*, ii. 310. [7] Walpole to Mann, 30 Nov. 1743. [8] *Corresp. H. Walpole* (Yale ed.), xviii. 550 n. 12. [9] *Structure*, 364, 430.

R.R.S.

PHILPOTT, Nicholas (?1695–1732), of Newton, Herefs.

WEOBLEY   22 Nov. 1718–1727

b. ?1695, 1st s. of Nicholas Philpott of Hereford and Vowchurch, Herefs. *educ.* Merton, Oxf. 22 Apr. 1714, aged 18. *m.* bef. Apr. 1727, Elizabeth.

Philpott's father, related to the Duke of Chandos, was prominent in Hereford politics, unsuccessfully contesting the city in 1715. In 1718 he himself successfully contested Weobley on an undertaking by Lord Coningsby (q.v.) that the Government would pay half his expenses. In Parliament he voted with the Administration on the repeal of the Occasional Conformity and Schism Acts and the peerage bill. In a letter of 18 May 1719 to Sunderland, referring to the promise to pay half Philpott's expenses, Coningsby wrote:

> I can assure your Lordship that I have with his assistance carried that town out of the hands of the enemy not only for this time but for all succeeding elections. I therefore hope you will be pleased to give this gentleman the countenance he deserves not only for his readiness to engage in this affair but likewise for his steady behaviour in Parliament ever since he was elected.[1]

The letter enclosed

> An account of what money Mr. Philpott expended at his election of Weobley.

	£	s	d
To the two returning officers	42	0	0
To 52 voters at £10 each	520	0	0
To two to be neuter	10	0	0
To expenses before and at the election in public houses and other expenses	120	8	9
To gratuities to persons who had interest and were very serviceable at the election	30	0	0
	£722	8	9

Returned again in 1722, Philpott was put up in 1727 but withdrew on a compromise with the Tories. He died 6 July 1732, 'having shot himself, being lunatic'.[2]

[1] Sunderland (Blenheim) mss. [2] *Gent. Mag.* 1732, p. 876.

R.S.L.

PICKERING, Sir Edward, 4th Bt. (?1715–49), of Titchmarsh, Northants. and West Langton, Leics.

MITCHELL   9 Nov. 1745–1747

b. ?1715, 1st surv. s. of Sir Gilbert Pickering, 3rd Bt., M.P., by Elizabeth, da. and h. of Staveley Staunton of Birchmoor, Beds. *educ.* Ch. Ch. Oxf. 25 May 1732, aged 16. *unm. suc.* fa. 29 Feb. 1736.

The grandson of Sir Gilbert Pickering, 1st Bt., M.P., chamberlain to Cromwell, Pickering's father had been active on behalf of the Whigs in Leicestershire elections.[1] Through his mother he inherited 'a very great fortune'.[2] Returned for Mitchell in 1745, he voted against the Hanoverians in April 1746, when he was classed as 'doubtful'. Six months later Lord Sandwich referred to him as a 'professed opposer' of the Administration.[3] He did not stand in 1747 and died 10 July 1749.

[1] *Verney Letters of 18th Cent.* i. 245, 333. [2] *Add.* 24121, f. 166. [3] *Add.* 32805, f. 281.

E.C.

PIERS, William (1686–1755) of West Bradley, Som.

WELLS   30 May 1716–1722, 18 Apr. 1729–1734, 25 Mar. 1735–1741

b. 20 May 1686,[1] s. of William Piers of Wells by Catherine, da. of William Coward, recorder of Wells, sis. of William Coward (q.v.). *m.* Elizabeth, da. of Harvey Ekins of Weston Favell, Northants., 1s. 2da.

Descended from a leading Wells family, holding lands in the vicinity of the city, Piers was the mainstay of the Whig interest there. From 1715 to 1747 he stood for Wells at every general election but one, being always defeated at the poll, but three times returned on petition, in 1734 with the active support of Walpole.[2] Voting consistently with the Government, he appears in a list published by the Opposition of the division on the Spanish convention with the note 'his son in the army'.[3] After his last defeat in 1747 he presented a petition, but in the end withdrew it. He died in 1755.

[1] A. J. Jewers, *Wells Cathedral: Mon. Inscriptions and Heraldry,* 236. [2] *HMC Egmont Diary,* ii. 161, where he is referred to as 'Col.', presumably his rank in the militia. [3] *Gent. Mag.* 1739, p. 306.

S.R.M.

PIGOTT, Robert (1664–1746), of Chetwynd, Salop, and Chesterton, Hunts.

HUNTINGDONSHIRE   1713–1722, 7 Feb. 1730–1741

b. 1664,[1] 1st s. of Walter Pigott of Chetwynd by his 2nd w. Anne, da. of Sir John Dryden, 2nd Bt., M.P., of Canons Ashby, Northants. and Chesterton. *educ.* Ch. Ch. Oxf. 5 Dec. 1681, aged 16; I. Temple 1683. *m.* (settlement 15 May 1695) Frances, da. of William Ward of Willingsworth, Staffs., bro. of Edward, 7th Lord Dudley and 2nd Baron Ward, 5s. 3da. *suc.* fa.

at Chetwynd 1699 and to the Hunts. estates of his uncles John and Erasmus Dryden 1708 and 1710.

Sheriff, Salop 1696, Cambs. and Hunts. 1709–10.

Robert Pigott, who came of an old Shropshire family, inherited considerable estates in Huntingdonshire from his maternal uncles, John and Erasmus Dryden,[2] the first of whom had sat for that county in six Parliaments.[3] Returned as a Whig for the county in 1713, he was re-elected without opposition in 1715, voting for the Administration in all recorded divisions of that Parliament. He did not stand in 1722 or 1727 but came in again at a contested by-election in 1730 and unopposed in 1734, with the support of the 2nd Duke of Manchester.[4] Though absent on the excise bill in 1733 and the place bill in 1740, he voted with the Government against the bill for repealing the Septennial Act in 1734 and for the Spanish convention in 1739. At a by-election in November 1739 he was reported to be giving his interest to Charles Clarke (q.v.) who was successful against the 3rd Duke of Manchester's nominee.[5] In June 1740 Lord Sandwich, then in opposition, informed Sarah, Duchess of Marlborough, that at the forthcoming general election he would be 'obliged to side with people whom I cannot think friends to their country', that is with Pigott and Clarke, both Government supporters, as this would 'be an effectual means of breaking the lord lieutenant's [Manchester's] interest'.[6] In the event he did not stand, dying in December 1746.

[1] *Salop Arch. Soc. Trans.* (ser. 4), iii. 95. [2] *VCH Hunts.* ii. 380. [3] PCC 105 Barrett and 154 Smith. [4] *HMC 8th Rep.* ii. 110. [5] Newcastle to Devonshire, 30 Oct. 1739, Devonshire mss. [6] Sandwich to Sarah, Duchess of Marlborough, 25 June 1740, Marlborough mss.

R.S.L.

PILKINGTON, Sir Lionel, 5th Bt. (1707–78), of Stanley, Yorks.

HORSHAM   17 Dec. 1748–1768

bap. 20 Jan. 1707, 1st s. of Sir Lyon Pilkington, 4th Bt., by Anne, da. of Sir Michael Wentworth of Woolley, Yorks. *educ.* Westminster 1721; Ch. Ch. Oxf. 1725. *unm. suc.* fa. June 1716.

Sheriff, Yorks. 1740–1.

Pilkington, a member of the 1st Lord Egmont's musical circle,[1] took a leading part on the government side in the Yorkshire election of 1734, later contributing £50 towards a scrutiny.[2] Returned for Horsham as a government supporter by his neighbour and friend, the 7th Viscount Irwin (q.v.), he was one of the sponsors of the Leeds turnpike bill in 1751.[3]

He died 11 Aug. 1778.

[1] *HMC Egmont Diary,* i. 325, 337, 342. [2] *Wentworth Pprs.* 488; *Add.* 32689, f. 270. [3] *HMC Var.* viii. 174; *CJ,* xxvi. 80.

J.B.L.

PILSWORTH, Charles (*d.*1749), of Oving, nr. Aylesbury, Bucks.

AYLESBURY 1741–1747

?s. of Rev. Charles Pilsworth, rector of Charfield, Glos. *educ.* I. Temple, called 1715. *m.* (1) Parnell (*d.* Mar. 1741), da. of Francis Tyringham of Lower Winchendon, Bucks., sis. and h. of Francis Tyringham of Lower Winchendon, *s.p.*; (2) 17 May 1744, Elizabeth, da. of Sir Thomas Cave, 3rd Bt., of Stanford, Northants., sis. of Sir Thomas Cave, 5th Bt. (qq.v.), and niece of Ralph Verney (q.v.), 1st Earl Verney [I], of Middle Claydon, Bucks., *s.p.*

Charles Pilsworth was living at Oving by 1723, before his marriage to the heiress of an old Buckinghamshire family, through whom he later acquired the manor of Oving.[1] A practising lawyer with a considerable reputation among the local justices, he was described in 1733 as 'the oracle of this country'.[2] Returned for Aylesbury as a government supporter in 1741, he voted with the Administration in all recorded divisions, was summoned to the Cockpit meeting in 1742 through Winnington (q.v.), and was classed as 'Old Whig' in 1746. When two vacancies occurred among the judges in March 1745, Pilsworth wrote to his uncle, Lord Verney:

> This will be the fairest opportunity that can offer of pushing our point; for if the ministry will not comply now, I shall be convinced they never intend to do anything. If . . . they should appear to trifle with us, we must in such case find access to the King forthwith . . . I am determined to press this point at this juncture; if those seats are filled with younger lives, I can have no further expectations.

Verney replied:

> I have had some discourse with [Mr. Pelham] . . . he speaks very fair and wishes you may be a judge, but says it can't be now . . . I really believe the ministry are in earnest and will serve you another time.[3]

Before anything more was done, Pilsworth died, 4 Jan. 1749.

[1] *Bucks. Sessions Recs.* vi. 86, 112; Lipscomb, *Bucks.* i. 377, 519. [2] *Verney Letters of 18th Cent.* ii. 212–13; Alexander Denton to Walpole, 23 Dec. 1733, Cholmondeley (Houghton) mss. [3] *Verney Letters*, ii. 213–14.

R.S.L.

PINNEY, John Frederick (1719–62), of Racedown, nr. Bridport, Dorset.

BRIDPORT 1747–1761

b. 27 Jan. 1719, o. surv. s. of John Pinney of Nevis by Mary, da. and h. of Major William Helme of Antigua and Nevis.[1] *unm. suc.* fa. 1720 and cos. Azariah Pinney of Bettiscombe, Dorset 1760.

Inheriting one of the largest estates in Nevis, but brought up in England, Pinney first visited the island in 1739 to put his plantations in order, staying till 1742. During this time he was twice elected to the Charlestown assembly, which he apparently attended very irregularly. In 1747, now living permanently in Dorset, he was returned as a Tory *vice* George, Lord Deerhurst (q.v.), who transferred to Worcestershire on finding 'a purse of two hundred thousand pounds listed against me at Bridport and a very liberal hand to distribute the contents'.[2] He visited Nevis again in 1749 for the last time, but retained his estates and influence there. The 2nd Lord Egmont, in his electoral survey, 1749–50, calls him 'a very proper man' to sit for Bridport, as he could procure the assistance of West India merchants, who carried weight in elections.

He died 11 Nov. 1762.

[1] R. Pares, *A West India Fortune.* [2] Deerhurst to Edmund Lechmere, 18 June 1747, Lechmere mss, Worcs. RO.

R.S.L.

PITT, George (?1663–1735), of Strathfieldsaye, Hants.

STOCKBRIDGE	23 Nov. 1694–1695
WAREHAM	1698–1702
HAMPSHIRE	1702–1705
WAREHAM	1705–1710
HAMPSHIRE	1710–1713
WAREHAM	1713–1715
HAMPSHIRE	1715–1722
OLD SARUM	30 May 1726–1727

b. ?1663, 1st s. of George Pitt of Strathfieldsaye by Jane, 1st da. of John Savage, M.P., 2nd Earl Rivers, wid. of (1) George Brydges, 6th Baron Chandos of Sudeley; (2) Sir William Sedley, 4th Bt. *educ.* Wadham Oxf. 26 Mar. 1680, aged 16. *m.* (1) lic. 14 Mar. 1691, Lucy (*d.*17 Nov. 1697), da. of Thomas Pile of Baverstock, Wilts. and Shroton, Dorset, wid. of Laurence Lowe of Shaftesbury, 2s. 1da.; (2) by 1700, Lora, da. and h. of Audley Grey of Kingston Marwood, in Stinsford, Dorset, 4s. 5da. *suc.* fa. 1694. Director, South Sea Co. 1711–18.

George Pitt was descended from Sir William Pitt (*d.*1636), of a Dorset family, M.P. Wareham 1621–5, whose younger brother, Thomas Pitt of Blandford, Dorset, was ancestor of the great Pitts.[1] Sir William's son Edward, George's grandfather, bought Strathfieldsaye from the Dabridgecourts in 1629.[2] In addition to this estate, George Pitt inherited valuable colliery interests in north Durham, which had been acquired by his father in 1686.[3] For many years he was closely associated with his kinsman, Governor Thomas Pitt (q.v.), who entrusted him with 'paternal authority' over his children in 1706 and with the custody of the famous Pitt diamond in 1710. Returned for Wareham and Hampshire in 1715, each of which he had represented in alternate Parliaments under Anne, he opted to sit for the county, leaving Wareham for his son George (q.v.).

A Tory, he voted against the Administration in all recorded divisions, refusing to sign the loyal association in December 1715. Returned by Robert Pitt (q.v.) for Old Sarum in 1726,[4] he did not stand again, dying 28 Feb. 1735.

[1] Hutchins, *Dorset*, iv. 90. [2] *VCH Hants* iv. 59. [3] E. Hughes, *N. Country Life in 18th Cent.* 163, 167. [4] *HMC Fortescue*, i. 22, 33, 43, 56, 61, 78.

R.S.L.

PITT, George (aft. 1691–1745), of Shroton, Dorset, and Strathfieldsaye, Hants.

WAREHAM   18 Apr. 1715–1722
DORSET   25 Jan.–5 Aug. 1727

b. aft. 1691, 1st s. of George Pitt (q.v., above) of Strathfieldsaye by his 1st w. *m.* by 1721, Mary Louisa, da. of John Bernier of Strasburg, in Alsace, 4s. 2da. *suc.* to Dorset estates of his maternal gd.-fa. 1714 and fa. 1735.

George Pitt, a Tory, was returned for Wareham on his family's interest in 1715 at a by-election caused by his father's opting to sit for Hampshire. Refusing like his father to sign the loyal association, December 1715,[1] he voted against the septennial bill in 1716, but was absent from the divisions on the repeal of the Occasional Conformity and Schism Acts and the peerage bill in 1719. Unsuccessful at Wareham in 1722, he apparently changed sides, defeating the Tory, Thomas Horner (q.v.), at a by-election for Dorset in January 1727, with the help of Bubb Dodington (q.v.), who described him as 'scarcely capable'.[2] Before the general election Richard Edgcumbe (q.v.) reported to Walpole that Pitt had again changed sides:

> The end of it is, a total desertion from his old friends and a transfer of his interest to Chaffin (q.v.) and Horner; strange that he should take this conduct after the candles were lighted up, but stranger still that any thing of this kind should happen in Dorsetshire.[3]

He did not stand again. According to a petition of his brother-in-law, Henry Bernier, supported by an affidavit, dated 21 Mar. 1730, of Mary Louisa Pitt, he separated from his wife, 'who was forcibly abducted from London by her husband, George Pitt . . . and kept locked up at a seat of Pitt's at Melcombe, in Dorset.'[4] He died in October 1745.

[1] *HMC Fortescue*, i. 56. [2] *Dodington Diary*, 246. [3] Undated, Cholmondeley (Houghton) mss 3240. [4] *Cal. Treas. Bks. and Pprs.* 1729–30, pp. 353–4.

R.S.L.

PITT, George (1721–1803), of Strathfieldsaye, Hants.

SHAFTESBURY   1 July 1742–1747
DORSET   1747–1774

b. 1 May 1721, 1st s. of George Pitt (*d.* 1745, q.v.) of Strathfieldsaye, and nephew of John Pitt (q.v.). *educ.* Winchester 1731; Magdalen, Oxf. 1737; travelled in Italy. *m.* 4 Jan. 1746, Penelope, da. of Sir Henry Atkins, 4th Bt., of Clapham, Surr., sis. and h. of Sir Richard Atkins, 6th Bt., 1s. 3da. *suc.* fa. 1745; *cr.* Baron Rivers of Strathfieldsaye 20 May 1776; Baron Rivers of Sudeley Castle 16 Mar. 1802, with sp. rem. to bro. Sir William Augustus Pitt, K.B., M.P., and his gd.-s. William Horace Beckford.

Groom of the bedchamber 1760–70; envoy to Turin 1761–8; ld. lt. Hants 1780–Mar. 1782; ld. of the bedchamber Apr. 1782–*d.*; ld. lt. Dorset 1793–*d.*

George Pitt entered Parliament at a by-election soon after returning from his grand tour.[1] A Tory, he voted with the Opposition on the Hanoverians in 1742, 1744 and 1746. Two months before the dissolution that year Lord Ilchester wrote: 'If [Pitt] does stand [at Shaftesbury] it will be, I suppose, upon that interest which is called Lord Shaftesbury's.' He appears, however, to have stood chiefly on his own interest, as he did not obtain Lord Shaftesbury's formal support till 10 June.[2] Returned both for Shaftesbury and Dorset, he opted to serve for the county, where he was unopposed. In the 2nd Lord Egmont's electoral survey c.1749–50, Pitt is described as 'not proper', i.e. unsuitable for the Prince. He died 7 May 1803.

[1] Walpole to Mann, 24 June 1742. [2] Ilchester to Hen. Fox, Apr. 1747, Fox mss; see SHAFTESBURY.

R.S.L.

PITT, George Morton (1693–1756), of Twickenham, Mdx.

OLD SARUM   3 Nov. 1722–Jan. 1724
PONTEFRACT   1741–1754

b. 1693 at Fort St. George, in India, o.s. of John Pitt of Tarrant Preston, Dorset, consul at Masulipatam, by his 2nd w. Sarah Charlton, wid. of Thomas Wavell, second of council at Fort St. George. *educ.* St. Paul's. *m.* 8 Sept. 1743, Sophia, da. of Charles Bugden, sec. of the E. I. Co. at Fort St. George, wid. of George Drake, councillor and merchant at Fort St. George. *suc.* fa. 1703.

Registrar of excise office Jan.–Aug. 1724; second of council at Madras 1724–30; dep. gov. Fort St. David 1725–30; gov. Fort St. George 1730–35.

Pitt's father, who was for many years in the service of the East India Company, was first cousin to George Pitt (*d.* 1735, q.v.) of Strathfieldsaye. After an English education he became a merchant at Fort St. George. Brought in by his kinsman, Governor Thomas Pitt (q.v.), at Old Sarum in 1722, he vacated his seat early in 1724 by accepting a minor office. A few months later he went back to Madras, where he held important and lucrative positions under the East India Company for eleven years.[1] Resigning as governor in 1735 with a considerable fortune, he bought an estate at Twicken-

ham and looked for a seat in Parliament. This he
secured in January 1740 by buying up, for £9,600,
the whole of Sir William Lowther's (q.v.) interest at
Pontefract, consisting of 86 burgages and several
freeholds in the borough.[2] He and his ally, Lord
Galway (q.v.), who had a similar interest, with 22
additional burgages, jointly held, were thus able to
exercise complete control of Pontefract, for which
Pitt was twice returned unopposed, voting with the
Administration in all recorded divisions. He did not
stand in 1754, giving his seat to his friend Sambrooke Freeman, and died 9 Feb. 1756. Under his
will the Pontefract burgages passed to his daughter,
Harriet, afterwards wife of Lord Brownlow Bertie,
M.P., with remainder to his kinsman John Pitt (q.v.)
of Encombe, who sold them in 1766.[3]

[1] *Diary of Wm. Hedges*, ed. Henry Yule (Hakluyt Soc. lxxviii), iii.
Pitt ped. facing pp. xxix, lxxxix–xci, clix, clxi–clxii. [2] Joshua Wilson
to Visct. Galway, 30 Jan. 1740, and 'An account of Mr. Pitt's and
Lord Galway's estates at Pontefract', 1743, Galway Pprs. cited by
Colin Bradley, 'Parl. Rep. Pontefract, Newark and East Retford,
1754–68' (Manchester Univ. M.A. thesis). [3] PCC 47 Glazier.

R.S.L.

PITT, John (c.1698–1754).

HINDON	6 May 1720–1722
OLD SARUM	20 Jan. 1724–1727
CAMELFORD	1727–1734

b. c.1698, 3rd s. of Thomas Pitt of Boconnoc (*d.* 1726,
q.v.) and yr. bro. of Robert and Thomas Pitt (*d.* 1729),
1st Earl of Londonderry (qq.v.). *educ.* Eton 1708. *m.*
Mary, da. of Thomas Belasyse, 3rd Visct. Fauconberg,
s.p.

Capt. and lt.-col. 1 Ft. Gds. 1717; a.-d.-c. to the
King 1722–?7.

John Pitt, 'the good-for-nothing colonel' as his
father called him, was sent to 'the best school in
England', given a company in the Guards, made
a.-d.-c. to the King, with whom he became a
personal favourite, and brought into Parliament.
But, his great-nephew, the 1st Lord Camelford,
writes, 'he contrived to sacrifice his health, his
honour, and his fortune, to a flow of libertinism,
which dashed the fairest prospects'. Camelford
gives two examples of 'the profligacy of his character.
He retained by force a qualification in Parliament
with which his father had trusted him', i.e. refused
to surrender an estate conveyed to him on the usual
understanding that he would convey it back on
taking his seat. Having been forbidden his father's
house, he waited outside till an estate agent arrived
with some rents, on which he rushed in with his
sword drawn, making off with the money. Cut out
of his father's will, he filed a bill in Chancery
against the executors, which his elder brother,
Robert (q.v.), described as 'vexatious and malicious . . . brought contrary to my father's will,

tending to . . . throw odious and wicked imputations
on his memory, and to blast him in his grave'.
Returned by his nephew, Thomas (d. 1761, q.v.),
after Robert's death in 1727, he voted with the
Government, but was not put up again. He survived
for 20 years, sunk 'in contempt and obscurity',
dying 'at the thatched house by the turnpike at
Hammersmith', 9 Feb. 1754.[1]

[1] *HMC Fortescue*, i. 31, 73, 86; 'Family Characters and Anecdotes,'
by the 1st Ld. Camelford, Fortescue mss at Boconnoc.

R.R.S.

PITT, John (?1706–87), of Encombe, Dorset.

WAREHAM	1734–1747
	26 Jan. 1748–c.Nov. 1750
DORCHESTER	29 Jan. 1751–1761
WAREHAM	1761–1768

b. ?1706, 5th but 3rd surv. s. of George Pitt (*d.* 1735,
q.v.) of Strathfieldsaye, being 3rd s. by his 2nd w.
educ. Queen's, Oxf. 6 July 1722, aged 16. *m.* 26 Jan.
1753, Marcia, da. of Mark Anthony Morgan of
Cottelstown, co. Sligo,[1] 4s. 1da.

Ld. of Trade Dec. 1744–55, of Admiralty Nov.-Dec.
1756; surveyor gen. of woods and forests north and
south of the Trent 1756–63, 1768–86.

Returned as a Tory for the family seat at Wareham
in 1734, standing jointly with Henry Drax (q.v.),
John Pitt voted against the Government, speaking
for the motion for an increase in the allowance of
the Prince of Wales in 1737. One of the signatories
of the opposition whip of 20 Dec. 1743, he spoke
against the Hanoverians on 12 Jan. 1744.[1] Accepting
a place in the Broad-bottom Government formed
in December 1744, he voted for the Hanoverians in
1746. In 1747 he was opposed at Wareham by Drax,
who was backed by the Prince of Wales. There was
a double return, on which Horace Walpole reported
to Mann, 26 Jan. 1748:

> The House is now sitting on the Wareham election,
> espousing George Pitt's [q.v.] uncle, one of the most
> active Jacobites, but of the coalition and in place,
> against Drax, a great favourite of the Prince.

Awarded the seat, Pitt wrote to Pelham, 19 May
1750:

> I have received so pressing an invitation to represent
> the borough of Dorchester and from so large a
> number as could not be refused and puts my success
> there at the next general election out of all doubt.

Observing that this offer 'in all human probability
will secure me the borough for life', he asked for 'a
new mark of his Majesty's favour [to] enable me to
do him these further services',[2] i.e. for an office to
vacate his Wareham seat. On 20 Oct. 1750 Pelham
wrote to William Pitt:

> I find Jack Pitt is very anxious about quitting his
> seat in Parliament in order to be chosen at Dorchester.

You know the only difficulty. I have assured him I will do my best when the King comes over; had I left it to be managed at Hanover, I am morally sure it would not have ended well. But I hope, when I can speak myself, it will do. I must beg you to make him easy. I believe he is satisfied as to my intentions.[3]

Appointed to the stewardship of the Chiltern Hundreds, the first time that this sinecure was used to vacate a seat, he was returned unopposed for Dorchester. The 2nd Lord Egmont added a note against Dorchester to his electoral survey, c.1749–50: 'Jack Pitt . . . a most improper man, is to be avoided', on which the Prince commented 'surely'. Re-elected unopposed at Dorchester in 1754, he followed his kinsman, William Pitt (q.v.), into opposition in 1755. He died February 1787.

[1] Harley Diary; Add. 29597, f. 29; Yorke's parl. jnl. *Parl. Hist.* xiii. 463. [2] Newcastle (Clumber) mss. [3] *Chatham Corresp.* i. 53–54.

R.S.L.

PITT, Ridgeway, 3rd Earl of Londonderry [I] (?1722–65), of Soldon, Devon.

CAMELFORD   1747–1754

b. ?1722, 2nd s. of Thomas Pitt (*d.* 1729), 1st Earl of Londonderry [I] (q.v.), and 1st cos. of Thomas Pitt of Boconnoc (*d.* 1761, q.v.). *educ.* Westminster, Apr. 1730, aged 8; Bury St. Edmunds 1734; St. John's, Camb. 25 Sept. 1740, aged 18. *unm. suc.* bro. as 3rd Earl 24 Aug. 1734.

In 1747 Londonderry was included in a list of persons to be brought into Parliament by the Prince of Wales. The duty of finding him a seat fell to his first cousin, Thomas Pitt, the Prince's Cornish election manager, whose only hope of extricating himself from his desperate financial difficulties was a twenty year old suit in Chancery claiming £95,000 from Londonderry's estate. Pitt would have preferred to put his cousin up for Bossiney, but Londonderry successfully insisted on being nominated for Camelford, where he had the backing of Pitt's most influential supporter.[1] He did not stand again, dying 8 Jan. 1765, when all his honours became extinct.

[1] *HMC Fortescue*, i. 108, 110, 115, 133.

R.R.S.

PITT, Robert (?1680–1727), of Stratford, Wilts.

OLD SARUM	1705–1710
SALISBURY	1710–1713
OLD SARUM	1713–1722
OKEHAMPTON	1722–21 May 1727

b. ?1680, 1st s. of Thomas Pitt of Boconnoc (*d.* 1726, q.v.) and e. bro. of Thomas (*d.* 1729), 1st Earl of Londonderry, and John Pitt (qq.v.). *m.* 1704, Harriet, da. of Gen. the Hon. Edward Villiers of Dromana, sis. of John Villiers, 5th Visct. Grandison [I], 2s. 5da. *suc.* fa. 26 Apr. 1726.

Clerk of the household to the Prince of Wales 1716–*d.*

In 1715 Robert Pitt was re-elected for his father's borough of Old Sarum as a Tory who might often vote with the Whigs. He also stood for Salisbury, where he was defeated by two Tories, against whom he petitioned. His petition was heard at the bar of the House but was discharged at the request of both parties.[1] He was employed by his brother-in-law, James Stanhope (q.v.), as an intermediary with the Duke of Ormonde before the latter's flight to France.[2] Reporting the arrest of 'your bosom friend,' Edward Harvey of Coombe (q.v.), his father informed him, 27 Sept. 1715, that

I have heard since I came to town that you are struck in with your old hellish acquaintance, and, in all your discourse, are speaking in favour of that villainous traitor Ormonde.

Two days later, in a letter saying that Stanhope had told him that a letter from Robert, of no importance, had been found in Harvey's papers, Governor Pitt added:

Since last post I have had it reiterated to me that in all company you are vindicating Ormonde and Bolingbroke, the two vilest rebels that ever were in any nation, and that you still adhere to your cursed Tory principles.

On Robert's appointment, through Stanhope's influence, to a £500 a year post in the Prince of Wales's household, he was exhorted by his father, 21 Jan. 1716,

to let the King and Prince see that you are capable to serve 'em in this employ,

and

to shun the company of your old comrades as you would the plague, for they are most of them in actual rebellion, or abettors, or those of avowed indifference.

On learning that Robert did not intend to come to town his father wrote, 7 Feb. 1716:

I think you have already put a more than ordinary slight on the Prince's favour, and those that obtained it for you. I do not doubt but you still adhere to the advice of your old Jacobite friends.

His failure to attend Parliament for the septennial bill gave rise to 'not a few speculations on his behaviour to the Prince and the reason he forbears to come up at this time', but like his father he voted against the Government on the repeal of the Occasional Conformity and Schism Acts and the peerage bill in 1719. In 1720 he moved unsuccessfully that the final report of the secret committee on the South Sea bubble should be printed. With Archibald Hutcheson (q.v.) he introduced a bill for securing the freedom of elections, 14 Jan. 1722, which passed the Commons but not the Lords. But a bill of £2549 for Robert's election expenses at

Okehampton in 1722 produced an explosion from his father:

> You have been such a son to me as he [the estate agent concerned] has been a steward, who I will suddenly discharge as a cursed and ungrateful steward.

On his failure to come up to vote for Archibald Hutcheson on the Westminster election petition, he was denounced as 'a slinker'. And again:

> My resentments against you all have been justly and honourably grounded, and that you will find when my head is laid.[3]

In the event he succeeded to the bulk of his father's fortune, only to die a year later, 21 May 1727, of gout and the stone, leaving a series of lawsuits with his brothers to his son, Thomas (q.v.)[4]

[1] *CJ*, xviii. 141-2. [2] *HMC Egmont Diary*, i. 400-1. [3] *HMC Fortescue*, i. 51-52, 56-58, 67-69; *HMC Portland*, v. 614. [4] 'Family Characters and Ancedotes', by the 1st Ld. Camelford, Fortescue mss at Boconnoc.

R.R.S.

PITT, Thomas (1653–1726), of Stratford, Wilts. and Boconnoc, Cornw.

OLD SARUM	16 Jan. –14 Mar. 1689
SALISBURY	30 May 1689–1695
OLD SARUM	1695–1698
	1710–20 June 1716
THIRSK	30 July 1717–1722
OLD SARUM	1722–28 Apr. 1726

bap. 5 July 1653, 2nd s. of Rev. John Pitt, rector of Blandford St. Mary, Dorset by Sarah, da. of John Jay of Hemswood. *m.* c.1678/9, Jane, da. of James Innes of Reid Hall, Moray, 3 surv. s. 2. surv. da., one of whom m. James Stanhope and the other Charles Cholmondeley (qq.v.).

Gov. Fort St. George, Madras 1697–1709; commr. for building 50 new churches in and around London 1715; gov. Jamaica 1716–17.

A younger son, of a junior branch of the Pitts of Strathfieldsaye (qq.v.), Thomas Pitt, the founder of the Pitts of Boconnoc, went as a youth to India, where he made a great fortune, which he invested in estates scattered over half a dozen counties, carrying considerable electoral influence. In 1715 he was re-elected for Old Sarum, the site of which he had bought from the trustees of the Earl of Salisbury in 1691 for £1,000.[1] A member of the secret committee set up that year to enquire into the negotiation of the treaty of Utrecht, Governor Pitt, as he was known, supported the Government, one of whose heads was his son-in-law, James Stanhope (q.v.). In 1716 he vacated his seat by accepting the governorship of Jamaica to retrieve his finances, which had been impaired by gifts to his children amounting to upwards of £90,000; but next year he resigned the post without going there on selling the Pitt

diamond to the Regent of France for £125,000, with which he bought the estate of Boconnoc in Cornwall for £53,000.[2] Re-entering Parliament for Thirsk, he acted with the Opposition during the split in the Whig party, voting in January 1719 against the repeal of the Occasional Conformity and Schism Acts. Put down as to be approached through Stanhope on the peerage bill, he spoke and voted against it in December of that year, taxing its authors with 'mean tenderness to foreigners and designs against the liberties of their countrymen'. In March 1720 he moved the rejection of a bill providing for appeals from the Irish to the English House of Lords, describing it as 'calculated for no other purpose than to increase the power of the peers, which was already much too great'. At the opening of Parliament in December he took a leading part in opposing the Government's attempts to avert an inquiry into the South Sea scandal, moving that the House should order the immediate attendance of the directors, with 'their myrmidons'.[3]

At the general election of 1722 Pitt returned himself and his three sons, quarrelling bitterly with the eldest, Robert, about his election bill[4] and with the youngest, John, for refusing to return an estate conveyed to him to qualify him for Parliament.[5] 'The misfortune that all my sons have brought on me', he wrote in 1723, 'will very speedily carry my grey hairs to my grave, and I care not how soon it is, for I am surrounded with the plagues and troubles of this world'. He died 28 Apr. 1726, leaving everything to his eldest son, subject to a number of legacies, including £200 a year to his grandson, William (q.v.), whom he pronounced 'a hopeful lad'.[6]

[1] *VCH Wilts.* vi. 66, 206; *HMC Fortescue*, i. 89. [2] *HMC Fortescue*, i. 59, 61–62, 89, 90–92. [3] Coxe, *Walpole*, ii. 203. [4] *HMC Fortescue*, i. 67. [5] 'Family Characters and Anecdotes', by the 1st Ld. Camelford, Fortescue mss at Boconnoc. [6] *HMC Fortescue*, i. 69, 73, 76; *Diary of Wm. Hedges*, ed. H. Yule (Hakluyt Soc. lxxviii), iii. p. clxv.

R.R.S.

PITT, Thomas (c.1688–1729), of Pall Mall, London.

WILTON	1713–1727
OLD SARUM	1727–Feb. 1728

b. c.1688, 2nd s. of Thomas Pitt of Boconnoc (*d.* 1726, q.v.) and bro. of Robert and John Pitt (qq.v.). *educ.* Mr. Meure's acad. 1704. *m.* 10 Mar. 1717, Lady Frances Ridgeway, da. and coh. of Robert, 4th Earl of Londonderry [I], 2s. 1da. *cr.* Baron of Londonderry [I] 3 Jan. 1719; Earl of Londonderry [I] 8 Oct. 1726.

Capt. Killigrew's regt. of Drags. 1709; col. regt. of Horse 1715–26, 3 Ft. 1726–d.; gov. Leeward Is. 1728–d.

Mayor, Wilton 1716–17.

Entering the army in 1709, with a troop of dragoons bought for 1,100 guineas, Thomas Pitt was brought in for Wilton, adjoining his father's estate of Stratford. From 1715 he voted regularly with the Government, serving with his regiment in the rebellion.[1] Marrying one of the heiresses of the Earl of Londonderry, 'he bought', according to his nephew, the 1st Lord Camelford, 'the honours that were extinct in her father'. He is said to have lost over £50,000 in the South Sea bubble. Camelford describes him as a man 'of no character, and of parts that were calculated only for the knavery of business, in which he overreached others, and at last himself'.[2] This seems to relate to a petition filed in Chancery against him in November 1727 by his elder brother, Robert (q.v.), as the residuary legatee of their father, alleging that Londonderry owed the estate £95,000, but that, having improperly secured possession of the Governor's papers, he had not only denied the debt but counter-claimed for £10,000.[3] Both brothers died within the next three years, Londonderry on 12 Sept. 1729 in the Leeward Islands, where he had gone as governor; but the litigation which they had started was still dragging on twenty years later.

[1] *HMC Fortescue*, i. 13, 18, 38, 54. [2] 'Family Characters and Anecdotes', by the 1st Ld. Camelford, Fortescue mss at Boconnoc; J. H. Plumb, *Walpole*, i. 332. [3] *HMC Fortescue*, i. 85.

R.R.S.

PITT, Thomas (c.1705–61), of Boconnoc, Cornw.

OKEHAMPTON   1727–1754
OLD SARUM   1754–Mar. 1755, 30 Mar.–
              17 July 1761

b. c.1705, 1st s. of Robert Pitt (q.v.) and bro. of William Pitt (*d.* 1778, q.v.), Earl of Chatham. *educ.* Eton c.1718–21. *m.* (1) c.1731, Christian (*d.* 5 June 1750), da. of Sir Thomas Lyttelton, 4th Bt. (q.v.), of Hagley, Worcs., sis. of George Lyttelton (q.v.), 2s. 2da.; (2) c.1 July 1761, Maria, da. of Gen. Murray. *suc.* fa. 1727.
    Assay master of the stannaries Mar. 1738–Feb. 1742, lord warden Feb. 1742–Mar. 1751; recorder, Camelford 1735–*d.*

Soon after coming of age, Thomas Pitt succeeded to large entailed estates giving him the nomination of both Members for Old Sarum, and an interest sufficient, with careful attention, to command one and at times two seats at both Okehampton and Camelford. Determined to carve out for himself a parliamentary career, he felt the need for money as well as landed property, ignoring family claims which had been made on his grandfather's death.

My father, [his son, the 1st Ld. Camelford wrote] seized whatever fell into his hands without account either belonging to my grandfather or grandmother, keeping at arms length every demand upon him, till somehow or other these litigations seem to have worn themselves out and slept by the acquiescence of all parties.[1]

Though the general election came only three months

after his succession, he was active in all the constituencies where he had inherited an interest. Unsure of his strength at Okehampton, he had himself returned for Old Sarum as well, where he also brought in his uncle, Lord Londonderry. Electing to serve for Okehampton, he chose Matthew Chitty St. Quintin to join Londonderry. Another uncle, Col. John Pitt, represented him at Camelford. In his first Parliament, except for voting against the motion granting the King £115,000 for civil list arrears in April 1729, he supported the Administration. But in the next he followed his wife's uncle, Lord Cobham, into opposition, carrying with him his brother, William, and his two brothers-in-law, George Lyttelton and Robert Nedham, whom he had brought in at Old Sarum and Okehampton, leaving Sir Thomas Lyttelton (Camelford) as the only Member returned by him who continued to support Walpole. A 'dull', 'ill-informed', speaker, he made no mark in the House, concentrating instead on electioneering.[2] Owing to his electoral activities, he was forced in 1737 to obtain an Act of Parliament enabling him to sell Swallowfield to John Dodd (q.v.) for £20,770. Next year, he increased his dwindling income by accepting an office from the Prince of Wales, the beginning of a connexion which was ultimately to reduce him to bankruptcy, exile, and black despair.

At the general election of 1741, Pitt acted as Cornish election manager for the Prince, in alliance with Lord Falmouth (Hugh Boscawen, q.v.) and the local Tories under Sir William Carew (q.v.), against the government manager, Richard Edgcumbe (q.v.). It was largely owing to his efforts that the Opposition won 27 out of 44 Members for Cornwall, the first time in this period that the Government had suffered defeat in that county. With his additional four seats at Old Sarum and Okehampton, he could claim to have played a major part in reducing Walpole's parliamentary majority to a figure which proved inadequate. As a reward, the Prince promoted him to be warden of the stannaries.

From 1735 to 1742 Pitt's politics had conformed to those of the Cobham group, consisting of William Pitt, Lyttelton, and the Grenvilles, who had also been closely associated with the Prince. But on Walpole's fall, he went over with Frederick to the Administration, while the Cobhamites (though Lyttelton and William Pitt remained in the Prince's service), continued to oppose. They eventually entered the Government in 1744 and 1746, but he parted company with them again in 1747, when he reverted to opposition with his royal master, for whom he again acted as chief election agent in Cornwall at the general election that year. Underestimating the importance of Falmouth's conversion to the Administration and without Tory co-operation, he faced the campaign with high hopes of repeating the victory of 1741. To his brother-in-law Ayscough, the Prince's clerk of the closet, he wrote that he saw 'great reason to hope for success':

> I will be as active and diligent as possibly I can. I will spare no pains, nor scruple running any risk to promote the service of my master, who has bound me to him by the indissoluble tie of gratitude for favours and honours bestowed on me . . . You tell me I am to spare neither money nor pains: to the utmost of my power I shall not, but the latter will hold out much longer than the former . . . No men can attack to any purpose without ammunition sufficient for the attack.

But, in the event, instead of the sixteen Members he had hoped to return, he had to be content with twelve. Mournfully he reported:

> I shall be ashamed to look the Prince in the face after the hopes that I had raised in him. I am vexed to the soul. What can I say? That I have been betrayed by villains that I had reason to depend on . . . This I can say, that nothing has been wanting in me; but my success has been far short of the expense of money and trouble . . . My uneasiness at present is so great that I hope never to be desired again to undertake the same kind of work. I would not, almost upon any consideration, undergo the same anxiety of mind, which success could hardly have recompensed me for . . . I am most damnably mortified . . . I shall hide myself at Boconnoc, for I am ashamed of making appearance in the world.

Comforted somewhat by a letter from the Prince, thanking him for his zeal and trouble, assuring him that he had 'shown the enemy a better generalship than they can boast of', and hoping to see him soon at Cliveden 'with his gun', he began to talk of the future, claiming that even where success had eluded him a foundation had been laid. But next year, hard pressed by his creditors, and challenged at both Camelford and Okehampton by the Duke of Bedford, his situation was 'enough to make a man mad'.[3] 1749 and 1750 were spent in devising complicated schemes for borrowing enough money to stave off the bankruptcy to which his borough-mongering had reduced him. He and his brother-in-law, Ayscough, attempted to secure a lease of the tin farm in the duchy of Cornwall, obtaining petitions from the miners to call a stannaries parliament to be presided over by Pitt as lord warden to ratify the deal. Though Dodington opposed the scheme as a 'scandalous job', Pitt 'lured [the Prince] to it by shewing to him new acquisitions in the Cornish elections'. The parliament of tinners met in the summer of 1750, but refused to be guided by the lord warden either as to their place of meeting or any of the business they were to transact, ending in a complete fiasco.[4]

According to Horace Walpole, Pitt was 'baffled by an opposition erected by the Boscawens, under the auspices of the ministry'.[5] Neither loans from Ayscough nor the Prince's grant, in return for the right to nominate both Members at Old Sarum, of £3,000 and an annual salary of £1,500, proved adequate.[6]

The final blow was Frederick's death on 20 Mar. 1751. If the Prince had lived to come to the throne, Pitt was to have been appointed to the lucrative office of vice-treasurer of Ireland, with a peerage, retaining the stannaries.[7] Now, deprived of his patron, overwhelmed with debts and lawsuits, threatened in his boroughs, and informed by his brother, William, that the King had no further use for his services, he was obliged, as he afterwards put it, 'to look about him'.[8] He opposed the regency bill in May 1751, proposing 'to leave out such words as precluded the Princess from disposing of offices'. He then opened negotiations with the Pelhams for the disposal of his only negotiable asset, his electoral interest at Old Sarum, Okehampton, and Camelford, which he ultimately pawned to the Government for £2,000 and a pension of £1,000 a year during pleasure.

> Sorry I am to say [wrote Camelford] that, dividing . . . in their political systems, in which my father was shipwrecked at the time that his brother rose to the top of everything, there was not a moment through the course of their lives when these obligations [of William to Thomas] seem to have been remembered, though the situation of my father when his brother was first minister was so reduced as to solicit in vain the appointment to the Swiss Cantons as an object of his ambition.[9]

He died 17 July 1761.

[1] 'Family Characters and Anecdotes', by the 1st Ld. Camelford, Fortescue mss at Boconnoc. [2] Walpole, *Mems. Geo. II*, i. 27; Yorke's parl. jnl. *Parl. Hist.* xiii. 140. [3] *HMC Fortescue*, i. 110, 120, 122, 127, 132–3. [4] *Dodington Diary*, 68–73, 75–80; *A State of the Proceedings of the Convocation of Parliament for the Stannaries* (1751). [5] *Mems. Geo. II*, i. 142. [6] *HMC Fortescue*, i. 133–5. [7] 'Family Characters'. [8] R.N. Aldworth to Duke of Bedford, 20 Dec. 1753, Bedford mss. [9] 'Family Characters'; Add. 32724, f. 214.

J.B.O./E.C.

PITT, William (d. 1725) of Cricket Malherbie, Som.

BRIDGWATER   19 Apr. 1720–1722

1st s. of Samuel Pitt of Cricket, Som. *m.* Oct. 1717, Jane, da. of William Hockmore of Combinteignhead, Devon, wid. of one Palmer of Sharpham Park, Som., 1s. *suc.* fa. 1712.

Returned for Bridgwater as a Whig after a contest at the by-election following the death of George Dodington (q.v.), Pitt did not stand in 1722, when his cousin Samuel Pitt, a London merchant, unsuccessfully contested the borough. He died about

June 1725. His wife subsequently married George Speke (q.v.) of Dillington, whom Pitt had appointed one of his executors.[1]

[1] PCC 142 Romney; *Som. Wills* (ser. 2), p. 37; (ser. 3), p. 122.

S.R.M.

PITT, William (1708–78), of Hayes, Kent.

OLD SARUM	18 Feb. 1735–1747
SEAFORD	1747–1754
ALDBOROUGH	1754–Dec. 1756
BUCKINGHAM	7–11 Dec. 1756
OAKHAMPTON	11 Dec. 1756–July 1757
BATH	9 July 1757–4 Aug. 1766

b. 15 Nov. 1708, 2nd s. of Robert Pitt (q.v.) and bro. of Thomas Pitt (*d.* 1761, q.v.). *educ.* Eton 1719–26; Trinity, Oxf. 1727; Utrecht. *m.* 16 Nov. 1754, Lady Hester Grenville, da. of Richard Grenville (q.v.) of Wootton, Bucks., 3s. 2da. *cr.* Earl of Chatham 4 Aug. 1766.

Cornet of Cobham's Horse 1731–6; groom of the bedchamber to Prince of Wales 1737–45; P.C. 28 May 1746; jt. vice-treasurer [I] Feb.–May 1746; paymaster gen. May 1746–55; sec. of state, southern dept. Dec. 1756–Apr. 1757, July 1757–61; ld. privy seal July 1766–Oct. 1768.

A younger brother with only £200 a year, William Pitt at the age of 22 acquired a cornet's commission costing £1,000, the money, according to the 2nd Lord Egmont,[1] being provided by Walpole, presumably in return for the support of William's elder brother, Thomas (q.v.), who brought four Members, including himself, into the 1727 Parliament. But in the next Parliament, to which Thomas returned his brother, both Pitts went into opposition, William making a distinguished maiden speech against the Government on a place bill, 22 Apr. 1735.[2] By the following session he was known as 'a very pretty speaker, one the Prince is particular to, and under the tuition of Lord Cobham',[3] with whose nephews, George Lyttelton and the Grenvilles (qq.v.), he formed a political group, nick-named 'Cobham's cubs'.

On 29 Apr. 1736, when the House of Commons addressed the King on the Prince of Wales's marriage,

three very remarkable speeches were made by Mr. Grenville and Mr. Lyttelton, two of Lord Cobham's nephews, and Cornet Pitt, who got up one after another in the House of Commons to compliment the Prince's character and the Princess's family and to insinuate, not in very covert terms, that the King had very little merit to the nation in making this match, since it had been owing to the Prince demanding it of his father, and the voice of the people calling for it too strongly not to be complied with.[4]

Dismissed by the King from the army for this speech at the end of the session, Pitt was compensated next year by a place in the Prince's household.

In Parliament he continued to act with Lyttelton and Grenville against the Government, notably in the debate of 9 Mar. 1739 on the Spanish convention, when they are described as 'young gentlemen who took great personal liberties'.[5]

After Walpole's fall the Cobham group parted company with the Prince, who supported the new Administration, while they remained in opposition. When Parliament re-assembled on 16 Nov. 1742, Pitt made a speech of which the Prince said that 'Pitt might as well have spit in his face as he spoke as he did'.[6] The King might have said the same of Pitt's speech on 10 Dec. against the grant for the Hanoverian troops in British pay. 'It is scarcely possible', Lord Rosebery writes, 'to conceive sarcasms more calculated to afflict the sovereign in his tenderest susceptibilities than those which Pitt now launched, even as we read them in an imperfect report; they are, indeed, so masterly in this way as almost to prove their authenticity'.[7] When Pelham became head of the Treasury in August 1743, Walpole, now Earl of Orford, urged him to strengthen himself by coming to terms with Pitt. 'Pitt', he wrote, 25 Aug., 'is thought able and formidable, try him and show him'. And again, 18 Sept., 'Pitt may be put into the Treasury, a monstrous advancement that. He will be useful there, or it takes out his sting'.[8]

In the next session, Pitt, now a member of the opposition shadow-cabinet, attacked Carteret as 'an execrable, a sole minister', 'the Hanoverian troop-minister, a flagitious task-master', whose 'sixteen thousand Hanoverians were all the party he had'. Nor did he spare George II, deriding the dangers which the Address congratulated him on escaping from at Dettingen; describing him as 'hemmed in by German officers and one English minister without an English heart'; and calling on Parliament to 'snatch him from the gulf where an infamous minister has placed him'. In the debate of 18 Jan. 1744, again on the Hanoverian troops, he appealed to the Pelhams, as 'the amiable part of the Administration, to give up so odious a point, which (if carried), would do them no service in the nation, and only tend to advance another's [Carteret's] power in the Closet'.[9]

Pitt's speech paved the way to a junction with the Pelhams, which was effected in November 1744, when Carteret, now Granville, was forced to resign, most of his supporters in the Government being turned out to make room for the heads of the Opposition. The results of the junction were manifested on 23 Jan. 1745, when Pitt's 'fulminating eloquence silenced all opposition' to the vote for the employment of 28,000 British troops in Flanders. The post earmarked for him at his own request was that of secretary at war, but owing to the King's personal objection to him he remained out of office till the Pelhams made his appointment 'into some honourable employment' one of the conditions of their own return to office in Feb. 1746. Even then George II objected so strongly to Pitt's appointment to the War Office, declaring that 'that fellow should never come into his Closet', that it was necessary to substitute some post not involving personal relations with the Sovereign.[10] He was accordingly appointed to a lucrative sinecure, which he soon exchanged for the Pay Office, where he followed Pelham's example of refusing to take the perquisites.[11]

Thus at the age of 37, after 11 years in Parliament, Pitt, in his own words, entered 'the stream of promotion, which by its natural current and the right of succession in the graduation of office . . . commonly bears men to fortune'. Entering the stream at a place reached by both Walpole and Pelham before him at a comparable age and in much the same time, he could reasonably expect to arrive in due course at the same destination, that of first minister. In this expectation he put up with eight years 'at the oar of parliamentary drudgery'[12] under Pelham. Only Murray, the future Lord Mansfield, could compare with him in mastery of the House of Commons: 'they alone', Chesterfield told his son in 1751, 'can quiet and inflame the House; they are so attended to in that numerous and noisy assembly, that you might hear a pin drop when either is speaking'.[13] But when Pelham's death in 1754 opened the way to Pitt's promotion, George II, in referring the choice of a successor to the Cabinet, said significantly that 'he hoped they would not think of recommending to him any person who had flown in his face'. The royal veto was allowed to prevail, leaving Pitt, as he himself put it, stuck 'fast aground' in 'the stream of cabinet promotion . . . , exposed to the ridiculous mortification of seeing everybody pass by me that navigates the same river.'[14] He died 11 May 1778.

[1] Draft of an unpublished pamphlet written about 1757 containing an account of Pitt's career, Add. 47097/8. [2] *HMC Egmont Diary*, ii. 171. [3] *HMC Carlisle*, 172. [4] Hervey, *Mems.* 553. [5] Coxe, *Walpole*, iii. 516. [6] Ilchester, *Ld. Holland*, i. 93. [7] *Chatham*, 188. [8] Coxe, *Pelham*, i. 91–93; Newcastle (Clumber) mss. [9] Owen, *Pelhams*, 199 and n.3; Yorke's parl. jnl. *Parl. Hist.* xiii. 141–2, 471, 473. [10] Yorke's parl. jnl. 1055–6; Owen, 301 n. 3. [11] 'Family Characters and Anecdotes', by the 1st Ld. Camelford, Fortescue mss at Boconnoc. [12] R. Phillimore, *Lyttelton*, ii. 267, 466. [13] *Letters*, 11 Feb. 1751. [14] Yorke, *Hardwicke*, ii. 205-6.

R.R.S.

PLEYDELL, Edmund Morton (?1693–1754), of Milborne St. Andrew, Dorset.

DORCHESTER 1722–13 Feb. 1723
DORSET 1727–1747

b. ?1693, 4th but 1st surv. s. of Edmund Pleydell, M.P., of Midgehall, Wilts. by Anne, da. and h. of Sir John Morton, 2nd Bt., M.P., of Milborne St. Andrew. *educ.* Balliol, Oxf. 10 Apr. 1712, aged 18. *m.* by 1724, Deborah, da. of William Kyffyn of Denb., 4s. 3da. *suc.* fa. 1726.

Edmund Pleydell's father was M.P. for Wootton Bassett and grandson of Sir Charles Pleydell of Midgehall, who died in 1642. His mother's family, to whom he was heir, had lived at Milborne since the fifteenth century.[1] Unseated on petition at Dorchester in 1723, he was returned for the county as a Tory in the next three Parliaments, in which he voted consistently against the Administration. Not standing again, he died 16 Mar. 1754.

[1] Hutchins, *Dorset*, i. 196; ii. 594, 599.

R.S.L.

PLUMER, Richard (c.1689–1750).

LICHFIELD	1722–1734
ST. MAWES	1734–1741
ALDEBURGH	1741–1747
WEYMOUTH AND MELCOMBE REGIS	1747–25 Nov. 1750

b. c.1689, 3rd surv. s. of John Plumer of Blakesware, Herts. by Mary, da. of William Hale of King's Walden, Herts.; bro. of Walter and William Plumer (qq.v.). *unm. suc.* to fa.'s Kent and Surrey estates 1719.

Ld. of Trade 1721–7, 1735–49.

Richard Plumer was appointed to the board of Trade a year before being brought into Parliament on the interest of the Chetwynds, one of whom was also on the board. On being turned out at George II's accession to make room for Sir Orlando Bridgeman (q.v.), he wrote to Sir Robert Walpole, 31 July 1727:

I have received the news of my being dismissed from my employment, which I could not do at first without some concern, but as I hope it is for his Majesty's service I submit to it patiently and take this first opportunity of returning you thanks for your favour in continuing me so long in it, and do assure you that I have always acknowledged it with the utmost gratitude. I hope I shall meet with no opposition at this place, and I now only desire I may succeed when I have an opportunity of convincing you by my behaviour in Parliament, that I acted upon principle, and with no other motive.[1]

He voted with the Administration on the civil list arrears in 1729, against them on the Hessians in 1730, the army in 1732, and the excise bill in 1733, and with them on the repeal of the Septennial Act in 1734.

In 1734 Walpole wrote to the widow of John Knight (q.v.), who controlled one seat at St. Mawes:[2]

I am obliged to you in taking my recommendation to your interest at St. Mawes. I beg leave to acquaint you that Mr. Richard Plumer is a gentleman very acceptable, and one that I should be glad of serving upon this occasion. I take this compliment, Madam, as a very personal obligation to myself.

Returned for St. Mawes, Plumer recovered his seat at the board of Trade in 1735, thereafter of course voting consistently with the Administration. In 1741 he was brought in for Aldeburgh, and in 1747 for Weymouth by Dodington on the nomination of Henry Pelham, at a cost of some five or six hundred pounds.[3] On 18 Nov. 1750 Dodington had an interview with Pelham to discuss arangements at Weymouth 'if Mr. Plumer should die (who was that day cut for stone)'.[4] He died a week later, 25 Nov. 1750.

[1] Cholmondeley (Houghton) mss. [2] 4 Apr. 1734, Stowe mss 142, f. 104. [3] Hartington to Devonshire, 16 June 1747, Devonshire mss. [4] *Dodington Diary*, 84.

R.R.S.

PLUMER, Walter (?1682–1746), of Cavendish Sq. and Chediston Hall, Suff.

ALDEBURGH   3 Dec. 1719–1727
APPLEBY   24 Jan. 1730–1741

b. ?1682, 1st surv. s. of John Plumer; bro. of Richard and William Plumer (qq.v.). *educ.* Eton 1698; Peterhouse, Camb. 26 Apr. 1699, aged 16; G. Inn 1702. *m.* Elizabeth, da. of Thomas Hanbury of Kelmarsh, Northants., *s.p. suc.* to fa.'s Berks., Essex and Mdx. estates and to his Bank of England stock 1719.

Plumer was the son of a wealthy London merchant, who bought Blakesware in 1685 and the manors of Eastwick and Gilston a few years later. Soon after succeeding to his patrimony he stood with government support for Aldeburgh in Suffolk, spending money liberally against Lord Strafford's interest. Writing to one of the Aldeburgh electors, Strafford described him as a 'gentleman of the Inns of Court', adding, 'though his father had a large estate he left it to his younger brother, not to him.'[1] Returned against Strafford's candidate, within a week of taking his seat he made his maiden speech in support of the peerage bill, continuing to support the Government for the rest of that Parliament.

Returned unopposed at the general election, Plumer was one of the leading ministerial supporters in the Commons who attended a private meeting in Walpole's house at the beginning of that Parliament about the suspension of the Habeas Corpus Act, which he opposed. During the next two sessions he spoke against the Government on the army estimates.[2] In 1725 he was appointed to the committee for drawing up the articles of Lord Macclesfield's impeachment, of which he was one of the managers.

Plumer did not stand for Aldeburgh in 1727, presumably because he had lost the government interest there. In 1730 he was brought in by Lord Thanet (Sackville Tufton, q.v.) for Appleby, which he continued to represent till he retired in 1741. He quickly established himself as one of the leading spokesmen of the opposition Whigs, taking a particularly active part in securing the repeal of the salt duty in 1730 and in opposing its re-imposition in 1732. It was alleged that

> the secret why he is against the Court and so strenuous against the revival of the salt duty, it is that he has an estate where salt works may be carried on, but by the former Act establishing that duty, no new works were to be made; the revival therefore of that duty deprived him of opening works, but had the duty been re-imposed by a new Act with a clause that he might work, he had not been against it.

But he did not belong to the extreme wing of the Opposition. When the more violent members of his party were for insisting on the formal rejection of the excise bill, he was among those who 'expressed themselves satisfied with attaining their end, the dropping the bill, and thought the mortification enough that Sir Robert had failed in his attempt', after which he obtained more votes than any other opposition Member in the ballot for a committee on frauds in the customs. On the Princess Royal's marriage, he took the opportunity of dissociating himself from the Tories by warmly supporting the Address and a handsome portion. A strong supporter of the nonconformists, moving for the repeal of the Test Act in 1736, he made his last recorded speech on a similar motion in 1739.

Plumer had a caustic tongue. On a report in 1737 that Walpole had offered to make him secretary at war he was said to have observed that he would not accept 'unless a sum of money be given him, merely saying Sir William Yonge [q.v.] has made that office to stink and he must be paid for perfumes to sweeten it'.[3] When Pelham turned Sandys and Rushout (qq.v.) out of the Treasury by promoting them in 1743, Plumer delighted Horace Walpole by the comment:

> Zounds, Mr. Pulteney took those old dishclouts to wipe out the Treasury and now they are going to lace them and lay them up.[4]

He died 2 Mar. 1746.

[1] Add. 22248, f. 90. [2] *Knatchbull Diary*, 12 Nov., 9 Dec. 1724, and p. 115. [3] *HMC Egmont Diary*, i. 246, 361, 367, 371–2; ii. 366; iii. 47. [4] To Mann, 30 Nov. 1743.

R.R.S.

PLUMER, William (?1686–1767), of Blakesware, Herts.

YARMOUTH I.o.W.   10 Feb. 1721–1722
HERTFORDSHIRE   1734–1741, 1 May 1755–1761

b. ?1686, 2nd surv. s. of John Plumer; bro. of Richard
and Walter Plumer (qq.v.). *educ.* Bishop's Stortford;
Peterhouse, Camb. 9 May 1702, aged 15; G. Inn 1702,
called 1708, bencher 1728. *m.* 9 Oct. 1731, Elizabeth,
da. of Thomas Byde of Ware Park, Herts., 2s. 4da.
suc. fa. 1719, bro. 1746.

Plumer was brought into Parliament as a government supporter in 1721, but did not stand in 1722.
At the Hertfordshire county election that year he
supported Charles Caesar (q.v.), subject to 'the
obligation I owe to my particular friends', i.e. the
local Whigs.[1] He again supported Caesar in 1727.
In 1734 he was chosen as a candidate for the county
at the general meeting of the gentlemen, clergy, and
freeholders.[2] He was returned, defeating Caesar,
who complained that the 'Tory gentlemen in
Hertfordshire were grossly imposed upon . . . to
choose a gentleman in my room who there is all the
reason in the world to believe will never or at least
very seldom vote with those I always did',[3] that is
to say with the Opposition, but there is no record
of his voting. He is included in a list of absent
ministerial supporters on 18 Nov. 1739.[4]

He died 12 Dec. 1767.

[1] Cottrell Dormer letter bk. A. 23, Rousham mss, ex inf. L. M.
Munby. [2] See HERTFORDSHIRE. [3] Cottrell Dormer letter bk.
C. 32. [4] Cholmondeley (Houghton) mss.

A.N.N.

PLUMPTRE, John (1679–1751), of Plumptre House, Nottingham.

NOTTINGHAM	25 Dec. 1706–1713, 1715–1727
BISHOP'S CASTLE	1727–1734
NOTTINGHAM	1734–1747
ST. IVES	11 Dec. 1747–29 Sept. 1751

b. 9 Feb. 1679, 1st s. of Henry Plumptre of Nottingham
by his 2nd w. Joyce, da. of Henry Sacheverell of
Barton, Notts., wid. of John Milward of Snitterton,
Derbys. *educ.* M. Temple 1696; Queens', Camb. 1697.
m. bef. 1708, Annabella, da. of Sir Francis Molyneux,
4th Bt., M.P., of Teversall, Notts., by Diana, sis. of
Scrope, 1st Visct. Howe, M.P., 7s. 2da. *suc.* fa. 1693.
  Commr. for stating army debts 1715–20; treasurer
of the Ordnance 1720–*d.*

John Plumptre belonged to an ancient Nottingham family, who had sat for the town under Richard
II and Elizabeth, still lived in it at Plumptre House,
but were otherwise indistinguishable from the
neighbouring county families with which they inter-
married. Returned as a Whig for Nottingham in
1706, he lost his seat in 1713, recovering it in 1715
with the support of the future Duke of Newcastle,[1]
thus beginning a connexion which lasted to the end
of his life. Though one of Newcastle's first and

staunchest adherents in the county, not above
accepting and asking favours from him—as he said
in applying for a living for a son, 'a man with nine
children must sometimes risk a small indecency'[2]—
he was in no sense a dependant. He owed his seat
primarily to his own local influence.

With a break from 1727 to 1734, when Newcastle
arranged for him to take a temporary seat at Bishop's
Castle[3] to facilitate a compromise at Nottingham,
Plumptre continued to represent the borough till
1747, consistently supporting the Government,
except in 1717, when he voted against them on
Lord Cadogan (q.v.), and in 1733 on the excise bill,
which he opposed. For over 30 years he held a
place in the Ordnance with a salary of £500 p.a.,
which according to Henry Pelham he might have
exchanged

> for almost any other, except the three or four first
> employments, but he chose rather to stay where he
> knew he was pleased than to run the risk of meeting
> with what he, upon trial, might not like so well.[4]

He spoke on 17 Mar. 1725 for a motion to prevent
the universities from purchasing advowsons, and on
4 Feb. 1730, objecting to a motion for a vote of
thanks for a sermon to the House on the anniversary
of the execution of Charles I as

> an ambiguous, dubious discourse, that might be taken
> by two handles, . . . no ways consonant to the dignity
> of the day, and not very respectful to the audience he
> preached before, so a division and carried against it
> by 93 to 48. The text was 'take the wicked from before
> the King and his throne shall be established in
> righteousness'.[5]

Plumptre lost his Nottingham seat at a three
cornered contest in 1747 between the previous Tory
Member, himself, and a rival Whig candidate, the
3rd Lord Howe (q.v.), his relation by marriage, in
which he found that 'on a poll I should make a
figure merely despicable'. He therefore withdrew,
notifying his withdrawal to the Tory candidate,
but not to Lord Howe's people, 'the ungentle-
manlike and the ungrateful behaviour of that family
towards me not entitling them from the very beginning of this affair to any such civility from me to
them'.[6] Accommodated, no doubt through Newcastle's good offices, with a seat at St. Ives, he was
chairman of a committee on fees in 1751,[7] dying
that year, 29 Sept.

[1] Add. 32686, f. 25; 33060, ff. 13, 16, 18. [2] To Newcastle, 29
Sept. 1740, Add. 32695, f. 158. [3] Cholmondeley (Houghton) mss
42/13; Duke of Chandos to Capt. Oakely, 13 Aug. 1727, Chandos
letter bks. [4] C. Nugent, *Mem. of Robert, Earl Nugent*, 254. [5] *Knatchbull Diary*. [6] To Newcastle, 15 and 27 June 1747, Add. 32711,
ff. 395–6, 576. [7] *CJ*, xxvi. 270, 290.

R.R.S.

POLE, Sir William, 4th Bt. (1678–1741), of Colcombe Castle, nr. Colyton, and Shute, nr. Honiton, Devon.

NEWPORT	1701–1702
CAMELFORD	17 Jan. 1704–1708
NEWPORT	1708–1710
DEVON	1710–June 1712
BOSSINEY	1713–1715
HONITON	17 Mar. 1716–1727
	15 Mar. 1731–1734

bap. 17 Aug. 1678, 1st s. of Sir John Pole, 3rd Bt., M.P., mayor of Honiton 1685, by Anne, da. of Sir William Morice, M.P., of Werrington, Devon, sis. of Sir William Morice, 1st Bt., M.P. *educ.* New Coll. Oxf. 1696. *m.* by 1733, for 'many years',[1] Elizabeth, da. of Robert Warry of Shute, Devon, 1s. 1da. *suc.* fa. 13 Mar. 1708.

Master of the Household 1712–14.

Pole was descended from an old Honiton family, who purchased Colcombe from the Courtenays in the early sixteenth century; leased Shute, subsequently the family seat, in the time of Elizabeth;[2] were largely instrumental in securing the re-enfranchisement of Honiton in 1640; and represented the borough at intervals for almost 100 years.[3] Returned for it as a Tory at a by-election in 1716, he voted against the Administration in all the three chief divisions of this Parliament. His name was sent to the Pretender in 1721 as a probable supporter in the event of a rising.[4] Re-elected after a contest in 1722, when he was also returned for Newport, he was unsuccessful at the poll in 1727, but recovered his seat on petition. In his will, drafted in 1733, he made it his 'earnest request and recommendation' to his son that he 'will never stand as a candidate or if chosen will never be prevailed upon to represent or serve in Parliament for the borough of Honiton.'[5] He did not stand again, dying of 'gout in his stomach', 31 Dec. 1741.[6]

[1] PCC 165 Trenley. [2] Lysons, *Devon*, i. pp. cix–cx; ii. 131; A. J. Jewers, 'The Churches of Colyton & Shute', *Dev. Assoc. Trans.* xxxiii. 714; Hoskins, *Devon*, 374, 476. [3] A. Farquharson, *Hist. Honiton*, 37. [4] Stuart mss 65/16. [5] PCC 165 Trenley. [6] M. F. Bridie, *Story of Shute*, 138.

S.R.M.

POLHILL, David (1674–1754), of Chipstead, Kent.

KENT	11 Jan. –21 Sept. 1710
BRAMBER	18 Feb. 1723–1727
ROCHESTER	1727–1741, 22 Feb. 1742–
	15 Jan. 1754

b. 1674, 2nd but 1st surv. s. of Thomas Polhill of Chipstead, Kent, and Clapham, Surr. by Elizabeth, da. of Henry Ireton of Attenborough, Notts. *m.* (1) 3 Sept. 1702, Elizabeth (*d.* 4 June 1708), da. of John Trevor of Glynde, Suss., *s.p.*; (2) 20 Aug. 1713, Gertrude (*d.* 1714), da. of Thomas Pelham, M.P., 1st

Baron Pelham, sis. of Thomas Pelham Holles, 1st Duke of Newcastle, *s.p.*; (3) Elizabeth, da. of John Borrett of Shoreham, Kent, 4s. 1da. *suc.* fa. 1683.

Sheriff, Kent 1714–15; keeper of the records in the Tower of London 1731–*d.*

A fervent Whig, who stood 11 times for Parliament, Polhill was first returned for his county at a by-election shortly before the dissolution of 1710, only to be defeated at the general election on the 'cry of Sacheverell and the danger of the Church'. In 1715, his son writes,

> my father's interest in the county was at that time so great, that Lord Westmorland was apprehensive he might be a dangerous rival to his brother Col. John Fane [q.v.] who I think, was either a candidate, or chosen knight of the shire that year, and, it being the first year of the accession of the house of Hanover to this throne, wanting a man of courage, temper, and a friend to that illustrious family for high sheriff, they pitched upon David Polhill . . .
> In 1722 he was again a candidate for the county with Sir George Oxenden [q.v.], and they would have been chosen, but for the jealousy of some great men (my father's pretended friends). The nobility, with the Duke of Dorset at their head, could not bear to see so much popularity, attended with so much real merit in a plebeian and Col. Fane setting up on the same (the Whig) interest they broke that interest.

When in 1731 the Duke of Dorset's son, Lord Middlesex (q.v.), stood for Kent, Polhill supported him, which

> occasioned a memorable conversation between the Duke of Dorset and my father.—'How is this', said the Duke, 'Mr. Polhill, I opposed you in favour of Col. Fane ten years ago. He now opposes my son and you support him.' 'It is, my Lord (replied my father) because your son is a Whig, and no private resentments shall ever induce me to act against my principles.'

Meanwhile Polhill, after sitting for Bramber, had been brought in by the Administration for Rochester, presumably through the influence of his brother-in-law, the Duke of Newcastle. He also obtained a post in the Tower worth £500 a year to himself, and a commissionership of excise, worth £800 a year, for his brother. With one brief interruption in 1741, when he lost his seat to the popular hero, Admiral Vernon (q.v.), he continued to sit for Rochester, voting with the Government, till his death 15 Jan. 1754, in his eightieth year.[1]

[1] Based on a note by Polhill's son, Charles, 10 Nov. 1770, Polhill mss, Sevenoaks pub. lib. Kent.

R.R.S.

POLLEN, John (?1702–75), of Andover, Hants.

ANDOVER 1734–1754

b. ?1702, 3rd s. of John Pollen, M.P., of Andover, but 1st by 3rd w. Mary, da. of Edward Sherwood of East Hendred, Berks. *educ.* C.C.C. Oxf. 17 Oct. 1719, aged 17; L. Inn 1718, called 1726, bencher 1746. *m.*

8 July 1731, Hester, da. of Ellis St. John (formerly Mews) of Farley and Dogmersfield Park, Hants, sis. of Paulet St. John (q.v.), 2s. 4da.

2nd justice Carm. circuit 1742–53, c.j. 1753–*d.*

A member of a prominent local family, Pollen, a practising lawyer, was returned as a Whig for Andover on his own interest in 1734. He voted with the Administration in every recorded division, except on the place bill of 1740, from which he was absent. Made a Welsh judge in 1742, in 1749 he applied to Hardwicke for the chief justiceship of his circuit, should it fall vacant, writing:

> I have been now near seven years in the circuit have done far the greatest part of the business alone and hope I have not demeaned myself so as to deserve any complaint against me. I flatter myself likewise that through the course of sixteen years attendance in Parliament my conduct has been such as not to be made an objection against me.[1]

In 1753 he obtained this office, which he held until his death, 24 July 1775.

[1] Add. 35590, f. 263.

P.W.

POLLINGTON, Baron, *see* SAVILE, John

POLLOCK, Sir Robert, 1st Bt. (c.1665–1735), of Pollock, Renfrew.

SCOTLAND 1707–1708
RENFREWSHIRE 1710–1722

b. c.1665, 1st s. of Robert Pollock of Pollock by his 2nd w. Jean, da. of Cornelius Crawford of Jordanhill, Renfrew. *educ.* Glasgow 1679. *m.* (1) contr. 25 and 30 Jan. 1686, Annabella (*d.* bef. 15 May 1691), da. of Sir George Maxwell of Nether Pollock, Renfrew, wid. of John Cathcart of Carleton, Ayr, *s.p.*; (2) Annabella, da. of Walter Stewart of Pardovan, 4s. 3da. *suc.* fa. 1673; *cr.* Bt. 30 Nov. 1703.

M.P. [S] Renfrewshire 1700–7.
Lt. indep. tp. Scotch horse 1689; capt. 7 Drags. bef. June 1691; maj. Lord Murray's Ft. 1694; half pay 1698; maj. Earl of Hyndford's Drags. 1703; lt.-col. Drags. 1706; lt.-col. Lord Carmichael's Drags. 1710; col. of Drags. 1712; half-pay 1713; gov. Fort William 1715–25.

Pollock, who was created a baronet for his services and suffering at the Revolution,[1] was returned for the third time for his county as a Whig in 1715. Appointed governor of Fort William, he commanded the garrison there throughout the rebellion, sending back much information to Montrose, though 'mortified' at so many 'ungrate and unnatural' rebels 'passing under his nose'.[2] After the rebellion he was said by a Jacobite agent to have supported a petition to allow wives and widows of English Jacobites to retain their jointures out of the estates forfeited by their husbands but to have opposed a similar petition on behalf of their counter-

parts in Scotland, to the surprise of English Members.[3] Voting consistently with the Government, which 'probably lost him some of those who formerly were his friends',[4] he was defeated in 1722, soon afterwards resigning his military governorship in return for a pension of £300 p.a.[5] He did not stand again, dying 22 Aug. 1735.

[1] Crawfurd, *Shire of Renfrew*, 291–2. [2] *HMC 3rd Rep.* 380. [3] *HMC Stuart*, vi. 106. [4] *Caldwell Pprs.* (Maitland Club lxxi), i. 238. [5] Chas. Cathcart to Walpole, 12 Sept. 1724, Cholmondeley (Houghton) mss.

J.M.S.

POLWARTH, Lord, *see* HUME CAMPBELL, Hugh

PONSONBY, William, Visct. Duncannon (c.1704–93)

DERBY 8 Mar. 1742–1754
SALTASH 1754–Nov. 1756
HARWICH 13 Dec. 1756–4 July 1758

b. c.1704, 1st surv. s. of Brabazon, 1st Earl of Bessborough [I], and 1st Baron Ponsonby, by his 1st w. Sarah, da. of James Margetson of Sysonby, Leics., wid. of Hugh Colvill of Newtown, co. Down. *educ.* Grand Tour. *m.* 5 July 1739, Lady Caroline Cavendish, da. of William Cavendish (q.v.), 3rd Duke of Devonshire, 5s. 4da. *suc.* fa. 4 July 1758.

M.P. [I] 1725–58.
P.C. [I] 19 Nov. 1741; sec. to ld. lt. [I] 1741–4; ld. of Admiralty 1746–56, of Treasury 1756–9; jt. postmaster gen. 1759–1762, 1765–6; P.C. 12 July 1765.

Duncannon was returned for Derby in 1742 on the interest of his father-in-law, the Duke of Devonshire, who secured a seat on the Admiralty board for him in 1746 and an English barony for his father in 1749.[1] He died 11 Mar. 1793.

[1] Walpole, *Mems. Geo. II*, i. 196.

R.R.S.

POOLE, Sir Francis, 2nd Bt. (c.1682–1763), of Poole, Cheshire, and The Friars, Lewes, Suss.

LEWES 6 Dec. 1743–15 Feb. 1763

b. c.1682, 3rd but 1st surv. s. of Sir James Poole, 1st Bt., by Anne, da. of Thomas Eyre of Hassop, Derbys. *m.* 13 Mar. 1723, Frances, da. of Henry Pelham (q.v.) of Stanmer, 2s. 1da. *suc.* fa. bet. 1725 and 1736.

Dep. paymaster Minorca to 1747.

Poole came of an ancient Roman Catholic family. His father, who was arrested for high treason in 1690 but released on bail a few months later, is shown on a register of Roman Catholic non-jurors compiled under an Act of 1715 as being at that date 'beyond the seas'.[1] Under the same Act Poole registered himself as a Roman Catholic non-juror, but he must have conformed before 1723, when he was married by the bishop of Chichester at St. Giles-in-the-Fields to Frances Pelham, first cousin to the Duke of Newcastle. Some years after his marriage he left Poole Hall in Cheshire to establish himself at Lewes, for which he was brought into Parliament by Newcastle in 1743. 'A good-humoured, downright, hearty John Bull',[2] he was a faithful follower of the Pelhams, to whom he owed much of his income. His estate brought in only about £800 p.a.,[3] but when he came to live in Lewes, Pelham, then paymaster general of the forces, made him deputy paymaster of the forces in Minorca (£550 p.a.), which was supplemented on his return to Parliament by a secret service pension of £200 p.a., subsequently increased to £300.[4] His office was transferred to his eldest son, Henry, in 1747, when under the Place Act of 1742 it became incompatible with a seat in the House. He died 15 Feb. 1763 at the age of 81.[5]

[1] CSP Dom. 1689-90, pp. 521, 527; E. E. Estcourt & J. O. Payne, *English Catholic Non-jurors in 1715*, p. 22. [2] Horsfield, *Sussex*, i. 211. [3] Thos. Pelham to Hen. Pelham, 25 Dec. 1722, Add. 33084, ff. 201 et seq. [4] Hen. Poole to Newcastle, 3 May 1759, Add. 32890, f. 460. [5] *Suss. Arch. Colls.* xxxiv. 166.

R.R.S.

POORE, Edward (?1704–80), of the Close, Salisbury, Wilts.

SALISBURY 1747–1754
DOWNTON 13 Dec. 1756–1761

b. ?1704, 1st s. of Edward Poore of Andover, Hants. *educ.* Magdalen Hall, Oxf. 4 Dec. 1721, aged 17; L. Inn 1723, called 1729, bencher 1751. *m.* 22 Nov. 1731, Rachel, da. of George Mullins, M.D., of the Close, Salisbury, 2s. *d.v.p.* 4da.

Dep. recorder, Salisbury 1743–55; 2nd justice, Carmarthen circuit 1753–*d.*

Edward Poore's father was the eldest brother of Abraham Poore of Enford and Combe, Wilts., grandfather of Sir John Methuen Poore, 1st Bt. A local lawyer, he was returned as a government supporter for Salisbury in 1747. On 27 Oct. 1750 Lord Feversham (Anthony Duncombe, q.v.) forwarded to Pelham an application from Poore for post office patronage in Salisbury, observing that Poore could not 'support himself without your favour properly bestowed in particular cases'.[1] He died 19 May 1780.

[1] Newcastle (Clumber) mss.

R.S.L.

POPHAM, Edward (?1711–72), of Littlecote, Wilts.

GREAT BEDWYN 5 Apr. 1738–1741
WILTSHIRE 1741–14 July 1772

b. ?1711, 2nd but 1st surv. s. of Francis Popham, M.P., of Littlecote by his cos. Anne, da. of Alexander

Popham of Bourton on the Hill, Glos. by Brilliana, sis. of Robert Harley, M.P., 1st Earl of Oxford and Earl Mortimer.[1] *educ.* Ch. Ch. Oxf. 28 Mar. 1729, aged 17. *m.* Rebecca Huddon, 2s. 1da. *suc.* fa. 1735.

The Pophams regularly represented Somerset and Wiltshire constituencies after acquiring Littlecote from the Darells in the sixteenth century. Having succeeded to the family estate, said to be worth £6,000 p.a.,[2] Edward Popham was returned at a contested by-election for Great Bedwyn in 1738, standing as a Tory on the Bruce interest. He was afterwards returned five times for the county unopposed, voting consistently against the Administration. The 2nd Lord Egmont wrote of him in his electoral survey, c.1749–50: 'I believe will be thoroughly with us, has a very large property but excessively encumbered as I have heard'. He died 14 July 1772.

[1] *HMC Portland*, v. 521. [2] *Gent. Mag.* 1735, p. 559.

R.S.L.

PORTER, Aubrey (c.1660–1717), of Bury St. Edmunds, Suff.

BURY ST. EDMUNDS 1 Dec. 1705–25 Apr. 1717

b. c.1660, 3rd s. of George Porter by Lady Diana Goring, da. of George Goring, M.P., 1st Earl of Norwich, wid. of Thomas Covert, of Slaugham, Suss. *m.* Kezia, da. of Sir Thomas Hervey, M.P., of Ickworth Suff., sis. of John Hervey, M.P., 1st Earl of Bristol, 1s.

Page of honour 1671; capt. Lord Windsor's regt. of Horse 1703, lt.-col. 1708, half pay 1713.

The grandson of Endymion Porter, M.P., one of Charles I's courtiers, and the son of a royalist officer, who made his peace with Parliament, Aubrey Porter owed his seat to his brother-in-law, Lord Bristol. Re-elected unopposed as a Whig in 1715, he voted for the septennial bill in 1716, dying 25 Apr. 1717.

R.R.S.

PORTMAN, Henry (*d.* 1728), of Bryanston, Dorset, and Orchard Portman, Som.

ST. MAWES 1679–1690
TOTNES 1690–1695
ST. MAWES 21 Nov. 1696–1698
TAUNTON 1698–1700
WELLS 1701–1708
SOMERSET 1708–1710
TAUNTON 1710–30 Aug. 1715

5th s. of Sir Edward Seymour, 3rd Bt., M.P., of Berry Pomeroy, Devon by Anne, da. of Sir John Portman, 1st Bt., of Orchard, Som. *m.* (1) Penelope, da. of Sir William Haslewood of Maidwell, Northants., *s.p.*; (2) Meliora, da. of William Fitch of High Hall, Dorset, *s.p.* *suc.* to estates of cos. Sir William

Portman, 6th Bt., 1690, and assumed name of Portman.

Ranger of Hyde Park 1703–d.

Portman was returned as a Tory from 1679 to 1715, when he was unseated on petition. He died 23 Feb. 1728 at an advanced age.[1]

[1] Pol. State, xxxv. 212.

S.R.M.

PORTMAN, Henry William (c.1709–61), of Bryanston, Dorset, and Orchard Portman, Som.

TAUNTON 1734–1741
SOMERSET 1741–1747

b. c.1709, 1st s. of William Portman (formerly Berkeley, of Pylle, Som., bro. and h. of Maurice Berkeley, q.v.) by Anne, da. of Sir Edward Seymour, 4th Bt., of Berry Pomeroy, Devon, niece of Henry Portman (q.v.). m. c.1737, Anne, da. of William Fitch of High Hall, Dorset, 1s. suc. fa. 1737.

On the death of Henry Portman (q.v., formerly Seymour), the Portman estates, said to be worth over £8,000 a year,[1] devolved upon his nephew William Berkeley of Pylle, who assumed the name and arms of Portman by Act of Parliament. His son, who was returned as a Tory for Taunton on a compromise in 1734 and for Somerset in 1741, voted consistently against the Government, retiring in 1747 on grounds of ill health.[2] Before the 1745 rebellion his name was sent to the French as one of the most considerable of the Pretender's supporters in England, from the size of his estates and the large number of his tenants employed in the woollen manufacture.[3] The second Lord Egmont in his electoral survey, c.1749–50, described him as 'a very odd man, has the best Tory interest'. He died 19 Jan. 1761, aged 52.

[1] AEM & D. Angl. 82, ff. 4–23. [2] Portman to Hardwicke, 20 Nov. 1749, Add. 35603, f. 188. [3] Stuart mss 248/111.

S.R.M.

POTENGER, Richard (?1690–1739), of Reading and Compton, Berks.

READING 1727–26 Nov. 1739

b. ?1690, 1st s. of Nicholas Potenger of Pangbourne, Berks. and the Inner Temple. educ. I. Temple 1704, called 1711; Trinity, Oxf. 20 Oct. 1705, aged 15. m. Apr. 1714, Anne Mason, 1s.

Recorder, Reading 1720–d.; 2nd justice, Chester 1735–d.

The Potenger family, originally of Burghfield, near Reading, acquired in the seventeenth century the manor of Maidenhatch, in Pangbourne, and lands in Compton, to which Richard Potenger, a lawyer, eventually succeeded.[1] As recorder of the borough, he was successful at Reading in 1727 and 1734 against a Tory. Re-elected without a contest in 1735

on appointment as a Welsh judge, he voted with the Administration on the Hessians in 1730 and the army in 1732, but against the excise bill in 1733. He died 26 Nov. 1739.

[1] VCH Berks. iii. 305; iv. 18.

R.S.L.

POTTER, Thomas (?1718–59), of Ridgmont, Beds.

ST. GERMANS 1747–1754
AYLESBURY 1754–July 1757
OAKHAMPTON 13 July 1757–17 June 1759

b. ?1718, 2nd s. of Rt. Rev. John Potter, bp. of Oxford (abp. of Canterbury 1737–47), by a da. of one Venner. educ. Ch. Ch. Oxf. 18 Nov. 1731, aged 13; M. Temple 1736, called 1740. m. (1) 17 Feb. 1740, Anne (d. 4 Jan. 1744), da. of Rev. Thomas Manningham, rector of Slinfold, Suss., 1s.; (2) 14 July 1747, Ann, da. of Francis Lowe of Brightwell, Oxon., 2da. suc. fa. 1747.

Principal registrar of the province of Canterbury; sec. to Princess of Wales 1748–51; jt. paymaster gen. 1756–7; jt. vice-treasurer [I] 1757–d.

A handsome, clever youth, Thomas Potter, while still under his father's roof at Lambeth Palace, started on a life of dissipation. His letters to Charles Lyttelton (later dean of Exeter and bishop of Carlisle) cannot all 'be printed as they stand'; but what can suffices. On 19 Feb. 1740:

Oh, my dear Charles, . . . I am no more what I was, no more the careless, the cheerful, the happy man thou knowest, but unhappy, miserable beyond remedy. In short I am—married, and married to a woman I despise and detest. My story you shall know in a few words. In Westminster Abbey cloisters you remember Miss Manningham . . . The friends when the matter came to a crisis refused to do anything except I would marry her.

Potter denied having made any promises; they appealed to his father who 'absolutely laid his commands' on him: he would never do anything for Thomas till he married her.

What could I do? . . . On Sunday the ceremony was read over me . . . I never can nor will live with her . . . Dear Charles, do not hear me abused. Tell me what the world says and thinks of me, and tell me truly. I think they cannot blame me for any thing but marrying.

But he was again prepared to obey and live with his wife if his rich father made a settlement on him. He wrote a letter to his brother-in-law, to be shown to the Archbishop, 'seemingly without my knowledge':

. . . many of the world condemn me as having carried my obedience further than duty required. But I am far from being concerned at having incurred any censure of that sort. It was not a self-interest and a servile obedience that I ever paid to my father's commands; it proceeded from principle, and if I may use such an expression, from affection.

And to Lyttelton, on 10 June 1740:

. . . if I found he [the Archbishop] would not enable me to live in the condition I might reasonably expect, I would rather have chose to bear the censure of the world for not living with my wife, than have let such a proof of the only failing his Grace has in his character be known.

When she died in January 1744, he felt 'deprived of what was most dear to him in the world', and hardly knew how to lament her as she deserved.[1]

The Archbishop died in October 1747, leaving to Potter his fortune of nearly £100,000, his eldest son having incurred his displeasure 'by marrying below his dignity'.[2]

Meanwhile Potter had joined the Prince of Wales's party. In a list compiled in June 1747 by Ayscough, the Prince's election manager and Charles Lyttelton's brother-in-law, 'of persons to be brought into Parliament by his Royal Highness, who are not able to bring in themselves', Potter appears among those 'not fixed' as yet.[3] 'Pray send me the names of the gentlemen His Royal Highness honours with his recommendation to me',[4] wrote Richard Eliot to Ayscough on 15 June; and on 2 July Potter was returned for St. Germans. He also stood for Callington but came out bottom of the poll. The House met on 10 Nov., and on the 20th Potter delivered his maiden speech.

> The Prince [Horace Walpole wrote to Mann on 24 Nov.] has got some new and very able speakers; particularly a young Mr. Potter . . . who promises very greatly; the world is already matching him against Mr. Pitt.

In another account Walpole describes him as 'a young man of the greatest good nature, though he had set out with two of the severest speeches that ever were made against the ministry and the Grenvilles'. His violence against the ministry was attributed to his father's 'not being able to get him to be a teller of the Exchequer.'[5] At the end of 1748 he was appointed secretary to the Princess of Wales. In 1749 Horace Walpole refers to him as making 'some figure in the rising opposition' headed by the Prince, though owing to a bad constitution he was seldom able to be in town. At a meeting between the Prince's party and the Tories that year

> Potter with great humour, and to the great amazement of the Jacobites, said he was very glad to see this union, and from thence hoped that if another attack like the last rebellion should be made on the royal family, they would all stand by them. No reply was made to this.[6]

In 1751 he spoke against the Government on the Address, 17 Jan., the navy estimates, 22 Jan., and the army, 11 Feb. In the ways and means committee, 20 Mar., 'he opened in an able manner' a 'scheme for an additional duty of two shillings on spirits', in support of which he had

produced several physicians and masters of work-houses to prove the fatal consequences of spirituous liquors which laid waste the meaner parts of the town and were now spreading into the country.

Pelham however opposed the proposal on the ground that 'imposing new duties would greatly diminish the revenue'. Resigning his appointment after the Prince's death, he spoke for the Government on the subsidy treaty with Saxony, 22 Jan. 1752.[7] On 30 Mar. 1753 he introduced a bill for a national census, which passed the Commons but was rejected by the Lords. In the same year, 26 Nov., he opposed the repeal of the Jewish Naturalization Act in a speech declaring himself unconnected with parties. Subsequently attaching himself to Pitt, he died 17 June 1759.

[1] M. Wyndham, *Chrons. of 18th Cent.* i. 99, 101–4, 107. [2] Nichols, *Lit. Anecs.* i. 177–8. [3] *HMC Fortescue*, i. 108. [4] Eliot mss at Port Eliot. [5] *Mems. Geo. II*, i. 70 n.; Harrowby mss 21 (L.Inn), 20 Dec. 1747. [6] To Mann, 4 Mar. and 3 May 1749. [7] *Mems. Geo. II*, i. 8, 12, 31, 66, 69–70, 92, 243.

L.B.N.

POULETT, Hon. Peregrine (1708–52), of Hinton St. George, Som.

| BOSSINEY | 24 May 1737–1741 |
| BRIDGWATER | 1747–28 Aug. 1752 |

b. 10 Dec. 1708, 2nd s. of John Poulett, M.P., 1st Earl Poulett, by Bridget, da. and coh. of Hon. Peregrine Bertie of Waldershare, Kent; twin bro. of John, 2nd Earl Poulett, and bro. of Hon. Vere Poulett (q.v.). *unm.*

Peregrine Poulett was the son of the 1st Earl Poulett, 'a man of grest estate', who had been lord steward in Anne's last Tory Government but had gone over to the Court in 1733 on his eldest son's being made a lord of the bedchamber and raised to the Lords. Returned after a contest for Bossiney in 1737, he voted with the Government on the Spanish convention in 1739 and the place bill in 1740. He did not stand again till 1747, when he was brought in for Bridgwater as a government supporter by his elder brother, Lord Poulett, in place of his younger brother, Vere, who had gone over to the Opposition. He died 28 Aug. 1752.[1]

[1] Hervey, *Mems.* 242.

S.R.M.

POULETT, Hon. Vere (1710–88), of Hinton St. George, Som.

| BRIDGWATER | 1741–1747 |

b. 18 May 1710, 3rd s. of John Poulett, M.P., 1st Earl Poulett; bro. of Hon. Peregrine Poulett (q.v.). *educ.* Ch. Ch. Oxf. 1729; L. Inn 1733. *m.* 4 Mar. 1755, Mary, da. and coh. of Richard Butt of Overton, Arlingham, Glos., 2s. *suc.* bro. as 3rd Earl 5 Nov. 1764.

Recorder, Bridgwater 1764; ld. lt. Devon 1771–*d.*

Vere Poulett was put up in 1741 at Bridgwater against Bubb Dodington with the strong support of Walpole, who wrote personally on his behalf to Sir William Pynsent (q.v.), asking him to give his interest to Poulett against Dodington.[1] In spite of this Poulett concluded an election pact with Dodington, with whom he was returned.[2] He supported the Administration till the beginning of 1744, when he spoke and voted against the Hanoverians. On 23 Jan. 1745 he showed that he had broken completely with the ministry by proposing that money should be voted to maintain the army in Flanders for two months only and that in default of a satisfactory undertaking from the Dutch to enter the war as principals the land war should be abandoned. He again spoke and voted against the Hanoverians in April 1746.[3] Having quarrelled with his eldest brother, Lord Poulett, he was replaced at Bridgwater in 1747 by his other brother, Peregrine, on whose death in 1752 Henry Pelham refused to hear of Vere's reinstatement at Bridgwater, observing to Dodington that

> Mr. Vere had left them unhandsomely and had treated him ill personally, wherever he could be heard. He was indeed for the union of the family, but he would have nothing to do with Mr. Vere, from his personal behaviour, though he could very well live and treat with those who opposed and even personally opposed him; which, considering those he had about him, was, I thought, saying in effect, that he would take a blow from a strong man, but not from a weak one.[4]

He did not stand again, dying 14 Apr. 1788.

[1] 24 Mar. 1741, Hoare mss. [2] See BRIDGWATER. [3] Owen, *Pelhams*, 208–9, 252, 306 n. 3. [4] *Dodington Diary*, 157.

S.R.M.

POWELL, Sir Christopher, 4th Bt. (?1690–1742), of Wierton House, in Boughton Monchelsea, Kent.

KENT   19 Feb. 1735–1741

b. ?1690, 2nd s. of Barnham Powell by Elizabeth, da. of James Clitherow of Boston, Mdx.; gd.-s. of Sir Nathaniel Powell, 2nd Bt., of Wierton. *educ.* Queen's, Oxf. 15 July 1709, aged 19. *m.* 1728, Frances Newington, *s.p. suc.* bro. as 4th Bt. 1708.

Returned unopposed as a Whig in succession to Lord Vane (q.v.), Powell voted with the Opposition. He did not stand in 1741, dying 5 July 1742.

A.N.N.

POWELL, Mansel (c.1696–1775), of Eardisley Park, Herefs.

WEOBLEY   1 July–9 Dec. 1747

b. c.1696, 1st s. of Rev. Roger Powell, rector of Moreton-on-Lugg, Herefs. by his w. Eleanor.[1] *m.* Jan. 1734, Martha, da. of Henry Hoare (q.v.) of Stourhead, Wilts., *s.p. suc.* fa. 1728.

     Sheriff, Herefs. 1733–4.

In 1738 Mansel Powell, a Hereford attorney, and others, acquired the property of a wealthy client, William Barnsley of Eardisley Park, by a forged will disinheriting Barnsley's only son, a lunatic. He enjoyed the estates until 1749 when the will was proved a forgery and a decree of restitution to young Barnsley was made in Chancery by Lord Hardwicke, under which Powell and his co-defendants had to pay costs and refund all the rents and other money they had received from the estate.[2] In the meantime, Powell had bought a controlling interest with Barnsley's money at Weobley,[3] where he was returned in 1747. Unseated on petition, he sold his interest to Lord Weymouth and did not stand again. He died 5 June 1775, aged 79.[4]

[1] M. I. at Moreton-on-Lugg. [2] *Gent. Mag.* 1750, pp. 364–70; Add. 36182, ff. 32 et seq. [3] See WEOBLEY. [4] M.I.

J.B.L.

POWELL, Thomas (c.1701–52), of Nanteos, Card.

CARDIGAN BOROUGHS	1 Apr. 1725–1727
CARDIGANSHIRE	22 Mar. 1742–1747

b. c.1701, 1st s. of William Powell by Averina, da. of Cornelius Le Brun of Cologne by Anne, da. and coh. of Col. John Jones of Nanteos. *educ.* M. Temple 1718. *m.* Mary, da. of Thomas Frederick of Westminster, sis. of Sir John Frederick, 1st Bt., *s.p. suc.* fa. 1738.[1]

Powell, whose father was one of the leaders of the Welsh Jacobites (see Pryse, Lewis), acquired Nanteos through his mother. Returned in 1725 as a Tory for Cardigan Boroughs, where he controlled Tregaron, he stood unsuccessfully for the county in 1727. He stood again for the Boroughs at a by-election in May 1729, when on a double return the seat was awarded to his opponent. The House of Commons also disfranchised the freemen of Tregaron, thus destroying his interest there. In 1732 the 1st Lord Egmont reports that at Drury Lane, during the performance of a dull play, Powell appeased a 'great tumult' in the audience and persuaded the manager to give them their money back.[2] In 1741 he contested the county, for which he was seated on petition after the fall of Walpole, voting regularly against the Government till he retired in 1747. He died 'of an apoplectic fit in the street', 17 Nov. 1752.[3]

[1] Meyrick, *Card.* 889. [2] *HMC Egmont Diary*, i. 216. [3] *Gent. Mag.* 1752, p. 536.

E.C.

POWLETT, Charles, Mq. of Winchester (1685–1754).

LYMINGTON   7 Dec. 1705–1708
HAMPSHIRE   1708–1710
CARMARTHENSHIRE   1715–12 Apr. 1717

b. 3 Sept. 1685, 1st s. of Charles Powlett, M.P., 2nd Duke of Bolton, by his 2nd w. Frances, da. of William Ramsden of Byram, Yorks.; bro. of Lord Harry and half-bro. of Lord Nassau Powlett (qq.v.). *educ.* Enfield. *m.* (1) 21 July 1713, Lady Anne Vaughan (*d.* 20 Sept. 1751), da. and h. of John Vaughan, M.P., 3rd Earl of Carberry [I], *s.p.*; (2) 20 Oct. 1751, Mrs. Lavinia Beswick, said to be da. of a lt. in the navy, actress, known as Lavinia Fenton, by whom he had had 3 illegit. s., *s.p. legit. cr.* Lord Pawlet of Basing, 12 Apr. 1717. *suc.* fa. as 3rd Duke 21 Jan. 1722; K.G. 10 Oct. 1722.

Gent. of the bedchamber to Prince of Wales 1714–17; gov. Milford Haven and v.-adm. of S. Wales 1715–33; ld. lt. Carm. 1715–33, Glam. 1715–33, Hants 1722–33, 1742–*d.*, Dorset 1722–33; col. R. Horse Gds. 1717–33; warden of the New Forest 1722–33, 1742–*d.*; P.C. 1 June 1725; gov. I.o.W. 1726–33, 1742–6; capt. of gent. pensioners 1740–2; lt.-gen. 1745; high steward, Winchester.

Powlett was returned in 1715 as a Whig for Carmarthenshire, where he had acquired an interest through his first wife. When the Whig party split in 1717 he adhered to the Government, resigning his place with the Prince's household in return for a peerage and the colonelcy of the Royal Horse Guards. The death of his father, the second Duke of Bolton, made him one of the principal landowners in Hampshire, controlling one seat at Winchester, one at St. Ives, and, in alliance with a local family, the Burrards, two at Lymington. From 1722–33 and 1740–6 he was the electoral manager for the Government in Hampshire, described as 'that noble person with whom his Majesty has thought proper to entrust the care of the country'.[1]

In 1733 Bolton was dismissed from all his offices for voting against the excise bill.

> The Duke of Bolton [Hervey writes] was at this time governor of the Isle of Wight, ranger of the New Forest, and had a regiment, yet with all this the Duke of Bolton was not satisfied. For, being as proud as if he had been of any consequence besides what his employments made him, as vain as if he had some merit, and as necessitous as if he had no estate, so he was troublesome at court, hated in the country, and scandalous in his regiment. The dirty tricks he played in the last to cheat the government of men, or his men of half-a-crown, were things unknown to any colonel but his Grace, no griping Scotchman excepted. As to his interest in Parliament by the Members he nominally made there, these were all virtually made by the Court, as they were only made by him in consequence of the powerful employments he held from the Court.

In 1740 he made his peace with Walpole, who gave him a seat in the Cabinet, though 'without a right to it from his office of captain of the band of pensioners'.[2] At the same time he was given a pension of £1,200, increased to £2,000 in 1742, as compensation for his failure to secure the post of master of the Ordnance.[3] In 1746 he was again dismissed from his offices, except his lord lieutenancy, for adhering to Granville.[4]

During 1746 Bolton failed in an attempt to extend his electoral influence by ousting the Burrard interest from the Lymington corporation. In 1750, he unsuccessfully applied to Newcastle for the office of master of the horse.[5] On the death of his first wife in 1751 he married Lavinia Fenton, with whom he had lived since he fell in love with her on seeing her as Polly Peachum in the 'Beggar's Opera' in 1728. His devotion to her is commemorated in the family pew at Wensley in Yorkshire, an exact replica of the box from which he first saw her.[6] He died 26 Aug. 1754.

[1] Lady Sundon, *Mems.* i. 218. [2] Hervey, *Mems.* 175–6, 925. [3] *HMC Egmont Diary*, iii. 140; *Cal. Treas. Bks. and Pprs. 1739–41*, p. 567; *1742–5*, p. 136. [4] R. Lodge, *Private Corresp. Chesterfield and Newcastle*, 111. [5] Bolton to A. Stone, 19 June 1747, Add. 32711, f. 413; to Newcastle, 2 Sept. 1750, Add. 32722, f. 287. [6] Ex inf. Lord Bolton.

P.W.

POWLETT, Charles (c.1718–65).

LYMINGTON   31 Dec. 1741–Dec. 1754
            25 Dec. 1754–9 Oct. 1759

b. c.1718, 1st surv. s. of Lord Harry Powlett and bro. of Harry Powlett (qq.v.). *educ.* Winchester 1728–9; Corpus Christi, Camb. 1735. *unm.*, 1 da. K.B. 27 Aug. 1753; *styled* Mq. of Winchester 1754–59; *suc.* fa. as 5th Duke of Bolton 9 Oct. 1759.

Ensign 1 Ft. Gds. 1737; lt.-col. army 1745; lt. Tower of London 1754–60; ld. lt. Hants 1758–63; P.C. 22 Dec. 1758; bearer of Queen's orb at coronation 1761.

Mayor, Lymington 1743, 1744, 1745, 1762, 1764.

Charles Powlett was returned on his family's interest at Lymington in 1747 in succession to his uncle, Lord Nassau Powlett (q.v.). Like his father he supported the Administration, voting with the Government in all recorded divisions. He was re-elected for Lymington in 1747, although his uncle, the 3rd Duke of Bolton (Charles Powlett, q.v.), whose efforts to gain complete control of the borough he had opposed, attempted at the last minute to have him replaced by somebody who would have been as agreeable to the Government, and more convenient to himself.[1] At a date unknown he obtained from Henry Pelham a secret service pension of £500 a year which ceased on his appointment as lieutenant of the Tower.[2]

He shot himself on 5 July 1765.

[1] Bolton to A. Stone, 19 June 1747, Add. 32711, f. 413. [2] Namier, *Structure*, 217.

P.W.

POWLETT, Charles Armand (c.1694–1751), of Leadwell, Oxon.

NEWTOWN I.o.W.	25 Apr. 1729–1734
CHRISTCHURCH	3 Apr. 1740–14 Nov. 1751

b. c.1694, 2nd s. of Lord William Powlett by his 1st w. and bro. of William Powlett (qq.v.). *m.* 12 June 1738, Elizabeth, da. of Thomas Lewis of Stamford, Notts., wid. of Richard Dashwood of Leadwell, Oxon. K.B. 26 June 1749.

Ensign 1 Ft. 1710; capt. 27 Ft. 1715; maj. 29 Ft. 1717; a.-d.-c. to Charles, 2nd Duke of Bolton, when ld. lt. [I] 1717–18; lt.-col. 10 Drags. 1720; lt.-col. 1 tp. Horse Gren. Gds. 1733; dep. gov. I.o.W. 1733–*d.*; col. 9 Marines 1740–7; brig.-gen. 1745; maj.-gen. 1747; col. 13 Drags. 1751.

Mayor, Lymington 1731.

Defeated at Newtown in 1727, but returned for it on petition in 1729, Powlett consistently voted with the Government. He did not follow his cousin, Charles Powlett (q.v.), 3rd Duke of Bolton, into opposition in 1733, which accounts for his defeat at St. Ives in 1734. Returned for Christchurch at a by-election in 1740, he again voted with the Administration in all recorded divisions. On 18 Nov. 1748 he applied to Newcastle for the Bath as one who had 'ever stood steady to H.M., your family, and the present Administration; if the head of my family has took a different turn, that can never be laid to me'. A month later, 10 Dec., he wrote to Newcastle expressing the hope that

> the very great expense I have been at in the elections and my steady attachment to the present Administration will plead in my behalf and I dare say Mr. Pelham, for whom I have a sincere regard and esteem, will do me the justice to acknowledge, that I never voted against anything he espoused, though often strongly solicited to act a different part, which I ever scorned . . . It is the first favour I have begged of your Grace.[1]

After receiving the red ribbon in June 1749, he begged Newcastle to

> mention me to his Majesty, as being now not only without any regiment, but without half pay, having a small thing of £330 a year as deputy governor of the Isle of Wight. I have paid above four thousand pounds for my late commission besides great sums in elections, which has hurt my fortune . . . My attendance in Parliament and the zeal our family have ever showed, I hope will plead some merit. My late regiment was broke when I was abroad, where I spent £1,000 more than the allowance.[2]

In 1750 the 2nd Lord Egmont described him as 'a very zealous contributor of noise and disturbance when any of our friends speak'.

He died 14 Nov. 1751.

[1] Add. 32717, f. 323, 405. [2] 24 July 1749, Add. 32718, f. 343.

P.W.

POWLETT, Lord Harry (1691–1759), of Edington, Wilts.

ST. IVES	1715–1722
HAMPSHIRE	1722–26 Aug. 1754

b. 24 July 1691, 2nd s. of Charles Powlett, M.P., 2nd Duke of Bolton, by his 2nd w.; bro. of Charles Powlett, Mq. of Winchester, and half-bro. of Lord Nassau Powlett (qq.v.). *m.* Catherine, da. of Charles Parry of Oakfield, Berks., 2s. 2da. *suc.* bro. Charles Powlett as 4th Duke of Bolton 26 Aug. 1754.

A.-d.-c. to Lord Galway in Portugal 1710; capt. Col. Molesworth's Drags. 1715–18; gov. Kinsale 1719. Ld. of Admiralty 1733–42; lt. Tower of London 1742–54; ld. lt. Glam. 1754–5, Hants 1754–8; P.C. 9 Jan. 1755.

Mayor, Lymington 1713, 1725, 1741, 1757.

After serving in Portugal as aide-de-camp to Lord Galway, Powlett took part as a captain of dragoons in the siege of Preston in 1715. Returned that year on his family's interest at St. Ives, he voted with the Government in every recorded division throughout his parliamentary career. In 1722 he was returned for Lymington but chose to sit for the county, which he served without interruption until be became Duke. He was also returned for Yarmouth in 1734, writing to Newcastle, 9 May, 'we are so hard pushed at our elections here that we are obliged to adjourn the poll to the Isle of Wight'.[1] After his elder brother's dismissal he remained loyal to Walpole who gave him a seat on the Admiralty board. He lost this place on Walpole's fall but was compensated by being made lieutenant of the Tower of London. He spoke in favour of the Hanoverians in December 1742 and was listed an 'Old Whig' in 1746. He died 9 Oct. 1759.

[1] Add. 32689, f. 235.

P.W.

POWLETT, Harry (1720–94).

CHRISTCHURCH	26 Nov. 1751–1754
LYMINGTON	17 Jan. 1755–1761
WINCHESTER	1761–5 July 1765

b. 6 Nov. 1720, 2nd s. of Lord Harry Powlett and bro. of Charles Powlett (qq.v.). *educ.* Winchester 1728–9; acad. in Portsmouth dockyard 1733. *m.* (1) 7 May 1752, Mary Munn (*d.* 31 May 1764) of Eltham, Kent, 1da.; (2) 8 Apr. 1765, Katherine, da. of Robert Lowther, M.P., of Mauds Meaburn, Westmld., sis. of James Lowther, M.P., 1st Earl of Lonsdale, 2da. *suc.* bro. Charles Powlett as 6th Duke of Bolton 5 July 1765.

Lt. R.N. 1739, capt. 1740, r.-adm. 1756, v.-adm. 1759, adm. 1770.

P.C. 10 Dec. 1766; gov. I.o.W. 1766–70, 1782–91; v.-adm. Hants and Dorset 1767; ld. lt. Hants 1782–93.

Mayor, Lymington 1761, 1768, 1771, 1773.

Harry Powlett made the navy his career, earning his promotion more by virtue of his family connexions than by his own merit. Entered at the academy in Portsmouth dockyard by his father when lord of the Admiralty, he was promoted captain while his father was still in office. Serving at Cartagena in 1743, Toulon in 1744, and subsequently in the East Indies, he was a prosecution witness against Admirals Lestock in 1745 and Griffin in 1750. In retaliation Griffin accused Powlett of misappropriating stores, of gross breaches of discipline, of not engaging the enemy and of abject cowardice when engaged. When, after many delays, a court martial was held on 1 Sept. 1752, Griffin could produce no witnesses and Powlett, who had been returned on his family's interest at Christchurch on the death of Charles Armand Powlett (q.v.), was acquitted.[1] He died 25 Dec. 1794.

[1] Charnock, *Biog. Navalis*, v. 5–7.

P.W.

POWLETT, Lord Nassau (1698–1741).

HAMPSHIRE 22 June 1720–1727
LYMINGTON 1727–1734
5 May–24 Aug. 1741

b. 23 June 1698, 3rd s. of Charles Powlett, M.P., 2nd Duke of Bolton, but 1st by his 3rd w. Henrietta Crofts, nat. da. of James Scott, 1st Duke of Monmouth; half-bro. of Charles Powlett, Mq. of Winchester, and Lord Harry Powlett (qq.v.). *m.* Dec. 1731, Lady Isabella Tufton, da. and coh. of Thomas Tufton, M.P., 6th Earl of Thanet, who subsequently *m.* Sir Francis Blake Delaval (q.v.), 3s. 2da. K.B. 27 May 1725.
Cornet 12 Drags. 1715; capt. 6 Drag. Gds. 1718, R. Horse Gds. 1721; auditor gen. of revenue [I] 1723–*d.*; mayor, Lymington 1723, 1730.

Returned for Hampshire on the elevation to the peerage of John Wallop (q.v.), Powlett voted with the Administration till 1733, when he followed his brother, Charles Powlett (q.v.), 3rd Duke of Bolton, into opposition, voting against the excise bill. He did not stand in 1734, but regained his seat in 1741, dying that year, 24 Aug.

P.W.

POWLETT, Norton (?1680–1741), of Rotherfield Park, nr. Alton, and Amport, Hants.

PETERSFIELD 1705–1734

b. ?1680, o.s. of Francis Powlett, M.P., of Amport, Hants by Elizabeth, da. and h. of Sir Richard Norton, 2nd Bt., of Rotherfield Park, Hants. *educ.* C.C.C. Oxf. 26 May 1698, aged 17. *m.* 1699, Jane, da. of Sir Charles Morley of Droxford, Hants, 8s. 3da. *suc.* fa. 1696.

Norton Powlett was returned as a Whig for Petersfield on his own interest for nearly thirty years. From 1715 he voted with the Administration in every recorded division. Defeated at Petersfield in 1734, he stood there again in 1741, when the 3rd Duke of Bolton wrote to Sir Robert Walpole: 'I am convinced that Mr. Norton Powlett will insist upon standing at Petersfield after having been for many years at so great an expense and trouble to support the Whig interest in that town'.[1] Again unsuccessful, he died 6 June 1741.

[1] 14 Feb. 1741, Cholmondeley (Houghton) mss.

P.W.

POWLETT, Norton (?1705–59).

WINCHESTER 26 Jan. 1730–1734

b. ?1705, 1st s. of Norton Powlett (q.v.). *educ.* Exeter, Oxf. 17 Dec. 1722, aged 17. *m.* 20 Jan. 1756, Anne Chute, wid. *s.p. suc.* fa. 1741.
Sheriff, Southampton 1738.

Norton Powlett was returned for Winchester in January 1730 on the interest of Charles Powlett (q.v.), 3rd Duke of Bolton, after the death of the Duke's uncle, Lord William Powlett (q.v.). He voted against the Administration on the Hessians in 1730 but with them on the army in 1732. He did not follow the Duke into opposition in 1733, when he voted for the excise bill, abstaining from the division on the repeal of the Septennial Act in 1734. Not standing again, he died 14 Mar. 1759.

P.W.

POWLETT, Lord William (c.1667–1729), of St. James's, London.

WINCHESTER 1689–1710
LYMINGTON 1710–1715
WINCHESTER 1715–25 Sept. 1729

b. c.1667, 2nd s. of Charles Powlett, M.P., 1st Duke of Bolton, by his 2nd w. Mary, nat. da. of Emanuel Scrope, 1st Earl of Sunderland, wid. of Henry Carey, Lord Leppington. *m.* (1) in Holland, Louisa, da. of Mq. de Mompouillon, 2s. 2da.; (2) lic. 26 Oct. 1699, Anne, da. and coh. of Randolph Egerton of Betley, Staffs., 1da.
Mayor, Lymington 1701, 1702, 1703, 1724, 1728. Teller of the Exchequer 1715–*d.*

One of the spokesmen in the Commons for the Whig lords of the Junto under Queen Anne, Powlett obtained a lucrative sinecure at George I's succession. Returned in 1715 for Winchester on the interest of his brother, the 2nd Duke of Bolton, he voted with the Administration in every recorded division, introducing a motion for laying heavier penalties on the Earl of Oxford in 1717 and speaking for the peerage bill in 1719. In 1721 he spoke in favour of bringing in a bill to allow the Quakers to affirm. In 1725 he opposed the restitution of Bolingbroke's estates, introducing a motion to prevent him sitting in either House or holding any office under the Crown. In March 1728 a bill was passed to discharge him from liability for £4,191 which had been stolen from his office as one of the tellers of the Exchequer in 1724.[1] He died 25 Sept. 1729, aged 62.

[1] *CJ*, xviii. 61, 63, 70, 262; Add. 36136, ff. 213–18, 233.

P.W.

POWLETT, William (?1693–1757), of Chilbolton and Easton, Hants.

LYMINGTON   13 May 1729–1734
WINCHESTER   1741–1747
WHITCHURCH   1754–28 Feb. 1757

b. ?1693, 1st s. of Lord William Powlett by his 1st w. and bro. of Charles Armand Powlett (qq.v.). *educ.* Wadham, Oxf. 27 Oct. 1710, aged 17. *m.* 10 Feb. 1721, Lady Annabella Bennet, da. of Charles Bennet, 1st Earl of Tankerville, 1s. 1da. *suc.* fa. 1729.
    Mayor, Lymington 1718, 1721.

William Powlett was returned for Lymington on the interest of his cousin, Charles Powlett (q.v.), 3rd Duke of Bolton, at a contested by-election in 1729. In his first Parliament he supported the Government till 1734, when he followed the Duke into opposition by voting against them on the repeal of the Septennial Act. Defeated at Winchester in 1734, but returned for it after a contest in 1741, he voted against the Government till 1746, when he voted with them on the Hanoverians, being classed as 'doubtful'. Again defeated at Winchester in 1747 and at a by-election in 1751, he was returned unopposed for Whitchurch on the interest of his brother-in-law, Lord Portsmouth (John Wallop, q.v.), in 1754, dying 28 Feb. 1757.

P.W.

POWNEY, Peniston (?1699–1757), of Ives Place, Maidenhead, Berks.

BERKSHIRE   5 Dec. 1739–8 Mar. 1757

b. ?1699, 1st s. of John Powney, M.P., of Old Windsor, Berks. by Hannah, da. of John Whitfield of Ives Place, Maidenhead. *educ.* ?Eton c.1716; Queen's, Oxf. 5 July 1716, aged 17; M. Temple 1712. *m.* 16 Oct. 1742, Penelope, da. and h. of Benjamin Portlock of Bedford, 1s. and other issue. *suc.* fa. 1704.
    Verderer of Windsor forest 1736–*d.*

Powney was a large landowner in Berkshire, which he represented as a Tory without opposition for nearly twenty years, consistently voting against the Government. His only reported speech was against the Hanoverians, 18 Jan. 1744.[1] One of the prominent Tories who agreed to support the Prince of Wales's programme in 1747,[2] he was put down by the 2nd Lord Egmont for a seat on the Admiralty board on Frederick's accession. The connexion

proved expensive. In 1784 his son, Peniston Portlock Powney, M.P., told the younger Pitt:

> I estimate myself a loser of 20,000 pounds by my father's connection with the late Prince of Wales to whom he was a friend and great assistant. The honours and emoluments promised to my father sank as well as the money with him.

This represented 'a large loan undischarged by Frederick, Prince of Wales, who incurred this debt during his residence at Cliveden'.[3]
    He died 8 Mar. 1757.

[1] Yorke's parl. jnl. *Parl. Hist.* xiii. 463. [2] Add. 35870, ff. 129–30. [3] Chatham Pprs. PRO.

A.N.N.

POWYS, Richard (c.1707–43), of Hintlesham Hall, Suff.

ORFORD   1734–1741

b. c.1707, o.s. of Richard Powys of Hintlesham, principal clerk of the Treasury and half-bro. of Sir Littleton Powys, judge of King's bench, and of Sir Thomas Powys, M.P., of Lilford, attorney-gen. 1687–9, by Elizabeth, da. of John Singleton, citizen and dyer of London. *educ.* Westminster; Trinity, Camb. 1724. *m.* 30 May 1735, Lady Mary Brudenell, da. of George Brudenell, 3rd Earl of Cardigan, 2da. *suc.* fa. 1724.

Of an ancient Welsh family, Powys succeeded to the manor of Hintlesham, which his father had bought in 1720 from a victim of the South Sea bubble. Returned in 1734 for Orford as a Tory, standing jointly with Price Devereux (q.v.), he voted against the Government but did not stand again. A man of extravagant tastes, he converted Hintlesham from a Tudor into a Georgian mansion. He died 10 Sept. 1743, so badly off that he is said to have been buried by royal charity at Hampton Court. His widow sold Hintlesham to Sir Richard Lloyd (q.v.).[1]

[1] Copinger, *Suffolk Manors*, vi. 56.

R.R.S.

PRAED, *see* **MACKWORTH PRAED**

PRATT, John (c.1685–1770), of Wildernesse, nr. Sevenoaks, Kent.

SANDWICH   1741–1747

b. c.1685, 4th but 1st surv. s. of Sir John Pratt, M.P., c. j. of King's bench 1718–25, by his 1st w. Elizabeth, da. and coh. of Rev. Henry Gregory of Middleton Stoney, Oxon. *educ.* I. Temple 1700. *m.* (1) Elizabeth, da. of Sir Jeffrey Jeffreys of Brecknock Priory, Brec., 1s. 1da.; (2) 10 Apr. 1725, Dorothy, da. and h. of Robert Tracy of Coscombe Court, Glos., 1s. *suc.* fa. 1725.

Descended from an old Devonshire family, who had lost their estates in the Civil War, Pratt inherited

Wildernesse, bought by his father in 1705. Returned for Sandwich in 1741 on the interest of Sir George Oxenden (q.v.), who wrote that the neighbouring farmers had 'certainly carried the election for my partner, Mr. Pratt',[1] he voted consistently against the Administration. He did not stand again. After his death, 24 July 1770, his property eventually went to the family of his half-brother, Charles Pratt, Lord Camden.

[1] Namier, *Structure*, 101.

P.W.

PRENDERGAST, Sir Thomas, 2nd Bt. (c.1700–60), of Gort, co. Galway.

CHICHESTER   13 Mar. 1733–1734

b. c.1700, o.s. of Brig-Gen. Sir Thomas Prendergast, 1st Bt., by Penelope, da. of Henry Cadogan of Liscarton, co. Meath, sis. of William Cadogan (q.v.), 1st Earl Cadogan. *educ.* Clare, Camb. 1719; I. Temple 1721. *m.* 11 Jan. 1739, Anne, da. and h. of Sir Griffith Williams, 6th Bt., of Marle, Caern., *s.p. suc.* fa. 11 Sept. 1709.
M.P. [I] 1733–*d.*
P.C. [I] 17 Aug. 1733; postmaster gen. [I] 1754–*d.*

Dubbed by George II 'an Irish blockhead',[1] Prendergast took advantage of being first cousin of the Duchess of Richmond to bombard her husband, the 2nd Duke (Charles Lennox, Lord March, q.v.) with applications for a seat in Parliament or a lucrative Irish job.[2] Returned as a government supporter by Richmond for Chichester at a by-election in 1733, he had not been a week in the House before he voted against the Administration on the city of London's petition against the excise bill, because he had been 'disobliged' by a non-committal reply to his application to be appointed postmaster general of Ireland.[3] He never obtained another seat, though he contested Shoreham unsuccessfully in 1734 and Caernarvonshire, where he had acquired an estate through his wife, in 1747; but his importunity was at last rewarded in 1754 by the Irish postmastership. He died 23 Sept. 1760.

[1] Hervey, *Mems.* 162. [2] Lord March, *A Duke and his Friends*, i. 206–7, 323–6; Cadogan 5 Sept. 1728, Prendergast 15 Feb. 1733, Devonshire 24 Aug. 1741, Newcastle 5 July 1743, to Richmond, Richmond mss. [3] *HMC Egmont Diary*, i. 360.

R.R.S.

PRICE, Richard, of Broomfield, Essex.

SUDBURY   1734–1741

After the death of John Knight, M.P. for Sudbury, in October 1733, Price, described as 'a rich citizen', unsuccessfully asked Walpole to support his candidature for the vacancy, stating that one of the leading men in Sudbury 'was his factor, did all his

business for him, and had promised him to use all his interest for him in the next election'.[1] Defeated at the ensuing by-election, but returned at the general election after a contest, he voted against the Government on the Spanish convention in 1739 and the place bill in 1740. He did not stand again. Nothing more is known of him except that he leased a house at Broomfield, which he improved 'so as to be fit for a gentleman's house'.[2]

[1] *Letter Bks. of J. Hervey, 1st Earl of Bristol*, iii. 107. [2] Morant, *Essex*, ii. 78.

R.R.S.

PRICE, Uvedale (1685–1764), of Foxley, Herefs.

WEOBLEY   1713–1715, 1727–1734

b. 17 Sept. 1685, 1st surv. s. of Robert Price, M.P., baron of the Exchequer and judge of the common pleas, by Lucy da. and coh. of Robert Rodd of Foxley. *educ.* St. Paul's; St. John's, Camb. 1704; L. Inn 1706; Grand Tour (France, Italy) 1709–12. *m.* 1714, Anne, da. and coh. of Lord Arthur Somerset, 2nd s. of Henry Somerset, M.P., 1st Duke of Beaufort, 1s. 3da. *suc.* fa. 1733.
Steward of the courts, Denbigh to 1740.

The son of a successful lawyer, M.P. for Weobley in five Parliaments under James II and William III, Price was returned for Weobley as a Hanoverian Tory in 1713, but did not stand in the next reign. Re-elected unopposed in 1727, he voted with the Government in all recorded divisions, except on the Hessian troops in 1730, when he voted with the Opposition. He did not stand again, dying 17 Mar. 1764.

A.N.N.

PRIDEAUX, Sir Edmund, 4th Bt. (?1646–1720), of Netherton, Devon.

TREGONY   1713–6 Feb. 1720

b. ?1646, 1st s. of Sir Peter Prideaux, 3rd Bt., M.P., of Netherton by Elizabeth, da. of Sir Bevil Granville of Stowe, Cornw., sis. of John Granville, M.P., 1st Earl of Bath. *educ.* Oriel, Oxf. 18 Apr. 1663, aged 16; I. Temple, called 1680. *m.* (1) 23 Feb. 1673, Susanna (*d.* Oct. 1687), da. of James Winstanley of Branston, Leics., wid. of John Austin of Derhams, Mdx., 2s. 1da.; (2) c.1695, Elizabeth (*d.* 1 May 1702), da. and coh. of Hon. George Saunderson of South Thoresby, Lincs., 1s.; (3) 5 Sept. 1710, Mary, da. of Spencer Vincent, alderman of London, wid. of Sir John Rogers, 1st Bt., of Wiscombe, Devon, *s.p. suc.* fa. 22 Nov. 1705.

Of an ancient family, who had long represented Cornish and Devonshire boroughs, Prideaux was patron of the living of Tregony, whose incumbent exercised an important electoral influence in the borough.[1] Returned for Tregony in 1715 as a Tory who might often vote with the Whigs, he voted with the Administration, except on the peerage bill in 1719, when he was absent. He died 6 Feb. 1720.

[1] Lysons, *Magna Britannia* (1738), i. 361; J. Wolrige to Sir Robt. Walpole, 1 July 1727, Cholmondeley (Houghton) mss.

E.C.

PRINGLE, John (c.1674–1754), of Haining, Selkirk.

SCOTLAND 1707–1708
SELKIRKSHIRE 1708–1 July 1729

b. c.1674, 2nd s. of Andrew Pringle of Clifton, Roxburgh by Violet, da. of John Rutherford of Edgerston, Roxburgh. *educ.* ?Edinburgh Univ. 1688; adv. 1698; ?Utrecht. *m.* 22 Nov. 1713, Anne, da. of Sir James Murray, M.P. [S], of Philiphaugh, Selkirk, Lord Philiphaugh, S.C.J., ld. clerk register, sis. of John Murray of Philiphaugh (q.v.), 3s. 3da.

M.P. [S] Selkirkshire 1703–7.

Commr. of the equivalent 1707–13 Jan. 1715; one of the keepers of the signet [S] 1711–13; ld. of session, Lord Haining, 1729–*d.*

Pringle, whose father bought Haining for him in 1701, was re-elected in 1715 for Selkirkshire on the interest of his brother-in-law, John Murray, its hereditary sheriff. Absent from the division on the septennial bill in 1716, he voted with the Administration in all other recorded divisions, including that on Lord Cadogan, 4 June 1717.[1] He retained his seat for Selkirkshire until his elevation to the bench in 1729.

He died 19 Aug. 1754.

[1] *More Culloden Pprs.* ii. 173–4.

J.M.S.

PROBY, John (c.1698–1762), of Elton Hall, Hunts.

HUNTINGDONSHIRE 27 Oct. 1722–1727
STAMFORD 1734–1747

b. c.1698, 1st s. of William Proby of Elton and Ranes, Bucks., sometime of Fort St. George, India, by Henrietta, da. of Robert Cornewall of Berrington, Herefs. *educ.* Jesus, Camb. 1715. *m.* 5 Jan. 1720, Jane, da. of John Leveson Gower, M.P., 1st Baron Gower, sis. of John, 1st Earl Gower, 5s. 1da. *suc.* fa. 1739.

Proby was descended from Sir Peter Proby, M.P., of Ranes, lord mayor of London 1622–3 and bailiff of Elton, whose grandson, Sir Thomas Proby, 1st Bt., M.P., acquired the manor of Elton by marriage c.1664.[1] In nine Parliaments between 1679 and 1710 his family represented Huntingdonshire, for which he himself was returned on his own interest as a Tory at a by-election in 1722. He did not stand again till 1734, when he was brought in for Stamford, ten miles from Elton, by Lord Exeter at a stormy election, during which Proby and William Noel (q.v.), the other Tory candidate, were said to have 'led their riotous mobs in person'.[2] He was one of the Tories who withdrew on the motion for the removal of Walpole in February 1741 but acted with the Opposition till 1745, when he was induced by

his brother-in-law, Lord Gower, who had recently gone over to the Government, to support William Montagu (q.v.), the brother and candidate of Lord Sandwich, one of the heads of the Huntingdonshire Whigs, at a by-election for that county.[3] Next year, though once again voting with the Opposition on the Hanoverians, he was classed by the Administration as 'doubtful', i.e. as a possible supporter. At the general election of 1747 he stood down in favour of his son, John (q.v.), to whom he handed over Elton in 1749,[4] thereafter taking no further part in public life. He died 15 Mar. 1762.

[1] *VCH Hunts.* iii. 160. [2] See STAMFORD. [3] Sandwich to Bedford, 18 Sept. 1745, Bedford mss. [4] *VCH Hunts.* loc. cit.

R.S.L.

PROBY, John, jun. (1720–72), of Elton Hall, Hunts. and Glenart, co. Wicklow.

STAMFORD 1747–1754
HUNTINGDONSHIRE 1754–1768

b. 25 Nov. 1720, 1st s. of John Proby (q.v.). *educ.* Westminster 1736; Jesus, Camb. 1737; I. Temple 1740. *m.* 22 Aug. 1750, Elizabeth, da. of Joshua Allen, 2nd Visct. Allen [I], sis. and (1745) coh. of John, 3rd Visct. Allen [I], 1s. 1da. *suc.* to Elton 1749 and fa. 1762; *cr.* Baron Carysfort [I] 23 Jan. 1752; K.B. 23 Mar. 1761.

Ld. of Admiralty Apr.–July 1757, 1762–5; P.C. [I] 4 Aug. 1758.

Described by the 2nd Lord Egmont in his electoral survey as the 'creature' of Lord Gower, Proby succeeded his father at Stamford in 1747. Classed in the new Parliament as a government supporter, he seconded the Address at the opening of the session of 1751. When later that year he announced that he intended to stand for Huntingdonshire at the next general election, his cousin, Lord Trentham (q.v.), was asked by Lord Sandwich to use his influence to persuade him to stand jointly with Sandwich's brother, William Montagu (q.v.).[1] 'All my friends', Sandwich told Trentham,

are astonished that Mr. Proby should hesitate a moment about accepting so advantageous an offer but if I may say so, among friends, his vanity leads him to wish to come in upon an independent interest and not to be obliged to me or any one else for his election. This (remember what I say) is what he cannot effect, and if he should be misled so far as to throw us into confusion, nothing is clearer to me that he will be the victim of it.

In the event Proby, now Lord Carysfort, was returned for the county unopposed with Coulson Fellowes (q.v.), standing as joint candidates with Sandwich's support.

He died 18 Oct. 1772.

[1] Sandwich to Trentham and to the Duke of Bedford, 15 Dec. 1751, Bedford mss.

R.R.S.

PROCTOR, George (1704–51), of Clewer, Berks.

DOWNTON   28 Nov. 1746–5 Apr. 1751

bap. 7 Oct. 1704, 1st s. of Henry Proctor, a Welsh judge, of Clewer by Ann Doughty,[1] prob. da. of Rev. Thomas Doughty, D.D., rector of Clewer and canon of Windsor. *educ.* Eton (K.S. 1719); King's, Camb. 1723, fellow 1726–46; M. Temple 1726, called 1728. *unm. suc.* fa. 1745.

Steward of the honor and castle of Windsor and keeper of the seals of the courts of record there[2] 1733–*d.*

Proctor, a lawyer, whose family had long connexions with the Middle Temple, was brought into Downton as a government supporter by Anthony Duncombe (q.v.). He died 5 Apr. 1751.

[1] *Faculty Office Marriage Lics.* (Index Lib. xxii), 193; [2] *Cal. Treas. Bks. and Pprs.* 1731–4, p. 524.

R.S.L.

PROCTOR, see also BEAUCHAMP PROCTOR

PROWSE, Thomas (c.1707–67) of Compton Bishop, Som.

SOMERSET   26 Nov. 1740–1 Jan. 1767

b. c.1707, o.s. of John Prowse, M.P., of Compton Bishop by his 2nd w. Abigail, da. of Rt. Rev. George Hooper, bp. of Bath and Wells. *m.* 1 Mar. 1731, Elizabeth, da. of John Sharpe of Grafton Park, Northants., 3s. 5da. *suc.* fa. 1710.

Recorder, Wells 1745–52; recorder, Axbridge.

Prowse's grandfather, a Somerset country gentleman, married a coheiress of the ancient family of Newborough, who brought him the estate of Berkley. Under Anne his father was returned for the county, which Prowse himself represented unopposed in five Parliaments. A moderate Tory, he withdrew on the motion for the removal of Walpole in February 1741, and was one of the opposition members of the secret committee elected by the Commons in April 1742 to inquire into Walpole's Administration. During the invasion crisis of February 1744 he dissociated himself from a factious opposition motion against the immediate suspension of the Habeas Corpus Act, walking out in the middle of its proposer's speech. He voted against the Hanoverians in all the three recorded divisions on them, speaking second for the Opposition in that of April 1746; but on 5 Dec. he did not directly oppose the vote for 15,000 British troops in Flanders, merely suggesting that a decision might be deferred until it was known what contribution was to be expected from Britain's allies during the forthcoming campaign. Though no Jacobite, he was angry with the Government for allowing evidence to be given at Lovat's trial in 1747 inculpating Lord Barrymore, Hynde Cotton and Watkin Williams Wynn (qq.v.), asking the Speaker

if some notice ought not to be taken of it in the House. Mr. Onslow intimated that he believed the parties concerned would not choose it. Prowse replied 'That I cannot help; others know themselves best'.[1]

After the peace Prowse twice spoke in favour of reducing the army to 15,000 men, 7 Nov. 1749 and 27 Nov. 1751. Horace Walpole, 4 Mar. 1749, wrote to Mann that the Tories were 'now governed by one Prowse, a cold plausible fellow, and a great wellwisher to Mr. Pelham', to whom he compared him in affecting to be candid and in being 'a man of some sense without parts'. In the 2nd Lord Egmont's list of offices he is put down for surveyor general of woods in a future reign. His other reported speeches during this Parliament were on the regency bill of 1751, which he criticized for giving too much power to the council, 16, 17 May 1751; against subsidy treaties in peacetime, 29 Jan. 1752, and a bill for settling foreign Protestants on estates in Scotland forfeited in the late rebellion, 28 Feb. 1752; and for the repeal of the Jewish Naturalization Act, 27 Nov. 1753, and an inquiry by the House of Commons into the management of the lottery for establishing the British Museum, 4 Dec. 1753.[2] His subsequent career was prejudiced by ill health, which prevented him from accepting nomination for the Speakership in 1761. He died 1 Jan. 1767.

[1] Owen, *Pelhams*, 215, 306 n. 3; Mahon, iii. p. lxxviii. [2] Coxe, *Pelham*, ii. 94; Walpole, *Mems. Geo. II*, i. 124–5, 139–40, 213, 254, 257, 363; Add. 47097/8.

S.R.M.

PRYSE, Lewis (?1683–1720), of Gogerddan, Card.

CARDIGANSHIRE	10 Dec. 1701–1702
CARDIGAN BOROUGHS	1705–1708
CARDIGANSHIRE	1708–1710
	1715–23 Mar. 1716

b. ?1683, o.s. of Thomas Pryse of Glanfraed, Card. by Margaret, da. of Lewis Owen, M.P., of Peniarth, Merion. *educ.* Jesus, Oxf. 1 Apr. 1699, aged 15. *m.* Ann, da. and h. of John Lloyd of Aberllefenni, Merion., 2s. 4da. *suc.* cos. Sir Carbery Pryse, 4th Bt., M.P. Cardiganshire 1690, at Gogerddan 1694.

Pryse, whose family had represented Cardiganshire since the seventeenth century, was successful at the general election of 1715, but was expelled next year for refusing to take the oaths.[1] The lord lieutenant of the county wrote to Paul Methuen (q.v.), that he and William Powell (father of Thomas, q.v.) were

the greatest incendiaries and most disaffected persons in the principality of Wales [and] . . . the managers of the correspondence between the malcontents in North and South Wales [whose agents] so terrified the people in general, that neither the commissions issued out by me, nor even the orders of the Privy Council, could either in the time of the rebellion or since be put into execution, and had I gone down without the grant of some regular forces I had nothing to expect but to have been murdered.[2]

In 1717 at the time of the new Jacobite plot (see Caesar, Charles) Lord Mar, the Pretender's secretary of state, wrote to Pryse, 7 Apr., asking him and his friends to prepare for a landing of the Duke of Ormonde in the west country.[3] He died 11 Aug. 1720, lamented by the English Jacobites as a man 'who ruled all his shire'.[4]

[1] *CJ*, xviii. 411. [2] 4 Jan. 1717, SP Dom. 35/8, f. 68. [3] NLW Nanteos mss ex inf. P. D. G. Thomas. [4] Stuart mss 65/16.

E.C.

PRYSE, Thomas (?1716–45), of Gogerddan, Card.

CARDIGAN BOROUGHS   1741–21 May 1745

> *b.* ?1716, o.s. of John Pryse of Glanseryn, Mont. by Mary, da. of David Lewis of Dolhaidd, Carm. *educ.* Westminster, Oct. 1724 (aged 8)–1728; Oriel, Oxf. 9 June 1732, aged 15; L. Inn 1732. *m.* Maria Charlotte, da. and eventually h. of Rowland Pugh of Mathafarn, Mont., 1s. *suc.* Lewis Pryse (q.v.) at Gogerddan 1720.

Pryse was returned for Cardigan as a Tory on his family's interest, voting against the Government in all recorded divisions. After Walpole's fall a local adherent wrote to him: 'I congratulate you and the rest of the Patriots on your late victory'.[1] One of the signatories of the opposition whip of 10 Nov. 1743,[2] he died 21 May 1745, described as 'of a free, hospitable temper, and a great promoter of agriculture . . . a strenuous assertor of the liberties of his country, and zealous for suppressing the barbarous practice of his countrymen in rifling and plundering shipwrecks'.[3]

[1] John Adams to Thos. Pryse, 11 Feb. 1742, NLW Gogerddan mss. [2] Owen, *Pelhams*, 198. [3] *Gent. Mag.* 1745, p. 332.

P.D.G.T.

PUGH, John (?1675–1737), of Mathafarn, Mont.

CARDIGANSHIRE   1705–1708
MONTGOMERY BOROUGHS   1708–1727

> *b.* ?1675, 1st s. of William Pugh of Mathafarn by Margaret, da. of John Lloyd of Ceiswyn and Aberllefenni, Merion. *educ.* Jesus, Oxf. 13 June 1691, aged 15; I. Temple, called 1700. *m.* bef. 1711, Elizabeth, da. of John Scudamore, M.P., 1st Visct. Scudamore [I], *s.p.*

Under George I Pugh, a Tory, is not recorded as voting. In 1719 he was committed to the custody of the serjeant at arms for defaulting on a call of the House.[1] In 1721 Montgomeryshire was described to the Pretender as 'under the jurisdiction of Lord Hereford and Mr. Pugh of Mathafarn, both worthy men and firm, to be relied on'.[2] He did not stand in 1727, when there was a double return for Montgomery, in the proceedings on which he appeared as

a witness for the Tory candidate.[3] He died 30 Nov. 1737.

[1] *CJ*, xix. 61. [2] Stuart mss 65/16. [3] *CJ*, xxi. 138.

P.D.G.T.

PULTENEY, Daniel (?1674–1731), of Harefield, Mdx.

TREGONY   23 Mar.–10 Oct. 1721
HEDON   7 Nov. 1721–1722
PRESTON   1722–7 Sept. 1731

> *b.* ?1674, 1st s. of John Pulteney, M.P., surveyor of crown lands, by Lucy Colville of Northants.; 1st cos. of William Pulteney (q.v.). *educ.* Westminster; Ch. Ch. Oxf. 15 July 1699, aged 15; Grand Tour (Holland, Germany) 1704–6. *m.* 14 Dec. 1717, Margaret, da. and coh. of Benjamin Tichborne, yr. bro. of Henry Tichborne, 1st Baron Ferrard of Beaulieu [I], (her yr. sis. *m.* Charles Spencer, 4th Earl of Sunderland), 3s. *d.v.p.* 4da. *suc.* fa. 1726 in estate and as clerk to the council in Ireland under a reversion granted by Queen Anne.
> Envoy extraordinary to Denmark 1706–15; ld. of Trade 1717–21, of Admiralty 10 Oct. 1721–5.

Speaker Onslow regarded Daniel Pulteney as the founder of the opposition to Walpole's Administration. In his autobiographical notes he wrote:

> He who first endeavoured to form this opposition into a system or regular method of proceeding, with a view only to ruin Mr. Walpole, and for that purpose, to unite people of every character and principle, and in which he took the most indefatigable pains, was Mr. Daniel Pulteney, in all other respects almost a very worthy man, very knowing and laborious in business especially in foreign affairs, of strong but not lively parts, a clear and weighty speaker, grace in his deportment, and of great virtue and decorum in his private life, generous and friendly; but, with all this, of most implacable hatred where he did hate, violent, keen and most bitter in his resentments, gave up all pleasures and comforts, and every other consideration to his anger.[1]

Pulteney served as envoy to Denmark in the reign of Queen Anne. Recalled on the accession of George I, in 1717 he was appointed to the board of Trade, going in November 1719 as one of H.M. commissaries to France, where he received the board's thanks 'for the exact information he has constantly sent them'.[2] He longed to return to England, where he had 'expectations' from his brother-in-law, Lord Sunderland, and from his cousin William Pulteney, who wrote to him (7 May 1720):

> You may depend upon it, that I will take care of you; and if it should happen, that there should be a vacancy at Hedon, before a new Parliament, you shall certainly be brought in, if not, 'tis not a great while you have to wait.[3]

In December 1720, he confided to a friend:

> I am preparing to return to London, my leave came this week . . . Mr. Craggs [James Craggs, jun. q.v.]

says in a private letter to me, I hope your stay here will be short, and that we shall hit upon something that may be to your satisfaction; the first part of the sentence seems to imply a return to France, but the latter can't be understood that way.

He went on to criticize Walpole's scheme for dealing with the financial crisis caused by the collapse of the South Sea bubble:

After a good deal of private management, in which the public was very little considered, Mr. Walpole has produced a scheme for the South Sea, which in my poor opinion, is liable to many objections, one I think very material. It obliges the proprietors of, and sub-scribers to, the South Sea, to take one-fourth of their stock in Bank and another fourth in East India stock at a fixed rate . . . I don't like either of these stocks, must I take them against my will and contrary to my judgement? This is compulsive disposal of private property, which, I believe, was never practised before by a Parliament.

In March 1721 he was brought in by the Government for Tregony, where he was faced with an opposition, which he believed to be inspired by Walpole, thus showing, as he wrote, 'how sincere he is to his brother minister, Sunderland, upon whose account only he could think of opposing me'. He bitterly resented the attacks made on Sunderland by the committee appointed by the House of Commons to inquire into the South Sea Company's affairs, writing on 13 April 1721:

I am told the secret committee intend to make another attack on Lord Sunderland and for this purpose to enter upon matters foreign to those they were employed about . . . credit will not revive, nor money circulate so long as terrors are kept over people . . . those, who are to be punished, should be punished quickly, and the rest set free from all apprehensions.

In June 1721, when the House of Commons was considering 'proper means to restore public credit', he expressed the opinion

that the first consideration should have been to do something to please the people in general, by easing them of some burdensome tax, as that on candles, and the matter might have been managed so as to give the King the opportunity of recommending such a popular act; this seemed to be necessary, not only with respect to the elections for the next Parliament, but to consequences more important and, I fear, not very distant. But what can we hope for, when in a time of common calamity and common danger we look only to ourselves and are divided by private resentments, by ambition and by avarice.[4]

Promoted to the Admiralty board in October 1721, at the ensuing by-election he was returned by William Pulteney for Hedon, which he exchanged for Preston at the general election of 1722. Sunderland's death in April 1722 was a crushing blow to him.

His animosity to Mr. Walpole [Onslow writes] arose from his intimacy with my Lord Sunderland, to whom

he was brother-in-law by having married the sister of my Lord Sunderland's last wife. He was in the depth of all that Lord's political secrets as far at least as he trusted anybody, and was designed by him to be secretary of state in the scheme he formed of a new Administration, if he had lived long enough to have once more overset Mr. Walpole and my Lord Townshend. But my Lord Sunderland's death putting an end to the other's hopes, so soured his mind that from the moment of his disappointment, I verily believe he scarcely thought of anything else but to revenge it in an opposition to him who had been the chief opponent of his friend and patron. This was at first carried on in whispers and insinuations and raising private prejudices against Mr. Walpole, for he still continued one of the commissioners of the Admiralty and so still voted with the Administration.[5]

On 7 Nov. 1723 he wrote:

I . . . should think myself at present more likely to lose what I have, than get better; at least, I am sure it would be so if Mr. Walpole can do it, since he seems determined to remove everyone who continued in the King's service when he thought fit to leave it.

And again on 22 Feb. 1725:

A seat there may be agreeable enough to one who can and will act independently, but I had rather have a place of £500 a year out of Parliament than one of £1000 and be in it; I think the difficulties to an honest man increase daily, and after all I can find no true satisfaction in life without an easy conscience.[6]

According to Onslow he was largely responsible for William Pulteney's decision to go into opposition, whereupon he himself resigned his own office 'which he had great joy in being disentangled from, that he might, as he soon did, act openly and without reserve against the Ministry in everything'. In a letter to Townshend on 10 Dec. 1725 Walpole forecast the main lines of the new Opposition:

The Pulteneys build great hopes upon the difficulties they promise themselves will arise from the foreign affairs, and especially from the Hanover treaty. I had a curiosity to open some of their letters, and find them full of this language . . . *Wise Daniel* fills all his inland correspondence with reflection of the same kind, and gives all their fools great hopes of doing wonders: their two only topics are the civil list and the Hanover treaty.[7]

Pulteney's first recorded speech in opposition was made on 9 Feb. 1726 when he moved that a committee be appointed to state the public debt since 1714 and

took upon him to explain how the debt of the navy accrued and thought it was through mismanagement. He said since 1721 the navy debt was increased £400,000 by not granting the extra repairs that were annually demanded and by arrears of the seamen's wages and endeavoured to prove this mismanagement in 4 years.

Walpole answered 'he was very glad he had that gentleman's assistance now, for when he was in the office of Admiralty, though it was his duty, he never took notice of that practice'. Pulteney then 'insinuated as if what had been appropriated to the navy had been applied to other uses', which Walpole denied and 'defied any one to prove'. The motion was defeated.[8] He was one of the chief opposition speakers in the debate on the treaties of Hanover and Vienna on 16 Feb. 1726. The same year he, William Pulteney and Bolingbroke jointly founded the *Craftsman*, of which they became the directing triumvirate.

At the general election of 1727 a candidate chosen by the King himself was sent to Preston to keep out Pulteney but found his interest so strong that there was 'not the least room either to hope success or give vexation'.[9] Returned unopposed, Pulteney continued in violent opposition. He opened the debate on the Hessian troops on 31 Jan. 1729, arguing that a 'great army' raised against a threatened invasion was unnecessary in time of peace.[10] On 3 Feb. 1730 he declared that

> the continuing these troops is so great a charge to Great Britain, and so unnecessary to her service and security, so evidently designed for the defence alone of the Hanover dominions, and so certain an entail upon these nations of a standing army for interest which Great Britain has no concern to support, that the House ought to receive the motion with contempt and disdain, and reject it without a debate.

In the same month, he was one of the organizers of an opposition manoeuvre to raise unexpectedly the question of the repairs carried on by the French to the port of Dunkirk by producing eye-witnesses at the bar of the House of Commons. Another of his moves to embarrass Walpole was to instigate an agitation by the Dissenters for the repeal of the Test Act, since if Walpole 'complied with the Dissenters and consented to the repeal he would lose the Churchmen; if he complied not he would lose the Dissenters'.[11] He became, in Onslow's words, 'a sort of magazine for all the materials necessary to the work' of the Opposition, until he 'fell at last a martyr' to his quarrel with Walpole;

> for his not succeeding in it preyed upon his spirits, which and with his living much with the Lord Bolingbroke (as an enemy to Mr. Walpole) threw him into an irregularity of drinking that occasioned his death.[12]

He died 7 Sept. 1731.

[1] *HMC 14th Rep. IX*, 465. [2] *Bd. Trade Jnl.* 1718–22, p. 133. [3] *HMC Var.* viii. 287; Coxe, *Walpole*, ii. 186. [4] *HMC Var.* viii. 289, 305, 330, [5] *HMC 14th Rep. IX*, 466. [6] *HMC Var.* viii. 367, 386. [7] *HMC 14th Rep. IX*, 466; Coxe, *Walpole*, ii. 492–3. [8] *Knatchbull Diary*. [9] See PRESTON. [10] *Knatchbull Diary*. [11] *HMC Egmont Diary*, i. 24, 35–39, 83; ii. 244. [12] *HMC 14th Rep. IX*, 465–6.

E.C.

PULTENEY, Harry (1686–1767).

HEDON   5 Nov. 1722–1734, 24 Nov. 1739–1741
KINGSTON-UPON-HULL   2 May 1744–1747

b. 14 Feb. 1686, 2nd s. of Col. William Pulteney of Misterton, Leics. by his 1st w. Mary Floyd; bro. of William Pulteney (q.v.). *educ.* Westminster. *unm. suc.* bro. 1764.

Ensign 1 Ft. Gds. 1703; lt. and capt. 2 Ft. Gds. 1709, capt. and lt.-col. 1715, 2nd maj. and col. 1733, 1st maj. 1734; col. 13 Ft. 1739; brig.-gen. 1742; maj.-gen. 1743; equerry to the King 1743; gov. Hull 1743–d.; lt.-gen. 1747; gen. 1765.

Pulteney, an army officer, who had been taken prisoner at Almanza, was returned for Hedon in 1722 by his famous brother, William (q.v.), with whom he shared the representation of the borough unopposed till 1734, though from 1725 William was leading the Whig Opposition while his brother voted consistently with the Government. In 1732 William, who for some time had refused to see Harry 'because he votes with the Court',

> sent him word that if ever he expected anything of him, or to change a word with him, he must vote against the Court. But the Colonel, for whom he never did anything, expecting nothing from him, though he should oblige him in it, could not hazard his employment by complying.[1]

He was not put up by his brother in 1734, but on a vacancy in 1739 he was again returned unopposed for Hedon. In 1741 William, faced with an opposition by Luke Robinson (q.v.) at Hedon, threatened not to put up Harry again unless Robinson withdrew his candidature. From friendship for Harry, Walpole pressed Robinson to withdraw, pointing out that he would only turn out Colonel Pulteney and refusing to name a candidate to join with Robinson against William.[2] Robinson however was obdurate, with the result that Harry was out of Parliament till 1744, when he was brought in for Hull, of which he had been appointed governor. Sent to Flanders in March that year to make arrangements for the return of the British force there in the event of a French invasion,[3] he voted for the Hanoverians in 1746. He did not stand again.

In 1764 Pulteney succeeded to the vast fortune of his brother, who had no one else to leave it to.[4] He died unmarried 26 Oct. 1767, leaving that fortune to the daughter of his first cousin, Daniel Pulteney (q.v.), the wife of William Johnstone, afterwards Sir William Pulteney, Bt.

[1] *HMC Egmont Diary*, i. 246. [2] Luke Robinson to Walpole, 3 and 16 Feb. 1741, Cholmondeley (Houghton) mss. [3] *HMC Egmont Diary*, iii. 290. [4] *Chesterfield Letters*, 2603.

R.R.S.

PULTENEY, William (1684–1764).

HEDON   1705–1734
MIDDLESEX   1734–14 July 1742

b. Apr. 1684, 1st s. of Col. William Pulteney of
Misterton, Leics. and bro. of Harry Pulteney (q.v.).
educ. Westminster; Ch. Ch. Oxf. 1700; Grand Tour.
m. 27 Dec. 1714, Anna Maria, da. and coh. of John
Gumley (q.v.) of Isleworth, Mdx., 1s. 2da. all *d.v.p.*
suc. fa. 1715; *cr.* Earl of Bath 14 July 1742.
    Sec. at war 1714–17; P.C. 6 July 1716–1 July 1731,
and from 20 Feb. 1742; ld. lt. E. Riding, Yorks.
1721–8; cofferer of the Household 1723–5; in Cabinet
council without office 1742–6; first ld. of the Treasury
10–12 Feb. 1746; ld. lt. Salop 1761–*d.*

Pulteney was the heir to the Pulteney estate,
lying between St. James's Street and the Green
Park, held from the Crown on a 99-year lease,
bringing in £10,000 a year.[1] His grandfather, Sir
William Pulteney, M.P. for Westminster, had
vested the estate in trustees, one of whom was
Henry Guy, M.P. for Hedon, secretary to the
Treasury till he was sent to the Tower for taking a
bribe. Guy died in 1710, leaving his fortune to
Pulteney, who soon afterwards acquired another by
his marriage to the daughter of a wealthy glass
manufacturer.

Returned for Hedon on Guy's interest at the first
opportunity after coming of age, Pulteney began his
career as one of Walpole's chief political associates,
obtaining office with him at George I's accession,
and resigning to accompany him into opposition in
1717. The first sign of a rift between them appeared
in 1718, when Pulteney did not conceal his disapproval of Walpole's conduct in joining the Tories
to force a reduction of the army.[2] By 1720 the rift
was so wide that Walpole not only excluded Pulteney
from the negotiations for a reunion of the Whig
party, but did not procure him a place in the
reconstituted Government, merely offering him a
peerage, which was indignantly refused. Pulteney
showed his resentment by accusing Walpole in the
Commons of changing his mind according as he was
in or out of office (14 July 1721) and of allowing his
attitude to financial questions to be affected by his
investments in the Bank of England (16 Feb. 1722).
He was temporarily appeased with a lord lieutenancy, the conversion of his lease of the Pulteney
estate into a freehold, and a lucrative office, but in
1724 he was mortally offended at being passed over
in favour of the Duke of Newcastle for the post of
secretary of state.[3] In the following session, on a
proposal for discharging a civil list debt, he vented
his resentment in a violent personal attack on
Walpole, accusing him of increasing his fortune 'by
indirect means and corruption' and of squandering
public money on 'pensions, bounties, or other

II—BB

gratuities' to Members of Parliament. After opposing
the proposal at every stage, he ended by voting for
it,[4] which did not save him from dismissal at the
end of the session.

Pulteney now entered upon the great period of
his career, his seventeen-year opposition to Walpole.
'Formed by nature for social and convivial pleasure',
Chesterfield wrote of him,

> resentment made him engage in business. He had
> thought himself slighted by Sir Robert Walpole, to
> whom he publicly vowed not only revenge, but utter
> destruction . . . He was a most complete orator and
> debater in the House of Commons; eloquent, enter-
> taining, persuasive, strong, and patriotic as occasion
> required; for he had arguments, wit, and tears, at his
> command.

Onslow, who presided over their long parliamentary
duel, considered that Pulteney 'certainly hurt Sir
Robert more than any of those who opposed him'.[5]

In 1726 Pulteney, with his cousin, Daniel (q.v.),
and Bolingbroke, founded the *Craftsman*, which
became the organ of the Opposition. In 1727, on a
motion aimed personally at Walpole, he declared
that 'this Administration had done more to introduce
corruption than ever was done before' and that he
would pursue it 'to destruction', an expression
which he subsequently explained was to be understood in a purely parliamentary sense.[6]

At George II's accession, when the King put his
civil list up to auction, the highest bidder was
Pulteney, but his bid was not accepted. 'Denied
leave to stand candidate upon the interest of the
Court for Westminster, never consulted in the closet,
and always very coldly received in the drawing-room,'
he returned to opposition. In 1729, taunted with
opposing the Government because he was out of
employment and wanted to get in again, he declared

> that he was so far from desiring employments that he
> took pains to get rid of that he had, and, should any
> be offered him again, his refusal would show that he
> did not accuse the Administration out of any such
> view.

Later that year he told Lord Hervey (q.v.), whom
he was trying to bring over from the Court, that the
time was ripe for 'a parliamentary popular Government', that is, a republic, or at least a change of
King, 'putting a new one under new restrictions.'
Lashing himself into a rage, he predicted that dur-
the forthcoming session,

> as stout as our shitten monarch pretends to be, you
> will find we shall force him to truckle and make his
> great fat-arsed wife stink with fear.[7]

Next year he joined with Sir William Wyndham
(q.v.) to form an organized Whig-Tory Opposition,
christened 'the Patriots'.

In 1731 he published a pamphlet couched in terms

so offensive not only to Walpole but to the King that he was struck out of the Privy Council.[8]

During the excise bill crisis in 1733 the leaders of the Opposition were so confident of Walpole's fall that they drew up a ministry to succeed him, in which Pulteney figured as first lord of the Treasury and chancellor of the Exchequer. But in 1736 Walpole was still going strong, while Pulteney, partly from ill-health, partly 'from being weary of the opposing part he had so long unsuccessfully acted', hardly attended the House of Commons. Next year he

> listened to and encouraged a sort of treaty that was underhand carrying on to make him a peer, buy his silence, and give him rest, but when it came to [the point] he could not stand the reproach he thought he should incur by striking this bargain, and, with that irresolution that was always the predominant defect in his conduct, went on without having courage sufficient either to quite make it or quite break it.[9]

His attitude was not changed by the opposition successes at the general election of 1741, after which he declared that

> he was weary of being at the head of a party; he would rather row in the galleys; and was absolutely resolved not to charge himself with taking the lead.[10]

According to Speaker Onslow, it was owing to Pulteney's fear of the Pretender,

> and not a little too because of his great fortune, which might be at stake, that he had often some checks of conscience, and very melancholy apprehensions, lest his violence against the Administration of Sir Robert Walpole, and joining for that purpose with those supposed to be the enemies to the Government, might not weaken the foundations of it, and give too much advantage to them who were thought to mean its destruction.[11]

When, on Walpole's fall, Pulteney was invited by the King to form a new Administration, with himself at the Treasury, he refused to accept any employment, contenting himself with a seat in the Cabinet. He explained a year later:

> When I declined accepting (though extremely pressed by all my friends) of any employment whatsoever on the late change of affairs in England, . . . I had then taken a pretty firm resolution never to concern myself with public affairs any more. I had been long tired with a tedious and disagreeable opposition, and was resolved, whenever I could get fairly and honourably out of it, never to engage on either side any more; that is, I was resolved to have as little to do with Courts as possibly I could, and determined to have nothing to do against them. This insignificant situation for myself I have at length happily compassed and I am resolved most indolently and steadfastly to persevere in.

In the ensuing negotiations, instead of insisting on a total change of Government, he stipulated for a majority in the Cabinet, but succeeded in securing the admission of only five opposition representatives compared with 13 members of the late ministry. In his own words,

> When the late minister came to be at last fairly run down and got the better of . . . almost everybody in the Opposition expected some employment and a total change of hands; scarce any person (though never so inconsiderable) but had carved out some good thing for himself, and many there were who thought they had a right to be consulted in the proper changes that were to be made. When this was found not to be the case and that the negotiation was fallen absolutely into Lord Carteret's and my hands, many were disappointed and dissatisfied. A schism was immediately made by some of the most considerable of our friends, and some were persuaded to forsake us, who happened to have the management of affairs in our hands, for no other reason but because we had got it. This . . . soon weakened us and gave strength to the Court again; but what is the hardest of all is that these very people, who thus deprived us of the power of extending the bottom and providing for many of them, grew angry with us that more were not preferred, though they were the only means of hindering it.[12]

His 'authority, weight, consideration, and power . . . in the House of Commons' remained so great that there was 'no withstanding it', till at the end of the session, having obtained places for all his personal followers, he agreed to take a peerage, thus reducing himself to 'an absolute nullity', 'a mere lord with one vote, and his influence in the House of Commons quite at an end'.[13]

Pulteney, now Earl of Bath, made more than one attempt to recover the opportunity which he had thrown away in 1742. Only eighteen months after refusing the Treasury he applied for it when it fell vacant on the death of Lord Wilmington (Spencer Compton, q.v.), who had been put into it as a stopgap. But his application was unsuccessful, as was his attempt in February 1746 to form an Administration, which collapsed in 48 hours for lack of parliamentary support. He spent the rest of his life in retirement, consoling himself with the pleasures of avarice, to which he had always been notoriously, indeed scandalously, addicted. When he died, 7 July 1764, he was worth £400,000 in money and £30,000 a year in land, half from his own and half from an estate which he had virtually stolen from the Newport family.[14]

[1] *Survey of London*, xxix. 26–28; Sir Dudley Ryder's diary, 18 Oct. 1739, Harrowby mss. [2] *Letters of Lady Mary Wortley Montagu*, i. 138; Mahon, ii. p. lxi. [3] Coxe, *Walpole*, i. 356–7, 717; Hervey, *Mems.* 9. [4] *Knatchbull Diary*, 9, 16 Apr. 1725. [5] Chesterfield, *Characters* (1777 ed.) 24–26; HMC *14th Rep. IX*, 467. [6] *Knatchbull Diary*, 7 Mar. 1727, 3 Apr. 1728. [7] *HMC Egmont Diary*, iii. 339; Hervey, 31, 37, 106–7. [8] Coxe, i. 361–5. [9] Hervey, 169–70, 529, 667. [10] Coxe, iii. 576. [11] *HMC 14th Rep. IX*, 466. [12] Bath to Stair, 11 Feb. 1743, Add. 35458, ff. 24–25. [13] Hervey, 945, 949, 953. [14] *Chesterfield Letters*, 2603; see under NEWPORT, Henry.

R.R.S.

PURVIS, George (1680–1741), of Darsham, Suff.

ALDEBURGH   21 Jan. 1732–8 Mar. 1741

> b. 27 July 1680, 1st s. of George Purvis of Darsham by Margaret, da. of George Dakins, wid. of one Berry, bro. of Adm. Sir John Berry. m. 3 Feb. 1712, Elizabeth Allen of Yoxford, Suff., 3s. 1da. suc. fa. 1715.
> Capt. R.N. 1709; commr. of the navy 1735–d.

Purvis was the protégé of Sir Charles Wager (q.v.), under whom he served in the West Indies and at Gibraltar and after whom he named his eldest son. Returned for Aldeburgh, where he managed the Admiralty interest, he voted with the Government in all recorded divisions till his death 8 Mar. 1741.

R.R.S.

PYE, Henry (1709–66), of Faringdon, Berks.

BERKSHIRE   26 Nov. 1746–2 Mar. 1766

> b. 29 July 1709,[1] 1st s. of Henry Pye of Faringdon by his 2nd w. Anne, da. of Sir Benjamin Bathurst, M.P., sis. of Benjamin Bathurst (q.v.). educ. Balliol, Oxf. 1725. m. 1743, Mary, da. of Rev. David James, rector of Woughton, Bucks., 3s. 1da. suc. fa. 1749.

Pye, whose great-grandfather, Sir Robert Pye, auditor of the Exchequer under James I and Charles I, bought Faringdon in 1623, represented his county as a Tory without opposition till his death, 2 Mar. 1766, leaving his son, H.J. Pye, M.P., the poet laureate, an estate encumbered with debts amounting to £50,000.

> [1] Noble, *Mem. House of Cromwell*, ii. 110.

L.B.N.

PYNSENT, William (c.1679–1765), of Burton, Curry Rivell, Som. and Urchfont, nr. Devizes, Wilts.

TAUNTON   30 Aug. 1715–1722

> b. c.1679, 1st s. of Sir William Pynsent, 1st Bt., M.P., of Urchfont, Wilts. by Patience, da. of John Bond, alderman of London. m. Mary, da. and coh. of Thomas Jennings of Burton, Som., wid. of Edmund Star of New Court, 1s. 3da. all d.v.p. suc. fa. as 2nd Bt. 1719.
> Sheriff, Som. 1741–2.

The first Sir William Pynsent, whose mother was an heiress and whose uncle, a legal official, made him his heir, bought an estate at Urchfont, near Devizes, which he represented in the Convention Parliament.[1] His son, the second baronet, having acquired another estate at Burton in Somerset through his wife, was returned on petition as a Whig for Taunton in 1715. He voted for the septennial bill and the repeal of the Occasional Conformity and Schism Acts, and was put down as to be approached through Sir John Eyles (q.v.) on the

peerage bill, on which he did not vote, thereafter ceasing to attend. He was said to be ready to retire from the House as soon as the Government enabled him to vacate his seat by providing him with an office of profit, which he would give up immediately,[2] but in the event he remained a Member till the end of the Parliament. Though never standing again, he continued to play a part in Somerset politics, offering his interest at Taunton in 1734 to Sir Charles Wyndham (q.v.)[3] and giving his 'very considerable interest' at Bridgwater in 1741 to Bubb Dodington, in spite of a personal appeal from Walpole.[4] He died 8 Jan. 1765, aged 85, leaving his whole fortune to William Pitt (q.v.), a total stranger, to whom he was not related. His will, dated 20 Oct. 1761, gives no reason for the bequest, merely observing: 'I hope he will like my Burton estate, where I now live, well enough to make it his country seat'. Horace Walpole writes of him:

> He was said to have had parts and humour, not many scruples, living to her death with his only daughter, in pretty notorious incest.[5]

> [1] *Wilts. Arch. Mag.* xlvi. 39–40. [2] See TRENCHARD, John. [3] Sir W. Wyndham to Pynsent, 16 Feb. 1734, Hoare mss. [4] Walpole to Pynsent 26 Mar. 1741; Dodington to Pynsent 5 June 1745, ibid. [5] PCC 29 Rushworth; Walpole, *Mems. Geo. III*, ii. 32–33, including words omitted from the printed vol.

S.R.M.

PYTTS, Edmund (?1696–1753), of Kyre, nr. Tenbury, Worcs.

WORCESTERSHIRE   1741–24 Nov. 1753

> b. ?1696, o.s. of Samuel Pytts, M.P., of Kyre by his 1st w. Frances, da. of Samuel Sandys, M.P., of Ombersley, Worcs. educ. Balliol, Oxf. 21 May 1713, aged 16. m. (1) settlement 24 Jan. 1727,[1] Susanna (d. 2 Apr. 1742), da. of Jonathan Collet of Upton, Essex, merchant, sometime in the service of the E. I. Co., 4s. 4da.; (2) 12 Dec. 1752, Anne, da. of Sir Streynsham Master of Codnor Castle, Derbys., wid. of Gilbert, 4th Earl of Coventry, s.p. suc. fa. 1729.

Pytts, whose family acquired Kyre in 1576,[2] owned large estates in Worcestershire, for which he was returned in 1741, after unsuccessfully contesting Ludlow in 1727. A Tory, he voted against the Administration in all recorded divisions. Re-elected unopposed in 1747, he was described by the 2nd Lord Egmont in his electoral survey, c.1749–50, as 'most heartily well with us, and thinks himself under eternal obligations for our stand for him in the turnpike bill [for Worcestershire in 1749] against Lord Sandys [q.v.]'. He died 24 Nov. 1753.

> [1] Jonathan Collet's will, PCC 145 Edmunds; *Kyre Park Charters* (Worcs. Hist. Soc.), 137. [2] *Kyre Park Charters*, 22–23.

R.S.L.

PYTTS, Edmund (1729–81), of Kyre, nr. Tenbury, Worcs.

WORCESTERSHIRE 26 Dec. 1753–1761

b. 23 Feb. 1729, 1st s. of Edmund Pytts (q.v.) of Kyre by his 1st w. *educ.* prob. Eton 1742–5; L. Inn 1745. *unm. suc.* fa. 1753.

Sheriff, Worcs. 1771–2.

Edmund Pytts, a Tory, succeeded his father as Member for the county. He died 13 Dec. 1781.

R.S.L.

QUARENDON, Visct., *see* LEE, George Henry

RAMSAY, *see* BALFOUR RAMSAY

RAMSDEN, John (1699–1769), of Byram and Longley Hall, Yorks.

APPLEBY 1727–1754

bap. 21 Mar. 1699, 1st s. of Sir William Ramsden, 2nd Bt., of Byram and Longley Hall by Elizabeth, da. of John Lowther, 1st Visct. Lonsdale, sis. and coh. of Henry, 3rd Visct. Lonsdale. *educ.* Clare, Camb. 1718. *m.* (lic. 8 Aug. 1748) Margaret, da. and h. of William Norton of Sawley, Yorks., wid. of Thomas Liddell Bright of Badsworth, Yorks., 2s. 2da. *suc.* fa. as 3rd Bt. 27 June 1736.

Ramsden was returned for Appleby by his uncle, the 3rd Viscount Lonsdale, with whose family he was also connected by his sister's marriage to Sir William Lowther, 2nd Bt. (q.v.). An independent Whig, he voted with the Government on the civil list arrears in 1729, the excise bill in 1733, and the repeal of the Septennial Act in 1734, but against them on the Spanish convention in 1739, figuring in ministerial lists of absent opposition Members on 21 Nov. 1739 and 18 Nov. 1740.[1] He was put down on Pelham's list for the ballot of 26 Mar. 1742 for the secret committee on Walpole, to which he was not elected, and included in the Cockpit list of October that year. But he voted against the Government on the Hanoverians in the following December and again in 1744, abstaining from the division on them in 1746, when he was classed as 'doubtful'. At the opening of the next Parliament he was classed as a government supporter. Though he himself remained independent, one of his brothers had a place in the secretary of state's office, another was a commissioner of the wine licence office, and a third was lieutenant governor of Carlisle and equerry to the King. He did not stand again, and died 10 Apr. 1769.

[1] Cholmondeley (Houghton) mss 66.

R.R.S.

RANDYLL, Morgan (b. 1649), of Chilworth, nr. Guildford, Surr.

GUILDFORD 1679–1681, 1690–1705, 1708–1710, 3 Feb. 1711–1722

b. 7 Oct. 1649, 1st s. of Vincent Randyll by Dorothy, da. of John Duncombe. *educ.* Wadham, Oxf. 1666; M. Temple 1670, called 1677. *m.* 5 Feb. 1678, Anne, da. and coh. of Sir Thomas Gould of St. Mary Aldermanbury, London, 2da. of whom one married Gilbert Vane, 2nd Baron Barnard. *suc.* fa. 1673.

Randyll's grandfather, Sir Edward Randyll of Albury, acquired Chilworth by marrying the only child of Sir John Morgan (*d.* 1621). The family owned considerable property round Guildford, including two gun-powder mills. A Tory, and a member of the October Club, Randyll voted consistently against the Administration after 1715. Owing to a succession of contested elections he 'became so much in debt . . . that in 1720 he sold his estate . . . to . . . one of the directors of the South Sea Company for £29,335'.[1] He contested Guildford again in 1722, but was defeated by Thomas Brodrick, put up by Lord Onslow (qq.v.).[2] On 14 July 1738 his grandson, Henry Vane (q.v.), wrote to the 2nd Lord Oxford:

My grandfather Randyll's . . . unhappy affairs oblige him to go to the Fleet to prevent a worse prison. I hope your Lordship will sign the enclosed note . . . for £25, a sum absolutely necessary to pay the warden's fees and buy a few necessaries.[3]

The date of his death is unknown.

[1] Manning & Bray, *Surr.* ii. 118. [2] *HMC 14th Rep. IX*, 517. [3] Harley mss.

A.N.N.

RASHLEIGH, Jonathan (1693–1764), of Menabilly, Cornw.

FOWEY 1727–24 Nov. 1764

b. 19 Jan. 1693, 4th s. of Jonathan Rashleigh, M.P., and bro. of Philip Rashleigh (q.v.). *m.* 11 June 1728, Mary, da. of Sir William Clayton, 1st Bt. (q.v.), of Morden, Surr., 9s. 4da. *suc.* bro. 1736, and cos. Sir Coventry Carew, 6th Bt. (q.v.), at Helset, Cornw. 1748.

Rashleigh represented Fowey on his family's interest as a Tory, voting consistently against the Government until his death, 24 Nov. 1764.

E.C.

RASHLEIGH, Philip (1689–1736), of Menabilly, Cornw.

LISKEARD 1710–1722

bap. 13 July 1689, 1st surv. s. of Jonathan Rashleigh, M.P., of Menabilly by Jane, da. of Sir John Carew, 3rd Bt., M.P., of Antony, Cornw.; bro. of Jonathan Rashleigh (q.v.). *educ.* Winchester. *unm. suc.* fa. 1702.

Recorder, Fowey 1714–*d.*

Philip Rashleigh came of a leading merchant family in Fowey, which they represented almost without interruption from 1586 until 1698 and continuously from 1727 until 1802. Returned for Liskeard as a Tory in 1715, he was absent from the divisions on the septennial bill in 1716 and on the Occasional Conformity and Schism Acts in 1719, but voted against the peerage bill. In 1715 a treasonable pamphlet addressed to him was seized in the post at Exeter on government orders,[1] and in 1721 his name was sent to the Pretender as a Jacobite supporter.[2] He did not stand in 1722, dying 12 Aug. 1736.

[1] E.W. Rashleigh, *Hist. Fowey*, 30. [2] Stuart mss 65/16.

E.C.

RAYMOND, John (c.1712–82), of Tower Hill, London, and Hatchlands, Surr.

WEYMOUTH AND MELCOMBE REGIS 1741–1747

b. c.1712, s. of Samuel Raymond, brewer, of London by Anne, da. of Nicholas Skinner of Firbeck, Yorks. *m.* (1) 10 Nov. 1735, Britannia (*d.* 2 May 1743), da. of James Lamb of Hackney, haberdasher, 1s. 2da.; (2) 21 June 1744, Mary, also da. of James Lamb, 3da. *suc.* fa. 1730.

In 1741 John Raymond, a London brewer, described by Sir Robert Walpole as 'a Dissenter who is to find money',[1] was put up for Weymouth by George Bubb Dodington (q.v.). Returned as an opposition Whig, he voted against the Government in all recorded divisions till 1746, when he was absent from the division on the Hanoverians. Not standing again, he died 21 Jan. 1782, having for 24 years held the office of brewer to the board of victualling.[2]

[1] Sir Dudley Ryder's diary, 9 Aug. 1740, Harrowby mss. [2] *Gent. Mag.* 1782, p. 47.

R.R.S.

RAYMOND, Sir Robert (1673–1733), of Lincoln's Inn, and Abbots Langley, Herts.

BISHOP'S CASTLE   1710–1715
YARMOUTH I.o.W.   1715–12 Apr. 1717
LUDLOW   26 Mar. 1719–1722
HELSTON   1722–31 Jan. 1724

b. 20 Dec. 1673, o.s. of Sir Thomas Raymond of Tremnals, Essex, judge of the King's bench, by Anne, da. of Sir Edward Fish, 2nd Bt., of Southill, Beds., sis. and coh. of Sir Edward Fish, 3rd Bt. *educ.* Eton; G. Inn 1 Nov. 1683, aged 9; Christ's, Camb. 1689; called G. Inn 1697, transferred to L. Inn 1710. *m.* Anne, da. of Sir Edward Northey (q.v.) of Woodcote Green, Epsom, Surr., attorney-gen., 1s. *suc.* fa. 1683; kntd. 20 Oct. 1710; *cr.* Lord Raymond, Baron of Abbots Langley, Herts. 15 Jan. 1731.

Solicitor-gen. May 1710—Oct. 1714; counsel for the university of Cambridge 1718; attorney-gen. May 1720–Jan. 1724; judge of King's bench Jan. 1724; commr. of the great seal 7 Jan.–4 June 1725; l.c.j. of King's bench 2 Mar. 1725–*d.*; P.C. 12 Apr. 1725; gov. of Charterhouse 1730–*d.*

Raymond became solicitor-general on the victory of the Tories in 1710, losing his office on the accession of George I. Returned as a Tory in 1715, he was one of the chief opposition speakers in the debate on the Address, 23 March; defended Harley, now Lord Oxford, from the charge of high treason in July; and spoke against the septennial bill, 24 Apr. 1716. Unseated on petition 12 Apr. 1717, he was approached on 17 Apr. by Lord Chief Justice Parker, afterwards Lord Chancellor Macclesfield, on behalf of the Government, offering to arrange for him to be found another seat. At first Raymond declined the offer on the ground that

> if I should be so brought in by the interest of the great man [Sunderland] your Lordship inclined to me, who was thought so instrumental in turning me out, very odd constructions might be put upon it, and used to the prejudice of my reputation, which would entirely disable me from doing any service in Parliament.[1]

However, he allowed himself to be put up at the end of the month by the Government for a by-election at Cockermouth, where he was defeated. Brought in for Ludlow in 1719 on the recommendation of the Duke of Chandos, he was appointed attorney-general next year in succession to Nicholas Lechmere. At the general election of 1722, after Sunderland had unsuccessfully tried to place him at Coventry, a seat was found for him by the Administration at Helston.[2]

As attorney-general Raymond was placed in the invidious position of having to conduct the proceedings arising out of the Atterbury plot, including the bill of pains and penalties against his old and intimate friend Atterbury, till the final stage of the bill when he withdrew, eliciting the comment from a Tory:

> This was pure grimace. Sense of decency, out of regard to past friendship, should surely have tied his tongue at least upon former occasions, as well as have obliged him to [be] absent upon this.[3]

Branded as an apostate, his position in the Commons became so untenable that he abandoned politics for the bench at the cost of becoming temporarily a mere puisne judge, an unprecedented step for an attorney-general. On the removal of Lord Chancellor Macclesfield in January 1725, he was appointed one of the three commissioners of the great seal, becoming lord chief justice of the King's bench two months later. In that capacity, he set an example, which was followed by the other chief justices and judges, by not accepting annual presents from the head of the King's bench prison. In 1730 the select committee set up by the House of Commons to investigate the conditions of the gaols reported that

> the King's Bench prison is much better regulated than any other prison the committee have enquired into; which they cannot but ascribe to the care of the Lord Chief Justice Raymond, who, from not accepting any presents or fees from the marshall of the said prison, hath kept the said marshall strictly to the performance of his duties, and his lordship hath heard and relieved the complaints of the prisoners.[4]

Raised to the peerage in 1731, he died 19 March 1733.

[1] Stowe 1750, f. 181. [2] Chandos letter bks.9 Nov., 2 Dec. 1721; corporation of Coventry to Sunderland, 30 Nov. 1721, Sunderland (Blenheim) mss. [3] HMC Portland, vii. 360. [4] CJ, xxi. 579.

E.C.

READE, George (1687–1756), of Shipton-under-Wychwood, Oxon.

TEWKESBURY 1722–1734

b. 1687, 4th s. of Sir Edward Reade, 2nd Bt., of Shipton Court by Elizabeth, da. of Edward Harby of Adstone, Northants.; bro. of Sir Thomas Reade, 4th Bt. (q.v.). m. Jane, da. of Charles Nowes, barrister, of Wood Ditton, Camb., s.p.[1]

Lt. and capt. 1 Ft. Gds. 1703, capt.-lt. and lt.-col. 1708, capt. 1709, 2nd maj. and col. 1729; col. 29 Ft. 1733–9, 9 Ft. 1739–49; lt.-gen. 1747; col. 9 Drag. Gds. 1749–d.

Returned for Tewkesbury after a contest in 1722 and re-elected unopposed in 1727, Reade voted consistently with the Government. He died 28 Mar. 1756, leaving £35,000 in trust for the purchase of lands of inheritance for his nephew Sir John Reade, 5th Bt.[2]

[1] Compton Reade, Redes of Barton Court, Berks. 50–54. [2] PCC 117 Glazier.

S.R.M.

READE, Sir Thomas, 4th Bt. (c.1684–1752), of Shipton-under-Wychwood, Oxon.

CRICKLADE 1713–1741, 24 Dec. 1741–1747

b. c.1684, 2nd s. of Sir Edward Reade, 2nd Bt., of Shipton Court, and bro. of George Reade (q.v.). m. 29 Oct. 1719, Jane Mary, da. of Sir Ralph Dutton, 1st Bt., M.P., of Sherborne, Glos., 1s. suc. e. bro. Sir Winwood Reade, 3rd Bt., 30 June 1692.

Clerk of the household to Prince of Wales c.1722–7; clerk of the Green Cloth 1727–d.

Reade's estates were some 20 miles from Cricklade, for which he was returned five times, after contesting Oxfordshire unsuccessfully in 1710. He is described by Hearne in 1710 as 'a young gentleman that never had any literary education; he is a staunch Whig, a loose debauchee and has little or nothing of religion'.[1] After 1715 he regularly voted with the Government, except on the peerage bill in 1719. On his death, 25 Sept. 1752, Henry Pelham

referred to him as 'an old servant of the King's, and a very honest man, but he has been declining for many years'.[2]

[1] Hearne, Colls. (Oxf. Hist. Soc.), ii. 348. [2] To Newcastle, 29 Sept. 1752, Add. 32729, f. 396.

R.S.L.

REBOW, Sir Isaac (1655–1726), of Head St., Colchester, Essex.

COLCHESTER 1689–1690, 12 Nov. 1692–21 Nov. 1702, 14 Dec. 1702–6 May 1714, 1715–1722

bap. 15 July 1655, o.s. of John Rebow of Colchester, merchant, by Sarah, da. of Francis Tayspil of Colchester, bay [baize]-maker. m. (1) bef. 1682, Mary, da. of James Lemyng of Greyfriars, Colchester by Mary da. and coh. of Sir William Batten, M.P., surveyor gen. of the navy, 1s.; (2) Dec. 1685, Mary, da. of Thomas Maccro, apothecary, of Bury, Suff., 2da.; (3) lic. 19 Nov. 1694, Elizabeth, da. of Sir William Wiseman, 1st Bt., of Rivenhall, Essex, wid. of John Lamotte Honeywood, M.P., of Markshall, Essex, s.p. Kntd. 26 Mar. 1693. suc. fa. 1699.

V.-adm. Essex 1693–6, 1702; mayor, Colchester 1716.

Descended from Flemish Protestant refugees and the grandson of a weaver, Rebow made a fortune in the clothing industry, becoming one of the leading men in Colchester,[1] for which he was returned at the Revolution as a Whig. He was knighted by William III, who used to stay at his house on the way to and from Harwich.[2] Re-elected in 1715, he consistently supported the Government. Defeated in 1722, he petitioned, but though twice renewed his petition was not heard. He died 6 Sept. 1726, leaving the bulk of his estates to his grandson, Isaac Lemyng Rebow (q.v.).[3]

[1] Essex Rev. vi. 174–5; J. H. Round, Hist. and Antiquities of Colchester Castle (1882), pp. 128–9. [2] Luttrell, iii. 65, 216; iv. 698. [3] PCC 192 Plymouth.

E.C.

REBOW, Isaac Lemyng (?1705–35), of Head St., Colchester, Essex.

COLCHESTER 1734–3 Mar. 1735

b. ?1705, 2nd s. of Lemyng Rebow of Fulham, Mdx. by Abigail, da. of Charles Chamberlain, alderman of London. educ. Fulham sch.; Trinity, Camb. 10 May 1722, aged 17; I. Temple 1727. m. 1729, Mary da. of Matthew Martin (q.v.) of Alresford Hall, Essex, 1s. suc. gd.-fa. 1726.

Rebow succeeded his grandfather, Sir Isaac Rebow (q.v.), as head of the Whig interest at Colchester,[1] for which he was returned unopposed in 1734, jointly with his father-in-law, Matthew Martin. He died 3 Mar. 1735.

[1] Essex Arch. Soc. Trans. n.s. xiv. 16–17.

E.C.

REVELL, Thomas (*d.*1752), of Fetcham Park, Surr.

DOVER   1734–26 Jan. 1752

m. (3) 12 May 1738, Jane, da. of Hon. William Egerton, yr. bro. of Scrope Egerton, 1st Duke of Bridgwater, 1da.
Victualling agent at Lisbon 1716;[1] commr. of victualling 1728–June 1747.

Revell, of whose origins and first two marriages nothing is known, started his career as victualling agent at Lisbon in 1716,[1] rising to become a commissioner of victualling at £500 p.a. Awarded a lucrative contract for victualling the garrison of Gibraltar[2] in 1733, he was able by 1735 to buy Fetcham Park. During the remainder of his life he made a considerable fortune out of such army contracts. When, on his standing in 1734 at Dover, his fellow commissioners 'agreed to have four hundred head of oxen killed at Dover . . . Thomas Revell . . . bought the offals of the said four hundred oxen and ordered them to be given to the poor inhabitants.'[3] He consistently supported the Administration but in 1747 resigned his office which, under the Place Act of 1742, was about to become incompatible with a seat in the Commons. He died 26 Jan. 1752, leaving his daughter Jane, still a minor, a fortune of over £20,000.

¹ Add. 15936, f. 90. ² Cal. Treas. Bks. and Pprs. 1731–4, p. 400. ³ St. James's Evening Post, 29 Jan. 1734.

P.W.

REYNELL, Richard (*c.*1681–1735), of East Ogwell and Denbury, nr. Ashburton, Devon.

ASHBURTON   1702–1708, 17 Mar. 1711–1734

b. c.1681, 3rd but 1st surv. s. of Thomas Reynell, M.P., of East Ogwell by his 2nd w. Elizabeth, da. of James Gould, merchant, of London, wid. of William Vincent of Exeter. *unm. suc.* fa. 1699.

Reynell came of an old Devonshire family, owning the manors of East and West Ogwell and Denbury, with property in Ashburton,[1] which he represented for 33 years. Though he was classed as a Whig in 1715, all his recorded votes were against the Government. Defeated in 1734, he died next year (buried 14 June). In his will he directed that his estates should be sold to pay his debts and legacies, and to purchase 'lands in South Britain' for his niece, the wife of Joseph Taylor (q.v.), and her son, his godson.[2]

¹ Lysons, Devonshire, i. p. ccxi; ii. 163–4, 374–5; PCC 48 Pett. ²PCC 131 Ducie.

S.R.M.

REYNOLDS, Francis (*d.*1773), of Strangeways, Manchester, Lancs.

LANCASTER   24 Apr. 1745–12 Aug. 1773

o.s. of Thomas Reynolds of South Mimms, Mdx. and Strangeways, director of South Sea Co. 1715–22, by his w. Mary. *m.* 17 Jan. 1729, Elizabeth, da. of Matthew Ducie Moreton, 1st Baron Ducie, wid. of Richard Symms of Blackheath, 2s 1da. *suc.* fa. 1741.
Surveyor of woods in the north of the duchy of Lancaster 1740–61; provost marshal of Barbados 1741–61; clerk of the Crown to duchy of Lancaster 1741–61.

Inheriting Strangeways in 1711, Reynold's father was granted the office of provost marshal of Barbados in 1715 with reversion to his son, who after contesting Preston unsuccessfully in 1741 was returned for Lancaster in 1745, continuing to sit for it till his death. He voted with the Administration on the Hanoverians, 11 Apr. 1746, writing to Newcastle 25 June: 'I have taken no step but under your Grace's favour and protection'.[1] The 2nd Lord Egmont wrote of him c.1749–50: 'This man is thoroughly attached to the Pelhams and should be routed by all means'.

He died 12 Aug. 1773.

¹ Add. 32707, f. 350.

E.C.

REYNOLDS, James (1686–1739), of Lincoln's Inn.

BURY ST. EDMUNDS   16 May 1717–16 Mar. 1725

b. 6 Jan. 1686, 4th s. of James Reynolds of Helion Bumpstead, Essex and Bury St. Edmunds, Suff., being o.s. by his 2nd w. Bridget Parker. (His 1st w. was Judith, da. of Sir William Hervey, M.P., gd.-fa. of the 1st Earl of Bristol). *educ.* Bury g. s.; Queens', Camb. 1702; M. Temple 1703; L. Inn 1705, called 1712. *m.* (1) Mary (*d.* 18 July 1736), da. of Thomas Smith of Thrandeston Hall, Suff., *s.p.*; (2) July 1737, Alicia Rainbird, *s.p.*
Recorder, Bury St. Edmunds 1712–25; serjeant-at-law 1715; university counsel, Cambridge 1718; justice of King's bench 1725–30; ld. chief baron of the Exchequer 1730–8 (res.).

Reynolds, who was connected with the Herveys through his father's first wife, was returned in succession to Lord Bristol's brother-in-law, Aubrey Porter (q.v.). He was counsel for the Prince of Wales in 1718, when the judges were asked for their opinion as to whether the care and education of the Prince's children belonged to the King. Absent from the division on the repeal of the Occasional Conformity and Schism Acts, he voted against the peerage bill in 1719. At the end of 1723 Lord Bristol suggested to him that he should make room for John, Lord Hervey (q.v.), by applying for a judgeship, to which he was appointed a little over a year later.[1]

He died 9 Feb. 1739.

¹ Letter Bks. of J. Hervey, 1st Earl of Bristol, ii. 339.

R.R.S.

RIALTON, Visct., *see* **GODOLPHIN, William**

RICE, Edward (*d.* 1727), of Newton, Carm.

CARMARTHENSHIRE   1722–18 Dec. 1724

> s. of Griffith Rice, M.P., of Newton by Catherine, da. and coh. of Philip Hoby of Neath Abbey, Glam. *m.* Lucy, da. of John Morley Trevor (q.v.) of Glynde, Suss. 1s. 2da.

Rice belonged to one of the leading Whig families of Carmarthenshire, which his father represented 1701–10. In Sunderland's plan for the 1722 Parliament, drawn up c.May 1721, he was listed to replace Sir Thomas Stepney (q.v.) for Carmarthenshire. He was returned, with the support of the Duke of Bolton[1] (Charles Powlett, q.v., Marquess of Winchester), but was unseated on petition. He died *v.p.* 3 Apr. 1727.

[1] See CARMARTHENSHIRE.

R.R.S.

RICH, Sir Robert, 4th Bt. (1685–1768), of Roos Hall, Suff.

DUNWICH   1715–1722
BERE ALSTON   4 Feb. 1724–1727
ST. IVES   1727–1741

> b. 3 July 1685, 2nd s. of Sir Robert Rich, 2nd Bt., M.P., ld. of Admiralty 1691–9, by Mary, da. of Sir Charles Rich, 1st Bt., of Mulbarton, Norf. *m.* 28 Sept. 1714, Elizabeth, da. and coh. of Col. Edward Griffith, clerk of the Green Cloth to Queen Anne and sec. to Prince George of Denmark, 3s. 2da., one of whom m. George Lyttelton (q.v.). *suc.* bro. Oct. 1706.
> Ensign 1 Ft. Gds. June 1700; capt. 24 Ft. Aug. 1704; capt. and lt.-col. 1 Ft. Gds. Mar. 1708; col. regt. of Ft. Feb. 1710, regt. of Drags. 1715–17, 13 Drag. Gds. Nov. 1722, 8 Drag. Gds. Sept. 1725; brig.-gen. Mar. 1727; col. 6 Drag. Gds. Jan. 1731, 4 Drag. Gds. May 1735–d.; maj.-gen. 1735; lt.-gen. 1739; gen. 1745; f.m. 1757.
> Page of honour to William III 1700–Aug. 1702; groom of the bedchamber to George II as Prince of Wales and King, Mar. 1718–59 (res.); gov. Chelsea Hospital 1740–d.

After serving under Marlborough, Rich was returned in 1715 for Dunwich, which his father had represented 1689–99. A Whig, he voted for the septennial bill in 1716, but was one of the army officers who were deprived of their regiments for voting against the Government in the division on Lord Cadogan (q.v.) in 1717.[1] Though appointed in 1718 to the household of the Prince of Wales, who was then in opposition, he voted with the Government on the repeal of the Occasional Conformity and Schism Acts and on the peerage bill in 1719. Defeated at Dunwich in 1722, but subsequently brought in for Bere Alston and St. Ives by his friend, Sir John Hobart (q.v.), he was given another regiment, thereafter voting with the Government in all recorded divisions. Retiring from Parliament in

1741, he served with his regiment in the war of the Austrian succession and was present at Dettingen. He died 1 Feb. 1768, worth £100,000.[2]

[1] *Pol. State*, xiv. 80.   [2] *HMC Carlisle*, 238.

S.R.M.

RICHARDS, Bisse (?1715–55), of Wimbledon, Surr.

HINDON   1747–29 Dec. 1755

> b. ?1715, s. of John (or Richard)[1] Richards of St. Andrew's Holborn by Eleanor, da. of George Bisse of Martock, Som. *educ.* Merton, Oxf. 10 May 1732, aged 16; L. Inn 1737. *unm.* *suc.* uncle Stephen Bisse (q.v.) 1746.

Bisse Richards, having inherited a fortune from his maternal uncle in 1746, was returned unopposed for Hindon in 1747 as a government supporter. He died 29 Dec. 1755.

[1] *Misc. Gen. et Her.* (ser. 3), iv. 122–3; Foster, *Al. Ox.* 1715–86, p. 1191.

R.S.L.

RICHARDS, George (*d.*1746), of Long Bredy, nr. Bridport, Dorset.

BRIDPORT   1741–25 Nov. 1746

> o.s. of George Richards of Long Bredy by his w. Anne Parker. *m.* (settlement 11 Nov. 1737) Eleanor, da. of Thomas Brodrepp of Melplash, nr. Bridport, 2s. *suc.* fa. 1724.

George Richards was the son of a Spanish merchant who had bought Long Bredy from the Hurdings and was sheriff of Dorset in 1710. His succession to the manor was unsuccessfully challenged in 1726 by relations, who, having abstracted the page recording his father's marriage from the Litton Cheney register, asserted his illegitimacy.[1] In January 1740 his father-in-law and the Earl of Coventry (q.v.) signed indentures for constructing a new harbour south of Bridport, to which Richards contributed part of the cost; and it was presumably on the Earl's interest that he was returned for the borough in 1741,[2] defeating a government supporter. An opposition Whig, he voted against Walpole's nominee for the chairman of the elections committee, December 1741, abstained on the Hanoverians in 1742 and 1746, and voted against them in 1744. He died 25 Nov. 1746.

[1] Hutchins, *Dorset*, ii. 184, 499.   [2] Ibid. 17; *Proc. Dorset Nat. Hist. and Antiq. Field Club*, xxxiii. 187.

R.S.L.

RICHMOND WEBB, *see* **WEBB, Borlase,** *and* **WEBB, John**

RIDER, Sir Barnham (?1683–1728), of Boughton Monchelsea, nr. Maidstone, Kent.

MAIDSTONE　30 June 1716–1722, 1 June 1723–1727

b. ?1683, o.s. of Thomas Rider, M.P., of Covent Garden and Boughton Monchelsea by Philadelphia, yst. da. of Sir Robert Barnham, 1st Bt., M.P., of Boughton Monchelsea. *educ.* M. Temple 1697; St. John's, Oxf. 16 Nov. 1703, aged 20. *m.* c.29 Nov. 1717,[1] Susan, da. of V.-Adm. James Littleton (q.v.) of North Ockendon, Essex, 2s. 2da. *suc.* fa. c.1704. Kntd. 20 Oct. 1714.

Rider's mother inherited Boughton Monchelsea from her father, Sir Robert Barnham, who represented Maidstone in Parliament. The family owned premises in Broad Street, London, which were leased to the navy pay office.[2] Knighted at George I's accession and returned for Maidstone at a contested by-election in 1716, Rider voted with the Administration, except on the peerage bill which he opposed. In a list of payments in the Sunderland papers,[3] his brother is shown as receiving a payment of £200 through 'Mr. Stanhope', presumably Charles (q.v.). Defeated in 1722 but returned at a by-election in 1723, he was again defeated in 1727, dying 21 Nov. 1728, before his petition came up.

[1] *Hist. Reg.* 1717, chron. p. 47. [2] *Cal. Treas. Bks.* xix. 59; xx. 347. [3] Sunderland (Blenheim) mss D. II, 4.

A.N.N.

RIDGE, Thomas (c.1671–1730), of Portsmouth, Hants.

POOLE　1708–15 Feb. 1711, 1722–1727

b. c.1671, 1st s. of Richard Ridge of Portsmouth, brewer, by Jane Fox of St. Margaret's, Westminster. *m.* Jan. 1697, Elizabeth, da. of Humphrey Ayles of St. Botolph's, Aldgate, 5s. 1da. *suc.* fa. 1691.

Queen's cooper at Portsmouth.

Thomas Ridge, who came of a Portsmouth family, inherited a large brewery there from his father. Returned for Poole as a Whig in 1708, he was expelled from the House of Commons in February 1711 for 'great frauds and abuses' in the supply of beer to the fleet.[1] He was again returned in 1722, did not stand in 1727, and died 10 Feb. 1730.

[1] *CJ*, xvi. 500–2.

R.S.L.

RIDLEY, Matthew (1711–78), of Heaton Hall, Northumb.

NEWCASTLE-UPON-TYNE　1747–1774

b. 14 Nov. 1711, 2nd s. of Richard Ridley, merchant, mayor of Newcastle 1713 and 1732, of Heaton Hall by Margaret, da. of Matthew White, mayor of Newcastle 1703, of Blagdon, Northumb. *educ.* Westminster 1724; St. John's, Oxf. 1727; G. Inn 1728, called 1732, bencher 1749. *m.* (1) 1735, secretly, Hannah (*d.*7 Nov. 1741), da. of Joseph Barnes, recorder of Newcastle, 1s.; (2) 18 Nov. 1742, his 1st cos. Elizabeth, da. of Matthew White of Blagdon, sis. and h. of Sir Matthew White, 1st Bt., 8s. 4da. *suc.* fa. 1739.

Mayor, Newcastle 1733, 1745, 1751, 1759; gov. Merchant Adventurers 1739.

Ridley's grandfather was a successful Newcastle merchant. His father, who married the daughter of a wealthy Newcastle merchant and coal-owner, bought Heaton, where he built the present Hall. Admitted to the Hostman's Company in December 1727 and to the Merchant Adventurers in October 1731, in 1732 he was made an alderman during the mayoralty of his father, who had built up a powerful party in the corporation.[1] Next year he was elected mayor, the youngest man to have held that office. In 1741 he stood unsuccessfully for Newcastle. During the rebellion of 1745, as mayor of Newcastle, he took prompt measures to defend the town against the rebels, receiving an express from the Duke of Newcastle in September,

> authorising me to form companies of his Majesty's well affected subjects in this place, and to grant commissions to officers for the command of the same. Also that stores of arms and ammunition are ordered hither fòrthwith, that the place may be put into the best posture of defence against the enemies of his Majesty in case they make an attempt upon it.[2]

He subsequently received the King's particular thanks from the Duke of Cumberland.[3] Returned unopposed on a compromise as a government supporter in 1747, he spoke, 8 May 1753, in favour of a bill for establishing a census.

He died 6 Apr. 1778.

[1] Add. 27420, f. 59. [2] Ridley to Duncan Forbes (q.v.), *Culloden Pprs.* 223. [3] Brand, *Newcastle*, ii. 511.

E.C.

RIGBY, Richard (1722–88), of Mistley Hall, Essex.

CASTLE RISING　24 Oct. 1745–1747
SUDBURY　1747–1754
TAVISTOCK　1754–8 Apr. 1788

b. Feb. 1722, o.s. of Richard Rigby of Paternoster Row, London and Mistley Hall, Essex by his w. Anne Perry. *educ.* Corpus Christi, Camb. 1738; M. Temple 1738; Grand Tour. *unm.* *suc.* fa. 1730.

Ld. of Trade Dec. 1755–Jan. 1760; sec. to ld. lt. [I] Jan. 1757–Mar. 1761; master of the rolls [I] Nov. 1759–*d.*; P.C. [I] June 1760; jt. vice-treasurer [I] Dec. 1762–July 1765, Jan.–June 1768; paymaster gen. June 1768–Mar. 1782.

The son of a woollen draper, who became factor to the South Sea Company, Rigby inherited as a minor an estate in Essex, with a rent roll of £1,100 a year.[1] Coming of age in 1743, he joined White's in 1744, at the same time as his great friend, the younger Horace Walpole, whose brother, the 2nd Earl of Orford, brought him into Parliament in 1745, in spite of being asked by Oxford university not to do so, as a punishment for assaulting a proctor. His political mentor was Thomas Winnington (q.v.), who, according to Horace Walpole, taught him

> to think it sensible to laugh at the shackles of morality, and having early encumbered his fortune by gaming he found his patron's maxims but too well adapted to retrieve his desperate fortunes.[2]

After Winnington's death in 1746, Rigby, like Horace Walpole, went over to the Prince of Wales, who

> promised to assist him with £1,000 if he would go down to stand for Sudbury on his interest, which he did, and though so populous a town, and in which he did not know one man, he carried his election[3]

against a government candidate, much to Pelham's annoyance.[4] When a petition was brought against him, accusing him of carrying the election by bringing down a party of prize fighters to intimidate the returning officer and the electors, he defended himself with such vigour that the matter was allowed to drop.

In addition to the £1,000, of which only £900 was paid, Frederick had promised to make Rigby a groom of his bedchamber, but, after keeping him waiting for two years, gave the post to William Trevanion (q.v.) in 1749.[5] On this Rigby broke with the Prince, transferring his allegiance to the Duke of Bedford, who lent him money to pay his debts.[6] His and Horace Walpole's names were struck out of a Leicester House list, dated 29 Apr. 1749, of persons to receive office on the Prince's accession, in which Rigby had figured as a clerk of the Green Cloth.[7] Thenceforth he became Bedford's accredited representative in the House of Commons, sitting for the Duke's pocket borough of Tavistock till his death, 8 Apr. 1788.

> [1] *Gent. Mag.* 1788, pp. 369–70. [2] Walpole to Hanbury Williams, 25 June 1746; *Mems. Geo. II*, iii. 66–67. [3] *Corresp. H. Walpole* (Yale ed.), xxx. app. 5. [4] Pelham to Horace Walpole sen., 4 Sept. 1747, Add. 9186, f. 105. [5] *Corresp. H. Walpole*, ut supra. [6] *Gent. Mag.* ut supra. [7] Add. 47092.

R.R.S.

RIVETT, Thomas (c.1713–63), of Derby.

DERBY   20 Dec. 1748–1754

> *b.* c.1713, o.s. of Thomas Rivett, mayor of Derby, by Elizabeth, da. of A. Eaton of Derby. *educ.* I. Temple 1731–2, called 1739. *m.* 26 Apr. 1749, Anne, da. of Rev. Peter Sibley, of Ilam, Som., 2s. 1da. His da. m. John Carnac (q.v.).
> Sheriff, Derbys. 1757–8.

On the death of John Stanhope (q.v.) in 1748, his kinsman, Thomas Stanhope, was put up for Derby by the Duke of Devonshire and Lord Chesterfield, joint patrons of the borough. The corporation undertook to support Stanhope; but eight days before the election the Duke of Devonshire was informed by his friends on that body that one of their number,

Thomas Rivett, 'the Duke's chief friend and manager' at Derby, had unexpectedly

> declared himself a candidate, which has broke into your Grace's interest . . . We shall need the assistance of all the outvoters. Are afraid the election will be very precarious and also expensive.

And a day later:

> The opposition made by Mr. Rivett . . . is very surprising to us all . . . As affairs are now circumstanced if anything could be done to prevail upon Mr. Rivett to decline standing, it would be very well, and seems to be the only chance we have.[1]

The Duke replied:

> I am afraid the election will be very precarious if Mr. Rivett persists; which I imagine he now is so engaged that he cannot be prevailed upon not to do; and to attempt to persuade without hope of success might not be so proper . . . it is evident to me by the names that have been sent up it is not for Mr. Rivett's sake that this is done and it would be surprising if anyone that sincerely wishes him well should advise him to it. Instances have been frequent of families suffering greatly by being chose for towns where they reside. It must be a large estate to support the expense that must attend it. As to these gentlemen that used to be in the Whig interest and have now set up Mr. Rivett, I suppose the pretext is that they do not know Captain Stanhope and that he is not of the county and that some of the county should have been set up.

Rivett's return by a large majority was most embarrassing to the Duke, who foresaw that he would be suspected of having 'acted a double part' in the affair.[2] This unfounded suspicion was voiced by the 2nd Lord Egmont, who in his electoral survey, c.1749–50, wrote: 'Rivett may be gained to act independently of the Duke, since it can never be owned that he owes his election to the Duke of Devonshire, who played false to Chesterfield at the last choice'. At the next general election Rivett was persuaded not to stand by the promise of 'a place in some of the inferior commissions, and in the meantime £300 a year' from the secret service money.[3] He died, still in receipt of his pension, 6 Apr. 1763.

> [1] Walpole to Mann, 26 Dec. 1748; mayor of Derby and others to Devonshire, 6 Dec., T. Gisborne and others to Devonshire, 12 Dec. and J. Gisborne jun. and others to Devonshire, 13 Dec. 1748, Devonshire mss. [2] To Gisborne, 15 Dec. 1748, ibid. [3] Namier, *Structure*, 435 n. 2.

E.C.

ROBARTES, Hon. Francis (1650–1718), of Truro, Cornw. and Twickenham, Mdx.

BOSSINEY	8 Mar. 1673–1679
CORNWALL	1679–1681, Aug. 1685–1687
LOSTWITHIEL	1689–1690
CORNWALL	1690–1695
TREGONY	1695–1702
BODMIN	2 Dec. 1702–1708
LOSTWITHIEL	20 Dec. 1709–1710
BODMIN	1710–3 Feb. 1718

bap. 6 Jan. 1650, 4th s. of John Robartes, 1st Earl of Radnor, by his 2nd w. Letitia Isabella, da. of Sir John Smith of Bidborough, Kent. *educ.* Chelsea sch.; Christ's, Camb. 1663. *m.* (1) lic. 13 July 1678, Penelope, da. of Sir Courtenay Pole, 2nd Bt., M.P., of Shute, Devon, *s.p.*; (2) Lady Anne Fitzgerald, da. of Wentworth, 17th Earl of Kildare [I], wid. of Hugh Boscawen of Tregothnan, Cornw., 2s.

Commr. of revenue [I] 1692–1704; P.C. [I] Mar. 1692; teller of the Exchequer 1704–10; commr. of revenue [I] Oct. 1710–14; vice-pres. of Royal Society.

A composer of music and a distinguished scholar, Robartes was returned for Bodmin as a Whig in 1715 by his nephew Charles Bodvile Robartes, M.P., 2nd Earl of Radnor, voting for the septennial bill in 1716. He died 3 Feb. 1718. His eldest son, John, succeeded to the Radnor title in 1741.

E.C.

ROBERTS, Gabriel (*b.* c.1665), of Ampthill, Beds.

MARLBOROUGH 1713–1715, 13 May 1717–1727
CHIPPENHAM 1727–1734

b. c.1665, 2nd s. of William Roberts of St. Katherine Cree, London, citizen and vintner, by Martha, da. of Francis Dashwood, Turkey merchant and alderman of London, sis. of Sir Samuel Dashwood, M.P., ld. mayor of London 1702–3, and Sir Francis Dashwood, 1st Bt., M.P., of West Wycombe, Bucks. *m.* (1) 25 Aug. 1687, at Fort St. George, India, Elizabeth, da. of Charles Proby, sometime of Fort St. George, sis. of William Proby of Fort St. George and Elton, Hunts., *s.p.*; (2) Mary, da. of Sir Francis Wenman, 1st Bt., M.P., of Caswell, Oxon., sis. of Richard Wenman, M.P., 1st Visct. Wenman of Tuam [I], 1s.

Receiver of sea customs at Fort St. George 1688–9; dep. gov. of Fort St. David, Madras, 1702–3, 1704–9; second of council at Fort St. George 1702–9; director S. Sea Co. 1724–33.

Gabriel Roberts, of a Beaumaris family, was the grandson of Lewis Roberts of the East India Company, merchant and writer, and nephew of Sir Gabriel Roberts, deputy governor of the Levant Company, who died in 1715, aged 85. Having entered the East India Company's service as a writer, he arrived at Fort St. George in June 1683.[1] Returning to England in 1689, he was again sent out in 1701, taking his seat as second of council to Governor Thomas Pitt (q.v.) on 11 June 1702. When Pitt left India in October 1709, Roberts resigned his post at Fort St. David but did not himself leave for England till 1711.[2] He appears to have acquired a property at Ampthill belonging to the Bruces, by whom he was returned as a Tory at Marlborough in 1713. He lost his seat there at the general election of 1715, but recovered it on petition in May 1717. He now supported the Administration, voting for the repeal of the Occasional Conformity and Schism Acts and the peerage bill, on which he was classed as 'doubtful,' to be spoken to by Sunderland.

Re-elected in 1722 for Marlborough, he transferred in 1727 to Chippenham, voting with the Opposition on the arrears of the civil list in 1729 but thereafter with the Government. He did not stand again and the date of his death is not known. His son was not John Roberts, Henry Pelham's secretary, as suggested in the *DNB*, but Philip, the father of Wenman Coke (q.v.), ancestor of the earls of Leicester.

[1] H. D. Love, *Vestiges of Old Madras*, i. 483; Lipscomb, *Bucks.* iii. 132; *Recs. of Ft. St. George, Diary and Consultation Bk.* 1688, p. 109. [2] *Diary and Consultation Bk.* 1689, p. 17; 1702, p. 48; *Recs. of Ft. St. George, Despatches from England*, 1701–6, p. 47; *Despatches to England*, 1702–11, pp. 8, 113, 117, 143.

R.S.L.

ROBERTS, John (*d.* 1731), of Plas Newydd, Denb.

DENBIGH BOROUGHS 1710–1713, 1715–1722

1st s. of Hugh Roberts of Havod-y-Bwch, Denb. by Anne, da. and h. of Richard Wynn Jones of Plas Newydd. *m.* (1) 1693, Susannah (*d.* 19 Jan. 1722), da. and eventually h. of William Parry of Llwyn Ynn, Denb., 3s. *d.v.p.* 1da.; (2) Jane, da. of Sir Walter Bagot, 3rd Bt., M.P., of Blithfield, Staffs., wid. of Morris Jones of Llanrhyadr, Denb.[1]

Sheriff, Denb. 1705–6.

Roberts was brought in as a Tory by the Myddeltons of Chirk Castle, near which he owned an estate.[2] Absent from the division on the septennial bill in 1716, he voted against the repeal of the Occasional Conformity and Schism Acts and the peerage bill in 1719. His name was sent to the Pretender in 1721 as a probable supporter in the event of a rising.[3] Also in 1721 the South Sea committee of the House of Commons disclosed that he was one of the Members who had been credited with stock by the Company without paying for it, in his case £1,000 at 178 on 1 Mar. 1720, with the right to sell it back to the Company whenever he chose, receiving the increase in the price as 'profit'.[4] In 1722 he had to give up his seat to Robert Myddelton (q.v.), on whose behalf he actively canvassed.[5] He died 4 Sept. 1731, leaving an estate of about £2,000 p.a. to his daughter.[6]

[1] W. M. Myddelton, *Chirk Castle Accounts*, 372n.; J. W. Lloyd, *Powys Fadog*, iii. 42; iv. 184. [2] NLW, Chirk Castle mss E. 455–60. [3] Stuart mss 65/16. [4] *CJ*, xix. 573–8. [5] Chirk Castle mss E. 469, 674. [6] *Hist. Reg.* 1731, chron. p. 42.

P.D.G.T.

ROBERTS, *see also* COKE, Wenman

ROBINS, John (c.1714–54), of Stafford.

STAFFORD 1747–1754

b. c.1714, 1st s. of William Robins, mayor of Stafford 1719, 1731, 1740, by Catherine, da. of William Abnett, mayor of Stafford 1706, 1720. *educ.* M. Temple 1731, called 1737. *suc.* fa. 1744.[1]

In 1747 John Robins, a lawyer, stood single for Stafford against two government candidates, one of whom withdrew, recognising that it was impossible to defeat him.[2] Classed as Opposition he was regarded by the 2nd Lord Egmont as a possible supporter in the next reign.

In 1752 Robins became involved with Anne, daughter of William Northey (q.v.) and widow of John Whitby, a Staffordshire gentleman who died in the previous year. Finding herself with child and apparently abandoned by Robins, she privately married, 23 Sept., an elderly neighbouring admirer, Sir William Wolseley, 5th Bt. Soon afterwards she received a proposal of marriage from Robins, to whom she was married in October, the clergyman being persuaded on the ground of her condition to antedate the marriage to June in order to preserve her character. She then brought an action against Wolseley, alleging that he had forcibly married her by doping her into insensibility, while Robins swore to the marriage in June, producing the marriage register in evidence. The court decided against her; the clergyman then confessed; Robins, who fled to France, died shortly afterwards, 17 Dec. 1754; but the lady, who also absconded, lived to marry a fourth husband, Christopher Hargrave, a Chancery solicitor.[3]

[1] *Staffs. Parl. Hist.* (Wm. Salt Arch. Soc.), ii. (2), pp. 259–60. [2] Anson to Bedford, 23 June 1747, Bedford mss. [3] *Gent. Mag.* 1755, p. 191; *Corresp. of Edmund Burke* (1961 ed.), iii. 373 n. 5.

A.N.N.

ROBINSON, George, of Lombard St., London and More Place, Bucks.

GREAT MARLOW 14 May 1731–3 Apr. 1732

Nothing is known of Robinson's career before 1727, when he was 'a broker in Exchange-alley', with a record of ruining his clients. Among these were three directors of the Charitable Corporation, a semi-philanthropic concern, which lent small sums to poor persons on pledges at legal interest, to prevent them from falling into the hands of pawn-brokers. All three having become heavily indebted to Robinson, on account of stock exchange losses which they were unable to meet, they entered into a partnership with him and one Thomson, the Corporation's warehouse keeper, in a scheme for borrowing money from the Corporation on fictitious pledges 'to stockjob and make fortunes by', meaning 'to return that money to the Company's account when their turns were served'.[1] By 1731 £356,000 was drawn out in this way by Thomson and paid to Robinson without arousing the suspicions of the other directors. About £200,000 of this was locked up in shares of the Corporation, which had been bought for re-sale on a rise but could not be sold because Robinson had pledged them to his own creditors. Nearly £500,000 of York Buildings Company stock was bought and sold by Robinson at a handsome profit, for none of which he ever accounted to his partners. Considerable sums were expended on keeping up the price of shares purchased and paying blackmail to persons who had guessed what was going on. None of the partners appears to have made much out of these transactions except Robinson, who bought an estate near Great Marlow, carrying with it an interest in that borough, for which he was returned at a by-election towards the end of the session of 1731.

Robinson did not take his seat that session and before the next one he and Thomson had fled the country to avoid an inquiry, which had become inevitable. A fortnight after his flight he was made a bankrupt on the application of the Corporation, to whom he owed £46,000 in his capacity of its banker and agent, in addition to the defalcations of the partnership. In February 1732 he was ordered by the House of Commons to attend in connexion with charges brought against him at a select committee, which had been appointed to inquire into the Corporation's affairs. In March an Act was passed providing that if he did not appear before the end of the month he would be declared a felon and his property forfeited to the Crown. On his failure to comply he was expelled the House; a motion was passed declaring him to have been guilty of breaches of trust and fraudulent practices; his property was made over to the Corporation for the relief of the sufferers; and next year the estate at Great Marlow was sold by public auction.[2] The date of his death is unknown.

[1] *HMC Egmont Diary*, i. 267–8; *Reports of Committee of House of Commons on the Charitable Corporation*, 1732, 1733, passim; Cholmondeley (Houghton) mss 68; see also GRANT, Sir Archibald, SUTTON, Sir Robert, and BOND, Denis.

R.R.S.

ROBINSON, Luke (*d.* 1773), of Elloughton on Brough, nr. Hull, Yorks.

HEDON 1741–4 Mar. 1742, 11 Feb. 1747–1754

3rd s. of Charles Robinson of Kingston-upon-Hull. *educ.* G. Inn 1720, called 1722, bencher 1743. *m.*, 1s. 3da.

Shortly before the general election of 1741 Robinson, a practising barrister, of a Hull family, invited Walpole to name a candidate to join with him in contesting Hedon, a borough controlled by William Pulteney (q.v.). He wrote:

I do not in the least doubt succeeding, and electing such person with me as I shall join, as I could easily convince you. Mr. Pulteney has not any personal interest there, or but very little, 'tis his money must do whatever he doth there, and though he should spend £10,000 I am very well satisfied he will not be able to carry one Member against me, and as to a petition, I am not under any concern about that, for I assure myself of a legal majority, and I do not suppose that the House will go an extraordinary length against justice to oblige Mr. Pulteney.

When Walpole refused, on the ground of his friendship for Pulteney's brother, General Harry Pulteney (q.v.), one of the sitting Members, Robinson replied:

I cant in my poor judgment think it can by any means be for your service to permit Mr. Wm. Pulteney to keep the borough, if you can prevent it, but you are the best judge of that; however I am determined to push it quite through and do not in the least doubt of carrying both the Members by an unquestionable majority, and therefore I am not in the least afraid of a petition. I am now only to beg the favour of you to leave me at my liberty to join such gentleman as I think proper. The gentleman I propose to join is heartily in your interest, and one you cannot have any objection to.[1]

Robinson's election partner was Francis Chute, who was returned with him against Pulteney's candidates. After Walpole's fall Pulteney, now in command of the House of Commons, not only had them unseated but caused Robinson to be prosecuted for bribery, of which he was convicted at the York assizes in 1743, thereby incurring a penalty of £500 under the anti-bribery Act of 1729.[2] He stood again unsuccessfully for Hedon at by-elections in 1744 and 1746, each time petitioning, but withdrawing his petition on the first occasion. In 1746 his petition was heard at the bar of the House of Commons, where ministers wanted to show the King that Pulteney, now Lord Bath, 'had not the interest he boasted'. After the sitting Member, Bath's brother-in-law, had been voted not duly elected, the question was raised whether Robinson was not incapacitated from sitting by his conviction for bribery. Pelham, Pitt, Fox, Legge, and Hume Campbell spoke for him, opposed by Bootle, Dr. Lee, Gundry, Lord Strange, and Prowse. The debate lasted till 11 at night, when he was awarded the seat by 139 to 104, the Prince's people and 'the all-opposing Tories' voting in the minority.[3] Re-elected in 1747 after a contest, he was granted a secret service pension of £800 a year, which he lost when he was defeated at Hedon in 1754.[4] He did not stand again, dying in 1773 (will proved 21 Aug.)[5]

[1] 3 and 16 Feb. 1741, Cholmondeley (Houghton) mss. [2] Gent. Mag. 1743, p. 388; L. Twells, Lives of Pocock etc. ii. 6. [3] HMC Polwarth, v. 202. [4] Add. 33038, f. 415. [5] PCC 342 Stevens.

R.R.S.

ROBINSON (afterwards **ROBINSON MORRIS**), **Matthew** (1713–1800), of Monks Horton, nr. Hythe, Kent.

CANTERBURY 1747–1761

b. 6 Apr. 1713, 1st s. of Matthew Robinson of Edgeley and West Layton, Yorks. by Elizabeth, da. of Robert Drake of Cambridge, gd.-da. and h. of Thomas Morris of Monks Horton; bro.-in-law of Edward Montagu (q.v.). educ. Westminster 1723–9; L. Inn 1730; Trinity Hall, Camb. 1731, fellow 1734–d. unm. suc. mother to Monks Horton 1746 and took add. name of Morris; fa. 1778; cos. Richard as 2nd Baron Rokeby [I] 10 Oct. 1794.

The brother of Mrs. Montagu, the well-known blue-stocking, Robinson was returned for Canterbury in 1747 after succeeding to his mother's Kentish estates. Classed as Opposition, he co-operated with Leicester House in the attacks on General Philip Anstruther (q.v.) in March 1751, till they were suspended by the death of the Prince of Wales.[1] He also spoke on the regency bill. In the following session he supported opposition motions to reduce the army and the land tax,[2] and opposed the forfeited estates bill.[3] Re-elected in 1754, when he was classed as 'Whig, against',[4] he died 30 Nov. 1800.

[1] Add. 47073. [2] Walpole, Mems. Geo. II, i. 141–2, 213, 218. [3] Add. 32726, f. 221. [4] Add. 33034, f. 177.

R.R.S.

ROBINSON, Nicholas (d. 1753), of Thicket, Yorks.

WOOTTON BASSETT 1734–1741

4th s. of Humphrey Robinson of Thicket by Rebecca, da. of Nicholas More of Austhorpe, Yorks. m. 4 Feb. 1728, Sarah, da. of William Vavasour of Weston, Yorks., wid. of William Collingwood, s.p. suc. bro. at Thicket.
    Lt. R.N. 1727, capt. 1735.

Nicholas Robinson was descended from a merchant and alderman of London, whose son settled at Thicket about the beginning of the seventeenth century.[1] Returned as a Whig for Wootton Bassett in 1734, he voted for the Spanish convention in 1739, and was absent from the division on the place bill in 1740. Defeated in 1741, he did not stand again. While in Parliament he was captain of a sloop to prevent smuggling, at £500 p.a.[2] On 16 June 1743 he was court martialled at Sheerness and fined 12 months' pay for defrauding the Government of £138. 18s. by false accounts.[3] He died 1 Feb. 1753.

[1] Fam. Min. Gent. (Harl. Soc. xxxix), 990; Genealogist, n. s. xxvi. 226–8. [2] Gent. Mag. 1739, p. 307. [3] Charnock, Biog. Navalis, iv. 302–3.

R.S.L.

ROBINSON, Thomas (1695–1770), of Newby, Yorks.

THIRSK 1727–1734
CHRISTCHURCH 30 Dec. 1748–1761

> *b.* 24 Apr. 1695, 4th s. of Sir William Robinson, 1st Bt. (q.v.). *educ.* Westminster 1708; Trinity, Camb. 1712, fellow 1718; M. Temple 1723. *m.* 13 July 1737, Frances, da. of Thomas Worsley of Hovingham, Yorks., 2s. 6da. K.B. 26 June 1742; *cr.* Baron Grantham 7 Apr. 1761.
> Sec. Paris Embassy 1723–30; ambassador at Vienna 1730–48; jt. plenipotentiary Aix-la-Chapelle 1748; ld. of Trade 1748–9; master of the great wardrobe 1749–54, 1755–61; P.C. 29 Mar. 1750; sec. of state, southern dept. Mar. 1754–Nov. 1755; jt. postmaster gen. 1765–6.

Robinson owed his appointment to Paris in 1723 to the Duke of Newcastle, with whom he had been intimately connected ever since they were at Westminster school.[1] Returned in 1727 for Thirsk on the Frankland interest, his eldest brother, for whom the seat had originally been intended, having resigned his pretensions to him,[2] he was absent, presumably on account of his diplomatic duties, from all the recorded divisions of that Parliament. He did not stand in 1734, by which time he had become ambassador at Vienna, where he served for 18 years.

In 1746 Robinson informed Newcastle and Pelham that his wife's uncle, Frederick Frankland (q.v.), would be calling on them to discuss the question of his standing at the forthcoming general election for York, which his father had represented for nearly a quarter of a century.[3] There would, he understood,

> be little difficulty in recovering our old family interest in that town were I present, but this last can neither consist with my duty or inclination to persevere in my constancy to go through with the foreign work which I have upon my hands at this court.

While willing to sacrifice the opportunity of re-entering Parliament to the needs of the public service, he ventured to point out that as soon as 'the great business of a general peace shall be over' he was anxious to return home; and that although

> my private inclination would most certainly lead me to look rather after absolute ease and commodiousness, such as my great friends might possibly secure for an old faithful servant, yet were the mite of a single vote for Parliament to be of any use, upon my return, at its due time, to his Majesty's service, there was nothing that I would not risk in the fatigue of that new duty.

To Pelham he added:

> As the crisis of my little fortunes is very probably at no great distance, and the present incident about the York election gives me such an indispensable occasion to breathe out my most secret desires for the sake of my little numerous family, I cannot but conjure you in particular to be thinking of me, for one moment, with Mr. Frankland, in that light, which he is always thinking of me and mine in; my absence, and long

disuse as to private interests at home, make me very unfit to think for myself.

In the event Robinson did not stand, remaining at Vienna till 1748, when he was sent to Aix-la-Chapelle to act as Newcastle's watchdog on Sandwich. After the conclusion of the peace negotiations he was brought into Parliament by Pelham, with a seat at the board of Trade (£1,000 p.a.), from which he was soon afterwards transferred to the great wardrobe (£2,000 p.a.). 'Believe me, Sir', he wrote in thanks to Pelham,

> with such a great disuse of my mother tongue, and with a habitude of thinking more than of speaking, which is so necessary to us foreigners, nothing but a good heart and the mite of a single vote is to be expected from me ...[4]

Notwithstanding these disabilities, Newcastle in 1750 confessed that 'if I were to choose for the King, the Parliament, and myself I would prefer Sir Thomas Robinson to any man living' to be secretary of state.[5] On Pelham's death Newcastle appointed him to that post, carrying with it the leadership of the House of Commons, both of which he thankfully surrendered to return to his old post in 1755. He died 30 Sept. 1770.

[1] Newcastle to Rockingham, 18 Sept. 1766, Add. 32977, ff. 91–95. [2] Robinson to Newcastle, 22 July 1727, Add. 32687, f. 223. [3] Robinson to Pelham and Newcastle, 19 Nov. N.S. 1746, Newcastle (Clumber) mss; Add. 32688, f. 190. [4] Robinson to Pelham, 16 Dec. N.S. 1748, Newcastle (Clumber) mss. [5] Coxe, *Pelham*, ii. 387.

R.R.S.

ROBINSON, Thomas (?1702–77), of Rokeby, Yorks.

MORPETH 1727–1734

> *b.* ?1702, 1st s. of William Robinson of Rokeby by Anne, da. and h. of Robert Walters of Cundall, Yorks.; cos. of Matthew Robinson (q.v.). *educ.* Exeter, Oxf. 22 June 1721, aged 18; M. Temple 1722; Grand Tour. *m.* (1) 25 Oct. 1728, Lady Elizabeth Howard (*d.*10 Apr. 1739), da. of Charles, 3rd Earl of Carlisle, wid. of Nicholas Lechmere (q.v.), 1st Baron Lechmere, *s.p.*; (2) 31 May 1743, at Barbados, Elizabeth Booth, wid. of Samuel Salmon of Barbados, ironmonger, *s.p. suc.* fa. 1720; *cr.* Bt. 10 Mar. 1731.
> Ensign 1 Ft. Gds. 1727; res. 1731; commr. of excise Nov. 1735–Feb. 1742; gov. of Barbados 1742–Apr. 1747.

Robinson was descended from a London merchant, who bought a Yorkshire estate in 1610. An amateur architect, he completely rebuilt the family seat at great expense, improving its name from Rookby to Rokeby. Returned for Morpeth in 1727 on the interest of George Bowes (q.v.), for which he paid £1,200,[1] he voted regularly with the Government, sending valuable accounts of debates to his father-in-law, Lord Carlisle. His first speech, 11 Mar. 1731, was against a proposal that common soldiers should be entitled to obtain their discharge after a certain period of service. In 1732 he introduced a petition from the sufferers of the frauds in the Charitable Corporation, becoming chairman of the committee set up by the Commons to investigate the affair. He spoke for the Government on the army in 1732 and 1733, observing that he was the only 'Member out of employment' who had done so.[2] In 1733 he spoke for the excise bill, according to his brother-in-law, Charles Howard (q.v.), 'so fast nobody could hear him, and towards the last, the House not being very silent, he was a little out'. However, in the debate on the repeal of the Septennial Act in 1734 Howard reported that Robinson's speech had 'gained the approbation of everybody, and I hope will be of real service to him, so that he will make a voyage to Cornwall, or have some employment'.[3] The voyage to Cornwall referred to the fact that, having no prospect of being re-elected for Morpeth, his only hope of returning to Parliament was by way of a government seat in that county. He did not obtain a seat but in 1735 he was made a commissioner of excise at £1,000 a year. In 1736 he asked the 1st Lord Egmont to put him up for a trusteeship of the Georgia Society but when Egmont proposed him several objected on the ground that 'he would give us a great deal of trouble', so it was decided to tell him that no trustees were being elected that year.[4] Having ruined himself by his improvements at Rokeby, he was appointed governor of Barbados in 1742 with a salary of £2,000 a year. Next year he married a West Indian heiress, who refused to accompany him when he was recalled in 1747 at the request of the local house of assembly, who complained, *inter alia*, that he had been diverting defence funds to rebuilding Government House. He was never employed again but in 1750 he obtained a pension of £500 a year.

A noted pest to persons of high rank or office, he is said to have been very troublesome to the Earl of Burlington, and when in his visits to him he was told his lordship had gone out, would desire to be admitted to look at the clock, or play with a monkey that was kept in the hall, in hopes of being sent for by the Earl. This he had so frequently done that all the household were tired of him. At length it was concerted amongst the servants that he should receive a summary answer to his usual questions; and accordingly, at his next coming, the porter, as soon as he had opened the gate, and without waiting for what he had to say dismissed him with these words, 'Sir, his lordship is gone out, the clock stands, and the monkey is dead'.

Before his death, 3 Mar. 1777, his extravagance forced him to sell Rokeby.[5]

[1] See MORPETH. [2] *HMC Egmont Diary*, i. 158, 219–20, 315. [3] *HMC Carlisle*, 105, 133. [4] *HMC Egmont Diary*, ii. 247, 372. [5] Add 33029, ff. 9–17, 37; Churchill, *Poetical Works* (1804), ii. 183.

R.R.S.

ROBINSON, Sir William, 1st Bt. (?1654–1736), of Newby, Yorks.

NORTHALLERTON	1689–1695
YORK	1698–1722

b. ?1654, 1st s. of Thomas Robinson, Turkey merchant, of York by Elizabeth, da. of Charles Tancred of Arden, Yorks. *educ.* St. John's, Camb. 6 Feb. 1671, aged 16; G. Inn 1674. *m.* 8 Sept. 1679, Mary, da. of George Aislabie of Studley Royal, Yorks., sis. of John Aislabie (q.v.), 5s. 1da. *suc.* fa. 1676; uncle Sir Metcalfe Robinson, 1st Bt. (1660 creation, M.P. York 1660–79, 1685–7), to Newby 1689; *cr.* Bt. 13 Feb. 1690.

Sheriff, Yorks. 1689–90; alderman, York 1698, res. 1718, ld. mayor 1700.

Robinson was descended from an eminent Hamburg merchant, twice M.P. for York and lord mayor of the city under Elizabeth. Succeeding to the estates of his uncle, who had represented York under Charles II and James II, he sat for the city as a Whig uninterruptedly for nearly a quarter of a century. Returned at the top of the poll in 1715, he voted with the Government on the septennial bill in 1716. In 1719 he voted against them on the repeal of the Occasional Conformity and Schism Acts, and was put down as 'doubtful', to be spoken to by Aislabie, in a list drawn up by Craggs before the peerage bill, on which he did not vote. During the debates on the South Sea bubble, he wrote to Lord Carlisle, 12 Jan. 1721:

I wish the Parliament is able to afford suitable remedies to the present malady; the calamity is so universal that infinite numbers must suffer, [even] if we were unanimous in applying proper plaisters to the hurts done to all degree of people by the vile practice of the directors. There seems a spirit in both Houses to pursue them to condign punishment. Though Mr. Walpole's scheme was carried in our House by a great majority, yet I find the city does not relish the project of ingrafting nine millions to the Bank and India Companies believing the stock cannot rise above 200, which will not answer the expectations of the poor annuitants, nor the subscription people; but if some further aid of Parliament could be had to raise the stock to 300, most people would sit down tolerably easy under their respective losses.

He did not stand in 1722, writing 'I am just wore out in the city's service, so decline the fatigue of Parliament'.[1] He died 22 Dec. 1736.

[1] *HMC Carlisle*, 27.

R.R.S.

RODNEY, George Brydges (1719–92), of Great Alresford, Hants.

SALTASH	13 May 1751–1754
OKEHAMPTON	24 Nov. 1759–1761
PENRYN	1761–1768
NORTHAMPTON	1768–1774
WESTMINSTER	1780–June 1782

bap. 13 Feb. 1719, 1st surv. s. of Henry Rodney of Walton-on-Thames, Surr. by Mary, da. and coh. of Sir Henry Newton, envoy to Tuscany and later judge of the court of Admiralty. *educ.* Harrow c.1730. *m.* (1) 31 Jan. 1753, Jane (*d.* 28 Jan. 1757), da. of Hon. Charles Compton of Eastbourne, Suss., sis. of Charles Compton, 7th Earl of Northampton, 2s.; (2) 1764, Henrietta, da. of John Clies of Lisbon, merchant, 2s. 3da. *suc.* fa. 1737; *cr.* Bt. 22 Jan. 1764; K.B. 14 Nov. 1780; Baron Rodney of Rodney Stoke, Som. 19 June 1782.

Entered R.N. as King's letter boy 1732, lt. 1739, capt. 1742; gov. Newfoundland 1749–50; r.-adm. 1759; c.-in-c. Leeward Is. 1761–3; v.-adm. 1762; gov. Greenwich Hospital 1765–70; r.-adm. of Great Britain 1771; c.-in-c. Jamaica 1771–4; c.-in-c. Leeward Is. and Barbados 1779; v.-adm. of Great Britain 1781.

Rodney belonged to the younger branch of a good Somersetshire family, related to James Brydges, 1st Duke of Chandos, who in 1739 recommended him to Admiral Haddock (q.v.). A year later Chandos advised him to approach Sir Charles Wager (q.v.) rather than Walpole for promotion, as he was 'a very young lieutenant' and there were 'many on the list before him'.[1] Making 'a fortune by very gallant behaviour'[2] during the war, he was taken up by the Duke of Bedford, the first lord of the Admiralty. After the peace he was put up by Bedford for Launceston at a by-election in 1750, but withdrew on finding his prospects hopeless. A few months later he wrote to his patron:

> Your Grace having honoured me with your protection during the late war, and still continuing to bestow favour on me, obliges me to take this method of expressing my gratitude, and to assure your Grace that the fortune I made, by your kind assistance, shall ever be devoted to your service, and that nothing shall ever influence me to desert the interest I have the honour to embark in.[3]

A year later, he was returned for Saltash on the Admiralty interest. He died 24 May 1792.

[1] C. H. Baker, *Jas. Brydges, Duke of Chandos*, 219. [2] Walpole to Mann, 26 Dec. 1748. [3] Rodney to Bedford, 22 and 24 Jan. and 10 May 1750, Bedford mss.

E.C.

ROGERS, Sir John, 2nd Bt. (1676–1744), of Blachford, in Cornwood, Devon.

PLYMOUTH 1713–1722

bap. 14 June 1676, o. surv. s. of Sir John Rogers, 1st Bt., of Blachford, common councilman of Plymouth 1684–*d.*,[1] M.P. Plymouth 1698–1700, by Mary, da. of Spencer Vincent, alderman of London, of Lombard St., London. *m.* 9 May 1698, Mary, da. of Sir Robert Henley of the Grange, nr. Farnborough, Hants, prothonotary of the King's bench, 5s. (3 *d.v.p.*) 5da. *suc.* fa. Apr. 1710.

Recorder, Plymouth 1713, mayor 1722–3, 1741–2.

Rogers, whose family had settled in Plymouth by the seventeenth century, was descended from the

Rev. John Rogers, the first martyr of Queen Mary's reign. Amassing a fortune from pilchard curing, his father purchased a considerable estate in the town, including apparently the manor of West Hooe, and was made a baronet in 1698.[2] Returned as a Whig for Plymouth in Anne's last Parliament and re-elected in 1715, Rogers voted erratically, opposing the septennial bill in 1716, supporting the repeal of the Occasional Conformity and Schism Acts, but opposing the peerage bill in 1719. He did not stand again, withdrawing at the last moment, but was active in Plymouth politics until his death 21 Jan. 1744.

[1] *HMC 9th Rep.* 281, 282. [2] Add. 24121, f. 200; Lysons, *Devonshire*, i. cxv; H. F. Whitfield, *Plymouth*, 158.

S.R.M.

ROGERS, John (1708–73), of Blachford, in Cornwood, Devon.

PLYMOUTH 13 June 1739–17 Jan. 1740

bap. 31 Aug. 1708, 1st s. of Sir John Rogers, 2nd Bt. (q.v.). *educ.* New Coll. Oxf. 1724. *m.* 28 Oct. 1742, Hannah, da. of Thomas Trefusis (q.v.) of Trefusis, Cornw., *s.p. suc.* fa. as 3rd Bt. 21 Jan. 1744.

Mayor, Plymouth, March 1728–9, 1743–4, recorder, ?1744; sheriff, Devon 1755–6.

John Rogers stood for the mayoralty of Plymouth in 1728, when passion rose so high that he and the rival candidate, George Treby (q.v.), drew their swords upon one another. On a tie, he was declared elected by a *mandamus* from the King's bench.[1] Returned against a government candidate, Charles Vanburgh (q.v.), in 1739, he was unseated in favour of his opponent and did not stand again. He died 20 Dec. 1773.

[1] H. F. Whitfield, *Plymouth*, 167; R. W. S. Baron, *Mayors and Mayoralties of Plymouth*, 42.

S.R.M.

ROGERS, Nathaniel.

KINGSTON-UPON-HULL 13 Mar. 1717–1727

s. of Alderman John Rogers, mayor of Hull 1652, by Elizabeth, da. of Edward Nelthorp of Barton-on-Humber, Yorks.[1]

Alderman, Hull.

Rogers succeeded his brother-in-law, William Maister (q.v.), at Hull, voting against the Government in the division of 4 June 1717 on Cadogan (q.v.), with them on the repeal of the Occasional Conformity and Schism Acts, and against them on the peerage bill in 1719. Re-elected in 1722, he voted for the government candidate, Sir Henry Hoghton (q.v.), at a by-election in 1724, after 'wishing himself damned if he or his voted thus'.[2]

He did not stand in 1727. The date of his death is unknown.

[1] Ex inf. F. Spencer. [2] J. R. Boyle, 'Story of a Parl. Election', *Hull Times*, 3 Jan. 1903.

R.R.S.

ROLLE, Henry (1708–50), of Stevenstone, nr. Barnstaple, Devon.

DEVON   2 June 1730–1741
BARNSTAPLE   1741–8 Jan. 1748

b. 7 Nov. 1708, 1st s. of John Rolle (q.v.). *educ.* Winchester 1723; New Coll. Oxf. 1725. *unm. suc.* fa. 1730; *cr.* Lord Rolle, Baron of Stevenstone 8 Jan. 1748.

Henry Rolle succeeded his father as a Tory knight of the shire in 1730. In his first Parliament he three times, in successive sessions, 1732–4, introduced a bill for obliging Members after their election to swear in the House to their qualifications, each time being defeated. On 2 Feb. 1733 he spoke against the army estimates, declaring the Pretender to be 'no more than a raw head and bloody bones, but of excellent use' to the ministry as a pretext for 'raising taxes and armies'. Later in the same session he spoke in favour of a 'violent motion' for the outright rejection of the excise bill after Walpole had withdrawn it. He voted against the Government in all recorded divisions.

In the next Parliament Rolle's only reported speech was against the repeal of the Test Act in March 1739.[1] Abstaining from the divisions on the Spanish convention that year and the place bill of 1740, he voted against the motion for Walpole's removal in February 1741. At the general election of 1741 he went over to the Government, writing to Newcastle in February 1742 as 'one who has lost so great an interest by espousing that of the Court', an allusion to his loss of the county seat. Returned unopposed on his own interest for Barnstaple, he voted consistently with the Administration, being put down to Pelham in the Cockpit list of October 1742. While absent from Parliament owing to ill health in March 1743, he wrote to Newcastle referring to 'that Government which is subsisting and for which I have the most inviolable respect, and will spend both my life and fortune to support'. Classed as an 'Old Whig' in 1746, he was raised to the peerage shortly after the general election of 1747, at which he had been re-elected unopposed. In 1748 he came into collision with the lord lieutenant of Devonshire, the 2nd Earl of Orford, over local ecclesiastical patronage. Both appealed to Newcastle, Rolle invoking 'an expense of seven thousand pounds for supporting the government interest at Barnstaple', while Orford asserted that

'since being made a peer Rolle has only once voted and then against the Government'.[2]

Rolle died 17 Aug. 1750.

[1] *HMC Egmont Diary*, i. 315, 332, 346, 360; ii. 31; iii. 47. [2] Add. 32699, f. 50; 32702, f. 185; 32714, f. 444; 32715, f. 154.

S.R.M.

ROLLE, John (1679–1730), of Stevenstone, nr. Barnstaple, Devon.

SALTASH   25 Jan. 1703–1705
DEVON   1710–1713
EXETER   1713–1715
BARNSTAPLE   1715–1722
EXETER   1722–1727
DEVON   1727–6 May 1730

bap. 8 Dec. 1679, 2nd s. of John Rolle by Lady Christiana Bruce, da. of Robert Bruce, M.P., 1st Earl of Ailesbury, and gd.-s. of Sir John Rolle, K.B., M.P. for Barnstaple. *educ.* Queens', Camb. 1696; ? I.Temple Feb. 1697, called June 1705. *m.* Isabella Charlotte, da. of Sir William Walter, 2nd Bt., of Sarsden, Oxon., 4s. 7da. *suc.* e. bro. Robert Rolle, M.P., 1726.

The Rolles, originally wealthy London merchants, purchased Stevenstone in the reign of Henry VIII, becoming one of the richest families in Devonshire, where they owned more than forty manors in 1706.[1] A Tory and a member of the October Club, John Rolle was returned for Barnstaple unopposed on his family's interest in 1715, subsequently sitting for Exeter and the county. He was one of the west country gentlemen in touch with Atterbury's agents during the plot of 1722.[2] His only recorded vote after George I's accession was against the Government on the Hessian troops, shortly before his death, 6 May 1730.

[1] T. Moore, *Devonshire*, 538–9. [2] *Report of the Committee of the House of Commons to examine Christopher Layer and others* (1723), App. F. 11.

S.R.M.

ROLLE, Samuel (1646–1719), of Heanton Satchville, Devon.

CALLINGTON   12 Dec. 1665–1679
DEVON   1680–1681, 1689–1701
CALLINGTON   1701–Nov. 1719

bap. 5 Nov. 1646, 1st s. of Robert Rolle of Heanton Satchville, M.P. Devon 1654, 1656, 1659 and Callington 1660, by Lady Arabella Clinton, da. of Theophilus, 4th Earl of Lincoln. *m.* (1) lic. 7 Feb. 1671, Frances, da. of John Roy, London merchant, *s.p.*; (2) 26 Oct. 1704, Margaret, da. of Roger Tuckfield of Raddon, 2s. *d.v.p.* 2da.

Great-nephew of Henry Rolle, M.P., lord chief justice, Rolle was returned for Callington on his family's interest. No vote of his is recorded after 1715. A member of the October Club, reputed to be a 'furious Jacobite', he held in particular aversion his neighbour John Harris (q.v.) whom he called 'the Hanover rat'.[1] But after his death in November 1719 his widow married Harris, while his sole surviving daughter Margaret married Robert Walpole, later 2nd Earl of Orford.

[1] T. Moore, *Devonshire*, 541–2.

E.C.

ROLT, Edward (1686–1722), of Sacombe, Herts., Harrowby, Lincs., and Spye Park, nr. Chippenham, Wilts.

St. Mawes	1713–1715
Grantham	1715–1722
Chippenham	22 Mar.–22 Dec. 1722

b. 1686, o.s. of Sir Thomas Rolt of Sacombe and Harrowby, sometime pres. of Surat, by Mary, da. of Dr. Thomas Cox, physician in ordinary to Charles II, wid. of Thomas Rolt of Milton Ernest, Beds.[1] *educ.* Merton, Oxf. 7 Nov. 1701, aged 15; L. Inn 1702. *m.* c.1708, Anne, da. of Henry Bayntun, M.P., sis. and h. of John Bayntun of Spye Park, 6s. 2da. *suc.* fa. 1710.

Rolt's father was the son of Edward Rolt of Pertenhall, Bedfordshire, by Mary, daughter of Sir Oliver Cromwell of Hinchingbrooke, Huntingdonshire, the Protector's uncle.[2] After many years in the service of the East India Company, he came home in 1682, buying the Sacombe estate in 1688 for £22,500.[3] Returned in 1715 as a Tory for Grantham, where he owned property, he voted against the Government, except on the septennial bill, when he was absent. He is mentioned in the 6th report of the South Sea committee as having accepted £5,000 stock from the Company on 1 Mar. 1720, in the same circumstances as Sir Robert Chaplin (q.v.), and another £800 on 23 Mar.[4] In 1721 his name was sent to the Pretender as a probable supporter in the event of a rising.[5]

Before the 1722 election Lord Cardigan wrote to Lord Gower:

> I am apt to believe that £300 will do, in case Rolt can be brought to join heartily with anyone . . . I have a project in my head to turn out Rolt, in case he does not do us justice.[6]

He was defeated at Grantham, where he stood jointly with Lord Cardigan's candidate,[7] but was returned for Chippenham, near which his wife had inherited from her brother in 1716 an estate said to be worth nearly £3,000 a year.[8] He died of smallpox 22 Dec. 1722.

[1] *Lics. Vic.-Gen.* (Harl. Soc. xxx), 206; *Lics. Fac. Office* (Harl. Soc. xxiv), 79; *Beds. N. & Q.* iii. 58, 365. [2] *Genealogist*, n.s. xvii. 145–9; Cussans, *Herts.* Broadwater, 161. [3] *HMC Lords*, ii. 353–4. [4] *CJ*, xix. 574, 578. [5] Stuart mss 65/16. [6] Undated, Leveson Gower letter bk. vii. f. 16. [7] I. Garner to John Heathcote, 18 Mar. 1722, I Ancaster 13/B/2, Lincs. Archives Office. [8] *Bland-Burges Pprs.* ed. Hutton, 6.

R.S.L.

ROLT, *see also* **BAYNTUN ROLT**

ROOS, *see* **STANWIX, John**

ROSE, Hugh (1684–1755), of Kilravock, Nairn.

Nairnshire	1708–1710
Ross-shire	1734–1741

b. 1684, 1st s. of Hugh Rose of Kilravock, M.P. [S], by Margaret, da. of Sir Hugh Campbell of Calder, M.P. *m.* (1) 1704, Elizabeth (*d.*1714), da. of Ludovick Grant of Grant, 2s. 1da.; (2) Jean, da. of John Rose of Broadley, 2s. 4da. *suc.* fa. 1732.
Sheriff, Ross 1732–4.

Rose came of an ancient Nairnshire family, who had recently acquired property in Ross-shire,[1] where he was returned in 1708, but was unseated on petition, taking his seat for Nairnshire. In 1715 he unsuccessfully contested Cromartyshire. He did not stand at the next two general elections, actively supporting the candidature of his brother-in-law, Duncan Forbes (q.v.), for Inverness Burghs, where he controlled Nairn.[2] Resigning his sheriffdom of Ross in 1734 to be returned unopposed for that county with the support of Forbes, he voted with the Government on the Spanish convention in 1739 and the place bill in 1740. Defeated in 1741, he stood again unsuccessfully at a by-election in 1746. During the Forty-five he entertained the Young Pretender and the Duke of Cumberland in turn. In 1747 he contemplated standing for Inverness Burghs but desisted.[3]

He died in May 1755.

[1] *Family of Kilravock* (Spalding Club, 1848), 379–427. [2] *More Culloden Pprs.* iii. 88–89. [3] See INVERNESS BURGHS.

R.R.S.

ROSS, Hon. Charles (*d.*1732), of Balnagowan, Ross.

Ross-shire	3 Mar. 1709–1722, 1727–5 Aug. 1732

2nd s. of George, 11th Lord Ross of Halkhead [S], being o.s. by his 2nd w. Lady Jean Ramsay, da. of George, 2nd Earl of Dalhousie [S]. *unm.*
Cornet, King's Regt. Scots Horse 1685; capt. 5 Drags. by 1689, lt.-col. 1694, col. 1695–1715, 1729–*d.*; brig.-gen. 1702; maj.-gen. 1704; lt.-gen. 1707; col.-gen. of all Drag. forces 1711; gen. 1712.

Ross, a professional soldier, who had served under Marlborough, was re-elected unopposed in 1715 for Ross-shire, where his brother, Lord Ross, had presented him with the estate of Balnagowan.[1] A Tory, he spoke against the Address at the opening of the new Parliament, as reflecting on the late Queen, defended the impeached Tory ministers, and opposed an increase of the army to meet a possible invasion, 26 July 1715. About this time he was among the army officers who were dismissed or required to sell their regiments on security grounds.[2] Continuing to speak and vote against the Government, he was elected to the secret committee set up by the House of Commons to inquire into the South Sea Company's affairs after the collapse of the bubble. On 23 Jan. 1721 he told the House that the committee had 'already discovered a train of deepest villainy and fraud that hell ever contrived to ruin a nation'. On 14 Apr. he drew the notice of the House to an extraordinary commission empowering the deputy sheriff of Inverness-shire 'to seize goods and chattels, take up and imprison any person north of the river of Tay, without giving reason therefor, and confine them during his pleasure'. As a result the commission, which was intended by the Squadrone to influence elections in their favour, was rescinded.[3] On 12 May he disclosed that an attempt had been made to bribe him on behalf of John Aislabie (q.v.) by Aislabie's brother-in-law, Thomas Vernon (q.v.), for which he was thanked by the House. He took part in the debates on the amounts to be allowed the South Sea directors out of their confiscated estates. On 16 Apr. 1722 he strenuously opposed Walpole's bill empowering the South Sea Company to sell some of their assets. Defeated at the general election of 1722, he presented a petition, which was shelved, a motion instructing the elections committee to hear it at an early date being defeated by Walpole.

> There were 28 Tories in the majority against Mr. Ross, some on account of Thomas Vernon's [q.v.] affair, and others supposed to have been in the South Sea account, Mr. Ross having been of the secret committee, and discovered some to have had stock taken in for them.

Going over to the Government, he was re-elected unopposed in 1727, speaking for a vote of credit, 7 May 1728,[4] and recovering his regiment in 1729. He continued to speak[5] and vote with the Government till his death, 5 Aug. 1732, leaving his estate to his great-nephew, Charles Ross (q.v.).

[1] A. Ross, *Clan Ross*, 34–35. [2] *Pol. State*, x. 98. [3] Stuart mss 52/57; *Knatchbull Diary*, 18 Jan., 22 Feb. 1723. [4] *Knatchbull Diary*, 24 Oct. 1722; Appendix C. 126–7. [5] *HMC Egmont Diary*, i. 12, 31, 144, 220.

J.M.S.

ROSS, Hon. Charles (1721–45), of Balnagowan, Ross.

ROSS-SHIRE   1741–30 Apr. 1745

b. 9 Feb. 1721, 2nd s. of George, 13th Lord Ross of Halkhead [S], by Lady Elizabeth Kerr, da. of William, 2nd Mq. of Lothian [S]. *unm. suc.* gt.-uncle Gen. Charles Ross (q.v.) to Balnagowan 1732.
   2nd lt. Col. Douglas's regt.of Marines Dec. 1739; lt. and capt. 3 Ft. Gds. 1741.

While still under age Ross, 'a very handsome

young man,'[1] was returned for Ross-shire, where he had inherited his great-uncle's estate. In the division of 16 Dec. 1741 on the chairman of the elections committee, Horace Walpole writes:

> Young Ross, son of a commissioner of customs, and saved from the dishonour of not liking to go to the West Indies, when it was his turn, by Sir Robert's giving him a lieutenancy, voted against us.[2]

A month later, shortly before Walpole's resignation, the 1st Lord Egmont heard

> that Lord Ross had been sent for up from Scotland to influence his son, Mr. Charles Ross, but Mr. Ross had a very good estate independent of his father.[3]

In October 1742 he was included in the Cockpit list of ministerial supporters; but in the division of 10 Dec. 1742 on the Hanoverians he is shown among the opposition absentees, and on 6 Dec. 1743 he was one of the army officers who supported an opposition motion for disbanding the Hanoverians, telling

> a story of a drunken quarrel between an English groom and a Hanoverian soldier on their march into winter quarters, after which the latter had been acquitted by his commanding officer before the party aggrieved had an opportunity of being heard, and producing his evidence.

Denying an imputation that his speech reflected on the King, he said that 'the instance he gave happened after that great person left the army'. The instance, according to the 1st Lord Egmont, 'appeared to the House very frivolous'.[4] He again voted against the Hanoverians in 1744. His death in action at Fontenoy, 30 Apr. 1745, is commemorated in Collins's 'Ode to a Lady', Miss Elizabeth Goddard, Ross's fiancée.

[1] Edw. Digby to John Ward, 16 Apr. 1743, Rylands, Crawford mss. [2] To Mann, 16 Dec. 1741. [3] *HMC Egmont Diary*, iii. 243, 278. [4] Yorke's parl. jnl. *Parl. Hist.* xiii. 140; *HMC Egmont Diary*, ii. 278.

R.R.S.

ROSS MACKYE, *see* **MACKYE**

ROWLEY, William (c.1690–1768), of Tendring Hall, Suff.

TAUNTON   27 Feb. 1750–1754
PORTSMOUTH   1754–1761

b. c.1690, s. of William Rowley of Whitehall. *m.* bef. 1729 (with a 'great fortune'), Arabella, da. and h. of Capt. George Dawson of co. Derry, 4s. *d.v.p.* 1da. K.B. 12 Dec. 1753.
   Entered R.N. 1704, lt. 1708, capt. 1716, r.-adm. 1743, v.-adm. 1744, adm. 1747; ld. of the Admiralty June 1751–Nov. 1756, Apr.–July 1757; adm. of the Fleet 1762.

Rowley entered the navy as a volunteer, serving under Captain, later Sir John, Norris (q.v.). His career was undistinguished until 1741, when he joined the Mediterranean fleet, taking part in

February 1744 in the engagement off Toulon in which he was one of the few flag-officers concerned whose conduct was not called into question. Appointed in August that year to the command of the Mediterranean fleet in succession to Thomas Mathews (q.v.), he presided over a court martial which was conducted with extraordinary partiality to the officer concerned, the son of Sir John Norris.[1] On 30 Apr. 1745 the House of Commons, during its inquiry into the Toulon action, passed a resolution that the trial was 'partial, arbitrary, and illegal'. The Admiralty found that the proceedings were improper and that Rowley was unfit to remain in command. Recalled in July, he never went to sea again.

Notwithstanding this affair Rowley was promoted to be admiral in 1747. In 1749 he was one of a number of admirals and captains who signed an address to the Admiralty against a new article of war subjecting half-pay officers to courts martial and were summoned to the Admiralty, where he spoke against the article.[2] In 1750 he was brought into Parliament by Lord Egremont (Sir Charles Wyndham, q.v.) who wrote on 9 Feb. to Newcastle:

> I pitched upon him, not only from my own personal regard and friendship to him, but likewise from knowing that your Grace honoured him with your protection; and also from my hopes that . . . it might not be disagreeable to the King to have him in Parliament.[3]

Next year he was appointed by the influence of Lord Granville to a seat on the Admiralty board.[4]

He died 1 Jan. 1768.

[1] H. W. Richmond, *Navy in the War of 1739–48*, ii. 141, 252–3.
[2] D. Erskine, *Augustus Hervey Diary*, 81. [3] Add. 32720, f. 90.
[4] Walpole, *Mems. Geo. II*, i. 194.

S.R.M.

ROWNEY, Thomas (?1667–1727), of St. Giles's, Oxford.

OXFORD 1695–1722

b. ?1667, 1st s. of Thomas Rowney, an Oxford attorney. *educ.* St. John's, Oxf. 15 May 1684, aged 16; I. Temple, called 1694. *m.* (lic. 27 May 1691) Elizabeth, da. of Edward Noel of St. Clement Danes, Mdx., 2s. 1da. *suc.* fa. 1694.

Returned unopposed as a Tory for Oxford in 1715, Rowney voted against the Administration in all recorded divisions. During the riots at Oxford on George I's birthday in 1716,

> the major of the regiment ordered the soldiers to go round the town and break all the windows that were not illuminated . . . Poor Tom Rowney's windows were broke, and he himself upon his coming out was insulted by several soldiers who flourished their naked swords over him, but did not cut him.

It was said that if his

> servants had not forced him into his house, he had certainly been murdered. Tom had been at the tavern that afternoon with his Corporation, which made him a little more brave [than] usual.

His name was sent to the Pretender in 1721 as a probable supporter in the event of a rising. He was asked to stand with his son in 1722, but declined, also refusing to stand for the county in 1727.[1] On his death, 26 Aug. 1727, Hearne, the Oxford antiquary, wrote:

> His distemper was an apoplexy, with which he was struck on Sunday last, as he was at dinner at the mayor of Oxford . . . [He] was a very rich man, and some years ago did some service to the poor, when corn being at ten shillings or more a bushel, he sold great quantities to them for four or five shillings a bushel, which I have heard mentioned in his commendation. But as for other acts of charity, I know of none, on the contrary I have often heard him railed at for a stingy, close, miserly man. Yet 'tis certain that he was generally looked upon as an honest Tory, and when he was Member of Parliament, he constantly attended in the Parliament House, a thing which cannot be said of many other Tory Members.[2]

In his will he left £300 towards rebuilding the town hall, as 'some acknowledgement for the trust reposed in me by the city of Oxford, though it was never any profit to me'.[3] The town hall was completed by his son in 1751.

[1] *HMC Portland*, vii. 217–18, 329, 450; Stuart mss 65/16.
[2] Hearne, *Colls.* (Oxf. Hist. Soc.), ix. 344. [3] PCC 61 Brook.

E.C.

ROWNEY, Thomas (?1693–1759), of Dean Farm, Oxon.

OXFORD 1722–27 Oct. 1759

b. ?1693, s. of Thomas Rowney (q.v.). *educ.* poss. Eton 1706–7; St. John's, Oxf. 5 July 1709, aged 16; I. Temple 1709. *m.* 10 Mar. 1756, Miss Trollope. High steward, Oxford 1743–*d.*

Rowney succeeded his father at Oxford as a Tory, voting against the Administration in every recorded division. The second Lord Egmont wrote of him in his electoral survey, c.1749–50:

> It is remarkable of this man, who is a rough clownish country gentleman, always reputed a rank Jacobite, and has drunk the Pretender's health 500 times, that when the Pretender's son came into England he was frightened out of his wits, and ordered his chaplain to pray for King George which he had never suffered him to do in his life before.

He was one of the Tory gentlemen who refused to join the county association in defence of the Hanoverian succession during the 1745 rebellion.[1] He died 27 Oct. 1759.

[1] R. J. Robson, *Oxfordshire Election of 1754*, p. 2.

E.C.

ROYSTON, Visct., *see* **YORKE, Hon. Philip**

RUDGE, Edward (1703–63), of Evesham Abbey, Worcs.

AYLESBURY 21 Feb. 1728–1734
EVESHAM 1741–1754, 23 Apr. 1756–1761

b. 22 Oct. 1703, o.s. of John Rudge (q.v.). *m.* 8 Apr. 1729, Elizabeth, da. and coh. of Matthew Howard of Hackney, Mdx., *s.p. suc.* fa. 1740.

Rudge's sister married Sir William Stanhope (q.v.), on whose interest he was returned as a Whig for Aylesbury in 1728, voting against the Government except on the repeal of the Septennial Act, when he was absent. He did not stand in 1734. Returned unopposed for his father's former seat at Evesham in 1741, he unexpectedly voted with the Government on the Bossiney election petition,[1] but reverted to opposition on the chairman of the elections committee and was not included in the Cockpit list of October 1742. For the rest of this Parliament he voted with the Government, classed in 1746 among Lord Bath's followers.

At the opening of the 1747 Parliament Rudge was classed as Opposition, but in 1753 he was described by his fellow Member for Evesham, Sir John Rushout, as one who had 'not much attended Parliament, always voted with the Government, and is now making interest for the Whig candidates in Oxfordshire'.[2] He died 6 June 1763.

[1] Coxe, *Walpole*, iii. 582. [2] Sir Dudley Ryder's diary, 13 Sept. 1753, Harrowby mss.

A.N.N.

RUDGE, John (1669–1740), of Mark Lane, London, and Evesham Abbey, Worcs.

EVESHAM 11 Mar. 1698–1701, 1702–1734

b. 15 Oct. 1669, 1st surv. s. of Edward Rudge, M.P., London merchant, by Susanna, da. of Sir John Dethick of London. *m.* 10 Jan. 1699, Susanna, da. and h. of John Letten of London, 1s. 1da. *suc.* fa. 1696.

Mayor, Evesham 1691; director, Bank of England 1699–1711, 1715–40 (with statutory intervals), dep. gov. 1711–13, gov. 1713–15; dep. gov. South Sea Co. 1721–30.

Rudge's father, a London merchant, purchased the manor of Evesham in 1664, sitting for the borough in the 1681 and 1690 Parliaments. Rudge, a leading figure in the city of London, represented Evesham with one short interruption for 35 years. Classed as Whig in 1715, he voted against the Administration in every recorded division of George I's reign. Under George II his only recorded vote was against the repeal of the Septennial Act in 1734. He lost his seat at the general election that year, and died 22 Mar. 1740.

A.N.N.

RUSH, John (by 1704–67), of Benhall Lodge, nr. Saxmundham, Suff.

WALLINGFORD 1741–1747

b. bef. Mar. 1704,[1] 1st surv. s. of Samuel Rush (q.v.), by his 2nd w. *unm. suc.* fa. 1725; bought Benhall, 1738.[2]

John Rush was returned at a contested election for Wallingford in 1741 probably as a Tory. He voted consistently against the Government, did not stand again, and died 12 May 1767.

[1] PCC 73 Romney. [2] Aldred, *Manor of Benhall*, 11; Copinget, *Suffolk Manors*, vi. 76.

R.S.L.

RUSH, Samuel (c.1670–1725), of the Park, Southwark, Surr.

SHAFTESBURY 31 Jan.–3 May 1715

b. c.1670, 1st s. of Samuel Rush of Clapham, Surr., vinegar distiller, by Hannah, da. of Ralph Creffield of Colchester. *m.* (1) Elizabeth, da. of William Brown of London, leather seller, at least 2s. 2da.; (2) Martha, da. of William Clark of London, brewer, at least 3s. 2da.[1] *suc.* fa. 1711.

Samuel Rush, a vinegar distiller, whose grandfather, William Rush of Colchester, had started the family business of vinegar making in Castle Street, Southwark, in 1641,[2] was returned in 1715 as a Tory for Shaftesbury, where he was a stranger, but was unseated on petition. He was also unsuccessful at Colchester in 1715 and Southwark in 1722. He died 13 Mar. 1725.

[1] Manning & Bray, *Surr.* iii. 366–7; Morant, *Essex*, ii. 300–1. [2] *VCH Surr.* ii. 398.

R.S.L.

RUSHOUT, Sir John, 4th Bt. (1685–1775), of Northwick Park, Worcs.

MALMESBURY 20 Apr. 1713–1722
EVESHAM 1722–1768

b. 6 Feb. 1685, 4th s. of Sir James Rushout, 1st Bt., M.P., of Northwick Park by Alice, da. of Edward Pitt of Harrow, wid. of Edward Palmer. *educ.* poss. Eton 1698. *m.* 16 Oct. 1729, Lady Anne Compton, da. of George, 4th Earl of Northampton, 1s. 2da. *suc.* nephew as 4th Bt. 21 Sept. 1711.

Cornet R. Horse Gds. 1705, lt. 1706, capt. 1710, ret. 1712; high steward, Malmesbury 1715–16, 1743–50; ld. of the Treasury Feb. 1742–Aug. 1743; treasurer of the navy 1743–4; P.C. 19 Jan. 1744.

Rushout's grandfather was a Flemish merchant, naturalized in 1634. His father bought an estate near Evesham, which he represented for nearly twenty years. In an account of his own career he writes:

When I first came into the army I was a younger brother, I served six or seven years in the Blue Regiment of Horse Guards and was promoted to the command of a troop in the year 1710 which I quitted with great regret two years afterwards when the Duke of Ormonde had the command and was garbling the army with a view to defeat the Hanoverian Succession, and I had reason to expect I should not have been allowed to have continued in it. About the same time my family estate fell to me, and I was elected into Parliament.[1]

He sat for Malmesbury till 1722, when he was unseated there on petition but was also returned for Evesham, which he and his son thenceforth represented without a break till 1796.

In the first Hanoverian Parliament Rushout voted against the septennial bill, for the repeal of the Occasional Conformity and Schism Acts, and was absent on the peerage bill. In the next Parliament he initiated the House of Commons inquiry into the Atterbury plot, and in 1725 sponsored the complaint leading to Lord Macclesfield's impeachment, of which he was a manager. Following his friend, Pulteney, into opposition, he spoke against a vote of credit, 25 Mar. 1726, and introduced a bill against election bribery, 27 Apr., which passed the Commons but was lost in the Lords. In 1727 he rose at the end of a finance debate,

> and after having said some reflecting things in an awkward manner as if the Treasury were answerable for mismanagement in every office concluded with a motion and a personal question on Sir Robert Walpole[2].

His defection was attributed to an unsuccessful application which he had made for the post of treasurer of the Household.[3]

For the rest of Walpole's Administration Rushout remained in opposition, closely associated with his nephew, Samuel Sandys, and Phillips Gybbon (qq.v.) as Pulteney's chief supporters. He acted as Pulteney's second in his duel with Lord Hervey in 1731, when he also chaired a select committee of the House of Commons, whose report led to the passing of the Molasses Act. During the excise bill crisis in 1733 he was put down as secretary at war in the list of a new ministry prepared by the opposition leaders.[4] On 20 Feb. 1736

> a bill for further regulating elections was presented by Sir John Rushout to the House. This bill went as far as a committee and there dropped, there being so many various opinions of gentlemen for the sake of their particular interests in their boroughs.

He spoke in favour of an increased allowance to the Prince of Wales on 22 Feb. 1737.[5] He was a frequent and boring speaker, with a trick of always putting out one leg and looking at it while speaking.[6]

On Walpole's fall Rushout, Sandys, and Gybbon became Pulteney's representatives on the new Treasury board, where they combined to outvote the first lord, Wilmington.[7] Elected to the secret committee of enquiry into Walpole's Administration, he defended Scrope (q.v.), the secretary of the

Treasury, for refusing to give evidence, eliciting Horace Walpole's comment: 'I don't think there is so easy a language as the ministerial in the world, one learns it in a week!'[8] But old habits died hard, for at the opening of the next session

> Sir John Rushout . . . actually forgot he was lord of the Treasury. He got up to speak and when he came to the point of Hessian and Hanoverian troops was against 'em, and went so far as to say he saw as little occasion for them this year as there was the last. Mr. Pelham and Winnington stared him in the face, which put him in mind who he was, so he said the heat of the House overcame him, and so sat down.[9]

On the day of Wilmington's death, 2 July 1743, a servant of Rushout's was sent to the King in Hanover with a letter from Pulteney, now Lord Bath, applying for the vacancy. When Pelham was appointed to it, Rushout and Bath's other adherents on the Treasury board were 'awkward and cold', seeming to be only waiting for an opportunity to treat Pelham as they had treated Wilmington.[10] But in November an overture from Bath to Pelham through Rushout led to an agreement, under which he and Sandys were replaced on the Treasury board by Pelham's nominees, subject to suitable compensation, in Rushout's case the lucrative office of treasurer of the navy. Turned out with most of Bath's followers a year later to make room for the leaders of the Opposition, he spoke against the Queen of Hungary's subsidy on 18 Feb. 1745 with a view to sowing dissensions between the Old Whigs and the Government's new allies.[11] He also revenged himself for his dismissal by refusing to make any payments from the sums standing in his account as treasurer of the navy, thus putting a stop for 8 or 9 months to the payment of all the seamen who had not received their pay up to the date of his dismissal.[12]

When Bath and Granville made their abortive attempt to form an Administration in February 1746, they found that 'in the Commons . . . they had no better man to take the lead than poor Sir John Rushout'.[13] Joining the Leicester House party in the next Parliament, he was put down for a peerage and the pay office when the Prince came to the throne. After Frederick's death in 1751 he attached himself to Newcastle 'in the hopes of a peerage'.[14] He died, still unennobled, in his ninetieth year, 2 Feb. 1775.

[1] Add. 32862, f. 218.   [2] *Knatchbull Diary*, 15 Jan. 1723 and 23 Jan. 1725, 7 Mar. 1727.   [3] *HMC Egmont Diary*, i. 245.   [4] *CJ*, xxi. 641–2, 685; Hervey, *Mems.* 170.   [5] Harley Diary.   [6] *Corresp. H. Walpole* (Yale ed.), xvii. 332 n. 23.   [7] Walpole, *Mems. Geo. II*, i. 178 n.   [8] To Mann, 24 June 1742.   [9] Hen. Finch to Ld. Malton, 18 Nov. 1724, Wentworth Woodhouse mss.   [10] Coxe, *Pelham*, i. 83, 101.   [11] Yorke's parl. jnl. *Parl. Hist.* xiii. 1175.   [12] '3rd Report of the Commissioners for examining . . . the Public Accounts, 1781', *CJ*, xxxviii. 248 et seq.   [13] H. Walpole to Mann, 14 Feb. 1746.   [14] Add. 32868, f. 218.

R.R.S.

RUTHERFORD, James (*d.*1747), of Bowland, Midlothian.

SELKIRKSHIRE 13 Feb. 1730–1734

o.s. of Robert Rutherford of Bowland by Anne, da. of Sir John Murray of Philiphaugh. *m.* Isabella, da. of John Sharplaw of Roxburgh, 1s.
Commissary of Peebles 1733.

John Rutherford, whose father bought Bowland in 1697, succeeded his cousin, John Pringle, as Member for Selkirkshire in 1730, voting consistently with the Administration. He did not stand in 1741, dying in August 1747.

P.W.

RUTHERFURD, John (1712–58), of Edgerston, Roxburgh.

ROXBURGHSHIRE 1734–Jan. 1742

bap. 12 June 1712, 1st surv. s. of Sir John Rutherfurd of Rutherfurd and Edgerston by his 1st w. Elizabeth, da. of William Cairncross of West Langlee, Roxburgh. *educ.* L. Inn 1731; adv. 1734. *m.* 27 Nov. 1737, Eleanor, da. of Sir Gilbert Elliot (q.v.), 2nd Bt. [S], of Minto, Roxburgh, Lord Minto, S.C.J., 3s. 4da.
Capt. of an indep. co. of Ft. in New York, Dec. 1741; member of council of New York 1745–*d.*; maj. New York Forces 1746, and of Royal Americans, Jan. 1756–*d.*

John Rutherfurd, whose father was the head of an old Roxburgh family, was returned unopposed for his county soon after he came of age. When the Prince of Wales broke with the King in September 1737, Rutherfurd, as a member of the Squadrone or anti-Argyll faction in Scotland, received a circular letter from Lord Marchmont, then in opposition, urging his attendance at the opening of the new session.[1] He voted against the Spanish convention in 1739, and was one of the opposition Whigs who voted against the motion of 13 Feb. 1741 to dismiss Walpole.[2] Again returned unopposed in 1741, he was said to have been won over from the Opposition by the grant of an army commission in December, thereby vacating his seat.[3] James Oswald (q.v.), hearing 'poor John Rutherfurd's character taken to pieces', wrote that he

has continued extremely firm in doing justice to his country on every occasion. But the state of his private affairs has now forced him to accept of a place, which vacates his seat in the House. He was sensible he could no longer act a part independently himself, and therefore was willing another to be chosen in his room, who may both attend better, and act more freely than he himself would for the future have been able to do.[4]

He proceeded at once to join his company in America, where he settled at Albany, New York, writing on 10 Jan. 1743:

I find my retirement here perfectly agreeable . . . dividing my time equally for mathematics, philosophy,

politics, etc. without being interrupted in any shape by family cares or public affairs, as hitherto I have always been . . . I think myself very happy in being out of the bustle.[5]

Becoming later a member of the New York council, he remained in America, rarely returning to Scotland, till his death in action at Ticonderoga, 8 July 1758.

[1] *HMC Polwarth*, v. 142. [2] Coxe, *Walpole*, iii. 563. [3] *HMC Egmont Diary*, iii. 243. [4] *Mems. Jas. Oswald*, 27–29. [5] *Cadwallader Colden Pprs.* (New York Hist. Soc. Colls.), ii. 249; iii. 1 et passim.

R.S.L.

RYDER, Dudley (1691–1756), of Tooting, Surr.

ST. GERMANS 1 Mar. 1733–1734
TIVERTON 1734–1754

b. 4 Nov. 1691, 2nd s. of Richard Ryder of Hackney, Mdx., mercer, by his 2nd w. Elizabeth, da. of William Marshall of Lincoln's Inn. *educ.* Dissenting acad. Hackney; Edinburgh and Leyden Univ.; M. Temple 1713, called 1719; L. Inn 1725, bencher 1733. *m.* Nov. 1733, Anne, da. of Nathaniel Newnham of Streatham, Surr. and sis. of Thomas and Nathaniel Newnham (qq.v.), 1s. Kntd. 12 May 1740.
Solicitor-gen. Dec. 1733–7; attorney-gen. Jan. 1737–54; c.j. of King's bench May 1754–*d.*; P.C. 1754.

Ryder owed his start in political life to Lord Chancellor King, like himself the son of a non-conformist tradesman, who is said to have introduced him to Walpole.[1] Brought into Parliament by the Government for a Cornish borough at the beginning of 1733, he was appointed solicitor-general in the legal promotions following his patron's retirement at the end of that year. In 1734 he was transferred to Tiverton, which he represented for the rest of his parliamentary career, using government patronage to found a strong family interest. Soon after the opening of the new Parliament he refused to support an attempt by Walpole to decide a hotly contested election petition in favour of the defeated government candidates, one of whom was Ryder's brother-in-law, Thomas Newnham (q.v.).[2] Promoted attorney-general in 1737, he turned down an offer of the mastership of the rolls in 1738, after unsuccessfully applying for an increase in its salary of under £1,300 a year.[3] Towards the end of Walpole's Administration he composed in his diary the following appreciation of his character and capacity as a public man:

My present character in the world as to ability is, I believe, that I am a good lawyer and some parts. As to the belief that I am thoroughly honest and of great humanity and candour, I am sometimes tempted to attack the enemies of the Administration in a severe manner, but I check myself in that design. I am more fitted to act the part of candour, mildness, sincerity and good nature and reasoning. My own disposition leads me to this. It will give me more credit in the world. It will better hide my infirmity and want of ability in any respect, and I think my talents are rather better adapted to it. It will better, likewise, secure me against enemies, and fall in more with my talents, which are not formed for hustle and controversy, management and design. It is indeed as much the reverse as can well be. I should therefore keep out of all scrapes, all enmities. Nor am I much fitted for friendship, and therefore in such disputes should want zealous friends, and have none or few but such as are so for their own ends or from public considerations and from my public character.[4]

Ryder continued in office under Pelham, to whom he was strongly recommended by Walpole as 'very able and very honest'.[5] Some years later Horace Walpole describes him as

a man of singular goodness and integrity; of the highest reputation in his profession, of the lowest in the House, where he wearied the audience by the multiplicity of his arguments; resembling the physician who ordered a medicine to be composed of all the simples in a meadow, as there must be some of them at least that would be proper.[6]

In 1749 Hardwicke again offered him the rolls, observing that he thought the salary ought to be made equal to that of the chief justice of the common pleas, that is at least £4,000 a year, 'but that the King would be averse to this on account of the great load on the civil list'. On raising the question of a peerage, Ryder was referred to Pelham,

who foresaw difficulty with the King. Objections would be made that a new office is to be brought into the peerage, which would give expectations to future masters of the rolls, and make a number of lords from the law.

Asked by Newcastle, who wanted the attorney's post for William Murray (q.v.), whether he would accept the rolls with a peerage at the existing salary, Ryder replied that he would, but withdrew next day on finding that his wife was 'much against my acceptance of this without additional salary, and thinks my sleepy disposition will make me unfit for the office'.[7]

Ryder remained attorney-general till 1754, when he accepted the chief justiceship of the King's bench, though the King refused his application for a peerage.[8]

It is £6,000 a year for life [George II afterwards said to Hardwicke], and I will not make a precedent that when I advance a man from the bar to that office he should think he has an immediate claim to a peerage. I had a very good opinion of Ryder, (who had served me very long and very well) and loved him; but you know that I refused to make him a peer till above two years after he was chief justice. *That* should come afterwards, after there has been some experience of a man in that office.[9]

In Ryder's case it came too late, for he died 25 May 1756, a day after the warrant for his peerage was signed, but before he had kissed hands for it.

[1] Campbell, *Lives of the Chief Justices*, ii. 235. [2] *HMC Egmont Diary*, ii. 167; Hervey, *Mems.* 418. [3] Diary, 23 Dec. 1739, Harrowby mss. [4] Ibid. 22 Aug. 1741. [5] Orford to Pelham, 25 Aug. 1743, Coxe, *Pelham*, i. 93. [6] Walpole, *Mems. Geo. II*, i. 123–4. [7] Diary, 16–27 Dec. 1749. [8] Ibid. 8 Apr. 1754. [9] Yorke, *Hardwicke*, ii. 302.

R.R.S.

SABINE, John (1712–76), of Tewin, Herts.

BOSSINEY   11 Dec. 1741–18 Mar. 1742

b. (by 24 June) 1712, 1st s. of Joseph Sabine (q.v.) by his 2nd w. *educ.* Westminster Apr. 1727, aged 14; Trinity Hall, Camb. 1731. *m.* (1) 6 May 1742, Susanna Osborne of Essex, 1s. 1da.; (2) Anne, 4s. 1da.[1] *suc.* fa. 1739.

Ensign 23 Ft. 24 June 1712, 1st lt. 1731, capt. 1738; capt. and lt.-col. 1 Ft. Gds. 1742.

Sabine, who was commissioned in his father's regiment soon after birth, was returned for Bossiney on petition by the Administration in 1741, but was unseated on a further petition after the fall of Walpole. After his father's death he transferred to the 1st Foot Guards, fought in the war of the Austrian succession, and left this regiment before 1749.[2] He died 14 July 1776.

[1] PCC 373 Bellas. [2] *N. & Q.* (ser. 2), ii. 404; Dalton, *Eng. Army Lists*, vi. 101.

E.C.

SABINE, Joseph (c.1661–1739), of Tewin, Herts.

BERWICK-UPON-TWEED   1727–1734

b. c.1661, perhaps s. of Walter Sabine and gd.-s. of Avery Sabine (*d.*1648), alderman and mayor of Canterbury.[1] *m.* (1) Hester, da. of Henry Whitfield of Bishop's Stortford, Herts., *s.p.*; (2) Margaretta, da. of Charles Newsham, sis. of John Newsham (q.v.) of Chadshunt, Warws., 2s. 3da.

Capt.-lt. Sir Henry Ingoldsby's Ft. Mar. 1689; capt. of a grenadier co. bef. Oct. 1689; maj. 23 Ft. 1691, lt.-col. 1695, col. 1705–*d.*; brevet-col. 1703; brig-gen. 1707; maj.-gen. 1710; lt.-gen. 1727; gen. 1730. Gov. Berwick-upon-Tweed and Holy Is. 1719–30; gov. Gibraltar 1730–*d.*

Sabine belonged to a branch of the Sabines of Patrixbourne in Kent. Entering the army at the Revolution, he served in Ireland under William III, who probably granted him the estates he held in co. Kildare.[2] Under Marlborough he was wounded at the battle of Schellenberg in 1704, and won great distinction at Oudenarde.[3] On the advent of the Tories to power, he paid his court to Strafford and Ormonde, through whom he obtained a promise that some provision would be made for him at the conclusion of the peace.[4]

During the rebellion of 1715 Sabine came over from Ireland with his regiment to Scotland, where he was left the chief command by General Cadogan (q.v.) in May 1716. In July following, the Duke of Atholl complained of 'the conduct of General Sabine and other King's officers, in regard to rebel prisoners and . . . of the plundering and other impositions made by the troops' in Perthshire.[5] Having purchased Tewin in 1715, he spent £40,000 on rebuilding and furnishing it with such magnificence that George I, 'under the pretext of hunting, visited it twice'.[6] Returned in 1727 on the government interest for Berwick,[7] of which he was governor, he voted with the Administration till 1730, when he went as governor to Gibraltar, where he died 24 Oct. 1739, aged 78. He was buried at Tewin.

[1] Dalton, *Geo. I's Army*, i. 347 n. 1. [2] PCC 52 Browne. [3] J. W. Fortescue, *Hist. Br. Army*, i. 498–500; Luttrell, vi. 325. [4] Sabine to Ld. Strafford, 22 July 1714, Add. 22211, ff. 174–5. [5] *HMC 12th Rep. VIII*, 71. [6] César de Saussure, *A Foreign View of England in the reigns of Geo. I and Geo. II*, 307–8. [7] E. Hughes, *N. Country Life in the 18th Cent.* 271 n. 2.

E.C.

SACKVILLE, Charles, Earl of Middlesex (1711–69).

EAST GRINSTEAD	1734–Jan. 1742
SUSSEX	14 Jan. 1742–1747
OLD SARUM	17 Dec. 1747–1754
EAST GRINSTEAD	1761–10 Oct. 1765

b. 6 Feb. 1711, 1st s. of Lionel Cranfield, 1st Duke of Dorset, by Elizabeth, da. and coh. of Gen. Walter Colyear (bro. of David, 1st Earl of Portmore [S]); bro. of Lord George and Lord John Sackville (qq.v.). *educ.* Westminster 1720–8; Ch. Ch. Oxf. 1728; Grand Tour. *m.* 30 Oct. 1744 (with £130,000)[1] Grace, da. and h. of Richard Boyle, 2nd Visct. Shannon [I] (q.v.), *s.p.*; *styled* Lord Buckhurst till 1720 and Earl of Middlesex 1720–65. *suc.* fa. as 2nd Duke of Dorset 10 Oct. 1765.

Ld. of the Treasury 1743–7; master of the horse to Prince of Wales 1747–51; P.C. 10 Feb. 1766; ld. lt. Kent 1766–*d*.

In 1734 Lord Middlesex contested Kent unsuccessfully but was returned for the family borough of East Grinstead, which he represented till 1742, when Newcastle arranged for him to be brought in as knight of the shire at a by-election for Sussex.[2] During the last weeks of Walpole's Administration he and his brother, Lord John, abstained from divisions on contested election petitions.[3] Returning to his allegiance after Walpole's fall, he was appointed to the Treasury board when Pelham reconstituted it on becoming chancellor of the Exchequer. The only member of the board not to resign in February 1746, he was allowed to retain his place on Pelham's return to office, but next year he joined the new Opposition launched by the Prince of Wales. Dismissed from the Treasury, he was not re-nominated for Sussex at the general election, nor, having quarrelled with his father, was he returned for East Grinstead. After unsuccessfully contesting Queenborough and Seaford on the Prince's interest he was

brought in for Old Sarum by Frederick's election manager, Thomas Pitt (q.v.). Appointed master of the horse to the Prince, he co-operated with Bubb Dodington (q.v.) at Leicester House, where his wife, the Prince's reputed mistress, was mistress of the robes to the Princess and his brother, Lord John, was a lord of the bedchamber.[4] In 1750 he intervened unsuccessfully against his father at East Grinstead.[5] When the heir-apparent's household was reconstituted after Frederick's death in 1751

> the King offered the Princess a master of the horse, but told her it must be a nobleman, and there was one to whom he had an objection: this was Lord Middlesex. She desired none; if she had been disposed to contend, it would not have been of all men in favour of the Lord in question.[6]

Remaining in opposition, he voted in favour of a reduction of the army in November 1751.[7] In 1752 Dodington negotiated a reconciliation between him and the Duke of Dorset, who consented to see him 'on condition that he would form no pretention to have his debts paid, or to a seat in Parliament, or to a place'.[8] His debts appear to have been due to subsidising opera, to which he was passionately addicted. On 4 May 1743 Horace Walpole wrote to Mann:

> Lord Middlesex is the impresario, and must ruin the house of Sackville by a course of these follies. Besides what he will lose this year, he has not paid his share to the losses of the last, and yet is singly undertaking another for next season, with the almost certainty of losing between four or five thousand pounds to which the deficiencies of the opera generally amount now. The Duke of Dorset has desired the King not to subscribe; but Lord Middlesex is so obstinate, that this will probably only make him lose a thousand pound more.

He died 5 or 6 Jan. 1769.

[1] Walpole to Mann, 16 Aug. 1744. [2] Hen. Pelham to Newcastle, 29 May 1741, Add. 32697, f. 13. [3] Owen, *Pelhams*, 31, 33. [4] Walpole, *Mems. Geo. II*, i. 76; Pelham to Middlesex, 14 and 20 June 1747, Newcastle (Clumber) mss. [5] Hardwicke to Newcastle, 3 Aug. 1750, Add. 32722, f. 42. [6] *Mems. Geo. II*, i. 96–97. [7] Coxe, *Pelham*, ii. 207. [8] *Dodington Diary*, 185.

R.R.S.

SACKVILLE (afterwards GERMAIN), Lord George (1716–85), of Stoneland Lodge, Suss. and Drayton, Northants.

DOVER	1741–1761
HYTHE	1761–1768
EAST GRINSTEAD	1768–11 Feb. 1782

b. 26 Jan. 1716, 3rd s. of Lionel Cranfield, 1st Duke of Dorset; bro. of Charles, Earl of Middlesex, and Lord John Sackville (qq.v.). *educ.* Westminster 1723–31; Trinity, Dublin, 1731; Irish bar 1734. *m.* 3 Sept. 1754, Diana, da. and coh. of John Sambrooke (bro. of Sir Samuel Sambrooke, or Vanacker-Sambrooke, 3rd Bt., M.P.), 2s. 3da. *suc.* fa. in estate of Stoneland Lodge 1765; and to Drayton on *d*. of Lady Elizabeth Germain in 1769, taking name of Germain; *cr.* Visct. Sackville 11 Feb. 1782.

M.P. [I] 1733-69.

Capt. 6 Drag. Gds. 1737; lt.-col. 28 Ft. 1740; col. army 1745; col. 20 Ft. 1746-9, 12 Drags. 1749-50, 6 Drag. Gds. 1750-7; maj.-gen. 1755; col. 2 Drag. Gds. 1757-9; lt.-gen. of the Ordnance 1757-9; lt.-gen. 1758; c.-in-c. British forces, Germany Oct. 1758; dismissed the service 1759.

Ranger, Phoenix Park 1736-*d.*; clerk of the Council [I] 1737-*d.*; P.C. [I] 19 Sept. 1751; chief sec. [I] 1751-5; P.C. [GB] 27 Jan. 1758-25 Apr. 1760, 20 Dec. 1765-*d.*; jt. vice-treasurer [I] Dec. 1765-July 1766; first ld. of Trade Nov. 1775-Nov. 1779; sec. of state for American dept. Nov. 1775-Feb. 1782.

When the Duke of Dorset went to Ireland as lord lieutenant in 1731 he took Lord George Sackville with him, bringing him into the Irish Parliament at the age of 17, appointing him to two Irish sinecures, and giving him a commission in a regiment on the Irish establishment, from which he exchanged into an English regiment in 1740. Returned for Dover in 1741 by the Duke of Dorset as warden of the Cinque Ports, he served in Flanders and Scotland, was wounded at Fontenoy, and was commended by the Duke of Cumberland for showing 'not only his courage but also a disposition to his trade that I don't always find in those of a higher rank.'[1] In Parliament he is described as defending Cumberland 'in a masterly manner' against attacks on his adminis-tration of the army.[2] When Dorset went back to Ireland in 1751, Sackville, as his chief secretary, and Archbishop Stone, the primate, became the real rulers of the country, where they aroused violent opposition, marked by attacks on their personal characters.

> The chronicle is rather scandalous [Horace Walpole wrote to Mann, 13 May 1752]. Lord George, the Duke's third son and governor, a very brave man and a very good speaker, is supposed to have a seraglio which is not at all in the style of a country that is famous for furnishing rich widows with second husbands. His friend, the primate . . . is accused of other cardinalesque dispositions too.

Horace Walpole elaborates this theme in a passage omitted from the published edition of his *Memoirs of George II*:

> Yet in so Cyprian an isle was the metropolitan himself accused of wayward passions, more consonant to the life of a cardinal than to the supremacy of so orthodox a flock. His friend, Lord George, was suspected of the same heresy, for certainly in both it was mere matter of suspicion, and had brought over a young Scotch officer, who being professed to be aide-de-camp to the primate, was picked out as the centre at which all the arrows of satire were discharged.

In 1755 Sackville returned to England with the prospect of rising to the top of the tree, either in politics or in the army. Four years later his career seemed to have been irrevocably closed by Minden,

but he made a new one in the next reign. He died 26 Aug. 1785.

[1] *HMC 4th Rep.* 281. [2] Walpole, *Mems. Geo. II*, i. 38.

R.R.S.

SACKVILLE, Lord John Philip (1713-65).

TAMWORTH 1734-1747

b. 22 June 1713, 2nd s. of Lionel Cranfield, 1st Duke of Dorset; bro. of Charles, Earl of Middlesex and Lord George Sackville (qq.v.). *educ.* Westminster 1721-c.29. *m.* 1 Jan. 1744, Lady Frances Leveson Gower, da. of John, 1st Earl Gower, 2s. 1da.

Capt. 37 Ft. 1734; lt. Dover Castle 1734-46; equerry to Queen Caroline 1736; capt. and lt.-col. 2 Ft. Gds. 1740-6; ld. of the bedchamber to Frederick, Prince of Wales, 1745-9.

Before coming of age, Lord John Sackville was brought into Parliament for Tamworth on the interest of his brother-in-law, the 2nd Viscount Weymouth. Like his elder brother he ratted on Walpole by refusing to attend election petitions. In 1743 Lord Wilmington (Spencer Compton, q.v.), who had been expected to leave him his Sussex estates, worth £3-£4,000 a year, died leaving him nothing.[1] In 1744 he was obliged to marry the Duchess of Bedford's sister, two days after she had given birth to a child by him at Woburn. The Prince of Wales offered to intercede for the couple with their enraged parents, undertaking to make up Sackville's allowance to £800 a year, if his father should allow him less,[2] a pledge which he carried out by making him a lord of his bedchamber in 1745, thus securing him as a recruit to his party. Next year Sackville deserted from the Guards, who had been ordered abroad, having just been released from arrest for absenting himself from duty on the day of embarkation. After being confined in a private asylum kept by the head of the Bethlehem (Bedlam) hospital for lunatics,[3] he was sent into exile near Lausanne, where Shelburne met him in 1760,

> living upon a very poor allowance and but very meanly looked after. He was very fond of coming among the young English at Lausanne, who suffered his company at times from motives of curiosity, and sometimes from humanity. He was always dirtily clad, but it was easy to perceive something gentlemanlike in his manner and a look of birth about him, under all his dis-advantages. His conversation was a mixture of weak-ness and shrewdness, as is common to most madmen. When he heard of his brother Lord George's behaviour at the battle of Minden, he immediately said, 'I always told you that my brother George was no better than myself'.[4]

He died 3 Dec. 1765.

[1] Ld. John Sackville to Bedford, 2 July 1743, Bedford mss. [2] Bedford to Ld. Gower, 1 Jan., Ld. John Sackville to Bedford, 27 Feb. 1744, ibid. [3] Ld. de Vere Beauclerk to Bedford, 15 and 20 Sept. 1746, ibid. [4] Fitzmaurice, *Shelburne*, i. 237-8.

R.R.S.

ST. AUBYN, Sir John, 3rd Bt. (?1702–44), of Clowance, and St. Michael's Mount, Cornw.

CORNWALL   1722–15 Aug. 1744

b. ? 1702, 1st s. of Sir John St. Aubyn, 2nd Bt., M.P., by Mary, da. and coh. of Peter de la Hay of St. Margaret's, Westminster. *educ.* Exeter, Oxf. 12 June 1718, aged 15. *m.* 3 Oct. 1725 (with £20,000), Catherine, da. of Sir Nicholas Morice, 2nd Bt., of Werrington, Devon, coh. to her bro. Sir William Morice, 3rd Bt. (qq.v.), 1s. 4da. *suc. fa.* 20 June 1714.

While still under age St. Aubyn, whose family had long represented Cornish boroughs, was returned for the county, which he continued to represent unopposed until his death. An extreme Tory, he was to have been one of the leaders of the rising planned for the 1722 elections; he was in contact with Jacobite agents acting for Atterbury; and in 1730 the Pretender was asked 'to write to Sir John St. Aubyn to acknowledge his sense of his service'.[1]

In Parliament St. Aubyn is described as 'constant in his attendance and application to the business of the House of Commons; he soon learnt to speak well, but spoke seldom, and never but on points of consequence'. He is recorded as speaking against the Hessians, 3 Feb. 1730, in support of a bill excluding pensioners from the House, 17 Feb. 1731, against an army of 18,000 men, 2 Feb. 1733, and against its augmentation by 1,800 men, 6 Feb. 1734.[2] On 13 Mar. 1734, he seconded the opposition motion for the repeal of the Septennial Act. The following report of his speech was sent to the Pretender:

That although septennial parliaments might be looked on as no hardship to those who might perhaps be paid for doing what they ought not to do, yet it certainly was a hardship to tie down country gentlemen to so long and expensive a service of their country. That not only the length of Parliament, but the time for the meeting of the sessions of Parliament seemed to be calculated by ministers to deter country gentlemen from attempting to serve in them; that they were obliged to attend in them at the very time when their country affairs required their presence elsewhere, and while they were attending the sessions of Parliament, the election-mongers, and agents of the ministry were buying them out of their natural interest in the country . . . That no man could say these practices were so frequent before the septennial bill passed. That he lived in a country where he had a misfortune to be too well informed of them, for the many boroughs that were in his county there were but few represented by any man who had ever been in the county that long . . . Men were not to be debauched all at once . . . it would always take some time for a minister to find out who were the men to be seduced, and what was the proper bait for each man. That one man might be pleased with a place or employment. Honours or ribbons might be the properest baits for others. All which might be accomplished in seven years, but could not possibly in one, or even in three . . . Long

Parliaments like country ponds gathered filth and corruption, and became nauseous to every by-stander, but frequent new Parliaments remain clear and uncorrupted like water just come from the fountain-head.[3]

He also spoke against the bill restricting the number of livings held by the two Universities, 5 Apr., and 'very strongly' against the Quakers' tithe bill, 30 Apr. 1736.[4]

In 1739 St. Aubyn discussed the possibility of a rising without foreign assistance with Thomas Carte, the Jacobite historian, who wrote to the Pretender:

Sir John St. Aubyn gave me a commission to assure your Majesty and the Duke of Ormonde when I had a safe opportunity of doing so that whenever your Majesty or his Grace will think fit to land in England, though but with your single persons, he would venture himself with the power he could raise to support the attempt, for he did not desire a man from abroad, being satisfied there was strength enough in the kingdom to overpower the standing forces and effect your Majesty's restoration.

Carte went on to say that in the

parish of Camborne and the three next continuous thereto viz. Ludgvan, Redruth and St. Agnes, there are not less than 2800 tinners, fighting-men all devoted to that gentleman and zealous in your Majesty's cause. Sir John has assured me he does not doubt of putting himself at the head of 8 or 10,000 of these any day in the world, and they are the best men we have in England.[5]

He was abroad for most of 1740 but returned in time to witness the defeat of the motion of February 1741 for Walpole's dismissal, of which he wrote:

Such insolence in administration, such wantonness in power, which surely nothing could produce but that mistaken vote of innocence, which so lately happened . . . [yet] this is the man against whom we want evidence to advise his removal, when at my very door there are such glaring proofs, which, in less corrupt times, would deprive him of his head.

At the 1741 election, he was among the Cornish gentry who agreed to contribute in proportion to their estates to a fund for gaining the venal boroughs in the county. He seconded the two motions for a secret committee to inquire into Walpole's Administration, to which he was unanimously elected, 'an honour neither then nor before (as far as the records of Parliament can reach) ever conferred on any [other] Member, as Mr. Speaker Onslow on the spot observed'.[6] His last recorded speech was in the debate against the Hanoverian troops of 10 Dec. 1742, on which Thomas Carte reported to the Pretender:

Sir John St. Aubyn, than whom none is more universally esteemed in the House or better beloved in the country, prefaced his speech with the remarkable words, viz. that he considered that day as the last day of liberty in England, and the last day of freedom of debate in that House, and therefore it was high time to speak out, for there was no mincing matters in such an extremity . . . he accordingly declared it to be his sentiment that we lived under a Prince who being used to arbitrary power in his dominions abroad, was minded to establish it here: that all his measures were calculated for that end and this of Hanover troops in particular. This speech made him in a moment the darling toast of the city of London . . . I give the words here as I had them from his own mouth.[7]

In 1743 he was among the Members to whom the plan for a French invasion was communicated, described as

> Le chevalier Jean St. Aubin, député au Parlement pour la province de Cornouailles est, par rapport a son esprit, son jugement, son érudition, sa probité, le beau rôle qu'il joue au Parlement, et la vertu qui parôit dans toutes ses actions, estimé universellement par tout le royaume, mais il est encore plus considérable dans sa province par sa demeure au fort du pais d'étain à Clowance dans la paroisse de Chambron.[8]

He did not live to see the Forty-five, dying of a fever, 15 Aug. 1744.

[1] *Rep. from the Cttee. to examine Christopher Layer and others* (1723), App. F. 11; Stuart mss 133/151, 216/111. [2] *Quarterly Rev.* cxxxix. 376; *HMC Egmont Diary*, i. 31, 134, 140, 317; ii. 24. [3] Stuart mss 169/156. [4] *Harley Diary.* [5] Stuart mss 216/111. [6] Ibid. 219/91; *Quarterly Rev.* cxxxix. 378. [7] Stuart mss 249/113. [8] AEM & D. Angl. 82, ff. 4–23, 62–109.

E.C.

ST. AUBYN, Sir John, 4th Bt. (1726–72), of Clowance and St. Michael's Mount, Cornw.

LAUNCESTON	1747–1754
	30 Dec. 1758–21 Feb. 1759
CORNWALL	1761–12 Oct. 1772

b. 12 Nov. 1726, o.s. of Sir John St. Aubyn, 3rd Bt. (q.v.). *educ.* Oriel, Oxf. 1744. *m.* 4 June 1756, Elizabeth, da. of William Wingfield of Washington, co. Dur., 1s. 5da. *suc.* fa. 15 Aug. 1744.

St. Aubyn inherited from his mother the manor of Stoke Damerel, a highly valuable property, including the whole of modern Devonport, Morice Town and Plymouth docks.[1] Though under age he was returned at Launceston as a Tory in 1747 on the interest of his uncle, Sir William Morice (q.v.), but was not put up in 1754 by his Whig cousin Humphry Morice (q.v.). Under George III he represented the county as a Tory, voting with the Opposition.

He died 12 Oct. 1772.

[1] *Parochial Hist. Cornw.* i. 268.

E.C.

ST. CLAIR, Hon. James (1688–1762), of Sinclair, Fife, and Balblair, Sutherland.

DYSART BURGHS	27 Oct. 1722–1734
SUTHERLAND	6 May 1736–1747
DYSART BURGHS	1747–1754
FIFESHIRE	1754–30 Nov. 1762

b. 1688, 2nd s. of Henry St. Clair, 10th Ld. Sinclair [S], by Barbara, da. of Sir James Cockburn, 1st Bt., of Cockburn. *m.* Janet, da. of Hon. Sir David Dalrymple, 1st Bt. (q.v.), of Hailes, wid. of Sir John Baird, 2nd Bt., of Newbyth (*d.* 30 Sept. 1745), *s.p. suc.* fa. 1723 (*vice* e. bro. John, Master of Sinclair, attainted 1716) in the family estates, which he surrendered on his bro.'s pardon 1736, and to which, on John's death in 1750, he again suc. as titular 12th Ld. Sinclair.

Ensign 1 Ft. 1694, capt. 1708, half-pay 1713; capt. and lt.-col. 3 Ft. Gds. 1714, 2nd maj. 1722, 1st maj. 1723; brevet col. 1722; lt. gov. Berwick and Holy Island 1733; col. 22 Ft. 1734–7, 1 Ft. 1737–*d.*; brig.-gen. 1739; maj.-gen. 1741; lt.-gen. 1745; gen. 1761.

St. Clair, a professional soldier commissioned at the age of six, represented his native district of burghs as an Argyll and Walpole Whig, until turned out by the Squadrone in 1734. Having secured another seat on the interest of his kinsman, William, 17th Earl of Sutherland, he 'made it his constant practice to support his Majesty's measures' throughout successive Administrations.[1] After serving under Cumberland in Flanders, and in England during the Forty-five, he was appointed commander-in-chief of the expedition intended against Canada in 1746. David Hume, his kinsman and secretary, wrote 24 July 1746:

> The General . . . though rigorous in exacting obedience . . . has insinuation and address to gain the sea officers and colonies. All our captains were exceedingly taken with his civilities.

On the cancellation of the American venture, the force made an unsuccessful attack on the French coast at L'Orient, St. Clair's conduct of which was strongly criticized.[2]

Defeated at Sutherland in 1747, St. Clair was obliged to return to Dysart Burghs, which he had intended for his nephew, Sir Harry Erskine (q.v.), as part of a scheme concerted with his friend James Oswald (q.v.) to gain control of the county and boroughs of Fife.[3] In 1748 he was sent as special envoy to Vienna and Turin, taking with him as aides David Hume and Erskine. Though described by Horace Walpole as 'Scotchissimé . . . and not very able', he seems to have carried out this military and diplomatic mission successfully.[4]

In 1749 St. Clair, through Argyll, secured the return of Sir Harry Erskine, who in 1751 attacked General Philip Anstruther (q.v.). Having by this incurred the hostility of the Duke of Cumberland, St. Clair in 1752 was refused the colonelcy of the 3rd Guards, which was given to Lord Rothes, Anstruther's supporter in Fifeshire politics.[5] When in 1753 Anstruther put up his secretary, Major Moncrieff, as candidate for Fifeshire at the impending general election, St. Clair, exchanging constituencies with Oswald, stood for Fifeshire, sending Erskine to oppose Anstruther in his own stronghold, Anstruther Burghs. He wrote to Oswald, 1 Aug. 1753:

> Our affairs in the county stand extremely well, Major Moncrieff's attempt being laughed at by all the free-holders except those depending on the Anstruthers . . . though joined by the party of the Earls of Rothes and Leven and supported by the War Office.

On being informed through Oswald that Pelham would give the government interest to Anstruther, St. Clair wrote a protest, which he asked Oswald to convey to Pelham 'in the genteelest manner' possible:

> 'Tis not from the vote against the gate of Edinburgh that this attack has taken its rise; 'tis from the General's behaviour towards us . . . to render both me and my nephew his implacable enemies . . . He sent his agents to insinuate that as we were descended from Jacobite families we must be looked on as disaffected to his Majesty and his Government . . . I never could have imagined my adversary's military services could have weighed more with his Majesty than mine; I did not know his parliamentary services were greater. I doubt . . . if Mr. Pelham will find his personal attachment to him is so great or so sincere . . . it must not be supposed that after Mr. Anstruther's insolent, outrageous and injurious behaviour he shall be suffered to tread me and my relations underfoot with impunity. I have given the strongest assurances to our friends in the Eastern [Anstruther] burghs that I never will abandon them . . . Were I to desist, I should give the world reason to believe that I acquiesce in the aspersions spread by his emissaries.[6]

Returned for the county as a government supporter, attached to Argyll, he retained his seat till his death, 30 Nov. 1762.

[1] St. Clair to Newcastle, 19 Apr. 1752, Add. 32726, ff. 446, 448. [2] *New Letters of David Hume* (ed. Klibansky & Mossner), 20; *Letters of David Hume* (ed. Greig), i. 228–9; Yorke, *Hardwicke*, i. 636–7. [3] Jas. Oswald to G. Grenville, 1 Aug. 1747, Grenville mss; Lady Morton to Morton, 13 Aug. 1747. Morton mss SRO.; *Mems. Jas. Oswald*, 333 et seq. [4] Walpole to Mann, 12 Jan. 1748; *Letters of David Hume*, i. 108 et seq.; St. Clair to Newcastle, 9 and 12 Oct. 1748, Add. 32814, f. 362; 32815, ff. 1 et seq. [5] Walpole, *Mems. Geo. II*, i. 44, 56; St. Clair to Newcastle, 19 Apr. 1752, Add. 32726, ff. 446, 448; Newcastle to St. Clair, 29 Apr., 10 May 1752, Add. 32727, f. 19. [6] Oswald mss; St. Clair to Oswald, 26 Jan. 1754, *Mems. of Jas. Oswald*, 330 et seq.

E.H.-G.

ST. JOHN, Hon. John (1702–48), of Lydiard Tregoze, Wilts.

WOOTTON BASSETT   1727–1734

b. 3 May 1702,[1] 3rd but 2nd surv. s. of Henry St. John, M.P., 1st Visct. St. John, being 2nd s. by his 2nd w. Angelica Magdalena, da. of Claude Pelissary, treasurer-gen. of the navy to Louis XIV, wid. of Phillip Wharton[2] (nephew of Philip, 4th Baron Wharton). *educ.* Eton 1717[3] and in Paris 1720. *m.* (1) 17 Apr. 1729, Anne (*d.* 14 July 1747), da. of Sir Robert Furnese, 2nd Bt. (q.v.), of Waldershare, Kent, sis. and coh. of Sir Henry Furnese, 3rd Bt., 3s. 3da.;

(2) 19 June 1748, Hester, da. of James Clarke of Wharton, Herefs., *s.p.* *suc.* fa. under sp. rem. as 2nd Visct. St. John 8 Apr. 1742.
Comptroller of customs in London Apr. 1740–*d.*

When John St. John was a child his elder half-brother, Bolingbroke, was attainted and excluded by special remainder from succeeding to the peerage which their father was said to have bought from the Duchess of Kendal in 1716. Five years later Lord St. John invested another £4,000 in the Duchess to acquire the reversion of a customs sinecure worth £1,200 a year for the lives of his two younger sons, John and Holles.[4] In 1720 John St. John was sent to Paris to complete his education under the eye of Bolingbroke, who wrote of him:

> We do not at all despair of licking our young cub into form very soon. The truth is he is extremely raw, but he seems to have docility and parts enough to make an honest man, provided he comes to have what is essential to a good character.[5]

Returned on the family interest for Wootton Bassett, at the first opportunity after coming of age, he voted with the Opposition except on the repeal of the Septennial Act in 1734. He never stood again but in the crisis of 1737 over the Prince of Wales's allowance he is described as 'a great advocate for the Prince, and intimate in consultations with' him.[6] On his father's death at the age of 89 he succeeded not only to the title but to Lydiard Tregoze, which Bolingbroke, in his own words, had

> abandoned . . . to him that he might restore the family seat, and that by living there decently and hospitably he might restore a family interest, too much and too long neglected. He may perhaps do the first in time . . . as to the last I doubt more of it. They have made themselves a proverb in the country already for their stinginess.

When St. John's wife died in 1747 Bolingbroke commented to their sister: 'I wish that the prejudices and habits which his late wife gave him and which are none of the best do not stick by him'.[7] Marrying again, he died abroad in November 1748.[8]

[1] His horoscope, Egerton mss 2378, f. 40. [2] PCC 38 Cann. [3] Add. 34196, f. 2. [4] *Lady Cowper Diary*, 113; Walpole to Mann, 26 Dec. 1748; *Cal. Treas. Bks. and Pprs.* 1739–41, p. 423. [5] Bolingbroke to Henrietta St. John, 23 July 1720, Add. 34196, ff. 11–12. [6] *HMC Egmont Diary*, ii. 359. [7] Bolingbroke to Henrietta Knight, 10 Aug. 1745, 13 Aug. 1747, Add. 34196, ff. 147, 149. [8] PCC 32 Lisle.

R.S.L.

ST. JOHN, Paulet (1704–80), of Farley Chamberlayne and Dogmersfield Park, Hants.

WINCHESTER   1734–1741
HAMPSHIRE   1741–1747
WINCHESTER   28 May 1751–1754

b. 7 Apr. 1704, 1st s. of Ellis St. John (formerly Mews) of Farley Chamberlayne by his 2nd w. Martha, da.

and eventually h. of Edward Goodyear of Dogmersfield Park. *educ.* Oriel, Oxf. 1722. *m.* (1) 2 Aug. 1731, Elizabeth (*d.* 21 Dec. 1733), da. of Sir James Rushout, 2nd Bt., M.P., of Northwick Park, Worcs., *s.p.*; (2) 1 Oct. 1736, Mary (*d.* 17 Dec. 1758), da. of John Waters of Brecon, wid. of Sir Halswell Tynte, 3rd Bt. (q.v.), 3s.; (3) 13 Feb. 1761, Jane, da. and h. of R. Harris of Silkstead, Hants, wid. of William Pescod of Winchester, *s.p.*   *suc.* fa. 1729; *cr.* Bt. 9 Oct. 1772.

Sheriff, Hants, 1727–8; woodward, New Forest 1764; mayor, Winchester 1772.

Descended from a Winchester family, St. John inherited considerable estates in Hampshire from his father, who had married two heiresses. Unsuccessful for Winchester at a by-election in 1730, he was returned for it as a government supporter at the general election of 1734, voting with the Administration on the Spanish convention in 1739. Returned for the county in 1741, he was put down to Pelham in the Cockpit list of Oct. 1742, but thenceforth he seems to have gone into opposition, for his only recorded vote was against the Hanoverians in 1744, and by 1746 he was no longer classed among government supporters. Declining to stand for the county in 1747,[1] he was returned once more at a contested by-election for Winchester in 1751 on the interest of the Duke of Chandos (Henry Brydges, q.v.) but did not stand again. He died 8 June 1780.

[1] Ld. Castlemaine to Bedford, 7 June 1747, Bedford mss.

P.W.

ST. LEGER, Arthur Mohun, 3rd Visct. Doneraile [I] (1718–50).

Winchelsea   1741–1747
Old Sarum   17 Dec. 1747–Aug. 1750

b. 7 Aug. 1718, o. surv. s. of Arthur St. Leger, 2nd Visct. Doneraile [I], by his 1st w. Mary, da. and h. of Charles, 4th Baron Mohun of Okehampton. *m.* (1) 3 Apr. 1738, Mary (*d.* 11 Aug. 1738), da. and h. of Anthony Sheppard of Newcastle, co. Longford, *s.p.*; (2) 3 June 1739, Catherine, da. of Clotworthy Skeffington, 4th Visct. Massereene [I], *s.p.* *suc.* fa. 13 Mar. 1734.

Ld. of the bedchamber to Prince of Wales 1747–*d.*

'A young man of great parts, but of no steadiness in courage, conduct, or principles',[1] Doneraile was returned in 1741 by the Government for Winchelsea. When a petition was presented against him he

spoke as well as ever anyone spoke in his own defence, insisted on the petition being heard [at the bar of the House], and concluded with declaring that *his cause was his defence and impartiality must be his support.*

He then agreed with the Opposition that if they would promise to withdraw the petition he would vote for them on the Westminster election.

His friends reproached him so strongly with his meanness that he was shocked, and went to Mr. Pulteney to get off; Mr. Pulteney told him he had given him his honour and he would not release him, though Lord Doneraile declared it was against his conscience.

In the end he voted with the Opposition on the Westminster petition. In spite of promising to vote straight in future, he ratted once more on the Chippenham election petition,[2] the loss of which by only one vote led to Walpole's resignation.

After Walpole's fall, Doneraile supported the Government till the Pelhams replaced the Bath-Granville section of the Administration by the leaders of the Opposition at the end of 1744. He then reverted to opposition, distinguishing himself by his skilful attempts to stir up trouble between the old corps of Whigs and their new allies.[3] During the rebellion of 1745 he made an effective attack on the Government's mis-management of the scheme for authorizing some noblemen to raise regiments at their own expense. In 1746 he voted for the Hanoverians as a follower of the Prince of Wales, who made him a lord of his bedchamber in April 1747.

Doneraile was defeated at Winchelsea in the general election of 1747, but was returned for Old Sarum at a by-election by the Prince's election manager, Thomas Pitt (q.v.). He disappointed Frederick by not speaking oftener in the House of Commons,[4] possibly owing to the consumption which carried him off in Lisbon, August 1750.

[1] Walpole, *Mems. Geo. II*, i. 747 and n.   [2] Walpole to Mann, 24 Dec. 1741; Coxe, *Walpole*, iii. 590.   [3] Owen, *Pelhams*, 254, 261. [4] Walpole, *Mems. Geo. II*, ut supra.

R.R.S.

ST. QUINTIN, Matthew Chitty (?1701–83), of Harpham, Yorks.

Old Sarum   1 Mar. 1728–1734

b. ?1701, yr. s. of Hugh St. Quintin of Amsterdam, merchant, by Catherine, da. of Matthew Chitty; bro. of Sir William St. Quintin, 4th Bt., and nephew of Sir William St. Quintin, 3rd Bt. (qq.v.). *educ.* Greenwich and Dr. Newcome's acad. at Hackney; Sidney Sussex, Camb. 17 Apr. 1718, aged 16; M. Temple 1718. *unm.*

Matthew Chitty St. Quintin was brought in at Old Sarum by Thomas Pitt (q.v.) at a by-election in 1728, after standing unsuccessfully for his uncle's former seat at Hull in 1727. In Parliament he voted for the Administration in all recorded divisions. Defeated at St. Mawes in 1734, he did not stand again. He died 8 May 1783.

R.S.L.

ST. QUINTIN, Sir William, 3rd Bt. (c.1662–1723), of Harpham, Yorks.

KINGSTON-UPON-HULL   1695–30 June 1723

b. c.1662, 1st surv. s. of William St. Quintin by Elizabeth, da. of Sir William Strickland, 1st Bt., M.P., of Boynton, Yorks. *unm. suc.* fa. and gd.-fa. as 3rd Bt. c.Nov. 1695.

Commr. of customs 1698–1701, of revenue [I] 1706–13; ld. of Treasury 1714–17; jt. vice-treasurer [I] 1720–*d.*

Sir William St. Quintin sat for Hull as a Whig in 11 successive Parliaments. Appointed to the Treasury board at George I's accession, he lost his post in 1717, when he followed Walpole into opposition. Obtaining a lucrative Irish sinecure on Walpole's return to office, he died 30 June 1723.

R.R.S.

ST. QUINTIN, William (?1699–1770), of Harpham Yorks.

THIRSK   1722–1727

b. ?1699, 1st s. of Hugh St. Quintin of Amsterdam, merchant; bro. of Matthew Chitty St. Quintin and nephew of Sir William St. Quintin, 3rd Bt. (qq.v.). *educ.* Greenwich and Dr. Newcome's acad. at Hackney; Sidney Sussex, Camb. 17 Apr. 1718, aged 18; M. Temple 1718. *m.* 11 June 1724, Rebecca, da. and h. of Sir John Thompson, ld. mayor of London 1736–7, 4s. 4da. *suc.* fa. 1702 and uncle as 4th Bt. 30 June 1723.

Sheriff, Yorks. 1729–30.

Returned as a government supporter on the Frankland interest in 1722, William St. Quintin did not stand again. He died 9 May 1770.

R.S.L.

SALUSBURY, *see* BRERETON

SAMBROOKE, Sir Jeremy Vanacker, 4th Bt. (?1703–40), of Bush Hill, nr. Enfield, Mdx.

BEDFORD   30 Jan. 1731–5 July 1740

b. ?1703, o.s. of Sir Samuel Sambrooke, 3rd Bt., M.P., by Elizabeth, da. of Sir Nathan Wright of Caldecote, Warws., ld. keeper of the great seal. *educ.* Dr. Uvedale's sch. at Enfield; I. Temple ?1716; Trinity, Camb. 7 July 1720, aged 17. *unm. suc.* fa. 27 Dec. 1714.

Sir Jeremy Sambrooke, whose father succeeded to the baronetcy under special remainder on the death of his maternal uncle Sir John Vanacker, 2nd Bt., came of a wealthy family of merchants, long connected with the East India Company and Madras. In 1731 he was reputed to be worth £12,000 a year.[1] Having acquired considerable estates in the north of Bedfordshire from 1719,[2] he stood as a Tory at several by-elections, but was unsuccessful at Queen-

borough in February 1728, Wendover in March 1728, and Queenborough again, January 1729.[3] However, at Bedford in January 1731, with the support of the young 3rd Duke of Bedford and a lavish expenditure of money, he defeated his Whig opponent, Dr. Thomas Browne, who had hoped to gain a majority through the creation of a large number of voting freemen.[4] Re-elected unopposed in 1734, he voted against the Administration in all recorded divisions till his death 5 July 1740.

[1] *Diary of Benjamin Rogers* (Beds. Hist. Rec. Soc. xxx), 23. [2] *VCH Beds.* iii. 105, 137, 177. [3] See QUEENBOROUGH. [4] See BEDFORD.

R.S.L.

SAMBROOKE, John (c.1692–1734).

DUNWICH   4 Apr. 1726–1727
WENLOCK   1727–1734

b. c.1692, 3rd s. of Sir Jeremy Sambrooke of Bush Hill, nr. Enfield, Mdx., merchant, by Judith, da. of Nicholas Vanacker of Erith, Kent, merchant; bro. of Sir Samuel Sambrooke, 3rd Bt., M.P. *educ.* St. Catherine's, Camb. 1709. *m.* May or June 1717,[1] Elizabeth, da. of Sir William Forester, M.P., of Dothill Park, Salop, by Mary, da. of James Cecil, 3rd Earl of Salisbury, *s.p.*

John Sambrooke, a Turkey merchant, was returned as a Whig for Wenlock on the interest of his brother-in-law, William Forester (q.v.). He gave all his known votes against the Government, writing in 1733 that

> there never was anyone who acted in Parliament with more disinterested views than I have done, or more for what I thought the Whig interest. It is true I have very often (but far from always) voted against what has been proposed by the ministry, and it is as true when I did so, that I have always thought them in the wrong, and acting contrary to the interest of their country and Whig principles.

This conduct gave him an undeserved Tory reputation, with the result that in 1733 Lord Bradford, the leader of the Shropshire Whigs, openly opposed his re-election, while two extreme Tories, Lord Gower and Watkin Williams Wynn (q.v.), who owned property in the borough, offered to support him and William Forester. Sambrooke pleaded with Forester to persuade Bradford to withdraw his opposition, claiming that he was a true Whig, that Bradford's brother-in-law James Cocks and his friend St. John Charlton (qq.v.) had the same voting record, and that Orlando Bridgeman (q.v.), whom Bradford now thought of for Wenlock, had earned the same reputation as himself. He also suggested that Sir Robert Walpole might persuade Bradford to change his mind, but this was impossible, for the quarrel had become so public that Bradford could not retract, nor Walpole ask him to do so.[2] Sambrooke did not stand in 1734, dying 19 May, three weeks after the election.

[1] PCC 143 Ockham. [2] Sambrooke to Forester, 16 Sept., 4 Oct. 1733, and Margaret Forester to Forester, 12 Oct. 1733, Willey Park mss.

J.B.L.

SAMWELL, Sir Thomas, 2nd Bt. (1687–1757), of Upton, Northants., and Atherstone-on-Stour, Warws.

COVENTRY 1715–1722

bap. 14 Apr. 1687, o.s. of Sir Thomas Samwell, 1st Bt., M.P., of Upton by Anne, da. and h. of Sir John Godschalk of Atherstone-on-Stour. *educ.* Corpus Christi, Camb. 1704; Grand Tour (Netherlands, Germany, Italy, Switzerland, France). *m.* (1) 22 Mar. 1710, Millicent (bur. 11 May 1716), da. and h. of Rev. Thomas Fuller of Hatfield, Herts., 2s. 4da.; (2) 26 Jan. 1721, Mary, da. of Sir Gilbert Clarke of Chilcote, Derbys., wid. of William Ives of Bradden, Northants., 1s. 1da. *suc.* fa. March 1694.

Samwell, whose family acquired Upton in 1600, was returned for Coventry as a Whig in 1715 with his cousin Adolphus Oughton (q.v.). He voted with the Administration on the septennial bill in 1716 but went into opposition with Walpole in 1717, voting against the Government in all subsequent divisions. He did not stand again. According to his monumental inscription at Upton:

truly sensible of the falsehood, ingratitude and corruption of mankind, he preferred retirement to the glare and splendour of a court, and looked upon a private station as the true post of honour.

In 1745 he and his two sons accepted commissions in Lord Halifax's regiment, raised during the rebellion.[1] He died 16 Nov. 1757.

[1] Baker, *Northants.* i. 227.

E.C.

SANDFORD, Sir Richard, 3rd Bt. (1675–1723), of Howgill Castle, Westmld.

WESTMORLAND 1695–1700
MORPETH 31 May–11 Nov. 1701
WESTMORLAND 1701–1702
MORPETH 1705–1713
APPLEBY 1713–2 Apr. 1723

b. 8 Sept. 1675, o.s. of Sir Richard Sandford, 2nd Bt., by Mary, da. of Sir Francis Bowes of Thornton, co. Dur. *educ.* Christ's, Camb. 1692. *unm. suc.* fa. 8 Sept. 1675.
Warden of the mint 1714–17.

Sandford came of one of the most ancient families of Westmorland, which his ancestors had frequently represented. Returned as a Whig for the county before coming of age, he sat from 1713 for Appleby, where he owned 13 burgages.[1] At George I's accession he obtained a place, which he lost in 1717 for voting against the Government in the division on Lord Cadogan (q.v.), thenceforth voting against them in all recorded divisions. On his death, 2 Apr. 1723, his estates passed to his sister, the wife of Robert Honywood (q.v.).

[1] B. Bonsall, *Sir Jas. Lowther and Cumb. and Westmld. Elections,* 20.

R.R.S.

SANDYS, Hon. Edwin (1726–97), of Ombersley, Worcs.

DROITWICH 16 Dec. 1747–1754
BOSSINEY 1754–1761
WESTMINSTER 27 Apr. 1762–21 Apr. 1770

b. 18 Apr. 1726, 1st s. of Samuel Sandys (q.v.). *educ.* Eton 1742; New Coll. Oxf. 1743. *m.* 26 Jan. 1769, Anne Maria, da. of James Colebrooke, London mercer, wid. of William Payne King of Fineshade Abbey, Northants., sis. of Sir James and Robert Colebrooke (qq.v.), *s.p. suc.* fa. as 2nd Ld. Sandys 21 Apr. 1770.
Ld. of Admiralty Apr.–July 1757.

Defeated by one vote at Droitwich in 1747, Sandys was returned on petition as a government supporter.

He died 11 Mar. 1797.

R.R.S.

SANDYS, Samuel (1695–1770), of Ombersley, Worcs.

WORCESTER 7 Mar. 1718–20 Dec. 1743

b. 10 Aug. 1695, 1st s. of Edwin Sandys, M.P. Worcs. 1695–8, by Alice, da. of Sir James Rushout, 1st Bt., M.P., of Northwick Park, Worcs., sis. of Sir John Rushout, 4th Bt. (q.v.). *educ.* New Coll. Oxf. 1711. *m.* 9 June 1725, Letitia, da. and eventually coh. of Sir Thomas Tipping, 1st Bt., M.P., of Wheatfield, Oxon., 7s. 3da. *suc.* fa. 1699 and gd.-fa. to family estates 1701; *cr.* Lord Sandys 20 Dec. 1743.
Chancellor of the Exchequer in Feb. 1742–Dec. 1743; P.C. 16 Feb. 1742; cofferer of the Household Dec. 1743–Dec. 1744; c.j. in eyre south of Trent, Dec. 1755–Dec. 1756, north of Trent 13 Feb. 1759–Mar. 1761; Speaker of the House of Lords Nov. 1756–July 1757; first ld. of Trade 21 Mar. 1761–Feb. 1763.

'A tall thin young gentleman', of an old Worcestershire family, Sandys was returned in 1718 at the age of 22 as a Whig for Worcester, which he represented for 25 years. His only recorded vote in this Parliament was against the repeal of the Occasional Conformity and Schism Acts in 1719. By the opening of the next Parliament in 1722 he was among the leading ministerial supporters in the Commons who were invited to private meetings at Walpole's house to hear the King's speech and to discuss the business of the forthcoming session. In 1725 he followed Pulteney into opposition, speaking with him against the Government in a debate on supply, 4 Mar. His defection was attributed to his failure to obtain the post of secretary at war, for which he was said to have applied, presumably in 1724, when it was filled by Henry Pelham.[1]

During the next two Parliaments Sandys was second-in-command to Pulteney, the leader of the Whig opposition, whose other chief lieutenants were Sandys's uncle, Sir John Rushout, and Phillips Gybbon (qq.v.). Speaking in most important debates, frequently introducing bills against place-men and pensioners, and distinguished for his knowledge of the journals of the House of Commons, he was put down for Speaker in the list of a new ministry drawn up by the opposition leaders during the excise bill crisis of 1733. When in 1737 Pulteney was toying with the idea of coming to terms with the Court, Sandys was understood to be ready 'to act under the new scheme and to be a manager for the Court', as Speaker. Though the negotiation came to nothing, it gave rise to a distrust of the Whig opposition leaders, reflected in the failure of the Tories to support Sandys's motion for Walpole's removal in 1741, and in the remark of their leader, Shippen (q.v.), that 'those men with long cravats', meaning Sandys, Rushout, and Gybbon, who wore voluminous neck-cloths, 'only desire places'. Nor were these suspicions confined to Tory circles. After the opposition successes at the general election of 1741, Chesterfield (Philip Dormer Stanhope, q.v.) predicted that Pulteney would use them only 'to get in with a few by negotiation and not by victory with numbers', adding:

> The interested Whigs, as Sandys, Rushout and Gybbon . . . are as impatient to come into court as he can be; and, persuaded that he has opened that door a little, will hold fast by him to squeeze in with him, and think they can justify their conduct to the public by following their old leader, under the colours (though false ones) of Whiggism.[2]

After Walpole's fall these suspicions were justified to the extent that Pulteney, while refusing office for himself, negotiated an agreement with the Court, without consulting the opposition parties, on terms providing for the continuation of the existing ministry, minus Walpole, subject to a comparatively few changes, including the appointment of Sandys to be chancellor of the Exchequer, with Rushout and Gybbon as lords of the Treasury. At a party meeting Sandys defended his conduct, taking the line that

> the King had done him the honour to offer him that place; why should he not accept it? If he had not, another would; if nobody would, the King would be obliged to employ his old minister again, which he imagined gentlemen present would not wish to see; and protested against screening [Walpole].

On being told some days later that 'the nation would expect some popular bills, or it would be said all the turn given to affairs was only to get places',

> he said that all men knew that parties attempted many things of this kind in opposition which they never meant to carry, but it was necessary to amuse the people. But that these [popular bills] in general he should oppose and so must every minister, and that as Sir Robert used to say, they were but the flurries of a day.

In March he introduced a place bill, which was the only popular measure to be passed by the Lords. On 23 Mar. he and Pulteney spoke in favour of the appointment of a secret committee to inquire into Walpole's Administration, Sandys declaring that 'he was always for inquiries into ministers' conduct, and should expect, if in his station he did anything amiss, to be called to account for it'. As a result, the 1st Lord Egmont wrote, 'the Country party entertain a more favourable opinion of Mr. Pulteney and Mr. Sandys'. But they soon effaced this impression by voting against motions for repealing the Septennial Act and for protesting against the rejection by the Lords of a bill indemnifying witnesses against Walpole. Sandys and Rushout also spoke against taking action against John Scrope (q.v.), the sec-retary of the Treasury, for refusing to give in-formation to the secret committee on Walpole about the disposal of secret service money.[3]

At the opening of the next session, Sandys completed his political volte-face by voting against a revival of the secret committee, telling 'his friends at a meeting the night before at his house that this motion . . . must be opposed, for otherwise the King would dismiss the ministry'. 'The whole debate ran,' Horace Walpole reported to Mann, 2 Dec. 1742, 'not upon Robert Earl of Orford but Robert Earl of Sandys. He is the constant butt of the party; indeed he bears it notably.' A few days later, in defiance of the instructions of his con-stituents, he spoke against a new place bill, causing Egmont to observe: 'so it seems the new ministry are above regarding the resentment of their old friends and the clamours of the people'.[4]

At the Treasury board Sandys and his friends combined to outvote the first lord, Wilmington (Spencer Compton, q.v.), on whose death in 1743 his successor, Henry Pelham, in order to avoid being placed in a similar disagreeable position, decided to transfer Sandys and Rushout to other posts. 'They press', he wrote, 'for the two best', Sandys for the pay office, failing which he 'insisted on being a peer and cofferer', while Rushout became treasurer of the navy. 'Zounds' exclaimed an old opposition hand, Walter Plumer, 'Mr. Pulteney took those old dishclouts to wipe out the Treasury, and now they are going to lace them and lay them up'.[5] A year later Sandys, Rushout, and Gybbon were all turned out to make room for the leaders of the Opposition. Never again playing a significant part in politics, though twice resurrected by Newcastle and Bute for brief spells of minor office, Sandys died, 21 Apr. 1770, of injuries received from the overturning of his chaise on Highgate Hill.

[1] *HMC Egmont Diary*, i. 83, 245; *Knatchbull Diary*, 115. [2] *Corresp. H. Walpole* (Yale ed.), xvii. 249–50 n. 5; Hervey, *Mems.* 170; *HMC Egmont Diary*, ii. 366; Coxe, *Walpole*, i. 672; iii. 580. [3] Walpole to Mann, 18 Feb., 26 May, 24 June 1742; *HMC Egmont Diary*, iii. 256, 263; Owen, *Pelhams*, 110; A. S. Foord, *His Majesty's Opposition, 1714–1830*, p. 144. [4] *HMC Egmont Diary*, iii. 268. [5] Pelham to Devonshire, 1 Dec. 1743, Devonshire mss; Walpole to Mann, 30 Nov. 1743.

R.R.S.

SARGENT, John (1715–91), of May Place, Crayford, Kent.

MIDHURST 25 Jan. 1754–1761
WEST LOOE 19 Jan. 1765–1768

b. 1715, o.s. of John Sargent, storekeeper of the King's Yard, Deptford, by his w. Mary? Arnold.[1] *m.* Rosamund Chambers, 2s.
    Director, Bank of England 1753–67 (with statutory intervals).

John Sargent, a merchant trading with North America,[2] was brought in by Lord Montagu, the patron of Midhurst, at the request of Henry Pelham.[3] He died 20 Sept. 1791.

[1] *Genealogist*, n.s. xxxiii, 189–94; John Sargent sen. to Newcastle, 16 June 1747, Add. 32711, f. 387; PCC 197 Busby. [2] *APC Col.* iv. 648. [3] Sargent to Newcastle, 2 July 1760, Add. 32908, ff. 21–22.

J.B.L.

SAUNDERS, Charles (c.1713–75), of Hambledon, nr. Fareham, Hants.

PLYMOUTH 6 Apr. 1750–1754
HEDON 1754–7 Dec. 1775

b. c.1713, s. of James Saunders of Bridgwater, Som.[1] *m.* 26 Sept. 1751, a da. of James Buck, a London banker, *s.p.* K.B. 16 May 1761.
    Entered R.N. 1727, lt. 1734, capt. 1741, r.-adm. 1756, v.-adm. 1759; lt.-gen. of marines 1759; adm. 1770.
    Treasurer of Greenwich Hospital 1754–66; comptroller of the navy 1755–6; ld. of Admiralty 1765–6; P.C. 10 Sept. 1766; 1st ld. of Admiralty Sept.–Dec. 1766.

Saunders entered politics under the patronage of Lord Anson (q.v.), with whom he had sailed round the world. In 1747 he was put up for Hedon by Anson but was defeated.[2] Returned in 1750 for Plymouth on the Admiralty interest, he is described by Horace Walpole as declaring his intention of voting against the clandestine marriages bill in 1753 'for the sake of the sailors, having once given 40 of his crew leave to go on shore for an hour, and all returned married', but as being 'compelled by Lord Anson, the chancellor's son-in-law and his patron, to vote for it'.[3] At the following election he was returned by Anson for Hedon, which he represented until his death, 7 Dec. 1775.

[1] E. Salmon, *Life of Adm. Sir Charles Saunders*, 14. [2] Anson to Bedford, 21 June 1747, Bedford mss; T. Keppel, *Life of Keppel*, 105; Salmon, 61. [3] H. Walpole, *Mems. Geo. II*, i. 345.

S.R.M.

SAUNDERS, Sir George (c.1671–1734), of St. Olave's, Hart St., London.

QUEENBOROUGH 20 Feb. 1728–5 Dec. 1734

b. c.1671. *m.* Anne, da. of Charles Dartiquenave, sis. of Charles Dartiquenave[1] of St. James's, Westminster, paymaster of the board of Works, 1da. who m. Hon. William Egerton (q.v.). Kntd. 8 Oct. 1720.
    Volunteer R.N. 1689, lt. 1694, capt. 1705; commr. of victualling 1721–7; commr. of the navy 1727–9; comptroller of the navy treasurer's acct. 1729–*d.*; r.-adm. 1731.

Saunders, whose parentage has not been ascertained, was in the merchant service before joining the navy, in which he served afloat with distinction for 31 years. In September 1715 he was sent by Admiral Sir George Byng (q.v.) to Havre and Paris to complain of ships suspected of carrying arms for the Pretender.[2] He was with Byng in the Baltic in 1717, and was chosen by him to be first captain, or captain of the fleet, in the operations against Spain off Sicily and Naples, 1718–20. This appointment was described by Pattee Byng (q.v.) as 'a rank of consideration and distinction, to which [Saunders] had been nominated by my father from particular friendship to him; and as he knew him to be an active, good officer, and a thinking man, he had much of his esteem'. Saunders was present at Byng's victory off Cape Passaro, 31 July 1718, was sent to negotiate a treaty with the Order of Malta, October 1719, and arranged the armistice with Spain, May 1720.[3] For these services he was knighted by the King at Hanover, while returning home, and given successive shore appointments which he continued to hold as an admiral.

Returned for Queenborough on the Admiralty interest at a by-election in 1728 and again in 1734, he consistently supported the Administration till his death, 5 Dec. 1734.

[1] PCC 123 Brown, 270 Wake; Metcalfe, *Vis. Suff.* 9. [2] *Byng Pprs.* (Navy Recs. Soc. lxx), iii. 142 et seq. [3] *Pattee Byng's Jnl.* (Navy Recs. Soc. lxxxviii), 121, 180 et seq., 270.

R.S.L.

SAUNDERSON, *see* **LUMLEY** (afterwards SAUNDERSON), **Hon. Thomas**

SAVILE, Sir George, 7th Bt. (1678–1743), of Rufford, Notts.

YORKSHIRE 19 June 1728–1734

bap. 18 Feb. 1678, s. of Rev. John Savile, rector of Thornhill, Yorks. by his 2nd w. Barbara, da. and coh. of Thomas Jenison of Newcastle. *educ.* Ch. Ch. Oxf. 1696; M. Temple 1691. *m.* 19 Dec. 1722, Mary, da. of John Pratt of Dublin, 1s. 2da. *suc.* cos. as 7th Bt. 1704.
Sheriff, Notts. 1706–7.

Though residing in Nottinghamshire at Rufford Abbey, acquired by marriage at the beginning of the sixteenth century, Savile came of a Yorkshire family, with extensive estates in the West Riding. In spite of non-residence, he was returned unopposed on the Whig interest for Yorkshire, at a by-election caused by the elevation to the peerage of his friend and kinsman, Sir Thomas Wentworth (q.v.). In Parliament he voted with the Opposition on the civil list arrears in 1729 and was absent from the division on the Hessians in 1730. In 1731 he introduced a bill to enact that proceedings in courts of justice should be in English, which passed into law, 'notwithstanding the opposition of the whole body of lawyers'.[1] He voted again with the Opposition on the army in 1732, was absent on the excise bill in 1733, but voted with the Government on the repeal of the Septennial Act in 1734, when he declined to stand for re-election. Shortly after retiring from Parliament he separated from his wife, the reputed natural daughter of Henry Petty, 1st Earl of Shelburne (q.v.), on account of an affair between her and William Levinz (q.v.). Discussing the question of divorce proceedings he told the 1st Lord Egmont that

he knew not how to venture it, for Mr. Levinz was a Tory, and the lawyers of the spiritual courts were all such, and he had experience how far party governed their judgments. To sue therefore for a divorce might be attended with ill success.[2]

He died 16 Sept. 1743.

[1] *Chandler,* vii. 82–83. [2] *HMC Egmont Diary,* ii. 218, 223–7, 338.

R.R.S.

SAVILE, John (1719–78), of Methley Hall, nr. Leeds.

HEDON 1747–1754
NEW SHOREHAM 4 Dec. 1761–1768

b. Dec. 1719, o.s. of Charles Savile of Methley Hall by Alathea, da. and coh. of Gilbert Millington of Felley Priory, Notts. *educ.* King's, Camb. 1739. *m.* 20 Jan. 1760, Sarah, da. of Francis Blake Delaval (q.v.), sis. of Sir Francis Blake Delaval, M.P., and Sir John Hussey Delaval, M.P., 3s. *suc.* fa. 1741; K.B. 2 May 1749; *cr.* Baron Pollington [I] 8 Nov. 1753; Earl of Mexborough [I] 11 Feb. 1766.

Returned for Hedon jointly with Luke Robinson (q.v.),[1] after a contest, Savile supported the Government, from whom he obtained an Irish peerage in 1753. He died 12 Feb. 1778.

[1] Joseph Hill to Rockingham, undated, Rockingham mss.

R.R.S.

SAVILL, Samuel (c.1700–63), of Colchester, and Stisted Hall, Essex.

COLCHESTER 26 Feb. 1742–1747

b. c.1700, 2nd s. of John Savill, mercer, of Colchester. *m.* Sarah, da. of Edward Husbands of Little Horkesley, Essex, 2da. *suc.* bro. John to Stisted Hall 1735.[1]

Returned for Colchester on petition in 1742, Savill voted against the Administration in all recorded divisions. His name was sent to the French Government in 1743 as a faithful supporter of the House of Stuart.[2] He did not stand in 1747, and died 2 Apr. 1763.

[1] Morant, *Essex,* ii. 391; *Essex Review,* vi. 186; Venn, *Al. Cant.* pt. 1, iv. 22. [2] AEM & D. Angl. 82, ff. 149–57; see under GRAY, Charles.

E.C.

SAWBRIDGE, Jacob (c.1665–1748), of Olantigh, Kent, and Hackney, Mdx.

CRICKLADE 1715–23 Jan. 1721

b. c.1665, 1st s. of Isaac Sawbridge by Katherine Bathrom. *m.* c.1698, Elizabeth, da. and h. of John Fisher, 3s. 1da. *suc.* fa. 1679.
Director, South Sea Co. 1711–21.

Starting life with a 'very considerable fortune',[1] Jacob Sawbridge became a partner in the firm of Turner, Sawbridge, and Caswall, bankers, operating under the name and charter of the Sword Blade Company. He was an original director of the South Sea Company, who banked with his firm. Returned as a Whig in 1715, he voted against the septennial bill, for the repeal of the Occasional Conformity and Schism Acts, but against the peerage bill on which he had been put down as to be spoken to by Craggs senior and his own partner, Sir George Caswall (q.v.).

When the South Sea frauds came out at the beginning of 1721 Sawbridge, with the other directors in the Commons, was expelled the House, committed to the custody of the serjeant at arms, and examined by the South Sea committee of the Commons. He was questioned by the committee as to entries in the books of his firm purporting to show that £50,000 of the £574,000 South Sea stock which was supposed to have been issued as bribes to Members of Parliament, etc. (see under Caswall, George) had been sold at a profit of £250,000 for Charles Stanhope (q.v.), secretary to the Treasury, whose name had been subsequently altered in the books to 'Stangape'. In his evidence he exonerated Stanhope from any share in or knowledge of this transaction, declaring that he, Sawbridge, had bought the stock for himself and his partners and had entered it under a fictitious name so that their staff should not know that it belonged to them.[2]

On the introduction of the bill confiscating the estates of the late directors and other guilty parties for the relief of their victims, Sawbridge petitioned the House for lenient treatment on the ground that whatever he had done 'that may have given offence hath been through ignorance and inadvertency, without any private or unlawful views or designs'.[3] He was allowed to keep only £5,000 out of a fortune of £77,000, a proportion which shows that the Commons classed him among the more rascally of the directors. In common with all the directors he was also incapacitated from sitting in Parliament or holding public office.

Sawbridge died 11 July 1748. Among his grandchildren were John Sawbridge, M.P., the radical lord mayor of London, and Mrs. Macaulay, who inserted a vindication of him in her *History of England*.

[1] *Case of Mr. Jacob Sawbridge.* [2] *CJ*, xix. 430–1. [3] Ibid. 524–5.

R.R.S.

SAYER, Exton (c.1691–1731), of Doctors' Commons, London.

HELSTON 13 May 1726–1727
TOTNES 1727–21 Sept. 1731

b. c.1691, 1st s. of George Sayer of Doctors' Commons by Mary, da. and coh. of Everard Exton, proctor of Doctors' Commons. *educ*, L. Inn 1709; Trinity Hall, Camb. 1709, LL.B. 1713, LL.D. 1718; Doctors' Commons 1718. *m.* 6 Feb. 1724, Catherine, da. of William Talbot, bp. of Durham, sis. of Charles Talbot (q.v.), 1st Baron Talbot, *s.p. suc.* fa. 1727.
Fellow of Trinity Hall 1714–24; chancellor of Durham dioc. 1724–*d.*; judge advocate, court of Admiralty 1726–*d.*; surveyor gen. of crown lands 1730–*d.*

On Sayer's marriage in 1724 he resigned his fellowship at Trinity Hall to become spiritual chancellor to his father-in-law, the Bishop of Durham, from whom he obtained valuable leases of ecclesiastical coal-bearing lands.[1] A famous advocate in Doctors' Commons, in 1725 he acted as counsel for Lord Chancellor Macclesfield, to whom he was a 'particular friend'.[2] Brought into Parliament as a ministerial nominee, he quickly became

one of the leading government spokesmen. On 26 Feb. 1730 he led for the Government in resisting an opposition sponsored petition to end the monopoly of the East India Company, and in the great Dunkirk debate next day he was put up by Walpole to sidetrack Sir William Wyndham's motion by rising before it could be seconded to move an alternative motion, which was adopted.[3] A promising political career was cut short by his death from a riding accident, 24 Sept. 1731.

[1] E. Hughes, *N. Country Life in 18th Cent.* 308. [2] Howell, *State Trials*, xvi. 886. [3] *HMC Egmont Diary*, i. 66–67, 72–73; *Knatchbull Diary*.

E.C.

SCAWEN, Sir Thomas (c.1650–1730), of Walbrook, London, and Horton, Bucks.

GRAMPOUND 1708–1710
LONDON 1715–1722

b. c.1650, 6th s. of Robert Scawen, M.P., of Horton by Catherine, da. of Cavendish Alsopp, merchant; bro. of Sir William Scawen (q.v.). *m.* (lic. 4 Sept. 1691) Martha, da. of Abraham Wessell, London merchant, 5s. 4da. Kntd. 25 Sept. 1714. *suc.* bro. to Horton 1722.
Prime warden, Fishmongers' Co. 1708–10; alderman, London 1712; director, Bank of England 1705–19, 1723–*d.* (with statutory intervals), dep. gov. 1719–21, gov. 1721–3.[1]

An eminent merchant, trading with Flanders,[2] Scawen was returned for London as a government supporter in 1715, after standing for it unsuccessfully in 1713. He voted with the Government except on the peerage bill, which he opposed, but did not stand again. Three years before his death, 22 Sept. 1730, he was passed over for lord mayor because he had not qualified by serving as sheriff.[3] As his eldest son Thomas (q.v.) had been already provided for by Sir William Scawen (q.v.), he left him only the manor of Horton, bequeathing the rest of his property, consisting of estates at Reigate and Cheam in Surrey, together with his personal property, to his three younger sons.[4]

[1] *N. & Q.* clxxix. 60. [2] *Bd. of Trade Jnl.* 1715–18, p. 222. [3] A. A. Beaven, *Aldermen of London*, ii. p. xxvi. [4] PCC 290 Auber.

R.R.S.

SCAWEN, Thomas (d. 1774), of Carshalton, Surr.

SURREY 12 Apr. 1727–1741

b. aft. 1695, 2nd but 1st surv. s. of Sir Thomas Scawen (q.v.). *m.* 8 June 1725, Tryphena, da. and h. of Lord James Russell of Maidwell, Northants. (5th s. of William, 1st Duke of Bedford), 2s. *suc.* uncle Sir William Scawen (q.v.) 1722; fa. 1730.

At the end of the 1727 Parliament, Scawen was returned as an opposition Whig for Surrey, where he had inherited the property of his uncle, Sir

William Scawen (q.v.). At the ensuing general election he joined interests with the other outgoing Member, John Walter, against Arthur Onslow (q.v.). When it became clear that the poll was going in Onslow's favour, Walter agreed to give up, apparently on condition that his expenses should be paid by Scawen. The sheriff however ruled that the poll must proceed, with the result that Scawen obtained a small majority over Walter by the second votes of Onslow's supporters.[1] Re-elected unopposed with Onslow in 1734, he voted regularly with the Opposition. He did not stand again but in 1747 he used his interest at Mitchell (see under Scawen, Sir William) to bring in Thomas Clarke (q.v.) for that borough at the request of Lord Chancellor Hardwicke. He died 11 Feb. 1774.

[1] *HMC 14th Rep.* IX, 518-19.

R.R.S.

SCAWEN, Sir William (c.1647–1722), of Walbrook, London, and Carshalton, Surr.

NEW WINDSOR   20 Nov. 1693–1698
GRAMPOUND   1698–1702
SURREY   1705–1710
                24 July 1721–1722

b. c.1647, 4th s. of Robert Scawen, M.P., of Horton, Bucks. and bro. of Sir Thomas Scawen (q.v.). *m.* (lic. 2 Dec. 1684) Mary, da. of Sir William Maynard, 1st Bt., *s.p. suc.* bro. to Horton 1691. Kntd. 29 Oct. 1692.
    Director, Bank of England 1694–5, 1699–1722 (with statutory intervals), dep. gov. 1695–7, gov. 1697–9; director, E.I. Co. 1710–12.

Sir William Scawen was descended from a Cornish family, whose estate of Molinick, carrying an interest in the borough of Mitchell, he inherited. His father, a successful London attorney, bought the manor of Horton, Bucks. in 1658.[1] A merchant, army clothing contractor,[2] and financier, who made a fortune in the wars of William III, he bought the manor of Carshalton and other properties in Surrey, for which he sat as a Whig 1705–10, and again 1721–2. He died 18 Oct. 1722, leaving £7,000 to each of his three younger nephews, the sons of his brother Thomas (q.v.), and all his real property in Buckinghamshire, Surrey, Yorkshire, Cornwall and Ireland to his eldest nephew, Thomas Scawen (q.v.), with £10,000 from his personal estate to be spent on rebuilding the house at Carshalton according to plans already made, which were never carried out.[3]

[1] G. W. J. Gyll, *Wraysbury*, 216–20. [2] *Cal. Treas. Bks.* xxxii. 37. [3] PCC 233 Marlborough.

R.R.S.

SCLATER, Thomas (?1664–1736), of Catley, Cambs.

BODMIN   1713–1715
CAMBRIDGE   27 Jan.–27 May 1715
                1722–22 Aug. 1736

b. ?1664, s. of Edward Sclater of Kingston-upon-Hull, Yorks. *educ.* St. Paul's; Trinity, Camb. 13 June 1682, aged 17; G. Inn 1694, called 1703, bencher 1724. *m.* c.1716, Elizabeth (*d.* Dec. 1726), sis. and h. of Peter Standley of Paxton Place, Hunts., and assumed name of Bacon, *s.p. suc.* to estates of his gt.-uncle Sir Thomas Sclater, 1st Bt., of Catley, Cambs. 1684.

Thomas Sclater, a practising barrister, assumed the name of Bacon about 1716, on marrying a considerable heiress who was in his charge. Much increasing her fortune, as well as the estate which he had inherited from his great-uncle, he bought several large estates in Cambridgeshire and elsewhere, rebuilt Catley House, and amassed a valuable collection of books, which was sold by auction after his death. Urged by Harley to stand for Cambridge University in 1710, he refused on the ground that he would split the church vote.[1] After sitting for Bodmin in Anne's last Parliament, he was brought in for Cambridge by Sir John Hynde Cotton (q.v.) in 1715, but was unseated on petition, declining to stand for the county at a by-election in 1718. From 1722 he represented Cambridge as a Tory, on Cotton's interest, voting against the Government in all recorded divisions. He died intestate, 22 Aug. 1736, leaving a fortune said to amount to £200,000.[2] He presented four maces to the Cambridge corporation.

[1] *HMC Portland*, vi. 148–9; v. 93–94. [2] *Gent. Mag.* 1736, p. 488.

R.R.S.

SCOTT (SCOT), David (1689–1766), of Scotstarvet, Fife.

FIFESHIRE   1741–1747
ABERDEEN BURGHS 27 Mar. 1751–1 Dec. 1766

b. 1689, o.s. of David Scot of Scotstarvet, by his 2nd w. Elizabeth, da. of John Ellis of Elliston. *educ.* adv. 1712. *m.* 26 Nov. 1716, Lucy, da. of Sir Robert Gordon, M.P. [S], 3rd Bt., of Gordonstown, 2s. 2da. *suc.* fa. 1718.

Scott stood for Anstruther Burghs in 1722, when there was a double return, on which the seat was awarded by the Commons to his opponent. Returned for his county in 1741, he voted with the Opposition till Walpole's fall, after which, influenced by his nephew, William Murray (q.v.), later Lord Mansfield, he went over to the Government. 'All the rest are with us', John Drummond (q.v.) wrote of the opposition Members for Scotland, 30 Nov. 1742, 'particularly Scot, now Murray is solicitor-general'.[1]

Though he voted consistently with the Administration he was classed in 1746 as 'doubtful'. Despite 'threats, promises, and great men's letters',[2] he was defeated at Fife by James Oswald (q.v.) in 1747. Next year he was put up unsuccessfully by Lord Panmure (William Maule, q.v.) for Aberdeen Burghs, where he was returned unopposed on his opponent's death in 1751. In 1753 the Duke of Argyll informed Pelham that, having been asked by the Aberdeen council to recommend a Member, he proposed to reply that in his opinion 'their present Member has behaved himself very well, with some little touch upon the merit of his relation', Murray.[3] He held the seat without a contest till his death, 1 Dec. 1766.

[1] To Earl of Morton, Morton mss, SRO. [2] Oswald to G. Grenville, 1 Aug. 1747, Grenville mss. [3] 28 Oct. 1753, Newcastle (Clumber) mss.

R.R.S.

SCOTT, Francis, Lord Dalkeith (1721–50).

BOROUGHBRIDGE   22 Apr. 1746–1 Apr. 1750

b. 19 Feb. 1721, 1st s. of Francis, 2nd Duke of Buccleuch [S], by Lady Jean Douglas, da. of James, 2nd Duke of Queensberry [S] and 1st Duke of Dover [GB]. *educ.* Eton 1732; Ch. Ch. Oxf. 1739. *m.* 2 Oct. 1742, Lady Caroline Campbell, da. and coh. of John, 2nd Duke of Argyll [S] and 1st Duke of Greenwich [GB], 4s. 2da.

Returned by the Duke of Newcastle at a by-election in 1746, Dalkeith wrote to Henry Pelham on the eve of the dissolution of Parliament in 1747:

> If the Duke of Newcastle is so good as to bring me again into Parliament, there will not be one person in the House of Commons a more steady friend to him and of his family, for the civilities I have already received from the Pelhams are sufficient to bind me to them forever. As to yourself I shall be silent, for if I was to say half what I think it would look like flattery, and a flatterer I abhor.[1]

Duly re-elected, he died of smallpox, 1 Apr. 1750.

[1] 9 June 1747, Newcastle (Clumber) mss.

R.R.S.

SCOTT, James (c.1672–1747), of Commieston, Kincardine.

KINCARDINESHIRE   1713–1734

b. c.1672, 2nd s. of Hercules Scott of Brotherton, Kincardine by Jane, da. of Sir James Ogilvy of New Grange, Forfar. *m.* Apr. 1712, Margaret, 1st da. of Hugh Wallace, M.P. [S], of Ingliston, Forfar, 1s. 1da.
Ensign and lt. 3 Ft. Gds. 1692, lt. and capt. 1693, capt. and lt.-col. 1694, 2nd maj. 1713, 1st maj. 1717, lt.-col. comdg. regt. 1723–43; col. of Ft. 1712; brig.-gen. 1735; maj.-gen. 1739; lt.-gen. 1743.

James Scott, related to James Scott of Logie and Robert Scott of Dunninald (qq.v.), was descended, as were all the Scotts in Angus, from the family of

Balwearie, Fife. A professional soldier, he had the remarkable distinction of serving for 51 years in the same regiment, including nearly 20 years in command. Returned four times for his county, he voted with the Administration in all recorded divisions. The secret committee of inquiry into the South Sea bubble disclosed in 1721 that he had accepted £1,000 stock from the Company without paying for it.[1] Standing down in 1734 for his son, who was not elected, he died in 1747.

[1] *CJ*, xix. 569, 572.

R.S.L.

SCOTT, James (1671–1732), of Logie, Forfar.

SCOTLAND   1707–1708
ABERDEEN BURGHS   1710–8 Feb. 1711
FORFARSHIRE   30 July 1716–17 Jan. 1733

b. 1671, 1st s. of James Scott, M.P. [S] 1693–1702, of Logie by Agnes, da. of Sir Alexander Falconer, 1st Bt., of Glenfarquhar, Kincardine. *m.* Isabella, da. of Sir Alexander Bannerman, 2nd Bt., of Elsick, Kincardine, 3s. 6da. *suc.* fa. bef. 1722.
M.P. [S] Forfarshire 1698–1702, Montrose Burgh 1702–7.

Of an ancient Forfarshire family, Scott, who had sat for the county with his father before the Union, was returned unopposed for it as a Whig in succession to John Carnegie, expelled for taking part in the rebellion of 1715. He voted with the Government in the division on Lord Cadogan (q.v.) in June 1717[1] but against them on the peerage bill in 1719. In an undated list of payments by Sunderland to Members of Parliament or their relations c.1720–1, he is shown as receiving £300.[2] Unopposed in 1722, he was attacked at Dundee in 1725 by a mob who 'accused him as an accessory to the malt tax bill and then fell upon him in so violent a manner that had he not been rescued by some soldiers, who casually were there, he must have been put to death'.[3] Re-elected in 1727 after a contest, he voted with the Government on the Hessians in 1730 but was absent from other reported divisions. He died in October 1732.

[1] *More Culloden Pprs*. ii. 173. [2] Sunderland (Blenheim) mss. D. II, 4. [3] *More Culloden Pprs*. ii. 266–7.

R.R.S.

SCOTT, Robert (1705–80), of Dunninald, Forfar.

FORFARSHIRE   1 Mar. 1733–1734

b. 1705, 2nd s. of Patrick Scott of Rossie, Dunninald and Usan by Margaret, da. of Sir Archibald Hope of Rankeillour, Fife, ld. of session (Lord Rankeillour). *educ.* adv. 1726. *m.* 1740, Anne, da. of John Middleton (q.v.) of Seaton, Aberdeen, 2s. 1da.

Scott, who succeeded his kinsman, James Scott (q.v.) of Logie, voted with the Government on the excise bill in 1733. Defeated in 1734 and again at a by-election in 1735, he died 27 Dec. 1780.

R.R.S.

SCOTT, Walter (1724–93), of Harden, Roxburgh, and Mertoun, Berwicks.

ROXBURGHSHIRE   1747–Apr. 1765

b. 31 Dec. 1724, 1st s. of Walter Scott of Harden by his 3rd w. Ann, o. da. of John Scott of Gorrenberry; gd.-s. of Walter Scott, Earl of Tarras [S]. *educ.* Glasgow Univ. 1743–4. *m.* 18 Apr. 1754, Lady Diana Hume (*de jure* Baroness Polwarth [S] 1822), 3rd da. of Hugh, 3rd Earl of Marchmont [S], 1s. 1da. *suc.* fa. 1746.
Receiver gen. and cashier of the excise in Scotland, Apr. 1765; trustee for fisheries and manufactures in Scotland, Nov. 1769.

The representative of a senior branch of the Buccleuch family, Scott was returned for his county in 1747 with the backing of the Marquess of Lothian, who supported the Government;[1] but in a list prepared by Pelham for the next general election in Scotland he is shown as 'opposing'.[2] He died 25 Jan. 1793.

[1] Lothian to Newcastle, 27 Aug. 1747, Add. 32712, f. 438.
[2] Newcastle (Clumber) mss.

E.H.-G.

SCROPE, John (c.1662–1752), of Wormsley, in Stokenchurch, Bucks.

RIPON   1722–1727
BRISTOL   1727–1734
LYME REGIS   1734–9 Apr. 1752

b. c.1662, o.s. of Thomas Scrope of Wormsley and Bristol, merchant, by Mary, da. of Thomas Hooke of Bristol, merchant.[1] *educ.* M. Temple 1686, called 1693, bencher 1719. *unm. suc.* fa. 1704.
Baron of the Exchequer [S] 1708–24; commr. of the great seal in England Sept.–Oct. 1710; sec. to the Treasury 1724–d.; recorder, Bristol 1727–35.

John Scrope was the grandson of Adrian Scrope, M.P., the regicide, whose estates, forfeited after his execution in 1660, were granted back to Scrope's father in 1661.[2] Said to have been in Monmouth's rebellion in 1685, carrying intelligence to Holland dressed as a woman,[3] he became a prosperous lawyer, giving up his practice in 1708 to accept a judicial post in the Exchequer court of Scotland.[4] In December 1716 he was one of the judges appointed to try the Jacobite prisoners who had been brought from Scotland to Carlisle for trial in England. Entering Parliament unopposed for Ripon in 1722 on the Aislabie interest, he was appointed by Walpole to succeed William Lowndes (q.v.) at the Treasury in 1724, a post which he retained till his death.

In debate Scrope usually confined himself to money matters, on which he was short and to the point. His first recorded speech was on 7 Dec. 1724, when, in the committee of ways and means, he moved the duty on malt, 'as usual with an exception to Scotland, with a hint that as they could not or would not pay the malt tax, there might be an equivalent'.[5] In April 1727 he moved a vote of credit which was then tacked on to a malt bill. Transferring to Bristol in 1727, he 'had a majority very near double to either of the others, for both Whig and Tory voted for him'.[6] He was also successful at Winchelsea but opted to serve for his native city. In the new Parliament he spoke against a proposal, made in February 1729, to place a further duty of 6*d.* a gallon on malt 'to discourage the pernicious use of spirits', his grounds being that 'he did not see how this consideration of making spirits could be brought into the malt bill, but thought it might deserve a particular bill.' He spoke in February 1730 against receiving a petition from the African Company. Having presented a petition from the Bristol weavers complaining of the illegal export of Irish wool to foreign countries in February 1731, he was elected chairman of a select committee set up to consider this and other similar petitions, on whose recommendation he introduced a bill for taking off the duty on the import of Irish yarn into Great Britain. During the debates on the bill he opposed a proposal to take away the right accorded to Irish seamen of carrying 40 shillings worth of woollen goods, observing that the 'liberty was given to prevent the seizing ships on every occasion, for before it was common to do so upon finding a single coat aboard'. In March 1732 he answered Pulteney's objections to the revival of the salt duty. Next year he spoke for a clause in the sugar colonies' relief bill prohibiting the importation of sugar into Ireland except through Great Britain, and a proposal to draw £500,000 out of the sinking fund for current expenditure.[7] His voting for the excise bill and against the repeal of the Septennial Act in 1734 cost him his seat at Bristol in the general election that year, though he had the support of the common council.[8] Walpole, however, through the interest of Henry Holt Henley (q.v.), had found him another seat at Lyme Regis, where he was duly returned on the votes of the honorary freemen, among whom his 'coachman came down from his box in his livery and voted for him.'[9] Thereafter by patronage he obtained complete control of the borough. Two years later he was obliged to vote for a motion for the repeal of the Test Act, having been elected on condition that he would do so, though he disapproved of the decision to raise the matter in Parliament, which he attributed to the late Daniel Pulteney's (q.v.) 'design to distress Sir Robert Walpole'.[10] When after Walpole's fall the House of Commons set up a secret committee to inquire into his Administration, Scrope was summoned before the committee to give evidence as to the use of secret service money, but refused to take the necessary oath, stating

> that he had laid his case before the King and was authorized to say 'that the disposal of money issued for secret service, by the nature of it, requires the utmost secrecy, and is accounted for to his Majesty only; and therefore his Majesty could not permit him to disclose anything on that subject.'

Described by Horace Walpole as 'a most testy little old gentleman', who had pulled the nose of Micajah Perry (q.v.) during the excise bill debates, Scrope was 'inflexible', telling the committee

> that he was fourscore years old and did not care if he spent the few months he has to live in the Tower or not; that the last thing he would do should be to betray the King and next to him the Earl of Orford.[11]

When the Duke of Bedford, who wanted Scrope's post for Henry Legge (q.v.), pressed for his removal on the ground that 'all impartial persons must wish to see him removed' from office, Pulteney answered that this was

> absolutely impracticable. Mr. Scrope is the only man I know that thoroughly understands the business of the Treasury and is versed in drawing money bills. On this foundation he stands secure and is immovable as a rock; besides I really take him for an exceeding honest man.[12]

He did not resign with the Pelhams in 1746, but was allowed to retain his post on their return to office.

On 10 Apr. 1752, Pelham wrote to Newcastle that

> old Scrope ... died yesterday ... leaving a vast fortune to Frank Fane [q.v.]; he will have in all at least £2,000 a year in land and above £100,000 in money, all in his own disposal, without any entail on his brothers or even a recommendation.

On the same date Lord Hardwicke told Newcastle that he heard that Scrope's fortune was 'not so vast as people have imagined, he having dealt very little in the funds.'[13]

[1] *Merchants and Merchandise in 17th Cent. Bristol* (Bristol Rec. Soc. xix), 33; *Bristol Marriage Bonds* (Bristol & Glos. Arch. Soc. Rec. Ser. i), 10. [2] *VCH Bucks.* iii. 99. [3] Walpole to Mann, 17 June 1742, note by H. W. [4] *Cal. Treas. Bks.* xxii. 327; xxiv. 186. [5] *Knatchbull Diary*, 7 Dec. 1724. [6] Jas. Pearce to Humphry Morice, 9 Sept. 1727, Morice mss 398. [7] *HMC Egmont Diary*, i. 51, 140, 184, 334; iii. 344-5. [8] Seyer, *Mems. Bristol*, ii. 580. [9] Diary of Lady Sarah Cowper, 5 May 1734, Cowper (Panshanger) mss, Herts. RO. [10] *HMC Egmont Diary*, ii. 243-4. [11] *CJ*, xxiv. 299; Walpole to Mann, 17 June 1742. [12] *Bedford Corresp.* i. 5, 7. [13] Add. 32726, ff. 393, 395.

R.S.L.

SCUDAMORE, James, 3rd Visct. Scudamore [I] (1684–1716), of Holme Lacy, Herefs.

HEREFORDSHIRE 1705–1715
HEREFORD 1715–2 Dec. 1716

bap. 15 July 1684, 2nd but 1st surv. s. of John Scudamore, M.P., 2nd Visct. Scudamore [I], by Lady Frances Cecil, o. da. of John, 4th Earl of Exeter. *educ.* Gloucester Hall, Oxf. 1695. *m.* by 7 Mar. 1706, Frances, da. and h. of Simon Digby, M.P., 4th Baron Digby of Geashill [I], 1da. *suc.* fa. as 3rd Visct. [I] July 1697.

Of an ancient Herefordshire family, who had often represented the county and borough of Hereford, Scudamore sat for the county in four Parliaments under Anne. In 1715 he was returned as a Tory for the borough, though in 1710 he had 'got a fall from his horse in riding hastily to Hereford about some electioneering business, which impaired his understanding, and at length occasioned his death',[1] 2 Dec. 1716.

[1] W. R. Williams, *Herefs. M.P.s*, 59; *HMC Portland*, iv. 570.

A.N.N.

SCUDAMORE, *see also* **FITZROY** (afterwards **FITZROY SCUDAMORE), Charles**

SEBRIGHT, Sir Thomas Saunders, 4th Bt. (1692–1736), of Beechwood, Herts.

HERTFORDSHIRE 1715–12 Apr. 1736

b. 11 May 1692, 1st s. of Sir Edward Sebright, 3rd Bt., of Besford, Worcs. by Anne, da. and coh. of Thomas Saunders of Beechwood. *educ.* Jesus, Oxf. 1705. *m.* Nov. 1718, Henrietta, da. of Sir Samuel Dashwood, M.P., ld. mayor of London, 2s. *suc.* fa. 15 Dec. 1702.

Sebright's father, a Worcestershire baronet, acquired by marriage an estate in Hertfordshire, for which Sebright himself was returned soon after coming of age. He was one of the Members who were credited by the South Sea Company with stock without paying for it, while the South Sea bill was before Parliament in 1720.[1] A high Tory, he voted against the Government in all recorded divisions, including that on the partial pardon of Bolingbroke, whom he detested for betraying the Pretender. In 1731 he introduced a bill to prevent the carrying of excessive weights on public roads, which was defeated on the third reading. He was one of the reputed Jacobites in the opposition list for a committee on frauds in the customs in 1733.[2] A book collector, whose library is often referred to by Hearne, the antiquary, he continued to represent his county till his death, 12 Apr. 1736.

[1] *CJ*, xix. 573. [2] Mahon, *Hist. of England* (1858), ii. p. xxiii; *Knatchbull Diary*, 48; *CJ*, xxi. 704, 732; *HMC Egmont Diary*, i. 365.

A.N.N.

SEDLEY, Sir Charles, 2nd Bt. (?1721–78), of Nuthall, Notts.

NOTTINGHAM 26 May 1747–1754
1774–23 Aug. 1778

b. ?1721, 1st s. of Sir Charles Sedley, 1st Bt., of Northfleet, Kent by Elizabeth, da. of William Frith of Nuthall. *educ.* Westminster Apr. 1732, aged 10; Univ. Coll. Oxf. 22 Feb. 1739, aged 17. *unm. suc.* fa. 18 Feb. 1730.

Descended from an illegitimate son of the Restoration dramatist, Sedley, whose father stood for Newark unsuccessfully in 1727, belonged to one of the leading Tory families in Nottinghamshire. Returned as a Tory for Nottingham at a contested by-election in May 1747, he was re-elected unopposed at the immediately following general election, but did not stand in 1754, remaining out of Parliament till 1774, when he was again returned for Nottingham. He died 23 Aug. 1778, leaving his property to an illegitimate daughter, who married Henry Venables Vernon, afterwards 3rd Lord Vernon.

R.R.S.

SELWYN, Charles (1689–1749), of West Sheen, Surr.

MITCHELL 1722–1727
GLOUCESTER 16 Feb. 1728–1734
LUDGERSHALL 1741–1747

b. 1689, 2nd s. of Lt.-Gen. William Selwyn, M.P., of Matson, Glos., gov. of Jamaica, by Albinia, da. of Richard Bettenson of Scadbury, Kent, sis. and coh. of Sir Edward Bettenson, 2nd Bt.; bro. of John Selwyn sen. (q.v.). *m.* (1) Mary Cook, wid. of William Houblon, *s.p.*; (2) Anna Maria, da. of Thomas Hyde and wid. of John Geddes, *s.p.*
Ensign 2 Ft. 1692; capt. 22 Ft. 1703; lt. and capt. Coldstream Gds. 1708; maj. 3 Ft. 1711–c.15; gent. usher to the Princess of Wales 1714–27; equerry to the Queen 1727–37; mayor, Gloucester 1736.

Commissioned at the age of three, Charles Selwyn was brought in for Mitchell in 1722 as a government nominee. In the next Parliament, after a double return, he represented Gloucester on the interest of his brother, voting with the Administration in all recorded divisions, except on the excise bill, when he was absent. Returned for Ludgershall by his brother in 1741, he deserted Walpole after his defeat on the chairman of the elections committee, 16 Dec., absenting himself on the Westminster election petition, 22 Dec., and on the secret committee, 21 Jan. 1742. It was said that 'after his brother had chose him he made him pay £1,000, which he is resolved to have back again some way or other'.[1] In 1742 he spoke against the Address, 16 Nov., and voted against the

Hanoverians, 10 Dec. He spoke in favour of an opposition pensions bill in 1743, and again voted against the Hanoverians in 1744. On 26 Feb. 1745, described by Philip Yorke (q.v.) as 'a very contemptible fellow',[2] and by Horace Walpole to Mann, 29 Mar., as 'a dirty pensioner, half turned patriot, by the Court being overstocked with votes', he moved for an inquiry into the naval miscarriage off Toulon. At the end of 1745 he transferred his allegiance to the Administration for a short time, supporting the address of thanks on 17 Oct. and voting for the Hanoverians in 1746, when he was classed as 'doubtful'. But on 18 Nov., in a speech opposing the Address, he called for a militia bill and the repeal of the Septennial Act, referring to Pitt as a prostitute to venality and the purchased slave of a corrupt ministry. No doubt owing to his political conduct he was not put up by his brother in 1747. He died 9 June 1749.

[1] Sir R. Wilmot to Devonshire, 12 Jan. 1742, Devonshire mss.
[2] Yorke's parl. jnl. *Parl. Hist.* xiii. 1202.

P.W.

SELWYN, George Augustus (1719–91), of Matson, Glos.

LUDGERSHALL 1747–1754
GLOUCESTER 1754–1780
LUDGERSHALL 1780–25 Jan. 1791

b. 11 Aug. 1719, 2nd but 1st surv. s. of John Selwyn of Matson; bro. of John Selwyn jun. (qq.v.). *educ.* Eton 1728–32; Hertford, Oxf. 1739 and 1744; I. Temple 1737; Grand Tour with George Montagu (q.v.) 1739–44. *unm. suc.* fa. 1751.
Surveyor of meltings and clerk of irons in the mint 1740–d.; registrar of court of Chancery, Barbados 1753–d.; paymaster, board of works 1755–82; mayor, Gloucester 1758, 1765; surveyor gen. of crown lands 1784–d.

Expelled from Oxford in 1745 for profaning the sacrament at a tavern, George Selwyn was returned for his father's pocket borough of Ludgershall in 1747. On his father's death in 1751 he inherited most of the family property, carrying complete control of two seats at Ludgershall and a strong interest at Gloucester. In 1752 Pelham wrote to Newcastle at Hanover recommending the grant of a pension to Selwyn's mother, 'the oldest servant of the late Queen,' who had been 'left by her husband in extreme bad circumstances'. The grounds for the recommendation were that

what kindness he did design her, by a flaw in his will does not stand good and her son is not of a nature to give her any dependence on his goodwill, further than he is obliged to do. Besides, his own circumstances are not great, were he disposed never so well.[1]

In 1753 he succeeded to a colonial sinecure, of which his father had bought the reversion in 1724.[2]

He died 25 Jan. 1791.

[1] Add. 32729, f. 396. [2] *CSP Col.* 1724–5, p. 167.

P.W.

SELWYN, John (1688–1751), of Matson, Glos.

TRURO	1715–Feb. 1721
WHITCHURCH	1727–1734
GLOUCESTER	1734–5 Nov. 1751

b. 20 Aug. 1688, 1st s. of Lt.-Gen. William Selwyn, M.P., of Matson, gov. of Jamaica; bro. of Charles Selwyn (q.v.). *m.* by 1709, Mary, da. of Gen. Thomas Farrington of Chislehurst, Kent, 2s. 1da. *suc.* fa. 1702.

Ensign and lt. 3 Ft. Gds. 31 Dec. 1688; capt. and lt.-col. 1 Ft. Gds. 1707; col. of a regt. of Ft. 1709–11; col. 3 Ft. 1711–13; commr. of the equivalent 1715–17; clerk of the household to Prince of Wales Jan. 1716–18; groom of the bedchamber to George II as Prince of Wales and King 1718–30; receiver gen. and comptroller of customs 1721–7; mayor, Gloucester 1727, 1734; treasurer of the Queen's Household 1730–7; paymaster of marines 1747–8; treasurer to Prince of Wales May 1751–*d.*

Commissioned in the Guards almost at birth, Selwyn served in Flanders as aide-de-camp to Marlborough. Returned for Truro on the Boscawen interest and appointed a commissioner of the equivalent[1] in 1715, he obtained a post in the Prince's household in 1716 by the influence of Lord Townshend,[2] whom he followed into opposition in 1717, at the cost of losing his commissionership. On the reunion of the Whig party in 1720, he was given a lucrative customs post, which disqualified him from sitting in Parliament. In 1727 he transferred it to a brother to hold for him, returning himself for Whitchurch, where, in 1726, he had bought property giving him control of one seat.[3] In 1730 he became treasurer to Queen Caroline, his wife being her favourite bedchamber woman. In 1733 he bought the manor of Ludgershall, carrying the nomination of both Members, thereafter sitting for Gloucester, which he controlled through the city's reservoirs, situated on his property at Matson.[4] He was a member of the gaols committee of the House of Commons in 1729–30; spoke in defence of the new colony of Georgia in a debate on the army estimates, 3 Feb. 1738; and voted regularly with the Government. In the published list of the division on the Spanish convention in 1739, he is shown as lately holding offices worth £4,600 a year.[5]

When Walpole fell in 1742, Selwyn advised him not to take the pension of £4,000 a year offered him by the King in view of the outcry against it. In November 1744 he was sent by the King with a message to Walpole in Norfolk asking him to advise

on the question of Granville's dismissal.[6] In December 1746 he succeeded Sir Charles Hanbury Williams as paymaster of marines, arranging for his son, John (q.v.), to hold it for him temporarily, presumably to avoid a by-election at Gloucester. He lost the post when the marines were disbanded in 1748, but in 1751, Horace Walpole writes,

> old John' Selwyn (who had succeeded to the confidence of Lord Townshend, Sir Robert Walpole and Mr. Pelham, as they succeeded one another in power, and had already laid a foundation with Mr. Fox) was appointed treasurer to the Prince, as he and his son were already to the Duke and Princesses. He was a shrewd silent man, humane, and reckoned very honest—he might be so—if he was, he did great honour to the cause, for he had made his court and his fortune with as much dexterity as those who reckon virtue the greatest impediment to wordly success.[7]

He died 5 Nov. 1751.

[1] See BOTELER, John. [2] *Lady Cowper Diary,* 52. [3] John Selwyn's notebook, Hants RO 4175/384. [4] Hervey, *Mems.* 607; *Cal. Treas. Bks. and Pprs.* 1731–4, p. 449; Walpole to Rich. Bentley, Sept. 1753. [5] *HMC Egmont Diary,* i. 45, 55; *Gent. Mag.* 1739, p. 307. [6] Walpole to Mann, 18 June 1744; Coxe, *Pelham,* i. 189. [7] *Mems. Geo. II,* i. 94–95.

P.W.

SELWYN, John (c.1709–51).

WHITCHURCH	1734–27 June 1751

b. c.1709, 1st s. of John Selwyn of Matson, Glos.; bro. of George Augustus Selwyn (qq.v.). *educ.* Clare, Camb. 1728. *unm.*

Treasurer to Duke of Cumberland and the Princesses 1737–*d.*; treasurer of the late Queen's pensions 1737–*d.*; paymaster of the marines Dec. 1746–7; groom of the bedchamber to George, Prince of Wales, May 1751–*d.*

Selwyn, who was returned for Whitchurch on the interest of his father, voted with the Administration in every recorded division, except on the Hanoverians in 1746, when he was absent. On 24 Jan. 1738 he seconded the Address;[1] on 8 Mar. 1739 he spoke in favour of the Spanish convention;[2] and on 29 Jan. 1740 he spoke against the place bill. He died shortly before his father, 27 June 1751.

[1] *HMC Egmont Diary,* ii. 462. [2] Coxe, *Walpole,* iii. 517.

P.W.

SERGISON, Thomas (1701–66), of Cuckfield Place, Suss.

LEWES	1747–13 Dec. 1766

b. 20 Feb. 1701, 2nd but 1st surv. s. of Thomas Warden of Cuckfield, mercer, by Prudence, da. and h. of Michael Sergison, niece of Charles Sergison, M.P., of Cuckfield Place. *m.* (settlement 19, 20 Apr. 1732) Mary, da. of William Pitt, 3da. *suc.* fa. 1718; gt.-uncle, Charles Sergison, to Cuckfield estate, taking the name of Sergison.

In 1732 Thomas Warden inherited a large estate

in Sussex, including a good deal of house property at Lewes, from his great-uncle, Charles Sergison, whose name he assumed. Next year 'the Tory gentlemen' of the neighbourhood set him up for Lewes[1] in opposition to the Duke of Newcastle's candidates. Narrowly defeated in 1734, he stood again unsuccessfully in 1741 and once more at a by-election in 1743 when, after much vacillation, he allowed his supporters to put him up, only to withdraw before the poll. Sergison, Newcastle's agent, reported on the last occasion,

> by his unaccountable proceedings in this affair has riveted your Grace's interest, and done more service than his friendship would have done, for though the natural interest he has [in Lewes] from property is considerable and his estate in the county makes it there so, yet such is the disposition, irresolution, and closeness of the man, that with as many hundreds as he has thousands per year, without vanity I would engage to bring more votes to a county election.

Still, when sounded by Sergison in 1746 with a view to an agreement, Newcastle's agent was strongly in favour of coming to terms. Newcastle at first took the line that if he brought Sergison in for Lewes it would look as if he had been 'forced'; tried to induce him to accept instead a seat at one of his Yorkshire boroughs; and asked for 'a declaration how he would vote in the House'. To this Sergison replied that he would 'only accept of being chose for the county or Lewes', pointing out that since he admittedly could not be returned there without Newcastle's consent 'whilst you are in power, . . . no one of common sense could say you was forced'. As to a declaration, he said that he

> should never declare beforehand how he should vote and chose to do more than he engaged for rather than engage for more than he should do, but could say this with great truth, that if he went into the House prejudiced any way it would be in your favour . . . and that he thought [he] could be able to do you more service by sometimes voting against than always with you.

From this position he would not budge and in the end Newcastle accepted him on his own terms.[2]

For the rest of Sergison's life he sat for Lewes without opposition as Newcastle's candidate. In 1751 he was included in a private whip sent by Newcastle to his parliamentary followers in the House. He seems to have asked for no favours for himself but to have looked after his relations.[3] Politically, he was as good as his word, adhering to Newcastle till his own death on 13 Dec. 1766.

[1] Newcastle to the bp. of Bangor, 4 Sept. 1733, Add. 32688, f. 257. [2] W. Poole to Newcastle, 10 Dec. 1743, Add. 32701, f. 306; 2 Nov. 1746, Add. 32709, f. 154; 15 Apr. 1747, Add. 32710, f. 440. [3] Newcastle to Jas. Pelham, 30 Jan. 1751, Add. 32724, f. 105; Namier, *Structure*, 22.

R.R.S.

SEYMOUR, Algernon, Earl of Hertford (1684–1750).

MARLBOROUGH   27 Nov. 1705–1708
NORTHUMBERLAND   1708–23 Nov. 1722

b. 11 Nov. 1684, 2nd but 1st surv. s. of Charles Seymour, 6th Duke of Somerset, by his 1st w. Elizabeth, da. and h. of Joceline Percy, 5th Earl of Northumberland, wid. of (i) Henry Cavendish (afterwards Percy), Earl of Ogle, and (ii) Thomas Thynne, M.P., of Longleat, Wilts.; bro. of Lord Percy Seymour (q.v.). *m.* Mar. 1715, Frances, da. and coh. of Hon. Henry Thynne, M.P. (s. and h. of Thomas Thynne, M.P., 1st Visct. Weymouth), 1s. *d.v.p.* 1da. *suc.* mother (in error) as Lord Percy 23 Nov. 1722; fa. as 7th Duke of Somerset 2 Dec. 1748; *cr.* Baron Warkworth of Warkworth Castle, Northumb. and Earl of Northumberland 2 Oct. 1749; Baron Cockermouth and Earl of Egremont 3 Oct. 1749.
Ld. lt. Suss. 1706–*d.*; col. 15 Ft. 1709–15; gov. Tynemouth castle 1710–*d.*; gent. of the bedchamber to Prince of Wales 1714–Dec. 1717; col. 2 Life Gds. 1715–40; brig.-gen. 1727; gov. Minorca 1727–42; maj.-gen. 1735; lt.-gen. 1739; col. R. Horse Gds. 1740–Feb. 1742, Mar. 1742–*d.*; gov. Guernsey 1742–*d.*; gen. 1747.

At the accession of George I, Lord Hertford, an army officer, was appointed to a post in the Prince of Wales's bedchamber. Returned in 1715 as a Whig for Northumberland, where his mother had inherited the Percy estates, he proposed Spencer Compton (q.v.) as Speaker on 17 Mar. following. In January 1716 he moved for the impeachment of Lord Kenmure, one of the rebel lords. He voted against the Government on Lord Cadogan (q.v.) in June 1717 but on the breach between George I and the Prince of Wales later that year he resigned his place in the Prince's bedchamber.[1] He moved the Address in November 1719, and on 16 Oct. 1722 took the chair at a committee of the whole House on the bill to suspend the Habeas Corpus Act. On his mother's death in November of that year he was summoned (in error) to the House of Lords as Lord Percy.[2] In 1749 George II created him Earl of Northumberland with remainder to Sir Hugh Smithson (q.v.), husband of his daughter Elizabeth, the heiress to the Percy estates, and Earl of Egremont, with remainder to Sir Charles Wyndham (q.v.), heir to his Sussex and Cumberland estates under the will of his father, the 6th Duke of Somerset. He died 7 Feb. 1750.

[1] *HMC Portland*, v. 543. [2] See *CP*.

E.C.

SEYMOUR, Sir Edward, 6th Bt. (1695–1757), of Maiden Bradley, Wilts. and Berry Pomeroy, Devon.

SALISBURY   1741–1747

bap. 17 Jan. 1695, 1st s. of Sir Edward Seymour, 5th Bt., M.P., by Letitia, da. of Sir Francis Popham, K.B., M.P., of Littlecote, Wilts.; e. bro. of Francis Seymour (q.v.). *educ.* Magdalen, Oxf. 1712. *m.* 5 Mar. 1717, Mary, da. and h. of Daniel Webb of Monkton Farleigh and Melksham, Wilts., 4s. 1da. *suc.* fa. 29 Dec. 1740 and distant kinsman as 8th Duke of Somerset 7 Feb. 1750.

Ld. lt. Wilts. and c.j. in eyre, north of Trent 1752–*d.*

Returned as a Tory for Salisbury in 1741, Seymour voted against the Administration in all recorded divisions but did not stand again. He succeeded in 1750 to the dukedom of Somerset (though not to the estates), as head of the senior line of the Seymours, whose right to the dukedom had been postponed, at its creation in 1547, to that of the junior line now extinct. He was chief mourner at the funeral of Frederick, Prince of Wales, in April 1751, in which month he applied unsuccessfully through Newcastle for the lord lieutenantship of Devonshire.[1] He died 12 Sept. 1757.

[1] Newcastle to Somerset, Apr. 1751, Add. 32724, f. 227.

R.S.L.

SEYMOUR, Francis (1697–1761), of Sherborne House, Dorset.

GREAT BEDWYN   29 Apr. 1732–1734
MARLBOROUGH   1734–1741

bap. 1 Oct. 1697,[1] 2nd s. of Sir Edward Seymour, 5th Bt., M.P.; yr. bro. of Sir Edward Seymour (q.v.), afterwards 8th Duke of Somerset. *m.* 30 July 1728, Elizabeth, da. of Alexander Popham, M.P., of Littlecote, Wilts., wid. of Edward Richard Montagu (q.v.), Visct. Hinchingbrooke, mother of John, 4th Earl of Sandwich, and Hon. William Montagu (qq.v.), 2s. 1da. *suc.* to Sherborne House and the personal estate of his paternal gt.-uncle Henry Seymour Portman, M.P., of Orchard Portman, Som. 1728.

Francis Seymour was returned as a Tory for Great Bedwyn and Marlborough on the Bruce interest. A petition against him and Edward Lisle (q.v.) in March 1735 was unsuccessful

notwithstanding the utmost efforts of Sir Robert Walpole, who stayed the hearing out . . . [and] who had (as I have heard) declared before the Parliament met that no members of Lord Bruce's recommending, if returned, should keep their seats.[2]

In the same year, according to Sarah, Duchess of Marlborough, Seymour, when at the opera, was requested by the King to take off his hat but refused to do so on the grounds that

he was ill and could not do it for fear of catching cold . . . he had paid for his place and he would not prejudice his health . . . he should have thought it very wrong to have done anything of that sort in the King's palaces, but there were no kings at operas or playhouses where everybody might sit as they pleased.[3]

He voted against Walpole's Administration in all recorded divisions, did not stand again, and died 23 Dec. 1761.

[1] *Coll. Top. et Gen.* v. 39. [2] *HMC Egmont Diary*, ii. 167. [3] *Letters of a Grandmother*, ed. G. Scott Thomson, 151–2.

R.S.L.

SEYMOUR, Lord Percy (1696–1721).

COCKERMOUTH   18 Jan. 1718–4 July 1721

b. 3 June 1696,[1] 2nd surv. s. of Charles Seymour, 6th Duke of Somerset; bro. of Algernon, Earl of Hertford (q.v.). *educ.* Eton 1706–14; Trinity, Camb. 4 May 1714, aged 18. *unm.*

Seymour was put up for a vacancy at Cockermouth by his father, the Duke of Somerset. There was a double return, on which he was awarded the seat by the House of Commons. In 1719 he voted with the Government on the repeal of the Occasional Conformity and Schism Acts, and on the peerage bill. He died of smallpox, 4 July 1721.

[1] Chester, *Westminster Abbey Reg.* 304.

R.R.S.

SEYMOUR, see also PORTMAN, Henry

SHAFTO, John (?1693–1742), of Whitworth, nr. Durham.

DURHAM   26 Jan. 1730–3 Apr. 1742

b. ?1693, 2nd s. of Mark Shafto of Whitworth by Margaret, da. of Sir John Ingleby, 2nd Bt., of Ripley, Yorks.; yr. bro. of Robert Shafto (q.v.). *educ.* Lincoln, Oxf. 9 May 1710, aged 16; L. Inn 1711, called 1718. *m.* 20 May 1731, Mary, da. and h. of Thomas Jackson of Nunnington, Yorks., 2s. 2da. *suc.* bro. 1729.

John Shafto, a Tory, succeeded to his brother's seat at Durham in 1730 after a close contest. Unopposed in 1734 and 1741, he voted against the Government in all recorded divisions. He died 3 Apr. 1742.

R.S.L.

SHAFTO, Robert (?1690–1729), of Whitworth, nr. Durham.

DURHAM   3 Mar. 1712–1713, 1727–Dec. 1729

b. ?1690, 1st s. of Mark Shafto of Whitworth and bro. of John Shafto (q.v.). *educ.* Lincoln, Oxf. 17 June 1708, aged 17. *m.* 1723, Dorothy, da. of Henry Dawnay, 2nd Visct. Downe [I], and sis. of John Dawnay (qq.v.), *s.p. suc.* fa. 1723.

Robert Shafto was great-grandson of Mark Shafto, a younger son of the Northumberland family of Benwell, who bought Whitworth about 1650. Returned as a Tory at a by-election for Durham in 1712, soon after he came of age and while his father was sheriff, he did not stand again till 1727, when he was unopposed. He died in December 1729.

R.S.L.

SHANNON, Visct., *see* **BOYLE, Richard**

SHATTERDEN, *see* **DRAX, Henry**

SHAW, Sir John, 3rd Bt. (?1679–1752), of Greenock, Renfrew, and Carnock, Stirling.

RENFREWSHIRE	1708–1710
CLACKMANNANSHIRE	1722–1727
RENFREWSHIRE	1727–1734

b. ?1679, 1st s. of Sir John Shaw, 2nd Bt., by Eleanor, da. and eventually coh. of Sir Thomas Nicolson, 2nd Bt., of Carnock. *educ.* Glasgow 1694. *m.* 15 Mar. 1700, Margaret, 1st da. of Hon. Sir Hew Dalrymple, 1st Bt., M.P. [S], of North Berwick, Haddington, ld. pres. of ct. of session, and aunt of Sir Hew Dalrymple, 2nd Bt. (q.v.), 1da. *suc.* fa. Apr. 1702.

Shaw, whose family owned estates in Clackmannan, became closely associated with the growth of Greenock as a rival to Glasgow on the Clyde, where he himself was responsible for financing the building of the harbour.[1] Connected with Argyll, under whom he fought in the Fifteen rebellion at the battle of Sheriffmuir,[2] he was returned as a Whig for Clackmannanshire in 1722. A government supporter, he voted for the bills of pains and penalties against those involved in the Atterbury plot but protested to Walpole against appointing Englishmen to fill offices in Scotland.[3] He was active on behalf of the Government in the malt tax riots in 1725, when the magistrates of Glasgow refused to act against the mob and new commissions of the peace had to be issued. Duncan Forbes (q.v.), the lord advocate, wrote to him, 5 July:

> As I am sensible of the interest you have with the gentlemen of your neighbourhood, I must beg the favour of you that you with as many neighbours as you can persuade to be wise, would forthwith come into Glasgow, qualify as justices of the peace and assist in the commitment of such of the rioters, as shall be presented to you upon proper informations. You have certainly heard that a good body of troops, foot and dragoons are ordered into Glasgow . . . My earnest request to you is that, without losing one moment's time you would order your affairs so as to be at Glasgow on the day the troops arrive, to the end that you may give countenance to the justices accepting and acting.

When he arrived Forbes found him 'very hearty'.[4] In the summer of that year, Shaw, who for several years had been pressing for vigorous measures to prevent the running of Irish victuals into Scotland, was granted a commission authorizing him 'to burn

all boats that shall bring meal or grain from Ireland to Scotland'.[5] Returned for Renfrewshire in 1727, he voted with the Administration on the army in 1732 and on the excise in 1733. In 1734 he stood unsuccessfully for Clackmannanshire. During the Forty-five he and his wife mobilized local support for the forces under General John Campbell (q.v.), raising the militia in Greenock in spite of threats from the rebels.[6]

He died 5 Apr. 1752.

[1] Sir J. Marwick, *River Clyde and the Clyde Burghs*. [2] *HMC 2nd Rep.* 26; A. Williamson, *Old Greenock*, 66. [3] *HMC 2nd Rep.* 26. [4] *More Culloden Pprs.* ii. 253–4, 272. [5] *HMC 2nd Rep.* 26; *Cal. Treas. Pprs.* 1720–8, p. 366. [6] Campbell to Lady Shaw, 24 Dec. 1745, and Lady Shaw to Campbell, 28 Dec. 1745 and 3 Jan. 1746, Mamore mss 58, 62 and 71, NLS; Sir J. Fergusson, *Argyll in the Forty-Five*, 60.

E.C.

SHELBURNE, Baron *later* **Earl of,** *see* **PETTY, Henry**

SHELLEY, Sir John, 4th Bt. (1692–1771), of Mitchelgrove, Suss.

ARUNDEL	1727–1741
LEWES	6 Dec. 1743–1747

b. 5 Mar. 1692, 1st s. of Sir John Shelley, 3rd Bt., by his 2nd w. Mary, da. and eventually coh. of Sir John Gage, 4th Bt., of Firle, Suss. *m.* (1) 21 May 1717, Catherine (*d.* Sept. 1726), da. of Sir Thomas Scawen (q.v.) of Horton, Bucks., 2da.; (2) 16 Mar. 1727, Margaret, da. of Thomas Pelham, M.P., 1st Baron Pelham of Laughton, sis. of Thomas Pelham-Holles, 1st Duke of Newcastle, and Hon. Henry Pelham (q.v.), 1s. 3da. *suc.* fa. 25 Apr. 1703.

Sir John Shelley came of an ancient Sussex family, settled at Mitchelgrove, near Arundel, since the beginning of the fifteenth century. A Roman Catholic, who conformed in 1716, he married a sister of the Duke of Newcastle as his second wife in 1727, in which year he was returned head of the poll for Arundel. Throughout his parliamentary career he consistently supported the Government.

Though incurring some local odium by voting for the excise bill,[1] Shelley was re-elected unopposed in 1734, but in 1741 he came out bottom of the poll. At the beginning of 1742 he had several long conversations with the 1st Lord Egmont about 'the bad situation of affairs and apprehended a civil war, for if the Parliament is obstinate to have Sir Robert Walpole out, the King is no less determined not to part with him'. He impressed Egmont as 'a man of very good sense', who, being 'brother-in-law to the Duke of Newcastle, and very well with him', must be assumed to have been in some degree expressing the Duke's views.[2]

In 1743 Shelley was brought back into Parliament by Newcastle. Next year his wife, through whom he was accustomed to correspond with his brother-in-law, asked Newcastle to make him a lord of the Treasury:

As you have now got the better of all opposition . . . [she wrote] Sir John Shelley thinks this a proper time to mention to you that you must be sensible of his having been many years in Parliament and always attached to the Administration without having received any marks of royal favour, never having had or asked any employment for himself during the whole time, and had he been allowed what his birth entitled him to, what everybody must think him so well qualified for, he would not have thought of an employment now. I hope these good reasons won't have the less weight by his being so near a relation to you.[3]

But his private life was beginning to excite comment. At a dinner party a few months later Lady Towns-hend announced:

I have been at Hampstead this morning, and I met Sir John Shelley, who had got a very shabby man with him, but the fellow was handsome; he looked so ashamed, that I fancy it was but just over.[4]

Dropped at the next general election, he spent the last 24 years of his life in retirement, dying 6 Sept. 1771.

[1] Lady Shelley to Newcastle, 23 Aug. 1733, Add. 32688, f. 164. [2] *HMC Egmont Diary*, iii. 235–41, 244. [3] 26 Nov. 1744, Add. 32703, f. 439. [4] Horace Walpole to Geo. Montagu, 12 July 1745; see also Walpole to Mann, 3 May 1749.

R.R.S.

SHELLEY, John (?1730–83), of Mitchelgrove, Suss.

EAST RETFORD	24 Dec. 1751–1768
NEWARK	1768–1774
SHOREHAM	1774–1780

b. ?1730, o.s. of Sir John Shelley, 4th Bt. (q.v.). *educ.* Westminster 1745–8; Peterhouse, Camb. 17 Sept. 1748, aged 18. *m.* (1) 27 Aug. 1769, Wilhelmina (*d.* 21 Mar. 1772), da. of John Newnham of Maresfield Park, Suss., 1s.; (2) 14 Feb. 1775, Elizabeth, da. of Edward Woodcock of Lincoln's Inn, 3da. *suc.* fa. as 5th Bt. 6 Sept. 1771.
    Keeper of the recs. in Tower of London 1755–*d.*; clerk of the pipe in the Exchequer 1758–*d.*; P.C. 3 Dec. 1766; treasurer of the Household 1766–77.

At the age of 21 Shelley was brought into Parliament by his uncle, the Duke of Newcastle, who later endowed him with the sinecures of keeper of the records in the Tower and clerk of the pipe, both for life. A place in the customs, being incompatible with a seat in the House of Commons, was held in trust for him, bringing his emoluments to upwards of £1,500 p.a. He died 11 Sept. 1783.

R.R.S.

SHEPHEARD, Samuel (*d.* 1748), of Exning, Suff., nr. Newmarket, Cambs.

MALMESBURY	1701
CAMBRIDGE	1708–1715, 27 May 1715–1722
CAMBRIDGESHIRE	19 Nov. 1724–1747
CAMBRIDGE	1747–24 Apr. 1748

b. c.1676, 2nd s. of Samuel Shepheard, M.P., of London by Mary, da. of Edward Chamberlayne of Princethorpe, Warws. *suc.* e. bro. 1739.
    Director, E.I. Co. 1717–21.

Shepheard was the son of a wealthy London merchant, M.P. for the city of London 1705–8, one of the founders and original directors of the new East India Company and head of the South Sea Company, who was described to Harley in 1710 as 'for shipping and foreign trade by far the first in England'.[1] After sitting for Malmesbury in the 1701 Parliament, of which both his father and his elder brother were also Members, he was returned for Cambridge in 1708, sharing the representation of the borough with Sir John Hynde Cotton, the head of the Cambridgeshire Tories, till 1715. 'Resolved', in Lady Cotton's words, 'to be a Cambridgeshire country gentleman', he was on terms of the 'most intimate and cordial' friendship with her husband,[2] as well as with the heads of other leading county families, including especially John Bromley, one of the knights of the shire, who appointed him guardian to his son and heir, Henry (q.v.).

In Anne's last Parliament Shepheard, a Hanover-ian Tory, parted political company with Cotton. Opposed by the Tories at Cambridge in 1715, he was defeated at the poll but was seated on petition. Classed as a Whig who would often vote with the Tories, his only recorded votes in this Parliament were against the septennial bill in 1716 and the peerage bill in 1719. He did not stand in 1722.

In 1723 Shepheard applied to Walpole's brother, Horace (q.v.), for government support in standing for the county at a by-election likely to take place in the near future on the death of Lord Oxford, whose son and heir, Lord Harley, had been returned with Cotton for Cambridgeshire in 1722. His letter has not survived, but its terms can be inferred from those of Horace Walpole's forwarding it to his brother:

I leave the enclosed letter from Samuel Shepheard with you because its possible he may write to you upon the contents; I am sure he is very well disposed, and worth obliging, and the probability of Lord Oxford's not holding long, makes it a public consideration; because as matters stand in Cambridge-shire, I believe Shepheard by the influence of Bromley's estate is the only person that can rout Cotton's interest, and if he can really be seconded by the interest of the Jenyns [qq.v.] I think he cannot fail.[3]

Returned after a close contest with a Tory candidate, he was re-elected with his former ward, Henry Bromley, in 1727 against Cotton and another Tory, who both gave up before the end of the poll. For the next 20 years he sat for the county without opposition.

Not content with this victory, Shepheard took advantage of it to revive a vexatious claim against Cotton's property. The estate of Madingley had been granted in 1543 to the Hyndes, from whom the Cottons had acquired it by marriage, on condition of paying £10 a year to the knights of the shire for their expenses.[4] The attempt to revive this antiquated claim, which had long been dropped, and to make Cotton pay the arrears, together with other provocations, gave rise to much ill-feeling, culminating in an assault by Cotton on Shepheard at quarter sessions. Cotton has left an account of this incident:

I pressed to have a chief constable restored, who had been turned out the sessions before upon an insinuation that 'twas his own desire, which he had assured me was not so. Therefore I thought the bench ought in justice to restore him if they had not some other reason to remove him, which I said I hoped they would give if they had any. Shepheard said he was against restoring him. I asked his reason; he said he would give none, I said I believed the only reason he had was that he would not be corrupted by him the last election, upon which he told me I lied. I said I heard him but I knew where I was; he then (I suppose to provoke me to resent it there) repeated the lie to me twice by saying *you lie*, I tell you before the face of the country *you lie*. I then said 'flesh and blood can bear it no longer' and struck him. The justices interposed, and I went off from the bench. They immediately sent the under sheriff after me with order if I would not return to take me as his prisoner, I returned, and they bound me in £10,000 bail and my sureties in £10,000 more to appear at the assizes, but just before I was bound over the chairman asked who would prosecute, Mr. Shepheard said he would, the chairman not hearing him asked again upon which Shepheard answered he had told him twenty times already he would.[5]

In the end the justices settled the affair by making Shepheard withdraw and apologize, on which Cotton expressed his regret.

Shepheard now proceeded to attack Cotton in his stronghold at Cambridge. Enormously rich, thinking nothing too much to spend on elections,[6] and supported by Henry Bromley, whose expenditure was equally extravagant, he soon succeeded in gaining a majority in the venal corporation on whom Cambridge elections depended. Giving up the unequal struggle in 1741, Cotton took refuge in a seat at Marlborough, leaving Shepheard and Bromley, now Lord Montfort, masters of the field.

Shepheard fought his last election campaign in 1747, when he transferred himself to Cambridge, creating consternation by insisting that his old friend Christopher Jeaffreson (q.v.) should be his fellow Member instead of Lord Dupplin (q.v.), whom he had for some time wanted to oust. 'Lord Montfort is gone to him to try to accommodate, but God knows whether that will do with such a humourist', Lord Hardwicke wrote to his son, Philip Yorke, who was standing for the county, telling him to 'make court' to Shepheard 'and remember not to appear too fond of Dupplin before him.'[7] Two days later Soame Jenyns (q.v.) was able to report that Montfort's negotiations were going on successfully with Shepheard, who was or would be very soon perfectly satisfied.

He goes with Montfort to the Duke of Grafton's to assist at the Suffolk election about which he is extremely warm and anxious, which I look upon as a lucky incident, it being likely to keep him employed and consequently in good humour; for being master of too easy a victory here, both in town and county, he is like Alexander, uneasy only for want of new worlds to conquer.[8]

He either voted with the Opposition or abstained in all the chief extant divisions of his time, except on the place bill of 1740 and the Hanoverians in 1742, when he voted with the Government. Nevertheless he was classed in 1746 as an Old Whig and in 1747 as a government supporter.

On 24 Apr. 1748 Shepheard died of an apoplectic stroke at Hampton Court on his way back from Bath. He never married, though for many years he had lived with a woman whom he had bought by a form of conveyance of her from her husband, eventually discarding her for infidelity.[9] He left his fortune, subject to various legacies, to a natural daughter, Frances, on condition that she did not marry an Irishman, a Scotchman, a peer, or the son of a peer, except the son of his old friend, Lord Montfort. She married the nephew and heir to the title of the 8th Viscount Irwin, by whom she had three daughters, who assumed the additional name of Shepheard. One of them married the Marquess of Hertford, became the Regent's mistress, and was the mother of the nobleman immortalized by Thackeray in *Vanity Fair*, a fact which adds an additional if unintentional point to the exchanges about sheep and shepherds between Becky Sharp and Lord Steyne.

[1] *HMC Portland*, iv. 559. [2] 'Memoir of Cottons', by J. J. Antrobus, Cotton mss in possession of Col. C. H. Antrobus. [3] Sept. 1723, Cholmondeley (Houghton) mss. [4] 'Memoir of Cottons'. [5] Cotton mss. [6] Philip Yorke to Hardwicke, 28 June 1747, Add. 35351, f. 117. [7] 16 June 1747, ibid. f. 103. [8] To Hardwicke, 18 June 1747, Add. 35679, f. 7. [9] *Knatchbull Diary*, 28 Feb. 1730.

R.R.S.

SHEPPARD, James (c.1681–1730), of Watton Court, nr. Honiton, Devon.

HONITON   18 Feb. 1711–1715, 1727–10 Apr. 1730

b. c.1681, 1st s. of James Sheppard of Honiton, attorney-at-law, by Mary Walrond of Payhembury, nr. Honiton. *educ.* M. Temple 1700, called 1705. *m.* (lic. 16 Mar. 1704) Elizabeth Fowler, 3s. 5da. Kntd. 14 May 1729.

Recorder, Honiton 1713; serjeant-at-law 1724–*d.*

The Sheppards, a Honiton family, held several properties in southern Devonshire, including the manor of Watton, near Honiton, which they acquired in 1632.[1] A Tory and member of the October Club, Sheppard sat for Honiton in Anne's last two Parliaments, but was defeated for it in 1715 and 1722. In 1727 he was returned after a contest, apparently as a government supporter, since he voted with the Administration on the civil list in 1729 and the Hessians in 1730. In the debate of 25 Feb. 1730 on the application of the surplus of the sinking fund, he spoke in favour of lessening the duty on soap to relieve the woollen industry.[2] After his death from gaol fever, 10 Apr. 1730, aged 49,[3] he was declared by the House of Commons to have been not duly elected, 15 Mar. 1731.[4]

[1] *Trans. Devon Assoc.* lxiv. 54. [2] *HMC Egmont Diary*, i. 62. [3] *Devon and Cornw. N. & Q.* xi. 316; *Pol. State*, xxxix. 448. [4] *CJ*, xxi. 671.

S.R.M.

SHIPPEN, William (1673–1743), of Norfolk St., London.

BRAMBER   29 Dec. 1707–15 Jan. 1709
            8 Dec. 1710–1713
SALTASH   1713–1715
NEWTON   1715–1 May 1743

bap. 30 July 1673, 2nd s. of Rev. William Shippen, D.D., rector of Stockport, Lancs. *educ.* Stockport g.s.; B.N.C. Oxf. 1687; Westminster 1688; Trinity, Camb. 1691; M. Temple 1693, called 1699. *m.* (lic. 17 July 1712, with £70,000) Frances, da. of Sir Richard Stote of Jesmond Hall, Northumb., serjeant-at-law, coh. to her bro. Bertram Stote, *s.p.*

Commr. of public accounts (£500 p.a.) and for stating army debts (£500 p.a.) 1711–14.

William Shippen, with only a modest income of his own, married an heiress. An ardent Jacobite, he took a leading part in the commission of accounts set up in 1711 to discredit the late Whig Government, presenting to the House of Commons the evidence for the commission's charges of peculation against Marlborough. Returned in 1715 for Newton on the interest of the Legh family, into which his elder brother had married, he quickly established himself as one of the most prolific opposition speakers, sending his speeches to the *Political State*

for publication.[1] At the end of the session of 1717 Atterbury reported to the Pretender that Shippen's 'services in the House of Commons can never be sufficiently acknowledged'. He was rewarded with a letter of appreciation from the Pretender which for some time he was unable to answer, having been sent to the Tower for describing the King's speech opening the next session as 'rather calculated for the meridian of Germany than that of Great Britain', and the King as 'a stranger to our language and constitution'. His imprisonment was an inconvenience in more ways than one to Atterbury, who had entrusted him with raising the money required to finance a projected Swedish invasion for the restoration of the Stuarts, and also with a plan for disrupting the Anglo-French alliance, which had now to be dropped. Its effect on Shippen, according to a Jacobite agent, was that for some time after his release he 'spoke often and well to the nature of the thing, but no personal reflections. In short, [he] has taken wise advice not to go to the Tower again'.[2] However, by 1719 he had recovered sufficiently to risk another gibe at the royal family, observing

> when it was urged in the debate in relation to the schism bill that it was unnatural to deprive parents of the education of their children [that] since it was now the case of the greatest subject in England [the Prince of Wales], he did not see why others should complain.[3]

After the collapse of the South Sea Company, in whose stock he had refused to speculate,[4] though offered £4,000 stock by Craggs with the prospect of a £10,000 profit, he provoked Craggs into offering to fight him for asserting that he knew some ministers who were no less guilty than the directors. He spoke and voted against Sunderland on the charge of accepting bribes from the Company, replying to Tories who objected that this was playing Walpole's game that he would 'be against them all in their turns. Overturn, overturn all Whigs'.[5] Later in the year a representative of the Scotch Tories, who had met him to concert plans for the general election, reported to the Pretender that Shippen had told him that Sunderland had recently made advances 'with great earnestness' to the English Tories, which they had 'utterly rejected',

> resolving to enter into no concert with any of the two contending powers at court, but to stick together and wait till it pleased God some event might occur, that would give them an occasion to do you and the country service.[6]

On the discovery of Atterbury's plot in 1722 Shippen's house was searched for papers but, though his name was mentioned in the ensuing trials, he himself was not arrested. During the proceedings in Parliament in 1723 against Atterbury and his accomplices he insinuated that the arrest of John Freind (q.v.) on a charge of high treason had been due to his recent attacks on ministers in connexion with the plot and that it was therefore an interference with freedom of speech in Parliament. On a bill of pains and penalties against another of the conspirators he pointed out

> how slender the evidence was and that people without doors might say it was extorted, suborned and bought, and was going on in that strain but was taken down by the Speaker.[7]

In the budget debate of 1726 he made a personal attack on Walpole, accusing him of stock jobbing.

> He went on with great violence and insolence, he said he would do anything to bring such a bear to the stake; that as much as he detested a bill of pains and penalties, he would readily come into it to make such a monster spew up his ill-gotten wealth.[8]

On George II's accession Shippen was one of the few Tory leaders who did not go to court to pay their 'condolence and congratulations on the new King'. Walpole's motion for an increased civil list was 'unopposed by anybody but Mr. Shippen, the head of the veteran staunch Jacobites'. Shippen, a Jacobite observed in 1728, 'keeps his honesty at a time when almost everybody is wavering.'[9] When Pulteney in 1729 agreed to the Address after saying that he would oppose it, Shippen hinted that he had been 'softened' by a report that he was to be sent to the Tower for an attack on the Government in the *Craftsman*. Next year he sailed close to the wind with another near-seditious speech on the army:

> Shippen said that at this rate he saw no prospect of being free from a government by a standing army; that he hoped the German constitution of ruling by an army was not to be introduced here, and that in England a King who should propose to govern by an army was a tyrant. This bold and audacious speech struck the House mute, till Sir William Yonge [q.v.] got up and said such things were not proper to be heard, and were intolerable, that the House ought to make him explain himself, not but that he believed the House understood his meaning. Shippen said something to extenuate his expression, but not to much satisfaction. Sir Robert Walpole said what was proper, and concluded that it was believed there would have been a long debate, but what Shippen had said had so shocked gentlemen that he could find nothing wiser than go to the question immediately.

On the excise bill in 1733 he dissociated himself from a 'violent motion' by Wyndham, directed to securing the formal rejection of the excise bill, expressing himself as satisfied with Walpole's announcement that it was to be dropped. Later in the same session he not only spoke 'obstinately' against the Princess Royal's marriage portion, which neither Pulteney nor Wyndham opposed, but

when the question was put for agreeing with the motion, said No, as did Sir John Cotton [q.v.], and one or two more, that it might not appear in the votes that the House was unanimous in this affair, an ill-natured and scandalous procedure.[10]

In the following session he and his 'squadron' again parted company from their Whig allies by refusing to support a motion for making army officers not above the rank of colonel irremovable except by court martial.[11]

During Shippen's last years his activity fell off and his political position became increasingly isolated. He did not conceal his dislike of the leaders of the opposition Whigs, declaring that 'Robin and I are two honest men; he is for King George and I for King James; but those men in long cravats [meaning Sandys, Rushout and Gybbon (qq.v.)] only desire places, either under King George or King James'.[12] Nor was he now prepared to go as far as the extremist members of his own party. When in 1740 an emissary from the Pretender came over to sound the English Jacobites as to a rising, combined with a French invasion, Shippen displayed such alarm 'upon the prospect of real business' that it was considered advisable to leave him out of the consultations.[13] On the opposition Whig motion for Walpole's removal in 1741 he walked out, declaring that 'he would not pull down Robin on republican principles'.[14] He took little part in the closing scenes of Walpole's Administration. His last recorded speeches were made on the King's speech opening Walpole's last Parliament, when 'the Jacobites, with Shippen and Lord Noel Somerset [q.v.] at their head, were for a division, Pulteney and the Patriots against one'; and on the army estimates of 1742, which were voted without a division, 'Shippen alone, unchanged opposing'.[15] He died 1 May 1743.

[1] *Pol. State*, xxxvii. p. vii. [2] *HMC Stuart*, v. 558, 287, 325, 419; vi. 260; vii. 574. [3] *HMC Portland*, v. 576. [4] *HMC Popham*, 253; Egerton 2618, ff. 221–6. [5] Stuart mss 53/13. [6] *Lockhart Pprs*. ii. 69–71. [7] *Knatchbull Diary*, 5 Apr. 1723. [8] *HMC Portland*, vii. 420. [9] Stuart mss 108/44, 122/109; Hervey, *Mems*. i. 34. [10] *HMC Egmont Diary*, i. 11, 361, 371–2; iii. 331. [11] *HMC Carlisle*, 132. [12] Coxe, *Walpole*, i. 671–2. [13] Stuart mss 221/109, 223/124. [14] Yorke, *Hardwicke*, i. 252. [15] Walpole to Mann, 10 Dec. 1741 and 25 Feb. 1742.

E.C.

SHIRLEY, Hon. Robert (1700–38), of Spring Gardens, Westminster.

STAMFORD 1727–1734

b. 27 May 1700, 11th s. of Robert Shirley, 1st Earl Ferrers, being 1st s. by his 2nd w. Selina, da. of George Finch of London; bro. of Hon. Sewallis Shirley (q.v.). *unm.*

Descended from an old Warwickshire family, Shirley, on his father's death in December 1717, inherited Ettington, Warwickshire, as well as part of his father's Irish estates.[1] Returned for Stamford in 1727 on the interest of Lord Exeter (Brownlow Cecil, q.v.), he voted against the Administration in every recorded division, did not stand again, and died 12 July 1738, leaving his Irish property to his sister.[2]

[1] E. P. Shirley, *Stemmata Shirleiana*, 162. [2] PCC 185 Brodrepp.

P.W.

SHIRLEY, Hon. Sewallis (1709–65).

BRACKLEY   22 Mar. 1742–1754
CALLINGTON   1754–1761

b. 19 Oct. 1709, 14th s. of Robert Shirley, 1st Earl Ferrers, being 4th s. by his 2nd w.; bro. of Hon. Robert Shirley (q.v.). *m.* 25 May 1751, Margaret, *suo jure* Baroness Clinton, da. and h. of Samuel Rolle (q.v.) of Heanton, Devon, wid. of Robert Walpole, 2nd Earl of Orford, *s.p.*

Comptroller of the Household to Queen Charlotte 1762–5.

Sewallis Shirley, 'no great genius', but a noted lady-killer,[1] was returned by the 1st Duke of Bridgwater for Brackley at a by-election in 1742 in the place of the former Member, Dr. George Lee (q.v.), who had been refused re-election by the Duke on vacating his seat by accepting office. During this Parliament he voted with the Opposition but in 1747, Brackley having come under the control of Col. Richard Lyttelton (q.v.), the stepfather of the new Duke of Bridgwater, a minor, Shirley adapted his politics to Lyttelton's, and was classed in the new Parliament as a government supporter. On the death of the 2nd Earl of Orford in 1751 he married his widow, with whom, according to her brother-in-law, Horace Walpole, he had been living since 1746.[2] She returned him for Callington in 1754 but two months later they separated and he was not put up for Callington again. He died 31 Oct. 1765.

[1] Horace Walpole to Mann, 15 Sept. 1746; *HMC Egmont Diary*, ii. 248. [2] To Mann, ut supra.

R.R.S.

SHUTE, *see* BARRINGTON, John

SHUTTLEWORTH, James (1714–73), of Gawthorpe Hall, Lancs. and Forcett Park, Yorks.

PRESTON   1741–1754
LANCASHIRE   1761–1768

bap. 6 Dec. 1714, 1st surv. s. of Richard Shuttleworth (q.v.). *m.* 25 May 1742, Mary, da. and h. of Robert Holden of Aston Hall, Derbys., 4s. 3da. *suc.* fa. 1749. Sheriff, Yorks 1760–1.

In 1741 Shuttleworth successfully contested Preston, where his father had been cultivating an

interest.[1] A Tory, who voted against the Government in all recorded divisions, he was re-elected unopposed in 1747. The second Lord Egmont wrote of him in his electoral survey c.1749–50: 'will be with us in the manner of his father'. He died 28 June 1773.

[1] See PRESTON, and W. Dobson, *Parl. Rep. Preston*, 17.

E.C.

SHUTTLEWORTH, Richard (1683–1749), of Gawthorpe Hall, Lancs. and Forcett, Yorks.

LANCASHIRE   1705–22 Dec. 1749

bap. 3 Sept. 1683, 1st s. of Sir Richard Shuttleworth, M.P., of Gawthorpe Hall and Forcett by Katherine, da. and h. of Henry Clerke, pres. of Magdalen, Oxf.; father-in-law of John Crewe, jun. (q.v.). *educ.* Grand Tour 1702. *m.* 20 Apr. 1703, Emma, da. and h. of William Cole of Laughton, Leics., 5s. 3da. *suc.* fa. 1687.

'Father' of House of Commons 1748–9.

Shuttleworth's family, who had been seated at Gawthorpe since the fifteenth century, had represented Preston and Clitheroe in the seventeenth century. Returned for Lancashire as a Tory against the Derby interest in 1705,[1] he continued to represent the county for the rest of his life. A member of the October Club and of the Jacobite Club at Preston, with two relations in the 1715 rebellion,[2] he consistently voted against every Administration after the accession of George I. He is only once recorded as speaking, on the gin bill in 1736.[3] Shortly before his death, 22 Dec. 1749, the second Lord Egmont wrote of him in his electoral survey:

Is reputed one of the strongest Jacobites in England—but has talked surprisingly in favour of a reconciling scheme to destroy all Jacobites, of late, and will certainly be with us for a time.

[1] *HMC Portland*, iv. 183. [2] K. Whittle, *Account of Preston*, 50; C. Hardwick, *Hist. Preston*, 252. [3] *HMC Egmont Diary*, ii. 257.

E.C.

SIBTHORP, Coningsby (1706–79), of Canwick Hall, Lincs.

LINCOLN   1734–1741, 1747–1754, 1761–1768

b. 1706, 2nd s. of John Sibthorp, M.P. for Lincoln, by Mary, da. and coh. of Humphrey Browne. *educ.* Westminster 1718; Hart Hall and Magdalen, Oxf. 1724–8. *unm. suc.* bro. 1727.

Sheriff, Lincs. 1733–4.

In 1727 Sibthorp inherited Canwick Hall, one mile from Lincoln, for which he was returned as a Tory in 1734, voting against the Administration except on the motion for the removal of Walpole in February 1741. He lost his seat in that year, but recovered it in 1747, with the support of Lord

Scarbrough (Thomas Lumley, q.v.). He died 20 July 1779.

P.W.

SKINNER, Matthew (1689–1749), of St. John the Baptist's, Oxford.

OXFORD 1734–Nov. 1738

b. 22 Oct. 1689, s. of Robert Skinner of Welton, Northants., and the Inner Temple, judge of the Marshalsea court, by Anne, da. of William Buckby, serjeant-at-law, recorder of Daventry, Northants. *educ.* Westminster (Q.S.) 1704; Ch. Ch. Oxf. 1709; L. Inn 1709, called 1716. *m.* 1719, Elizabeth, da. of Thomas Whitfield of Watford Place, Herts., 2s.

Common pleader, city of London 1719–22; recorder, Oxford 1721–*d.*; serjeant-at-law 1724, King's serjeant 1728, prime serjeant 1734; c.j. Chester Nov. 1738–*d.*

Skinner was the great-grandson of Robert Skinner, bishop of Oxford and of Worcester. On his election to be recorder of Oxford in May 1721, Hearne reported: 'Mr. Skinner carried it above three to one . . . [he] is a very honest gentleman, and an excellent lawyer.' After unsuccessfully contesting Andover in 1727, he was chosen unanimously as a Tory for Oxford in 1734, with the support of the Earl of Abingdon and 'the most reputable persons, both of the university and city'.[1] But he soon went over to the Government, speaking, 16 May 1737, in favour of the bill against the provost and city of Edinburgh after the Porteous riots. He left the House on being appointed chief justice of Chester a year and a half later. In July 1746 he was counsel for the Crown in the prosecution of the rebels on the northern circuit, and led for the Crown at Lord Balmerino's trial before the House of Lords the same year when, according to Horace Walpole, he made 'the most absurd speech imaginable'.[2] He died 21 Oct. 1749.

[1] Hearne, *Colls.* (Oxf. Hist. Soc.), vii. 246; xi. 330–1. [2] To Mann, 1 Aug. 1746.

E.C.

SKRYMSHER, *see* **BOOTHBY SKRYMSHER**

SLINGSBY, Henry (?1693–1763), of Scriven, nr. Knaresborough, Yorks.

KNARESBOROUGH 17 May 1714–1715
                   1722–18 Jan. 1763

b. ?1693, 1st s. of Sir Thomas Slingsby, 4th Bt., by Sarah, da. of John Savile of Methley, nr. Leeds. *educ.* Univ. Coll. Oxf. 13 Oct. 1710, aged 17. *m.* 1729, Mary, da. of John Aislabie of Studley, Yorks., chancellor of the Exchequer 1718–21, sis. of William Aislabie (qq.v.), *s.p. suc.* fa. as 5th Bt. Nov. 1726.

Slingsby was descended from Sir Henry Slingsby, M.P., who was executed in 1658 for participating in a plot against the Commonwealth Government. Returned as a Tory on his family's interest at Knaresborough, he was defeated at the general election of 1715, but recovered his seat in 1722, voting regularly with the Opposition. In 1743 an emissary sent by the French Government to England to concert measures for a Jacobite rising combined with a French invasion next year, recommended that he should be one of a council to be set up to advise the Young Pretender on his arrival in England.[1] He was not appointed but was one of the few to whom the military details of the proposed French landing were communicated.[2] He continued to represent Knaresborough without opposition till his death, 18 Jan. 1763.

[1] Stuart mss 254/152. [2] AEM & D Angl. 82, ff. 62–109.

R.R.S.

SLOPER, William (?1658–1743), of West Woodhay, Berks.

GREAT BEDWYN	1715–1722
CAMELFORD	1722–1727
GREAT BEDWYN	26 Mar. 1729–1741
WHITCHURCH	2 Jan. 1742–14 Jan. 1743

b. ?1658, s. of William Sloper of Great Bedwyn, Wilts. *educ.* New Coll. Oxf. 5 June 1679, aged 20. *m.* bef. 1708, Rebecca Abbott, 2s.

Clerk to paymaster gen. by 1702; dep. paymaster gen. 1714–20; dep. cofferer of the Household by 1730–*d.*

In 1714 William Sloper bought the estate of West Woodhay,[1] not far from his native town of Great Bedwyn. Returned unopposed in 1715 for Great Bedwyn, which he represented for most of his parliamentary career, he voted with the Government in all recorded divisions of this Parliament. As deputy paymaster general he handled Walpole's official accounts both while and after he held the office of paymaster, including a transaction involving the sale of £9,000 South Sea stock in January 1720 on which Walpole made a profit of nearly £3,700.[2] Turned out on Walpole's return to the Pay Office in 1720, he took an active part in the parliamentary proceedings following the collapse of the South Sea bubble, attacking the directors, 15 Dec. 1720, and carrying a resolution, 19 Dec., that 'the present calamity was mainly owing to the vile arts of stock jobbers'. Elected to the secret committee set up in January 1721 by the Commons to investigate the affair, he was one of the three members of the committee who abstained from voting on the case of Charles Stanhope (q.v.),[3] but he strongly supported severity in the cases of Sir John Blunt and John Aislabie (q.v.). He opposed Walpole's engraftment scheme, 7 Feb., and opened the debate on the relief to be extended to subscribers to the Company's stock, 2 May. In the same session he also spoke against the Government on the Bere Alston election, 11 May, and on a proposal for defraying the civil list arrears, 12 July; joined in protests against obnoxious newspaper articles, which led to the prosecution of the publisher, 28 May; and backed a petition for a Quaker relief bill, 13 Dec. 1721. In the next Parliament he spoke against the Government on the suspension of the Habeas Corpus Act, 16 Oct. 1722; the special levy on Papists, 26 Nov. 1722; the army, 22 Jan. 1724; and on the civil list arrears, 17 Apr. 1725.

After George II's accession, when Sloper obtained a place under Walpole's brother, Horace, no more anti-government speeches by him are reported. He became a member of the council of the Georgia Society in January 1733, attending meetings regularly till 1741. On 12 Feb. 1734 he spoke in favour of the abolition of the duty on Irish yarn, observing that

> no Member of this House will speak for the advantage of Ireland but as it concurs with the interest of England, and yet we ought to look on that people as part of ourselves . . . What millions have been lost to England by the prohibition of Irish manufacture 36 years ago.[4]

On 29 Apr. 1737 he opposed Sir John Barnard's financial proposals. In the final debate of 9 Mar. 1739 on the convention with Spain, 'old Sloper' 'was asleep till the House was begun to be told, and they would not let him go out after he was awake, so he voted against his inclinations',[5] i.e. against the convention. His last recorded speeches were for repealing the Test Act, 30 Mar. 1739, and for an increase in the army, 10 Dec. 1740. He did not stand in 1741, but was brought in for Whitchurch at a by-election in January 1742. He died 14 Jan. 1743.

[1] HMC 15th Rep. VII, 217. [2] J. H. Plumb, Walpole, i. 306–8. [3] HMC Var. viii. 300. [4] HMC Egmont Diary, ii. 28–29. [5] Coxe, Walpole, iii. 519–20.

R.S.L.

SLOPER, William (1709–89), of West Woodhay, Berks.

GREAT BEDWYN 15 Dec. 1747–Dec. 1756

b. 28 Apr. 1709, 2nd but 1st surv. s. of William Sloper (q.v.) of West Woodhay. *educ.* Westminster 1722; Trinity, Camb. 1725. *m.* 20 Sept. 1728,[1] Catherine, da. of Maj.-Gen. Robert Hunter, sis. of Thomas Orby Hunter (q.v.), 2s. *suc.* fa. 1743.
   Ld. of Trade Dec. 1756–Mar. 1761; dep. paymaster of the forces at Gibraltar 1761–*d.*

After an early marriage William Sloper formed a connexion in 1737 with Susannah Maria Cibber,

the well-known actress, apparently with the connivance of her husband, Theophilus Cibber, the actor. Cibber, however, brought two actions against Sloper in 1738 and 1739 for *crim. con.* and detention of his wife, as a result of which he obtained damages of £20 and £500. By Susannah, Sloper had a son and a daughter, who both died young.

In 1747 Sloper stood as a Whig for his father's old borough, for which he was seated by the House of Commons after a double return, largely owing to the efforts on his behalf of Henry Fox (q.v.).[2] Attaching himself to Fox, he was again returned in 1754, but resigned his seat on appointment to office in 1756 and did not stand again. He died July 1789.

[1] Hist. Reg. 1728, chron. p. 51. 13 Nov. 1727 according to the Supplement to the Rec. of Old Westminsters. [2] Ilchester, Lord Holland, i. 144.

R.S.L.

SMELT, Leonard (c.1683–1740), of Kirkby Fleetham, nr. Northallerton, Yorks.

THIRSK 6 May 1709–1710
NORTHALLERTON 1713–30 May 1740

b. c.1683, 1st s. of Leonard Smelt of Kirkby Fleetham by Grace, da. of Sir William Frankland, 1st Bt., M.P., of Thorkleby, Yorks.; bro. of William Smelt (q.v.). *educ.* Jesus, Camb. 1700. *m.* Elizabeth Whitaker,[1] *s.p. suc.* fa. 1710.
   Commr. for stating army debts 1715–22; clerk of deliveries in the Ordnance 1722–33; clerk of the Ordnance 1733–*d.*

Returned for Thirsk on the interest of the Franklands in 1709, Smelt sat from 1713 for Northallerton, voting with the Government except on Lord Cadogan (q.v.) in 1717 and on the peerage bill in 1719. In 1721 he applied to Lord Sunderland for a vacant place in the victualling office, writing:

> I have the misfortune to be very little personally known to your Lordship, but I flatter myself that my behaviour in Parliament (where I have sat many years and have interest enough to sit there as long as I live) has been in no respect undeserving of his Majesty's favour and of your Lordship's patronage.[2]

Given a post in the Ordnance, he died 30 May 1740.

[1] PCC 184 Browne. [2] 28 June 1721, Sunderland (Blenheim) mss.

R.R.S.

SMELT, William (1690–1755), of Leases, Yorks.

NORTHALLERTON 1 Dec. 1740–Apr. 1745

b. 10 Jan. 1690, yr. s. of Leonard Smelt of Kirkby Fleetham, Yorks.; bro. of Leonard Smelt (q.v.). *m.* Dorothy, da. of Cornelius Cayley of York, 4s. 4da. *suc.* bro. 1740.
   Receiver gen. of casual revenue, Barbados 1745–*d.*

William Smelt succeeded his brother at Northallerton, voting with the Government. In 1745 he sold the family interest at Northallerton to Henry Lascelles (q.v.), in favour of whom he vacated his seat by accepting a colonial appointment.[1] He died 14 Sept. 1755.

[1] See 'A London West-India Merchant House 1740–69', by R. Pares, *Essays presented to Sir Lewis Namier*, ed. Pares & Taylor, 78.

R.R.S.

SMITH, Edward (?1704–62), of Edmondthorpe, Leics.

LEICESTERSHIRE   1734–15 Feb. 1762.

b. ?1704, 1st s. of Rev. Roger Smith of Husbands Bosworth, Leics. by Judith Tomlinson. *educ.* Melton Mowbray; Rugby 1714; Magdalene, Camb. 18 Apr. 1722, aged 17. *m.* Margaret, da. of Edward Horsman of Stretton, Rutland, 1s. *d.v.p. suc.* cos. Sir Edward Smith, 2nd Bt., at Edmondthorpe 1721; and fa. 1736.

Smith, whose family had settled at Edmondthorpe in the seventeenth century, contested Rutland unsuccessfully as a Tory at a by-election in 1730. Returned unopposed for Leicestershire as a Tory in 1734 and re-elected after a contest in 1741, he voted against the Walpole and Pelham Administrations in all recorded divisions, though withdrawing on the motion for the dismissal of Walpole in February 1741. During the election campaign in 1740 his interest in the county was said to be 'exceedingly good and his manner of canvassing inimitable'.[1] He is described in the 2nd Lord Egmont's electoral survey, c.1749–50, as 'a good natured Tory who does not love attendance, but will be with us, if his friends are'. He continued to represent Leicestershire till his death, 15 Feb. 1762.

[1] Braye mss, Leicester Mus. 23 D. 57–3029.

E.C.

SMITH, James (?1681–?1734), of Black Torrington, Devon, and Common Leigh, Som.[1]

TAUNTON   30 Aug. 1715–1727

b. ?1681, s. of James Smith of Torrington, Devon. *educ.* Exeter, Oxf. 7 Apr. 1698, aged 16; I. Temple 1699.

Returned on petition as a Whig, Smith voted with the Government in all recorded divisions, except on the peerage bill, which he opposed. Re-elected after a contest in 1722, he did not stand again, dying perhaps in 1734.[2]

[1] PCC 47 Bolton. [2] *Cal. Wills & Admons. in Court of Archdeacon of Taunton* (Index Lib. xlva), 100.

S.R.M.

SMITH, John (?1655–1723), of South Tidworth, Hants.

LUDGERSHALL	1679, 1681, 1689–1690
BERE ALSTON	15 Dec. 1691–1695
ANDOVER	1695–1713
EAST LOOE	1715–2 Oct. 1723

b. ?1655, s. of John Smith of South Tidworth. *educ.* St. John's, Oxf. 18 May 1672, aged 16; M. Temple 1674. *m.* (2) 7 Nov. 1683, Anne, da. of Sir Thomas Strickland, 2nd Bt., M.P., of Boynton, Yorks.,[1] 4s. 3da. survived him.[2] *suc.* fa. 1690.

Ld. of Treasury May 1694–Nov. 1699; P.C. 23 May 1695; chancellor of the Exchequer Nov. 1699–Mar. 1701; Speaker of the House of Commons Oct. 1705–Nov. 1708; commr. for the union of Scotland and England 1706; chancellor of the Exchequer Nov. 1708–Aug. 1710; teller of the Exchequer Oct. 1710–July 1712, Nov. 1715–*d.*

Smith, a prominent Whig politician under Anne, was reinstated as teller of the Exchequer when the Whigs returned to power in 1715, speaking for the septennial bill in 1716 and the army on 4 Mar. 1717. Though 'one of the chief men in place'[3] he opposed the vote for measures against Sweden in April 1717, later speaking and voting against the Government in the debate of 4 June on Lord Cadogan (q.v.). On 4 Dec. following he spoke for the army estimates, two days later severely censuring the strictures on the King's speech by Shippen, who, he declared, 'at last had pared his apples so thin that he had cut his fingers'. He was reported to have refused the treasurership of the navy in March 1718. After supporting the Address on 11 Nov. 1718, he joined Walpole in speaking and voting against the repeal of the Occasional Conformity and Schism Acts in January 1719, and against the peerage bill in December of that year. He spoke for the army estimates on 19 Dec. 1720; opposed Walpole's engrafting scheme on 10 Jan. 1721; on 10 Mar. 1721 answered Sir George Caswall's (q.v.) defenders 'with a great deal of warmth';[4] and on 18 May advocated severe punishment for Sir John Blunt as the chief promoter of the South Sea scheme. He seconded an opposition motion for limiting the suspension of the Habeas Corpus Act to six months on 16 Oct. 1722, spoke again for the army estimates, on 26 Oct., and on 11 Mar. 1723 supported the drawing up of a bill of pains and penalties against Atterbury.

He died 2 Oct. 1723.

[1] Foster, *London Marriage Licences.* [2] PCC 217 Richmond. [3] *Letters of Lady Mary Wortley Montagu*, i. 138; *HMC Portland*, v. 542. [4] *HMC Portland*, v. 547 558, 576, 612, 618.

E.C.

SMITH, Thomas (d.1716).

GLASGOW BURGHS   1710–19 Jan. 1716

1st surv. s. of Thomas Smith, apothecary, of Glasgow. *educ.* Glasgow Univ. ?1693. *m.* by 1709, Janet Cross, 1s. *suc.* fa. by 1707.

Bailie of Glasgow by 1707; dean of guild, Glasgow 1709–11, 1713–15; commr. for stating army debts 1715–*d.*

At George I's accession, Thomas Smith, a Glasgow merchant, who had been returned as a Whig for Glasgow in 1710, conveyed a message of loyalty from the Glasgow magistrates to the King through the Duke of Montrose. He also presented plaids from the Glasgow town council to the Princess of Wales: 'I had the honour to kiss her hand, and when I was going out of her closet she said 'Pray, Mr. Smith, forget not to return my hearty thanks to the magistrates of Glasgow for their fine present'.[1] Re-elected in 1715, he died 19 Jan. 1716, described by the Speaker, Spencer Compton (q.v.), as an honest and useful Member of the House of Commons.[2] His widow petitioned the Glasgow town council on behalf of herself and her son, left in financial straits because, though her husband's expenses in London had been paid by the city, he did, by excessive 'care and application' to his parliamentary duties 'in a manner . . . sequestrate himself to public business', to the detriment of his own affairs. On 14 Sept. 1716 the council voted two thousand marks (about £115) to help to bring up young Thomas, then aged seven.[3]

[1] *Extracts from Glasgow Burgh Recs.* iv. 542. [2] SRO, Clerk of Penicuik mss, box 120/3171. [3] *Glasgow Recs.* iv. 582, 597–8 & n.

J.M.S.

SMITH, Thomas (d. 1728), of South Tidworth, Hants.

MILBORNE PORT	7 May 1709–1710
EAST LOOE	1710–1713
EYE	1715–1722
TREGONY	1727–3 Aug. 1728

1st s. of John Smith (q.v.). *unm. suc.* fa. 1723.

Clerk of the Council in extraordinary Mar. 1706–12;[1] vice-chamberlain to Queen Caroline 1727–*d.*

Returned for Eye as a Whig in 1715 on the Cornwallis interest, Smith voted against the septennial bill and the repeal of the Occasional Conformity and Schism Acts but for the peerage bill. He did not stand in 1722 but was brought in for Tregony on the Treasury interest there at George II's accession, when he obtained a court office. He died 3 Aug. 1728.

[1] Luttrell, vi. 27.

E.C.

SMITH STANLEY, see STANLEY (afterwards SMITH STANLEY), James

SMITHSON, Hugh (?1661–1740), of Tottenham High Cross, Mdx. and Armin, Yorks.

MIDDLESEX   1701, 1702–1705, 1710–1722

b. ?1661, o.s. of Anthony Smithson of Tottenham High Cross and Armin by Susanna, da. of Sir Edward Barkham, 1st Bt., M.P., of South Acre, Norf. *educ.* Charterhouse; St. John's, Camb. 29 Mar. 1680, aged 18; G. Inn 1681. *m.* (1) 16 Apr. 1691, Hester, da. of Michael Godfrey of Woodford, Essex, sis. of Peter Godfrey (q.v.), 3s. 4da. *d.v.p.*; (2) 26 Dec. 1717, Constantia, da. of Henry Hare, M.P., 2nd Baron Coleraine [I], *s.p.*

Smithson, who had inherited estates worth £3,000 p.a. in Middlesex and Yorkshire,[1] was a Tory and a member of the October Club. Re-elected for Middlesex in 1715, he voted against the Administration in all recorded divisions but did not stand again. In July 1740, when his cousin and heir, Sir Hugh Smithson (q.v.), was about to marry Lady Elizabeth Seymour, her grandfather, the 6th Duke of Somerset, insisted that the Tottenham and Armin estates should be included in the marriage settlement. This Smithson refused to do, declaring,

> it was true he was no duke, nor boasted of any such great alliances; but that in point of honourable dealing he would yield to no man. That he had given his word that he would leave certain of his estates to Sir Hugh Smithson, and that was sufficient; and he would not be tied down by any lawyers.[2]

He died shortly afterwards, 4 Sept. 1740, leaving his estates to Sir Hugh.

[1] Duke of Leeds to Duke of Somerset, 9 Jan. 1740, Duke of Northumberland's mss at Alnwick. [2] Cowslade's jnl., ibid.

E.C.

SMITHSON, Sir Hugh, 4th Bt. (1715–86), of Stanwick, Yorks. and Tottenham, Mdx.

MIDDLESEX   15 May 1740–7 Feb. 1750

b. 19 Dec. 1715, o.s. of Langdale Smithson of Stanwick (o.s. of Sir Hugh Smithson, 3rd Bt.) by Philadelphia, da. of William Revely of Newby Wiske, Yorks. *educ.* Ch. Ch. Oxf. 1730. *m.* 16 July 1740, Lady Elizabeth Seymour, da. and h. of Algernon Seymour (q.v.), 7th Duke of Somerset, 2s. 1da. *suc.* gd.-fa. Sir Hugh Smithson, 3rd Bt., 2 Mar. 1733; his cos. Hugh Smithson (q.v.) at Tottenham High Cross, Mdx. and Armin, Yorks. 1740; his fa.-in-law the 7th Duke of Somerset as Baron Warkworth and Earl of Northumberland 7 Feb. 1750, taking name of Percy in lieu of Smithson; K.G. 29 Mar. 1757; *cr.* Duke of Northumberland 22 Oct. 1766, Lord Lovaine, Baron of Alnwick 28 Jan. 1784.

Sheriff, Yorks. 1738–9; trustee, British Museum 1753–*d.*; ld. of the bedchamber 1753–63; ld. lt. Northumb. 1753–*d.*; v.-adm. Northumb. 1755; P.C. 22 Nov. 1762; ld. chamberlain to the Queen 1762–8; ld. lt. Mdx. 1762–*d.*; ld. lt. [I] 1763–5; v.-adm. N. America 1764; master of the horse 1778–80.

Smithson was descended from a London merchant, who was made a baronet by Charles II. He was brought up a Roman Catholic, but entered the Church of England on becoming heir to his grandfather.[1] In 1740 he became engaged to Lady Elizabeth Seymour, who was to have a portion of £10,000 from her grandfather, the 6th Duke of Somerset. The Duke of Leeds wrote on behalf of Smithson, asking for Somerset's consent, 9 Jan. 1740:

> I know him to be a gentleman of great honour and worth, and one that is endowed with all those qualifications which are necessary to make an honest man, a sincere friend and an agreeable companion, having made the best use of every part of his education and being naturally of an extreme good and natural temper . . . As it is usual upon these occasions to mention estates, I will inform your Grace that Sir Hugh has at present better than £4,000 a year entirely in his power . . . He will likewise inherit at the death of a relation who is upwards of fourscore years of age [Hugh Smithson, q.v.], very near if not quite three thousand pounds a year more, and who while living is ready to come into any settlements as to that part of the estate, as is Sir Hugh himself with regard to his part.

Somerset was dissatisfied with the marriage settlement, writing to his granddaughter:

> you are descended by many generations from the most ancient families in England and it is you who doth add ancient blood to Sir Hugh Smithson's family. He adds not so ancient blood to your family.

He insisted that Hugh Smithson's (q.v.) Yorkshire and Tottenham estates should be included in the settlement, but Hugh Smithson refused.[2] In the end Somerset reluctantly consented to the marriage. While these negotiations were in progress, Smithson was returned for Middlesex as a Tory with the support of the Duke of Somerset.[3] He withdrew with most of the Tories in the division on the dismissal of Walpole in February 1741, was re-elected unopposed for the county three months later, having succeeded to his cousin's estates, and voted against the Hanoverians in 1742 and 1744.

On the death of Lord Beauchamp, Lady Elizabeth's brother, in 1744, she became heir to the Percy estates. At the end of the year, Somerset, who had conceived a violent dislike for Smithson, petitioned the King to create him, Somerset, Earl of Northumberland with remainder to Sir Charles Wyndham (q.v.) to the exclusion of Smithson and Lady Elizabeth. Smithson's father-in-law, Lord Hertford (q.v.), sent Smithson to George II with a letter of protest, on which

> the King immediately called him to his closet and allowed him to explain the case which he listened to with the greatest attention and humanity, and said it was far from his intention to do a hardship to my Lord Hertford.[4]

As a result, the King held up the patent. From then on, acting through Lord Hertford, Smithson worked to secure the reversion of the earldom of Northumberland for himself. He gradually abandoned Toryism. During the rebellion he was praised for his 'zealous behaviour for his religion, his King and his country'.[5] He was absent from the division on the Hanoverian troops of April 1746, when he was classed as 'doubtful', but he spoke on the government side in the debate on the bill to abolish hereditary jurisdictions in Scotland in April 1747.[6] He was successful for the county with another government supporter in 1747 against two Tories, writing to Newcastle:

> I am not less sensible of the honour of your Grace's congratulations upon my success, than I am grateful for your Grace's assistance and goodness in promoting it, and shall be happy to find that my endeavours have in any degree contributed to his Majesty's service, which I shall always esteem as inseparable from the interest of my country and shall never think any expense or trouble too great to defeat the designs of those who act upon different principles.

After the death of the 6th Duke of Somerset in 1748, Lord Hertford, now Duke of Somerset, applied to the King for the earldom of Northumberland with remainder to Smithson and his male heirs by Lady Elizabeth. Newcastle replied, 21 July 1749:

> According to my promise to Sir Hugh Smithson, I laid before the King your Grace's request as to the limitations of the title of Earl of Northumberland. His Majesty . . . told me that he was very ready to grant the earldom of Northumberland to your Grace and to Lady Elizabeth Smithson and her heirs male, but that he did not think it proper to go any farther . . . The King is very sorry, that, in this instance, he cannot comply with what is asked in favour of Sir Hugh Smithson though upon any other proper occasion, his Majesty will be ready to show him any mark of his regard.

But three months later George II relented, granting the patent with remainder to Smithson, who succeeded his father-in-law to the earldom a year later, asking Newcastle

> to represent my most dutiful and inviolable attachment to his Majesty, and the grateful sense I shall always retain of the great honour his Majesty out of his unbounded goodness has been pleased to confer upon me and my family and that I shall certainly take the most early opportunity that decency and my unfeigned grief for so great a loss will permit, to throw myself at his Majesty's feet, whose service upon all occasions I shall zealously endeavour to promote and to prove myself a most dutiful and loyal subject to his Majesty.[7]

He died 6 June 1786.

[1] F. Brenan, *House of Percy*, ii. 433. [2] Somerset to Lady Betty Seymour, 8 July 1740, and Cowslade's jnl., Duke of Northumberland's mss at Alnwick. [3] H. Finch to Ld. Malton, 18 Nov. 1742, Fitzwilliam mss; Somerset to Smithson, 26 May 1740, Northumberland mss. [4] 27 Sept. 1744, Northumberland mss. [5] T.

Duncombe to Lady Hertford, 22 Jan. 1746, ibid. [6] Add. 35876, f. 250. [7] Add. 32712, ff. 36–37; 32714, ff. 239, 319; 32718, f. 330; 32719, f. 117; 32720, ff. 88–89.

E.C.

SMYTHE, Sydney Stafford (1705–78), of Old Bounds, Bidborough, and Sutton at Hone, Kent.

EAST GRINSTEAD   1747–June 1750

b. 1705, 1st s. of Henry Smythe of Old Bounds by Elizabeth, da. of Dr. John Lloyd, canon of Windsor. educ. Kensington (Mr. Coxe); St. John's, Camb. 1 July 1721, aged nearly 16; I. Temple 1724, called 1729, bencher 1747. m. May 1733, Sarah, da. of Sir Charles Farnaby, 1st Bt., of Kippington, Kent, 1s. suc. fa. 1706. Kntd. 7 Nov. 1750.

Steward and judge of court of palace of Westminster 1740–50; K.C. 1747; baron of the Exchequer June 1750; serjeant-at-law 1750; commr. of the great seal Nov. 1756–June 1757, Jan. 1770–Jan. 1771; chief baron of the Exchequer 1772–7; P.C. 3 Dec. 1777.

In 1733 Smythe, a practising lawyer, was recommended to Sir Philip Yorke (q.v.) by the Duke of Dorset as

> a very sensible young fellow and I hope will deserve any favour you are pleased to show him; he is related to the Duke of Newcastle and my Lord Leicester; he is not easily distinguished by his surname which is a very common one, but his christian name is not so.[1]

He was brought in by the Duke as a Whig for East Grinstead in 1747, vacating his seat in 1750 on being made a baron of the Exchequer. In April 1754 he declined promotion in another court writing: 'I am so well pleased with the court in which I am placed, that I have at present no desire of removing from it.' He again declined promotion on the death of the lord chief baron in 1755.[2]

He died 2 Nov. 1778.

[1] 22 Sept. 1733, Add. 35585, f. 193. [2] To Hardwicke, 27 Apr. 1754, 20 Sept. 1755, Add. 35592, f. 331; 35593, f. 254.

J.B.L.

SNELL, John (1682–1726), of Lower Guiting, Glos.

GLOUCESTER   1713–Sept. 1726

b. 1682, 1st s. of Thomas Snell of Gloucester, mayor of Gloucester 1699. educ. I. Temple, called 1704. m. (settlement 6 Apr. 1713) Anna Maria, da. and h. of Robert Huntingdon, bp. of Raphoe, niece and principal h. of Sir John Powell, M.P., of Gloucester, c. j. of Queen's bench, 1s. 1da.

Snell, who purchased Lower Guiting early in the eighteenth century, acquired most of the property of his uncle, Sir John Powell, in Gloucester, under the terms of his marriage settlement in 1713,[1] when he was returned for Gloucester as a Tory. Re-elected after a contest in 1715, he voted consistently against the Government, speaking frequently, notably in the debate of 24 Apr. 1716 on the septennial bill, when he replied to a speech in its favour by Patrick Haldane (q.v.):

Snell took him up, and after a smart discourse against the bill, said he did not wonder that a gentleman who had given up the liberties of his own country in order to sit here, was so ready to give up those of England too. Mr. Smith rose up upon this, took it upon him to repeat the words which he called scandalous reflections that deserved the utmost resentment of the House before they proceeded any further. Lord Coningsby insisted the same. The Speaker called to Snell to explain himself, which he said he might do; but Snell sitting still, Mr. Smith pronounced the words again, and said as before. Upon that, Snell pretending to mitigate the thing, turned the reproach from Mr. Haddon [Haldane] in particular, upon the whole Scotch nation. Then Sir David Dalrymple made a most severe speech wherein he called him insolent 3 or 4 times. Lord Coningsby then moved the words should be taken in writing and laid upon the table. Mr. Baillie, a Scotch Member, flung out his hand with expressions of great contempt to Snell, who, he said, could not maintain his words in another place with gentlemen that were better than himself. The Speaker confessed that Snell had made his fault worse by pretending to explain it, but he conceived that a hurry of expressions in so awful an assembly might have brought him to say things he had no intention to say. Snell thanked him for the justice he did him, for that was his case, he confessed and if he had said anything whereby to deserve the displeasure of that House, he was sorry for it and asked pardon; and thus it ended.[2]

In December 1717 he was among the Members who urged that Shippen should be allowed to explain his reflections on the ministry before his committal to the Tower. On 11 Feb. 1719 he moved for a list of pensions granted since 1715, which was seconded by Shippen. In 1721 his name was sent to the Pretender as a probable supporter in the event of a rebellion.[3]

In the next Parliament Snell was again a frequent speaker. He opposed an increase of the army, 23 Nov. 1724,[4] was appointed one of the managers of the trial of the Earl of Macclesfield in 1725, spoke 'very strongly' against the Treaty of Hanover, 18 Feb. 1726, and opposed a vote of credit, 25 Mar. 1726.[5] He died in September the same year.

[1] PCC 168 Leeds, 210 Plymouth; Rudder, Glos. 464. [2] A. Corbière to Horace Walpole, 27 Apr. 1716, Cholmondeley (Houghton) mss. [3] Stuart mss 65/16. [4] Knatchbull Diary. [5] Stuart mss 90/128 92/44.

S.R.M.

SNEYD, William (c.1693–1745), of Bishton, Staffs.

LICHFIELD   24 Apr.–10 Dec. 1718

b. c.1693, 1st s. of Ralph Sneyd of the Birches, Staffs. by Elizabeth, da. and h. of John Bowyer of Bishton. educ. Clare, Camb. 1710; M. Temple 1710, called 1719. m. 8 Oct. 1724, Susanna, da. and h. of John Edmonds, London merchant, of Hendon Place, Mdx. by Susanna, da. of Sir William Hedges, gov. of Bengal, 2s. 3da. suc. fa. 1729.

Sneyd, whose grandfather had represented

Newcastle-under-Lyme in James II's only Parliament, was the cousin of Ralph Sneyd of Keele, M.P. Staffordshire 1713–15, who led the Jacobite riots in the county in 1715.[1] In 1718 he was returned as a Tory for Lichfield but was unseated on petition. He died 11 Feb. 1745.

[1] *Staffs. Parl. Hist.* (Wm. Salt Arch. Soc.), ii(2), p. 221.

E.C.

SOMERSET, Lord Charles Noel (1709–56).

MONMOUTHSHIRE   17 May 1731–1734
MONMOUTH   1734–24 Feb. 1745

b. 12 Sept. 1709, 3rd s. of Henry Somerset, 2nd Duke of Beaufort, by his 2nd w. Lady Rachel Noel, da. and coh. of Wriothesley Baptist Noel, M.P., 2nd Earl of Gainsborough. *educ.* Westminster 1717; Univ. Coll. Oxf. 1725, D.C.L. 1736. *m.* 1 May 1740 (with £3,000),[1] Elizabeth, da. of John Symes Berkeley of Stoke Gifford, Glos., sis. and eventually h. of Norborne Berkeley (q.v.), Lord Botetourt, 1s. 5da. *suc.* e. bro. Henry as 4th Duke of Beaufort 24 Feb. 1745.

Gov. and guardian, Foundling Hospital 1739; high steward, Hereford; gov. Christ's Hospital 1745; steward, anniversary dinner of independent electors of Westminster 1746.

At a by-election in 1731 Somerset was returned for Monmouthshire, which his family traditionally represented, but at the next general election he transferred to Monmouth, where his brother had a strong interest. 'A most determined and unwavering Jacobite',[2] he was active in the House, speaking in favour of the repeal of the Septennial Act in March 1734, and against the Address in January of the following year. He opposed the repeal of the Test Act in March, and the mortmain bill in April 1736, and moved for a reduction in the army in February 1738. In December 1741, he and Shippen unsuccessfully pressed for a division on the Address, against the advice of Pulteney.[3]

After Lord Gower, hitherto the head of the Tory party, joined the Broad-bottom Government in December 1744, Somerset, now Duke of Beaufort, in Newcastle's words,

> set himself up, and the Tories have taken him, for the head of their party. In consequence of which, they have excluded Lord Gower from a negotiation depending about justices of peace [for the inclusion of Tories into the commissions], [and] put it into the hands of the Duke of Beaufort.[4]

Beaufort, meeting Lord Hardwicke, stated that 'the lords and gentlemen with whom he had met or consulted, were uneasy that nothing was done in the affair of justices of the peace' and asked that new commissions should be issued for six specific counties 'as an earnest of what should be done in other counties'. But the Pelhams excluded him from the negotiations on the matter, which they

conducted with Lord Gower.[5] His brother, the 3rd Duke, had been privy to the negotiations with France which led to the Forty-five,[6] and he himself joined wholeheartedly in the project, sending assurances of support to the French in August 1745, and pressing a month later 'for a body of troops to be landed near London'. Lord Lovat declared that 'if the Duke of Beaufort had not promised to raise £12,000, he would not have concerned himself',[7] but the Government took no action against him.

On the eve of the dissolution of 1747, Beaufort was one of the prominent Tories who agreed to support the Prince's programme.[8] In May 1749 Horace Walpole reported a meeting 'between the Prince's party and the Jacobites':

> The Duke of Beaufort opened the assembly with a panegyric on the stand that had been made this winter against so corrupt an administration; and hoped it would continue, and desired harmony.[9]

In September 1750 he and Lord Westmorland (John Fane, q.v.) jointly presided at a meeting of English Jacobites held during the Young Pretender's secret visit to London in September 1750.[10] He died 28 Oct. 1756.

[1] Stuart mss 222/109. [2] Walpole to Mann, 29 Mar. 1745. [3] *HMC Egmont Diary*, ii. 55; *HMC Carlisle*, 146–7, 192; Harley Diary, 15 Apr. 1736; Walpole to Mann, 10 Dec. 1741. [4] To Chesterfield, 26 Mar. 1745, Add. 32804, ff. 286–7. [5] Add. 35602, ff. 46, 55; see Owen, *Pelhams*, 262–3. [6] AEM & D Angl. 82, ff. 62–109. [7] Murray of Broughton, *Memorials* (Sc. Hist. Soc. xxvii), 57n. 510; Stuart mss 268/5. [8] Add. 35870, ff. 129–30. [9] To Mann, 3 May 1749. [10] *The Times*, 29 Dec. 1864.

E.C.

SONDES, Visct., *see* WATSON, Edward

SOUTHWELL, Edward (1705–55), of King's Weston, nr. Bristol, Glos.

BRISTOL   12 Dec. 1739–1754

b. 16 June 1705, 1st s. of Rt. Hon. Edward Southwell, M.P., of Dublin and King's Weston by his 1st w. Lady Elizabeth Cromwell, da. and h. of Vere Essex, 4th Earl of Ardglass [I]. *educ.* Westminster 1715–16; Queen's, Oxf. 1721; travelled abroad 1723. *m.* 21 Aug. 1729 (with £10,000), Catherine, da. of Edward Watson (q.v.), Visct. Sondes, sis. and h. of Thomas Watson (q.v.), 3rd Earl of Rockingham, 2s. 1da. *suc.* fa. 1730.

M.P. [I] 1727–55.

Jt. clerk of the Crown and prothonotary of King's bench [I] (with his father) 1715–17; jt. sec. of the Council [I] (with his father) 1720–30, sole sec. 1730–*d.*

Edward Southwell, described by his cousin, the 1st Lord Egmont, as 'a very sober virtuous man', belonged to an Anglo-Irish family, who held high official positions under successive sovereigns.[1] Returned, presumably as a Whig, for the neighbouring town of Bristol in 1739, he spoke and voted with the Opposition on the place bill in 1740, but against the motion for Walpole's removal in 1741. He also sponsored a bill for prohibiting the insurance of enemy ships and goods and opposed a bill for strengthening the power to press seamen. In the next Parliament he continued to act with the Opposition till 1744 when, 'though very seldom vot[ing] with the Court', he spoke against motions for inquiries into the Hanoverians and the state of the naval forces.[2] He spoke in favour of a proposal for replacing the land tax by doubling the tax on places and pensions in December 1744 and voted for the Hanoverians in 1746, when he was classed by the Government as 'opposition Whig'.

At the opening of the Parliament of 1747 Southwell was put down as Opposition, but in January 1749 he voted with the Administration in the committee of supply.[3] About this time his kinsman, the 2nd Lord Egmont, wrote in his electoral survey:

> Southwell is a weak man. Has an affectation of being supposed to act according to his conscience, which directs him to vote one day for a proposition in a committee, and the very reverse the next day and in the House. They think him an honest man at Bristol but they have no opinion of his understanding and I believe if occasion were, he might be easily changed— But if not he will be as often for us as against us!

Southwell's last recorded speech was made on the regency bill, May 1751, in favour of continuing the sitting Parliament until the end of the young King's minority.[4] He did not stand in 1754, dying 16 Mar. 1755.

[1] *HMC Egmont Diary*, i. 119. [2] Coxe, *Walpole*, iii. 563–4; *HMC Egmont Diary*, iii. 192; *CJ*, xxiii. 674, 700; Owen, *Pelhams*, 212–13; Yorke's parl. jnl. *Parl. Hist.* xiii. 648. [3] R. Hoblyn to Southwell, 23 Jan. 1749, Add. 11759, f. 230. [4] Walpole, *Mems. Geo. II*, i. 145.

S.R.M.

SPEKE, George (*d.*1753), of White Lackington and Dillington, Som.

MILBORNE PORT   1722–1727
TAUNTON   1727–1734
WELLS   25 Mar. 1735–1747

b. c.1686, o.s. of John Speke of White Lackington and Dillington, M.P. Taunton 1690–8, by his 2nd w. Elizabeth, da. of Robert Pelham of Compton Valence, Dorset. *m.* (1) Alicia, da. of Nicholas Brooking, 2da. (1 *d.v.p.*); (2) Feb. 1732, Jane,[1] da. and coh. of William Hockmore of Combe-in-Teignhead, Devon, wid. of (i) one Palmer of Sharpham Pk., Som., and (ii) William Pitt of Cricket Malherbie, Som., *s.p.*; (3) July 1737, Anne, da. of William Peere Williams (q.v.) of Grey Friars, Chichester, Suss., sis. of Sir Hutchins Williams, 1st Bt., and wid. of Sir William Drake, 6th Bt., of Ashe, Devon, 1s. *d.v.p.* 1da.

The son of one of the most wealthy and influential landowners in Somerset, George Speke unsuccessfully contested the county election in 1715. Sitting thereafter for Somerset boroughs, he voted con-

sistently with the Administration, except on the division on the Spanish convention in 1739, when he was absent. On 18 Feb. 1737 he spoke late in support of the government motion for continuing an army of 17,704 men, adding that

> he was for it as sick men take physic, because necessary, though very bitter in going down and disagreeable to the palate.

On 30 Mar. 1737, immediately after the House had agreed to a bill for a general reduction of interest on the national debt to 3%, he spoke in favour of an opposition motion which sought to pledge the House to a reduction of taxes once interest was settled uniformly at that level. On 30 Mar. 1739 he supported a motion for the repeal of the Test Act.[2]

On 14 June 1740 Newcastle wrote to Pelham, referring to the impending general election:

> Sir Robert Walpole is a good deal uneasy and I think with reason at Mr. Dodington's [q.v.] behaviour [he was then lord lieutenant of Somerset], who has declared against Speke at Wells and Olmius [q.v.] at Weymouth. Sir Robert has wrote to him about Olmius (I should rather have wrote about Speke).[3]

He was in fact successful at Wells in 1741, continuing to support the Administration. He lost his seat in 1747 and died 2 Jan. 1753, leaving his daughter Mary £10,000 and the rest of his property, worth more than £4,000 a year, to his daughter Anne, who married Lord North.[4]

[1] PCC 90 Henchman. [2] *HMC Egmont Diary*, ii, 352; iii. 47. [3] Newcastle (Clumber) mss. [4] PCC 61 Searle; *HMC Hastings*, iii. 118.

S.R.M.

SPENCER, Hon. John (1708–46), of Wimbledon Park, Surr. and Althorp Park, Northants.

NEW WOODSTOCK   22 Jan. 1732–19 June 1746

b. 13 May 1708, 4th s. of Charles Spencer, M.P., 3rd Earl of Sunderland, by Lady Anne Churchill, da. and coh. of John, 1st Duke of Marlborough. *educ.* Eton c.1722; Grand Tour (France, Switzerland, Italy) 1725–7. *m.* 14 Feb. 1734, Lady Georgina Caroline, da. of John Carteret, 2nd Earl Granville, sis. of Robert Carteret (q.v.), Lord Carteret, 1s. 1da. *suc.* bro. Charles, 3rd Duke of Marlborough, at Althorp 1734 under will of 1st Duke of Marlborough, and grandmother Sarah, Duchess of Marlborough, 1744.

Ranger, Windsor Park 1744–*d.*

John Spencer, who was not quite eight when his mother died, was brought up by his grandmother Sarah, Duchess of Marlborough, becoming a great favourite with her.[1] Soon after he came of age she began to think of getting him into Parliament, writing on 27 Feb. 1730, when she was expecting a vacancy at St. Albans, which did not materialize:

> I design to set up the only grandson I have now that is a commoner, John Spencer, who has a very considerable fortune for a younger brother, and I will make it as good as most elder brothers.[2]

In 1732 she returned him for Woodstock.

When the Duchess quarrelled with his brother Charles, 5th Earl of Sunderland, later 3rd Duke of Marlborough, she told Spencer

> that if he expected to be my heir, he must live with me as my son, which I own did imply that he was not to correspond with his brother.

On his refusal to comply she declared that

> since John Spencer likes it better to depend upon a vain, extravagant brother than to have had a great estate from me, by only acting like a man of sense and true principles, he may please himself, for I shall concern myself no more about him.

But she soon relented, herself asking his pardon. On his marriage to Carteret's daughter, she wrote to his sister the Duchess of Bedford:

> I propose more satisfaction and advantages in marrying your brother to the daughter of such a man than a sheet of this paper can contain. I think your brother John has good nature, sense, frankness in his temper (which I love), and in short, a great many desirable things in him; but still he wants a great deal to get through this world in the manner that I wish he should do. And as young men won't taste even the best advice without being delivered with good breeding and good sense, I know of nothing so desirable in the present case as the kindness and assistance of a father-in-law, who, I think must always make a considerable figure whatever way the world turns.[3]

When he took his bride to court,

> Lord Carteret and his lady, the Earl of Sunderland and his countess and several others attended on the occasion, and as is usual expected the honour to kiss hands, but the King turned his back to them all, nor did the Queen (who usually makes amends for the King's reservedness) say anything to them, only . . . at last came up to Mr. Spencer, and only said to him, 'I think, Mr. Spencer, I have not seen you since you was a child'; to which he answered as coldly, 'No, Madam, I believe not', and so they all came away displeased.[4]

Before the general election of 1734 the Duchess wrote:

> I believe . . . that I might possibly succeed in setting up John for Surrey . . . The expense should not hinder me from that undertaking, but I can't think it is so proper to have him stand there or indeed anywhere as at Woodstock, where, if I can, I would settle so as to have that place always, as it ought to be, in the Marlborough family.

The Duke of Bedford annoyed her by putting him up for Bedfordshire 'to the prejudice of his election at Woodstock, which place I always thought most natural for him to stand for'.[5] Returned for both places, he chose to sit for Woodstock, which he represented till his death, voting against the Administration.

In 1744 Spencer succeeded to the personal estate of his grandmother, on condition that he should not 'accept or take from any King or Queen of these realms any pension or any office or employment, civil or military' except the rangership of Windsor Park.[6] He died 19 June 1746, aged 38,

> in possession of near £30,000 a year, merely because he would not be abridged of those invaluable blessings of an English subject, brandy, small beer, and tobacco.[7]

[1] G. Scott Thomson, *Letters of a Grandmother*, 11–13. [2] *HMC Verulam*, 121. [3] Lord Ilchester, *Lord Hervey and his Friends*, 292–3; *Letters of a Grandmother*, 83, 104, 110. [4] *HMC Egmont Diary*, ii. 34. [5] *Letters of a Grandmother*, 95, 113. [6] PCC 259 Anstis. [7] Walpole to Mann, 20 June 1746.

E.C.

STANHOPE, Charles (1673–1760), of Elvaston, Derbys.

MILBORNE PORT	6 July 1717–1722
ALDBOROUGH	1722–1734
HARWICH	1734–1741

b. 1673, 2nd surv. s. of John Stanhope of Elvaston, Derbys. by Dorothy, da. and coh. of Charles Agard of Foston, Derbys.; bro. of William Stanhope (q.v.), 1st Earl of Harrington. *educ.* I. Temple, called 1703. *unm. suc.* bro. Thomas Stanhope, M.P., to family estates 1730.

Under-sec. of state 1714–17; sec. to Treasury 1717–21; treasurer of the chamber 1722–7.

Charles Stanhope was the cousin and protégé of James Stanhope (q.v.), 1st Earl Stanhope, who as secretary of state made him his under-secretary in 1714. On Walpole's resignation in 1717 he served as secretary of the Treasury under Lords Stanhope and Sunderland successively and was brought into Parliament. When it was decided that Walpole should return to the Treasury, Charles Stanhope was recommended by Lord Stanhope for a vacancy on the Treasury board. But, as he subsequently wrote to the King,

> some uneasiness not being removed which [Walpole] had conceived against me during the time of his quitting your service and my faithful and zealous continuance in it both as under secretary of state and secretary to the Treasury, it was ordered by your Majesty that Mr. [Henry] Pelham [q.v.] should come into the Treasury in the place designed for me, and that I should succeed him as treasurer of the Chamber.[1]

Before these changes had been carried into effect, the secret committee set up by the Commons to investigate the South Sea bubble presented a report charging Charles Stanhope, Sunderland, the first lord of the Treasury, and Aislabie, the chancellor of the Exchequer, with accepting bribes from the South Sea Company. The first charge against Stanhope related to a sum of £250,000, representing the proceeds of the sale of £50,000 South Sea stock credited to him by the books of the Sword Blade Company, the South Sea Company's bankers. As one of the partners of the Sword Blade Company took full responsibility for this transaction, declaring that Stanhope's name had been used without his knowledge or consent, this charge was withdrawn, though the facts left little doubt that the money was intended for bribing Members of Parliament.[2] The second charge was embodied in a resolution moved on 28 Feb. 1721

> that during the time that the proposal made by the South Sea Company and the bill relating thereto were depending in this House, £10,000 stock was taken in, or held, by Mr. Knight, late cashier of the said Company, for the benefit of Charles Stanhope Esq., one of the secretaries of the Treasury, and a Member of this House, without any valuable consideration paid, or security given, for the acceptance of or payment for the said stock; and that the difference arising by the advanced price thereof was paid to the said Charles Stanhope Esq., out of the cash of the South Sea Company.

The 'difference' paid to Stanhope was over £50,000. Stanhope's reply to this charge was that

> for some years past he had lodged all the money he was master of in Mr. Knight's hands and whatever stock Mr. Knight had taken in for him he had paid a valuable consideration for it.

The ministry exerted all its influence on his behalf, The King himself was said to have written personally to two influential members of the secret committee, Sir Joseph Jekyll and Lord Molesworth (qq.v.), 'desiring it as a favour that nearly concerned him that they would not vote against Mr. Stanhope'. A third member of the committee, William Sloper (q.v.), absented himself from the division. A relation, Philip Dormer Stanhope (q.v.), the future Lord Chesterfield, made an effective appeal to the memory of Lord Stanhope, who had died suddenly on 5 Feb., following an apoplectic fit in the House of Lords. By these means 'between forty and fifty who could not bring themselves to give negatives were however prevailed to withdraw before the question', which was lost by three votes.[3]

Stanhope's acquittal aroused such indignation both in and outside Parliament that it was considered advisable to defer his appointment as treasurer of the chamber till the rising of the House. When that time came the King, in spite of Stanhope's protests to him personally, decided that the appointment should be postponed again till the end of the Parliament 'for fear of giving uneasiness to some favourers of the secret committee'. This, Carteret wrote to Newcastle, 22 Aug. 1721,

> has mortified Lord Sunderland and me not a little, but when Mr. Walpole has taken upon him that all South Sea matters shall be kept out of Parliament next session we could not persist in a point which would bring us to answer for any ill event in Parliament that should happen upon such an occasion . . . I

wish Charles Stanhope took this matter more patiently than he does . . . It is a blow to him, I confess, but not entire ruin, as he with too much melancholy calls it.[4]

The appointment was duly announced on the very day of the dissolution in 1722, Stanhope being subsequently returned by Newcastle for Aldborough as his seat at Milborne Port was not safe.

On George II's accession Stanhope, whose claims were strongly pressed by his family, was recommended by Walpole for a seat on the Admiralty board. But the new King had found among his father's papers a memorial by Sunderland, in the handwriting of his secretary, Charles Stanhope, making drastic proposals for dealing with him at the height of the quarrel in the royal family during the previous reign. One passage is said to have run:

> Il faut l'enlever; et my Lord Berkeley [the 1st Lord of the Admiralty] le prendra sur un vaisseau, et le conduira en aucune partie du monde que votre Majesté l'ordonnera.

On this George II 'absolutely refused to prefer him . . . with some expressions of resentment against Sir Robert Walpole for having recommended him'.[5] Stanhope however attributed his failure to secure office to Walpole, of whom he thenceforth became a secret enemy. So long as he owed his seat to Newcastle he supported the Government, voting for them in all recorded divisions, except on the civil list arrears in 1729; but when returned on his own account for Harwich in 1734 he went over to the Opposition, voting against the Government on the Prince of Wales's allowance in 1737[6] and on the convention in 1739, though he withdrew on the motion for the removal of Walpole in February 1741. He did not stand again, dying 16 Mar. 1760, aged 87.

[1] 19 Aug. 1721, Add. 32686, f. 183. [2] See SAWBRIDGE, Jacob, and CASWALL, Sir George. [3] CJ, xix. 429–32, 437, 462; Chandler, vi. 236; Stuart mss 52/137; Thos. Brodrick to Ld. Midleton, 7 Mar. 1721, Midleton mss; Coxe, Walpole, ii. 209. [4] Add. 32686, ff. 181, 183, 186, 191. [5] Coxe, i. 300; ii. 627 et seq.; Hervey, Mems. 849; see also Introductory Survey, p.32. [6] HMC Egmont Diary, ii. 90–1, 360.

R.R.S.

STANHOPE, Hon. Charles (1708–36).

DERBY   3 Feb. 1730–20 Feb. 1736

> b. 6 Sept. 1708, 4th s. of Philip Stanhope, 3rd Earl of Chesterfield, by Elizabeth, da. of George Savile, M.P., 1st Mq. of Halifax; bro. of Hon. John, Philip Dormer, Lord Stanhope, and Hon. Sir William Stanhope (qq.v.). educ. Grand Tour 1728. unm.
> Ensign 13 Ft. 1720; lt. and capt. 1 Ft. Gds. 1723, ret. bef. 1730.

Charles Stanhope, although the youngest son, inherited under the will of his grandfather, the 2nd

Lord Chesterfield, a large estate entailed after him upon his other brothers.[1] In 1730 he was returned unopposed for Derby by his brother, Philip Dormer, Lord Chesterfield, whom he followed into opposition in 1733, voting against the Government on the excise bill and on the repeal of the Septennial Act in 1734. Re-elected after a contest, he died 20 Feb. 1736.

[1] PCC 5 Fagg.

R.R.S.

STANHOPE, James (1673–1721), of Chevening, Kent.

NEWPORT I.o.W.	7 Mar.–2 July 1702
COCKERMOUTH	1702–7 Apr. 1711
	15 May 1711–1713
WENDOVER	13 Mar. 1714–1715
COCKERMOUTH	1715–Apr. 1717
NEWPORT I.o.W.	25 Apr.–3 July 1717

b. 1673, 1st s. of Hon. Alexander Stanhope (yr. s. of Philip, 1st Earl of Chesterfield) by Katherine, da. of Arnold Burghill of Thinghill Parva, Herefs. educ. Trinity, Oxf. 1688. m. 24 Feb. 1713, Lucy, yr. da. of Thomas Pitt (q.v.) of Blandford, Dorset, 3s. 4da. cr. Visct. Stanhope of Mahon 3 July 1717; Earl Stanhope 14 Apr. 1718.

A.-d.-c. to Duke of Schomberg in service of Savoy 1691, sgt. 1692, capt. 1693; capt. 28 Ft. 1694; capt. and lt.-col. 1 Ft. Gds. 1695; second sec. to Paris embassy 1698 and sec. to his fa. at The Hague 1700–1; col. 11 Ft. 1702–5; brig.-gen. 1704; envoy extraordinary to Charles III of Spain May 1706–Dec. 1707, May 1708–Dec. 1710; maj.-gen. 1707; c.-in-c. of British forces in Spain Mar. 1708–Dec. 1710, when he was forced to capitulate at Brihuega; lt.-gen. 1709; col. regt. of Drags. 1710–12; sec. of state, southern dept. Sept. 1714–Dec. 1716, northern dept. Dec. 1716–Apr. 1717, Mar. 1718–d.; P.C. 29 Sept. 1714; ambassador to Vienna Nov.–Dec. 1714; first ld. of Treasury and chancellor of the Exchequer Apr. 1717–Mar. 1718; ambassador to Paris and Madrid June–Sept. 1718, to Paris, Jan. and Mar.–Apr. 1720, and to Berlin July 1720; one of the lds. justices of the realm May–Nov. 1719, June–Nov. 1720.

While attached to the Paris embassy in 1698, Stanhope contracted a friendship with the Duke of Orleans through the Duke's tutor, the future Cardinal Dubois, which paid dividends when he became secretary of state and Orleans regent, with Dubois as his foreign minister.[1] He owed his appointment as secretary of state to Lord Townshend, the head of the new Whig ministry, to whom he had been recommended by Walpole's brother, Horace (q.v.),

knowing indeed that he had a fruitful and luxurious genius in foreign affairs, which I hoped he would have suffered to be checked and pruned by Lord Townshend's prudence, but I never imagined that he would have proved wild, mad, and ungrateful.

Returned at the general election by his father's friend, the Duke of Somerset, he became the junior member of the ruling triumvirate in the Government, the others being his 'old sworn friends',[2] Townshend and Walpole. In the Commons, where he was regarded as one of Walpole's chief lieutenants, he is said to have 'made many remarkable false steps in managing the business of the House'. According to Edward Wortley (q.v.), writing about October 1715,

Mr. Stanhope, who has doubled his fortune in one year, as he thinks, by the favour of Lord Townshend, will always second what he does; and perhaps his want of judgment, or want of skill, in the affairs of the House, may give him a great opinion of Mr. Walpole . . . what he says are commonly Mr. Walpole's words.[3]

Yet little over a year later Stanhope, irked by Townshend's checks on his diplomatic activities and attracted by the promise of a peerage, lent himself to a palace intrigue resulting in Townshend's dismissal, Walpole's resignation, and their replacement by their enemy, Lord Sunderland, as secretary of state, and by Stanhope at the Treasury. On learning of Stanhope's conduct Townshend wrote to him:

My heart is so full with the thoughts of having received this treatment from you, to whom I have always been so faithful a friend, that you will excuse my not saying more at this time. I pray God forgive you; I do.

And Walpole:

What could prevail on you to enter into such a scheme as this, and appear to be chief actor in it, and undertake to carry it through in all events, without which it could not have been undertaken, is unaccountable. I do swear to you that Lord Townshend has no way deserved it of you . . . Believe me, Stanhope, he never thought you could enter into a combination with his enemies against him.

Stanhope's transfer to the Treasury vacated his seat at Cockermouth, for which the Duke of Somerset, now in opposition, was not prepared to re-elect him. 'Stanhope hath no interest in the nation' the Duke wrote on hearing of Townshend's dismissal:

He is to make friends when he is made a lord, for that part of the scheme one may dive into, that he is no more to expose himself to the contempt of the House of Commons.[4]

However, a vacancy in one of the Isle of Wight boroughs enabled him to return for a short time to the Commons, where in a financial debate on 20 May 1717

he ingenuously owned his incapacity for the affairs of the Treasury, which were so remote from his studies and inclination that therefore he would fain have kept the employment he had before, which was both more easy and more profitable to him; but he thought it his duty to obey the King's commands.

He went on to make a personal attack on Walpole, saying that

> he would endeavour to make up by application, honesty, and disinterestedness what he wanted in abilities and experience. That he would content himself with the salary and lawful perquisites of his office; and, though he had quitted a better place, he would not quarter himself upon anybody to make it up; that he had no brothers, nor other relations, to provide for; and that upon his first entering into the Treasury he had made a standing order against the late practice of granting reversions of places.

These remarks led to an altercation so violent that to prevent a duel the House passed a resolution forbidding the two statesmen to carry the dispute further.

At the end of the session Stanhope was duly raised to the Lords. He retained his Treasury posts, contrary to the unwritten rule that the chancellor of the Exchequer should sit in the House of Commons, till the following March, when he returned to the field of foreign affairs, which he thenceforth dominated, basing his policy on the Anglo-French alliance, a reversal of the previous policy of both countries, effected by himself in collaboration with his old friend, Dubois. He died suddenly, 5 Feb. 1721, on the eve of succeeding Marlborough as captain general, of an apoplectic fit brought on by the violence of his reply to an attack on the Government in the House of Lords, or, according to another account, by 'a great debauch . . . at the Duke of Newcastle's,' where 'they drank excessively of new tokay, champagne, visney, and barba water, thirteen hours it is said'.[5]

¹ St. Simon, *Mems.* (ed. Boislisle) xviii. 50; B. Williams, *Stanhope*, 154. ² Coxe, *Walpole*, ii. 48, 143–6. ³ 'Account of the court of Geo. I', by Edward Wortley Montagu, in *Letters of Lady Mary Wortley Montagu* (1887), i. 18–19. ⁴ Coxe, ii. 126, 143–6, 148; *HMC Stuart*, iii. 447. ⁵ Williams, 439–45; *HMC Portland*, v. 616.

R.R.S.

STANHOPE, Hon. John (1705–48), of Blackheath, Kent.

NOTTINGHAM   1727–1734
DERBY   13 Mar. 1736–4 Dec. 1748

b. 5 Jan. 1705, 3rd s. of Philip Stanhope, 3rd Earl of Chesterfield; bro. of Hon. Charles, Philip Dormer, Lord Stanhope, and Hon. Sir William Stanhope (qq.v.). *unm. suc.* yr. bro. Charles 1736.
Sec. to embassy at The Hague 1728–32; ld. of Admiralty Feb. 1748–*d.*

John Stanhope was brought in by the Duke of Newcastle for Nottingham on a compromise in 1727. From 1728 to 1732, he was secretary to his brother, Philip Dormer, Lord Chesterfield, ambas-

sador at The Hague. In 1733 he followed Chesterfield into opposition, voting against the excise bill, his only recorded vote in this Parliament. When the question of his re-election came up, Newcastle was informed that

> ever since the last election he has so totally neglected the town that both sides seem to be set as one man against him; and Lord Chesterfield has about a fortnight ago completed the disgust by chasing through the town on his way to Scarborough without taking notice of anybody here.[1]

He was not put up for Nottingham but in 1736 he was returned on his family's interest at Derby, in succession to his younger brother, Charles, whose fortune he also inherited. He continued to follow Chesterfield politically, voting against the Government till 1744, when Chesterfield joined the Administration, after which he became a government supporter. When Chesterfield resigned in 1748, John Stanhope was made a lord of the Admiralty, which, Chesterfield wrote,

> he never would have been as long as I had continued in, the resolution being taken to exclude all those who might otherwise have been supposed to have come in upon my interest. As I retire without quarrelling, and without the least intention to oppose, I saw no reason why my brother should decline this post; and I advised him to accept of it, and the rather as it was the King's own doing.[2]

He died 4 Dec. 1748

> of a fit of the gout, which he had had about a month in his hands, and feet, and which fell at last upon his stomach and head.[3]

¹ John Plumptre to Newcastle, 21 July 1733, Add. 32688, f. 30. ² To Dayrolles, 23 Feb. 1748, *Letters of Chesterfield*, ed. Dobrée, 1109. ³ Chesterfield to his son, 6 Dec. 1748, ibid. 1269.

R.R.S.

STANHOPE, Philip Dormer, Lord Stanhope (1694–1773).

ST. GERMANS   3 May 1715–1722
LOSTWITHIEL   1722–May 1723

b. 22 Sept. 1694, 1st s. of Philip Stanhope, 3rd Earl of Chesterfield; bro. of Hon. Charles, John and Sir William Stanhope (qq.v.). *educ.* Trinity Hall, Camb. 1712–14; Grand Tour 1714–15. *m.* 14 May 1733, Petronille Melusine von der Schulenberg, *suo jure* Countess of Walsingham, illegit. da. of George I by Ermingarde Melusina, *suo jure* Duchess of Kendal, *s.p. legit. suc.* fa. as 4th Earl 9 Feb. 1726; K.G. 18 June 1730.
Gent. of the bedchamber to Prince of Wales 1715–27; ld. of the bedchamber 1727–30; capt. yeoman of the guard 1723–5; P.C. 26 Feb. 1728; ambassador to The Hague 1728–32; ld. steward of the Household 1730–3; ld. lt. [I] Jan. 1745–Oct. 1746; one of the lds. justices of the realm May 1745; sec. of state, northern dept. Oct. 1746–Feb. 1748.

On the accession of George I, the future Lord

Chesterfield abandoned the grand tour to return to England, was introduced to the new King by his kinsman, James Stanhope (q.v.), and was appointed a gentleman of the Prince's bedchamber.[1] Returned for St. Germans on the recommendation of James Stanhope, he wrote that 'from the day I was elected to the day that I spoke I thought nor dreamed of nothing but speaking'.[2]

After his maiden speech on 5 Aug. 1715, calling for Ormonde's impeachment, a Tory Member, drawing him aside, threatened to reveal his being still under age if he voted as he had spoken, whereupon he 'answered nothing, but making a low bow, quitted the House directly and went to Paris'.[3] He spoke for the septennial bill in 1716. As a member of the Prince's household he voted against the Government during the split in the Whig party, 1717–20, except in the case of the peerage bill, on which he was put down by Craggs as 'con' and by Sunderland as 'pro', eventually voting for it along with the other Stanhopes in the Commons. Lady Cowper reported in 1720:

> the Prince has been so rough with little Lord Stanhope about voting in the South Sea affair [the proposals of the South Sea Company to take over the national debt], that he has talked of resigning for a good while.[4]

In March 1721, reporting the proceedings against Charles Stanhope (q.v.), Thomas Brodrick (q.v.) commented:

> Lord Stanhope . . . carried off a pretty many by mentioning in the strongest terms the memory of the late lord of that name.[5]

At the opening of the next Parliament he moved the re-election of Spencer Compton as Speaker.[6] He did not stand for re-election on vacating his seat by accepting the office of captain of the yeomen of the guard in 1723. Succeeding to the peerage in 1726, he went into opposition over the excise bill in 1733, thereafter holding office only from 1745 to 1748, when he retired.

He died 24 Mar. 1773.

[1] Maty, *Mems. Life Ld. Chesterfield*, i. 19. [2] Letter to his son, 15 Mar. 1754. *Letters of Chesterfield*, ed. Dobrée, 2102. [3] Maty, i. 21–22. [4] *Lady Cowper Diary*, 136. [5] Coxe, *Walpole*, ii. 209. [6] *Knatchbull Diary*, 9 Oct. 1722.

E.C.

STANHOPE, William (c.1683–1756).

DERBY	1715–1722
STEYNING	24 Apr.–5 Aug. 1727
DERBY	1727–6 Jan. 1730

b. c.1683, 3rd surv. s. of John Stanhope of Elvaston, Derbys.; bro. of Charles Stanhope (q.v.). *educ.* Eton; I. Temple, called 1704. *m.* c.1718, Anne, da. and h. of Col. Edward Griffith, 2s. *cr.* Baron Harrington 6 Jan. 1730; Earl of Harrington 9 Feb. 1742.

Lt. and capt. 2 Ft. Gds. 1703; capt. and lt.-col. 3 Ft. Gds. 1710; col. regt. of Ft. 1711–12, regt. of Drags. 1715–18, 13 Drags. 1725–30; maj.-gen. 1735; lt.-gen. 1739; gen. 1747; envoy, Madrid 1717–18, Turin 1718–20, Paris 1719, Madrid 1720; ambassador, Madrid 1721–7, 1729–30, Aix la Chapelle 1727, Soissons Feb. 1730; vice-chamberlain of the Household 1727–30; P.C. 31 May 1727; sec. of state, northern dept. 1730–42, 1744–6; ld. president of the Council 1742–5; one of the lds. justices of the realm 1743, 1745; ld. lt. [I] 1746–51.

William Stanhope, in Horace Walpole's words, 'raised himself from a younger brother's fortune to the first posts in the Government, without either the talent of speaking in Parliament or any interest there'.[1] Beginning his career in the army, he was returned on his family's interest for Derby in 1715, voting with the Government in every recorded division. Appointed envoy and then ambassador to Spain, he did not stand again till 1727, when he returned to England, resuming his seat at the general election, after sitting a few months for Steyning. He was then sent abroad again to take part in the peace negotiations which resulted in the conclusion of the treaty of Seville, for which he was rewarded with a peerage and a secretaryship of state.

> There was something very singular [Hervey writes] both in this man's acquisition of fame and in his loss of it; for when he was at the court of Spain, without doing anything there that might not have been transacted by a common clerk, all parties at home flattered and courted him . . . [But] as soon as he came over and was made secretary of state, the sound of his name began to die away. He was forgotten in his eminence, seen every day, and never mentioned.[2]

He retained his post by the favour of the King, which he lost when he resigned with the Pelhams in 1746. He died 8 Dec. 1756.

[1] *Mems. Geo. II*, i. 4. [2] Hervey, *Mems.* 174.

R.R.S.

STANHOPE, Hon. Sir William (1702–72), of Eythrope, Bucks.

LOSTWITHIEL	26 Jan.–5 Aug. 1727
BUCKINGHAMSHIRE	1727–1741, 1747–1768

b. 20 July 1702, 2nd s. of Philip Stanhope, 3rd Earl of Chesterfield; bro. of Hon. Charles, Hon. John and Philip Dormer, Lord Stanhope (qq.v.). *m.* (1) 27 Apr. 1721, Susanna (*d.* 7 Oct. 1740), da. of John Rudge (q.v.) of Wheatfield, Oxon., 1da., who m. Welbore Ellis (q.v.); (2) 29 May 1745, Elizabeth (*d.* 25 Feb. 1746), da. of Sir Ambrose Crowley, M.P., alderman of London, *s.p.*; (3) 6 Oct. 1759, Anne Hussey, da. of Francis Blake Delaval, sis. of Francis Blake (qq.v.) and John Hussey Delaval, M.P., *s.p.* K.B. 27 May 1725.

The younger brother of the famous Lord Chesterfield, Stanhope was the favourite of his father, who settled upon him, on his marriage, his Buckingham-shire estates, worth £8,000 a year.[1] In January 1727 he stood unsuccessfully for Hertford but was returned unopposed for a government seat at Lostwithiel. At the ensuing general election that year he was returned for Buckinghamshire and Aylesbury, opting to serve for the county, for which he was re-elected in 1734. No votes of his are recorded till 1732, after which, like his brothers, he voted regularly against the Administration. As a member of the Whig Opposition he frequented the court of Frederick, Prince of Wales, which the Prince's mistress, Lady Archibald Hamilton, had so filled with her relations, that one day Stanhope addressed every person he did not know there as Mr. or Mrs. Hamilton.[2] After this he was given to understand that his presence there was not 'quite agreeable'.[3]

Stanhope did not stand again till 1747, when he was once more returned as an opposition Whig for Buckinghamshire. In 1748 he bitterly attacked the Grenvilles in Parliament on a bill for transferring the summer assizes from Aylesbury to Buckingham; but the virulent oration later published under his name was composed by Horace Walpole from his own undelivered speech on that occasion.[4] He appears to have renewed his affiliations with the Prince of Wales, for he figures as joint vice-treasurer of Ireland in the 2nd Lord Egmont's lists of persons to receive office on Frederick's accession. He died 7 May 1772.

[1] Maty, *Mems. Life Ld. Chesterfield*, i. 269. [2] Horace Walpole's ms notes in B.M. copy of above, i. 269. [3] Walpole to Mann, 7 Jan. 1742. [4] H. Walpole, *Corresp.* (Yale ed.), xiii. 21.

E.C.

STANHOPE, Hon. William (1719–79), of Elvaston, Derbys.

AYLESBURY   1741–1747
BURY ST. EDMUNDS   1747–8 Dec. 1756

b. 18 Dec. 1719, 1st s. of William Stanhope (q.v.), 1st Earl of Harrington. *educ.* ?Eton 1732. *m.* 11 Aug. 1746, Lady Caroline FitzRoy, da. of Charles, 2nd Duke of Grafton, 2s. 5da. *styled* Visct. Petersham 1742–56. *suc.* fa. as 2nd Earl 8 Dec. 1756.

Ensign 10 Ft. 1738; capt. 14 Ft. 1739; capt. and lt.-col. 3 Ft. Gds. 1741; col. 2 tp. Horse Grenadier Gds. 1745–*d.*; maj.-gen. 1755; lt.-gen. 1758; gen. 1770; customer, port of Dublin 1748–*d.*

Lord Petersham, a professional soldier, was present at Fontenoy, where he was 'slightly wounded' and 'most commended'.[1] Returned for Aylesbury in 1741 on the interest of Sir William Stanhope (q.v.), he voted with the Administration in all three divisions on the Hanoverians but with the opposition minority on 15 Dec. 1743 for George Grenville's

compromise motion in favour of a stricter alliance with the Dutch.[2] In 1747 he succeeded his brother-in-law, Lord Euston (q.v.), at Coventry but elected to sit for Bury St. Edmunds, where he had also been returned by the Duke of Grafton, whose daughter he had married, though

neither he nor his father, Lord Harrington, have a single foot of land to make any settlement with. Lord Harrington's elder brother, Mr. Charles Stanhope [q.v.], who is unmarried, has a good estate but will not do anything upon this occasion to oblige his nephew, whose sole subsistence is his commission.[3]

Two years later Horace Walpole wrote that

Sir William Stanhope has just given a great ball to Lady Caroline Petersham, to whom he takes extremely since his daughter married herself to Mr. [Welbore] Ellis [q.v.]; and as the Petershams are relations, they propose to be his heirs.[4]

Because of his peculiar gait Lord Petersham was nicknamed 'Peter Shambles' and Walpole also refers to 'his nose and legs twisted to every point of crossness'.[5] In later life he took little part in politics and was known chiefly for his libertinism. He died 1 Apr. 1779.

[1] Walpole to Mann, 11 May 1745. [2] Owen, *Pelhams*, 205. [3] *Malmesbury Letters*, i. 39–40. [4] Walpole to Mann, 7 June 1748. [5] Walpole to Montagu, 23 June 1750.

R.S.L.

STANLEY, Sir Edward, 5th Bt. (1689–1776), of Bickerstaffe, Lancs.

LANCASHIRE   1727–13 Apr. 1736

b. 17 Sept. 1689, 1st s. of Sir Thomas Stanley, 4th Bt., M.P., of Bickerstaffe by his 1st w. Elizabeth, da. and h. of Thomas Patten, M.P., of Preston, Lancs. *educ.* Macclesfield sch. Cheshire; Sidney Sussex, Camb. 1707. *m.* 14 Sept. 1714, Elizabeth, da. and h. of Robert Hesketh of Rufford, Lancs., 3s. *d.v.p.* 6da. *suc.* fa. 7 May 1714; his distant cos. James Stanley, M.P., 10th Earl of Derby, as 11th Earl, 1 Feb. 1736.

Sheriff, Lancs. 1722–4; mayor, Preston 1731–2; ld. lt. Lancs. 1742–57, 1771–*d.*

Returned unopposed for Lancashire as an opposition Whig, Stanley voted consistently against the Government. Three speeches of his are recorded: for a pension bill, 31 Jan. 1733, moving for a committee to inquire into frauds in the customs, 19 Apr. 1733, and for the repeal of the Septennial Act, 13 Mar. 1734.[1] After succeeding to the earldom, he took little part in national politics. During the Forty-five, as lord lieutenant, he complained that he was sent no advice or information by the Government:

That I should be forgot is no wonder, having never had any interest, and very little acquaintance among the great ones, however what I can do for the service of my king and country shall never be wanting.[2]

On receiving orders from the Government to call out the militia he wrote to Newcastle, 15 Nov. 1745:

> I wish our militia could be made of use . . . but as our 14 days' pay (which being known not to be strictly legal was unwillingly paid by some towns) will expire on the 25th, which I fear is sooner than the King's troops can arrive among us, I hope, if it be the opinion of the Council, that the other 14 days be ordered.

Although an Act of Parliament was passed to meet this difficulty, he disbanded the militia, explaining, 24 Nov.:

> I think it can scarce be expected by anybody that a raw undisciplined militia, consisting of foot, without any one that knows how to command, would be able to prevent the advance of an army seven or eight times their number, and this not only the opinion of me, but of several deputy lieutenants and officers who happen to be with me. Liverpool is certainly not tenable, nor is there any place of strength for us to have retired to . . . As for myself, I am going to Manchester, my present purpose being to proceed to London, not seeing how it is in any way in my power or any of the friends of the Government, to be longer serviceable to the country in which my fortune lies, or the nation in general, and therefore I think I am at liberty to save myself from the hands of those whose religion of course makes them enemies to the constitution, under which they live, with which sort of person this country does but too much abound.[3]

His political attitude is shown in a letter he wrote to Thomas Bootle (q.v.) in 1747:

> You judge right in imagining a Whig Parliament would be my choice, and much to my satisfaction, could such a number of independents as would fill the House be found in Britain, but I have seen enough to observe that such a blessing is not to be hoped for, and am therefore pretty indifferent who are our representatives, so long as there is no danger of a Tory Parliament, and so long as the only contest is who shall hold their places, or who shall undermine them, which seems to have been the sole aim of our great men for many years past.[4]

He retained the lord lieutenancy until 1757, when he resigned it to his son, Lord Strange (q.v.), on whose death in 1771 he resumed it till his own, 22 Feb. 1776.

[1] *HMC Egmont Diary*, i. 365; ii. 55. [2] To Ld. Cholmondeley, 29 Sept. 1745, mss at Lancs. RO. [3] Add. 32705, ff. 314, 372. [4] 14 June 1747, Bootle mss, Royal archives, Windsor.

E.C.

STANLEY, Hans (1721–80), of Paultons, nr. Romsey, Hants, and Ventnor, I.o.W.

ST. ALBANS 11 Feb. 1743–1747
SOUTHAMPTON 1754–12 Jan. 1780

b. 23 Sept. 1721,[1] o.s. of George Stanley of Paultons by Sarah, da. of Sir Hans Sloane, 1st Bt., of Chelsea, and coh. with her sis., w. of Charles Cadogan (q.v.), 2nd Baron Cadogan. *educ.* Hackney; Switzerland.[2] *suc.* fa. (who committed suicide) 1734. *unm.* One of his sisters m. Welbore Ellis (q.v.).

Ld. of Admiralty Sept. 1757–July 1765; envoy to Paris May–Sept. 1761; P.C. 26 Nov. 1762; gov. and v.-adm. I.o.W. 1764–6, 1770–*d.*; ambassador designate to Russia 1766–7; cofferer of the Household Dec. 1766–Mar. 1774, Oct. 1776–*d.*

Hans Stanley's grandfather, a Southampton merchant and alderman, bought Paultons and his father unsuccessfully contested Lymington in 1729. Returned for St. Albans as an opposition Whig, he was one of the signatories of the opposition whip of 10 Nov. 1743.[3] He spoke twice in the debates on the Hanoverian troops in January 1744, stating

> in express terms that the King had been obviously guilty of partiality to the worst of mercenaries. Mr. Pelham reprimanded him very mildly and excused him as a young man; he then resumed his speech and was as abusive as he had been before.[4]

He remained in opposition till the end of the Parliament. He did not stand in 1747, though on 18 May he was made a freeman of Southampton,[5] together with his cousin A. L. Swymmer (q.v.), possibly with a view to his contesting the borough. By this time he had gone over to the Government. Shortly after the general election he was nominated by Pelham to contest a by-election at Shaftesbury on Lord Ilchester's (Stephen Fox, q.v.) interest against William Beckford (q.v.), who, however, arranged a compromise under which Stanley withdrew.[6] Like his father he died by his own hand, 12 Jan. 1780.

[1] Sloane-Stanley mss. [2] Yorke, *Hardwicke*, iii. 320; Stanley to Ld. Palmerston, 28 Oct. 1763, Palmerston mss. [3] Owen, *Pelhams*, 198. [4] Hartington to Devonshire, 19 Jan. 1744, Devonshire mss; Yorke's parl. jnl. *Parl. Hist.* xiii. 390, 393, 463. [5] Reg. of Burgesses Admission, 1697–1835, Southampton City recs. [6] See SHAFTESBURY.

L.B.N.

STANLEY (afterwards **SMITH STANLEY**), **James**, Lord Strange (1717–71).

LANCASHIRE 1741–1 June 1771

b. 7 Jan. 1717, 1st s. of Sir Edward Stanley (q.v.), 11th Earl of Derby. *educ.* Westminster 1729; Leyden Univ. 1735; Grand Tour c.1737. *m.* 17 Mar. 1747 (with £100,000), Lucy, da. and coh. of Hugh Smith of Weald Hall, Essex, and assumed name of Smith bef. Stanley, 3s. 4da.

Ld. lt. Lancs. 1757–*d.*; P.C. 15 Dec. 1762; chancellor of the duchy of Lancaster Dec. 1762–*d.*

'A Whig in principle' but one who 'always acts according to the dictates of conscience',[1] Strange, throughout his thirty years as knight of the shire for Lancashire was the extreme type of independent Member. Horace Walpole in 1749 described him as 'of a party by himself, yet voting generally with the Tories'; a short time later, as 'a busy young lord, very disinterested, often quick, as often injudicious, and not the less troublesome for either', and as 'the most absurd man that ever existed with a very clear head'.[2] Philip Yorke (q.v.) in 1745 referred to his 'cavilling acuteness';[3] the 2nd Lord Egmont, in his electoral survey c.1749–50, wished 'he was called to the House of Lords for he will always trouble the waters in the Commons'; and George III wrote about him in March 1763 as 'forever running counter'.[4]

Strange made his first reported speech in May 1742, when he moved that the rejection by the Lords of the bill indemnifying witnesses against Walpole was 'an obstruction to justice and might prove fatal to liberties of the nation'.[5] In the next session he supported a new place bill and opposed taking Hanoverian troops into British pay. During the threatened French invasion in February 1744 and the rebellion of 1745 he strongly rallied to the House of Hanover: 'though I never flattered him [the King] I will freely lose my life rather than see him supplanted by any of that rascally family'; but he opposed the voluntary subscription for raising troops, which he compared to the benevolences of Charles I.[6] After the rebellion he continued in opposition to the Pelhams, calling the resignations of February 1746 'a plot against the King's sovereignty'. He was critical of the regency bill, in 1751 asking

> if it was probable that there would be no dissensions in the council of regency, which was to be composed of the present ministry? Survey them; with what cordiality have they concurred in all measures for some years! May not it happen, that if the Regent should refuse to employ some person recommended by them, the junto may threaten to resign? An insult, such as within my own time I have almost seen offered to a crowned head! We shall see all that repeated scramble for power, that I have two or three times seen acted over. Can the Duke [of Cumberland] be removed by address of Parliament? I won't say that he is most likely to do mischief, but certainly he is most capable of doing it. As to the praemunire clause, the person who drew it deserves to incur it.

He spoke against the subsidy treaty with Saxony, 22 Jan. 1752. But in December 1751 he supported the Government in continuing the land tax at 3s. in the pound,[7] remarkable in a knight of the shire who usually acted with the Opposition.

He died v.p. 1 June 1771.

[1] Bute Register, Add. 36796. [2] To Horace Mann, 4 Mar. 1749; *Mems. Geo. II*, i. 108; ii. 145. [3] Yorke's parl. jnl. *Parl. Hist.* xiii. 1051. [4] Sedgwick, *Letters Geo. III to Bute*, i. 198. [5] Coxe, *Walpole*, i. 715. [6] To Jas. Oswald, 20 Aug. 1745, Oswald mss; Yorke, *Hardwicke*, i. 418. [7] *Mems. Geo. II*, i. 130–1, 219, 243.

E.C.

STANWIX, John (1693–1766), of Carlisle, Cumb.

CARLISLE   1741–26 Jan. 1742, 26 Nov. 1746–1761
APPLEBY   1761–Oct. 1766

bap. 19 Mar. 1693,[1] s. of Rev. John Roos, rector of Widmerpool, Notts., by Matilda, da. of Thomas Stanwix of Carlisle. *m.* (1) Ann (d. 17 Mar. 1754), da. of Henry Holmes, 1s. 1da; (2) 20 Apr. 1763 (with £12,000), a da. of Marmaduke Sowle of Dublin, *s.p. suc.* fa. 1704 and to estates of uncle Thomas Stanwix (q.v.) 1725, taking name of Stanwix.

Ensign 1706; lt. 1706; capt. 28 Ft. 1722; maj. 10 Marines 1741; lt.-col. 71 Ft. 1745; half pay 1749; gov. Carlisle 1752–d.; dep. q.m.g. 1754–6; col. 1756; col. comm. 60 Ft. 1756–61, serving with his regt. in America 1756–60; brig.-gen. (America) 1757; maj.-gen. 1759; lt.-gen. 1761; col. 49 Ft. 1761–4; lt. gov. I. of W. 1763–d.; col. 8 Ft. 1764–d.

Alderman, Carlisle; equerry to the Prince of Wales 1749–51.

Standing as a government supporter for Carlisle in 1741 with the backing of the corporation,[2] Stanwix was returned by the mayor, who declared the poll closed before most of his opponent's supporters had voted. On petition he came to a compromise with his defeated opponent, John Hylton (q.v.), that Hylton was 'to come in on terms of indemnity to the mayor'.[3] Returned at a by-election in 1746, he was listed in 1747 as Opposition and in 1749 was appointed to the Prince of Wales's household. On Frederick's death, according to the 2nd Lord Egmont, he 'declared to the Court . . . that he had been long tired with the minority, and would never give another vote against them as long as he lived or the first vote he gave should be with them, for which the courtiers expressed great contempt for him'.[4] When the appointments to the Princess's household were discussed, he was ruled out on the ground that the King 'dislikes Stanwix extremely'.[5] However, in 1752 Pelham recommended him for the post of governor of Carlisle, writing on 17 July to Newcastle at Hanover, 'if I remember right the King desired to be put in mind of Stanwix when anything happened in the military way . . . I think him a very nice man, at least as much so as any in the army'.[6] He was drowned, probably on 29 Oct. 1766, with his wife and daughter, on the way back to England from Ireland.

[1] Stanwix ped., Portland mss. [2] *HMC Carlisle*, 196–7. [3] Coxe, *Walpole*, iii. 584. [4] Add. 47073. [5] Newcastle to Pelham, 10 Apr. 1751, Newcastle (Clumber) mss. [6] Add. 32728, f.286.

R.R.S.

STANWIX, Thomas (c.1670–1725), of Carlisle, Cumb.

CARLISLE   1702–Mar. 1721
NEWPORT I.o.W.   2 Aug. 1721–1722
YARMOUTH I.o.W.   1722–14 Mar. 1725

b. c.1670, o.s. of Thomas Stanwix of Carlisle by Grace, da. of Thomas Fairfax of Parkhead, Cumb.[1] *m.* Susannah, *s.p.*

Capt.-lt. 13 Ft. 1691, capt. 1692; capt. 14 Ft. 1693, Earl of Arran's Horse 1694, 6 Drag. Gds. by 1702;

lt.-col. Ld. Henry Scott's Ft. 1704; brevet col. 1705; lt. gov. Carlisle 1705–d.; col. of newly raised regt. of Ft. 1706; served in Portugal, took part in the battle of the Caya 1709; brig.-gen. 1710; gov. Gibraltar 1710–15, Chelsea Hospital Jan. 1715–June 1720; col. of newly raised regt. of Ft. 1715–17, 30 Ft. July–Aug. 1717, 12 Ft. Aug. 1717–d.; gov. Kingston-upon-Hull Mar. 1721–d.; mayor, Carlisle 1715.

Stanwix was a native of Carlisle, which he represented for nearly 20 years, building up a strong personal interest. For most of that time he was attached to the 3rd Earl of Carlisle, who recommended him to Marlborough for the lieutenant governorship of Carlisle in 1705.[2] Appointed governor of Chelsea Hospital on George I's accession, he was mayor and commandant of Carlisle during the rebellion of 1715;[3] voted for the septennial bill in 1716; spoke for the Government in the army debate of December 1717; and voted with them on the repeal of the Occasional Conformity and Schism Acts but against them on the peerage bill in 1719. About this time he fell out with Lord Carlisle, who was assured by Lord Sunderland that 'no regard or favour shall be had to Stanwix, his behaviour of late having not deserved much of that'.[4] On Walpole's return to the Pay Office in 1720 Stanwix was turned out of his Chelsea post to make way for Charles Churchill (q.v.), but next year he was compensated with another governorship. His acceptance of the post was held by the House of Commons to vacate his seat, which he lost at the ensuing by-election. He stood again at the general election with the support of Lord Lonsdale,[5] but was narrowly defeated. On both occasions he was brought back into Parliament by the Government for Isle of Wight boroughs. He died 14 May 1725, leaving his property in Carlisle to a nephew, John Roos, who took the name of Stanwix (q.v.).

[1] J. Foster, *Vis. Cumb.* 128; Stanwix ped., Portland mss. [2] Marlborough's *Dispatches*, i. 597. [3] R. C. Jarvis, *Jacobite Risings of 1715 and 1745*, p. 157 n. 7. [4] *HMC Carlisle*, 23. [5] Ld. Lonsdale 'to my tenants in Burgh Barony who are freemen of Carlisle', 28 Dec. 1721, Lowther mss.

R.R.S.

STANYAN, Abraham (c.1670–1732), of St. Martin-in-the-Fields, London.

BUCKINGHAM   1715–Oct. 1717

b. c.1670, 1st s. of Lawrence Stanyan[1] of Monken Hadley, Mdx., merchant, farmer and commr. of the revenue [I], by Dorothy, da. and coh. of Henry Knapp of Woodcote, or Rawlins, in South Stoke, Oxon., sis. of Mary, w. of Sir Richard Temple, 3rd Bt., M.P., of Stowe, Bucks., and aunt of Richard Temple, M.P., 1st Visct. Cobham. *unm. suc.* fa. 1725.[2]

Sec. of embassy to Sir William Trumbull at Constantinople 1690–1, to the Earl of Manchester at Venice 1697–8, and Paris 1699–1700; clerk to Privy Council extraordinary 1699; envoy extraordinary to Switzerland 1705–14, and to the Grisons 1707–14; special commr. to mediate between the Emperor and Savoy 1712–13; ld. of Admiralty 1714–17; envoy extraordinary and plenipotentiary to the Emperor 1716–18; clerk in ordinary to Privy Council 1717–20; ambassador to Turkey 1717–30; commr. of privy seal Jan.–June 1731.

Abraham Stanyan, a career diplomat, entered the secretary of state's office as a clerk, distinguishing himself under Queen Anne as envoy to Switzerland, of which he published an account on his return to England in 1714. A Whig and member of the Kit-Cat club, he was made a lord of the Admiralty on George I's accession and returned for Buckingham on the interest of his cousin, Lord Cobham. Vacating his seat in October 1717 on appointment to a Privy Council clerkship, a few weeks later he was appointed ambassador to Turkey, where he remained for over twelve years. His successor there, Lord Kinnoull, described him as 'a well-behaved, complaisant gentleman of an indolent temper . . . whose life [at Constantinople] . . . has been upon a sofa with the women'.[3] After his final return to England in 1730 he held office for a few months as commissioner of the privy seal *ad interim*. He died 9–11 Sept. 1732, leaving to Lord Cobham the 'large diamond brilliant ring I usually wear [as a] small token of my gratitude in acknowledgment of the friendship he has constantly honoured me with'.[4]

[1] *HMC Downshire*, i. 319. [2] O. G. Knapp, *Hist. Fam. of Knapp*, 83–87. [3] Wood, *Hist. Levant Co.* 174–5. [4] PCC 255 Bedford.

R.S.L.

STAPLETON, Sir William, 4th Bt. (?1698–1740), of Rotherfield Greys, Oxon.

OXFORDSHIRE   1727–12 Jan. 1740

b. ?1698, 1st s. of Sir William Stapleton, 3rd Bt., of Nevis by Frances, da. and coh. of Sir James Russell, gov. Nevis. *educ.* Ch. Ch. Oxf. 17 Apr. 1714, aged 15. *m.* 28 Apr. 1724, Catherine, da. and h. of William Paul of Braywick, Berks. by Lady Catherine Fane, da. of Vere Fane, M.P., 4th Earl of Westmorland, 3s. 2da. *suc.* fa. Dec. 1699.

Stapleton was the grandson of Sir William Stapleton, who followed Charles II into exile in France, and after the Restoration was appointed deputy-governor of Montserrat and captain-general of the Leeward Islands, with a baronetcy.[1] In February 1725 Stapleton invited several other Tories to a dinner, during which the Duke of Wharton publicly drank the Pretender's health and boasted of the facility of a restoration with French help.[2] At the general election of 1727, Dr. Stratford of Christ Church reported:

Our knighthood of the shire went a begging . . . One Sir William Stapleton, a West Indian, formerly of Christ Church, a rake then as I hear he is still, is to be [the] man. He has but little estate in Oxfordshire, and that by his wife Mrs. Paul.[3]

Returned unopposed, he voted against the Administration in every recorded division. His only recorded speech was made on the resolutions for a bill for the relief of the sugar colonies, 21 Feb. 1733, when he successfully opposed the importation of rum from the North American colonies into Ireland as detrimental to the sugar colonies. He was the only unofficial member of the committee appointed to draft the bill, known as the Molasses Act.[4]

He died at Bath 12 Jan. 1740.

[1] Oliver, *Antigua*, iii. 102. [2] *HMC Var.* viii. 385. [3] *HMC Portland*, vii. 450. [4] *HMC Egmont Diary*, i. 335.

E.C.

STAPYLTON, Sir Miles, 4th Bt. (?1708–52), of Myton, Yorks.

YORKSHIRE 1734–Apr. 1750

b. ?1708, o.s. of Sir John Stapylton, 3rd Bt., M.P., by Mary, da. and h. of Frances Sandys of Scroby, Notts. *educ.* Westminster 1724; Univ. Coll. Oxf. 16 Nov. 1726, aged 18. *m.* May 1738, Ann, da. of Edmund Waller (q.v.), 1da. *suc.* fa. 25 Oct. 1733. Commr. of customs Apr. 1750–*d.*

Sir John Stapylton, a wealthy country gentleman, was killed by a fall from his horse on the way to attend a meeting at York, where he was to be adopted as the Tory candidate for the county at the impending general election. The Yorkshire Tories thereupon adopted his son and heir, Miles, who was returned at the head of the poll, after a hard-fought and costly contest. After Walpole's fall his political course conformed with that of his father-in-law, Edmund Waller, with whom he voted against the Government on the Hanoverians in 1742 and 1744, but for them on the same question in 1746 as a 'New Ally'. His only recorded speech was on 1 Feb. 1744, when he moved unsuccessfully to address the King for all letters and papers relating to the treaty of Worms and that with Prussia.[1] For a short time he appears to have joined the party of the Prince of Wales, figuring as a lord of the Treasury in the 2nd Lord Egmont's lists of persons to receive office on Frederick's accession. Towards the end of 1749 he went over to the Government in circumstances described by Henry Pelham:

Sir Miles Stapylton some time ago expressed his regard for the King and those who have the honour to serve him, and indeed in the most frank and gentlemanly manner declared his intention to support that interest in all places. I soon found that it would be convenient to him if he could have an employment

that would ease him from the trouble and expense of Parliament.[2]

In April he was given such an employment in the form of a commissionership of customs, thereby automatically forfeiting his seat, which was filled at his suggestion by another converted Tory, Henry Pleydell Dawnay, 3rd Viscount Downe [I] (q.v.).

He died 14 May 1752.

[1] Yorke's parl. jnl. *Parl. Hist.* xiii. 635; *CJ*, xxiv. 539. [2] To Ld. Rockingham, 25 Nov. 1749, Rockingham mss.

R.R.S.

STEELE, Richard (1672–1729), of Llangunnor, Carm.

STOCKBRIDGE	1713–18 Mar. 1714
BOROUGHBRIDGE	1715–1722
WENDOVER	1722–1727

bap. 12 Mar. 1672, o.s. of Richard Steele of Monks-town and Dublin, attorney, by Eleanor, da. of one Sheyles, wid. of Thomas Symes, or Sims, of Dublin. *educ.* Charterhouse, as nominee of the Duke of Ormonde 1684–9; Ch. Ch. Oxf. 1689; postmaster Merton, Oxf. 1691–2. *m.* (1) c.May 1705, Margaret (*d.* 21 Dec. 1706) da. of John Ford of St. Andrew Overhills, Barbados, sis. and testamentary h. of Maj. Robert Ford of St. Andrew's, Barbados, wid. of John Stretch of St. James's, Barbados, *s.p.*; (2) 9 Sept. 1707, Mary, da. and h. of Jonathan Scurlock of Llangunnor, 2s. 2da. *suc.* fa. c.1677. Kntd. 9 Apr. 1715.

Volunteer 2 tp. Life Gds. c.1693; sec. to Ld. Cutts 1696–7; ensign, Coldstream Gds. 1697; capt. 34 Ft. 1702–c.1705; gentleman waiter to the Prince Consort 1706–8; gazetteer 1707–10; commr. of stamps 1710–13; surveyor, royal stables at Hampton Court 1714–c.1717; supervisor, Theatre Royal, Drury Lane, Jan. 1715–Jan. 1720, May 1721–*d.*; commr. for forfeited estates 1716–25.

Richard Steele, the Whig essayist and dramatist,[1] took a prominent part in the political warfare against the Tories under Queen Anne, bringing out the *Tatler*, 1709–11, and, with his friend Joseph Addison (q.v.), the *Spectator*, 1711–12. Expelled by the Tory House of Commons in March 1714 for uttering seditious libels, he again obtained minor preferment after the Hanoverian succession, receiving a patent for the management of the theatre at Drury Lane and a royal bounty of £500 in January 1715.[2] Through the Duke of Somerset he was offered a 'very precarious and uncertain' seat at Great Bedwyn but he accepted a nomination from the young Earl of Clare, afterwards Duke of Newcastle, for Boroughbridge where, with the help of Clare's agent, Charles Wilkinson, and William Jessop (q.v.), he was returned in February 1715.[3] Shortly afterwards he was knighted on the presentation to the King of a congratulatory address, composed by himself, from Lord Clare and the deputy lieutenants of Middlesex. Early in May 1715 he was asked to take charge of official anti-Jacobite propaganda, especially that relating to the impeachment of the Tory ex-ministers. He was, however, like Addison, dissatisfied with the rewards for his services to the Hanoverian cause, complaining to Lord Clare on 25 May that in the late reign he had lost £3,000

> and an acceptable character by choosing a side . . . I will never hereafter do more than my part without knowing the terms I act upon and I think what I have said deserves a good establishment for life . . . I cannot turn so much time that way and be supported by assistants equal to the work for less than £1,000 a year. And before I enter upon the argument I hope to receive £500 or be excused from so painful, so anxious and so unacceptable a service.

The £500 was forthcoming[4] and Steele brought out a second series of the pro-Government *Englishman*, July–November 1715, but the 'establishment' of £1,000 a year did not materialize.

In Parliament Steele supported the Administration in a number of speeches but was prepared on occasion to put an independent point of view because, as he wrote to his wife, 'I have always an unfashionable thing called conscience in all matters of judicature or justice'.[5] Despite his attacks on the Jacobites in the *Englishman*, Steele, with characteristic humanity, was among those Whigs who, on 22 Feb. 1716, presented a petition to the House from the womenfolk of the condemned rebel lords, for whom, in a rousing speech, he urged respite of sentence and clemency. When describing the working of a triennial Parliament in a debate on the septennial bill in 1716, he said that the first year was spent in vindictive decisions and animosities about the late elections; the second session entered into business but rather in a spirit of contradiction to what former Parliaments had brought to pass; the third session languished and the approach of the next election terrified the Members into a servile management. After Walpole had presented his scheme for reducing the national debt in March 1717, Steele told his wife that 'I happened to be the only man in the House who spoke against it because I did not think the way of doing it just. I believe the scheme will take place and, if it does, Walpole must be a very great man'. It was said that his objections 'must have been put into his head by some stockjobber; for . . . he has no more skill in, than liking to, the affair of accounts and funds'.[6] He was one of a group that met in March and April 1717 to promote the interests of the Dissenters, but at the same time 'was reported a Tory'; for when the Duke of Norfolk and others presented a petition to the House of Commons on 26 March for the relief of Roman Catholics, he

stood up and said to this purpose . . . I cannot but be of opinion that to put severities upon men merely on account of religion is a most grievous and unwarrantable proceeding. But indeed the Roman Catholics hold tenets which are inconsistent with the being and safety of a Protestant people; for this reason we are justified in laying upon them . . . penalties . . . but, Sir, let us not pursue Roman Catholics with the spirit of Roman Catholics but act towards them with the temper of our own religion.[7]

After the split in the Whig party in April 1717 he continued to support the Administration, speaking for the army estimates, December 1717 and January 1718, and voting for the repeal of the Occasional Conformity and Schism Acts in January 1719. Two months later, however, he went into opposition over the projected peerage bill, producing in support of his views the *Plebeian*, which was answered by Addison's *Old Whig*. In December 1719 he was the first to speak against the committal of the bill, arguing 'in a very masterly speech'[8] that they were safer under the prerogative in the King than they could be under an aristocracy. Newcastle, with whom Steele had for some time been at odds over the management of Drury Lane, took the opportunity, probably at the instigation of Craggs and Stanhope (qq.v.), to revoke his licence at the theatre. Sir John Vanbrugh wrote on 18 Feb. 1720 that

> Sir R. Steele is grown such a malcontent that he now takes the ministry directly for his mark and treats them in the House for some days past in so very frank a manner that they grow quite angry, and 'tis talked as if it would not be impossible to see him very soon expelled the House. He has quarrelled with the lord chamberlain, that a new licence has been granted to Wilks, Cibber and Booth, which . . . [has] left him with his patent but not one player. And so the lord chamberlain's authority over the playhouse is restored and the patent ends in a joke.[9]

Steele next turned his attention to the South Sea Company which he attacked in pamphlets and in his new periodical the *Theatre*, January to April 1720; and in March he followed Walpole in opposing the proposals of the company for reducing the national debt. After the crash and during the debate on the South Sea directors, 12 Dec. 1720, he observed that

> this nation, which two years ago possessed more weight and greater credit than any other nation in Europe, was reduced to its present distress by a few cyphering cits, a species of men of equal capacity, in all respects . . . with those animals who saved the capitol, who were now to be screened by those of greater figure.

However, as with the Jacobite lords in 1716, Steele soon ceased to belabour a beaten foe. In March 1721 he spoke against forcing Robert Knight, the absconding South Sea cashier, to give evidence; and in April and June he joined Walpole in urging leniency for John Aislabie[10] and Sir Theodore Janssen (qq.v.). When Walpole replaced Sunderland at the Treasury, Steele, after applying to both men and to Henry Pelham (q.v.) for their good offices with Newcastle, was restored to his place at Drury Lane on 2 May 1721. As his seat at Boroughbridge was clearly lost to him, he now turned to Sunderland, his first patron of the *Gazette* days, for political backing. With money from this source and presumably on the interest of Richard Hampden (q.v.), who also needed Sunderland's patronage, Steele transferred to Wendover for the 1722 election, at which he defeated the sitting member, Sir Roger Hill (q.v.), then aged 80, by 71 votes.[11] Lord Perceval (q.v.) commented on 27 Mar. 1722 that

> Sir R. Steele got his election by a merry trick. He scooped an apple and put ten guineas into it, and said it should be deposited for the wife of any of the voters that should be the first brought to bed that day 9 months. Upon this, several that would have been against him and who lived some miles from the town, posted home to capacitate their wives to claim the apple, and the next morning the election passed in his favour before they returned.[12]

In the new Parliament Steele took little active part, withdrawing in 1724, harassed by debts and ill-health, to his dead wife's property in Wales, where he died 1 Sept. 1729.

[1] See G. A. Aitken, *Life of Rich. Steele*; W. Connely, *Sir Rich. Steele*; and R. Blanchard, *Corresp. of Rich. Steele*. [2] *Cal. Treas. Bks.* xxix. 328. [3] *Corresp.* 97–101, 308–10. [4] Ibid. 101–2, 310–1. [5] Ibid. 338. [6] Ibid. 333; Oldmixon, *Hist. England*, iii. 635. [7] *Pol. State*, xiii. 417–19; *Corresp.* 338. [8] Coxe, *Walpole*, i. 120. [9] *Corresp.* 145–54, 541; *HMC 2nd Rep.* 71. [10] Coxe, i. 142; ii. 215. [11] *Corresp.* 162–3, 174–5, 541. [12] *HMC 7th Rep.* 247–8.

R.S.L.

STEELE, William (*d.*1748), of Lamorbey, in Bexley, Kent.

HINDON   1741–1747

m. (settlement 14 June 1723) Mary Turner, 3s. 4da. Director, E.I. Co. 1742–*d.*

William Steele, a merchant, of unknown parentage, was returned unopposed at Hindon, a venal borough, in 1741. Voting with the Administration in all recorded divisions, he was classed as an Old Whig in 1746, but did not stand again. He died shortly before 9 July 1748, appointing his friend John Selwyn (q.v.) to be his executor.[1]

[1] PCC 226 Strahan.

R.S.L.

STEPHENS, Samuel (1728–94), of St. Ives, Cornw.

ST. IVES   9 Dec. 1751–1754

bap. 1728, 1st surv. s. of John Stephens of St. Ives by Mary, da. of Samuel Phillips of Pendrea, Cornw. *educ.* Helston sch.; Trinity, Camb. 1746. *m.* June 1762,

Anne, da. and h. of Richard Seaborn of Bristol, 3s. 3da. *suc.* fa. 1764.

Mayor, St. Ives 1761, 1763, 1765.

The Stephens family, who had been settled at St. Ives since the fifteenth century, were Presbyterians, deriving their wealth from the local fishery and mines. They had acquired considerable property in and around the town, playing a prominent part in its affairs. Stephens's father acted for many years as electoral agent for John Hobart (q.v.), 1st Earl of Buckinghamshire. Stephens studied for the church, but came home after the death of his elder brother[1] and in 1751 was put up for St. Ives by his father. Lord Buckinghamshire went down to oppose him, charging him with 'being no friend to the Government nor Administration' and enlisting the officers of the port against him,[2] whereupon the head of his college wrote to Newcastle:

> During my connexions with him I had all the reason possible to imagine him a most loyal subject and a zealous friend to his Majesty and his government ... My friend Mr. White who was his schoolmaster in Cornwall and is now very well acquainted with him writes me word that no method of injuring Mr. Stephens could be so improper as to charge him with disaffection, and observes very justly that it is a strange paradox to reckon the son of a Dissenter an enemy to the Government.[3]

He was successful, but did not stand in 1754. After his father's death, he decided to live like a gentleman, disposing of everything connected with trade or the fishery, and began to build a splendid mansion in the town, Tregenna Castle. He also pulled down the local Presbyterian chapel and withdrew his support from its minister. In 1774 he stood unsuccessfully for the borough, where he had acquired much unpopularity by his conduct.[4] He died at Bath, 1 Mar. 1794.

[1] *Parochial Hist. Cornw.* ii. 262; G. C. Boase, *Coll. Cornubiensia*, 927. [2] Sam. Stephens to P. Yonge, 14 Nov. 1751, Add. 32725, ff. 422–3. [3] 21 Nov. 1751, ibid. f. 420. [4] *Parochial Hist. Cornw.* and *Coll. Cornubiensia*, ut supra.

E.C.

STEPHENS, Thomas (?1672–1720), of Lypiatt, nr. Stroud, Glos.

GLOUCESTERSHIRE   1713–24 Feb. 1720

b. ?1672, 1st s. of Thomas Stephens, M.P., of Lypiatt by Anne, da. of Thomas Child of Northwick, Worcs. *educ.* Ch. Ch. Oxf. 14 July 1688, aged 16. *m.* bef. 1699, Anne, da. of John Neale, M.P., of Dean, Beds. 2s. 4da.[1] *suc.* fa. 1708.

Thomas Stephens was descended from the younger branch of an old Gloucestershire family, seated at Lypiatt since the early seventeenth century.[2] Both his father and grandfather had represented Gloucestershire, where the family held extensive property, in addition to land in neighbouring counties. Returned as a Whig under Anne, and re-elected unopposed in 1715, he voted against the septennial bill but for the repeal of the Occasional Conformity and Schism Acts and the peerage bill. He died of smallpox,[3] 24 Feb. 1720.

[1] PCC 122 Shaller. [2] Fenwick & Metcalfe, *Vis. Glos. 1682-3*, pp. 176-7; Rudder, *Glos.* 430-1, 713. [3] *Hist. Reg.* 1738, chron. p. 10.

S.R.M.

STEPHENS, William (1671-1753), of Bowcombe, nr. Newport, I.o.W.

NEWPORT I.o.W.   1702-1722
NEWTOWN I.o.W.   1722-1727

b. 28 Jan. 1671, 1st s. of Sir William Stephens of Bowcombe, lt.-gov. of I.o.W., by Elizabeth, da. of Henry Hillary of Dorset, grazier. *educ.* Winchester 1684-8; King's, Camb. 1689; M. Temple 1691. *m.* 1697, Mary, da. of Sir Richard Newdigate, 2nd Bt., M.P., of Arbury, Warws., 7s. 2da. *suc.* fa. 1697.

Col. militia; commr. of victualling 1712-14; agent for York Buildings Co. in Scotland 1728-35; sec. to trustees of Georgia 1737-41; pres. Savannah, Georgia 1741-3; gov. Georgia 1743-51.

Stephens inherited the manor of Bowcombe, which had been bought by his grandfather in 1671.[1] A Tory under Anne, he was re-elected for Newport in 1715 on his own interest, voting against the Administration in all recorded divisions. His name was sent to the Pretender in 1721 as a probable supporter in the event of a rising. In 1722, having lost his interest at Newport to the Government, he was returned for Newtown by Sir Robert Worsley (q.v.). In 1724 he was described to the Duke of Bolton (Charles Powlett, q.v.), lord lieutenant of Hampshire, as 'one of those men that always opposed your interest on your elections, and all your friends down to this day; he is one of those men that meets and belongs to the Tory club'.[2] In 1728, ruined by extravagance, he sold all his property and absconded, until his friends found him the job of agent for the York Buildings Company in North Scotland at a salary of £200 p.a. In 1732 he declined an invitation from the Isle of Wight Tories to stand again for Newport. Losing his job in 1735, when the Company sold their assets, he went to South Carolina as agent for a friend. On his return, he was made secretary to the Georgia Trustees, Lord Egmont describing him as 'a very sensible man'.[3] He became president of Savannah County in 1741 and governor of the whole of Georgia in 1743. Retiring in 1751 with a pension of £80, he died in great poverty, August 1753.

[1] *VCH Hants*, v. 228. [2] Thos. Stephens, *The Castle Builders*, 43-44, 154; Stuart mss 65/16. [3] *HMC Egmont Diary*, ii. 368.

P.W.

STEPHENSON, Edward (1691-1768), of Dawley, Mdx.

SUDBURY   1734-1741

bap. 8 Oct. 1691, at Crosthwaite, Cumb., 1st s. of Edward Stephenson of Keswick, Cumb. by Rebecca, da. of John Winder of Lorton, Cumb. and London. *m.* 30 Apr. 1741, Anne, da. of William Jennings of Gt. Russell St., Bloomsbury, and Fort St. George, India, *s.p.*

Writer, E.I. Co.'s service 1708, factor 1714; third in embassy to Delhi 1714-17; chief of factory at Balasor 1717-18; chief at Patna and later at Cassimbazar 1719-29; member of council at Fort William 1720; pres. and gov. Fort William 17-18 Sept. 1728; sheriff, Essex 1742-4.

Edward Stephenson arrived in Bengal early in 1710, securing rapid promotion. On the death of the governor in 1728 the presidency of Fort William devolved on him, but he was superseded next day by another governor, who arrived from England with a new commission.[1] Returning to England in 1730, he bought an estate at Great Bardfield, in Essex,[2] less than 20 miles from Sudbury, for which he was returned in 1734 after a contest, voting against the Administration, but did not stand again. He bought Dawley from Bolingbroke in 1738 for £26,000 and sold it soon after 1748.[3] From 1755 to 1765 he was listed in directories as a merchant of Queen Square, Bloomsbury, where he died, 7 Sept. 1768.

[1] *Jnl. of Asiatic Soc. of Bengal*, lxvii. i. 167-74; C. R. Wilson, *Early Annals of Bengal*, ii and iii passim. [2] Morant, *Essex*, ii. 520. [3] Pope to Swift, 17 May 1739; Lysons, *Mdx.* 127-8.

P.W.

STEPNEY, Sir Thomas, 5th Bt. (?1668-1745), of Llanelly, Carm.

CARMARTHENSHIRE   23 May 1717-1722

b. ?1668, o.s. of Sir John Stepney, Bt., of Prendergast, Pemb. by Justina, da. and h. of Sir Anthony Van Dyck. *m.* (settlement 8 Dec. 1691) Margaret, da. of John Vaughan of Llanelly, sis. and coh. of Walter Vaughan, 1s. 2da. *suc.* fa. c.1681.
Sheriff, Pemb. 1696-7.

Stepney married the co-heiress of a branch of the Vaughans of Golden Grove, who had represented Carmarthenshire in most Parliaments during the seventeenth century. Returned unopposed as a Whig in succession to the Marquess of Winchester (Charles Powlett, q.v.), who had married the heiress of the main branch of the family, he voted against the Government on the repeal of the Occasional Conformity and Schism Acts and the peerage bill in 1719, when he was put down by Craggs as to be approached through Lord William Powlett (q.v.). He did not stand again. He was buried 19 Jan. 1745, aged 76.

R.R.S.

STERT, Arthur (*d.* 1755), of Membland, nr. Modbury, Devon.

PLYMOUTH 1727–1754

m. 1s. *d.v.p.* 2da.[1]

Commr. for settling merchants' losses with Spain 1730–42.

Stert, whose family had been settled in the vicinity of Plympton, near Plymouth, since the early sixteenth century, purchasing Membland from the Champernownes in 1723,[2] sat as a government supporter for Plymouth, where he had a 'precarious' interest of his own with the corporation.[3] Appointed under the treaty of Seville a commissioner for settling the claims of merchants against Spain, he was responsible for assessing the compensation payable to them under the convention of 1739, on which he was examined by the House of Commons. Commenting on his performance, a government supporter wrote:

> They say he is an able man, but he has not the gift of utterance; he did not answer the questions put to him with readiness or clearness, but yet, I think, did give answers which might satisfy those who were not resolved not to be satisfied.[4]

He was recommended by Walpole after his fall to Pelham, who procured him a secret service pension and employed him in west country elections.[5] He died 2 Feb. 1755.

[1] *PCC* 147 Paul. [2] *Western Antiquary*, x. 97; *Trans. Devon Assoc.* lxviii. 355. [3] 3 Mar. 1722, Sunderland (Blenheim) mss. [4] Coxe, *Walpole*, iii. 515–16; *HMC 14th Rep. IX*, 244. [5] Walpole. *Mems. Geo. II*, i. 167; Add. 33038, ff. 352, 415; Stert to Pelham, 16 Dec. 1753, Newcastle (Clumber) mss.

S.R.M.

STEUART, James (*d.*1757), of St. George's, Hanover Sq., London.

WEYMOUTH AND MELCOMBE REGIS 1741–1747

s. of John Steuart and nephew of Gen. William Steuart of St. George's, Hanover Sq., and of Ireland. *m.* bef. 1744, Mary, da. of John Taylor of Portsmouth, 1s. *suc.* to half the estate of his uncle, Gen. Steuart 1726.[1]

Capt. R.N. 1709, r.-adm. 1742, v.-adm. 1743, adm. 1747, adm. and c.-in-c. of the fleet 1750–*d.*

In 1715 Steuart commanded a squadron on the west coast of Scotland engaged in helping the military to round up the rebels, but his next twenty-five years were passed in complete obscurity.[2] He was still a post captain in 1740, when he was put up by George Bubb Dodington (q.v.) for Weymouth at the forthcoming general election as a friend of the Duke of Argyll.[3] Though returned as an opposition candidate, by the opening of the session of 1742–3 he was regarded as a government supporter; his only recorded vote was for the Hanover-

ians in 1744; and in 1746 he was classed as Old Whig. Meanwhile, thanks to the outbreak of war and his own seniority, his advancement was as rapid as it previously had been slow. Beginning the war as a captain of some thirty years standing, he ended it as a full admiral and the third senior officer of the navy.

In 1747 Steuart wrote to Henry Pelham and the Duke of Bedford, then the first lord of the Admiralty, about his prospects of re-election. 'The state of affairs is this', Pelham explained to Bedford:

> Mr. Dodington and I have agreed to nominate two persons each; Mr. Dodington would not name Mr. Steuart for one of his, and I did not see the necessity of my naming him for one of ours. Dodington, therefore, made the best excuse to him he could, and I must own, in my sense, not an improper one. For during these three or four years Mr. Steuart has had a command at Portsmouth which has kept him from attending Parliament as much as if he had been in the West Indies; besides, to whom does he belong? Not to your Grace, otherwise than as his profession obliges him; and as to your humble servant I have no knowledge of him but what was acquired by House of Commons acquaintance.[4]

Steuart did not obtain a seat. He died 30 Mar. 1757, having risen by seniority to the post of commander-in-chief of the fleet.

[1] *PCC* 89 Plymouth, 136 Herring. [2] *Byng Pprs.* (Navy Recs. Soc. lxx), iii. 194–5; Charnock, *Biog. Navalis*, iv. 18–19. [3] Sir Dudley Ryder's diary, 9 Aug. 1740, Harrowby mss. [4] *Bedford Corresp.* i. 216.

R.R.S.

STEUART, William (1686–1768), of Weyland and Seatter, Orkney.

INVERNESS BURGHS 1713–1722
AYR BURGHS 1722–1734
ELGIN BURGHS 1734–1741

b. 25 May 1686, o.s. of Thomas Steuart, commissary and stewart clerk of Orkney, by his 2nd w. Isobel, da. of Andrew Young of Castle Yards, Orkney, niece of Sir Thomas Moncreiffe, 1st Bt., of Moncreiffe, Perth. *educ.* King's Coll. Aberdeen 1701; adv. 1707. *m.* 30 Apr. 1741, Frances, e. da. of Dr. George Cheyne of Bath, *s.p.*

Principal clerk of the Exchequer [S] 1705–8; jt. King's remembrancer of the Exchequer [S] 1708–*d.*; sec. to Prince of Wales for Scotland 1714–27; director, E.I. Co. 1716–19; paymaster of pensions 1731–42; overseer of the King's swans by 1739.

Steuart was the confidential agent of the 2nd Duke of Argyll and his brother, Lord Ilay. During the Fifteen he was the recipient of a long letter from Argyll justifying his conduct in the rebellion, written just before Sheriffmuir.[1] Hervey relates in his memoirs that about 1724 Argyll and Ilay had a quarrel, after which, for many years, they never spoke to one another, but by the means of a Mr. Stuart, who went between them, an adroit fellow and a common friend to them both, they acted as much in concert as if they had been the most intimate and most cordial friends.[2]

An example of this form of intercourse is a long letter to Steuart from Ilay reporting on his proceedings at Edinburgh during the malt tax agitation in 1725, which was presumably intended to be shown to Argyll.[3] Lord Chancellor King states that Steuart in 1725

> acquainted me that all the lists of the justices of the peace for the several counties of Scotland had been settled, by the direction of Lord Townshend, by Lord Ilay, with the Members of the House of Commons, and that the settling these lists had taken up three months' time.[4]

Returned to Parliament for nearly thirty years on the Argyll interest, to which he also owed offices worth £1,400 a year in 1739,[5] Steuart voted with the Government from 1715, except on the motion of 4 June 1717 against Argyll's rival, Lord Cadogan (q.v.), till he retired in 1741. When Argyll went into opposition in 1739, Steuart adhered to Ilay, who wrote through him to Walpole from Scotland: 'I have desired Mr. Stewart to ask you for the 500 which I am now laying out, and I fear 100 more.'[6] He died 13 Sept. 1768, leaving £2,000 to the 4th Duke of Argyll.

[1] Dalton, *Geo. I's Army*, i. 10–16. [2] Hervey, *Mems.* 297. [3] Coxe, *Walpole*, ii. 456–62. [4] Peter, Lord King, *Notes of Domestic and Foreign Affairs*, 10. [5] *Gent. Mag.* 1739, p. 307. [6] 16 Sept. 1740, Cholmondeley (Houghton) mss.

J.M.S.

STEWART, Archibald (1697–1780), of Edinburgh and Mitcham, Surr.

EDINBURGH 1741–1747

b. 1697, yr. s. of Sir Robert Stewart, 1st Bt., M.P. [S], of Allanbank, Berwick, being o.s. by his 2nd w. Helen, da. of Sir Archibald Cockburn of Langton, Berwick. *m.* bef. 1728, Grizel, da. of John Gordon of Edinburgh, wine merchant, 4s. 5da.

Lord provost, Edinburgh 1744–5.

In February 1718 Archibald Stewart was admitted a burgess of Edinburgh, where he became a prosperous wine merchant. Returned as an opposition Whig for the city in 1741, he voted against Walpole's nominee for the chairman of the elections committee in December. After Walpole's fall he continued in opposition, voting with the group known as the Duke of Argyll's gang[1] against the Hanoverians in 1742 and 1744. For the 'faithful and diligent discharge of his duty in Parliament and promoting the interest of the country and particularly that of the Royal Burghs', he received the thanks of the convention of Royal Burghs, of which he was then praeses, on 3 July

1745.[2] Two months later he failed, as lord provost, to organize an effective defence of Edinburgh against Prince Charles Edward, who entered the city without opposition on 17 Sept. According to Alexander Carlyle, who was present as a volunteer,

> there was not a Whig in the town who did not suspect that [Stewart] favoured the Pretender's cause; and however cautiously he acted in his capacity as chief magistrate, there were not a few who suspected that his backwardness and coldness in the measure of arming the people, was part of a plan to admit the Pretender into the city . . . if that part of the town council who were Whigs had found good ground to have put Stewart under arrest, the city would have held out.[3]

However, Murray of Broughton, the Young Pretender's secretary, considered him to be

> the only man in the city who . . . appears to have exerted himself the most to bar the enemy's entry . . . [to] a place not only open almost on all hands, but . . . that in forty-eight hours time might have been starved.[4]

Stewart was afterwards arrested and taken before the Privy Council in London on 7 Dec. The consent of the House of Commons to his detention having been obtained on 10 Dec., he was imprisoned in the Tower from 13 Dec. 1745 till 23 Jan. 1747, when he was released on bail of £15,000. Charged with neglect of duty and misbehaviour in the execution of his office, he was found 'not guilty' on 2 Nov. 1747 after a protracted trial in Edinburgh, the lord chief justice clerk, Andrew Fletcher (Lord Milton) commenting to Newcastle that 'the behaviour of the Jacobites . . . on this occasion has been most insolent and does not abate'.[5] After his acquittal he transferred his business to London, where he had acquired premises at 11 Buckingham Street, Strand, in 1743. For himself he leased a large country villa at Mitcham, equipped, according to his cousin, with 'the nicest water-closet [and] a cold bath'.[6] He died at Bath, 24 Jan. 1780.

[1] John Drummond to Ld. Morton, 2 and 11 Dec. 1742, Morton mss, SRO. [2] T. Hunter, *Recs. of the Convention of Royal Burghs, 1738–59*, p. 179. [3] Alex. Carlyle, *Autobiog.*, 122–3. [4] Murray of Broughton, *Memorials* (Sc. Hist. Soc. xxvii), 195. [5] *Williamson's Diary* (Cam. Soc. ser. 3. xxii), 120; Howell's *State Trials*, xviii. 863–1068; *Albemarle Pprs.* (New Spalding Club xxv), ii. 468–9. [6] *Survey of London*, xviii. 69; *Coltness Coll.* 123–4.

R.S.L.

STEWART, Hon. Charles (1681–1741), of West Malling, Kent.

MALMESBURY 25 Jan. 1723–1727
PORTSMOUTH 10 Feb.1737–5 Feb. 1741

b. 1681, 5th s. of William Stewart, 1st Visct. Mountjoy [I], by Mary, 1st da. of Richard Coote, 1st Baron Coote of Coloony [I]. *unm.*

M.P. [I] 1715–27.

Ent. R.N. bef. 1697, capt. 1704; plenipotentiary to Morocco and cdr. of a squadron against Sallee, in the Mediterranean, 1720-1; c.-in-c. Jamaica station 1729-32; adm. 1729; v.-adm. 1734; 2nd-in-command to Sir John Norris (q.v.) in the Channel 1734.

Charles Stewart lost his right hand at the age of 16 in an engagement against the French, for which he was granted a naval pension of £100 in February 1699.[1] On his mission to Morocco in 1721 he was able to negotiate the release of a large number of English prisoners there. From Michaelmas 1724 he received a further pension of £300 on the Irish establishment.[2] He appears to have been attached to the 2nd Duke of Argyll, on whose interest he was returned for Malmesbury in 1723. In 1732 Argyll was expected by Sir Charles Wager (q.v.) to ask that Stewart should be returned at the next general election for Portsmouth,[3] for which he was in fact returned at a by-election in 1737, voting against the Spanish convention in 1739, presumably under Argyll's influence, but with the Administration on the place bill of 1740. He died 5 Feb. 1741.

[1] Charnock, *Biog. Navalis*, iii. 304; *CSP Dom.* 1699-1700, pp. 68, 74. [2] *CJ* [I], v. 325. [3] To Walpole, 8 Dec. 1732, Cholmondeley (Houghton) mss.

R.S.L.

STEWART, Hon. James (c.1699-1768), of Auchleland, Wigtown.

WIGTOWN BURGHS	1734-1741
WIGTOWNSHIRE	1741-1747
WIGTOWN BURGHS	1747-1754
WIGTOWNSHIRE	1754-1761

b. c.1699, 2nd s. of James Stewart, 5th Earl of Galloway [S], by Lady Catherine Montgomerie, da. of Alexander, 9th Earl of Eglintoun [S]; bro. of Hon. William Stewart (q.v.). *educ.* Eton 1715.[1] *unm.*
Ensign 3 Ft. Gds. 1720, lt., capt.-lt. 1734, capt. and lt.-col. 1736, 2nd maj. and col. 1744, 1st maj. 1745, lt.-col. 1748; col. 37 Ft. 1752-*d.*; maj.-gen. 1754; lt.-gen. 1758.

James Stewart, a professional soldier, served in the Scots Guards for 32 years, being present at Fontenoy. Returned on his family's interest for Wigtown Burghs in 1734, after a contest in which his father and brother, Lord Garlies, took an active but illegal part, he voted with the Administration on the Spanish convention in 1739 and the place bill of 1740. Moving in 1741 to the county to provide a seat for his younger brother William (q.v.), he voted for Walpole's candidate for the chairman of the elections committee in December. Under the new Administration he was absent on the Hanoverians in 1742 and 1744, but voted for them in 1746, when he was classed as an Old Whig. Meanwhile Lord Garlies, then in opposition, succeeded to the earldom of Galloway and the

family interest on his father's death in February 1746. Finding that James was to be opposed in the county for the 1747 election, Galloway, who had gone over to the Administration, transferred him to the Burghs, where he was unopposed. James went back to the county in 1754 but did not stand again. He died 27 Apr. 1768.

[1] *Mems. Sir John Clerk of Penicuik* (Sc. Hist. Soc. xiii), 87.

R.S.L

STEWART, Hon. John (c.1673-1748), of Sorbie, Wigtown.

| SCOTLAND | 1707-1708 |
| WIGTOWNSHIRE | 1708-1710, 3 Mar. 1711-1727 |

b. c.1673, 3rd s. of Alexander Stewart, 3rd Earl of Galloway [S], by Lady Mary Douglas, da. of James, 2nd Earl of Queensberry [S]; uncle of James and William Stewart (qq.v.). *educ.* Glasgow 1687. *unm.*
M.P. [S] Wigtownshire 1702-7.
Ensign 3 Ft. Gds. 1691, capt.-lt. Apr. 1692, capt. and lt.-col. July 1692, 2nd lt.-col. 1704, 1st lt.-col. and col. of Ft. 1710; brig.-gen. 1710; ret. 1717.

John Stewart was a professional soldier who served with his regiment in Spain during the war of the Spanish succession and was afterwards with the Duke of Argyll in Catalonia. After representing his county under Queen Anne, he was again returned unopposed as a Whig on his family's interest in 1715 and 1722, voting with the Administration on the septennial bill and the repeal of the Occasional Conformity and Schism Acts. In 1719 Craggs considered that he should be approached through Argyll, Sunderland marked him as doubtful, and he was absent on the peerage bill in December. He did not stand again and died in April 1748.

J.M.S.

STEWART, Hon. John (c.1709-96), of Pittendriech, Edinburgh.

| ANSTRUTHER EASTER BURGHS | 1741-1747 |

b. c.1709, 2nd s. of Francis Stewart, 7th Earl of Moray [S], by his 2nd w. Jean, da. of John Elphinstone, 4th Lord Balmerino [S]. *m.* (1) *d.* 15 Jan. 1764, *s.p.*;[1] (2) Jean Home, *s.p.*[2]
Capt. Earl of Loudoun's Highlanders 1745-7; ent. service of States-General 1747;[3] lt.-col. Earl of Drumlanrig's regt. 1747; col. Lt.-Gen. Charles Halkett's regt. 1754; col.-commdt. Maj. Gen. Charles William Stewart's regt. 1758; col. of the same 1760-95; maj. gen. 1772.

John Stewart, who had long family connections with Fife and Elgin, stood against Ilay's candidates for Elginshire and Anstruther Easter Burghs in 1741. Successful for the latter, presumably because of the unpopularity in Scotland of the sitting Member, Philip Anstruther (q.v.), a government supporter, he voted against Walpole's nominee for the chairman of the elections committee in December 1741. One of the group of Scotch Members known as the Duke of Argyll's gang,[4] he voted against the Hanoverians in 1742 and 1744. Receiving a commission in a newly raised Highland regiment in 1745, he was taken prisoner at Prestonpans, 21 Sept., but was forcibly released in January 1746, when he rejoined his regiment.[5] He was absent from the division on the Hanoverians in the following April, when he was claimed by the Administration as a 'New Ally'. Removed in May 1747 'from Lord Loudoun's regiment for his behaviour this winter, which indeed has been very imprudent', he was appointed two months afterwards lieutenant-colonel of a new regiment which Lord Drumlanrig was raising in Scotland for the Dutch.[6] He did not stand again for Parliament but remained for many years in the service of the States-General, before returning to Scotland where he died 13 Aug. 1796.

[1] Scots Peerage, ix. 140. [2] Restalrig Burial Reg. (Sc. Rec. Soc. xxxii), 31, 59. [3] Scots Brigade in Holland (Sc. Hist. Soc. xxxv), ii. 413. [4] John Drummond to Ld. Morton, 2 and 11 Dec. 1742, Morton mss, SRO. [5] Origins of the Forty-five (Sc. Hist. Soc. ser. 2. ii), 363–4; More Culloden Pprs. v. 30. [6] HMC Polwarth, v. 245.

R.S.L.

STEWART, John (d.1769), of Castle Stewart, Wigtown.

WIGTOWNSHIRE   1747–1754

1st s. of William Stewart of Castle Stewart by Isabel, da. of Sir William Maxwell, 1st Bt., of Monreith, Wigtown. m. by Sept. 1733, Jean, da. of Adam Craik of Duchrae, Kirkcudbright, 3s. suc. fa. 1722.

An officer in the custom house till 1747; clerk of the pipe in the Exchequer [S] 1751–d.

The great-grandson of the 2nd Earl of Galloway,[1] Stewart gave up his customs post in 1747 to stand for his county as a government supporter on the interest of his kinsman, the 6th Earl of Galloway, who put him in the hands of Argyll and Pelham.[2] Receiving a place in 1751, he was unopposed at the ensuing by-election, mentioning to Claudius Amyand (q.v.) the 'favours I have received' from Newcastle and Pelham.[3] He may have been the Mr Stuart who in 1754 was receiving a secret service pension of £200 a year, which was not continued.[4] With Argyll's support he expected to be returned again in 1754, but Galloway was hostile to the Duke and, combining with the Dalrymples, put up his brother, Colonel James Stewart (q.v.),[5] thus forcing John Stewart to withdraw. Four days before the election John Dalrymple (afterwards 5th Earl of Stair) wrote to Lord Loudoun: 'Castle Stewart could never have been able to carry the shire without

Colonel Stewart for the burghs; he has no interest earthly, independent of Galloway'.[6] He did not stand again and died shortly before 6 July 1769.

[1] P. H. M'Kerlie, Lands and their Owners in Galloway, i. 314–17; ii. 315; iii. 151, 387; v. 360. [2] Argyll to Pelham, 6 Aug. 1747, Newcastle (Clumber) mss. [3] 31 July 1751, Add. 32724, f. 502. [4] Add. 33038, f. 415. [5] Corresp. of Ld. Loudoun, Apr. 1754, with John Dalrymple and others, Loudoun mss. [6] 28 Apr. 1754, ibid.

R.S.L.

STEWART, Hon. William (c.1706–?48).

WIGTOWN BURGHS   1741–1747

b. c.1706, 3rd s. of James Stewart, 5th Earl of Galloway [S], and yr. bro. of Hon. James Stewart (q.v.). educ. Glasgow Univ. 1721. unm.

Ensign 1729; capt. 12 Drags. 1737.

Provost, Whithorn 1741.

In 1741 William Stewart, a professional soldier like his brother, stood unsuccessfully for Kircudbright Stewartry but was returned unopposed for Wigtown Burghs on his family's interest. He voted for Walpole's candidate for the chairman of the elections committee in December; was absent on the Hanoverians in 1742 and 1746; voted against them in 1744, his eldest brother, Lord Garlies, being then in opposition; and in 1746 was classed as an Old Whig. He did not stand again. The date of his death is not known, but possibly it was he—it could not have been his brother James—who died on 3 May 1748.[1]

[1] Gent. Mag. 1748, p.236.

R.S.L.

STILES, see **HASKINS STILES**

STONE, Andrew (1703–73).

HASTINGS   1741–1761

b. 4 Feb. 1703, 1st s. of Andrew Stone of Lombard St., London, goldsmith, by his w. Anne Holbrooke. educ. Westminster 1715–22; Ch. Ch. Oxf. 1722–6. m. 7 July 1743, Hannah, da. of Stephen Mauvillain of Tooting, Surr., 1s. d.v.p. suc. fa. 1711.

Private sec. to Duke of Newcastle 1732–4; under-sec. of state 1734–51; jt. transmitter of state papers 1739–41; keeper of the state paper office 1742–d.; sec. of Barbados 1742–d; ld. of Trade 1749–61; sub-governor to Prince of Wales 1751–6; registrar of Chancery, Jamaica 1753–d.; sec. to Prince of Wales 1756–60; treasurer to Queen Charlotte 1761–d.

The son of one of the founders of Martin's bank, Stone was educated on the foundation of Westminster and Christ Church, like William Murray (q.v.), with whom he became closely connected. After taking his degree he remained at Oxford till 1732, when his brother-in-law, William Barnard, then chaplain at Claremont, introduced him to the Duke of Newcastle. 'I have had the charmingest man with me at Claremont I ever saw', Newcastle wrote of Stone to the Duchess. 'He has more learning, more parts, and as agreeable as any man I ever saw in my life . . . He has wrote very pretty things upon the Queen's hermitage and four or five lines in Latin upon Claremont, most exceedingly so'. Three weeks later Newcastle announced: 'I have made my bargain with my friend Stone. He is to be with us and to have £200 p.a.'[1]

In Stone Newcastle acquired an excellent secretary, able, industrious, cautious, and self-effacing. Soon promoted under-secretary of state, he was *ex officio* brought into Parliament, though quite without political ambitions. He became not only Newcastle's 'first commis', who wrote his despatches for him,[2] but his constant companion, spending every week-end at Claremont. When Stone married, Newcastle inquired whether 'the necessary attendance on the business of your office will not be as much time as you can conveniently spare from your family without spending any part of it in this place'.

> You know [he wrote] the confidence I have now for many years had in you, and you cannot be ignorant of the satisfaction I have had in your conversation which I have found always agreeable and in many respects useful to me.
>
> You know also my way of life, and my inclinations, make it necessary for me to have with me one in whom I can confide and with whom I can spend my leisure hours with pleasure at this place. Such a one I have ever found in you.

It would be a great abatement, Stone replied, to the happiness he expected from his marriage, if he thought it would

> in any material degree prevent me from paying that attendance which I have now for several years had the honour and happiness to do . . . After this summer I shall be able to obey your Grace's commands and to follow my own inclinations by attending your Grace as usual at Claremont, which I am sure may be made easy for me in every respect by some small relaxation of office attendance in town when not called by particular business.[3]

In return Newcastle, who believed 'that men so intrusted, as our commis must be, ought to be well rewarded',[4] loaded Stone with sinecures, bringing in over £4,000 a year.

After nearly twenty years of drudgery under Newcastle, Stone, of whom George II had a high opinion, was appointed sub-governor of the future George III when, at the age of twelve, he became heir apparent on the death of his father, Frederick, Prince of Wales, in 1751. The Prince's governor was Lord Harcourt, who at the end of 1752 was replaced by Lord Waldegrave, in circumstances described by Waldegrave himself:

> The King, soon after his return from Hanover in

November 1752, found great confusion in the Prince of Wales's family. Earl Harcourt and the bishop of Norwich, the one governor, the other preceptor to H.R.H., were both much displeased. The persons they chiefly accused were Mr. Stone the sub-governor; Mr. Cresset, treasurer to the Prince, also secretary and first minister to the Princess of Wales; and Scott, the sub-preceptor.

> The crimes objected against them were: Jacobite connexions, instilling Tory principles, and Scott was moreover pronounced an atheist on the presumptive evidence of being a philosopher and a mathematician.

> The real fact was this: The bishop of Norwich, who, from having been the first chaplain to an archbishop, and afterwards chaplain at court, thought himself equally qualified to govern both church and state, persuaded Harcourt, an honest, worthy man, but whose heart was better than his head, that they as governor and preceptor must be the sole directors of the young Prince, and that not even the Princess herself ought to have the least influence over him.

> Harcourt having approved the proposal, they formed their plan of operations, and began to carry it into execution. But the plot was soon discovered; the Princess took the alarm, Stone and Cresset were consulted, and Harcourt and the bishop were soon defeated without the least difficulty.

> This passed while the King was in Germany. On his Majesty's arrival they made their last effort, that Stone, Cresset and Scott might be turned out for the reasons already mentioned. They also endeavoured to raise jealousies against the Princess, as secretly favouring the Opposition formed by her late husband. But again failing in their attempt, they both resigned their employment.

Waldegrave goes on to say that 'though Harcourt and the bishop succeeded so ill at court', their charges were artfully used to raise a clamour against the Pelhams on the ground that

> we were governed by Jacobites, that Stone and Murray, the Duke of Newcastle's two cabinet counsellors, were known Jacobites at Oxford, and that if they had changed their old principles they still adhered to their old connexions.

While this clamour was at its height, Henry Liddell (q.v.), Lord Ravensworth, informed the Pelhams that he had evidence that Stone and Murray as young men had frequented circles where disaffected healths were habitually drunk. His charges were investigated by the Cabinet, who reported to the King that they were completely groundless and ought not in any way to prejudice the characters of the accused persons. The attack was then transferred to the House of Lords, where it petered out after a series of tributes had been paid to Stone and Murray by members of the Cabinet, who had been released from their privy counsellor's oaths so that they could give an account of the inquiry.[5]

Thenceforth Stone was left in peace to perform his duties as sub-governor, which, according to the Princess, amounted to very little. In August 1755 she told Bubb Dodington (q.v.) that as to Mr. Stone, if she was to live forty years in the house with him, she should never be better acquainted with him than she was. She once desired him to inform the Prince about the constitution; but he declined it, to avoid giving jealousy to the bishop of Norwich; and that she had mentioned it again, but he still declined it, as not being his province. Pray, madam, said I, what is his province? She said she did not know, unless it was to go before the Prince upstairs, to walk with him sometimes, seldomer to ride with him, and, now and then, to dine with him—but when they did walk together the Prince generally took that time, to think of his own affairs and to say nothing.[6]

Lord Waldegrave's verdict on his colleagues, including Stone, was that though they 'were men of sense, men of learning, and worthy good men, they had but little weight and influence'.[7]

Stone remained in the Prince's service till the end of George II's reign, after which he was made treasurer to Queen Charlotte. He died 17 Dec. 1773.

[1] 8, 19, 29 Aug. 1732, Add. 33073, ff. 66, 69, 73. [2] Hervey, *Mems.* 581. [3] Newcastle to Stone, 13 June 1743, Stone to Newcastle, 22 June 1743, Add. 32700, ff. 211, 232. [4] Newcastle to Sir Robt. Walpole, 19 Nov. 1738, Add. 32691, f. 476. [5] Sedgwick, *Letters from Geo. III to Bute*, xxii et seq. [6] *Dodington Diary*, 357. [7] Waldegrave, *Mems.* 10.

R.R.S.

STONHOUSE, Sir John, 3rd Bt. (?1672–1733), of Radley, Berks.

BERKSHIRE 1701–10 Oct. 1733

b. ?1672, 1st s. of Sir John Stonhouse, 2nd Bt., M.P., by Martha, da. and h. of Robert Brigges. *educ.* Queen's, Oxf. 12 Apr. 1690, aged 17; I. Temple 1690. *m.* (1) 1695, Mary (*d.*1705), da. and h. of Henry Mellish of Sanderstead, Surr., 1s. *d.v.p.* 3da.; (2) 29 Aug. 1706, Penelope, da. of Sir Robert Dashwood, 1st Bt., 3s. 6da. *suc.* fa. 1700.
Steward and bailiff of the hundreds of Ock and Moreton, Berks. 1706;[1] comptroller of the Household 1713–14; P.C. 7 Apr. 1713.

Descended from a court official, who purchased Radley in 1560,[2] Stonhouse represented his county as a Tory for over thirty years, voting after 1715 against the Government in most recorded divisions, but being twice taken into custody by the serjeant at arms for defaulting in a call of the House.[3] In 1721 his name was sent to the Pretender as a probable supporter in the event of a rising.[4] He died 10 Oct. 1733.

[1] *Cal. Treas. Bks.* xx. 706. [2] *VCH Berks.* iv. 412. [3] *CJ*, xix. 61; xxi. 375. [4] Stuart mss 65/16.

R.S.L.

STRADLING, Sir Edward, 5th Bt. (?1672–1735), of St. Donat's Castle, Glam.

CARDIFF BOROUGHS 1698–1701, 1710–1722

b. ?1672, 2nd but 1st surv. s. of Sir Edward Stradling, 4th Bt., by Elizabeth, da. of Anthony Hungerford of

Black Bourton, Oxon. *educ.* Ch. Ch. Oxf. 18 July 1684, aged 12. *m.* 5 June 1694, Elizabeth, yr. da. of Sir Edward Mansel, 4th Bt., M.P., of Margam, Glam., 2s. *suc.* fa. 5 Sept. 1685.
Sheriff, Glam. 1709–10.

Stradling owed his Cardiff seat as much to his own influence in Glamorgan, where his rent-roll was said to be £5,000,[1] as to the support of his brother-in-law, Thomas, Lord Mansel, a former M.P. for the boroughs and the county. Described in 1715 as a Tory who might often vote with the Whigs, he voted with the Opposition in all recorded divisions. In 1721 his name was sent to the Pretender as a probable supporter in the event of a rising.[2] He retired from Parliament in favour of his eldest son Edward in 1722 and died 5 Apr. 1735.

[1] *Gent. Mag.* 1738, p. 546. [2] Stuart mss 65/16.

P.D.G.T.

STRADLING, Edward (1699–1726), of St. Donat's Castle, Glam.

CARDIFF BOROUGHS 1722–3 Oct. 1726

b. 30 Mar. 1699,[1] 1st s. of Sir Edward Stradling, 5th Bt. (q.v.). *educ.* Ch. Ch. Oxf. 1716. *unm.*

Edward Stradling succeeded his father on the Tory interest at Cardiff Boroughs in 1722 but no votes of his have been recorded. He died in his father's lifetime 3 Oct. 1726.

[1] Birch, *Penrice and Margam mss*, ii. 108.

P.D.G.T.

STRANGE, Lord *see* STANLEY (afterwards SMITH STANLEY), James

STRANGE, John (c.1696–1754), of Leyton Grange, Essex.

WEST LOOE 9 Feb. 1737–1741
TOTNES 25 Jan. 1742–18 May 1754

b. c.1696, 1st s. of John Strange of Fleet St., London by his 2nd w. Mary Plaistowe. *educ.* M. Temple 1712, called 1718. *m.* Susan, da. and coh. of Edward Strong of Greenwich, 2s. 7da. surv. Kntd. 12 May 1740.
K.C. 1736; solicitor-gen. 1737–42; recorder, London 1739–42; P.C. 17 Jan. 1750; master of the rolls 1750–*d.*

Strange received his legal training in Salkeld's office, where Hardwicke, Lord Jocelyn, and Sir Thomas Parker had also started. He was counsel for the defence when Macclesfield was impeached in 1725, and by 1729 had begun to compile the *Law Reports* published after his death. On his appointment as solicitor-general he was brought into Parliament by the Government, producing evidence for, seconding, and speaking on the bill against the city of Edinburgh after the Porteous riots, May–June 1737.[1] In 1738 he declined the mastership of the rolls on the ground that

> (besides my objection of want of experience in a court of equity which I know not how to get over) considering the dignity of the post on the one hand and the great diminution of the profits on the other, I cannot with justice to my numerous family so far consult my own ease or any personal accession of honour as to accept the favour that is intended me.[2]

In February 1741 he spoke against the motion for the dismissal of Walpole. He was not returned in May 1741, but was brought in at a by-election for Totnes, though the mayor received a letter 'from the Prince and signed by two of his lords, to recommend a candidate in opposition to the solicitor-general'.

Though Strange was one of the five members on the government list who were elected to the secret committee to inquire into Walpole's conduct, he voted on the committee for the indemnity bill.[3] Before the end of the year he resigned all his appointments. According to his own account,[4]

> having received a considerable addition to my fortune and some degree of ease and retirement being judged proper for my health I . . . resigned my offices . . . and left off my practice at the House of Lords, council table, delegates, and all the courts in Westminster Hall except the King's Bench and there also at the afternoon sitting. His Majesty when at a private audience I took my leave of him expressed himself with the greatest goodness towards me and honoured me with his patent to take place for life next to his attorney-general.

Subsequently his successor William Murray (q.v.) declared that Strange 'from a warmth and generosity of friendship peculiar to him, resigned the office which he then held, that I might succeed him in it'.[5]

Strange was counsel for the prosecution against Francis Townley and Lord Balmerino for high treason in 1746, and in 1747 was manager for the impeachment of Lord Lovat. He continued to support the Government, and in 1750 was made master of the rolls. He died 18 May 1754.

[1] *Parl. Hist.* x. 265, 274–82. [2] To Hardwicke, 28 Aug. 1738, Add. 35586, f. 83. [3] Walpole to Mann, 22 Jan. and 20 May 1742. [4] *Strange, Reports*, 1176. [5] 23 Feb. 1753, Add. 33050, f. 335.

A.N.N.

STRANGWAYS, John (?1688–1716), of Dewlish, Dorset.

BRIDPORT   1 Feb.–10 May 1715

b. ?1688, 3rd but 2nd surv. s. of Thomas Strangways, M.P., of Melbury, Dorset by Susanna, da. and h. of John Ridout; yr. bro. of Thomas Strangways (q.v.), *educ.* L. Inn 1704; Hart Hall, Oxf. 19 Aug. 1706, aged 18. *unm.*

While at Oxford in 1708, John Strangways accidentally shot and killed a friend with whom he was out shooting.[1] Returned on his brother's interest in 1715 as a Tory for Bridport, he was unseated three months later and died 5 May 1716.

[1] Luttrell, vi. 309.

R.S.L.

STRANGWAYS, Thomas (?1683–1726), of Melbury, Dorset.

BRIDPORT   1705–1713
DORSET   1713–23 Sept. 1726

b. ?1683, 2nd but 1st surv. s. of Thomas Strangways, M.P., of Melbury, and bro. of John Strangways (q.v.). *educ.* Hart Hall, Oxf. 8 Aug. 1700, aged 17. *m.* 1710, Mary, da. and h. of Edward Vaughan of Llangwydden, Mont., *s.p. suc.* fa. 1713.
Recorder, Bridport 1707–*d.*, high steward 1714–*d.*

Thomas Strangways was descended from Henry Strangways who acquired Melbury through marriage in the time of Henry VII.[1] He and his father represented the county for over 47 years in 17 successive Parliaments. His grandfather, uncle and father were all successively high stewards of Bridport. A Tory and member of the October Club under Queen Anne, he voted against the Administration in all recorded divisions of the 1715 Parliament. Edward Harley (q.v.) wrote on 11 Jan. 1719 that ' . . . Mr. Strangways with several others are allowed by everybody to have distinguished themselves very handsomely against' the repeal of the Occasional Conformity and Schism Acts.[2] He was a member of the secret committee appointed by the House of Commons in January 1721 to inquire into the affairs of the South Sea Company. His name was sent to the Pretender in 1721 as a probable supporter in the event of a rising;[3] and in March 1723 he opposed the motion for a bill of pains and penalties against Atterbury. On the bill to restore Bolingbroke's estates in 1725, the Duke of Wharton reported that 'Strangways and others were absent, which I believe was owing to an unguarded promise they had made not to oppose it.'[4]

He died 23 Sept. 1726.

[1] Hutchins, *Dorset*, ii. 660, 662–3. [2] *HMC Portland*, v. 575. [3] Stuart mss 65/16. [4] To the Pretender, 1 May 1725, ibid. 82/3.

R.S.L.

STRANGWAYS HORNER, *see* HORNER

STRATHNAVER, Lord, *see* SUTHERLAND, William

STRICKLAND, Sir William, 3rd Bt. (1665–1724), of Boynton, Yorks.

MALTON	1689–1698, 1701–1708
YORKSHIRE	1708–1710
OLD SARUM	3 Aug. 1716–1722
MALTON	1722–12 May 1724

b. Mar. 1665, s. of Sir Thomas Strickland, 2nd Bt., M.P., by Elizabeth, da. and coh. of Sir Francis Pile, 2nd Bt., M.P., of Compton Beauchamp, Berks. *educ.* Exeter, Oxf. 1680. *m.* 28 Aug. 1684, Elizabeth, da. and h. of William Palmes, M.P., of Lindley, Yorks., 1s. *suc.* fa. 20 Nov. 1684.

Muster-master gen. 1720–*d.*

Strickland was the grandson of one of the leading supporters of the parliamentary cause in Yorkshire during the civil war, who was summoned to Cromwell's House of Lords. Brought into Parliament at the Revolution by his father-in-law for Malton, and subsequently sitting for his county, he was an active supporter of the Whig junto, playing his part in the stormy debates on Fenwick's attainder and on the case of *Ashby v. White*. After some years out of Parliament he re-entered the House for the Pitt borough of Old Sarum in 1716. On the breakdown of the impeachment of Lord Oxford in 1717, he moved unsuccessfully for proceeding by a bill of attainder, declaring that he looked upon Lord Oxford as an enemy to his country. On 17 Mar. 1718 he moved an address which Walpole described as having the air of a declaration of war on Spain. In 1719 he voted for the repeal of the Occasional Conformity and Schism Acts but on the peerage bill he was put down as 'doubtful', to be spoken to by Stanhope and Sunderland, and was 'talked of' for a place in December that year, when they were 'very busy to get friends for their bill'.[1] Though he voted against it, he obtained the place on the re-union of the Whig party in June 1720. He died 12 May, 1724.

[1] *HMC Polwarth*, ii. 403.

R.R.S.

STRICKLAND, William (c.1686–1735) of Boynton, Yorks.

MALTON	14 Dec. 1708–1715
CARLISLE	1715–1722
SCARBOROUGH	1722–1 Sept. 1735

b. c.1686, 1st s. of Sir William Strickland, 3rd Bt. (q.v.). *m.* Catherine, da. of Sir Jeremy Sambrooke of Bush Hill, Enfield, Mdx., sis. of Sir Samuel Vanacker Sambrooke, 3rd Bt., M.P., 1s. 1da. *suc.* fa. as 4th Bt. 12 May 1724.

Commr. of revenue [I] 1709–11 and 1714–25; ld. of Treasury 1725–7; treasurer to the Queen 1727–30; sec. at war 1730–9 May 1735; P.C. 11 June 1730.

Brought in by Lord Carlisle for Carlisle in 1715,

Strickland voted for the septennial bill in 1716 but against the Government in the division of 4 June 1717 on Lord Cadogan (q.v.). Like his father, he voted for the repeal of the Occasional Conformity and Schism Acts but against the peerage bill in 1719. In 1722 he stood successfully for Scarborough, where Walpole's brother, Horace, as a secretary to the Treasury, had given him the Treasury patronage in preference to the former Whig Member.[1] On 12 Feb. 1725 he seconded the motion for Lord Macclesfield's impeachment, of which he was one of the managers. In the changes following Pulteney's dismissal in the following April he secured a seat at the Treasury board, thenceforth becoming one of the chief government spokesmen. Appointed treasurer to the Queen on George II's accession and secretary at war in 1730, he continued to take a leading part in debates till he was prevented by illness from attending Parliament in 1733. He retained his post, with Walpole deputizing for him at the War office, till May 1735, when he was relieved of his duties.[2] He died 1 Sept. 1735.

[1] Undated letter from Wm. Thompson (q.v.), Marlborough mss.
[2] *HMC Carlisle*, 96, 97, 151; Coxe, *Walpole*, i. 752; Hervey, *Mems.* 450.

R.R.S.

STRICKLAND, William (1714–88), of Beverley, Yorks.

BEVERLEY	1741–1747

bap. 9 Oct. 1714, 2nd s. of Walter Strickland of Beverley (bro. of Sir William Strickland, 3rd Bt., q.v.) by his w. Elizabeth Peirson of Mowthorpe, Yorks. *m.* (1) Katherine (*d.* Dec. 1741), da. and coh. of Edward Charles Henshaw of Eltham, Kent, *s.p.*; (2) 25 May 1752, Diana, da. and coh. of Col. James Moyser of Beverley, 1s. 1da.

Lt. 1 tp. Horse Gren. Gds. 1732; capt. 2 tp. 1743.

On 12 May 1741 Lady Isabella Finch wrote to her brother-in-law, Lord Malton (Sir Thomas Wentworth, q.v.): 'the Patriots rejoice in Strickland's success at Beverley, by which I conclude he'll prove a worthless coxcomb'.[1] He was absent from the division on the chairman of the elections committee on 16 Dec. 1741 owing to the death of his wife, and was one of those who went away without voting on the Westminster election six days later.[2] Put down as a government supporter in the Cockpit list of October 1742, he did not vote in the division of 10 Dec. 1742 on the Hanoverians. On the opposition motion of 7 Dec. 1743 for disbanding the Hanoverians, Strickland, who had served at Dettingen, joined in the attacks on the Hanoverians, telling a story about some straw taken by them from the English troops, which appeared to the House as 'very frivolous'.[3] He voted against the Hanoverians in 1744 but for them in 1746, when he was classed by Newcastle as doubtful. He did not stand in 1747 and died 3 June 1788.

¹ Rockingham mss. ² Coxe, *Walpole*, iii. 583; Hartington to Devonshire, 22 Dec. 1741, Devonshire mss. ³ *HMC Egmont Diary*, iii. 278; Walpole to Mann, 11 Dec. 1743; Yorke's parl. jnl. *Parl. Hist.* xiii. 141.

R.R.S.

STRODE, William (c.1712–55), of Ponsbourne, Herts. and Mapledurham, Oxon.

READING 26 Nov. 1740–17 Feb. 1741
1741–1747, 1754–29 Apr. 1755

b. c.1712, 1st s. of Samuel Strode of Ponsbourne, citizen and barber-surgeon of London, by his w. Anne Richbell. *educ.* Grand Tour (France, Flanders, Holland) c.1730–2. *m.* 4 Feb. 1736, Lady Anne Cecil, da. of James, 5th Earl of Salisbury, 2s. 3da. *suc.* fa. 1727.

Strode's father, a Leadenhall Street broker, who acted for the South Sea Company, bought estates in Hertfordshire and elsewhere.¹ Returned as a Tory for Reading at a contested by-election in 1740, he was unseated on petition. Recovering his seat unopposed at the general election, he voted against the Administration in all recorded divisions. He did not stand in 1747 but was again returned at the top of the poll in 1754, when he was gravely ill.² He died 29 Apr. 1755.

¹ Nichols, *Lit. Anecs.* iv. 276; viii. 510; PCC 25 Brook. ² *HMC 5th Rep.* 364–5.

R.S.L.

STUART, James (?1681–1743), of Torrance, Lanark.

AYR BURGHS 1734–1741

b. ?1681, 1st s. of Alexander Stuart of Torrance by Isabel, da. of Sir Patrick Nisbet, 1st Bt., of Dean, Edinburgh; bro. of Patrick Stuart (q.v.). *educ.* Glasgow Univ. 1687. *unm. suc.* fa. 1733.
Ensign 1 Ft. 1704; capt.-lt. and lt.-col. 3 Ft. Gds. 1724, capt. 1725–*d.*; gent. usher 1727–*d.*

After serving in Flanders and Spain during the war of the Spanish succession, James Stuart was present at Sheriffmuir as a.-d.-c. to the Duke of Argyll. Obtaining a Household place at George II's accession, he was returned by Argyll for Ayr Burghs in 1734, but is not recorded as voting in Parliament. He was not put up in 1741 and died 3 Apr. 1743.

R.R.S.

STUART, Patrick (?1682–1760), of Torrance, Lanark.

LANARKSHIRE 18 May 1750–1754

b. ?1682, 2nd s. of Alexander Stuart of Torrance and bro. of James Stuart (q.v.). *educ.* Glasgow Univ. 1697. *unm. suc.* bro. 1743.
Ensign 1 Ft. 1704, lt. 1707, capt.-lt. 1726, capt. 1727, ret. aft. 1740.

In 1750 Stuart, a retired army officer, who had served under Marlborough, was returned for Lanarkshire at a by-election after a contest. Reporting the result of the election to the young Duke of Hamilton, then abroad, William Mure (q.v.) explained that the Duke's friends had fixed on

> our old friend the Captain as the only person who, by his connexions, and other considerations, could unite the jarring interests of the shire and preserve your Grace's interest in your absence. He received with horror the first proposition of drawing him from his retirement into public life; but at length they . . . prevailed, and he sent his circular letters round the county, acquainting us that he stood upon Duke Hamilton's interest, and assuring us that it would be safe in his hands.¹

He is shown in Newcastle's lists of March 1754 as drawing a secret service pension of £200 p.a.,² which was stopped after the general election that year, when he did not stand.

He died in 1760.

¹ *Caldwell Pprs.* (Maitland Club lxxi), ii (1), pp. 88–91. ² Add. 33038, ff. 352, 415.

E.C.

STUART MACKENZIE, Hon. James (?1719–1800), of Rosehaugh, Ross, and Belmont, Angus.

ARGYLLSHIRE	3 Feb. 1742–1747
BUTESHIRE	1747–1754
AYR BURGHS	1754–1761
ROSS-SHIRE	1761–1780

b. ?1719, 2nd s. of James Stuart, 2nd Earl of Bute [S], by Lady Anne Campbell, da. of Archibald, 1st Duke of Argyll [S] and sis. of John and Archibald, 2nd and 3rd Dukes. *educ.* Eton 1728–32; Grand Tour; Leyden 1737. *m.* 16 Feb. 1749, his cos. Lady Elizabeth Campbell, da. of John, 2nd Duke of Argyll [S], 2ch. *d.* young. *suc.* fa. in the estate of Rosehaugh 1723, under the entail of his gt.-gd.-fa. Sir George Mackenzie, and took add. name of Mackenzie.
Envoy extraordinary, Turin 1758–61; P.C. 4 Sept. 1761; ld. privy seal [S] Apr. 1763–May 1765, Aug. 1766–*d.*

Stuart Mackenzie was brought up under the guardianship of his uncles, the 2nd Duke of Argyll and Lord Ilay, later 3rd Duke of Argyll. He was returned for Argyllshire in February 1742 on the interest of the 2nd Duke, with whose followers in the House of Commons he voted against the Government in the following session. He did not vote in the session of 1743–4, when he was abroad with the Barberina, a celebrated opera dancer, with whom he had fallen in love when she came to

London for the season of 1742–3. They planned to marry at Venice, but were foiled by Lord Ilay, now Duke of Argyll, who arranged through his friend, Lord Hyndford, the British ambassador at Berlin, for her to be arrested at Venice and sent under escort to Berlin to fulfil a contract which she had made to dance there during the forthcoming season, and for Mackenzie to be deported from Prussia as soon as he arrived in pursuit of her.[1] On his return to England he is described as 'ill with love, spitting blood,' and very angry with Argyll, who wrote: 'I have no hope for him, for I am told he continues to talk like a madman'.[2] He was absent from the division on the Hanoverians in April 1746, classed by the Government as 'doubtful'. Returned for Buteshire on his family's interest in 1747, he married his first cousin, the daughter of the 2nd Duke of Argyll, in 1749. In the next reign he succeeded the 3rd Duke as the manager of affairs in Scotland.

He died 8 Apr. 1800.

[1] John Drummond to Ld. Morton, 4 Dec. 1742, Morton mss. SRO; *Letters and Jnls. of Lady Coke*, i. pp. lii–iv. [2] Walpole to Hanbury Williams, 17 July 1744; Argyll to Andrew Fletcher, Ld. Milton, 27 Oct. 1744, Milton mss.

R.R.S.

STYLE, Sir Thomas, 4th Bt. (?1685–1769), of Wateringbury, Kent.

BRAMBER 27 Jan.–1 June 1715

b. ?1685, s. of Sir Thomas Style, 2nd Bt., M.P., by his 2nd w. Margaret, da. of Sir Thomas Twisden, 1st Bt., M.P. *educ.* Enfield, Mdx.; Trinity, Camb. 13 Sept. 1704, aged 19. *m.* Elizabeth, da. of Sir Charles Hotham, 4th Bt. (q.v.), 4s. 2da. *suc.* half-bro. as 4th Bt. 12 Feb. 1703.
Sheriff, Kent 1709–10.

Style was descended from Sir John Style, a London alderman, who bought the estate of Langley, in Beckenham, at the end of the fifteenth century. About the beginning of the seventeenth century his great-grandfather bought Wateringbury, which Style rebuilt.[1] Returned as a Tory in 1715, he was unseated on petition and did not stand again. He died 11 Jan. 1769.

[1] Hasted, *Kent*, v. 112.

R.R.S.

SUNDON, Baron, *see* **CLAYTON, William** (*b.*1671)

SUTHERLAND, William, Lord Strathnaver (1708–50).

SUTHERLAND 1727–27 June 1733

b. 2 Oct. 1708, 1st surv. s. of William Gordon,

II—GG

afterwards Sutherland, M.P., Lord Strathnaver, by Catherine, da. of William Morrison, M.P., of Prestongrange, Haddington. *educ.* Grand Tour (France and Hanover) c.1726–7. *m.* (contract 17 Apr. 1734) Lady Elizabeth Wemyss, da. of David, 3rd Earl of Wemyss [S], 1s. 1da. *suc.* bro. 12 Dec. 1720, and gd.-fa. as 17th Earl of Sutherland [S] 27 June 1733.
Rep. peer [S] 1734–47; ld. of police [S] 1734–44, 1st ld. 1744–7.

Lord Strathnaver was the grandson and heir of the 16th Earl of Sutherland, who advised him, while he was on the Grand Tour in 1727, to go to Hanover to pay his court to Frederick, the new Prince of Wales, in the hope of becoming a gentleman of his bedchamber.[1] Though he was only 18, his grandfather put him up for Sutherland at the general election that year, expressing the hope to the Duke of Argyll that the resolution that the eldest sons of peers of Scotland should not sit in the House of Commons would not be invoked, as Strathnaver was a grandson, not a son.[2] Taking his seat without difficulty, he voted with the Administration on the Hessians in 1730 and on the excise bill in 1733. In 1730 he claimed repayment for arms surrendered to the Government, under the Act for disarming the Highlands, but his claim was deferred on the ground that 'some of the receipts for arms produced for the Lord Strathnaver are attended with very suspicious circumstances'.[3] On succeeding his grandfather as Earl of Sutherland in 1733, he was said to have made a bargain with Walpole and Ilay under which, in return for voting for the court list of representative peers, he was made one of them himself, appointed a lord of police in Scotland at £800 p.a., and granted a pension of £1,200 p.a.[4] Promoted to be first lord of police in 1744, during the Forty-five he raised two independent companies on behalf of the Government, and was present at the battle of Culloden.[5] Having apparently connected himself with Frederick, Prince of Wales, he lost his post in 1747, writing to Newcastle, 30 July 1747:

I had the honour of your Grace's letter acquainting me that his Majesty thought it for his service to give the police to the Earl of Marchmont [q.v. under Hugh Hume Campbell, Lord Polwarth] . . . At the same time, I must beg leave to acquaint your Grace that it surprised me, as I cannot charge my conscience with anything I ever did contrary to the King's interest or that of his royal House . . . The last time I had the honour to see your Grace you was so good as promise to speak to Mr. Pelham concerning the money I expended during the late wicked rebellion. As the reference was made to His Royal Highness the Duke, I was at the expense of sending my principal servant to Flanders to have the Duke's determination. His Royal Highness has been pleased to return me a very favourable answer and will interest himself to get me freed of an expense incurred with cheerfulness to serve my King and country.[6]

He left the management of his estates in Scotland to his mother, preferring to live 'near the Court, upon which I have still some pretensions'. Two years later, he reported to his uncle, James St. Clair (q.v.):

> I have no great hopes of getting justice since his Majesty and ministry are displeased at me . . . I design to go to Tonbridge next month, for [to] Scotland I will not return on any account. I hope . . . to satisfy the world of my behaviour for his Majesty's service, though perhaps to the ruin of my family, and then shall go to foreign parts, where I hope to be better used.

He died at Montauban in France, 7 Dec. 1750, leaving debts amounting to £15,797.[7]

[1] Sir W. Fraser, *Sutherland Bk.* ii. 33, 226. [2] Ibid. i. 364. [3] *Cal. Treas. Pprs.* 1729–30, pp. 456, 458. [4] *HMC Polwarth*, v. 110–11; *Cal. Treas. Pprs.* 1731–4, p. 508. [5] *Sutherland Bk.* i. 405–24. [6] *HMC Fortescue*, i. 117–18; Add. 32712, f.278. [7] *Sutherland Bk.* i. 429–30; ii. 273.

E.C.

SUTTON, Richard (1674–1737), of Scofton, Notts.

NEWARK   1708–10, 28 Jan. 1712–23 July 1737

b. 16 Jan. 1674, 2nd s. of Robert Sutton of Averham, Notts. (nephew of Robert Sutton, M.P., 1st Baron Lexington), by Katherine, da. of Rev. William Sherborne, D.D., of Pembridge, Herefs.; yr. bro. of Sir Robert Sutton (q.v.). *m.* Catherine de Tolmer of Bruges, 2s. 1da.
Ensign, Visct. Castleton's regt. of Ft. 1690, capt. 1693, maj. 1697, half-pay 1698; maj. 8 Ft. 1701, lt.-col. 1702; brevet-col. 1704; lt. gov. Hull 1707–11; col. regt. of Ft. 1709–12; brig.-gen. 1710; gov. Hull 1711–15; col. 19 Ft. 1712–15; c.-in-c. Bruges 1713–14; clerk of the Green Cloth 1724–6; maj.-gen. 1727; envoy to Hesse-Cassel 1727–9 and 1730–1, Brunswick Wolfenbüttel 1729, 1730–1, and Denmark 1729; col. 19 Ft. (again) 1729–*d.*; gov. Guernsey 1733–5; lt.-gen. 1735.

Entering the army at the age of 16, Sutton served in Flanders under William III and Marlborough.[1] He was returned for Newark, where his cousin, Lord Lexington, a prominent Jacobite, had a strong interest. Classed as a Tory in 1713, but as a Whig in 1715, he was one of the high ranking army officers who, on the outbreak of the Fifteen rebellion, were dismissed or required to resign their regiments on security grounds, either because of Lexington's treasonable activities, or because he himself had been connected with Bolingbroke and the Duke of Ormonde during the last years of the late reign.[2] Going into opposition, he voted against the septennial bill in 1716, and the repeal of the Occasional Conformity Act in 1719, but seems to have made his peace with the Government by the end of that year, when he voted for the peerage bill. Nevertheless in 1722 he declared against one of the government candidates for Nottinghamshire, the other being his brother, Sir Robert Sutton (q.v.), apparently in anger with the Duke of Newcastle for not supporting his son's candidature at Retford.[3]

After Sunderland's death, Sutton attached himself to Walpole, whose son tells the following story:

> General Sutton . . . was one day sitting by my father at his dressing. Sir Robert said to Jones, who was shaving him, 'John, you cut me'—presently afterwards, 'John, you cut me'—and again with the same patience . . . 'John, you cut me'. Sutton started up and cried, 'By God! if he can bear it, I can't; if you cut him once more, damn my blood if I don't knock you down'.[4]

Re-employed and reinstated in his military appointments, he thenceforth voted with the Government, speaking for them on army matters.[5] In the affair of the Charitable Corporation Sir Robert Sutton is said to have been prejudiced by 'the character of his brother, the general, as worthless a man, without question, as ever was created'. On his death the 1st Lord Egmont wrote:

> Last Saturday, 23rd inst. [July 1737] died General Richard Sutton, governor of Hull, and Guernsey, of whom it is said that 'Satan, governor of Hell, is dead'. He was indeed an atheistical, debauched man.[6]

[1] Dalton, *Geo. I's Army*, i. 55–58. [2] *Pol. State*, x. 98. [3] Newcastle to the Duchess, 28 Mar. 1722, Add. 33073, f.15. [4] Horace Walpole to Conway, 21 June 1760. [5] *HMC Egmont Diary*, i. 126, 158. [6] G. Sherburn, *Pope's Corresp.* iv. 493; *HMC Egmont Diary*, ii. 425.

R.R.S.

SUTTON, Sir Robert (?1671–1746), of Broughton, Lincs.

NOTTINGHAMSHIRE   1722–4 May 1732
GREAT GRIMSBY   1734–1741

b. ?1671, 1st s. of Robert Sutton of Averham, Notts., and bro. of Richard Sutton (q.v.). *educ.* Trinity, Oxf. 25 May 1688, aged 16; M. Temple 1691. *m.* 10 Dec. 1724, Judith, da. and coh. of Benjamin Tichborne, wid. of Charles Spencer, M.P., 3rd Earl of Sunderland, 2 surv. s. *suc.* fa. by 1691. Kntd. 18 June 1701; K.B. 27 May 1725.
Sec. and resident at Vienna 1697–1700; ambassador to Constantinople 1700–17; jt. mediator at Peace of Passarowitz 1717–18; ambassador at Paris 1720–1; P.C. 9 May 1722; member of committee of management, Charitable Corporation 1725–32; assistant, R. African Co. 1726–32, sub-gov. 1726–7, 1730–1.

'Reverend Sutton' as Pope was to refer to him, began life in straitened circumstances. Taking deacon's orders,[1] he became chaplain to his cousin, Lord Lexington, ambassador at Vienna in 1694, but gave up the church on being appointed secretary to the embassy in 1697. By Lord Lexington's influence he was promoted in 1700 to be ambassador at Constantinople, where the British representative was also the paid agent of the Levant

Company, with ample opportunities for enriching himself.[2] At the end of 17 years at Constantinople, followed by a profitable mediation at Passarowitz and a final spell as ambassador at Paris, Sutton had made enough money to fight and win a costly county election, to marry the dowager Countess of Sunderland, and to embark on a new career as a Member of Parliament, a privy councillor, and a knight of the newly revived order of the Bath, with a house in Grosvenor Square, another in the country, and estates in Lincolnshire and Nottinghamshire worth nearly £5,000 p.a.[3] In Parliament he moved the Address in 1726, but voted against the Government on the civil list arrears in 1729. On 16 Feb. 1730 he was one of some 60 ministerial supporters who caused the defeat of the Government on a bill excluding pensioners from the House of Commons, in his case by leaving the House before the division. Two days later he presented a petition from the Royal African Company, of which he was sub-governor.[4] He was also on the managing committee of the Charitable Corporation, which had been granted a charter in 1707 to lend small sums to poor persons on pledges at legal interest so as to prevent them from falling into the hands of private pawnbrokers. In 1728 and 1730 he succeeded in obtaining licences from the Government to increase the Corporation's authorized capital from £100,000 to £300,000 and then to £600,000. On the announcement of each increase the Corporation's shares rose sharply, enabling Sutton and others with advance information to make thousands by stagging the new issues. In 1731 he defended the Corporation in the House of Commons against attacks made on it by the city of London and other parties for unfair trading practices and contraventions of its charter, under pressure from the Bank of England giving a public pledge, which was promptly evaded, that the Corporation would desist from the practice of issuing its own notes.[5]

Early in 1732 the disclosure of extensive frauds and losses in the Charitable Corporation led to an inquiry by a select committee of the House of Commons, mainly composed of extreme members of the Opposition. In April 1732, the committee presented a report showing that the Corporation's losses were due to defalcations by some of its directors, made possible by the negligence of their colleagues, who throughout 'had nothing in their view but to enhance the prices of their shares'. Sutton himself was not one of the directors implicated in the defalcations, but the report pointed out that he had obtained the first licence for increasing the Corporation's capital on a false

statement that the authorized capital had been exhausted, and that the grant of both applications had been 'kept secret for some months for the private advantage of some of the committee [of management] and assistants and their agents, during which time great numbers of shares were bought by them'. In his evidence before the parliamentary committee he took the line that he had made the statement in good faith on information supplied to him by his colleagues; that he did not know that the grant of the licences had been concealed; that 'he had but little share in the management of the Corporation, and when he entered upon it frequently afterwards declared that he neither would nor could attend the execution of ordinary business'. In this he was borne out by a colleague who testified to his practice of reading newspapers at board meetings.[6]

In the debate, 3 May, on this report the chairman of the select committee, Samuel Sandys (q.v.), after moving and carrying a series of resolutions condemning the fraudulent practices disclosed by the Committee, went on to charge Sutton personally with several of these practices. The House then adjourned so that Sutton might have time to prepare his defence. Next morning, the 1st Lord Egmont wrote,

> I went early to the House [of Commons] to secure a place. We proceeded on Sir Robert Sutton who, after a defence of six hours, was ordered to withdraw, and then Mr. Sandys, recapitulating the particulars of Sir Robert, showed the weakness of some and falseness of others [and] made a motion that . . . Sir Robert Sutton had been guilty of promoting and abetting and carrying on the fraudulent practices of the Charitable Corporation.

Appeals for some mitigation of the severity of the motion were made by Sir Paul Methuen and Henry Pelham, on the ground that Sutton, though guilty of the grossest negligence, was a man of high character, who was not only admittedly innocent of wilful fraud, but as a large shareholder in the Corporation was one of the heaviest losers by the frauds. In reply John Barnard, a member of the select committee, said that there were

> no words in the question that were not strictly true; that Sir Robert was not only remiss and negligent, but the patron of the Corporation. That his application and credit alone obtained the two licences for augmenting their capital to £300,000 and £600,000.

After pointing out that the first licence had been obtained on a false statement Barnard continued:

> He left it to the House's consideration how criminal a thing it was for Sir Robert to . . . impose falsities on the King; and make his sacred Majesty a participant in the ruin of his subjects. That his guilt was greater in that he was at that time a Privy Councillor,

and his good character before is an objection to him in this case, since he made use of it to seduce numbers of people to trust him with their fortunes, and then not only betrayed them to others, but bought up their shares at low prices to sell them out dear, for which purpose he kept the licences for augmentation of the capital secret for some months. He thought the motion was rather too charitable than too severe.

Carried without a division, the motion was followed by Sutton's expulsion from the House. According to Egmont,

the Tories and discontented Whigs were resolved to a man to leave the House abruptly, if a division had passed this day against Mr. Sandys' motion, which had been of most dangerous consequence to the Ministry, and perhaps to the nation. It would have been represented to the nation that the majority of the House were corrupted by the court, and that honest men could not sit any longer there. Sir Robert [Walpole] was informed of it late last night and for that reason made no opposition.

As Parliament was about to rise, the question of the punishment of Sutton and others who had been similarly censured was deferred; but a motion was carried declaring that they 'ought to make a just satisfaction' for the losses which they had occasioned, and an Act was passed prohibiting them from leaving the country and from alienating their property, which was to be inventoried, till the end of the next session.[7]

Towards the end of the next session Sandys, now armed with a report based on the confession of one of the parties to the defalcations, resumed his attack with a motion that Sutton had been guilty of 'many notorious breaches of trust and many indirect and fraudulent practices'.

Had this been carried [Egmont writes], nothing had been bad enough for him, and we should have moved for a bill of pains and penalties, to render him forever incapable of holding a place of profit or trust, and to give his estate to the proprietors of the Corporation, sufferers by his breach of trust. Sir Robert Walpole, who thought this too severe, though he spoke not, yet influenced the court party to speak in Sir Robert Sutton's favour, who were likewise joined by some of the malcontents on account of relation or particular friendship . . . to him, such as Sir Paul Methuen, Lord Morpeth etc.

An amendment declaring Sutton to have been guilty of 'neglect of duty' only was carried by 148 to 89 which, Egmont writes, 'put the minority in such a passion that after the numbers were reported, above 50 rose together from their seats and in a passion left the House'.[8]

In 1734 Sutton re-entered Parliament for Great Grimsby, the refuge of shady business men, where he owned considerable property and employed the mayor as his electoral agent.[9] He played no further part in politics or business, and

did not stand again. The verdict of the House of Commons was subsequently endorsed by Lord Hardwicke in his judgment in the case of *Charitable Corporation v. Sir Robert Sutton and others* in 1742, and also in an opinion on a petition by the Corporation to the House of Lords in 1743, in which he stated that

it is now fully known both from the enquiries in Parliament and in the court of Chancery that the whole iniquity was carried on by five only who entered into respective partnerships and that Sir Robert Sutton and the other defendants were equally imposed on with the rest and were themselves the greatest sufferers as their property in the Corporation was larger.[10]

In these circumstances Pope, on representations from Warburton, who was under obligations to Sutton, agreed that in future editions of his works allusions to 'reverend Sutton' should be amended to 'reverend bishop' or 'bishops'.[11]

He died 13 Aug. 1746.

[1] *Pope's Poems*, Twickenham ed. iii (2), p. 97, n. 107. [2] A. C. Wood, *Hist. Levant Co.* 134–5. [3] *Inventory of Lands and Goods of Sir Robert Sutton*, 1732. [4] *HMC Egmont Diary*, i. 50–51. [5] 'Report of the Committee of the House of Commons on the Charitable Corporation,' *Parl. Hist.* viii. 1103, 1124–5, 1147–8; *Inventory*, ut supra. [6] *HMC Egmont Diary*, i. 221; *Parl. Hist.* viii. 1120, 1124–5, 1129; *CJ*, xxi. 912–13. [7] *HMC Egmont Diary*, i. 266–8, 270–2. [8] Ibid. 368; *CJ*, xxii. 131. [9] Tennyson d'Eyncourt mss B.24, Lincs. AO. [10] Add. 35876, ff.200–4. [11] G. Sherburn, *Pope's Corresp.* iv. 492–6.

R.R.S.

SUTTON, *see also* MANNERS SUTTON

SWANTON, Francis (?1666–1721), of Salisbury, Wilts.

SALISBURY 1715–25 Apr. 1721

b. ?1666, 1st s. of William Swanton, M.P., of the Close, Salisbury by his 1st w. Elizabeth, da. of Emanuel Gauntlett of Salisbury.[1] *educ.* Magdalen Hall, Oxf. 14 Nov. 1684, aged 18. *suc.* fa. 1681.
Dep. recorder, Salisbury 1712–*d.*

Francis Swanton, whose father had been recorder of Salisbury and M.P. for the city, came of a family with long connexions with the Middle Temple. Returned as a Tory in 1715, he voted against the Government in all recorded divisions. His name was sent to the Pretender early in 1721 as a probable supporter in the event of a rising.[2] He died 25 Apr. 1721.

[1] Phillipps, *Vis. Wilts.* 1677, p. 17. [2] Stuart mss 65/16.

R.S.L.

SWANTON, Thomas (d. 1723), of London.

SALTASH 1722–18 Jan. 1723

m. Elizabeth, 4s. 2da.
Lt. R.N. by 1690; capt. 1695; commr. of the navy

at Plymouth 1715–16; comptroller of the store-keepers' accounts 1716–18; comptroller of the navy 1718–d.

During the war of the Spanish succession Swanton served under Sir Clowdisley Shovell, M.P., in the Mediterranean.[1] Appointed commissioner of the navy on George I's accession, he stood unsuccessfully for Saltash at a by-election in December 1718, but carried his election in 1722 on the Admiralty interest, which he managed.[2] He died shortly afterwards, 18 Jan. 1723, leaving £8,000 in South Sea stock to be shared by his children,[3] two of whom entered the Royal Navy, Thomas, who was a captain in 1741, and Robert, who became an admiral in 1762.

[1] Charnock, *Biog. Navalis*, iii. 111. [2] Thos. Coram to Sir Chas. Wager, 3 Oct. 1723, copy in Buller mss at Antony. [3] PCC 18 Richmond.

E.C.

SWIFT, Samuel (d. 1718), of Claines, in Worcester.

WORCESTER   5 Dec. 1693–7 Feb. 1694
             1695–8 Feb. 1718

b. c.1659, 1st. surv. s. of William Swift of Worcester, merchant and sugar baker, grocer and draper, by Martha, da. of John Beauchamp of Newland, Worcs. m. by 1682, Sarah, o. da. of Thomas Shewring of Worcester, 1s. 1da. suc. fa. 1689.
    Alderman, Worcester, mayor 1684–5; sheriff, Worcs. 1692–3.

Swift, a Worcester merchant and grocer,[1] represented his native city as a Tory for nearly 23 years without a break. There is no record of his voting or speaking from 1715 till his death, 8 Feb. 1718.

[1] W. C. Metcalfe, *Vis. Worcs.* 1682–3, pp. 90–91.

R.S.L.

SWINFEN, Richard (?1678–1726), of Swinfen, Staffs.

TAMWORTH   1708–1710, 23 Jan. 1723–22 July 1726

b. ?1678, 1st s. of Francis Swinfen, draper, of Shrewsbury by his w. Jane Doughty. educ. Pembroke, Oxf. 10 Nov. 1694, aged 16; M. Temple 1696. unm. suc. fa. 1693 and gd.-fa. to Swinfen 1694.
    Recorder, Tamworth.

Of an ancient Staffordshire family, Swinfen was the grandson of John Swinfen, M.P. Stafford 1645–8 and 1660, Tamworth 1659, 1661–79, 1681, and Bere Alston 1690–4, who played an active part on the parliamentary side in the civil war and was one of the Members chosen to draw up the exclusion bill in 1679. A Whig, he was returned on petition for Tamworth in 1723, which he had represented

in the previous reign, dying before the next general election, 22 July 1726.

R.R.S.

SWYMMER, Anthony Langley[1] (?1724–60), of Mold, Flints. and Longwood House, nr. Winchester.

SOUTHAMPTON   1747–4 Jan. 1760

b. ?1724, o.s. of Anthony Swymmer of St. Thomas-in-the-East, Jamaica, member of the Council there, by his 2nd w. Milborough. educ. Winchester; Peterhouse, Camb. 7 Nov. 1741, aged 17.[2] m. 5 Jan. 1748, Arabella, da. and coh. of Sir John Astley, 2nd Bt. (q.v.), of Patshull, Staffs., s.p. suc. fa. 1730.

A member of a good Bristol merchant family, Swymmer, who was born in Jamaica, where his grandfather owned a plantation,[3] was returned for Southampton as a Tory in 1747. In March 1752, when a scheme was afoot for a restoration of the Stuarts with Prussian help, he went over to Paris with his father-in-law, Sir John Astley (q.v.), meeting the Young Pretender, and bringing a paper from England for the Jacobite Earl Marischal, then Prussian ambassador to France. He and his wife then travelled to Rome, with a recommendation to the Pretender's secretary, who described him as 'a most agreeable companion, and which is more a perfect honest man [i.e. Jacobite]', adding: 'If you will make him happy . . . let him know H.R.H. [the Young Pretender] is well, for surely no man on earth loves him better nor would do more to serve him'.[4]

He died 4 Jan. 1760 in Jamaica.

[1] The genealogical particulars here given supersede those in Namier & Brooke, *House of Commons 1754–90*. [2] T. A. Walker, *Peterhouse Adm. Bk.* 279. [3] V. L. Oliver, *Caribbeana*, iv. 227–32, where there is some confusion. [4] 28 Sept., 29 Nov. 1752, Stuart mss 336/7, 338/69; A. Lang, *Pickle the Spy*, 190, 213, who misdates a letter.

E.C.

SYDENHAM, Humphrey (1694–1757), of Combe, nr. Dulverton, Som. and Nutcombe, Devon.

EXETER   1741–1754

b. 24 Oct. 1694, 1st s. of Humphrey Sydenham of Combe by his 1st w. Eliza, da. of George Peppin of Dulverton. educ. Exeter and Uffculme sch.; Sidney Suss. Camb. 1713; I. Temple 1712, called 1728. m. by 1724, Grace, da. and h. of Richard Hill of the Priory, nr. Exeter, 1s. 3da. (2 d.v.p.). suc. fa. 1710; gt.-gt.-uncle Sir John St. Barbe, 1st Bt., M.P., 1723.

Sydenham, a lawyer, who kept his chamber in the Inner Temple till his death, belonged to an old Somerset family seated at Dulverton since the sixteenth century, with extensive property on the Devonshire and Somerset border.[1] Returned as a Tory for Exeter in 1741, he is described as 'extremely nettled at several passages in the instructions' sent by the Exeter corporation to their Members to promote a bill to restore triennial Parliaments and a place bill, declaring that if they were printed he would 'complain to the House of a breach of privilege.'[2] Voting consistently against the Government, he seconded Thomas Carew's motion for annual Parliaments, 29 Jan. 1745; supported Sir Francis Dashwood's amendments to the address on the rebellion, 18 Oct. 1745; and opposed the Hanoverians on 14 Apr. 1746, and the second reading of the bill for continuing the suspension of the Habeas Corpus Act, 19 Nov. 1746.[3] In 1751, described by Horace Walpole as 'a mad High-Church zealot', he opposed the regency bill, on which he

> spoke for the undiminished prerogative, quoted Greek and said that subjects had never before attempted to make peers; and that the commissions of judges determine at the King's death.

In the debates on the arrest of Alexander Murray, he made 'a speech worthy the ages of fanaticism, comparing Murray to prophet Daniel . . . and alleg[ing] the example of the Dissenters who do not kneel at the Sacrament'. On 5 Dec. 1751, on the report from the committee of supply fixing a 3s. land tax, he

> affected to cry and ask pardon for quoting a ludicrous epitaph on so melancholy an occasion, but which he could not help thinking applicable to the great minister of these times who hath so burdened land:—
> Lie heavy on him, land; for he
> Laid many a heavy load on thee.[4]

Early in 1753 Sydenham is said to have

> wanted a tax on swords and full bottom wigs, which last do not amount to 40 in the kingdom. The Speaker and the attorney-general, who were the only wearers of them then in the House, pulled off their hats and made him due reverence.[5]

Later in the year he antagonized the Exeter corporation by supporting the Jewish naturalization bill. Refusing to retract,[6] in spite of the popular outcry against this measure, he was dropped by his party and did not stand in 1754. He died 12 Aug. 1757, leaving his property to his son with no less than ten remainders, so that it should be certain to pass to the nearest male heir.

[1] G. F. Sydenham, *Hist. Sydenham Fam.* 89–91 et passim. [2] *HMC Exeter*, 245–6. [3] Coxe, *Pelham*, i. 220; Owen, *Pelhams*, 284, 306–7; *Bedford Corresp.* i. 189. [4] H. Walpole, *Mems. Geo. II*, i. 50, 141, 211–12, 219. [5] *HMC 1st Rep.* 51. [6] Sir Francis Drake to Pelham, 6 Sept. 1753, Newcastle (Clumber) mss.

S.R.M.

SYMMONS, John (1701–64), of Llanstinan, Pemb.

CARDIGAN BOROUGHS 20 Mar. 1746–1761

b. 12 Sept. 1701, 4th s. of John Symmons of Llanstinan by Martha, da. of George Harries of Tregwynt, Pemb. *m.* by 1744, Maria, da. of Charles Philipps of Sandyhaven, Pemb., 2s. *suc.* bro. 1741.

A member of the Society of Sea Serjeants, a reputedly Jacobite organization in South Wales, Symmons represented Cardigan as a Tory. He died in September 1764.

P.D.G.T.

TAAFFE, Theobald (c.1708–80), of Hanover Sq., London.

ARUNDEL 1747–1754

b. c.1708, 1st s. of Stephen Taaffe of Dowanstown, co. Meath by his 2nd w. Mabel, da. of Henry, 2nd Visct. Barnewall [I].[1] *m.* Susanna, yst. da. of Henry Lowe of Goadby Marwood, Leics., *s.p. suc.* fa. 1730.

Taaffe came of an Irish Roman Catholic family, distantly connected with the Earls of Carlingford. Marrying a wealthy Englishwoman, who inherited half the Jamaican property of her brother, Samuel Lowe (q.v.),[2] he settled in England, with a house in Hanover Square and an estate near Midhurst in Sussex, building up an interest in the neighbouring borough of Arundel, for which he was returned as an opposition Whig after a contested election in 1747. In 1750 he was one of the boon companions of the Duke of Bedford and Lord Sandwich, who were spending their whole time that summer in 'riot and gaming'.[3] On 22 Nov. 1751 Horace Walpole described him to Mann as

> an Irishman, who changed his religion to fight a duel, as . . . you know, in Ireland a Catholic may not wear a sword. He is the hero who having betted Mrs. Woffington five guineas on as many performances in one night, and demanding the money which he won, received the famous reply, *double or quits*. He is a gamester, usurer, adventurer, and of late has divided his attentions between the Duke of Newcastle and Madame de Pompadour, travelling with turtles and pineapples in post-chaises, to the latter, flying back to the former for Lewes races—and smuggling Burgundy at the same time.

Towards the end of 1751 Taaffe and Edward Wortley Montagu, who had been acting as faro bankers to the French ambassadress in London, transferred their activities to Paris, where they were arrested and imprisoned on charges of cheating and robbing a Jew with whom they had been gambling (see Edward Wortley Montagu, jun.). Released on representations from the British Embassy, after a series of actions and counteractions Taaffe went to Hanover 'to pay his duty to H.M. and to remove any bad impressions' that Newcastle, who was in attendance there, might have received from this affair.[4] In 1754 he stood again for Arundel but came out bottom of the poll.

Returning to France, where he was presented at court, he attached himself to the Prince de Conti, a notorious gambler and libertine.[5] In 1755 he won a large sum of money in Paris from Sir John Bland, M.P., who committed suicide after being arrested at Taaffe's instigation in consequence of the dishonouring of the bills which he had given for the debt.[6] Three years later he himself was sent to the Bastille for suspicious behaviour, but was released on the intervention of Choiseul.[7] At the beginning of 1761 he was said to be living at the French court on the best footing.[8] In March of that year he visited London, professing to bring a message to Henry Fox from Choiseul to the effect that if England was inclined to peace on reasonable terms the French Government were ready to send someone to open negotiations. Fox, knowing Taaffe only as a 'sharper', consulted Selwyn, the Paris banker, who reported that he was very able and well-informed about France, had been extremely intimate and influential with the late Marshal Belle Isle, and had not played for four years. In the end Fox 'dismissed' Taaffe.[9]

In 1763 Edward Gibbon reported from Paris that Taaffe was again in prison there, this time for debt.

> He has settled with his English creditors and given up his estate at Jamaica for the payment of his debts. He wants to compromise with his other creditors, who are very numerous, but as they are convinced he wants to cheat them and that he only offers the same estate after the other debts are cleared which cannot be in less than ten or fifteen years they will hear of no compromise . . . Mr. Taaffe's scheme is to keep another estate in Jamaica clear of his creditors. They on their side want to starve him into giving up that estate likewise.[10]

Towards the end of 1767 Lord Clive's agents were approached by 'an extraordinary adventurer', namely Taaffe, with an offer of three seats in two Cornish boroughs, Helston and Grampound, for £7,000, the fourth seat to be reserved for Taaffe 'for his trouble in the management'. The proposals were described as 'a plan of poor Charles Townshend's, moderate in expense, but abortive to his use by his death'; but it was subsequently found that this was untrue. In the end the negotiations were broken off owing to Taaffe's insistence on receiving the money at once, instead of after the elections, and to his inability to furnish satisfactory security, his estates in Jamaica, worth about £3,000 a year, being vested for the payment of his debts in trustees, who allowed him £500 a year. According to Clive's agents, when Taaffe was informed of the decision it was 'not easy to conceive the astonishment, rage, and fury that ensued'.[11]

Nothing more is known of Taaffe till 1777, when he claimed to have been cured of his gout by a London quack through a treatment which would have killed any man less strong.[12] He died in 1780.

[1] Information supplied by College of Arms. [2] R. M. Howard, *Longs of Jamaica*, i. 58–59. [3] Dupplin to Newcastle, 21 Aug. 1750, Add. 32722, f.208. [4] Albemarle to Newcastle, 20/31 Aug. 1752, Add. 32839, f.378. [5] Duc de Luynes, *Mems.* xiv. 7. [6] *H. Walpole Corresp.* (Yale ed.) ix. 172–3. [7] W. H. Smith, *Letters to and from Mme Du Deffand* (1938), p. xiv. [8] Walpole to Mann, 27 Jan. 1761. [9] Fox to Shelburne, 13, 14 and (?) 15 Mar. 1761, Lansdowne mss. [10] *Letters*, i. 143. [11] Letters to Ld. Clive from Geo. Clive, Chase Price, John Walsh, Thos. Rider and Hen. Mountfort, Oct. and Nov. 1767, Clive mss, Powis Castle. [12] Walpole to Lady Upper Ossory, 17 Dec. 1777.

R.R.S.

TALBOT, Charles (1685–1737), of Castell-y-Mynach, Glam.

TREGONY 15 Mar. 1720–1722
DURHAM 1722–5 Dec. 1733

bap. 22 Dec. 1685, 1st s. of William Talbot, bp. successively of Oxford, Salisbury and Durham, by his 1st w. Katherine, da. of Richard King of Upham, Wilts., alderman of London. *educ.* Eton c.1700; Oriel, Oxf. 1702; I. Temple 1707, called 1711; L. Inn 1719, bencher 1726. *m.* c.June 1708,[1] Cecil, da. and h. of Charles Mathews of Castell-y-Mynach and gt. gd.-da. and h. of David Jenkins of Hensol, Glam., 5s. *suc.* fa. 1730; *cr.* Baron Talbot of Hensol 5 Dec. 1733.

Fellow of All Souls, Oxf. 1704; solicitor-gen. 1726–33; P.C. 29 Nov. 1733; lord chancellor 1733–*d.*

Charles Talbot came of a Worcestershire family descended from the 2nd Earl of Shrewsbury. The son of a Whig bishop, he was at first destined for the church but on the advice, it is said, of Lord Chancellor Cowper, he turned to the law. In his early days he went the Oxford circuit, also practising in the court of Chancery. He was brought in at a by-election at Tregony in 1720, but removed in 1722 to Durham, where he was returned at the top of the poll on the interest of his father, the newly translated bishop of that diocese. In Parliament he consistently supported the Administration, speaking frequently on the constitutional and legal aspects of business before the House. His first recorded speech was in October 1722, when he seconded the nomination of Spencer Compton (q.v.) as Speaker. In the following March he supported the motions to bring in bills of pains and penalties against the bishop of Rochester and his associates. After his promotion to solicitor-general in 1726 he formed a strong legal team for seven years with his friend Sir Philip Yorke (q.v.), the attorney-general. Re-elected unopposed for Durham in 1727, he spoke at length in February 1730 against a merchants' petition, sponsored by John Barnard (q.v.), to lay open the East Indies trade by redeeming the funds of the East India Company, observing that

> the question was whether the Parliament should take away the privileges purchased by the Company. That by the perusal of the Acts it seemed to him a perpetuity of trade was granted them, but he would not declare it positively as his opinion . . . As to laying the trade open, it is visibly the sense of all nations that an East India trade cannot be carried on but by a company.[2]

In April 1733 he strongly upheld Walpole's objections to hearing the city of London's petition against the excise bill by counsel. On the death of the lord chief justice, Lord Raymond (q.v.), followed by the resignation of the lord chancellor, Lord King, both in 1733,

> Sir Philip Yorke and Mr. Talbot were destined to succeed them. But . . . these two morsels without any addition were not enough to satisfy these two cormorant stomachs . . . Sir Philip Yorke, being first in rank, had certainly a right to the chancellor's seals; but Talbot, who was an excellent Chancery lawyer and knew nothing of the common law, if he was not chancellor would be nothing. Yorke therefore, though fit for both these employments, got the worst, being prevailed upon to accept that of lord chief justice, on the salary being raised from £3,000 to £4,000 a year for life, and £1,000 more paid him out of the chancellor's salary by Lord Talbot. This was a scheme of Sir Robert Walpole's, who . . . was always fertile in expedients and thought these two great and able men of too much consequence to lose or disoblige either.

Hervey describes him as having

> as clear, separating, distinguishing, subtle, and fine parts as ever man had . . . no man's were more forcible. No one could make more of a good cause than Lord Hardwicke, and no one so much of a bad one as Lord Talbot. The one had infinite knowledge, the other infinite ingenuity; they were both excellent but very different . . . both great pleaders, as well as upright judges; and both esteemed by all parties, as much for their temper and integrity as for their knowledge and abilities.[3]

He died 14 Feb. 1737.

¹ HMC 7th Rep. 507. ² HMC Egmont Diary, i. 67–68. ³ Hervey, Mems. 242–3; Yorke, Hardwicke, ii. 501.

R.S.L.

TALBOT, Hon. John (c.1712–56), of Lincoln's Inn.

BRECON   1734–1754
ILCHESTER   1754–23 Sept. 1756

b. c.1712, 3rd s. of Charles, 1st Baron Talbot of Hensol, and bro. of Hon. William Talbot (qq.v.). educ. L. Inn 1734, called 1737. m. (1) 30 May 1737, Henrietta (d. Sept. 1747), da. and coh. of Sir Matthew Decker, 1st Bt. (q.v.), s.p.; (2) 4 Aug. 1748, Catherine, da. of John Chetwynd (q.v.), 2nd Visct. Chetwynd [I], 4s.
Recorder, Brecon 1734–45; puisne justice of Chester 1740–d.; ld. of Trade Dec. 1755–d.

Returned for Brecon on the Tredegar interest, Talbot, a lawyer, voted for the Government in all recorded divisions. In 1742 he was on the court list for the ballot on members of the committee of inquiry into Walpole's Administration, to which he was one of the few Old Whigs elected. Nevertheless, he voted and spoke for the bill indemnifying witnesses who gave evidence to the committee incriminating themselves.[1] Otherwise he continued to act with the Government till his death, 23 Sept. 1756.

¹ Walpole to Mann, 1 Apr. and 20 May 1742.

P.D.G.T.

TALBOT, John (?1717–78), of Lacock Abbey, Wilts.

MARLBOROUGH   1747–1754

b. ?1717, 1st s. of John Ivory Talbot (q.v.) of Lacock Abbey. educ. Westminster June 1726, aged 8; Oriel, Oxf. 8 Feb. 1735, aged 17. m. 19 Dec. 1742, Elizabeth, da. of James Stone of Badbury Manor, Wilts., s.p. suc. fa. 1772.
Sheriff, Wilts. 1763.

Returned unopposed as a Tory on the Bruce interest at Marlborough in 1747, Talbot did not stand again. He died 1778.

R.S.L.

TALBOT, Hon. William (1710–82), of Hensol, Glam.

GLAMORGAN   1734–14 Feb. 1737

b. 16 May 1710, 1st surv. s. of Charles Talbot, 1st Baron Talbot of Hensol, and bro. of Hon. John Talbot (qq.v.). educ. Eton 1725–8; Exeter, Oxf. 1728, D.C.L. 1736; L. Inn 1728. m. 21 Feb. 1734, Mary ('is and will be worth above £70,000'), da. and h. of Rt. Hon. Adam de Cardonnel, M.P., of Bedhampton Park, Hants, 1s. d.v.p. 1da. (separated 1742).[1] suc. fa. 14 Feb. 1737; cr. Earl Talbot 19 Mar. 1761, Baron Dinevor, with a sp. rem. 17 Oct. 1780.
Lord steward of the Household 1761–d.; P.C. 25 Mar. 1761; lord high steward of England at George III's coronation 22 Sept. 1761.

In March 1734 Talbot was elected a trustee of the Georgia Society, of which he became a common councillor from March 1737 to March 1738, when he resigned. Standing as a Whig for Glamorgan in 1734 on the interest of his father, the lord chancellor, whose wife had inherited an estate in the county, he won the seat from the hitherto dominant Tories. In February 1735, when Sir William Wyndham (q.v.) moved that a committee be appointed to examine the ordinances of the navy, Talbot voted against the Administration, 'which was much taken notice of'. After succeeding to the peerage he refused, March 1738, to sign two applications to the Government from the Georgia Society, 'because he would not apply to Sir Robert Walpole for anything'.[2] In 1747 he and Sir Francis Dashwood (q.v.) were commissioned by the Prince of Wales to invite the Tories to 'coalesce and unite' with him;[3] in 1749 they were among the friends for whom Bubb Dodington (q.v.) obtained promises of places on the Prince's accession, Talbot being put down for master of the jewel office;[4] and on George III's accession they were both given high office by Bute, who made Talbot lord steward. On the occasion of his appointment Horace Walpole wrote of him:

> This Lord had long affected a very free spoken kind of patriotism on all occasions. He had some wit, and a little tincture of a disordered understanding, but was better known as a boxer and a man of pleasure than in the light of a statesman. The Duchess of [Beaufort] had been publicly divorced from her husband on his account, and was not the only woman of fashion who had lived with him openly as his mistress. He was strong, well-made, and very comely, but with no air, nor with the manners of a man of quality.[5]

He died 27 Apr. 1782.

[1] N. & Q. (ser. 2) i. 326; Walpole to Mann, 18 July 1742. [2] HMC Egmont Diary, ii. 66, 154, 372, 469, 483-4. [3] Owen, Pelhams, 312-15. [4] Dodington Diary, 6-7; Add. 47097/8. [5] Mems. Geo. III, i. 36.

E.C.

TALBOT, see also IVORY TALBOT

TAYLOR, Charles (?1693-1766), of Maridge, nr. Totnes, Devon.

TOTNES   1747-1754

b. ?1693, 1st s. of Charles Taylor of Ugborough and Totnes, Devon. educ. Wadham, Oxf. 27 Aug. 1709, aged 16; M. Temple 1710, called 1717, bencher 1749. m. 8 Dec. 1725, Ann Pearse, 4s.
    Dep. remembrancer in the court of Exchequer June 1729-d.; dep. recorder, Totnes 1728-36.

Taylor was the son of a Totnes attorney, town clerk of the borough,[1] who bought the neighbouring estate of Maridge in 1699.[2] Returned in 1747 by the corporation against a ministerial candidate, he was classed as Opposition, attaching himself to the Duke of Bedford.[3] He was said by a government agent to have owed his election 'to the recommendation and interest of [Browse] Trist', recorder of the borough,

> which he, Mr. Taylor, his coz. Jonathan Taylor, an alderman then, now dead, and Mr. Alderman Philips were so conscious of that they wrote a letter (I may rather call it a promissory note) and directed it to Mr. Trist and his brother Dyer wherein they take notice of, and all agree that the election of Mr. Charles Taylor was owing to Mr. Trist's interest and therefore did therein promise that they would at any future

election support Mr. Trist and his interest with their votes and interest.[4]

Notwithstanding this promise he stood for re-election in 1754 against Trist, but came out bottom of the poll and did not stand again. He died 6 July 1766.

[1] Account of the Corporation of Totnes in Newcastle (Clumber) mss. [2] Lysons, Devon, ii. 543. [3] John Proby jun. to Bedford, 13 July 1751, Bedford mss. [4] Harris to A. Stert, 15 Dec. 1753, Newcastle (Clumber) mss.

S.R.M.

TAYLOR, Joseph (?1679-1759), of Stanmore, Mdx. and the Inner Temple.

PETERSFIELD   28 Jan.-9 May 1727, 1727-1734

b. ?1679 (aft. 16 Sept.), prob. posth. s. of Joseph Taylor of Queen St., London, merchant and draper, by his 2nd w. Hannah Rolt.[1] educ. M. Temple 1697; I. Temple, called 1707. ?unm. s.p. legit. suc. fa. at birth.
    Clerk of Bridewell and Bethlehem Hospitals 1707-d.

Taylor, a Tory lawyer, was described in 1712 as 'the solicitor, clerk of Bridewell, our Dean's creature',[2] i.e. of Francis Atterbury, then dean of Christ Church, Oxford, and preacher at Bridewell. He acted as counsel to Lord Oxford during his impeachment in 1715; and was also legal adviser and executor to Edward Gibbon's (q.v.) father,[3] on whose interest he contested Petersfield as a Tory unsuccessfully in 1722. Returned for it at a by-election in 1727, but unseated on petition, he was re-elected unopposed at the general election of that year, voting against the Government. On 23 Feb. 1733 he spoke against Walpole's motion to issue £500,000 out of the sinking fund towards the supply for the coming year, saying

> there were some people, the more they owed, the more advantage they made, and the richer they might be reckoned; these were the bankers or goldsmiths of London. But he much doubted if that could possibly be the case of the nation. He believed the more the nation owed the poorer it was and the longer it owed the poorer it would grow.

Consulted by Lord Chesterfield (Philip Dormer Stanhope, q.v.) as to the means of securing payment of a legacy of £50,000 left to his wife by her reputed father, George I, whose son, George II, had suppressed the will, he is said to have achieved this object by threatening to bring the matter before the ecclesiastical court.[4]

The Petersfield seat was taken by Edward Gibbon in 1734 and Taylor did not stand again. He died 19 May 1759, aged about 80, leaving his estate to his 'kinswoman, Mrs. Charlotte Williamson who lives with me', probably the sister of another legatee, William Williamson, 'formerly my clerk and now [1741] at Carolina', who is described by the 1st

Lord Egmont as Taylor's 'bastard son . . . bred an attorney'.[5]

[1] *Lic. Vic.-Gen.* 1660–79 (Harl. Soc. xxiii), 293; PCC 168 King. [2] *HMC Portland*, vii. 87. [3] *Letters of Edw. Gibbon*, i. 232, 236 and app. III. [4] Stuart mss 160/46.; R. Glover, *Mems.* 55–56 n. [5] PCC 217 Arran; *HMC Egmont Diary*, iii. 65.

R.S.L.

TAYLOR, Joseph (?1693–1746), of East and West Ogwell, Denbury, Devon.

ASHBURTON 16 Apr. 1739–1741

b. ?1693, o.s. of Capt. Joseph Taylor, R.N., of Plymouth, Devon by his w. Mary. *educ.* Exeter, Oxf. 24 Oct. 1710, aged 17; M. Temple 1712. *m.* 16 Aug. 1726, Rebecca, da. of John Whitrow of Dartmouth by Mary, da. of Thomas Reynell, M.P., and half-sis. of Richard Reynell (q.v.), 2s. 1da. *suc.* fa. 1733.[1]

In 1734 Taylor contested Ashburton unsuccessfully in conjunction with his wife's uncle, Richard Reynell (q.v.), who died in 1735, leaving his estates to be sold for the benefit of Taylor's wife. Next year he purchased these estates as the 'absolute estate of inheritance—in Devon or elsewhere' which he was required to settle upon her and his eldest son under the terms of his marriage settlement.[2] Returned unopposed for Ashburton in 1739, presumably as an anti-ministerial Whig, he was one of the Members who withdrew from the House before the division on the motion for Walpole's dismissal in February 1741. He did not stand again, dying 6 May 1746.

[1] *Trans. Devon Assoc.* xxxii. 248. [2] PCC 193 Edmunds.

S.R.M.

TAYLOR, William (c.1697–1741), of Middle Hill, Broadway, Worcs.

EVESHAM 1734–1741

b. c.1697, 2nd s. of Francis Taylor of South Littleton, Worcs. by Elizabeth, da. of William Rawlins of Pophills, Warws. *educ.* I. Temple 1722, called 1724; M. Temple 1725. *unm.*
Recorder, Evesham; town clerk, Worcester.

Taylor, a successful lawyer, acquired lands at Middle Hill, Broadway, where he built a mansion in 1724.[1] Returned for Evesham as a Tory in 1734, after contesting it unsuccessfully in 1727, he voted against the Government on the Spanish convention in 1739 and the place bill in 1740. According to a memorandum sent to the Pretender in 1739, he was ready to use his interest in Worcestershire to promote any scheme for the restoration of the Stuarts, was 'very loyal, and does not want courage'.[2] Withdrawing with many other Tories before the division on the motion for Walpole's dismissal,

13 Feb. 1741,[3] he died soon afterwards, 17 Apr., aged 44.

[1] *VCH Worcs.* iv. 40; Nash, *Worcs.* i. 146. [2] Stuart mss 216/111. [3] Coxe, *Walpole*, iii. 563.

E.C.

TEMPEST, John (1710–76), of Sherburn, nr. Durham.

DURHAM 23 Apr. 1742–1768

bap. 28 Apr. 1710, 1st s. of John Tempest, M.P., of Old Durham by Jane, da. and h. of Richard Wharton of Durham. *educ.* Durham; St. John's, Camb. 1728. *m.* 9 May 1738, cos. Frances, da. of Richard Shuttleworth (q.v.) of Gawthorpe, Lancs., 1s. 1da. *suc.* fa. 1738.
Mayor, Hartlepool 1747 and 1758; alderman, Durham 1749.

John Tempest's great-grandfather and father had represented the county of Durham and his grandfather the city, for which he himself was returned unopposed as a Tory at a by-election in 1742. Voting twice against the Administration on the Hanoverians, he was re-elected after a contest in 1747. He died 12 May 1776.

R.S.L.

TEMPLE, Henry, 1st Visct. Palmerston [I] (c.1673–1757), of East Sheen, Surr. and Broadlands, Hants.

EAST GRINSTEAD 1727–1734
BOSSINEY 1734–1741
WEOBLEY 1741–1747

b. c.1673, 2nd but 1st surv. s. of Sir John Temple of East Sheen, Speaker of the Irish House of Commons (yr. bro. of Sir William Temple, 1st Bt.), by Jane, da. of Sir Abraham Yarner, muster-master gen. [I]. *educ.* Eton c.1689–93; King's, Camb. 1693. *m.* (1) 10 June 1703, Anne (*d.* 8 Dec. 1735), da. of Abraham Houblon of Langley, Bucks., gov. of Bank of England, sis. of Sir Richard Houblon, 3s. 2da.; (2) 11 May 1738, Isabella, da. of Sir Francis Gerard, 2nd Bt., wid. of Sir John Fryer, 1st Bt., of Wherwell, Hants, *s.p. suc.* fa. 1705; *cr.* Baron Temple and Visct. Palmerston [I] 12 Mar. 1723.
Jt. chief remembrancer of the court of Exchequer [I] 1715, sole from 1740–d.

'Little Broadbottom Palmerston', as Sir Charles Hanbury Williams (q.v.) called him,[1] came of a distinguished Anglo-Irish family, to whose merits, apparently, rather than to his own, he owed the Irish peerage which was given him at the age of 50.[2] A placeman, who had been granted the reversion of his office when a boy in 1680, provided with seats in different parts of the country, he voted for successive Administrations in all recorded divisions. As a member of the Irish lobby in the House, he took part in discussions on a proposal to remove the duty on Irish yarn in 1731.[3]

He died 10 June 1757, aged 84.

[1] *Works*, ii. 265. [2] Lodge, *Irish Peerage*, v. 243. [3] *HMC Egmont Diary*, i. 161–2.

R.S.L.

TEMPLE, Hon. Richard (c.1726–49), of Broadlands, Hants.

DOWNTON   17 Dec. 1747–8 Aug. 1749

b. c.1726, o. surv. s. of Henry Temple, 1st Visct. Palmerston [I] (q.v.). *educ.* Clare, Camb. 1743. *m.* 18 May 1748, Henrietta, da. of Thomas Pelham (q.v.) of Stanmer, Suss., 1s.

Richard Temple was brought in for Downton at a contested by-election as a government supporter. He died *v.p.* of smallpox 8 Aug. 1749.

R.S.L.

TENCH, Fisher (?1673–1736), of Low Leyton, Essex.

SOUTHWARK   1713–20 Apr. 1714, 3 May 1714–1722

b. ?1673, o. surv. s. of Nathaniel Tench, merchant, of Fenchurch St., London, and Low Leyton, gov. of Bank of England 1699–1701, by Anne, da. of William Fisher, alderman of London, sis. and h. to her bro. Thomas Fisher. *educ.* Sidney Sussex, Camb. 22 July 1690, aged 17; I. Temple 1690. *m.* in or bef. 1697, Elizabeth, da. of Robert Bird of Staple Inn, 5s. 4da. *suc.* fa. 1710; *cr.* Bt. 8 Aug. 1715.

Sheriff, Essex 1711–12.
Director, South Sea Co. 1715–18.

Tench inherited an estate at Low Leyton in Essex, where he built himself a fine house designed by Inigo Jones and decorated by Sir James Thornhill (q.v.). Returned unopposed for Southwark as a Whig in 1715, and created a baronet by George I six months later, he voted for the septennial bill in 1716 but against the Government on Lord Cadogan in 1717. As a director of the South Sea Company he defended the response of the Company in May 1717 to Walpole's scheme for reducing the interest on the national debt. On 22 Jan. 1719 he applied to James Craggs (q.v.) for lottery tickets, explaining that

> I ask not one for myself but for the principal persons in my borough, who as they were hearty friends to me on my election, so are now the most zealous for the present establishment.[1]

In that year he voted for the repeal of the Occasional Conformity and Schism Acts and the peerage bill. He was defeated for Southwark in 1722, and again at a by-election in 1724.

In 1725, Tench was appointed one of the managers of the Charitable Corporation,[2] of which his second son, William, became cashier. When in

1732 Samuel Sandys (q.v.), the chairman of the select committee set up to investigate the Corporation's affairs, 'passed over' Tench as 'not justly to be censured', the 1st Lord Egmont remarked that although Tench left the Corporation when he found evidence of irregularities he 'suffered his son to remain cashier till his death [in 1731] who was guilty of frauds', and that he must have known 'of his son's roguery, because he affirmed in a gentleman's hearing that his son's employment as cashier was worth him £600 a year, though his salary was but £150; and further that Robinson [George, q.v.] gave his son £100 a year, which could not be but that he might abet Robinson in his rogueries'.[3] He did not stand again, and died 31 Oct. 1736.

[1] Stowe 246, f.210. [2] See BOND, Denis, and SUTTON, Sir Robert. [3] *HMC Egmont Diary* i. 270.

E.C.

THISTLETHWAYTE, Alexander (?1717–71), of Southwick, nr. Fareham, Hants.

HAMPSHIRE   8 May 1751–1761

b. ?1717, 1st s. of Alexander Thistlethwayte of Compton Valence, Dorset by Mary, da. and h. of Richard Whithed of Southwick and Norman Court, Hants; bro. of Francis Whithed (q.v.). *educ.* Wadham, Oxf. 27 June 1735, aged 17. *m.* (1) 1741, Catherine, da. of E. Randall of Salisbury, 3da.; (2) Mary Rolls, wid., da. of William Strong of Chalk, Kent. *suc.* fa. 1728; and to Whithed estates on the d. of his yr. bro. Francis 1751.

Thistlethwayte was returned as a Whig for Hampshire on the death of his younger brother, Francis Whithed, in 1751. He and his brother Robert were called 'the brute brothers'[1] by Horace Walpole for their slowness in paying the small annuity left by Francis Whithed to his illegitimate daughter in Florence.

He died 15 Oct. 1771.

[1] Walpole to Mann, 22 Apr. 1751.

P.W.

THISTLETHWAYTE, *see also* **WHITHED**

THOMAS, Sir Edmund, 3rd Bt. (1712–67), of Wenvoe Castle, Glam.

CHIPPENHAM   1741–1754
GLAMORGAN   1761–10 Oct. 1767

bap. 9 Apr. 1712, 1st s. of Sir Edmund Thomas, 2nd Bt., by Mary, da. of John Howe, M.P., of Stowell, Glos. *educ.* Westminster 1725; M. Temple 1728; Queen's, Oxf. 1730. *m.* May 1740, Abigail, da. of Sir Thomas Webster, 1st Bt. (q.v.), of Battle Abbey, Suss., wid. of William Northey and mother of William Northey (qq.v.), 3s. *suc.* fa. 1723.

Groom of the bedchamber to the Prince of Wales

1742–51; clerk of the household to the Princess Dowager 1756–7; jt. treasurer to the Princess 1757–61; ld. of Trade Mar. 1761–Apr. 1763; surveyor gen. of woods north and south of Trent 1763–d.

Thomas's marriage to William Northey's widow gained him influence in Wiltshire, for which his uncle John Howe (q.v.), afterwards Lord Chedworth, sat till 1741. His return, with Edward Bayntun Rolt (q.v.), for Chippenham in that year led to the unsuccessful petition by the defeated court party candidates on which Walpole resigned.[1] Taken into the Prince's service, he at first supported the new Administration, speaking in favour of the motion for continuing British troops in Flanders on 11 Jan. 1744.[2] In 1747 he followed Frederick into opposition, supporting the 2nd Lord Egmont's motion of 7 Feb. 1749 for laying before the House copies of all proposals made for peace with France between 1744 and 1747.

In Egmont's list of future office holders on Frederick's accession Thomas is variously placed as a lord of the Admiralty, second secretary to the Admiralty, groom of the bedchamber with £800 p.a., and auditor to the Queen or Prince. On Frederick's death in 1751 Sir Thomas Webster wrote to Newcastle asking that Thomas, Webster's son-in-law, should be given a place with Prince George,[3] but the King had already shown his disfavour to this.[4] However, he wrote shortly afterwards to his friend Sir John Cust (q.v.):

[I] have (between friends) all the reason in the world to be satisfied of [H.] R. H. ['s] good and gracious intentions towards me, from which I have reason to hope for the earliest good effects.[5]

Later in the year he applied for an interview with Newcastle[6] but he was not given a place till 1756, when he was out of Parliament. He died 10 Oct. 1767.

[1] See BAYNTUN ROLT and CHIPPENHAM. [2] Yorke's parl. jnl. *Parl. Hist.* xiii. 393. [3] Webster to Newcastle, 12 Apr. 1751, Add. 32724, f.231. [4] Newcastle to Pelham, 10 Apr. 1751, Newcastle (Clumber) mss. [5] Thomas to Cust, 11 June 1751, *Recs. Cust Fam.* (ser. 3), p. 143 [6] Thomas to Newcastle, 24 Nov. 1751, Add. 32725, f.435.

R.S.L.

THOMOND, Earl of, *see* **WYNDHAM O'BRIEN**

THOMPSON, Edward (1696–1742), of Marston, Yorks.

YORK 1722–5 July 1742

bap. 26 Feb. 1696, 1st surv. s. of Edward Thompson of Marston by Lucy, da. and h. of Bradwardine Tindal of Brotherton, Yorks. *educ.* New Coll. Oxf. 1714. *m.* (1) 1724, Arabella (*d.* 1734), da. of Edmund Dunch (q.v.) of Little Wittenham, 1da.; (2) 15 May 1737, Mary, da. and coh. of William More of Oswaldkirk, Yorks., 1da.

Commr. of revenue [I] May 1725–d.; ld. of Admiralty Apr. 1741–d.

Edward Thompson was the grandson of Sir Henry Thompson, M.P. York 1673–81 and lord mayor of the city 1663 and 1672, whose brother Edward was also lord mayor of York 1683 and sat for it 1688–98 and 1700. Returned himself for York after a contest in 1722, he seconded a motion that a committee of the House of Commons should examine Christopher Layer in the Tower, 15 Jan. 1723; spoke against the special tax on the property of Papists, 6 May 1723; moved the Address in terms of 'most elaborate flattery', 12 Nov. 1724; and was one of the managers of Lord Chancellor Macclesfield's impeachment 1725.[1] In that year he was appointed a commissioner of Irish revenue, thereafter speaking frequently for the Government, specializing on Irish affairs.[2] In 1734 he managed the Yorkshire petition, spending £60 a day on bringing witnesses to London and maintaining them there.[3] About this time he separated from his wife on account of her intrigue with his intimate friend, Sir George Oxenden (q.v.). He was opposed at York in 1741, but headed the poll, as he wrote to the Duke of Newcastle, 'against the power of the magistracy, the partiality of the returning officers, the fury of the mob, the papist influence, and the rage of faction'.[4] He died, ruined by his election expenditure,[5] 5 July 1742.

[1] *Knatchbull Diary.* [2] *HMC Egmont Diary*, ii. 26, 69, 164. [3] *HMC Carlisle*, 164; W. W. Bean, *Parl. Rep. of Six Northern Counties*, 1113. [4] Add. 32697, f.24. [5] J. Ibbetson to Newcastle, 1 July 1747, Add. 32712, f.7; Sir Thos. Robinson to Pelham, 19 Nov. 1746, Newcastle (Clumber) mss.

R.R.S.

THOMPSON, Sir Peter (1698–1770), of Mill St., Bermondsey, and Market St., Poole, Dorset.

ST. ALBANS 1747–1754

b. 30 Oct. 1698, 3rd s. of Capt. Thomas Thompson of Poole by Amata, da. of John Edwards of Moseley, Hants. *unm. suc.* e. bro. James 1740; kntd. 27 Nov. 1745.

Sheriff, Surr. 1745–6.

Peter Thompson was an eminent merchant in Bermondsey, engaged in the Hamburg and Newfoundland trade.[1] When sheriff of Surrey during the Forty-five, he was knighted on presenting a loyal address to the King. In 1747 he was brought into Parliament at St. Albans as a government supporter by his friend James West (q.v.), the newly appointed recorder of Poole, of which Thompson was a freeman.[2] Though he did not stand again, he developed a considerable political influence in his native town, where he normally resided. In 1751 he supported opposition in the Poole corporation to Joseph Gulston (q.v.).[3] Nine years later he reminded Gulston

of his great neglect of the Poole turnpike bill in June 1757, and desired his reasons for so doing which I expected ere I would promise him my vote and interest . . . In my humble opinion when Members of Parliament don't attend the business of their boroughs in Parliament, they ought to be reminded in decent language or decent scribble.[4]

In 1764 he was described by Thomas Erle Drax (q.v.) as 'the person who has most personal weight' in the borough.[5] A well-known antiquary and collector, fellow of the Royal Society and of the Society of Antiquaries, he formed a valuable library and museum in his house at Poole. He died 31 Oct. 1770.

[1] Hutchins, *Dorset*, i. 49, 66–67. [2] West to Newcastle, 26 June 1747, Add. 32711, f.546. [3] John Masters to Gulston, 21 Oct. 1751, Newcastle (Clumber) mss. [4] Thompson to West, 20 Dec. 1760, West mss at Alscott. [5] Letter dated 26 Mar. 1764, Grenville mss. (JM).

R.S.L.

THOMPSON, Richard (*d.* c.1735), of Coley, Reading, Berks.

READING 15 Mar. 1720–1722, 1727–1734

s. of William Thompson by his w. Elizabeth. *m.* Jane Nicoll,[1] 3da.
Col. in the Jamaica militia; member of the Jamaica assembly; member of the council of Jamaica 1704–11; sheriff, Berks. 1719–20.

Richard Thompson, a Jamaica merchant, was said to be the grandson of Sir Samuel Thompson of Bradfield, Berks., sheriff of London in 1688 and kinsman of the 1st Lord Haversham.[2] Having bought the manors of Whitley and Coley on the outskirts of Reading,[3] he informed the board of Trade in February 1711 that he did not intend to return to Jamaica, where he was replaced on the local council.[4] While serving as sheriff for the county he was returned as a Whig for Reading at an unexpected contested by-election in March 1720. Later in that year he was one of the eight patentees of the Royal Mining Company, formed to develop gold and silver mines in Jamaica, who invested their subscribers' funds in the South Sea Company and went into liquidation. Defeated at Reading in 1722, but successful in 1727, he voted for the Administration on the army in 1732 and the excise bill in 1733. He did not stand in 1734 and was apparently dead by Michaelmas 1736.[5]

[1] Her admon., PCC 14 May 1728. [2] Constance, Lady Russell, *Swallowfield and its Owners*, 233; Le Neve, *Knights* (Harl. Soc. viii), 45. [3] *VCH Berks*. iii. 364–5, 367. [4] *APC Col.* 1680–1720, p. 812; *CSP Col.* 1710–11, pp. 363–4. [5] R. M. Howard, *Longs of Jamaica*, i. 68–70, 72–73.

R.S.L.

THOMPSON, William (?1680–1744), of Humbleton, Yorks.

SCARBOROUGH 1701–1722, 26 Jan. 1730–June 1744

b. ?1680, s. of Francis Thompson, M.P., of York by Arabella, da. and h. of Sir Edmund Alleyn, 2nd Bt., of Hatfield Peverell, Essex. *educ.* St. John's, Oxf. 6 July 1695, aged 15. *unm. suc.* fa. 1693.
Gov. of Scarborough castle 1715–44; warden of the mint 1718–29; commr. of the victualling office 1729–*d.*

William Thompson, a Yorkshire country gentleman, sat throughout his parliamentary career for Scarborough, which his family had represented almost uninterruptedly since 1660, sometimes holding both seats. A Whig, from 1715 he voted regularly with the Government. But when, shortly before the general election of 1722, he asked Walpole's brother, Horace (q.v.), then secretary to the Treasury, to put down one of his constituents for some employment in the local customs when a vacancy occurred,

he sent for me to come to him, being in the secretary's room alone. He told me, Will. Strickland [q.v.] stands for Scarborough, and has already desired to have a minute entered for the next vacancy that happened at or near Scarborough, and they must assist him. I answered with some surprise that I had served in Parliament twenty one years and done my best for his Majesty's interest, therefore was sorry an opposer should be countenanced against me. He replied, No, that 'twas not against me, but [John] Hungerford [q.v.]; that if what I asked was granted it might be making interest for him. My answer was, that he did not want it, so much as myself, for upon a contest between us 10 years ago I carried my election but by one vote and that by the death of some friend, since, the majority of those who choose when vacancies happen among our voters, being more for him than me, had taken care to elect such men as he could depend on: and therefore to wound Hungerford must be through my body, considering how matters stand now there. This I think was the substance of all that's material that passed between us; but at my going away he said he would let the board know what I requested, but seeing every day how much my opposer was caressed, I went no more.[1]

He did not stand in 1722 but was re-elected in 1730, continuing to support the Government as a placeman till his death in June 1744.

[1] Undated and presumably addressed to Sunderland's secretary as it began 'Sir', Sunderland (Blenheim) mss.

R.R.S.

THOMPSON, William (?1676–1739), of the Middle Temple.

ORFORD 29 Jan. 1709–1710
IPSWICH 1713–1 Apr. 1714, 1715–15 Nov. 1729

b. ?1676, 2nd s. of Sir William Thompson, serjeant at law of the Middle Temple, by Mary Stephens of Bermondsey.[1] *educ.* Brentwood g. s., Essex; Trinity,

Camb. 25 Apr. 1691, aged 14; M. Temple 1688, called 1698; L. Inn 1719. *m.* (1) lic. 16 Feb. 1701, Joyce Brent, wid., of St. Clement's Danes, Mdx., *s.p.*; (2) 1711, Julia, da. of Sir Christopher Conyers, 2nd Bt., wid. of Sir William Blackett, 1st Bt., M.P., of Newcastle-upon-Tyne, *s.p.* Kntd. 18 July 1715.

Recorder, Ipswich 1707–*d.*, and of London 1715–*d.*; solicitor-gen. 24 Jan. 1717–17 Mar. 1720; cursitor baron of the Exchequer 1726–9; serjeant-at-law 1729; baron of the Exchequer 1729–*d.*

Thompson was recorder of Ipswich, which he represented for most of his parliamentary career, and of London, for which he defeated Serjeant Pengelly (q.v.). One of the managers of the impeachment of Sacheverell in 1709 and of Lord Wintoun in 1716, he was appointed solicitor-general in 1717, but was dismissed in 1720 for bringing against the attorney-general, Nicholas Lechmere (q.v.), charges of corruption which the House of Commons, after an inquiry, resolved to be 'malicious, false, scandalous and utterly groundless'.[2] Re-elected unopposed in 1722, he spoke 'with great vehemence' against the Pretender's declaration, 10 Nov. 1722, following this up with speeches supporting the special tax on Papists, 13 Nov., and the bill of pains and penalties against one of the Atterbury conspirators, 22 Mar. 1723. In 1724 he was granted a patent giving him precedence in the courts next to the law officers of the Crown and a pension of £1,200 a year.[3] In 1725, after a speech by Pulteney attacking pensions to Members of Parliament, Thompson

> owned he had a pension and commended himself much for his merits and services for which he had it, and that the ministers knew he had deserved it of his Majesty: the House made a jest of him and the Speaker took him down, by saying gentlemen should neither make personal reflections nor personal commendations in the course of their debates (it seems his merit was discovering to the ministers what his son-in-law, Sir W. Blackett [q.v.] told him about the rebellion when it was said the cash was lodged in his hands and the hanging three poor young lads at the riot at Read's Mug house).[4]

Next year he accepted a minor post in the court of Exchequer. He vacated his seat in 1729 on being promoted to be a baron of the Exchequer and died 27 Oct. 1739.

[1] *Marriage Licences, Vic. Gen. 1660–79* (Harl. Soc. xxiii), 149; PCC 103 Bond. [2] *CJ*, xix. 305–10. [3] Foss, *Judges of England*, viii. 175. [4] *Knatchbull Diary*, 9 Apr. 1725; for the riot see *Pol. State*, xii. 221 et seq.

R.R.S.

THORNHAGH, John (c.1721–87), of Osberton and Shireoaks, Notts. and South Kelsey, Lincs.

Nottinghamshire 1747–1774

b. c.1721, o. surv. s. of St. Andrew Thornhagh of Osberton by Letitia, da. of Sir Edward Ayscough of

Stallingborough and South Kelsey, Lincs. *educ.* Queens', Camb. 1739. *m.* 23 July 1744, Arabella, da. of Sir George Savile, 7th Bt. (q.v.), sis. and coh. of Sir George Savile, 8th Bt., M.P., 3da. *suc.* fa. 1742, and to Shireoaks under will of his god-fa. Sir Thomas Hewett 1756, and took name of Hewett.

Thornhagh came of a wealthy family of Whig country gentlemen. His grandfather represented East Retford on his own interest from 1688–1705 and the county from 1705–10. Of his father, who never stood but played an influential part in county politics, Newcastle wrote: 'My opinion has always been, ever since I knew Nottinghamshire, that if Mr. Thornhagh could be prevailed upon to stand, he would be the most proper person'.[1] With the support of both parties he was unanimously chosen in 1747 to stand for Nottinghamshire, which he represented without a contest for twenty-seven years. Classed as a government supporter in 1747, throughout his career he remained connected with Newcastle, both in national and in county politics. Independent and disinterested, he often sought favours for his constituents, but never for himself.[2]

He died 17 May 1787.

[1] Newcastle to Duke of Kingston, 1 July 1738, Add. 32691, f.216. [2] Add. 32976, ff.117, 128–9.

R.R.S.

THORNHILL, Sir James (c.1675–1734), of Thornhill, Dorset.

Weymouth and Melcombe Regis 1722–1734

b. c.1675, s. of Walter Thornhill of Wareham by Mary, da. of Col. William Sydenham, gov. of Weymouth castle. *m.* Judith, 1s. 1da. who m. William Hogarth. Kntd. 2 May 1720.

King's history painter 1720–*d.*; serjeant-painter 1720–32.

Thornhill was born at Weymouth of an ancient Dorset family. Having made a fortune by his painting, he purchased and re-built his ancestral seat at Thornhill. Returned without opposition for Weymouth, to whose church he presented an altarpiece painted by himself, he voted regularly with the Government. He died 13 May 1734, acclaimed as 'the greatest history painter this kingdom ever produced'.[1]

[1] *Gent. Mag.* 1734, pp. 174–5.

R.R.S.

THORNTON, William (?1712–69), of Cattal, nr. York.

York 1747–1754, 1 Dec. 1758–1761

b. ?1712, s. of Sir William Thornton of York by his w. Elizabeth. *educ.* Mr. Jackson's sch., York; St. John's, Camb. 27 Mar. 1731, aged 18. *m.* (1) Isabella (*d.* 25 Feb. 1748), o. da. of William Norton of Sawley,

Yorks.;[1] (2) 11 July 1749, Mary, da. of John Myster of Epsom, Surr., 1s. 1da.

Thornton, whose father had been knighted for presenting an address from Yorkshire on the Union in 1707, raised at his own expense a company of foot in the Forty-five, taking part in the battle of Falkirk. Returned as a government supporter for York in 1747, he went into opposition in 1751, speaking against the Administration on the navy estimates, 23 Nov., the army, 28 Nov., and the land tax, 5 Dec.[2] In 1752 he published a pamphlet entitled *The Counterpoise: being thoughts on a militia and a standing army*, following this by a bill for improving the militia, which did not get beyond the report stage.[3] He did not stand in 1754 and died 10 July 1769.

[1] M.I. at Kirk Deighton, ex inf. K. Workman. [2] Walpole, *Mems. Geo. II*, i. 213, 218. [3] C. Collyer, 'The Rockinghams and Yorkshire Politics, 1742–61', *Thoresby Misc.* xii (1954), 371–2.

R.R.S.

THRALE, Ralph (c.1698–1758), of Streatham, Surr.

SOUTHWARK   1741–1747

b. c.1698, s. of Ralph Thrale of Offley, Herts. by Anne, sis. of Edmund Halsey (q.v.). *m.*, 1s. (Henry Thrale, M.P.), 3da.
      Brewers' Co. 1732, master 1748; sheriff, Surr. 1733–4.

The son of 'a hardworking man at Offley', Thrale was brought to London by his uncle, Edmund Halsey, the owner of the Anchor brewery at Southwark, who 'said he would make a man of him, and did so but . . . treated him very roughly', making him work 'at six shillings a week for twenty years'. He soon 'made himself so useful . . . that the weight of the business fell entirely on him', and he was expected to succeed to the brewery.[1] But he fell out with his uncle by marrying 'a wench that Halsey wanted to have for his own pleasure', and was cut off.[2] On Halsey's death in 1729, the Anchor brewery was put up for sale. According to Mrs. Piozzi, Thrale's daughter-in-law,

> to find a purchaser for so large a property was a difficult matter, and after some time, it was suggested that it would be advisable to treat with Thrale, a sensible, active, honest man, who had been long employed in the house, and to transfer the whole to him for £30,000, security being taken upon the property. This was accordingly settled. In eleven years Thrale paid the purchase money. He acquired a large fortune. But what was most remarkable was the liberality with which he used his riches.[3]

Returned as an opposition Whig for Southwark, the brewers' constituency, he voted against the Government on the chairman of the elections committee in 1741 and on the Hanoverians in 1744,

was absent from other recorded divisions, did not stand again, and died 8 Apr. 1758.

[1] Mrs. Piozzi, *Autobiog.* i. 7–9. [2] K. C. Balderston, *Thraliana*, i. 299–300. [3] Mrs. Piozzi, loc. cit.

E.C.

THURSBY, *see* **HARVEY THURSBY**

TILSON, Christopher (1670–1742), of St. Margaret's, Westminster, and Hampton Poyle, Oxon.

CRICKLADE   1727–1734

b. 24 Jan. 1670, s. of Nathaniel Tilson of London. *educ.* St. Paul's. *m.* (1) bef. 1706, Mary (*d.* 30 Aug. 1737), da. of George Humble, sis. of Sir John Humble, 4th Bt.; (2) *d.* Sept. 1739, *s.p.*
      Clerk of the Treasury Feb. 1685–*d.*; clerk of commrs. of appeal in the excise (£100 p.a.) Apr. 1693; receiver gen. of crown land revenues 1699.[1]

Tilson, who spent nearly 58 years at the Treasury, was the brother of George Tilson,[2] under-secretary of state for the northern department 1710–38, and grandson of Henry Tilson, bishop of Elphin, in Ireland. Buying the manor of Hampton Poyle in 1723,[3] he was returned for Cricklade in 1727, voting with the Administration, but did not stand again. He was chosen one of the directors of the Chelsea Waterworks in 1730 and deputy governor in 1733.[4] Questioned on 30 June 1742 by the secret committee of the House of Commons as to the sums issued for secret service while Walpole was at the Treasury, he replied

> that he looked on all these monies to be of the same nature, that they are all without account, except as to what related to the solicitor of the Treasury, nor is there any entry in the Treasury of the application of any of these sums of money.[5]

On his death, 25 Aug. 1742, Horace Walpole wrote that 'old Tilson . . . was so much tormented' by the secret committee on Walpole that 'it turned his brain and he is dead'.[6]

[1] M. I. at Hampton Poyle; *HMC Lords* n.s. vi. 398. [2] PCC 259 Trenley. [3] *VCH Oxon.* vi. 5, 162. [4] *HMC Egmont Diary*, i. 90, 345. [5] *CJ*, xxiv. 246. [6] To Mann, 28 Aug. 1742.

R.S.L.

TONSON, Richard (*d.* 1772), of Water Oakley, nr. Windsor, Berks.

WALLINGFORD   1747–1754
NEW WINDSOR   18 May 1768–9 Oct. 1772

2nd s. of Jacob Tonson, publisher, by a da. of Samuel Hoole of London, bookseller. *suc.* bro. Jacob 1767. *unm.*

The great-nephew of Jacob Tonson, Dryden's publisher and secretary of the Kit-Cat Club, Tonson was the last of a family of wealthy booksellers. He himself was merely a sleeping partner in the business, living the life of a country gentleman at his Berkshire seat, which had come to him from his father and to which he added a gallery for Kit-Cat portraits inherited from his elder brother.[1] Brought in for Wallingford by Chauncy Townsend (q.v) in 1747, he was classed as a government supporter. His recorded political activities are nil. He did not stand again till 1768, dying 9 Oct. 1772.

[1] Nichols, *Lit. Anecs.* i. 292–9.

E.C.

TOWER, Christopher (?1694–1771), of Hunts-moor Park, Bucks.

LANCASTER 1 May 1727–1734
AYLESBURY 1734–1741
BOSSINEY 11 Dec. 1741–18 Mar. 1742

b. ?1694, 1st s. of Christopher Tower of Huntsmoor Park, dep. collector of customs for London, by his 1st w. Elizabeth, da. of Richard Hale of New Windsor; bro. of Thomas Tower (q.v.). *educ.* Trinity, Oxf. 7 May 1712, aged 17. *m.* (1) 1719, Jane (*d.* 20 Nov. 1739), 2nd da. of William Proctor of Epsom, Surr., 2da. of whom Jane m. her cos. Sir William Beauchamp Proctor, 1st Bt. (q.v.); (2) 25 Oct. 1746, Jane, 1st da. and coh. of George Tash of Delaford, 1s. *suc.* fa. 1728.

Director, Bank of England 1734–40 (with statutory intervals).

Christopher Tower's paternal grandparents came from Wyredale and Tatham, near Lancaster,[1] where he was returned as a Whig at a by-election in 1727, heading the poll at the ensuing general election. In June 1732, he and his brother Thomas, both consistent government supporters, were granted the reversion of the two lucrative posts of auditor of the imprest,[2] which they never enjoyed. With his brother, in February 1734, he absented himself from the division on a place bill, of which he approved, to avoid disobliging the ministry. Having succeeded his father at Huntsmoor, he transferred to Aylesbury for the general election of 1734. A trustee of the Georgia Society, he did not become a common councilman till March 1738, when he began to attend board meetings regularly. Like his brother he came to be regarded by the board as one of Walpole's 'creatures', absenting himself for political reasons from an important meeting in December 1740, soon after which he seems to have given up attending.[3] Put up by the Administration for Bossiney at the general election that year, he was defeated at the poll but was returned on petition in time to vote on 16 Dec. 1741 for Walpole's candidate for chairman of the elections committee. Unseated on a further petition after Walpole's fall, he did not stand again and died 26 Sept. 1771.

[1] Lipscomb, *Bucks.* iv. 530. [2] *Cal. Treas. Bks. and Pprs.* 1731–4, p. 356. [3] *HMC Egmont Diary*, ii. 23, 37, 471; iii. 168, 194.

R.S.L.

TOWER, Thomas (?1698–1778), of Weald House, Essex, and the Inner Temple.

WAREHAM 26 Feb. 1729–1734
WALLINGFORD 1734–1741

b. ?1698, 2nd s. of Christopher Tower and yr. bro. of Christopher Tower (q.v.). *educ.* Harrow c.1711; Trinity, Oxf. 22 May 1717, aged 18; I. Temple 1717, called 1722, bencher 1751. *unm. suc.* fa. at Mansfield, Bucks., and mat. uncle Richard Hale in his Bucks. and Essex estates, both in 1728;[1] bought Weald House 1759.

Original trustee and common councilman for Georgia 1732; sheriff, Essex 1760.

Thomas Tower, a lawyer, entered Parliament soon after succeeding to his father's and uncle's estates. A consistent government supporter, closely attached to Walpole, to whose recommendation he owed his Wareham and probably his Wallingford seats, he absented himself, together with his brother, Christopher, from the division on a place bill in 1734 because, though approving it, they 'were not willing to disoblige the ministry', who were warmly against it. After serving on the gaols committee of the House of Commons, he became for some years a keen member of the governing board of the Georgia Society. When at the beginning of 1739 Walpole seemed to be planning to avoid war with Spain by giving up Georgia, Tower's intimacy with Walpole gave rise to suspicions among his colleagues on the board that 'he was not so zealous and true to the trust as he ought to be'.

> They thought Mr. Tower would, to oblige Sir Robert, who never cared for our colony, hazard the colony itself, and acquaint him with all our proceedings in too open a manner, and saw him so constantly vote for the measures of the ministry, that it lost us the favour of that party which opposed the Court.

These suspicions were confirmed when he with other of 'Sir Robert Walpole's creatures' absented themselves from a meeting to approve a publication by the board showing the value of Georgia to Great Britain, in case they should be expected to give it 'a better support, either with Sir Robert or in the House, than they care to give'. A few days later, when the time came to prepare the annual petition to Parliament for a grant-in-aid of the colony, he is said to have 'slunk away' to avoid being asked to present the petition to Walpole.[2] Soon after this he seems to have given up attending. He did not stand again, and died 2 Sept. 1778.

[1] *VCH Bucks.* iii. 291, 323. [2] *HMC Egmont Diary*, i. 45; ii. 37; iii. 20–21, 168–9.

R.S.L.

TOWNSEND, Chauncy (1708–70), of Austin Friars, London.

WESTBURY   16 Mar. 1748–1768
WIGTOWN BURGHS   23 Dec. 1768–28 Mar. 1770

bap. 23 Feb. 1708,[1] o.s. of Jonathan Townsend, London brewer, by Elizabeth, da. of Richard Chauncy, London merchant and Welsh mining adventurer. *m.* c.1730, Bridget, da. of James Phipps of Westbury, Wilts., gov. of Cape Coast castle, 7s. 5da.[2] *suc.* fa. 1710.

Chauncy Townsend, who lost his father at the age of two, was apprenticed to Richard Chauncy & Co., linen-drapers, his maternal grandfather's business. Admitted to the Mercers' Company in 1730,[3] he appears in commercial directories up to 1740 as a linen-draper, subsequently as a merchant. He had extensive connexions in America, about which he wrote to the Duke of Newcastle, 28 Mar. 1740: 'I correspond and am conversant with the most considerable persons of New England which has given me a considerable knowledge of that Government'.[4] He obtained contracts for provisioning the garrison of Ruatan, off Honduras, and troops in Nova Scotia in 1744;[5] had a further contract for supplying coal to Louisbourg in 1747;[6] and before 1750 was working coalmines in the Swansea district, which he greatly extended, employing mining engineers.[7] In the early '40s he appears to have lent £4,000 to Frederick, Prince of Wales.[8]

Townsend was connected with Wallingford and Westbury through his cousin, Joseph Townsend (q.v.), who represented Wallingford 1740–1 and Westbury 1741–7, and through his wife, whose brother had stood unsuccessfully for Westbury. According to his own account, 'in 1747 . . . on my assuring Mr. Pelham I could carry both [boroughs] with his support he desired me to undertake them and if I carried them he would help me out to my satisfaction'.[9] He was defeated but was returned on petition. In the House, as a holder of government contracts, he consistently supported the Administration under George II. He died 28 Mar. 1770.

[1] Freshfield, *Reg. Book of the Parish of St. Christopher-le-Stocks*, 37. [2] *Misc. Gen. et Her.* (n. s.) iv. 125–31. [3] *N. & Q.* (ser. 11), v. 2. [4] Add. 32693, f. 121. [5] *Cal. Treas. Bks. and Pprs.* 1742–5, pp. 472–74, 517–27. [6] T29/31. [7] C. Wilkins, *S. Wales Coal Trade*, 48–49. [8] Daniel Avery to Lord Gage, 20 Feb. 1749, Newcastle (Clumber) mss. [9] To James West (q.v.), 26 June 1754, Add. 32735, f. 573.

R.S.L.

TOWNSEND, Isaac (c.1685–1765), of Old Windsor, Berks. and Thorpe, Surr.

PORTSMOUTH   28 Dec. 1744–1754
ROCHESTER   28 Mar. 1757–21 Nov. 1765

b. c.1685, nephew of Sir Isaac Townsend, commr. of the navy, of Portsmouth. *m.* Elizabeth, da. of William Larcum, surgeon, of Richmond, 1s. 1da.

Entered R.N. c.1698, capt. 1720, r.-adm. 1744, v.-adm. 1746, adm. 1747; gov. Greenwich Hospital 1754–*d.*; e. bro. of Trinity House 1751.

On attaining flag rank after some forty years' service, Townsend was returned for Portsmouth on the Admiralty interest in 1744. In 1745 he took or destroyed 30 French merchantmen bound from Europe for Martinique, driving ashore their convoy of two men of war.[1] Absent from the division on the Hanoverians in 1746, he was classed as a government supporter in 1747. He died 21 Nov. 1765.

[1] *Gent. Mag.* 1745, p. 628.

P.W.

TOWNSEND, Joseph (by 1704–63), of Honington, Warws.

WALLINGFORD   22 Dec. 1740–1741
WESTBURY   1741–1747
WALLINGFORD   1747–1754

b. bef. 6 May 1704,[1] 1st s. (but not h.) of Joseph Townsend (*d.* 1728) of Winchester St., London, brewer, by his 1st w., Mary ?Shipsey.[2] *m.* 11 Oct. 1737, Judith, da. and coh. of John Gore (q.v.) of Bush Hill, Mdx. *suc.* his yr. half-bro. Thomas Beacon Townsend 1737.

Townsend, whose father by 'long experience of his temper and behaviour' left him only an annuity of £200, a 'very reasonable provision . . . for a person of no trade or employment', was through his younger brother's death enabled to marry and to buy the Honington estate in 1737.[3] Chauncy Townsend (q.v.) was his cousin, James Oswald (q.v.) his brother-in-law, and, through his wife's family, he had other important parliamentary connexions. He entered Parliament for Wallingford at a contested by-election in 1740, apparently as a last minute nominee of Walpole's;[4] in 1741 transferred to Westbury, where Chauncy Townsend had an interest; and went back to Wallingford in 1747, when Chauncy replaced him at Westbury. Voting with the Administration in all recorded divisions, he was classed as an Old Whig in 1746 and a government supporter in 1747.

After 1747 Townsend's health declined.[5] He did not stand again, and died 8 July 1763.

[1] PCC 365 Brook. [2] See *Misc. Gen. et Her.* (n. s.) iv. 125. [3] *VCH Warws.* v. 94. [4] Robt. Hucks to Walpole, 5 Feb. 1741, Cholmondeley (Houghton) mss. [5] Add. 32735, f. 573.

R.S.L.

TOWNSHEND, Hon. Charles (1700–64).

GREAT YARMOUTH   1722–22 May 1723

b. 11 July 1700, 1st s. of Charles Townshend, 2nd Visct. Townshend, by his 1st w. Elizabeth, da. of

Thomas Pelham, M.P., 1st Baron Pelham, half-sis. of the Duke of Newcastle and Henry Pelham (q.v.); bro. of Hon. Thomas, William, and Roger Townshend (qq.v.). *educ.* Eton; King's, Camb. 1718; Grand Tour.[1] *m.* 29 May 1723, Etheldreda, da. and h. of Edward Harrison (q.v.) of Balls Park, Herts., niece of George Harrison (q.v.), 4s. 1da. *summ.* to Lords in his fa.'s barony of Townshend of Lynn Regis (but styled Lord Lynn) 22 May 1723; *suc.* fa. as 3rd Visct. 21 June 1738.

Ld. of the bedchamber 1723–7; master of the jewel office 1730–9; ld. lt. and custos rot. Norf. 1730–8.

The son of a distinguished father, and the father of a still more famous son, Townshend himself played little part in national politics. He was returned in 1722 on his family's interest for Yarmouth but soon vacated his seat on being raised to the House of Lords. After succeeding his father as 3rd Viscount he proved a source of dissension in Norfolk politics. On 5 Sept. 1747 Thomas Coke (q.v.), Earl of Leicester, who had managed Norfolk for Walpole, wrote to Hardwicke (Philip Yorke, q.v.):

It grieves me much to see the Whig interest in this county in so very bad a way, but I must take share to myself, for Lord Townshend's son [George, q.v.] could not have had the least chance to have been representative here had I not put him into the place of my own son [Edward Coke, q.v.], which I did hoping thereby to establish the Whig interest the more by making his family, which for some time had not stirred, active on the Whig cause; but it has taken the contrary effect, he has chiefly applied to the Tories. Mr. Townshend, his son, when here never visited but the Tories, and now his Lordship recommends as justice of the peace . . . one of the most distinguished Tories. . . . In Lord Orford's [Robert Walpole] time with great reluctance he, at the request of the principal Whig gentlemen, got Lord Townshend removed from being lord lieutenant for his desire to bring in Tory justices, and will your Lordship now, contrary to the desire of the present lord lieutenant, and I will venture to say of the principal Whig gentlemen of the county, let him introduce them into the commission now?[2]

He died 12 Mar. 1764.

[1] Ex inf. Prof. J. H. Plumb. [2] Add. 35602 f. 314.

R.R.S.

TOWNSHEND, Hon. Charles (1725–67), of Adderbury, Oxon.

GREAT YARMOUTH	1747–Nov. 1756
SALTASH	14 Dec. 1756–1761
HARWICH	1761–4 Sept. 1767

b. 27 Aug. 1725, 2nd s. of Hon. Charles Townshend (q.v., afterwards 3rd Visct. Townshend, *d.* 1764) and bro. of Hon. George Townshend (q.v.). *educ.* Clare, Camb. 1742; Leyden 1745–6; L. Inn 1742, called 1747. *m.* 18 Sept. 1755, Lady Caroline Campbell, da. and coh. of John, 2nd Duke of Argyll [S] and 1st Duke of Greenwich, wid. of Francis Scott, Lord Dalkeith (q.v.) and mother of Henry Scott, 3rd Duke of Buccleuch [S], 2s. *d.v.m.* 1da. She was *cr.* 19 Aug. 1767, Baroness of Greenwich.

Ld. of Trade June 1749–Apr. 1754, of Admiralty Apr. 1754–Dec. 1755; treasurer of the chamber Nov. 1756–Mar. 1761; sec. at war Mar. 1761–Dec. 1762; first ld. of Trade Feb.–Apr. 1763; paymaster gen. May 1765–July 1766; chancellor of the Exchequer July 1766–*d.*

Returned for Yarmouth in 1747 at the age of 21, Charles Townshend lost no time in pressing his claim for promotion. In April 1748 he told his father that he hoped to relieve him of part of the burden of maintaining him by acquiring 'a creditable post at the board of Trade', or, better still, at the Admiralty, which 'would strengthen and establish immovably' the Townshend interest at Yarmouth. In December he asked Pelham for a seat on the Admiralty board,[1] but had to content himself with the board of Trade, where he 'distinguished himself on affairs of trade and in drawing plans and papers'.[2] He moved the Address on 16 Nov. 1749. On 8 Mar. 1753, in a debate on Jamaica, he argued in favour of making the island bear the cost of its own defence works, maintaining that it was wrong that the mother country should be sacrificed to the interests of the colonies.[3] He attacked Hardwicke's clandestine marriage bill two months later, when Horace Walpole describes him as

a young man of unbounded ambition, of exceeding application, and, as it now appeared, of abilities capable of satisfying that ambition . . . His figure was tall and advantageous, his action vehement, his voice loud, his laugh louder . . . He spoke long and with much wit, and drew a picture, with much humour . . . of his own situation as the younger son of a capricious father, who had already debarred his son from an advantageous match.[4]

Horace Walpole concluded that Charles Townshend 'seemed marked by nature' to become one of the leaders of the Government of his country. Thus before the end of his first Parliament he had developed and displayed the views and qualities which produced the disastrous Townshend duties a few months before his premature death, 4 Sept. 1767.

[1] *HMC Townshend*, 363, 366–7. [2] Walpole, *Mems. Geo. II*, i. 340. [3] AECP Angl. 436, ff. 10–15. [4] Walpole, loc. cit.

R.R.S.

TOWNSHEND, Hon. George (1724–1807), of Raynham, Norf.

NORFOLK	1747–12 Mar. 1764

b. 28 Feb. 1724, 1st s. of Hon. Charles Townshend (q.v., afterwards 3rd Visct. Townshend, *d.* 1764) and bro. of Hon. Charles Townshend (q.v.). *educ.* Eton c.1740; St. John's, Camb. 1741; Grand Tour. *m.* (1) 19 Dec. 1751, Lady Charlotte Compton, *s.j.*

Baroness Ferrers (*d.* 14 Sept. 1770), da. of James, 5th Earl of Northampton, 4s. 4da.; (2) 19 May 1773, Anne, da. of Sir William Montgomery, 1st Bt., of Magpie Hill, Tweeddale, 2s. 4da. *suc.* fa. as 4th Visct. 12 Mar. 1764; *cr.* Mq. Townshend 31 Oct. 1787.

Joined army 1743; capt. 7 Drag. Gds. Apr. 1745, 20 Ft. May 1745; a.-d.-c. to Duke of Cumberland Feb. 1746–8; capt. and lt.-col. 1 Ft. Gds. Feb. 1748–Nov. 1750 (ret.); col. May 1758; col. 64 Ft. June–Dec. 1759, 28 Ft. Oct. 1759–July 1773; P.C. 2 Dec. 1760; maj.-gen. 1761; lt.-gen. of the Ordnance Apr. 1763–Aug. 1767; ld. lt. [I] Aug. 1767–Sept. 1772; lt.-gen. 1770; master-gen. of the Ordnance Oct. 1772–Mar. 1782, Apr.–Dec. 1783; col. 2 Drag. Gds. 1773–*d.*; gen. 1782; ld. lt. Norf. 1792–*d.*; f.m. 1796.

Townshend joined the army in Flanders as a volunteer in the summer of 1743. According to an army officer he was 'very good-natured as well as droll' and 'behaved with a good deal of spirit at the battle' of Dettingen, but

> does not like the army and is determined not to be of the profession, and says his father sent him only that he may get a commission, and so not need an allowance.[1]

Commissioned two years later, he became aide-de-camp to the Duke of Cumberland. In 1747, while serving in Flanders, he was put up by his father for Norfolk, which he represented, unopposed, on a compromise with the Tories, till he succeeded to the title. Horace Walpole describes him as

> a very particular young man, who, with much oddness, some humour, no knowledge, great fickleness, greater want of judgement, and with still more disposition to ridicule, had once or twice promised to make a good speaker.

He is said to have been placed by his uncles, the Pelhams, with the Duke of Cumberland to counteract the influence of his mother, who hated Cumberland. But the treatment was unsuccessful, for his first recorded speech on the mutiny bill, in February 1749, was in support of the attack made on Cumberland by another young officer, Richard Lyttelton (q.v.), whose charges against the Duke 'were the more believed by the defection of . . . one of his aide-de-camps'. On the mutiny bill next year he moved that commanding officers should be deprived of the power of punishing non-commissioned officers and private soldiers, which should be vested exclusively in courts martial. The motion, a scarcely veiled attack on Cumberland, supported by the Prince of Wales's party, was defeated. At the end of 1750 he resigned from the army, apparently on being refused leave to stay in Norfolk to cultivate the Whig interest there.[2] Connecting himself with the Prince of Wales, he moved on 4 Mar. 1751 'a long, inflammatory' motion,[3] drafted for him by Frederick's chief adviser, Lord Egmont, on the case of General Anstruther (q.v.). On the Prince's death less than three weeks later, he made

his peace with Pelham, but not with Cumberland, 'drawing caricatures of him and his court',[4] as well as of other politicians. The first great English caricaturist, he died 14 Sept. 1807.

[1] *HMC Astley*, 271, 309. [2] Walpole, *Mems. Geo. II*, i. 39–40; Walpole to Mann, 4 Mar. 1749. [3] *Dodington Diary*, 94–95, 113–14. [4] *Mems. Geo. II*, loc. cit.

R.R.S.

TOWNSHEND, Hon. Horatio (c.1683–1751), of New Ormond St., London.

GREAT YARMOUTH 1715–1722
HEYTESBURY 1727–1734

b. c.1683, 3rd s. of Horatio Townshend, M.P., 1st Visct. Townshend, by his 2nd w. Mary, da. of Sir Joseph Ashe, 1st Bt., M.P., of Twickenham, Mdx.; bro. of Charles, 2nd Visct. Townshend. *educ.* Eton 1692–8. *m.* by 1720, Alice, da. of John Starkie of Huntroyde, Lancs., 1s. 3da.

Director, South Sea Co. 1715–18, Bank of England 1722–32 (with statutory intervals), dep. gov. 1732–3, gov. 1733–5, director 1735–6; commr. of excise 1735–*d.*

As the brother of the 2nd Lord Townshend, Horatio Townshend, a wealthy London merchant, played a part in Norfolk politics under Anne.[1] Returned in 1715 on the Walpole-Townshend interest as a Whig for Great Yarmouth, he was replaced there by his nephew, Charles, later 3rd Visct. Townshend (q.v.) in 1722, but brought in again in 1727 for Heytesbury by his kinsman Edward Ashe (q.v.), supporting the Administration in all recorded divisions, except on the peerage bill in 1719, which he opposed. He did not stand in 1734 but in December 1735 was given a lucrative place which he held till his death, 4 Oct. 1751.

[1] Plumb, *Walpole*, i. 102–3, 164.

R.S.L.

TOWNSHEND, Hon. Roger (1708–60).

GREAT YARMOUTH 14 Feb. 1738–1747
EYE 1747–Feb. 1748

b. 5 June 1708, 4th s. of Charles, 2nd Visct. Townshend, and bro. of Hon. Charles, Thomas and William Townshend (qq.v.). *educ.* Eton. *unm.*

Cornet 4 Hussars 1726; capt. 3 Drag. Gds. 1729; capt. and lt.-col. 1 Ft. Gds. 1741; a.-d.-c. to the King at Dettingen 1743; gov. Yarmouth castle 1745–*d.*; receiver gen. of customs 1748–*d.*

Townshend voted with the Opposition in his first Parliament but thereafter with the Administration. Originally returned on his family's interest at Yarmouth, he transferred in 1747 to Lord Cornwallis's pocket borough of Eye, vacating his seat next year on being appointed to an office disqualifying him from the House of Commons. He died 7 Aug. 1760.

R.R.S.

TOWNSHEND, Hon. Thomas (1701–80), of Frognal, Kent.

WINCHELSEA 1 Nov. 1722–1727
CAMBRIDGE UNIVERSITY 1727–1774

b. 2 June 1701, 2nd s. of Charles, 2nd Visct. Townshend, and bro. of Hon. Charles, William and Roger Townshend (qq.v.). *educ.* Eton 1718; King's, Camb. 1720; L. Inn 1720. *m.* 2 May 1730, Albinia (*d.* 7 Sept. 1739), da. of John Selwyn (q.v.) of Matson, Glos., 3s. 2da.
Under-sec. of state to his fa. 1724–30; teller of the Exchequer 1727–*d.*; sec. to ld. lt. [I] 1739–45.

Son of Walpole's brother-in-law and nephew of the Pelhams, Thomas Townshend served as private secretary and under-secretary to his father, who procured him a life sinecure worth at the time of his death nearly £7,000 a year.[1] After sitting for Winchelsea, he was returned in 1727 for both Hastings and Cambridge University, choosing the latter, which he represented for the next forty-seven years, after 1734 without opposition. He and his fellow member, Edward Finch, founded the Members' prizes in 1752.

Townshend went out with his father in 1730 but continued to support the Government. In 1739 he was appointed secretary to the Duke of Devonshire, the lord lieutenant of Ireland. On 8 Sept. 1739 Henry Pelham wrote to Devonshire:

> Poor Mrs. Townshend died yesterday in the afternoon which has put her whole family in the greatest distress; he is, as you may imagine, in as great affliction as is possible for any man to be, and of consequence at present utterly incapable of business . . . The thoughts of men in his condition may alter, but to your Grace I venture to say, that in my own opinion he will scarce ever come out into any public way again . . . I know your good nature will make you pity this unhappy young man, who besides having lost a very good companion, has lost one [who] managed their whole affairs, and to whom he left everything.[2]

As Pelham forecast, Townshend never again took any active part in politics. He died 21 May 1780.

[1] *CJ*, xxxviii. 708. [2] Devonshire mss.

R.R.S.

TOWNSHEND, Hon. William (1702–38).

GREAT YARMOUTH 11 June 1723–28 Jan. 1738

b. 9 June 1702, 3rd s. of Charles Townshend, 2nd Visct. Townshend, and bro. of Hon. Charles, Thomas and Roger Townshend (qq.v.). *m.* 29 May 1725, Henrietta, da. of Lord William Powlett (q.v.), 1s. 2da.
A.-d.-c. to the King with the rank of col. Jan. 1724, renewed 1727; capt.-lt. 3 Drag. Gds. Feb. 1727–*d.*; groom of the bedchamber to the Prince of Wales 1729–*d.*; usher of the Exchequer 1730–*d.*

Succeeding to the family seat at Yarmouth on coming of age, Townshend was appointed groom of the bedchamber to the Prince of Wales when Frederick was brought over to England from Hanover at the beginning of 1729. By 1733 he had become a great favourite with the Prince, whose views on the excise bill were generally supposed to be indicated by Townshend's voting against it. For this the King offered Walpole to make the Prince dismiss Townshend, but the offer was refused. When the Prince, on his marriage, asked for permission to appoint Townshend's wife as one of the Princess's women of the bedchamber, the King told the Queen to reply that

> as Mr. Townshend was the most impertinent puppy in the Prince's whole family, he was determined not to reward him for being so; and that it was more favour than either the servant or the master deserves that he himself was not turned out.

In the end she was appointed without the King's permission. Discussing the Prince's entourage in 1737, George II described Townshend as 'a silent, proud, surly, wrong-headed booby'.[1] On Townshend's death, 28 Jan. 1738, his cousin, Horace Walpole, succeeded to his sinecure at the Exchequer.

[1] Hervey, *Mems.* 176, 554, 748, 817.

R.R.S.

TRACY, Robert (?1706–67), of Stanway, nr. Tewkesbury, Glos.

TEWKESBURY 1734–1741
WORCESTER 11 Feb. 1748–1754

b. ?1706, 1st s. of John Tracy of Stanway, Glos. by Anne, da. of Sir Robert Atkyns, chief baron of the Exchequer. *educ.* New Coll. Oxf. 10 Nov. 1724, aged 18. *m.* 7 Aug. 1735, Anna Maria, da. of Sir Roger Hudson, director of South Sea Co., *s.p.* *suc.* fa. 1735.

Robert Tracy belonged to a branch of an ancient Gloucestershire family, who in 1532–3 obtained a crown grant of the manor of Stanway, part of the lands of the abbey of Tewkesbury. Returned for Tewkesbury after a contest in 1734 as a government supporter, he became a trustee and common councilman of the Georgia Society in 1734, having several meetings with Walpole in 1739–40 to obtain increased financial assistance from Parliament for the colony.[1] He voted for the Spanish convention in March 1739; spoke against an opposition motion asking for papers relating to the war with Spain, 29 Nov.; absented himself, on 29 Jan. 1740, from a division on the place bill, which the corporation of Tewkesbury had instructed him to support;[2] spoke against an opposition motion for a call of the House two days later; and supported Sir Charles Wager's (q.v.) seamen's bill in 1741.

'At the earnest solicitation' of the leading

Gloucestershire Whigs, Tracy agreed to declare himself a candidate for the county at the next general election, 'without regarding any ill consequences it might have as to my interest at Tewkesbury', for which he also intended to stand. Announcing his decision to Walpole, he wrote:

I returned but yesterday from Tewkesbury race, and find indeed the people are disgusted with my declaration and some call it a desertion, but my old friends still stick by me, and . . . I will poll the borough to the last man, against any opposition whatsoever.

He added that the people of Tewkesbury

damn the convention and all who espoused it, so that I suffer for righteousness sake and, if it be a shame, glory in it since I voted for it merely from conscience and a firm persuasion that what I did was for the true interest of my country. I can't help having a just contempt for men so misled, and am determined notwithstanding this behaviour to try my fate both for town and county, since as to the latter, all the Whigs of property and distinction do look upon it as a critical time, and that we have a good chance for retrieving the Whig interest. If I should prove an instrument in their hands of accomplishing their design, no body can be more sensible of the honour, or more sincerely rejoiced at so fortunate an event.[3]

In the end he stood for neither the county nor the borough.

Soon after Walpole's fall Tracy went to see him at his house at Richmond, where he 'found only three young sparks reading a bawdy book which scandalized him much, being Sunday'.[4] In 1744 he wrote to the lord chancellor protesting against proposals for conciliating the Tories by giving them greater representation on commissions of the peace in certain counties, including Gloucestershire:

The general notion which prevailed upon Lord Orford's going out, of uniting all parties under the cant term of Broad Bottom is to me absurd and ridiculous.

At the general election of 1747 he stood for Worcester city, where he was subjected to such vilification that he issued a broadsheet printing a denial by his opponents of having accused him of rape.[5] He came out bottom of the poll but was returned on petition as a government supporter. According to the 2nd Lord Egmont's electoral survey, c.1749–50,

Tracy for a time made some particular advances to us, endeavouring to set himself right in opinion as to some former behaviour—but he seems grown violent and sour against us since so that we must have no thoughts of him.

Placed by Egmont among the twelve 'most obnoxious men of an inferior degree' in the Commons, he returned to the charge about Tory J.P.s, writing to Hardwicke on 10 Sept. 1750:

If more Tories should be admitted the county may be thrown into confusion, and the Whig interest totally subverted.[6]

In 1751 Tracy applied for his wife to be made guardian to Miss Nicoll, a wealthy ward in Chancery, to whom he was distantly related. According to Horace Walpole, whose friend, John Chute, was also a candidate for this position, the 'bait' in Tracy's case was the allowance of £1,000 a year authorized by the court for her maintenance.

Mr. Tracy [Walpole writes] persisting in endeavouring to force Miss Nicoll into his power, absolutely against her consent, her friends found it necessary to represent the impropriety of placing her with a gentleman who had so far damaged his fortune as to be reduced to keep his parliamentary residence at a milliner's, and with his wife, whose intellects were in as crazy a condition as her husband's fortune.

After hearing Tracy's counsel, Lord Chancellor Hardwicke rejected his application without calling on Miss Nicoll's.[7]

In 1752 Tracy spoke for the Government on an opposition motion against subsidy treaties in peace time.[8] Next year, after seconding the Address, he applied to Pelham for financial assistance from the Government towards the cost of standing again for Worcester at the forthcoming general election, writing:

I hope I have not deserved so ill of the King and his Administration by my behaviour either at Worcester or Tewkesbury, and for the whole tenour of my conduct since I first came into Parliament.[9]

Pelham advanced him £1,000 from the secret service money but feared the election would cost £4 or 5,000 and 'seemed desirous to break off engagements . . . , if he had known how to extricate himself'.

After Pelham's death Newcastle noted on 18 Mar.:

Mr. Tracy has had £1,000 for his election, demands £3,500 [sic] more—offers to desist for £2,000—to be chosen at another place—and if not chosen will return £1,000,

with the comment, 'will lay it before the King'. On 24 Mar. Tracy wrote to Newcastle:

I beg your immediate answer whether the £2,500 will be paid, £1,000 tomorrow, and the remaining £1,500 when I go down; if these terms are not agreed to, and you will be pleased to determine tonight whether you will or will not make them good, I shall trouble neither the King nor your Grace any further, nor shall I be with you on Thursday morning, but will stand the poll for Worcester unassisted by your Grace, and free, I thank God, from all obligations. Your Grace must be peremptory tonight, or you will see me no more.
P.S. Tomorrow I shall begin executing the plan necessary to secure my election and will be put off no longer.[10]

Newcastle managed to extricate himself and Tracy stood down.

In 1761 Tracy again put up for Worcester but,

finding no subscription towards his election, as he expected, wrote to his friends of his intention of dropping the opposition, and they in answer told him that as he stood for the city on his own voluntary offer, so he was left to his claim to proceed or not as he thought proper.

It was thought that his design was

not to carry on a real opposition, for that would be chargeable, but to keep up the appearance of one, in order to create what expence he can to the other candidates; a design no way worthy to be supported by his friends.[11]

In the event he stood and was defeated.

He died 28 Sept. 1767.

[1] *HMC Egmont Diary*, iii. 19, 21, 170. [2] Corporation of Tewkesbury to Lord Gage and Robt. Tracy n.d. [1739], Lechmere mss, Worcester RO. [3] Tracy to Sir Robt. Walpole, 21 Sept. 1739, Cholmondeley (Houghton) mss. [4] *HMC Egmont Diary*, iii. 256–7. [5] Tracy to Hardwicke, 25 Apr. 1744, Add. 35601, f. 317; Nicholas Taylor to Hardwicke, 4 July 1747, Add. 35589, f. 281 et seq. [6] Add. 35603, f. 251. [7] *H. Walpole Corresp.* (Yale ed.), xiv. 199, 215, 224, 229, and see WALPOLE, Hon. Horatio. [8] Walpole, *Mems. Geo. II*, i. 254. [9] Add. 32733, f. 421. [10] Namier, *Structure*, 197, 210, 203. [11] Add. 33055, f. 292.

A.N.N.

TRACY, *see also* **KECK**

TRAVERS, Samuel (?1655–1725), of Hitcham, nr. Windsor, Bucks.

BOSSINEY	1690–1695
LOSTWITHIEL	1695–1700
BOSSINEY	1708–1710
NEW WINDSOR	14 Apr. 1715–1722
ST. MAWES	1722–17 Sept. 1725

b. ?1655, 2nd s. of Rev. Thomas Travers, rector of St. Columb Major, Cornw., by Elizabeth, da. of William Rous, M.P., of Halton, Cornw. by Mary, da. of Richard, 1st Baron Robartes, wid. of her cos. Francis Rous of Wotton-under-Edge, Glos. *educ.* Exeter, Oxf. 17 June 1674, aged 19; M. Temple 1679, called 1683, bencher 1693. *unm. suc.* cos. Giles Thorpe at Waltham Place, Berks. 1706.[1]

Surveyor gen. of land revenue March 1693–1710; surveyor gen. of Blenheim 1705–16; auditor to Prince of Wales 1715–*d.*

The nephew of Walter Travers, a Puritan divine, Travers's father, having been ejected from his living in 1662, became chaplain to John Robartes, 1st Earl of Radnor, a staunch Presbyterian, whose niece he had married. Travers himself was brought up under the protection of the Robartes family, with whose support he represented Bossiney and Lostwithiel as a Whig under William and Anne. In 1708 he was granted a 31-year duchy of Cornwall lease of Tintagel castle,[2] subsequently establishing a controlling interest for one seat at Bossiney. His work as surveyor general had brought him into connexion with the borough of Windsor,[3] in the vicinity of which he purchased Hitcham in 1712.[4]

Returned for Windsor on petition in 1715, he was appointed a member of the Prince's household, voting for the septennial bill in 1716. Next year he went into opposition with the Prince's party, voting against the Government on Lord Cadogan (q.v.) in June 1717, the repeal of the Occasional Conformity and Schism Acts, and the peerage bill in 1719. Brought in by the ministry for St. Mawes in 1722, he died 17 Sept. 1725, leaving his lease of Tintagel castle to his 'good friend' Walter Carey (q.v.); a sum of money to erect a statue to 'the glorious memory of my master King William III', which was eventually put up in St. James's Square; £500 p.a. for the foundation of what became the College of Naval Knights at Windsor; and the remainder of his estate to Christ's Hospital to educate boys 'in the study and practice of mathematics'.[5]

[1] S. Smith-Travers & R. Hone, *The Devonshire Family of Travers*; *Herald and Gen.* iv. 109–112. [2] Maclean, *Trigg Minor*, i. 203. [3] See Tighe & Davis, *Annals of Windsor*, ii. 468, 489–91. [4] S. Travers to Mr. Joynes, 24 Oct. 1712, Add. 19609 f. 133. [5] *Gent. Mag.* 1731, pp. 442–3.

E.C.

TREBY, George (?1684–1742), of Plympton, Devon.

PLYMPTON ERLE	1708–1727
DARTMOUTH	1727–8 Mar. 1742

b. ?1684, 1st s. of Sir George Treby, M.P. Plympton Erle 1677–81, 1689–92, Speaker of the House of Commons, c. j. of common pleas, by his 3rd w. Dorothy, da. of Ralph Grainge of the I. Temple. *educ.* Exeter, Oxf. 3 Apr. 1701, aged 16; M. Temple 1692. *m.* Charity, da. and coh. of Roger Hele of Holwell, Devon, 2s. 3da. *suc.* fa. 1700.

Commr. for forfeited estates June 1716–19; sec. at war 1718–24; teller of the Exchequer Apr. 1724–Aug. 1727; master of the Household 1730–40; ld. of Treasury Oct. 1740–Feb. 1742.

The son of an eminent Whig lawyer and politician, with a strong electoral interest in the west country, Treby was returned at the first opportunity after coming of age for Plympton, where his family controlled one seat. During the split in the Whig party, 1717–20, he spoke (12 May 1717) against a Tory motion, supported by Walpole, for an extreme high churchman to preach before the House, voted against Lord Cadogan (q.v.), 4 June 1717, and was appointed secretary at war in 1718. When, after Sunderland's death, Townshend and Walpole were engaged in a struggle for power with Carteret, Treby was regarded in 1722 as Carteret's choice as secretary of state in place of Townshend.[1] In 1723 Townshend suggested to Walpole that the best way of getting rid of him would be to appoint him to a vacancy for the vice-treasurership of Ireland, by which 'a way might have opened for bringing Mr.

[Henry] Pelham into the war office'. In the event 'an opportunity of disposing of Treby and putting in Pelham' occurred in the following year when a tellership of the Exchequer fell vacant.[2]

On George II's accession Treby was deprived of his tellership.[3] Two days later he wrote to Walpole about the elections in the west of England which he was managing for the Government, adding:

No one can have a greater duty to his Majesty nor a greater regard for the present Ministry than myself. I was many years in Parliament when the Hanover succession was struck at and I had then the honesty to vote as you did. My father Sir George Treby was exempted by name out of King James II's Act of Grace and by many actions showed himself a friend to the Protestant Succession. I have taken some pains and been at some expense to promote the same interest at Plympton, Plymouth, Totnes and Dartmouth and I can truly say his Majesty has not a more faithful subject.

In 1730 he returned to office as master of the Household.

At the general election of 1734 Treby acted as government manager not only for the four boroughs mentioned in his 1727 letter, but also for Oakhampton and Ashburton in conjunction with Sir William Yonge (q.v.).[4] In 1740 he was transferred to the Treasury, where he remained till he was turned out on Walpole's fall in February 1742. He died shortly afterwards, 8 Mar. 1742.

[1] *HMC Portland*, vii. 312. [2] Coxe, *Walpole*, ii. 256, 278. [3] Add. 36127, f. 11. [4] Treby to Walpole, 4 Aug. 1727 and 30 Apr. 1734, Cholmondeley (Houghton) mss.

R.R.S.

TREBY, George (c.1685–aft. 1727).

DARTMOUTH 1722–1727

b. c.1685, o.s. of James Treby; nephew of Sir George Treby, M.P., and cos. of George Treby of Plympton (q.v.).[1]

Lt. in Col. Roger Townshend's Ft. Apr. 1706; capt. Col. de Magny's Portuguese regt. of Ft. 1709; capt. 10 Drag. Gds. 1715; capt. and lt. col. 1 Ft. Gds. Jan. 1720, res. Mar. 1727.

Capt. and gov. Dartmouth castle 1720.

Treby was returned unopposed on the Treasury interest for Dartmouth, no doubt through the influence of his cousin, George Treby of Plympton (q.v.). He did not stand again. The date of his death is unknown.

[1] PCC 29 Dyer; PCC 61 Buckingham.

S.R.M.

TREBY, George (?1726–61), of Plympton, Devon.

PLYMPTON ERLE 14 Dec. 1747–5 Nov. 1761

b. ?1726, 1st s. of George Treby of Plympton (q.v.). *educ.* Exeter, Oxf. 26 Apr. 1743, aged 16; Grand Tour (Italy) 1746.[1]

Treby was returned unopposed on his family's interest for Plympton as a government supporter. He died 5 Nov. 1761.

[1] L. Lewis, *Connoisseurs & Secret Agents*, 134.

S.R.M.

TREFUSIS, Robert (1708–42), of Trefusis, Cornw.

TRURO 1734–1741

b. 22 Mar. 1708, o.s. of Samuel Trefusis (q.v.). *educ.* Pembroke, Camb. 1724, fellow 1733–7. *m.* 18 Mar. 1737, Elizabeth, da. of Gilbert Affleck (q.v.) of Dalham Hall, Suff., 1s. 1da. *suc.* fa. 1724.

Defeated at Penryn in 1734, Trefusis was returned unopposed for Truro on the Boscawen interest, voting against the Administration on the Westminster bridge bill, 31 Mar. 1736,[1] to which the common council of the city of London was bitterly opposed, on the Spanish convention in 1739, and on the place bill in 1740. He did not stand in 1741, dying in August 1742.

[1] Harley Diary.

E.C.

TREFUSIS, Samuel (1676–1724), of Trefusis, nr. Penryn, Cornw.

PENRYN 1698–1713, 15 Mar. 1714–1722

bap. 6 Oct. 1676, 2nd s. of Francis Trefusis of Trefusis by Bridget, da. of Robert Rolle of Heanton Satchville, Devon. *educ.* St. Edmund Hall, Oxf. 1695. *m.* (1) 13 Dec. 1702, Alice, da. and h. of Sir Robert Cotton, M.P., 1s. 1da.; (2) 9 July 1719, Margaret, da. of James Craggs, postmaster gen., sis. of James Craggs (q.v.), *s.p. suc.* e. bro. Francis Trefusis 1692.

Trefusis, a member of one of the oldest Cornish families, had been responsible for building a large portion of Flushing, the port serving Penryn, where he was returned unopposed on his own interest in 1715. Classed as a Whig who would often vote with the Tories, he supported the septennial bill in 1716 but was absent from other recorded divisions. On 30 Apr. 1721, in the course of a debate on the motion that his father-in-law's estate should be forfeited he said

that neither he nor Mr. Newsham [q.v.] were at all prepared, not expecting that this affair would have come on this day . . . and therefore he desired the House would give them time to get their witnesses,

adding that

he had never been used to speak in the House, or but very rarely . . . which he hoped the House would take into consideration and allow them counsel to speak for them: that by Mr. Craggs's death, his estate was devolved to them and Mr. Eliot [Edward, q.v.], in right of their wives, the deceased's three daughters: that there was no manner of crime laid to their charge, and since Mr. Craggs was dead, and could not answer for himself, he hoped the House would allow them time and counsel.

Despite Walpole's intervention in his favour, a motion for allowing counsel was dropped, and it was resolved that all estates acquired by Craggs after December 1719 should be confiscated.[1] He did not stand in 1722 and died 4 Apr. 1724.

[1] Chandler, vi. 243-4.

E.C.

TREFUSIS, Thomas (1687-1754), of Penryn, Cornw.

GRAMPOUND   9 Feb. 1739-1741

bap. 16 Aug. 1687, 4th s. of Henry Trefusis of Constantine by his w. Elizabeth. *m.* 1716, Hannah, da. of John Addis of Mevagissey, Cornw., 2da.

Lt. R.N. 1711, capt. 1736; commr. of victualling May 1740-June 1744; commr. of the navy at Port Mahon 1744-7; superannuated r.-adm. 1748.

Trefusis, a naval officer, was returned at Grampound by the Administration, voting with them on the Spanish convention in 1739 and on the place bill in 1740. He was defeated at Grampound in 1741, petitioning unsuccessfully. In June 1744 he was appointed extra commissioner of the navy resident at Port Mahon, a temporary office created as the scene of naval operations was transferred to the Mediterranean. He came home towards the end of 1747, and in July 1748 was placed on the superannuated list with the rank and half pay of a rear-admiral.[1] He died 21 Apr. 1754.

[1] Boase & Courtney, *Bibliog. Cornub.*; Charnock, *Biog. Navalis*, iv. 309-10; HMC Du Cane, 142, 167, 171, 173, 184.

E.C.

TRELAWNY, Charles (?1706-1764), of Coldrenick, nr. Liskeard, Cornw.

LISKEARD   25 Mar. 1740-1754

b. ?1706, 2nd s. of Edward Trelawny, dean of Exeter, by Elizabeth, da. of Thomas Darell of Chawcroft, Hants; bro. of Darell Trelawny (q.v.). *educ.* Westminster 1715-21; Ch. Ch. Oxf. 15 Dec. 1722, aged 16. *unm. suc.* bro. Darell 1727.

Assay master of the stannaries 1742-*d.*   •

Chosen for Liskeard by Richard Eliot (q.v.) in March 1740, Trelawny was unable to take his seat as the return had been stolen in a robbery of the western mail. Edward Harley (q.v.) reports:

As this was an entire new case, the House were at a loss how to proceed. Some Members proposed to hear *viva voce* evidence of the election and return and upon this to admit Mr. Trelawny, . . . but this proposal of admitting *viva voce* evidence to supply a record would not be listened to. Then it was proposed that the lord chancellor should make a facsimile, but this was not approved. The House not knowing what

to do, adjourned the consideration to a day when the sessions would be over.

During

the next sessions, 19 Nov. 1740, the matter was again heard, and several persons [including the sheriff of the county] examined in relation to it, when it was ordered *nem. con.* that the deputy clerk of the Crown do file among the returns of Members to serve in this present Parliament for the county of Cornwall, the counterpart of the indenture, executed by the sheriff of Cornwall, of the return of Charles Trelawny Esq. to serve as a burgess for the borough of Liskeard, it appearing to this House, that the writ and the principal part of the aforesaid indenture were taken away, in coming up to the clerk of the Crown, by highwaymen, who destroyed the same by burning them.[1]

Like Eliot, a member of the Prince of Wales's party, holding from 1742 a duchy of Cornwall office, he followed the Prince's lead in Parliament, voting with the Opposition till Walpole's fall, after which he supported the new Administration, till the Prince reverted to opposition in 1747. Going over to the Government on Frederick's death in 1751, he was allowed by Pelham to retain his office in return for standing down in favour of Philip Stanhope, Lord Chesterfield's illegitimate son, in 1754.[2] On his death, 6 Oct. 1764, Coldrenick passed to his maternal cousin, Henry St. George Darell, who assumed the name of Trelawny.

[1] Harley Diary; *CJ*, xxxiii. 525, 535-6. [2] Edw. Eliot to Pelham, 12 Feb. 1754, Newcastle (Clumber) mss.

E.C.

TRELAWNY, Darell (1695-1727), of Coldrenick, nr. Liskeard, Cornw.

LOSTWITHIEL   25 Aug.-14 Oct. 1727

b. ?1695, 1st s. of Edward Trelawny of Coldrenick, dean of Exeter, and bro. of Charles Trelawny (q.v.). *educ.* Ch. Ch. Oxf. 26 Mar. 1713, aged 17. *unm. suc.* fa. 1726.

Trelawny was descended from Sir Jonathan Trelawny, M.P., of Trelawne (*d.* 1604), who left Coldrenick to his second son, Edward. Unsuccessful for Callington and Truro in 1722, he was defeated at Lostwithiel in January 1727, but was returned for it by the Administration at the ensuing general election, dying shortly afterwards, 14 Oct. 1727, on his way to Lisbon by way of Falmouth for the recovery of his health.[1] He left his estates to his brother Charles (q.v.), whom he entrusted to the guidance of his 'good friends' Lord Falmouth and John Laroche (qq.v.), directing that should his brother die without issue, he should 'not think of giving any part of his estate' to his cousins, the Trelawnys of Trelawne [Sir John and Edward, qq.v.], since they 'have behaved towards me and my family in such a manner as if they thought me and my family no part of theirs, and as if we were beneath them' but that his maternal relatives, the Darells, should inherit.[2]

[1] *Pol. State*, xxxiv. 419. [2] PCC 26 Brook.

E.C.

TRELAWNY, Edward (1699–1754), of Hengar, Cornw.

WEST LOOE   20 Jan. 1724–Dec. 1732

bap. 9 July 1699, 4th s. of Sir Jonathan Trelawny, 3rd Bt., bp. of Winchester, by Rebecca, da. and coh. of Thomas Hele of Bascombe, Devon; bro. of Sir John Trelawny, 4th Bt. (q.v.). *educ.* Westminster 1713–17; Ch. Ch. Oxf. 1717. *m.* (1) *s.p.*; (2) 8 Nov. 1737, Amoretta (*d.* Nov. 1741), da. of John Crawford, 1s. *d.v.p.*; (3) 2 Feb. 1752, Catherine, wid. of Robert Penny, attorney-gen. of Jamaica, *s.p. suc.* uncle Brig.-Gen. Charles Trelawny at Hengar 1731.[1]
    Commr. of victualling Jan. 1726–32; commr. of customs [S] Dec. 1732–7; gov. Jamaica June 1737–Sept. 1752; col. 49 Ft. Dec. 1743–53.

Returned for East Looe on the Trelawny interest, Trelawny was given a job in the victualling office. He spoke on the Government's side in a debate on supply on 21 Feb. 1727, but voted against the Administration on the civil list arrears in 1729, the Hessians in 1730, and the army in 1732, writing subsequently that he would not be thought of 'as a party man, which I think I am as little as any one, perhaps too little to please any one'.[2] A friend of Sir Charles Wager's (q.v.), he vacated his seat on being given a place in the customs at Edinburgh by Walpole in 1732, when his sister described him as 'much fallen away . . . and but in an ill state of health' which, she believed, proceeded 'from uneasiness: his not rising where he would be and conscience not agreeing together, and wish his new place may be for life'.[3] In 1734, having left Scotland to join the Imperial army against the French in the war of the Polish succession, he was elected in his absence for both East and West Looe, on which he wrote to Thomas Robinson (q.v.) from Wiesenthal, 3 July 1734:

The elections, you know, are void of course upon account of my place. If Sir Charles does not get me out before a new election can be made, I can't receive the benefit of the Looers' favour so voluntarily bestowed on the mad volunteer: but I have left everything to Sir Charles Wager and whether I am to be senator, commissioner, or neither, I shall be easy under his decision and management.[4]

Both elections were declared void. In November 1735 his elder brother, Sir John (q.v.), being deeply in debt, Edward gave £5,000 of his own money to pay the creditors, Wager putting up the rest of the sum required by way of mortgage, on the security of Trelawne and other Cornish estates, including the properties at East and West Looe, which were made over to Edward.[5] In 1737 he was appointed governor of Jamaica, repaying the whole of the mortgage to Wager and Wager's widow by 1744 out of his salary.[6] During his absence he entrusted the management of his electoral interest at the Looes to Wager's protégé, Francis Gashry (q.v.), filling the seats with government nominees in return for suitable payment to himself, except in 1741 when he insisted that his nephew James Buller (q.v.), a Tory, and his friend Benjamin Keene (q.v.) should be returned.[7]

Trelawny took part in the campaign in the West Indies with Admiral Vernon (q.v.), to whom Pulteney wrote (27 Mar. 1740):

Pray make my compliments to Mr. Trelawny: when I consider how my country has been used for many years, and what a poor figure she has made, it is the greatest joy to me to consider that her honour will be retrieved and her trade restored, by the union of two such worthy men as he and you, similar in your characters, for honour, bravery and disinterestedness.

In the summer of 1742, he had a violent quarrel with Sir Chaloner Ogle (q.v.), during which Vernon reported, he 'drew his sword, turned as pale as the wall with rage, and looked as wild as a madman'.[8] In 1748 he took part in the capture of Port Louis in San Domingo. In November 1751 he arranged to marry the widow of the late attorney-general in Jamaica with a fortune 'reported to be between £30,000 and £40,000' in Jamaican money.[9] Shortly afterwards, he asked to be relieved of his post owing to ill-health,[10] leaving Jamaica in November 1752, with the thanks of the House of Assembly for his 'just administration' and the 'many important services' he had rendered to the island.[11] He died 16 Jan. 1754, bequeathing Trelawne and the Looe properties to his brother, Sir John, for life, and afterwards to his cousin and brother-in-law, Harry Trelawny, of Butshead, Devon, later the 5th Bt.[12]

[1] PCC 316 Isham. [2] To Wager, 1 June 1740, Add. 28558, f. 13. [3] *Trelawny Corresp. Letters between Myrtilla and Philander*, 92. [4] Add. 32791, f. 202. [5] *Trelawny Corresp.* 106–7; Add. 19030, f. 350; PCC 60 Pinfold. [6] Add. 19030, f. 350. [7] See Edw. Trelawny to Francis Gashry, 19 July 1753, Vernon-Wager mss in library of Congress; Wager to Keene, 25 Feb. 1737, Add. 32794, f. 161, and Wager to mayor of East Looe, 24 Mar. 1741, East Looe Town Trust. [8] *Vernon Pprs.* (Navy Recs. Soc. xcix), 79–80, 263. [9] Edw. Trelawny to Pelham, 2 Nov. 1751, Newcastle (Clumber) mss. [10] Edw. Trelawny to Chas. Knowles (q.v.), 6 Mar. 1752, Add. 32724, f. 409. [11] *Jnl. of the House of Assembly of Jamaica*, 25 Nov. 1752. For his governorship, see R. Pares, *War and Trade in the West Indies*. [12] PCC 60 Pinfold.

E.C.

TRELAWNY, John (1691–1756), of Trelawne, nr. Looe, Cornw.

WEST LOOE	20 Apr. 1713–1715
LISKEARD	1715–1722
WEST LOOE	1722–1727
EAST LOOE	1727–1734

b. 26 July 1691, 1st s. of Sir Jonathan Trelawny, 3rd Bt., bp. of Winchester, and bro. of Edward Trelawny (q.v.). *m.* Agnes, da. of Thomas Blackwood of Scotland, *s.p. educ.* Ch. Ch. Oxf. 1708. *suc.* fa. as 4th Bt. 19 July 1721.

Groom of the bedchamber to the Prince of Wales 1714–?17.

Trelawny was descended from Sir Jonathan Trelawny (*d.* 1604), who purchased Trelawne near the Looes in 1599.[1] His family's long-standing parliamentary influence reached its peak in the time of his father, the bishop of Winchester, who when Trelawny came of age, made over to him the Cornish estates and the management of the electoral interest,[2] comprising control of four seats at East and West Looe, as well as an interest at Liskeard. Returned as a Whig for Liskeard in 1715, he voted with the Government in all the recorded divisions of that Parliament, giving up a place in the household of the Prince of Wales when the Prince went into opposition in 1717. Transferring to West Looe in 1722 and East Looe in 1727, he voted for the Hessians in 1730 but was absent from other recorded divisions.

Trelawny did not stand in 1734, when he was already in deep financial difficulties, making over his estates and parliamentary interest the following year to his brother, Edward (q.v.), in return for the payment of his debts.[3] According to John Buller (q.v.) he received from the Government 'an allowance of £500 a year, and a present of £1,000 the year of the general election',[4] the Trelawny seats being placed at Walpole's disposal. On the death of his brother Edward in 1754 he recovered Trelawne until his death on 2 Feb. 1756, when it passed to another branch of the family.[5]

[1] *Cam. Misc.* ii (5), p. 3. [2] *HMC Portland*, v. 193. [3] PCC 60 Pinfold; Add. 19030, f. 350. [4] Namier, *Structure*, 321. [5] PCC 60 Pinfold.

E.C.

TREMAYNE, Arthur (1701–1796), of Sydenham, Devon.

LAUNCESTON	1727–1734

b. 23 Feb. 1701, o.s. of Arthur Tremayne of Sydenham by Grace, da. of Sir Halswell Tynte, 1st Bt., M.P., of Halswell, Som. *educ.* Westminster 1715; Trinity, Camb. 1721. *m.* Dorothy Hammond of Wiltshire, 1s. *suc.* fa. at Sydenham 1709 and gt.-gd.-fa. at Collacombe 1709.

Sheriff, Devon 1739–40.

Of an ancient royalist Cornish family, Tremayne inherited a very large fortune from his great-grandfather.[1] A Tory and a friend of the Morices of Werrington, who probably returned him at Launceston, he voted against the Government in every recorded division. He did not stand again, and died at an advanced age in 1796.

[1] Sir Nicholas Morice to Humphry Morice, 10 July 1709, Morice mss at Bank of England.

E.C.

TRENCHARD, George (c.1684–1758), of Litchet Matravers, nr. Poole, Dorset.

POOLE	1713–1741, 1747–1754

b. c.1684, 1st s. of Sir John Trenchard, M.P., sec. of state 1692–5, of Litchet Matravers by Philippa, da. of George Speke of White Lackington, Som. *educ.* Jesus, Camb. 1705; M. Temple 1702. *m.* his cos. Mary, da. and h. of Col. Thomas Trenchard, M.P., of Wolveton, Dorset, 3s. 2da. *suc.* fa. 1695.

Ensign, Earl of Monmouth's Ft. 1693, Col. Henry Mordaunt's Ft. 1695, out by 1702.

George Trenchard was five times returned for Poole, which his father, secretary of state under William III, had also represented. A Whig, after 1715 he voted consistently with the Administration except on the peerage bill in 1719, which he opposed. His only reported speech was on 2 June 1721, in the committee on the South Sea sufferers bill, when he moved that Sir Theodore Janssen (q.v.) be allowed £50,000 out of his estate. Before the 1754 election he gave his interest at Poole to Sir Richard Lyttelton (q.v.), on condition that his son John should be made a commissioner of taxes.[1]

He died 31 Mar. 1758.

[1] Add. 38335, f. 55.

S.R.M.

TRENCHARD, Henry (1668–1720), of Fulford, Devon.

DORCHESTER	1713–28 Mar. 1720

bap. 1668, s. of George Trenchard of Charminster, Dorset by his w. Mary. *m.* 20 Feb. 1705, Mary, da. and h. of John Tuckfield of Little Fulford, Devon, wid. of Francis Fulford of Fulford, Devon, *s.p. suc.* fa. 1686.

Cornet, Mq. of Winchester's vol. regt. of Horse 1690; lt. in (his cos.) Thomas Erle's (q.v.) regt. of Ft. 1694, half-pay 1698; lt. 34 Ft. 1702.

The first cousin once removed of George Trenchard (q.v.), Henry Trenchard was re-elected for Dorchester in 1715 without a contest. Though a member of a strongly Whig family, he himself was classed as a Tory. No vote of his is recorded. He died 28 Mar. 1720.

S.R.M.

TRENCHARD, John (?1668–1723) of Abbot's Leigh, Som.

TAUNTON 1722–16 Dec. 1723

b. ?1668, 1st s. of William Trenchard of Cutteridge, Wilts. by Ellen, da. and h. of Sir George Norton of Abbot's Leigh, Som. *educ.* Trinity, Dublin 29 May 1685, aged 16; I. Temple, called 1689. *m.* (1) da. of Sir Thomas Scawen (q.v.), who cut her own throat Nov. 1718, *s.p.*[1]; (2) lic. 19 Nov. 1719, Anne, da. of Sir William Blackett, 1st Bt., M.P., of Wallington, sis. of Sir William Blackett, 2nd Bt. (q.v.), *s.p. suc.* fa. 1710.

Commr. of forfeited estates [I] 1699.

Distantly related to Sir John Trenchard, M.P., secretary of state to William III, Trenchard, a Somerset landowner, made his reputation at the end of William III's reign as the most effective of the Whig pamphleteers who raised an outcry against a standing army, and as the author, in his capacity as a member of the forfeited Irish lands commission, of a vitriolic report reflecting on the King. He seems to have taken no further part in politics till a letter from him to an unknown person shows that he made overtures to Sunderland to succeed William Pynsent (q.v.) at Taunton, which in the past had been represented by Sir John Trenchard. The letter is undated but the references to Pynsent's not attending and to Sunderland's acting on 'principles of liberty' suggest that it was written soon after the repeal of the Occasional Conformity and Schism Acts in 1719, the subject of Pynsent's last recorded vote. Trenchard wrote:

> When I was last to wait upon your Lordship you informed me that Lord Sunderland continued in the disposition to bring me into the House and the only obstacle to it was that he could not readily find a proper place for a gentleman of Mr. Pynsent's condition: I confess I always doubted it, and do so now more than ever since there are reasons to believe the Court are upon a new plan of politics, but I have now an opportunity to try the sincerity of great men's promises, for Mr. Pynsent is content to quit the House upon any terms, and will accept any place to do it which he will give up again immediately, so that your Lord can have no objection but what must be personal to me, for Mr. Pynsent never attends.
>
> If my Lord continues to act upon the principles of liberty he is sure of my utmost assistance and there can scarce such a circumstance of affairs happen, but my attachment to the present ministry will be greater than to any who now appear to oppose them.[2]

Not getting Pynsent's seat, he later in the year wrote a pamphlet against the peerage bill. In 1720 he began his collaboration with Thomas Gordon, a Scotch journalist, in the *Independent Whig*, where they attacked the High Church party, and in the *London Journal*, a precursor of the *Craftsman*, in the famous 'Cato Letters', where they called 'for public justice upon the wicked managers of the

late fatal South Sea scheme'.[3] When in August 1721 they were about to print the reports of the secret committee set up by the House of Commons to inquire into the scheme, the Government had the papers seized and broke the printing press. Soon after this, negotiations began which ended in the *London Journal* becoming a government newspaper, with Gordon going over into the pay of the Government.[4] In Sunderland's plans for the 1722 Parliament drawn up c.October 1721 Trenchard is put down to replace Pynsent at Taunton. Returned there as an independent Whig, he opposed Walpole's proposal to remit two millions owed to the Government by the South Sea Company, 12 Dec. 1722. On 29 Jan. next, in a debate on the frauds on the tobacco duty, he denounced the 'great frauds made by the North Britons upon the English', moving that they should be subjected to discriminatory regulations, but failed to find a seconder. On 3 Feb. he moved for an inquiry into the collection and payment of the malt duty in Scotland, declaring that 'the Scotch had cheated us in everything'; but 'like an irresolute man did not insist on his motion' after Walpole had described his speech as 'inflammatory' and tending to break the Union.[5] On 11 Mar. he opposed proceedings against one of the Atterbury plot conspirators by a bill of pains and penalties, arguing that the proper procedure was by a bill of attainder, but again found no support. He died 16 Dec. 1723, shortly before the opening of the next session.

[1] PCC 47 Bolton; *HMC Portland*, v. 573; *N. & Q.* (ser. 2), xi. 215. [2] Undated, addressee unknown, Sunderland (Blenheim) mss. [3] *Cato's Letters* (1733 ed.), p. xlii. [4] C. B. Realey, 'The London Journal and its Authors', *Bull. Univ. Kansas*, v. no. 3, pp. 1–34. [5] *Knatchbull Diary*, which credits another speaker with a speech on 6 May attributed by Chandler to Trenchard.

E.C.

TRENTHAM, Visct., *see* **LEVESON GOWER, Granville**

TREVANION, John (c.1667–1740), of Carhayes, nr. Tregony, Cornw.

TREGONY 1705–1708
BODMIN 1708–1710
CORNWALL 1710–1722

b. c.1667, 1st s. of Charles Trevanion of Carhayes, M.P. Tregony 1679–85, by Jane, da. and coh. of Sir Maurice Drummond, gent. usher. *m.* (1) Anne (*d.* Nov. 1725), da. and coh. of Francis Blake of Ford Castle, Northumb., *s.p.*; (2) 29 Mar. 1726, Barbara, da. of William, 4th Baron Berkeley of Stratton, 1s. 2da. *suc.* fa. 1703.

Under Queen Anne Trevanion, a Tory and a member of the October Club, who had an interest of his own at Tregony and had been active in

Cornish elections, had been 'highly discontented that his expectations . . . [had] not been answered' by Harley.[1] He was chosen for the county in 1715, at the same time acting against the Whigs at Bodmin.[2] Shortly afterwards he went over to the Administration, speaking and voting in favour of the septennial bill in 1716. He voted against the repeal of the Occasional Conformity and Schism Acts but for the peerage bill in 1719. His conversion brought him no office but lost him his seat for the county. He died 15 Aug. 1740, aged 73, leaving an estate of £4,000 p.a.[3]

[1] *HMC Portland*, v. 233. [2] *Cal. Treas. Pprs.* 1708–14, p. 284. [3] *Gent. Mag.* 1740, p. 413.

E.C.

TREVANION, William (1727–67), of Carhayes, nr. Tregony, Cornw.

TREGONY 1747–24 Jan. 1767

b. 15 Mar. 1727, o. surv. s. of John Trevanion (q.v.). *educ.* ?Eton; Ch. Ch. Oxf. 1744. *m.* 19 May 1758, Ann, da. and h. of George Barlow (q.v.) of Slebech, Pemb., *s.p. suc.* fa. 1740.

Groom of the bedchamber to Prince of Wales Apr. 1749–Mar. 1751; auditor of the duchy of Cornw. June 1751–*d.*

In 1747 Trevanion was returned on his family's interest at Tregony against the candidates of the Prince of Wales. 'Mr. Trevanion', wrote Thomas Pitt (q.v.), the Prince's election manager in Cornwall, 3 July 1747, 'is most certainly not of age . . . but the difficulty is to find proof of it'.[1] Classed as a government supporter he went over to the Prince of Wales, whose household he joined in 1749, but rejoined the Pelhams after the Prince's death, when he was given a duchy of Cornwall office of £220 p.a.

He died 24 Jan. 1767.

[1] *HMC Fortescue*, i. 120.

E.C.

TREVELYAN, Sir John, 2nd Bt. (?1670–1755), of Nettlecombe, Som.

SOMERSET 1695–1698, 1701
MINEHEAD 1708–10 Sept. 1715, 23 May 1717–1722

b. ?1670, 1st surv. s. of Sir George Trevelyan, 1st Bt., of Nettlecombe by Margaret, da. and h. of John Willoughby of Ley Hill, Devon. *educ.* Wadham, Oxf. 15 Oct. 1687, aged 17. *m.* (1) 1693, Urith (*d.* 26 Apr. 1697), da. of Sir John Pole, 3rd Bt., M.P., of Shute, 1da. *d.v.p.*; (2) 1700, Susanna, da. and h. of William Warren of Stallensthorn, Devon, 3s. 5da. *suc.* fa. 1671.

Sheriff, Som. 1704–5.

Sir John Trevelyan, of a family seated at Nettlecombe since the reign of Henry VII, was a member of the October Club. Returned for Minehead in

1715 on the interest of his neighbours, the Luttrells of Dunster Castle, he was unseated on petition but recovered his seat on petition after the ensuing by-election in 1717. No votes of his are recorded nor did he not stand again. His name was included in the list of leading English Jacobites sent to the Pretender in 1721.[1] He subsequently married one of his daughters to Alexander Luttrell (q.v.), who died in 1737, appointing him a trustee for his daughter and heir Margaret. Shortly after her marriage in 1747, her husband, Henry Fownes Luttrell, M.P., wrote to Francis Luttrell, bencher of the Middle Temple and one of the few surviving representatives of the family:[2]

> I am extremely sorry I am obliged to trouble you with a letter on such a subject . . . What obliges me to do it now, is, that I am going to revive the cause in Chancery against Sir John Trevelyan and Mr. Bampfylde [q.v.], two surviving trustees under Mr. Luttrell's will, and a term of 500 years being created in the same will to them, for the payment of his debts. Now Sir John out of a particular dislike to me, refuses even to act in the said trust, or assign over the term, thinking thereby to distress me, by keeping me out of the rents and profits of the estate for which purpose, to get the power vested in myself, I have revived the cause . . .

Francis Luttrell expressed himself as not surprised to learn

> how ill Sir John hath treated you, which is no wonder. Can you expect better usage when his own son (nay his heir apparent) hath such reason to enter the lists with him. God be thanked he doth not come in my way.[3]

Trevelyan died 25 Sept. 1755, aged 85.

[1] Stuart mss 65/16. [2] Maxwell-Lyte, *Dunster Castle* (1909 ed.), i. 225. [3] Add. 41843, f. 116.

S.R.M.

TREVOR, Hon. John (1695–1764), of St. Anne's Hill, Surr.

NEW WOODSTOCK 4 July 1746–22 Mar. 1753

b. 25 Aug. 1695, 2nd s. of Thomas Trevor, M.P., 1st Baron Trevor, c. j. of common pleas 1701–14, by Elizabeth, da. and coh. of John Searle of Finchley, Mdx.; cos. of John Trevor (q.v.). *educ.* Corpus Christi, Camb. 1711; I. Temple 1712, called 1718. *m.* 30 May 1732, Elizabeth, da. and h. of Sir Richard Steele (q.v.), 1da. *suc.* bro. Thomas as 3rd Baron 22 Mar. 1753.

C.j. Carm., Card. and Pemb. 1724–53; bencher, I. Temple, 1725; K.C. 1730.

Trevor's father, one of the Tory peers created in 1712, was dismissed on the accession of George I, but went over to the Government, becoming 'as zealous a servant to the Hanover family as any of those who had never been otherwise'.[1] His half-brother Robert, envoy at The Hague, contested Oxford University unsuccessfully for the Whigs in

1737. He himself was returned for New Woodstock as a government supporter in 1746 by his brother-in-law, the 3rd Duke of Marlborough, sitting until he succeeded his elder brother to the peerage in 1753. He died 27 Sept. 1764.

¹ Hervey, *Mems.* 85.

E.C.

TREVOR, John (?1717–43), of Glynde, Suss.

LEWES 13 Feb. 1738–Sept. 1743

b. ?1717, o. surv. s. of John Morley Trevor (q.v.) of Glynde. *educ.* Eton 1725; Ch. Ch. Oxf. 2 Apr. 1734, aged 17; Grand Tour c.1737–8. *m.* 1740, Elizabeth, da. of Sir Thomas Frankland, 3rd Bt. (q.v.), of Thirkleby, Yorks., *s.p. suc.* fa. 1719.

Ld. of Admiralty Mar. 1742–*d.*

Trevor was on the grand tour when he received a letter from his cousin, the British minister at The Hague, telling him that the Duke of Newcastle was nominating him for a vacant seat at Lewes which, it was understood, would cost him nothing, and that ministers desired him to return at once to England for the meeting of Parliament.[1] In a letter to Newcastle announcing his immediate return he explained why he had hitherto been reluctant to accept the Duke's offer to bring him in for Lewes:

The way of life I have hitherto led made me think myself incapable of success in the borough of Lewes at present, and though under your Grace's protection I don't despair it, I had rather this affair . . . had happened when I had been more known in the town and I then should not have been so heavy on your Grace's hands.[2]

Returned at a by-election, he voted with the Government on the Spanish convention in 1739 and the place bill in 1740. In 1739 Newcastle through his agent suggested to him that he should buy some houses at Lewes which were to be had for £700. Trevor replied:

Though it would be so extremely inconvenient to me to take up any sum of money that I have debarred myself of many indulgences merely for the want of it, yet would I give no direct denial till I had first given your Grace this trouble, and I assure you, my Lord, that the thoughts of my being an additional weight to your Grace's expense upon these occasions gives me much greater uneasiness than a seat in Parliament can ever give me pleasure, which consideration, I own would make it much more agreeable to me to contribute any little interest that I may have towards the benefit of someone whose inclination it might be perhaps to push the thing more immediately, though I defy any person upon the whole to appear better inclined than him on whom your Grace has already conferred the honour of a candidate.[3]

Re-elected after a contest in 1741, Trevor voted with the Government on the chairman of the elections committee. After Walpole's fall he was one of the two members of the old corps who were appointed to the new Admiralty board. His appointment, Horace Walpole wrote, 'is much disliked, for he is of no consequence for estate, and much less for parts, but is a relation of the Pelhams'.[4] He voted for the Hanoverians, December 1742. In June 1743 he began to show signs of insanity, 'doing nothing but dance and sing and write challenges all day'. In July, though under the charge of a doctor, he attempted to commit suicide.[5] He died some time in September 1743, leaving Glynde to his cousin, Dr. Richard Trevor, bishop of Durham, the brother of John Trevor (q.v.).[6]

¹ *HMC 14th Rep. IX*, 9. ² 13 Jan. 1738, Add. 32691, f. 17. ³ 11 Oct. 1739, Add. 32692, f. 368. ⁴ To Mann, 23 Mar. 1742. ⁵ *HMC Astley*, 250, 268, 281, 292. ⁶ Horsfield, *Suss.* ii. 116.

R.R.S.

TREVOR, John Morley (1681–1719), of Glynde, nr. Lewes, Suss.

SUSSEX 1705–1708
LEWES 5 May 1712–Apr. 1719

b. 31 Aug. 1681, 1st s. of John Trevor of Trevalyn, Denb. by Elizabeth, da. and h. of George Clarke, wid. of William Morley of Glynde, Suss. *educ.* Ch. Ch. Oxf. 17 Dec. 1697, aged 16. *m.* lic. 23 Mar. 1702, Lucy, da. of Edward Montagu of Boughton, Northants. by Elizabeth. sis. of Sir Thomas Pelham, 4th Bt., M.P., of Halland, Suss., 3s. 9da. *suc.* fa. 1686.

Trevor belonged to a Denbighshire family, who acquired Glynde by marriage in 1679. After sitting as a Whig for Sussex he was brought in for Lewes with the support of the future Duke of Newcastle, whose first cousin he had married. His only recorded vote after 1715 was against the septennial bill in 1716, but in a list drawn up after his death in 1719 he is classed among Newcastle's parliamentary followers. He was buried 12 Apr. 1719.

R.R.S.

TROTMAN, Samuel (1650–1720), of Siston Court, Glos.

BATH 20 Feb. 1707–6 Feb. 1720

b. 23 Feb. 1650, 1st s. of Samuel Trotman, barrister-at-law, of Bucknell, Oxon. by his 2nd w. Mary, da. of Samuel Warcup of English, Oxon. *educ.* Exeter, Oxf. 1663; I. Temple, called 1671, bencher 1682. *m.* (1) indenture 5/6 Dec. 1677, Dorothea, da. and coh. of Robert Dring of Isleworth, Mdx., 1da.; (2) lic. 15 Dec. 1691, Elizabeth, da. of Hon. William Mountagu, chief baron of the Exchequer, wid. of Sir William Drake of Shardeloes, nr. Amersham, Bucks., 1da. *d.v.p. suc.* fa. 1685.

Gov. St. Bartholomew's Hospital 1719.

Trotman belonged to an ancient Gloucestershire family. His father purchased Siston Court not far from Bath in 1651, settling it on him, with the manors of Shelswell and Newton Purcell in Oxfordshire, on his marriage in 1677.[1] He represented Bath as a Tory for thirteen years, voting against the septennial bill in 1716, but was absent from the other recorded divisions of that Parliament. He died 6 Feb. 1720.

[1] PCC 12 Cann; *Glos. N. & Q.*, v. 334.

S.R.M.

TROTMAN, Samuel (1686–1748), of Bucknell, Oxon.

NEW WOODSTOCK 1722–1734

b. 7 Mar. 1686, 1st s. of Lenthall Trotman of Bucknell by Mary, da. of Thomas Phillips of Ickford, Bucks. *educ.* Trinity, Oxf. 1702; I. Temple, called 1710. *m.* 16 Oct. 1712, his cos. Dorothea, da. of Samuel Trotman (q.v.) of Siston Court, Glos., *s.p. suc.* fa. 1710.

Trotman, whose family had been seated at Bucknell since 1652, was returned for Woodstock against the Duchess of Marlborough's candidates in 1722, with the support of the Tory Earl of Abingdon. Unopposed in 1727, he is not recorded as voting, and did not stand again. He died 2 Feb. 1748.

E.C.

TUCKER, Edward (d. 1739), of Weymouth, Dorset.

WEYMOUTH AND MELCOMBE REGIS
30 Jan. 1727–10 Mar. 1737

s. of Edward Tucker of Weymouth by his w. Joane. *m.*, 2s. 3da. *suc.* fa. 1707.[1]
Mayor, Weymouth 1702, 1705, 1716, 1721, 1725, 1735; supervisor of the Portland quarries 1714–27, 1737–*d.*

Tucker, a Weymouth merchant, whose father, a merchant adventurer of Weymouth, was imprisoned as a Quaker in 1665,[2] held a government lease of some of the quarries at Portland. At George I's accession he obtained the post of supervisor of the Portland quarries,[3] carrying considerable electoral influence in the borough of Weymouth and Melcombe Regis, which returned four Members. Allying himself with Bubb Dodington (q.v.), who looked after their interests at Westminster, leaving Tucker to manage the borough, he was returned unopposed for it in 1727, transferring his post, which was incompatible with a seat in the Commons, to one of his sons. In Parliament he voted with the Government on the army in 1732 and the repeal of the Septennial Act in 1734, but was absent from the other recorded divisions. Shortly before the general election of 1734 Walpole received a warning from a friend in Weymouth that it was important

> for the people there to see that Mr. Tucker cannot dispose of everything in the town as he is daily persuading them that he can and consequently has his principal sway there by being thought to have it alone. For in short that consideration and the Portland stone are what support his power there—personally he is not popular and the people want but a small gleam of encouragement to revolt.

The letter added:

> Mr. Tucker is and has been long dangerously ill and by what I know of his infirmities rheumatism palsy and dropsy cannot live long.[4]

He and his son, John, who was also returned for Weymouth and Melcombe Regis in 1735, were among the five 'friends' whom Walpole asked Dodington to speak to about the opposition motion of 22 Feb. 1737 for an increase in the allowance of the Prince of Wales. After the division, in which, led by Dodington, they all voted with the Government against the motion, Dodington told Walpole that 'the connexion between these gentlemen and me was such that we should not have differed in opinion', if he had decided to vote for the motion.[5] Next month he vacated his seat by resuming his Portland place. He died 5 Apr. 1739.

[1] PCC 118 Henchman. [2] H. J. Maule, *Weymouth*, 83. [3] *Gent. Mag.* ix. 307. See also *Cal. Treas. Bks. and Pprs.* 1742–5, pp. 69, 717. [4] L. Chaplain to Sir Robt. Walpole, 4 Dec. 1733, Cholmondeley (Houghton) mss. [5] *Dodington Diary*, 466, 468.

R.R.S.

TUCKER, John (d. 1779), of Weymouth, Dorset.

WEYMOUTH AND MELCOMBE REGIS
28 Feb. 1735–1747, 1754–June 1778

1st s. of Edward Tucker (q.v.). *m.* Martha, da. of George Gollop of Berwick, Dorset, *s.p. suc.* fa. 1739.
Mayor, Weymouth 1726, 1732, 1754, 1763, 1772; cashier to treasurer of the navy 1744–9; paymaster of the marines ?1757–*d.*; keeper of the King's private roads 1770–*d.*

John Tucker entered Parliament for the seat vacated by George Bubb Dodington's decision to sit for Bridgwater. Like his father, he followed Dodington,[1] accompanying him into opposition in 1740[2] and combining with him to wrest the control of Weymouth and Melcombe Regis from Walpole in 1741.[3] He remained in opposition till Dodington became treasurer of the navy in 1744, appointing him his cashier; was classed by the Government as 'New Ally' in 1746; did not stand in 1747, when his post became incompatible with a seat in the Commons under the Place Act of 1742; and lost his post in 1749, when Dodington went over to the Prince of Wales. About 1749–50 Egmont described him to Frederick as the 'absolute creature' of

Dodington, who left all his property at Weymouth and Melcombe Regis to him.[4] He died 9 Oct. 1779.

[1] *Dodington Diary*, 466, 468. [2] Sir Dudley Ryder's diary, 9 Aug. 1740, Harrowby mss. [3] *CJ*, xxiv. 293-5. [4] PCC Boycott 264.

R.R.S.

TUCKFIELD, John (c.1719-67), of Little Fulford, nr. Crediton, Devon.

EXETER   1747-6 Dec. 1767

b. c.1719, s. of Roger Tuckfield of London. *m.* 18 Mar. 1741, Frances, da. and coh. of William Gould of Downes House, nr. Crediton, *s.p.*; her sis. Elizabeth m. James Buller (q.v.). *suc. cos.* Roger Tuckfield (q.v.) at Raddon 1739.[1]

Tuckfield's family purchased Little Fulford, now known as Shobrooke Park, at the beginning of the seventeenth century.[2] When the severe winter of 1740 had caused so many deaths and so much illness in Exeter that the building of a hospital was proposed, Tuckfield provided the land and building materials. The Devon and Exeter Hospital, as it was named, was opened in January 1743, with Tuckfield as chairman of the court of governors.[3] A freeman of Exeter since 1741, he was returned as a Tory for the city in 1747 on the corporation interest.

He died 6 Dec. 1767.

[1] Vivian, *Vis. Devon*, 422; *Trans. Dev. Assoc.* lxii. 214. [2] C. Worthy, *Devon Wills*, 418. [3] Jenkins, *Exeter*, 201-3.

R.R.S.

TUCKFIELD, Roger (?1685-1739), of Raddon Court, Devon.

ASHBURTON   21 Jan. 1708-17 Mar. 1711
            1713-26 Mar. 1739

b. ?Apr. 1685, 1st s. of Roger Tuckfield of Raddon Court by Margaret, da. of William Davy of Dura, Devon, barrister. *educ.* Exeter, Oxf. 8 Aug. 1700, aged 15. *unm. suc. fa.* 1687.[1]

The Tuckfields, originally wealthy clothiers, had been seated at Raddon since the sixteenth century. In 1702 they purchased a moiety of the manor of Ashburton,[2] obtaining control of the borough, for which Roger Tuckfield sat, with one short interruption, from the first by-election following his coming of age till his death. Classed as a Whig in 1715, he was absent from the division on the septennial bill but supported the repeal of the Occasional Conformity and Schism Acts in 1719. He was classed as 'doubtful' by Sunderland on the peerage bill, 'to be spoken to' by Carteret, but he was absent from the division on the bill. No further vote of his is recorded during the remaining 20 years of his parliamentary career. He died 26 Mar. 1739, leaving Ashburton to his sister, the wife of

John Harris (q.v.), on whose death in 1754 it was inherited by her daughter, the wife of the 2nd Earl of Orford, while Raddon went to his cousin John Tuckfield (q.v.).[3]

[1] Vivian, *Vis. Devon*, 270; PCC 172 Foot. [2] Lysons, *Devonshire*, i. clviii; ii. 13; *Trans. Dev. Assoc.* xiv. 448; *Magna Britannia* (1715), i. 524; G. D. Stawell, *Quantock Fam.* 170-5, app. xvi n. 10. [3] Lady Orford to Jas. Buller, 5 Apr. 1754, Buller mss at Antony, Cornw.; PCC 92 Henchman.

S.R.M.

TUFNELL, Samuel (1682-1758), of Langleys, Essex.

MALDON   20 May 1715-1722
COLCHESTER   1727-1734
GREAT MARLOW 1741-1747

b. 15 Sept. 1682, o.s. of John Tufnell, brewer, of St. Mary's Undershaft, London, and Monken Hadley, Mdx. by Elizabeth, da. of John Jolliffe, M.P., merchant and alderman of London. *educ.* Merton, Oxf. 1698; M. Temple 1699, called 1703, bencher 1740; Grand Tour (Holland, Germany, Italy, Switzerland) 1703-5. *m.* 19 Dec. 1717 (with £10,000), Elizabeth, da. of George Cressener of Earl's Colne, Essex, 3s. 2da. *suc. fa.* 1699; uncle, Sir William Jolliffe (q.v.), to Pleshey, Essex 1750.

Capt. of troop of Essex militia 1715; commr. of the equivalent[1] 24 July 1717-18 Apr. 1719; commr. for settling commerce at Antwerp June 1732-Feb. 1742.

Tufnell was the grandson of Richard Tufnell, a prosperous brewer, M.P. Southwark 1640. At the age of 17 he succeeded to the family estate, subject to the trusteeship of his uncles, Sir William Jolliffe and Sir Edward Northey (qq.v.), till he came of age. He was called to the bar but, though he became a bencher, there is no evidence of his having practised.[2] In 1710 he purchased the manor of Langleys, not far from Maldon, for which he stood as a Whig in 1715, jointly with Sir William Jolliffe, succeeding on petition. He made his first recorded speech in support of the septennial bill in 1716, sending a copy to the editor of the *Political State*,[3] in which it is printed. At a meeting of M.P.s in March 1717, called to consider the introduction of a bill to repeal the laws against the Dissenters, he recommended that the matter should be postponed.[4] In June 1717 he opposed the motion to postpone the trial of Lord Oxford, saying that he had originally supported the impeachment on a charge of high treason on the assurance of Walpole, as chairman of the secret committee set up to inquire into the late Tory Government, that there were just grounds for it. Walpole then

> let drop an insinuation, as if many who followed his opinion in the business of the impeachments, did it rather out of compliment to his power, than to his person,

whereupon Tufnell,

resenting this innuendo, immediately repelled the dint of it, by appealing to that honourable Member 'whether he ever made his court to him?' 'And whether he had not paid him more respect since he was out, than when he was in place?'

During the split in the Whig party he was given a temporary place which lapsed in April 1719, after which he spoke against the peerage bill. After the collapse of the South Sea bubble in 1720 he supported Walpole's efforts to damp down the proceedings against its authors, speaking with him on behalf of Sir George Caswall (q.v.) on 10 Mar. 1721 and on 2 June seconding a motion for allowing one of the directors to retain a substantial part of his confiscated estate. A few days later the secret committee of the Commons on the South Sea affair presented a report containing the names of a number of Members, including Tufnell, who, while the South Sea bill was before the House, had allowed themselves to be put down by the Company for stock without paying for it on the understanding that if the bill went through and the stock consequently rose, they would be entitled to receive the difference.[5] The amount allotted to Tufnell was £5,000 at 182, but it is not known what he made on the transaction, nor was the matter pursued by the Commons. In January 1722 he is reported as complaining of 'a scandalous list that was handed about', in which he was named as one of the Members 'who received South Sea stock for giving their votes for the South Sea bill', and as professing to be able to clear himself.[6]

Tufnell was out of Parliament till 1727 when he successfully contested Colchester as a Walpole Whig, voting for the excise bill and against the repeal of the Septennial Act. In 1732 he was appointed a commissioner, with an allowance of £4 a day, to treat with the commissioners of the Emperor and the States General on commercial and other matters arising out of the treaty of Vienna.[7] The negotiations opened in 1737 at Antwerp, where Tufnell remained, with occasional visits to England, till they ended inconclusively on the outbreak of the war of the Austrian succession.[8]

Tufnell did not stand in 1734 but was returned on Walpole's nomination for Great Marlow in 1741,[9] continuing to vote regularly with the Government till he retired in 1747. He died 28 Dec. 1758.

[1] See BOTELER, John. [2] F.W. Steer, *Samuel Tufnell of Langleys*, 17. [3] *Pol. State*, xxxvii. p. vii. [4] W. Michael, *England under Geo. I*, i. 50. [5] *CJ*, xix. 569, 578. [6] *Hist. Reg.* 1722, p. 53. [6] *Cal. Treas. Bks. and Pprs.* 1731-4, p. 230. [8] Steer, 62-73. [9] Sir Wm. Clayton to Walpole, 4 Feb. 1740, Cholmondeley (Houghton) mss.

E.C.

TUFTON, Sackville (1688-1753), of Newbottle, Northants.

APPLEBY 1722-30 July 1729

b. 11 May 1688, 1st surv. s. of Hon. Sackville Tufton by Elizabeth, da. and h. of Ralph Wilbraham of Newbottle. *m.* 11 June 1722, Lady Mary Saville, da. and coh. of William, 2nd Mq. of Halifax, 2s. 2da. *suc.* fa. 1721; uncle as 7th Earl of Thanet 30 July 1729.

The Tuftons were a Kent family who had acquired by marriage the vast Clifford estates in Westmorland, including the castle at Appleby, where they controlled one seat. Returned unopposed as a Tory on the family's interest for Appleby in 1722, Sackville Tufton unsuccessfully attempted to gain control of the other seat at a by-election in 1723, putting up Lord Hillsborough (q.v.), 'because he will spend money, by which Tufton saves his own'.[1] In 1725 he concluded an agreement with the 3rd Viscount Lonsdale for their joint lives, under which each of them was to recommend one Member for Appleby and no attempt was to be made to alter the balance of power in the borough.[2] His only recorded vote in the Commons before he succeeded to the title was against the Government on the civil list arrears in 1729. He died 4 Dec. 1753, after sending for his tailor to ask him if he could make him a suit of mourning in eight hours; if he could he would go into mourning for his brother-in-law, Lord Burlington (who had died on 3 Dec.), but that he did not expect to live twelve hours himself.[3]

[1] Ld. Finch to Ld. Nottingham, 11 Apr. 1723, Finch mss at HMC. [2] See APPLEBY. [3] Horace Walpole to Bentley, 19 Dec. 1753.

R.R.S.

TURNER, Sir Charles, 1st Bt. (1666-1738), of Warham, Norf.

KING'S LYNN 1695-24 Nov. 1728

bap. 11 June 1666, s. of William Turner, attorney at law, of North Elmham, Norf. by Anne, da. of John Spooner. *educ.* Scarning and Norwich; Caius, Camb. 1681; M. Temple 1684. *m.* (1) Apr. 1689, Mary (*d.* Apr. 1701), da. of Robert Walpole, M.P., of Houghton and sis. of Sir Robert Walpole (q.v.), 1s. *d.v.p.* 4da.; (2) Mary, da. of Sir William Blois of Grundisburgh, Suff., wid. of Sir Nevil Catelyn of Kirby Cane, *s.p.* Kntd. 22 Mar. 1696; *cr.* Bt. 27 Apr. 1727.

Ld. of Treasury 1707-13, of the Admiralty 1714-17, of the Treasury 1720-30; chairman of committees of supply and ways and means 1728-*d.*; teller of the Exchequer 1729-*d.*

The Turners were one of the leading families in Lynn, which they represented in every Parliament for nearly 80 years. Returned as a Whig for Lynn in 1695, Turner from 1702 shared the representation of the borough with his brother-in-law, Robert Walpole, of whom he was a loyal and trusted supporter. He obtained office with Walpole in 1714, speaking for the septennial bill in 1716; followed him into opposition in 1717, at the cost of losing his place; and was one of the friends whom Walpole put into the new Treasury board when he returned to office in 1720. When in 1724 William Farrer (q.v.) was taken ill in the chair of the ways and means committee, Turner deputized for him,[1] succeeding him in the money chair in 1728. On his death at Houghton, 24 Nov. 1738, Walpole wrote that he had lost 'the oldest friend and acquaintance I had in the world'.[2]

[1] *Knatchbull Diary*, 2 Dec. 1724. [2] Coxe, *Walpole*, iii. 517.

R.R.S.

TURNER, Cholmley (1685–1757), of Kirkleatham, Yorks.

NORTHALLERTON   1715–1722
YORKSHIRE   1 Feb. 1727–1741, 21 Jan. 1742–1747

bap. 20 July 1685, 1st s. of Charles Turner of Kirkleatham by Margaret, da. of Sir William Cholmley, 2nd Bt., of Whitby, Yorks., sis and coh. of Sir Hugh Cholmley, 3rd Bt. *educ.* New Coll. Oxf. 1701. *m.* 1709, Jane, da. of George Marwood of Little Busby, Yorks., 1s. 1da. *d.v.p.*[1]
   High steward, York 1725.

Turner was a wealthy country gentleman, with properties in Northallerton and along Tees side, as well as lead mining interests in the North Riding.[2] Returned as a Whig for Northallerton in 1715, he followed Walpole into opposition in 1717, voting against the Government in all recorded divisions. He did not stand in 1722, but was successful in 1726 at a by-election for Yorkshire, which he thenceforth represented, with one short interruption, for the rest of his parliamentary career. In the 1727 Parliament he took a very independent line, speaking on the opposition side in a debate on foreign affairs, 5 Feb. 1729,[3] and voting against the Government on the Hessians in 1730, the army in 1732, and the excise bill in 1733, but for them on the repeal of the Septennial Act in 1734. Complaining that 'he was so wrong-headed there was no holding him', Walpole wondered whether he would like a red ribbon.[4] He announced his intention of not standing in 1734 but changed his mind on receiving an invitation from the Whig county meeting at York, which he accepted, the 3rd Earl of Carlisle told Walpole, 'although he had writ to me the day before that he desired not to stand'.[5] Re-elected after a hard contest, he voted with the Government on the navy estimates in February 1735, when it was 'thought the petition which is lodged against [him] will make him do right while that is depending'.[6] He also voted for the Spanish convention in 1739. He refused to stand in 1741 but when a by-election

occurred he was induced to submit himself to 'the command of the gentlemen', as expressed by his unanimous adoption at another general Whig meeting, 'the most numerous that has been seen a great while'.[7] Returned after a contest, he was on the court list for the secret committee of inquiry into Walpole's Administration, to which he was elected, never attending its meetings.[8] His only vote in this Parliament was for the Hanoverians in 1744. In 1747 he finally retired, giving as his reason that there were 'so many noblemen' who were 'thought to have the interest and direction of this county'.[9] On his retirement he received a secret service pension of £500 a year from Pelham, which was not renewed when Newcastle succeeded to the Treasury.[10] He died 9 May 1757.

[1] *Top. & Gen.* i. 507–8. [2] C. Collyer, 'The Yorks. election of 1734,' *Proc. Leeds Philosophical Soc.* vii. 55–56. [3] *HMC Egmont Diary*, iii. 345. [4] *HMC Carlisle*, 127. [5] 8 Nov. [1733], Cholmondeley (Houghton) mss. [6] *HMC Carlisle*, 151. [7] C. Collyer, 'The Yorks. election of 1741', *Proc. Leeds Philosophical Soc.* vii. 141. [8] Walpole to Mann, 1 and 22 Apr. 1742. [9] C. Collyer, 'The Rockinghams & Yorks. politics 1742–61', *Thoresby Misc.* xli. 358. [10] Add. 33038, f. 415.

R.R.S.

TURNER, Sir Edward, 2nd Bt. (1719–66), of Ambrosden, Oxon.

GREAT BEDWYN   1741–1747
OXFORDSHIRE   23 Apr. 1755–1761
PENRYN   1761–31 Oct. 1766

b. 18 Apr. 1719, o. surv. s. of Sir Edward Turner, 1st Bt., of Ambrosden, merchant and director of the E.I. Co., by Mary, da. and h. in her issue of Sir Gregory Page, 1st Bt. (q.v.). *educ.* Eton 1725–32; Balliol, Oxf. 1735; L. Inn 1745. *m.* 8 Sept. 1739, Cassandra, da. of William Leigh of Adlestrop, Glos., 6s. 3da. *suc.* fa. 19 June 1735 and to £100,000 on *d.* of his uncle John Turner 1760.
   Freeman, Oxford 1742–51.

The son and heir of a wealthy merchant, Turner succeeded as a boy to a large fortune. Returned as a Tory on coming of age on the Bruce interest at Great Bedwyn, he 'acted with a good deal of violence in opposition'.[1] He spoke against the Hanoverians in January 1744 and April 1746, soon afterwards writing to a friend:

> Hang the Parliament! Why should I have stayed boiling in London any longer? When a vote of credit for so large a sum as £50[0],000 can be swallowed so easily by those who were formerly noted for great delicacy in their political food, what can raise our admiration? In short, my patience is worn out in seeing politists swallow down ministerial pudding piping hot without so much as blistering their tongues.[2]

On 12 Dec. 1746 he and Lord Strange (q.v.) moved to postpone voting the deficiencies of the civil list, only securing 32 supporters.[3]

Turner stood again for Great Bedwyn in 1747 but on a double return was unseated by the Commons after a hard struggle.[4] In 1749 he tried unsuccessfully to get himself adopted as a prospective candidate for Oxford city, should one of the sitting Members, Lord Wenman, stand for the county at the next general election. About this time the 2nd Lord Egmont in his electoral survey wrote of him under Oxford:

> A pert, warm little man, busy, with a turn to find fault. While he was in Parliament no two people agreed so well together or acted more in concert than he and my Lord Strange. He will have a very great estate—for I understand Gregory Page's fortune will be added to his own.

In 1751 he was one of three rival Tory candidates for Oxford University, of which he had been created an honorary doctor in 1714, resigning his freedom of the city to qualify himself for election, but coming bottom of the poll.[5] In 1752 Lord Harcourt assured Newcastle that he had 'always heard from those who knew him he was neither Tory or Jacobite'.[6] At the general election of 1754 he stood on the 'new' or Whig interest against Lord Wenman for the county, for which he was seated on petition by the Commons after a double return.

He died 31 Oct. 1766.

[1] R. J. Robson, *The Oxfordshire Election of 1754*, p. 13. [2] Yorke's parl. jnl. *Parl. Hist.* xiii. 463; *An 18th Cent. Corresp.* (ed. Dickens & Stanton), 121–2. [3] Hartington to Devonshire, 13 Dec. 1746, Devonshire mss. [4] Ilchester, *Lord Holland*, i. 144. [5] W. R. Ward, *Georgian Oxford*, 189–91. [6] Robson, op. cit.

R.S.L.

TURNER, Sir John, 3rd Bt. (1712–80), of Warham, Norf.

KING'S LYNN   9 Feb. 1739–1774

bap. 19 June 1712, o.s. of Sir John Turner, 2nd Bt., M.P. (bro. of Sir Charles Turner, q.v.), of Warham by Anne, da. of Thomas Allen, London merchant. *educ.* Greenwich sch.; Christ's, Camb. 1730; M. Temple 1729, called 1736, bencher 1766. *m.* (1) 20 Oct. 1746, Miss Stonehouse (*d.* 1749), *s.p.*; (2) Frances, da. and coh. of John Neale (q.v.) of Allesley, Warws., 2da. *suc.* fa. 6 Jan. 1739.
Ld. of Treasury May 1762–July 1765.

Turner succeeded his uncle, Sir Charles Turner, as M.P. for King's Lynn, voting with the Government in every recorded division. He died 25 June 1780.

R.R.S.

TURNER, *see also* **HORSEMONDEN TURNER**

TURNOR, Sir Edward (?1646–1721), of Hallingbury, Essex.

ORFORD   1701–29 Jan. 1709, 1710–3 Dec. 1721

b. ?1646, 1st s. of Sir Edward Turnor, M.P., of Little Parndon, Essex, Speaker of the House of Commons 1661–70, by Sarah, da. and h. of Gerard Gore, alderman of London. *educ.* Christ's, Camb. 17 Feb. 1662, aged 15; M. Temple 1661, called 1672. *m.* May 1667, Lady Isabel Keith, da. of William, 7th Earl Marischal [S], 2s. 5da. *suc.* fa. 1676. Kntd. 6 Feb. 1664.

Turnor came of an ancient Suffolk family, who had moved to Essex, where his father bought Hallingbury.[1] Re-elected in 1715 for Orford as a Tory, he voted against the Government in every recorded division. His name was sent to the Pretender in 1721 as a probable supporter in the event of a rising.[2] He died 3 Dec. 1721.

[1] Morant, *Essex*, ii. 495–6. [2] Stuart mss 65/16.

R.R.S.

TWISDEN, Sir Roger, 5th Bt. (1705–72), of Bradbourne, Kent.

KENT   1741–1754

b. 4 Apr. 1705, 2nd s. of Sir Thomas Twisden, 3rd Bt. (q.v.). *educ.* Trinity, Oxf. 1722. *m.* 10 Jan. 1737, Elizabeth, da. of Edward Watton of Addington, Kent, wid. of Leonard Bartholomew of Oxenhoath, Kent, 4s. 2da. *suc.* bro. as 5th Bt. 30 July 1737.
Cornet 3 Hussars 1736–7.

A Tory, but not a Jacobite, Twisden obtained an army commission in 1736 which he resigned on succeeding his brother next year. Returned unopposed for the county in 1741, he voted with the Opposition. During the Forty-five he served in the Kent militia, becoming a captain in 1746. He was again unopposed in 1747, but declined standing in 1754 because of ill-health.[1] Between 1761 and 1768 he made several unsuccessful attempts to secure his eldest son's return for Kent.

He died 7 Mar. 1772.

[1] Sir J. R. Twisden, *Twisden Fam.* 399.

A.N.N.

TWISDEN, Sir Thomas, 3rd Bt. (1668–1728), of Bradbourne, Kent.

KENT   1722–1727

b. 10 Nov. 1668, 1st s. of Sir Roger Twisden, 2nd Bt., M.P., by Margaret, da. of Sir John Marsham, 1st Bt., of Whorne's Place, Cuxton, Kent. *educ.* I. Temple 1684; Grand Tour (Holland, Germany, Italy, France) 1693. *m.* 17 July 1701, Anne, da. and h. of John Musters of Colwick Hall, Notts., 4s. *suc.* fa. 28 Feb. 1703.

Twisden's family had purchased Bradbourne in 1656 and had represented Maidstone and Rochester in Parliament. While travelling in France with his father in 1698 he is said to have visited and kissed the hand of James II's son. On his marriage in 1701 his father handed over to him the Bradbourne estate where he rebuilt the house in the style of Sir Christopher Wren.[1] Returned for his county as a Tory in 1722, he did not stand in 1727, dying 12 Sept. 1728.

[1] Sir J. R. Twisden, *Twisden Fam.* 380–9.

E.C.

TYLNEY, Earl, *see* CHILD, Sir Richard

TYLNEY, Frederick (?1653–1725), of Tylney Hall, Hants.

WINCHESTER	1690–1700
STOCKBRIDGE	1701–1702
SOUTHAMPTON	1702–1705
WHITCHURCH	17 Jan.–17 Feb. 1708, 5 May–21 Dec. 1708, 1710–1715, 25 May–26 June 1721

b. ?1653, s. of Francis Tylney of Rotherwick, Hants by Dorothy, da. of Robert Henley of Bramshill. *educ.* Queen's, Oxf. 22 Oct. 1669, aged 16. *m.* 7 Sept. 1688, Anne, da. of George Pitt of Strathfieldsaye, Hants, 1da. *suc.* fa. 1684.

Commr. to inquire into encroachments in the New Forest 1691–4.

Descended from a wealthy Hampshire family seated at Rotherwick since 1629,[1] Tylney, a Tory, was defeated at Whitchurch in 1715. Recovering the seat at a by-election in 1721, but unseated on petition a month later, he was defeated at the general election of 1722. He died 2 Oct. 1725, his property passing after the death of his daughter, Anne, Baroness Craven, to his niece, whose husband, Sir Richard Child (q.v.), Viscount Castlemaine, adopted the name of Tylney.

[1] *VCH Hants*, iv. 99.

P.W.

TYNTE, Sir Halswell, 3rd Bt. (1705–30), of Halswell, nr. Bridgwater, Som.

BRIDGWATER 1727–12 Nov. 1730

b. 15 Nov. 1705, 1st s. of Sir John Tynte, 2nd Bt., of Halswell, Somerset, by Jane, da. of Sir Charles Kemys, 3rd Bt., M.P., of Cefn Mably, Glam., sis. of Sir Charles Kemys, 4th Bt. (q.v.); bro. of Sir Charles Kemys Tynte, 5th Bt. (q.v.). *educ.* New Coll. Oxf. 1723. *m.* 28 Sept. 1727, Mary, da. of John Walters of Brecon, 2da. *d.v.p. suc.* fa. Mar. 1710.

Tynte, whose family had been settled in Somerset since the beginning of the seventeenth century,[1] was returned unopposed for Bridgwater on his family's interest shortly after coming of age. A Tory, he voted against the Administration in the division on the Hessian troops, dying 12 Nov. 1730.

[1] Collinson. *Som*, ii. 317–18.

S.R.M.

TYNTE, *see also* KEMYS TYNTE

TYRCONNEL, Visct., *see* BROWNLOW, Sir John

TYRRELL, James (c.1674–1742), of Shotover, Oxon.

BOROUGHBRIDGE 1722–30 Aug. 1742

b. c.1674, o.s. of James Tyrrell of Oakley, Bucks. by Mary, da. and h. of Sir Michael Hutchinson of Fladbury, Worcs. *unm. suc.* fa. 1718.

Capt.-lt. Earl of Macclesfield's Horse 1694; 5 Drag. Gds. by 1707; brevet lt.-col. 1707; col. of a regt. of Ft. 1709; half-pay 1713; col. of a regt. of Drags. July 1715–Nov. 1718; col. 17 Ft. 1722–d.; brig.-gen. 1727; maj.-gen. 1735; lt.-gen. 1739; gov. Pendennis castle 1737, Gravesend and Tilbury 1737–d., Holy Island and Berwick May 1742–d.

Groom of the bedchamber to George I 1714–27.

The son of a wealthy Whig country gentleman, who was an intimate friend of John Locke's and the author of a number of political and historical works, Tyrrell served in the wars of William III and Marlborough. Obtaining a court place at George I's accession, he was brought into Parliament by the Duke of Newcastle for one of his pocket boroughs, voting consistently with the Government till his death 30 Aug. 1742.

R.R.S.

TYRWHITT, Sir John, 5th Bt. (?1663–1741), of Stainfield, Lincs.

LINCOLN 1715–1727, 5 Jan. 1728–1734

b. ?1663, o. surv. s. of Sir Philip Tyrwhitt, 4th Bt., M.P., of Stainfield, Lincs. by Penelope, da. of Sir Erasmus de la Fountain of Kirkby Bellars, Leics. *m.* 24 Feb. 1691, Elizabeth, da. and coh. of Francis Phillips of Kempton Park, Sunbury, Mdx., 2da.; (2) lic. 5 Aug. 1704, Mary da., of Sir William Drake of Shardeloes, Bucks., 1s. 4da. *suc.* fa. July 1688.

Sheriff, Lincs. 1693–4.

Descended from an old Lincolnshire family seated at Stainfield since the sixteenth century, Tyrwhitt is described as 'of good natural parts but debauched'.[1] Returned for Lincoln as a Whig on his family's interest in 1715, he voted with the Administration on the septennial bill in 1716, but against them on the repeal of the Occasional Conformity and Schism Acts in 1719. He was classed by Sunderland as 'doubtful' in a list drawn up before the peerage bill, and to be spoken to by Newcastle and Craggs, but he voted against it. Unsuccessful for Lincoln in 1727, he regained his seat at a by-election in 1728, but no further votes of his are recorded. He died November 1741.

[1] *Her. & Gen.* ii. 126.

P.W.

TYRWHITT, Sir John de la Fountain, 6th Bt. (1708–60), of Stainfield, Lincs.

LINCOLN 1741–1747

> *b.* 6 Mar. 1708, o.s. of Sir John Tyrwhitt (q.v.) by his 2nd w. *educ.* Eton 1718–25. *unm.* *suc.* fa. Nov. 1741.
>
> Sheriff, Lincs. 1750–1.

Returned, apparently as a Whig, for Lincoln in 1741, Tyrwhitt voted consistently against the Administration, signing the opposition whip of 10 Nov. 1743.[1] He did not stand again and died 22 Aug. 1760, entailing his estates on his cousin Thomas Drake.[2]

[1] Owen, *Pelhams*, 178. [2] *Notices and Remains of Fam. of Tyrwhitt*, 48.

P.W.

UPPER OSSORY, Earl of, *see* **FITZPATRICK, John**

URQUHART, Alexander (*d.* 1727). of Newhall, Ross.

CROMARTYSHIRE 1715–1722
ROSS-SHIRE 1722–1727

> 1st s. of John Urquhart of Newhall by Jean, da. of Colin Mackenzie of Redcastle, Ross; bro.-in-law of Sir Kenneth Mackenzie, M.P. [S], of Scatwell, Ross. *m.* Anna, da. of Col. Thomas Hamilton of Olivestob, Haddington, 1s. 1da. *suc.* fa. by 1715.
>
> Ensign 15 Ft. 1708; capt. Stanwix's Ft. 1710; half-pay 1714.

Though returned for Cromartyshire on the recommendation of the Duke of Montrose, the secretary of state for Scotland, and classed as a Whig in 1715,[1] Urquhart was a Tory, voting against the Administration in all recorded divisions. Professing 'great zeal' for the Pretender's service, 'he found means to be well known to the Earl of Sunderland', for whom he acted as an intermediary with the Jacobites. When in March 1721 Sunderland was threatened with impeachment for his part in the South Sea bubble, he gave Urquhart

> full power to assure the Tories that if they would be his friends in keeping off the impeachment his enemies design against him, he would order things to their desire . . . that the House of Commons shall be entirely of their own making so that the Tories shall have a way open for England to do the thing [a restoration] herself, and if the Tories do not make use of the opportunity, 'twill be none of Lord Sunderland's fault.

When the case came before Parliament in April 'as many of the Tories joined Lord Sunderland as saved him'. In August Sunderland sent Urquhart to Scotland, where he applied to leading Jacobites, 'endeavouring . . . to give us a good impression of Sunderland's designs, that we might . . . influence the Tories to favour his interest at the election of

the new Parliament'. In reply to inquiries whether these overtures should be accepted, the Pretender wrote to his friends: 'I am satisfied Captain Urquhart is a sincere well-wisher of mine', but advised them against trusting Sunderland too far. He also gave Urquhart a commission as lieutenant-colonel in January 1722. After Sunderland's death Urquhart became 'as great a depender on' Walpole,[2] who secured the shelving of a petition against his return for Ross-shire by his relation, Sir William Gordon (q.v.), in 1722.[3] During the South Sea bubble he had speculated heavily, borrowing money to buy South Sea stock, which he pawned to the Sword Blade Company as security for a loan. When the stock was at its highest he attempted to redeem it, but the Sword Blade Company refused to return it, whereupon he brought an action against them, which was settled by a payment to him of £25,000. On this his creditors pressed for repayment, which he refused, taking refuge under his parliamentary privilege. In 1725 they petitioned the House of Commons for relief, with the result that he had to agree to waive his privilege to enable them to bring an action against him for the recovery of their money.[4] He died bankrupt and intestate in 1727, Newhall passing to his relatives, the Gordons of Invergordon, his principal creditors.[5]

[1] Sir W. Fraser, *Earls of Cromarty*, ii. 158. [2] *Lockhart Pprs.* ii. 67–68, 69, 78, 81; Stuart mss 52/105, 53/13; Ruvigny, *Jacobite Peerage*, 244. [3] *Knatchbull Diary*, 24 Oct. 1722. [4] *Ibid.* 12 Apr. 1725; *Case of Creditors of Alex. Urquhart*; *Case of Alex. Urquhart*; *Further Case of the Creditors of Alex. Urquhart*; *CJ*, xx. 464, 486, 496. [5] H. Tayler, *Fam. of Urquhart*; 251.

P.W

URQUHART, Duncan (*d.* 1742), of Burdsyards, Morayshire.

INVERNESS BURGHS 21 July 1737–1741

> 1st s. of Capt. Robert Urquhart, M.P., of Burdsyards by Mary, da. of Duncan Forbes of Culloden, M.P. *unm.* *suc.* fa. 1741.
>
> Ensign 10 Ft. 1726, lt. 1731; lt. and capt. 2 Ft. Gds. 1738; provost of Forres.

Descended from the Urquharts of Cromarty, Urquhart was returned for Inverness Burghs in 1737 by his uncle, Duncan Forbes (q.v.). He voted with the Administration on the Spanish convention in 1739 and the place bill in 1740, did not stand in 1741, and died 11 Jan. 1742.

P.W.

VANBRUGH, Charles (1680–1740), of St. James's, Westminster.

PLYMOUTH 17 Jan.–2 Nov. 1740

> *bap.* 27 Feb. 1680, 6th s. of Gyles Vanbrugh, sugar baker, of St. Nicholas Acon, London, and of Chester,

by Elizabeth, da. of Sir Dudley Carleton of Imber Court, Surr.; bro. of Sir John Vanbrugh, the architect and dramatist, and Philip Vanbrugh, commr. of the navy at Plymouth 1739–*d. m.* 19 June 1721, Ann Burt of Knightsbridge, 1s.[1]

Capt. R.N. 1709.

Charles Vanbrugh served under Byng at Cape Passaro in 1718, in which year his brother, Sir John Vanbrugh, designed the gun-wharf at Plymouth.[2] He stood unsuccessfully for Plymouth on the Admiralty interest[3] at a by-election in 1739, but was seated on petition, voting with the Government on the place bill next year. He died 2 Nov. 1740.

[1] PCC 310 Browne. [2] Lysons, *Mag. Brit.* Devon, ii. 459. [3] *Cal. of Vernon-Wager mss in Lib. of Congress*, 59.

S.R.M.

VANE, Hon. Henry (c.1705–58), of Raby Castle, co. Dur.

LAUNCESTON	31 May 1726–1727
ST. MAWES	1727–1741
RIPON	1741–1747
DURHAM CO.	1747–27 Apr. 1753

b. c.1705, 1st s. of Gilbert Vane, 2nd Baron Barnard, by Mary, da. and coh. of Morgan Randyll (q.v.) of Chilworth, Surr. *educ.* privately. *m.* 2 Sept. 1725, Lady Grace Fitzroy, da. of Charles Fitzroy, 2nd Duke of Cleveland and Southampton, 3s. 3da. *suc.* fa. as 3rd Baron 27 Apr. 1753; *cr.* Visct. Barnard and Earl of Darlington 3 Apr. 1754.

Jt. vice-treasurer and paymaster gen. [I] 1742–4; P.C. [I] 18 Sept. 1742; ld. of Treasury 1749–55; jt. paymaster of forces 1755–6.

Mayor, Hartlepool 1748, Durham 1755; ld. lt. and v.-adm. co. Durham 1750–8.

Descended from Sir Henry Vane, who purchased Raby, Barnard Castle, and other estates in Durham during the reign of Charles I, Vane unsuccessfully contested that county as a Whig on his family's interest in 1722. Brought in by the ministry for Launceston at a by-election in 1726, he was put up again for Durham county in 1727, but stood down to avoid splitting the Whig vote, on the understanding that the ministry would find him another seat.[1] Having been duly returned by the Government for St. Mawes, he went into opposition, attaching himself to Pulteney, his wife's first cousin. He never spoke in the House, being prevented from doing so by 'a monstrous tongue which lolled out of his mouth'.[2] In the shadow Government drawn up by the Opposition in 1733 he was put down for Lord Hervey's post of vice-chamberlain, on which George II observed: 'I should have made a fine charge for that silly cur'.[3] Re-elected for St. Mawes in 1734, on the Boscawen interest, in 1739 he again declared his intention of

standing for Durham county at the next general election[4] but once more withdrew, this time to be returned for Ripon on the Aislabie interest. After Walpole's fall Pulteney procured him a lucrative Irish sinecure,[5] which he lost when his patron's adherents were turned out in December 1744. Returned as a government supporter for Durham county in 1747, he now attached himself to his kinsman, the Duke of Newcastle, cultivating him so assiduously that in 1749 a vacancy on the Treasury board was

> filled . . . with that toad-eater and spy to all parties, Harry Vane: there is no enumerating all the circumstances that make his nomination scandalous and ridiculous.

When not at the Treasury he was said to have been entirely employed in opening and shutting the door for the Duchess of Newcastle's latest favourite, 'a common pig, that she had brought from Hanover'.[6] Rewarded by Newcastle with an earldom, he died 6 Mar. 1758.

[1] Bp. of Durham to Geo. Bowes, 4 July 1727, Exton Sayer to Geo. Bowes, 18 July 1727, Add. 40748, ff. 28, 31. [2] Horace Walpole's ms notes, ex inf. W. S. Lewis. [3] Hervey, *Mems.* 170. [4] Bp. of Durham to Sir Robt. Walpole, 1739, Cholmondeley (Houghton) mss. [5] Hervey, *Mems.* 951, 955. [6] Walpole to Mann, 23 Mar. and 25 June 1749.

E.C.

VANE, Henry (?1726–92).

DOWNTON	24 Nov. 1749–27 Apr. 1753
DURHAM CO.	19 May 1753–6 Mar. 1758

b. ?1726, 1st s. of Henry Vane (q.v.), 1st Earl of Darlington. *educ.* Westminster 1736–44; Ch. Ch. Oxf. 28 May 1744, aged 17. *m.* 19 Mar. 1757, Margaret, da. of Robert Lowther of Mauds Meaburn, Westmld., gov. of Barbados, sis. of James Lowther, M.P., 1st Earl of Lonsdale, 1s. 2da. *styled* Visct. Barnard 1754–8; *suc.* fa. as 2nd Earl 6 Mar. 1758.

Ensign 1 Ft. Gds. 1745, lt. and capt. 1747; capt. and lt.-col. 2 Ft. Gds. 1750; ret. 1758; col. in army (during service) 1779; ld. lt. co. Durham 1758–*d.*; master of the jewel office 1763–82; gov. Carlisle 1763–*d.*

Henry Vane was brought in for Downton at an unopposed by-election in 1749 by Anthony Duncombe (q.v.), Lord Feversham. He sat there till 1753, when he applied for the Chiltern Hundreds to stand for Durham County in place of his father, who had succeeded to the peerage as Lord Barnard. On 20 May 1753 Lord Barnard wrote to Newcastle:

> Yesterday we had our election for this county . . . Harry was chose without any opposition and I believe . . . with the general approbation of the whole county, and I think there was not one gentleman not present or did not send me an excuse, and about six hundred freeholders.[1]

Returned unopposed in 1754, he was classed as a government supporter. He died 8 Sept. 1792.

[1] Add. 32731, f. 474.

E.C.

VANE, William, 1st Visct. Vane [I] (c.1680–1734), of Fairlawn, Kent.

DURHAM CO.	1708–1710
STEYNING	1727–1734
KENT	15–20 May 1734

b. c.1680, 2nd surv. s. of Christopher Vane, M.P., 1st Baron Barnard, by Lady Elizabeth Holles, da. of Gilbert Holles, M.P., 3rd Earl of Clare, sis. and coh. of John Holles, M.P., 1st Duke of Newcastle. *m.* (settlement 15 Nov. 1703), Lucy, da. and coh. of William Jolliffe of Caverswall Castle, Staffs., 3s. *cr.* Visct. Vane [I] 13 Sept. 1720. *suc.* fa. at Fairlawn 1723.

Vane was first returned under Anne for Durham, where his family possessed large estates. After this he remained out of Parliament until 1727 when, having succeeded to his father's Kent estates and unsuccessfully attempted to secure the Whig nomination for that county, he found himself a seat at Steyning,[1] voting consistently against the Government. Defeated at Steyning in 1734, he was returned as an opposition Whig for Kent, dying of apoplexy a few days later, 20 May 1734.

[1] Thos. Robinson to Geo. Bowes, 20 July 1727, Add. 40748, f. 35.

J.B.L.

VAN HULS, William Charles (aft. 1649–1722), of Whitehall, London.

BRAMBER	21 Mar.–11 June 1722

b. aft. 1649,[1] s. of Samuel van Huls (*d.* 1687), sec. to the Prince of Orange, by Sara Maria, da. of John le Maire, minister at Amsterdam. *unm.*

King's letter carrier for life 1697, res. 1700; clerk of the robes and wardrobe 1700–*d.*

Van Huls was private secretary to William III, who gave him a court place for life.[2] Returned for Bramber after a contest, he died before taking his seat, 11 June 1722. His only brother Samuel van Huls, burgomaster of The Hague, was his sole heir and executor.[3]

[1] J. P. de Bie & J. Loosjers, *Biogr. Voordenboek van Protest. Godgel. in Ned.* iv. 407–8. [2] *Cal. Treas. Bks.* xiv. 310; xvi. 169; Luttrell, iv. 304. [3] PCC 42 Marlborough.

R.R.S.

VANSE, Patrick (c.1655–1733), of Barnbarroch, Wigtown.

WIGTOWNSHIRE	1710–3 Mar. 1711
WIGTOWN BURGHS	1715–1722

b. c.1655, 1st s. of Alexander Vanse of Barnbarroch by Margaret, da. of William Maxwell of Monreith, Wigtown. *m.* (1) Margaret, da. of Sir James Campbell of Lawers, Perth, 1s. 1da.; (2) 28 Feb. 1715, Barbara, da. of Patrick Macdowall of Freugh, Wigtown, 2s. 3da. *suc.* fa. c.1712.

In the French service c.1673–89;[1] capt. Inniskilling regt. c.1690–92; lt.-col. Lord Mark Kerr's Ft. c.1708–12; half-pay 1713.

Patrick Vanse, a professional soldier, of an old Wigtownshire family, succeeded his cousin, Sir Alexander Maxwell, 2nd Bt., for Wigtown Burghs at the age of 60 in 1715, voting with the Administration in all recorded divisions, including that on Lord Cadogan in June 1717.[2] He did not stand again and died 27 Jan. 1733, 'owing to the breaking out of a wound he received' in Spain.[3]

[1] Dalton, *English Army Lists*, iii. 207.. [2] *More Culloden Pprs.* ii. 173. [3] W. Balbirnie, *Account of Fam. of Vanse*, 22.

J.M.S.

VAUGHAN, Edward (d.1718), of Llwydiarth, Mont.

MONTGOMERYSHIRE	1679–1681, 1685–1687,
	1689–Dec. 1718

s. of Howel Vaughan of Glanllyn, Merion. by Elizabeth, da. of Humphrey Jones of Ddol, Flints. *m.* 1672, Mary,[1] da. and coh. of John Purcell, M.P., of Nantycribba, by Eleanor, da. of Sir Robert Vaughan of Llwydiarth, 1s. 2da. *suc.* Edward Vaughan, M.P., to estates of Llwydiarth and Llangedwyn, Denb. 1661; fa. 1669.

Custos rot. Merion. 1711; sheriff, Mont. 1688.

A life long Tory, but not a Jacobite, Vaughan was the adopted heir of his wife's uncle, Edward Vaughan, M.P., from whom he inherited large estates in Montgomeryshire.[2] Returned for his county in 1715 for the sixteenth consecutive time, he voted against the septennial bill in 1716. He died December 1718, his property going to his son-in-law, Watkin Williams Wynn (q.v.).

[1] PCC 94 Browning. [2] *Mont. Colls.* xiv. 376–8, 388.

P.D.G.T.

VAUGHAN, John (1693–1765), of Derwydd, Carm., and Shenfield, Essex.

CARMARTHENSHIRE	21 Nov. 1745–1754

b. 1693, 1st surv. s. of Richard Vaughan of Terracoyd, Carm. by his 2nd w. Elizabeth, da. and eventually h. of Sir William Appleton, 5th Bt., of Shenfield, Essex. *m.* (1) Ellen, da. and coh. of Nicholas Partridge of Doddinghurst, Essex, 1s.; (2) Elizabeth, da. and h. of John Vaughan of Court Derllys, Carm., wid. of Thomas Lloyd of Danyrallt, Carm. and coh. of her uncle, Richard Vaughan (q.v.) of Derwydd. *suc.* fa. 1728; cos. Anne, Duchess of Bolton, to Golden Grove, Carm. estate 1751.

Chamberlain, Brec., Glam., and Rad. 1745–*d.*

Vaughan was returned on the interest of the Golden Grove estate, which he inherited in 1751. Succeeding to his predecessor's office, he voted with the Government for the Hanoverians in 1746, when he was put down as Old Whig. Classed as a government supporter in the next Parliament, he did not stand again. He died 27 Jan. 1765.

P.D.G.T.

VAUGHAN, John, 2nd Visct. Lisburne [I], (c.1695–1741), of Crosswood, Card.

CARDIGANSHIRE 1727–1734

b. c.1695, 1st s. of John Vaughan, 1st Visct. Lisburne, M.P. Card. 1694–8, by Lady Malet Wilmot, da. of John Wilmot, 2nd Earl of Rochester. *m.* (1) Anne (*d.* 31 July 1723), da. of Sir John Bennet, serjeant-at-law, *s.p.*; (2) Feb. 1726, Dorothy Waller, wid., da. of Capt. Richard Hill of Henblas, Mont., 1s. 1da.[1] *suc.* fa. 20 Mar. 1721.
Ld. lt. and custos rot. Card. 1721–d.

Lisburne's father had taken vigorous measures against the Jacobites as lord lieutenant of his county during and just after the Fifteen rebellion, asking for the help of regular troops.[2] Returned as a Whig for Cardiganshire in 1727, he voted with the Government on the excise bill in 1733 and the repeal of the Septennial Act in 1734, but did not stand again. Holding estates under the Crown, he was being prosecuted by the Treasury for arrears of rent in 1737, but was granted a stay of execution in May 1738.[3] He died 15 Jan. 1741.

[1] See *CP.* [2] Ld. Lisburne to Paul Methuen, 4 Jan. 1717, SP Dom. 35/8, f. 68. [3] *Cal. Treas. Bks. and Pprs.* 1735–8, pp. 377, 482, 546.

E.C.

VAUGHAN, Richard (?1655–1724), of Derwydd, Carm.

CARMARTHEN 1685–1687, 1689–26 Oct. 1724

b. ?1655, 1st s. of John Vaughan of Court Derllys by Rachel, da. of Sir Henry Vaughan, M.P., of Derwydd. *educ.* Jesus, Oxf. 23 May 1672, aged 16; G. Inn 1673, called 1680, bencher 1706. *m.* (lic. 12 July 1692) Arabella, da. of Sir Erasmus Philipps, 3rd Bt., M.P., of Picton Castle, Pemb., sis. of Sir John Philipps, 4th Bt. (q.v.), *s.p. suc.* uncle Sir Henry Vaughan, M.P., to Derwydd 1676.
Recorder, Carm. 1683–6, 1688–1722; c.j. Carm. circuit 1715–d.

Vaughan, who came of a junior branch of the Vaughans of Golden Grove, the leading Whig family in Carmarthenshire, represented Carmarthen for nearly 40 years. Though made a Welsh judge in 1715, he was absent from the division on the septennial bill in 1716, and voted against the Government on the repeal of the Occasional Conformity and Schism Acts and on the peerage bill

in 1719. He died 27 Oct. 1724, his estates going to his niece, the wife of John Vaughan (q.v.).

P.D.G.T.

VAUGHAN, Richard (c.1665–1734), of Corsygedol, Merion.

MERIONETH 29 Apr. 1701–28 Mar. 1734

b. c.1665, 2nd s. of William Vaughan of Corsygedol by Anne, da. of Griffith Nanney of Nannau, Merion. *m.* Margaret, da. and h. of Sir Evan Lloyd, 2nd Bt., of Bodidris, Denb., 2s. 3da. *suc.* bro. to Corsygedol 1697.
Constable, Harlech castle 1704–16.

In 1701 Richard Vaughan succeeded to the Merioneth seat vacated by the death of his brother-in-law, Hugh Nanney. A life-long Tory, he did not vote in any of the recorded divisions after 1715. He died 28 Mar. 1734.

P.D.G.T.

VAUGHAN, William (?1707–75), of Corsygedol, Merion.

MERIONETH 1734–1768

b. ?1707, 1st s. of Richard Vaughan (q.v.). *educ.* Chester and Mortlake schools; St. John's, Camb. 22 Dec. 1726, aged 19. *m.* 2 Dec. 1732, his cos. Catherine, da. and coh. of Hugh Nanney, M.P., of Nannau, Merion., 1da. *d.v.p. suc.* fa. 1734.
Custos rot. Merion. 1731–69; ld. lt. 1762–d.

William Vaughan, like his father, a Tory, voted steadily against Walpole, though at a by-election in Caernarvonshire in 1740 he supported his Whig relations, the Wynns of Glynnllivon, against Watkin Williams Wynn (q.v.). Absent from the division on the Hanoverian troops in December 1742, earning a reprimand from his constituents—'we had no representative present to declare our sense of so extraordinary a measure'—and an admonition—'in a word, exert an English spirit, in opposing all the bad designs of men with foreign hearts'[1]—he voted against them in 1744 and 1746. In 1747 he was classed by the Administration as Opposition. He died 12 Apr. 1775.

[1] *Gent. Mag.* 1743, p. 34.

P.D.G.T.

VAUGHAN, William Gwyn (?1681–1753), of Trebarried, Brec.

BRECONSHIRE 30 Aug. 1721–1734

b. ?1681, 2nd s. of Gwyn Vaughan of Trebarried by Mary, da. of William Lucy, bp. of St. Davids 1660–77. *educ.* Queen's, Oxf. 12 May 1698, aged 16. *m.* Frances, da. and h. of John Vaughan of Hergest, 6s. 2da. *suc.* bro. Thomas 1694.

Vaughan was returned as a Tory in 1721, when his name was sent to the Pretender as a probable supporter in the event of a rising.[1] A list of payments totalling £2,000 to Members of Parliament, apparently prepared by Sunderland for George I about this time, contains the item: 'à M. Vaughan, beaufrère de M. Morgan de Tredegar, £200'. He spoke against the Government on the Hessians in 1730,[2] and on the army estimates, 15 Feb. 1733, voting against the excise bill that year and for the repeal of the Septennial Act in 1734. Defeated in 1734 by an opposition Whig, he did not stand again. He died 31 Aug. 1753.

[1] Stuart mss 65/16. [2] *Knatchbull Diary*, 5 Feb. 1730.

P.D.G.T.

VENABLES VERNON, George (1710–80), of Sudbury, Derbys. and Kinderton, Cheshire.

LICHFIELD   20 May 1731–1747
DERBY   1754–Apr. 1762

b. 9 Feb. 1710, 1st s. of Henry Vernon (q.v.) by his 1st w. *m.* (1) 22 June 1733, Mary (*d.* 23 Feb. 1740), da. and coh. of Thomas, 6th Baron Howard of Effingham, 3s. 2da.; (2) 22 Dec. 1741, Anne (*d.* 22 Sept. 1742), da. of Sir Thomas Lee, 3rd Bt. (q.v.), of Hartwell, Bucks.; (3) 10 Apr. 1744, Martha, da. of Hon. Simon Harcourt, M.P., sis. of Simon, 1st Earl Harcourt, 3s. 4da. *suc.* to Kinderton under will of his mat. gt.-uncle Peter Venables 1715 and assumed name of Venables before Vernon 1715; fa. 1719; *cr.* Baron Vernon of Kinderton 12 May 1762.

Sitting unopposed as a Tory for Lichfield from 1731 to 1747, Vernon consistently voted with the Opposition till 1744, when he went over to the Administration with the Leveson Gowers, voted in favour of sending Hessian troops against the rebels in December 1745,[1] and was classed by the Government as a 'new ally' in 1746. Reverting to opposition, he fought a bitter, expensive, and unsuccessful contest at Lichfield against the combined Gower and Anson interests at the general election of 1747.[2] After the violent Tory demonstration at Lichfield races in September that year, his brother-in-law, Lord Harcourt, wrote to him:

You cannot conceive what a noise the Lichfield hunting meeting makes in town, where people make no ceremony of treating the company as Jacobites.

I was under no uneasiness or apprehension of your being there, for I love and honour you too much to think you capable of such an action. Everybody's eyes were upon you, and his Majesty told me in a little sort of private conference that he was very glad you was not at that, for he must and ought to consider that company as his declared enemies; upon which I assured him that whatever ill-treatment you might have received from your former friends, you were, however, incapable of entertaining a disloyal sentiment, or of doing anything that had the appearance of

disrespect towards him; besides which, I told him that in the time of the rebellion you had exerted yourself very much in behalf of his Majesty and his cause.[3]

Shortly afterwards Thomas Anson reported to Lord Anson (qq.v.) on 17 Oct. 1747 that Vernon

has entirely quitted his old connexions, which will appear soon by most plentiful abuse from that quarter. He now seems fixed and easy.[4]

He died 21 Aug. 1780, said to be worth £4,000 p.a.[5]

[1] Ilchester, *Lord Holland*, i. 121–2. [2] See LICHFIELD. [3] E. W. Harcourt, *Harcourt Pprs.* iii. 37. [4] Add. 15955, f. 62. [5] *Staffs. Parl. Hist.* (Wm. Salt Arch. Soc.) ii (2), p. 234.

E.C.

VERE, Thomas (c.1681–1766), of Thorpe Hall, Norf.

NORWICH   19 Feb. 1735–1747

b. c.1681, s. of George Vere, merchant, of Norwich. *m.* (1) Elizabeth (*d.* 23 Sept. 1714), da. of Stephen Day, 1da.; (2) Frances, sis. and h. of Sir Peter Seaman, mayor of Norwich, 1 surv. s.
Alderman of Norwich 1722, mayor 1735.

A Norwich merchant, exporting woollen goods, Vere in 1731 gave evidence on the export of Irish cambrics to a select committee of the House of Commons on the woollen industry.[1] Returned for Norwich as a government supporter at a by-election in 1735, he spoke a month later for taking off the duties on the importation of Irish yarn into Great Britain. About this time he instituted prosecutions against persons wearing fustians, which were affecting the sales of Norwich woollen goods. The prosecutions were based on the ground that fustians came under the Act of 1721, prohibiting the wearing of dyed calicoes (see under Page, Sir Gregory). On a petition from Manchester fustian manufacturers an Act was passed exempting fustians from the 1721 Act. In 1739, on a bill for relieving the woollen trade, he moved several amendments, including one to extend the Wool Registration Act to Ireland, which was unopposed, and another to increase the penalties on the export of woollen cloth etc. from Ireland, which was opposed by Sir John Barnard, who held that the prohibition of the export of manufactured wool in Ireland was the root of the decay of the English wool industry.[2] In 1739 there was a movement to oust him at the next general election, which was attributed to his having 'neglected opportunities of making himself acceptable',[3] but he was re-elected in 1741 after a contest. One of Walpole's last acts before resigning was to appoint Vere's son to a vacant commissionership of the salt office.[4] He continued to support the Government till the end of the Parliament, when he failed to secure re-nomination for Norwich. 'I am sorry for Vere', Pelham wrote, 'he should not have wanted help if I had known how to have conveyed it to him'.[5] He died, never having stood for Parliament again, 28 June 1766, aged 85.

[1] *CJ*, xxi. 573. [2] *HMC Egmont Diary*, ii. 162; iii. 36–37; Harley Diary, 9 and 16 Feb. 1736. [3] J. Fowle to 'old' Horace Walpole, 10 Nov. 1739, Walpole (Wolterton) mss. [4] *Gent. Mag.* 1742, p. 108; *Cal. Treas. Bks. and Pprs.* 1742–5, p. 212. [5] Pelham to 'old' Horace Walpole, 4 July 1747, Add. 9186, f. 105.

R.R.S.

VERNEY, John, 1st Visct. Fermanagh [I] (1640–1717), of Middle Claydon, nr. Buckingham, Bucks.

BUCKINGHAMSHIRE   1710–1715
AMERSHAM   1715–23 June 1717

b. 5 Nov. 1640, 2nd but 1st surv. s. of Sir Ralph Verney, 1st Bt., M.P., of Middle Claydon by Mary, da. and h. of John Blacknall of Wasing and Abingdon, Berks. *educ.* at Blois in France 1648–53 and schools at Barn Elms and Kensington 1653–8.[1] *m.* (1) 27 May 1680, Elizabeth (*d.* 20 May 1686), da. of Ralph Palmer of Little Chelsea, Mdx., 1s. 3da.; (2) 10 July 1692, Mary (*d.* 24 Aug. 1694), da. of Sir Francis Lawley, 2nd Bt., M.P., of Spoonhill, Salop, 1s.; (3) 8 Apr. 1697, Elizabeth, da. of Daniel Baker of Penn House, Bucks., alderman of London, *s.p.* *suc.* fa. as 2nd Bt. 24 Sept. 1696; *cr.* Visct. Fermanagh and Baron Verney of Belturbet [I] 16 June 1703.

Lord Fermanagh was the grandson of Sir Edmund Verney, knight marshal and standard bearer to Charles I, who was M.P. for Buckingham, Aylesbury and Chipping Wycombe and was killed at Edgehill in 1642.[2] His father represented Aylesbury in the Short and Long Parliaments until 1643 and Buckingham in three Parliaments, 1681–90. A younger son, apprenticed in 1659 to Gabriel Roberts, a Levant merchant, for twelve years he was a factor at Aleppo.[3] Returning to England in 1674, he set up as a merchant on his own account until he succeeded to the baronetcy in 1696. In his seventieth year he entered Parliament for his county as a Tory, but refused for reasons of age and health to stand for it again in 1715.

My happiness [he wrote] is that I have no place to be removed out of and I am too much for the Church of England to be put into any, so I shall live quietly under my own vine and remain an honest Sacheverellian.

Signing the compromise for the county arranged by the local Whig and Tory leaders,[4] he was persuaded to stand on the Drake interest at Amersham, where he was unopposed, voting against the septennial bill in 1716. He died 23 June 1717.

[1] *Verney Mems. during 17th Cent.* ii. 87–107. [2] Ibid. passim; *Verney Letters of 18th Cent.* i. passim. [3] *Verney Mems.* ii. 97, 261–273. [4] *Verney Letters*, i. 315–16, 317.

R.S.L.

VERNEY, Hon. John (1699–1741), of Compton Verney, Warws.

DOWNTON   1722–1734, 4 May–5 Aug. 1741

b. 23 Oct. 1699, 5th s. of George Verney, 12th Lord Willoughby de Broke, by Margaret, da. and h. of Sir John Heath of Brasted, Kent. *educ.* New Coll., Oxf. 1714; M. Temple 1715, called *ex gratia* 1721, bencher L. Inn 1728. *m.* 16 Sept. 1724, Abigail, da. of Edward Harley of Eywood, Herefs., auditor of the imprest (q.v.), 1s. 2da.

2nd justice of Brec. circuit 1726–32; K.C. 1727; attorney-gen. to Queen Caroline 1729–37; c.j. Chester 1733–8; master of the rolls 1738–*d.*; P.C. 12 Oct. 1738.

Verney was returned as a Tory for Downton by his brother-in-law Anthony Duncombe (q.v.). He spoke on 22 Jan. 1724 against the Government on a motion for maintaining the existing strength of the army, but supported them on a similar motion on 28 Jan. 1726, at the end of the year being made a Welsh judge. Shortly before the announcement of his appointment a Tory wrote to the second Earl of Oxford (Edward, Lord Harley, q.v.), with whom Verney was connected by marriage: 'It looks as though there was some rub in the way. I hope he has not managed like some indiscreet ladies to have scandals without joy'.[1] A few days after his re-election he spoke for the Government on an opposition motion about the despatch of a fleet to the Baltic.

At the general election of 1727 Verney stood for Radnor as well as for Downton, writing to Walpole:

Mr. Duncombe's election at Salisbury being very doubtful makes me the more solicitous for my success at Radnor . . . the returning officer, who is Mr. [Thomas] Lewis's [q.v.] brother, has declared he will return him right or wrong . . . It would be a great uneasiness to me to petition, because Radnorshire is one of the counties in my commission and possibly ill-natured people might reflect upon me for it . . . I am persuaded that the least word from you will make [Lewis] desist, for he has a place in the Custom House . . . Duke Chandos sees Mr. Lewis every day and can easily prevail upon him to do anything you think proper.[2]

He was defeated at Radnor, but kept his seat at Downton.

In the new Parliament Verney is described as speaking in a financial debate on 4 Mar. 1728 'very ridiculously, and of that which it was plain he was utterly ignorant, and Barnard lashed him'.[3] In 1730 and 1731 he spoke in support of the Hessians and against a petition for abolishing the monopoly of the East India Company. On 8 Feb. 1733 he opposed receiving a petition from the York Buildings Society on the ground that 'the law would redress any abuses of this nature', but his advice was not accepted by the House.[4]

Verney was out of the next Parliament, as his

Downton seat was taken by Duncombe for himself, while he was again defeated at Radnor. In 1738 he applied to Hardwicke for the vacant post of master of the rolls, to which he was appointed. Early in 1741 he offered to resign on grounds of ill-health, adding: 'I propose to stand next Parliament for Downton, where I shall be elected without any difficulty'.[5] He was returned but died 5 Aug. 1741, before Parliament met.

[1] *HMC Portland*, vii. 445. [2] 5 Aug. 1727, Cholmondeley (Houghton) mss. [3] *HMC Portland*, vii. 458. [4] *HMC Egmont Diary*, i. 30, 69, 126, 325. [5] Add. 35586, ff. 73, 87, 329.

R.S.L.

VERNEY, Ralph, 2nd Visct. Fermanagh [I] (1683–1752), of Middle Claydon, nr. Buckingham, Bucks.

AMERSHAM 10 July 1717–1727
WENDOVER 1741–4 Oct. 1752

b. 18 Mar. 1683, 1st s. of John Verney, 1st Visct. Fermanagh [I] (q.v.), by his 1st w. *educ.* Mrs. Morland's sch. at Hackney c.1695–1700; Merton, Oxf. 1700. *m.* 24 Feb. 1708, Catherine, da. and coh. of Henry Paschall of Baddow, Essex, 2s. 2da. *suc.* fa. 23 June 1717; *cr.* Earl Verney [I] 22 Mar. 1743.

On leaving Oxford Ralph Verney had rooms for some years in the Middle Temple but does not seem to have been admitted to the Inn. Succeeding his father on the Drake interest at Amersham in 1717, he voted as a Tory against the repeal of the Occasional Conformity and Schism Acts and the peerage bill in 1719. His name was sent to the Pretender in 1721 as a probable supporter in case of a rebellion. Re-elected in 1722, he did not stand in 1727, when he was described as 'being unconcerned for any party',[1] nor in 1734; but he began to develop an interest at Wendover, eventually acquiring control of that borough from John Hampden (q.v.),[2] with whom he was returned for it from 1741. Voting consistently with the Administration, he obtained an Irish earldom in 1743, being classed as an Old Whig in 1746 and as a government supporter in 1747. The second Lord Egmont, in his electoral survey c.1749–50, wrote against Wendover:

> Earl Verney can bring in two. He lives a close sort of life, does not know very much of the world, and seems a man to be gained with what will cost little. At least he will not give himself up to a faction against any Administration, if they have but common address.

On which the Prince of Wales commented: 'L.C. Justice Willes and Potter [qq.v.] know how to deal with him'.

He died 4 Oct. 1752.

[1] Stuart mss 65/16; *Verney Letters of 18th Cent.* i. 100–1; ii. 100[.] [2] See WENDOVER.

R.S.L.

VERNEY, Ralph, 2nd Earl Verney [I] (1714–91), of Claydon House, Bucks.

WENDOVER 17 Jan. 1753–1761
CARMARTHEN 1761–1768
BUCKINGHAMSHIRE 1768–1784
1790–31 Mar. 1791

b. 1 Feb. 1714, 2nd but o. surv. s. of Ralph Verney, 1st Earl Verney [I] (q.v.). *educ.* Brentford from 1721; M. Temple 1729; Christ's, Camb. 1733. *m.* 11 Sept. 1740, Mary, da. and h. of Henry Herring, merchant and director of the Bank of England, of Egham, Surr., *s.p.* *styled* Lord Fermanagh 1743–52. *suc.* fa. 4 Oct. 1752.
P.C. 22 Nov. 1765.

Verney inherited a large estate in Buckinghamshire and the control of both seats at Wendover, where he succeeded his father in January 1753 as a government supporter. About this time he bough[1] the manor of Stokke, in Great Bedwyn, Wilts.,t with a view to establishing an interest there in opposition to Lord Bruce before the 1754 election. He died 31 Mar. 1791.

[1] Narrative of the purchase of Stokke manor, Savernake mss.

R.S.L.

VERNON, Bowater (1683–1735), of Hanbury Hall, Worcs.

BISHOP'S CASTLE 1722–26 Apr. 1726

b. 21 May 1683, 1st s. of William Vernon of Caldewell, Worcs. by Phoebe, da. of Rev. Samuel Bowater of Shrawley, Worcs. *m.* (1) 1721, Mathia (*d.* June 1721 'three weeks after her marriage'),[1] da. of George Wheeler, under-treasurer of I. Temple, *s.p.*; (2) Jane, da. and coh. of Thomas Cornwallis of Abermarlais, Carm., 1s. 2da. *suc.* fa. 1709; Thomas Vernon (q.v.) 1721.

On inheriting the fortune of Thomas Vernon (q.v.), Bowater Vernon stood for Bishop's Castle, announcing that 'he had brought down money to carry the election if that would do it'.[2] Described as a 'South Sea man', who was resolved to outbid the Duke of Chandos, 'let him offer what he will',[3] he was returned after a contest as a government supporter.[4] After sitting for four years he was unseated on petition, the elections committee finding that all but one of his 52 voters had been bribed, at a total cost of nearly £700.[5] He did not stand again, dying 30 Nov. 1735.

[1] Nash, *Worcs.* i. ped. facing 549. [2] *CJ*, xx. 682. [3] *HMC Portland*, vii. 314. [4] *HMC Townshend*, 137. [5] *CJ*, xx. 681–2.

J.B.L.

VERNON, Sir Charles (c.1683–1762), of Farnham, Surr.

CHIPPING WYCOMBE 27 Jan. 1731–1734
17 Feb. 1735–1741
RIPON 1747–1761

b. c.1683, 3rd s.[1] of Sir Thomas Vernon, M.P., London merchant and director E.I. Co., by his w. Anne; bro. of Thomas Vernon (q.v.). *m.* bef. 1717, Anne Catherine, da. of George Vernon of Farnham, 4s. 2da. Kntd. 27 Oct. 1717.

Vernon, a Turkey merchant, was returned unopposed in 1731 and 1735 on the interest of his nephew, Edmund Waller (q.v.). Presumably a Tory, like his brother, he consistently voted against the Administration, though withdrawing on the motion for the dismissal of Walpole in February 1741. Both seats at Wycombe were required by the Wallers in 1741, but in 1747 he was returned at Ripon on the interest of his son-in-law, William Aislabie (q.v.), the brother-in-law of Edmund Waller, and classed as 'Opposition'. He died 4 Apr. 1762, aged 78.

[1] PCC 73 Young.

E.C.

VERNON, Edward (1684–1757), of Nacton, nr. Ipswich, Suff.

PENRYN	1722–1734
PORTSMOUTH	21 Feb.–27 Apr. 1741
IPSWICH	1741–30 Oct. 1757

b. 12 Nov. 1684, 2nd s. of Rt. Hon. James Vernon, M.P., sec. of state 1696–1700, of Watford, Herts. by Mary, da. of Sir John Buck, 1st Bt., of Hamby Grange, Lincs. *educ.* Westminster 1692–1700. *m.* c.1729, Sarah, da. of Thomas Best of Chatham, brewer, 3s. *d.v.p.* Entered R.N. 1700, capt. 1706, v. adm. 1739, adm. 1745.

Vernon served throughout the war of the Spanish succession, for part of the time in the West Indies, where, seeing a merchant ship celebrating the Pretender's birthday, 'he put the captain in chains, and brought him to England . . . which cost him a thousand pounds, being prosecuted by the owners of that vessel for damages'.[1] Returned unopposed in 1722 for Penryn, which his father had represented, he supported the Government, speaking on 26 Oct. 1722 for an augmentation of the army, and on 26 Nov. for a special levy on papists. During the international crisis following the treaty of Hanover, he commanded a ship in the Baltic in 1726 and 1727 under Sir John Norris (q.v.).

In the new Parliament, Vernon took an independent line, generally speaking and voting against the Government. On 6 May 1728, on a bill for encouraging naval recruitment, he proposed unsuccessfully a number of clauses for improving the arrangements as to pay, sickness, etc., alleging that the fleet recently sent under Admiral Hosier to blockade Porto Bello had been paid short, in Jamaica money, not sterling,

> and the difference betwixt one and the other was great, and the men suffered and mutinied often on

receiving it, but the difference was put in somebody's pocket, and that Hosier's squadron was victualled with stinking provision and made distempers among the men.

On 21 Jan. 1729, in the debate on the Address, he declared that the orders given to Hosier 'were given by those who understood nothing of the sea' and that Porto Bello could have been taken by 300 men. He returned to the charge on 31 Jan., when the matter was taken up by the leaders of the Opposition. Next session, as a member of the Commons gaols committee, he seconded a motion on 26 Jan. 1730 for the printing of the trials of the officers of the Fleet prison, hinting that the judges had been partial to them.[2] In the Dunkirk debate on 12 Feb. he made a 'passionate speech' for an inquiry, bringing

> in the Pope, the Devil, the Jesuits, the seamen, etc. so that the House had not patience to attend him, though he was not taken down. He quite lost his temper and made himself hoarse again.

In 1731 he spoke, *inter alia*, against the treaty of Seville, on the ground that it would prevent us from protecting British merchants; for a motion to prevent the translation of bishops, observing that he hoped shortly to introduce a bill for turning them out of the Lords; and in favour of inserting a clause in the Mutiny Act to allow common soldiers to claim their discharge after a certain term of years, characterising 'the present keeping soldiers for their lives in the service' as 'making slaves of them'. On 10 Feb. 1732 he was severely rebuked by the Speaker for describing a bill to revive the salt duty as 'only to ease the rich at the expense of the poor', adding that 'ninety nine in a hundred of the people would not bear the tax, and that he should expect, if he voted for it, to be treated like a polecat and knocked on the head'. Later in the session the Speaker had to intervene to prevent a duel between Vernon and Sir John Eyles (q.v.), the head of the South Sea Company, who took as directed against himself a speech by Vernon 'insinuating that the directors of the company had carried on a private trade contrary to their oaths and hurtful to the company'. In 1733 he spoke against the excise bill, giving as his chief reason that if it passed the royal family 'must necessarily lose the affection of the subject'. In the last session of the Parliament, on a motion for 20,000 seamen, he proposed that the figure should be increased to 30,000, because 'a powerful navy is the natural security of England . . . Let France get the superiority at sea, and this kingdom will be lost in one campaign'.

Defeated at Penryn and at Ipswich in 1734, Vernon retired to his Suffolk estate until 1739 when, seeing that war with Spain was imminent, he offered his services to the Admiralty, on condition of being restored to his rank.[3] Sir Charles Wager (q.v.) wrote to Newcastle in December 1738:

> He is certainly much properer than any officer we have to send, being very well acquainted in all that part of the West Indies, and is a very good sea officer whatever he may be or has been in the House of Commons.[4]

He was at once appointed admiral of the Blue, with orders to proceed in command of a squadron to the West Indies. On learning of the appointment, the 1st Lord Egmont wrote:

> He is a remarkable brave man, sober, well experienced, and zealous for the honour and interest of his country, as he showed both in war and in the House of Commons, where he sat when I was in Parliament, and for opposing the Ministry was put by his rank on the promotion of Admirals . . . The seamen and the city will be well pleased at his promotion.[5]

His capture of Porto Bello made him a national hero, thanked by both Houses and courted by both the Government and the Opposition. In February 1741 he was brought in on the Admiralty interest at Portsmouth, where he was renominated at the general election on the opposition interest, at the same time being put up for London, Westminster, Rochester, Ipswich and Penryn. Congratulating him on being returned for the last three, Pulteney wrote:

> You are certainly, at this time, the most popular and best loved man in *England*. All places that send members to Parliament have been struggling to have you for their representative, and, I dare say, you might have been chosen in twenty more places that you are.

At the same time he begged him to defer deciding for which of the three he would sit, explaining that if he were to choose one, there was a danger that the other two might be recaptured by the Government.[6]

Vernon was recalled from the West Indies at the end of 1742, after quarrelling with the commander of the land forces sent out to co-operate with him, contrary to his advice to the Government to confine themselves to naval operations there. On his arrival he refused an offer of the Bath; was presented with the freedom of the city of London in a gold box; and had

> half an hour in audience with the King, to whom he said that his Majesty's security lay in being master of the sea, and that when he ceased so to be, his land army could not preserve him, at which words, he said, the King gathered himself up, and seemed not pleased, answering that soldiers were necessary. I was resolved, said the Admiral, to take that opportunity of letting the King know what no Ministry will tell him, for they flatter the King in his passions.[7]

Electing to sit for Ipswich, he at once opened fire on the Government.

> I was not in the House at Vernon's frantic speech [Horace Walpole wrote to Mann, 4 May 1743]; but I know he made it, and have heard him pronounce several such: but he has worn out even laughter, and did not make impression enough on me to remember . . . that he had spoken.[8]

In February 1744 he was one of only two opponents of an augmentation of the army and navy against the threatened French invasion, taking the line that the navy alone required attention. A few days later he was among the warmest supporters of a feeble attempt to put off the suspension of the Habeas Corpus Act. After the invasion threat was over, he joined in an opposition motion for an inquiry into the navy by a select committee, which was rejected.[9]

In April 1745 Vernon, now the senior active admiral, was appointed to the command of a fleet assembled in the Downs to guard against another threatened French invasion but he became involved in so acrimonious a correspondence with the Admiralty about his own rights and powers that he was superseded in December at his own suggestion. He retorted by publishing his correspondence with the Admiralty, for which he was dismissed from the service in April 1746.

For the rest of his life Vernon, whom the war had made a wealthy man, was re-elected for Ipswich. In Parliament he continued to revile the Government in language which, according to a lampoon inspired by his becoming a director of the new British Herring Fishery Company, was felt by the House, 'sick of his noise', to make it appropriate that he should have a job at Billingsgate.[10]

He died 30 Oct. 1757.

[1] *HMC Egmont Diary*, iii. 77. [2] *Knatchbull Diary; HMC Egmont Diary*, iii. 331–2, 339. [3] *HMC Egmont Diary*, i. 43, 143, 153, 158, 220, 263, 349–50; ii. 17; iii. 77. [4] Add. 32691, f. 504. [5] *HMC Egmont Diary*, iii. 77. [6] *Vernon Pprs.* (Navy Recs. Soc. xcix), 237, 240. [7] *HMC Egmont Diary*, iii. 271, 280. [8] Walpole to Mann, 4 May 1743. [9] Owen, *Pelhams*, 214–15; Walpole to Mann, 1 Mar. 1744. [10] Walpole, *Mems. Geo. II*, i. 100–1 n. 1.

E.C.

VERNON, Henry (1686–1719), of Sudbury, Derbys.

STAFFORDSHIRE   1713–1715
NEWCASTLE-UNDER-LYME   29 Jan.–2 June 1715

b. Apr. 1686, o. surv. s. of George Vernon of Sudbury by his 3rd w. Catherine, da. of Sir Thomas Vernon, M.P., London merchant, sis. of Sir Charles and Thomas Vernon (qq.v.). *m.* (1) Anne (*d.* Apr. 1714), da. and h. of Thomas Pigot of Chetwynd, Salop, niece and h. of Peter Venables of Kinderton, 1s. 1da.; (2) Matilda, da. of Thomas Wright of Longstone, Derbys., *s.p. suc.* fa. 1702.

The Vernons of Sudbury acquired Swynnerton and Hilton in Staffordshire by marriage in 1557. Vernon's grandfather left Sudbury to his eldest son, George, Vernon's father, and Hilton to his 2nd son, the grandfather of Henry Vernon of Hilton (q.v.).

Returned as a Tory in 1715, but unseated on petition, Vernon died 25 Feb. 1719.

E.C.

VERNON, Henry (1718–65), of Hilton Park, Staffs.

LICHFIELD   29 Jan.–8 Apr. 1754
       15 Jan. 1755–1761
NEWCASTLE-UNDER-LYME   1761–Dec. 1762

b. 13 Sept. 1718, 1st s. of Henry Vernon, M.P. Stafford 1711–15, of Hilton Park by Penelope, da. and coh. of Robert Philips of Newton Regis, Warws.; bro. of Richard Vernon, M.P., and 2nd cos. of George Venables Vernon (q.v.). *educ.* Westminster 1728–33; Trinity, Camb. 1736; L. Inn 1739; Grand Tour (France) with Sir John Hynde Cotton, 4th Bt. (q.v.), 1739. *m.* Dec. 1743, Lady Henrietta Wentworth, da. of Thomas Wentworth, 3rd Earl of Strafford, 3s. 5da. *suc.* fa. 1732.
Commr. of excise Dec. 1762–*d.*

Put up for Lichfield as a Whig by Lord Gower at a by-election in 1753, Vernon was returned on petition. He died 25 May 1765.

E.C.

VERNON, Thomas (bef. 1683–1726), of Twickenham Park, Mdx.

WHITCHURCH   1710–8 May 1721
       1722–22 Aug. 1726

b. bef. 1683, 1st s.[1] of Sir Thomas Vernon, M.P., London merchant and director E.I. Co.; bro. of Sir Charles Vernon (q.v.). *m.* Jane, 3da. *suc.* fa. 1711. Ld. of Trade 1713–14.

A Turkey merchant and army bread contractor, Vernon was a Tory under Anne. Returned on his own interest for Whitchurch in 1715 as a Tory who might often vote Whig, he voted against the Administration in all recorded divisions. On 8 May 1721 he was expelled from the House of Commons for attempting to influence General Ross (q.v.), a member of the secret committee on the South Sea bubble, in favour of his brother-in-law, John Aislabie (q.v.), before the debate on the 'South Sea sufferers' bill. Defeated at the ensuing by-election for Whitchurch, he recovered his seat at the next general election, dying 22 Aug. 1726.

[1] PCC 73 Young.

P.W.

VERNON, Thomas (1654–1721), of Hanbury Hall, Worcs.

WORCESTERSHIRE   1715–5 Feb. 1721

b. 25 Nov. 1654, 1st surv. s. of Richard Vernon of Hanbury Hall by Jane, da. of Rev. Thomas Carter of Dinton, Bucks. *educ.* M. Temple 1672, called 1679, bencher 1703. *m.* (lic. 5 Jan. 1680) Mary, da. of Sir Anthony Keck, a Chancery lawyer and commr. of the great seal 1689, *s.p.* *suc.* fa. 1679.

Thomas Vernon's family had been settled in Worcestershire since 1580, when his great-grandfather was presented to the rectory of Hanbury. He himself was an eminent Chancery lawyer, whose law notes were posthumously published under the direction of Lord Chancellors Macclesfield and King, and subsequently re-issued at Lord Eldon's suggestion. In 1733 Lord Cobham suggested to Pope as an example of a ruling passion 'Counsellor Vernon retiring to enjoy himself with £5000 a year which he had got, and returning to the Chancery to get a little more when he could not speak so loud as to be heard'.[1] Having greatly added to his family's property in Worcestershire he was returned for that county as a Whig. A member of the secret committee set up by the House of Commons to inquire into the late peace negotiations, he voted with the Government, except on the peerage bill which he opposed. He died 5 Feb. 1721, leaving his property to Bowater Vernon (q.v.), his first cousin once removed.

[1] DNB.

A.N.N.

VERNON, Thomas (1724–71), of Hanbury Hall, Worcs.

WORCESTER   13 May 1746–1761

b. 7 June 1724, o.s. of Bowater Vernon (q.v.) by his 2nd w. *educ.* University Coll. Oxf. 1742. *m.* Emma, da. of James Cornewall, M.P., of Berrington, Herefs. (bro. of Velters Cornewall, q.v.), 1s. *d.v.p.* 1da. *suc.* fa. 1735.

Returned without a contest in 1746, Vernon headed the poll in 1747 as an opposition Whig. In the 2nd Lord Egmont's electoral survey, c.1749–50, he is shown as 'sure' of re-election and as a supporter in the future reign. He seems to have agreed to stand at the next election on a joint interest with Robert Tracy (q.v.), who in calculating the probable cost reckoned that half of the £1200 for '200 London votes' would be borne by Vernon.[1] In the end Tracy stood down but Vernon was returned unopposed. He died 9 Dec. 1771.

[1] 11 Dec. 1753, Add. 32733, f. 421.

E.C.

VERNON, *see also* **VENABLES VERNON**

VILLIERS, Hon. Thomas (1709–86), of The Grove, Watford, Herts.

TAMWORTH 1747–3 June 1756

b. 1709, 2nd s. of William Villiers, M.P., 2nd Earl of Jersey, by Judith, da. and h. of Frederick Herne, London merchant. *educ.* Eton 1725; Queens', Camb. 1728. *m.* 30 Mar. 1752, Lady Charlotte Capel (coh. of her mother), da. of William Capel, 3rd Earl of Essex, by Lady Jane Hyde, da. of Henry Hyde, M.P., 4th and last Earl of Clarendon, 3s. 1da. *cr.* Baron Hyde 3 June 1756; Earl of Clarendon 14 June 1776.

Envoy to Poland 1738–43; minister to Austria 1742–3; envoy to Poland 1744–6, to Prussia Feb.–Sept. 1746; ld. of the Admiralty 1748–56; P.C. 9 Sept. 1763; jt. paymaster gen. 1763–5; chancellor of duchy of Lancaster 1771–82, 1783–6; jt. paymaster gen. 1786–*d.*

Villiers was appointed to Poland in 1738 on the recommendation of Queen Caroline, at the instance of his brother, Lord Jersey.[1] He retired in 1746, feeling that 'he would be happier in an honourable retreat than in the enjoyment of a foreign employment', but making it clear that he expected to be provided for.[2] Returned in 1747 for Tamworth on the interest of his cousin, the 2nd Viscount Weymouth, he was submitted with Sir Peter Warren (q.v.) for a vacancy on the Admiralty board by Pelham to the King, who chose Villiers. Though Horace Walpole calls Villiers 'a very silly fellow',[3] he managed to remain in lucrative posts for most of the time till he died, Earl of Clarendon, 11 Dec. 1786.

[1] Coxe, *Walpole*, iii. 370. [2] To Ld. Harrington, 22 Apr. 1746 SP For. 88/68. [3] To Mann, 26 Dec. 1748.

R.R.S.

VINCENT, Henry (c.1686–1719), of Trelavan, nr. Fowey, Cornw.

FOWEY 1708–1 Nov. 1719

b. c.1686, 1st surv. s. of Henry Vincent, M.P., of Trelavan, commr. of victualling, by Rebecca Serle of Wanstead, Essex; bro. of Nicholas Vincent (q.v.). *m.* 4 Jan. 1706 (with £19,000), Anne, da. and h. of Henry Stevens of Chelsea, wid., 1s. *d.v.p.* *suc.* fa. 1717.[1]

Commr. of victualling 1711–18; dep. paymaster of the tin 1714–*d.*

Vincent belonged to a Cornish family of good standing, who had represented Grampound, Lostwithiel, Mitchell and Truro, as well as Fowey, where they had founded the grammar school. His grandfather, Walter Vincent, M.P., baron of the Exchequer under Charles II, had purchased Trelavan in 1669. He and his father, whom he succeeded as commissioner of victualling, were

Tories under Queen Anne, acting as agents for Lord Lansdowne, who managed Cornish elections under Harley in 1713.[2] In 1715 he appears to have acted in the same capacity for the new Whig ministry, under whom he not only retained his office but secured one for his younger brother, Nicholas (q.v.). Classed as a Whig who would often vote with the Tories, he voted for the septennial bill, but against the repeal of the Occasional Conformity and Schism Acts. Owing to illness, he resigned his place in the victualling office in 1718, dying of a fever at Aix-la-Chapelle 1 Nov. 1719, aged 33.[3]

[1] Thos. Tonkin's Hist. Cornw. f. 119, R. Inst. of Cornwall. [2] *HMC Portland*, v. 233–4, 241. [3] Tonkin, op. cit.

E.C.

VINCENT, Henry (?1685–1757), of Stoke d'Abernon, Surr.

GUILDFORD 21 Feb. 1728–1734

b. ?1685, 4th but 1st surv. s. of Sir Francis Vincent, 5th Bt., M.P., by Rebecca, da. of Jonathan Ashe, London merchant. *educ.* C.C.C. Oxf. 11 Oct. 1703, aged 18. *m.* Elizabeth, da. of Bazaliel Sherman of London, Turkey merchant, 2s. 5da. *suc.* fa. 10 Feb. 1736.

Henry Vincent, of an old Surrey family, who had represented the county, was brought in for Guildford at a by-election by the Onslows, to whom he was distantly related. He voted consistently with the Administration, but was not put up again in 1734. In 1741 he stood for Surrey, asking Walpole to recommend him to several influential persons in that county,[1] but gave up before the poll. He died 20 Jan. 1757.

[1] 28 Jan. 1741, Cholmondeley (Houghton) mss.

R.R.S.

VINCENT, Nicholas (c.1687–1726), of Trelavan, nr. Fowey, Cornw.

FOWEY 7 Dec. 1719–1 July 1726

b. c.1687, 2nd s. of Henry Vincent of Trelavan, M.P.; bro. of Henry Vincent (q.v.). *unm.* *suc.* bro. 1719.

Commr. of leather duties 1714–18, of land taxes 1714–19; assay-master of the stannaries 1720–*d.*

On Henry Vincent's death his brother, Nicholas, succeeded him both as Member for Fowey and as government agent for Cornwall under Hugh Boscawen (q.v.), later Lord Falmouth. He is shown in Sunderland's plans for a new Parliament as responsible for Lostwithiel, Truro, Bodmin, Helston, Camelford, Grampound, Tregony, Mitchell, and St. Mawes. During the 1722 election campaign he toured the west country with Boscawen.[1] It was said that he 'bore the greatest sway in his country of any commoner of his time', and ran through a fortune of 'at least £30,000 besides what he had acquired himself'. He died 'more of trouble of mind than any other distemper' 1 July 1726, aged 39,[2] leaving his estates mortgaged to John Knight (q.v.).

[1] Blenheim (Sunderland) mss; *HMC Portland*, vii. 307; Chandos to Parker, 27 Feb. 1722, to Vincent 20 Mar., 11 Apr. 1722, Chandos letter bks. [2] Thos. Tonkin's Hist. Cornw. f. 119, R. Inst. of Cornwall.

E.C.

VYNER, Robert (c.1685–1777), of Gautby, Lincs.

| GREAT GRIMSBY | 1710–1713 |
| LINCOLNSHIRE | 12 Feb. 1724–1761 |

b. c.1685, o.s. of Thomas Vyner, M.P. (nephew to Sir Robert Vyner, 1st Bt., ld. mayor of London, and h. to his Lincs. and Cheshire estates) by Anne, da. of Sir Francis Leeke, 1st Bt., M.P., of Newark, Notts. *m.* (1) Margaret, da. of Sir Thomas Style, 2nd Bt., M.P., of Wateringbury, Kent, 1s. 2da.; (2) 3 June 1758, Mrs. Delicia de Pipre of Upper Brook St., London, *s.p.* *suc.* fa. 1707.

Vyner inherited the Lincolnshire and Cheshire estates acquired by his great uncle, Charles II's banker. Returned in 1710 for Grimsby, which his father had represented 1699–1701, he did not stand again till 1721, when he was defeated at Grimsby. In 1724 he was returned as an independent Whig for Lincolnshire, for which he continued to sit without opposition till he retired in 1761. One of the most prolific speakers of his time, he acted consistently against every Administration, though voting against the motion for Walpole's removal in February 1741. In 1730 the 1st Lord Egmont wrote of him:

This gentleman denied himself to be a Jacobite and insisted he was for nothing but his country; he speaks to figure in the House and with spirit, and always divides with the Tories and does not want for sense nor words in private discourse, in which last he is a little redundant, for he swears like a dragoon.[1]

He himself defined his position in an election letter to another independent Whig, Josph Banks (q.v.), 8 Sept. 1740:

The principles on which we tender our services, setting aside the cant words of the country interest, are independency and uncorruption.[2]

In 1749–50 the 2nd Lord Egmont in his electoral survey describes Vyner as 'a whimsical man, full of projects of reformation, especially about the army and militia'. Horace Walpole observed in 1751 that 'the House generally suffered him to be singular in his opinion'.[3] He died 10 Apr. 1777.

[1] *HMC Egmont Diary*, i. 32. [2] Spalding Gentlemen's Soc. mss. [3] *Mems. Geo. II*, i. 124.

P.W.

WADE, George (1673–1748), of Abbey Courtyard, Bath, Som.

| HINDON | 1715–1722 |
| BATH | 1722–14 Mar. 1748 |

b. 1673, 3rd s. of Jerome Wade of Kilavally, co. Westmeath. *unm.*

Ensign 10 Ft. 1690, lt. 1693, capt.-lt. 1694, capt. 1695, maj. 1703; lt.-col. 17 Ft. 1703; brevet-col. 1704; adjt.-gen. to forces in Portugal 1704; col. 33 Ft. 1705; brig.-gen. Spanish army 1707; brig.-gen. 1708; maj.-gen. Spanish army 1708; maj.-gen. 1714; col. 3 Drag. Gds. 1717–*d.*; 2nd-in-c. expedition against Vigo 1719; c.-in-c. Scotland 1724–40; lt.-gen. 1727; gov. Berwick 1732, and Fort William, Fort George and Fort Augustus 1733; gen. of Horse 1739; lt.-gen. of Ordnance 1742–*d.*; P.C. 24 June 1742; f. m. 1743; c.-in-c. Flanders 1743–45; c.-in-c. north of England during Jacobite rebellion 1745.

The grandson of a Cromwellian army officer, who settled in Ireland, Wade served with distinction in the wars of William III and Marlborough. Returned as a Whig for Hindon in 1715, he transferred in 1722 to Bath, where he had been stationed in the Fifteen rebellion, making his residence there and building up an impregnable position in the city, based on personal prestige. He even succeeded in polling all 30 votes in 1734, an unequalled feat. In this he was helped by the well-known Bath postmaster, Ralph Allen, who had married his illegitimate daughter and became so influential in the city and corporation that he was known widely as 'the man of Bath'. There was no question of bribery though he spent money freely on charities, corporation feasts and the abbey, and had the portraits of the corporation painted at his own expense.

In Parliament Wade voted assiduously with the Administration, missing only one out of 14 recorded divisions between 1716 and 1746. He spoke frequently on army matters in support of the Government; when Pulteney complained, 27 Jan. 1732, that the British received far more pay than the French and Germans, he replied that 'it is well known that what [the German army] come short of ours in pay they do more than make up by plundering, oppressing and raising contributions upon the countries where they are quartered'. He was capable of taking an independent line on other subjects. In opposing on disciplinary grounds an opposition motion, 13 Feb. 1734, that an officer not above the rank of colonel should not be removed except by court martial or an address of Parliament, he said:

Though I have generally joined in opinion with . . . the Administration, yet I have likewise upon many occasions differed from them . . . When the famous

South Sea scheme was in agitation in this House, though it was brought in by a minister and strongly supported . . . yet I had the honour to be one of the 55 who divided against it . . . I had upon that occasion messages sent to me and was threatened to be stripped of all my military employments, but those threats had no weight with me.

On 28 and 30 Mar. 1737 he spoke on Sir John Barnard's (q.v.) proposals for reducing the interest on the National Debt to 3%, unsuccessfully moving an amendment to substitute $3\frac{1}{2}$ for 3.

For 16 years Wade was commander-in-chief in Scotland, where he opened up the Highlands by constructing 250 miles of military roads. He was responsible for putting down the Glasgow riots against the malt tax in 1725, when one of his officers was found guilty of murder by a local jury. With this in mind he defended the officer in command at Edinburgh for refusing to intervene in the Porteous riots without a written request from the magistrates, observing, in the debate on the bill for punishing Edinburgh, 16 May 1737, that had he done so 'he might have stopped the riots but then he would have risked his life', for 'the aversion of the people of that country to the gentlemen of the army' was so great that there was 'no room to suppose he would have met with much favour . . . had his conduct been brought to trial in the civil court'. He was for 'making an example of the city of Edinburgh for the part her citizens acted in this inhuman affair.'

After the outbreak of war with Spain in 1739 Wade defended the Government's proposals for raising new troops.[1] On 2 Mar. 1741 he spoke against a clause in a press bill providing that volunteers should be entitled to £6 a year for life, arguing that pressed men should share this bounty. In Jan. 1742 he was summoned to the last meeting of Walpole's war cabinet.[2] He was included in the court list of candidates for the secret committee on Walpole's Administration, but was not elected to it.

In 1743 Wade, though old and asthmatic, was made commander-in-chief of the army in Flanders, impressing George II as 'a very able officer but . . . not alert'.[3] Resigning early in 1745, he was called on to take command of the forces sent against the rebels, but was soon superseded. He died 14 Mar. 1748, leaving about £100,000, most of it to his natural children.[4]

[1] HMC 14th Rep. IX, 62; Coxe, Walpole, iii. 558. [2] SP Dom. various 3, 8 Jan. 1742. [3] Walpole to Mann, 6 Aug. 1744. [4] C. Dalton, Geo. I's Army, ii. 22.

R.S.L.

WAGER, Sir Charles (c.1666–1743), of Kilmenath, nr. West Looe, Cornw. and Parson's Green, London.

PORTSMOUTH	23 Jan. 1710–3 Feb. 1711
WEST LOOE	1713–1715
PORTSMOUTH	1715–1734
WESTMINSTER	1734–1741
WEST LOOE	1741–24 May 1743

b. c.1666, nr. West Looe,[1] posth. s. of Charles Wager of Deal, Kent, capt. R.N., by Prudence, da. of William Goodsonn of Ratcliffe, Mdx., v.-adm. in Cromwell's navy. m. (lic. 8 Dec. 1691) Martha, da. of Anthony Earning, capt. in Cromwell's navy, of Limehouse, Mdx., s.p. suc. fa. at birth. Kntd. 8 Dec. 1709.

Lt. R.N. by 1690, capt. 1692; freeman, West Looe 1699; r.-adm. 1708, v.-adm. 1716, adm. 1731; v.-adm. Great Britain 1742; comptroller of the navy Feb. 1715–18; ld. of Admiralty Mar. 1718–33, 1st ld. Jan. 1733–Mar. 1742; P.C. 25 Jan. 1733; treasurer of the navy Dec. 1742–d.

The son of a captain in Cromwell's navy, described by Pepys as one of the bravest officers he ever knew, Wager was said by the 1st Lord Onslow to have been

of the most gentle and humane disposition I ever knew, and spent almost the whole he got in the most generous acts of charity and compassion . . . His father . . . dying when his son was young, and the mother marrying a quaker, he was bred up among that people; by which he acquired the simplicity of his manners, and had much of their fashion in his speech as well as carriage. And all this, with his particular roughness of countenance, made the softness of his nature still more pleasing, because unexpected at his first appearance.[2]

He served in the Mediterranean in 1703–4 with Sir George Byng (q.v.), later Lord Torrington, under Sir Clowdisley Shovel. In May 1708 he intercepted the Spanish treasure fleet off Cartagena, capturing a galleon 'worth 200,000 pieces of eight' (about £50,000) in 'coined and uncoined gold and silver',[3] a large share of which he retained as prize-money. Returning to England a wealthy man, he acquired an estate near his birth place, West Looe, which he represented as a Whig in the 1713 Parliament. Transferring to Portsmouth on the Admiralty interest in 1715, he became a lord of the Admiralty in 1718, making a 'very short unintelligible' speech in a debate on the South Sea Company in June 1721.[4] Sent with a squadron to the Baltic to prevent a war in the north, he accomplished his mission so successfully that Townshend wrote to him:

His Majesty has commanded me to let you know from him that he was before persuaded you was a very good admiral, but he now sees that you are likewise an able minister.[5]

His next assignment was to command a fleet off the Spanish coast during the siege of Gibraltar in 1727.

Returning to England in April 1728, he took part on 6 May in a debate on a bill for encouraging naval recruitment, in which he opposed proposals of his former subordinate, Edward Vernon (q.v.), for improving the living conditions of seamen, saying 'it was impossible better care could be taken than was'. On 12 Mar. 1729 he defended the conduct of the Administration in a debate on the Spanish depredations, observing

> that the merchants might be mistaken in some things in their complaints, for what was said yesterday at the bar [of the House] was impossible to be true, and as they were not on oath they might say what they pleased.[6]

He spoke against a proposal for ending the monopoly of the East India Company on 26 Feb. 1730, and next day in a debate on Dunkirk, which he seemed, to the 1st Lord Egmont (q.v.), to treat 'as a thing of too little consequence'. In a debate on a pension bill on 17 Feb. 1731, he

> said he was against all disqualifying bills, that the Act which obliged every member to have an estate at least of three hundred pounds a year in land had disqualified ninety-nine persons of a hundred in the kingdom . . . he did not know why gentlemen who had served their country well should be discouraged from sitting in the House; in all other countries they met with regard, but here as soon as the benefit was reaped from their services, they were looked on as the vilest of men.[7]

At the Admiralty, he was already carrying out the duties of first lord, for

> though Lord Torrington had the name and the appearance of it, Sir Charles, by giving way in some things not essential, and by suggesting matters in such a way that the other imagined the first thought was his own, kept all in order, without ever having any squabble.

On 12 July 1731 Wager wrote to Walpole:

> You are sensible that our chief at the Admiralty can last but a little time longer, and I believe you are sensible that we shall not like to have a man put over us that must be instructed in what he must say when he goes to court; and what mistakes he may make would fall upon us.
>
> There are two objections against my being at the head of the Admiralty, if I should chance to outlive the present head; one is that it is necessary the head should be a lord (not an Irish lord) for which . . . I may without much vanity, look upon myself as well qualified as some of them . . . Indeed I have no estate suitable to that dignity; but a man that is an officer does not like to have anybody put over his head, and if that can be prevented I shall be very well content.[8]

So as 'to be able to say' that he was 'not altogether an upstart, but descended from an ancient family, though they never had but a small estate', he claimed kinship with the heiress of the Wagers of Charlton Kings, Gloucestershire, who, suitably plied with presents, was ready to acknowledge the

relationship, even consulting him on family matters.[9] Thus equipped with a pedigree, he succeeded Torrington as first lord, though he was not given a peerage. A year later, in a debate on the navy, Vernon, censuring English subservience to France, referred to him as

> a gentleman . . . whose consummate courage, conduct, and generosity had rendered him the darling and glory of his country; what vexation must he have felt in his breast to be forced to submit to those dishonourable orders he received to idle away his time at Spithead in doing nothing for his country's service but feasting and keeping a Bartholomew fair on board.[10]

In the winter of 1736, in spite of being 'very much decayed' by a recent illness, Wager conveyed George II back to England from Hanover. It was reported that, the weather being bad,

> the King had declared if Sir Charles Wager would not sail, his Majesty would go in a packet-boat, that he had told Sir Charles go; and that Sir Charles, in his laconic Spartan style, had told him he could not; that the King had said: 'let it be what weather it will, I am not afraid'; and that Sir Charles Wager had replied, 'if you are not, I am'; that his Majesty had sworn he had rather be twelve hours in a storm than twenty-four more at Helvoetsluys; upon which Sir Charles had told him he need not wish for twelve, for four would do his business; and that, when the King by the force of importunity, had obliged Sir Charles Wager to sail, Sir Charles had told him: 'well, Sir, you can oblige me to go, but I can make you come back again'.[11]

Appointed one of the plenipotentiaries to adjust differences with Spain in February 1739, he defended the Spanish convention in March.[12] After the declaration of war against Spain, in order to relieve the chronic shortage of seamen, he introduced on 5 Feb. 1740 a bill establishing a register of seamen on the French model, which was dropped in face of bitter opposition, but passed next year in a modified form.[13] He was beginning to show his age, 74: at a meeting of the cabinet on 28 Apr. 1740 to decide the future destination of the fleet, Hervey describes him as muttering something

> most of it so inarticulately, that it seemed like sounds without words, and where the articulation was plain, it seemed words without sense.[14]

In 1741 Wager stood for Westminster, which he had represented since 1734.

> Two days before the election [he wrote to Vernon] . . . when Lord Sundon [q.v.] and I dreamed of no opposition, you and Mr. Edwin [Charles, q.v.] were set up . . . and, at the election, a poll demanded for you both which continued six days, with such mobs and riots as never were seen before . . . I had the good fortune to be obliged to attend the King to Holland the three last days, and returned in five days when the poll was closed, and Lord Sundon and I declared to be duly elected.

Pulteney, writing to Vernon of the 'most scandalous practices and violent acts of power' made use of by the Administration there, added:

> Your friend Sir Charles Wager, had nothing to do in this, which I am heartily glad of, because I esteem him much, and know him to be a very valuable man, extremely amiable in his character of private life, and a well wisher to his country in his public capacity.[15]

Unseated in one of the critical divisions on election petitions before the fall of Walpole, he took his seat for West Looe, for which he had also been returned. Subsequently the secret committee appointed to inquire into Walpole's Administration investigated the payment of £1,500 of secret service money by Wager to the high bailiff of Westminster as compensation for being taken into custody of the House and other losses.[16] In January 1742 he had an audience with the King during which he 'begged he might quit his employment, finding age and infirmities had impaired his faculties, to which the King replied, I don't see that, and you shall serve me on'. He resigned with Walpole on 11 Feb., although he seems to have been the only member of the Admiralty board for whose dismissal the Opposition had not pressed.[17] According to Horace Walpole, he refused an invitation to return to the Admiralty a fortnight later,[18] but he accepted the treasurership of the navy at the end of the year. He died 24 May 1743, leaving his fortune to his wife.[19]

[1] *Hist. Surv. Cornw.* i. 38; Burnet, *Hist. of his own Time* (1833 ed.), v. 390 n. [2] *Diary*, ed. Wheatley, v. 126; vii. 355. [3] *Cal. Treas. Pprs.* 1708–14, p. 79. [4] Coxe, *Walpole*, ii. 218. [5] J. F. Chance, *Alliance of Hanover*, 343. [6] *Knatchbull Diary.* [7] HMC Egmont *Diary*, i. 68, 73, 140. [8] Coxe, iii. 128, 116–17. [9] *Glos. N. & Q.* i. 35–36, 119–20. [10] HMC Egmont *Diary*, ii. 17. [11] Hervey, *Mems.* 637. [12] HMC Egmont *Diary*, iii. 18; Coxe, iii. 517. [13] 14 Geo. II, c.38. [14] *Mems.* 927. [15] *Original Letters to an Honest Sailor* (1746), pp. 38, 43. [16] *CJ*, xxiv. 331. [17] HMC Egmont *Diary*, iii. 236; Vaucher, *Walpole et la Politique de Fleury*, 428. [18] To Mann, 25 Feb. 1742. [19] PCC 184 Boycott.

E.C.

WALCOT, Humphrey (1672–1743), of Bitterley, Salop.

LUDLOW 1713–1722

b. 1672, 4th s. of John Walcot, M.P., of Walcot, Salop by his 2nd w. Elizabeth, da. of Sir George Clerke of Watford, Northants. *m.* (1) Margaret (*d.* 6 Nov. 1715), da. of Edmund Pearce of Wilcott, Salop, *s.p.*; (2) c.1720, Anne, da. and h. of George Curteis of Otterden, Kent, wid. of Thomas Wheler (*d.s.p.* 1716), 1s. 3da.

Dep. paymaster of forces 1712–13; assistant, R. African Co. 1717–22, dep. gov. 1720, sub gov. 1721.[1]

Humphrey Walcot belonged to an ancient Shropshire family, with large estates between Ludlow and Bishop's Castle, carrying an interest in both boroughs. A merchant, apprenticed in 1691 to a British firm in Cadiz, he was related to James Brydges, M.P., paymaster of the forces abroad 1705–13, created Duke of Chandos 1719, whose sister married his elder brother in 1696. Soon after this marriage he settled at Stanmore, near Cannons, the future seat of Brydges, with whom he became closely associated, both officially and in business on the board of the Royal African Company, in which his holding in 1716 amounted to £32,000.

In 1709 Walcot bought his brother's estate of Bitterley Court,[2] near Ludlow, which he contested unsuccessfully in 1710. He was returned for it as a Tory in 1713 but as a Whig who would often vote with the Tories in 1715, giving his interest at Bishop's Castle to Lord Harley (q.v.).[3] From 1715 he voted against the Government in all recorded divisions. He also looked after the interests of the African Company, at whose request he appears to have been instrumental in securing the rejection of a petition from its creditors to the Commons for an enquiry into its affairs in 1720.[4] Though supported by Chandos, who had bought the manor of Bishop's Castle from the Harleys in 1718, he lost his seat in 1722 and did not stand again.[5] He died in October 1743.

[1] R. African Co. court bks. T70/101. [2] J. R. Burton, *Hist. Walcot Fam.* 78–79. [3] Chandos to Walcot, 15 and 21 Sept. 1714, 28 Dec. 1714, 13 Jan. and 5 Feb. 1715, Chandos letter bks. [4] General court, 27 Jan. 1720, T70/101, ff. 190–6; *CJ*, xix. 280. [5] Chandos to J. Baldwyn, 9 Nov., 11 Dec. 1721, to Sir F. Charlton, 28 Feb. 1722, Chandos letter bks.

J.B.L.

WALCOT, John (1697–1765), of Walcot, Salop.

SALOP 1727–1734

bap. 24 June 1697, 1st s. of Charles Walcot of Walcot (e. bro. of Humphrey Walcot, q.v.) by his 2nd w. Anne, 4th da. of James Brydges, 8th Baron Chandos of Sudeley, sis. of James Brydges, M.P., 1st Duke of Chandos. *educ.* Magdalen, Oxf. 1715. *m.* 15 May 1732, Mary, da. of Sir Francis Dashwood, 1st Bt., M.P., of West Wycombe, Bucks., 2s. *suc.* fa. 1726.

In 1727 John Walcot rounded off his estates by purchasing the manor of Bishop's Castle from his uncle, the Duke of Chandos, for £7,000,[1] thus acquiring the chief interest in that borough. With an income of £3,000 a year, burdened with a debt of £22,000, he stood for the county against Chandos's advice to wait till he had paid off the debt.[2] Returned as a Tory, he voted against the Government.

Though Walcot did not stand again he continued to support his interest at Bishop's Castle, plunging deeper into debt. By 1742 he owed over £33,000 and was forced to procure a private Act of Parliament to raise money on his wife's portion.[3] Before the election of 1747 he borrowed £8,500 on mortgage from his banker, Samuel Child (q.v.), who was standing for Bishop's Castle. After a close contest in 1753 it was said that if his candidate, Dashwood King, failed to send him a remittance, Walcot 'would have done asking votes in Bishop's Castle'.[4] The end came in 1761, when his debts had risen to over £48,000. He was forced to conceal himself from his creditors, leaving his son and lawyer to sell his property to Lord Clive for the vastly inflated price of £92,000.[5]

He died in 1765.

[1] Chandos to Walcot, 3 Apr. 1727, Walcot mss, Salop RO. [2] *Gent. Mag.* 1732, p. 776; Walcot mss; Chandos to Walcot, 17 July 1727, Chandos letter bks. [3] 15 & 16 Geo. II, c.31; J. R. Burton, *Hist. Walcot Fam.* 85. [4] Walcot mss; S. Griffiths to Corbyn Morris, 27 Feb. 1753, Newcastle (Clumber) mss. [5] Account of Abraham Jones, 14 May 1764, Walcot mss.

J.B.L.

WALDEGRAVE, Hon. John (1718-84).

ORFORD 1747–1754
NEWCASTLE-UNDER-LYME 1754–28 Apr. 1763

b. 28 Apr. 1718, 3rd s. of James, 1st Earl Waldegrave, by Mary, da. of Sir John Webb, 3rd Bt., of Hatherop, Glos. *m.* 7 May 1751, Lady Elizabeth Leveson Gower, da. of John, 1st Earl Gower, sis. of Granville Leveson Gower (q.v.), 1st Marquess of Stafford, and Gertrude, Duchess of Bedford, 3s. 5da. *suc.* bro. as 3rd Earl 28 Apr. 1763.

Ensign 1 Ft. Gds. 1735, lt. and capt. 1739; capt. and lt.-col. 3 Ft. Gds. 1743, 2nd maj. 1748, 1st maj. 1749; a.-d.-c. to Duke of Cumberland 1747; col. army 1747; col. 9 Ft. 1751–5, 8 Drags. 1755–8; maj.-gen. 1757; col. 5 Drag. Gds. 1758–9; lt.-gen. 1759; col. 2 Drag. Gds. 1759–73; gov. Plymouth 1761–*d.*; gen. 1772; col. 2 Ft. Gds. 1773–*d.*

Groom of the bedchamber 1747–63; master of the horse to the Queen 1770–*d.*; ld. lt. Essex 1781–*d.*

Brought in by the Government for Orford in 1747, Waldegrave was made a lord of the bedchamber, no doubt through the influence of his brother, Lord Waldegrave, 'a personal favourite of the King'. In 1751 he married the sister of the Duchess of Bedford without the consent of her father, Lord Gower, who was so much incensed with Lord Sandwich for allowing the marriage to be performed at his apartments in the Admiralty that he broke with him and did not resign with the Duke of Bedford when Sandwich was dismissed a month later. At the beginning of 1752 Bedford is reported to have come to town 'resolved to make use of the remains of the King's favour to ask a pension for . . . Lady Elizabeth Waldegrave',[1] which however was not granted till some years later.

Waldegrave died 22 Oct. 1784.

[1] Walpole, *Mems. Geo. II*, i. 92, 188, 242.

R.R.S.

WALDEN, Lord, see HOWARD, Henry (*b.* 1707)

WALKER, Thomas (c.1664–1748), of Wimbledon, Surr.

WEST LOOE 26 Jan. 1733–1734
PLYMPTON ERLE 21 Feb. 1735–1741
HELSTON 1741–1747

b. c.1664, bro. of Peter Walker and bro.-in-law of Stephen Skynner, West India merchant, of Wanstead, Essex; prob. s. of Edward Walker of St. Sepulchre's, London, by Susanna Winchurst.[1] *unm.*

Commr. of customs Nov. 1714–31; surveyor gen. of crown lands Oct. 1731–*d.*

At George I's accession Walker was appointed to a commissionership of customs, which he exchanged in 1731 for a post not disqualifying him from sitting in the House of Commons. Beginning a parliamentary career at the age of 69, he sat as a government nominee for Cornish boroughs, voting consistently with the ministry. He made his only known speech in 1733, when as an ex-commissioner of customs he defended the then commissioners against aspersions on them by the Opposition.[2] He died 22 Oct. 1748, aged 84, 'most immensely rich', Henry Pelham reported to Newcastle, 'most people say £300,000, I believe not much less'.[3] Horace Walpole describes him as 'a kind of toad-eater to Sir Robert Walpole and Lord Godolphin, a great frequenter of Newmarket, and a notorious usurer'.[4]

[1] PCC 346 Strahan, 49 Auber; *Marriage Lic. Vic.-Gen.* (Harl. Soc. xxxi), 143; *Fac. Office Marriage Lic. Index Lib.* xxxiii), 22. [2] Stuart mss 160/129. [3] 1 Nov. 1748, Add. 32717, f. 245. [4] Note to letter to Mann, 24 Oct. 1748.

E.C.

WALLER, Edmund (c.1699–1771), of Hall Barn, Beaconsfield, Bucks.

GREAT MARLOW 1722–1741
CHIPPING WYCOMBE 1741–1754

b. c.1699, 1st s. of Dr. Stephen Waller by Judith, da. of Sir Thomas Vernon, M.P., of Farnham, Surr., and 2nd w. of John Aislabie (q.v.); bro. of Harry Waller (q.v.). *educ.* Eton 1707. *m.* bef. 1720, Mary, da. of John Aislabie, 4s. 2da. *suc.* uncle Edmund Waller in Glos. estates c.1700, and fa. 1707.

Cofferer of the Household Dec. 1744–Dec. 1746.

Descended from the seventeenth century poet and politician, Waller owned estates near both Great Marlow and Chipping Wycombe, carrying considerable influence in both boroughs. As a youth of 21, he was used by Aislabie (his stepfather and father-in-law) as a cover for his own speculations in South Sea stock. The facts came out when the South Sea committee of the House of Commons, on examining the books of the Sword Blade bank, found entries totalling nearly £800,000 representing Waller's stock exchange transactions between March and November 1720, with a credit balance of £77,000 due to him in respect of these transactions.

On further investigation it transpired that £33,000 of the £77,000 admittedly belonged to Aislabie, who himself is reported afterwards to have said that the correct figure was £53,000.[1]

Returned as a Whig in 1722 on the family interest at Marlow, Waller helped his brother, Harry (q.v.), to capture Wycombe in 1726, spending more 'to get one borough than would buy a score'.[2] Following Pulteney into opposition, he was one of the anti-ministerial tellers on the Petersfield election petition in 1727, thenceforth becoming a prolific speaker against Walpole's Administration.

On Walpole's fall Waller was offered a seat on the Treasury board but 'refused until the whole party were agreed and satisfied in the measures to be pursued'.[3] Elected to the secret committee of inquiry into Walpole's Administration, he moved the opposition address against the Hanoverians on 10 Dec. 1742, signed the opposition whip sent out in November 1743, and served on the committee of six set up to co-ordinate opposition activity in the Commons during the next session. In 1744 he was one of the 'junto' of nine opposition leaders who were united 'upon one principle, which was to get into place', an aim achieved on the formation of the Broad-bottom Administration in December 1744.[4] Appointed cofferer of the Household in this Government, he did not resign with the Pelhams in February 1746 but was not dismissed on their return to office. In December 1746, having become so deaf that he had ceased to attend the House, he gave up his post in return for the appointment of his younger son, Edmund (q.v.), to a life sinecure vacated by the death of George Berkeley (q.v.), carrying with it a well paid deputyship for his brother Harry.

In the next Parliament Waller was classed by the Government as Opposition and by the 2nd Lord Egmont among the Prince's supporters, which did not prevent him from applying to Newcastle for a company in the army for his eldest son.[5] He gave up his seat in 1754, spending the rest of his life in retirement.

Horace Walpole describes Waller as

a dull obscure person, of great application to figures and the revenue, which knowledge he could never communicate. He spoke with a tone which yet was the least cause of the unintelligibility of his speeches. Lord Chesterfield went for six weeks to his country house to be instructed in the public accounts, and when he came back said he had been *beating his head against a Waller*.[6]

He died 25 Apr. 1771.

[1] *CJ*, xix. 432, 519; *Hist. Reg.* 1721, p. 309 et seq. [2] *HMC Var.* vi. 5. [3] *HMC Egmont Diary*, iii. 250. [4] Owen, *Pelhams*, 198–9; R. Glover, *Mems.* 30. [5] 6 Nov. 1747, Add. 32713, f. 389. [6] *Corresp.* (Yale ed.), xvii. 352 n. 25.

R.R.S.

WALLER, Edmund, jun. (?1725–88), of Beaconsfield, Bucks.

CHIPPING WYCOMBE 1747–1754, 10 Dec. 1757–1761

b. ?1725, 2nd but 1st surv. s. of Edmund Waller (q.v.). *educ.* St. Mary Hall, Oxf. 3 Feb. 1744, aged 18; L. Inn 1745. *m.* 22 Feb. 1755, Martha, da. of Rowland Philipps of Orlandon, Pemb., 2s. 2da. *suc.* fa. 1771.
Master, St. Katherine's Hospital 1747–*d.*

In January 1747 Waller was appointed to the lucrative life sinecure of St. Katherine's Hospital, apparently in compensation for his father's surrender of office. Yet when he and his father were returned for the family borough of Chipping Wycombe at the general election a few months later, they were classed as Opposition. Having taken to the bottle, he was replaced in 1754 by his elder brother John, on whose death he was again returned, sitting until the next general election when his younger brother, Robert, replaced him. His father left the bulk of his estate to him, but so tied it up in the hands of trustees as to make it impossible for him to squander it.[1]

He died 8 Aug. 1788.

[1] L. J. Ashford, *High Wycombe*, 183.

R.R.S.

WALLER, Harry (c.1701–72), of Lincoln's Inn and Grosvenor St., London.

CHIPPING WYCOMBE 17 Mar. 1726–1747

b. c.1701, 2nd s. of Dr. Stephen Waller; yr. bro. of Edmund Waller (q.v.). *educ.* I. Temple 1716, called 1725; L. Inn 1721. *m.* 4 Aug. 1744, Elizabeth, da. of Sir John Stapylton, 3rd Bt., M.P.
Dep. master St. Katherine's Hospital Feb. 1747–*d.*

After unsuccessfully contesting Wycombe and St. Ives in 1722, Harry Waller was returned in 1726 as a government supporter[1] on petition at a by-election for Wycombe, where his family had a major interest. Following his elder brother into opposition, he voted consistently against the ministry till Edmund obtained a place in 1744, after which Harry was classed by the Government as 'New Ally'. On the motion for the removal of Walpole in February 1741 he withdrew. He retained his seat till 1747, when he was replaced by his nephew, Edmund Waller junior (q.v.), under whom he had obtained a profitable office. He died 29 July 1772.

[1] *Knatchbull Diary*, 7 Feb. 1726.

R.R.S.

WALLINGFORD, Visct., *see* **KNOLLYS, William**

WALLIS, William (c.1657–1737), of Wormley-bury, Herts.

STEYNING 1705–1708, 1710–17 Feb. 1711,
                        1713–1715,   12 Apr. 1717–1722

b. c.1657, parentage unknown, *s.p.*
  Groom of the privy chamber to William III bef.
1700 and gent. of the privy chamber at his *d.* 1702.

According to an obituary William Wallis was

a great favourite of the late King William, and was in
all the wars in Flanders with him; and being advanced
to a high station upon his coming to England, was
possessed of an estate in Hertfordshire of £30,000,
but being unfortunately engaged for the receiver-
general of excise in the beginning of the reign of
Queen Anne, his estate was seized upon for the
revenues of excise. He was present in the chamber
when the late King William died, and has since been
supported by the nobility and gentry of the kingdom.[1]

He bought lands in Datchworth, Hertfordshire, in
1693 and Wormleybury in 1697, being then of
Holborn, Middlesex.[2] He also owned houses in
Steyning, for which he was returned as a Whig
under Anne. Defeated in 1715, but awarded the
seat on petition, he was granted a lease of the
forest of Arkengarthdale, Yorkshire, valued at
£300,[3] voted with the Government, and was again
defeated in 1722. Shortly afterwards he sold his
houses in the borough to the Duke of Chandos. In
1733 he wrote a begging letter to Chandos, whose
secretary replied that the Duke was sorry for his
misfortunes, but that Wallis

must be sensible how shameful a price you extorted
from him when he made an agreement with you for
the few houses you had at Steyning, and for which he
has not to this day any of the most material writings
necessary to make out his title,

and that therefore he could only send him £5.[4]

He died 4 Feb. 1737, aged 80, in the rules of the
Fleet.[5]

[1] *Hist. Reg.* 1737, p. 127. [2] *VCH Herts.* iii. 79, 488. [3] *Cal. Treas.
Pprs.* 1714–19, p. 306; PCC 71 Lake. [4] 6 Dec. 1733, Chandos letter
bks. [5] *Hist. Reg.* loc. cit.

J.B.L.

WALLOP, Hon. Bluett (1726–49).

NEWPORT I.o.W.   1747–6 June 1749

b. 27 Apr. 1726, 4th s. of John Wallop (q.v.), 1st Earl
of Portsmouth, bro. of Hon. Charles and John Wallop
(qq.v.). *unm.*
  Page of honour to George II 1743–5; equerry to
Duke of Cumberland 1746–8; capt. 3 Ft. by 1746.

Bluett Wallop served in Flanders in 1743 and
1744 as a page of honour to the King and at Culloden
in 1746 as equerry to the Duke of Cumberland.
Returned as a government supporter for Newport
in 1747 on the interest of his father, then Governor
of the Isle of Wight, he died on 6 June 1749.

P.W.

WALLOP, Hon. Charles (1722–71).

WHITCHURCH 1747–1754

b. 12 Dec. 1722, 3rd s. of John Wallop (q.v.), 1st Earl
of Portsmouth; bro. of Hon. Bluett and John Wallop
(qq.v.). *educ.* Winchester 1732–9; Corpus Christi,
Camb. 1740–3. *unm.*

Charles Wallop was returned for Whitchurch as
a government supporter on the interest of his
father in 1747 but did not stand again. He died
11 Aug. 1771.

P.W.

WALLOP, John (1690–1762), of Hurstbourne Park, nr. Whitchurch, and Farleigh Wallop, Hants.

HAMPSHIRE 1715–11 June 1720

b. 15 Apr. 1690, 3rd s. of John Wallop of Farleigh
Wallop by Alicia, da. and coh. of William Borlase of
Great Marlow, Bucks. *educ.* Eton 1708; Geneva
1708–9; Grand Tour (Italy and Germany) 1710. *m.*
(1) 20 May 1716, Lady Bridget Bennet (*d.* 12 Oct.
1738), da. of Charles, 1st Earl of Tankerville, 6s. 4da.;
(2) 9 June 1741, Elizabeth, da. of James Griffin, M.P.,
2nd Baron Griffin, wid. of Henry Grey (q.v.) of
Billingbear, Berks., *s.p. suc.* e. bro. Bluett Wallop
at Hurstbourne and Farleigh Wallop 1707; *cr.* Baron
Wallop and Visct. Lymington 11 June 1720, Earl of
Portsmouth 11 Apr. 1743.
  Hereditary bailiff, Burley (New Forest); ld. of
Treasury Apr. 1717–June 1720; c.j. in eyre north of
Trent 1732–34; ld. lt. and v.-adm. Hants 1733–42;
gov. and v.-adm. I.o.W. 1734–42, 1746–*d.*

Wallop belonged to an old Hampshire family,
who controlled one seat at Andover and one at
Whitchurch. Returned as a Whig for the county in
1715, he adhered to Sunderland on the split in the
Whig party in 1717, when he was rewarded with a
seat at the Treasury board, in spite of which he
voted against the Government on the repeal of the
Occasional Conformity and Schism Acts in 1719.
He lost his place on Walpole's return to office in
1720, but was compensated with a peerage. In 1731
he sent a message to the Queen through her favourite, Mrs. Clayton (wife of William Clayton, q.v.),
suggesting that he should replace the Duke of
Bolton (Charles Powlett, q.v.) as the government
electoral manager in Hampshire. His application
produced no results at the time, but when the Duke
went into opposition in 1733 Wallop, now Lord
Lymington, succeeded him as lord lieutenant and
vice-admiral of Hampshire, and governor of the
Isle of Wight. Losing all his appointments on
Walpole's fall, he was created Earl of Portsmouth as
compensation in 1743. He died 22 Nov. 1762.

[1] Lady Sundon, *Mems.* i. 218–22.

P.W.

WALLOP, Hon. John (1718–49).

ANDOVER 1741–19 Nov. 1749

b. 3 Aug. 1718, 1st s. of John Wallop (q.v.), 1st Earl of Portsmouth; bro. of Hon. Bluett and Charles Wallop (qq.v.). *educ.* Winchester 1731–4; Ch. Ch. Oxf. 1735. *m.* 12 July 1740, Catherine, da. and h. of John Conduit (q.v.) of Cranbury Lodge, Otterbourne, Hants, 4s. 1da. *styled* Visct. Lymington 1743–*d.*

Page of honour to the King 1739; mayor, Lymington 1739–40.

Returned for Andover on the family interest, John Wallop voted with the Administration on the chairman of the elections committee in 1741 but against the Hanoverians in 1744, abstaining from the corresponding divisions in 1742 and 1746. Classed as a government supporter in 1747, he died *v.p.* 19 Nov. 1749.

P.W.

WALLWYN, James (?1689–1766), of Longworth, Herefs.

HEREFORD 2 Apr. 1723–1727

b. ?1689, o.s. of James Wallwyn of Longworth by Ann, o. da. and h. of Sir William Bowyer. *educ.* Wadham, Oxf. 14 Jan. 1707, aged 17. *m.* Anne, da. and h. of Richard Taylor, 1s. 3da. *suc.* fa. 1705.

Sheriff, Herefs. 1732–3.

Wallwyn belonged to a cadet branch of an old Herefordshire family settled in the county from the fourteenth century. Returned as a Tory at a by-election in 1723 and put up again in 1727, he withdrew on a compromise with the Whigs. He did not stand again, and died 29 June 1766.

A.N.N.

WALPOLE, Hon. Edward (1706–84), of Frogmore, Berks.

LOSTWITHIEL 29 Apr. 1730–1734
GREAT YARMOUTH 1734–1768

b. 1706, 2nd s. of Sir Robert Walpole (q.v.); bro. of Hon. Horatio Walpole (q.v.) of Strawberry Hill. *educ.* Eton 1718; King's, Camb. 1725; L. Inn 1723, called 1727; Grand Tour (Italy 1730).[1] *unm.*, 1s. 3da. K.B. 27 Aug. 1753.

M.P. [I] 1737–60.

Master of pleas in the Exchequer 1727, and clerk of the pells 1739, for life; jt. sec. to Treasury 1730–9; P.C. [I] 1737; sec. to ld. lt. [I] 1737–9.

Brought into Parliament in 1730, Edward Walpole, aged 24, was appointed joint secretary of the Treasury in succession to his uncle, old Horace Walpole, whom he also succeeded at Yarmouth in 1734. From 1737 he combined this post, dealing with the political side of the Treasury work under his father, with that of secretary to the Duke of Devonshire as lord lieutenant of Ireland, reporting to him debates at Westminster affecting Irish affairs. He resigned both posts in 1739, on appointment to a life sinecure at the Exchequer worth £3,000 a year, which by 1782 was producing £7,000 a year.[2] In addition he had £400 a year from another life sinecure, and, after his father's death, a further £300–£400 a year from a third one held in trust for him as it was incompatible with a seat in the House of Commons.[3] He voted with the Government of the day in all recorded divisions, making his only known speech on 3 Dec. 1742 against an opposition place bill. In 1743 he talked of retiring from Parliament at the next general election,[4] but eventually agreed to continue, 'a trouble and expense taken upon me entirely for the service of the Government, without which motive it suits my genius much more to live quite retired in obscurity'.[5] In 1751 a gang of Irish blackmailers were given heavy sentences for conspiring to extort money from him by threatening to accuse him of sodomy.[6] In 1753 he applied for a K.B., explaining that

> I should like to be employed abroad in his Majesty's service, to which purpose this kind of trapping has its subserviency.[7]

He obtained the K.B. but not an appointment. In later life he became a recluse. He died 12 Jan. 1784.

[1] J. H. Plumb, *Walpole*, ii. 86 n. 2. [2] *CJ*, xxxviii. 708. [3] Coxe, *Walpole*, i. 730–1; *Cal. Treas. Bks.* xxx. 296; *Corresp. H. Walpole* (Yale ed.), xiii. 15. [4] J. Fowle to 'old' Horace Walpole, 30 July 1743, Walpole (Wolterton) mss. [5] To Newcastle, 19 June 1747, Add. 32711, f. 418. [6] *Gent. Mag.* 1751, pp. 328, 334, 521–2. [7] To Newcastle, 23 Aug. 1753, Add. 32732, f. 516.

R.R.S.

WALPOLE, Galfridus (1683–1726), of Westcomb House, Blackheath, Kent.

LOSTWITHIEL 1715–21 Mar. 1721

b. 1683, 3rd surv. s. of Robert Walpole, M.P., of Houghton, Norf. by Mary, da. and h. of Sir Geoffrey Burwell of Rougham, Suff.; bro. of Sir Robert Walpole and Horatio Walpole of Wolterton (qq.v.). *m.* Cornelia Hays of London, *s.p.*

Capt. R.N. 1706; treasurer of Greenwich Hospital 1715–21; jt. postmaster gen. 1721–*d.*

Galfridus Walpole, a naval officer, lost his right arm in an action in the Mediterranean in 1711.[1] Brought into Parliament and provided with a sinecure in 1715 by his brother, Robert, whom he followed into opposition in 1717, without losing his place, he vacated his seat in 1721 on appointment to the office of joint postmaster general, which disqualified its holder from sitting in the House of Commons. He died 7 Aug. 1726.

[1] Charnock, *Biog. Navalis*, iii. 376.

R.R.S.

WALPOLE, Horatio (1678–1757), of Wolterton, Norf.

LOSTWITHIEL	10 Jan.–21 Sept. 1710
CASTLE RISING	11 Dec. 1710–1715
BERE ALSTON	1715–Nov. 1717
EAST LOOE	2 Dec. 1718–1722
GREAT YARMOUTH	1722–1734
NORWICH	1734–4 June 1756

b. 8 Dec. 1678, 2nd surv. s. of Robert Walpole, M.P., of Houghton, Norf.; bro. of Robert Walpole, 1st Earl of Orford, and Galfridus Walpole (qq.v.). *educ.* Eton 1693–8; King's, Camb. 1698, fellow 1702–14; L. Inn 1700. *m.* 21 July 1720, Mary Magdalen, da. and coh. of Peter Lombard of Burnham Thorpe, Norf., 4s. 3da. *cr.* Baron Walpole of Wolterton 4 June 1756.

Sec. to envoy to Spain 1706–7, to chancellor of Exchequer and sec. of state 1707–9, to embassy at The Hague May 1709–March 1711; under-sec. of state 1708–10, 1714–15; commr. of revenue [I] 1713–16; minister to The Hague Jan.–Apr. 1715, Oct. 1715–Oct. 1716, May–July 1722; sec. to Treasury 1715–17, 1721–30; surveyor and auditor gen. of the revenue in America (for life) 1717; sec. to ld. lt. [I] 1720–21; P.C. [I] 1720; envoy to Paris 1723, ambassador extraordinary May 1724–7, ambassador extraordinary and plenip. 1727–30; plenip. and jt. ambassador, congress of Soissons 1728; cofferer of the Household 1730–41; P.C. 12 Nov. 1730; ambassador and plenip. to The Hague Apr. 1734–Nov. 1739; teller of the Exchequer 1741–*d.*

At George I's accession Horace Walpole was appointed under-secretary to his brother-in-law, Lord Townshend, but soon exchanged this post for that of secretary to the Treasury under his brother, Robert, obtaining the reversion of a valuable colonial sinecure for life which soon fell in. In 1717 he followed his brother into opposition, speaking against the Government on the repeal of the Occasional Conformity and Schism Acts and on the peerage bill in 1719. After an interlude as secretary to the lord lieutenant of Ireland on the reunion of the Whig party in 1720, he was reinstated at the Treasury, dealing with patronage and elections,[1] when his brother became first lord again in 1721. Sent to Paris by Walpole and Townshend in 1723 to counteract the activities of their rival, Carteret, he was appointed ambassador next year, coming over to England each session to defend the Government's foreign policy in the House of Commons. As ambassador he was on excellent personal terms with Cardinal Fleury, the French first minister, who never forgot his action in calling on him at a time when Fleury was supposed to have been disgraced at court. On the death of George I he came over to England with a letter from the Cardinal which, by re-affirming the policy of Anglo-French co-operation established in the late reign, contributed to the new King's decision to retain the existing ministry, consisting in practice, according to Hervey, of the two Walpole brothers, Townshend, and Newcastle.[2]

When Townshend resigned in 1730, Horace Walpole was brought home as cofferer of the Household to assist his brother in the House of Commons, where he seems to have acted as deputy leader. In 1731 he took an active part in the proceedings of an important select committee of the House, set up to consider petitions from all over the country, including his present and future constituencies of Yarmouth and Norwich, complaining of the harm done to the woollen manufacturing industry by the illegal export of Irish yarn to France and other foreign countries. On 12 Apr. he moved for a bill, which passed the Commons but was rejected by the Lords, taking off the duty on the importation of Irish yarn into Great Britain, with a view to inducing the Irish to bring it to this country instead of smuggling it abroad. He also supported a bill, which passed into law, allowing unenumerated goods from the plantations to come direct to Ireland without first passing through England. When Sir Robert Walpole complained that he had not heard of this bill, the 1st Lord Egmont (q.v.) explained on behalf of the Irish Members of the House, who had been negotiating about the bill with Horace Walpole, that

> it was only out of respect that we did not in the multitude of his business trouble him with it, presuming he was sufficiently acquainted with the thing by his brother.

Next year he seconded a motion, which led to an Act, taking away a concession allowing Irish seamen to carry with them 40s. worth of woollen goods on the ground that

> the Irish had made a compact with the English that upon giving them the advantage of the linen trade they should quit the woollen, but the Irish had broken the agreement, to the very great prejudice of our manufacturers.

In 1733 he introduced the bill, which eventually became the Molasses Act, for assisting the sugar colonies.[3] Nevertheless his nephew's statement that 'he was a dead weight on his brother's ministry' is confirmed by Hervey, who describes him at this time as

> a very good treaty dictionary, to which his brother often referred for facts necessary for him to be informed of and of which he was capable of making good use. But to hear Horace himself talk on these subjects unrestrained, and without being turned to any particular point, was listening to a rhapsody that was never coherent, and often totally unintelligible. This made his long and frequent speeches in Parliament uneasy to his own party, ridiculous to the other, and tiresome to both. He loved business, had great application, and was indefatigable, but from having

a most unclear head, no genius, no method, and a most inconclusive manner of reasoning, he was absolutely useless to his brother in every capacity but that which I have already mentioned of a dictionary.

In 1734, finding that 'he made no figure in Parliament, or rather a ridiculous one',[4] he returned to diplomacy as ambassador at The Hague, continuing to come over each session. In 1739 he moved an address of thanks for the Spanish convention in a two hours speech, also introducing another bill for taking off the duty on Irish yarn, which this time passed both Houses.[5] At the end of this year, tiring of diplomacy, he came home for good, occasionally attending meetings of the war cabinet.[6] In 1741 he exchanged his cofferership for a tellership of the Exchequer, a life sinecure, worth £3,000 a year.

On the fall of the Administration in 1742 there was a move to impeach not only Robert but Horace Walpole,

> who being auditor of the plantations, an office fairly not worth above £7 or £800 per annum, is supposed by secret practices and a kind of force upon the plantations, to make it worth £8 or £9,000 per annum,

Discussing this possibility with Sir John Shelley (q.v.), Egmont remarked that he 'found some Members, who wish well to Sir Robert, his brother, very ready to give up this man, and even to vote for confiscating his estate'. Shelley replied that

> he was not surprised at it, he having neither the love or esteem of any man, being conceited, overbearing, excessive covetous, and never having done one good thing that is known in his life. That not contented with his several great employments, he asked and obtained £2,000 per annum under pretence of keeping a table to entertain Members, and by discoursing with them at such times to keep them steady to the court, but his dinners were so scandalous that few cared to dine with him.[7]

When a secret committee was set up by the Commons to inquire into the late Administration, he went down to Wolterton, where he burned numerous documents, including his private correspondence with his brother, fearing that the committee would order the seizure of his papers.[8] However, the storm blew over, though the 2nd Lord Egmont noted under Norwich in his electoral survey, c.1749-50:

> Old Horace Walpole—to be routed if possible. An early inquiry into the frauds of the revenue may reach him in the affair of the sugars and if clearly proved that he was concerned he may not only be expelled but obliged to refund a great sum.

In 1743 he fought a duel with William Richard Chetwynd (q.v.) for saying that he deserved to be hanged. The duel took place at the bottom of the stairs leading out of the lobby of the House of Commons, where they drew.

> Chetwynd hit him on the breast, but was not near enough to pierce his coat. Horace made a pass, which the other put by with his hand, but it glanced along his side—a clerk, who had observed them go out together so arm-in-armly, could not believe it amicable, but followed them, and came up just time enough to beat down their swords as Horace had driven him against a post, and would probably have run him through at the next thrust.[9]

In 1747 he was still one of the men of business who were invited to Pelham's house to hear the King's speech read before the opening of Parliament.[10] At the end of a long speech against the Government on the Bavarian subsidy treaty in 1751, for which he nevertheless voted, he announced that in future he would confine himself 'to those low trifles . . . , woollen manufacture and the improvement of our trade'.[11] His only subsequent speeches in this Parliament were in support of a bill throwing open all ports to Irish wool, which under the 1739 Act had been restricted to certain specified ports, and against the repeal of the Jewish Naturalization Act.

He died 5 Feb. 1757.

[1] See STRICKLAND, Sir William, 4th Bt., and SHEPHEARD, Samuel. [2] St. Simon, *Mems.* (Boislisle ed.), xv. 199 et seq; Hervey, *Mems.* 29–31. [3] *HMC Egmont Diary*, i. 150, 173, 178–9, 183–4, 239, 334; *CJ*, xxii. 71. [4] Walpole, *Mems. Geo. II*, i. 140; Hervey, 284–5. [5] Coxe, *Walpole*, iii. 316; *HMC Egmont Diary*, iii. 31, 36. [6] *EHR*, xxxiv. 296 et seq. [7] *HMC Egmont Diary*, iii. 239–40. [8] Coxe, *Lord Walpole*, ii. 46. [9] Walpole to Mann, 14 Mar. 1743. [10] Owen, *Pelhams*, 143 n. 4. [11] Coxe, *Lord Walpole*, ii. 340.

R.R.S.

WALPOLE, Hon. Horatio (1717-97), of Strawberry Hill, Mdx.[1]

CALLINGTON	1741–1754
CASTLE RISING	1754–Feb. 1757
KING'S LYNN	24 Feb. 1757–1768

b. 24 Sept. 1717,[2] 3rd s. of Sir Robert Walpole (q.v.); bro. of Hon. Edward Walpole (q.v.). *educ.* Eton 1727–34; King's Camb. 1735; Grand Tour (France, Switzerland, Italy) 1739–41. *unm. suc.* nephew as 4th Earl of Orford 5 Dec. 1791.

Inspector gen. of exports and imports Dec. 1737–Feb. 1738; usher of the Exchequer, clerk of the estreats, and comptroller of the pipe 1738–*d.*

Before entering Parliament, Horace Walpole was provided with life sinecures worth about £2,000 a year. On his father's death in 1745 he inherited a share of a place in the customs granted to Robert Walpole in 1716 for the lives of his two elder sons, Robert and Edward (q.v.), with power to dispose of the income as he pleased. The two elder sons having been otherwise handsomely provided for, this power was exercised in favour of Horace, to the extent of £1,000 out of the £1,800 a year produced by the place, the remainder, subject to an annuity of £200 a year to a family dependant, being divided equally between Horace and Edward, who was to inherit the whole if Horace predeceased him. Thus £1,300 out of Horace's income of £3,300 a year depended on the lives of his two brothers, the younger of whom was 11 years older than himself.[3]

Returned for a family borough while on the grand tour, Horace Walpole made his maiden speech, 23 Mar. 1742, against the motion for a secret committee of inquiry into his father's Administration. Chosen to second the vote for the Hanoverian troops on 18 Jan. 1744, he is described as speaking 'extremely well', 'with deserved applause from everybody', paying an 'elegant' Latin compliment to the King on the battle of Dettingen. After his father's death in 1745 he took a more independent line in Parliament, speaking on 25 Oct. that year against the Government on a motion for recalling all British troops from Flanders to deal with the rebellion, which a number of other ministerial Members also supported; voted, 1 Nov., against them, in company with his friends Henry Fox and Thomas Winnington, on a proposal to give permanent commissions to officers of newly raised regiments, which cut across party lines; but stayed away when the question came up again, not wishing 'to give hindrance to a public measure (or at least what was called so) just now'.[4] In the division of 11 Apr. 1746 on the Hanoverians he voted with the Government, who in the Parliament elected in 1747 classed him as a supporter.

In fact since February 1747 Horace Walpole had been secretly contributing to the anti-government propaganda put out by the new Opposition launched in January that year by the Prince of Wales. During the next two and a half years he published 18 anonymous newspaper articles, which he sent to the editors without a name, attacking the Pelhams 'for the misfortunes which have happened to the kingdom under the present Administration'; for 'unconstitutionally' dissolving Parliament before the completion of its term so as to 'pack' its successor; for setting up the Duke of Newcastle against the Prince of Wales for the chancellorship of Cambridge University; and generally for 'engrossing power', making themselves into 'maires du palais', and 'laying illegal restraints on the royal will'. These activities came to an end in October 1749, when one of his articles, 'occasioned by the very tyrannic behaviour of the Duke of Cumberland', led to the prosecution of the printer. At the same time his unpublished pamphlet, *Delenda est Oxonia*, accusing the ministry of planning an attack on the liberties of the university, similar to that of James II, 'which had given rise to the Revolution', was seized at the

printer's. Presumably in return for these services he figures in the 2nd Lord Egmont's lists of persons to receive office on the Prince's accession, in one of which, dated 29 Apr. 1749, he is put down for a seat on the council of Prince George, the future George III, who was to be lord high admiral, a post last held by Prince George of Denmark, on whose council Sir Robert Walpole had begun his ministerial career in 1705.[5]

In Horace Walpole's *Short Notes* of his life he states that his reason for these activities was that 'Mr. Pelham had used my father and his friends extremely ill, and neglected the Whigs to court the Tories'. This however did not prevent him from accepting an invitation by Pelham to move the Address at the opening of the session of 1751, which may account for the deletion of his name from another of Egmont's lists of a future Admiralty council. Nor did it prevent him a few weeks later, when the death of his eldest brother, Lord Orford, left him dependent on the life of his only surviving brother, Edward, for the £1,300 a year produced by the customs place, from applying to Pelham to add his name to the patent granting that office. Pelham

> replied civilly, he could not ask the King to add my life to the patent; but if I could get my brother Edward to let my life stand in lieu of his, he would endeavour to serve me. I answered quickly, 'Sir, I will never ask my brother to stand in a precarious light instead of me', and, hurrying out of his house, returned to two of my friends who waited for me, and said to them 'I have done what you desired me to do but, thank God, I have been refused'.

About this time he began his *Memoirs* of 1751, which contain a violent attack on the Pelhams and Hardwicke (i. 158 et seq.).[6]

Horace Walpole's attack on Hardwicke arose from a scheme which he had concocted with his friend, John Chute, for marrying the new Lord Orford, a youth of 21, 'whose intellects were never very sound and which were afterwards much disordered' (iii. 185 n.), to Chute's cousin, Miss Nicoll, a 16-year old ward in Chancery, with 'an immense fortune', estimated at over £150,000. When Miss Nicoll, whom Chute had already once abducted but returned to her legal guardian after an interview with Hardwicke, upset the scheme by refusing to apply to the court to be transferred to the guardianship of Chute's sister-in-law, Chute's behaviour to her became so outrageous that in July 1751 her lawyers obtained an order from Hardwicke, as Lord Chancellor, prohibiting Chute and his sister-in-law from seeing her except in the presence of her new chosen guardian.[7] Beside himself with rage at the loss of this rich prize, Horace Walpole inserted in his *Memoirs* of 1751 a scarifying portrait of Hardwicke, on which his editor, Lord Holland, justly observes that his 'resentments blind his judgment and disfigure his narrative' (i. 160 n.).

When Parliament re-assembled in January 1752, Horace Walpole resumed his clandestine attempts 'to traverse Mr. Pelham's measures' and 'to blow up an opposition underhand', by inciting the Duke of Bedford, with whom he was connected through his friend, Richard Rigby (q.v.), to attack the Government in the Lords (i. 242–53, 262–75). On 25 Nov. 1752, shortly before the opening of the next session, he renewed his application to Pelham, asking him to give him the reversion of the customs place. Pelham told him

> that as to granting a reversion, that was what he had never done and what the King did not love to grant. That if he did ask it, the King would probably mention what I have already for my life; however, if I desired it, he would mention it to the King though he did not believe it would succeed. I replied, he knew best, and took my leave.[8]

A little over a fortnight later he proceeded, in his own words, to 'sow seeds of discontent in a rank soil, which did indeed produce an ample crop'. The 'seeds' were contained in an anonymous memorial purporting to have been signed by 'several noblemen and gentlemen of the first rank and fortune' but actually concocted by himself alone. Modelled on a leaflet recently circulated by Leicester House against the Duke of Cumberland, which had created enough stir to be burned by the common hangman (i. 9–12, 427–9), it accused the Pelhams of entrusting the education of the future George III to 'none but the friends and pupils of the late Lord Bolingbroke,' who were bringing him up on 'books inculcating the worst principles of government and defending the most avowed tyrannies', and of being themselves the tools of a 'dangerous faction, who intend to overthrow the Government and restore the exiled and arbitrary House of Stuart'. The 'rank soil' was Lord Ravensworth (Henry Liddell, q.v.), to whom Horace Walpole sent the memorial as being 'rather a factious and interested than an honest Whig'. The 'crop' was charges of drinking disaffected healths some 20 years ago, brought by Ravensworth against Andrew Stone and William Murray (qq.v.), the 'dangerous faction' referred to in the memorial, which were found by a Cabinet inquiry to be false and malicious. A debate in the Lords on the affair initiated by Bedford merely gave the Cabinet ministers in that House an opportunity of publicly re-affirming this verdict (i. 298–332).

After Pelham's death in 1754, Horace Walpole, still classed by the Government as a supporter, entered into a negotiation in April 1755 with the new head of the Treasury, Newcastle, for the sale of the customs place for £20,000, subsequently reducing the price to £14–15,000, but 'the affair went off' owing to Edward Walpole's asking too much for his share. In 1758 he tried to get Newcastle to allow him to exchange his share of the place for the office of master of the mint, worth £1,200 a year, for his life, if and when it fell vacant, pointing out that this would give Newcastle a 'very fair pretence for asking [the King] at the same time for one or two lives in the custom house place', which 'would be a great provision for a younger son of my Lord Lincoln', Newcastle's nephew and heir, but nothing came of this either.[9] Deciding about this time to retire from politics, he inserted at the end of his *Memoirs* of 1758, finished in 1759, a self-portrait, confessing that 'a propensity to faction', aggravated by 'prejudices contracted by himself', had kept him 'balanced for a few years between right and wrong', till 'virtue extinguished this culpable ardour'. Among the objects 'of his greatest prejudices', he mentions Pelham and Hardwicke, from whom 'he had received trifling offence' and for whom 'he avows he had strong aversion'; and his former friend, Henry Fox, from whom 'he had felt coldness and ingratitude', evidently referring to Fox's failure to include the reversion among the favours which he obtained for his friends in return for allying himself with Newcastle in September 1755. But, though admitting that 'he had too much weakness to resist doing wrong', he claims that 'one virtue he possessed in a singular degree—disinterestedness and contempt of money—if one may call that a virtue, which really was a passion' (iii. 158–63). Nevertheless in his *Memoirs* of 1763 he confesses to being 'much provoked' on learning that Bute had given the reversion to his secretary, Charles Jenkinson, M.P.,

> and took occasion of fomenting the ill-humour against the Favourite, who thus excluded me from the possibility of obtaining the continuance of that place in case of my brother's death.

By this time he had persuaded himself that he had refused an offer by Fox to try to procure him the reversion from Newcastle in 1755, because 'I will never accept that reversion from the Duke', later improved into 'because it is a greater favour than I will ever accept from any man'. By 1771 he had succeeded in convincing himself of the rectitude of the political conduct which in 1759 he had confessed to have been 'culpable'. The occasion for this favourable reconsideration of the anonymous memorial etc. was the publication in 1770 of Burke's *Thoughts on the Cause of the Present Discontents*, which set him to work on constructing an alternative theory of his own. In his opinion, Burke had made the mistake of 'not going back far enough'.

> The canker had begun in the Administration of the Pelhams and Lord Hardwicke, who, at the head of a proud aristocracy of Whig lords, had thought of nothing but establishing their own power; and who, as it suited their occasional purposes, now depressed and insulted the Crown and royal family, and now raised the prerogative. Their factious usurpations and insolence were even some excuse for the maxim taken up by Frederick, Prince of Wales, by the Princess dowager, and the reigning King, of breaking that overbearing combination: and so blinded were the Pelhams by their own ambition that they furnished the Princess with men whose principles and abilities were best suited to inspire arbitrary notions into her son, and to instruct him how to get rid of his tyrants, and establish a despotism that may end in tyranny in his descendants.

In short, Stone and Murray 'were the real sources of those discontents which Burke sought but never discovered', though Walpole's penetration had detected them at the time, as his earlier *Memoirs* showed. By 1778 he was suggesting that Murray, now Lord Mansfield, had 'drawn out the steps of James II, and recommended them one by one, in order to ruin the House of Hanover by the same measures that paved their way to the throne'.[10]

Walpole's theory, by justifying his political activities, enabled him to raise the veil originally drawn over them in his *Memoirs* of 1751–60, in the body of which he gives no indication of his responsibility for the culpable behaviour described in them, only disclosing it in foot-notes added many years later. In 1775 he carried his self-deception a stage further by persuading himself that he had received and refused an offer of the reversion from Lord North. When it was pointed out to him that the reversion had already been granted, he assented, observing that Bute

> would have been overjoyed to have given me my place for my life, but I would not accept it; and so the reversion was given to Jenkinson,

notwithstanding which he describes himself as 'much pleased with this offer'. By 1782 he had come to believe that his application to Pelham in 1751 was 'the first and last favour I ever asked of any minister for myself'. On his brother's death in 1784 he wrote, referring to his imaginary offers from Fox and North:

> I had twice been offered the reversion for my own life, and positively refused to accept it, because I would receive no obligation that might entangle my honour and my gratitude and set them at variance.[11]

Thus Horace Walpole came to believe not only that his anonymous lies had been far-sighted warnings but that his rejected solicitations had been improper proposals, which he had virtuously refused.

In a review of the *Memoirs of the Reign of George II*, Croker drew attention to such of these facts as were then available, in the hope of preventing Walpole from 'poisoning the sources of history'. In this he was unsuccessful. Popularized by Macaulay's second essay on Chatham, which was based on the then unpublished *Memoirs* of 1760–71, the story that George III was brought up on the neo-Tory doctrines of the *Patriot King* became for a time part of the canon of English history.[12]

He died 2 Mar. 1797.

[1] The references in the text are to Walpole, *Mems. Geo. II.* [2] *Corresp. H. Walpole* (Yale ed.), xiii. 3. [3] Ibid. 15; *Cal. Treas. Pprs.* 1714–19, p. 296; Walpole to Conway, 20 July 1744; West to Newcastle, 5 Apr. 1755, Add. 32854, f. 57. [4] Hartington to Devonshire, 19 Jan. 1744, Devonshire mss; Yorke's parl. jnl. *Parl. Hist.* xiii. 462; *Corresp.* (Yale ed.), xxx; Walpole to Mann, 18 June 1744, 4 and 15 Nov. 1745. [5] *Corresp.* (Yale ed.), xiii. 18 n. 116, 22–23 n. 144, 146; Add. 47092. [6] *Corresp.* (Yale ed.), xiii. 19; Add. 47097/8; Walpole, *Works*, ii. 366–7. [7] *Corresp.* (Yale ed.), xiii. app. 1. [8] Walpole to Pelham, 25 Nov. 1752 and annexures. [9] West to Newcastle, ut sup.; Walpole to Newcastle, 12 Nov. 1758. [10] *Mems. Geo. III.* i. 167, 210; iv. 90–95; to Mason, 28 Aug. 1778. [11] *Last Jnls.* i. 488–9; *Works*, ut sup.; to Mason, 2 Feb. 1784. [12] *Quarterly Rev.* xvi. 178–215; *Croker Pprs.* i. 271; G. O. Trevelyan, *Life of Lord Macaulay* (1883), iv.156.

R.R.S.

WALPOLE, Hon. Horatio (1723–1809).

KING'S LYNN 1747–5 Feb. 1757

b. 12 June 1723, 1st s. of Horatio Walpole (q.v.) of Wolterton, 1st Baron Walpole of Wolterton. *educ.* L. Inn 1736; Corpus Christi, Camb. 1741; Grand Tour (Italy 1746–7)[1]. *m.* 12 May 1748, Lady Rachel Cavendish, 3rd da. of William, 3rd Duke of Devonshire, 4s. 2da. *suc.* fa. as 2nd Baron Walpole of Wolterton 5 Feb. 1757; uncle Horatio Walpole (q.v.), 4th Earl of Orford, as Baron Walpole of Walpole 2 Mar. 1797; *cr.* Earl of Orford 10 Apr. 1806.

Returned for King's Lynn on the Walpole interest in 1747, Horatio Walpole was classed as a government supporter. He died 24 Feb. 1809.

[1] *Corresp. H. Walpole* (Yale ed.), xix. 59, 192, 232, 238.

R.R.S.

WALPOLE, Robert (1676–1745), of Houghton, Norf.[1]

CASTLE RISING 1701–1702
KING'S LYNN 1702–17 Jan. 1712,
11 Feb.–6 Mar. 1712, 1713–6 Feb. 1742

b. 26 Aug. 1676, 1st surv. s. of Robert Walpole, M.P., of Houghton; bro. of Galfridus and Horatio Walpole (qq.v.). *educ.* Eton 1690–6; King's, Camb. 1696–8. *m.* (1) 30 July 1700, Catherine (*d.* 20 Aug. 1737), da. of John Shorter, a Baltic merchant, of Bybrook, Kent, 3s. 2da.; (2) bef. 3 Mar. 1738, Maria, da. of Thomas Skerrett, 2da. (illegit.). *suc.* fa. 1700. K.B. 27 May 1725; K.G. 26 May 1726; *cr.* Earl of Orford 6 Feb. 1742.

One of the council of ld. high adm. 1705–8; sec. at war 1708–10; treasurer of the navy Jan. 1710–

Jan. 1711; P.C. 29 Sept. 1714; paymaster of the forces Oct. 1714–15 and June 1720–1; first ld. of the Treasury and chancellor of the Exchequer Oct. 1715–Apr. 1717, 3 Apr. 1721–11 Feb. 1742.

High steward, Yarmouth 1733, King's Lynn 1738–d.

At George I's accession Walpole took the lead in the House of Commons, with the office of paymaster general, which he soon exchanged for those of first lord of the Treasury and chancellor of the Exchequer, sharing the chief power in the Administration with his brother-in-law, Lord Townshend. When Townshend was ousted by Sunderland in 1717, Walpole followed him into opposition, where they were joined by the heir-apparent, later George II, causing 'such a defection from the Court, especially in the House of Commons, that it was with the utmost difficulty the ministers carried on their affairs in Parliament'.[2] On the reconciliation of the rival Whig leaders in 1720, Walpole returned to the pay office till 1721, when he and Townshend recovered their former offices. He remained at the Treasury for the next 21 years, at first as junior partner to Townshend, on whose 'superior favour at court', based on the King's mistress, the Duchess of Kendal, 'as much Queen of England as ever any was,'[3] his own power depended.

> For as the Duchess of Kendal never loved Sir Robert Walpole, and was weak enough to admire and be fond of Lord Townshend, so in any nice points that were to be insinuated gently and carried by favour . . . the canal of application to the royal ear always had been from Lord Townshend to the Duchess, and from the Duchess to the King. (84)

The situation was reversed at the accession of George II, after which

> everything that passed to the present King through the Queen (who was to the son at least what the Duchess of Kendal had been to the father) was suggested by Sir Robert, and nothing pushed or received by her from any other hand. (84)

George II himself, who had come to the throne intending to have no first minister and with a strong prejudice against Walpole, was gradually converted by the Queen to the view that

> it was absolutely necessary, from the nature of the English Government, that he should have but one minister; and that it was equally necessary, from Sir Robert's superior abilities, that he should be that one . . . Instead of betraying (as formerly) a jealousy of being thought to be governed by him; instead of avoiding every opportunity of distinguishing and speaking to him in public, instead of hating him whilst he employed him, and grudging every power with which he armed him, he very apparently now took all occasions to declare him his first, or rather his sole, minister, singled him out always in the drawing-room, received no application (military affairs excepted) but from him, and most certainly, if he loved anybody in the world besides the Queen, he

had not only an opinion of the statesman, but an affection for the man. (152–3)

Townshend was greatly mortified by

> seeing and feeling every day that Sir Robert Walpole, who came into the world, in a manner, under his protection and inferior to him in fortune, quality, and credit, was now, by the force of his infinitely superior talents, as much above him in power, interest, weight, credit, and reputation. All application was made to him. His house was crowded like a fair with all sorts of petitioners, whilst Lord Townshend's was only frequented by the narrow set of a few relations and particular flatterers; and as Lord Townshend in the late reign had nothing but personal favour at Court to depend upon in any disputes that might arise between him and Sir Robert, he could not but grieve to find that resource in the new reign entirely taken away, the scene quite inverted, and himself as much dependent now upon Sir Robert's personal interest as Sir Robert had formerly been upon his. (83–84)

When it became clear that, in Walpole's words, the firm of Townshend and Walpole had turned into Walpole and Townshend, Townshend resigned, leaving Walpole undisputed first, or rather sole, minister.

After Townshend's retirement in 1730 the effective Government consisted of the King, the Queen, and Walpole, who settled all important matters before referring them to 'those ciphers of the Cabinet' 'to give their sanction to' and 'to have their share in being responsible for what in form and appearance only they ever had any share in advising or concerting' (470, 777–8). The Queen's role was to persuade the King to accept proposals which he would not take from Walpole. For example:

> Sir Robert communicated this scheme secretly to the Queen, she insinuated it to the King, and the King proposed it to Sir Robert as an act of his own ingenuity and generosity. (242)

Even when she did not agree with Walpole, his arguments,

> conveyed through the Queen to the King, so wrought upon him, that they quite changed the colour of his Majesty's sentiments, though they did not tinge the channel through which they flowed. When Lord Hervey told Sir Robert he had made this observation, Sir Robert said it was true, and agreed with him how extraordinary it was that she should be either able or willing to repeat what he said with energy and force sufficient to convince another without being convinced herself. (360–1)

In telling her that without her support he found it impossible 'to persuade the King into any measure he did not like' (375), he was paying her a compliment which events were to show to have been only too true.

Despite a new schism in the Whig party, origin-ated by Pulteney in 1725, Walpole's position seemed so impregnable that at the beginning of 1737 Pulteney seriously considered giving up the struggle. The situation was changed that year by a fresh quarrel in the royal family, which once more placed the heir-apparent at the head of the Whig Opposition. No one was more aware than Walpole, from his experience in the late reign, of the difficulties which this would inevitably bring upon his Administration. 'There,' he said, 'is all the Prince's family [household], be they more or less, thrown in every question into the Opposition; and how is the loss of those votes to be replaced?' (772). But 'the passions of the King and Queen'—for on this occasion he 'found her not as usual an auxiliary by his side, but another opponent'—'made Sir Robert Walpole afraid of offering or giving in to any palliating schemes' (786). He therefore reluctantly acquiesced in a rupture, with consequences which only became fully apparent at the general election of 1741, when the Government won only 17 seats in the venal Cornish boroughs, compared with 32 in 1734, largely owing to the activities of the Prince, whose party of 21, all dependent on him either for their places or for their seats, virtually held the balance in the new House of Commons.

In November 1737, two months after the rupture between the King and the Prince, the death of the Queen deprived Walpole of his most useful ally at court. Discussing the effects of her death with Hervey, who argued that it would rather increase than diminish Walpole's power, because his 'credit before was through the medium of the Queen, and all power through a medium must be weaker than when it operates directly', Walpole said that though it was true that the King

will hear nobody but me, you do not know how often he refuses to hear me when it is on a subject he does not like; but by the Queen I can with time fetch him round to those subjects again; she can make him do the same thing in another shape, and when I give her her lesson, can make him propose the very thing as his own opinion which a week before he had rejected as mine. The many opportunities and the credit she has with him, the knowledge of his temper, the being constantly at him, and the opinion he has both of her judgment and her pursuit of his interest and his pleasure as her first objects, make this part easy for her; but I have not the same materials to act it, and cannot do without somebody that has leisure to operate slowly upon him, which is the only way he can be effectually operated upon. For he is neither to be persuaded nor convinced; he will do nothing to oblige anybody, nor ever own or think he has been in the wrong; and I have told the Queen a thousand times that it is not to be wondered at that he should be of that mind, when she, whom he believed sooner than any other body in the world, never heard him broach the most absurd opinion, or declare the most

extravagant design, that she did not tell him he was in the right. (904–5)

Walpole's fears were soon justified by the King, who after the Queen's death became increasingly unmanageable. The most serious consequence of his intractability was the defection of the Duke of Argyll, who considered that as the only officer of the rank of field marshal he should have been

set at the head of the army, and imputed his not being so to Sir Robert Walpole, though in reality, had Sir Robert loved him as much as he hated him, it would not have been in his power to do it; in the first place, as he had little power in military affairs, and in the next, because the King determined to have nobody at the head of the army but himself, would do everything there by his own authority, and without any advice, and last of all, because, if his Majesty would have given any authority or taken any advice in these matters, he disliked the Duke of Argyll so much that he was the last man in England to whom he would have delegated the one, or from whom he would have received the other. (707–8)

At the beginning of 1739 Argyll, though a member of the Cabinet, manifested his displeasure by attacking the Spanish convention in the Lords, where he continued to act with the Opposition, without resigning his offices. On 29 Apr. 1740, Walpole's brother, Horace (q.v.), wrote:

There has been and is still a good deal of motion about the Duke of Argyll's behaviour; it was resolved to let him have the command of a camp this summer, for there will be three encampments. The King acquainted him with it himself, he accepted it, but has since insisted that by the title of marshal he should be called commander-in-chief of all the forces. This has been refused by his Majesty with indignation. I suppose a reconciliation with his Grace is absolutely become impracticable.[4]

A few days later Argyll was dismissed from all his offices, at the cost of throwing him into opposition, with the result that the Government won only 19 seats in Scotland at the ensuing general election, compared with 34 in 1734.

Argyll's defection was followed by that of Bubb Dodington (q.v.) owing to Walpole's inability to hold out any hopes of his obtaining a peerage, because the King, apart from being 'in nothing so hard to be persuaded as to make peers', had a personal objection to him for having set the Prince against his parents. Dodington's defection cost Walpole another five seats, making a total of 35 lost not on any point of policy or principle, nor because any of the applications in question was unreasonable but purely because, without the backing of the Queen, he was unable 'to persuade the King into any measure he did not like.' Dependent on the royal favour, he was forced to discard from his majority to keep his court cards.

The loss of these 35 seats, counting 70 in a

division, left Walpole with an unworkably small majority, which soon showed signs of turning into a minority by defeats on election petitions. During the Christmas recess he attempted to win over the Prince's party by persuading the King with great difficulty to offer his son the extra £50,000 a year for which he had originally gone into opposition. On the Prince's refusal to consider any terms so long as Walpole remained in office

> all the Cabinet Council . . . told the King his affairs could not go on as long as Sir Robert continued in post, and that it would be most advisable for himself and the King that he should quit. The King told them all he would never part with him till he himself desired it.

Walpole's first reaction was 'that he was determined to stand it out to the last', but after further reverses on election petitions even his staunchest supporters recognized that the game was lost. On 31 Jan. 1742 he decided to retire, communicating his decision to 'some particular persons in the House' on 2 Feb.,[5] and sending to the Duke of Devonshire, who was in Ireland as lord lieutenant, 'a short view of this great revolution'.

> I must inform you that the panic was so great among what I should call my own friends, that *they all* declared my retiring was become absolutely necessary, as the only means to carry on the public business, and this to be attended with honour and security, etc.[6]

After settling the lines of the new Administration he resigned with an earldom, a patent of precedence for his illegitimate daughter, and a pension of £4,000 a year, which he did not take up till 1744, when the outcry against it had subsided.[7] An attempt by a secret committee of the House of Commons to collect material for his impeachment on grounds of corruption petered out owing to the refusal of the Treasury officials to give evidence as to the disposal of secret service money. During the struggle for power between the old and new sides of the Administration he supported the claim of Henry Pelham to succeed Wilmington as head of the Treasury, and continued to advise him after his appointment.[8] Later in 1743 he prevailed on the new ministry to continue the Hanoverian troops, who but for his intervention would have been given up. His last political act was to advise the King not to persist in supporting Carteret, now Lord Granville, against the demand of the Pelhams for his dismissal.[9] Four months later, 18 Mar. 1745, he died, killed by a remedy for the stone.

Walpole's long predominance was due to a combination of the qualities of a parliamentarian, a courtier, and a man of business, in all three of which capacities he was 'much superior to his contemporaries' (17). Chesterfield, an opponent, describes him as the

> best parliament-man, and the ablest manager of Parliament, that I believe ever lived. An artful rather than an eloquent speaker, he saw, as if by intuition, the disposition of the House, and pressed or receded accordingly. So clear in stating the most intricate matters, especially in the finances, that, whilst he was speaking, the most ignorant thought that they understood what they really did not.[10]

Both George II and the Queen

> were possessed with an opinion that Sir Robert Walpole was, by so great a superiority, the most able man in the kingdom, that he understood the revenue, and knew how to manage that formidable and refractory body, the House of Commons, so much better than any other man, that it was impossible for the business of the Crown to be well done without him. (177–8)

His skill as a courtier is shown by his early realisation that George II was governed by his wife. While others were paying court to the mistress, Walpole, in his own words, 'had the right sow by the ear'.[11] As a man of business

> he had great skill in figures, the nature of the funds, and the revenue; his first application was to this branch of knowledge; but as he afterwards rose to the highest posts of power, and continued longer there than any first minister in this country since Lord Burleigh ever did, he grew, of course, conversant with all the other parts of government and very soon equally able in transacting them. The weight of the whole Administration lay on him, every project was of his forming, conducting, and executing. From the time of making the treaty of Hanover all the foreign as well as domestic affairs passed through his hands; and, considering the little assistance he received from subalterns, it is incredible what a variety and quantity of business he dispatched. But as he had infinite application and long experience, so he had great method and a prodigious memory, with a mind and spirit that were indefatigable; and without every one of these natural as well as acquired advantages, it would indeed have been impossible for him to go through half what he undertook. (17)

Walpole's long Administration is marked by no reformist measures.

> More anxious to keep his power than to raise his fame . . . he knew, whatever happened, he could be nothing greater than what he was; and, in order to remain in that situation, his great maxim in policy was to keep everything else as undisturbed as he could, to bear with some abuses rather than risk reformations, and submit to old inconveniences rather than encourage innovations. From these maxims . . . he would never lend his assistance nor give the least encouragement to any emendation either of the law or the church . . . From this way of reasoning he opposed the inquiry into the South Sea affair, the bill to vacate the infamous sale of Lord Derwentwater's estate, the examination of the House

of Commons into the affairs of the charitable corporations and the abuses in the gaols . . . This apprehension, long experience and thorough knowledge of this country and this Government had taught him; and in this way of thinking, the unsuccessful deviation he had made from it in the excise scheme had . . . more than ever confirmed him. (364–5)

The worst charge brought against him was that of deliberately lowering the standard of public morality.

Money . . . was the chief engine of his Administration; and he employed it with a success that in a manner disgraced humanity . . . When he found anybody proof against pecuniary temptations, which, alas, was but seldom, he had recourse to a still worse art; for he laughed at and ridiculed all notions of public virtue.[12]

Admitting that he 'gave [money] away liberally at home', George II added: 'He was a great man, he understood the country'.[13] His creation of the positions of leader of the Opposition and of minister for the House of Commons is discussed in chapters II and III of the Introductory Survey.

[1] The references in the text are to Hervey's *Mems.* [2] *HMC 14th Rep. IX,* 509. [3] *Lady Cowper Diary,* 58. [4] *HMC 14th Rep. IX,* 46. [5] Walpole to Mann, 4 Feb. 1742. [6] Coxe, *Walpole,* iii. 591–2. [7] Harrowby mss 10 (L. Inn), 8 Jan. and 2 Feb. 1742; Walpole to Mann, 18 June 1744. [8] Owen, *Pelhams,* 170–2. [9] Coxe, *Walpole,* i. 736–7; iii. 602; Yorke, *Hardwicke,* i. 336. [10] Chesterfield, *Characters,* 31. [11] Hardwicke, *Walpoliana,* 6. [12] Chesterfield, 32. [13] Coxe, *Pelham,* ii. 440.

R.R.S.

WALTER, Sir John, 3rd Bt. (c.1674–1722), of Sarsden, Oxon.

APPLEBY 13 Dec. 1694–1695, 23 Dec. 1697–1700
OXFORD 11 Dec. 1706–11 June 1722

b. c.1674, 1st surv. s. of Sir William Walter, 2nd Bt., by his 1st w. Mary, da. of John Tufton, 2nd Earl of Thanet. *educ.* Queen's, Oxf. 21 Aug. 1691. *m.* c.1700,[1] Elizabeth, da. of Sir Thomas Vernon, M.P., London merchant, *s.p. suc.* fa. 5 Mar. 1694.
Clerk comptroller of the Green Cloth 1711–14.

Walter was the great grandson of Sir John Walter, M.P., of Wolvercot, Oxon., lord chief baron of the Exchequer and a benefactor of Jesus College, Oxford. His grandfather, the first baronet, had represented the county under Charles II. Re-elected unopposed as a Tory for Oxford in 1715 and 1722, he voted against the Administration in every recorded division. He died 11 June 1722, leaving £1,000 to his friend Lord Harcourt, and his whole estate to his wife, with reversion to his brother, who succeeded him to the baronetcy.[2] His widow subsequently married Harcourt.

[1] *HMC Cowper,* ii. 407. [2] *HMC Portland,* vii. 328–9.

E.C.

WALTER, John (*d.*1736), of Busbridge, nr. Godalming, Surr.

SURREY 15 Dec. 1719–1727

s. of Richard Walter of Barbados, merchant. *m.* 22 Apr. 1697, Lucy, da. of Col. Abel Alleyne of Barbados, member and speaker of the assembly there, 8s. 3da.

Between 1708 and 1715 John Walter, a rich West Indian, bought the manor of Busbridge and other properties in Surrey. After contesting Haslemere unsuccessfully in 1715, he was returned as a Tory for the county in 1719, heading the poll in 1722. In 1727 he joined with Thomas Scawen against Arthur Onslow (qq.v.), but gave up during the poll, apparently on the understanding that Scawen should pay all the election expenses, which were supposed to be 'very large', and 'not suited, as it was thought, to Mr. Walter's circumstances at that time'.[1] He died 12 May 1736.

[1] *HMC 14th Rep. IX,* 518–19.

R.R.S.

WALTER, Peter (c.1663–1746), of Stalbridge, Dorset.

BRIDPORT 10 May 1715–1727
WINCHELSEA 23 Apr. 1728–1734

b. c.1663. *m.* bef. Jan. 1694, Diana, niece of Richard Newman of Fifehead Magdalen, Dorset, 1s.
Clerk of the peace, Mdx. 1724–*d.*

The parentage of Peter Walter, the 'very noted money scrivener',[1] i.e. moneylender, is unknown, but he probably came of a Dorset family. By 1694 he was the trusted clerk of Richard Newman, whose niece he married and who made him his executor in 1695.[2] By 1707 he had become steward for life to John Holles, Duke of Newcastle,[3] whose successor obtained for him a lucrative place. He also acted as agent for many of the nobility, including the 2nd and 3rd Earls of Essex and the 1st Earl of Uxbridge,[4] whose name, Paget, he gave to his only son. Returned on petition in 1715 for Bridport, where he unseated a Tory, he voted for the Administration in all recorded divisions. He did not stand there for the 1727 election but was found a seat at Winchelsea in the following year.

By taking up mortgages and then foreclosing on the estates, Walter built up a large fortune. He was thus able to buy for himself Stalbridge and other valuable properties, chiefly in Dorset and Somerset, including those of Michael Harvey (q.v.). For his unscrupulous methods he was portrayed by Fielding as 'Peter Pounce'; Swift wrote of him as

That rogue of genuine ministerial kind,
Can half the peerage by his arts bewitch,
Starve twenty lords to make one scoundrel rich;[5]

and Pope:

If Peter deigns to help you to your *own*:
What thanks, what praise, if Peter but supplies!
And what a solemn face if he denies!
. . .
And lies to every Lord in everything,
Like a King's favourite—or like a King.[6]

He died 19 Jan. 1746, 'reputed worth £300,000'.[7]

[1] *Gent. Mag.* 1746, p. 45. [2] PCC 143 Bond. [3] *Cal. Treas. Pprs.* 1702–7, p. 561; Walter to Ld. Pelham, 4 Dec. 1713, Add. 33064, f. 27. [4] *Cal. Treas. Bks.* xxiv. 511; *HMC Portland*, vii. 422; *Cal. Treas. Pprs.* 1714–19, p. 89. [5] *Epistle to Mr. Gay.* [6] *Second satire of Dr. John Donne.* [7] *Gent. Mag.* 1746, p. 45.

R.S.L.

WALTER, Peter (1715–53), of Stalbridge, Dorset.

SHAFTESBURY 1741–1747

b. 1715,[1] 1st s. of Paget Walter of Stalbridge by Elizabeth, da. of Edward Mervyn of Salisbury. *m.* by 1738, Christian, da. of Thomas Bedwell, 1da. *suc.* fa. (who *d.v.p.*) aft. 1740 and gd.-fa. Peter Walter (q.v.) 1746.

Peter Walter was returned unopposed on a compromise as a Whig for Shaftesbury in 1741, standing on his own and his father's interest, 'in nowise interfering with Mr. [Stephen] Fox' (q.v.),[2] who was created Lord Ilchester on the day of the election. In Parliament he voted for Walpole's candidate for the chairman of the elections committee, 16 Dec. 1741; but a month later the Duke of Newcastle wrote to his wife that 'young Peter Walter, influenced by the old one, voted against us'[3] on Pulteney's motion of 21 Jan. 1742 to examine all papers relevant to the recent conduct of the war, which Walpole carried by three votes only. Under the new Administration he voted against the Hanoverians in 1742 but for them in 1744 and 1746, when he was classed as 'doubtful'. Early in 1746 he succeeded to Stalbridge and to most of his grandfather's large estates and fortune. He again offered himself as a candidate at Shaftesbury in 1747 but stood down before the poll, Lord Ilchester writing to Henry Fox (q.v.) in June:[4]

Mr. Walter is very ill at his house at Stalbridge, keeps his bed with the gout in his stomach, and yesterday 'twas reported he would desist . . . he is at present far behind and Mr. [George] Pitt [q.v.] has gained ground of him very considerably.

However, the 2nd Lord Egmont in his electoral survey c.1749–50 noted against Shaftesbury: 'Peter

Walter, as Mr. Dodington [q.v.] says he can influence him', to which the Prince added 'not to be depended upon'. He died in October 1753. Under his will,[5] in which he totally ignored his wife and daughter, he left Stalbridge and other properties to his brother Edward in tail male, with remainder to Henry Bayly, afterwards 10th Lord Paget, who succeeded to them in 1780 and was created Earl of Uxbridge in 1784. The reasons for this disposition to a stranger are unknown, but see Peter Walter *supra*.

[1] *Misc. Gen. et Her.* n.s. ii. 6, 8. [2] Peter Walter to Newcastle, 6 Oct. 1740, Add. 32695, f. 205. [3] 23 Jan. 1742, Add. 33073, f. 205. [4] Hen. Fox mss. [5] PCC 283 Searle.

R.S.L.

WANDESFORD, Christopher, 2nd Visct. Castlecomer [I] (1684–1719), of Kirklington, Yorks.

MORPETH 1710–1713
RIPON 1715–23 June 1719

bap. 2 Mar. 1684, 1st s. of Christopher Wandesford, M.P., 1st Visct. Castlecomer [I], by Elizabeth, da. of Hon. George Montagu of Horton, Northants. *educ.* Trinity, Dublin 1702. *m.* 1717, Frances, da. of Thomas Pelham, M.P., 1st Baron Pelham of Laughton, sis. of Thomas, 1st Duke of Newcastle, 1s. *suc.* fa. 15 Sept. 1707.
M.P. [I] 1707.
P.C. [I] 25 Apr. 1710; gov. Kilkenny 1715–*d.*

The Wandesford family had estates in Yorkshire within ten miles of Ripon, which the first Lord Castlecomer represented 1679–81 and for which his son, after sitting as a Whig for Morpeth under Anne, was returned in 1715, having also been elected for Morpeth. In July 1717 he moved and carried an address for excepting Lord Oxford from the Act of Grace and was chairman of the Commons committee appointed to draft it. In March 1718 he was announced to have been appointed[1] secretary at war but received an unfavourable report from his agent as to his prospects of re-election:

I cannot tell what to think of them in case you should have occasion to be elected again, for I find a great many of the burrowmen that was our staunch friends before that will not give us their interest again. Our recorder and some others have said of late that your Lordship will never be chose for this place any more . . . I know . . . that as your Lordship did not upon any account take notice of them when here has given an occasion of general disgust, but if Mr. Aislabie will give you his interest heartily there would be no great hazard in it.[2]

In the event he was not appointed. Next year he was one of the Whigs who unexpectedly joined Walpole in voting against the Government on the repeal of the Occasional Conformity and Schism Acts.[3] Classed by Craggs as Opposition but as 'pro' by Sunderland on the peerage bill, he died 23 June 1719.

[1] *Pol. State*, xv. 376 and errata. [2] H. B. MacCall, *Wandesfordes of Kirklington and Castlecomer*, 301-2. [3] *HMC Portland*, v. 576.

A.N.N.

WARBURTON, Sir George, 3rd Bt. (1675–1743), of Warburton and Arley, Cheshire.

CHESHIRE   1702–1705, 1710–1722

bap. 1 June 1675, 1st s. of Sir Peter Warburton, 2nd Bt., by Martha, da. and h. of Thomas Dockwra of Putteridge, Herts. *m.* 18 June 1700, Diana, da. of William Alington, M.P., 1st Baron Alington of Wymondeley, 1s. *d.v.p.* 1da. (m. Sir Richard Grosvenor, q.v.). *suc. fa.* c.1698.

A high church Tory[1] and a member of the October Club under Anne, Warburton was re-elected for Cheshire as a Tory in 1715, voting against the Government in all recorded divisions. In 1721 his name was sent to the Pretender as a probable supporter in the event of a rising.[2] He did not stand again and died 23 June 1743, leaving an estate of upwards of £2,000 p.a. to his nephew, who succeeded him as 4th Bt.[3]

[1] See 'Diary of Henry Prescott', 25 May 1705, in *Cheshire Sheaf*, 3 July 1940. [2] Stuart mss 65/16. [3] *Gent. Mag.* 1743, p.389.

E.C.

WARBURTON, *see also* HENRY WARBURTON

WARD, John (*d.*1755), of Hackney, Mdx.

BLETCHINGLEY	1701–1708
REIGATE	1710–1713
LUDGERSHALL	24 Mar. 1714–1715
WEYMOUTH AND	
MELCOMBE REGIS	1722–16 May 1726

Bro. of Joshua Ward (q.v.). *m.* Rebecca? Knox, 1s. Director, E.I. Co. 1712–15, 1718–26.

John Ward of Hackney, a wealthy and unscrupulous business man, who appears to have been a Whig under Anne,[1] was returned unopposed for Weymouth in 1722, after standing unsuccessfully for it in 1710 and 1713, and for Aldeburgh in 1718. He made his only reported speech on 21 Feb. 1724, against a petition from the subscribers to the Bahama Company[2] (see Guise, John). Next year he became involved in a dispute with the executors of the late Duke of Buckingham, from whom he had leased some alum works in Yorkshire for 19 years in 1705. The lease entitled Ward to require the Duke to buy up to 740 tons of alum a year at £10 a ton, the normal price being £15. Ward's practice was to require the Duke to take up his full quota of alum each year on the ground that there

had been a slump in the market for it; to persuade him to store the alum so purchased at Ward's works pending a recovery in the price; and to sell it himself on the open market, thus being paid twice over for it, once by the purchaser and once by the Duke. Before the fraud was discovered the Duke had been cheated out of over £70,000, of which only £10,000 was recovered from Ward.[3]

When the lease expired the Duke's executors, acting on behalf of the new Duke, a minor, instituted proceedings in Chancery against Ward for failing to comply with a covenant requiring him to leave 351 tons of alum on going out. Ward's defence was that he had been released from this covenant by a note from the Duke, which was proved to relate to another matter but to have been altered by Ward to suit his purpose. On losing his case he set up a claim to parliamentary privilege. When this claim was rejected by the Commons he appealed against the Chancery decree to the House of Lords, who not only rejected his appeal but ordered the attorney-general, Sir Philip Yorke (q.v.), to prosecute him for forgery.[4] He was convicted, expelled from the House of Commons, and, after evading justice for eight months by absconding, was brought up and sentenced to a fine of £500, to stand in the pillory for an hour, and to give security for his good behaviour for nine years. A large crowd, including many members of both Houses, gathered in Palace Yard to witness his ordeal, at the end of which, though protected from pelting by a strong body of constables, he was taken down bleeding at the mouth and senseless for some hours.[5] A few weeks later he had recovered sufficiently to write to Yorke that he had instructed his solicitor to retain him in an impending case, adding that he freely forgave him.[6]

Ward's subsequent career is summarized in Pope's note to the line bracketing him with another contemporary scoundrel, Colonel Charteris:

He was suspected of joining in a conveyance with Sir John Blunt, to secrete fifty thousand pounds of that director's estate, forfeited to the South Sea Company by Act of Parliament. The company recovered the fifty thousand pounds against Ward; but he set up prior conveyances of his real estate to his brother and son [Ralph and Knox Ward] and concealed all his personal, which was computed to be one hundred and fifty thousand pounds. These conveyances being also set aside by a bill in Chancery, Ward was imprisoned, and hazarded the forfeiture of his life, by not giving in his effects till the last day, which was that of his examination. During his confinement, his amusement was to give poison to dogs and cats, and to see them expire by slower or quicker torments. To sum up the *worth* of this gentleman, at the several eras of his life, at his standing in the pillory he was *worth above two hundred thousand pounds*; at his commitment to

prison, he was *worth one hundred and fifty thousand,*
but has been since so far diminished in his reputation
as to be thought *a worse man* by *fifty or sixty thousand.*[7]

He died 30 July 1755, predeceased by his only
son, Knox Ward, Clarenceux king of arms, an
office purchased for some £3,000 in 1725, when
Ward was salting away his assets from his creditors.[8]

[1] W. A. Speck, 'The choice of a Speaker in 1705', *Bull. Inst.
Hist. Res.* xxxvii. 44. [2] *Knatchbull Diary.* [3] Duchess of Buckingham
to Sir Phil. Yorke, undated, Add. 35585, f. 251; *Case of the late and
present Dukes of Buckingham with John Ward of Hackney*, Add.
36148, f. 81. [4] *CJ*, xx. 439-40; *LJ*, xxii. 513b. [5] *Brice's Weekly Jnl.*
24 Feb. 1727. [6] 13 Apr. 1727, Add. 35585, f. 58. [7] *Moral Essays*,
iii. line 20. [8] De Gols and Read, assignees of the estate and effects
of John Ward, late of London, merchant and a bankrupt, *v.* Knox
Ward and others, Add. 36153, f. 141 et seq.

R.R.S.

WARD, Sir John (c.1650–1726), of Clay Hall, Epsom, Surr.

| LONDON | 1708–1710, 1715–1722 |
| DUNWICH | 7 Dec. 1722–12 Mar. 1726 |

b. c.1650, 2nd s. of John Ward, commr. of customs, of
Tanshelf, nr. Pontefract, Yorks. by Elizabeth, da. of
Thomas Vincent of Barnborough, Yorks. *m.* 17 Apr.
1684, Mary, da. of Sir William Bucknell of Oxhey
Place, Herts., 1s. 10da. Kntd. 25 Sept. 1714.
   Merchant Taylors' Co. 1709–*d.*, master 1709–10;
alderman, London 1709, sheriff 1715–16, ld. mayor
1718–19; director, Bank of England 1694–9 (with
statutory intervals), dep. gov. 1699–1701, gov. 1701–3,
director 1703–*d.*; director, E.I. Co. 1703–7, 1709–11.

The nephew of Sir Patience Ward, lord mayor of
London 1681–2, Ward was returned for the city
on the government list, voting for the septennial
bill in 1716. During the split in the Whig party
from 1717 to 1720 he voted with the Opposition.
On 3 Aug. 1721 he presented a petition on behalf
of the proprietors of the redeemable funds, and in
December of that year he supported the Quaker
affirmation bill.[1] He did not stand for London in
1722, but was returned at a by-election that year
for Dunwich, which he represented until his death,
12 Mar. 1726.

[1] *Pol. State*, xxii. 633.

E.C.

WARD, John (1704–74), of Sedgley Park, Staffs.

| NEWCASTLE-UNDER-LYME | 1727–1734 |

b. 6 Mar. 1704, 1st s. of William Ward (q.v.). *educ.*
King's, Camb. 1722. *m.* (1) 26 Dec. 1723, Anna
Maria (*d.* 12 Dec. 1725), da. of Charles Bourchier of
Clontarf, co. Dublin, 1s. (John, M.P., 2nd Visct.
Dudley and Ward); (2) 1 Jan. 1745, Mary, da. and h.
of John Carver of Hanover Sq., 2s. (2nd s. William,
M.P., 3rd Visct. Dudley and Ward). *suc.* fa. 1720;
cos. as 6th Baron Ward of Birmingham 21 May 1740;
cr. Visct. Dudley and Ward 21 Apr. 1763.
   Grand master of freemasons 1742–3; steward of

anniversary dinner of independent electors of Westminster 1748; recorder of Worcester.

Returned unopposed as a Tory at Newcastle-
under-Lyme in 1727, Ward consistently voted
against the Administration till he lost his seat in
1734. During the negotiations which led to the
Forty-five rebellion, his name was sent to the
French by the English Jacobites as one of their
most influential and wealthiest members.[1] In the
tumultuous county election of 1747, when he took
an active part in the campaign against the Leveson
Gowers, who had deserted the Tories, Lord
Gower complained to Newcastle that Ward was
'endeavouring to undermine' his interest in the
county 'by all the little low dirty tricks you can
imagine'.[2]

He died 6 May 1774.

[1] AEM & D Angl. 82, ff. 4–23. [2] Add. 32709, f. 61.

E.C.

WARD, John (1670–1749), of Capesthorne, Cheshire, and the Inner Temple.

| NEWTON | 7 Dec. 1703–1715 |
| THETFORD | 1715–1722 |

b. 13 June 1670, 1st s. of Philip Ward of Capesthorne
by Penelope, da. and coh. of Charles Edmunds of
Preston, Northants. *educ.* Ch. Ch. Oxf. 1684; G. Inn
1689, called 1693; I. Temple 1698, bencher 1711. *m.*
(settlement Aug. 1694) Thomazia, da. of Thomas
Terrick of Yorks., 1s. *d.v.p.* 3da. *suc.* fa. 1687.
   Q.C. 1711; puisne justice of Chester 1711–14.

A leading Hanoverian Tory, Ward was returned
for Thetford in 1715 on the interest of Sir Thomas
Hanmer (q.v.), over whom he had great influence.[1]
On 9 Apr. 1715 he seconded Stanhope's motion for
appointing a committee to inquire into the conduct
of the late ministry, declaring that 'though his
principle was that Kings can do no wrong, yet he
was of opinion, that ministers were accountable for
their maladministration'.[2] In June, however, he
opposed the impeachments of Ormonde and
Strafford and the contention that the charge against
Oxford in the 11th article of the secret committee's
report amounted to treason. He was one of the
chief speakers for the Opposition in the debates on
the septennial bill and the repeal of the Occasional
Conformity and Schism Acts. In 1721 he supported
Walpole's motion that John Aislabie (q.v.) should
be allowed to keep everything he possessed before
1719. He did not stand in 1722, devoting himself
entirely to his legal career until his death, 17 Mar.
1749.

[1] HMC Portland, vii. 181. [2] Chandler, vi. 18.

E.C.

WARD, Joshua (1685–1761).

MARLBOROUGH   1715–13 May 1717

b. 1685, bro. of John Ward (*d.* 1755, q.v.).

Ward was returned for Marlborough in 1715 by one of two rival mayors, who obtained possession of the precept and affixed Ward's return to it, though no one had voted for him. Classed as a Whig, he voted against the septennial bill before being unseated on petition, the elections committee reporting that 'Mr. Ward not appearing nor any counsel for him the Committee were not informed upon what pretence he was chosen'.[1] In 1725 he was a co-defendant with his brother in a suit brought by the Duchess of Buckingham over some alum works which they had leased from her late husband,[2] but he was not involved in the subsequent proceedings against John Ward for forgery. After some years in France, where he practised with great success as a quack doctor, he returned in 1734 to England where he made a fortune out of Ward's Pill, a reputed panacea consisting largely of antimony, which purged, sweated, and vomited all at once. The 1st Lord Egmont gives the following picture of his consulting room in 1735:

> I went this morning to see Mr. Ward, who does such famous cures with his drop, pill and powder. His rooms were all full of poor people, with a few of better sort, who came to be cured of blindness, deafness, cancers, king's evil, and other disorders wherein the physicians could not help them. I talked with several persons who had been a long time blind, but by his means had in a great measure recovered their sight, and one lady told me she had the palsy that took away her speech for seven years, and it had cost her 200 guineas to five doctors, who successively treated her in vain, among whom were Sir Hans Sloane and Dr. Jurin, but in taking Mr. Ward's medicine 14 times she was perfectly cured, as I might see by her telling me her story.
>
> Afterwards Sir Edward Lawrence told me of his own knowledge that a gentleman who had been several years blind now sees by the help of Mr. Ward as well as ever. Some who were born deaf and dumb have been made by him both to hear and to speak.[3]

Ward died 21 Nov. 1761, bequeathing the secret of his pill to his friend and admirer, John Page (q.v.), but its efficacy expired with its owner.

[1] *CJ*, xviii. 481, 547. [2] *LJ*, xxii. 513b. [3] *HMC Egmont Diary*, ii. 152.

R.R.S.

WARD, William (1670–1720), of Sedgley Park, Staffs.

STAFFORDSHIRE   1710–1713, 1715–25 Oct. 1720

b. 1670, o. surv. s. of Hon. William Ward of Sedgley Park (3rd s. of Humble Ward, 1st Baron Ward of Birmingham, by Frances, *suo jure* Baroness Dudley) by Anne, da. of Thomas Parkes of Willingsworth,

Staffs. *m.* Mary, da. of Hon. John Grey, M.P., of Enville, Staffs., sis. of Henry, 3rd Earl of Stamford, 3s. 4da.

Ward, whose father-in-law, John Grey, had represented Staffordshire from 1689 until 1698, was returned unopposed in 1715. Though classed as a Whig, he appears to have been a moderate Tory, who consistently voted against the Government till his death, 25 Oct. 1720.

E.C.

WARDEN, *see* SERGISON

WARDOUR, William (1686–1746), of Whitney Court, Herefs.

CALNE   1727–1734
FOWEY   4 July 1737–17 July 1746

b. 12 July 1686, 1st s. of William Wardour of Whitney Court, clerk of the pells, by Anne Sopia, da. and coh. of Robert Rodd of Foxley, Herefs. *educ.* Queen's, Oxf. 1704. *unm.* *suc.* fa. 1699.

Returned unopposed for Calne in 1727, Wardour voted against the Administration on the civil list in 1729 and on the Hessians in 1730, but with them on the army in 1732, the excise bill in 1733, and the repeal of the Septennial Act in 1734. Defeated at Mitchell that year, he was returned for Fowey by the Administration in 1737, thereafter voting with them in all recorded divisions, except on the chairman of the elections committee, 16 Dec. 1741, when he voted against Walpole's candidate. He died 17 July 1746.

E.C.

WARRE, Sir Francis, 1st Bt. (?1659–1718), of Hestercombe, nr. Taunton, Som.

BRIDGWATER   1685–1687, 1689–1695, 29 Nov. 1699–1700
TAUNTON   17 Mar. 1701–30 Aug. 1715

b. ?1659, o.s. of Sir John Warre, M.P., of Hestercombe by Unton, da. of Francis Hawley, M.P., 1st Baron Hawley of Duncannon [I], wid. of John Malet of Enmore, Som. *educ.* Oriel, Oxf. 16 Oct. 1674, aged 15. *m.* (1) Anne (d. 24 Dec. 1690), da. and h. of Robert Cuffe of St. Michael Church, Som., 1s. *d.v.p.*; (2) Margaret, da. of John Harbin, merchant, of London and Yeovil, Som., 1s. *d.v.p.* 1da. *suc.* fa. 1669; *cr.* Bt. 2 June 1673.

Recorder, Bridgwater 1685, Taunton 1701; capt. Duke of Monmouth's Ft. 1678; col. Taunton Regt.; vice-adm. Som. and Bristol; dep. lt. Som.

Warre, whose family had been seated at Hestercombe since 1375, was one of the largest landowners in Somerset.[1] After representing Somerset boroughs as a Tory in ten Parliaments he was re-elected for Taunton in 1715 but unseated on petition. In September 1715 he gave Sir William Wyndham (q.v.) a letter from Lord Lansdowne about arrangements for the rebellion projected in the west country, which was found by the officer sent to arrest Wyndham. Arrested but released a few months later,[2] he died at Ghent 1 Dec. 1718.

[1] Collinson, *Som.* iii. 259–63; Rev. F. Brown, *Som. Wills*, iv. 131 n.2. [2] *HMC Stuart*, ii. 204.

E.C.

WARREN, Borlase (1677–1747), of Stapleford, Notts.

NOTTINGHAM 1713–1715, 1727–15 May 1747

bap. 25 Sept. 1677, o.s. of Arthur Warren of Stapleford, Notts. by Anne, da. and eventually h. of Sir John Borlase, 1st Bt., M.P., of Bockmer, Bucks. *m.* 1702, Ann, da. of Sir John Harpur, 3rd Bt., of Calke, Derbys., 7s. 7da. *suc.* fa. 1697.
Sheriff, Notts. 1703–4.

Returned for Nottingham as a Tory in 1713, Warren lost his seat in 1715. His name was sent to the Pretender in 1721 as one likely to support a rising.[1] After failing by a small margin to recapture his seat in 1722, he was returned for it on a compromise in 1727. He was re-elected without opposition in 1734 and again in 1741, when he was

so liberal of his drink in the morning that, not long after he was got to his inn, his own mob grew very troublesome to him, beginning first to plunder the victuals, ale and wine, then whatever else they could lay their hands on, breaking bottles, glasses, pots, chairs etc., till at last his friends were forced to send for the mayor and aldermen . . . to come with their constables and quell them, and Mr. Warren made his escape in Mr. Musters' coach . . .[2]

He consistently voted with the Opposition till his death, 15 May 1747.

[1] Stuart mss 65/16. [2] John Plumptre to Newcastle, 13 May 1741, Add. 32696, f. 518.

R.R.S.

WARREN, Sir Peter (c.1703–52), of Cavendish Sq., London, and Westbury, Hants.

WESTMINSTER 1747–29 July 1752

b. c.1703, 3rd s. of Michael Warren of Warrenstown, co. Meath, by Catharine, da. of Sir Christopher Aylmer, 1st Bt., of Balrath, co. Meath, wid. of Sir Nicholas Plunket. *m.* July 1731, Susanna, da. of Stephen de Lancey, a French Huguenot, of Caen and New York, sis. of James de Lancey, c.j. and lt.-gov. of New York, 1s. *d.v.p.* 4da. K.B. 29 May 1747.
Entered R.N. 1716, midshipman 1719, lt. 1723, capt. 1727, r.-adm. 1745, c.-in-c. Western squadron 1747, v.-adm. 1747.

Of an Irish Roman Catholic family, Warren entered the navy under the care of his uncle Admiral Matthew Aylmer (q.v.), becoming a Protestant.[1] He served successively under his cousin, Sir John Norris, Sir Charles Wager, and Lord Anson (qq.v.), to the last of whom he wrote 'I pin my whole faith upon you, and determine, if you will give me leave, to stand or fall with you'.[2] In 1742 he was appointed to the Leeward Islands station, where he captured over 20 prizes, including one valued at £250,000.[3] He commanded the fleet at the capture of Louisbourg in 1745, earning a tribute from the Duke of Bedford, the first lord of the Admiralty:

Commodore Warren has behaved, in the whole affair, so much like an officer who has nothing so much at heart as his Majesty's service, and so much to the satisfaction of us who employed him, as well as to that of all the officers who had the pleasure to serve under him, and has kept up so good an agreement, by his prudent conduct, with the officers that commanded the land forces, that I should think myself highly deficient in my duty to the King was I not to represent how much I thought it was for his Majesty's service to reward so much merit in a conspicuous manner.[4]

Refused a baronetcy on the ground he had no heir, he was made a rear-admiral. In that year he took several more valuable prizes from the French. In the spring of 1747 he was second-in-command at the victory off Cape Finisterre under Anson, whom he succeeded as commander of the Channel fleet. Suffering from a 'scorbutic disorder',[5] he saw little more active service before the peace.

Having failed to obtain the governorships of New York and of New Jersey 1745–6, Warren then expressed his intention 'to get into Parliament and perhaps venture to open my mouth with more temper though less eloquence than our friend Mr. Vernon [Edward, q.v.].' He was returned for Westminster on the interest of the Duke of Bedford, who provided him with the necessary property qualification.[6] He asked Anson for a seat on the Admiralty board, writing:

I beg you will assure his Grace the Duke of Bedford and yourself that I shall ever, upon all occasions adhere with a most firm and an unchangeable attachment to his Grace's and your interest and service.[7]

Pelham put him forward in 1748, but the King turned him down. In March 1749 he was one of the high naval officers who 'vehemently opposed' the navy bill.[8] He figures in the Leicester House lists of the new Government to be formed on the Prince's accession as third commissioner of a council presided over by Prince George as lord high admiral. He spoke against an opposition motion for an inquiry into the state of Dunkirk, 5 Feb. 1750, and supported the Saxony subsidy in January 1752.[9] In the summer of 1752 he went over to Ireland to complete the purchase of some estates there, dying in Dublin of a violent fever. 29 July.[10]

[1] T. Warren, *Hist. and Gen. of Warren Fam.* 188-9.   [2] Add 15957, f. 179.   [3] Charnock, *Biog. Navalis*, iv. 185.   [4] *Bedford Corresp.* i. 28-29.   [5] Add. 15957, ff. 160, 168, 170.   [6] Ex inf. Julian Gwyn, from the following: Warren to Clinton, 28 Aug. 1745, Clinton mss, Wm. L. Clements Lib.; Warren to Newcastle, 7 June 1746, Warren to Charles Knowles, 10 Nov. 1746, Gage mss; Add. 15955, f. 141. Anson to Bedford, 21, 23 June 1747, Bedford mss.   [7] 9 Aug. 1747, Add. 15957, f. 208.   [8] Walpole to Mann, 26 Dec. 1748, 4 Mar. 1749.   [9] Walpole, *Mems. Geo. II*, i. 243.   [10] *Warren Fam.* 1-2.

E.C.

WARRENDER, George (c.1658–1721), of Lochend, Haddington, and Bruntsfield, Edinburgh.

EDINBURGH   1715–4 Mar. 1721

b. c.1658, o.s. of George Warrender by Margaret Cunynghame, a relation of Sir James Cunynghame (q.v.). *m.* (1) 13 Apr. 1680, Margaret (*bur.* 2 June 1699), da. of Thomas Lawrie, Edinburgh merchant, 1 surv. s. 1da.; (2) proclamation 10 Dec. 1699, Grissel, da. of Hugh Blair, Edinburgh merchant, 3s. 5da. *suc.* fa. ?1661; *cr.* Bt. 2 June 1715.
Ld. provost, Edinburgh 1713–15.

Warrender, a successful merchant dealing in foreign trade, purchased Bruntsfield in 1675, later buying adjacent properties, and acquiring Lochend. In 1705 he was one of a syndicate to whom a three years' farm of the customs and foreign excise of Scotland was assigned.[1] A staunch Whig, who had been fined for nonconformity under James II,[2] he was created a baronet at George I's accession, which he had proclaimed at Edinburgh in his capacity of lord provost. Returned for Edinburgh in 1715 after a contest with an Argyll candidate, he was in London during the early stages of the Fifteen, but came north in August, feeling that 'his presence would be of greater importance at Edinburgh at such a juncture than it would be in Parliament'.[3] In 1716 he applied for compensation for his losses during the rebellion, claiming that he had been 'put to great charge and was obliged to lay aside a large and gainful share of his trade'.[4]

In Parliament Warrender voted with the Government in every recorded division, including that on the opposition motion of 4 June 1717, censuring Argyll's rival, Lord Cadogan (q.v.). After this vote he was reported by one of the followers of the Duke of Argyll to have been

> in a terrible fright because of the temper he fears the town are in on account of his behaviour in the House . . . The poor man had impudence enough to deny facts, as the only method he fancies is left to save his bacon.[5]

Always anxious lest some incident in Edinburgh—a clash with the excise officers or an address to repeal the Act of Union—should create an unfavourable impression on the Government, he advised the magistrates 'to shun extremes and to consider the need we have of favour'.[6]

He died a year before the next general election, 4 Mar. 1721.

[1] *Cal. Treas. Bks.* xxii. 91.   [2] W. K. Dickson, *Warrender Letters* (Sc. Hist. Soc. ser. 3, xxv), p. xxiii.   [3] M. Wood, *Lord Provosts of Edinburgh*, 61.   [4] *Cal. Treas. Pprs.* 1714–19, p. 222.   [5] *More Culloden Pprs.* ii. 173–4, 181.   [6] *Warrender Letters*, 27–28.

J.M.S.

WARTON, Sir Michael (?1648–1725), of Beverley, Yorks.

BOROUGHBRIDGE	22 Oct. 1675–1679
KINGSTON-UPON-HULL	1679–1681
BEVERLEY	1689–1702, 1708–1722

b. ?1648, 1st s. of Michael Warton, M.P. Beverley 1660–87, by Susannah, da. of John Poulett, M.P., 1st Baron Poulett. *educ.* Cheam, Surr.; St. John's, Camb. 17 Feb. 1665, aged 16; G. Inn 1667. *unm.* Kntd. 30 June 1666. *suc.* fa. 1688.
Ld. of Admiralty 1689–90.

Of an old Beverley family, who had sat for the borough since the sixteenth century, Warton was classed as a Whig in the list of the 1715 Parliament prepared for George I, in which it is stated that 'il refusa l'offre de la reine qui l'avoit nommé pour un des douze pairs. Le Roy lui a aussi offert mais il s'en est excusé'. He was gazetted a baron in the coronation honours list but was allowed to decline.[1] He is not recorded as voting in that Parliament, and was one of a number of Members who were committed to the custody of the serjeant-at-arms for defaulting from a call of the House, 9 Dec. 1719.[2] He did not stand in 1722. In 1723 he wrote to his old friend, Harley, 1st Earl of Oxford, complaining that 'a distemper in the guts . . . tyrannises over the poor remains of life my fever has left, worse than this Walpolish government over an agonising free people'.[3] He died 25 Mar. 1725, leaving his real property to his heirs at law. One of these was Michael Newton (q.v.), to whom he also left all his personal estate, subject to legacies, including liberal benefactions to Beverley. Another was Charles Pelham (q.v.).

[1] *Pol. State*, viii. 345–6.   [2] *CJ*, xix. 61.   [3] *HMC Portland*, v. 634.

R.R.S.

WATSON, Edward, Visct. Sondes (?1686–1722).

CANTERBURY	1708–1710
NEW ROMNEY	20 Apr. 1713–1722

b. ?1686, 1st s. of Lewis Watson, M.P., 1st Earl of Rockingham, by Lady Catherine Sondes, o. surv. da. and h. of George Sondes, M.P., 1st Earl of Feversham. *educ.* Merton, Oxf. 1 June 1703, aged 16. *m.* 21 Mar.

1709, Lady Catherine Tufton, da. and coh. of Thomas Tufton, M.P., 6th Earl of Thanet, 2s. 2da.

Gent. of the bedchamber to Prince of Wales 1718–*d*.

A Whig, whose father had been created an Earl on the Hanoverian succession, Sondes went over to the Opposition in 1718, when he was given a place in the Prince's household. He died *v.p.* 20 Mar. 1722.

A.N.N.

WATSON, Hon. Lewis (1728–95), of Lees Court, Kent.

BOROUGHBRIDGE	23 Apr. 1750–1754
KENT	1754–22 May 1760

b. 28 Nov. 1728, 2nd s. of John Monson (q.v.), 1st Baron Monson, by Lady Margaret Watson, da. of Lewis Watson, M.P., 1st Earl of Rockingham. *educ.* Westminster 1737–45; Grand Tour. *m.* 12 Oct. 1752, Grace, da. and coh. of Henry Pelham (q.v.) and niece of Thomas, 1st Duke of Newcastle, 3s. *suc.* cos. Thomas Watson (q.v.), 3rd Earl of Rockingham, to Watson estates in Northants. and Kent 26 Feb. 1746 and assumed name of Watson; *cr.* Baron Sondes of Lees Court 22 May 1760.

Jt. auditor of the imprest Feb. 1754–85.

While Watson was on the grand tour with his kinsmen, Lord Malton, later Lord Rockingham, and Thomas Pelham jun. of Stanmer (q.v.), he was returned by the Duke of Newcastle, whose niece he subsequently married. On 4 Oct. 1750 Newcastle reported from Hanover to Henry Pelham, that he had just had 'a very mortifying slight'. He had arranged to present Watson, Malton, Pelham, Lord Downe (q.v.) and three other young Englishmen of quality on their travels.

> I acquainted H.M. with it beforehand. He flew out— what did they come there to trouble him for? I answered, to show their zeal and attachment. 'Let them show it in Parliament' etc. When they were presented in the circle, before all the foreign ministers and all the court, H.M. said not one word to any one, but a little to Lord Malton, and a little, very little, to Lord Downe. I fear the effect of this unhappy incident.[1]

In 1754 Pelham procured him the life sinecure of auditor of the imprest, which was abolished by Act of Parliament in 1785, subject to the payment to him of £7,000 a year 'in lieu of the profits and emoluments of the said office' till his death, 30 Mar. 1795.

[1] Add. 32723, f. 13.

R.R.S.

WATSON, Thomas (c.1701–66), of Grindon Bridge, Northumb.

BERWICK-UPON-TWEED	27 Nov. 1740–Dec. 1765

b. c.1701, s. of Thomas Watson of Berwick by his w. Margaret Clerk. *m.* Barbara Forster, *s.p.*

Mayor, Berwick 1727, 1729, 1732, 1734, 1736, 1739; commissary of musters in south Britain 1732; dep. commissary for Danish and Hessian troops in British pay 1741.

Thomas Watson was an influential member of the corporation of Berwick, for which he was returned, voting regularly with the Government. Up to 1754 his fellow Member was Lord Barrington, with whom he fell out c.1749–50, when the 2nd Lord Egmont wrote in his electoral survey for the Prince of Wales, 'I am assured that Watson will be able to turn out Barrington and bring in a proper person'. In March 1754 he is shown in a list of secret service pensions as receiving one of £500 a year.[1] He died 7 Jan. 1766.

[1] Add. 33038, f.415.

R.R.S.

WATSON, Hon. Thomas (1715–46).

CANTERBURY	1741–4 Dec. 1745

b. 30 Dec. 1715, 2nd s. of Edward Watson, Visct. Sondes (q.v.). *educ.* Eton 1725; L. Inn 1732. *unm.* *suc.* bro. as 3rd Earl of Rockingham 4 Dec. 1745. Ld. lt. Kent 1745–*d.*

Returned for Canterbury on the 'country interest' as an opposition Whig, Watson voted consistently against the Administration. Despite his politics he was appointed lord lieutenant of the county on succeeding to the peerage, but he enjoyed his honours for little over two months, dying 26 Feb. 1746. He left his estates to his cousin, Lewis Monson, who subsequently assumed the name of Watson (q.v.).

A.N.N.

WATSON WENTWORTH, Hon. Thomas (1665–1723), of Wentworth Woodhouse, Yorks.

BOSSINEY	21 Mar.–11 Nov. 1701
HIGHAM FERRERS	22 Nov. 1703–1713
MALTON	1713–1722
HIGHAM FERRERS	1722–6 Oct. 1723

b. 17 June 1665, 3rd s. of Edward Watson, 2nd Baron Rockingham, by Anne, da. of Thomas Wentworth, M.P., 1st Earl of Strafford, sis. and coh. to William, 2nd Earl of Strafford. *educ.* Ch. Ch. Oxf. 1683. *m.* (lic. 18 July 1689) Alice, da. of Sir Thomas Proby, 1st Bt., M.P., of Elton Hall, Hunts., 1s. *suc.* 1695 to Wentworth Woodhouse and the bulk of the estates of his uncle, the 2nd Earl of Strafford, taking the name of Wentworth after Watson.

Succeeding to the bulk of the great Wentworth estates in Yorkshire, Northamptonshire, and Ireland, Thomas Watson Wentworth sat for 20 years for his boroughs of Malton and Higham Ferrers. Classed in 1715 as a Whig who would often vote with the Tories, he voted against the Government in every recorded division except on Lord Cadogan (q.v.). He died 6 Oct. 1723.

R.R.S.

WATSON WENTWORTH, Thomas (1693–1750), of Wentworth Woodhouse, Yorks.

MALTON   1715–1727
YORKSHIRE   1727–28 May 1728

b. 13 Nov. 1693, o.s. of Hon. Thomas Watson Wentworth (q.v.). *educ.* St. John's, Camb. 1707. *m.* 22 Sept. 1716, Mary, da. of Daniel Finch, M.P., 2nd Earl of Nottingham and 7th Earl of Winchilsea, 1 surv. s. 4 surv. da. *suc.* fa. 6 Oct. 1723; K.B. 27 May 1725; *cr.* Baron Malton 28 May 1728; Earl of Malton 19 Nov. 1734; *suc.* cos. Thomas Watson (q.v.), 3rd Earl of Rockingham and 5th Baron, as 6th Baron Rockingham, 26 Feb. 1746, the earldom becoming extinct; *cr.* Mq. of Rockingham 19 Apr. 1746.
Ld. lt. W. Riding and custos rot. N. Riding of Yorks. 1733–*d.*

Returned in 1715 for the family borough of Malton, Wentworth, like his father, was classed as a Whig who would often vote with the Tories. In his first Parliament all his recorded votes were against the Government, except on the septennial bill, which he supported. On succeeding his father he set himself up as the leader of the Yorkshire Whigs, to whose 'confederacy' he was described as 'a noble and significant recruit'. At a by-election for the county in the last year of George I his influence powerfully contributed to the return of the Whig candidate; at the general election following he himself took the other seat; and on his elevation to the peerage in 1728 he nominated his successor. His position as the head of the government interest in Yorkshire was recognized by his appointment to the lord lieutenancy of the West Riding in 1733, when he was raised to an earldom. Thenceforth his electoral influence declined. Accused of attempting 'to dictate to the country', he lost one seat in 1734, aggravating the setback by instituting costly, unpopular, and unsuccessful petition proceedings; in 1741 both seats went to the opposition interests, headed by his rival for the leadership of the Yorkshire Whigs, the Earl of Carlisle; and though by 1750 both seats had been recovered for the Government, neither of the Members was his nominee.[1] Created a marquess in 1746 to avoid giving him a garter,[2] he was considered by the 2nd Lord Egmont about 1750 as 'to be had' by the promise of a dukedom, 'if it were worth while', a view with which the Prince of Wales agreed.[3] Soon afterwards 'the little Marquis' died, 'drowned in claret',[4] 14 Dec. 1750.

[1] C. Collyer, 'Yorks. election of 1734', *Proc. Leeds Philosophical Soc.* 1952; 'Yorks. Election of 1741', ibid. 1953; 'The Rockinghams

and Yorks. politics', *Thoresby Soc. Misc.* 1954. [2] Walpole to Geo. Montagu, 2 Aug. 1746. [3] Add. 47097, f. 8. [4] Walpole to Mann, 19 Dec. 1750.

R.R.S.

WATTS, Thomas (*d.*1742), of Enfield Chase, Mdx.

MITCHELL   1734–1741
TREGONY   1741–18 Jan. 1742

s. of William Watts of Shanks House, Cucklington, Som. *m.* Susannah, da. of Benjamin Gascoyne of Chiswick, sis. of Sir Crisp Gascoyne, ld. mayor of London, 2s.[1]
Sec. Sun Fire Office 1723–34, cashier 1726–41.

A member of a good Somersetshire family, Watts joined the Sun Fire Office in 1720, soon becoming its 'ruling genius' and a leading man in the city.[2] Returned as an opposition Whig by Lord Falmouth (q.v.) for Mitchell in 1734, he opposed the Westminster bridge bill on 31 Mar. 1736,[3] was absent from the division on the Spanish convention in 1739, and voted against the Administration on the place bill of 1740. In 1741 he was returned as an opposition candidate for Tregony, retiring from the Sun Fire Office in July with an annuity of £200 p.a. in recognition that

> many of the good regulations made in this office and more particularly the scheme and success of the subscription stock (from which era we may date the establishment and good fortune of the office) were owing in a great measure to the contrivances and good services of Mr. Thomas Watts.[4]

He died 18 Jan. 1742, leaving two sons who, in turn, succeeded him as secretary to the board.

[1] PCC 38 Trenley. [2] F. B. Relton, *Fire Insurance Companies*, 286. [3] Harley Diary. [4] E. Baumer, *Early Days of the Sun Fire Office*, 51.

E.C.

WEARG, Sir Clement (c.1686–1726), of the Inner Temple, London.

HELSTON   10 Mar. 1724–6 Apr. 1726

b. c.1686, 1st s. of Thomas Wearg of the Inner Temple by Mary Fletcher of Ely, Cambs. *educ.* Peterhouse, Camb. 1706; I. Temple 1706, called 1711, bencher 1723. *m.* 1 Oct. 1723, Elizabeth, da. of Sir James Montagu, chief baron of the Exchequer, *s.p.* Kntd. 4 Feb. 1724.
Solicitor-gen. Feb. 1724–*d.*

Wearg, a successful lawyer, was counsel for the Crown in the proceedings against Atterbury and his fellow conspirators 1722–3. Defeated for Shaftesbury in 1722, he was brought in for Helston by Lord Godolphin in 1724,[1] when he was appointed solicitor-general in succession to Sir Robert Raymond (q.v.), to whose seat he also succeeded. He managed the impeachment of Lord Chancellor Macclesfield in 1725, in which year he gave legal support to Bolingbroke's petition for the restoration of his estates. He died of a violent fever 6 Apr. 1726.[2]

[1] G. Clarke (q.v.) to Edw. Nicholas (q.v.), 21 Jan. 1724, Egerton 2540, f. 254. [2] *Pol. State*, xxxi. 430–1.

E.C.

WEAVER, Arthur (c.1719–59), of Morville, nr. Bridgnorth, Salop.

BRIDGNORTH   1747–1754

b. c.1719, o.s. of John Weaver (q.v.) of Morville. *educ.* I. Temple 1736. *m.* 25 Aug. 1754, Susannah, da. of David Papillon (q.v.) of Acrise, Kent, *s.p. suc.* fa. 1747.

Weaver was returned as a government supporter on his own and the Whitmore interest in 1747, in place of William Whitmore (q.v.) of Lower Slaughter. He did not seek re-election and died 5 Apr. 1759.

J.B.L.

WEAVER, John (c.1672–1747), of Morville, nr. Bridgnorth, Salop.

BRIDGNORTH   1713–1734

b. c.1672, 1st s. of Arthur Weaver of Morville, Salop by Maria Careswell of Shifnal, Salop. *educ.* I. Temple 1689, called 1697. *m.* Sarah Acton, 1s. *suc.* fa. 1710. Recorder, Bridgnorth 1725–35.

Weaver, through his grandfather's marriage with the heiress of the Smythes of Morville, had an interest at Bridgnorth. Returned as a Whig on his own and the Whitmore interest in the 1715 Parliament, he voted with the Government, except on the peerage bill, which he opposed. On the death of William Whitmore (q.v.) of Apley he was elected recorder of the borough as a stop-gap during the minority of Thomas Whitmore (q.v.). In his last Parliament, during which he was taken into the custody of the serjeant at arms for defaulting on a call of the House in 1733,[1] he voted against the Administration. He died 9 Jan. 1747.[2]

[1] *CJ*, xxi. 375. [2] J. F. A. Mason, 'Recorders of Bridgnorth', *Salop Arch. Soc. Trans.* liv. 197–9.

J.B.L.

WEBB, Borlase Richmond (c.1696–1738), of Biddesden, in Ludgershall, Wilts.

LUDGERSHALL   1722–1734

b. c.1696, 2nd s. but h. of John Richmond Webb (q.v.) of Biddesden by his 1st w. *educ.* Turin acad. 1716.[1] *m.* 6 July 1727, Hester Newton, *s.p. suc.* fa. 1724.
    Ensign 8 Ft. 1701, capt. 1705–15.

Borlase Webb, who was given a commission in his father's regiment as a small boy, left the army with him in 1715. Returned with his father as a

Tory for Ludgershall in 1722 he was again successful in 1727, voting against the excise bill in 1733. Under his father's will he succeeded to the family estates to the exclusion of his elder brother Edmund. Defeated in 1734, he died 3 Mar. 1738.

[1] *HMC Stuart*, iii. 162.

R.S.L.

WEBB, John Richmond (1667–1724), of Biddesden, in Ludgershall, Wilts.

LUDGERSHALL	16 Jan. 1695–1698
	11 Feb. 1699–1705
	17 Jan. 1706–1713
NEWPORT I.o.W.	1713–1715
LUDGERSHALL	1715–5 Sept. 1724

b. 26 Dec. 1667,[1] 3rd but 2nd surv. s. of Col. Edmund Richmond Webb, M.P., of Rodbourne Cheney, Wilts. by his 1st w. Jane, da. of John Smith of St. Mary Aldermanbury, London, and Tidworth, Wilts. *m.* (1) lic. 3 Feb. 1690, Henrietta (*d.* June 1711), da. and coh. of William Borlase, M.P. (yr. bro. of Sir John Borlase, 1st Bt., M.P.), wid. of Sir Richard Astley, 1st Bt., 3s. 4da.; (2) 20 May 1720, Anne Skeates, wid., said to be illegit., 1s. 2da.
    Cornet 3 Drags. 1685; capt. and lt.-col. Gren. Gds. 1689; col. 8 Ft. 1695–1715; brig.-gen. 1704; maj.-gen. 1706; lt.-gen. 1709; capt. and gov. I.o.W. 1710–15; cdr. forces in England 1712.

A distinguished soldier, who had served under Marlborough, Webb came of a Wiltshire family, with a strong interest at Ludgershall, where he was returned as a Tory to twelve successive Parliaments, including that of 1713, when he chose to sit for Newport in the Isle of Wight, of which he had been appointed governor by the Tory Government in 1710. After George I's accession, attempts were made to secure his dismissal as a Tory from his military posts, but the King re-appointed him to them on condition that he made his peace with Marlborough,[2] whom he wrongly believed to have tried to deprive him of the credit for his brilliant action at Wyendael in 1708. Re-elected after a contest with his brother in 1715, when he was classed as a Whig who would often vote with the Tories, he took his seat on 29 March after the House had decided that it had not been vacated by his re-appointment as governor of the Isle of Wight by letters patent which had passed the great seal since his election (see under Stanwix, Thomas).[3] On 11 June 1715 it was reported that he had been dismissed from his military posts for voting with the Tories in Parliament and that similar action was to be taken against other Tory officers in the House. He was one of the high-ranking officers who were dismissed the service or ordered to sell their regiments in July, when the Government was taking emergency measures against the impending rebellion.[4] He was not involved in the rebellion but in April 1716 he was consulted by Atterbury on a plan for landing Swedish troops in England, on which he declared

> that if he had 6,000 regular troops, he would undertake to beat all the forces which could on a sudden be brought together in England . . . He desired timely notice when and where the descent will be made, that he might draw his money out of the funds and bring a good purse with him to the field.

In January 1717 the Pretender sent him a letter of thanks for his devotion to the cause; and in the spring of 1717 he was said to 'wait but a call anywhere'.[5] After his name had been sent to the Pretender in 1721 as a probable supporter in the event of a rising, he was sent a commission to act as one of the generals in the rebellion planned for the summer of 1722, when the Pretender wrote: 'I extremely confide in his advice and assistance in matters of which he has so much experience'. In the course of the ensuing trials, his name was mentioned as one of the promoters of the plot.[6]

Webb's only recorded speech after George I's accession was made in November 1718, in support of a motion for translating the text of treaties from Latin into English. He

> said he was not ashamed to own his ignorance; that he was never brought up in a university but in the army ever since he was 16 and had never looked in a grammar since, and that he did not understand one word that was read, and therefore insisted that they should be turned into English and not forced to vote for what they did not know.[7]

His only recorded vote was against the peerage bill in 1719. At the general election of 1722 he was again opposed by his brother, who petitioned, renewing his petition till Webb's death 5 Sept. 1724.

[1] H. I. Richmond, *Richmond Fam. Recs.* ii. 235. [2] *Wentworth Pprs.* 422, 426, 430; *Pol. State*, viii. 331. [3] *CJ*, xviii. 29, 30. [4] *Verney Letters of 18th Cent.* i. 339; *Pol. State*, x. 98. [5] *HMC Stuart*, ii. 67–68; iii. 378, 475–6; iv. 333. [6] Stuart mss 59/17, 60/55, 65/16, Howell's *State Trials*, xvi. 179. [7] *HMC Stuart*, vii. 568.

E.C.

WEBB, Robert (c.1719–65), of Taunton, Som. and Marylebone, Mdx.

TAUNTON   1747–1754

b. c.1719, 1st s. of Nathaniel Webb of Montserrat and of Taunton, Som. by his 1st w. Bethiah, da. of William Gerrish. *educ.* M. Temple 1736, called 1741; I. Temple 1745. *unm.*[1] *suc.* fa. 1741.

Webb's father, of a Somerset family, who made his fortune as a merchant in the West Indies,[2] bought considerable properties in and around Taunton. Returned unopposed for Taunton on the dissenting interest in 1747, standing jointly with

Sir Charles Wyndham (q.v.),[3] he was classed as a government supporter. At the general election of 1754 he withdrew, refusing to face the expense of a contest. He died 9 Sept. 1765.

[1] PCC 357 Rushworth. [2] Oliver, *Antigua*, iii. 214. [3] Egremont to Newcastle, 12 July 1754, Add. 32736, f. 23; *HMC 15th Rep. VII*, 124–5.

S.R.M.

WEBSTER, Sir Thomas, 1st Bt. (c.1679–1751), of Copped Hall, Essex and Battle Abbey, Suss.

COLCHESTER   18 Dec. 1705–27 Jan. 1711,
                     1713–6 May 1714,   1722–1727

b. c.1679, 1st s. of Sir Godfrey Webster of Fenchurch St., London, and the Nelmes, Havering, Essex by Abigail, da. and coh. of Thomas Jordan of the Mere, Staffs. by Mary, da. and coh. of Henry Whistler of Epsom, Surr. *educ.* M. Temple 1697. *m.* Jane, da. and h. of Edward Cheek of Sandford Orcas, Som., 2s. 3da. *suc.* fa. 1720; *cr.* Bt. 21 May 1703.
   Sheriff, Essex 1703–4; verderer of Waltham forest 1718–*d.*

The son of a wealthy London clothier,[1] Webster purchased the estate of Copped Hall for over £20,000 from Charles Sackville, 6th Earl of Dorset, in 1700; Battle Abbey from Anthony Browne, 6th Viscount Montagu, in 1721;[2] and property including several burgages at East Grinstead.[3] Returned as a Whig for Colchester in 1722, he did not stand again, dying 30 May 1751.

[1] PCC 147 Shaller. [2] T. Wright, *Hist. Essex*, ii. 460–1; *VCH Suss.* ix. 106. [3] W. H. Hills, *Hist. East Grinstead*, 50.

E.C.

WEBSTER, Whistler (aft. 1699–1779), of Battle Abbey, Suss.

EAST GRINSTEAD   1741–1761

b. aft. 1699,[1] 1st s. of Sir Thomas Webster, 1st Bt. (q.v.), of Copped Hall, Essex, and Battle Abbey. *m.* 20 Nov. 1766, Martha, da. of Rev. Richard Nairne, dean of Battle, *s.p. suc.* fa. 30 May 1751.

After contesting Hastings unsuccessfully in 1734,[2] Webster was returned in 1741 unopposed at East Grinstead, where his father (q.v.) had acquired an interest. Voting consistently against the Government, he was classed as Opposition in 1747. Despite this he wrote to Newcastle, 12 Apr. 1751, asking for a place in Prince George's establishment for his brother-in-law, Sir Edmund Thomas (q.v.).[3]

He died 21 Sept. 1779.

[1] PCC 147 Shaller, 130 Lynch. [2] John Collier to Newcastle, 18 Apr. 1734, Add. 32689, f. 200. [3] Add. 32724, f. 231.

A.N.N.

WEIR, Daniel (167?–1724), of Stonebyres, Lanark.

LINLITHGOW BURGHS   1722–21 May 1724

b. 167?, 2nd s. of James Weir of Stonebyres by Rachel, yr, da. of Sir William Carmichael, Master of Carmichael. *m.* 14 Sept. 1713, Elizabeth, da. of Sir John Hamilton, M.P. [S] of Halcraig, Lanark (Lord Halcraig, S.C.J.), 2s. *suc.* bro. William to Stonebyres c.1712.

Cornet, Earl of Hyndford's Drags. c.1702, lt. 1709, capt. 1710, half-pay 1713; capt. Gen. Palmes's Drags. 1716–17.

The Weirs of Stonebyres, cadets of the family of Weir of Blackwood, probably acquired their lands during the fifteenth century. Assessed as a 'gentleman' for the poll-tax in 1695,[1] Daniel Weir joined his uncle's regiment about 1702. On succeeding to the family estates he went on half-pay, drilling his tenants regularly during the Fifteen on behalf of the Duke of Argyll.[2] At the 1722 election he was returned for Linlithgow Burghs by the casting vote of the dubiously elected representative of Linlithgow, the presiding burgh.[3] He died 21 May 1724, before the petition against him was heard.

[1] J. B. Greenshields, *Annals of Lesmahagow*, 82, 176, [2] W. Hunter, *Biggar and the House of Fleming*, 562, [3] See LINLITHGOW BURGHS.

R.S.L.

WEIR, *see also* **HOPE WEIR**

WENMAN, Philip, 3rd Visct. Wenman [I] (1719–60), of Thame Park, Oxon.

OXFORD   21 Nov. 1749–1754

b. 23 Nov. 1719, 1st s. of Richard, 2nd Visct. Wenman [I], by Susanna, da. of Seymour Wroughton of Eastcott, Wilts. *educ.* Abingdon g.s.; Oriel, Oxf. 1737. *m.* 13 July 1741, Sophia, da. of James Herbert of Tythrop and Kingsey, Bucks., sis. and h. of Philip Herbert (qq.v.), 4s. 3da. *suc.* fa. 28 Nov. 1729.

Wenman's family had large estates in Oxfordshire, which they had represented since the sixteenth century. A commission of idiocy was issued against his father in 1718,[1] and he himself was described as 'of not much greater capacity'.[2] Refusing to join the county association in defence of the Hanoverian succession during the 1745 rebellion,[3] he is called a Jacobite in the 2nd Lord Egmont's electoral survey, c.1749–50. Returned as a Tory for Oxfordshire at a by-election in 1749, he also fought the great Oxfordshire election of 1754 on behalf of his party. He died 16 Aug. 1760.

[1] *HMC Portland*, v. 571. [2] *VCH Oxon.* vii. 177. [3] R. J. Robson, *Oxfordshire Election of 1754*, p.2.

E.C.

WENTWORTH, Godfrey (1704–89), of Woolley, Yorks.

YORK   1741–1747

b. 17 Oct. 1704, 3rd but 1st surv. s. of Godfrey

Wentworth of Woolley by Anne, da. of Giles Clarke of Lyon's Inn, London. *educ.* Wakefield sch.; St. John's, Camb. 1722. *m.* 1728, his 1st cos. Dorothy, da. of Sir Lyon Pilkington, 4th Bt., 3s. 3da.; marriage dissolved by Act of Parliament 1758. *suc.* uncle William Wentworth 1729.

Alderman, York, ld. mayor 1759.

Wentworth belonged to a junior branch of the Wentworth Woodhouse family, who had been seated at Woolley since the end of the sixteenth century. Returned for York as a Tory after a contest in 1741, he voted against the Government, for which he was thanked by the corporation in February 1742.[1] He did not stand again, and died 18 Jan. 1789.

[1] *Gent. Mag.* 1742, p. 96.

R.R.S.

WENTWORTH, Thomas (?1693–1747), of Sunninghill, Berks.

WHITCHURCH   18 Feb. 1743–1747

b. ?1693, 3rd but 2nd surv. s. of Sir Mathew Wentworth, 3rd Bt., of Bretton, Yorks. by Elizabeth, da. of William Osbaldeston of Hunmanby, Yorks.; bro. of Sir William Wentworth, 4th Bt. (q.v.). *educ.* Univ. Coll. Oxf. 28 Jan. 1710, aged 16. *m.* 3 July 1720, Elizabeth, da. and coh. of Robert Lord of London, s.p.

Lt. 1st tp. Horse Gren. Gds. Mar. 1715; capt. and lt.-col. 1 Ft. Gds. Oct. 1715; lt.-col. 23 Ft. 1718; adjt.-gen. of all forces and col. of Horse 1722; col. 39 Ft. 1732–7, 24 Ft. 1737–45; brig.-gen. 1739; maj.-gen. 1741; lt.-gen. 1745; col. 5 Drag. Gds. 1745–*d.*; ambassador, Turin 1746–*d.*

When Sir William Wentworth voted against the Government on the motion for an increase in the Prince of Wales's allowance in 1737, Thomas Wentworth, a professional soldier, wrote to his kinsman, Lord Malton (Thomas Watson Wentworth, q.v.):

My brother thought fit on that occasion to leave his old friends and to join the minority, which has put me under a difficulty . . . Your Lordship may easily imagine that my hopes of being removed to an older regiment will by this accident be very much weakened.[1]

He was second-in-command and later commander-in-chief of the land forces on the unsuccessful expedition to Cartagena in 1740, quarrelling violently with Admiral Vernon (q.v.). Returned as a government supporter for Whitchurch in 1743 on the Wallop interest, he voted with the Administration on the Hanoverians in 1744, subsequently serving in Flanders. In 1745 he accompanied Marshal Wade (q.v.) on his march to Newcastle. He did not vote on the Hanoverians in 1746, dying November 1747.

[1] 28 Feb. 1737, Rockingham mss.

P.W.

WENTWORTH, Sir William, 4th Bt. (1686–1763), of Bretton, Yorks.

MALTON 19 May 1731–1741

bap. 29 Oct. 1686, 2nd but 1st surv. s. of Sir Mathew Wentworth, 3rd Bt., of Bretton; bro. of Thomas Wentworth (q.v.). *m.* 23 June 1720, Diana, da. of Sir William Blackett, 1st Bt., M.P., sis. and coh. of Sir William Blackett, 2nd Bt., 5s. 4da. *suc.* fa. Feb. 1706.

Wentworth, who was returned by his kinsman, Lord Malton (Thomas Watson Wentworth, q.v.), voted with the Government till 1737, when he was asked on behalf of the Prince of Wales to support the motion proposing an increase in the Prince's allowance. 'His brains are most puzzled on this affair', Lady Isabella Finch reported to Lord Malton, 'but [he] declared if he knew your opinion he would follow that'.[1] In the end he voted for the Prince, to the consternation of his brother, Thomas Wentworth (q.v.).[2] According to Lady Isabella, 'poor Sir William . . . is very sorry now he gave his vote in the manner he did, but he was tricked into it'.[3] He did not vote on the Spanish convention in 1739 or on the place bill in 1740, was not put up again, and died 1 Mar. 1763.

[1] 22 Feb. 1737, Rockingham mss. [2] 28 Feb. 1737, ibid. [3] 26 Feb. 1737, ibid.

R.R.S.

WENTWORTH, *see also* WATSON WENTWORTH

WEST, James (1703–72), of Alscott Park, Glos.

ST. ALBANS 1741–1768
BOROUGHBRIDGE 1768–2 July 1772

b. 2 May 1703, o.s. of Richard West of Priors Marston, Warws. and St. Swithin's, London by his w. Mary Russell of Strensham, Worcs. *educ.* Balliol, Oxf. 1719; I. Temple 1721, called 1728, bencher 1761; L. Inn 1738. *m.* 15 Aug. 1738, Sarah, da. of Sir Thomas Steavens, timber merchant, of Eltham, Kent, and h. of her bro. Thomas, 1s. 2da. Sec. to chancellor of the Exchequer, Dec. 1743–May 1752; jt. sec. to Treasury May 1746–Nov. 1756, July 1757–May 1762; recorder, Poole 1746–*d.*, St. Albans Apr. 1758–July 1760; high steward, St. Albans 1759–*d.*; treasurer, R. Soc. 1736–68, president 1768–*d.*

West came of a Warwickshire family, descended from Thomas West, 8th Lord de la Warre.[1] His father, who seems to have gone into business as a packer in London, left him £1,000 a year.[2] As a young man, practising at the bar, he became known as an antiquary, amassing a valuable collection of manuscripts, deeds and charters, many of which perished in a fire at his chambers in the Inner Temple in 1736. Next year, at the request of his friend and fellow collector, Edward Harley, 2nd

Earl of Oxford, he became one of the trustees in whom Lady Oxford's estates were vested for the payment of debts totalling nearly a quarter of a million. In this capacity he was responsible for the sale of the Harleian manuscripts to the British Museum in 1753 for £10,000.[3]

In 1738 West married a wealthy timber merchant's daughter, who ultimately brought him a fortune of £100,000.[4] At the next general election he was recommended by Thomas Martin (q.v.) to Walpole as likely to be 'of great use to you, having a very large clear fortune and a very extensive acquaintance'.[5] Returned unopposed for St. Albans, which he represented for the next 27 years, he was included by Pelham in the court list for the secret committee set up to inquire into Walpole's Administration, to which he was not elected. He was also one of the court Members chosen to serve as commissioners of public accounts under an opposition bill, which was rejected by the Lords.[6] On Wilmington's death in 1743, he sent Pelham an anonymous letter urging him to accept the Treasury,

as it is the only means of calling back the wavering and fixing the minds of the old and constant friends of the government which have been not a little warped by seeing men in opposition too much supported by yours and your family's interest . . .

It is this, Sir, will give strength to your party (for parties there must, there will, and for the safety of this country, there always ought to be) will inspire them with industry and courage. They will be convinced that to preserve themselves they must follow and adhere to you and the others will in time learn that a faithful service of their King and country may be as beneficial as an unwearied opposition to both. The strength of opposition will decline and you will have the power by reasonable means to lead them to reasonable ends.

Forgive me, Sir, for this trouble and this presumption, which nothing should have extorted but love to you and love to my country. I have the honour to sit in Parliament with you and though I sometimes wait on you, have not the honour of an intimacy sufficient to mention these things to you.

I should set my name but some impressions may make you think that the effect of flattery which is the result of my truest judgement.[7]

The anonymity was merely formal; the letter, in West's handwriting, is endorsed in Pelham's papers as from West.

In December 1743 West became secretary to Pelham as Chancellor of the Exchequer, on the understanding that he should be made joint secretary to the Treasury as soon as alternative provision could be found for John Jeffreys (q.v.). On the reconstruction of the Government at the end of 1744 he pressed Pelham to fulfil his promise:

I hope you will forgive me if upon learning Mr. Jeffreys is the only person of that set in the House of Commons who is to continue his employment and from a thorough conviction that his being kept in your own department by your own power and authority is of great disservice to you in the thoughts of many men as well friends as others, I represent to you what is said.

Almost everybody asked yesterday in the House and more will ask tomorrow what public reason could be given for keeping in a friend of Lord Bath's that does not hold as strong for any person displaced. Whether the same interest exerted for any other might not have kept them in, or whether his merit, peculiar abilities in his province, skill in figures, or interest and credit with the moneyed part of this kingdom have supported him when no other could stand.

The regard and countenance you have been so good to honour me with has given foundation to many of my friends in both Houses of Parliament, in the law, and in the city to look upon me as intended by you for something in the Treasury, and though I have never suffered anything to drop from me yet perhaps the nature and condition of the place you gave me was by them thought some earnest of the other.

Should I be so happy to succeed, as gratitude was ever the strongest passion of my heart, I should think myself obliged to obey every command of yours; and though I would pawn my life to you to make myself absolute master of the business in a very short time, yet my behaviour to Mr. Scrope [q.v.] should be such in every instance as you should dictate and approve.

In a postscript he wrote:

May I add Mr. Jeffreys in the time he has had his place has received more from it than the value of mine in perpetuity. Happy man! Would be continued by Lord Bath, is continued by you. Is not Jeffreys kept in to keep West out in complaisance to the froward unreasonable temper and views of Scrope; if so must wait till Scrope dies. The party are determined to force Jeffreys out.[8]

Pelham replied from Esher on 26 Dec.:

I received your letter yesterday morning, not long before I set out for this place and as it gave me the greatest concern I can assure you, it made my short retreat here much less agreeable to me. I never thought the little employment you held under me, gave me any merit with you, but have always declared, that I thought your acceptance of it entitled you to all the regard and assistance from me that my public station could enable me to shew you. Confidence and friendship I have demonstrated in its full extent, and whenever I shew that, I want nothing but opportunity to extend it further to the advantage of the man I wish well to. But to be told that I must displace a man so immediately under my direction as the secretary of the Treasury, and that there are even those who resolve to unite, till they can force me to it, is not a way of working upon my temper. If those who ask what public reason is to be given for my keeping in Mr. Jefferies, would by that insinuate that there may be a private one, you know me enough to answer yourself; that such insinuations I most heartily despise; but for your own private information, I can tell you, that no one, except Lord Harrington, and he very slightly, has said one word to me about him. It was not out of any personal regard to others that made me keep him in, when I first came at the head

of the Treasury, nor will that have the least share in influencing me, in case I should continue him now. I have known the man long, I think him a good retired inoffensive creature, and as such had no desire to shew resentment to him on the account of others; nor did I imagine the public could think itself at all interested in his situation one way or other. That I always intended you should succeed whenever any vacancy was made there, is undoubtedly true, but to be told I must make one whether I will or no is a little hard; and let the person who is the object of these gentlemen's resentment be never so inconsiderable, you cannot but see, it is I am struck at, and were I to yield upon such sort of threats I had much better give up the game at once, and retire where I have long wished myself to be. You see, Sir, I write to you with openness and freedom, I have always valued your friendship, and shall continue to do so, but hope you will not exact that of me at present, which I think, in these circumstances, I cannot do with honour. I am exceedingly concerned to hear that your being with me should at all lessen your practice in the profession of the law, I truly thought it was not the employment, but your own option that led you to another course of life. I must entreat you to reflect upon what has passed, see how I stand, either complying or refusing, one way contemptible, the other unkind. Neither of which I wish to be, for let your reputation be what it will, I cannot bring myself to think *you* mean what *others* say, nor shall I easily persuade myself that you have in the least changed that favourable opinion which you voluntarily have shown of me.[9]

It was not till 1746 that West succeeded to the post, and then only on condition that he allowed Jeffreys £1,000 p.a. till Pelham could provide for him, meanwhile retaining his secretaryship to the chancellor of the Exchequer (£500 p.a.) as compensation. This arrangement lasted till Scrope's death in 1752, after which Jeffreys was quartered on the new joint secretary, Nicholas Hardinge (q.v.).[10] After Pelham's death West attached himself to Newcastle. He died 2 July 1772.

[1] Blore, *Rutland*, 101. [2] Foster, *Al. Ox.* 1715–86, iv. 1527; *Gent. Mag.* 1731, p. 500; Brooke, *Chatham Administration*, 287. [3] West to Lord Oxford, 6 Jan. 1736, Lady Oxford to West, passim, West mss at Alscott. [4] Brooke, loc. cit. [5] Martin to Walpole, 27 Dec. 1740, Cholmondeley (Houghton) mss. [6] Walpole to Mann, 1 Apr. and 26 May 1742. [7] Newcastle (Clumber) mss. [8] West mss. The letter exists in draft only. [9] Ibid. 26 Dec. 1744. [10] West to Newcastle, 17 Jan. 1758, Add. 32877, f. 168.

R.R.S.

WEST, Hon. John (1693–1766).

GRAMPOUND 1715–1722

b. 4 Apr. 1693, o.s. of John West, 6th Baron de la Warr, by Margaret, da. and h. of John Freeman, London merchant, wid. of Thomas Salwey, merchant. *educ.* Eton 1707; Grand Tour. *m.* (1) 25 May 1721 (secretly), Lady Charlotte MacCarthy (*d.*7 Feb. 1735), da. of Donogh, 4th Earl of Clancarty [I], 2s. 3da.; (2) 15 June 1744, Anne, da. of Nehemiah Walker, a sea captain of Mdx., wid. of George Nevill, 13th Lord Abergavenny, *s.p. suc.* fa. as 7th Baron de la Warr 26 May 1723; K.B. 27 May 1725; *cr.* Visct. Cantelupe and Earl de la Warr 18 Mar. 1761.

Standard bearer, gent. pensioners 1712–14; guidon and 1st maj. 1 tp. Horse Gds. 1715, lt. and lt.-col. 1717; capt. and lt.-col. 1 Ft. Gds. 1730; col. 1 tp. Horse Gds. 1737–d; brig.-gen. 1743; maj.-gen. 1745; lt.-gen. 1747; gen. of Horse 1765.

Clerk extraordinary to Privy Council 1712–23; verderer, Windsor Park 1718; ld. of the bedchamber 1725–7; P.C. 12 June 1731; treasurer of the Household June 1731–7; ambassador, Saxe Gotha, Mar. 1736; gov. Levant Co. 1736–d.; gov. New York July–Sept. 1737; gov. Gravesend and Tilbury 1747–52; gov. Guernsey 1752–d.

Returned as a Whig for Grampound, West voted with the Administration in every recorded division, except that on Lord Cadogan in June 1717, when he voted with the Whig Opposition. He did not stand in 1722. After his accession to the peerage in 1723, he became one of the principal ministerial representatives in the Lords.[1] On his appointment to escort the Princess of Saxe Gotha to England for her marriage with the Prince of Wales in 1736, Hervey observed that West, now Lord de la Warr,

if the King chose him to prevent the Prince's having any jealousy of the future bride's affections being purloined on the way by him who was sent to attend her to England, was the properest man his Majesty could have pitched upon; for, except his white staff and red ribband as knight of the Bath, I know of nothing belonging to the long, lank, awkward person of Lord Delaware that could attract her eyes; nor do I believe there could be found in any of the Goth or Vandal courts of Germany a more unpolished ambassador for such an occasion.[2]

He died 16 Mar. 1766.

[1] Hervey, *Mems.* 713. [2] Ibid. 548–9.

E.C.

WEST, Richard (c.1691–1726), of Ridge, Herts.

GRAMPOUND 13 Mar. 1721–1722
BODMIN 1722–3 Dec. 1726

b. c.1691, s. of Richard West, London merchant. *educ.* I. Temple 1708, called 1714, bencher 1719. *m.* Apr. 1714, Elizabeth, da. of Gilbert Burnet, bp. of Salisbury, 1s. 1da.

K.C. 1717; counsel to board of Trade 1724; ld. chancellor [I] 1725–d.

The author of a pamphlet in support of the peerage bill in 1719,[1] West was returned as a Whig for Grampound in 1721 and for Bodmin in 1722. On 26 Oct. 1722 he supported a motion to increase the army by 4,000 men. A month later, and again in May 1723, he spoke against a bill for raising £100,000 from Papists. In 1724 he introduced the bill regulating the elections in the city of London and curbing the power of the common council.[2] He was one of the managers of the trial of Lord Chancellor Macclesfield in 1725, soon after which he was appointed lord chancellor of Ireland. Falling ill 'with a great cold and fever' in November 1726, he

died on 3 Dec., leaving 'little more than would answer his debts on both sides of the water'. His family were granted a pension.[3]

[1] *An Inquiry into the Manner of creating Peers.* [2] *Knatchbull Diary*, 16 Dec. 1724. [3] *Letters of Hugh Boulter*, i. 105–6, 123, 145.

E.C.

WEST, Temple (1713–57), of Upper Grosvenor St., London.

BUCKINGHAM 17 Jan. 1753–1754

b. 1713, yr. s. of Rev. Richard West, D.D., prebendary of Winchester and archdeacon of Berkshire, by Maria, 1st da. of Sir Richard Temple, 3rd Bt., M.P., of Stowe, sis. of Richard Temple, M.P., 1st Visct. Cobham, and of Hester, 1st Countess Temple; cos. of the Lytteltons and Grenvilles (qq.v.). *m.* Frances, o. da. of Adm. Sir John Balchen, sis. and h. of Capt. George Balchen, R.N., 3s.

Lt. R.N. 1734, capt. 1738; cashiered 1745; reinstated 1746; commodore and c.-in-c. at the Nore 1748; r.-adm. 1755; second in command to Adm. John Byng (q.v.) in the Mediterranean 1756; ld. of Admiralty Nov. 1756–Feb. 1757, July 1757–d.; v.-adm. 1756.

Entering the navy as a volunteer in September 1727, Temple West received his first command in 1737. Court martialled and cashiered for taking an inactive part in Admiral Thomas Mathews's (q.v.) action off Toulon on 11 Feb. 1744, he was soon reinstated, no doubt through the influence of his cousin, George Grenville (q.v.), a member of the Admiralty board. On 3 May 1747 he was flag-captain to Admiral Peter Warren (q.v.) in Admiral George Anson's (q.v.) battle off Finisterre. During a period ashore he was brought in as a stop-gap for Buckingham in January 1753 at a by-election caused by the accession of his cousin Richard Grenville (q.v.), Lord Cobham, to the peerage, but did not stand again. As second in command to Admiral John Byng (q.v.) he was superseded after the action off Minorca in May 1756, but was appointed to the Admiralty board under Lord Temple next November. Following Byng's court-martial, at which he gave evidence, he struck his flag and later resigned from the Admiralty, writing to Temple on 27 Jan. 1757 that he was 'fully resolved to forego anything rather than serve on terms which subject an officer to the treatment shewn Admiral Byng'.[1] He resumed his post in July but died a few weeks later, 9 Aug. 1757.

[1] Charnock, *Biog. Navalis*, iv. 422.

R.S.L.

WESTBY, Wardell George (d.1756), of Ravenfield, Yorks.

MALTON 1727–May 1731

1st s. of Thomas Westby, M.P., of Ravenfield by his 1st w. Margaret, da. of George (?Matthew) Wardell of Holderness, Yorks. *m.* 30 May 1723, Charlotte, da. of Hon. John Darcy, sis. of Robert Darcy, 3rd Earl of Holdernesse, 1da. *suc. fa.* 1747.

Commr. of customs 1731–*d.*

On Westby's marriage his father gave up to him the estate of Ravenfield, which had been in the family since the early seventeenth century, but he was ultimately forced to sell it owing to the extravagance of his wife.[1] Returned for Malton on the Wentworth Woodhouse interest, he voted with the Government till 1731, when he vacated his seat on being appointed to a commissionership of customs, which he retained till his death, 9 Dec. 1756.

[1] J. W. Clay, *Dugdale's Vis. Yorks.* i. 253 n.1.

R.R.S.

WESTCOTE, Baron, *see* LYTTELTON, William Henry

WESTERN, Thomas (c.1693–1733), of Preston, Suss.

SUDBURY 1715–1722

b. c.1693, s. and h. of Thomas Western jun. of London, merchant, by Ann, da. of Capt. Fisher. *educ.* St. Catherine's, Camb. 1708; G. Inn 1708; I. Temple 1710. *m.* Mary, da. of Sir Richard Shirley, 2nd Bt., sis. and coh. of Sir Richard Shirley, 3rd Bt., of Preston, Suss., 1s. *suc.* cos. to Rivenhall, Essex, 1730.

Western was the grandson of an ironmaster, who died in 1707, said to be worth £200,000.[1] Himself a London merchant, he acquired through his wife the estates of the Shirleys, buying her sister's moiety in 1721 for £6,275.[2] Returned unopposed in 1715 as a Whig for Sudbury, he seconded the Address 17 Dec. 1718, but voted against the Government in all recorded divisions. He did not stand again, dying 7 Apr. 1733, aged about 40.[3] His great-grandson was Charles Callis Western, M.P., created Lord Western.

[1] Luttrell, vi. 130. [2] Horsfall, *Suss.* i. 169. [3] C. F. Smith, 'The Western family of Rivenhall', *Essex Rev.* x. 8.

R.R.S.

WESTFALING, Herbert Rudhale (?1671–1743), of Rudhall, Herefs.

HEREFORD 12 Mar. 1717–1727

b. ?1671, s. of Herbert Westfaling, M.P., of Rudhall by Ann, da. of Sir Thomas Edwards, 1st Bt., of Greete, Salop. *educ.* Magdalen Hall, Oxf. 22 Mar. 1689, aged 17; G. Inn 1688. *m.* (lic. 12 Jan. 1695) Anne, da. and h. of Charles Chappell of Battersea, 5s. *suc. fa.* 1705.

Commr. for stating army debts 1720–2.

Westfaling was descended from Herbert Westfaling, bishop of Hereford 1585–1602. His father, M.P. Hereford 1660 and 1661–79, inherited the house and a considerable part of the estates of the Rudhales, one of the oldest Herefordshire families, into which the Westfalings had married. Westfaling himself was closely connected, both in politics and business, with the Duke of Chandos, who referred to him as 'cousin Westfaling'.[1] Returned as a Whig for Hereford in 1717, after contesting it unsuccessfully with the support of Chandos and Lord Coningsby (q.v.) in 1715,[2] he voted for the peerage bill in 1719. He was re-elected unopposed in 1722, when Chandos instructed his local agent to exert himself to the utmost for him.[3] In 1727 he stood with Chandos's son, Lord Carnarvon (q.v.), but withdrew on a compromise to secure Carnarvon's election.[4] He did not stand again, dying November 1743.

[1] Baker, *Jas. Brydges, 1st Duke of Chandos*, 80, 290. [2] Chandos to Westfaling and Ld. Coningsby, 31 Dec. 1714, Chandos letter bks. [3] Chandos to Capt. Herring, 8 Mar. 1722, ibid. [4] Chandos to Sir Robt. Walpole, 19 Aug., and to Westfaling, 25 Aug. 1727, ibid.

R.S.L.

WHEATE, Sir Thomas, 1st Bt. (1667–1721), of Glympton Park, Oxon.

NEW WOODSTOCK   1690–1695

                    1708–16 Mar. 1714

       24 Mar. 1714–25 Aug. 1721

b. 6 Sept. 1667, o.s. of Thomas Wheate of Glympton Park by Frances, da. of Sir Robert Jenkinson, 1st Bt., M.P., of Walcot, Oxon. *m.* bef. 1688, Anne, da. and coh. of George Sawbridge of London, bookseller, 2s. 2da. *suc. fa.* 1668; *cr.* Bt. 2 May 1696.

Sheriff, Oxon. 1696–7; storekeeper of the Ordnance Mar. 1717–*d.*

Wheate's grandfather, William Wheate of Coventry, bought Glympton, four miles from Woodstock, in 1633.[1] Returned for Woodstock as a Whig in 1715, he voted with the Administration in every recorded division. According to Sarah, Duchess of Marlborough, he would 'not have been chose at Woodstock but for the Duke of Marlborough, who paid all the expense for him' and saved him 'from great distress by giving him a place in the Ordnance' in 1717.[2] He died 25 Aug. 1721.

[1] *Oxfordshire Rec. Soc.* v. 26. [2] To Lady Abingdon, 12 July 1727, Marlborough mss.

E.C.

WHEATE, Sir Thomas, 2nd Bt. (1693–1746), of Glympton Park, Oxon.

NEW WOODSTOCK 1722–1727

bap. 2 Mar. 1693, 1st s. of Sir Thomas Wheate, 1st Bt. (q.v.). *educ.* Wadham, Oxf. 1712. *m.* c.1724, Mary, da. and coh. of Thomas Gould of Oak End, Iver, Bucks., 4da. *suc.* fa. 25 Aug. 1721.

> Cornet, Col. William Stanhope's Drags. 1715.

By the influence of the Duke of Marlborough Wheate secured a commission in a regiment raised for the rebellion of 1715,[1] which was disbanded in 1718. On his father's death in 1721 he contested Woodstock unsuccessfully against the Duchess of Marlborough's candidate but was returned for it against her interest in 1722.[2] When he stood again in 1727 the Duchess complained to Lord Abingdon of Wheate's and his father's 'ingratitude', expressing the hope that Abingdon, who had an interest in the borough, would not support him.[3] In reply she was assured that Lord Abingdon was 'no ways desirous of putting upon your Grace a man so disagreeable as Sir Thomas Wheate'.[4] He came out bottom of the poll, did not stand again, and died 1 May 1746.

[1] Duchess of Marlborough to Lady Abingdon, 12 July 1727, Marlborough mss. [2] See NEW WOODSTOCK. [3] To Lady Abingdon, 12 July 1727, Marlborough mss. [4] 15 July 1727, ibid.

E.C.

WHETHAM, Thomas (c.1665–1741), of Turnham Green, Mdx.

BARNSTAPLE   1722–1727

b. c.1665, 1st s. of Nathaniel Whetham, barrister, I. Temple (1st s. of Col. Nathaniel Whetham, gov. of Northampton and Portsmouth for the parliamentary army), by Elizabeth, da. of Adrian Scrope of Wormesley, Oxon. *m.* Mary, da. of Edward Thompson of Marston, Yorks., 1s. 1da. *suc.* fa. 1667.

> Ensign 15 Ft. 1685; capt.-lt. Sir James Leslie's Ft. 1694, capt. 1694; maj. 11 Ft. bef. 1700; col. 27 Ft. 1702–25; brig.-gen. 1707; c.-in-c. Canada 1709; maj.-gen. 1710; c.-in-c. Scotland 1712; col. 12 Ft. 1725–*d.*; lt.-gen. 1727; gen. 1739.
> Gov. Berwick and Holy Island 1740.

After serving in Scotland, the West Indies and Spain under William III and Anne, Whetham commanded the left wing of the army at Sheriffmuir in the rebellion of 1715. Returned as a Whig for Barnstaple after a contest in 1722, he did not stand again. In or about 1739 he purchased the manors of Kirklington and Hockerton in Nottinghamshire for £25,000.[1] He died 28 Apr. 1741.

[1] PCC 140 Spurway; Thoroton, *Notts.* iii. 99.

S.R.M.

WHICHCOT, Thomas (?1700–76), of Harpswell, Lincs.

LINCOLNSHIRE   20 Feb. 1740–1774

b. ?1700, 1st s. of George Whichcot, M.P., by Frances Katherine, da. of Sir Thomas Meres, M.P., of Kirton, Lincs., sis. and coh. of Sir John Meres. *educ.* Brigg; Magdalene, Camb. 16 May 1719, aged 18. *m.* (1) 27 Nov. 1729, Eliza Maria (*d.*1732), da. of Francis Anderson of Manby, Lincs., 1da. *d.v.p.*; (2) settle-

ment 21 May 1734, Jane, da. of John Tregagle of Trevolder, Cornw., 1da. *suc.* fa. 1720.

Whichcot, whose family had been settled at Harpswell since the early sixteenth century and whose father had represented Lincolnshire 1698–1700 and 1705–10, was returned for the county in 1740 as an independent Whig. Though opposing the motion for the removal of Walpole in February 1741, he voted with the Opposition till 1744, when he went over to the Government, speaking and voting in favour of the Hanoverians on 18 Jan.[1] Classed as a government supporter in 1747, he is described in the 2nd Lord Egmont's electoral survey c.1749–50 as to be 'routed for he is a dangler after Pelham'. On 26 Mar. 1753 he spoke against a bill to permit the export of Irish wool. He died 30 Sept. 1776.

[1] 19 Jan. 1744, Hartington to Devonshire, Devonshire mss.

P.W.

WHICHCOTE, Francis (c.1692–1775), of Quy Hall, Cambs. and Aswarby, Lincs.

CAMBRIDGESHIRE   27 Nov. 1718–1722

b. c.1692, o. surv. s. of Sir Paul Whichcote, 2nd Bt., by Jane, da. and coh. of Sir Nicholas Gould, 1st Bt., of the city of London. *educ.* St. Catherine's, Camb. 1708; Trinity Hall, Camb. 1711; I. Temple 1714. *m.* (1) 1717,[1] Mary (*d.*19 Sept. 1726), da. of Joseph Banks (q.v.) of Revesby Abbey, Lincs., *s.p.*; (2) 1 Mar. 1737, Frances, da. of Edward Hall and wid. of Sir Nevile Hickman, 4th Bt., of Gainsborough, Lincs., 2s. *suc.* fa. as 3rd Bt. Dec. 1721.

> Commr. for stating army debts 1720–2.

When Whichcote was returned unopposed for the vacancy caused by the death of John Bromley, an Oxford Tory wrote to Lord Harley (q.v.): 'I am hard put to it to excuse my Lord Harley for letting a Whig come in to the county of Cambridge'.[2] He voted with the Government, lost his seat at the next general election, and did not stand again. Soon afterwards he sold Quy to James Martin (q.v.), thereafter living at Aswarby. He died 27 Oct. 1775.

[1] *Banks. Pprs.* (Lincoln Rec. Soc. xlv), 48. [2] *HMC Portland*, vii. 246.

R.R.S.

WHITE, John (1699–1769), of Wallingwells, Notts.

EAST RETFORD   26 Jan. 1733–1768

b. 2 Dec. 1699, 1st s. of Thomas White (q.v.). *unm.* *suc.* fa. 1732.

In 1733 White succeeded his father unopposed at Retford, which he represented for 35 years, travelling to London each session in a coach and six, attended by a concourse of servants and outriders.[1] Elected a trustee and a common councillor of the Georgia Society (see Oglethorpe, James Edward), he offended some of his colleagues by leaving the House in 1734 to avoid being put on a committee appointed to consider a petition from the Society on the ground that it might lead to a private bill costing £1,400, though told by another trustee that he had never known one to cost more than £100. 'A professed Dissenter', 'no friend to church establishment', he resigned from the council, though remaining a trustee, in 1736, along with Robert More (q.v.), owing to disagreement with the Society's policy of appropriating land in Georgia to the endowment of the Church of England. In the same year he spoke and voted against a proposal that Parliament should contribute £4,000 towards the repair of Henry VII's chapel. In the debates on the mortmain bill that session (see Jekyll, Sir Joseph), he is described by a Tory as one of the 'Georgians', i.e. of the Georgia trustees, 'the spawn of the gaols committee', who were foremost in invectives against the universities, charity schools, Queen's Anne's bounty, and the clergy generally. In 1739 he introduced a motion for the repeal of the Test Act.[2] He voted with the Government on the Spanish convention that year but was absent from the division on the place bill in 1740.

Re-elected in 1741, after a costly contest, leading to a petition against the other sitting Member, William Mellish, White wrote to Newcastle that unless the petition were 'attended with success . . . the best and last bidder must always have success in that corporation. The sums given for votes have been monstrous . . . and every step taken that can unhinge the borough'.[3] Soon after Parliament met, his absence from the important division on the chairman of the elections committee produced a friendly remonstrance from Newcastle, pointing out that 'my declining, out of regard to you, so late as yesterday morning, to promise to support Mr. Mellish in his petition was the single reason for his voting against us; and I am afraid as the division was so near, my conduct in that respect may be blamed'.[4] White explained that his absence had been due to illness, continuing:

The loss of your question I am heartily sorry for, but it would give me much greater concern should any of the gentlemen in the Opposition think I meant it as a court to them . . . I never was guilty of such a conduct nor never will be; and desire to be in the situation I am in for no other reason than to be able to give a hearty assistance to those persons and those measures which I have always to my utmost espoused. I . . . beg to assure your Grace that you will on every occasion find me honestly, steadily, and affectionately attached to your Grace. I . . . beg you will assure Sir Robert Walpole he may depend upon me and I beg you will add that he knows me much less than he does the rest of mankind if he ever once doubted it.[5]

He voted with the Government in all other recorded divisions of this Parliament. Described by Horace Walpole as an 'old Republican',[6] he died 7 Sept. 1769.

[1] *Mems. House of White of Wallingwells*, 33. [2] *HMC Egmont Diary*, i. 344; ii. 228 et seq., 233, 236, 373; Harley Diary, 15 Apr. 1736, 30 Mar. 1739. [3] 9 May 1741, Add. 32696, f. 494. [4] 17 Dec. 1741, Add. 32698, f. 409. [5] 17 Dec. 1741, ibid. ff. 407-8. [6] *Mems. Geo. III*, ii. 106.

R.R.S.

WHITE, Thomas (1667–1732), of Wallingwells, Notts.

EAST RETFORD   11 Jan.–15 Apr. 1701
          1701–28 Nov. 1702, 1708–11 Jan. 1711
          1715–30 Sept. 1732

b. Aug. 1667, 2nd but 1st surv. s. of John White, M.P., of Tuxford, Notts. by Jane, da. of Sir Thomas Williamson, 1st Bt., of East Markham, Notts. *educ.* Christ's, Camb. 1686. *m.* 28 July 1698, Bridget, da. and h. of Richard Taylor, M.P. for East Retford 1690–8, of Wallingwells, Notts., 2s. 3da. *suc.* fa. 1713.
          Clerk of the Ordnance 1718–d.

White came of an old Nottinghamshire family, tracing their descent as landed gentry back to the beginning of the fifteenth century. Both he and his father, several times M.P. for the county, were friends and followers of John Holles, Duke of Newcastle, the leader of the Nottinghamshire Whigs, whose heir, Lord Pelham, subsequently himself Duke of Newcastle, used to refer to White as his 'first friend' in the county.[1]

In 1699 White acquired through his wife the estate of Wallingwells, carrying with it an interest in the neighbouring town of Retford, for which he was returned as a Whig at five general elections between 1701 and 1710, though three times unseated on petition. From 1715 he held the seat continuously for the rest of his life, securing a place in the Ordnance worth £600 p.a. He voted with the Government in all recorded divisions till his death, 30 Sept. 1732.

[1] Newcastle to John White, 13 Oct. 1767, Add. 33003, f. 386.

R.R.S.

WHITHED, Francis (?1719–51), of Southwick Park, Hants.

HAMPSHIRE   1747–30 Mar. 1751

b. ?1719, 2nd s. of Alexander Thistlethwayte of Compton Valence, Dorset and Winterslow, Wilts. by Mary, da. of Richard Whithed of Norman Court, Hants; bro. of Alexander Thistlethwayte (q.v.). *educ.* Wadham, Oxf. 26 Feb. 1737, aged 17. *unm.*, 1da. *suc.* uncle Richard Whithed at Southwick Park 1733 and assumed name of Whithed.
          Ranger, Bere forest, Hants.

Whithed's uncle left him large estates in Hampshire, in which he was confirmed by the court of Chancery against an attempt by his elder brother, Alexander Thistlethwayte (q.v.) to dispute the will.[1] He lived in Italy from 1740 to 1746 with his cousin John Chute, making friends with young Horace Walpole (q.v.) and the poet Gray, on their grand tour. Returned for Hampshire in 1747 as a government supporter, he died 30 Mar. 1751, leaving his estates to his two brothers, subject to small bequests to his Italian mistress and daughter.[2]

[1] B. Whitehead, *Whitehead Fams.* 24. [2] PCC 128 Busby.

P.W.

WHITLOCK, Sir William (c.1636–1717), of Phyllis Court, Henley, Oxon.

WEST LOOE	1659
GREAT MARLOW	14 Dec. 1689–1695
OXFORD UNIVERSITY	22 Nov. 1703–22 Nov. 1717

b. c.1636, 2nd s. of Sir Bulstrode Whitlock, M.P., of Fawley Court, Bucks. and Chilton, Wilts. but 1st s. by his 2nd w. Frances, da. of William Willoughby, 6th Baron Willoughby of Parham. *educ.* M. Temple 1647, called 1655, bencher 1671. *m.* 1671, Mary, da. of Sir Thomas Overbury of Bourton on the Hill, Glos., 5s. 8da. *suc.* fa. at Phyllis Court 1675. Kntd. 10 Apr. 1689.

K.C. 1689–95; Q.C. 1702–14.

Whitlock, a successful lawyer, began his career with 'much the same principles with his father',[1] an eminent Cromwellian official, but subsequently became a high Tory. Returned unopposed for the University of Oxford in 1715, he was put down as 'a recognised Jacobite' in the list of that Parliament drawn up for George I, which describes him as being well heard by the House of Commons, 'car il ne manque jamais de faire rire'. He spoke against the Address in March 1715, suggesting that the Whig ministry would start a new war and increase the land tax to 6s. in the pound. On 5 Apr. he described the dissolution proclamation, urging the electors to choose as members 'such as showed a firmness to the Protestant succession, when it was most in danger', as 'unprecedented and unwarrantable'. In August he, Shippen, Sir William Wyndham, and John Hungerford are described as the only Tory speakers against the impeachment of the late Tory ministers. 'The others do not speak, though they vote, and a good many do not attend the House'.[2] He also spoke against the septennial bill in April 1716. Known as 'old shoe strings',[3] from his attachment to the fashions of a former age, he died 22 Nov. 1717, aged 81.

[1] Hearne, *Colls.* (Oxf. Hist. Soc.) vi. 109. [2] Egmont Diary, 9 Aug. 1715, Add. 47087. [3] HMC Portland, vii. 231.

E.C.

WHITMORE, Thomas (1711–73), of Apley, nr. Bridgnorth, Salop.

BRIDGNORTH 1734–1754

b. 21 Dec. 1711, 2nd but 1st surv. s. of William Whitmore of Apley and bro. of William Whitmore (qq.v.). *m.* Anne, da. of Sir Jonathan Cope, 1st Bt. (q.v.), of Bruern Abbey, Oxon., 3da. *suc.* fa. 1725; *cos.* Catherine Pope 1754. K.B. 28 May 1744.

Recorder, Bridgnorth 1735–*d.*

Returned on the family interest for Bridgnorth soon after coming of age, Whitmore spoke against a place bill in 1735, but voted against the Spanish convention in 1739, having been 'got within the last hour by the Prince' who 'was the whole while in the House, applauding all abuse and canvassing the Members'.[1] He did not vote on the place bill in 1740. In the next Parliament he was put down in the Cockpit list of October 1742 as 'Pelham', voted with the Administration in all recorded divisions, and was classed in 1746 as Old Whig. During the 1745 rebellion he enlisted in Lord Powis's (H. A. Herbert, q.v.) regiment of militia.[2] He was one of the group of Shropshire Whigs led by Lord Powis, who in 1748 unsuccessfully applied to the Duke of Newcastle on Whitmore's behalf for the office of governor of North Carolina for his younger brother George.[3] In 1753 Whitmore himself wrote to Newcastle asking that he would place his brother 'in some post, as he has nothing but the small younger brother's fortune to live upon'.[4] After his retirement from Parliament in 1754 the struggle for George's preferment was brought to a successful conclusion by his other brother William (q.v.).[5] He died 15 Apr. 1773.

[1] Harley Diary, 22 Apr. 1735; Coxe, *Walpole*, iii. 609. [2] Owen and Blakeway, *Hist. Shrewsbury*, i. 507. [3] 7 June 1748, Add. 32715, f. 174. [4] 1 Apr. 1753, Add. 32731, f. 324. [5] Namier, *Structure*, 249–52.

J.B.L.

WHITMORE, William (?1681–1725), of Lower Slaughter, Glos., and Apley, nr. Bridgnorth, Salop.

BRIDGNORTH 1705–1710, 1713–24 May 1725

b. ?1681, 1st s. of Richard Whitmore of Lower Slaughter by Anne, da. of Sir John Weld, M.P., of Willey, Salop. *educ.* Ch. Ch. Oxf. 16 Apr. 1698, aged 16. *m.* 1707, Elizabeth, da. of his 1st cos. Roger Pope, M.P., of Woolstaston, Salop, 6s. *suc.* cos. Sir William Whitmore, 2nd Bt., M.P., at Apley 1699.

Dep. lt. Salop 1715; recorder, Bridgnorth 1716–*d.*

The Whitmores were an ancient Shropshire family, who made their fortunes as London merchants in the sixteenth century. Returning to the county in 1582, they bought the Apley estate, 3 miles from Bridgnorth, later acquiring property in and around the borough. Under the early Stuarts they sat for the borough, after the Restoration establishing their influence so firmly that from 1660 to 1870, with only a single break, 1710–13, they or their nominees invariably held one seat, and during 41 years both seats.

William Whitmore had the distinction of being the only member of his family ever to lose an election at Bridgnorth, that of 1710. A staunch Whig, he married into a prominent Bridgnorth burgess family who had provided several Members for Bridgnorth in the previous century. Re-elected unopposed in 1715 and 1722 he gave all his recorded votes for the Government. In 1717 he presented the borough with a water-engine to replace the water supply installed by his great-grandfather, Sir William Whitmore, 1st. Bt.[1]

He died 24 May 1725.

[1] J. F. A. Mason, 'Borough of Bridgnorth 1157–1957', *Salop Arch. Soc. Trans.* liv. 196–7.

J.B.L.

WHITMORE, William (1714–71) of Lower Slaughter, Glos.

BRIDGNORTH   1741–1747, 1754–22 July 1771.

b. 14 May 1714, 3rd but 2nd surv. s. of William Whitmore of Lower Slaughter, and Apley, Salop, and bro. of Thomas Whitmore (qq.v.). *unm.*, 1s. 2da.
Capt. 2 Ft. 1735; maj. 1743; capt. and lt.-col. 3 Ft. Gds. 1745; col. army 1751; col. 53 Ft. 1755–*d.*; maj.-gen. 1758; lt.-gen. 1760; warden of the mint 1766–*d.*

William Whitmore was brought in at Bridgnorth by his elder brother, Thomas Whitmore. Like his brother one of Lord Powis's group of Shropshire Whigs, he voted with the Government. He did not stand in 1747, but succeeded Thomas Whitmore at Bridgnorth in 1754. He died 22 July 1771.

J.B.L.

WHITTINGTON, Isaac (c.1709–73) of Orford House, Ugley, Essex.

AMERSHAM   15 Feb. 1754–1761

b. c.1709, s. of Isaac Whittington, citizen and haberdasher of London. *educ.* I. Temple 1728. *m.* (1) 12 Feb. 1736, Miss Fenwick of Bedford Row, Holborn, Mdx., 1da.; (2) 20 Dec. 1759, Miss Hawood, *s.p.*
A clerk in Chancery c.1730–*d.*

Isaac Whittington, a practising lawyer, whose grandfather came from Leominster, Herefordshire, was probably related through his first wife to William Drake (q.v.) of Shardeloes, whose brother, the Reverend Thomas Drake, rector of Amersham, married Whittington's daughter in 1755. Brought in as a Tory for Amersham on the Drake interest at a by-election early in 1754, he died 25 Apr. 1773.

R.S.L.

WHITWELL, *see* **GRIFFIN**

WHITWORTH, Charles, 1st Baron Whitworth [I] (1675–1725), of Batchacre Park, in Adbaston, Staffs.

NEWPORT I.O.W.   1722–23 Oct. 1725

bap. 14 Oct. 1675, 1st s. of Richard Whitworth of Batchacre Park by Anne, da. of Rev. Francis Mosley of Wilmslow, Cheshire; bro. of Francis Whitworth (q.v.). *educ.* Westminster 1690; Trinity, Camb. 1694; ?M. Temple 1694. *m.* (contract 9/20 June 1720) Madeleine Jacqueline, da. of Albert Henri De Sallengre de Grifoort, receiver-gen. of Walloon Flanders, *s.p.* *suc.* fa. 1719; *cr.* Baron Whitworth [I] 9 Jan. 1721.
Resident, Imperial Diet 1702–4; chargé d'affaires, Vienna 1703–4; envoy, Russia 1704–9, ambassador 1709–12; spec. envoy, Prussia May–June 1711; ambassador, Poland June–Oct. 1711, Vienna July–Sept. 1711; minister, Imperial Diet 1714–16; envoy, Berlin 1716–17, The Hague 1717–21; minister, Berlin 1719–22; jt. ambassador, congress of Cambrai 1722–5.

One of the leading British diplomatists of the time, Whitworth wrote to his old friend, George Tilson, under-secretary of the northern department, asking him

> to sound my Lord Stanhope, whether it would not be seasonable to bring me into the House on this occasion, as Mr. secretary Craggs promised me last summer on a new election. Whilst I am abroad, it is but a vote lost, and when I come home, it will keep me in countenance at least, if it does not make me useful.[1]

After Stanhope's death Whitworth raised the matter with Sunderland at the end of 1721.

> I see by all advices a new Parliament will probably be called. In that case, my poor Lord Stanhope and the late Mr. secretary Craggs had assured me, I should be brought into the House. To be in England without it I should make but a very indifferent figure, and neither be able to serve my friends nor my country; and I would not be useless in any place. The Parliaments by the late Act are like to last long, and I hope I am not destined to be always kept abroad, since the foreign business will be of less importance by the general peace. I am therefore obliged to have recourse to your Lordship's friendship and protection for being named at some court borough. Had I been at home for three or four months I should not have troubled your Lordship or the Government on this occasion; but after so long an absence I can pretend to no personal interest at this distance, being known to very few, if not quite forgot.

The result was an offer from Lord Cadogan (q.v.) to bring him in for Newport, which he accepted, though aggrieved at finding that he would have to pay about £600 for the seat instead of getting it free from the Government.[2] Abroad as joint ambassador to the congress of Cambrai during most of his short term in Parliament, he died 23 Oct. 1725 and was buried in Westminster Abbey.

[1] Add. 37383, f. 192. [2] Add. 37387, ff. 65, 377–8; 37388, f. 146.

S.R.M.

WHITWORTH, Charles (c.1721–78), of Leybourne, Kent, and Blackford, nr. Minehead, Som.

MINEHEAD	1747–1761
BLETCHINGLEY	1761–1768
MINEHEAD	1768–1774
EAST LOOE	14 Oct.–Dec. 1774
SALTASH	3 Jan. 1775–22 Aug. 1778

b. c.1721, o.s. of Francis Whitworth (q.v.). *educ.* Westminster 1730–8; L. Inn 1738. *m.* 1 June 1749, Martha, da. of Richard Shelley, commr. of the stamp office, niece of Sir John Shelley, 4th Bt. (q.v.), 3 surv. s. 4 surv. da. *suc.* fa. 1742; kntd. 19 Aug. 1768.

For a short time served in the army; lt.-gov. Gravesend and Tilbury 1758–*d.*; chairman of committees of supply and ways and means May 1768–*d.*

In 1747 Whitworth was returned for Minehead, having since his father's death 'maintained that interest as entirely as he enjoyed it, with a view to offer myself the first opportunity'. On his father's death he had raised the question of the reversion of the West Indian sinecure which George I had intended to give him (see Whitworth, Francis), but had been persuaded to desist, on a promise from Newcastle, with whom he was distantly connected by his marriage, to provide for him. In 1750 he began to press Newcastle for the fulfilment of this promise:

As your Grace has frequently done me the honour to testify your readiness to serve me, I have taken all opportunities of waiting upon your Grace, but have never troubled your Grace for anything, being sensible your Grace would have confirmed your assurances, if an opportunity had offered, therefore take the liberty to trouble your Grace, as your Grace . . .

Next year he applied to Newcastle for a place in the establishment of the new Prince of Wales, later George III:

I entreat your Grace that you will not suffer an old friend to whom you have made such kind professions to be left out on such an occasion, as the honour of being in this young Prince's family is what as a young man I should covet preferable to anything.

On 13 Sept. 1753 he asked Newcastle for the post of warden of the mint, following this up with a letter of 17 Oct. beginning:

I flatter myself I am not out of your Grace's thoughts, so am persuaded though not apprised, of your Grace's good services to procure me the honour of the employment I took the liberty to apply for.[1]

His persistence was rewarded with a secret service pension of £400 a year, which he exchanged in 1758 for a minor military post. He ultimately found his

niche as the paid chairman of the committees of supply and ways and means, for which his published work, *A Collection of the Supplies and Ways and Means from the Revolution to the Present Time* (1763), had qualified him.

He died 22 Aug. 1778.

[1] Namier, *Structure*, 419 et seq.

S.R.M.

WHITWORTH, Francis (1684–1742), of Leybourne, Kent, and Blackford, nr. Minehead, Som.

MINEHEAD	24 May 1723–6 Mar. 1742

b. 9 May 1684, 6th s. of Richard Whitworth of Batchacre Park, in Adbaston, Staffs. and yr. bro. of Charles, 1st Baron Whitworth [I] (q.v.). *educ.* Westminster 1701. *m.* c.1720, Joan Windham of Clarewell, Glos., 1s.

Sec. Barbados 1719–*d.*; surveyor of woods and forests north and south of Trent 1732–*d.*

In 1722 Whitworth stood for Minehead on an assurance from Lord Carteret that he would be supported by the Government. Defeated after a hot contest, he presented a petition only to find, as his elder brother (q.v.) put it, that though 'his endeavours at Minehead had been approved by the ministry, and that he had by great expense and pains in that town broke the interest of a party always contrary to the Government', he was 'discouraged by a great man [Walpole] from prosecuting his right in Parliament' and 'over-persuaded to withdraw it'.[1] However, he was returned for the borough at a by-election the following year, retaining the seat in 1727, when a petition against him was disposed of by a government motion closing the elections committee in order to prevent its being heard.[2] About this time he strengthened his interest by buying an estate near Minehead, which he represented for the rest of his life.[3]

Early in George II's reign Whitworth applied for the reversion of a colonial sinecure, which he had obtained in the late reign, to be granted to his son, on the ground that George I had consented to this but had died before he had signed the warrant. The application was unsuccessful, but in 1732 he obtained the surveyorship of woods and forests, worth £1,000 a year.[4]

Whitworth made his first recorded speech, in support of the Hessian troops, on 3 Feb. 1731. On 12 Apr. following he spoke against a proposal to take off the duty on Irish yarn, expressing the views of his constituents, who, depending on wool manufacture, feared Irish competition, based on low wages. Actuated by similar considerations, on 10 Mar. 1732 he moved successfully for a bill to stop the importation of hops from New England into Ireland free of duty, 'by which the demand in that kingdom for English hops is greatly lessened'. He spoke on the Charitable Corporation bill on 15 May; seconded the army vote in the next session; and 'had very contumelious usage' by the mob outside the House on the withdrawal of the excise bill; 'such language, he said, that was not fit for him to repeat to the House'. On 10 May 1733 he opposed a petition from the trustees for Georgia for more money. According to the 1st Lord Egmont,

> he said the gentlemen concerned in the trust were doubtless disinterested, and meant well, but they did not know the scarcity of inhabitants in the country; he therefore was against sending any English men over, but was for some good laws to regulate our poor and make them useful. We might try what we could do by private subscription, but he was against giving public money. I did not wonder at it [Egmont added] for he told me this morning that he was against enlarging our colonies, and wished New England at the bottom of the sea.

Both his last two recorded speeches, in 1734 and 1735, are concerned with the local interests of Minehead.[5]

Re-elected unopposed in 1741, he was absent from the division on the chairman of the elections committee on 16 Dec. 1741, presumably owing to illness, dying shortly afterwards, 6 Mar. 1742.

[1] Add. 37388, ff. 34, 132; 37390, ff. 103, 277. [2] *HMC Egmont Diary*, i. 81. [3] C. E. H. Chadwyck Healey, *West Somerset*, 222. [4] Add. 33057, f. 501; *Gent. Mag.* 1739, p. 307. [5] *HMC Egmont Diary*, i. 126, 177, 234–5, 275, 362, 373; ii. 26, 162–3; *CJ*, xviii. 686; Stuart mss 159/155.

S.R.M.

WIGLEY, James (1700–65), of Scraptoft Hall, nr. Leicester.

LEICESTER   27 Apr. 1737–21 June 1765

b. 10 Aug. 1700, 2nd surv. s. of Sir Edward Wigley of Scraptoft by Letitia, da. and h. of Arthur Cressey of Brigsley, Lincs. *educ.* Rugby 1713; Magdalen, Oxf. 1718. *m.* Martha, da. and h. of Richard Ebourne of Allesley, Warws., *s.p. suc.* bro. 1716.

Wigley came of a family settled in Leicestershire since the sixteenth century, with extensive estates in the county. Returned as a Tory for Leicester on the corporation interest at a by-election in 1737, he voted against the Administration except on the motion for the dismissal of Walpole in February 1741, when he was among the Tories who withdrew. Re-elected unopposed in 1741, he continued to vote against the Government in all recorded divisions except on the Hanoverians in 1746, when he was absent. The 2nd Lord Egmont wrote of him, c.1749–50: 'Much such another man as Smith' [Edward, q.v.] i.e. 'a good natured Tory who does not love attendance.'

He died 21 June 1765.

E.C.

WILBRAHAM, Randle (?1695–1770), of Rode Hall, nr. Congleton, Cheshire.

NEWCASTLE-UNDER-LYME   26 Nov. 1740–1747
APPLEBY   1747–1754
NEWTON   1754–1768

b. ?1695, 2nd surv. s. of Randle Wilbraham of Nantwich, Cheshire by Mary, da. of Sir Richard Brooke, 2nd Bt., of Norton Priory, Cheshire. *educ.* B.N.C. Oxf. 10 Oct. 1711, aged 16; L. Inn 1711, called 1718, bencher 1743. *m.* 24 Aug. 1722, Dorothy, da. of Andrew Kenrick, barrister, of Woore, Salop, 2s. 3da. (da. Mary *m.* Charles Gray, q.v.).

Vice-chamberlain, Chester; dep. steward, Oxford University.

Wilbraham, a Tory, was returned by Lord Gower at a by-election in 1740 and again in 1741. He remained in opposition after Lord Gower went over to the Government in 1744. During the trial of the rebel lords in 1746, Horace Walpole reported (to Mann, 1 Aug. 1746) that Lord Balmerino asked to be defended by Wilbraham,

> a very able lawyer in the House of Commons, who, the Chancellor said privately, he was sure would as soon be hanged as plead such a cause. But he came as counsel to-day (the third day), when Lord Balmerino gave up his plea as invalid, and submitted, without any speech.

In 1747 he was brought in by his kinsman, Lord Thanet, for Appleby. The 2nd Lord Egmont wrote of him in his electoral survey, c.1749–50, 'Must have some lift in the law considerable. He has strongly declared for us', adding that he was one of the lawyers who 'have highly the esteem of the Tories, beyond all of their profession, except Fazackerley' (Nicholas, q.v.). He made his first recorded speech, 1 June 1753, against an amendment to Hardwicke's marriage bill.[1]

He died 3 Dec. 1770.

[1] Add. 32732, f. 3.

E.C.

WILKINSON, Andrew (1697–1784), of Boroughbridge Hall, Yorks.

ALDBOROUGH   19 Feb. 1735–Sept. 1765
              1768–May 1772

b. 1697, s. of Charles Wilkinson of Aldborough and Boroughbridge by Deborah, da. of Richard Cholmley of Bramham, Yorks. *educ.* Clare, Camb. 1715; M. Temple 1719. *m.* 2 Sept. 1723, Barbara, da. of William Jessop (q.v.) of Broomhall, Yorks., 7s. *suc.* fa. 1735.

Receiver of land tax for W. Riding 1727–34; clerk of deliveries in the Ordnance May 1741–May 1746; chief storekeeper of the Ordnance May 1746–Dec. 1762, Sept. 1765–May 1778.

Andrew Wilkinson's father, Charles, the Yorkshire estate agent of successive Dukes of Newcastle, was appointed receiver-general of the land tax for

Yorkshire, Northumberland and Durham, jointly with his nephew, Thomas (q.v.), in 1718. From Thomas's death that year, Charles was sole receiver till he resigned in 1727, when Northumberland and Durham were detached from Yorkshire, which was divided into two parts, Andrew becoming receiver for the West Riding.[1] Soon afterwards it came out that Charles had become indebted to the Government for over £30,000, of which only part proved recoverable, most of the family property having been settled on Andrew when he married in 1723.[2]

Because of Charles Wilkinson's defalcations—he spent the rest of his life as a Crown debtor in Newgate, where he died in November 1735[3]—the Treasury hesitated to renew Andrew's appointment, but relented on receiving a letter from his father-in-law, William Jessop (q.v.), offering to stand security for him. Succeeding his father as Newcastle's estate agent and manager for Aldborough and Boroughbridge, he claimed before the general election of 1734 that he was 'importuned' by many Boroughbridge voters to stand for the borough and that this would strengthen the Duke's interest. Newcastle wished him to wait till the Aldborough seat of his father-in-law, Jessop, became vacant, pointing out that if he were returned he would have to give up his place, which was not compatible with a seat in the House of Commons. Resigning his office, he was returned on Jessop's death a few months later, subsequently being provided with another place by Newcastle. The 2nd Lord Egmont listed him, c.1749–50, as 'one of the most obnoxious men of inferior degree'.[4] He died 29 Mar. 1784.

[1] Cal. Treas. Bks. xxxii. 355; Cal. Treas. Bks. & Pprs. 1729–30, pp. 428, 468; T 1/274, f. 229. [2] Lond. Mag. 1735, p. 628. [3] Cal. Treas. Bks. & Pprs. 1729–30, pp. 89, 95. [4] Wilkinson to Newcastle, 18 Mar. and 7 Apr. 1734, Add. 32689, ff. 172, 184; T. Lawson-Tancred, Recs. of a Yorks. Manor, 278–81; Cal. Treas. Bks. & Pprs. 1731–4, p. 545.

R.R.S.

WILKINSON, Thomas (1686–1718), of Boroughbridge Hall, Yorks.

BOROUGHBRIDGE   1715–Jan. 1718

b. 1686, 1st s. of Andrew Wilkinson of Boroughbridge Hall by Mary, da. of Richard Cholmley of Bramham, Yorks. educ. G. Inn 1703; Jesus, Camb. 1704. m. cos. Elizabeth, da. of Charles Wilkinson of Aldborough, s.p. suc. fa. 1711.
Jt. receiver-gen. of land tax for Yorks. Dur. and Northumb. Jan. 1718–d.

In 1654 Thomas Wilkinson's family bought an estate in Boroughbridge, where they were among the principal burgage-holders. In the early eighteenth century they attached themselves to John Holles, Duke of Newcastle, and after his death in 1711 to his heir, Thomas Pelham, created Duke of

Newcastle in 1715, whose property was contiguous to their own. Shortly before the general election of 1713 Pelham wrote to his Yorkshire estate agent, Thomas Wilkinson's uncle, Charles Wilkinson:

> As the interest at Boroughbridge entirely depends upon your nephew, I take for the greatest obligation the favour he does me, in letting me recommend one there, and shall always be ready to do all in my power to support his interest.[1]

Returned for Boroughbridge in 1715, Thomas voted for the septennial bill in 1716, vacating his seat in 1718 on being appointed to an office incompatible with membership of the House of Commons. He died the same year, leaving his property to his uncle Charles, who was also his father-in-law and the father of Andrew Wilkinson (q.v.).

[1] T. Lawson-Tancred, Recs. of a Yorks. Manor, 190–1, 249–50.

R.R.S.

WILLES, Edward (1723–87), of Lincoln's Inn, London.

OLD SARUM	28 May–18 June 1747
AYLESBURY	1747–1754
LEOMINSTER	21 Mar. 1767–Jan. 1768

bap. 6 Nov. 1723, 2nd surv. s. of Sir John Willes, l.c.j. of common pleas, and yr. bro. of John Willes (qq.v.) of Astrop, Northants. educ. Worcester, Oxf. 1738; L. Inn 1741, called 1747, bencher 1757. m. 23 Sept. 1752, Anne, da. of Rev. Edward Taylor of Sutton, Wilts., 3s.
K.C. 1756; solicitor-gen. 1766–8; serjeant-at-law 1768; justice of King's bench 1768–d.

Edward Willes, who came into political life about the same time as his brother John, was brought in for Old Sarum by Thomas Pitt (q.v.) shortly before the general election of 1747, at which he was returned for Aylesbury on the Prince of Wales's interest, being classed as Opposition. During a debate in February 1748, on a bill for transferring the summer assizes from Aylesbury to Buckingham, it was alleged by George Grenville (q.v.) that Willes's father, the lord chief justice, had deliberately brought back the summer assizes to Aylesbury, holding them there himself during the recent election, in order to procure his son's return by a grateful electorate.[1] The 2nd Lord Egmont noted in his memorandum book, under 13 Sept. 1749, that 'Chief Justice Willes made me strong assurances of his friendship and gave up his two sons to my direction in Parliament'.[2] In his electoral survey about that time, he wrote against Aylesbury: 'Edward Willes to continue'. Willes did not stand in 1754, when he was succeeded by his brother. He died 14 Jan. 1787.

[1] Parl. Hist. xiv. 222–3. [2] Add. 47073.

R.S.L.

WILLES, John (1685–1761), of Lincoln's Inn and Astrop, Northants.

LAUNCESTON 17 Mar. 1724–May 1726
WEYMOUTH AND MELCOMBE REGIS 9 June 1726–1727
WEST LOOE 1727–Feb. 1737

b. 29 Nov. 1685, 1st s. of Rev. John Willes, canon of Lichfield, by Anne, da. of Sir William Walker, mayor of Oxford. *educ.* Lichfield g.s.; Trinity, Oxford 1700; L. Inn 1708, called 1713, bencher 1719. *m.* Margaret, da. and coh. of Charles Brewster of Worcester, 4s. 4da. Kntd. 23 Jan. 1737.

K.C. 1719; 2nd justice of Chester 1726, c.j. 1729; attorney-gen. 1734; serjeant-at-law 1737; l.c.j. of common pleas 1737–*d.*; commr. for great seal 1756–7.

Lord Carteret used to say that he had make Willes chief justice:

> I will tell you how: I knew him at Oxford: Queen Anne's Ministry had caught him scribbling libels: I had even then an interest with men in power—I saved him from the pillory—now, you know, if he had stood in the pillory, Sir Robert Walpole could never have made him a judge.[1]

He first came to the fore in 1721, when, during the proceedings on a by-election at Minehead, a motion that 'John Willes of Lincoln's Inn had been guilty of a crime in having caused the writ to be delivered to a candidate' was negatived without a division'.[2] He put up for Bishop's Castle in 1722, but withdrew in favour of the Duke of Chandos's candidate, on the understanding that Chandos would find him another seat and pay all expenses. After a great deal of trouble Chandos arranged for him to be put up on Edward Eliot's (q.v.) interest for Launceston,[3] where he was defeated but returned on petition. Only three speeches of his have been recorded. On 30 Mar. 1732, as a lawyer, he unsuccessfully opposed the resolution to declare void the sale of the Radclyffe annuity and the Derwentwater estate.[4] He spoke at length against the repeal of the Septennial Act in March 1734; and on 28 Feb. 1735 he supported the subsidy to Denmark. In spite of his disreputable private life—his passion for gaming, according to Horace Walpole 'was notorious, for women, unbounded'[5]—he was rapidly advanced in his profession by Walpole. When the chief justiceship of the common pleas fell vacant in 1737, the 1st Lord Egmont writes,

> there were two that put in for it, Judge Denton [q.v.] and Sir John Willes, attorney-general. Denton exposed his long service, to which Sir Robert Walpole replied: 'I confess it, but you don't whore; Willes must have it.' 'I did not know,' answered Denton, 'that whoring is a necessary qualification for a chief justice,' and going his way made no scruple to relate the story. Willes accordingly got it, who does not care who knows his attachment to women. An acquaintance of his told him, he heard that one of his maids was delivered of a bastard. 'What is that to me?' said

Willes. 'Aye, but', said the other,' 'tis reported you are the father.' 'Then what is that to you,' replied the other.[6]

After Walpole's fall Willes attached himself to Leicester House, who put him down for the great seal in the future reign.

He was offered the great seal as lord keeper in 1757, but missed it by stipulating for a peerage with it, which was refused by George II.[7] He died 15 Dec. 1761.

[1] Walpole, *Mems. Geo. II*, i. 169–70. [2] *CJ*, xix. 717. [3] Chandos to Oakeley, 27 Nov. 1721, to Carter, 27 Feb., to Brinsden 7 Mar., to Vincent 17 Mar. and to John Willes 17 Mar. and 17 Apr. 1722, Chandos letter bks. [4] *HMC Egmont Diary*, i. 248. [5] *Mems. Geo. II*, i. 89. [6] *HMC Egmont Diary*, iii. 270. [7] Yorke, *Hardwicke*, ii. 407–8.

R.R.S.

WILLES, John (?1721–84), of Astrop, Northants.

BANBURY 26 Nov. 1746–1754
AYLESBURY 1754–1761

b. ?1721, 1st surv. s. of Sir John Willes, l.c.j. of common pleas 1737–61, and bro. of Edward Willes (qq.v.). *educ.* Worcester, Oxf. 3 Mar. 1738, aged 16; L. Inn 1734. *m.* 15 July 1754, Frances, da. and h. of Thomas Freke, Bristol merchant, 1s. 3da. *suc.* fa. 1761.

Filazer for Mdx. in court of common pleas 1752–*d.*

Returned for Banbury by Francis, Lord North (q.v.), Willes, a follower of the Prince of Wales, was classed as Opposition. At the opening of the Parliament, he spoke in favour of the re-election of Speaker Onslow. In 1748, on a bill for transferring the summer assizes from Aylesbury to Buckingham (see Willes, Edward), Horace Walpole reported to Mann, 11 Mar., that Pelham attacked Willes's father, accusing him of ingratitude.

> The eldest Willes [John] got up extremely moved, but with great propriety and cleverness told Mr. Pelham that his father had no obligation to any man now in the ministry; that he had been obliged to one of the greatest ministers that ever was [Walpole], who is now no more; that the person who accused his father of ingratitude was now leagued with the very men who had ruined that minister, to whom he (Mr. Pelham) owed his advancement, and without whom he would have been nothing.

The 2nd Lord Egmont wrote in September 1749: 'Chief Justice Willes . . . gave up his two sons to my direction in Parliament. Willes hopes his eldest son would have some place—dropped that he would prefer the board of Trade to the Admiralty for him',[1] and he was put down for the board of Trade in the next reign. He wrote to his friend, John Wilkes, 15 Mar. 1753:

> I am involved in a very troublesome affair: I have the management of a turnpike bill in which the borough of Banbury is very nearly concerned, and I shall not get it through the House in less than a

fortnight, and am to oppose a bill for an enclosure; these two silly things keep me in hot water and prevent my going out of town.[2]

He died 24 Nov. 1784.

[1] Add. 47073. [2] Add. 30867, ff. 73–74.

E.C.

WILLIAMS, Sir Edward (1659–1721), of Gwernyfed, Brec.

BRECONSHIRE 17 Feb. 1697–1698
1705–July 1721

bap. 6 Nov. 1659, 2nd s. of Sir Thomas Williams, 1st Bt., M.P., of Elham, Kent by his 1st w. Anne, da. of John Hogbeane of Elham. *m.* (lic. 9 July 1675) Elizabeth, da. and h. of Sir Henry Williams, 2nd Bt., M.P., of Gwernyfed, 4s. 2da. Kntd. by 1675.

A member of the October Club, Williams, who had acquired the important Gwernyfed estate at his marriage, was classed as a Tory on his return in 1715, but appears to have changed sides, as he voted for the septennial bill in 1716. No other votes of his are recorded but on the peerage bill in 1719 he was put down by Sunderland as 'pro', and by Craggs as 'doubtful', to be approached through 'Wroth and Coventry', presumably Robert Wroth (q.v.) and Lord Coventry. He died July 1721.

P.D.G.T.

WILLIAMS, Hugh (?1694–1742), of Chester.

ANGLESEY 10 Apr. 1725–1734

b. ?1694, 1st s. of John Williams of Chester by Catherine, da. of Sir Hugh Owen, 2nd Bt., M.P., of Orielton, Pemb.; bro. of Kyffin Williams (q.v.). *educ.* Jesus, Oxf. 3 June 1712, aged 17; G. Inn 1713, called 1718. *m.* (1) Ursula, da. of Sir John Bridgeman, 3rd Bt., of Castle Bromwich, Warws., *s.p.*; (2) Susannah, da. of Edward Norris (q.v.), *s.p.* *suc.* fa. to estates of Bridge House, Chester, Bodelwyddan, Flints. and Nantanog, Anglesey.

After unsuccessfully contesting Chester as a Whig in 1722, Williams was returned in 1725 for Anglesey by the Bulkeleys, the leading Tory family in the county, probably on the recommendation of his first cousin, Watkin Williams Wynn (q.v.), who considered him 'the only person at present in Lord Bulkeley's interest that can in all likelihood meet with success'.[1] In 1727 the Bulkeleys again brought him in on the ground that he 'had done such service that should be remembered by the county and family, and was preferable to any rival'.[2] Voting with the Government in every recorded division, he spoke in March 1732 against a motion to make a holding in the funds as good a qualification for Parliament as land; in support of a bill invalidating the sale of the Derwentwater estate; and on 13 Feb. 1734 against a proposal to make

officers not above the rank of colonel irremovable except by court martial.[3] By voting for the excise bill he made himself so unpopular in Anglesey that in 1734, having lost the support of the Bulkeleys and Watkin Williams Wynn, he withdrew before the poll, once more contesting Chester unsuccessfully.

He died 14 Jan. 1742.

[1] UCNW, Penrhos mss 1335; see also ANGLESEY. [2] Penrhos mss. 1358. [3] *HMC Egmont Diary*, i. 240, 248.

P.D.G.T.

WILLIAMS, Sir John (167?–1743), of Stoke by Nayland, Suff.

ALDEBURGH 8 May 1730–1734

b. 167?, 2nd s. of Reginald Williams of Stoke by Nayland, by his 2nd w. Sarah, da. of Sir Thomas Dyke of Horeham, Suss., sis. of Sir Thomas Dyke, 1st Bt., M.P. *m.* (settlement 4 Mar., lic. 8 Mar. 1709) Mary,[1] da. of Richard Onslow, 1st Baron Onslow, Speaker of the House of Commons, sis. of Thomas Onslow, 2nd Baron Onslow (qq.v.), 3s. Kntd. 23 June 1713.
Director, South Sea Co. 1711–15; sub-gov. R. Exchange Assurance 1720; Mercers' Co. 1723–*d.*, master 1723; alderman, London 1723, sheriff 1729–30, ld. mayor 1735–6.

A wealthy London merchant, 'at the head of the Turkey trade', Williams was said to be 'the greatest exporter of cloth in England'.[2] One of the promoters of the insurance company known in 1720 as 'Onslow's Bubble', which survives today as the Royal Exchange Assurance,[3] he stood unsuccessfully for Minehead in 1723 and London in 1727. A prominent Tory in the city of London, he was a member of the committee of the common council to prepare the city petitions to the Commons and to the Lords against the city elections bill. He was also on the committee which drew up a loyal address upon the accession of George II, couched in such offensive terms that the lord mayor, Sir John Eyles (q.v.), refused to present it. Returned as a Tory for Aldeburgh in 1730, he was one of the members of the woollen manufacture committee of the House of Commons who supported the taking off the duties on the import of Irish yarn in 1731. He voted regularly against the Government, receiving the thanks of the common council for his 'strenuous opposing' of the excise bill.[4] He seems to have been regarded at Aldeburgh as parsimonious, though according to his own account he offered to build a ship at the local yard and to buy all or part of the season's herring catch.[5] He did not stand again but continued active on the Tory side in the common council, who at the end of his mayoralty thanked him

for his constant attendance, his judicious and faithful discharge and great dispatch of the several duties of that high station, his vigilant care in preserving the peace and quiet of this city, for the easy access he has given to our fellow citizens upon all occasions and more especially for the frequent opportunities he hath given this court of meeting together for the dispatch of the public business.[6]

On 4 May 1743 Thomas Carte, the Jacobite historian, reported:

Sir John Williams has been for some time languishing of a dropsy and been tapped several times, and his death is daily expected.[7]

He died three days later, 7 May 1743.

[1] PCC 250 Boycott. [2] PCC 72 Ent; *Gent. Mag.* 1743, p. 274; *HMC Egmont Diary*, i. 130. [3] *CJ*, xix. 344. [4] 29 Jan. 1724, 22 Mar. 1725, 9 and 22 June 1727, 18 Apr. 1733, Jnl. vol. 57; *HMC Egmont Diary*, i. 131. [5] Williams to Strafford, 3 July 1731, Add. 22248, f. 145. [6] 26 Oct. 1736, Jnl. vol. 58. [7] Stuart mss 249/113.

E.C.

WILLIAMS, Kyffin (c.1697–1753), of Bodelwyddan, Flints.

FLINT BOROUGHS   1747–30 Oct. 1753

b. c.1697, 2nd s. of John Williams of Chester, and yr. bro. of Hugh Williams (q.v.). *m.* (1) 20 Dec. 1736, a da. of John Barlow of Lawrenny, Pemb. and sis. of Hugh Barlow (qq.v.), *s.p.*; (2) bef. May 1744, Frances, da. of Sir Henry Bunbury, 3rd Bt., of Stanney, Cheshire, sis. of Sir Charles Bunbury, 4th Bt. (qq.v.), *s.p.* *suc.* e. bro. Hugh 1742.

Kyffin Williams owed his seat primarily to the interest of his cousin, Sir Watkin Williams Wynn (q.v.), though he was, like his elder brother Hugh, a government supporter, classed as such in 1747.

He died 30 October 1753.

P.D.G.T.

WILLIAMS, Sir Nicholas, 1st Bt. (1681–1745), of Edwinsford, Carm.

CARMARTHENSHIRE   18 Dec. 1724–19 July 1745

b. 1681, 1st s. of Sir Rice Williams of Edwinsford by his 2nd w. Mary, da. of John Vaughan of Llanelly, Carm. *educ.* Eton 1698; Queens', Camb. 1698; I. Temple 1699, called 1705. *m.* 19 June 1712, Mary (articles of separation 25 June 1720),[1] da. of Charles Cocks, M.P., of Worcester, *s.p.* *suc.* fa. 1694; *cr.* Bt. 30 July 1707.

Chamberlain, Brec. Glam. and Rad. 1734–*d.*; ld. lt. and custos rot. Carm. 1735–40.

Williams, who won his seat on petition, voted regularly for the Walpole ministry, from which he obtained legal offices, carrying a salary of £500 each, for himself and his brother Thomas, chamberlain from 1731 of the other South Wales circuit. After Walpole's fall he voted with the new Administration on the Hanoverians in 1742. He died 19 July 1745, aged 64.

[1] Sir F. D. Williams-Drummond, *Annals of Edwinsford*, 37.

P.D.G.T.

WILLIAMS, Richard (?1699–1759), of Penbedw, Denb.

FLINT BOROUGHS   22 Mar. 1742–1747

b. ?1699, 3rd s. of Sir William Williams, 2nd Bt., M.P., of Llanforda, Salop and Glascoed, Denb. by Jane, da. and h. of Edward Thelwall of Plasyward, Denb.; bro. of Robert Williams and Watkin Williams Wynn (qq.v.). *educ.* Balliol, Oxf. 11 July 1717, aged 18. *m.* (2) Charlotte, da. and coh. of Richard Mostyn of Penbedw, 1s.; (3) bef. 1742, Annabella, da. and h. of Charles Lloyd of Drenewydd, Salop, 4s. 4da. Inherited estate of Penbedw from 2nd w.

Richard Williams stood for Flint on the Tory interest in 1741 reluctantly, on the insistence of his brother, Sir Watkin Williams Wynn. Awarded the seat on petition, he voted against the Hanoverians in 1742 and 1744, but was absent from the division on them in 1746, and did not stand again. He died 12 Apr. 1759.

P.D.G.T.

WILLIAMS, Robert (?1695–1763), of Erbistock, Denb.

MONTGOMERYSHIRE   12 Dec. 1740–1741
                                    2 Apr. 1742–1747

b. ?1695, 2nd s. of Sir William Williams, 2nd Bt., M.P., of Llanforda, Salop, and Glascoed, Denb.; bro. of Richard Williams and Watkin Williams Wynn (qq.v.). *educ.* Jesus, Oxf. 9 Dec. 1711, aged 16; G. Inn 1711, called 1718, bencher 1737. *m.* Muriel, da. of Arthur Williams of Ystymcolwyn, *s.p.*

Recorder, Oswestry.

A member of the Jacobite Cycle of the White Rose, Robert Williams stood unsuccessfully for Montgomery Boroughs in 1727. He was brought into Parliament in 1740 by his elder brother, Sir Watkin Williams Wynn, to whom he surrendered his seat in 1741 in order to ensure him a place in the House. Resuming his seat in April 1742, he received an address from a general county meeting held in August commending his parliamentary conduct and enjoining him to bring Walpole to justice.[1] One of the signatories of the opposition 'whip' in November 1743,[2] he voted against the Government in all recorded divisions. He did not stand again, and died 18 May 1763.

[1] *Gent. Mag*, 1742, p. 487. [2] Owen, *Pelhams*, 198.

P.D.G.T.

WILLIAMS (afterwards WILLIAMS WYNN), Watkin (?1693–1749), of Wynnstay, Denb.

DENBIGHSHIRE   30 June 1716–1741
MONTGOMERYSHIRE   1741–23 Feb. 1742
DENBIGHSHIRE   23 Feb. 1742–20 Sept. 1749

b. ?1693, 1st s. of Sir William Williams, 2nd Bt., M.P., of Llanforda, Salop and Glascoed Denb.; bro.

of Richard and Robert Williams (qq.v.). *educ.* Jesus, Oxf. 18 Dec. 1710, aged 17. *m.* (1) 20 Nov. 1715, Anne (*d.*14 Mar. 1748), da. and h. of Edward Vaughan (q.v.) of Llwydiarth, Mont., 1s.; (2) 19 July 1748, Frances, da. of George Shakerley of Hulme, Cheshire, 2s. *suc.* to estates of Llwydiarth and Glanllyn, Mont. and Llangedwyn, Denb. through his 1st w. on *d.*1718 of her fa. and 1725 of her sis.; to estates of Wynnstay, Denb. and Rhiwgoch, Merion. on *d.* of his mother's cos. Sir John Wynn, 5th Bt., M.P., Jan. 1719, when he assumed add. name of Wynn; and fa. as 3rd Bt. 20 Oct. 1740.

Wynn was the grandson of Sir William Williams, James II's solicitor-general, who prosecuted the seven bishops. In 1716 he was returned on his father's interest at a by-election for Denbighshire, continuing to represent it but for a brief interval for the rest of his life. In 1718 he inherited his father-in-law's estates, carrying a major electoral influence in Montgomeryshire; and in 1719 Wynnstay and other extensive property in North Wales from a distant kinsman, subject to his taking the name of Wynn. A member of the Cycle of the White Rose, a secret Welsh Jacobite society, he was included in a list of leading Jacobites sent to the Pretender in 1721. He 'audaciously burnt the King's picture' during the general election of 1722, when he was largely responsible for the return of nine Tories out of eleven Members for North Wales. Opposing a loyal address from his county on the discovery of the Atterbury plot, he supported Kelly, the chief agent of the plot, during his imprisonment in the Tower. His vast estates, great electioneering activity, and personal popularity soon made him the head of the North Wales Tories, so dominating Welsh politics that he was called Prince of Wales.[1]

No speech of Wynn's is recorded till 7 Mar. 1727 when he seconded an opposition motion attacking Walpole on a Treasury matter.[2] At the general election of 1727 he had his brother, Robert Williams, returned for Montgomery Boroughs, but the return was petitioned against on the ground that the right of election lay in the freemen of the county town only. In the debate on the petition in April 1728, Wynn observed:

If a right of election supported by two Acts of Parliament, founded upon the union between England and Wales, several ancient returns evidently admitting the right, several resolutions made upon a formal hearing at the Bar of this House . . . is to be broken through, I must appeal to the gentlemen, whose seat in this House can be secure? . . . That scandalous practice of corruption and bribery I thank God has not crept amongst us, but if the number of electors are to be reduced, I am afraid our people could not withstand so great a temptation.[3]

In 1729 he introduced a bill to prevent bribery at elections which passed into law with an amend-

ment by the Lords making the last determination of the House as to the right of election in every constituency final.[4] In 1730 he spoke 'popularly but not much to the argument' against the taking of Hessian troops into British pay and in favour of a reduction in the size of the army, returning to the theme in 1732, 1733, and again in 1738, when his performance is described as 'very weak'. He supported a bill for enforcing the existing land qualification for Members in 1732 and 1733;[5] spoke in favour of the repeal of the Septennial Act in 1734; was one of six Members appointed to bring in a place bill in 1735, when he sent word to the Pretender that he would be 'always ready' to serve him both with his life and his fortune; and opposed the mortmain bill and the repeal of the Test Act in 1736. In 1737, on the motion for an increased allowance for the Prince of Wales,

Sir R. Walpole told Mr. Watkin Williams that if he or Mr. Shippen (q.v.) would vote against it and bring over some of the Tories to do the same he would get £20,000 to be given to Lady Derwentwater [see Bond, Denis], which he refused to do and told Sir R. Walpole that though he should be very glad that poor lady might have something out of her husband's forfeited estate, yet he could neither apply for her or anyone else in so mean a manner.

He spoke against the Address in 1738 and seconded the place bill in 1740. According to Horace Walpole, he always began his speeches with 'Sir, I am one of those'.[6]

In 1740 an emissary from the Pretender, sent to sound the English Jacobite leaders as to their attitude towards a project for a Jacobite rising combined with a French invasion, reported that Wynn was 'hearty and may certainly be depended on'. Thenceforth he became deeply involved in Jacobite schemes, which culminated in the rebellion of 1745.

In 1741, on the motion for Walpole's dismissal, Wynn and another Jacobite, Sir John Hynde Cotton (q.v.), now joint leaders of the Tory party in the Commons, went 'about the House to solicit their friends to stay the debate' but failed to prevent a considerable body of Tories from abstaining.[7] At the general election, on which he spent over £20,000,[8] his candidates for Denbigh Boroughs and Flint Boroughs were defeated, and he himself temporarily lost his seat for Denbighshire, taking refuge in Montgomeryshire till the return was reversed on petition. He participated in the final assaults on Walpole, seconding the successful opposition candidate for the chairmanship of the committee of elections and speaking in support of Pulteney's motion for an inquiry into the conduct of the war.

After Walpole's fall Wynn did his best to secure that the Duke of Argyll, who had had dealings with the Pretender, should become commander-in-chief. On Argyll's refusal to accept this office unless his Tory friends were given places

> Sir Watkin Williams Wynn, with a considerable number of other Parliament men, repaired to his Grace, and exposed to him that unless matters were in a further way of settlement, they should all break to pieces next Thursday, when Parliament was to meet; that when the question about the army should come on, he and the rest were determined to oppose continuing the same number, unless his Grace were at the head of it, and therefore they pressed him hard to accept his Majesty's offer to restore him to his posts.

They not only released Argyll from his pledge to them but even offered to accompany him to court, and when he kissed hands

> above a hundred Lords and Commons, among whom were the chiefs of the Tory party, Sir Watkin Williams Wynn, Sir John Cotton, etc., waited on the King, whose rooms had not been seen from the beginning of the reign so crowded.[9]

The army was duly voted without a division, but next month, on the King's refusal to appoint Cotton to the board of Admiralty, Argyll resigned and Wynn reverted to opposition.

At the opening of the next session in November 1742 Wynn, supported by Pitt, attacked the policy of the new Administration. He followed this up by unsuccessfully moving for the revival of the secret committee on Walpole, seconding a place bill, which was rejected, and voting against the Hanoverian troops. He appears in a list of 'persons of distinction' drawn up for the French Government in the spring of 1743 with the comment: 'il jouït de £18,000 sterling de rente en terres qu'il fait valoir'; and a marginal note: 'indécis dans cette affaire á cause de ses richesses mais au fond bien intentionné'.[10] In the summer of 1743 he and other leading Jacobites met emissaries from the Pretender, their opposite numbers in Scotland, and the French Government to discuss arrangements for a Jacobite rising supported by a French invasion next year. They 'all declared their readiness to give what assistance was in their power, provided a considerable body of troops were landed in England, but would not consent to give any writing under their hand'. When the necessity of raising money was mentioned Wynn said that 'it was natural to expect a large contribution from him, being possessed of a very great fortune, but . . . he was obliged to live at a vast expense, and had it less in his power to be assisting in that way than if his income was smaller'.[11] The French emissary reported that Wales was 'entirely at the orders of

the Dukes of Beaufort and Powis, Lord Bulkeley [q.v.], Sir Watkin Williams and those who think with them, and they have all undertaken to hold themselves in readiness to take to the saddle as soon as the first signal is given by Lord Barrymore [q.v.]', the Pretender's general. Despite fears that many supporters would be loath to turn out in cold weather, the invasion date was fixed for the end of February, when the main business of the House would be over and Wynn and his friends could leave for their counties without exciting suspicion.[12]

Shortly before Parliament re-assembled in December 1743 Wynn became one of the Tory representatives on a committee appointed by the Opposition to co-ordinate their activities in the Commons during the coming session. When Lord Barrymore was arrested at the end of February 1744 on a charge of being implicated in the threatened invasion, Wynn and his Tory colleagues on the committee protested but did not press the matter to a division. At the height of the invasion crisis he nearly defeated the Government on the Denbigh Boroughs petition, which had belatedly come up, only losing it after a protracted struggle, during which the Government majority fell to one.[13] He was almost certainly the 'gentilhomme anglois député par le parti Tori'—referred to as W—who went over in October 1744 to persuade the French Government to make another attempt and was given favourable assurances from the King of France for the English Jacobites.[14]

On the formation of the Broad-bottom Administration at the end of 1744, Wynn was offered a peerage. He is said to have replied that

> as long as his Majesty's ministers acted for the good of their country, he was willing to consent to anything; that he thanked his Majesty for the earldom he had sent him, but he was very well content with the honours he had and was resolved to live and die Sir Watkin.

He followed this by speaking and voting with the Government for the first time in his life. He supported the despatch of an army to Flanders, saying 'that he did not doubt that all his friends would do the same, and that the whole nation would be unanimous in it, because we must all stand or fall together, there being no medium'.[15] Meanwhile he was sending assurances to the Pretender that 'all your Majesty's friends will stand to the engagements of last year', were 'impatient for H.R.H.'s arrival with a body of troops', and answered 'for his success'.

In August 1745, when England was stripped of troops and the war was going badly, Wynn and the other heads of the English Jacobites sent an appeal to the French government for a French invasion, pledging themselves to raise the Pretender's standard in the various parts of the country the moment the French disembarked. On learning that the Young Pretender had already landed in Scotland without French support they made no move, beyond pressing 'loudly and vehemently for a body of troops to be landed near London as the most effectual means to support the Prince, and the only method by which a dangerous and ruinous civil war can be avoided'.[16] In Parliament, when Pitt and his friends attacked the Government for the inadequacy of the steps taken to deal with the rebellion, 'Sir Watkin nor none of his friends meddled in the debate [Lord Hartington q.v. wrote], but left it for us and our new friends to dispute it'.[17] When the rebels reached Derby, Wynn and Barrymore sent an oral message to Prince Charles assuring him that his English friends were ready to join him in the capital, or to rise in their own counties, whichever he preferred. The message never reached the Prince as he had left Derby two days before it arrived there.

Next year Murray of Broughton, turning King's evidence, disclosed to the Government treasonable conversations between the English Jacobite leaders and the Pretender's representative in 1743. 'The moderation of Mr. Pelham and the Cabinet ministers', Hardwicke records, 'then satisfied with having brought the leaders of the rebellion to the block, and having the rest at their mercy, did not choose to push inquiries further'. However, at Lord Lovat's trial in 1747 Murray was allowed to mention the 1743 conversations in his evidence, giving the names of Wynn, Cotton and Barrymore. 'The Tories', Hardwicke adds, 'at first seemed very angry with us for letting the names of Sir Watkin etc. slip out of Murray's mouth, and Prowse, a Tory, but no Jacobite, asked Speaker Onslow if some notice ought not to be taken of it in the House. Mr. Onslow intimated that he believed the parties concerned would not choose it'.[18] Nor did they.

In December 1747 Wynn sent a message to the Young Pretender that 'the whole body of your loyal subjects in England', wished

for nothing more than another happy opportunity wherein they may exert themselves more in deeds than in words, in the support of your Royal Highness's dignity and interest and the cause of liberty, and that if they failed joining your Royal Highness in the time you ventured your sacred person so gloriously in defence of their rights, it was owing more to the want in them of concert and unanimity than of real zeal and dutiful attachment. They beg leave to represent most earnestly to your Royal Highness that if the foreign succours of men and arms so often promised by your faithful allies can be obtained in the present circumstances they will join

the remains of the injured Scotch to be revenged of the others of their misfortunes.[19]

In the meantime he was one of the prominent Tories who agreed to support the Prince of Wales's programme in 1717.[20] His last public action was to attend and speak at a joint meeting between the two opposition parties, at which one of the Prince's friends, 'to the great abashment of the Jacobites, said, he was very glad to see this union, and from thence hoped, that if another attack like the last rebellion should be made on the royal family, they would all stand by them. No reply was made to this'.[21]

On 20 Sept. 1749 Wynn died of a fall from his horse when hunting. 'This accident will in all probability change the whole face of things in that part of the world', wrote Henry Pelham, 'and a great stroke it is for the King and his family. . . . The cause in general must be the better for the loss of such a man'.[22]

[1] Stuart mss 65/16, 178/6; Yorke, *Hardwicke*, i. 76. [2] *Knatchbull Diary*. [3] 'The Montgomery Boroughs constituency 1660–1728', *Bull. of Bd. of Celtic Studies*, Nov. 1963, pp. 301–2. [4] *CJ*, xxi. 265, 301; 2 Geo. II. cap. 24. [5] *HMC Egmont Diary*, i. 26, 240, 346; *HMC Carlisle*, 66, 193. [6] Harley Diary; NLW, Wynnstay mss C. 97, 341F; *Corresp. H. Walpole* (Yale ed.), xvii. 243 n. 8; Stuart mss 194/10. [7] Mahon, iii. 29–30 and app. p.v. [8] NLW, Wynnstay mss 341 F; Add. 32919, f. 267; 35600, f. 232. [9] *HMC Egmont Diary*, iii. 254–5. [10] Stuart mss 248/151. [11] Murray of Broughton, *Memorials* (Sc. Hist. Soc. xxvii), 55, 456. [12] AEM & D Angl. 82, ff. 49–57; J. Colin, *Louis XV et les Jacobites*, 49–50. [13] Owen, *Pelhams*, 199, 214–16. [14] Stuart mss 260/6, 260/107. [15] *HMC Hastings*, iii. 49; Stuart mss 261/54; Mahon, iii. app. p. lx. [16] Sempill to the Pretender, 28 Dec. 1744 and 13 Sept. 1745, Stuart mss 261/54, 268/5. [17] Owen, 286 n. 4. [18] Mahon, iii. 277 and app. p. lxxii et seq.; Yorke, i. 582. See also BARRY, James. [19] Stuart mss 288/172. [20] Add. 35870, ff. 29–30. [21] Walpole to Mann, 3 May 1749. [22] Pelham to Hartington, 30 Sept. 1749, Devonshire mss.

E.C.

WILLIAMS, William Peere (?1664-1736), of Hoddesdon, Herts., and Northolt, Mdx.

BISHOP'S CASTLE 1722-1727

b. ?1664, o.s. of Peere Williams of Hoddesdon, clerk of estreats 1652–75, by his w. Joanna Oeiles, a Dutchwoman. *educ.* Trinity, Oxf. 10 May 1679, aged 14; G. Inn 1680, called 1687, bencher 1722. *m.* Oct. 1697, Anne, da. of Sir George Hutchins, King's serjeant and commr. of the great seal 1690–3, 4s. 2da. *suc.* fa. by 1700.[1]

An eminent lawyer and law reporter who defended one of the rebel lords, the Earl of Winton, on his impeachment in 1716, Williams was frequently employed by the Duke of Chandos on legal business, including the marriage treaty of Lord Carnarvon (q.v.) with Lady Mary Bruce. His name was sent to the Pretender in 1721 as a probable supporter in the event of a rebellion.[2] At Bishop's Castle his return was entirely due to the influence of Chandos, he himself not appearing at the election. Soon afterwards Chandos suggested that Williams should buy his Radnorshire and Bishop's Castle estates, with a rental of £1,500 a year, observing: 'you will have the command of a borough (though I cannot say without some expense attending each election), the lordship of Bishop's Castle (for which you now serve) being a part of this estate, and many of the tenants voters'.[3] However, Williams preferred to buy the manor of Northolt from Chandos.[4] His only recorded speech in Parliament was on 23 Mar. 1726, when he supported a motion for vesting the estates of Richard Hampden (q.v.) in trustees. He did not stand again, and died 10 June 1736, reputed to be worth £150,000.[5]

[1] PCC 71, 76 Eedes. [2] Stuart mss 65/16; C. H. & C. Baker, *James Brydges, 1st Duke of Chandos*, 252. [3] 23 Apr. 1722, Chandos letter bks. [4] Lysons, *Environs of London*, iii. 309. [5] *Gent. Mag.* 1736, p. 356.

J.B.L.

WILLIAMS, *see also* HANBURY WILLIAMS

WILLIMOT, Robert (*d*.1746), of Mincing Lane, London, and Coombe, Surr.

LONDON   1734–1741

m. bef. 1715, Elizabeth, da. and coh. of John Lambert of Garratts, in Banstead, Surr., a distant relative of Daniel Lambert (q.v.), 3da.[1] Kntd. 18 Feb. 1744.
    Coopers' Co. 1736-*d*, master 1743; alderman, London 1736, sheriff 1741–2, ld. mayor 1742–3; pres. Bethlehem Hospital and Bridewell 1741–6.

Returned for London as a Tory[2] in 1734, Willimot, an underwriter, made his first reported speech on the navy estimates, 7 Feb. 1735, saying 'he hoped this House would pour down national vengeance upon the head of that man who should advise his Prince to enter this war without the Dutch', for which Pulteney called him 'the Dutch orator'.[3] On 19 Mar. that year he reported the resolutions of a committee appointed to consider how to prevent the smuggling of wool from England and Ireland to France and of woollen goods from Ireland to Lisbon;[4] and a year later he was one of the minority of twelve to vote against the Westminster bridge bill.[5] On 3 Mar. 1738 he supported the merchants' petition on the Spanish depredations, saying he had in his hand a letter giving details of several English sailors held in chains by the Spaniards.[6] He spoke and voted against the Spanish convention in March 1739, and received the thanks of the common council for his support of the place bill on 18 June 1740. In March 1741 he opposed a bill, which was eventually dropped, to regulate and check frauds in marine insurance. He did not stand in 1741 but continued on several key committees of the corporation of London, including those set up on 25 Jan. 1742 to prepare a petition on merchants' losses, and

on 10 Feb. following to draw up instructions for the London Members. At the end of his mayoralty he received the thanks of the common council

> for his constant attendance, his judicious and faithful discharge of the duties of that high station, for the easy access given to his fellow citizens, and for the frequent opportunities he gave this court of meeting together for the dispatch of the public business of this city.[7]

He was knighted on presenting the city's loyal address to the King on the threatened French invasion in February 1744.[8] He died 19 Dec. 1746.

[1] PCC 27 Potter; *Reg. St. Dunstan-in-the-East* (Harl. Soc.), iii. 36, 38, 53. [2] Stuart mss 254/154. [3] *HMC Carlisle*, 149–50. [4] *HMC Egmont Diary*, ii. 162. [5] Harley Diary, 31 Mar. 1736. [6] Chandler, x. 101; Coxe, *Walpole*, iii. 517. [7] Jnl. vol. 58. [8] *HMC Egmont Diary*, iii. 286.

E.C.

WILLOUGHBY, Hon. Francis (1692–1758), of Wollaton, Notts.

NOTTINGHAMSHIRE   1713–1722
TAMWORTH   1722–1727

b. 29 Sept. 1692, 1st s. of Thomas Willoughby, M.P., 1st Baron Middleton, by Elizabeth, da. and coh. of Sir Richard Rothwell, 1st Bt., M.P.; bro. of Hon. Thomas Willoughby (q.v.). *educ.* Eton 1706–7; Jesus, Camb. 1709–12. *m.* 25 July 1723, Mary, da. and coh. of Thomas Edwards (q.v.) of Filkins, Oxon., 2s. 1da. *suc.* fa. as 2nd Baron 2 Apr. 1729.

Francis Willoughby came of a wealthy Tory family, with estates in Nottinghamshire and Warwickshire, carrying interests at Newark and Tamworth. A few weeks before coming of age he was returned on the Tory interest for Nottingham-shire, which his father had represented 1698–1702 and 1705–10. Re-elected unopposed in 1715, he was defeated after a close contest in 1722 but returned on his family's interest for Tamworth. He did not stand in 1727, two years later succeeding to the peerage. He continued for the rest of his life to play a leading part in Nottinghamshire politics as the head of the Tory interest in the county.[1]

He died 31 July 1758.

[1] See NOTTINGHAMSHIRE and NEWARK.

R.R.S.

WILLOUGHBY, Hon. Thomas (1694–1742), of Birdsall, Yorks.

CAMBRIDGE UNIVERSITY   19 Dec. 1720–1727
TAMWORTH   1727–1734

b. 11 June 1694, 2nd s. of Thomas Willoughby, M.P., 1st Baron Middleton, and yr. bro. of Hon. Francis Willoughby (q.v.). *educ.* Eton; Jesus, Camb. 1711. *m.* 1719, Elizabeth, da. and h. of Thomas Sotheby of Birdsall, Yorks., 5s. 4da.
    High steward, Tamworth.

Willoughby sat as a Tory for Cambridge University till 1727, when he was returned on his father's interest at Tamworth. He is recorded as voting only once, against the excise bill.

He died 2 Dec. 1742.

R.R.S.

WILLS, Charles (1666–1741).

TOTNES 29 Dec. 1718–25 Dec. 1741

bap. 23 Oct. 1666, 1st s. of Anthony Wills of St. Gorran, Cornw. by his w. Jenofer. *unm.* K.B. 17 June 1725.

Ensign, Col. Thomas Erle's regt. of Ft. 1689; capt. 19 Ft. 1691; maj. Col. Thos. Saunderson's regt. of Ft. 1694, lt.-col. 1697, half-pay 1698; lt.-col. 36 Ft. 1701; adjt.-gen. to Earl of Peterborough in Spain 1705; col. 30 Ft. 1705–16; brig.-gen. 1707; maj.-gen. 1709; lt.-gen. 1715; col. 3 Ft. 1716–26, 1 Ft. Gds. 1726–*d.*; gen. 1730; gen. comdg. the Ft. 1739.

Gov. Berwick-upon-Tweed 1715, Portsmouth 1718; lt.-gen. of the Ordnance 1718–*d.*; P.C. 9 May 1719.

After a distinguished military career culminating in the surrender to him at Preston of the rebel army in 1715,[1] Wills was returned by the Duke of Bolton for Totnes, which he continued to represent till his death. In a loyal address in 1727 the Totnes corporation boasted that

our borough now sends to your senate, a Wills; who as he has been the scourge of perfidious rebels at home, will, we doubt not, on occasion, with like courage and success, vanquish and confound all your Majesty's faith-breaking enemies abroad.[2]

Wills, who in 1722 was said to have been a follower of Lord Cadogan's (q.v.),[3] voted consistently with the Administration. In September 1726 it was reported that he was about to become a peer and in September 1739 he seems to have expected to be made a field marshal, but neither promotion was in fact conferred,[4] perhaps owing to 'the remarkable passages which happened at the review of the footguards' in July 1737, when the King told 'Gen. Wills that he lied, who thereupon turned his horse about and rode off the field'.[5] He died 25 Dec. 1741 and was buried in Westminster Abbey.

[1] C. Dalton, *Geo. I's Army*, i. 59–70. [2] *The Totnes Address Versified. To which is annex'd the Orig. Address* (7th ed. 1727), p. 10. [3] *HMC Portland*, vii. 329. [4] *Pol. State*, xxxii. 300; Dalton, i. 69. [5] *Stuart mss* 201/40.

S.R.M.

WILLY, William (?1703–65), of New Park Devizes, Wilts.

DEVIZES 1747–22 May 1765

b. ?1703, 2nd s. of George Willy of New Park, mercer. *unm.*

Director, E. I. Co. 1746–54.

Willy was a London merchant of Barge Yard, Bucklersbury. His brother was mayor of Devizes in 1749 and 1758, and his brother-in-law, a Devizes clothier, was mayor in 1744. Returned as a Whig for Devizes in 1747, he was classed as a government supporter, though the 2nd Lord Egmont, in his electoral survey c.1749–50, noted that 'Willy seems inclined very much to us'. He died 22 May 1765, aged 61, and was succeeded at Devizes by his nephew, James Sutton.

R.S.L.

WILLYS, Sir William, 6th Bt. (c.1685–1732), of Fen Ditton, Cambs.

NEWPORT I.o.W. 31 Jan.–5 Aug. 1727
GREAT BEDWYN 1727–14 Apr. 1732

b. c.1685, 2nd s. of William Willys of Austin Friars, London, Hamburg merchant (4th s. of Sir Thomas Willys, 1st Bt.), by his 2nd w. Catherine, da. of Robert Gore of Chelsea, merchant, wid. of George Evelyn (*d.v.p.* 1676) of Wotton, Surr. *unm. suc.* bro. as 6th Bt. 17 July 1726.

Sir William Willys headed the poll at Great Bedwyn in 1727, presumably with the support of his brother-in-law, Francis Stonehouse of Hungerford and of Stokke, in Great Bedwyn, a former Member for the borough, who had married Mary Evelyn, Willys's half-sister.[1] He voted with the Administration in all recorded divisions till his death, 14 Apr. 1732.

[1] Muskett, *Suff. Manorial Fams.* ii. 102; *Coll. Top. et Gen.* v. 35, 361; *Evelyn Diary*, ed. E. S. de Beer, v. 358 n.6, 7.

R.S.L.

WILMER, William (?1692–1744), of Sywell, Northants.

NORTHAMPTON 7 June 1715–1727
1734–2 Apr. 1744

b. ?1692, 1st s. of William Wilmer of Sywell by his w. Dinah Lancaster. *educ.* Queen's, Oxf. 16 May 1711, aged 18. *m.* 5 Aug. 1720, Lady Mary Bennet, da. of Charles, 1st Earl of Tankerville, 3s. 1da. *suc.* fa. 1706.

Wilmer, whose family had been seated at Sywell since the beginning of the seventeenth century, succeeded to the Northampton seat vacated by George Montagu (q.v.) on his accession to the peerage as Lord Halifax in 1715. A Whig, he voted with the Government on the septennial bill and the repeal of the Occasional Conformity and Schism Acts, but against them on the peerage bill. In 1722 Halifax was pressed by the Tories

to let his brother [Edward Montagu, q.v.] and Mr. Wykes [q.v., the sitting Tory Member] be the two Members and to dispose of Mr. Wilmer somewhere else.

Replying that

if the county would have been content with one

Whig and one Tory he would have been contented for one of each party for the town, but since there were to be two Tories for the county he hoped to have two Whigs for the town,

Halifax put up Wilmer with Edward Montagu, who were returned after a contest.

In 1727 Halifax came to an agreement with Lord Northampton, the other chief local Whig magnate, that their brothers should be jointly returned for the borough.

> Mr. Wilmer and the mob at Northampton are so exasperated that he is resolved to stand by himself, and they say they will choose him in spite of Lord Halifax; what this will end in nobody knows, but at present there is great confusion at Northampton, and a good deal of money spent, which is all the mob aim at.

At the ensuing contest Wilmer was defeated by Edward Montagu and George Compton.

At the next general election Wilmer stood with Edward Montagu against George Compton, whose brother, Lord Northampton, had fallen out with Lord Halifax. This time Wilmer was returned with Compton, Montagu losing his seat.[1] Re-elected unopposed with Compton in 1741, he voted with the Government on the Convention in 1739, the chairman of the elections committee in 1741, and the Hanoverians in 1742. He died 3 Apr. 1744.

[1] E. G. Forrester, *Northants. County Elections 1695–1832*, pp. 43, 45, 57.

R.R.S.

WILSON, Daniel (1680–1754), of Dallam Tower, Westmld.

WESTMORLAND   1708–1722, 1727–1747

> b. 8 Mar. 1680,[1] 2nd but 1st surv. s. of Edward Wilson of Parkhouse, Lancs. by Katherine, da. of Sir Daniel Fleming of Rydal Hall, Westmld. m. 1716, Elizabeth, da. of William Crowle, merchant, of Hull, 4s. 2da. suc. fa. 1720.
> Sheriff, Lancs. 1727–8.

The fortunes of the Wilsons were founded by a wealthy Kendal manufacturer, who died childless in 1653, bequeathing his estates to a kinsman, Thomas Wilson. Thomas's son bought the manor of Haverbrack, including a house known as Dallam Tower, which his grandson, Daniel, rebuilt in 1723.[2] A staunch Whig, who claimed that he 'never was backward, but all of a piece',[3] he represented his county for 34 years, during which, after 1715, all his recorded votes were for the Government, except on the peerage bill. In 1737 his brother-in-law, George Crowle (q.v.), told Walpole that considering

> the great expense he has already been at for 30 years always in support of the constitution both in Parliament and at home without the least assistance or bounty from the Crown, I am almost persuaded another instance will not be found of any gentleman

of his fortune and figure in life, particularly by his natural interest and character in that county.[4]

He stood down in favour of his son, Edward (q.v.), in 1747 and died 31 May 1754, leaving the reputation of 'an extremely honest man, a good neighbour, and fond of peace and quietness'.[5]

[1] *HMC Le Fleming*, 394. [2] *Beetham Repository* (Cumb. & Westmld. Antiq. & Arch. Soc. Tract ser. no. 7), pp. 138–42. [3] To Jas. Craggs, 31 Dec. [1718], Stowe mss 246, f. 156. [4] 7 May 1737, Cholmondeley (Houghton) mss. [5] *Beetham Repository*, 141.

R.R.S.

WILSON, Edward (?1719–64), of Dallam Tower, Westmld.

WESTMORLAND   1747–1754

> b. ?1719, 1st s. of Daniel Wilson (q.v.). educ. Queen's, Oxf. 27 June 1738, aged 18. m. 19 June 1746, Dorothy, da. and coh. of Sir William Fleming, 1st Bt., of Rydal Hall, Westmld., 4s. 7da. suc. fa. 1754.

Returned unopposed for Westmorland, Edward Wilson, like his father, was classed as a government supporter. He did not stand in 1754, but stood unsuccessfully in 1761 'to support the independency of the county'.[1] He died in 1764.

[1] B. Bonsall, *Cumb. & Westmld. Elections*, 55–56.

R.R.S.

WINCHESTER, Mq. of, *see* **POWLETT, Charles**

WINDHAM, William (c.1674–1730), of Earsham, Norf.

SUDBURY   1722–1727
ALDEBURGH   1727–22 Apr. 1730

> b. c.1674, 2nd s. of William Windham of Felbrigg, Norf. by Catherine, da. of Sir Joseph Ashe, 1st Bt., M.P., of Twickenham, Mdx.; e. bro. of Joseph Windham Ashe (q.v.). educ. Eton c.1685. m. Sept. 1705, Anne, da. of Sir Charles Tyrrell, 2nd Bt., of Heron, Essex, 2s. 1da.
> Cornet 6 Drag. Gds. 1698, capt. 1702, lt.-col. 1706, res.1712; lt.-gov. Chelsea Hospital 1726–d.

The younger son of a Norfolk squire by the daughter of a wealthy merchant, Windham served under Marlborough, losing a leg at Blenheim. In 1720 he bought an estate at Earsham, where he built a house out of his profits from the South Sea bubble.[1] Entering Parliament in 1722 for the venal borough of Sudbury, he obtained a place, whose salary was raised from £200 to £400 'in view of his sufferings in the service'.[2] Returned on the Treasury interest for Aldeburgh in 1727, no doubt through the influence of his first cousin, Lord Townshend, he died 22 Apr. 1730.

[1] R. W. Ketton-Cremer, *Norf. Portraits*, 70, 79. [2] C. G. T. Dean, *Chelsea Hospital*, 211.

R.R.S.

WINDHAM, William (c.1706–89), of Earsham, Norf.

ALDEBURGH 1747–1761
HELSTON 4 Feb. 1766–1768

b. c.1706, 1st s. of William Windham of Earsham and nephew of Joseph Windham Ashe (qq.v.). *m.* Apr. 1734, Mary, da. of Charles Howard, wid. of Henry Scott, 1st Earl of Delorain [S], 1s. *suc.* fa. 1730.

Sub-gov. to Duke of Cumberland 1731; afterwards comptroller of his household till the Duke's death in 1765.

Appointed sub-governor to the ten-year-old Duke of Cumberland, Windham married the governess of the younger Princesses, a lady who

engrossed the dalliance of the King's looser hours, his Majesty having chosen, not from any violence of passion, but as a decent convenient, natural, and unexceptionable commerce, to make the governess of his two youngest daughters his whore, his two eldest daughters convenient [i.e. to make a convenience of their apartment], and the guardian of his son's youth and morals his cuckold.[1]

Returned for Aldeburgh in 1747 on Pelham's recommendation,[2] classed as a government supporter, he died 4 May 1789.

[1] Hervey, *Mems.* 745. [2] Pelham to Bedford, 28 Dec. 1746, Bedford mss.

R.R.S.

WINDHAM ASHE, Joseph (1683–1746), of Twickenham, Mdx.

DOWNTON 1734–1741, 4 Jan. 1742–30 July 1746

bap. 11 Aug. 1683,[1] yr. s. of William Windham of Felbrigg, Norf. and bro. of William Windham (*d.* 1730, q.v.). *m.* 1715, Martha, o. surv. da. and h. of Sir James Ashe, 2nd Bt., M.P., of Twickenham, 1da., assuming surn. name of Ashe 1733.

Cashier to salt commissioners c.1718–Apr. 1734.[2]

Windham Ashe was related on his father's side to the Windhams of Norfolk and through his mother and wife to the Ashes of Heytesbury, whose name he assumed on his wife's succession to her father's property in 1733. This included a lease of the manor of Downton, carrying with it the appointment of the returning officer of that borough, for which he was returned as a government supporter in 1734. In 1741 he stood unsuccessfully on the government interest for Bishop's Castle, having been displaced from Downton by Anthony Duncombe (q.v.), who had gained control of that borough and required the seat for his brother-in-law John Verney (q.v.). On Verney's death in 1742 Ashe was brought in for Downton by Duncombe, to whom he soon afterwards transferred the lease of the manor. On 18 Jan. 1743 he was committed to the custody of the serjeant at arms for defaulting on a call of the House—the last Member for 30

years to be punished for this offence.[3] He continued to support the Government till his death, 30 July 1746.

[1] R. S. Cobbett, *Memorials of Twickenham*, 49. [2] *Cal. Treas. Bks. and Pprs.* 1731–4, p. 545. [3] *CJ.* xxiv. 383.

R.S.L.

WINDSOR, Hon. Andrews (1678–1765), of Southampton.

BRAMBER 1710–1715
MONMOUTH 13 May 1720–1722

b. 1678, 4th s. of Thomas Windsor, 1st Earl of Plymouth, being 3rd s. by his 2nd w. Ursula, da. and coh. of Sir Thomas Widdrington, M.P., Speaker of the House of Commons, of Cheeseburn Grange, Northumb.; yr. bro. of Hon. Dixie Windsor (q.v.). *unm.*

Cornet, R. Horse Gds. 1698; capt. and lt.-col. 1 Ft. Gds. 1703; brevet-col. 1706; col. 28 Ft. 1709–15; brig.-gen. 1711.

A professional soldier, who had fought at Blenheim, Ramillies and Malplaquet, Windsor represented Bramber as a Tory on the interest of his elder brother, Lord Windsor, under Queen Anne. Narrowly defeated in 1715 for Monmouth on the Duke of Beaufort's interest, he was one of the Tory officers who were dismissed on the outbreak of the rebellion that year. Returned unopposed for Monmouth at a by-election in 1720, he once more contested Bramber in 1722 but was unsuccessful. He did not stand again, dying about November 1765.[1]

[1] *Lond. Mag.* 1765, p. 598; PCC 164 Tyndall.

P.D.G.T./R.S.L.

WINDSOR, Hon. Dixie (?1673–1743), of Gamlingay, Cambs.

CAMBRIDGE UNIVERSITY 1705–1727

b. ?1673, 2nd s. of Thomas Windsor, 1st Earl of Plymouth, by his 2nd w.; bro. of Hon. Andrews Windsor (q.v.). *educ.* Westminster; Trinity, Camb. 26 June 1691, aged 17, fellow 1697. *m.* Dorothy, da. and eventually coh. of Sir Richard Stote of Jesmond Hall, Northumb., *s.p.*

Capt.-lt. Lord Windsor's regt. of Horse 1706; storekeeper of the Ordnance 1712–17.

Dixie Windsor, the brother-in-law of William Shippen (q.v.), represented Cambridge for 22 years. A moderate Tory, he was allowed to retain his place in the Ordnance for some time after George I's accession. A member of the secret committee on the South Sea affair, he made his only recorded speech in favour of Sir John Blunt on the question of the allowances to be made to the South Sea directors out of their forfeited estates.

Windsor lost his seat in 1727 when, according to

Cole, the Cambridge antiquary, a number of his supporters, headed by Dr. Gooch, the master of Caius, afterwards bishop of Ely, decided to go over to the Government. At the general election that year, Cole writes,

> a prebend of Canterbury being vacant, which Dr. Gooch afterwards was promoted to, at which time Mr. Windsor and Dr. Gooch coming down from London together in the same coach, and seemingly as great friends as ever, after Mr. Windsor had been in the university and found there was a strong party formed against him, he came to Dr. Gooch's lodge in Caius college, whom he found shaving himself, and complaining to the Doctor, whom he supposed to be most hearty in his cause, that he found the university much altered, and that if the court party would set up a broomstick he believed they would vote for him, to Mr. Windsor's no small surprise, the Doctor turned about, and very gravely told him, 'and so must I'.[1]

Windsor made an unsuccessful attempt to recover his seat in 1734, when he was also defeated at Bramber. He died 20 Oct. 1743.

[1] Add. 5833, f. 233.

R.R.S.

WINDSOR, Hon. Herbert (1707–58).

CARDIFF BOROUGHS   1734–8 June 1738

> bap. 1 May 1707, 1st surv. s. of Thomas Windsor, M.P., 1st Visct. Windsor [I] and Baron Mountjoy [GB], by Charlotte, da. and h. of Philip Herbert, 7th Earl of Pembroke, wid. of John Jeffreys, 2nd Baron Jeffreys. m. 16 Apr. 1737, Alice (worth £60,000), da. of Sir John Clavering, 3rd Bt., of Axwell, co. Dur., sis. and coh. of Sir James Clavering, 4th Bt., 2s. 2da. suc. fa. as 2nd Visct. and 2nd Baron 8 June 1738.

Windsor stood unsuccessfully for Bramber in 1734, when he was brought in unopposed as a Tory on his family's interest for Cardiff. On succeeding his father in 1738, he was called to the Upper House as Lord Mountjoy. He died 25 Jan. 1758.

P.D.G.T.

WINFORD, see GEERS

WINNINGTON, Edward, see JEFFERIES (formerly WINNINGTON)

WINNINGTON, Francis (b.1704), of Broadway, Worcs.

DROITWICH   9 Dec. 1747–1754

> b. Feb. or Mar. 1704, 1st s. of Francis Winnington of Broadway, Worcs. (e. bro. of Edward Jefferies, formerly Winnington, q.v.) by Anne, da. of Thomas Jackson of London. educ. Westminster, Jan. 1717, aged 12; Trinity, Oxf. 29 Mar. 1721, aged 17; M. Temple 1722, called 1728. m. Susannah Courtney, 2da.
>
> Solicitor to Admiralty 1733–June 1747.

Francis Winnington was the first cousin of Thomas Winnington (q.v.), to whom he presumably owed his appointment as solicitor to the Admiralty in 1733. He resigned this post to stand for Droitwich in 1747 to preserve the family interest there till his nephew, Edward Winnington, Thomas Winnington's heir, came of age. Returned on petition, he is probably the Mr. Winnington who lost a secret service pension of £200 a year in 1754,[1] when he did not stand. The date of his death is unknown.

[1] Add. 33038, f. 352.

R.R.S.

WINNINGTON, Thomas (1696–1746), of Stanford Court, Worcs.

DROITWICH   31 Jan. 1726–1741
WORCESTER   1741–23 Apr. 1746

> b. 31 Dec. 1696, 2nd but 1st surv. s. of Salwey Winnington, M.P., of Stanford Court (e. bro. of Edward Jefferies, formerly Winnington, q.v.) by Anne, da. of Thomas Foley, M.P., of Witley Court, Worcs., sis. of Thomas Foley, M.P., 1st Baron Foley, and sis.-in-law to Robert Harley, M.P., 1st Earl of Oxford. educ. Westminster; Ch. Ch. Oxf. 1713; M. Temple 1714. m. 6 Aug. 1719, Love, da. of Sir James Reade, 2nd Bt., of Brocket Hall, Herts., sis. and coh. of Sir John Reade, 3rd Bt., s.p.s. suc. fa. 1736.
>
> Recorder, Worcester 1727–d.; ld. of Admiralty 1730–6, of Treasury 1736–41; P.C. 27 Apr. 1741; cofferer of the Household 1741–3; paymaster gen. 1743–d.

When Thomas Winnington died Horace Walpole described him as 'one of the first men in England, from his parts and from his employment' who had 'left nobody equal to him, as before nobody was superior to him except my father'. In 1752 he wrote of Winnington in his memoirs:

> His jolly way of laughing at his own want of principles had revolted all the graver sort . . . He had infinitely more wit than any man I ever knew, and it was as ready and quick as it was constant and unmeditated. His style was a little brutal; his courage not at all so; his good-humour inexhaustible: it was impossible to hate or to trust him.

His final estimate about 1759 was:

> Winnington had unluckily lived when all virtue had been set to notorious sale, and in ridicule of false pretences had affected an honesty in avowing whatever was dishonourable.[1]

Winnington was brought up as a Tory.

> His father still living [wrote Thomas Carte, the Jacobite historian, in 1734], and his eldest brother now dead I know perfectly well, they were both very honest men [i.e. Jacobites]. This who is now the eldest son and heir to a very noble estate besides a good one in possession[2] was bred up in the same sentiments.[3]

Succeeding his uncle Edward Jefferies (q.v.) at Droitwich, where his family controlled one seat, he quickly made his reputation as a rising member of the Opposition. But on 31 Jan. 1729, ten days after speaking on the Address against the Administration, in a debate on the army,

> Mr. Winnington, a Tory, and one I never knew on the Ministry's side before, said the point before us was whether to continue the same number of troops as the year before, therefore he would not go back to consider how we came into the present bad situation. That he thought the best method to get out of it was to show vigour and not disband forces at a time when all other nations augment theirs. His speech was premeditated and long.

Shortly after this volte-face he showed the thoroughness of his defection by discharging his duties as chairman of a committee of the whole House with such pro-government bias that most of the opposition Members walked out. 'That young dog,' Sir John Hynde Cotton (q.v.) exclaimed to Walpole, 'promised that he would always stand by us'.[4]

By the next session Winnington had become one of the leading government spokesmen. He spoke fifth for the Government in the full-dress debate of 4 Feb. 1730 on the Hessians; on 16 Feb. he was one of the five chief government speakers who were 'violently against' an opposition bill for excluding pensioners from the House of Commons; in the Dunkirk debate on 27 Feb. he figured in a ministerial manoeuvre to side-track the opposition motion; and on 18 Mar. he was entrusted with a motion closing the elections committee prematurely in order to prevent it from hearing a petition against a government supporter. At the end of the session he was made a lord of the Admiralty, a position for which he had no obvious qualifications. When in 1731, on a fresh opposition pensions bill, he called Pulteney to order for talking about places, observing that 'he never knew before that places were pensions', Pulteney raised 'a prodigious laugh' at Winnington's expense by retorting that 'if a person enjoys an office he knows nothing of, he looked on that office to be no more than a pension'. In 1732 he introduced a bill for assisting the sugar colonies, which led to the Molasses Act of 1733; in the debate on the city of London's petition against the excise bill, 'in which the great speakers on both sides appeared', he spoke first for the Government; and generally he was, 'from his party-knowledge and application, of infinite use to Sir Robert Walpole in the House of Commons'.[5]

In the next Parliament Winnington and his friends, Hanbury Williams and the two Fox brothers (qq.v.), combined under Hervey to push their claims to promotion. In 1735 Hervey strongly pressed Walpole to appoint Winnington to a vacancy on the Treasury board but was told, 'you know I am the only friend (yourself excepted) he has in the Court, and that both the King and Queen have great prejudices against him'. When Winnington showed his resentment at being passed over by 'voting in public with Sir Robert and talking in private against him', Hervey 'insisted on his making the option of either quitting his employment . . . or . . . being thoroughly reconciled. He advised the last, and his advice was followed'.[6] Promoted to the Treasury next year, Winnington helped Walpole to defeat Sir John Barnard's (q.v.) scheme for reducing the interest on the national debt in 1737, answered Pulteney extremely well on the Spanish convention in 1739, and secured another step in 1741, when he succeeded old Horace Walpole as cofferer of the Household.

At the general election of 1741 Winnington was returned for Worcester as well as Droitwich, choosing to sit for Worcester. In the new Parliament he, Pelham, and Yonge (q.v.), Walpole's chief assistants in the Commons, stood by their leader, ably defending him in the great debate of 21 Jan. on Pulteney's motion for a committee of inquiry into the Administration. On 19 Feb., after Walpole's resignation, they showed

> that the old courtiers and their party in the House of Commons were resolved to stick together and keep up their strength: for in the committee that sat . . . till one o'clock in the morning, upon the Colchester election, Hen. Pelham, Sir Will. Yonge, Mr. Winnington, etc. battled it in favour of the sitting members, who were Sir Robert Walpole's friends.

On 2 Mar., supporting Pelham in opposing a motion indicting the late Government for failing to protect shipping, Winnington himself was personally attacked as one of the 'guilty' men. Though politically loyal to Walpole, he was persuaded by his mistress, Lady Townshend, not to visit him after his fall, thus offending 'the steady Old Whigs'.[7]

Along with Pelham and Yonge, Winnington retained his post under the new Administration, whose policy he defended on the Address at the opening of the next session, and again in the debate of 10 Dec. 1742 on the Hanoverians. On Pelham's appointment to be head of the Treasury in August 1743, Walpole, now Lord Orford, wrote to him that 'Winnington must be had in the way that he can, or will be had'. Succeeding to Pelham's former post of paymaster general, he was re-elected for Worcester, in spite of a letter from the local corporation denouncing his political conduct.[8]

During the struggle between Granville and the Pelhams George II relied on Winnington to replace

Pelham as leader of the House of Commons. In September 1745 he suggested Winnington for the post of secretary of state in a new government excluding the Pelhams: in November Newcastle referred to Winnington as one of George II's 'confidants': in the controversy over the raising of new regiments against the rebels he voted against the Government at the King's instigation or at least with his open approval; and the attempt to form a Bath-Granville ministry at the beginning of 1746 was based on George II's belief that Winnington would consent to undertake the management of the House of Commons. But Winnington, 'though far from being a friend to Mr. Pelham, and wishing well to Lord Granville, yet understood his own interest too well' to accept. Warning George II that 'the new ministry could neither support him nor themselves, and that they could not depend upon more than thirty-one lords and eighty commoners,' he declared his intention of resigning with the rest of the Government; and was ultimately commissioned by the King, 'as the only honest man about him', to invite Pelham and his colleagues to return to their posts.

Winnington did not long survive his return to office. His death, Horace Walpole writes, was 'a cruel tragedy'. 'Not quite fifty, extremely temperate and regular, and of a constitution remarkably strong, hale and healthy', he contracted rheumatic fever and put himself in the hands of a quack, who bled and purged him to death in a few days.[9] He died 23 Apr. 1746 at the height of his powers and reputation.

[1] To Mann, 25 Apr. 1746; *Mems. Geo. II*, i. 174; iii. 67. [2] His wife's estate of Brocket, Herts. [3] Stuart mss 174/68. [4] *HMC Egmont Diary*, iii. 337; *Knatchbull Diary*, 13 Mar. 1729; *Mems. Geo. II*, i. 33. [5] *HMC Egmont Diary*, i. 28, 50, 72, 81, 136–7, 333–5, 358–9; *CJ*, xxi. 782; Hervey, *Mems.* 451. [6] *Mems. Geo. II*, i. 205; Fitzmaurice, *Shelburne*, i. 42; Hervey, 451–5. [7] Coxe, *Walpole*, i. 694; *HMC Egmont Diary*, iii. 255, 258; Walpole to Mann, 3 Mar. 1742; *Mems. Geo. II*, i. 174. [8] Owen, *Pelhams*, 149, 151; Coxe, *Pelham*, i. 91–93; *Gent. Mag.* 1742, p. 581. [9] Owen, 282, 289, 295; P. Yorke, *Hardwicke*, i. 371; *Mems. Geo. II*, i. 173; Walpole to Mann, 14 Feb., 25 Apr. 1746.

R.R.S.

WINSTANLEY, James (c.1667–1719), of Braunstone Hall, Leics.

LEICESTER 1701–22 Jan. 1719

b. c.1667, o.s. of Clement Winstanley of Gray's Inn and Braunstone by Catherine, da. of Sir Francis Willoughby, M.P. *educ.* Jesus, Camb. 1684; G. Inn 1688. *m.* c.1701, Frances, da. and coh. of James Holt of Castleton, Lancs., 4s. 5da. *suc.* fa. 1672.

Winstanley was the grandson of James Winstanley of Gray's Inn, recorder of Leicester 1653–62, who purchased the manor of Braunstone, two miles from Leicester, in 1650.[1] A moderate Tory, who

had voted against the French commercial treaty, he was re-elected unopposed for Leicester in 1715. He voted against the septennial bill in 1716, was absent from the division on the repeal of the Occasional Conformity and Schism Acts in 1719, and died a fortnight later, 22 Jan. 1719, aged 51.

[1] Nichols, *Leics.* iv. 629*.

E.C.

WITHER, Charles (1684–1731), of Oakley Hall, Hants.

WHITCHURCH 17 Feb–15 Apr. 1708
CHRISTCHURCH 1727–20 Nov. 1731

b. 24 July 1684, 1st s. of Charles Wither of Oakley Hall by Dorothy, da. of Sir William Smith, 1st Bt., M.P., of Radclive, Bucks. *educ.* Balliol, Oxf. 1700; Grand Tour (Holland). *m.* 17 July 1707, Frances, da. of Thomas Wavell of Winchester, 1s. *d.v.p.* 4da. *suc.* fa. 1697.
Sheriff, Hants 1707–8; commr. of woods and forests 1720–*d.*

Wither, whose family had been seated at Oakley Hall since 1626, stood unsuccessfully for Shaftesbury in 1722. Returned as a government supporter for Christchurch in 1727, he voted with the Administration on the Hessians in 1730, and died 20 Nov. 1731.

P.W.

WITTEWRONG, Sir John, 3rd Bt. (1673–1722), of Stantonbury, Bucks.

AYLESBURY 1705–1710
CHIPPING WYCOMBE 1713–30 Jan. 1722

bap. 11 July 1673, 1st surv. s. of Sir John Wittewrong, 2nd Bt., of Stantonbury by his 2nd w. Martha Seabrook, niece of Edward Backwell, goldsmith, alderman of London. *m.* c.1695, Mary da. of Samuel White, London merchant, 6s. 5da. *suc.* fa. 30 Jan. 1697.
Col. new regt. of Ft. [I] 1709–12; of another 1716–18.

Wittewrong was descended from a Flemish immigrant, who had settled in England in the sixteenth century, making a fortune as a brewer. His grandfather, the first baronet, fought on the parliamentary side in the civil war and sat for Hertfordshire in one of Cromwell's Parliaments. He himself sat successively for Aylesbury and Wycombe attached to Lord Wharton, who as lord lieutenant of Ireland procured for him the command of a newly raised regiment on the Irish establishment in 1709. On the raising of new regiments to deal with the rebellion of 1715 he presented a petition to the King stating that he had

always supported the Protestant succession and his Majesty's interest, for which he has spent great sums in the county of Bucks. Has served as a Member of Parliament for more than twelve years [actually six] and is still a Member.

During the last ministry much injustice was done him and he rejected several advantageous offers as his principles prevented his entering into the measures that were then on foot.

He has had the honour to serve as a colonel of infantry and he would rather be cashiered than sell out.

Notwithstanding such a character and his zeal for his Majesty, he has had the misfortune to be excluded from the new levies, several colonels of less standing than him have been preferred, and many persons have had civil employments without anyone having the least regard for the petitioner.

He therefore humbly prays for the command of a regiment, or to be put on the excise commission, or in such other employment as his Majesty shall think fit, so that the petitioner's enemies cannot have occasion to say that he is entirely neglected.[1]

Given a commission to raise a regiment on the Irish establishment, commanded by himself, he steadily voted with the Government. He died 30 Jan. 1722, soon after making a settlement of his estates jointly with his eldest son, who had been forced to flee the country for murder and died in the Fleet of wounds received from a fellow prisoner in 1743.[2] The estate was sold by Act of Parliament in 1727 to Sarah, Duchess of Marlborough.

[1] *HMC Townshend*, 133-4. [2] *VCH Bucks*. iv. 464.

R.R.S.

WODEHOUSE, Armine (c.1714-77), of Kimberley Hall, Norf.

NORFOLK 23 Mar. 1737-1768

b. c.1714, 1st surv. s. of Sir John Wodehouse, 4th Bt., M.P., by his 2nd w. Mary, da. of William Fermor, M.P., 1st Baron Leominster; bro. of William Wodehouse (q.v.). *educ.* Trinity Hall, Camb. 1730. *m.* 3 Oct. 1738, Laetitia, da. and h. of Sir Edmund Bacon, 6th Bt. (q.v.), of Garboldisham, Norf., 4s. *suc.* fa. as 5th Bt. 9 Aug. 1754.

Wodehouse, who succeeded his elder brother for Norfolk, was one of the Tories who withdrew on the motion for the dismissal of Walpole in February 1741, otherwise voting regularly against the Government in the Parliaments of 1734 and 1741. The second Lord Egmont in his electoral survey, c.1749-50, describes him as 'heartily with us', i.e. with Leicester House. He died 21 May 1777.

R.R.S.

WODEHOUSE, William (?1706-37), of Kimberley Hall, Norf.

NORFOLK 1734-13 Mar. 1737

b. ?1706, 1st s. of Sir John Wodehouse, 4th Bt., M.P., of Kimberley, Norf.; bro. of Armine Wodehouse (q.v.). *educ.* Caius, Camb. 1723. *m.* Frances, da. of Allen Bathurst, M.P., 1st Earl Bathurst, *s.p.*

The Wodehouses were the leading Tory family in Norfolk, which they had frequently represented. Wodehouse, whose father's name was sent to the Pretender in 1721 as a leading Norfolk Jacobite with an estate of £5,000 p.a.,[1] was returned for the county after a close and expensive contest in 1734, when he was also returned for Cirencester by his father-in-law, Lord Bathurst. Choosing to sit for Norfolk, he died *v.p.* of smallpox in London, 13 May 1737.

[1] Stuart mss 65/10.

R.R.S.

WOLLASTON, William (1693-1757), of Finborough, Suff.

IPSWICH 29 Jan. 1733-1741

b. 26 Apr. 1693, 2nd s. of Rev. William Wollaston of Shenton, Leics. and Finborough, Suff. by Catherine, da. and coh. of Nicholas Charlton, citizen and draper of London. *educ.* Sidney Sussex, Camb. 1710; King's, Camb. 1710; I. Temple 1709, called 1715. *m.* 6 Apr. 1728, Elizabeth, da. of John Francis Fauquier of Rich's Court, Lime St., London, dep. master of the mint and gov. of the Bank of England, 5s. 3da. *suc.* bro. Charlton at Finborough 1729.

Wollaston was descended from a wealthy Elizabethan wool merchant, whose son bought the manor of Finborough for £10,000 in 1656.[1] His father, the author of *The Religion of Nature*, was left the family estates, including Shenton in Leicestershire, by a first cousin once removed. Returned unopposed at a by-election for Ipswich, for which he was re-elected after a contest in 1734, he voted with the Government. He became a trustee of the Georgia Society in March 1734, but when a petition for a parliamentary grant for the colony came before the House in February 1739, he unexpectedly rose from his seat and left.[2] He voted with the Government on the Spanish convention in that year, was absent from the division on the place bill in 1740, did not stand again, and died 20 June 1757.

[1] Copinger, *Suff. Manors*, vi. 173. *HMC Egmont Diary*, i. 66, 69; iii. 28.

R.R.S.

WOODWARD, *see* KNIGHT, William

WORSLEY, Charles (aft. 1671-1739), of the Middle Temple, London.

NEWTOWN I.o.W. 1722-1727

b. aft. 1671, 2nd s. of Sir James Worsley of Pylewell Park, Hants by Mary, da. of Sir Nicholas Stuart, 1st Bt., of Hartley Mauditt; bro. of James Worsley and cos. of Sir Robert Worsley (qq.v.). *educ.* M. Temple 1690, called 1696, bencher 1723. *unm.*

Agent for Barbados 1723–7.

Returned for Newtown as a Tory in 1722 on the family interest, Charles Worsley, a practising lawyer, spoke on 16 Oct. 1722 against the bill to suspend the Habeas Corpus Act for a year. In 1723 he was made agent for Barbados,[1] no doubt on the recommendation of the governor, his cousin, Henry Worsley. He was the author of 'Master Worsley's Book' on the history and constitution of the Middle Temple. He did not stand again, and died 28 Aug. 1739.

[1] L. M. Penson, *Col. Agents of British W. Indies*, 250.

P.W.

WORSLEY, James (?1671–1756), of Pylewell Park, Hants.

NEWTOWN I.o.W.   1695–1701, 1705–1722,
                                1727–25 Apr. 1729, 1734–1741

b. ?1671, 1st s. of Sir James Worsley of Pylewell; bro. of Charles Worsley and cos. of Sir Robert Worsley (qq.v.). *educ.* New Coll. Oxf. 15 June 1688, aged 16; M. Temple 1691. *m.* 25 Feb. 1714, Rachel, da. of Thomas Merrick of St. Margaret's, Westminster. *suc.* fa. 1695; cos. Sir Robert Worsley as 5th Bt. 29 July 1747.

Woodward of New Forest 1710–14.

James Worsley inherited Pylewell Park in the New Forest from his father in 1695. Returned for Newtown in 1715 on his family's interest, he was classed like his cousin, Sir Robert Worsley, as a Tory who might often vote with the Whigs, but in fact he voted consistently against the Administration. He did not stand in 1722 but was returned in 1727, when his Whig opponent petitioned. On 26 Mar. 1729 Sir Edward Knatchbull (q.v.) reported,

> the motion for Lord William Powlett's son's [Charles Armand, q.v.] petition for Newton was made for hearing it at the bar [of the House], although but two days before the committee of elections had been closed with intention to hear no more, upon which Worsley, the sitting Member, had sent his witnesses out of town and they might be gone into other parts; however, on a division, it was carried by 160 against 147.[1]

He was unseated a month later. Re-elected unopposed in 1734, he spoke on 16 Feb. 1738 against a petition from the dean and chapter of Westminster for funds for the repair of the Abbey. He did not stand after 1741, by which time his family had lost their interest at Newtown. In 1747 he succeeded his cousin, Sir Robert Worsley, as fifth baronet, but Appuldurcombe and the other Isle of Wight property was left not to him but in trust for his son.[2] He died 12 June 1756.

[1] *Knatchbull Diary.* [2] PCC 219 Potter.

P.W.

WORSLEY, Sir Robert, 4th Bt. (?1669–1747), of Appuldurcombe, I.o.W., and Chilton Condover, Hants.

NEWTOWN I.o.W.   1715–1722

b. ?1669, 1st s. of Sir Robert Worsley, 3rd Bt., M.P., of Appuldurcombe by Mary, da. of Hon. James Herbert of Kingsey, Bucks., 2nd s. of Philip, 4th Earl of Pembroke; cos. of James and Charles Worsley (qq.v.). *educ.* Ch. Ch. Oxf. 17 Dec. 1684, aged 15. *m.* (lic. 13 Aug. 1690) Frances, da. of Thomas Thynne, 1st Visct. Weymouth, of Longleat, Wilts., 7 surv. da. *suc.* fa. 1676.

Dep. lt. Hants 1699–1702.

Sir Robert Worsley inherited the manor of Appuldurcombe, which had been in his family since 1527.[1] Returned for Newtown on his own interest in 1715, he explained his reasons for standing to his brother Henry, envoy to Portugal:

> I am told my standing has done you service, and indeed that was the only reason that made me first think of it . . . by offering myself, I kept out other pretenders, and had you been recalled, I was determined to transfer my interest to you.[2]

Classed as a Tory who might often vote with the Whigs, he voted against the Administration on the septennial bill and the repeal of the Occasional Conformity and Schism Acts, but with them on the peerage bill. He did not stand again and died 29 July 1747, leaving his mainland Hampshire property to Robert, Lord Carteret (q.v.), the son of his daughter, Frances.[3]

[1] *VCH Hants*, v. 171. [2] 28 Dec. 1714, Worsley mss. [3] PCC 219 Potter.

P.W.

WORTLEY MONTAGU, Edward (1678–1761), of Wortley, Yorks.

HUNTINGDON   1705–1713
WESTMINSTER   1715–1722
HUNTINGDON   1722–1734
PETERBOROUGH   1734–1761

b. 8 Feb. 1678, o. surv. s. of Hon. Sidney Wortley Montagu (q.v.) of Wortley. *educ.* Westminster; Trinity, Camb. 1693; M. Temple 1693, called 1699; I. Temple 1706; Grand Tour 1700–3. *m.* (lic. 17 Aug.) prob. 20 Aug. 1712, Lady Mary Pierrepont (the celebrated Lady Mary Wortley Montagu), da. of Evelyn, 1st Duke of Kingston, 1s. 1da. (who m. John, 3rd Earl of Bute [S]). *suc.* fa. 1727 and cos. James Montagu (q.v.) at Newbold Verdon, Leics. 1748.

Ld. of the Treasury 1714–15; ambassador to Turkey 1716–18.

In a memorandum written at the age of 70 Edward Wortley claims that

> in the four last years of Queen Anne he was one of the most active members and was successful in his endeavours to weaken those who were supposed to have formed a design to bring in the Pretender. In

concert with the Duke of Marlborough, Lord Godolphin and Lords Somers and Halifax, he brought in a place bill, on which occasion Sir T. Hanmer and his party divided against Lord Bolingbroke. He had the principal share in throwing out the bill of commerce with France.[1]

At George I's accession he was disappointed to receive only a lordship of the Treasury under his kinsman, Lord Halifax, instead of a secretaryship of state which he considered his due. Elected for Westminster in 1715, he lost his post after Halifax's death, when the Treasury board was reconstituted under Walpole, of whose conduct as leader of the House of Commons and appointment as first lord he strongly disapproved.[2] In compensation he was promised an auditorship of the imprest as soon as one became vacant. Meanwhile he was sent as ambassador to Constantinople, from which he was recalled as a failure after little more than a year, the blow being softened by the grant of a reversion to the auditorship. On his return he put in a claim for arrears of pay and for extraordinary expenses during his embassy. He states that Lord Sunderland, then at the head of the Treasury, offered him £10,000 in discharge of this debt, and the immediate possession of an auditorship, 'on condition he would be for the peerage bill, which he refused to be', speaking and voting against it. 'On this they paid him no more than £5,000', that is to say, his arrears of pay, but not his extraordinary expenses, and he was required to surrender his reversion to the auditorship. In 1721 he was elected to the secret committee of the House of Commons on the South Sea bubble.

After the Earl of Sunderland's death, Wortley refused to 'declare himself a friend to Sir Robert Walpole', though, according to his own account, offered 'carte blanche' if he would do so.[3] From 1727, when his father's death put him into possession of a vast fortune, he was in active opposition. On 3 Apr. 1728, after a speech by Pulteney in a debate on hawkers and pedlars,

> Sir R. Walpole answered him and took notice that the gentleman had put himself in a 'rant and ramble' in his discourse, upon which Wortley Montagu said he never knew such parliamentary discourse and language and took down the words, and said no man was above parliamentary censure, and for less words than those people in former parliaments had been called to the Bar and upon their knees asked pardon, and that he perceived by the gentleman's silence to whom it was applied, meaning Pulteney, that he designed to take notice of it in another manner, upon which the Speaker took him down to order, and said he dared say the gentleman intended no such thing, nor could the words bear that interpretation, and that, if any one deserved to be taken notice of in the House, it was he, and expressed himself with great warmth as if Wortley had designed to set

people by the ears, and Wortley was forced to explain and ask pardon of the House.[4]

In a debate on a bill to prevent loans to foreign princes without the consent of the King, on 24 Feb. 1730, he said that 'he was sorry to hear the King's name made use of to influence our debates [and] . . . that according to the bill it was put into the King's power to restrain all the trade of the kingdom'. Two days later he supported John Barnard's (q.v.) petition against the monopoly of the East India Company. He spoke against the Hessians on 8 Feb. 1731 and for the outright rejection of the excise bill on 11 Apr. 1733.[5]

In 1734 Wortley was returned for his father's seat at Peterborough, standing also for Yorkshire, with a view to keeping out one of the government candidates, in which he was successful, though he himself came out bottom of the poll. He was a member of a committee appointed to prepare a place bill, 19 Mar. 1735, and of another in March 1737 to propose a bill for giving effect to Barnard's scheme for converting the national debt, in support of which he had spoken. In 1741 he spoke strongly in support of the motion for Walpole's removal, proposing unsuccessfully that Walpole should be ordered to withdraw from the House during the debate.

After Walpole's fall Wortley is not recorded as voting till 1746, when he supported the Government on the Hanoverians but was classed as an opposition Whig, though according to his own account he 'constantly voted in support of the measures of the Government and acted the part of one attached nowhere unless to the King'.[6] In 1747 he instructed the mayor of Bossiney, where he had purchased property carrying with it a major interest in the borough,[7] to return him, together with such person as should be recommended by Thomas Pitt (q.v.), explaining that

> as I am likely to be chosen again for Peterborough, I should have named to you another person rather than myself, if I had fixed on a proper person. But as the dissolution of this Parliament will be earlier by almost a year than I supposed it would be, I am not yet prepared; and shall, after Parliament has met, recommend a proper person to serve in my place.[8]

Electing to sit for Peterborough, he was again classed as Opposition, but took no further active part in politics, though retaining his seat for the rest of the reign. A confirmed miser, about 1748 he considered applying to George II for compensation for the failure to pay the debt which he regarded as owing to him in respect of his embassy and to implement the promise to appoint him to an auditorship. In a long draft memorandum, parts of which have already been quoted, he assessed his financial loss as follows:

£10,000[9] doubled in 14 years   £20,000
£20,000 doubled in 14 years   £40,000
£1,500 a year for 28 years for interest upon
it may reasonably be computed at   £60,000

If the odds were five to one that the debt would not be recovered after 28 years the having run that hazard may be estimated at five to one and make the debt £500,000. If one half of this be due it is a sum too great to be asked.

The upshot was that he would be prepared to settle for a viscountcy, but he seems not to have pursued the matter. Devoting the rest of his long life to hoarding health and money, he died 22 Jan. 1761, leaving over a million to his only daughter, Lady Bute.

[1] In the possession of Prof. R. Halsband. [2] *Letters of Lady Mary Wortley Montagu*, ed. Ld. Wharncliffe, i. 122–8, 214–15. [3] *Letters of Joseph Addison*, ed. Graham, 376–8; *Cal. Treas. Pprs.* 1714–19, p. 413; 1735–8, p. 394; Wortley's memo. [4] *Knatchbull Diary*. [5] *HMC Egmont Diary*, i. 58, 128, 148, 360. [6] Wortley's memo. [7] Maclean, *Trigg Minor*, iii. 203, 245. [8] *HMC Fortescue*, i. 112. [9] This figure ignores his own statement that he had recovered £5,000 out of the £10,000 owing to him.

R.R.S.

WORTLEY MONTAGU, Edward, jun. (1713–76), of Boreham Wood, Herts.

HUNTINGDONSHIRE   1747–1754
BOSSINEY   1754–1768

b. 16 May 1713, o.s. of Edward Wortley Montagu (q.v.). *educ.* Westminster 1718?; Leyden. *m.* 1730, Sally (*d.*1776), *s.p. legit.*
    Cornet 7 Drag. Gds. 1743; capt.-lt. 1 Ft. 1745, capt. 1747, ret. 1748.
    Sec. at congress of Aix-la-Chapelle 1748.

Edward Wortley was sent abroad in 1730 for contracting a marriage to a woman reputed to be a laundress or washer-woman, who was immediately pensioned off but remained his lawful wife till shortly before her death. At the same time his father took legal steps to break the entail on the Wortley estates, thus making it possible to disinherit him.[1] After thirteen years as a remittance man on the continent, he entered the army, serving in Flanders till 1746, when he was seconded to the staff of his cousin, Lord Sandwich, British representative at the conference of Breda and the congress of Aix-la-Chapelle. His knowledge of foreign languages, including Dutch, made him useful to Sandwich, who described him to Newcastle as 'a treasure', securing his appointment as secretary at the Congress and his unopposed return for Huntingdonshire in 1747.

Wortley attended the opening of Parliament, but was recalled almost immediately to Aix by Sandwich. According to Edward Montagu (q.v.):

> His father has a little augmented his allowance, but has not made it sufficient for a knight of the shire. He has not yet admitted him into his company and he has orders to sit on a different side of the House from him.[2]

On the signature of the peace treaty in October 1748, Sandwich sent him with the news to the King at Hanover, where he raised the question of his future with Newcastle, the secretary of state in attendance. Newcastle, having recently quarrelled with Sandwich, at once wrote to the Duke of Cumberland at Allied Headquarters to forestall any application by Wortley:

> Mr. Wortley (lately called Mr. Montagu) will pay his duty to Your Royal Highness with my Lord Sussex [one of the hostages appointed under the Treaty for the return of Cape Breton]. He has a mind to go to Paris with my Lord Sussex. I am not against it, as I think he would be of use to the young man; but otherwise I should not wish to have a *Montagu* there at this time.
>
> He pushed at being secretary for the embassy. I told him plainly Mr. Yorke [Joseph, q.v.] was to go with the Duke of Richmond; perhaps the secretary to the embassy; or as second minister . . . And so I have put Wortley off tho' he still has it in his head.[3]

In August 1749, after the termination of his appointment, he went to Paris, where he came under the suspicion of the British embassy by visiting French ministers without informing the embassy. Hardwicke, however, on hearing of this incident, brushed it aside as relating to 'a strolling light-headed man'. In November 1750 he had to leave Paris, because of the arrival of his father, who had made it a condition of his allowance of £1,000 a year that they should never be in the same city together.[4] At the beginning of 1751 he reappeared in London, where he and Theobald Taaffe (q.v.), another adventurer, set up as faro bankers to Mme de Mirepoix, the French ambassadress.

> Our greatest miracle [wrote Horace Walpole] is Lady Mary Wortley's son, whose adventures have made so much noise; his parts are not proportionate, but his expense is incredible. His father scarce allows him anything: yet he plays, dresses, diamonds himself, even to distinct shoe-buckles for a frock, and has more snuff boxes than would suffice a Chinese idol with an hundred noses. But the most curious part of his dress, which he has brought from Paris, is an iron wig; you literally would not know it from hair—I believe it is on this account that the Royal Society have chosen him of their body.

He also contracted, 21 July 1751, a bigamous marriage with a Miss Elizabeth Ashe, prominent in London society at that time.[5]

In the summer of 1751 Wortley and Taaffe went to Paris, where in October they were arrested by the French authorities on charges by an English Jew, Abraham Payba, an absconding bankrupt, of cheating him out of large sums of money at play and, on his failure to pay up, of breaking into his lodgings and taking 50,000 livres worth of jewellery and other valuables.[6] Released on bail, Wortley and Taaffe brought counter-charges against Payba, who himself was arrested. In January 1752, they were acquitted and Payba was sentenced; but on appeal the judgment was annulled and Payba ordered to be released.[7] During these proceedings Wortley took a very good house in Paris, keeping a magnificent equipage, and living at great expense, though how he supported it was a mystery to the embassy, since it was thought that after this affair 'few people would choose to play with him for much money'.[8]

After this there was no question of Wortley's standing again for the county, but in 1754 his father returned him at Bossiney to protect him from his creditors. After many other vicissitudes, he died at Padua, 29 Apr. 1776.

^{E. Wortley Montagu to John Bridger, 24 July 1760, mss in possession of Sir Henry Shiffner, Bt. ² Sandwich to Newcastle, private, 22 Dec. (N.S.) 1747, Add. 32810, f. 323; 17 Mar. (N.S.) 1748, Add. 32811, f. 349; 31 May (N.S.) 1748, Add. 32812, f. 219; Geo. Paston, *Lady Mary Wortley Montagu*, 446-7, 451-2. ³ Newcastle to the King, 21 Oct., to Cumberland, 29 Oct., and Cumberland to Newcastle, 3 Nov. (all N.S.) 1748, Add. 32717, ff. 179, 147, 169. ⁴ Hardwicke to Newcastle, Sept. 1749, Add. 32719, f. 95; *Luynes Mems.* x. 366. ⁵ Walpole to Mann, 9 Feb. and 22 Nov. 1751 ⁶ Taaffe to Albemarle, 2 and 6 Nov. (N.S.) 1751, Add. 32832, f. 215; *London Gaz.* 15 and 16 June 1751. ⁷ Wortley Montagu to Albemarle, 29 Dec. (N.S.) 1751, Add. 32832, f. 215; Taaffe to Albemarle, 19 Jan. (N.S.) 1752, Add. 32833, f. 68; J. Jeffreys to Royston, 23 Aug. and 8 Sept. (N.S.) 1752, Add. 35630, ff. 48-51. ⁸ Jeffreys to Claudius Amyand, 5 Jan. (N.S.) 1752, mss in possession of Sir William Cornewall, Bt.}

R.R.S.

WORTLEY MONTAGU, Hon. Sidney (1650-1727), of Wortley, Yorks.

HUNTINGDON	1679-1681, 1689-1695
CAMELFORD	1 Apr. 1696-1698
PETERBOROUGH	1698-1710
HUNTINGDON	1713-1722
PETERBOROUGH	1722-1727

b. 28 July 1650, 2nd s. of Edward Montagu, M.P., 1st Earl of Sandwich, by Jemima, da. of John, 1st Baron Crew of Stene. *m.* c.1676, Anne Newcomen (*b.* 2 Sept. 1659), nat. da. and h. of Sir Francis Wortley, 2nd Bt. (*d.*1666), of Wortley, Yorks., and assumed add. name of Wortley, 5s. 2da.

Sidney Montagu, who took the name Wortley on marrying the heiress to the Wortley estates in S. Yorkshire, used his wife's fortune to acquire and develop extensive coal mining interests in Northumberland and Durham, where he and his relations had opportunities of acquiring leases of church lands on favourable terms, through his uncle

Nathaniel, Lord Crew, bishop of Durham 1674-1721. By the close of Anne's reign, he had become one of the greatest coal owners of the day, actively co-operating with other representatives of the industry in Parliament on matters affecting their joint interests, and on the directorate of a powerful coal cartel formed in 1709. In 1716 his defection led to the break up of the cartel, earning him considerable unpopularity among his former associates, who regarded him and his agent as

> two of the greatest rogues that ever a county was blessed withal. They will, by right or wrong, come at means to purchase estates, but at last must go to the devil.

Ten years later he joined with two other major coal proprietors, George Bowes and the Liddells (qq.v.), to form a new cartel, the Grand Alliance, 'which dominated the coal trade for the rest of the century'.[1]

A lifelong Whig, Wortley, in his son's words,

> was always zealous for the Protestant succession, voted for the exclusion of the Duke of York, voted for settling the Crown in the family, lived to be in Parliament after the King's [George II's] accession, and never asked anything for himself.[2]

Returned on his family's interest for Huntingdon and on his own for Peterborough, he voted for the septennial bill in 1716, but was absent from other recorded divisions.

In old age Wortley is described as

> a large, rough-looking man, with a huge, flapped hat, seated majestically in his elbow chair, talking very loud and swearing boisterously at his servants.[3]

He died 9 Nov. 1727, having survived his wife and his male children, except his second son, Edward (q.v.), who succeeded to all his coal mining interests as well as to the settled Wortley estates.

^{¹ E. Hughes, *N. Country Life in 18th Cent.* 168, 195, 235, 290-1. ² Ms memo by his son Edward (q.v.), owned by Professor R. Halsband. ³ *Letters of Lady Mary Wortley Montagu*, ed. Ld. Wharncliffe, i. 14.}

R.R.S.

WREN, Christopher (1675-1747), of Wroxall, Warws.

NEW WINDSOR	1713-14 Apr. 1715

b. 8 (or 18) Feb. 1675,[1] 2nd but 1st surv. s. of Sir Christopher Wren, M.P., surveyor gen. of the works, by his 1st w. Faith, da. of Sir Thomas Coghill of Bletchingdon, Oxon. *educ.* Eton c.1686-91; Pembroke, Camb. 1691; M. Temple 1694; Grand Tour 1698. *m.* (1) 1706,[2] Mary (*d.*10 Dec. 1712), da. of Philip Musard, jeweller to Queen Anne, 1s.; (2) 8 Nov. 1715, Constance, da. of Sir Thomas Middleton of Stansted Mountfitchet, Essex, wid. of Sir Roger Burgoyne, 4th Bt., of Wroxall, 1s. *suc.* fa. 1723.

Dep. clerk engraver of the works 1694-1702; chief clerk of the works 1702-16.

Wren was returned in 1713 as a Tory for New

Windsor, where his father was controller of works at the castle. Classed as a Tory who might often vote Whig, he was re-elected in 1715 but was unseated on petition, it being alleged *inter alia* that he had used his official position to influence voters.[3] He did not stand again, employing himself in collecting documents for the *Parentalia*, published in 1750 by his son Stephen, which is still the main authority for his father's life. He died 24 Aug. 1747.

[1] *Genealogists' Mag.* iii. 84; iv. 2–3; *Parentalia*, p. ix.   [2] Agnew, *Protestant Exiles*, i. 155.   [3] *CJ*, xviii. 63.

R.S.L.

WREY, Sir Bourchier, 6th Bt. (?1715–84), of Tawstock, nr. Barnstaple, Devon.

BARNSTAPLE   20 Jan. 1748–1754

b. ?1715, 1st s. of Sir Bourchier Wrey, 5th Bt., M.P., of Tawstock by Diana, da. of John Rolle of Stevenstone, Devon, sis. of John Rolle (q.v.) and wid. of John Sparke of Plymouth, Devon. *educ.* Winchester; New Coll. Oxf. 21 Oct. 1732, aged 17; Grand Tour (Italy, Germany, Holland) 1737–40.[1] *m.* (1) 10 July 1749, Mary (bur. 3 Sept. 1751), da. of John Edwards of Highgate, Mdx., *s.p.*; (2) 1 May 1755, Ellen, da. of John Thresher of Bradford, Wilts., 2s. *suc.* fa. Nov. 1726.

Wrey came of an old west country family, who in 1654 had inherited the Devonshire property of the Bourchiers, Earls of Bath.[2] The son of an active Jacobite,[3] he was introduced by his first cousin, Henry Rolle (q.v.), to Newcastle in 1742 as 'one who has a great interest in his county'.[4] According to Horace Walpole, who describes him as 'a very foolish knight', he hurried up to London from Exeter during the political crisis of February 1746, on hearing from his kinswoman, Lady Orford, 'that it was a brave opportunity for him to come up and make his own terms'.[5] Returned as a Whig for Barnstaple in 1748 in succession to Rolle, who had been created a peer, he became involved in a bitter quarrel with the 2nd Earl of Orford, lord lieutenant of Devonshire, over the disposal of a local crown living. Both parties appealed to Newcastle, Wrey writing, 2 June 1748, that he would appear

contemptible . . . in the face of all those gentlemen, who I ventured to oppose in person at the late elections for both Exeter and Barnstaple and in both places, with some honour perhaps and at no inconsiderable expense to myself and my relations, if I do not appear to merit from your Grace some little preference to those, who neither on those, or occasions of much higher importance [i.e. in 1745] have given us the least assistance in that county;

while Orford threatened to resign his lord lieutenancy if he were 'got the better of in this affair' by Wrey and Rolle, 'two such insignificant figures . . . as silly and as dirty fellows as ever were born',

both of whom had been 'bred up Jacobites from their cradles and will never give you another vote as soon as their turn is secured'.[6] He went to the Baltic ports in 1752 on behalf of the society for promoting the herring fishery;[7] voted against Hardwicke's marriage bill in 1753;[8] and declared himself a candidate for Exeter at the forthcoming general election, but withdrew before the poll.[9] He died 13 Apr. 1784.

[1] PCC 301 Rockingham.   [2] Lysons, *Devonshire*, i. pp. xcviii, cix.   [3] *Report from the Committee appointed by the House of Commons to examine Christopher Layer and others* (1723), App. F. 11.   [4] Add. 32699, f. 459.   [5] To Mann, 6 Mar. 1746.   [6] Add. 32715, ff. 147, 154.   [7] Wrey to Newcastle, 19 July 1752, Add. 32838, f. 333.   [8] C. Amyand to Newcastle, 4 June 1753, Add. 32732, f. 22.   [9] Wrey to Bedford, 2 Sept. 1753, Bedford mss; Sir F. Drake to Pelham, 6 Sept. 1753, Newcastle (Clumber) mss.

S.R.M.

WRIGHT, John (?1692–1766), of Oxford and Dry Sandford,[1] nr. Abingdon.

ABINGDON   1741–1747

b. ?1692, 2nd s. of William Wright (*d.*1721), recorder of Oxford and a Welsh judge,[2] by Dorothy, da. and coh. of John Finch of Fynes, in White Waltham, Berks.[3] *educ.* Exeter, Oxf. 6 Apr. 1709, aged 16; I. Temple 1711, called 1718, bencher 1746. *m.* by Mar. 1721,[4] Mary, da. of Francis Heywood of Holywell, Oxford and Forest Hill, Oxon., 2s. 2da.

Dep. recorder, Oxford 1719;[5] steward, manor of Shippon in St. Helen's, Abingdon, to the Prince of Wales by 1741 (£1. 6s. 8d. p.a.), of St. John's, Oxf. –*d.*[6]

Wright's brother was Sir Martin Wright, justice of the King's bench. His father stood unsuccessfully as a Whig for Oxford in 1695; William Wright, his grandfather, was Whig M.P. for Oxford 1679–81; described by Hearne as 'a great Whig',[7] he himself stood unsuccessfully for Oxford in 1722.[8] Returned for Abingdon in 1741, he was included in the Cockpit list of ministerial supporters, October 1742, though his only recorded vote was against the Government on the Hanoverians in January 1744. Classed among the 'doubtful' Old Whigs in 1746, he did not stand again. He died 1 Nov. 1766.

[1] *VCH Berks.* iv. 419.   [2] Williams, *Welsh Judges*, 145.   [3] Hearne, *Colls.* (Oxford Hist. Soc.), vii. 222; *VCH Berks.* iii. 173.   [4] Hearne, vii. 223; viii. 70; *VCH Oxon.* v. 127; Salter, *Oxford City Properties* (Oxf. Hist. Soc.), 193.   [5] Receiving his father's salary (Hobson, *Oxf. Council Acts, 1701–52*, p. 115).   [6] Costin, *St. John's Coll. Oxf. 1598–1860* (Oxf. Hist. Soc.), 214.   [7] Hearne, vii. 224.   [8] *HMC Portland*, vii. 317.

R.S.L.

WRIGHTE, George (c.1706–66), of Gayhurst, Bucks. and Brooksby Hall, nr. Leicester.

LEICESTER   1727–27 Jan. 1766

b. c.1706, 1st surv. s. of George Wrighte of Gayhurst and Brooksby, clerk of the Crown in Chancery, by Mary, da. and h. of Thomas Bedford of Doctors' Commons, register of Admiralty. *educ.* Emmanuel,

Camb. 1724; I. Temple 1715. *m.* May 1733, Barbara, da. of Sir Thomas Clarges, 2nd Bt., M.P., of Aston, Herts., 1s. 1da. *suc.* fa. 1725.

Wrighte was the grandson of Sir Nathan Wrighte (recorder of Leicester 1680–5 and 1688–96), keeper of the great seal 1700–5, who played an active part on the Tory side in the county election of 1715 (see under Leicestershire). His uncle, William, was recorder of Leicester 1729–62. Returned for Leicester as a Tory on the corporation interest in 1727, he voted against the Administration, except on the motion for the dismissal of Walpole in February 1741, when he was one of the Tories who withdrew. In his only recorded speech, made on 5 May 1738 in a debate on the Spanish depredations in America, he exonerated the Spanish government from responsibility, deprecating measures likely to provoke Spain into war.[1] The 2nd Lord Egmont wrote in his electoral survey, c.1749–50: 'I do not know Wrighte well, but I believe he will acquiesce in the measures of the Tories be they what they will'. To which the Prince of Wales added: 'I think he will, all his and her acquaintants are my friends'.

He died 27 Jan. 1766.

[1] *Parl. Hist.* x. 836.

E.C.

WRIGHTSON, William (c.1676–1760), of Newcastle-upon-Tyne.

NEWCASTLE-UPON-TYNE 1710–1722
NORTHUMBERLAND 20 Feb. 1723–15 Apr. 1724

b. c.1676, 2nd s. of Robert Wrightson of Cusworth, Yorks. by Sarah, da. of Sir Thomas Beaumont of Whitley Beaumont, Yorks. *m.* (1) Isabel (*d.*13 Mar. 1716), da. and h. of Francis Beaumont, merchant, of Newcastle, wid. of Thomas Matthews of Newcastle, *s.p.*; (2) 1722, Isabella, da. and coh. of William Fenwick of Bywell, Northumb. and sis of Margaret, w. of John Fenwick (q.v.), 1da. *suc.* bro. at Cusworth 1724.

Marrying into a wealthy Newcastle merchant family, Wrightson settled in the town.[1] Returned for Newcastle as a Tory in 1710, he voted against the Administration in every recorded division after George I's accession. His name was sent to the Pretender in 1721 as a supporter in the event of a rising to restore the Stuarts.[2] Defeated for Newcastle in 1722, he was returned in 1723 for the county, where his second wife had considerable estates. Unseated on petition in 1724, he did not stand again, dying 4 Dec. 1760, aged 84.

[1] R. Welford, *Men of Mark 'twixt Tyne and Tweed*, iii. 687.
[2] Stuart mss 65/16.

E.C.

WROTH, Robert (1660–1720), of Burpham, nr. Guildford, Surr.

GUILDFORD 1705–1708, 1710–3 Feb. 1711, 31 Dec. 1717–4 Feb. 1720

bap. 27 Aug. 1660, 2nd s. of Sir Henry Wroth of Durrants, Enfield, Mdx. by Anne Maynard, da. of William, 2nd Baron Maynard; gd.-s. of Henry Wroth by Jane Harris. *m.* 1687, Knightly, da. of Humphry Wyrley, prothonotary of court of common pleas, 2s. 3da. *suc.* aunt Mary, illegit da. of Sir Francis Wolley by Jane Harris and w. of Sir John Wyrley of Hamstead, Staffs. at Burpham 1676.[1]

Cornet, independent tp. of Horse 1685; ensign 4 Tp. Horse Gren. Gds. 1686, lt. 1687, capt. 1688; lt.-col. R. Horse Gds. 1703–8; brig.-gen. 1707; maj.-gen. 1710.
Clerk of the Green Cloth 1715–*d.*

Wroth owned an estate near Guildford, carrying with it a considerable interest in the borough, for which he sat in 1705 and again in 1710, when he was unseated 'for not being acceptable to those who were then in power', i.e. the Tory majority of the House of Commons. At George I's accession he was made a clerk of the Green Cloth by the 'procurement or assistance' of the 1st Lord Onslow (q.v.), for whose family he had always shown 'an unalterable attachment'.[2] Brought in for Guildford by the 2nd Lord Onslow (q.v.), at a by-election in 1717, he voted with the Administration till his death, 4 Feb. 1720.

[1] *Essex Arch. Soc. Trans.* n.s. viii. 145 et seq; Shaw, *Staffs.* ii. 115; *N. & Q.* (ser. 8), iv. 252; PCC 3 Bunce. [2] *HMC 14th Rep.* IX, 503.

R.R.S.

WROTTESLEY, Sir Richard, 7th Bt. (1721–69), of Wrottesley, Staffs.

TAVISTOCK 12 Dec. 1747–1754

b. 12 Apr. 1721, 5th s. of Sir John Wrottesley, 4th Bt., M.P., by Frances, da. of Hon. John Grey, M.P., of Enville, sis. of Harry, 3rd Earl of Stamford. *educ.* Winchester 1736–8; St. John's, Oxf. 1739. *m.* 6 Oct. 1739 (with £10,000), Lady Mary Gower, da. of John, 2nd Baron Gower and 1st Earl Gower, 1s. (Sir John Wrottesley, M.P.), 5da. *suc.* bro. Sir Walter Wrottesley, 6th Bt., Feb. 1732.

Clerk comptroller of the Green Cloth 1749–54; chaplain to George III, 1763; dean of Worcester 1765–*d.*

Wrottesley, whose father had been a prominent Jacobite,[1] went over to the Administration with the Leveson Gowers at the end of 1744. During the Forty-five rebellion he armed his servants and tenantry, and with a body of yeomanry set out to join his father-in-law, Lord Gower, who was raising a regiment. According to Tory neighbours, Wrottesley's force never went beyond the first public house on the road, less than a mile from Wrottesley.[2]

In 1747 Wrottesley was put up for Staffordshire as an administration candidate. On his defeat, Lord Gower wrote to the Duke of Bedford, 3 Aug. 1747:

> His heart is set upon being in Parliament, and I really think he deserves a seat there for his zeal, prudent behaviour, and activity in our contest, but he can have no chance now unless some of your great men that have persons chosen in two places will take compassion of him.[3]

In December the Duke of Bedford returned him for Tavistock.

In 1754 Wrottesley gave up his seat in Parliament and his post in the royal household to enter holy orders. He died 20 July 1769.

[1] Stuart mss 65/16. [2] *Wm. Salt. Arch. Soc. Colls.* n.s. vi (2), pp. 347-8. [3] Bedford mss.

E.C.

WYKES, William (aft. 1680–1742), of Haselbeach, Northants.

NORTHAMPTON   1710–1722

b. aft. 1680, 2nd s. of Randolph Wykes of Haselbeach by Sarah, da. and h. of William Clarke of Loddington, Leics. *m.* Grace Corrie of Creaton, Northants., *s.p. suc.* bro. 1706.

Wykes was the grandson of Randolph Wykes, grocer and citizen of London (*d.*1676), who acquired the manor of Haselbeach. His elder brother, Randolph, sheriff of the county 1702–3, died in 1706, aged 26.[1] Returned as a Tory for Northampton in 1710 after a contest, and re-elected in 1713 and 1715 unopposed, he voted against the Government in every recorded division after George I's accession. On 6 Aug. 1714 he proposed tacking to the bill for the new King's civil list a clause limiting the number of placemen in the Commons, but nobody seconded him. He also spoke against the land tax in January 1716[2] and the septennial and peerage bills. In 1722 the local Tory leaders unsuccessfully attempted to compromise the Northampton election, at which he was easily defeated. He did not stand again but took part in subsequent Northamptonshire elections.[3] He died 5 May 1742. Having been granted by the Northampton corporation a monopoly for laying a piped water supply for the town, he appointed his 'worthy and good friends', George Compton and Sir Edmund Isham (qq.v.), as two of the trustees of his waterworks, to see that they be kept in good repair and to prevent their ever falling 'into the hands of any person or persons of republican principles'.[4]

[1] Bridges, *Northants.* ii. 36–37, 45, 77. [2] A. Corbière to Horace Walpole, 27 Jan. 1716, Walpole (Wolterton) mss. [3] E.G. Forrester, *Northants. County Elections 1695–1832*, pp. 43, 49 n. 55. [4] PCC 262 Trenley.

R.R.S.

WYLDE, Thomas (?1670–1740), of the Commandery, Worcester.

WORCESTER   1701–1727

b. ?1670, 1st s. of Robert Wylde of the Commandery, Worcester by Elizabeth, da. of Rev. Thomas Dennis of St. Helen's, Worcester. *educ.* Ch. Ch. Oxf. 18 May 1686, aged 15; M. Temple 1691. *m.* (1) 23 Dec. 1696, Catherine, da. and coh. of Sir Baynham Throckmorton, 3rd Bt., M.P., of Clowerwall, Glos., 1s. 3da.; (2) 27 Feb. 1720, Anne, da. of Hon. Robert Tracy, justice of the common pleas, wid. of Charles Dowdeswell of Forthampton, Glos., 1da. *suc.* fa. 1708.

Commr. of revenue [I] 1715–27; commr. of excise Nov. 1727–*d.*

Of an old Worcester family, who had bought the property known as the Commandery in 1544, Wylde represented his native city as a Whig for 26 years without a break. Obtaining a place in 1715, he was absent from the division on the septennial bill in 1716, but voted with the Government on the repeal of the Occasional Conformity and Schism Acts and on the peerage bill in 1719. He lost his seat in 1727, when, having 'greatly impaired his fortune by electoral contests',[1] he exchanged his place for one incompatible with a seat in the House of Commons.

He died 12 Apr. 1740.

[1] W. R. Williams, *Worcs. Members*, 100.

A.N.N.

WYNDHAM, Charles (1710–63), of Orchard Wyndham, Som.

BRIDGWATER   7 Apr. 1735–1741
APPLEBY   1 Jan. 1742–1747
TAUNTON   1747–7 Feb. 1750

b. 19 Aug. 1710, 1st s. of Sir William Wyndham (q.v.). *educ.* Westminster 1719; Ch. Ch. Oxf. 1725; Grand Tour (Germany, France, Italy) 1728–30 with George Lyttelton and Henry Bathurst (qq.v.). *m.* 12 Mar. 1751, Alicia Maria, da. of George Carpenter, 2nd Baron Carpenter of Killaghy [I] (q.v.), 4s. 3da. *suc.* fa. as 4th Bt. 17 June 1740, and mat. uncle Algernon Seymour (q.v.), 7th Duke of Somerset, as 2nd Earl of Egremont 7 Feb. 1759.

Ld. lt. Cumb. 1751–9; custos rot. Cumb. 1751–*d.*; v.-adm. Cumb. 1755–*d.*; first plenip. to intended congress at Augsburg and P.C. 8 July 1761; sec. of state, southern dept. Oct. 1761–*d.*; ld. lt. Suss. 1762–*d.*

Wyndham was 'the son of the great Sir William Wyndham, and grandson of the old Duke of Somerset, whose prodigious pride he inherited more than his father's abilities, though he had a great deal of humour'.[1] Returned at a by-election for Bridgwater in 1735, after unsuccessfully contesting Launceston as a Tory in 1734, he voted with the Opposition. In 1741 he was tricked out of his seat by George Bubb Dodington, who, apparently through the good offices of Lord Gower, had also been returned by Lord Thanet for Appleby in case he failed at Bridgwater.

> The treachery I met with from Mr. Dodington [Wyndham told Gower] could not be suspected of any man, wherefore I beg that the protection you gave him may give you no uneasiness . . . However mortified I am at being out of Parliament, I am far from envying Mr. Dodington his seat for Bridgwater, if I was to have got it by the means he did, and he had long ago taken care that it was impossible for me to get it by any other. I humbly thank you for being so kind as to write to Lord Thanet about Appleby.[2]

The Prince of Wales, Lord Carteret, and all the heads of the Opposition were anxious that he should be adopted as a candidate for Westminster, should the sitting Member there be unseated on petition, as was expected.[3] But in the end he was returned for the seat vacated by Dodington at Appleby.

After Walpole's fall Wyndham went over to the Administration, attaching himself to Carteret, his kinsman. In the debate on the Hanoverians on 18 Jan. 1744, a Tory wrote:

> There was not an opprobrious word in the English language that was not made use of and applied to Hanover—and almost as much dirt flung at Lord Carteret, which only Sir Ch. Wyndham endeavoured to wipe off, but stuck himself in the mire and, plunged as deep in the mud as any hero in the *Dunciad*.[4]

A month later, he seconded the loyal address upon the threatened French invasion to restore the Stuarts.[5]

In 1747 Wyndham's change of party made it necessary for him to seek a new seat, which he found at Taunton. On the death of his uncle, the 7th Duke of Somerset, in 1750, he succeeded to the Percy estates at Cockermouth in Cumberland and to Petworth in Sussex. Having 'miscarried with Lord Granville' [Carteret], he paid 'assiduous court to Newcastle', then attached himself to Fox,[6] and under George III was made secretary of state by Bute. He died of apoplexy caused by over-eating, 21 Aug. 1763.[7]

[1] Walpole, *Mems. Geo. II*, i. 80. [2] 28 May 1741, Granville mss. [3] Egmont mss, Add. 47091, ff. 6-7. [4] *Orrery Pprs*. ii. 174-5. [5] Walpole to Mann, 16 Feb. 1744. [6] *Mems. Geo. II*, iii. 2. [7] Walpole, *Mems. Geo. III*, i. 224.

E.C.

WYNDHAM, Thomas (c.1686–1752), of Clearwell Court, Glos., Dunraven Castle, Glam. and Cromer, Norf.

TRURO 17 Mar. 1721–1727
DUNWICH 1727–1734

b. c.1686, 2nd s. of Francis Wyndham of Cromer, Norf. by Sarah, da. of Sir Thomas Darell. *educ.* Eton 1699; King's, Camb. 1705, fellow 1707; L. Inn 1706, called 1716. *m.* (1) cos. Jane (*d.*1723), da. and h. of William Wyndham of Dunraven Castle, Glam., niece and h. of Francis Wyndham of Clearwell Court, Glos., 2s.; (2) Anne, da. of Samuel Edwin (q.v.) of Llanmihangel Plâs, Glam., sis. and h. to Charles Edwin (q.v.), 3s. *suc.* e. bro. to Cromer 1745.

Sec. to chancellor of duchy of Lancaster 1716 for life; auditor to south part of duchy of Lancaster 1716–31; recorder, Gloucester 1727–34.

The 1st Lord Egmont writes of Thomas Wyndham:

> When a younger brother he obtained two places in the Duchy of Lancaster by the interest of Sir Robert Walpole, his neighbour in the country, and was brought into the House by his means when he had barely a qualification, notwithstanding which he turned against him and voted with the opposite party to the Court.[1]

In his first Parliament he supported the Government, seconding a motion for examining one of the Atterbury conspirators in the Tower in 1723, and seconding the Address in 1726, when he was described as a 'favourite of Walpole's'. In the next Parliament he went into opposition, because Walpole had not made him a lord of the Admiralty, speaking against the Government in the civil list arrears debate, 24 Apr. 1729.[2] According to Speaker Onslow, Walpole, 'to get him out of the House of Commons', offered him a commissionership of customs, which he accepted; 'but when he afterwards found it was in Scotland he refused to accept it', though he had actually kissed hands for it.[3] Thenceforth he voted against the Government in all recorded divisions, becoming one of the most frequent opposition speakers. In the debate on the Address in January 1730 he

> desired the Ministry would say whether our address bound us down to assist the King in defence of his Hanover dominions in case the Emperor or King of Prussia should attack them; if they would allow the sense of the House to be that we do not intend to engage the kingdom in any expense on that account, he would vote for the address, otherwise he must oppose it, but no reply was made to him.

On 4 Feb. he

> distinguished himself by the sharpness and freedom with which he spoke against the Hessians and the Ministry. He said, as an Englishman, he could not vote for them, nor could show his zeal for his Majesty better than by appearing warm in this affair. That his Majesty held his Crown by the Act of Succession, and this was an infringement of it, and consequently of his title.

After inveighing against standing armies

> he concluded that he had been misled by the opinion he had of men, but found such incapacity and insincerity in them, that he would for the future judge for himself, as every honest man must for the future do, if he will discharge his duty to those he represents, and preserve his country from slavery . . .

In 1731 he spoke third for the Opposition on a bill for excluding pensioners from Parliament, observing that

> if the casting an imputation on the House be a reason for opposing the bill now, it will always be a reason in future times, and we must give up the hopes of ever preventing corruption.

Next session he seconded an opposition motion for an inquiry into the qualifications of Members, saying

> we should consider with ourselves how much the Crown had gained on the subject of late years, and that a poor mercenary House of Commons was capable of corruption.

He also served on the inquiry into the frauds in the Charitable Corporation, carrying a motion for the committal of Sir Archibald Grant (q.v.) to the custody of the serjeant at arms. In 1733 he supported a motion that Sir Robert Sutton (q.v.) was guilty of fraud and breach of trust,[4] also speaking on the molasses bill, the qualification of Members bill, the sinking fund, and the excise bill. In the last session of the Parliament he spoke against the army and for a place bill.

Wyndham did not stand again but retired for the rest of his life to the considerable estates in Gloucestershire and Glamorgan which he had acquired through his first marriage. According to Horace Walpole, who states that he was 'known for his blunt humour', 'he always spoke with esteem of Sir Robert Walpole'.[5] He died 12 Dec. 1752.

[1] HMC Egmont Diary, i. 245. [2] Knatchbull Diary, 15 Jan. 1723, 20 Jan. 1726, and pp. 141–2; Stuart mss 132/159; Horace Walpole's notes on his article in Old England, 22 Aug. 1727, with W. S. Lewis. [3] J. Hatsell, Precedents and Proceedings, ii. 394. [4] HMC Egmont Diary, i. 5, 29–30, 135, 242, 245, 368. [5] Horace Walpole's notes ut sup.

E.C.

WYNDHAM, Thomas (c.1693–1777), of Tale, Devon.

POOLE 26 Apr. 1732–1741

b. c.1693, o.s. of Edmund Wyndham of Tale by Penelope, da. of John Dodington of Dodington, Som., sis. of George Dodington (q.v.). unm. suc. fa. 1723 and to disposable estate of cos. George Bubb Dodington (q.v.), Lord Melcombe, 1762.
Commr. of land tax 1762–d.

Thomas Wyndham belonged to the Kentsford branch of the Wyndhams and was last of the line of Tale. Returned unopposed on the government interest[1] for Poole at a by-election in 1732, probably by the influence of his first cousin, Bubb Dodington, then a lord of the Treasury, he was also successful there in 1734 but did not stand again. In Parliament he voted for the Administration in all recorded divisions till Dodington went into opposition in 1740. Described as a 'misanthrope',[2] Wyndham was Dodington's frequent companion at the villa of La Trappe, in Hammersmith, which he inherited from him and where he died, 19 Sept. 1777.

[1] Hutchins, Dorset, i. 30. [2] Rich. Cumberland, Mems. 138.

R.S.L.

WYNDHAM, Sir William, 3rd Bt. (?1688–1740), of Orchard Wyndham, Som.

SOMERSET 26 Apr. 1710–17 June 1740

b. ?1688, o.s. of Sir Edward Wyndham, 2nd Bt., M.P., of Orchard Wyndham by Catherine, da. of Sir William Gower, 4th Bt., M.P., of Stittenham, Yorks. by Jane, da. of John Granville, M.P., 1st Earl of Bath, and sis. of John Leveson Gower, M.P., 1st Baron Gower, educ. Eton 1698; Ch. Ch. Oxf. 1 June 1704, aged 15; Grand Tour (France, Italy). m. (1) 21 July 1708, Lady Catherine Seymour (d. 9 Apr. 1731), da. of Charles, 6th Duke of Somerset, 2s.; (2) 1 June 1734, Maria Catherine, da. of Peter de Jong, burgomaster of Utrecht, wid. of William Godolphin (q.v.), Mq. of Blandford, s.p. suc. fa. June 1695.
Master of the buckhounds 1711–12; sec. at war 1712–13; chancellor of the Exchequer and P.C. 1713–14.

Wyndham's career from first to last was dominated by Bolingbroke.

> He was [Hervey writes] a man of family, fortune, and figure, but pushed up to the employment of chancellor of the Exchequer, by the favour of Lord Bolingbroke, at a time when neither his years, his experience, his talents, his knowledge, nor his weight could give him any pretence to distinction.[1]

When at the beginning of the reign of George I Bolingbroke fled to take service under the Pretender, Wyndham became one of the heads of the rebellion in England planned for the summer of 1715, sending a message to the Pretender in July 'not to lose a day in going over'.[2] On the outbreak of the rebellion he escaped from a messenger sent to arrest him at Orchard Wyndham, but after a reward of £1,000 had been placed on his head he voluntarily surrendered himself, relying on the protection of his father-in-law, the Duke of Somerset, a member of the Government. Excusing his conduct, Bolingbroke wrote to the Pretender:

> I know the virtue of the man so well that I have not the least distrust of him, but I confess to you, Sir, my apprehension is, that after his escape, he tried the West, and found them not disposed to rise; in which case he had perhaps nothing left to do, but his father-in-law's credit to save himself as he could.[3]

In fact, the west country Jacobites had gathered at Bath as arranged, only to receive a message from Wyndham 'that he had surrendered his person to the Government and begged they would consider their own safety', whereupon 'after many imprecations, urged by their resentment for what they called his treachery, they dispersed several ways to their particular friends'.[4]

After a few months in the Tower Wyndham was released on bail, to find that Bolingbroke had been dismissed by the Pretender and that a fresh Jacobite rising with Swedish help was being planned (see Caesar, Charles). In August 1716 he joined in an appeal to the Pretender to land in England immediately with 5,000 regular forces and 20,000 stand of arms, adding a plea for Bolingbroke's reinstatement, as he was merely charged with negligence, not treason.[5] But in September he received a letter from Bolingbroke, now engaged in working his passage with the British Government, urging him at all costs to keep out of an enterprise foredoomed to failure.[6] About the same time the Pretender wrote to him justifying Bolingbroke's dismissal but earnestly desiring the continuance of Wyndham's valued friendship. Though Wyndham's reply was considered in Jacobite circles as satisfactory,[7] he seems in practice to have followed Bolingbroke's advice.

In 1720 Wyndham resumed his connexion with Bolingbroke in Paris, whence he sent his last letter to the Pretender, protesting his continued devotion to the cause. His name was also sent to the Pretender in 1721 as a probable supporter in the event of a rising.[8] Three years later Bolingbroke proposed to Walpole that he should ally himself with the Tories against Carteret and the followers of Lord Sunderland, stating that Wyndham and his close friends, Lords Bathurst and Gower, were now 'ready to enter into any measures' with Walpole and Townshend, being 'desirous to rid themselves of the disagreeable situation they were in by renouncing Jacobitism'.[9] The overture was rejected, but thenceforth Wyndham took every opportunity 'to declare himself a strong Hanoverian', which 'made the Jacobites not love him, though they did not care to separate from him'. He further antagonized them by supporting the bill restoring Bolingbroke's estates.

Walpole's rejection of Bolingbroke's overture, followed by his breach with Pulteney, led at the end of 1726 to the formation, under Bolingbroke's auspices, of a combined Whig-Tory opposition, in which Wyndham, now the recognized 'head of those calling themselves Hanover Tories',[10] acted as the mouthpiece of Bolingbroke, himself excluded from Parliament. In Speaker Onslow's words:

by frequent speaking in public, and great application to business, and the constant instruction he still received from his friend and as it were his master [Bolingbroke], especially in foreign affairs, he became

from a very disagreeable speaker and little knowing in business to be one of the most pleasing and able speakers of his time, wore out all the prejudices of party, grew moderate towards the dissenters, against whom he once bore a most implacable hatred, studied and understood the nature of government and the constitution of his own country, and formed such a new set of principles with regard to the public, and from them grew to think that the religion and liberties of the nation so much depended on the support of the present family to the throne, that he lost all confidence with the Jacobites and the most rigid of the Tories, and it is thought would have left them entirely if he could have stood the reproach of that in his county or could have maintained a prevailing interest there without them; and upon that footing would willingly have come into a new Whig Administration upon the exclusion of Sir Robert Walpole, with whom he would never have acted, and with the admission of some few of his Tory friends who in company with him would willingly also have left their party for such a change.[11]

His association with Bolingbroke, whose name was anathema to the Whigs, was frequently used by Walpole to discredit him, notably in the Dunkirk debate in February 1730, which Walpole turned in his favour by hinting 'that Bolingbroke was at bottom of this inquiry concerning Dunkirk, and had sent for the evidences produced by Sir William Wyndham'.[12]

Wyndham's professed attachment to the House of Hanover did not prevent him from taking part in the Jacobite negotiations with the French government in 1731-3 to restore the Stuarts. Lord Cornbury (Henry Hyde, q.v.), who conducted the negotiations, secured the Pretender's approval for a future Administration containing both Bolingbroke and Wyndham, who then proceeded to put forward a proposal that the Pretender's eldest son should be educated as a Protestant under the care of Ormonde either in France or in Switzerland, and that the Pretender himself should abdicate, pressing their views through Chavigny, the French ambassador at London. The proposal was indignantly rejected by the Pretender, who also resented a speech made by Wyndham in February 1733, saying

that whenever there appeared to be any just fears of the Pretender, he would then show by his actions, as he always had done, what his principles were. That he believed he stood in the opinion of mankind acquitted of any imputation of Jacobitism. . . that that was not the first time such insinuations had in that House been thrown out against him, but he would have gentlemen know, it was treatment he would no longer bear with.[13]

In the shadow cabinet drawn up by the opposition leaders during the excise bill crisis in 1733, Wyndham figured as secretary of state.[14] When the Prince of Wales went into opposition Wyndham became one of his chief advisers, taking with him 'Lord

Cornbury and some others whom he had drawn aside to embark in Prince Frederick's party'.[15] In February 1737 he spoke but did not vote in support of the motion for increasing the Prince's allowance, but in 1738 a scheme for a coalition between the Prince and the Tories broke down on Frederick's refusal to agree to Wyndham's stipulation that 'the Prince's people should join in reducing the army'.[16] In 1739 he headed the unsuccessful secession of the Opposition.

Wyndham was not admitted to the negotiations, initiated in 1739, for a Jacobite rising, supported by a French invasion, which led to the Forty-five. In April 1740, when Lord Barrymore (q.v.) was about to visit Paris to confer with the French government on this matter, a Jacobite agent reported to the Pretender that Wyndham was coming over to see Bolingbroke, and probably Cardinal Fleury. He continued:

> I shall prevent [warn] the Cardinal as to Sir William Wyndham. Though Lord Bolingbroke's behaviour has been all along such as you know, and though Sir William Wyndham has been for some years very unaccountable, yet they both seem to dread that any business of the King's [i.e. the Pretender] should be thought of without them.

Fleury was duly warned and gave all the 'assurances and satisfaction' required 'with reference both to Sir William Wyndham and Bolingbroke'.[17]

Wyndham died at Wells, 17 June 1740, survived by his master, Bolingbroke. Soon after his death his son, followed by his friends, Bathurst and Gower, went over to the Whigs.

[1] Hervey, *Mems.* 19–20. [2] *HMC Stuart*, i. 362, 392, 413–15, 532–3; iii. 557–9. [3] Mahon, i. pp. xxxiv–v. [4] Mrs. Delany, *Autobiog. and Corresp.* i. 17. [5] *HMC Stuart*, iv. 57. [6] Coxe, *Walpole*, ii. 308–9. [7] *HMC Stuart*, ii. 406–7; v. 309, 419, 439. [8] Stuart mss 49/12, 49/28, 65/16. [9] Coxe, ii. 264. [10] Hervey, 19, 20–21; Stuart mss 82/3, 90/128. [11] *HMC 14th Rep. IX*, 467. [12] *HMC Egmont Diary*, i. 74. [13] Stuart mss 156/158, 157/29, 161/42, 169/26. [14] Hervey, 170. [15] Stuart mss 224/112. [16] *HMC Egmont Diary*, ii. 462; *Dodington Diary*, 443–4. [17] Stuart mss 221/178, 222/9.

E.C.

WYNDHAM O'BRIEN, Percy (?1723–74), of Shortgrove, nr. Saffron Walden, Essex.

TAUNTON	16 Apr. 1745–1747
MINEHEAD	1747–1754
COCKERMOUTH	1754–1761
MINEHEAD	1761–1768
WINCHELSEA	1768–21 July 1774

b. ?1723, 2nd s. of Sir William Wyndham, 3rd Bt., and yr. bro. of Charles Wyndham (qq.v.), 2nd Earl of Egremont. *educ.* Winchester 1737–40; St. Mary Hall, Oxf. 17 Nov. 1740, aged 17; Grand Tour. *unm. suc.* to estates of Henry O'Brien, 7th Earl of Thomond [I], husband of his mother's sister, assuming add. name of O'Brien 1741; *cr.* Earl of Thomond [I] 11 Dec. 1756.

Ld. of Treasury Dec. 1755–Nov. 1756; P.C. 8 July 1757; treasurer of the Household July 1757–Nov. 1761, cofferer Nov. 1761–5; ld. lt. Som. 1764–73; recorder, Taunton 1765.

Succeeding as a minor to the name and estates of the Earls of Thomond, O'Brien was returned for Taunton on the Wyndham interest at a by-election in 1745 soon after he came of age. Voting for the Hanoverians in 1746, he was put down by the Government as a 'New Ally'. In 1747, when his Taunton seat was required for his elder brother, Sir Charles Wyndham, he 'forced himself' into Minehead as a courtier, getting 'everything that money could buy', without consulting the lord of the manor, who had a 'natural interest' there.[1] In the new Parliament he was classed, with his brother, as a government supporter. He died 21 July 1774.

[1] H. C. Maxwell-Lyte, *Dunster Castle*, i. 232–3.

R.R.S.

WYNN, John (1701–73), of Glynnllivon and Bodvean, Caern. and Melai, Denb.

CAERNARVONSHIRE	2 Jan. 1740–1741
DENBIGH BOROUGHS	1741–1747
CAERNARVONSHIRE	1754–1761
CAERNARVON BOROUGHS	1761–1768

b. Sept. 1701, o.s. of Sir Thomas Wynn, 1st Bt. (q.v.). *educ.* Queens', Camb. 1720. *m.* c.1735, Jane, da. and h. of John Wynne, M.P. Denbigh Boroughs 1713–15, of Melai, Denb. and Maenan, Caern., 4s. 3da. *suc.* fa. as 2nd Bt. 13 Apr. 1749.

Dep. cofferer of the Household Jan.–Dec. 1743; dep. treasurer, Chelsea Hospital 1744–54; surveyor gen. of mines in N. Wales; constable, Caernarvon castle, forester of Snowdon and steward of Bardsey 1727–61; custos rot. Caern. 1756–d.

Sheriff, Caern. 1732–3.

John Wynn entered the House for Caernarvonshire as a government supporter on a compromise negotiated by the Administration. He was absent from the division on the place bill in 1740 but voted with the Administration in every recorded division of the 1741 Parliament. Moving in 1741 to Denbigh, he was returned after a contest, followed by lengthy petition proceedings, which were ultimately decided in his favour against a Tory candidate supported by Sir Watkin Williams Wynn (q.v.). He did not stand in 1747, having obtained a lucrative post at Chelsea Hospital which the Place Act of 1742 had made incompatible with membership of the House as from the next general election. On his father's death in 1749 he would have stood for Caernarvon if given his father's place at the board of Green Cloth, but as he was not, he brought in his uncle, Sir William Wynn (q.v.). About 1749–50 the 2nd Lord Egmont in his electoral survey wrote of him:

This man has had a great deal of discourse with me. And I am satisfied that he will be thoroughly right with us. His attachments were to Winnington (q.v.), a little through him to Fox, but accidentally and only as keeping his employment, which Winnington got for him, to Pelham.

He died 14 Feb. 1773.

P.D.G.T.

WYNN, Richard (1655–1719), of Bedwell Park, Herts. and Charterhouse Yard, London.

BOSTON 1698–1700, 1705–26 Oct. 1719

b. 2 Mar. 1655, s. of Richard Wynn of London, merchant, by his w. Joyce. *educ.* St. Paul's; Christ's, Camb. 1673; I. Temple 1676, called 1682. *m.* (1) 23 Aug. 1676, Dorothy, da. of George Weldon of London, *s.p.*; (2) 1696, Sarah, da. of Richard Young of London, merchant, wid. of William Barrington of London, merchant, 2s. 2da.

The son of a London merchant, Wynn was related by marriage to Sir William Massingberd (q.v.), one of the leading Tories in Lincolnshire. Before 1696 he had purchased the manors of Folkingham and Threckingham, Lincolnshire, from the Earl of Lincoln for £24,491,[1] and in 1701 he bought Bedwell Park in Hertfordshire, which became his principal seat.[2] A Tory under Anne, he was returned for Boston in 1715, voting against the Administration till his death, 26 Oct. 1719.

[1] *HMC Lords*, n.s. ii. 262. [2] *VCH Herts.* iii. 460.

P.W.

WYNN, Thomas (1677–1749), of Glynnllivon and Bodvean, Caern.

CAERNARVON BOROUGHS 1713–13 Apr. 1749

b. Mar. 1677, 1st s. of Griffith Wynn of Bodvean by Catherine, da. of William Vaughan of Corsygedol, Merion.; bro. of Sir William Wynn (q.v.). *m.* bef. 1701, Frances, da. and coh. of John Glynn of Glynnllivon, l.c.j. of common pleas, 1s. 4da. *suc.* fa. 1680; *cr.* Bt. 25 Oct. 1742.

Equerry to Prince of Wales 1714–24; clerk of the household to Prince of Wales Oct. 1724–7; constable of Caernarvon castle, forester of Snowdon and steward of Bardsey 1724–7; clerk of the Green Cloth 1727–*d.*; equerry to George II 1727–*d.* Sheriff, Caern. Jan.–Dec. 1712.

Thomas Wynn founded the fortunes of his family by marrying the heiress to the Glynnllivon estate, building up a dominating position in Caernarvonshire politics. At George I's accession he received a post in the household of the Prince of Wales, to whom he owed the various places and titles subsequently conferred on himself and his brother, Sir William Wynn (q.v.). In 1721 the report of the secret committee of inquiry into the South Sea bubble disclosed that he was one of the members who had accepted stock from the Company without paying for it.[1] Except from 1717 to 1720,

when he followed his master into opposition during the quarrel in the royal family, he voted with the Government in every recorded division till his death, 13 Apr. 1749.

[1] *CJ*, xix. 575.

P.D.G.T.

WYNN, Sir William (1678–1754).

CAERNARVON BOROUGHS May 1749–20 May 1754

b. Mar. 1678, 2nd s. of Griffith Wynn of Bodvean; bro. of Sir Thomas Wynn, 1st Bt. (q.v.). *unm.* Kntd. 11 Oct. 1727.

Constable, Harlech castle 1716–*d.*; equerry to Prince of Wales 1724–7; standard bearer, gent. pensioners 1727, lt. 1740–*d.*

Wynn owed his knighthood and his places to the influence of his elder brother, whom he succeeded as equerry to the Prince of Wales, and on whose death he was brought into Parliament as a stop-gap by his nephew, Sir John Wynn (q.v.).

He died 20 May 1754.

P.D.G.T.

WYNNE, Sir George (1700–56), of Leeswood Hall, Flints.

FLINT BOROUGHS 1734–22 Mar. 1742

b. May 1700, 1st s. of John Wynne of Leeswood by Jane, da. of Humphrey Jones of Halkyn, Flints. *m.* 26 Apr. 1720, Margaret, da. of Evan Lloyd of Halkyn, 2s. 2da. *suc.* mother to Halkyn estate 1703; *cr.* Bt. 16 July 1731.

Sheriff, Flints. 1722–4; constable, Flint castle c. 1734–50.

Wynne was the son of a poor Welsh country gentleman, but as a child inherited from his mother an estate at Halkyn on which valuable lead deposits were discovered. Having secured control of the property after prolonged litigation with his father, he re-built and re-equipped the family house at Leeswood regardless of expense and embarked on a political career.[1] In 1727 he stood for Flint Boroughs, when there was a double return on which the seat was awarded to his opponent. Attaching himself to Walpole, he was rewarded with a baronetcy in 1731, and won the seat after an extremely expensive contest in 1734.

As a Member, Wynne was industrious, taking notes of debates, 'pushing fairly to be eminent', and regularly voting with the Government.[2] But on the eve of the general election of 1741 his extravagant expenditure and a falling off in his receipts from the lead mines had reduced him to such straits that he was forced to make the following desperate appeal to Walpole:[3]

It is with unspeakable grief that I am at length under the necessity of troubling you with so melancholy a letter as you will find this to be. You cannot be insensible, Sir, that I was the first person that attempted to (and the only one that could) stem the torrent of Jacobitism in Flintshire, and that has been able to make any head against your most inveterate personal enemies, and the present opposition that is now made to Sir Watkin is in consequence thereof. The great power and influence of Sir W. Williams, Sir Robert Grosvenor, Sir Thomas Mostyn, Sir John Glynne (qq.v.) etc., which I have so many years alone stood in opposition to, has brought my affairs into so bad a situation that unless you are pleased to give me some speedy and immediate relief, all that interest that I have at above thirty thousand pounds expense been rearing must quite sink, I myself and family become a sacrifice to your enemies and this on no other account but for my honest zeal in supporting your measures.

He then explained that a mortgage on one of his estates was in danger of being assigned to his arch-enemy, Sir Watkin Williams Wynn, 'which would put it in his hands to ruin me at once'.

> . . . So that, Sir, as soon as ever the Parliament is up, instead of being able to support my interest I am an undone man, a wife, and three children ruined for attachment to the service of my King and his minister. How to turn my self in so unhappy a condition I know not, I have no where to fly for protection but to that Government, in whose interest I have spent the greatest part of my estate in opposition to a most powerful and wealthy body. I must conjure you therefore, Sir, speedily to think of measures to support me against so great a subscription that the enemy have made to oppose me. The fifteen hundred pounds you were pleased to mention will not go above half way, three thousand pounds I doubt not will effectually crown the work. But then, Sir, this will not avail me to support the dignity of my family unless you are pleased to intercede with his Majesty to allow me a handsome place or pension to make me safe for so pressing are my affairs that they will admit of no delay. If I am not immediately supported I must fall a sacrifice and my poor family be entirely undone. For the sake of your own honour and interest as well as that of his Majesty take my affair, good Sir, under your immediate consideration. If I am so happy as to be supported by the Crown I shall be able to put my affairs into such a state of redemption that I shall be in a capacity to maintain my country interest with honour in opposition to those who are such enemies to his Majesty's measures and so strenuous to ruin me only for supporting them. My case you will please to consider, Sir, is very particular. I believe there is not another instance in the whole kingdom circumstanced as mine is, where one man has to deal with so powerful an interest as that of Sir Watkin, Sir Robert Grosvenor, Sir Thomas Mostyn, Sir John Glynne, and a great number of other gentlemen of good estates. On my success, Sir, depends totally the destruction of the Tory interest in North Wales, and if I do not succeed it will be so established that there will be no making head against it in future. The enemy have no other hope of success but the apprehension that I shall not be sufficiently supported

by the Court; they are too sensible if I am, that I should not only carry it for the borough but could overturn their interest for the county.

Walpole's response is unknown but may be presumed to have been helpful, for Wynne was once again returned after a hotly contested election. He took his seat in the House of Commons, and voted with the Government on the division on the chairman of the elections committee, 16 Dec. 1741. In March, however, he was unseated by the anti-Walpole majority of the House on petition, and within a year it was reported that his personal estate had been seized for debt.[4] For a time he was imprisoned in the King's Bench prison, but in the end he appears to have overcome his financial difficulties, dying at his house in Greenwich,[5] 5 Aug. 1756.

[1] *Flints. Hist. Soc. Publ.* ix. 6–13; Dodd, *Industrial Revolution*, 21; *Thraliana*, 336. [2] *HMC Puleston*, 318. [3] 12 Feb. 1741, Cholmondeley (Houghton) mss. [4] UCNW, Penrhos mss v. 698. [5] Palmer, *Wrexham*, 253n.

P.D.G.T.

WYNN, *see also* WILLIAMS (afterwards WILLIAMS WYNN), Watkin

WYVILL, Sir Marmaduke, 6th Bt. (1692–1754), of Constable Burton, Yorks.

RICHMOND   1727–14 Mar. 1728

b. 1692, s. of Sir Marmaduke Wyvill, 5th Bt., M.P. Richmond 1695–8, of Constable Burton by Henrietta Maria, da. of Sir Thomas Yarburgh of Balne Hall and Snaith, Yorks. *m.* 1716, Carey, da. of Edward Coke of Holtham, Norf., sis. of Thomas Coke (q.v.), 1st Earl of Leicester, *s.p. suc.* fa. 2 Nov. 1722.
Postmaster gen. [I] 1736–d.

Constable Burton, so-called because its former owners had been constables of Richmond castle, was acquired through marriage by the Wyvills in the reign of Edward VI.[1] In 1713 and 1715 Wyvill stood unsuccessfully for Richmond against the Yorke and Darcy interests. In 1722 his father forbade him to stand, on learning that his doing so would be disapproved by Lord Sunderland.[2] In 1727 he was successful but was unseated on petition. In 1736 his brother-in-law, Thomas Coke (q.v.), later Lord Leicester, the English postmaster general, appointed him postmaster general of Ireland, which disqualified him from sitting in the House of Commons. He is described as 'a great man for sheep in Yorkshire'.[3]

He died 27 Dec. 1754.

[1] C. Clarkson, *Richmond*, 68. [2] Sir Marmaduke Wyvill, 5th Bt., to Sunderland, 9 Mar. 1722, Sunderland (Blenheim) mss. [3] *HMC Egmont Diary*, ii. 247–8, 408.

R.R.S.

YATES, Thomas (*b*.1693), of Chichester, Suss.

CHICHESTER 1734–1741

bap. 9 Oct. 1693, o.s. of Henry Yates, M.P., of Warnham, Suss. by his w. Elizabeth Partherick. *m*. Margaret, da. of Sir John Miller, 2nd Bt., M.P., of Chichester, *s.p. suc*. fa. 1716.

Yates came of an old Sussex family. His father was M.P. for Horsham and he himself married the daughter of a former M.P. for Chichester, for which he was returned on the Tory interest in 1734, after contesting it unsuccessfully at a by-election in 1733. According to the Duke of Richmond, 'whoring lost Yates his first election'.[1] He voted against the Government, and did not stand again. The date of his death is unknown.

[1] Richmond to Newcastle, 2 Jan. 1741, Add. 32696, f. 16.

A.N.N.

YONGE, William (c.1693–1755), of Colyton, Devon.

HONITON 1715–1754
TIVERTON 1754–10 Aug. 1755

b. c.1693, 1st s. of Sir Walter Yonge, 3rd Bt., M.P., of Colyton by his 2nd w. Gwen, da. of Sir Robert Williams, 2nd Bt., M.P., of Penryn, Cornw. *m*. (1) 30 July 1716, Mary (div. 1724), da. of Samuel Heathcote of Hackney, sis. of Sir William Heathcote, 1st Bt. (q.v.), *s.p.*; (2) 14 Sept. 1729, Anne, da. and coh. of Thomas Howard, 6th Baron Howard of Effingham, 2s. 6da. K.B. 27 May 1725. *suc*. fa. as 4th Bt. 18 July 1731.
Commr. for stating army debts 1717–22, of Irish revenue 1723–4; ld. of Treasury 1724–7, 1730–5, of Admiralty 1728–30; recorder, Tiverton 1725–48; P.C. 6 Nov. 1735; sec. at war 1735–46; jt. vice-treasurer [I] 1746–*d*.

Sir William Yonge, Hervey writes,

was certainly a very remarkable instance how much character and reputation depend sometimes on unaccountable accident and the caprice of mankind; . . . for, without having done anything that I know of particularly profligate—anything out of the common track of a ductile courtier and a parliamentary tool—his name was proverbially used to express everything pitiful, corrupt, and contemptible.[1]

Returned for the family seat at Honiton soon after coming of age, he made his first reported speech for the Government on the septennial bill in 1716. During the split in the Whig party he adhered to Sunderland, obtaining a place in 1717. On the Shaftesbury election petition in 1719, when William Benson was unseated, Yonge was one of the ministerial 'underlings' who 'protracted the debate till two in the morning', though their chiefs had walked out after losing a motion for adjourning at eleven.[2] In a debate on the South Sea scheme, 23 Mar. 1720, he was one of the ministerial spokesmen

who narrowly secured the rejection of Walpole's motion for protecting holders of government loans by fixing the rate at which they might be converted into South Sea stock. Two days later he was among a number of Members who were credited by the South Sea Company with stock—in his case £3,000 at the current price of 350—which they did not pay for but were entitled to 'sell' back to the Company at any time, receiving as 'profit' any rise in the market price.[3] After Sunderland's death he attached himself to Walpole, under whom he became a lord of the Treasury and one of the chief government spokesmen in the Commons.

He had [Hervey writes] a great command of what is called parliamentary language and a talent of talking eloquently without a meaning and expatiating agreeably upon nothing, beyond any man, I believe, that ever had the gift of speech.

Horace Walpole, who describes his eloquence as 'astonishing', states that

Sir Robert Walpole has often, when he did not care to enter early into the debate himself, given Yonge his notes, as the latter has come late into the House, from which he could speak admirably and fluently, though he had missed all the preceding discussion.

His parliamentary talents are shown by an incident in the Dunkirk debate of 14 Mar. 1730, in which Sandys, replying to Walpole's aspersions on the last Tory Administration in Anne's reign,

desired the Journal of 13 Reg. Anne might be read to show what was the sense of the majority at that time upon a motion relating to Dunkirk. He thought the majority at that time, who were the Tories, had made a strong address to the Queen to interpose for the more effectual performance of the treaty in demolishing Dunkirk, which Louis XIV was slow in doing; but Mr. Sandys in this overshot himself. Sir William Yonge, who remembered the matter, immediately seconded him, and the Journal was read, whereby it appeared that when the motion was made by the Whigs of that Parliament, who were the minority, for addressing the Queen, the ministry caused the previous question to be put whether the motion should be put, and carried in the negative. This silenced Mr. Sandys, and made Sir Robert Walpole triumph.

Chesterfield refers to him as one who had

by a glibness of tongue singly, raised himself successively to the best employments of the kingdom; he has been lord of the Admiralty, lord of the Treasury, secretary at war, and is now vice-treasurer of Ireland, and all this with a most sullied, not to say blasted, character.[4]

Yonge lost his place on the accession of George II, who

used always to call him 'stinking Yonge',[5] and had conceived and expressed such an insurmountable dislike to his person and character that no interest nor influence was potent enough at this time to prevail with his Majesty to continue him . . . However, Sir Robert advised him, upon this disgrace, to be patient, not clamorous, to submit, not resent or oppose, to be as subservient to the Court in attendance and give the King his assistance as constantly and as assiduously in Parliament as if he was paid for it; telling him and all the world what afterwards proved true, that whatever people might imagine, Yonge was not sunk, he had only dived, and would yet get up again.[6]

So he did, even overcoming the King's prejudice sufficiently to become secretary at war, an office carrying access to the Closet on army business.

Yonge stood by Walpole to the end, excelling himself in a speech against the opposition motion of 21 Jan. 1742 for an inquiry into the conduct of the war. After Walpole's fall, his three chief lieutenants, Yonge, Pelham and Winnington, showed 'that the old courtiers and their party in the House of Commons were resolved to stick together' by keeping the House up to one o'clock in the morning on an election petition while they 'battled it in favour of the sitting Members, who were Sir Robert Walpole's friends'. He retained his place, much to the indignation of the Opposition, who talked of impeaching him.[7]

When Pelham became chancellor of the Exchequer at the end of 1743, Yonge was 'hurt' at not succeeding him as paymaster general. To make up for this Pelham procured the King's consent for a pension of £600 a year on Ireland for Lady Yonge, as charity.[8] Owing to failing health he gave up the war office for a lucrative sinecure in 1746. He died 10 Aug. 1755.

[1] Hervey, *Mems.* 35–37. [2] *HMC Portland*, v. 577. [3] *CJ*, xix. 569. [4] Hervey, loc. cit.; Walpole, *Mems. Geo. II*, i. 23 n. 1; *HMC Egmont Diary*, i. 43; *Chesterfield Letters*, 2084. [5] See PLUMER, Walter. [6] Hervey, loc. cit. [7] Walpole to Mann, 22, 25 Jan. 1742; *HMC Egmont Diary*, iii. 253, 255. [8] Pelham to Devonshire, 1 Dec. 1743, Newcastle (Clumber) mss.

R.R.S.

YORKE, Hon. Charles (1722–70), of Tittenhanger, Herts.

REIGATE 7 Dec. 1747–1768
CAMBRIDGE UNIVERSITY 1768–20 Jan. 1770

b. 30 Dec. 1722, 2nd s. of Philip Yorke (q.v.), 1st Earl of Hardwicke; bro. of Hon. John, Joseph and Philip Yorke (qq.v.). *educ.* Dr. Newcome's, Hackney; Corpus Christi, Camb. 1739; M. Temple 1735; L. Inn 1742, called 1746, bencher 1745. *m.* (1) 19 May 1755, Catherine (*d.*10 July 1759), da. and h. of William Freeman of Aspenden, Herts., 1s.; (2) 30 Dec. 1762, Agneta, da. and coh. of Henry Johnson of Great Berkhampstead, Herts., 2s. 1da.
Clerk of the Crown in Chancery 1746–*d.*; K.C. 1754; solicitor-gen. to Prince of Wales 1754–6; solicitor-gen. 1756–61; attorney-gen. 1762–3, 1765–6; recorder, Dover 1764–*d.*; ld. chancellor 17 Jan. 1770–*d.*

On being called to the bar in 1746 Charles Yorke was appointed by his father to a Chancery sinecure worth £1,200 a year, the proceeds of which he

shared with his younger brother, John (q.v.), till Lord Hardwicke arranged for him to draw the whole income as a consolation for the recent destruction of his library by fire.[1] Succeeding his elder brother, Philip (q.v.), for the family seat in Reigate in 1747, he was chosen to second the Address in November 1748 and to move it in January 1753. He spoke on the regency bill in 1751, described by Horace Walpole as 'a young lawyer of good parts, but precise and affected'. Walpole also records that when Henry Fox made a personal attack on Lord Hardwicke during the debates on his marriage bill in 1753, 'Charles Yorke, the Chancellor's son, took this up with great anger, and yet with preciseness, beginning with these words, "It is new in Parliament, it is new in politics, it is new in ambition".'[2] About this time he was earning £1,000 a year at the bar[3] and acting as his father's legal secretary.

In 1754 Lord Hardwicke arranged for both the Prince of Wales's law officers to be promoted,[4] thus clearing the way for Charles Yorke's appointment to be solicitor-general to the Prince of Wales—the first rung on the ladder to his goal, the great seal. He achieved his ambition only to die three days later, 20 Jan. 1770, before the patent for his peerage had been completed.

[1] See YORKE, John. [2] *Mems. Geo. II*, i. 125, 343. [3] Yorke, *Hardwicke*, ii. 141 n.2. [4] See BATHURST, Hon. Henry.

R.R.S.

YORKE, John (1685–1757), of Gouthwaite and Richmond, Yorks.

RICHMOND 1710–1713, 5 Mar. 1717–1727
14 Mar. 1728–14 July 1757

bap. 16 Dec. 1685, 1st s. of Thomas Yorke (q.v.). *educ.* Eton 1698; Peterhouse, Camb. 1703. *m.* 5 Jan. 1732, Anne, da. of James Darcy, M.P., 1st Baron Darcy of Navan, 2nd cos. of Robert Darcy, 4th Earl of Holderness, *s.p. suc.* fa. 1716.

Yorke, who succeeded his father at Richmond in 1717, was an independent Whig. Up to 1741 all his recorded votes were against the Government, except on the two most unpopular measures of Walpole's Administration, the excise bill and the Spanish convention, for both of which he voted. In the next Parliament he is described as one of the 'capricious . . . or a sort of neutrals in party', who voted against the Government on the chairman of the elections committee,[1] but he voted for them on the Hanoverians in all three divisions. In the 2nd Lord Egmont's electoral survey, c.1749–50, he is described as 'a whimsical fellow but in the main will be with Government'.

He died 14 July 1757.

[1] Coxe, *Walpole*, iii. 583.

R.R.S.

YORKE, Hon. John (1728–1801), of Sonning, Berks.

HIGHAM FERRERS   21 Nov. 1753–1768
REIGATE   1768–1784

b. 27 Aug. 1728, 4th s. of Philip Yorke (q.v.), 1st Earl of Hardwicke, and bro. of Hon. Charles, Joseph and Philip Yorke (qq.v.). *educ.* Dr. Newcome's, Hackney; Corpus Christi, Camb. 1746; L. Inn 1746, called 1754. *m.* 1 Jan. 1762, Elizabeth, da. of Reginald Lygon of Madresfield, Worcs., 1da.

Clerk of the Crown in Chancery 1746–*d.*; chaffwax 1752–5; patentee for commissions of bankruptcy 1755–*d.*; ld. of Trade 1761–3, July–Dec. 1765, of Admiralty 1765–6.

At the age of 18 John Yorke and his brother, Charles (q.v.), were appointed by Lord Hardwicke jointly to a life sinecure in Chancery worth £1,200 a year.[1] When he was 22 his father applied through Newcastle to the King at Hanover to give him another Chancery sinecure, that of chaffwax, equivalent in value to his half share of the Crown office, so that Charles might enjoy the whole of the profits of that office. The King's reaction was:

My Lord Chancellor is getting every office that falls in the law for his own children;

but on his return to England he granted the application.[2] Three years later John exchanged the office for a joint share in another Chancery place, held by the poet Cowper's father, who died the next year, leaving John with the whole of the profits.[3]

He died 4 Sept. 1801.

[1] Walpole to Montagu, 5 Aug. 1746. [2] Yorke, *Hardwicke*, ii. 179 et seq. [3] *Gent. Mag.* 1755, p. 572.

R.R.S.

YORKE, Hon. Joseph (1724–92).

EAST GRINSTEAD   22 Jan. 1751–1761
DOVER   1761–1774
GRAMPOUND   1774–1780

b. 24 June 1724, 3rd s. of Philip Yorke (q.v.), 1st Earl of Hardwicke, and bro. of Hon. Charles, John and Philip Yorke (qq.v.). *educ.* Dr. Newcome's, Hackney. *m.* 23 Jan. 1783, Christiana Charlotte Margaret, Baroness de Stöcken, da. of Johan Henrik, Baron de Stöcken of Denmark, wid. of Baron de Boctzalaer of Holland, *s.p.* K.B. 23 Mar. 1761; *cr.* Baron Dover 18 Sept. 1788.

Ensign 2 Ft. Gds. 1741, lt. and capt. 1743; capt. and lt.-col. 1 Ft. Gds. 1745; a.-d.-c. to the Duke of Cumberland 1745–9; a.-d.-c. to the King 1749–58; col. army 1749; col. 9 Ft. 1755–9; maj.-gen. 1758; col. 8 Drags. 1759–60, 5 Drags. 1760–87; lt.-gen. 1760; gen. 1777; col. 11 Lt. Drags. 1787–9, 1 Life Gds. 1789–*d.*

Sec. to Paris embassy 1749–51; minister at The Hague 1751–61, ambassador 1761–80; P.C. 29 June 1768.

Entering the army, Joseph Yorke received rapid promotion, becoming a lieutenant-colonel before he was of age, and a.-d.-c. to the King, as a result of heavy pressure from his father,[1] at 25. Deciding after the peace of Aix-la-Chapelle to exchange a military for a diplomatic career, he was appointed minister to The Hague at the age of 26. Brought into Parliament by the Duke of Dorset[2] shortly before his appointment, he kept up his membership throughout his 30 years at The Hague, for the prestige which it brought him there, but there is no evidence that he ever attended.

He died 2 Dec. 1792.

[1] Yorke, *Hardwicke*, ii. 91–92, 169–71. [2] Hardwicke to Newcastle, 1 June 1750, Add. 32721, f. 3.

R.R.S.

YORKE, Philip (1690–1764), of Lincoln's Inn, and Carshalton, Croydon, Surr.

LEWES   21 Apr. 1719–1722
SEAFORD   1722–23 Nov. 1733

b. 1 Dec. 1690, s. of Philip Yorke of Dover by Elizabeth, da. of Richard Gibbon of Dover, wid. of her cos. Edward Gibbon of West Cliffe, Kent. *educ.* Samuel Morland's, Bethnal Green; M. Temple 1708, called 1715, bencher 1720; L. Inn 1724, bencher 1724. *m.* 16 May 1719, Margaret, da. of Charles Cocks, M.P., of Worcester, wid. of John Lygon of Madresfield, Worcs. and niece of Lord Chancellor Somers, 5s. 2da. Kntd. 11 June 1720. *cr.* Baron Hardwicke 23 Nov. 1733; Earl of Hardwicke 2 Apr. 1754.

Recorder, Dover 1718–*d.*; solicitor-gen. 1720–4; attorney-gen. 1724–33; c.j. of King's bench 1733–7; P.C. 1 Nov. 1733; ld. chancellor 1737–56; high steward, Cambridge Univ. 1749–*d.*

Philip Yorke, the son of a Dover solicitor, was brought up for the bar, where his pre-eminent ability quickly attracted the attention of Lord Chancellor Macclesfield.[1] On Macclesfield's recommendation he was brought into Parliament by the Duke of Newcastle in 1719 and made solicitor general in 1720, less than five years after being called.[2] In 1725, as attorney-general, he refused to be a manager of the impeachment of his old patron and benefactor, with whom he remained to the end on affectionate terms.[3] For his first ten years in the House his comparatively few recorded speeches are confined to legal matters. In 1729 he is mentioned as speaking in a debate on the Hessians; in 1730 he defended a bill, which he had drafted, prohibiting loans to foreign powers without a licence; and in 1732 he spoke in justification of maintaining the strength of the standing army at 18,000 men. He distinguished himself next year in the debates on the excise bill, delivering a powerful speech in its support on 14 Mar. and taking part on 10 Apr. in the debate on the City of London's petition against the bill, 'in which the great speakers on both sides appeared'. On 12 Apr., after Walpole had been mobbed in the lobby, Yorke made

> a warm and learned speech on the fatal consequences of such tumultuary behaviour, and aggravated it by the consideration that the person aimed at was one of the King's Council, a magistrate of high degree, and a member of the House; that if this was suffered to pass without a proper notice taken of it, there was an end of meeting there and even of the Legislature. He therefore proposed several resolutions, which all passed *nemine contradicente*, tending to the freedom of debates, and to the prevention of mobs gathering together to impede or promote bills passing in Parliament.

At the Cockpit meeting of government supporters called by Walpole on 23 Apr., the only speakers besides Walpole himself, were Yorke, Henry Pelham, and the Speaker.[4]

When the chief justiceship of the King's bench fell vacant at the end of March 1733, neither Yorke nor his friend, the solicitor-general, Talbot, 'two as great and eminent lawyers as this country ever bred', was willing to take it, Yorke on financial grounds—the salary was only £2,000—and Talbot because he was a purely equity lawyer and not an expert on the common law; but on Lord Chancellor King's resignation later in the year they both laid claim to the great seal.[5] Walpole, however, persuaded Yorke, who was equally qualified for both positions, to waive his superior claim in Talbot's favour and to take the lower but permanent office with an additional £2,000 a year.[6] He also received a peerage, dated before Talbot's,[7] taking the title of Lord Hardwicke from an estate in Gloucestershire which he had bought in 1725, apparently as an investment, for he never lived there.

On Talbot's death in 1737 Hardwicke succeeded to the great seal, with the reversion of a tellership of the Exchequer for his eldest son, which fell in the next year. In 1738, as a result of the death of his wife's uncle, Sir Joseph Jekyll (q.v.), he acquired control of a seat at Reigate. In 1740 he entered the territorial aristocracy by buying the estate of Wimpole in Cambridgeshire from the 2nd Lord Oxford for £86,740.[8] In the same year he married his eldest son to the grand-daughter and heiress of the Duke of Kent, on whose death shortly afterwards she succeeded to Wrest in Bedfordshire, becoming a Marchioness in her own right.

In a conversation with Sir Dudley Ryder, the attorney-general, on 18 Oct. 1739, Walpole said that

> Lord Hardwicke was one of the greatest men this nation ever bred, and if he himself should drop or quit, the public affairs must fall into his hands, though he seemed very unwilling to accept them.

Recurring to the subject in February 1740, he told Ryder that

he would now quit if he could put the administration of affairs into any other hand that was fit. That he saw none but the Chancellor fit for it. That he had often urged him to prepare himself for it, had given him opportunity of conversing with the King and gaining his confidence. But the Chancellor is much averse to it, and says he had rather retire and live at £1,000 a year than bear the fatigue that he, Sir Robert, goes through. On which, Sir Robert told him he must either take it, or it must in case of any accident to himself fall into hands that would never suffer him in the post he is, that they had friends of all sorts to provide for and doubly manned in the law and every other sort of preferment. But he has not yet been able to prevail on him to think of it.[9]

During the last days of his Administration Walpole complained that Hardwicke

> was acting a part to save himself, and had been promised not to be removed, but he was sure, if he himself was to be out, as the Prince would then be master of the King, the present Chancellor could not hold it and Murray [William, q.v.] would have the seal.[10]

In fact Hardwicke remained lord chancellor till he resigned in 1756 with his life-long friend, the Duke of Newcastle. He declined to accept his old or any other post in the Pitt–Newcastle Government, but continued a member of the effective cabinet till 1762, when he finally went out with Newcastle. At his death, 6 Mar. 1764, four of his sons, Philip, Charles, Joseph and John (qq.v.), were Members of Parliament. The fifth son, James, became bishop of Ely. His two daughters married Lord Anson (George Anson, q.v.), and Sir Gilbert Heathcote, 3rd Bt., one of the richest commoners in the country.

[1] Yorke, *Hardwicke*, i. 52, 63–64. [2] G. Harris, *Hardwicke*, i. 91, 98. [3] Yorke, i. 88–89; ii. 381. [4] *HMC Egmont Diary*, i. 358, 362, 366. [5] Harris, 230; Hervey, *Mems.* 242. [6] Sir Dudley Ryder's diary, 18 Oct. 1739, Harrowby mss. [7] Harris, 258–9. [8] Yorke, i. 108, 206. [9] Sir Dudley Ryder's diary, Harrowby mss. [10] Harrowby mss 10 (L. Inn), 8 Jan. 1742.

R.R.S.

YORKE, Hon. Philip (1720–90), of Wrest, Beds.

REIGATE	1741–1747
CAMBRIDGESHIRE	1747–1 Mar. 1764

b. 9 Dec. 1720, 1st s. of Philip Yorke (q.v.), 1st Earl of Hardwicke, and bro. of Hon. Charles, John and Joseph Yorke (qq.v.). *educ.* Dr. Newcome's, Hackney; Corpus Christi, Camb. 1737. *m.* 22 May 1740, Lady Jemima Campbell, da. of John, 3rd Earl of Breadalbane [S], 2da. She suc. gd.-fa. as Marchioness Gray 5 June 1740. *suc.* fa. as 2nd Earl 6 Mar. 1764.

Teller of the Exchequer 1738–*d.*; ld. lt. Cambs. 1757–*d.*; P.C. 17 Dec. 1760; high steward, Cambridge Univ. 1764–*d.*

Before Philip Yorke was 21 his father, Lord Hardwicke, had provided him with a life sinecure which by 1782 was worth £7,000 a year, married him to a great heiress, and returned him for Reigate. In his first Parliament he was chosen to second the Address in 1743, to move it in 1744, and to be a manager of Lord Lovat's trial in 1747. He also spoke for the Government on the continuing of British troops to Flanders in January 1744 and on the Hanoverians in April 1746. Between December 1743 and April 1745 he kept a diary of debates in both Houses, which has been described as 'the most trustworthy and impartial authority on the parliamentary history of the period'.[1]

In 1747 Yorke was chosen by the general meeting of the county to stand for Cambridgeshire, where his father's estate of Wimpole and near which his wife's of Wrest were situated. Though no opposition was expected, his father took the precaution of returning him again for Reigate, plying him with advice, from the care of his health to the question of treating the freeholders. 'You can't drink', Lord Hardwicke wrote, 'and need not do it much yourself. If you find yourself hot and dry, drink negus, I mean wine and warm water. And be sure to take care that your bed and sheets are *in all places* well aired'. On treating he was to be guided by Lord Montfort, who, as Henry Bromley, had represented the county in the last two Parliaments and was acting as Yorke's manager. Montfort decided that treating was essential, with the result that Yorke's return cost his father over £2,000—a 'monstrous' sum, Hardwicke complained, 'for an election without any opposition'.[2]

Though Hardwicke could bring his eldest son into Parliament, he could not make him a politician. An ample income, poor health, and bookish tastes, combined to disincline Philip Yorke (from 1754 Lord Royston) for an active public life. His ruling passion was collecting historical documents. Advising Horace Mann to cultivate Yorke, Horace Walpole wrote, 8 Sept. 1757:

> That family is very powerful; the eldest brother, Lord Royston, is historically curious and political: if, without its appearing too forced, you could at any time send him uncommon letters, papers, manifestoes, and things of that sort, it might do you good service.

He edited *Sir Dudley Carleton's Letters* (1757) and *Miscellaneous State Papers* (1778), published *Walpoliana* (1783), a collection of anecdotes about Sir Robert Walpole, and annotated Burnet.

He died 16 May 1790.

[1] *CJ*, xxxvii. 707; Yorke, *Hardwicke*, i. 577; Owen, *Pelhams*, 219, 306 n.3. [2] 16, 23 June, 6 Aug. 1747, Add. 35351, ff. 103, 112, 126.

R.R.S.

YORKE, Thomas (1658–1716), of Gouthwaite and Richmond, Yorks.

RICHMOND 1689–1690, 1695–1710, 1713– Nov. 1716

b. 29 June 1658, 1st s. of Sir John Yorke of Gouthwaite, M.P. Richmond 1661–3, by Mary, da. of Maulger Norton of St. Nicholas, nr. Richmond. *m.* 7 Dec. 1680, Catherine, da. and h. of Thomas Lister of Arnold's Biggin, Yorks., 3s. 4da. *suc.* fa. 1663.

Yorke's mother brought with her as a dowry some property at Richmond, which the family represented continuously for 66 years. Returned as a Whig in 1715, he died next year (buried 16 Nov.).[1]

[1] J. W. Clay, *Dugdale's Vis. Yorks.* ii. 282.

R.R.S.

YOUNGE, Hitch (?1688–1759), of Garlic Hill, London, and Roehampton, Surr.

STEYNING 26 Nov. 1740–30 Jan. 1759

b. ?1688. *unm.*

A wealthy merchant, engaged in the Spanish and Mediterranean trade, Younge supplied wheat to the Minorca garrison in 1734[1] and was the banker and London agent to Benjamin Keene (q.v.).[2] Returned for Steyning with the support of Charles Eversfield (q.v.) in 1740, he voted with the Government in all recorded divisions of the next Parliament. He died 30 Jan. 1759, leaving the bulk of his property to his sister Mary, the widow of his partner Bartholomew Clarke, whose only child married Jacob Bouverie (q.v.), 1st Viscount Folkestone.[3]

[1] *Cal. Treas. Bks. and Pprs.* 1735–8, pp. 31, 122. [2] *Private Corresp. of Sir Benjamin Keene*, ed. Lodge, 34–35. [3] PCC 79 Arran.

J.B.L.